THE BUILDINGS OF ENGLAND

FOUNDING EDITOR: NIKOLAUS PEVSNER

NORTHAMPTONSHIRE

BRUCE BAILEY

NIKOLAUS PEVSNER

AND
BRIDGET CHERRY

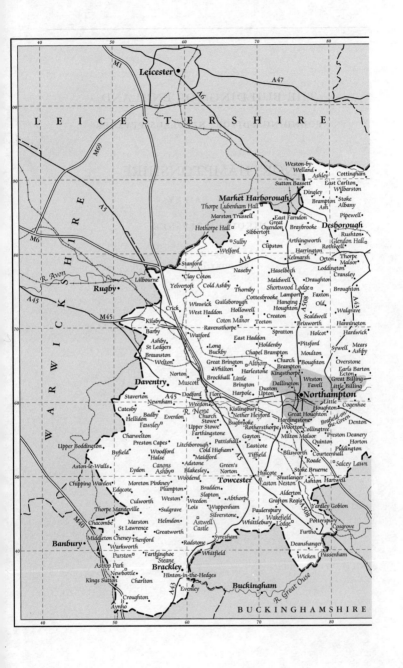

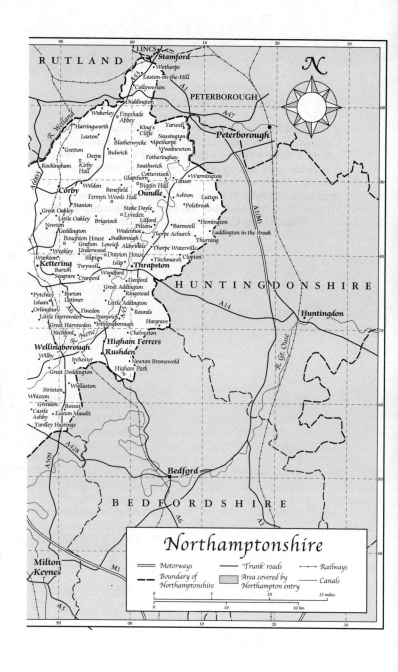

Northamptonshire

Northamptonshire

BY

BRUCE BAILEY

NIKOLAUS PEVSNER

AND

BRIDGET CHERRY

THE BUILDINGS OF ENGLAND

YALE UNIVERSITY PRESS
NEW HAVEN AND LONDON

YALE UNIVERSITY PRESS
NEW HAVEN AND LONDON

302 Temple Street, New Haven CT 06511
47 Bedford Square, London WC1B 3DP
www.pevsner.co.uk
www.lookingatbuildings.org.uk
www.yalebooks.co.uk
www.yalebooks.com

Published by Yale University Press 2013
2 4 6 8 10 9 7 5 3 1

ISBN 978 0 300 18507 2

Printed in China
through World Print
Set in Monotype Plantin

The print edition of
Northamptonshire
was dedicated to
MARGARET RASTAN

The print edition is dedicated to
the memory of
VERA ISHAM and RUPERT GUNNIS
for their inspiration and patronage
and
to the numerous Church Wardens
who have so valiantly opened their churches

CONTENTS

LIST OF TEXT FIGURES AND MAPS

Every effort has been made to contact or trace all copyright holders. The publishers will be glad to make good any errors or omissions brought to our attention in future editions.

PHOTOGRAPHIC ACKNOWLEDGEMENTS

The photographs were almost all taken by John Roan Photography. We are also grateful for permission to reproduce the remaining photographs from the sources as shown below.

© Country Life: 71, 91
© English Heritage Photo Library: 40
© Martin Charles, courtesy of the Ecclesiological Society: 113

MAP REFERENCES

The numbers printed in italic type in the margin against the place names in the gazetteer of the book indicate the position of the place in question on the index map (pp. ii–iii), which is divided into sections by the 10-km. reference lines of the National Grid. The reference given here omits the two initial letters which in a full grid reference refer to the 100-km. squares into which the county is divided. The first two numbers indicate the *western* boundary, and the last two the *southern* boundary, of the 10-km. square in which the place in question is situated. For example, Abthorpe (reference 6040) will be found in the 10-km. square bounded by grid lines 60 (on the *west*) and 70, and 40 (on the *south*) and 50; Yelvertoft (reference 5070) in the square bounded by the grid lines 50 (on the *west*) and 60, and 70 (on the *south*) and 80.

The map contains all those places, whether towns, villages, or isolated buildings, which are the subject of separate entries in the text.

FOREWORD AND ACKNOWLEDGEMENTS

Pevsner's *Northamptonshire* was first published in 1961. There was a partially revised edition by Bridget Cherry in 1973, following the removal of the entries for the Soke of Peterborough to a separate volume with Huntingdonshire. I have had the pleasure, I might say, privilege, of being involved in all three editions. The present revision has taken roughly three years: it could easily have taken five but lines have to be drawn. It is not solely my work, as the list of acknowledgements will make clear and it is impossible to credit all the help I have received. I have seen my role as coordinating editor rather than sole author and I have tried to pull together innumerable strands of information from a huge variety of sources.

Since 1973 Northamptonshire has been lucky in a number of intensive studies in various areas. The Royal Commission on Historical Monuments (RCHME) has produced a volume on the major country houses and outline work by the same authority has been done on the churches. There have been major studies of medieval and post-Reformation stained glass. The time seemed right therefore to embark on another revision.

I am very conscious that this is Pevsner's Northamptonshire and where possible I have tried to keep his words intact. This is especially so with regard to the parish churches. He had an acute eye for medieval architecture and I have found few instances where it has been necessary to challenge his views or adjust his comments. He was less at home with the country houses and the study by RCHME has led to a reassessment of a number of them. Inevitably the accounts of the towns have had to be extensively rewritten. They have all seen major redevelopment since 1973. It has been possible this time, with additional space, to extend the original coverage and include more detailed and wider descriptions of individual buildings and of those in towns and villages.

Over the years various correspondents have sent comments to the publishers. I must single out the 'star' correspondent as far as Northamptonshire is concerned and that is Dr Geoffrey Brandwood. The files contained numerous notes which he had sent in, but I owe him a special acknowledgement since he offered to check for me the files of the Incorporated Church Building Society at Lambeth Palace. Others whose names occurred frequently are Rodney Hubbuck and Jack Laundon. Several people have contributed throughout the project: Alan Brooks, Brian Giggins (notably on Towcester), Alan Mayes, Nick Hill (English Heritage), Crispin Powell (formerly of Northamptonshire Record Office), Jon-Paul Carr (Northamptonshire Libraries). In specialist areas I must thank Paul Sharpling who has collaborated with me on the later stained glass in the county,* Richard Marks for medieval stained glass and useful comments in other areas, Geoffrey Fisher for observations on church monuments (GF), Andrew Chapman for reviewing the archaeology of the county, Diana Sutherland for the passage on geology and building stones, Geoffrey Starmer for the passage on Industrial Northamptonshire and Dr David Parsons for reviewing the Anglo-Saxon entries.

Many owners have been generous in allowing me access to properties and for sharing their knowledge and I am especially grateful to the Duke of Buccleuch, Earl Spencer, Lady Heseltine, Lady Juliet Townsend, Edmund and the Hon. Mrs Brudenell, Mark Bradshaw (National Trust), David Allen, Clare Brooks, Christopher Davidge, the late J. Eades, David Hall, Charles Micklewright and Charles Stopford Sackville. For major assistance elsewhere: David & Angela Adams (Daventry), John Bailey (Finedon), John Barker and Alex Stevenson (Wellingborough), Edward Bartlett (Canons Ashby), Liz Brandon-Jones (Wicksteed Trust), Greg Bucknill (Southwick), Dale Dishon (Ashton Wold), Ptolemy Dean (Aynhoe Park and Easton Neston), George Drye and Neil Lyon (Lamport), Rosemary Eady (Pytchley), Mark Girouard (Kirby Hall), Paul and Janet Griffin (Wothorpe), Judith Hodgkinson (Kelmarsh Hall and Northampton), Beryl Hudson (Brackley), Enid Jarvis (Spratton), Alan Langley (East Farndon), Basil Morgan (Rockingham), Dr Mark Page & Matthew Bristow (Corby), David Pain (Rushton), Geoff Pullin (Badby), Robin Rowe and Stephen Forge (Oundle), Paul Sanders-Hewett (Draughton & Maidwell), Sally Strutt (Cransley Hall & Edgcote), Peter Inskip (Charlton and Lilford), Nicholas Williams (Thenford), Mike Rumbold (Weedon), Pete Smith and Kathryn Morrison (Apethorpe), Juliet Wilson (Fotheringhay) and Dr Roy Hargrave (the work of J. A. Gotch). Others who have helped in various ways: Paul Barnwell, Gill & David Lindsay and the staff at Northamptonshire Record Office.

I am most grateful to John Roan who has taken – and in not a few cases retaken – the photographs. I am only sad that space has precluded only a fraction of the splendid series he has taken being used.

Perhaps my greatest debt of gratitude is to my editor Charles O'Brien who has patiently dealt with my imperfect computer drafts but most importantly for his perceptive eye in noticing errors and for keeping the text on the rails. At Yale Catherine Bankhurst has steered the text through the press with Phoebe Lowndes dealing with illustrations. To them all I am grateful for their diligence and patience.

There are bound to be errors and omissions, dates and names inaccurately transcribed, and I can only hope that users of this volume will alert the publishers as scores of others have done in the past.

* The dates for stained glass in the gazetteer are often taken from documentary sources and may refer to manufacture or installation, so may not coincide with the date seen in the window itself. Paul's full catalogue of the post-Reformation glass in the county is due for publication by the Northamptonshire Record Society in 2014.

INTRODUCTION

To say that Northamptonshire is the county of squires and spires is not very original, but it is true all the same. Squires – that means that Northamptonshire is not only, as Camden put it, 'passing well furnish'd with noblemen's and gentlemen's houses', but that the nobility and gentry not only possess them but live in them, that many of these houses have remained in the same family for centuries, and that consequently the families belong as much to the houses as the houses to the families. The county is far enough from London to avoid developments which would make it less attractive to continue residence and near enough to London to make continued residence possible even in the C21. It is very gratifying to see how many of the major houses are being carefully kept up. Among the families that have been in residence for centuries there are e.g. the Montagus and Buccleuchs at Boughton, the Spencers at Althorp, the Comptons at Castle Ashby and the Brudenells at Deene. In other cases newcomers look after the houses equally exemplarily (e.g. at Cottesbrooke and Thenford). Yet other houses have been acquired by the state or are being used in different ways: Kirby (English Heritage), Canons Ashby (National Trust), Laxton (a Polish care home) and Rushton and Fawsley (both hotels). Apethorpe should be added, currently (2013) in the care of English Heritage. Only a few of the great and famous houses have been demolished, and these not recently. Holdenby was pulled down in 1651, Pytchley in 1828 and Blatherwycke in 1948. So much for squires; spires do not need much comment, and what architectural comment is necessary will be made later. Spires predominate in the E of the county but are rare in the W. This is connected with the fact that the E has a very fine hard limestone, while the W has softer stones and tends towards brick and timber.

Northamptonshire is altogether clearly divided into regions, first geological, secondly according to the influences exerted by adjoining counties. Before the Soke of Peterborough was removed in 1965, Northamptonshire bordered on more counties than any other in England, nine in all (Buckinghamshire, Bedfordshire, Huntingdonshire, Cambridgeshire, Lincolnshire, Rutland, Leicestershire, Warwickshire, Oxfordshire), and it partakes of the Home Counties character, the East Anglian and Lincolnshire character, and the Midland character, without, however – it must be admitted – enjoying any of the memorable scenic qualities one may connect with some of them. The traveller is not going to visit

Northamptonshire for its landscape. Its beauty spots are few. There is no coast or a spectacular range of hills. The highest point is on the w border towards Warwickshire: 804 ft (245 metres) near Arbury. Yet having said that the county is still very rural. There is much gentle rolling green countryside and woodland – it is after all a hunting county – and there are many attractive stone villages. The county's planners are to be congratulated in keeping most of the villages compact. There is hardly any ribbon development in Northamptonshire.

Northamptonshire, if sought out at all, will be sought out for its buildings. That makes it such a rewarding county, as far as this series of books is concerned – rewarding, though it has no old cathedral and no big city. The nearest cathedral town, Peterborough, is now outside the county, and Peterborough was made a cathedral only in 1541. Northampton until the 1950s had little more than 100,000 inhabitants. It is still a county of relatively small towns[*] and unforgettable villages and of country houses from the largest to the smallest. In the houses and the churches there is perpetual surprise and there are for the architectural historian perpetual puzzles.[†] The houses are decidedly weaker for the early than for the later centuries. They culminate, one is inclined to say, in the Elizabethan age, but do not lose interest to the end of the Georgian era. Late Georgian and Victorian new built houses are few. The churches on the other hand keep up an extremely high level of interest from the Early Anglo-Saxon centuries to the C14 and then begin to weaken, though there is some splendid Perpendicular work and very interesting C17 work, and there are several good Georgian interiors and some fine C19 and early C20 examples. For the period since 1850 there is more to be enjoyed from the secular buildings in the towns and in particular at Northampton. But before this architectural history can be traced, a few pages must be devoted to the soil from which building grows and to the, on the whole less important, periods which precede the Anglo-Saxon.

GEOLOGY AND BUILDING STONES
BY
D. S. SUTHERLAND

Northamptonshire along its length follows the band of Jurassic rocks that stretches across England sw to ne from the Dorset coast through the Cotswold hills to the Humber and into Yorkshire. The rocks formed as sediments on the floor of a shallow sea that covered much of Europe, lapping around islands

---

[*] The county population is (2011) bordering 785,000, of which Northampton has over 210,000, Kettering just over 90,000, Daventry some 80,000, Wellingborough nearly 76,000 and Corby just over 55,000.
[†] To the student the following are specially recommended as tests: Moulton, Raunds, Rothwell, Tansor and Woodford.

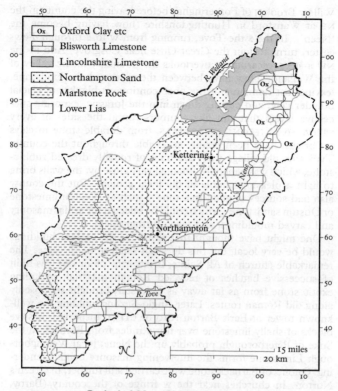

Ox — Oxford Clay etc
Blisworth Limestone
Lincolnshire Limestone
Northampton Sand
Marlstone Rock
Lower Lias

R. Welland

R. Nene

Kettering

Northampton

R. Tove

15 miles
20 km

Geological Map of Northamptonshire

of higher ground. But compared with the familiar limestone of the Cotswolds, the geology in Northamptonshire is more varied. Periodic changes in the shoreline gave a succession that oscillated between mud-rocks, sandstones and indeed, limestones, but also ironstones; and at times the sea retreated altogether, leaving Northamptonshire exposed to erosion, or covered inshore by wet marsh. The sequence of rocks may be variable, but the geological structure is very simple, the beds not quite horizontal, but tilted very slightly to the SE. The dip, though gentle, affects the outcrops so that the oldest (Lias) reaches the surface in the W, followed by successively younger rocks to the E. This pattern is interestingly displayed above ground by differences in the colour and character of buildings in the array of villages.

As long ago as 1712 John Morton observed 'how plentifully we are stor'd with Quarrystone' throughout the county – 'here of White Stone, there of Red'. Such abundance can be attributed to the work of the rivers. The Nene gathers itself together in the W near Weedon (where it is called the 'Nen') to form the main artery through the county, linking incoming valleys at Northampton, Wellingborough and Thrapston and receiving the long

Willow Brook N of Fotheringhay before leaving the county in the
NE at Wansford in Huntingdonshire (now having become the
'Neen'). In the S the Tove, running from W to E through Towcester, turns to join the Great Ouse near Cosgrove. And in the
NW a steep escarpment overlooks the boundary in the valley of
the Welland. They have between them created the landscape,
leaving just remnants of the once continuous blanket of glacial
boulder clay, and cutting down into the Jurassic, exposing successive layers that run like contours round the sides of every
valley. So BUILDING MATERIALS, from durable stone to clays
for bricks, have been readily accessible throughout the county.
Typically, old village walls are built of roughly dressed rubblestone, which was generally obtained very close by; the walls bring
to light a pleasing sample of the local geology. But the county
also had sources of good freestone – such as Weldon limestone
or Duston sandstone – which could be selected for ashlar masonry
and carved mouldings, and taken further afield.

One might have thought that stone for the earliest buildings
would be very local, but this does not seem to be the case. The
remarkable church of All Saints, Brixworth (C8 or C9) was built
of successive batches of recycled Roman material, including
exotic stone from as far away as Leicester, brought supposedly
along old Roman routes. Later Anglo-Saxons building the well-
known tower at Earls Barton (C10 or C11) transported massive
blocks of shelly limestone over thirty miles from Barnack in the
Soke of Peterborough, probably up the Nene; local Wellingborough Limestone forms the intervening masonry behind rendering. Quoins of Barnack stone were carried still further, to Green's
Norton. In churches near the W fringe of the county (Barby,
Crick, Newnham) pink or red sandstone from the Midlands
makes an appearance; in the S, Cotswold limestone (e.g. for the
W porch at Kings Sutton); and Ketton stone from Rutland is
used for the portico of All Saints, Northampton (1701). Otherwise, until canals and railways allowed easy transport, for example
from Bath, very little stone came from outside the county. Remnants of COB walling occur sporadically, mostly in the NW quadrant where Lower Lias or superficial deposits contribute little
building stone, but also in sandstone areas (Guilsborough, East
and West Haddon, Ravensthorpe, Hollowell). Villages on Liasdal
clay (e.g. Yelvertoft) are predominantly BRICK, but with stone
imported from adjacent outcrops.

In the western uplands overlooking the Cherwell valley and
among the headwaters of the Nene, villages are built of MARL-
STONE ROCK, a warm brown iron-rich limestone from the top of
the Middle Lias. The elegant churches of Kings Sutton and Middleton Cheney are built of it, and villages N to Ashby St Ledgers
and Crick. Rubblestone is common for church walls, but freestone was also available for interior piers. Around Byfield it is a
dark ironstone, once quarried as iron ore. Many Marlstone buildings show incompletely weathered stone, blocks having clove-
brown, purplish or greenish cores. The rock often contains fossils,
shells, brachiopods and belemnites, which can distinguish it from

rather similar brown building stone from the Northampton Sand. Hornton stone from Marlstone quarries near Edge Hill is often imported for restoration of Northamptonshire's brown stone buildings (e.g. Welsh House on Northampton's Market Square).

The later deposits of the Lias were clays, once the raw material for many brickworks. But the overlying Middle Jurassic produced a number of useful building stones, beginning with the NORTHAMPTON SAND FORMATION; it is not a sand, but includes sandy deposits that became cemented into sandstones. Most notably the rocks contain variable amounts of iron minerals, already oxidized by weathering in the ground, giving a selection of tawny, rusty and chestnut-coloured stones. Although often referred to as ironstone, not all the building stones are real ironstone, i.e. composed almost entirely of iron minerals. Some of the Northampton Sand did prove to be a workable ore, and from the C19 to the C20 it was quarried over a wide area between Towcester and Corby. The ironstone was also used for building. In Finedon and Wellingborough, where it was particularly durable, there are excellent examples from the C14 to the C20, in rather spice-like colours, with freestone for ashlar, even windowcases and door-cases, though most dressings are Weldon limestone. Northampton, however, has thick deposits of ferruginous sandstone, which provided rich brown building stone, some streaked with iron-rich layers, for the town's fine Norman churches and for rebuilding after the great fire of 1675. Good sandstones were quarried for centuries in the village of Harlestone, nearby at Duston, and SW at Eydon. In an area N and E of central Northampton more calcareous rocks occur within the Northampton Sand, and beige sandy limestone is seen in Boughton and Pitsford villages and in Abington. It was quarried at Kingsthorpe (for St Matthew's and other churches in Northampton), and good freestone was obtained at Mears Ashby, the village itself having mixed rubblestone of brown ironstone, golden limestone and very dark sandstone, from successive layers of the local Northampton Sand.

The E of the county by contrast is occupied by pale limestone villages, but several different limestones are separated in time geologically. The LINCOLNSHIRE LIMESTONE is the oldest, and though equivalent to the Inferior Oolite of the Cotswolds, it was laid down mainly in Lincolnshire, becoming thinner as it came into N Northamptonshire, and is missing SE of a line from Tansor to Kettering and Maidwell. It provided some of the best building stones. At the base is the sandy limestone yielding Collyweston 'slate', which was mined in underground galleries; this is not a true slate in the geological sense, but a cross-bedded limestone that, once it has been exposed to frost, happens to split easily into thin slabs, much favoured for roofing. Although very localized, the industry supplied huge quantities of stone slates for major buildings, not only in Northamptonshire, from the C14 until the late C20. The broad plateau of Lower Lincolnshire Limestone has furnished neat building blocks for attractive villages, most of them roofed with the local 'slate'. Quoins, windows and door cases are often of freestone, which comes from the Upper Lincolnshire Limestone. This stone is oolitic, that is, composed of spherical grains that formed on the sea floor; the distinctive texture is revealed with the help of a lens or magnifying glass. It has a patchy distribution, confined to channels that were scoured into the Lower Lincolnshire Limestone. The finest freestone in Northamptonshire was quarried at Weldon near Corby. It is a pale grey oolite with a few flakes of shell, and little visible cement. It was widely used for church windows, spires and towers (e.g. Titchmarsh, Whiston), and was transported outside the county to complete the glory of King's College Chapel in Cambridge. Many of Northamptonshire's great houses were built of Weldon stone (Deene, Kirby Hall, Rushton Hall, Boughton House and Lamport). Similar stone came from the village of Kingscliffe, and was used at Apethorpe. The churches of Fotheringhay and Lowick incorporate several of the freestones, and a good deal of oolitic Lincolnshire Limestone (from Weldon, and Ketton in Rutland) is seen in Oundle.

The Great Oolite Group begins with sands and soft clays, deposited mainly inshore with only periodic incursions of the sea. The thin WELLINGBOROUGH LIMESTONE formed in one of these episodes, and is characteristically full of oyster shell, a local building stone seen in Pytchley and Great Doddington. It thickens to the S, and was quarried at Helmdon in the C13 for the Eleanor Cross in Northampton (the cross in Geddington is Weldon stone), and the early C18 for Easton Neston. It continues further S as the Taynton Limestone.

The main limestone seen from Aynho and Brackley in the S, through E Northamptonshire to Fotheringhay in the N, is the BLISWORTH LIMESTONE (formerly called Great Oolite Limestone). As a building stone it varies, mainly providing light-coloured rubblestone for the many villages, but locally there was good freestone. Cosgrove had ancient quarries, some worked underground; they were known to John Morton in the early C18, and were the source of fine ashlar for Cosgrove Hall and probably also for Stoke Park (C17). The limestone at St Peter, Northampton (C12), is rather similar, cross-bedded, granular, shelly, and not oolitic. The limestone around the Nene valley includes more powdery-weathering rock, but good stone was available for the churches at Higham Ferrers, Stanwick and Raunds. From quarries close to Oundle came shelly limestone for ashlar buildings as well as rubblestone. In the central limestone area we also see some striking buildings in which limestone is combined with ironstone in stripes. Chichele's Bede House (C15) in Higham Ferrers churchyard is an example, and readily explained by the underlying geology. Higham Ferrers is built on the E slope of the Nene valley. The Nene for much of its length runs on Lower Jurassic Lias, among more recent deposits of gravel which as they are exploited leave a chain of lakes; in the valley sides are the strata of the Middle Jurassic, layers of stone alternating with soft sand or clay, with Northampton Sand ironstone low down, separated by about 10 metres from the overlying Blisworth

Limestone; higher ground then rises through Blisworth Clay, Cornbrash limestone and Kellaways beds to the Oxford Clay that stretches away E of the county.

An interesting stone that turns up sometimes in buildings is TUFA. Small patches of calcium carbonate can form locally near springs, sometimes hardening into a porous rock; a deposit at Weston Favell may be the source of tufa seen in Abington church. It is a major component in the stair-turret and tower at Brix-worth, but its origin could be outside the county. Church monuments for the most part are made of exotic stone, usually polished MARBLE from Europe, or recognizable Purbeck 'marble' from Dorset, alabaster from the East Midlands, or 'clunch' from the chalk of Cambridgeshire. But certain local limestone beds which were hard, sparry and full of fossil shells, as noted by Morton, could be polished like marble; they include Weldon Rag from the Lincolnshire Limestone, e.g. a Brudenell monument at Deene (1664), and similar ornamental stone with fossils obtained from the Blisworth Limestone at Raunds and Stanwick. Morton cited a Montagu monument at Weekley (1644) as an example of 'Rance [Raunds] Ragg'. A wall monument at Lowick for baby William Mordaunt (†1625) is of this same stone.

PREHISTORIC AND ROMAN NORTHAMPTONSHIRE

BY

ANDREW CHAPMAN

Prehistory

In the fifty years since the publication of the first edition of this guide, the processes of archaeological investigation have undergone several transformations that have resulted in a huge increase in the number of known and investigated archaeological sites, making the task of producing a concise summary of the current state of knowledge all the more difficult. In 1960 archaeological fieldwork was conducted by local amateur groups and the relatively small number of university or museum-based academic archaeologists. By the mid 1960s, freelance professional archaeologists were responding to the rapid pace of development with rescue archaeology, and in Northamptonshire Dennis Jackson in particular produced significant work on Iron Age settlements and other prehistoric sites threatened by ironstone and gravel quarrying. By the early 1970s there was a more systematic approach, with the formation of the Northampton Development Corporation Archaeological Unit and the Northamptonshire County Council Archaeology Unit, supported by local and central government grants, the goodwill of developers and schemes to provide temporary work for the unemployed. A major change occurred in 1990, when developers became responsible for funding necessary archaeological works. Local government archaeology units became commercial businesses competing to win tenders to carry out archaeological works defined within the developers' planning permissions, and this has produced an even greater increase in the quantity of fieldwork. The last decade has also seen a resurgence of local societies carrying out substantial fieldwork projects.

As recorded in the first edition of this book, the small number of known prehistoric sites was seen as a genuine reflection of a low level of activity across a county that 'was probably covered with dense forest . . . well into historical times'. Our knowledge of most periods has now expanded beyond all expectations as a result of the opportunities provided by the continuing expansion and redevelopment of our towns and the impact on the rural landscape of quarrying, new roads and out-of-town developments such as sprawling business parks. The techniques generating the new knowledge have been aerial photography, geophysical survey, fieldwalking and open area excavation. Coverage has been uneven, with the Nene valley attracting the greatest attention, while across the S of the county there has been less development to generate opportunities for fieldwork.

Understanding of the PALAEOLITHIC period remains largely dependent on the chance recovery of flint implements, typically during gravel quarrying. Fewer than one hundred stone artefacts of the Lower and Middle Palaeolithic, mainly Acheulian handaxes, have been recovered, and the only certain Upper Palaeolithic artefact is a reindeer antler 'Lyngby' axe found at Grendon quarry in 1982, dating to near the end of the last Ice Age, around 10,000 years ago. This would have been associated with glacial lake deposits that lie beneath the River Nene gravels between Northampton and Earls Barton/Grendon.

MESOLITHIC studies are also dependent on flint artefacts, and those recovered during fieldwalking and excavation attest to the wide roaming of these hunter gatherers, but it has also been possible to identify specific sites. In addition to the flint assemblage identified in the early C20 at Duston (Northampton), a substantial assemblage was gathered over years of fieldwalking at Honey Hill, near Cold Ashby, on the uplands in the W. Subsequently, a broader picture was provided by programmes of systematic fieldwalking, as in the Raunds area in the 1980s, indicating a general preference for the permeable geologies along the River Nene and its tributaries. While there are some upland sites, these still avoided the heavy claylands. A significant quantity of Late Mesolithic flint was recovered from the soils forming a Neolithic mound at West Cotton, Raunds, at the confluence of the Nene and the Raunds brook, and recent work at Irchester Roman town has recovered Mesolithic flints from buried soils beneath the Roman deposits, in a similar riverside location.

The appearance of the EARLY NEOLITHIC herding and farming communities in the upper Nene valley from 4000 B.C. was once marked only by the flint assemblage from Duston. Aerial photography has located possible Neolithic CAUSEWAYED ENCLOSURES, all around 220 yds (200 metres) in diameter, at

Briar Hill and Dallington (Northampton), and at Southwick in the NE of the county. The excavation in the 1970s of the Briar Hill enclosure, on the slopes below Hunsbury hill-fort, showed a history of Early Neolithic construction followed by later reuse, including small pits containing assemblages of pottery and flint dating to the Middle and Late Neolithic; a small Late Neolithic timber structure associated with grooved ware pottery, and perhaps the earliest timber building recorded in the county; pottery of the Early Bronze Age; and a Middle Bronze Age cremation cemetery.

While causewayed enclosures acted as focal points for the living, the burial places of the dead were also significant in the Neolithic landscape. There are possible but unproven LONG BARROWS in the SW of the county, but the only excavated example lay at Stanwick at the S end of the Raunds/Stanwick Neolithic and Bronze Age monument complex, which extended along the valley for 1¼ m., with the N end marked by a Neolithic turf mound 148 yds (135 metres) long. While no other long barrows are known along the River Nene, Early to Middle Neolithic OVAL BARROWS were a local variation that served the same function. The known examples at Grendon, Aldwinkle and Tansor (and Orton Longueville, Peterborough), together with the long barrow at Stanwick, were at intervals of 6½–8¾ m. along the Nene valley, perhaps marking territories.

Recent work in the vicinity of the Briar Hill (Northampton) enclosure has identified some elements of the broader Neolithic landscape. At Banbury Lane, 1 m. W of Briar Hill, a triple-ditched circular monument, 25 yds (23 metres) in diameter, excavated in 2011, had an entrance blocked by a pit filled with disarticulated human bone, dated to the MIDDLE NEOLITHIC (3300–3000 B.C.). This deposit of selected bones, mainly long bones and particularly thigh bones, appears to derive from the forcible dismemberment of the bodies of some 130 people. The scale of the assemblage tells us that there was a considerable local population, even if the nature of the catastrophe that befell them remains uncertain. At the domestic level, the chance find of a small Middle Neolithic cremation cemetery to the S of Briar Hill, at Milton Ham, is probably representative of the nature of local settlement, centred on family groups. Across the county there have also been finds of small clusters of pits dating to the Middle and LATE NEOLITHIC (3000–2500 B.C.) containing offerings of pottery sherds, animal bone and other items. These pits probably mark the temporary camps of people who were still at least seasonally nomadic while moving their herds to the best grazing.

A classic HENGE monument was excavated in 2011 on the uplands E of Corby, at Priors Hall, and another may lie within the Dallington causewayed enclosure. Traditionally, these have been regarded as monuments of the Late Neolithic, but evidence from across the country now suggests that the characteristic ditch and external bank may often date to the beginning of the EARLY BRONZE AGE (2500–1500 B.C.), often in association with Beaker pottery, as at Priors Hall. This period is, however, characterized

by the ROUND BARROW burial mound. It was formerly thought
that the sparse scatter of known examples, such as the Three Hills
barrows at Woodford overlooking the Nene valley, the group
within the hill-fort at Borough Hill, Daventry, others lost to
ironstone quarrying on the Jurassic ridge in the NE, and isolated
barrow mounds at Boughton, Sulgrave and other locations, indicated a low level of occupation. However, aerial photography has
now revealed the ditches of numerous plough-flattened barrows,
both single examples and forming small barrow cemeteries,
including many along the River Nene and its tributaries. Multi-
ditched round barrows at Raunds and Stanwick, 1 m. apart,
excavated in the 1980s, had richly furnished central inhumation
burials accompanied by highly decorated Beaker pots, flint
daggers, jet buttons and other items. These barrows and others
had been added to a Neolithic monument complex, as also
occurred at Grendon, Aldwinkle and Tansor. At Ashton, near
Oundle, in the 1980s and Warmington in the 1990s, the excavation of later period sites fortuitously located Beaker inhumation
burials in graves with no encircling ditches and perhaps, therefore, no substantial mounds. After 2000 B.C. cremation took over
from inhumation as the normal burial rite, with the ashes interred
within large pottery urns, often highly decorated. A barrow at
Earls Barton, excavated in the 1960s, belonged to the later centuries of the Early Bronze Age and overlay a cremation burial
accompanied by a Wessex-style bronze dagger.

Throughout the Early Bronze Age settlement evidence is
again limited to small clusters of pits containing small groups of
pottery sherds and other artefacts, similar to those of the later
Neolithic.

From the MIDDLE TO LATE BRONZE AGE (1500–700 B.C.)
and the EARLY IRON AGE (700–450 B.C.), there are hoards and
individual finds of BRONZE AXES and other metalwork, but as a
result of the scant evidence that they left behind, few burial and
settlement sites have been recognized. Middle Bronze Age CRE-
MATION CEMETERIES have been excavated at Briar Hill, Chapel
Brampton, on the A14 near Kelmarsh, and at the E end of the
Stanwick Long Barrow, but when not associated with an earlier
monument, discovering these clusters of ashes in small pits is a
matter of chance. A substantial circular ditched enclosure,
109 yds (100 metres) in diameter, excavated in the 1990s at
Thrapston, is probably a high-status settlement and is exceptional for this period. Late Bronze Age to Early Iron Age settlements tend to comprise loose scatters of small pits and post-holes,
as located by chance at Gretton, Great Oakley, Upton and Harlestone quarry, although extensive excavations at Raunds also
located a network of field boundary ditches, similar to those seen
around the Fen edge to the E.

The settlement at Harlestone quarry is adjacent to a PIT
ALIGNMENT, the most enigmatic landscape feature of the first
millennium B.C., with numerous examples recorded by aerial
photography. They comprise lines of pits, often consistently
square or circular, running for hundreds of yards, apparently

forming land boundaries. Many examples have been examined, as at Raunds, Wollaston, Upton and Briar Hill (Northampton), but they produce little in the way of finds, although a hoard of iron currency bars was associated with a pit alignment at Gretton. Radiocarbon dating indicates that they were functioning between the C8 and C5 B.C., although some were replaced by ditches in the Middle Iron Age or even as late as the Early Roman period, as at Wollaston.

Fifty years ago the known Iron Age HILL-FORTS at Arbury (Badby), Rainsborough (Newbottle), Borough Hill (Daventry) and Hunsbury Hill (Northampton) stood almost alone as representatives of Iron Age settlement. Further hill-forts, with largely levelled earthworks, at Guilsborough, Farthingstone, Irthlingborough and Whittlebury can now be added to the list, and others await confirmation. The origin of hill-forts, which formed the focal centres for tribal groups, lay in the Early Iron Age, although few have been well dated. Borough Hill (Daventry) was a focal point in the later Bronze Age, and the earthworks encircling the hilltop may have had a particularly early origin. Many hill-forts continued in use or were reused through the MIDDLE and LATE IRON AGE (450–50 B.C.). At Hunsbury, the interior was lost to ironstone quarrying in the C19 and numerous grain storage pits were discovered. These produced a major assemblage of finds including over one hundred rotary querns and distinctive burnished globular pottery bowls with curvilinear decoration, dating to the C1 B.C.

With the exception of a small ditched enclosure at Draughton, discovered during wartime airfield construction in the 1940s, ordinary DOMESTIC SETTLEMENTS remained almost invisible until the 1960s when aerial photography revealed how common they were, with perhaps one every half mile along the Nene valley. The characteristic settlement of the Middle and Late Iron Age was the family farmstead, comprising a single ditch enclosing a principal ROUND-HOUSE and perhaps one or two subsidiary round-houses and a stock corral. There were also larger settlements of ten to twenty round-houses, often unenclosed. These may have formed small villages but there is evidence to suggest that they functioned on a communal basis, with a central principal house, subsidiary houses (perhaps separated by gender and age), and specific areas for craft activities such as spinning and weaving, bone working and metalworking. The sudden appearance and rapid spread of settlement from around 450 B.C. reflects population growth that was at least partly caused by incomers from the S and, ultimately, the Continent, and the need for territorial definition can be seen in the long boundary ditches that often sat beside these settlements.

Understanding of these settlements has come from the pioneering excavations of Dennis Jackson, beginning in the mid 1960s, at Brigstock, Wakerley, Weekley and Twywell, and has continued through the work of the county unit and commercial archaeologists over the past two decades at Wollaston, Crick (Daventry Rail Freight Terminal), Earls Barton, Wilby Way,

Barton Seagrave, along the A43 new road SW of Towcester, and in numerous other more partial investigations.

Burial evidence in the Iron Age is limited to occasional crouched burials in disused storage pits. An older woman at Great Houghton had a lead collar, perhaps in imitation of silver, around her neck, but the remains of the majority of the population were not buried in the ground.

Northamptonshire, with its extensive deposits of ironstone, has produced evidence of iron smelting in the Iron Age, particular in the NE around Corby, and copper-alloy working also remained important, although the decorated bronze scabbard from Hunsbury (in Northampton Museum) and the decorated bronze mirror from Desborough (in the British Museum) are rare finds of high-quality metalwork.

By the CI A.D. Northamptonshire lay on the southern borders of the extensive territory of the *Corieltauvi*, centred on Leicester and extending across the East Midlands as far as the Humber. The Belgic culture coming in from the Continent with refugees from Roman Gaul, which dominated the territory of the *Catuvellauni* to the S, made some impact, with larger Belgic settlements at Duston and Irchester, but many of the smaller settlements show few signs of cultural change up to their abandonment following the Roman conquest.

Roman Northamptonshire

The ROMAN CONQUEST (A.D. 43) and occupation brought changes that are visible at all levels of the archaeological record. The construction of a national network of surfaced ROADS, initially driven by the need to enable rapid movement of troops and supplies, provided a permanent practical legacy, parts of which have endured to the present day, with Watling Street, linking London and Chester, still a major highway, the A5 trunk road. Within Northamptonshire two small walled towns lay on Watling Street, *Lactodorum*, the modern Towcester, and *Bannaventa*, near Norton. The only other road of comparable strategic importance is the Gartree Road, which crosses the N of the county near Corby, linking Leicester to Godmanchester on Ermine Street. Although its course is only partly defined, a further road system ran the length of the Nene valley, linking Towcester and *Bannaventa* to the small towns at Duston (Northampton), Irchester and Titchmarsh, the latter at the junction with the Gartree Road, before continuing N past the small town of Ashton (near Oundle) to *Durobrivae*, near Water Newton (Huntingdonshire).

The Roman small TOWNS have seen varying levels of investigation. At Towcester (*Lactodorum*) there is an ongoing process of investigation as parts of the town and its environs undergo redevelopment, but much of the small-scale work remains unpublished. The line of the W defences, created in the later C2, has long been known and partly survives in earthwork, and in the 1990s the line of the defences to the S was established, running along Richmond Road. To the N, the walled town of *Bannaventa* is part of a five-year investigation led by the Community Landscape and Archaeology Survey Project (CLASP). The geophysical survey of the entire town and its environs should provide the opportunity to reconstruct the Roman landscape in some detail. In the Nene valley, the walled town of Irchester (Chester Farm) had seen antiquarian interest, and from the 1950s onwards as the adjacent road, the A45, was upgraded, the town defences and areas of Late Iron Age settlement were examined. In the 2000s, development to the W saw excavation of more elements of Iron Age settlement as well as part of the Roman W suburb, where a row of industrial buildings stood beside a road running E towards the town. A programme of assessment has involved geophysical survey of the suburbs and the walled town, which has recovered detailed plans of individual buildings, and the square Romano-Celtic temple has also been reopened to establish how well it had survived antiquarian investigation. With the purchase of Chester Farm by the County Council, the Roman town will become a major heritage resource. In the E of the county, excavation within the Roman town at Ashton, near Oundle, in the 1980s in advance of road improvements, uncovered a Late Roman cemetery and stone buildings set alongside a road. It is suspected that the Roman town at Titchmarsh, on the junction with the Gartree Road, was of considerable importance, but much of the town has been lost, with little archaeological coverage.

It has only been in recent decades that aerial photography and excavation have provided a landscape of NATIVE SETTLEMENT. It appears that existing Iron Age settlements were largely abandoned after the Roman occupation and new settlements were created nearby. These typically comprise rectangular enclosures and trackways, although traces of rectangular timber houses are only rarely found. The later C1 saw the development of the simple row-type VILLA, with stone foundations, as at Quinton, Piddington, Brixworth and Redlands Farm, Stanwick. In the NE, timber round-houses appear to have remained in use longer, being replaced in the C2 by villas and timber-aisled halls. Through the C3 and C4 smaller villas might retain a simple row and corridor form, with a small bath suite at one end, as at Wootton Fields (Northampton), but others became more elaborate with the addition of wings and complex bath suites. The corridors had tessellated pavements and the reception rooms might have under-floor heating and mosaic pavements, as at Piddington, excavated by the Upper Nene Archaeological Society from since 1979, Whitehall Farm villa (near Weedon), excavated by CLASP through the 2000s, and others such as Cotterstock, Weldon and Thenford. Earlier excavation tended to focus on the villa buildings alone, while recent work is interested in establishing these building within their landscape, as at Stanwick, where the excavation of 10 ha (25 acres) in the 1980s located the villa and its estate buildings, including barns, small houses for the workers and a possible bailiff's residence, enabling the tenurial and social relationships of the villa to be reconstructed.

Work at Wollaston quarry in the 1990s located the trenches for a vineyard attached to a villa. The presence of local ironstone was the basis for an IRON SMELTING INDUSTRY, with production associated with several villas, such as Stanion and Wootton Fields (Northampton), although the most notably example is the industrial-scale production at Laxton. Small groups of Early Roman pottery kilns are common finds, as at Weston Favell and Delapré (Northampton) in the 1950s and the 2000s, while the Late Iron Age and Early Roman pottery industry at Rushden was on a grander scale, producing exotic slip-decorated ware.

RELIGIOUS LIFE in Roman Northamptonshire is seen through structures such as a square Romano-Celtic shrine within Irchester Roman town, and the circular and polygonal shrines at Brigstock and Collyweston, while at Stanwick a polygonal shrine was built over a Bronze Age round barrow. In the Late Roman period, the coming of Christianity is marked by lead tanks from Ashton and Rushton bearing the *chi-rho* motif.

MEDIEVAL NORTHAMPTONSHIRE

*Anglo-Saxon**

At the beginning of the C5 (A.D. 410) Rome left Britain to its own defences, and through the following century incoming ANGLO-SAXON settlers gradually achieved dominance and carved out what became the Anglo-Saxon kingdoms. Northamptonshire lay in the S of Mercia. In Northamptonshire this change is visible in the archaeological record through the abandonment of the Roman towns and villas, apart from the occasional small timber buildings and burials somewhere nearby, as seen at Wollaston, Whitehall Farm, Wootton Fields and Stanwick. A pattern of dispersed small settlements reappeared, as has been investigated in the Raunds area through extensive fieldwalking, and seen in excavations at Upton (Northampton) and on the Brixworth bypass, while several sunken-featured buildings have been found within the Briar Hill causewayed enclosure. There was also Early–Middle Saxon occupation at Northampton. Numerous Anglo-Saxon CEMETERIES have been investigated over the past century, as at Nassington, but there has been little recent work since the excavation at the end of the 1960s of the cemetery at Wakerley, which contained eighty-five burials accompanied by a wide range of grave goods. A single burial within a large grave on the margins of the floodplain below Wollaston, excavated in the 1990s, was accompanied by a sword, bowl and a helmet adorned with a crest depicting a boar; this was only the fourth Anglo-Saxon helmet to have been found in England, after those at Sutton Hoo, Suffolk; Benty Grange, Derbyshire; and Jorvik,

---

* I am grateful to Andrew Chapman and David Parsons for the opening paragraphs of this chapter.

York. A small cemetery near Great Houghton, however, dated to the later C7, is probably Early Christian. It pre-dates the appearance of cemeteries attached to churches, and may provide the earliest evidence for the conversion of the local population.

In the C9 that part of the county N and E of Watling Street was overrun by the Danes and incorporated in their territory, the Danelaw. Place names ending in -by, such as the Ashbys or Naseby, are Danish.

Brixworth must stand at the beginning of any survey of the great SAXON CHURCHES. As it was in all probability founded and built in the late C8 or early C9,* it is one of the largest and most orderly surviving buildings of its date N of the Alps. It was built with much Roman brick, used in the voussoirs of arches in a technically uninformed way. It has regular N and S arcades with tall and wide openings. Some of these definitely gave into *porticus*, i.e. separate side-chambers, rather than aisles. The chancel may have been divided from the nave by tripartite arcading, just as had been done a little earlier at Reculver in Kent and elsewhere in the S E of England. The form of the original E apse is unknown and the existing polygonal shape externally is a product of a major refurbishment, probably before the end of the C9. It is a rather late use of an Early Christian form from Syria. This apse was surrounded by a sunk, tunnel-vaulted passage forming what one now calls a ring crypt. Crypts with a passage running concentrically inside the line of the apse go back to Gregory the Great's adaptation *c.* 600 of the apsidal W end of Old St Peter's to give access to the saint's memoria. Archaeology has shown that this arrangement was widely adopted in early European churches. The precise layout represented by the Brixworth ring crypt is less common, but there is a close parallel at St Emmeram in Regensburg, which was in use by 791. At the W end Brixworth had a range of five compartments, the central one acting as an entry porch. This was retained in the C9 rebuilding, when a tower was constructed using the porch as its base. There are several other important Anglo-Saxon towers in Northamptonshire. Brigstock and Brixworth have a rounded projection from the W wall, the latter containing a barrel-vaulted staircase. Arcading with pilasters and triangle-heads ran along the exterior of the nave at Geddington. At Green's Norton is a triangular-headed Anglo-Saxon doorway in the E wall of the nave above the chancel arch, and there is some more minor Anglo-Saxon evidence, as there is in other Northamptonshire churches (e.g. at Nassington, Pattishall and Church Stowe). It should be remembered that just over the border in the Soke of Peterborough are Barnack and Wittering. One more major work of Anglo-Saxon architecture must be added: the tower at Earls Barton. Like Barnack, this is one of the most spectacular examples of the Late Saxon passion for a matchstick-like decoration of outer surfaces by lesenes or pilaster-strips and arches and triangles of the same unmoulded

---

* The traditional date of *c.* 675 has been disqualified by excavation (*see* Brixworth, p. 139).

rectangular section. Lesenes stand on arches quite unconcerned
with the structural sense of the arch and the lesene. Structural
motifs are converted into pure decoration. The tower is large and
broad and stands at the W end of the church. It was wider than
the part which followed to the E, and it has therefore been
assumed that this part was the chancel and that the tower represented the nave and not a W attachment to the nave. There is
however no indication of a W porch.

There were also Saxon churches at Northampton, one with a
dedication to St Gregory suggesting a foundation of the C7 or
C8. The other, to St Peter, was rebuilt in the mid C12 but in the
Saxon period it may have had almost minster status and had an
important shrine, probably that of the Anglo-Saxon prince St
Ragener, nephew of St Edmund, slain in battle in 870. At that
time the church was part of a large palace-like collection of
DOMESTIC BUILDINGS which was partially excavated in 1980–2.
There, E of the church, the major discovery was a substantial
timber hall of the C8, 98 ft (30 metres) long and 30 ft (9 metres)
wide, with a central hall and narrower end chambers. In the C9
the timber hall was rebuilt in stone and this, along with further
church building, used mortar produced in circular rotary mortar
mixers, which have also been found in association with early
churches at Monkwearmouth, Aelfric's abbey at Eynsham, Wall-
ingford, and on the Continent. To this evidence can be added
that of Anglo-Saxon halls at Sulgrave, revealed by excavation in
1967–76, and Furnells Manor, Raunds. At the latter, excavation
has revealed that post-built halls of the C9, with probable Scan-
dinavian connections, were replaced in the mid C10, following
the reconquest of the Danelaw, by a regular system of rectangular
plots that contained a stave-built timber hall and associated
ranges. A small stone church and a surrounding churchyard were
added in the later C10 and continued in use into the Norman
period, with the hall rebuilt as a timber aisled hall. A parallel
sequence occurred nearby at West Cotton (*see* Stanwick), where
a set of rectangular plots laid out in the mid C10 contained a
timber hall and ancillary buildings, accompanied by a watermill.
Soon after the Norman Conquest the timber hall was replaced
by a stone hall, with a detached kitchen range, dovecote and barn.

ANGLO-SAXON SCULPTURE is well represented in Northamptonshire, although the most important pieces now lie outside the
county. These are the Hedda Stone at Peterborough Cathedral,
which is assigned to the late C7, and belongs together stylistically
with a stone at Fletton outside Peterborough, a stone at Castor,
and some of the work at Breedon-on-the-Hill in Leicestershire.
One major piece is the grave slab in Northampton St Peter of
C10 or C11 date. This is thought to have been part of the shrine
of St Ragener, hence its elaborate decoration with its Green Man
type head and the intricate trails which issue from it. The symbolism of its various elements is a matter for discussion. There
is then the fine, if small, slab with an eagle, probably the symbol
of St John, at Brixworth may be late C8 and makes one regret
that not more is preserved. Fragments of Anglo-Saxon crosses

are abundant (Brixworth, Church Stowe, Dallington, Desborough, Lutton, Mears Ashby, Moreton Pinkney, Moulton, Nassington and Northampton St Peter), but none is of the first order.

Norman and Early English churches

The Norman style is essentially a style of clear demarcations, as is the Romanesque style everywhere in Europe – that Romanesque style of which the Norman is the English national variety. With the exclusion from the county not only of Peterborough, but also of the spectacularly decorated church at Castor, a survey of NORMAN CHURCHES has to begin with the two very impressive but exceptional examples in Northampton, Holy Sepulchre and St Peter, the former early to late C12, the latter of *c*. 1130–40. Holy Sepulchre, though only a parish church, is one of the few medieval round churches in England; St Peter is startlingly lavish (perhaps because of its proximity to the former castle of Northampton) and exhibits a motif usual in cathedrals, but highly unusual in parish churches: namely alternation of supports, a feature which incidentally occurs at Peterborough. Moreover – an equally unusual motif – there are shafts reaching right up to the roof to support the principal beams. The capitals are of many varieties, and there is in addition an extremely sumptuous tower arch – one of the many Norman arches in the county which, whether tower arch, crossing arch, or chancel arch, cannot here be enumerated.* The figured tympanum at Holy Sepulchre is early C12; of other tympana Barton Seagrave has an ill-assembled one, and the tympanum at Pitsford is stylistically significant in its sculpture. But Northamptonshire has on the whole little of Norman architectural sculpture. The best is at Wakerley where there are very fine historiated capitals by the workshop from Castor in the Soke of Peterborough.

The cruciform plan can be regarded as the most usual Norman plan, although it has in later centuries often been abolished or disguised, either by removing the crossing and its tower, removing the transepts or widening aisles until their walls were flush with those of the transepts. Crossing towers could carry bells. Kingscliffe was probably always cruciform, so too St Giles Northampton and Rothwell. Twywell, which is to this day essentially a Norman building, may have had a transept. Sometimes there was a central tower without transepts, as at Barton Seagrave. In other cases w towers were built (Gayton, Great Doddington, Harringworth, Nassington). St Peter Northampton and Spratton are two specially ornate examples. The motif used for enrichment is blank arcading, as it was also used inside the building, e.g. in the chancels of Earls Barton and Kings Sutton. Where village churches were very small, already the Norman age replaced towers for the bells by simple bellcotes. Northampton has a rare

10

11

* The Corpus of Romanesque Sculpture records over a hundred churches where there is something of the Norman period.

assembly of Norman church plans with the round form of Holy
Sepulchre, the basilica form of St Peter's and the cruciform plan
at St Giles and All Saints.

Returning to Norman SCULPTURE there is more figure-work
to be found on FONTS. As in all English counties, fonts were
preserved more faithfully than any other objects, and so Northamptonshire still possesses well over a dozen worthwhile Norman
examples. They were the work of the masons of the churches, as
is proved by that remarkable inscription at Little Billing (outer
Northampton) which commemorates *Wigberhtus artifex atq*
cementarius. As for scenes carved on fonts, West Haddon has the
Baptism of Christ, the Nativity, the Entry into Jerusalem, and
Christ in Glory. Braybrooke is an example of how absurd an
arrangement of figures the Norman carver and his clients were
ready to tolerate. The font at Crick rests on three kneeling figures,
an Italian motif, less surprising if one remembers the north
Italian influences noticeable in the Norman sculpture of Ely
Cathedral. Many more fonts have ornamental decoration only,
ranging from simple and repetitive intersected arcading, perhaps
with an additional trail of foliage (St John Brackley, East Haddon),
or lunettes with some stylized leaf enrichment (Paulerspury, Tiffield, Weedon Lois), to complicated, crazily entangled patterns
(Harpole).

Besides fonts it is DOORWAYS which were often preserved and
even re-erected when the rest of a wall or a church was remodelled. We do not know the reasons for this. Was it respect for
elaborate carving? One would like to think so; for much loving
care was lavished on the jambs and arches of doorways. Many of
them of course are naïve and lacking in accomplishment. As a
rule they belong to the later rather than the earlier C12. Ornamental motifs are the ubiquitous zigzag (Great Addington, Little
Harrowden, Spratton), again frequently used at right angles to
the surface as well as on it. If such zigzags meet at the angle the
impression is of lozenges broken round the angle (e.g. the C19
reconstruction of the crossing arch at St Giles Northampton). As
far as figure-work goes the motif of the beakhead and allied
motifs can be found here and there (Earls Barton, Pitsford,
Roade), though not often. Perhaps the most sumptuous doorway
is that of Castle Ashby, and here a late date is proved instructively
by the use side by side of the Norman motif of zigzag and the
E.E. motif of the dogtooth.

Northamptonshire has plenty of interesting instances of the
many ways in which the transition from Norman to E.E. could
be effected. They can be studied most profitably in the ARCADES
between nave and aisles. The hallmark of the C12 is the circular
pier with the square abacus. At Gretton for instance it appears
in the N arcade with scalloped capitals and round arches with roll
mouldings, i.e. at the Peterborough stage. The details are paralleled at Duddington. They are all still completely Norman. The
Transitional can then make itself felt in a variety of ways: the
keeling of shafts; the replacement of the scalloped by the waterleaf capital (Pilton, waterleaf side by side with dogtooth), and
then the crocket capital (Polebrook, N arcade, also together with

dogtooth) and the stiff-leaf capital; the replacement of the square by the octagonal and then the circular abacus (the latter already at Holy Sepulchre Northampton and then at Grendon and Woodford); and the replacement of the round by the pointed arch (Harringworth, with waterleaf responds). The latter however came sometimes very late (cf. Leicestershire and Rutland). At Barnwell Castle round-headed doorways exist of as late a date as the 1260s, perhaps because they appeared a safer, more solid form than the pointed arch. Similarly bell-openings of towers right into the late C13 often have twin pointed arches under one round arch. The details of the arches are of importance too. They develop from the unmoulded section of the Early Norman style by way of the heavy roll mouldings to a single-step section, slight chamfers, and finally the full double-chamfer which remained standard through the C13 and was still in use in the C14 and C15, when no special elaboration was aimed at. When the C13 wanted to be elaborate it could design the most complex mouldings with fine but strong rolls and deep hollows.

Exact dating within the stages between Norman and E.E. is impossible. All that can be said is that by the arrival of the early C13 the EARLY ENGLISH style was complete. There is plenty of evidence of the C13 in the county, both major and minor. In the famous W tower of Raunds the design is far from harmonious, and it would be hard to suggest what made the master mason choose this restless arrangement of motifs. He was obviously not satisfied with the simple blank arcading continued from Norman precedent in such towers as those of Brackley St John, Burton Latimer, Chelveston, Higham Ferrers, Mears Ashby, Moreton Pinkney, Stanwick and Wadenhoe. He desired something livelier even at the expense of jettisoning logic.

The tower of Raunds is crowned by a broach spire, and so we have arrived at a first form of Northamptonshire SPIRES. Broaches perhaps need an explanation. They are a device to link a square tower with an octagonal spire. The four broaches are a more or less steep pyramid, remaining a fragment because penetrated by the spire. Of the lower part of the spire proper only the four cardinal sides start at once. They begin in the middles of the sides of the pyramid. The relation of pyramid, i.e. broaches, to spire proper can vary from very large to very small broaches, and from a moderate steepness of the spire to needle-thinness. At Raunds e.g. the broaches are tall, at Warmington, at Barnwell and at Pilton they are small and low. The variation in outline caused by the proportions of broaches to whole spire must be studied in the field. Generally speaking the tower with broach spire tends to have a blunt, direct, unsophisticated character. Not all towers, of course, received their spires at once. Often one can trace a development through a century and more from the lower parts of the tower to the spire. Some few towers were finished by saddleback roofs and have preserved them (Cold Higham, Maidford, Rothersthorpe, Wadenhoe).

Among the parish churches of Northamptonshire the most beautifully and unifiedly E.E. is Warmington. Polebrook is as consistently E.E. but lacks unity. Hargrave is on a smaller scale.

16 Warmington has the very rare distinction – rare in English parish
churches – of a rib-vault over the nave, even if that vault is made
of timber, not of stone. The usual thing in England is the open
timber roof or the flat ceiling concealing the structural timber.
On a smaller scale C13 stone vaulting was occasionally used, e.g.
in the porches at Warmington and Woodford. They have blank
arcading too, and this overplayed motif is also to be found –
admittedly an effective display – in the porch at Weldon, the N
transept at Polebrook, and the chancels of Cogenhoe, Denford
and Newton Bromswold (Dec) and to a lesser extent at
Woodford.

The C13 churches of Northamptonshire have naves accompanied by aisles, with one delightful exception, the extremely rare
case of the unaisled, two-naved church of Hannington with its
beautiful tall circular piers. The circular pier is one of the accepted
C13 PIER TYPES, though more frequent at the beginning than the
end of the century when octagonal piers become common. The
C13 innovation is the quatrefoil pier, and this is used more often
than can be listed. But other freer forms also occur already in
the early C13, notably the alternating circular and square piers,
both with demi-shafts at Rothwell, and the piers with big keeled
shafts in the diagonals and thin coupled shafts in the cardinal
directions at Brafield. Rothwell, which is the largest parish church
in the county, was followed by others, and so the circular pier
with the demi-shafts is met at Loddington and Welford, the
square pier with demi-shafts at Burton Latimer. Another variant
is the pier of four shafts and four hollows, which became standard
in the Perp style, and which occurs in the tower arch at Higham
Ferrers and, strangely enough, set diagonally at Cogenhoe. The
date here is before 1281. The quatrefoil pier also appears with
thin rectangular shafts in the diagonals and fillets at Brackley St
John, and the extravagant multiplication of shafts – groups of
three in each of the cardinal directions – at Rothersthorpe, Flore
and Great Billing leads into the C14.

The quatrefoil was used as a blank ornamental motif too (e.g.
in the tower of Raunds) and as a shape for clerestory windows
(e.g. at Geddington), again leading into the C14. So far nothing
has been said about WINDOWS altogether. Here again the transition from Norman to E.E. is fluid. The step from the slender
round-headed to the slender pointed, or lancet, window was
taken at various moments in various places. The lancet then
remained the accepted shape for the major part of the C13. Plate
tracery in the form of a quatrefoil or a trefoil or a lozenge pierced
into the spandrel below two arches, e.g. of the bell-openings in
a tower, is frequent and nowhere exactly datable. Bar tracery
introduced into England from France at Westminster Abbey
c. 1245–50 appears some time c. 1260–70 at Peterborough in the
s transept and in many places later, often in conjunction with
less pure details in other windows. Already in the Peterborough
transept the details are no longer quite pure, and a leaning
towards variety and surprise can be felt which was going to
destroy the E.E. style and establish the Dec. Of characteristic late

C13 tracery forms with three or five stepped lancet lights under one tall two-centred arch are seen in exemplary form at Warmington. Y-tracery incidentally occurs as early as the first third of the century in the w porch of Peterborough, though in Northamptonshire, as in all England, it was not accepted until *c.* 1275–80. Pointed-trefoiled lights, an enrichment first to be seen in the Sainte Chapelle in Paris in the mid 1240s and in England immediately after in the cloister of Westminster Abbey *c.* 1250–60, also entered the area by *c.* 1300 (Stoke Albany, Thorpe Achurch). Square-headed windows are not entirely absent, but very rare. Geddington is a case in point.

Northamptonshire in the C13 was certainly in close touch with events in the centre. That is shown most impressively in the w tower of Higham Ferrers and its porch and SCULPTURE. The carvers who worked on it must have come from Westminster Abbey, an offshoot of the mid-C13 lodge there, and, as so much at the abbey is over-restored or restored away, Higham Ferrers is of great national importance for an understanding of E.E. sculpture, while bearing in mind the C17 reconstruction of its spire. There is nothing else in the county to compare with it, though the equally exquisite carving of the horizontally placed figures on the capitals at Cottingham, and the w tower of Brackley St Peter – comparable with the sculpture of Wells – deserve to be better known than they are.

The porch which houses most of the Higham Ferrers sculpture is unusually shallow. The shallow w porch is a feature in Northamptonshire. It occurs at Raunds, Rushden and Oundle. Ornamental sculpture of the C13 culminates in the foliage commonly called stiff-leaf. In Northamptonshire capitals there is much of the earlier type with upright leaves not venturing into too high a degree of detachment (e.g. Rothwell). A portal worth singling out is that of the w front of Canons Ashby priory church with its elaborate arcading. Stiff-leaf also plays round the rare crosshead with the Crucifixus at Rothersthorpe. Towards the end of the century foliage turns away from the conventions of stiff-leaf towards a more naturalistic and more varied interpretation of leaves. Of this Northamptonshire has no outstanding example. Where naturalistic leaves occur, they belong to the late C13. There are many C13 FONTS, with much variety of shape and decoration, though none of outstanding quality. A special type for example is that of Fawsley, Great Addington, Hargrave and Norton. They have heads sticking out from an unadorned bowl. The type is prepared in the Norman font at Wappenham, and has a parallel in the font at Harlestone, where the heads project not from the bowl but from the foot.

Fourteenth-century churches

The motif which marks the momentous change from E.E. to DECORATED is the ogee curve. The earliest ogee arches in England date from the years immediately after 1290 and were

Higham Ferrers, St Mary, western doorway.
Engraving, 1849

devised by the masons and carvers of the king's court. Northamptonshire received a share of these important pioneer pieces
because it was crossed by the funeral cortège of Queen Eleanor,
which in the winter of 1290–1 moved from Harby in Nottinghamshire to London and was in the next few years commemor-
ated by a number of tall crosses, or rather polygonal pillars
carrying crosses, which were erected where the sad procession
had halted for the night. Northamptonshire boasts the two best
medieval examples: one just s of Northampton and the other at

Geddington. The ogee motif is by no means prominent, but other motifs also show the change from the clarity and generous spacing of the E.E. decoration to the complexity, the crowding and the delectable confusion of the Dec. Thus e.g. the use of the triangular instead of the octagonal plan at Geddington is significant. It leads the eye round the pillar more easily, because there are fewer planes in the cardinal directions inviting the eye to halt. The sculptural style of the figures of the queen also, compared with that of the mid-C13 figures mentioned above, is less articulate and readier for an undulating play of surfaces or such details as the rippling hem of a mantle. In foliage the same change can be watched, though a little later. The naturalistic leaf is replaced by a more generally undulating, bossy or nobbly leaf, comparable (accidentally) with some kinds of seaweed, although Northamptonshire is not a county where rich foliage carving is common, probably because of the friable nature of the sandstones which abound.

It is in window TRACERY however that the change is most marked. By degrees what had been a harmonious and easily understood combination of lancet lights with quatrefoiled or sexfoiled circles becomes a pattern of ogee curves combined into mouchettes or shapes like leaves, until one's memory refuses to retain them individually. The results are fascinating or exciting or (to some) irritating; they are never reposeful as those of the Geometrical tracery of the later C13 had been. The climax was reached about the middle of the C14. Other motifs underwent less change. PIERS for instance remained very often octagonal and arches double-chamfered. A favourite arch moulding of the Dec style is the sunk quadrant. A new and eminently characteristic variation on the theme of the octagonal pier is to make its eight sides concave. This was done at Harlestone, where the church was complete in 1325, and also at Great Brington, Ravensthorpe and Sudborough. The square pier with four demi-shafts continued (Finedon), and so did the quatrefoil pier, though the moulded capitals have now more and closer and less deeply divided mouldings. Variations were not absent in the C13; they became more frequent and fanciful in the C14. One variation is the addition of thin shafts in the diagonals (Little Addington), another that of fillets on the four shafts (with the thin diagonal shafts as well, at Great Brington, with spurs in the diagonals, at Blakesley, and with filleted shafts in the diagonals, at Chipping Warden). The most successful variation was the introduction of a hollow between the four main shafts. This, as we have seen, had been done already in the C13. It is now found at Great Harrowden, Middleton Cheney and Walgrave. It became, in a thinner form, one of the standard pier sections of the Perp style. The Dec, so fascinated by flowing, gliding connexions between parts instead of the crisp, determined articulation of the E.E., often chose to do without capitals. Continuous mouldings had existed in England ever since the Norman style, but only the Dec had the conviction to make a major motif of them. Thus one finds e.g. double-chamfered arches carried down to the ground in piers of the same moulding (East Farndon, Lilbourne, Marston St Lawrence, Stanford, Stoke Bruerne) or the same motif with wavy instead of straight chamfers (Charwelton), or the sunk quadrant treated in the same way (Everdon).

The dating of tracery is complicated by what can only be called English conservatism. Pre-Dec remained in use in the Dec decades. Intersected tracery e.g. occurs still *c*. 1320 etc. at Higham Ferrers. Another typical case is at Wellingborough, where the lancet lights have ogee-arched heads, but the top of the window is still a circle filled with spherical quadrangles, i.e. another motif of *c*. 1300. Even more baffling is the chancel of Geddington. The forms are of the same stage as at Wellingborough, i.e. of *c*. 1300, except for ogee-headed lights, but an inscription which is preserved refers to the man who built the chancel and who died in 1369. So 1340 is about the earliest date one can assume. Straight-headed windows are often regarded as a sign of Late Perp date. That is not so: an E.E. example has been referred to, and the Dec style uses them in Northamptonshire certainly not rarely, and other counties also. They occur e.g. with the motif of ogee reticulation in the top parts, one of the most characteristic Dec motifs (e.g. Easton-on-the-Hill). Segmental heads are also typical (e.g. Byfield and Lilbourne). At Denford windows have square heads. The variety of patterns of tracery is legion. One charming motif is that here called the four-petalled flower. It can be seen e.g. at Bozeat. Specially interesting or enjoyable tracery conceits are at Milton Malsor (a square window with a wheel of radially placed arches), and at Blisworth, Brackley, Chipping Warden and Kings Sutton. One of the most sumptuous displays of flowing tracery is the E window of Gayton. Reticulated tracery abounds with especially grand windows at the E end of Higham Ferrers and St Giles Northampton. Finedon has almost every window with reticulated forms under ogee heads, but here there are no cusps and one wonders why. The explanation is probably reglazing at some later date. At Finedon there is record of refurbishment of the chancel in the C18 and the grand C13 E window at Raunds had no cusps before George Gilbert Scott put them back in 1873.

The delight of the C14 in 'leading the eye a wanton chase' must be largely responsible for the existence and the detailing of the strainer arches at Rushden and Finedon and also between the N aisle and N chapel at Easton Maudit. They are usually dated as late as *c*. 1400, but appear earlier. Their transparence and their upward-curved upper edge achieve that very surprise in unexpected vistas which guided the Dec designers in so much of what they did. The pleasure in the opening out of a vista freer and airier than they had been permitted before may have something to do with the remarkable width and openness of the new Dec aisle and Dec chancel chapel which were added at Higham Ferrers, duplicating the dimensions of the C13 nave and chancel. The date when this was done is about 1320–30.

The dating of the C14 in Northamptonshire is always a difficult task. Documented dates such as 1337 for the approximate beginning of the splendid chancel at Cotterstock are rare, and they prove no more than that e.g. reticulated tracery was used in 1320 (in the dated chancel at Harlestone) and still after 1354 (in the tower of Irthlingborough). However, even that is a warning. While the Perp style had replaced the Dec in the s transept and the chancel at Gloucester as early as the 1330s and in the chapter house of Old St Paul's in London in the same years, Dec went on in most places into the third quarter of the C14 and even beyond. It would therefore be foolhardy to assign dates to those churches which are consistently Dec throughout or nearly throughout. Such churches in Northamptonshire are Finedon, where they intended to vault the chancel, Byfield, Crick and Stanford.

21

One or two specially impressive or pretty motifs may be added as an appendix, one the steeply rising transverse arches in porches which carry the stone slates of the roof without any intermediate timberwork (Chacombe, Corby, Middleton Cheney), the other the foliage trails with knotty branches instead of soft stalks (capitals Radstone, doorway Kislingbury). Neither motif can be connected with any particular date.

The TOWERS AND SPIRES of the C14 are equally lacking in documentation which would allow one to date them. Yet they are the most memorable achievement of medieval parish church architecture in the county. A county of spires – the old saying has already been referred to. It is, like most such proverbial sayings, not strictly true. Northamptonshire has well over two hundred medieval parish churches, but no more than about eighty spires, including those which are no longer in existence, but recorded. Of those that exist more than three-quarters are in or near the Nene district.

There are two principal types, the broach spire and the recessed spire rising behind a parapet. Of the broach spires something has already been said. The recessed spire is another possibility of combining square tower and octagonal spire. There are yet others, and they will be described a little later. The broach spire, as we have seen, goes back to the early C13, the recessed spire begins a little later. Deene, of the second half of the C13, is one of the earliest in England. A sign of this early date is that it has broaches as well, as have Woodford, Denford and Newton-in-the-Willows. An even rarer mixture is the spire of Desborough, where the battlements fade into the broaches. Aesthetically speaking, it can safely be said that the recessed spire is the more perfect solution. The finest spires of Northamptonshire belong to this type. It is difficult to make a choice. Oundle must certainly be one of those selected (assuming it was rebuilt exactly in 1634), Kettering must be another, and Rushden a third. For sheer brilliance of effect Kings Sutton must be added. At Kettering the tower below is sumptuously decorated with friezes and the spire has crockets all up the edges of the spire, a motif which occurs in other places as well, and in broach spires as much as in recessed spires (Islip, Kings Sutton, Naseby, Oundle, Rushden, Southwick, Wakerley). Another decorative motif of spires, though

34

20

one which has an obvious functional reason, is lucarnes. They ventilate the spire and increase its resistance to wind, and they are used in one, two or three tiers. They can be set in the cardinal directions exclusively or in alternating directions, and they can be large or small, shallow or deep. Tall lower or lowest lucarnes are usually early, i.e. of the C13. They may start right at the foot of a spire (Raunds, Ringstead, Hargrave) or close to the foot (Warmington, Polebrook). They may even start lower than the broaches of a broach spire (Kingscliffe), and may be taller than the broaches (Deene). Lucarnes, especially upper ones, are not without aesthetic drawbacks; for unless detailed very sensitively, they tend to come out of the smooth and sleek outlines of a spire almost like pimples or warts. The broach spire, as the more robust form, can do with them with less damage than the Dec or Perp needle spire. If Dec and Perp are here thrown together, the reason is that few spires have enough details to permit safe dating.

So a morphological survey is more advisable than a chronological. The usual transition from tower to recessed spire is by a parapet or battlements and angle pinnacles. Very occasionally a broach spire adopts the pinnacles (Brixworth, Cottingham, Piddington, Wellingborough, Wollaston). Higham Ferrers, Rushden, Wilby, Easton Maudit and a few others have graceful flying buttresses to connect the spire with the pinnacles, and at Kings Sutton there is the additional combination of inner pinnacles close to the spire, so that the flying buttresses are thrown from inner to outer pinnacles.

Further enrichment of the outline is achieved where the change from square to octagon is not made between tower and spire but between the lower parts of the tower and the bell-stage. Moreover, not all towers where this was done added a spire. The prototype of the octagonal top stage was presumably the Ely Octagon of 1322 etc. The crossing of Peterborough had a wooden octagon as well, though it has long perished. It dated from almost the same years as the Ely Octagon. An example with a stone spire is Milton Malsor, but Barnack of the C13 and Helpston (both in the Soke) should also be noted. To these must be added Wilby, with flying buttresses between square and octagon and again from eight pinnacles to the spire; Nassington, where the change to the octagon is awkwardly performed halfway up the bell-stage; and Stanwick, where the tower is octagonal from the ground. The normal square-topped towers of Northamptonshire require little comment. An oddity is the tower at Ecton with its truncated pyramid roof on which stands an embattled and pinnacled recessed top stage.

One needs to add a note of caution when looking at spires. There is ample evidence that they have been the subject of damage and destruction by storms and especially lightning. It is clear that both tower and spire at Higham Ferrers were almost totally reconstructed following their collapse in 1631. Oundle spire was rebuilt in 1634, Raunds in 1822, and there must be other unrecorded examples.

Fifteenth-century churches

The PERPENDICULAR style on its own requires not much comment in Northamptonshire. The time of greatest activity in church building was over by the end of the C14. It had been the hundred and fifty-odd years from *c.* 1190 to *c.* 1350 or 1360. There are some proud Perp churches in Northamptonshire – none prouder than Fotheringhay, stately and transparent, and Lowick, elegant with a profusion of pinnacles, both with octagonal lanterns – but there is nothing to compare with the C15 and early C16 in Norfolk or Suffolk or Gloucestershire or Somerset, though the tower of Titchmarsh, with its sixteen pinnacles, is worthy of the last. Dates are now a little easier to come by. We know that Lowick was built by members of the Greene family who died in 1399 (nave and aisles), 1417 (chancel), and 1468 (Greene Chapel and W tower), and that Fotheringhay was built in the later C14 and C15. Of the splendid church which served a college founded in 1411 the chancel exists no longer. The nave with its large aisle and large clerestory windows and its flying buttresses gives an idea of the grand conception. The interior reminds one of the grandest in East Anglia. Dated also are the sumptuous S porch of Oundle built *c.* 1485, the Chambre Chapel at Aldwinkle All Saints founded in 1489, the S chapel at Blakesley for which money was left in 1500, the Chambre Chapel at Spratton built by 1505, the Spencer Chapel at Great Brington of before 1522, and the church at Whiston built shortly before 1534. The C16 phase of Perpendicular may well be more widespread than is generally realized.

Individual motifs and elements of these Perp churches do not call for much analysis. Octagonal piers continue, piers with four shafts and four hollows continue (Kettering and Weekley), at Harrington with a deep continuous wave connecting shafts and hollows, and continuous mouldings without any capitals or abaci between piers and arches also continue. Often the shafts towards the aisle openings have capitals but no other members. The varieties are better seen than described (Islip, Brampton Ash and Weldon forming one group; Stanion, Luddington and, most complicated of all, Fotheringhay another). The strainer arches of Rushden, Finedon and Easton Maudit have been mentioned earlier on. Capitals with foliage carving occur only occasionally, with Harrington a good example. Vaulted porches were a heritage from the C13. They now have not only diagonal ribs and ridge ribs but also tiercerons (Wellingborough etc.). The heavily timber-framed N porch of Marston Trussell on the Leicestershire border is unique in the county. Neither timber nor brick entered the field of church building. Window tracery is of the nationally accepted types without local specialities. It is at its grandest again at Fotheringhay, but even inside Fotheringhay there is no display of decoration that could be compared with e.g. Long Melford. A particularly rich ensemble is the monument to John Dycson †1445, rector of Yelvertoft, with its recess and the window behind it, externally as well as internally. At Whiston the relatively small church is a perfect complete Perp essay with tall arcades high enough to admit the light from the aisle windows without the use of a clerestory. Especially striking is its tower with alternating bands of silver limestone and golden sandstone. It has also the advantage of having its original roofs and pews.

In the N of the county is a fine series of towers, probably by the same builders as St John and St Martin Stamford, just across the Lincolnshire border, characterized by clasping buttresses, tall four-light (two plus two) bell-openings, a top frieze of quatrefoils or cusped lozenges, and usually big pinnacles (Aldwinkle All Saints, Bulwick, Easton-on-the-Hill, Geddington, Warkton). The group is quite large, but not all towers have all motifs.

Medieval church decoration, furnishings and monuments

The absence of WALL PAINTINGS from medieval churches (and indeed houses – see below) is much to be deplored. If we had all that crowded the walls we might like some churches less, but we would understand them better. In Northamptonshire there are many churches in which the faded traces of former cycles of frescoes have been laid bare. There is hardly anywhere enough for even the most moderate enjoyment although the little church at Slapton gives as good an impression of what interiors were like as any. Specially complete are the series of Ashby St Ledgers, Croughton and Holcot. Other churches with wall paintings are Burton Latimer, Great Doddington and Raunds. A series of late C16 panels at Burton Latimer are especially interesting since the origin of their design has been traced.

STAINED GLASS, never fading though easily broken, can take the place of wall paintings to give us an idea of the colourfulness of the medieval church. But Northamptonshire is not rich in stained glass. By far the most rewarding place not only in Northamptonshire but in England is Stanford, where a splendid array of good glass from the early C14 to the C16 survives. Lowick has sixteen figures from a C14 Jesse window, Rushden good C15 glass, Thenford minor remains. At Weldon is a complete early C16 South Netherlandish window with the Adoration of the Magi.

CHURCH FURNISHINGS are on the whole not of special interest. Of METALWORK only one piece can be introduced here, the precious processional cross at Lamport of the C15. As regards furnishings of stone, there are of course plenty of FONTS, but none, except for Stanion, deserves individual mention. Generally a word may be said for the groups of fonts (not only in Northamptonshire) which are decorated with a variety of blank tracery motifs, Dec as well as Perp, as if they were copied from some mason's pattern-book of window tracery. Canons Ashby and Preston Capes have such fonts. Much more interesting is the small stone RELIQUARY of about 1300 at Brixworth. Stone REREDOSES of the C14 are preserved at Barnwell, Great Billing, Spratton and Wilbarston – more than in most other counties. A Perp reredos is at Geddington. Of SEDILIA and PISCINA one must mention a fine C13 array at Rushden with trefoil-headed arches and gables over the sedilia, and two similar C14 sets with ogee arches under a square frame at East Haddon and Grafton Underwood. No PULPITS of stone need be placed on record. Perp pulpits of wood are more frequent, but again of current types. The best is that of Fotheringhay with its pretty rib-vaulted tester or sounding-board. At Hannington it is interesting to see that the same wood carver must have done the pulpit and the SCREEN. No Northamptonshire screens can compete with the South-West or East Anglia. Geddington may be singled out because it seems as early as the early to mid C14, Ashby St Ledgers because, with its four-light divisions and its ribbed coving, it is more sumptuous than most. Bozeat also has four-light divisions, and Braybrooke has its ribbed coving preserved. MISERICORDS have survived in quite a number of places, notably Great Oakley (from Pipewell Abbey), Higham Ferrers, Gayton, Great Doddington, Rothwell and Wellingborough. BENCHES and bench-ends are frequent but not particularly interesting. Kingscliffe has bench-ends and some stained glass from Fotheringhay. Benefield, Hemington and Tansor have stalls from the demolished chancel of the same church.

Medieval CHURCH MONUMENTS in Northamptonshire, on the whole, keep within the prosperous average of the country. There are few if any highlights. On the subject the most important remark to be made is more general and includes the post-medieval centuries. The county is uncommonly rich in FAMILY CHAPELS, an expression of the wealth in Northamptonshire which the growth and maintenance of country houses also attests. The Spencer monuments at Great Brington run from 1522 to the C19, the Knightley monuments at Fawsley from the early C16 to the mid C19, the Brudenells at Deene from 1531 to the C19, the Fermors at Easton Neston from 1550 to the C19, the Caves and their descendants at Stanford from 1558 to nearly 1900, the Montagus at Weekley and then Warkton from 1557 to the C19, the Langhams at Cottesbrooke from the C17 to the early C19, and the Comptons at Castle Ashby from 1828 to the C20.

There are many churches with remains of medieval coffin-lids ornamented with foliate crosses or double omega type patterns. Then of course there are the beautiful cross-legged knights of Purbeck marble at Castle Ashby, Dodford and Church Stowe. They date from the late C13 to the early C14. The same period was responsible for the oaken effigies of knights and ladies at Alderton, Ashton (Roade), Braybrooke, Cold Higham, Dodford, Gayton, Paulerspury and Woodford. Alabaster, a Derbyshire and Nottinghamshire material, was used both for incised slabs and fully carved effigies. Gardner counts sixteen alabaster monuments in the county. The earliest ones are of 1365–70 (Ashton, Orlingbury, Spratton), the finest Ralph Greene †1417 at Lowick (for which the contract has been preserved), Sir John Cressy at Dodford †1444, and the Earl of Wiltshire †1499 at Lowick. Among C14 monuments in stone the best is at Warkworth (c. 1350) with a particularly splendid effigy. The monument to

Archdeacon Sponne at Towcester (†1448) has a cadaver as well
as an effigy, a specifically English conception and arrangement
the earliest example of which is Bishop Fleming of Lincoln †1433.
Several Late Perp monuments follow the arrangement of the
Dycson at Yelvertoft, i.e. use recesses with a straight top cresting.
The recesses at Gayton, Harrington and Irthlingborough, all of
the first half of the C16, are of Purbeck marble or a similar grey
marble, possibly Alwalton. The most splendid canopied composition is however that of the tomb of Sir John Spencer †1522 at
Great Brington in a beautifully carved white stone. The painting
of effigies and surround are renewed here so as to give an impression of how gay such a Perp ensemble was in its original state.*

The earliest BRASS and one of the best in England is the St
Maur (†1337) at Higham Ferrers. Good C15 brasses are at Ashby
St Ledgers, Cotterstock, Great Harrowden and Lowick. In the
first four of these the figures stand under canopies. At Lowick
they wear heraldic attire and there is a kneeling figure in the same
at Ashby St Ledgers. The brass at Geddington (formerly Newton-in-the-Willows) is especially attractive. The figures kneel
below a large slender cross. An especially fine one of a priest
(†1401) is at Castle Ashby.

Medieval domestic architecture

The county is on the whole singularly poor in MONASTIC
REMAINS, though it should not be forgotten that the great Benedictine houses of Crowland and Thorney were originally just
across the border to the NE. Moreover, of the abbeys and priories
which existed in Northamptonshire hardly anything has come
down to our century. A list will bear that out. Recorded are two
Benedictine houses for monks and one for nuns, two Cluniac
houses for monks and one for nuns (the former including St
Andrew Northampton which has totally disappeared), one Cistercian house for monks (Pipewell, which has also totally disappeared) and two for nuns, six houses of Augustinian canons
(including St James Northampton and Fineshade) and one for
canonesses, two Premonstratensian houses (including Sulby),
two houses of the Knights Hospitallers (including Dingley), and
six houses of the mendicant orders at Northampton (Dominican,
Franciscan, Franciscan nuns, Carmelite, Austin and Sack). Of
all this no more need be singled out here than the probably
recognizable plan of Delapré (Cluniac nuns) at Northampton
and the C13 w front of Canons Ashby (Augustinian canons). In
addition there were the ambitious collegiate foundations of Cotterstock (1338), Irthlingborough (1388), Fotheringhay (1411),
Higham Ferrers (1422) and All Saints Northampton (1460) as
well as a number of hospitals.

CASTLES proper are rare in the county and with two exceptions
of minor interest. The chief exception is Barnwell Castle, built,

* For the angel under the arch *see* below, p. 41.

it is traditionally said, *c.* 1266. If that is so, it represents the earliest case in England of the most monumental type of medieval castle, that of a square or oblong plan with round angle towers, a type created on Roman patterns in Italy and France *c.* 1230 and taken over at Caerphilly Castle *c.* 1267 and Harlech Castle *c.* 1285. Barnwell Castle precedes Caerphilly by a few years. The gatehouse of Rockingham Castle, which in its present form dates from *c.* 1275–80, has round towers too. It was one of the most famous castles of Northamptonshire. Of the others – Northampton and Fotheringhay – all architecturally relevant evidence has disappeared. At Fotheringhay on the other hand a curious, quite sizeable house of about 1460, known as Garden Farmhouse, formerly a guest house associated with the castle, remains.

The complete disappearance of the college at Fotheringhay, the almost complete disappearance of that founded by Archbishop Chichele in his native Higham Ferrers, and the scanty remains of that established in 1388 at Irthlingborough deprive us of any vision of how such late medieval domestic building for clerics was arranged and equipped. The survival of Chichele's School, mid C15, and Bede House of 1428 is an inadequate though welcome substitute. The school is an oblong with large church windows and might just as well be a Lady Chapel; the Bede House has some of its fitments still *in situ*, and one can visualize the cubicles with their beds and cupboards and the raised chapel at the E end. Among the SMALLER HOUSES the one amazing example of secular architecture to survive is the Prebendal Manor at Nassington. Here we have a complete, if altered, early C13 hall house of which the hall remains, along with evidence of its solar and service wings. At Cottingham, the Royal George pub conceals another remarkable survival: the remains of a cruck-framed house dated (by dendrochronology) to 1262. This is very early. The only other cruck-framed building so far identified in the county is C15 (Nos. 19–21 High Street, Byfield). The Chantry House at Towcester, established by Archdeacon Sponne in 1447, must find its place here, as must the probable chantry house, known as the Priest's House, at Easton-on-the-Hill, built in the last decades of the C15.

Of the later medieval period the most rewarding, and indeed complex house, is Southwick Hall. It has a C14 tower which was added to a slightly earlier hall (rebuilt later). The ground floor of the tower is rib-vaulted (like the tower at Longthorpe near Peterborough). Such houses could be used in wartime but were built for residence. Astwell Castle of the C15 is of a similar type. Another almost complete C14 hall is at the so-called Monastery at Shutlanger. Here there are sooted timbers in the roof declaring an original central hearth. There are, of course, remnants of other early medieval hall houses elsewhere, of which the Old House at Stoke Albany and The Priory at Syresham are examples, both with doorways in the former screens passage wall surviving. In their plan several houses show the hall, chambers and service rooms in a single axis line, for example Hardwick, Loddington and Nassington. Even by *c.* 1300 at Drayton service rooms were on the same axis as the hall, with just the chamber range forming a cross-wing, but even this hardly extends beyond the width of the hall. Main chambers were without exception on the first floor or at any rate on a raised level, and usually above an undercroft. At Drayton the vaulted undercroft survives, while undercrofts may be implied at Yardley Hastings and Deene. At Brigstock even the hall was on a raised level. Medieval staircases are almost non-existent save for the one at Southwick. Kitchens, if not detached like those at Deene and Yardley Hastings, were often at a distance from the hall because of the incidence of damaging fires. Later phases of rebuilding often removed evidence of medieval layouts but a surprising number of remains of roof structures survive and to those houses already mentioned can be added Abbey Lodge at Farthinghoe.

Of the Northamptonshire MANSIONS of the Middle Ages by
36 far the most impressive is Drayton, of which the core – that is the hall, the largest in the county, undercroft and chamber – was built from *c*. 1300 onwards, and whose walls are still largely intact. The early house was then enlarged in the C15 with the chamber range becoming a three-storey tower block. Later building has overlaid this C14 and C15 work with equally interesting work of a different character, but the impression of the embattled and turreted mansion of the de Draytons and Greenes can still be conjured up. Drayton also had courts on both sides of the hall range, though the former entrance court on the W side only partially survives. It was also moated, though only a fragment of that arrangement can be traced today. Otherwise moats only survive as marks of a lost structure. To this must be added the remains of the service end of the *c*. 1320–40 hall at Yardley Hastings, originally almost as big as that at Drayton. For the C15 there is no major house until the Tudor age is reached. Then, of *c*. 1500 and after, there are the hall range and the Back Court, i.e. service court (*c*. 1530 etc.), at Apethorpe, the hall with the remarkable motif of a bow-fronted bay window at Rushton, the hall and the chamber over at Brigstock Manor House, the E range
39 at Deene Park with its canted bay window feature and roof of *c*. 1530, the remains of the hall with roof at Abington Abbey,
38 Northampton, and the hall with splendid bay window at Fawsley, also of *c*. 1530. The latter is the finest piece of late medieval domestic display in the county. The bay window and the other windows have uncusped arched lights, a motif characteristic of the time of Henry VIII but continued by conservative designers and patrons into the later C16 (Great Oakley Hall 1555, Canons Ashby after 1551, the hall range at Deene Park after 1549, and at Rushton even after 1575). Altogether it can be observed that the Renaissance, even as a fashion, was received only with much
37 hesitation. A house such as Canons Ashby shows no sign of it in all the work undertaken after 1551. Nor does it appear in the hall of Boughton House, another of large proportions, of the same time as Canons Ashby.

At Fawsley another house, known as the Dower House, smaller and more domestic in character, remains in the grounds. It dates

from the early c16, and is mostly of brick. It has the delightful
twisted and decorated chimneyshafts which are so characteristic
of EARLY TUDOR ARCHITECTURE. Here BRICK makes its first
appearance in this survey, although evidence of brickmaking has
been found at Lyveden c. 1480. It was also used at Canons Ashby
and at Winwick Manor House, again after 1550. The next appearance of brick in the county is not until the c18. The other building
material of regions poor in good stone is timber, and TIMBER
FRAMING therefore is also unusual in Northamptonshire, perhaps
surprisingly considering the large areas of forest that existed in
medieval times. Ashby St Ledgers has one timber-framed range
of some elaboration, but this comes from Ipswich and was re-
erected by the 2nd Lord Wimborne. Of other examples, one
might refer to the Court House at Kings Sutton, and houses at
Wellingborough, Braunston and Yelvertoft, the last two on the
Warwickshire border where this form of construction becomes
more usual. Timber pieces of interior decoration are rare too,
and no more needs a reference than the carved lintel of a fireplace
at Helmdon dated 1533, a fine room with linenfold of an unusual
design of c. 1500 at Deene, the linenfold panelling with various
Late Gothic as well as Renaissance motifs reassembled in a room
at Abington Abbey, Northampton, and the screen with various
bold linenfold motifs re-erected from outside the county at Cosgrove Priory, also of the time of Henry VIII.

THE REFORMATION TO THE LATE
SEVENTEENTH CENTURY

So the RENAISSANCE has been reached. The earliest documents
of the Italian style in England are the monuments to the Lady
Margaret and to Henry VII in Westminster Abbey begun in 1511
and 1512. In the stained glass of King's College Chapel, Cambridge, Italian motifs appear in 1515–17, at Hampton Court
actual Italian work in 1521. By 1530 Renaissance motifs, mostly
minor and mostly Englished in a somewhat provincial way,
become more abundant. What are the incunabula in Northamptonshire? Certainly among them is the parclose screen at Warmington which, with its ogee arches with Renaissance detail and
its linenfold panels side by side with pilasters, cannot be later
than the 1530s. It has unfortunately no inscribed or otherwise
known dates. But it was in the mid 1550s that things changed,
and now for a generation Northamptonshire becomes the architecturally most important county in England. Evidence of the
style of the third quarter of the c16 is more frequent and more
valuable here than anywhere else. Indeed, Northamptonshire
now set out on that triumphant procession of major country
house building which continued without a break into the c18. It
can safely be said that the history of domestic architecture in
England from 1560 to 1700 could be written with Northampton-

shire examples alone: with Kirby, Rushton and Lyveden, Deene,
Castle Ashby, Stoke Bruerne, Lamport Hall, Boughton and
Easton Neston and alongside these, although in the Soke of
Peterborough, Burghley and Thorpe Hall, both too important to
ignore.

The change in the 1550s to which reference has been made
and which initiates ELIZABETHAN ARCHITECTURE can be illustrated by comparing Canons Ashby of after 1551, which still has
the windows with arched lights as had been current under Henry
VIII, with the porch of 1558 and the gatehouse range of 1560 at
Dingley. The porch at Dingley is the earliest piece of Renaissance
architecture in Northamptonshire,* late if one compares with
Sutton Place in Surrey or Layer Marney in Essex, both of the
1520s. A sense of Italian Renaissance – or by then rather Franco-
Italian Renaissance – composition appeared for the first time in
England in Old Somerset House in the Strand in London, built
for himself by the Lord Protector Somerset in 1547–52. Here one
can also see for the first time a number of motifs which the Elizabethan style was gradually to adopt: the mullioned window
without arches to the lights, the frontispiece with superimposed
orders including columns (not only pilasters), the pediment, the
top balustrade. Other forms are pilasters with sunk panels ornamented with close arabesque, a shell pediment, strapwork, and
bulbous vase finials. Yet whoever designed the porch of 1558 at
Dingley was clearly aware of the innovations of the Somerset
circle. The outer entrance at Dingley is dated 1560 and carries a
most extraordinary inscription which refers to King Philip of
Spain as the king, and thus impressively illustrates how unmo-
lested influential Catholics still were in the early years of Elizabeth I. The doorway has a four-centred arch, and the same
arches occur inside in a short cloister. The attached columns of
this cloister have a curiously exaggerated taper, which, however,
the top floor of the frontispiece of Somerset House also had. The
cresting on the other hand – shaped gables and shell motifs – is
still of the playful kind typical of the earliest decades of Renaissance influence in England. It is reasonable to associate all these
items with the *Thorpes* of Kingscliffe and we need now to
consider what else can be associated with them.

The *Thorpes* worked the quarries at Kingscliffe and in the
church is a memorial to three generations, all Thomas. The first
cannot be dated, but the second Thomas died 1558, and the third
Thomas in 1596. It is the last who was master mason at Kirby
Hall and who was the father of John, whose collection of drawings (now in the Soane Museum) has made the name famous.
The earliest work attributable to them is in the 1550s at Deene
and at Dingley. The Deene example is the splendid external
showpiece on the E front. It is really a large bay window now with
all its lights blocked, using fat Ionic columns as mullions, together
with strapwork panels, and a truncated ogee gable, though this
may be a C17 addition, when the window was reset in its present

---

* The relevance of the 1555 date on the façade at Great Oakley is questionable.

position. At Dingley there is also a porch, originally fronting the
hall, but moved in the C19 onto a gable end. It has three superimposed orders like Somerset House, even if they are handled
with less assurance. The columnation 1. and r. of the door and
upper window is carried round the corner, an idea which we shall
find again. Here fat fluted columns appear as corners of buttresses. The windows have a cross of mullion and transom, set
within a wall decoration copied from a Roman ceiling taken from
Serlio. At the top are bulbous vase finials and a small shell gable.
Such bulbous finials and also the shell motif become almost a
trademark of the school. It is clear that the Thorpes employed a
number of stone-carvers and they appear now in a remarkable
series of funerary monuments and chimneypieces. The Griffin
Monument at Braybrooke of c. 1565–70 is an excellent example.
It is exuberant and overcrowded, with tapered vase-like Ionic
pilasters in different proportions. There is no effigy, just a mass
of decoration, heraldic standards at the top and once again a big
shell gable. At Boughton House (Drawing Room) there is a
chimneypiece brought from Hemington which has exactly the
same tiers of vase-like Ionic fluted columns, but this time slender
Corinthian columns either side the overmantel. At this point in
the late 1560s there seems to be an outside influence on the
workshop. Carving becomes crisper and designs just that bit
more sophisticated. Clearly related is another fireplace at
Boughton House (Audit Room) which must be c. 1550–60. Its
design is a curious mixture with Renaissance style heads and no
pure architectural elements, save that the overmantel pilasters
have a version of Corinthian. The pilasters themselves have arabesque infills. The fireplace seems to be carved from clunch and
is clearly from the same stable as the chimneypiece at Apethorpe
dated 1562, which is again of clunch. In this case the base pilasters have a series of circles and half-circles with a narrow pilaster
overlaying a wider one. Exactly the same forms appear on the
1571 hall chimneypiece at Deene. The finest example from the   42
workshop is the monument to William Markham at Little Oakley.   46
Here there are tall fluted Doric columns, beneath a Doric entablature. A pair of shields is surrounded by intricate strapwork
containing grotesque masks. These strapwork-edged shields with
grotesque heads become another characteristic of the workshop.
Above, a further heraldic panel is supported by lion's legs issuing
from acanthus fronds. These leafy legs are a motif of the school
to which we will return. Even more elaborate strapwork surrounds are on the two monuments which were erected at Fotheringhay for the Yorkist dukes in the 1570s, this time set between
pairs of Corinthian columns. The strapwork-edged shields and
grotesque heads again are paralleled at Deene. Also at Deene the
hall porch is equally crisp and assured, in total contrast to the
clumsy use of Ionic columns on the earlier E front feature. Then
in the 1570s the rich exuberance disappears and memorials
become more architectural. Whoever was the outside influence
seems to have gone. Just elements remain from what has gone
before with the addition of caryatids, large and small. At Fawsley

(Sir Valentine Knightley), c. 1570, for example, we have the
return of the Doric pilasters and frieze, the central supports being
caryatid-like figures on tapered supports, with claw feet, together
with the lion's leg side elements, the whole now surmounted by
a huge sarcophagus with gadrooning. The Doric order now
becomes dominant and there are versions outside the county
which seem to be from the same school. At Turvey, Beds., the
monument to the 1st Lord Mordaunt c. 1571 has just such Doric
architecture and caryatid-like figures. It can also be found at
Chicheley and at Hillesden, Bucks., both of these with the sarcophagus feature. However, this leads into an area still being
researched and at present little understood but is has been
possible to identify the mark used by one mason associated with
the last Thomas Thorpe, *Samson Frisby.** He is known to have
provided stonework in the early C17 at Apethorpe, Deene and
Kirby, as well as at Blickling Hall, Norfolk, Clare College,
Cambridge, and Quenby Hall, Leicestershire.

We need to return to more mainstream ideas and here we must
consider Kirby Hall. Kirby was begun in 1570 and when its
patron Sir Humphrey Stafford died in 1575 it was still not complete. It is, however, the use of the giant order for the very first
time in England which makes this building so important. While
there are naïve elements it is used with such assurance, especially
on the N courtyard façade, where it is integrated with a loggia,
that we must assume an outside influence. Kirby was acquired
by Sir Christopher Hatton, a young favourite of the Virgin Queen,
on Stafford's death but little seems to have been done to the
building until the early C17. Serlio remains a source for inspiration, notably in the plaster ceiling in the Tapestry Room at
Deene, of the later years of the C16, and also at the beginning of
the C17 at Wothorpe, where the curious long rectangular window
forms are copied directly from its pages. Large mullioned-and-
transomed windows are the most conspicuous motif inherited
from such houses as Longleat and Burghley, and in both cases
they seem to belong to the 1570s; so we find them at Kirby,
Deene and Castle Ashby. With them the mature Elizabethan style
was established.

Meanwhile what had been a matter of a few individual buildings up to 1570 developed into the broad stream of MATURE
ELIZABETHAN AND JACOBEAN DOMESTIC ARCHITECTURE.
Sir Christopher Hatton also built on a prodigious scale at Holdenby, where the completion date is probably that marked on the
garden archways, which are the only thing left of the house. They
are very similar to archways outside Kirby. The date at Holdenby
is 1583. Pytchley, an Isham mansion which has also disappeared
and of which only fragments survive in various places, seems to
have been completed in 1596. Of Newton, a Tresham mansion,

* I am grateful for discussions with Kathryn Morrison (RCHME) who has been,
with Jenny Alexander, collecting and analysing mason's marks on Northamptonshire buildings. See Jenny Alexander, 'Signed in Stone', *Country Life*, 13 February
2013, pp. 60–62 and also several articles by Jon Bayliss and J. Edis (2001) in the
Journal of the Church Monuments Society.

Pytchley Hall.
Drawing by G. Clarke, *c.* 1850

the dovecote is all that remains. Sir Thomas Tresham, convert to
Rome and a man equally enamoured of theology, architecture
and allegorical conceits, built the Market House at Rothwell in
1578 and added to Rushton, but is principally remembered for
the Triangular Lodge in the Rushton grounds and for Lyveden   43
New Bield, which is a Greek cross and was never completed. The   45
one symbolizes the Trinity, the other the Passion. (Of these conceits and of Tresham's troubled life more is to be found on pp.
405 and 569.) At Castle Ashby work started in 1574 and went on
into the C17. The Elizabethan plan with long projecting wings
and two staircase turrets attached to them is one familiar from
such mid-C16 houses as Melford Hall, Kentwell Hall and Rushbrooke, all three in Suffolk. Castle Ashby was remodelled *c.*   63
1600–35 and then received its delightful balustrade with lettering,
a feature of French origin also to be found at the same time e.g.
at Temple Newsam outside Leeds. A few years later still Castle
Ashby received its screen across the front, but this belongs
emphatically to the style which was to replace that of the Jacobean decades. The screen as such, however, again of French
descent, had been quite a usual Elizabethan and Jacobean motif.
Kirby Hall of course has it; other examples are among the Cambridge colleges. In Northamptonshire a late and ambitious
example is at Rushton, of the time (*c.* 1625–30) when the   53
Cokaynes had replaced the Treshams. To these should be added
another elaborate gateway of late C16 date at Winwick, though
this seems to emanate from a school of carving from outside the
county.

Of the Jacobean era the most important house in the county
is Apethorpe where in the 1620s a suite of apartments was created
especially for the use of James I. These have very fine plasterwork
and carved stone fireplaces. The E range of the house was rebuilt   52

with an open arcade on the ground floor and a long gallery above.
50 Also outstanding is Wothorpe, a secondary Cecil mansion or
rather lodge, impressive even in its ruined state, on a compact
plan similar to those of certain north country houses such as
Barlborough, Derbyshire and Wootton Lodge, Staffs. Gayton
Manor is also lodge-like but smaller and equally compact.

A few more Elizabethan and Jacobean houses must be referred
to in passing: extensions at Drayton of *c.* 1584 with a three-floor
wing and a large staircase tower, and the s front of Brockhall
Hall. Also Jacobean in style but less ambitious are Burton Latimer
Hall, Rushden Hall, the w front of Delapré, Lilford Hall (1635),
and the hall range at Ashby St Ledgers (with additions of 1652).
Lilford and Ashby St Ledgers have shaped gables in the later
work, and altogether it can be said that in more marginal building
in the county the Jacobean style was still unchanged after 1660.
TOWN HOUSES of the same years are few and far between. The
fire of 1675 did not leave many houses untouched at Northampton. The only noteworthy ones are the (rebuilt) Welsh House of
1595 and the late C16 Hazelrigg House. To these may be added
the Talbot Inn of 1626 at Oundle.

INTERIORS of these decades and of special value are oddly
65 rare. There is good Jacobean plasterwork at Apethorpe, Canons
Ashby, Castle Ashby and Deene. Also at Castle Ashby is the West
Staircase with its openwork panels, a motif which, about 1630,
occasionally took the place of turned balusters. The panels are
still of strapwork, though they include certain gristly details
which belong to the mid-C17 style. The East Staircase some
decades later has luscious openwork acanthus scrolls instead, and
that represents a different style.

Inigo Jones, John Webb and the court style

The moment has now come to turn to the great divide. *Inigo
Jones* was born in 1573. He is first met in 1603 as a painter, but
had then already visited Italy and there no doubt acquired the
knowledge of theatrical design and the deft hand at sketching
which are both his when he next appears, in 1605, as a designer
and draughtsman for a court masque. He developed into the
most brilliant English theatre designer of his age, on a par with
the best abroad. But out of feigned architecture he moved into
real architecture, and became Surveyor to the Prince of Wales in
1611 and Surveyor of the King's Works in 1613. In the same year
he went to Italy again, and this time closely studied Italian architecture and especially his idol, Andrea Palladio. In his earliest
works of architecture, such as the New Exchange in London of
1609, he was still essentially Jacobean, but in 1616 he designed
the Queen's Villa at Greenwich as a purely Palladian work and
in 1619 the Banqueting House in Whitehall for the king, equally
pure and equally Palladian. In Northamptonshire two works of
architecture are attributed to him, the s front or screen at Castle
Ashby and the pavilions at Stoke Bruerne, the former on no

better authority than that of Campbell's *Vitruvius Britannicus* and now considered the work of his assistant *Edward Carter*, the latter on the authority of John Bridges, the reliable C18 county historian who writes that Sir Francis Crane brought the design from Italy and that Inigo Jones helped him with it. This indeed is quite possible. The plan is that of Palladio's villas, i.e. a plan with a compact centre connected by quadrant wings to pavilions. Jones would have been sympathetic if Crane had made the suggestion to him to build on such a plan in England. It had not been done before in England, though it was just then also done in France and Holland, and who else but Jones would have had experience of it? The date of Stoke Park is 1629–35. The centre of the house was burnt and was apparently not built to Inigo's plan. It may have been an earlier building, altered. The pavilions are charac-   62
terized by giant pilasters, again a Palladio motif which about 1630–40 began to become popular in Holland and France, and again their first appearance since they were introduced in this county at Kirby in 1570, although their original inspiration is the Capitoline palaces by Michelangelo in Rome. The s front at Castle Ashby is characterized by a pediment and Venetian   63
windows, both Palladian as well as Jonesian elements. Certain impurities need not worry us overmuch. It is becoming more and more patent that Jones was not as pure an architect as e.g. Gotch had surmised more than a generation ago. The work on the N front at Kirby dating from 1638–40 and executed by *Nicholas Stone* is less convincing. With its Dutch, i.e. scrolly, pedimented gables, it is closer to a more popular trend of architecture in the second third of the C17 than to the courtly style of Inigo. An excellent example of this more popular trend is the gateway of 1653 at Apethorpe, another the garden temple of 1641 at Easton Neston, which could be Jonesian if it were not for one rather wild Jacobean intrusion.

The situation in the mid C17 in Northamptonshire, and indeed in England, was that Inigo Jones's battle was not won. Only few as yet followed him, among them first and foremost his pupil and kinsman *John Webb*. One of the best surviving works of Webb is in the county, Lamport Hall of *c.* 1655, built at first as no more   64
than a villa, in the succession of Inigo's villa for the queen at Greenwich. It contains a splendid two-storeyed hall, a staircase with the pierced acanthus panels, and an impressive large fire-place. Webb also designed fireplaces for Drayton and consider-able further work there is attributable to him: a castellated gate-tower with a pendentive domed stone ceiling and two delightful banqueting houses. He may well have designed parts of Watford Court where there were additions dated 1657 and 1659, but these, alas, are no longer standing. Howard Colvin has shown that this popular version of the mid-C17 possibilities is in its most elaborate, decidedly Mannerist form connected with *Peter Mills*, carpenter to the City of London. Mills was responsi-ble for the design of Thorpe Hall (Peterborough), which dates from 1653–6. The style of Thorpe Hall is reflected at Cotterstock Hall (1658), at Cobthorne, Oundle of similar date and in the   66

interior decoration at Chipping Warden Manor, and was reflected in a window of the now demolished Peacock Hotel at Northampton, but this was later. By an unknown architect, but perhaps *Anthony Ellis*, is the staircase of 1666 at Althorp, one of the grandest and most classical of those years in England, constructed of oak but originally stained to look like walnut. The graining of panelling such as pine to look like walnut was a fashion much in favour at this time and the King's Dining Room at Drayton still has such a scheme.

Post-Reformation church architecture

There is nothing whatever to report until after the death of Elizabeth I. There were enough churches in existence, the troubled decades before the Settlement were not propitious to church building, and the Settlement itself did not lead to church building enthusiasm either. So what can be referred to between 1620 and 1639 is confined to six items, none of them major. They show an almost unquestioning adherence to the Perp style and only occasional passages in the Jacobean or the coming classical idiom. Of 1620 much or most of the disused Gothic chapel at Furtho and the larger and more ambitious chapel of Sir Thomas Crewe close to Steane Park. This has Gothic windows and Gothic pier sections. Of 1621 is the Mildmay Chapel at Apethorpe, where the pier towards the chancel is Perp but the decoration decidedly classical, that is not really Jacobean. The chancel at Passenham is dated 1626 and has windows of a bastardized Perp design and a wagon roof. The tower of Apethorpe church with its recessed spire is also Perp and was rebuilt in 1633. The Hanbury Chapel at Kelmarsh of *c.* 1639 on the other hand has in its curious Geometric E window what can only be described as Carolean tracery. A number of rebuildings of parts of churches should be mentioned. By far the most impressive is the rebuilding of the tower and spire at Higham Ferrers. Here a local mason *Richard Atkins* did an extraordinarily fine job in recreating the effect of what had stood there before its almost total collapse in 1631. It is only when one examines the structure carefully that it becomes clear that almost everything which stands today is of the 1630s. In Northampton a similar fate occurred at St Giles's church but here the tower is more obviously not medieval, though its Gothic form is perfectly acceptable. The spire at Oundle is clearly dated 1634, again probably rehearsing what existed previously, and there are several church towers which show evidence of C17 work such as Wicken (1617), Passenham (*c.* 1626) and East Haddon (1673), together with others without a secure date.

In CHURCH FURNISHINGS the situation is reversed. Here the Gothic style survives only very occasionally, and one is indeed tempted to speak of revival rather than survival, when it occurs, and most of what was commissioned was done in the Elizabethan and Jacobean style with its Netherlandish sympathies. Again little is of before the death of Queen Elizabeth. There are two pulpits (of 1579 and 1584) at Rothersthorpe and Newbottle, both very simple and not with the broad, blank arches on short pillars which are so familiar as an Elizabethan and Jacobean motif in church as well as house. They decorate e.g. the pulpits at Catesby and at Alderton. The latter is dated 1631. The work at Passenham of *c.* 1626 is perhaps the most consistent that can be introduced here. The gallery front, the former chancel screen, is contemporary with the stalls, which have to one's amazement Jacobean misericords, and the wall paintings of single figures in niches are on the Venetian Cinquecento pattern. No other painting need be mentioned, only one stained glass job (at Apethorpe, 1621, entirely Flemish-looking), and little other woodwork. By far the most interesting screen is that at Geddington which is dated 1618 and repeats the Dec tracery of the window against which it stands, even if it embroiders on it with small Jacobean motifs. Other screens are at Clipston, a specially fine piece, at Marston St Lawrence (1610) made up from a reredos, and at Apethorpe. If to these the splendid organ case at Stanford, dating from the early C17, and the reredos of 1635 at Deene are added, all is listed that needs listing.

The development from the later Elizabethan age to the 1660s is paralleled in the development of FUNERAL MONUMENTS. The earliest of all Renaissance details is the Doric peplos worn by the angel in the apex of the arch of the Spencer tomb at Great Brington, erected immediately after 1522. The dress is that of the angels of the tomb of Henry VII. Then come minor decorative details on other tombs, introduced by the way and without any great conviction. Such are small coarse balusters taking the place of buttress shafts to separate panel from panel on the sides of tomb-chests. These motifs are to be found on the work of *Richard Parker* and the *Roileys* of Burton upon Trent. They are to be found in the Brudenell monument of 1531 at Deene and the monument of Lord Parr, uncle of Catherine Parr, at Horton (†1546). At Deene the panels still have the blank quatrefoils of the Perp style, and there are indeed several monuments with just the slightest hint of the Renaissance with the use of a twisted column (Fawsley †1534, Weekley †1557, Stanford †1558, Rushton †1559, Charwelton †1564). Parker at his best is a brilliant carver and the 1534 Knightley monument at Fawsley is a classic example, made the more so since it retains much of its original colour. The Roileys are but a shadow in his train and their carving is often lumpy and coarse and must have relied on the colour and gilding applied to it for effect, alas, all too often fragmentary now. The tombs at Edgcote are sad examples of their art.

New types are the memorials which form a group with kneeling figures in relief facing one another; occasionally names of sculptors are now known. One series with sumptuous foliage decoration is attributed to the workshop of *Garrett Hollemans* of Burton upon Trent but no doubt of Netherlandish extraction. The Saunders Monument at Harrington, dated 1588, is the finest since it is carved from alabaster. The others (at Nether Heyford †1556, Charwelton 1590, Thorpe Mandeville *c.* 1600) are carved

in clunch, an unusual material in Northamptonshire. There are
then the large standing memorials with no effigies at all but
relying on architecture for effect. This type appears now at Stanford (†1568), and on the monuments at Fotheringhay (1573) and
Little Oakley (c. 1575) already referred to in relation to the
Thorpe workshop. Three of the Spencer monuments at Great
Brington are by *Jasper Hollemans*, of Burton upon Trent, a series
here all made at the same time between 1599 and 1601, and one
monument at Steane is by *John & Matthias Christmas*. As regards
types of tombs, the free-standing tomb-chest or the tomb-chest
attached to the wall and with recumbent effigy or effigies on it
is still the most frequent (e.g. Great Brington, Sir John Spencer
†1586; 1st Lord Spencer 1599; Easton Maudit †1612). Sometimes effigies in tombs placed against a wall now lie, not side by
side, but one behind and a little higher than the other (e.g.
Stanford c. 1600, Easton Maudit †1635, Steane †1633, Maidwell
1634). Sometimes also the deceased is placed on his side propped
up on his elbow in a contemplative attitude (Paulerspury †1603,
Easton Maudit †1631). The architectural surround is most frequently an arch against the back wall with a cartouche under it,
with or without flanking columns and with a top achievement
(e.g. Great Brington †1586 by *Hollemans*, Cottesbrooke †1604,
Stanford †1613, and Easton Neston †1628, the latter also Hollemans, with its splendid display like a peacock's tail under the
back arch).

49   A great rarity is the Yelverton Monument at Easton Maudit
(†1631), where the flanking columns are replaced by caryatid
figures of bearded bedesmen, an echo of French *pleureurs* of the
C15. Some specially ambitious monuments have four, or six,
columns carrying a superstructure above the tomb-chest (Great
Brington †1599, again *Hollemans*, Weekley †1602, Easton Maudit
†1612*). To this type belongs the most sumptuous monument
in Northamptonshire and one of the most sumptuous of its time
60   in England, that of Sir Anthony Mildmay †1617 at Apethorpe,
with four life-size figures of the Virtues standing at the angles
and a circular lantern raised above the centre, the work of *Maximilian Colt*. Also attributed to Colt is the Hicklinge Monument
at Green's Norton of c. 1620–30, where the type with two kneeling figures facing each other is rejuvenated and enriched by a
baldacchino and two standing angels. The other most frequent
Elizabethan type is the kneeling figure (e.g. Marston Trussell
†1612, a monument to a merchant who had died at Moscow) or
the pair of kneeling figures facing one another across a prayer-
desk (e.g. Rushden †1608, Ashby St Ledgers †1634, Kelmarsh
†1639). Occasionally yet another type is seen which had been
established before, but only for clergymen and scholars: the frontally placed bust with an architectural surround or in a niche.
This occurs in a monument to a rector of Barnwell who died in
1620 and again at Broughton (1631) and Clipston (†1632) in the

---

* A note of caution as the supports here are almost certainly an C18 replacement.
They are interesting since they are constructed of the local fossily stone.

1630s. At the same time, or, to be more precise, in 1633, the Apreece Monument at Lutton shows three kneeling figures all placed frontally. These were, just as in domestic architecture, altogether the years of change. The monument to Henry Montagu †1625 at Barnwell All Saints, which consists of a tall obelisk with the small figure in a niche and many inscriptions, is a new and original conception. So is the monument to Temperance Browne at Steane. She died in 1634, and the monument shows her in her shroud sitting up in her coffin, awakened by the last trumpet. The conceit is influenced no doubt by Nicholas Stone's monument to John Donne at St Paul's, which was set up in 1631.

The tomb-chest with the recumbent effigy remains a current type, but when it is handled by *Nicholas Stone* (Church Stowe 1617–20, Great Brington c. 1636–8), the white marble effigy becomes eloquent and elegant and belongs no longer to the tribe of the stiff, silent effigies of the Jacobean style. Stone was trained in Holland and co-operated with Inigo Jones. The Stowe tomb is remarkable in that the effigy lies in a natural pose. By Stone also is a very fine, completely simple tablet of 1640 at Blatherwycke. Such classical tablets occur in other places as well and need not be by Stone (e.g. Weekley †1644). *John Stone*, in the footsteps of his father at his most metaphysical, appears in the monument of 1656 at Great Brington, where Sir Edward Spencer rises out of a big urn which is placed between a pillar and a column. Such curious conceits were a passing fashion of the second third of the century. A lasting effect on the other hand had the iconographical innovation of the same time which is illustrated by John Stone's monument of 1655 at Newbottle. This has two free-standing busts. The same motif can be seen at Norton attributed to *Cibber*, where the date of death is 1658. The free-standing bust was soon to become a favourite memorial. It must be kept separate from the bust in a niche, which we have found before, although even in this type the 1630s bring some amendment. The niche is replaced by an oval medallion (Broughton 1631; also Passenham †1649 and Clipston †1659), and the bust may develop into a three-quarter length (Ashby St Ledgers 1663, again attributed to *Cibber*). As regards the free-standing bust, a type of secular origin which would be very popular in the c18, it occurs, placed in front of an obelisk, already in a monument of the 1640s at Marholm (Soke of Peterborough) (†1646), and placed in an open segmental pediment, as was also usual in the c18, in a monument at Clipston (†1668). But the 1660s form a border, the border between the style of Jones, Webb, and Mills and that of Wren, and so we must for the moment leave monuments again.

Late seventeenth-century houses

Following the Civil War and Commonwealth period it might be expected that there would have been a wave of new building and brand new houses. In Northamptonshire this is not the case. A sense of tradition has always been strong in the county and there

was a desire to preserve the old houses rather than replace with
new. Owners added new suites of rooms or refurbished existing
apartments. Althorp, Boughton, Castle Ashby and Drayton are
examples. What is often called the Wren style in domestic architecture was not created by Sir Christopher Wren. It was used
e.g. by *Hugh May* before Wren had even finally turned to architecture from science. It is possible that May was the designer of
the alterations of the 1670s and 1680s at Dingley. This is well-
proportioned work, and stands for more that was done externally
to houses during those decades. The climax is no doubt the so-
called Versailles front of Boughton House built by the 1st Duke
of Montagu after 1684, again extremely simple and strictly
regular but excessively noble in scale and proportions. Dingley
and Boughton have sashed windows, an innovation at the time,
the latter being some of the earliest known. The usual windows
were those of cross-type, upright, with one mullion and one
transom, to be considered below.

A word may here be inserted on WINDOWS of the later C17
and early C18. In cottages the mullioned window of Tudor type
was not given up entirely until the end of the C17. Examples are
Old House, Little Everdon, of 1690, Stonehouse Farm at Weston
of 1694, the Manor House, Ecton also of 1694, and The Croft at
Staverton of 1700. The tendency was to change over from a
horizontal to a vertical shape, and that can already be noticed in
the mullioned windows of Hazelrigg House at Northampton and
Sycamore Farm at Blakesley of 1672. Upright two-light windows
occur e.g. at Aynho Grammar School in 1671, Rose Manor,
Guilsborough, in 1686, Walnut Farmhouse at Blakesley in 1689,
The Firs, Weedon, in 1692, the Post Office at Great Billing
(Outer Northampton) in 1703, and The Manor, Wappenham, in
1704. The cross-window replaces this type. It was used e.g. in
one of the earliest houses of the classical mid-C17 type in England,
Chevening in Kent, in 1638. Webb probably used it at Lamport,
and so it goes on to Chipping Warden Manor House, dated 1668,
and survives also at Purston, Harringworth Manor and Teeton.
Boughton e.g., except for the Versailles front, has cross-windows.
So have the stables of Lamport in 1680. Side by side often with
cross-windows one can find in the later C17 oval windows placed
vertically as well as horizontally. Examples of the former are
Guilsborough Grammar School (1668 etc.), Old House, Little
Everdon (1690), and Lodge Farmhouse at Little Houghton
(1702), and of the latter The Firs, Weedon (1692) and Alderton
Manor House (1695).

The typical SMALLER HOUSE of the late C17, if built at one go
and not merely an addition or remodelling, however grand, can
best be exemplified by the elder *William Smith*'s Stanford Hall
of 1697–1700, although it lies just across the Leicestershire
border. This is a simple oblong block of nine by seven bays with
a hipped roof, cross-windows and quoins. Little is done in the
way of decorative relief. On a smaller scale the same type is
represented by Finedon vicarage of 1688, and the core of Aynhoe,
built *c.* 1680–2 by *Edward Marshall*. The windows here have

pediments, and the middle window on the first floor an aedicular frame.

In complete contrast to this restraint in the exteriors is the splendid display of DECORATION inside. Here it is hard to choose what to single out, but there is the excellent plasterwork in the Sessions House at Northampton of 1684–8 by *Edward Goudge*, who appears in the accounts for Hampton Court in the early 1690s, likewise the superb overmantels at Castle Ashby, and the staircase railing of *c.* 1680 in the same house with its openwork leaf scrolls already pointed out. The grand staircases of Boughton and Drayton on the other hand are of stone and have wrought-iron railings, and the wrought-iron work can be very fine indeed. By far the most splendid IRONWORK in Northamptonshire is that of the various gates at Drayton (1699, 1701), attributable to *Tijou*. The walls and ceilings of the grand staircases of *c.* 1700 are painted somewhat grossly by foreigners then working in England. The Drayton staircase is by *Lanscroon* and that at Harrowden Hall is attributed to him; the Boughton staircase (and much else at Boughton) is by *Cheron*. 70

There remains to consider the elusive and enigmatic figure of *John Lumley*. Lumley was born in 1654, a member of a long established mason family who had worked quarries in Harlestone since medieval times. Nothing is known of his training but in 1686 he was made free of the London Masons' Company as a 'Foreign Member'. It seems certain that he was involved in the rebuilding of Northampton after the 1675 fire but no secure documentation has been found. In 1697 he was working at Burley-on-the-Hill, Rutland, and took over the role of surveyor from another minor Northamptonshire architectural figure, *Henry Dormer*. While the basic form of the house had already been created there is evidence that Lumley was involved in some details until the house was completed in 1700. He was still in correspondence with the Earl of Nottingham about the stables until 1705. His name then occurs in accounts for Aynhoe Park in 1698, although there is no known building phase at this time. He also seems to have had some involvement *c.* 1700–2 with the building of Cottesbrooke Hall, built to the designs of *Francis Smith* of Warwick. It may well be that the basic façade design by Smith, ending in tall pilasters, was one which Lumley may have taken on board. In 1703 he was made freeman of Northampton *gratis* in repayment of a debt owed him by the Corporation. It is unclear what this refers to, but the date coincides with work going on at All Saints church, most notably the portico, and he may well have been executive builder of this, even if it was designed by *Henry Bell* (*see* below). He then appears as surveyor at Park House, Ampthill, Beds., working for Lord Nottingham's friend, Lord Ashburnham, in 1704–7, and the design of the house is credited to him. Park House is a substantial red brick and stone house of the standard double-pile plan. In 1719 he is providing designs for the Westmorland Building at Emmanuel College, Cambridge, under the patronage of the 6th Earl of Westmorland, of Apethorpe. This connection almost certainly proves that 69

Lumley was responsible for the simple Orangery at Apethorpe built the year before. The Westmorland Building is a slightly ungainly building of three storeys with an elongated pair of Ionic pilasters for decoration. It is here tempting to include the N front of Castle Ashby, also of 1719, where similar plain tall pilasters occur. As far as is known he remained in Northampton until his death in 1721. Apart from those buildings noted there is nothing which can be attributed to him with certainty but there are, entering into the minefield of speculation, a number of buildings which may be his. The rather clumsy Emmanuel College façade could be compared with the N front of Orlingbury Hall for instance. His name has been suggested for Cosgrove Hall where the façades are of two storeys with Ionic and Corinthian pilasters for each storey. There are then houses where the name of Smith of Warwick has been suggested, such as Harrowden Hall and, over the Bedfordshire border, Hinwick House and Hinwick Hall. The latter has a rather naïve central tower with angle pilasters, and the former a Smith-like front with Corinthian pilasters. It may be significant that Hinwick House has a sculptural pediment signed prominently by the Northampton sculptor *John Hunt* who is not known to have had any association with the Smiths. Of simpler form one could add Grendon Hall and Cransley Hall, where the stable block has a broad tower with angle pilasters, and a not dissimilar stable block at Horton. One can only hope that some documentation may be found which can settle more solidly Lumley's *œuvre*, for he must have built many more building than we currently know.

In CHURCH ARCHITECTURE there is only one building in the class of the great houses, All Saints at Northampton of 1676–80, designed by *Henry Bell* of King's Lynn. It is certainly not a provincial design. Its ancestors are Inigo Jones, whose celebrated portico of Old St Paul's the architect borrowed, and Christopher Wren, whose plan of St Mary-at-Hill is all but copied; there are also echoes from Holland which Bell knew. All Saints is thus externally as well as internally a church of national importance, even if the curious tracery of the windows introduces a discordant note – is it provincial or inspired by Holland? The fittings and furnishings are equally worthwhile. The doorcases, the mayor's chair and the pulpit might be in any of the London City churches. The same incidentally can be said of the pulpit of *c.* 1700 at Abington, Northampton. Worth a mention are a group of *c.* 1660 fonts, notably those at Culworth (1662) and Rockingham (1669), and there are others undated.

Far more must be said of FUNERAL MONUMENTS of *c.* 1660 to *c.* 1700. The new passion for noble display presents itself as early as 1662 in the monument to Sir Hatton Fermor at Easton Neston attributed to *Pierre Besnier*. The effigies here stand upright, alive, not dead or asleep, and in self-conscious postures, not kneeling in prayer. In the Palmer Monument at East Carlton (†1673) by *Joshua Marshall* the figures also stand, but they are in their shrouds and appear inside a black cupboard-like recess, its doors open. The conceit harks back to Stone and his Dr Donne.

Standing figures also are the centre of the monument to Sir Creswell Levinz †1700 at Evenley attributed to *John Nost*, which has lost its architectural backcloth, and of three Rockingham monuments. The dates of death are 1695, 1713 and 1724. The first is by *Nost*, the second *William Palmer* and the third *Peter Scheemakers* and *Laurent Delvaux*. The huge monument to Dr Thomas Turner †1714 at Church Stowe is by *Thomas Stayner*, and here the standing doctor is matched by a figure of Faith, a characteristically worldly conceit. Other types were not of course given up, and one can for instance still see plenty of simple tablets with ornamental surrounds – in fact the cartouches of the late C17 with their brilliantly carved garlands and cherubs' heads are among the most enjoyable works of sculpture in the churches. The free-standing tomb-chest with recumbent effigies also survives, though it is becoming rare (Sir John Langham †1671, Cottesbrooke, by *Thomas Cartwright Sen.*), and the same is true of kneeling figures in pairs. Examples are Sir Samuel Jones †1672 at Courteenhall, probably by *William Stanton*, and the Earl of Thomond (erected 1700) by *John Bushnell* at Great Billing (Outer Northampton). The latter is a curious work, rather grotesque in its handling, the work of a great mind in decay, and it comes as no surprise to learn that Bushnell died insane the year after he made the Billing tomb. The *Stantons* did more work in the county and of importance is the collection at Lamport where we find all three generations of them: Thomas, William and Edward. Other good Stanton memorials are at Marston St Lawrence and Harlestone. Signed monuments become more frequent now, and bills survive more often to identify sculptors of unsigned tombs.

THE EIGHTEENTH AND EARLY NINETEENTH CENTURIES

Early eighteenth-century country houses

At the very beginning stands Easton Neston, begun in *Wren*'s office, remodelled by *Hawksmoor*, and completed by 1702. With its simple cubic shape and the even grandeur of its giant pilasters and giant columns and crowning balustrade it is perhaps the finest house of its date in England. Wren, Hawksmoor's master and protector, was certainly involved in the original design, and although the present appearance of Easton Neston is due to Hawksmoor, it is derived from Wren's late style, the style which influenced Hawksmoor before he turned to more Baroque ideals. There is no work by Vanbrugh in Northamptonshire, but *Thomas Archer* seems to have been responsible for the wings of *c.* 1707–10 and other work at Aynhoe Park. The door pilasters set at an angle and similar motifs seem indeed a safe guide. The same development from noble grandeur to Baroque wilfulness, though in a more playful and Continental mood, can be matched in *William Talman*'s hall front at Drayton, built 1702–4. This is just about

73 as Baroque as anything anywhere. A reaction against the Baroque, whether English or Continental, set in almost at once. It acted in the name of Palladio and Inigo Jones and was led by the 3rd Earl of Burlington. Its earliest works in London belong to the years between 1715 and 1720. In Northamptonshire it appears with *Gibbs*'s Kelmarsh of *c*. 1730–36, but it met with the opposition of those who believed in the more staid Baroque which the *Smiths* of Warwick, influenced by Buckingham House in London, had made their own. This Baroque is characterized by an ample use of giant pilasters. Cottesbrooke Hall of 1702–13, by *Francis Smith*, using the layout of a central block with two pavilions linked by quadrant wings, and Orlingbury Hall of *c*. 1706–10 and later Dallington Hall near Northampton and Bramston House, Oundle, belong to it. Cottesbrooke in addition demonstrates the double-pile plan which was the vogue of the moment – a novelty in the county for even at Easton Neston this is reflected rather than directly stated.

The Midland fashion of employing the Smiths inevitably spread into Northamptonshire. At Lamport they added wings onto the earlier Webb building, keeping in their exteriors remarkably tactfully to Webb's style. They added a new block onto the house at Fawsley, created a new house at Harlestone and began another at Hinton, Woodford Halse. It is likely that they were also involved at both Canons Ashby and Deene. Francis Smith in all probability designed new fronts at Abington Abbey, Northampton, and William Smith designed Edgcote, executed after his

87 death by *William Jones*. In *c*. 1740 the Earl of Westmorland called in *Roger Morris* to transform Apethorpe Hall into a grand Palladian mansion. We have to be grateful that the scheme never reached fruition or the grand suite of Jacobean apartments, for which the house has become famous, would all have disappeared. Morris built the stables at Althorp *c*. 1733 and is credited with a

89 striking façade on the Manor House, Woodnewton. *William Kent* began a new hunting lodge at Wakefield, Potterspury, *c*. 1745 for

90 the Duke of Grafton, with a plan deriving from Jones's Queen's House at Greenwich, but died before it was completed, the final work probably being undertaken by *Robert Taylor*. *Henry Flitcroft*, 'Burlington's Harry', designed the entrance hall of Lilford Hall. Purely Palladian also are Astrop of after 1735 again by the Smiths and the stables at Courteenhall of *c*. 1750 attributed to *John Carr* of York. Of Palladian interiors the first is perhaps the entrance hall at Althorp, also probably by Morris; of Rococo interiors the best are those at Lamport Hall of 1740, at Easton Neston of *c*. 1740, at Cottesbrooke Hall (especially the staircase), and at

92 Upton (with stucco work of 1737 by *Giuseppe Artari*). There are
85 good mid-C18 interiors also at Edgcote (1747–52), Cransley and Thenford. Thenford is dated 1761–5 and is somewhat puzzling in that it has, to crown its Palladian front, two hipped roofs side by side and a cupola between, a 1660- rather than a 1760-looking motif.

This seems the best place to introduce the partnership between *Samuel Warren* (1645–1709) and his son *Thomas* (1675–1735), both blacksmiths by trade. Samuel, however, developed a considerable skill in devising water mechanics used to provide a supply for several large houses. This activity is recorded by John Morton in his *Natural History of Northamptonshire* published in 1712. The elder Warren began his life at Weston Favell, then just E of Northampton. Morton states that he was responsible for 'The conveyance of water to my Lord Northampton's seat at Castle Ashby' and this is confirmed by payments in the archive there in 1698–9 to 'Mr Warren for laying the foundation of a waterhouse' and for his bill 'for an Ingon' in 1701. Morton also credits him with a similar system at Easton Neston where 'water is brought 2,000 yards with a 4 inches fall' – a remarkable achievement. It is almost certain that a similar system at Abington, Warren's neighbouring parish, where a water tower is dated 1678, is also his. Thomas assisted his father, although the only example of him doing such work so far discovered is at Aynho, where in 1724 he was paid for 'ye engine'. Thomas's main reputation is, however, as a wrought-iron smith. It is conceivable that he developed this skill at either Easton Neston in the 1690s or at Drayton around 1700 when the Tijou workshop was employed there. Such was his skill that it was recognized by Sir John Vanbrugh, who employed him at Blenheim 1709–11. He probably met Vanbrugh at Kimbolton, where a garden balustrade can be attributed to him. He did considerable work at Castle Ashby between 1704 and his death, such as 'a pair of gates for the bowling green' in 1727. Sadly none of this now survives. Thomas Warren is also recorded at Clare College Cambridge, 1713–15, and at Wimpole Hall, Cambs., in 1710–24. Doubtless much of the decorative ironwork in the county is his work. While it has elements of the Tijou style, his work relies more on sequences of scrollwork rather than repoussé. The church screen at Haselbech is one of his finest surviving pieces, to which can be added gates at Finedon church and Kislingbury rectory. He is buried in the churchyard at Castle Ashby, where he had set up his forge, under a slab inscribed 'fam'd for his skill in Mechanicks and Ironwork'.

Of SMALLER HOUSES there are a number of fine parsonages of the early C18 such as those at Easton-on-the-Hill and Yardley Hastings. Of more sophistication are that of 1727 at Lamport designed by *Francis Smith* of Warwick and another attributed to him at Kislingbury. In the towns, local gentry built fine houses such as those in Oundle (Bramston House and The Berrystead) and there are similar examples in Brackley and on the Market Square in Northampton.

On the the broader LANDSCAPE front *Capability Brown* is to be found at Wakefield, Fawsley and more obviously at Castle Ashby. Alongside the house is his Dairy and above the lake on the park boundary his charming Menagerie, assuming it is his and not Adam's. At Horton are the remains of a landscape attributed to *Thomas Wright* with one of the most delightful park

91   buildings in the Midlands, his Menagerie, together with a classical temple and an arched eyecatcher. A further classical temple
stands by the Oval at Althorp, but this is a visitor, having started
its life in the garden at the Admiralty. *Repton* designed the landscape at Harlestone and was involved with both landscape and
architecture at Courteenhall.

At about this time medievalism made its entry into Northamptonshire. Two especially good GOTHICK churches exist, Wicken
and East Carlton. The nave and aisles of Wicken were built in
1758 by the gentleman-architect *Thomas Prowse* in a rather
curious manner with quatrefoil piers and shallow vaults. The
chancel completed by his widow *c.* 1770, very probably to her
husband's design, has delicious fan-vaulting, just like the drawing
room at Arbury, Warwicks. East Carlton is a much more serious
job. It was built in 1788 to the designs of *John Wing Jun.* and it
shows that Wing had studied the medieval Dec style, the window
tracery and the tower being so convincing that the building at
first sight looks medieval. There is only one major Gothick
country house survival, the s front of Ecton Hall. It was built in
1756, i.e. two years before Mr Prowse's fan-vaults in the chancel
at Wicken. Designs exist signed by *William Hiorne* but it is very
likely that *Sanderson Miller* may also have been involved. To these
can be added the castellated follies round Boughton Park and
the group of cottages behind a castellated wall at Preston Capes
which were an eyecatcher for Fawsley. Most of these date from
c. 1770, although the Hawking Tower at Boughton Park was built
by 1756. There are also Gothic features on the somewhat later N
front of Brockhall Hall and the exceedingly pretty *c.* 1800 canal
bridge at Cosgrove.

Non-domestic secular architecture

We break this survey off just before the new and more elegant
style of Robert Adam sweeps the board of classical design and
the Gothic Revival begins to query its validity altogether, to look
at secular architecture other than domestic and at ecclesiastical
architecture and decoration.

Secular architecture other than domestic should indeed have
been introduced earlier, but so far it has been enough to mention
the odd market hall or school as the context of its style required.
Now the fact must be emphasized that such public, charitable
and scholastic buildings grow in frequency and importance as
the C16 moves into the C17 and the C17 into the C18. A list is
simple. For PUBLIC BUILDINGS it starts with Sir Thomas
Tresham's Market House at Rothwell, built by *William Grumbold*
c. 1578, culminates in the Sessions House at Northampton –
68   designed by *Henry Bell* of King's Lynn, built in 1676–8, and
provided with the masterly stucco ceilings by Goudge which have
already been mentioned – and ends for the time being with the
84   Brackley Town Hall of 1704–7, presented by the 1st Duke of
Bridgewater, and the modest Palladian Daventry Moot Hall of

1769. The list of SCHOOLS is a little longer, and some of them are of remarkable size considering their date. We start with the Finedon Boys' School endowed in 1595, the Daventry Grammar School of 1600, the Wellingborough (Old) Grammar School of 1620, and the school at Burton Latimer of 1622. The next group belongs to the mid C17. It begins with the Cottesbrooke School and Hospital of 1651, and goes on to two most generous and stately schools, Clipston Grammar School and Hospital of 1667–73 and Guilsborough Grammar School of 1668. This was for fifty boys, a remarkably large number for a C17 foundation. In style both are still closer to the early than the late C17. The Aynho Grammar School of 1671 has upright two-light windows, the Courteenhall Grammar School of 1680 cross-windows and a big, open segmental pediment above the doorway. Its arrangement of benches inside is preserved. Two of the schools in this list were combined with HOSPITALS. Hospitals as independent buildings were erected in 1591–3 at Rothwell (on an interesting plan) and at Weekley in 1611. After 1675 these charitable activities came more or less to a standstill, although a number of elementary schools were founded in the C18. Examples are Ashton, near Oundle, 1705; Finedon, 1714; Lowick, 1718–25; Kingscliffe Boys' School and Almshouses, 1749, and Girls' School, 1752–4; Ecton, 1752; and Culworth, 1794.

The first surviving NONCONFORMIST CHAPELS in the county are Georgian too,* i.e. those of the Congregationalists at Long Buckby (1771) and Potterspury (1780) and that of the Baptists at Thrapston (1787). There is also a Moravian chapel of 1810 at Culworth and a delightful Friends' Meeting House of 1819 at Wellingborough. Others might be mentioned, but many are too small and too uniform to call for special listing.

Church building and decoration

CHURCH BUILDING after 1720 makes a reasonable show. There is not much, but what there is has a great variety of interest. Chronologically arranged the list of C18 churches looks like this: Stoke Doyle 1722–5, by *Thomas Eayre*; Aynho 1723–5 by *Edward Wing*, but so much in the style of *Thomas Archer* that he may well have had a hand in it; Wollaston 1737, with giant Tuscan columns between nave and aisles; the chancel at Lamport by *William Smith* 1743, with splendid plasterwork by *J. Woolston* of Northampton; the chancel at Warkton of shortly after 1749, with its four niches to hold the spectacular monuments to which we shall turn presently; the large and townish parish church of Daventry 1752–8 by *David Hiorne*, the only larger Georgian church in the county, with a spire and giant Tuscan columns inside; and also his, Great Houghton of 1754 with its good, strong spire.

* Except for the Doddridge Congregational Chapel, Northampton, founded 1695, but this is not in its original state.

Georgian CHURCH FURNISHINGS hardly fill a paragraph: some fonts (the best being at Draughton, Oundle and Cottesbrooke), some decaying stained glass of 1732 at Apethorpe by *J. Rowell*, and an organ case at Finedon. That is all. The organ case, to be sure, is something special, by *Shrider*. There was one at Towcester, originally in the mansion of William Beckford's nabob father, but it has been removed.

For CHURCH MONUMENTS on the other hand the situation is reversed, and it is evident that space is lacking to introduce and classify them all. For some the index of artists must suffice (e.g. *E. Bingham* of Peterborough; *J. Hunt* of Northampton, who made the statue of Charles II for All Saints Northampton, and was an apprentice of Gibbons; and the *Cox* family, also of Northampton). Others are anonymous and will not even be found there. We start with the coming of Baroque classicism, that is Baroque sculpture in Palladian settings. This is what characterizes *Guelfi*'s Duchess of Richmond †1722 at Deene in its Kentian frame and the eight known monuments by *J. M. Rysbrack*. Three of these, at Edgcote, are purely architectural, two are architectural too but have a bust as well (Ecton 1732 and †1761). Three bust reliefs are on the monument at Hardingstone, two of *c.* 1746, the third added *c.* 1759, and an excellent bust is also on the fourth monument at Edgcote (1760). Of major importance is the Ward Monument at Stoke Doyle of *c.* 1720–2, an early but completely self-assured work by Rysbrack, even if its semi-reclining figure is still in the C17 and early C18 tradition. The quality of carving here is as good as Rysbrack ever achieved. The standing figure of Lady Arabella Oxenden †1734 at Rockingham is also almost certainly by him too. Another semi-reclining figure is by *Robert Hartshorne* (Thorpe Achurch †1719), clumsy compared with Rysbrack's, and there are two more at Lowick (†1705 and †1718, attributed to *William Woodman*). Traditionally attributed to *Scheemakers*, an attribution now considered dubious, is a bust belonging to the Isham Monument (†1737) at Lamport. The Scheemakers at Rockingham (†1724) has already been mentioned. *L.-F. Roubiliac* was without doubt the most brilliant Georgian sculptor in England, and Northamptonshire is lucky in possessing two of his most spectacular monuments. They face one another in the chancel of Warkton church, and one is hard put to decide whether the feminine charms of the monument to Duchess Mary of 1753 or the masculine vigour of the monument to Duke John of 1752 should be valued more highly. Both compositions are completely free, and with their serpentine or zigzag movement through space eminently characteristic of the Rococo. Roubiliac's Lynn Monument at Southwick (†1758) while simpler is not inferior to these two. *John Bacon*'s Langton Freke Monument at Kings Sutton (†1769) is clearly influenced by Roubiliac at his most dramatic, the Roubiliac of the Hargrave Monument in Westminster Abbey. It is an odd thing, being more a plaster model rather than a full-scale memorial. At Warkton, next to Roubiliac's Duke John, is the monument to the Duchess of Montagu of 1775, carved by *van Gelder*. It is the farewell to Baroque and Rococo; for though

79

80
82

van Gelder still composes according to Baroque formulae, his style lacks the *brio* and the scintillating chiselwork of Roubiliac, though his standing figure of an angel deserves admiration. Another *John Bacon* (an excellent monument at Ashby St Ledgers, 1784), several *Nollekens* (Whiston †1775, Great Brington †1783 to a design by *Cipriani*, Whiston †1792), and the curious painted monuments by *Mrs Creed* at Titchmarsh (early c18) are no more than a postscript. It is Robert Adam and his style that we must halt at.

83

Neoclassical country houses

It has already been said that in the field of domestic decoration the Adam style swept the board, but Northamptonshire has less to offer than many other counties and there is no major Neoclassical house. Of the houses of the period the most important are Eydon Hall by *James Lewis* (1789–91), *Samuel Saxon* and *Repton*'s Courteenhall of 1791–3, the exquisite anonymous Orangery at Barton Seagrave Hall, and *Robert Mitchell*'s work at Cottesbrooke Hall, which includes the lodges, bridge and gates as well as plasterwork inside. Repton's Sulby Hall, 1792–5 is, alas, no longer standing. While no original work by Adam is known in the county,* several houses have interiors in his style. The best examples are at Drayton, which date from the early 1770s and are the work of the elusive *William Rhodes*, a London plasterer of the first order. The dining room at Drayton is the finest Neoclassical interior in the county, and the drawing room there has a Palmyra ceiling. *Henry Holland* was responsible for beautifully restrained interiors at Althorp (1786–90), the younger *Dance* for the fine hall at Laxton Hall, and *Soane* for a delightful series of rooms at Aynhoe Park (1800–5). They are of course, with their idiosyncratic shallow arches and vaults, a good deal removed from the Adam style of a generation before.

93

94

Early nineteenth-century architecture

The Victorian age is now nearly with us, and no more need prevent us from exploring its Northamptonshire aspects than two or three notes about the style of the REGENCY and after. Again there is no major Regency house in the county but there are a number of smaller ones such as Bragborough at Braunston, Newnham Hall and Badby House. Northampton has a number of villas of the period, notably in Spencer Parade and Cheyne Walk, and occasionally a village produces an example, such as Scaldwell Grange at Scaldwell and Easton Hall, Easton-on-the-Hill. Of special note are an interesting sequence of model FARM-HOUSES built by the Duke of Grafton on his estates in the SE

* We should note his involvement with the landscape at Castle Ashby, where his signed plan survives.

97   corner of the county. They can be seen round Abthorpe, Blakes-
     ley, Green's Norton, Paulerspury, Shutlanger and Stoke Bruerne,
     and are at once recognizable by their spacious, regular and
     rational planning and their plain but sound architecture. They
     look Regency but were built as late as *c.* 1841–3. Another note
     must draw attention to a spacious and rationally planned enter-
96   prise, the Royal Ordnance Depot at Weedon, begun in 1804 and
     comprising originally of a tripartite group of quite stately domes-
     tic buildings, alas demolished, and two rows of long storehouses
     facing one another across the canal wharf, which is shut off from
     the canal by a portcullis.

     It remains to bring the history of CHURCH MONUMENTS up
     to date, i.e. to carry it on from about 1800 to the verge of the
     Victorian style. Most of the best monuments are now signed, but
     by no means all of them. As for the signed pieces, here are the
     works of the masters. *Flaxman* first with monuments at Grafton
     Regis (†1808), Great Billing (†1812) and Great Brington (†1814);
     Regnart second, a minor sculptor but one whose chef d'œuvre is
     in Northamptonshire (the reclining effigy of George Rush †1806
     at Farthinghoe); *Bacon Jun.* third, who did several monuments
     at Cottesbrooke including the fine free-standing vase on a ped-
     estal (1815) made in *Coade* stone; *Westmacott* fourth with one
     monument (†1809) at Marston St Lawrence and one (*c.* 1820)
     at Grafton Underwood; *Rossi* fifth with an early monument still
     in the Bacon style at Canons Ashby (†1797), one of curiously
     Victorian Quattrocento inspiration at Ecton (†1817), and a fine
     (attributed) Grecian monument at Canons Ashby (1818).
     Chantrey is well represented by monuments at Kelmarsh (†1807),
     Northampton Town Hall (from All Saints, 1817), Easton Neston
     (1819), Stoke Doyle (†1819), Whittlebury (†1820) and Great
     Brington (1833). The last empty niche in the chancel at Warkton
     was finally filled by a very monumental but very cold classical
     machine by *Campbell* (†1827). A monument (†1830) at Stanford
     is said to be by the Dutchman *Kessells*. Just within our range of
     dates also come four early monuments by Early Victorian sculp-
     tors, that by *Behnes* at Norton (†1825), one by *W. Pitts* at Whiston
     (†1835), and the two by *Baily* at Easton Neston (†1830 and 1835).
     By *Westmacott Jun.* are one (†1844) at Stanford and another at
     Lowick (†1843).

                    VICTORIAN AND EDWARDIAN
                            ARCHITECTURE

     Few buildings would find admittance in a national as against a
     county list. Mark Girouard's *Victorian Country House* only finds
     reference to Castle Ashby, Finedon Hall and Overstone Park.
     The work at Castle Ashby is a revamping of the Jacobean interior
     by *Wade* and the gardens by *M. D. Wyatt* and *E. W. Godwin. E. F.
     Law*'s Finedon was all but gutted when it was converted into

apartments, and *W. M. Teulon*'s Overstone now stands as a blackened fire-destroyed shell. Godwin is important, having won the competition for the new Town Hall in 1864 for Northampton, designed in a Ruskin *Stones of Venice* manner, and while his Germanic Rheinfelden on Billing Road has gone, the Gothic St Martin's Villas, opposite its site, are still there. *William Burn* was held in check at Lamport and his more lavish Jacobethan Whittlebury Lodge was demolished in 1972. *Salvin* was similarly held in check at Rockingham, adding a tower which adds much to the garden façade. At Fawsley he rebuilt an earlier wing and added more to another, but there Salvin's Tudor detracts rather than enhances the front. *E. F. Law*'s other major house is East Carlton Hall, where a sensible Georgian house was replaced by a rather monstrous and unwieldly essay in the French chateau manner. His revamping of Moreton Pinkney Manor was more sympathetic and has the advantage of a pleasant lodge and gateway. Law's other work was the rebuilding of parsonages, usually in a mild Elizabethan style, and there are several to choose from: Little Addington and Aldwinkle are two examples. At Althorp *Macvicar Anderson* was also restrained, working in a relatively quiet Neo-Georgian mode.

Victorian ESTATE HOUSING is prominent in a number of villages and proof of the care with which Northamptonshire landowners looked after their tenants. Precursor examples are the *cottage orné* village begun in 1800–10 by the *Reptons* at Laxton and the slightly later Gothick cottages at Hulcote on the Easton Neston Estate. Substantial and picturesque Spencer housing of *c.* 1848 is at Church Brampton, Chapel Brampton, Little Brington and Harlestone; Grafton housing of *c.* 1850 at Potterspury; Lady Overstone's housing at Sywell of the 1860s; Pulteney housing at Ashley also of the 1860s; and so on to the remarkable Rothschild housing of 1900 etc. at Ashton near Oundle.

98

When we come to the CHURCHES of the period there is more to say. This, of course, was the great age of church restoration and Northamptonshire's medieval churches were an obvious target. They had become well known to readers of J. H. Parker's publications, notably his *ABC of Gothic Architecture* and his *Glossary*, both of which abound in Northamptonshire examples. There is no doubt that many churches were in dire need of some attention and the text of *Churches of the Archdeaconry of Northampton* (1849), incidentally published by Parker, gives some indication of their condition. One of the first architects to turn his attention to Northamptonshire was *R. C. Hussey*, a pupil of Rickman in Birmingham. He rebuilt two churches in the 1840s (Orlingbury 1843, Braunston 1849). The first is a serious essay in the Dec style with a tall central tower and an E rose window. It is slightly less impressive a sight today since its pinnacles had to be reduced in height for safety reasons, but it still looks well. Braunston is a more prosperous model, also in the Dec style. Less satisfactory is his rebuilding of Weston-by-Welland in 1863, even if Kelly describes it as 'in exact facsimile'. His restorations are more gentle but Potterspury must stand out for the daring introduction of a triple chancel arch which does much for the interior of that church. *G. G. Scott* was born in 1839 just over the border at Gawcott near Buckingham; his father had the living at Wappenham and that church may have some of his earliest work. Scott's major restoration in the county is undoubtedly at Ashley (1867) where he was ably assisted by *Clayton & Bell* and *Bodley*. The beautifully restored interior of the chancel at Ashley is one of the triumphs of recent years. Architecturally more lavish but more predictable Scott are his restoration and eastern extension of the Church of the Holy Sepulchre in Northampton (1879). This is Scott in his favourite Early Dec manner which he repeated on a smaller scale in the chapel at St Andrew's Hospital (1863). Two of the most expensive High Victorian interiors are by *J. K. Colling* at Kelmarsh (1874) and at nearby Arthingworth (1872), and a third is also nearby at Haselbech (with the lavish chancel of 1881 by *F. Butler*). The restoration of Haselbech had begun under *William Slater* in 1859. Haselbech is where Slater was born, and indeed where he is buried, and this local connection doubtless accounts for why he and his partner *R. H. Carpenter* got so many commissions in the county. Their work while unremarkable is usually in excellent taste. They were especially tactful in their furnishings. *William Butterfield* appears three times in the county, at his most eccentric at Hellidon (1845–7), where he also built the rectory (1852), the other two restorations less obtrusive (Wootton in 1865 and Dodford in 1878–80). Other restorations often fell to favoured architects of the Peterborough diocese, notably *Edward Browning* of Stamford and *E. F. Law* of Northampton. Browning's work inevitably occurs more in the N of the county. He could be very self-effacing, such as the restoration at Rockingham, but occasionally can launch into something more extreme, as at Sibbertoft (1862–3). The Law firm (that is *E. F. Law* and his son *Edmund*) was very active around Northampton in both rebuilding and restoration. Their restorations can be a little overpowering, for example at Dallington (1883) and Great Billing (1867), but much seemed to depend inevitably on what funds were available. A new church by the firm is at Yardley Gobion (1863–4), a modest building in the Early Dec manner. Northampton boasts another worthy architect of the period, *Matthew Holding*. Holding was a pupil of *Charles Buckeridge* and when he died suddenly Holding was taken into the office of *J. L. Pearson*, just at the point when Pearson was working on designs for Truro and St Michael Croydon. Holding was much inspired by Pearson's work and this is nowhere more obvious than in his St Matthew Northampton (1891–3), the finest church interior of the period in the county with some splendid craftsmanship as well as architecture. His other churches in the town explore the styles of Gothic architecture: St Mary Far Cotton (1885), E.E.; Christ Church (1904), Transitional Dec/Perp; and Holy Trinity, Kingsthorpe (1909), Perp. The crescendo of the period is *Sir Ninian Comper*'s St Mary Wellingborough. This brings together in a stupendous way all the ideas of the Victorian era with an interior designed to bring one to one's knees. It was begun in

1908 and was structurally complete by 1930, though its interior decoration was never fully carried out, and perhaps it is better for this.

A final word on CHURCH MONUMENTS. *Tenerani*'s monuments at Castle Ashby, though the earlier is of 1836, must be seen in Victorian contexts. The second is an over-life-size seated angel of white marble and dates from 1866. The combination of sentimentality with overdone size is wholly Victorian. At Castle Ashby there is also a big *Marochetti* monument (†1858), and that is Gothic and reintroduces the motif of the recumbent effigy. Finally two monuments by *John Gibson* of Rome, at Fawsley (†1856) and Stanford (†1862), the latter probably actually carved by *Mary Thornycroft*. The former is in the Georgian tradition, the latter is again a big Victorian machine with Gothic background and recumbent effigy. That finishes the survey of monuments.

A mention must also be made of STAINED GLASS. With almost every parish church having some work done during the later C19 or early C20, there is inevitably a good quantity of it. The mecca for many enthusiasts will be Middleton Cheney, where the *Morris* company from the mid 1860s filled almost every window with fine designs. There is almost equally fine Morris glass at Guilsborough. St Matthew's Northampton is another church with a gallery of glass: *Clayton & Bell*, *Kempe*, *Hymers* and *Percy Bacon*. Barby should be mentioned since almost every window is by the *Kempe* firm. Higham Ferrers also has a fine Kempe Jesse window as well as important modern glass by *John Hayward*. Of Victorian glass there is the fine series of the 1860s at Watford by *Heaton, Butler & Bayne* and another window by them at Sibbertoft. *Christopher Whall* was born in Northamptonshire so should be noted, especially for his two windows at Apethorpe and a stunning war memorial window at Sywell; the splendid St Katherine at Irchester is by *Veronica Whall*.

The C19 architecture in the TOWNS is inevitably more eclectic in style. Northampton was a relatively modest country town until the arrival of the canal and the railway in the middle of that century. This set in motion the expansion of the boot and shoe industry and the prosperity of the town. To a lesser extent the same applies to the other major towns, Kettering and Wellingborough. Northampton's civic pride is nowhere better illustrated than by Godwin's Town Hall, already referred to. Alongside this arose some impressive shoe factories of which the finest, Manfields, like an Italian palace, on the Mounts (1857–9) has sadly gone. Expensive villas began to be built along Billing Road, Cheyne Walk and Cliftonville, nearly all by local designers (*Law, Holding, Dorman* etc.). Behind these fashionable rows arose streets of terraced houses interspersed with the occasional factory or Nonconformist chapel, and while much has been lost in Northampton the creation of a conservation area from Billing Road and N across the Kettering Road will ensure that what is left will survive. Rather better preserved, although not protected, is a similar area in Kettering, between the Stamford and Rockingham roads. Kettering in fact has still a good display of Late

104

108
109
Victorian and Edwardian architecture, not a little owed to its native architect *John Alfred Gotch*. The firm was founded in 1879 and gradually expanded; he took *Charles Saunders* into partnership in 1887 and then *Henry Surridge* in 1899. Once established Gotch to an extent cornered the architectural field in Kettering and the firm continues to this day, still using the three partners' names. Several main streets are lined with the firm's terraced rows of shops, offices and apartments, displaying in most cases Gotch's variant designs deriving from his great interest in English Renaissance architecture. Especially important are a series of Board Schools the firm designed in the town, nearly all in a varied Jacobethan manner with tall boiler chimneys rising like campaniles above the sites. There is another good example in Gretton.

109
Gotch also designed a number of villas such as Sunnylands in the Headlands and Elm Bank on Northampton Road. Outside Kettering are a number of sizeable houses such as Burdyke at Weekley (1902) and Armston House at Barnwell (1884). There are also other substantial villas by other architects along Rockingham Road, Kettering. In Wellingborough the local architects
105
were *Edward Sharman* and *Walter Talbot Brown*. Sharman was a fairly orthodox Gothic designer in his early days but later, when he had formed the firm of *Sharman & Archer*, and taken into partnership his son John, developed a grand Neo-Georgian manner, designing two important schools, the former School for Girls (1915) in Northampton (now one of the university buildings), and the former County High School in Wellingborough (1912), now part of Wrenn School. One of their finest buildings is the 1912
111
United Reformed church at Desborough, a most striking building somewhere between Neoclassical and Arts and Crafts.

Full blown Art Nouveau is hardly seen in the county but what one might call 'Turn of the Century' design gets a good showing, most notably in Northampton. The influence is Glasgow and it comes from two directions: first in the work of *Alexander Anderson*, who had early training there, and secondly from *Charles Rennie Mackintosh*. Anderson came to Northampton around 1893 and within a couple of years is producing some outstanding buildings. One of the grandest is for the Glasgow leather factors Malcolm Inglis, City Buildings (1900) in Fish Street, an extraordinary multi-storey building with an elaborate corner façade incorporating sculptural decoration and what was to become his very individual style of lettering. He went on to design several shoe-making factories, for firms like Crockett & Jones and Church's. He also had a very individual approach to house design which begins with a curved house built for himself in Abington Avenue (No.19) in 1895 and comes to fruition in a group of houses for the projected Alexandra Park estate in Christchurch Road, begun in 1905, with such names as The Nook, Hillcrest and the delightful Cottage and Bungalow in Sandringham Road, in reality neither exactly fitting their labels. Anderson was a friend of one of Northampton's foremost art patrons, the model maker Wenman Bassett-Lowke. In 1916 he had acquired a small terrace house in Derngate and asked Anderson to redesign the

internal layout. Bassett-Lowke was a keen follower of design
fashion and attended several international design exhibitions. For
the interior decoration of the Derngate house he approached
Charles Rennie Mackintosh, and Mackintosh produced some of
his most imaginative interiors. Despite the changing ownership
of the house these have in essence survived and, now fully
restored, represent not only a remarkable addition to Northampton's heritage but Mackintosh's only surviving interiors outside
Glasgow. Mackintosh also made alterations to a cottage at Roade
for Bassett-Lowke and the dining room interior was copied for
his brother-in-law's house in The Drive, Northampton. Elsewhere in the county there is less *c.* 1900 architecture of note. Of
national importance is *Voysey*'s The Hill, Thorpe Mandeville,
1897–8, even if not of the first order, but distinctive enough of
Voysey's style: battered rendered walls, a veranda, arched
entrance etc. The Arts and Crafts vernacular manner is represented by *Lutyens*'s work at Ashby St Ledgers, begun in 1904
and still being altered twenty years later, by which time vernacular had given place to a style more akin to his work in New Delhi.
Other examples are *C. H. Biddulph-Pinchard*'s Gate House of
1920–5 at Syresham and 1931 extensions at Purston by an
unknown architect. Another important example was *Walter
Cave*'s Littlecourt at Farthingstone (1905), but the main house
was demolished in the 1950s and only the stable block now
remains. There are a number of mock Elizabethan houses of the
early C20 with two especially grand examples: Hinton House,
Woodford Halse, 1900 by *James A. Morris* of Ayr, his only work
S of the border, and Thornby Hall, 1921–5 by *Charles S. Mordaunt*,
an architect who worked almost solely for his patron there. One
ought to record the work of *Gotch* around this time, most notably
in his restoration of houses like Rushton Hall and Drayton.

That brings us to the end of the survey of buildings up to 1914,
but before the narrative is continued into the rest of the C20, a
word is required about structures associated with Northamptonshire's industry and transport.

INDUSTRY AND TRANSPORT IN THE
NINETEENTH AND TWENTIETH CENTURIES

BY

GEOFFREY STARMER

The natural resources of stone, clay and iron ore in Northamptonshire were exploited from early times. The buildings associated with the working of stone were little more than sheds, but
the use of clay to produce BRICKS was practised at many sites in
the county, sometimes using clamps but usually by firing in kilns.
Generally, the bricks were of a dark red colour often impressed
with the name of the brickworks. In the 1930s there were brickworks at many places in the county, the major centres being

Blisworth, Corby, Duston, Higham Ferrers, Kettering, Northampton and Wellingborough, but since that time brickmaking
declined until the surviving brickworks at Raunds closed in 1974.
In Northamptonshire, the smelting of iron ore to produce IRON
seems to have been forgotten for several centuries until interest
revived in the mid C19. Blast furnaces and their associated
blowing houses were erected at eleven sites in the county:
Heyford, Stowe, Finedon, Irthlingborough, Islip, Hunsbury Hill,
Towcester, Cransley, Kettering, Wellingborough and Corby, but
apart from the last, all these sites have now been cleared of their
buildings. In addition to the iron-ore extraction sites adjacent to
the furnaces there were many iron-ore workings remote from the
furnaces they served. These required connection to the mainline
railway system and the railways, of gauges varying from 3 ft to
the standard 4 ft 8½ in., often involved bridges under the public
roads. Most of the ore was extracted from open pits but in some
locations it was worked underground, as at Islip, where one of
the ventilation shafts survives. Usually there were no significant
structures at these workings but at Wakerley cylindrical kilns over
33 ft (10 metres) high were erected in 1914–18 for calcining the
ore; although never used, they remain *in situ*. By the late 1960s
the only remaining iron-ore workings were at Corby, which
closed when the iron and steel works were shut down in 1980.

Farming and forestry were practised extensively in the county.
The subsequent processing of the products of these led to significant structures such as water-, wind- and later steam-powered
MILLS for flour, paper, tanning and sawing timber. The river
system of Northamptonshire provided power at over 170 sites.
Many of these WATERMILLS have been demolished and most of
the survivors have been converted to dwellings or other uses, e.g.
Duddington. WINDMILLS were introduced in the C12 and nearly
200 sites have been identified in Northamptonshire, although not
all would have had a windmill at any given time. There are no
remains of post mills and of the twelve upstanding remains of
tower mills one at Braunston has been well adapted to a dwelling,
but others have been so altered through house conversion that
they are hardly recognizable. In 1788 a Boulton & Watt steam
engine was installed in the watermill at Sulgrave. This seems to
have been the first steam engine in the county (the second,
another Boulton & Watt engine, was not erected until 1797 at the
Cotton Mill in Northampton). During the C19 other mills began
to use steam engines as supplementary power and by 1886 eight
mills were entirely dependent on steam power. One of these, built
in 1879 for Joseph Westley & Sons at Blisworth, is now converted
into apartments. Another, still in use by Whitworth Bros, millers,
was erected in 1886 at Wellingborough.

Barley was milled for animal food but it was also converted
into malt for BREWING. The increase in size of the common
brewers in towns led to the construction of large maltings nearby,
resulting in the closure of the small rural maltings, which were
soon adapted for other purposes and lost their distinctive conical
or pyramidal roofs. Some of the larger town maltings survive and

despite adaption for other use retain characteristic features, as can be seen at Kettering (Elworthy's, 1904), Northampton (St James' Road, 1887–8) and Oundle (ceased 1947 and converted to apartments under the name of Fotheringhay Mews). In earlier times brewing of beer from malt was at a domestic scale and *c*. 1820 this still accounted for half the beer brewed in England. The 1830 Beer Act seems to have encouraged small-scale brewing by removing the need for a lengthy licensing process. Since the product is a liquid, the different stages of brewing could be situated one above the other so that gravity provided the movement between the different stages of the process. This encouraged the construction of multi-storey buildings and large breweries were established in Northampton, Kettering, Oundle and Wellingborough. Surviving buildings include the former Anchor Brewery in Oundle (operated by Charles Frederick McKee 1886–1906) and the Hope Brewery (used by W. J. East & Co. Ltd 1888) in Milton Malsor. The Phipps Brewery at Northampton was rebuilt in Brutalist style in the 1970s for Carlsberg.

From the late C17 PAPER was made at eight sites in the county: Boughton 1717–1814; Hardingstone (Rush Mills) 1684–1897; Isham 1756–1821; Northampton (Town Mill) 1781–95; Northampton (Vigo) 1731–83; Ringstead 1782–1833; Woodford Upper Mill 1748–1835; and Yardley Gobion 1729–1851. In 1840, Mr Wise of Rush Mills obtained the first order from the Post Office for the supply of penny adhesive stamps.

Until the C17 BOOTS and SHOES were made in the county on the same scale as elsewhere. In 1642 a large order of footwear from Northamptonshire for the army required manufacture on a large scale and was the impetus for the subsequent development of the industry in the county. During the C18 footwear manufacture developed in Daventry, Kettering and Wellingborough, later in Higham Ferrers, Rushden and Raunds and subsequently in their surrounding villages. Initially shoemaking was entirely a hand process, with most of the work done at the workers' homes, leading in some places to outworkers' shops, usually single-storey, in the garden. Two-storey outworkers' workshops survive behind houses in East Street, Long Buckby. The manufacturer usually had little more than a warehouse from which work was issued out and taken in. Changes came in the latter part of the C19 with the increasing use of machinery, usually powered by internal combustion engines, and production undertaken almost entirely in factories. Most of the earlier shoe factories were of three storeys, with the top floor used for clicking (cutting out the components of the upper part of the shoe from fine leather) and closing (sewing together the components), the intermediate floor for lasting and attaching and finishing and the shoe room being carried out just above street level. Raw materials were stored at the bottom in rooms which were part above and part below street pavement level. Small-scale versions of this arrangement can be found in all the county's former shoemaking towns, e.g., Mill Street, Wellingborough, and Henry Street, Northampton. Larger examples survive in all the county's former footwear manufacturing centres. Especially impressive is the former Barratt Footshape Boot Works in Kingsthorpe Road, Northampton. Despite the marked decline in the industry during the second half of the C20, many of the factories remain in use although not all are for footwear manufacture.

There were many TANNERIES providing leather for shoe production and industrial purposes such as belts for driving machinery. Although most were mundane premises, the office building of W. Pearce & Company's former tannery at Great Billing is a remarkable example of Art Deco.

ENGINEERING developed in most of the county's towns, often biased towards items for the manufacture of footwear. Apart from a frontage office block, usually built multi-storey to create an impression, the main production areas were mainly single-storey, often covering a large area. Before the advent of electricity, when steam engines powered the machinery, tall chimneys were a prominent feature, but none of these survive. The lift-testing tower in Northampton, built in 1980–2 for the Express Lift Company, is all that remained after the works were closed in the 1990s and the rest of the site was demolished for the site to be developed for housing. Its survival is uncertain because of deterioration of the concrete.

Of the SERVICE INDUSTRIES, while electricity generation and gas production in the county on a commercial scale have declined, there is still evidence of small-scale undertakings, usually associated with country estates. An example of the supply of electricity and water on this scale survives in the former mill at Ashton, near Oundle, which provided for the Rothschilds' estate. The demand for water from the larger towns in the county caused the construction of reservoirs with PUMP HOUSES at Cransley (c.1900), Ravensthorpe (1890), Sywell (1906) and later Pitsford (1956), and of WATER TOWERS, such as the five-storey octagonal polychrome-brick water tower near the southern edge of Finedon (built 1904), now converted into a dwelling. At Cransley reservoir the buildings for the steam-driven pumps and the waterworks engineer's house are now private residences. Some small towns and larger villages, for example Long Buckby, had their own gasworks and others, as at Raunds, their own waterworks. Most of the larger towns had their own sewage treatment facilities situated at some distance, although as towns grew these facilities had to be moved even further away. Evidence for this is provided by the decorative chimney standing in isolation s of the Bedford Road from Northampton.

Northamptonshire's long narrow shape on a SW–NE axis ensured that whatever the form of TRANSPORT, most major routes from London to the Midlands and North passed through the county. During the C18 and early C19 a number of TURNPIKE ROADS were established in the county accompanied by the construction of TOLL HOUSES. Sadly most of these have been removed but those at Staverton and Weedon are good examples. The earlier use of inns as staging points gave way to bus stops, bus and COACH STATIONS as mechanical public transport developed. The Derngate coach station of 1935 in Northampton has gone but the former Birch Brothers' 1930s coach station in Rushden survives as a furniture showroom. Urban transport was improved in Northampton in 1881 with the opening of a horse-operated TRAMWAY with stables on the E side of Abington Street. The system was purchased by Northampton Borough Council in 1902, electrified in 1904 and closed in 1934. A tram depot was built on St James' Road with three high semicircular arched entrances for the double-deck tramcars and is now incorporated in Northampton Transport's bus garage. The cast-iron waiting shelters for intending tram passengers survive, well-painted, at Kingsthorpe and at the NE corner of the Racecourse.

The River Nene was made navigable up to Northampton in 1761 following a number of improvements including the building of locks which bypassed the weirs for the numerous mills on the river. Warehouses were built at several of the wharfs. The first CANAL to come into the county was the Oxford Canal, built by *James Brindley* and opened from Coventry to Banbury in 1778. In addition to the structures carrying the canal over valleys and through hills, there were toll houses, such as the one at Braunston Junction, and warehouses at some of the wharfs. The Grand Junction Canal, constructed by *William Jessop*, with *James Barnes* as resident engineer, opened in 1805. In 1814 the Old Grand Union canal from the Grand Junction at Norton through Welford to Leicester was opened and the Junction's branch from Gayton to Northampton opened the following year. Some businesses, anxious to make use of the canals, built their premises alongside, e.g. Joseph Westley & Sons, at Blisworth, see above.

Although a horse-operated railed way was used over Blisworth Hill between 1800 and 1805 while the canal tunnel was being built, the first mainline RAILWAY through Northamptonshire was

Blisworth, railway bridge.
Engraving, *c.* 1850

the London & Birmingham Railway, which was built under the direction of *George & Robert Stephenson*. This opened throughout in 1838 with stations in the county at Roade and Weedon; these have not survived. In 1848 the line became part of the London and North Western Railway (L&NWR). The significant structures of Roade cutting and Kilsby tunnel – 1½ m. long, with two 70-ft (21-metre) diameter ventilation shafts – remain in use today. Northampton gained its first railway station, situated s of the river on Bridge Street in Cotton End, in 1845 when the branch line from Blisworth to Peterborough was opened. This and many other pretty Neo-Tudor stations along the line were of 1845 by *John Livock*. Now only those at Oundle and Barnwell survive. This line closed to passengers in 1964 and to freight in stages until the final train, an enthusiasts' special, in 1957. The SW end of Northamptonshire was crossed by the Birmingham and Oxford Railway (later the Great Western Railway) which opened in 1850. A station was built at Aynho to *Brunel*'s design for small stations; it closed in 1964 and the platforms were removed, but the station building survives. In 1910 the Great Western Railway opened its direct route between Paddington and Birmingham; Aynho Park Platform was erected on this line, but this 'station' closed in 1963. To minimize conflicting movements at the junction of the line to Princes Risborough with the Oxford–Birmingham line a ten-bay Warren girder bridge was built at the time of the 1910 improvements. This carries the single northbound track of the line from Princes Risborough to Aynho over the Oxford to Banbury line, with which it makes a junction about ½ m. N.

The Midland Railway's Leicester & Hitchin Extension line which crossed Northamptonshire opened in 1857. From this, branches were opened to Huntingdon in 1866 (closed completely in 1978), Cransley in 1877 (closed 1963 but used for enthusiasts' specials in 1965 and 1968), and Higham Ferrers in 1892 (closed 1969). The stations at Kettering and Wellingborough, both of which have decorative cast-iron work, are still in use. Both were by the Midland's usual architect, *C. H. Driver*, but only at Wellingborough is the original building preserved, Kettering having been rebuilt in the 1890s. From the later 1870s, the main line was progressively quadrupled s of Kettering. When the overbridges were extended to accommodate the extra lines, blue bricks were used instead of red on the original.

In 1859 the L&NWR opened its line to Market Harborough, with a new station at Northampton, named Castle Station to distinguish it from the one in Bridge Street. This was rebuilt in 1881 when the loop line from Rugby to Roade passing through Northampton was built. In 1859 there were proposals for a line from Bedford via Northampton to Southam, but by 1865 this had contracted to the Bedford & Northampton Railway for its Parliamentary Bill, passed in 1870. This railway opened in June 1872 to St John's Street Station, accessed by Guildhall Road, built the same year, from the centre of Northampton. In 1885 this railway became part of the Midland Railway. St John's Street

Station closed on 3 July 1939 and was subsequently demolished after the layout at Hardingstone Junction had been reversed to allow trains from Bedford to run into Northampton (Castle) Station.

A branch line was opened by the L&NWR from its main line at Weedon to Daventry in 1888 and later extended to a junction with a line from Rugby to Leamington. Although the line was closed to passengers in 1958 and freight in 1963, bridges remain where it passed beneath roads across its route. The Great Central Railway (GCR)'s extension to London was opened in 1898, with extensive locomotive sheds at Woodford Halse, in the S of the county, turning the village into a railway town. In contrast to the railway stations on earlier lines, where there could be significant differences between the stations on the same line, those on the GCR through Northamptonshire were all of a similar design, with an island platform having buildings to provide the usual facilities, accessed from a footbridge or a subway from the ticket office at the level of the public access road. The last public railway to be built in the county was in 1910 from Aynho Junction (on the Oxford–Banbury line) to Ashendon Junction in Bucks (to join the GCR's line from Grendon Underwood, so providing a more direct line between Birmingham and Paddington).

Over time there were seventy-one railway stations in the county but now there are only five functioning: Northampton, rebuilt 1963–4, Long Buckby, Kettering, Wellingborough and Corby (rebuilt and opened in 2009).

THE INTERWAR PERIOD TO THE PRESENT DAY

After the lull of the First World War, with only sporadic building occurring, by 1920 things were on the move again. For the most inspiring achievement we return to Bassett-Lowke. In 1925 he was to commission a new house but could not locate Mackintosh and went instead to the German architect *Peter Behrens*. The result was what has been claimed as the first true 'Modern' house in Great Britain. Bassett-Lowke had some of the internal fittings from Derngate moved there and they fit surprisingly well. Perhaps what is most remarkable about New Ways is that it materialized from Behrens's sketchy drawings to be put into effect by Bassett-Lowke and his Northampton builder, *Henry Green*, and it is certainly as much a monument to both as to its designer. One other early C20 firm should be included, *Brown & Henson*, that is Sir John Brown and A. E. Henson, responsible in Northampton's Derngate for a block of flats, Bedford Mansions (1934–6), and in Cheyne Walk for the Barratt Maternity Home (1936), both of brick with horizontal streamlined format and very much of the 1930s.

In Kettering the engineer Charles Wicksteed gave a public park to his town in 1926 and alongside it in the 1930s began a development of housing. He employed *Gotch* to build the park pavilion but for the houses chose *John Brandon-Jones*. Only one or two houses were built to his design but they are distinct examples of the period: a pair form the corner of Lewis Road (1937) and there are a few more in Paradise Lane. In Rushden the shoe manufacturer John White employed *Albert Richardson* to alter his own house in Northampton Road and to build a new factory in Lime Street (1937–8) and new offices (1936) and a retirement complex for his workers at Higham Ferrers. One should also record the buildings of the Co-operative Wholesale Society and notably those by their architect *L. G. Ekins*. Of special note in Northampton is their former factory in Guildhall Road of 1932, with an impressive faience façade and a swirling staircase, and a large 1920 Neoclassical factory and office block in Christchurch Road.

Of early C20 planned development and civic buildings there is little of note. The finest example is the 1930s Lloyds estate built by Stewarts & Lloyds at Corby, either side of Rockingham Road. This was designed on a Garden City plan and despite some alterations and loss of a few gardens, the area still retains its original atmosphere, sufficient for it to have been designated as a conservation area. An earlier Garden Village was designed to be built in 1911 by *Gibson, Skipworth & Gordon* at Delapre, s of Northampton, but only a scatter of houses had been built by 1920 and the scheme was abandoned and the rest of the site developed in a more orthodox manner. In 1925 the Borough Council commissioned a development plan for the town from the landscape architects *Thomas Mawson & Son*, but nothing materialized (Mawson had also recommended a Garden Village at Delapre). Fortuitously several of his schemes for outer ring roads have come to fruition in recent times. Another attempt to create civic focus in Northampton occurred between 1938 and 1941 when three grand buildings were erected by *Prestwich & Sons* on the Mounts: a police station, fire station and flats, and a swimming bath. Although plain and simple in design they manage to look fresh still today and the baths with its parabolic arched interior is reckoned an icon of its age. It is not surprising to discover that Bassett-Lowke was instrumental in their erection.

In the field of CHURCHES one might note for monuments the sculptured animal frieze on the Bower Ismay memorial at Haselbech (†1924) by *A. H. Gerrard* and two memorials by *Lutyens*, the first the war memorial of 1926 at All Saints Northampton, with its two obelisks and stone flags, and the second at Ashby St Ledgers *c.* 1940. Of lesser status but worthy is the gravestone for Edith Sitwell at Weedon Lois by *Henry Moore*. One of Moore's most important early works is, of course, his Madonna and Child at St Matthew Northampton. This was commissioned in 1943 and is, apart from its noble undated beauty, historically important as the great sculptor's first step in the direction of increased concreteness for certain purposes. The placing of an image in a church was recognized by Moore as such a purpose, and the name of the rector who commissioned him and Sutherland must be recorded; for he was the first patron of both for work to be made with a view to being seen in public. He was the Rev. Walter Hussey, who went on to become Dean of Chichester, and it was Hussey who gave also to St Matthew's a classic work of art, *Graham Sutherland*'s virtually Expressionist Crucifixion of 1946.

Of early C20 stained glass one could single out the *Martin Travers* window of 1927 in St Mary Kettering. *Hugh Easton* is always worth looking at, and notably at Kelmarsh and the series in the Oundle School chapel. To these must be added *Evie Hone*'s Expressionist stained glass at Wellingborough parish church of 1955, *John Piper* and *Patrick Reyntiens*'s moving, also Expressionist glass at Oundle School chapel of 1955–6 and later at Wellingborough. Then there is the work of *Francis Skeat* such as the two windows of the 1980s at Earls Barton, another at Roade and others at Raunds and All Saints Wellingborough. Coming up to date the Northamptonshire artist *Chris Fiddes*, usually in collaboration with *Nicholas Bechgaard*, has designed windows at Stoke Bruerne 1988, Orlingbury 1994, Potterspury 1997 and Millennium windows at Bozeat and Potterspury. Several other churches have inserted windows to mark the Millennium such as the fine window at Winwick by *Jane Campbell* of 2003. 119

Buildings and planning since 1945

The development of Northampton was to progress along national trends until 1950 when the then Borough Architect *J. Lewis Womersley* produced his award-winning scheme for the Kings Heath Estate at Dallington on the W side of Northampton. The kidney-shaped plan with lines of houses edging an open space with a central shopping precinct was hailed as an icon for the future. Today alas it looks a little tired and its central shops have failed and are mostly boarded up. Two estates on the E side of the town, Eastfield and Thorplands, were also built in the 1950s, but both are now considered substandard. In 1968 Womersley was asked back together with *Hugh Wilson* to produce an expansion plan for the town (published 1969). This set in motion a development of the central area and notably the Market Square, which had a devastating effect. Despite ardent appeals by the then Civic Society many important buildings and indeed whole streets around the Square, especially on the N side, were lost, largely to accommodate the Grosvenor shopping precinct. The 1970s were a bad period for historic buildings in the town and losses spread beyond the Square (Albion Place, Abington Street and Wood Hill).* Following the Womersley and Wilson plan Northampton was designated as a Development Town and the Northampton Development Corporation was set up. The priority

---

* A good deal of the clearance was sadly recorded in the previous 1973 edition of this volume.

was to set in motion house building for London overspill, initially
on the E side of the town around Weston Favell and then S of
the town around Hunsbury. Initially building was under the
auspices of the Development Corporation but by the 1980s individual developers began to work on separate areas and in a more
standard form. Perhaps the main advantage of the outline plan
prepared by the Development Corporation on the E side of
Northampton was the incorporation of existing landscape features such as brooks and woodland, and this greatly adds to
the attractiveness and indeed success of the development. The
Eastern and Southern Districts were largely complete by the
1990s and attention moved to the area SW of the town between
St James, Dallington and Upton. Upton Park is still (2013) under
construction, again using a number of separate firms. The scheme
has created much publicity following the accolade given it by the
Prince of Wales. Whether its rather over-size outer-city style of
blocks will be looked upon in the future as suitable for a provincial town remains to be seen.

Equally expansive schemes have been applied in Wellingborough, Corby and Daventry. Kettering has been less affected by
these measures. Daventry has trebled in size. Its earliest new
housing was by the *City of Birmingham*'s *Architect*'s *Department*.
Corby, also a New Town, has had a new centre. Here the earliest
housing between 1965 and 1972 was by *John Stedman*. His work
at Kingswood, ingenious in its compact yet humane planning,
intriguing in its visual variety, was hailed as a notable example
of the kind of low-rise housing which was to become increasingly
popular, though that early promise has failed to fulfil its expectations. Just as in Northampton these early estates of the 1960s and
1970s are now the subject of regeneration schemes. In all these
towns the guiding force of the original architect teams who began
the development has, inevitably, become diffused as the demand
for housing increased with the later phases of development,
resulting in a varied sequence of firms taking commissions and
producing their own individual approaches to house design
which are less remarkable. Numerous SCHOOLS have been
rebuilt and remodelled and a whole array of new academies have
been created, most notably that at Corby by *Sir Norman Foster*.
Northampton now has its own university but its campus at
Moulton Park is a disparate array of buildings deriving from its
educational predecessors, so that its more recent buildings fail to
make much impact.

ROADS have had a major effect on the post-war landscape of
the county. The M1 motorway made its introduction across
Northamptonshire between 1958 and 1959. It was then that the
bridges designed by *Sir Owen Williams & Partners* made their
mark, as Pevsner himself wrote in 1961: 'The bigger ones are of
mass concrete with the simplest reinforcements, and impress by
a cyclopean rudeness rather than by elegance. Especially surprising are the supports between the traffic lanes in the N and S
directions: a kind of elementary columns, without base and
capital, but with an abacus – a curious period suggestion, not

called for in this forward-looking job.' Today they seem by famil-iarity less obtrusive. The lessons of landscaping which caused regret then have been learnt so that later motorways and dual-carriageways have been clothed with trees and in many cases with wild flowers. The M1 is still the only motorway in the county but a whole network of dual-carriageways now criss-crosses the landscape. The most intrusive is the A14, although this has totally transformed the access E–W, which formerly hardly existed. All the towns are now surrounded by bypasses and the SW to NE route, the A43 and A45, has largely been realigned. The result has been that around both towns and villages on these new routes have grown up a proliferation of industrial, distribution and retail parks. The most obvious examples are the E side of Corby, the S side of Wellingborough, N and E of Kettering, the S and W sides of Daventry and most disastrously W and N of the village of Weldon. The A45 from Northampton as far as Thrapston is almost totally lined with such areas.

Since the 1970s in the field of RESTORATION AND CONSERVA-TION there have been several major successes: in Northampton the refurbishment of the interiors of the Guildhall following its extension in 1991 under the direction of *Roderick Gradidge* and also the enhancement of the square in front; and most impor-tantly the restoration of the Mackintosh interiors at 78 Derngate by *John McAslan & Partners* from 1998 to 2003. Of the country houses the prime rescue has been that of Apethorpe Hall by English Heritage since 2004, to be followed by a detailed inves-tigation of its structure. Another rescue is ongoing at Lilford Hall. Both Fawsley Hall and Rushton Hall have been converted into hotels, with at the former a magnificent recreation of the Great Hall, whose roof timbers had been removed. Several house interiors have received improvement, most notably Aynhoe Park, Cottesbrooke, Lamport and Thenford. In the sphere of parks and gardens the major achievement has been the restoration at Lyveden of the water garden and New Bield, together with the replanting of the orchard. To this can be added the magnificent arboretum at Thenford, a parterre by *David Hicks* at Deene and the enhancement of the park at Wakefield. Opinions are divided about English Heritage's recreated C17 garden at Kirby Hall.

An interesting exercise is to choose a recent building to repre-sent each major town. For Northampton, while one might edge towards the Guildhall extension or even the Upton Park develop-ment, the final choice would have to be *Maurice Walton*'s 1980–2 'Lighthouse' – the Express Lifts Tower. For Kettering there is hardly any choice but the RCI. Headquarters (1990–1 by *Lister Drew Haines Barrow*), perched on the hill at the S entrance to the town from the A14, is an obvious candidate. In Daventry the 2009–11 Icon building by *Consarc* is again an obvious choice. However, the clear winner in this competition has surely to be Corby's 'Cube' (*Hawkins Brown* 2010), as challenging as it was, inevitably, over budget.

What of the landscape of the county of Northamptonshire as a whole today? For those looking at its buildings there is one saving grace. Despite the huge development of a number of its towns, its villages have remained almost entirely compact. There is hardly a shred of ribbon development. One moves from one village to another across acres of green countryside. The planners of Northamptonshire would do well to preserve this quality: it is very endearing.

FURTHER READING

Northamptonshire has two early county histories: Bridges and Baker. John Bridges began putting together his *History* around 1718 and commissioned Peter Tillemans and other artists to make a set of drawings of buildings for the illustrations between 1719 and 1721. Unfortunately Bridges died in 1724 and his text was not published until 1791, by which time the drawings had gone on a different route from the text manuscript, with only one or two ever being engraved. Bridges's *History and Antiquities of Northamptonshire* (ed. Peter Whalley), 2 vols, 1791, covers the complete county together with the Soke of Peterborough. Whalley's editing did not update Bridges's text so it needs to be used with caution, its publication date being irrelevant. The drawings eventually ended up in the British Museum but were published in *Northamptonshire in the Early Eighteenth Century: The Drawings of Peter Tillemans and others* (ed. Bruce A. Bailey), Northamptonshire Record Society, 1996, and while they are a selective collection they are a most useful source. George Baker was collecting material for a further county history in the first decades of the C19. Unfortunately only the southern half of the county had been published before his death in 1851, as *History and Antiquities of the County of Northampton*, vol. I, 1822–30, vol. II, 1836–41. Baker is especially useful for genealogical information. The *Victoria County History* (VCH) (4 vols, 1902–37) admirably covered the NE half of the county, from a line S of Northampton to the Soke of Peterborough. To these have been added vol. 5 (2002) which covers Cleley Hundred, that part of the county S of Northampton which stretches towards Buckingham, although it lacks the architectural character of its predecessors, most notably in the almost complete absence of any plans and on the whole rather sketchy information on buildings; and vol. 6, *Modern Industry* (2007). The National Heritage List for England of buildings of architectural and historic interest cover the whole county and can be accessed on the internet (www.britishlistedbuildings.co.uk or via www.english-heritage. org.uk).

The Royal Commission on the Historical Monuments of England (RCHME) began work on Northamptonshire in the 1960s largely from its Cambridge office. The work began while the Commission was still producing detailed inventory volumes, but during the process it was decided to stop producing them and revert to more general survey volumes. Four volumes of inventories of archaeological sites were published as part of *An Inventory of the Historical Monuments in the County of Northampton*: vol. 1, *North-east Northamptonshire*, 1975; vol. 2, *Central Northamptonshire*, 1979; vol. 3, *North-west Northamptonshire*, 1981; and vol. 4, *South-west Northamptonshire*, 1982. Vol. 5, 1985, covers *Archaeological Sites and Churches in Northampton*, and there is one complete inventory volume (vol. 6) covering in detail the parishes close to the Soke of Peterborough, *Architectural Monuments in North Northamptonshire*, 1984. Two volumes were projected covering the country houses and churches, but only the first was published: John Heward and Robert Taylor, *The Country Houses of Northamptonshire*, 1996. This is a hugely detailed survey of the major houses in the county with extensive illustrations and detailed plans. One or two lesser houses were not included in the published text but survey notes are held at the English Heritage Archive (fomerly the National Monuments Record) in Swindon. Apethorpe Hall has been the subject of more recent research, for which see *English Heritage Historical Review* vol. 2 (2007), vol. 3 (2008), vol. 4 (2009); and *English Heritage Research News*, No. 5 (2006–7). The survey notes for the churches, largely by Hugh Richmond, are also in the English Heritage Archive. Alas, therefore, RCHME ended up like Baker, only covering part of the county in depth. For the churches *Architectural Notices of the Churches of the Archdeaconry of Northampton*, 1849, comprising the hundreds of Guilsborough and Nobottle Grove NW of Northampton, which the Victoria County History has not yet covered, is still well worth looking at. Its writers had good eyes and even bearing in mind they wrote before the great phase of Victorian restoration, what they say can be illuminating. It has beautiful engraved illustrations and several good plans. RCHME also published *Nonconformist Chapels and Meeting-houses in Northamptonshire and Oxfordshire*, 1986. For the churches, invaluable is the Corpus of Romanesque sculpture in Britain and Ireland (www.crsbi.ac.uk) and for Victorian restorations the files of the Incorporated Church Building Society (Lambeth Palace Library, www.churchplansonline.org). Nearly all the major country houses have at one time or another been written up in *Country Life*. In addition three admirable books by J. Alfred Gotch deal with them: *A Complete Account of the Buildings Erected by Sir Thomas Tresham*, 1883; *The Old Halls and Manor Houses of Northamptonshire*, 1936; and *Squires' Homes and Other Old Buildings of Northamptonshire*, 1939. Highlighting lesser houses with early remains is Paul Woodfield, *The larger medieval houses of Northamptonshire*, Northamptonshire Archaeology, 16, 1991, pp. 153–95. There are many references in the journal *Vernacular Archaeology* of which important is N. Hill, The Royal George Cottingham, Northamptonshire, an early cruck building, Vol. 23, 2001, pp. 62–7. The historic gardens of the county have been admirably covered by Timothy Mowl and Clare Hickman's *The historic gardens of England: Northamptonshire*, 2008. For the wider landscape John M. Steane's *The Northamptonshire*

Landscape, 1974, is essential reading. Whellan's *History, Gazetteer and Directory of Northamptonshire*, in both the 1849 and 1874 editions, is always worth looking at.

In the field of archaeology, the Northamptonshire archaeological society has published a journal, *Northamptonshire Archaeology*, since 1966. This contains excavation reports, articles and notes, as well as providing summaries of archaeological work and reviews of other publications relating to archaeology of the county. In 2004 the society also published an overview spanning the Palaeolithic to post-medieval, *The Archaeology of Northamptonshire*, and in 2010 published the autobiography of one of the county's busiest field archaeologists of the 1960 and 70s, *Dennis Jackson: a Northamptonshire Archaeologist*. Northamptonshire Archaeology, the commercial archaeological contractor attached to the County Council, publishes in the county journal and also makes reports available online through the Archaeology Data Service (ADS), as do other commercial archaeologists operating in the county.

The best general historical introduction to the county is R. L. Greenall, *A History of Northamptonshire*, 2nd edn, 2000. Juliet Smith's *Shell Guide*, 1968, is on a smaller scale and more general and enjoyable. Greenall has also published books on Daventry (*Daventry Past*, 1999) and Kettering (*A History of Kettering*, 2003). For Northampton there is Cynthia Brown's *Northampton 1835–1985: Shoe Town, New Town*, 1990. This relies heavily on the various articles written by Victor Hatley between the 1950s and 1980s, usefully listed in the bibliography of Mrs Brown's volume. The Rushden & District History Society have amassed an enormous amount of information for that area and it is all available on their outstanding website (www.rushdenheritage.co.uk). The enterprising Northamptonshire Record Society produces an excellent annual journal, *Northamptonshire Past and Present*, as well as volumes based on manuscript sources such as militia lists, etc.; and their volume of the Tillemans drawings has already been noted. Also useful is *Hindsight*, the journal of the Northamptonshire Association for Local History. The Northamptonshire Industrial Archaeology Group has produced the excellent *A Guide to the Industrial Heritage of Northamptonshire*, 2001 (revised 2011), which has an invaluable gazetteer. Amongst the older volumes on architectural subjects are: a number of excellent books by R. M. Sergeantson on individual churches of Northampton (1897–1911); E. Sharpe, J. Johnson and A. H. Kersey, *The Churches of the Nene Valley*, 1880; A. Hartshorne, *Recumbent Monumental Effigies in Northamptonshire*, 1876; and F. Hudson and A. Hartshorne, *The Brasses of Northamptonshire*, 1853. There are of course two general volumes which are indispensable: Howard Colvin, *A Biographical Dictionary of British Architects 1600–1840*, 4th edn, 2008 and *A Biographical Dictionary of Sculptors in Britain 1660–1851*, 2009, a revision of the original dictionary by Rupert Gunnis by Ingrid Roscoe. Such general books as Mill Stephenson on brasses, Aymer Vallance on screens, and A. Gardner on alabaster monuments need not be referred to specially.

Attention must be drawn to the drawings of Northamptonshire buildings by George Clarke (1790–1868), a schoolmaster of Hanging Houghton who later went to live at Scaldwell. Clarke began sketching buildings in the 1820s but did not really become fully productive till around 1840. He drew almost every church in the county and most of the houses of any note, including many parsonages. From his sketches he then worked up Indian ink and wash drawings. So great was the demand for his drawings that he gave up being a schoolmaster and took to living off the income from the drawings. The great value of his drawings is that they show buildings before the great wave of Victorian alteration. Later in his life he used published engravings as a source so the later drawings can be less useful. Fortunately his sketchbooks survive in the Northamptonshire Record Office together with two large volumes of drawings which had belonged to the North-amptonshire Antiquarian Society. They also have many individ-ual drawings and a similarly large collection is held by Northamptonshire Libraries. The Northampton Library has an especially useful file of local illustrations and the local libraries in the towns have good collections too.

The research notes compiled for this edition and its predeces-sors will be deposited with the English Heritage Archive, Swindon, and may be freely consulted by prior arrangement with the public search room.

GAZETTEER

ABINGTON *see* INNER NORTHAMPTON: EAST

ABTHORPE

The old part of the village is around an attractive green, with the church occupying its w portion.

St John Baptist. By *Ewan Christian*, 1869–71. Quite large, with a spire on its stocky NW tower which also acts as the porch. The tower is a little stark, perhaps because it has no angle buttresses and the spire, which is of Northamptonshire broach form, is almost too heavy for it. The style of the church is Geometrical to Dec but lower parts of the walls survive from the old building, and above the E window there is still a 1747 date. The simple C19 interior is intact and refreshingly lime-washed. Four bay arcades and a barrel ceiling the whole length of the building, as there is no chancel arch. The fittings simple and just a few decorative tiles in the chancel. – FONT. A curious moulded baluster shape. A new font was made in 1709, which this could be, although it is recorded that a new font was acquired in 1840. – REREDOS. 1913 in the Dec style. – STAINED GLASS. E window by *Mayer* of Munich, 1913. – s chapel, 1959, by *J. Hardman & Co.* – MONUMENTS. Rev. Joseph Key †1783. A stone tablet with decorative surround like a picture frame, cherub head at the base. A nice example of local craftsmanship and very probably by *Middleton* of Towcester. Another large tablet records the Leeson and Nicoll charities, 1737 (*see* below).

Opposite the church, THE OLD READING ROOM, an ironstone house of 1682 with a gable end with mullioned windows of, from bottom to top, four, three, two lights. More mullioned windows in side wall and a later wing behind. The vista ends at the E end of the green with the former SCHOOL. The old part, the house, is of 1642 formed by a charity left by Jane Leeson. Sandstone and ironstone, of three bays with a central dormer. The windows are mullioned and of 3–2–3 lights. Schoolroom rebuilt in 1866, probably by *E. F. Law*. LEESON HOUSE just N of the school was originally the vicarage and part of the Leeson Charity. Part C17 but largely rebuilt in 1854 by *E. F. Law*.

ABTHORPE MANOR, 80 yds NW. One wing of a larger house, dated 1638, of sandstone and ironstone with some original mullions.

97 FOSCOTE HOUSE, HILL FARMHOUSE ¼ m. NE and CHARLOCK FARMHOUSE, ¼ m. SE. Built by the Grafton Estate *c*. 1840. Characterized by a three-bay house with widely spaced windows and a low-pitched, hipped slate roof, and in addition lower wings arranged in line with the house or at right angles to it. Foscote has a simple pedimented doorcase, while the other two have doorcases with Doric columns.

ACHURCH *see* THORPE ACHURCH

ADSTONE

5050

ALL SAINTS. A simple church appearing almost totally Victorian. Nave with bellcote and lower chancel. Probably of C12 origin including the rear arch of the N doorway, although this appears to be C13 outside. Early C13 S aisle of three bays. Low arcade with circular piers and octagonal abaci. Single-chamfered arches. In the nave W wall a lancet window. Heavily restored in 1843, when the chancel was added, and again in 1896. – Perp style REREDOS of 1931. – FONT. In a decorative Gothic style dated 1843 (cf. Blakesley). – Victorian CERAMIC PANELS for the Lord's Prayer and the Creed.

Former SCHOOL (Village Hall) and HOUSE, N of the church. 1846, Tudor manner, small but charming. Its porch declares it to have been built by the Corporation of the Sons of the Clergy.

OLD VICARAGE, E of the church. By *E. F. Law*, 1869–70. Neo-Elizabethan.

MANOR HOUSE. On the N side of the Green. Mid–late C17. Handsome, with a recessed centre, four-light mullioned windows in two storeys, and a hipped roof. Staircase with dumb-bell balusters. Some Jacobean panelling.

ALDERTON

7040

ST MARGARET. Late Perp W tower. Money was left for it in 1522 and 1528, but it was probably altered in the C17. The rest of 1847–8. The plans are signed by *Thomas Freeman* 'architect' and *John Wheeler*, builder, of Whittlebury, so it may be a reasonably accurate rebuilding, although there was originally a S aisle. The nave has reticulated windows and the chancel E window is a kind of flowing reticulated. – FONT. Octagonal, Perp. Stem and bowl in one, the stem panelled, the bowl with a frieze of leaves and small heads. – PULPIT. Dated 1631. With the usual panels with short broad blank arches and oblong panels with arabesques over. Back panel with a biblical inscription. Tester. – WEST GALLERY, dated 1837, incorporates Perp bench fronts or backs. – STALLS. Fleur-de-lys heads and clearly of 1848 (cf. Stoke Bruerne). Some C17 panelling is incorporated against the walls of the PEWS, which are interesting as they show status, the front pews being taller than those behind. – REREDOS with broad Gothic panels, also 1848. – Two fine Victorian Gurney (Romesse) STOVES. – STAINED GLASS. In the nave s and N windows, panels from the chancel E window of 1886, destroyed by a wartime bomb. – Chancel s, c. 1902, with figure of Faith by *Percy Bacon*. – MONUMENTS. Effigy of a cross-legged knight. Oak. Of the early C14, his head slightly turned (Sir William de Combemartyne †1318?). – Brass inscription in a stone frame for John Hesilrige †1655.

The small village has a number of most attractive thatched cottages such as Nos. 1–4 SPRING LANE. To the s is the so-called MANOR HOUSE, dated 1695. Symmetrical three-bay front with quoins and two horizontally oval windows above the doorway. The original manor house stood to the NW of the village and there are sparse remains there of a garden layout. It was large enough to host a visit of Queen Anne of Denmark in 1605.

THE MOUNT, just E of the church. A moderate ringwork of uncertain origin. Excavation in 2000 failed to produce conclusive evidence. It is assumed to be C12. There is a recorded grant for a castle in 1226.

ALDWINKLE

An attractive long village with good stone houses and much thatch, fine trees and two fine churches.

ST PETER. Well situated with many textbook C14 features, notably the w tower and spire. Three stages with stair-turret on s. w window with ogee top and almost Perp tracery. Circular window with renewed spiral of mouchettes. Further almost Perp tracery at bell-stage. Frieze of heads and animals and a string of tiny flowers over. Spire with tall broaches carrying small pinnacles on the top and three tiers of lucarnes. Windows around the church are a study in tracery. Some s aisle windows late C13, of two lights with Y-tracery and a circle in the spandrel. A large inserted Perp window, then another Dec with flowing tracery. Three tall windows in the chancel all Dec, reticulated, with a lowside opening, two lights with quatrefoil head and flowing curvilinear. Big five-light Perp E window. The s porch, like the tower, Late Dec. The N side has its original C14 vestry and further Dec windows, though their reticulated tracery owes much to the restoration of 1874–6 by *E. F. Law*, when this aisle was rebuilt. The main restoration was by *William Slater* in 1860 with further work by *W. Talbot Brown*, 1921. Internally the oldest elements are the W impost and the W pier of the three-bay N arcade. The pier is round and has a shallow capital with foliage and heads and a square abacus, i.e. belongs to the late C12. The rest of the arcade is of *c.* 1300 (quatrefoil pier, double-chamfered pointed arches), i.e. later than the S arcade which, with its round piers and round or octagonal abaci ornamented with nailhead and its responds on head corbels, is C13. C13 also the PISCINA in the N aisle on short triple shafts. Tower arch chamfered and supported on corbels with heads. Inside a pretty doorway to the staircase with shouldered ogee head. – SCREEN. Perp style, 1921 by *Talbot Brown*. – STAINED GLASS. Chancel S. Substantial remains of the original early C14 glass, especially the two figures of St Christopher and St George. Angels *c.* 1310–30, at the top of other windows. – Elaborate E window by *C. E. Kempe*, 1900, a little different from his usual production, very probably because he has a muted colour range to fit in with the C14 canopies at the top of the main lights. High up, to the l. and r., in the mouchettes, two kneeling figures of donor priests, *c.* 1370–80. – Other windows, 1875–8 by *Burlison & Grylls*. – S aisle centre (Millennium window) by *Benjamin Finn*, 2003. – MONUMENT. Mrs Davenant †1616. Much strap decoration and shields; no figures.

ALL SAINTS (Churches Conservation Trust). Especially fine W tower, a classic Perp piece. Clasping buttresses with a host of crawling creatures on all the set-offs (cf. Whiston and St John, Stamford, Lincs.). Doorway richly moulded with side-shafts and with tracery spandrels, W window with crocketed ogee top, tall bell-openings, two of two lights on each side, straight-headed, with transoms, set back in rectangular frames, quatrefoil frieze above, big gargoyles, four tall pinnacles. Then on the S side the Chambre Chapel, founded by the will of Elizabeth Chambre in 1489. Fine Perp. Three- and four-light windows. Battlements, originally with corner pinnacles, S door inserted later. Otherwise mixed features. Late C13 one chancel N window (bar tracery). Some minor Dec contributions, i.e. N aisle W and E windows, S aisle W window, S porch entrance (the porch itself has been taken down and the entrance shifted closer to the church). Other N aisle windows Perp. Perp vestry. The nave and aisles are also embattled.

The interior, wide open without fittings, is predominantly C13. Of the arcades one S pier seems earlier than the rest. All piers round with round abaci and double-chamfered pointed arches. The chancel arch on cone corbels with one capital with nailhead enrichment also C13. – COMMUNION RAIL. Jacobean, with vertically symmetrical balusters. – STAINED GLASS. Remains of *c.* 1489 in the Chambre Chapel and other windows. With many quarries with flowers and in N aisle grapes. – Chancel E, 1892 by *Heaton, Butler & Bayne*. – BRASS. William Aldwyncle †1463, a civilian figure of *c.* 2 ft (0.6 metres) length (chancel). – LYCHGATE, 1918 by *W. Talbot Brown*.

OLD RECTORY, behind St Peters. Faintly Tudor, 1867 by *E. F. Law*. Law did further work in 1874 and *Talbot Brown* in 1921. Near St Peter's also the attractive vernacular style VILLAGE HALL of 1907 by *Talbot Brown & Fisher*. Further E on the S side the BAPTIST CHAPEL of 1822, brick, with charming arched gateway. W in Main Street, THE HERMITAGE, *c.* 1820. A handsome three-bay, two-storey house of coursed limestone with a porch with Doric fluted columns and a pediment. Moving N a very distinctive house on the W side, No. 81, formerly a pub. Broad street frontage of stone, red brick and render. A wide central gable of two bays with a canopied doorway, and wings of one bay. Horizontal bands of red brick, and the same material for quoins and window lintels.

OLD RECTORY, opposite All Saints. Dryden's birthplace. Thatched, with canted bay window on the l. side. A faculty of 1821 describes the house as being 'out of repair' with proposal for a new drawing room and outbuildings. C14 walls incorporated inside.

MANOR HOUSE, SE of All Saints. 1881 by *R. W. Collier*, surveyor to the Lilford Estate and originally built for the Agent. Tudor style, much enlarged in 1994 by the *John Whyte Partnership*.

SW of All Saints TAVERN COTTAGE, with a plaque with the masons' arms, masons' tools; also an inscription, the initials J A and the date 1834.

BRIDGE. E of All Saints, of 1760, with three round arches.

ALTHORP

The estate was bought in 1508 by Sir John Spencer, a sheep farmer of Wormleighton in Warwickshire. He obtained leave in 1512 to create a park of 300 acres at Althorp. During alterations *c.* 1958, fragments of medieval pieces were found. They include a stiff-leaf capital, perhaps from the former church. About 1573 the house was enlarged, with a courtyard and two projecting wings. Neither the early nor the late C16 house has ever been destroyed, though no features of any eloquence belonging to them can be seen any longer. The remains of a large Tudor window and of several smaller ones were however discovered again *c.* 1958 in the N wall of the entrance hall. The next stage in the history of the building is the making of the grand staircase in the former courtyard. Bills in the Blenheim archive show that the work was directed by *Anthony Ellis*, a builder and carver, a pupil of Nicholas Stone, and begun in 1666. The Long Gallery was altered and panelled in 1682. Much more was done to the interior in the 1670s and 1680s. In 1688 John Evelyn called the house a palace and the state rooms such 'as may become a great prince'. Too little of this remains, and it seems hardly worth recording that we still have three staircases with strong turned balusters. Then between 1729 and 1733 came the splendid Palladian work on the stables and the interior by *Roger Morris*. It is among the most impressive at Althorp. It was begun for the 5th Earl of Sunderland, whose mother was Marlborough's daughter and who succeeded to the Marlborough title in 1734, and completed by his brother. This brother's son was created Earl Spencer in 1765. *John Vardy* built for him Spencer House in London in 1756–65, but when repairs to the roof became necessary at Althorp in 1772, he was dead, and the job went to *Sir Robert Taylor*. In 1787–91 *Henry Holland* gave the house more or less its present appearance. Part of his work was the provision of the functionally very desirable corridors on either side of the wings towards the forecourt. Finally, *c.* 1877, *Macvicar Anderson* made alterations inside and added the dining room, which projects to the E on the N side.

The house is of light grey brick, largely consisting of so-called mathematical tiles, i.e. tiles made to look like bricks, attached to the original exterior of red brick. All this dates from Holland's alterations. The house is two storeys in height. One approaches it from the S (or rather SE), where it has a double-stepped forecourt. The recessed centre is faced with Roche Abbey stone. It is of five bays with giant Corinthian pilasters and a pediment. The N side has nine bays and a three-bay pediment and on the ground floor three windows are distinguished by pediments. This exterior is dignified, but no more than that, and does not prepare for the glories of the interior, glories of architecture, furniture and painting. The latter two, alas, are outside the scope of *The Buildings of England*.

The interior of the house was much enhanced by the 7th Earl Spencer when in 1941 he had the interior of Spencer House in London stripped and chimneypieces and doorcase brought to Althorp. There are also chimneypieces from neighbouring Harlestone House, which the estate had bought in the 1820s, but which was demolished in 1939.

88 Splendid entrance hall, the WOOTTON HALL, the noblest Georgian room in the county. Roughly on the site of the Tudor hall. Dated 1733. It rises nearly to the full height of the house and has a deep coffered coving. In the corners big cartouches with eagles and leaves. Plain panels in the middle with frames adorned with Greek key. Charming frieze below with Diana, and 'affronted' cherubs, hounds and foxes. Grand doorway in the back wall with attached fluted Corinthian columns and an open pediment. Set into the walls, as an integral part of the decoration, large paintings of horses, grooms, hounds, etc., by *John Wootton*. In the private part, to the E, a small DINING ROOM with a C16 stone fireplace brought from Wormleighton *c.* 1925 and panelling of 1605 from the same house. Behind the hall, the SALOON, whose staircase, of the late 1660s, fills the space of the former courtyard. It is of a unique monumentality for its date in England. The STAIRCASE itself is of oak and rises in the middle of the room in one straight, wide flight, with an intermediate landing, until it reaches the end wall, where for a few steps it branches l. and r. to reach two doors on each

side. It then joins up with the comfortably wide gallery, or rather balcony, all along the walls. This balcony dates from Holland's alterations. When in 1669 Cosimo Medici III, the future Grand Duke of Tuscany, and Count Lorenzo Magolotti paid a visit to Althorp, Magolotti was especially taken with the staircase, which he found 'constructed with great magnificence' and described as 'dividing itself into two equal branches' and leading 'to the grand saloon from which is the passage to the chambers'. From this remark one can deduce that before Holland's balcony was added, the only access to the upper rooms on the garden side was through the door on the l. at the top of the stairs. This arrangement is shown in a plan in *Vitruvius Britannicus*, vol. II. The balustrading of the staircase and balcony is all of wood, with dumb-bell balusters. Originally the staircase was painted and grained to look like walnut; in Holland's time it was painted white. The present appearance of the staircase hall owes much to *Macvicar Anderson*. He enlarged the room to the W by adding to it a small ante-room, originally part of the interior courtyard. The decoration of the coved and coffered ceiling (which formerly had plain coffering) is also his, as are the heavy brackets beneath the balcony. At the W end of the staircase hall a chimneypiece from Spencer House, London, i.e. of 1758.

To the NE the SUNDERLAND ROOM. This still has Lord Sunderland's carved cornice. The two chimneypieces are from Spencer House, one by *Athenian Stuart*, the other by *John Vardy*. There follows the MARLBOROUGH ROOM, formed from two rooms 1910–11. The columns were introduced by *Jacksons* and the two fireplaces are from Spencer House, one of them, with heads of Homer and Hesiod, by *Peter Scheemakers*. The LIBRARY, at right angles to the Marlborough Room, i.e. facing W, is a tripartite apartment with screens of unfluted Ionic columns created by *Holland*, and the chimneypiece of his time, by *Deval*, survives. The ceiling in the Adam style is by *Macvicar Anderson*. He also added the central double doors. The BILLIARD ROOM (formerly Yellow Drawing Room) has a fine chimneypiece designed by Holland and made by *Deval* with circular, tapering, spiral-fluted shafts l. and r. and a Victorian ceiling by *Broadbent* of Leicester. By the same the ceiling in the SOUTH DRAWING ROOM. This, in *Holland*'s alterations, was the dining room with an ante-room. It has a doorcase by *Athenian Stuart* from Spencer House. Fireplace of 1802 by *Lancelot Wood*. One more room on the ground floor, in the private wing, must be mentioned: the BOUDOIR at the SE end of the E wing. It is a masterpiece of *Holland*'s, with panels painted by *Pernotin*. It was originally in the Garden Lobby area, but was moved to its present position by *Macvicar Anderson* when the dining room was created.

The most interesting room on the first floor is the CHAPEL in the E wing. This was seen and commented on as too small in 1675 by John Evelyn. The later C17 balustrade with the openwork foliage comes from the Duke of Marlborough's pew at St Albans. The doorcases are from Spencer House. Plain bolection chimneypiece by *Joshua Marshall*. Armorial glass in the windows, some dated 1588, largely from Wormleighton.

On the N side, the suite of five rooms made by Lord Sunderland, and later divided up, has been restored. The rooms have specially fine cornices. In the ANTE-ROOM chimneypiece by *Repton* from Harlestone House. In the GREAT ROOM two fireplaces from the time of *Holland*. They are by *Lancelot Wood*, from elsewhere in the house. In the KING WILLIAM BEDROOM a fireplace by *P. C. Hardwick, c.* 1850. In the W wing, in place of the Elizabethan Long Gallery is the seven-bay GALLERY made for Lord Sunderland in 1682–3. This has fine, large panelling, arranged so as to fit the C17 frames of the pictures of court beauties by *van Dyck*, *Lely*, and others. Fireplace from Spencer House by *Athenian Stuart*. The frieze is a copy from that of the Lysicrates Monument.

89   It might well be argued that the STABLES of the 1730s by *Roger Morris* are the finest piece of architecture at Althorp. They are of local ironstone with a deep Tuscan portico (two pairs of columns) – inspired without any doubt by Inigo Jones's St Paul Covent Garden and not by Palladio. Horace Walpole mentioned the 'pediments like Covent Garden Church, that for that purpose have good effect'. Typically English Palladian also the four corner towers or eminences, a motif familiar from Wilton and then Houghton, Holkham, Hagley, and other places. Circular and semicircular shapes among the windows – this Palladian as well as Anglo-Palladian motif. Very elegant interior with Tuscan columns supporting central groin-vaults. The aisles have transverse tunnel-vaults. In the SE corner a staircase survives from the late C17 stable block.

To the SW *Morris*'s GARDENER'S HOUSE, small, but decidedly grand. Golden ironstone ashlar with a 'Venetian' bay in the middle, derived directly from Palladio's Basilica at Vicenza. This bay is flanked by an arched bay on pillars l. and r. Pyramid roof with central chimney. At the back three bays and one and a half storeys. Doorway with pediment on brackets. In line with the Gardener's House to the S an ARCHWAY with quoins, a Greek frieze, and a broken pediment.

The formal GARDEN round the house and the stone pillars and ironwork to the forecourt are by *W. M. Teulon* and date from 1860–3. The gardener was *W. B. Thomas*. In the arboretum to the NE, by the lake known as the ROUND OVAL, a TEMPLE of wood with portico of four Roman Doric columns and a pediment. This originally stood in the garden of the Admiralty and was moved to Althorp in 1905, and to this position in 1926. It was adapted as a memorial to Diana, Princess of Wales in 1997. On the W side of the lake the DAIRY, of ironstone with a pyramid roof, now slated but originally thatched. This was built in 1786. Delightful interior with original *Wedgwood* tiles and dairy utensils.

Yet further NW the STANDING or FALCONRY, a curious, compact composition dated 1611 but in most of its details decidedly Vanbrughian. Oblong with a porch-like centre projection to the front and a broader projection at the back. Arched doorway; arcading on the first floor, which was originally open for watching the feats of falconry; top gable. To the l. and r. an arched window, again blank arcading on the first floor, again gables. The side elevations also have blank arcading and gables. The staircase is in the r. wing. It has stone walls and a moulded handrail partly recessed into the wall. The back with two gables and more Vanbrughian detail was added in 1901.

EAST LODGES. These may originate *c.* 1790 with Holland's alterations, but the work recorded by *Luke Kirshaw* in 1818 probably resulted in their present appearance. Portland stone, one-storeyed with raised pedimented centre. Doorways with Gibbs surrounds. Yellow brick quadrant walls. Big Victorian cast-iron gates.

BRINGTON LODGES. On w side of park. Of *c.* 1730, with gatehouses and banded piers with ball tops.

SWISS LODGE (former Station Lodge) On the A428. 1875, in an Arts and Crafts style by *Josiah Mander*, estate surveyor. Decorative details by *Farmer & Brindley*.

COTHERSTONE LODGE, just outside the park wall to the sw. 1879–80 by *W. H. Lascelles*, after a design by *R. Norman Shaw*. An early use of pre-cast concrete panels on a timber frame, the lower sections pebbledashed. Two rooms either side of a staircase and three bedrooms above in the eaves. It cost £195 and is the only example of its type now known to exist.

Planting began in the PARK in the C16, and there are still many fine trees and evidence of avenues. There is a whole series of dated planting stones around the park (1567–8, 1589, 1602–3, 1625, 1798, 1800, 1901). The park is entirely walled and a good deal of old walling survives, some parts dating from the C16.

APETHORPE   *0090*

ST LEONARD. Mostly Perp of 1420–30,* with the s chapel being turned into the Mildmay Chapel in 1621. This has windows with cusped, pointed lights, but no tracery, a three-bay arcade with debased Perp, emphatically pre-classical, piers, and above them ornate carved stonework of 1621. Heavy cartouches with gristly rather than strapwork surrounds, fat guilloche, big cherubs' heads and draperies. The tower, of fine ashlar, has the date 1633. Bell-openings round-arched with Y-tracery. Recessed spire. The tower arch has the same debased Perp as the chapel arcade. The one piece of evidence of an earlier church is a fragment of C12 chevron against a window in the N aisle. – FONT. C18 baluster with small marble bowl. –

* Dateable by dendrochronology, information Nick Hill.

REREDOS. Of wood, with pilasters, *c.* 1735. – PULPIT. Supplied in 1736. Heavily moulded panels with a little inlay. – TOWER SCREEN. Probably of *c.* 1633. With sturdy balusters and moulded panels. – PAINTING. Christ Walking on the Lake, by *R. S. Lauder.* – ARMS. Arms and a silk tabard C17, of Sir Anthony Mildmay and Sir Francis Fane. – STAINED GLASS. E window, the Last Supper, painted by *John Rowell* of High Wycombe, 1732. Restored by *Barley Studio*, York, 1994–5. – S chapel E window. Interesting work of 1621, English but entirely in the Flemish C16 style. The panels are: Adam and Eve, the Crucifixion, the Ascension and Christ in Majesty. – S aisle, two fine Brassey memorial windows of 1919 by the *Christopher Whall Studio.* – MONUMENTS. The huge monument to Sir Anthony Mildmay, †1617, dominates the church. It is almost too high to fit into the S chapel which houses it. Black-and-white veined marble. Recumbent effigies on a big sarcophagus, not fully coloured but just picked out with gilding. The four life-size figures of the Cardinal Virtues, Prudence, Fortitude, Wisdom and Justice, showing knowledge of classical sculpture, stand at the corners. Open draperies fall from a circular centre raised as a dome and lantern; on this a seated figure, and two more seated figures at the head and foot ends of the canopy. These represent Faith, Hope and Charity. The monument is among the best of its date in England and is confidently attributed to *Maximilian Colt.* There are similar kneeling versions of the Virtues on the documented Cecil tomb at Hatfield and standing Virtues on the monument at Dunbar, Scotland, also firmly attributed to Colt. – Sir Richard Dalton †1442, late C15 alabaster miniature effigy, fine if somewhat damaged. Above the head is a scene of the Annunciation to the Virgin. – John Leigh, †1627. Tablet with broken pediment rising in two shanks outward instead of inward. On one shank a seated figure, attributed to *William Wright* (GF). – Rowland Woodward, undated, attributed also to *Colt* (GF). – John Fane, infant son of Lord Burghersh, †1816. White marble effigy of a baby with bonnet, asleep on a couch.

STOCKS AND WHIPPING POST, in a wall recess of 1920, W of the church.

OLD SCHOOL. 1846 with an elaborate Gothic bargeboarded gable.

MANOR HOUSE (formerly the Agent's House), S of the church. 1711. Five bays, two storeys, cross-windows. Doorway with broad frame and pediment on brackets. C18 staircase with turned balusters. Rear extensions largely *c.* 1920. GATEPIERS, SCREEN WALLS & LODGE. The original entrance to the Hall by *Blomfield.*

The village shows much evidence of the influence of the Brassey Estate. In the decades following the acquisition of the Westmorland Estate by Leonard Brassey in 1904 much tidying was undertaken, largely under the direction of *H. F. Traylen* of Stamford, and many old cottages were replaced by new. The KING'S ARMS pub, for example, was rebuilt in 1913 and the

WAR MEMORIAL CROSS was designed in 1921. A set of alms-houses was also built (now a house on the N side of Main Street called TOMKINS). The Brassey Estate continues its good management, and in 2005–6 the ESTATE YARD was developed for housing with stone houses, some thatched.

LODGE FARM or CHEESEMAN'S LODGE, 1¼ m. SW. Former park lodge of C17 origin. Two storeys with a central four-centred arched doorway between mullioned windows. Extra bay on the r. in the same manner added c. 1864. Interior refitted in C19 but incorporating C17 balusters on the staircase.

WILLOWBROOK LODGE, ½ m. N. A house of 1931 built by the Brassey Estate in a late C17 style with rendered façades with exposed quoins and cross-mullion-transom windows. Tall chimneys, all rather colonial.

BLUE FIELD FARM, ½ m. NE. Also 1931. Interesting BARN. Slits in the end walls. Four posts inside, l. and r. of the cross-cartway through.

APETHORPE HALL. A large, impressive house with some of the finest Jacobean work in the country. The house and the manor belonged to Sir Guy Wolston in 1480s, and early in the C16 to his son-in-law Thomas Empson. They were bought in 1515 by Henry Keble, grocer of London. His grandson, Lord Mountjoy, sold them in 1543 to Henry VIII. In 1550 they went to Sir Walter Mildmay, the first to make additions to the Wolston house, then to his son Anthony who entertained James I in 1603 and in 1614, when James met for the first time George Villiers. In 1617 it passed to Anthony's grandson-in-law Sir Francis Fane, a favourite of James I, and so began a long association of the King with Apethorpe. Fane in 1622 began to create a series of apartments 'for the more commodious entertainment of His Majesty and his company at his repair unto these parts for his princely recreation there', that is for hunting. Timber was given from the Royal Forest for the purpose. He became Earl of Westmorland in 1624. In 1736 the 7th Earl, who had recently employed Colen Campbell to build a Palladian villa at Mereworth, Kent, brought in Campbell's assistant, *Roger Morris*, to begin a massive rebuilding with the intention of turning Apethorpe into a Palladian palace. It was to have towers at the four corners topped by pyramid roofs, à la Holkham or a large version of Morris's own stable block at Althorp. However, all that was done was to reface the S side of the courtyard and begin a new E wing. In the 1840s some alterations were made on the S side by *Bryan Browning* of Stamford. The estate remained with the Westmorlands till 1904, when it was bought by Leonard Brassey, M.P., later Lord Brassey of Apethorpe, nephew of the 1st Earl Brassey, a very rich man. He brought in *Sir Reginald Blomfield* who made further alterations and relaid the gardens. In 1949 it was sold and converted for use as a school. The school closed in 1982 and the house was bought by a private owner who never occupied it and allowed it to fall into serious decay. Following a public inquiry in 2004, it was compulsorily purchased by

English Heritage who put it back into repair, discovering much about its history in the process.

The house is built round two courtyards, the principal one being E of the other. It is thus an oblong, about 240 by 120 ft (73 by 37 metres) in size and very varied in appearance. The building history is complicated. The approach now is from the N, with an irregular front, as it contains work of four periods. The work of c. 1480 is at once recognizable. The GATEWAY with its four-centred arch and the three-light window above it belongs to those years, as does the wall to its r. But the gateway front was overlaid in 1653 with sumptuous decoration in a style wavering between the Jacobean and the new Inigo Jones–John Webb idiom. Before that time the doorway had of course a niche to the l. just like the one on the r. There is a coat of arms above the Perp arch, and thick, solid garlands hang down from it. Garlands also hang down to the l. and r. of the first-floor window. Nice scrolly volutes in various places. The fine composition is fragmentary, because to its immediate l. a new LIBRARY was built about 1740–50. This is quite unadorned and has irregularly placed sash windows. The library was dismantled and subdivided during the school occupation. Behind it is a wide stone passage with doors with Vanbrughian stonework, and at the end a C17 staircase with turned balusters. Also of c. 1653 is the fenestration of the kitchen with three tall windows with two transoms. The front further W looks cottagey.

Entering the E COURTYARD on the r. is a substantial part of the c. 1480 house, with at its core, what is the core still, the HALL RANGE between the two courts. Its façade is to the E court and has here a porch with the hall on its l. and a canted bay window at its S end. There are also rooms beyond to the S and the N where half the N range belongs to the same date. The work of c. 1480 has windows with arched lights. The porch entrance has a four-centred arch, the bay window a transom and arched lights also below it. The two small bay windows in the N and S corners of the hall range are mid-C16 additions. The parapet, the bold curved gables and the finials all belong to c. 1620–25, i.e. the time of Sir Francis Fane. The end on the N side is the gateway, with a pretty oriel towards the court, and stair-turret with an ogee cap to its E, and beyond the back of the Early Georgian library. The side of the hall range which turns towards the Back Court, i.e. the W court, was given a new, even frontage c. 1530–50. But behind this, inside the building, the back porch of the hall is still in existence, and also the walls of several rooms including the kitchen in the NE corner of the Back Court. This court is altogether, with the exception of the C18 Orangery on its S side, the work of c. 1530–50. Some windows still have arched lights, but most of them are simply straight-headed.

To continue with the court, the S SIDE is of the Mildmay period, redecorated in the 1620s, but refaced by *Roger Morris* c. 1740. It has a three-bay centre with Roman Doric columns

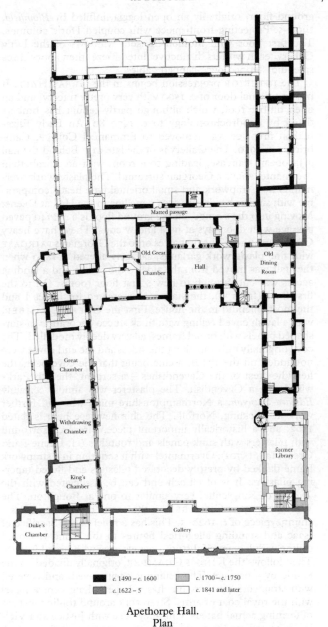

Apethorpe Hall.
Plan

c. 1490 – c. 1600   c. 1700 – c. 1750
c. 1622 – 5   c. 1841 and later

Matted passage

Old Great Chamber

Hall

Old Dining Room

Great Chamber

Withdrawing Chamber

King's Chamber

former Library

Duke's Chamber

Gallery

and a pediment. Four bays to the l., three to the r. At the E
end the cut-off parapet and cornice of the projected E range.
However, this fortunately survived and is a splendid example
of the work done for Sir Francis Fane *c.* 1620–5. Arcaded

ground floor, originally an open loggia, infilled by *Blomfield*, 1904–5. Projecting frontispiece with coupled Doric columns. The first floor with mullion-transom windows of the Long Gallery, each with its distinctive fluted frieze, then above three splendid stepped ogee-capped gables.

The INTERIOR progression begins in the GREAT HALL. It has an original door of *c.* 1500 with very pretty tracery, and an open timber roof, which although partly rebuilt has timbers dated by dendrochronology to *c.* 1470–80. An Early Elizabethan fireplace was removed to Emmanuel College, Cambridge, in 1950. The Gallery is of the late C17. Behind the hall a Jacobean staircase, leading to a room with an Elizabethan overmantel above a Georgian surround. The plasterwork overmantel has strapwork and small oriental type heads comparable with similar heads on 1570s panelling in the Hall at Deene. Moving into the s range, on the ground floor is a *c.* 1740 paved passage with doorways at its E and W ends. These have heavy Gibbs surrounds. The first gives onto the Georgian STAIRCASE with fine plasterwork garlands, savagely altered *c.* 1840 when the stair was moved from the side to the centre and a landing access was cut through to new s first-floor rooms. On to the first floor (from W), the state rooms created for James I and the most splendid in the house. First the GREAT CHAMBER, with a lavish coved ceiling with thick stucco decoration in star-shaped panels with broad frames, all very deeply modelled. The cove originally only ran along the sides, and the end coves were not added till the 1740s, a clue being that the cove bears the heraldic crest of the Cavendishes – a serpent, the 7th Earl's wife being a Cavendish. The plasterer was almost certainly *Edward Stanyon*, a Northamptonshire man, who did further work at Blickling, Norfolk. The chimneypiece here is dated 1562, and a historically important piece. Fireplace surround with pilasters with sunk panels and roundels (cf. Deene Park, Great Hall, 1570s). Overmantel with inscription in a strapwork frame flanked by prettily decorated pilasters and fluted tapering pilasters. It is of clunch and can be associated with the *Thorpes* of Kingscliffe; very similar to one at Boughton. The WITHDRAWING CHAMBER, in the centre of the range, has a chimneypiece of *c.* 1620–5. This has a relief of the Sacrifice of Isaac and standing allegorical figures to the l. and r. Coved ceiling with less fanciful stucco panels, also with broad frames. Then follows the KING'S CHAMBER, originally divided on the N side by a passage. The ceiling is again coved, and covered with strapwork patterns but has a large oblong centre panel with the royal coat of arms. Strapwork around trailing instead of forming actual panels. Chimneypiece with Justice and Vigilance seated under a canopy with curtains pulled open. A cherub appears at the top holding a coronet. Sir Francis Fane was raised to an earldom in 1624. Termini caryatids l. and r. Pretty hunting scene with little horsemen on the frieze above the fireplace opening. The SE corner room, The DUKE'S or PRINCE'S ROOM, has a flat plaster ceiling, again with broad bands, but is the one ceiling to have small pendants. Over-mantel with wide open pediment, two awkward figures seated on it, and above the open part of the pediment an accurate relief representation of a ship in full sail, again pedimented. The idea that the ship refers to Prince Charles's rash journey to Spain in 1623, when he hoped to win the Infanta, is considered implausible.* The main staircase in the E range is mostly a creation by *Blomfield* in 1922 incorporating some C17 woodwork.

The E side is almost entirely occupied by the LONG GALLERY. The plaster ceiling still has the thin ribs of the Elizabethan style. The walls are panelled and originally housed a series of large portraits. The chimneypiece has a spirited standing figure of King David in a niche. To his l. and r., on the shanks of an open pediment, two allegorical figures. In the broad frieze above the fireplace opening two sirens flanking an inscription and holding fat, compact, hanging garlands. The inscription reads:

Rare & ever to be wisht maye sound heere Instruments wch fainte sprites and muses cheere Composing for the Body, Soule and Bare Which sickness, sadness and Foule Spirits feare.

An intriguing feature of all these *c.* 1620 chimneypieces is that the architectural elements have several mason's marks, the same as those found elsewhere in the building, so cut by Northamptonshire masons. But does this also mean the carved work is by them? It looks more metropolitan, especially that on the Gallery fireplace.

One final feature needs to be mentioned. From the attics on the E side there is access to a roof walk. This runs the whole length of the façade and ingeniously runs behind the shaped gables, where within there are niches, perhaps just seats or possibly for lanterns.

It remains to consider the other external façades. The SOUTH FRONT is a mixture of Jacobean and Neo-Jacobean of 1904 by *Blomfield*. To the l. of the S façade in the S range of the Back Court is the ORANGERY, with an ashlar facade with parapet. This was built in 1718, by *John Lumley* of Northampton. Its original tall sash windows were replaced when the house was a school. By far the most impressive façade is the EAST FRONT. It is the most stately and coherent Jacobean piece in the county. It was not the entrance side – that remained to the N – but faced a garden with two summerhouses. In fact it was no more than a screen, though a specially ambitious one. It is symmetrical, of nine bays, in a fine varied rhythm. Two storeys, mullioned and transomed windows of 4–2–4–4–2–4–4–2–4 lights, parapet with three big shaped gables, two small semicircular gables, and two chimney-breasts and stacks. On the ground floor the centre is a projecting porch with coupled Tuscan

---

* See Adam White, 'The iconography of the State Apartment at Apethorpe Hall', *English Heritage Historical Review*, 3 (2008), p. 79.

columns, a metope frieze with excessively elongated metopes, and a balcony with vertically symmetrical balusters. To the l. and r. of the porch, below the adjoining windows, was originally an open arcaded loggia. The interior with its entrance hall was revised by *Blomfield* in 1913. In this stands a stone STATUE of James I, perhaps by *Cornelius Cure*. Its original place was the centre of the C17 S courtyard range. The porch has coupled Tuscan columns and a loggia also towards the court. But while there were two bays each to the outside, there are four plus four towards the court. The two loggias share their back wall but do not communicate. There is much evidence of mason's marks which points to the builders being the *Thorpes* of Kingscliffe. Confirmation of this has been the identification of the mark of one of the masons, *Samson Frisby*.* The forecourt gates and piers are all *Blomfield* of 1907.

The GARDENS were relaid by *Blomfield* at various dates between 1907 and 1912, although the S yew avenue derives from the C18. The LOGGIA in the W garden, overlooked by a huge cedar, has a reused C17 arcade. S are a LILY POND and some topiary. The GARDENER'S HOUSE is 1904–5. A lake SE of the church was created 1908–9.

DOVECOTE, NW of the Hall. Circular, with cupola, built in 1740.

₇₀₈₀

ARTHINGWORTH

ST ANDREW. The S arcade contains C12 work. One original pier, circular with a many-scalloped capital and a square abacus. Single-chamfered pointed arch. The second pier is C19 but, being a piece of wall with two responds, it represents no doubt original evidence as to the position of the W wall, before a S aisle existed. C13 S chapel arcade of two bays, octagonal pier, double-chamfered arches. Fine ashlar-faced W tower with setback buttresses. Pairs of two-light bell-openings, rounded heads, both under one big ogee arch (cf. Desborough, Haselbech etc.). The openings have transoms and cusping below them. Frieze of cusped lozenges. Battlements and square pinnacles which have lost or never had their tops. There is evidence for its building 1501–12. What is original of external features is Perp. The rest mostly of an expensive restoration in 1871–2 by *J. K. Colling*, recommended by Richard Naylor of Kelmarsh (q.v.). Colling was prevented from returning the church to C13 style by the patron, Henry Rokeby.†

Chancel interior with much foliage carving and furnishings and tiles of the same period, notably the REREDOS of alabaster

---

* See Introduction, p. 36.
† An entertaining sequence of letters from Colling arguing his case survives in the Arthingworth Parish collection (NRO).

by *Cornish*, builder of North Walsham, Norfolk. Columns of Devonshire marble and good painted panels with Passion flowers, wheat and grapes, Christ the Good Shepherd and some Apostles. – ORGAN. 1884. Splendidly decorated pipes. – STAINED GLASS. Chancel E, 1872, and S, 1874, both by *Heaton, Butler & Bayne*. – MONUMENT. Catherine Jekyll †1775. Of white and grey marble, a pretty composition. Oval medallion on an obelisk. In it an angel with a quill. Garlands hang down l. and r. of the medallion. The whole beautifully executed as one would expect of its sculptor, *Van Gelder* (*see* Warkton).

ARTHINGWORTH MANOR. NE of the church. Now two houses: the OLD MANOR and the MANOR. A large part of the mid-C18 old manor house was pulled down in 1967, revealing stone interior walls, which must have been part of an older manor house of the Rokebys. The house was formerly a long brick building of two storeys with two projecting wings ending in three-sided bay windows and projecting centre bay with pedimented doorway. The bones of this survive, with the W wing having been reduced to one storey. Interior altered 1933 and completely refitted *c.* 1990. Beautiful grounds landscaped in the 1970s with the advice of *John Codrington*, notably the WALLED GARDEN with its wrought iron gates.

The C18 STABLES, now called the MANOR, E of the house, were converted *c.* 1960 into a house by *Kellet & Partners*. The C18 staircase from the manor house has been incorporated. Small Victorian LODGE dated 1877.

A number of good houses in the village, notably BOSWORTH HOUSE (Kelmarsh Road), three tall storeys of brick, dated 1790.

ASHBY ST LEDGERS

ST LEODEGARIUS. A church whose architecture takes second place to its furnishings and monuments. Small Dec W tower; the N chapel windows (with arches upon arches) should be early C14 too. S aisle with big Perp windows, the traceried heads occupying about half their height. S doorway a large rather coarse C15 ogee surround. Perp arcades of four bays with octagonal piers and double-chamfered arches. Antiquarian manuscripts recording the lost glass suggest a date for the nave of *c.* 1470–90. The interior has one of the best collections of pre-Victorian restoration furnishings in the county. – ROOD SCREEN, C15. Tall, with four-light divisions and mullions reaching up into the apex of the arch; ribbed coving. Some colour on base panels. – PULPIT. Jacobean three-decker with C18 stairs. – BENCHES. Many C15; with much tracery. – Two large Jacobean PEWS in front of the chancel and C18 box pews along the S and N walls facing towards the nave. Also a raised pew at the W end. – WALL PAINTINGS. They were discovered

in 1927 and Professor *E. W. Tristram* worked on them in 1929.
They were renovated by *Eve Baker* in 1968. Alas they are now
mostly too faded to be enjoyed. Over the chancel arch and
running over both arcades, one of the most complete cycles in
England of the Passion of Christ, *c.* 1500. There are eighteen
scenes. Upper tier, N: Entry into Jerusalem, Christ washing St
Peter's feet, Last Supper, Agony in the Garden; E: Christ before
Pilate, Mocking of Christ, Crucifixion, Pieta; S: Christ carrying
the Cross, Nailing to the Cross, Crucifixion. Lower tier, N:
Crucifixion, Deposition; E: Betrayal, Resurrection; S: Resurrection, the Three Maries at the Sepulchre. In the S aisle E end,
a Flagellation of St Margaret of *c.* 1325. – In addition large St
Christopher with the Catesby arms, N wall. – S side of tower
arch: Death with pick and shovel (C16 or C17). Other walls
have remains of C17 text panels. – ALTAR RAILS. Georgian
balusters. – STAINED GLASS. In a S window of the nave a
bishop, *c.* 1470. Several windows with Catesby coats of arms
and other fragments, C14–C15. Chancel E, *c.* 1847 by *Ward &
Nixon.* Also by them the S window of *c.* 1850. N chapel, windows
with medallions by *J. Powell & Sons,* 1850. The single medallion
representing the Magnificat was designed by *J. Grieve.*

MONUMENTS. Brass to Thomas Stokes †1416 and wife,
13-in. (33-cm.) figures (S aisle). Another in S aisle for Rev.
William Smyght, priest in long surplice, 1510. – Large floor
slab with indents for Sir William Catesby †1471 and wives
(chancel). Only half of the male figure, in a shroud, remains.
Within the rails, William Catesby †1485 and wife, figures in
heraldic dress, under a double canopy. – Finely engraved brass
to Sir Richard Catesby †1553 (N aisle). Figure in heraldic
tabard. Another in the S aisle for George Catesby †1505, kneeling figure 18 in. (46 cm.) long. – In the chancel: Brian I'Anson
†1634. Alabaster. Two long kneeling figures, their children
below. – John I'Anson, 1663. Alabaster. Large oval medallion
with three-quarter figure. Wreath around the medallion, and
garlands. Convincingly attributed to *C. G. Cibber* (GF). – Joseph
Ashley †1738. Architectural tablet with three putto heads. –
Moses Ashley †1740. With bust in roundel. Pedimented top.
Both by *Nathaniel Hedges.* – John Bentley Ashley †1761 and
wife †1784. By *John Bacon,* 1785. A very fine standing monument. Two standing allegorical figures, amply draped, l. and r.
of the inscription. Above sarcophagus in front of obelisk. On
the sarcophagus stands a Roman oil-lamp. – James Ashley
†1798. Very simple, with urn in front of obelisk. – N chapel.
George Henry Arnold †1844. Sumptuous Gothic shrine
without effigy. Signed by *I. Wheeler* of Reading. – 2nd Lord
Wimborne †1939. In the churchyard, S of the church, with
steps down to it. A tall tapering cross, the arms and head very
little projecting. To its S an altar or sarcophagus. All by *Lutyens.*
ASHBY ST LEDGERS. A large mansion, the work of over three
centuries, but so happily informal in its grouping that it is
never overpowering. The estate had belonged to the Catesby
family in the later Middle Ages and the Elizabethan period,

was sold to Brian l'Anson, a London draper, in 1612, by his descendants to another London draper, Joseph Ashley, in 1703, and finally came to Ivor Guest, 2nd Lord Wimborne, in 1903. In spite of its long architectural history it is essentially a monument of the early C20 and *Sir Edwin Lutyens*, i.e. the C20 before it developed its own style. Of the transitional phase between historicism and the Modern Movement Ashby St Ledgers is a characteristic and convincing example. Lutyens worked at Ashby in four periods: 1904–5, 1909–12, 1923–4 and 1938–9. Between 1968 and 1969 the house was reduced in size by the demolition of Lutyens's N guest wing, and some internal alterations were carried out, notably the dividing by a floor of Lutyens's Great Hall (the Stone Hall). This work was done by *Jellicoe & Coleridge*. The house was sold in the mid 1970s and had a chequered history, but it was purchased back by the 3rd Lord Wimborne in 1997 and he put in hand a restoration and revival.

The approach is from the W, straight along, through gate-piers, into the forecourt. The original approach was from the church, at an angle through a GATEHOUSE of stone and timber framing. One passes then between the medieval STABLES on the W and the oblong DOVECOTE on the E, and reaches the FORECOURT. The forecourt tells the story of the house. What faces us is the hall range, Elizabethan or Jacobean, with regularly placed three-light windows in two storeys. The lights still have four-centred arches as their heads. But on the l. the display is continued round the corner by *Lutyens*. There is first the imitation Jacobean gable of the Stone Hall of 1909–10, then the big bay window added in 1938 to the first dining room of 1904, and then, half-hiding it, the later extension of the dining room (1924) with its rubble masonry, unrelieved cubic shapes, and only one window, a large canted bay window with three transoms in Lutyens's Castle Drogo manner. To the W of this range a passage leads N, through gatepiers and down through a half-timbered link by a wide Bramantesque stair, with the first half of the steps convex-semicircular and the second half concave-semicircular, so that the landing is a circle. This link connects with a C17 house of half-H plan, with gables to the N and dormers to the forecourt, which Lutyens converted into servants' rooms and nurseries.

Instead of continuing here it is better to return to the hall range and turn S round the range. The S view is specially fine. From l. to r. the gable end of the hall range rises but does not descend again, because of an addition made in 1652. This projects, two-stepped in plan, and consists of a flat-topped balustraded part and a big shaped gable at the r. end. The gable may be a remnant of the work of *C. S. Smith* of Leamington who in 1853 made sizeable additions to the house at the N end which were swept away by Lutyens but are recorded in drawings by George Clarke and an engraving. Below the gable a canted bay window; in the gable a stepped three-light window. In the Hall end wall a doorway with shouldered surround and cherub keystone of *c.* 1700, acting as overture to the garden here, which has four stone figures, badly weathered, of the seasons and a central one of Atlas, also probably *c.* 1700. The extension of 1652 turns the corner to the E and has a straight gable. The E front now exhibits a symmetrical Jacobean façade. This, however, is due to Lutyens, who in 1909 designed – probably not with much pleasure – the central part and the N gable repeating the S gable of 1652. Lutyens made this range the axis for his fine GARDEN with a sunk canal, herbaceous borders and, at r. angles to the N, an ingenious BRIDGE of three stone arches with a demonstratively heavy timber superstructure. Beyond the garden, by the lake, a marble statue of Apollo, apparently English, *c.* 1730, brought from the site of Ashby Lodge in 1972.

The N end of this Lutyens range is a little confusing. A bay window cuts across a large window behind. The window belongs to the Stone Hall, a room of 1909–10 continuing the axis of the dining room to the E. What is more confusing still is that the E front then runs on, recessed as against the Lutyens façade but projecting a little as against the E window of the Stone Hall, and that it runs on by means of a timber-framed C17 house which was bought by the 2nd Lord Wimborne at Ipswich and re-erected (against Lutyens's wishes as he records: 'not got my way'!). The IPSWICH HOUSE stood in Carr Street. It is of two storeys with an overhang, built of closely set uprights and occasional diagonal braces. Beyond this projected until 1968 Lutyens's NORTH WING of 1923–4. This had kitchen and servants' hall below, twelve servants' bedrooms on a mezzanine floor, and guest rooms and the master's bedroom above. It had a good masculine front with canted oriel windows and block-shaped chimneystacks. Now that this has been removed the Ipswich House acts as terminal to the E front. The N side is now a service approach. Turning S we are brought back by the Bramantesque stair into the forecourt and to the main entrance.

Of the INTERIORS the screen on the N side of the entrance hall introduces one to Lutyens's ingenuities. It leads down some steps to the newly created DINING ROOM and so to the STONE HALL of 1909. This was restored as a two-storey hall with open roof in 1998–2000 by *Martin Hillier* and *Mervyn Cable*. The axis turns here, and one passes from the W end of the Stone Hall through an arch into the dining room of 1904, now a GALLERY. This was designed by the decorators *Thornton Smith*. It has a tunnel-vault decorated by imitation Jacobean plasterwork. Beyond this is the DINING ROOM of 1924, with a coved plain ceiling and classical unfluted Doric columns. Chimneypiece with pedimented overmantel and marble fireplace surround. Finally the E range. In the STUDY in the SE corner good panelling of the first half of the C17, with primitive Corinthian pilasters and flat carving. Next to the study a C17 staircase. N of this Lutyens's MUSIC ROOM, then another C17 staircase, rebuilt, and N again the CARD

ROOM with late C17 panelling, not *in situ*, and a good chimneypiece.

In the village THE COTTAGE, a small Jacobethan house by *Lutyens*, 1912, built for Lord Wimborne's agent. H-shaped plan, with central projecting porch. Restored and extended in 1980s by *Roderick Gradidge*. Also by *Lutyens* a picturesque row of COTTAGES, 1908–9, with sweeping thatched roofs, asymmetrically placed windows, and Lutyens's typical battered buttresses and bold chimneys.

Former LODGES, 1 m. NW on the A361, originally for Ashby Lodge (demolished in the 1920s). Mid-C18, with an early C20 portico in between also by *Lutyens*. It was used as a clubhouse for Lord Wimborne's private golf club. Ashby Lodge had a R.C. chapel and when this was demolished a panel of glass was taken to St John's Hospital in Northampton (*see* p. 457).

ASHLEY

ST MARY. A grand church of ironstone and grey limestone, made the more impressive due to its almost total rebuilding by *G. G. Scott*, 1865–7, using *John Thompson* of Peterborough as builder. Very expensively done, for the Rev. Richard Pulteney, rector from 1853 till 1874 and squire as well. A faculty dated 1863 suggests that the organ chamber and vestry had already been added. Pre-restoration drawings by George Clarke suggest that, apart from the chancel, Scott followed what was there. The tower and spire were totally rebuilt when the church was extended W by one bay. The style is Dec with a pair of belfry windows with reticulated tracery and above the corbel table a broach spire. The base of the tower is ironstone but the top stages are limestone ashlar, as is the S porch. The old material reused indicates a date *c.* 1300. Quatrefoil piers, dogtooth hoodmould over the S doorway. The chancel, which Scott also extended E, has a section of its S wall intact with its doorway and a blocked rectangular lowside window. Its original height is also clear.

It is the interior which makes a visit to Ashley so memorable, especially that of the chancel. Impressive use of polished pink granite shafts in the chancel arch and of various colours in the triple arches between chancel and organ chamber. The whole of the walls painted by *Clayton & Bell*, who also did the STAINED GLASS. The WALL DECORATION is based on the Te Deum, with Apostles and Martyrs on the N wall, and Old Testament Prophets on the S. Christ in Majesty over the E window. As well as colour there is much gilding, notably on the REREDOS, of alabaster and other marbles, with its splendid crocketed gables. The painted decoration was beautifully restored by Bell's great grandson *Peter Larkworthy* in 1973. – PAVEMENT of coloured marbles and encaustic tiles. – Very

richly detailed CHANCEL RAIL of brass. – FONT a solid block
of pink marble. According to the Rev. L. E. Brown it cost
£2,000 in 1865–8. – The delightful Gothic CHANDELIERS of
iron are by *G. F. Bodley* and were also repainted in 1973. They
have tiny shields hanging from gold coronets.

The Rev. Richard Pulteney did a good deal also to beautify the
village. He was responsible for remodelling the MANOR
HOUSE (by *E. F. Law*, dated 1865), got *G. G. Scott* to design a
handsome Gothic SCHOOL (of 1858) and master's house (date
1865), all in white stone, and built a number of substantial
cottages, or rather semi-detached houses. *Law* designed some
of these in broad Tudor style in the 1860s and 1870s (there are
dates of 1860 and 1868).

ASHLEY COURT, Main Street. The rectory in Pulteney's time.
Part ironstone and probably late C17, but overwhelmed by
stone and brick additions of 1867–71, apparently by *E. F.
Law*. Most remarkable three timbered gables with pargetting
decoration.

YEOMANS, Green Lane. Medieval and later. L-shaped, one wing
cruck-framed, originally an open hall. Stone external walls.

0080

ASHTON
¾ m. E of Oundle

The village was the inspiration of the Hon. Charles Rothschild,
whose family had bought the estate in 1860. He had discovered
the place while on a butterfly hunting expedition with the vicar
of Polebrook. There existed a small hunting lodge and he per-
suaded his father, the 1st Lord Rothschild, to allow him to build
a new house. In 1900 he brought in *William Huckvale*, an architect who had worked for the family at Tring and who was to
spend nearly all his career working for them. His commission
included not only the house but a model farm, lodges, estate
buildings and, above all, the village.

CHAPEL AND SCHOOL. Built and endowed by the Creed family
of Oundle in 1705–6 'for bringing up and instructing the poor
of Ashton to read and write'. Oblong with four tall round-arched
windows of two lights. The first three belong to the chapel, the
fourth to the schoolroom, W front with a round-arched doorway
in a heavy oblong frame which incorporates sections of quatrefoil piers of *c.* 1300. Three-light window of stepped round-
arched lights under one big round arch and framed by volutes.
The interior is simple with a barrel-vault. – REREDOS with
fluted pilasters and pediment with Commandments Table, an
open bible and clouds and curtains, painted by *Elizabeth Creed*.
Doorways either side to the schoolroom and master's room.

The VILLAGE HOUSES are basically in the Tudor manner,
rock-faced and all thatched. They were built with local materi-

als and local labour. Every cottage, already in 1900, had filtered water supply, electricity and a bathroom. All wiring is underground, an all too rare luxury which has a considerable effect on the undisturbed unity of a street or a village. On the edge of the green is THE CHEQUERED SKIPPER (formerly The Three Horseshoes). Two stone gables, its entrance beneath a wooden pillared veranda. Gutted by fire in 1966 but faithfully rebuilt. One or two of the cottages are rebuildings of older structures but submerged in the unifying 1900 effect. At the w entrance to the village is the MANOR HOUSE, which was not altered. It is L-shaped with a large gabled wing on the r. The gable has remains of a C15 opening within it and some fragments of carving, but is otherwise totally C17 to C19.

ASHTON WOLD, about 1 m. E in well-wooded surroundings. In *Huckvale*'s Tudor style with straight-sided gables and mullioned-and-transomed windows, large and essentially symmetrical. Reinhabited in 1971 by Miriam Rothschild after a period of neglect and reduced in height by *Claud Phillimore*, turning the top floor into attics. Miriam Rothschild transformed the Edwardian garden into a wildflower garden and planted trees on the terraces. Subdivided since her death in 2005. STABLE BLOCK, NW, in a similar broad Tudor manner with a courtyard and its main range having a central gable above its carriage archway. Alongside a WATER TOWER, a curious design, with a castellated range and the tower having tapered buttresses, a square top and pyramidal roof. Amongst the many other buildings on the estate are the STEWARD'S HOUSE, near the stable block, like a little manor house with its three-bay façade with mullioned windows and central projecting gable with ball finials, a DAIRY of curved form with a tall thatched central building, its tiled interior still intact, and the HOME FARM complex.

ASHTON

1¼ m. SE of Roade

7040

ST MICHAEL. W tower of 1848 in the Dec style with saddleback roof by *R. C. Hussey* using the local builder *William Shakeshaft*. Restoration by *E. F. Law & Son*, 1895, when much was rebuilt. N arcade of two bays, with octagonal pier and double-chamfered arches, C13 or early C14. A C19 extra short bay for the organ. Dec chancel and N aisle windows, the latter worth a special glance for their lopsidedness. Very wide N aisle. Blackand-white marble chancel floor of 1911. – FONT. Small tub form, C12. – PULPIT. Jacobean, with two tiers of the well-known blank arches. – STAINED GLASS. Chancel E window of 1892 by *E. Horwood* of Somerset. – MONUMENTS. Effigy of a cross-legged knight. Of wood, early C14. Said to be Sir Philip de Lou. – Sir John de Herteshull *c.* 1365. A much battered alabaster effigy on a tomb-chest with panels and a ballflower frieze. The earliest alabaster effigy in the county. (Both restored by *Elliott Ryder Conservation* in 2009.) – Robert Marriott †1584 and family. Tomb-chest with brasses, the figures 2 ft 6 in. (76 cm.) long. – Captain Richard Lestocke †1715. Alabaster frame with military trophy at base.

MANOR HOUSE, NW of the church. C17 but on an older site with surrounding moat. Staircase with slim twisted balusters.

MANOR FARMHOUSE, Roade Hill, NE of the church. A long L-shaped building of various C17 phases. Central two-window section facing the road, mullions with label and porch. Gable end on r. of two storeys with two light mullioned windows. The l. range has further three light mullions. Later extensions behind.

ASTON-LE-WALLS

ST LEONARD. The oldest features are the bottom parts of the W tower – its W doorway, now hidden behind the early C16 W porch, an unusual feature in a village church, and a S window are round-headed – and the N doorway, with a single-stepped pointed arch but still a scalloped capital. The tower ends in C13 bell-openings, of two lights with a shaft between. The top stage was rebuilt 1909–10 following a partial collapse. C13 also the S doorway and the (somewhat later?) N and S windows (pairs of lancets, Y-tracery with a trefoil in the spandrel). Of *c.* 1300 the SEDILIA and the very pretty DOUBLE PISCINA (with a cinquefoil in fine bar tracery and foliate capitals) and the tomb-recess opposite (with a cinquecusped arch). Arcades of three bays. On the N a circular and then an octagonal pier, on the S an octagonal and then a circular one. Double-chamfered arches. The aisles are extremely narrow. Restored in 1875–7 and 1881–2 by *H. M. Townsend*. Doubtless of his time, the rather effective TILE floor and REREDOS of alabaster and marble in a C13 manner. – FONT. Square, Norman, three sides carved. On one a knot pattern, on the next intersected arches, on the third a very asymmetrical Tree of Life. – BENCHES. Square-headed with tracery panels between buttresses. – BRASS. Alban Butler †1609. A plate with him, his two wives and children all kneeling. – MONUMENTS. Effigy of a priest; early C14; stone (chancel N). – Elizabeth Orme †1692. Small bust at the top. The inscription ought to be read.

SACRED HEART & OUR LADY (R.C.). 1827, originally Gothic with thin details. – STAINED GLASS. Three of 1920–1 by *J. Vosch* of Brussels. One by *J. Hardman & Co.*, 1937.

MANOR HOUSE, Blacksmiths Lane. W front of *c.* 1700. Seven bays and two storeys with a hipped roof. Otherwise mainly late C17 with some evidence of C16 origins, such as moulded beams

and some doorways with pointed arched heads. Many mullioned windows. Staircase with turned balusters.

ASTROP PARK
¾ m. NE of Kings Sutton

5030

Built by Sir John Willes after 1735–7 by *Francis* and *William Smith*
of Warwick. The house was seven bays long, of two storeys.
Quoins, and also quoins to the five-bay centre, which has a
pediment. All windows with alternatingly triangular and segmental pediments. Doorway with Gibbs surround on the E
side. To this house *Sir John Soane* added one-storeyed wings
in 1805. These had two further floors added in the later C19,
bringing them to the height of the rest of the house. They were
removed in 1961 leaving rather blank rendered walls at either
end of the building. Soane is also responsible for the four pairs
of columns in the DINING ROOM. ENTRANCE HALL with
Doric columns and a fine marble chimneypiece of *Cheere* type
with pastoral reliefs against Siena marble background. Splendid STAIRCASE with three balusters each tread, twisted, fluted
and plain columns. Typical of the Smiths and very similar to
that at Chicheley, Bucks. Other rooms have evidence of C19
alterations, such as painted ceiling decoration. – KEEPER'S
LODGE, PHEASANTRY, and a COTTAGE by *W. Wilkinson* of
Oxford, 1868. – PARK partly landscaped by *Brown*, probably
when he was working at Aynho *c.* 1760.

ST RUMBALD'S WELL, S of the house in a valley. Astrop was the
site of a short-lived but famous spa, whose waters were discovered in the mid C17. Round-headed niche with large keystone
and rusticated quoins standing at the rear of a small basin. A
New Well was opened in October 1749 (*Northampton Mercury*),
and it could easily be of this date. The niche was probably used
as a seat and is thus represented in an amusing drawing of 1813
by Rowlandson. A replica without the side rustication stands
by the Newbottle road S of the park. It was created following
the purchase of the estate in 1865 by Sir William Brown, who
re-routed the road.

THE GATEHOUSE, Upper Astrop Road, on the S edge of the
park, with a tall round bay of early C19 character, had use as
a form of assembly rooms during the period of the spa.

ASTWELL CASTLE
1½ m. SW of Wappenham

6040

A fragment of what was, by the end of the C17, one of the larger
houses in the county. It is really a fortified manor house,

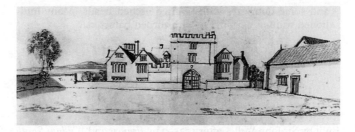

Astwell Castle.
Drawing by P. Tillemans, 1721

though battlements are prominent, originating with Thomas
Lovett, who in 1471 arranged to exchange Astwell for Rushton.
It passed at the end of the C16 to the Shirleys of Staunton
Harold, Leics., and was mostly demolished after their descendants, the Earls Ferrers, sold the estate in 1763. Drawings of it
c. 1720 by Peter Tillemans show a courtyard house with a moat.
What stands today is the three-floor tower of the C15 with the
lower attachment on its l. Both parts are embattled. The tower
has an archway with a four-centred head, two-light cusped
windows, and a higher stair-turret on the N side. The lower
building has a quatrefoil window to the S and one to the W. To
the W a house was added by George Shirley about 1606. Yet it
still has mullioned windows with arched lights. Inside a c. 1600
fireplace with a broad frieze of simple geometrical motifs above
the four-centred arch. The hall and other wings of the courtyard lay NW of the tower. Altered in the C19 and again in 1957
when the interior was remodeled.

5030   AYNHO

ST MICHAEL. An unusual sight: a fine medieval tower attached
to a striking C18 Baroque church. The tower is Dec. It has
diagonal buttresses with a niche to the NW and one to the SW,
a doorway with many fine continuous mouldings, a three-light
window, and two-light bell-openings under a straight hoodmould (cf. Kings Sutton). Beneath the W window niche,
perched on the sill, a somewhat weathered dragon, a remnant
of a statue of St Michael. Battlements and pinnacles. The body
of the building was rebuilt in 1723–5 by *Edward Wing*, a carpenter and builder at Aynho (and 'by the Pious care, Generous
encouragement and prudent management' of Mr Cartwright
of Aynhoe Park, as the architect says on a drawing). It is broad
and somewhat squat, in Helmdon stone, and much in the style
of Hawksmoor and Archer (cf. below). Seven bays treated as
a symmetrical composition – not as a procession from W to E.

Two storeys of windows, round-arched and segment-headed. Flat frames. Bays one and seven project a little and are emphasized by giant Doric pilasters. Bays three to five are again stressed by giant pilasters and have in addition a pediment. The centre of its footline is broken by an arch, a motif from Baalbek used for instance at St Alphege, Greenwich, but also already by Sir Christopher Wren, e.g. in the transept front of St Paul's. E end with four giant pilasters, three big round-arched windows, and a middle pediment. For a village mason/builder this is surprisingly competent, with a sense of proportion and balance which is very metropolitan. Did he have help from a higher authority?

The INTERIOR, just one large, uncomposed unit, is disappointing, largely due to the restoration of 1863 carried out by *Franklin*, a builder of Deddington. The ceiling is now flat but originally had a deep cove (see drawings hanging in the church and also the remaining coving in the s chapel). Fine, dignified WEST GALLERY on coupled Doric columns, each with a tiny section of frieze above. – Also original PULPIT and BOX PEWS, lowered in 1863. – LECTERN. Victorian, but unusually a pelican in piety. – FONT. 1860s, octagonal with quatrefoil panelled bowl. – STAINED GLASS. E window by *Thomas Willement*, 1857. With a very Victorian vine border and three religious roundels. – s wall. Two *Kempe* windows of 1898 and 1899. – MONUMENTS. Many tablets. The best are the two splendid ones either side the altar, identical, to Rebecca and Rhoda Chapman †1686 and 1694, who were related by marriage to the Cartwrights. Attributed to *William Stanton*, and both probably erected *c.* 1694, and that to Matthew Hutton, †1711, by *Edward Stanton*. – In the s chapel a fine free-standing tomb to members of the Cartwright family, erected 1654, almost certainly by *Edward Marshall* (G.F.).

AYNHOE PARK. The Aynho Estate was acquired by Richard Cartwright, a lawyer, between 1615 and 1616. It remained in Cartwright ownership till the late 1950s, when it was sold and the house divided into apartments. In 2004 it once more came into private ownership and has been successfully restored. The house represents essentially four periods: Jacobean, Carolean, the early C18 and the early C19. Three names are connected with it: *Edward Marshall*, master mason to the king from 1660 to 1673 and sculptor of monuments, *Thomas Archer*, one of the triad of truly Baroque English architects, and *Sir John Soane*. It is Soane's work which makes the house so important. The Jacobean house was of E-shape, facing s. It was set on fire in 1645, but much of it seems to have survived. *Marshall* filled in the space between the formerly projecting wings with their canted bay windows. The wings were of three storeys, the infilling piece of two. It looked like a separate five-bay house. All this we know from a drawing of 1683. Most of Marshall's work can still be seen in the present s front. The windows were of the cross-type and are now, it is true, sashed, but their pediments, triangular on the ground

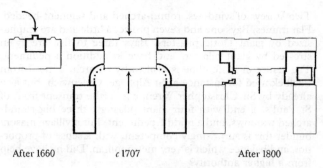

After 1660   c 1707   After 1800

Aynhoe Park.
Plan of development

floor, segmental on the first floor, are Carolean, and so is the
arched upper middle window with its characteristic surround
of two Corinthian columns carrying pieces of jutting-forward
entablature and decorated between these with garlands. The
quoins also date from the 1660s. The top storey, on the other
hand, which replaces Marshall's balustrade, belongs to the
work attributed to Archer, as does the entrance below the
central window and repeating its columned frame. (The pediment was added by Soane.) The columns are Tuscan. *Archer*
worked at Aynhoe from 1707 to 1714. He also refaced the
fronts of the former wings, removing e.g. their canted bay
windows. Moreover, he added seven-bay wings of one storey
which continue the line of the s facade. The windows are
arched, and the arches rest on pilasters. The inward-turning
volutes of their capitals ought to be noted as an Archer
mannerism copied by others of his generation (cf. the Bastards
of Blandford). Their central sections originally had a pediment. The two attachments were built for the library and the
Orangery. It was *Soane* who added the upper floor of the
Orangery and library and rebuilt the w end. His work at
Aynhoe dates from 1800 to 1805. His incised Grecian ornament is unmistakable. His square windows do not sit too
happily over Archer's arcade of windows below. The w façade
is worth noting. It is of four bays, the lateral ones having
blind rectangles above a niche on the ground floor. The two
central bays have tall round-arched windows on the ground
floor and square windows above, all beneath a triangular pediment. Pilasters which divide the façade are rusticated below
and have incised patterns above. In the centre of the façade
they become double and are partnered above the pediment
by a chimneystack. If the design is a little uneasy, the balance
is superb.

The N front is much simpler. It consists of a raised three-
storeyed five-bay centre with pediment, and three-bay, three-
storeyed side pieces. There is no display of decoration. The
only indications of the Carolean house are the mullioned

windows of the basement. Archer's principal contribution to
Aynhoe are the detached STABLES and OFFICES flanking the
entrance courtyard and placed at right angles to the N front.
They are of eleven bays and two storeys, with a slightly higher
pedimented five-bay centre. Unmistakably Archerish here are
the doorways. They are arched, and the arches stand on oddly
moulded shafts. Their mouldings are continued in the arch,
and the arch is separated from the shafts not by capitals but
by a block with hardly any detail. Moreover, the whole of this
is surrounded by a frame with diagonally placed, tapering
pilasters without proper capitals carrying an entablature the
centre of which curves back concavely. The whole group is
architecturally impressive, though visually somewhat forbidding, an impression due largely to the rendering of the brick
structure.

The wings were joined to the centre by Soane. The motif he
used is the triumphal arch, i.e. an open archway flanked by
blank bays with niches. The bays have Tuscan columns with
projecting fragments of entablature. The whole does not blend
well with the rest and cannot be called one of Soane's
successes.

The INTERIOR is Soane's triumph. All that remains of the
Archer period is the STAIRCASE to the E of the entrance hall.
It is a very handsome piece, of wood, with three slim balusters
for each tread: twisted – fluted – twisted. The tread-ends are
carved. The newel posts are fluted Corinthian columns. The
treads have some inlay. It has much in common with staircases
in the *Smith* of Warwick houses and it could well be by one of
their craftsmen. The decoration of the walls with attached
unfluted Ionic columns however is Soane's. He in 1801 had
planned a much more thorough remodelling of the staircase
with ashlar or imitation ashlar walls and a segmental tunnel-
vault. In the ENTRANCE HALL the screens of Roman Doric
columns are his. The only discordant note is the green onyx
chimneypiece, a late addition by the Cartwrights. A vaulted
corridor leads to Soane's STAIRCASE. It is a tall space rising
the whole height of the house, with a glazed skylight with strips
of orange glass to give some warmth of colour. The cast-iron
balustrade is extremely simple, but almost identical to that he
designed at Wimpole, Cambs. Next comes the ANTE-ROOM.
This almost square room has a shallow domed ceiling with
each wall given arched shapes and slender pilasters.

To appreciate fully what Soane is up to one should move r.
into the LIBRARY. It is only from here that the effect of the
enfilade is appreciated. Double doors can be opened to give a
vista along the whole length of the S front, and with the moving
shapes it is inspiring. The library itself is the most intimate
room, but this intimacy is achieved by masking by bookcases
two lobbies in the S corners of the room. Each wall has a trio
of arches, wider in the centre of each wall, that on the S becoming a bay. The frieze is one used by Soane elsewhere, a sequence
of tiny fans with beaded edges. Through the ante-room is the

EATING ROOM, a more orthodox room. It is entered through an apsed service space with Ionic columns and fitted serving tables. The SALOON, in the centre of the front, is Soane at his best. An exceedingly delicate design with shallow apsed ends, very shallow wall arches, and a groin-vault, the groins of which disappear towards the corner, and three arches on each of its long sides. The *enfilade* ends with a flight of curved steps into the brightly lit interior of the ORANGERY. One more Soane room should be mentioned: the COLD BATH, near the E end. But this was largely remodelled in 1952 and is now part of a kitchen. It has strangely swelling attenuated Tuscan columns carrying a groin-vault. The plan is, on a minute scale, the Byzantine plan of the inscribed cross.

The PARK was landscaped by *Capability Brown* in 1761–3. An ICE HOUSE of the Soane period survives in excellent condition (just to the E of the house, S of the churchyard wall). In the C18 there was a terraced layout S of the house, with a pool, leading to a long avenue vista recorded by Peter Tillemans in 1721.

The VILLAGE of Aynho is full of neat stone houses, all beautifully kept. Of individual buildings the following deserve notice.

GRAMMAR SCHOOL, Croughton Road. Founded by Mrs Mary Cartwright in 1654 but, because of a family dispute about the will, not built till 1665–71. Originally L-shaped with master's house forming the l. section and the school, with a room on each floor, the r. The façade much altered and renewed, especially the mullioned windows. Original doorway opposite the gateway. Four-centred with lozenge stops. The large windows of the house part *c.* 1900, in the place of two mullioned openings on each floor. One first-floor window blocked with inserted sundial (dated 1671). In the school part, on the ground floor, tall two-light mullioned windows – an early case of this motif. A second doorway, now blocked, may not be an original feature. On the w side several long rectangular openings, now mostly blocked indicate the original staircase position. One small portion of it survives. Long wing behind on the E, *c.* 1900. Much subdivision internally.

ALMSHOUSES, N of the Grammar School. 1822. Grey and brown stone. Two-storeyed, with tripartite windows and pedimented doorways. The centre bay carries a rather starved pediment.

VILLAGE HALL. 1928 by *F. J. Cooke* of Banbury. Just a simple triangular pedimented block with a lunette above its porch.

THE PEDIMENT, E of the Village Hall on the s side of Main Street. 1956–7 by *Raymond Erith*. A three-bay stone house of two storeys topped by a triangular pediment containing a circular window. The central window on the first floor is blind. Both fronts are identical. Drawing room fireplace with an inscription: 'The significance of the dwelling is in the dweller.' In the study an ogee-headed recess. The grounds were worked on 1959–73. Doric colonnaded SUMMERHOUSE and a

CROQUET SHED with a pyramidal roof topped by a short round
column surmounted by an urn finial. Erith died in 1974 and
his final designs for garden ornaments were carried out by
Quinlan Terry.

STOCKS. N of the E end of the road to Deddington (B4031).

The OXFORD CANAL cuts through the S part of the parish. In
1788 an extensive wharf was opened. One of its WHARF
HOUSES, with an overhanging roof, still stands in the midst of
the modern marina, just off the road to Deddington (B4031).
There are also two ACCOMMODATION BRIDGES. One, a single
stone elliptical arch *c.* 1780–90, is probably by *Samuel Simcock*.
The other is a lift bridge, also late C18. In the same area are
the remains of the former RAILWAY STATION, 1850 by *Brunel*.
To the N is a skewed Warren GIRDER BRIDGE of 1910, originally carrying a lesser line over the main line.

UPPER AYNHO GROUNDS, 2 m. SE. A tall, rather plain limestone farmhouse of three bays and two storeys, *c.* 1800 but
whose W double end gables have built into them large Gothick
arches with circular windows above, acting as an eyecatcher
from Aynhoe Park. It was called New Farm when the enclosure
was done in 1793. Two enormous barns to the N of the same
date.

BADBY   5050

Many nice stone houses and an attractive large green.

ST MARY. W tower of 1707 with arched windows and bell-
openings. The latter have the flat bands of Y-tracery which are
so characteristic of the C18. Lower down also a vertically
placed oval and a circular window. As for the body of the
church, much outside is due to the restoration by *E. F. Law &
Son*, 1880–1. The chancel windows seem of *c.* 1300, the E with
intersecting tracery and trefoils (cf. Newnham); the N aisle
windows certainly are, and the N arcade with its octagonal
piers, responds with ballflower, and double-chamfered arches
also fits the date. The S arcade, if anything, looks earlier.
Chancel arch broad continuous chamfers set on leaf corbels.
A step down into the chancel. The clerestory with its ten
extraordinarily closely set straight-headed two-light windows
is Perp, as is the S porch. – SEDILIA C13 with Dec PISCINA.
– PULPIT. Simple, C17. – COMMUNION RAIL. Slender balusters, mid-C18. – COMMANDMENT BOARDS. Victorian either
side the E window. Painted decorative lettering on metal. –
FONT. The bowl Perp style of 1880–1, but the base genuine.
– STAINED GLASS. Chancel S, late C15 roundel. – Nave N
clerestory. Inscription and arms, C15. – Chancel E of 1851. –
Chancel N of 1919 by *Burlison & Grylls*. – Chancel S of 1957,

designed by *Arthur Waller* and made by *G. Maile & Son*, and a
window of 1914–18 by *Burlison & Grylls*. – S aisle E, by *Ward
& Hughes*, 1881.

UNITED REFORMED CHURCH (formerly Congregational),
Chapel Lane. 1873, in a Lombardic Romanesque manner.

Former SCHOOL, on the green. Built *c.* 1812 by *James Wyatt*.
Ironstone, broadly Tudor, symmetrical. Five bays, one-storeyed, the centre a two-storeyed porch-tower. Cross-windows,
and in the tower a window with Y-tracery.

BADBY HOUSE, 1½ m. N. 1826 for Charles Watkin. S front of five
bays and two storeys. On the E side entrance with unfluted
Doric columns in antis. Cantilever staircase.

LANTERN HOUSE (or Fawsley Lodge), on the Banbury–Daventry road. Two-storeyed, octagonal, early C19. Probably by
Wyatt, but *Thomas Cundy* is also a candidate (*see* Fawsley).

BARROW. N of the village on the Daventry road, now much
spread by ploughing. This is all that remains of a group which
lay N of the village.

IRON AGE HILLFORT. On Arbury Hill, ½ m. W of the village,
lies a single-rampart hillfort roughly square with sides 600 ft
long. There is now practically no sign of a ditch and bank, and
apart from a slight feature in the NE corner no evidence survives for an entrance.

BARBY

ST MARY. Mostly of W Northamptonshire/Warwickshire pink
sandstone. The windows are nearly entirely C19. Inside, W of
the S doorway, a re-set small Anglo-Saxon window. The chancel
N windows belong to the late C13, the bell-openings and the
top frieze of the W tower too. Inside the chancel, arcade of
three bays to the S chapel. Low piers of quatrefoil section.
Double-chamfered arches. Probably late C13 or early C14. The
doorway and windows are all C19. There was a restoration in
1897–1900 by *W. & C. H. Bassett-Smith*. The nave is flanked by
two aisles. The N arcade has four bays with octagonal piers
carrying capitals with big faces, shields, etc., and double-chamfered arches. The heraldry is for the Zouche family who held
the manor from the 1270s to the C17. The S arcade was pulled
down and re-erected further S, a change credited to the C16
(Whellan records a date of 1600). This gives the interior an
uncomfortably lopsided appearance. Not that one comes to
notice this easily, for the interior is perhaps the darkest in the
county, because of a very complete set of STAINED GLASS by
Kempe & Co., from 1900 to the 1930s. It is a magnificent
display and shows the way the firm's art changed from pure
Kempe to the later work when Tower took over. The one
window not by the firm is at the W end of the N aisle, and that
is by *C. C. Powell*, 1938. – N aisle E. Nativity (restored), *c.* 1310.

– COMMUNION RAIL. Early C18. – REREDOS. Ceramic with painting, *c.* 1890. – LECTERN. A wonderfully modelled eagle, in bronze, almost in flight. What date? Perhaps *c.* 1900? It clearly was never intended originally to be a church lectern.

RECTORY. 1869. Red brick with yellow diapering. Gabled, Tudor – like so many others in the neighbourhood.

SCHOOL (VILLAGE HALL), Kilsby Road. The original building of 1865 is of red brick with blue brick patterns.

MOTTE of a castle, N of the village. There does not appear to be any bailey.

BARNWELL

A large an attractive village, enhanced by some good stone houses, a stream and trees.

ST ANDREW. Externally mostly of the later C13. The priest's doorway looks early but is probably remade out of bits from All Saints (*see* below). C13 W tower. Doorway with three orders of shafts and pretty fillets, W window of two lights with a quatrefoil over. A little higher up on the S side a circular window with dogtooth. Bell-openings wildly decorated with dogtooth and ballflower. Spire tall with small broaches. Three tiers of lucarnes. They show that by then the C14 was under way. C13 S doorway (shaft-rings, dogtooth, hoodmould on flower stops) and S aisle (E lancet – inside accompanied by two fine big Perp niches). Late C13 clerestory with two-light windows with pointed quatrefoils over. Corbel-frieze with closely set heads. Late C13 N aisle W window. The other N aisle windows after 1300, one with a big circle in the tracery filled by three spherical triangles, the other with reticulated tracery. Very good Dec N doorway. Two orders of shafts, but instead of capitals a frieze of nobbly leaves sprouting out of a face. Late C13 arcades inside, except for one raw earlier circular pier. The rest of quatrefoil section with fillets and double-chamfered arches. Tower arch triple-chamfered and dying against the imposts. Chancel arch with groups of three short detached shafts on corbels. At the E end of the N aisle a splendid Dec REREDOS, very unusual in composition. Tripartite with a wider centre. Extremely rich ogee arches with big cusps filled with big leaves. Finials and a frieze of fleurons and faces against the back wall. It was cut through in the C19. In the chancel Dec SEDILIA with little tipped-up vaults and flat ogee arches. The chancel, which has Perp windows, was completely remodelled by *E. Browning* in 1873. Of his time the rich Maw's tiled sanctuary floor. – FONT. Dec. Octagonal with eight flat crocketed gables and flowers at the foot, no doubt the same carver as the N aisle reredos. – PULPIT. Jacobean. – STAINED GLASS. Chancel S. At the top of a window dated 1844, canopies and saints (Nicholas, Clement and Gregory), *c.* 1400–25. Tower an assembly of bits, not all medieval. Chancel E, The Works of Mercy, by *Ward & Hughes*, 1865. By them also the chancel SW window of 1875–6. Chancel N window of *c.* 1850 by *Ward & Winston.* – MONUMENTS. Christopher Freeman †1610. Brass plate with small kneeling figures. – The Rev. Nicholas Latham †1620. Frontal demi-figure with a book on a desk representing the reading desk of a pulpit. Questionable colouring. – Henry Duke of Gloucester †1974, a modest stone tablet over the priest's doorway. – N aisle, a large bronze plaque with a profile head of Prince William of Gloucester †1972 signed *Roboz.* Nearby a painted memorial for Elizabeth Worthington 1665, like a small hatchment.

In the wall between the church and the former rectory, several C13 FRAGMENTS from All Saints (*see* below), including a window head with cusped intersected tracery and others of two lights with foiled circles.

ALL SAINTS, ¼ m. W on the S side of the stream. Pulled down in 1825. Only the chancel remains, with a C13 chancel arch and big Perp windows. It was left undisturbed because of the Montagu monuments. – REREDOS and PANELLING. Handsome C18, with Corinthian pilasters. Said to have been given by the 2nd Duke of Montagu in 1740. – MONUMENTS. Henry Montagu †1625, a most unusual and attractive monument covered with pathetic and quaint inscriptions. The monument is a tall obelisk on a base. Its lowest part is opened as a niche or tabernacle and in it stands a beautifully carved figure of Henry, who died at the age of three, dressed as a little man.

Barnwell, All Saints.
Drawing by G. Clarke, *c.* 1850

He holds a scroll which reads: 'Lord give me of ye water.' But
below we are told that he died 'immature per aquas'. The upper
parts of the obelisk have five tiers of heraldic shields. Immediately below the niche two big feet. On one it says: 'Not my
feete only', on the other 'but also my hands and head'. In the
middle an opening as of a village pump with the inscription:
'Poure on me the ioyes of thy salvation.' At the very foot of the
monument: 'Vita brevis, merces aeterna.' It has been attributed
to *William Wright* (GF). – Dame Letice Montagu †1611. Severe,
tall oblong monument without figures. Framed inscription and
framed shield above. At the top an obelisk on a disk with a
shell motif. Probably from the workshop of the *Thorpes* of
Kingscliffe. – Dorothy Creed †1714, painted by her mother
Elizabeth Creed (*see also* Titchmarsh). Oil on slate. At the top
an armorial lozenge and swags. Several other memorials and
ledger slabs.

LATHAM'S ALMSHOUSES, SE of St Andrew. Founded in 1601
and rebuilt in the appropriate style in 1874 by *Edward Browning*. Some good armorial glass thought to be by *Ward &
Winston*. E of the church, on the other side of the stream,
BIGLEY ALMSHOUSES, Tudor style 1838, rebuilt 1915.

STATION HOUSE, at the entrance to the village on the A605.
1845 by *Livock*. Much altered as a residence but still with part
of its platform canopy. The main station building is now at
Wansford (Nene Valley Steam Railway), near Peterborough.

BARNWELL CASTLE. The castle is of great architectural interest
and far too little known. If it was really built in or about 1266
by Berengar Le Moyne, who ceded it to Ramsey Abbey in
1276, then it represents the first example in Britain of the most
monumental type of castle architecture, the type with a more
or less square plan and round corner towers. The date is based
on the statement of a jury in 1276 that he had illegally built a
castle ten years earlies. The type is more famously represented
in Britain by Harlech of 1284 etc. and derives from France and
Italy where, on Roman town-planning precedent, it had been
used from about 1220 or 1230 onwards. Barnwell has four
mighty round corner TOWERS, the only irregularity being that
the NE and NW towers are really trefoiled to the outside, with
garderobe and staircase projections. This form appears earlier
on the Constable's Gate added to Dover Castle in the 1220s.
The other irregularity is that the GATEHOUSE is not in the
middle of its side, the E side, but immediately next to the SE
tower containing garderobes. The gatehouse again has two
round towers. The arches are double-chamfered; the gateway
inside has a pointed tunnel-vault. Grooves for the portcullis.
In the tower of the gatehouse ground-floor rooms with two
bays of vaults with single-chamfered ribs. Above the gateway
was a room with large windows. Otherwise the windows
are small and there are many cross-slits, some with two horizontal slits. At a later period the curtain wall was thickened
on its internal face by about a metre; the thickening was
carried across the towers, and new round-headed doorways

constructed. The unusual treatment of the towers and the high quality of the work suggests the designer had connections with the royal works.

In 1982 traces of wall paintings of religious figures *c.* 1300 were discovered in the ground-floor gatehouse chamber, N of the access, suggesting this was a chapel during the Ramsey Abbey period. To the NW of the castle are ditches and ponds of unknown use, but perhaps connected with an earlier moat.

At the Dissolution Barnwell was granted to Sir Edward Montagu of Boughton. He built a new house in the inner courtyard. Camden in 1586 calls it 'of late repaired and beautified with new buildings'. This was demolished in the 1680s. The present HOUSE was constructed around part of the lodgings of the Montagu mansion. It has a central section of three gables and the porch deriving from the C16 building, though the l. wing has been enlarged and there is much refacing. Some of the mullioned windows are original but others have been altered and made larger. Some of this work was done *c.* 1890 and much more in 1913 by *Gotch & Saunders* and even later. The Montagu-Buccleuchs held the estate till that year after which it passed through two or three ownerships. In 1935 it was acquired by Henry, 1st Duke of Gloucester, and he employed *Sir Albert Richardson* to refurbish parts of the interior. The Duchess did much to improve the garden layout. The Gloucester Estate still owns the property. The lateral extensions to the entrance side with the larger mullion-transom windows are the Gotch additions. The E front has a Georgian centre of two storeys with three bays of windows and a wide canted bay. The DRAWING ROOM has panelling designed by Richardson, inset with mid-C18 paintings of hunting scenes. More original than the main house are the range of STABLES and OUTBUILDINGS, largely late C16 to C17 but also including fragments of a C13 aisled barn.

ARMSTON HOUSE, 1¼ m. NE. A large gabled house of two storeys and attics in the Elizabethan manner of 1884 by *J. A. Gotch*. Low bays on the S and W sides. Alongside a farmhouse and two cottages in yellow and red brick, dated 1890, probably also Gotch.

BARTON SEAGRAVE

Really outer Kettering, with its village cut through by the A6003. Fortunately the old centre round the church is intact, but beyond housing estates have proliferated.

ST BOTOLPH. An impressive Norman parish church. Nave, central tower and chancel. Herringbone masonry. N doorway with one order of shafts and a tympanum which must be wrongly assembled. Two friezes. Below a head (of Christ?)

between two beasts. Above a jumble of stones with saltire crosses, stars, etc. The hoodmould also is decorated. Its DOOR is probably C16 or C17. One blocked upper N window. With a big shaft, saltire crosses in the abaci, and a strong roll moulding in the arch. The rest here of *c.* 1300, i.e. cusped intersected tracery and a clerestory of spherical triangles. In the tower, N side again, a Norman window, much like the nave window. The tower top Perp. In the chancel N side a similar Norman window. The chancel otherwise has two widely separated lancets on the S side and a splendid, if vastly restored, display of blank arcading. This is of the late C13, as the naturalistic foliage of the few original capitals proves. The arcading covers the E, N and S sides and even returns on the W side. It can do this because the chancel arch is Norman and narrow. With the Norman W arch of the tower it makes a good show. Tall shafts, primitive volute capitals, one also with primitive upright leaves, another with birds. Arches with roll mouldings and an outer billet frieze. All these Norman motifs together indicate a date *c.* 1120 or 1130. S arcade C13. Two bays, octagonal pier, double-chamfered arches. The aisle itself dates from the restoration of 1875–8 by *Carpenter & Ingelow*. – PULPIT. Jacobean panels. – FONT. Plain tub shaped, probably also C12. – READER'S DESK. With two good linenfold panels reused. – STAINED GLASS. W window, 1880s, by *Ward & Hughes*. – One N window by *Kempe*, 1890. – S aisle windows of 1893 and 1895 both by *Clayton & Bell*. – MONUMENTS. Jane Floyde †1616. Brass plate with kneeling figures. – John Bridges †1712. Tablet with pilasters and open segmental pediment. – John Bridges, the county historian, †1724 (above the N door). Tablet by *John Hunt*. – John Bridges †1741. Tablet of variegated marbles, with side volutes and a pretty pediment with a top consisting of two ogee curves and a crowning segmental curve. The Bridges family lived at the Hall.

Former RECTORY. Of *c.* 1700. Six bays, two storeys, hipped roof on modillion cornice. The S side of 1806 (*Gentleman's Magazine*).

MANOR HOUSE. An attractive small house of *c.* 1600 opposite the church.

BARTON SEAGRAVE HALL, N of the church, on the A road which cruelly cuts across what had been its garden. Eleven-bay S front of two storeys, all windows sashed and with flat frames. Porch doorway with segmental pediment on fluted Doric pilasters with a pediment of 1725. Rainwater heads also 1725. The building is, however, clearly structurally older. E-plan with two gables. The W wing contains structure of the late C16. The front was regularized by John Bridges, the county historian, who purchased the manor in 1665. He added the porch and E half of the front. Peter Tillemans drew the house in 1721 and shows it with wooden cross mullion-transom windows. Fine late C17 STAIRCASE with turned balusters and newels with ball finials also of his time. Lower wing on the E side. One-storeyed with pedimented dormers, the W front entirely Georgian in

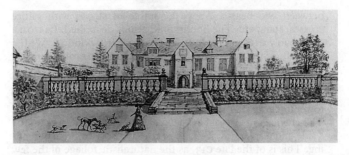

Barton Seagrave Hall.
Drawing by P. Tillemans, 1719

character. Five bays, two storeys, doorway with pediment on corbels. It also has a lower extension built in the late C18 as a library. Canted bay window. Further service buildings *c.* 1820–30. – ORANGERY, on the w lawn. An exquisitely beautiful little building again probably *c.* 1820. Five bays, the middle three in a shallow canted projection. These have round arches, the outer bays segmental arches. The arches are separated by immensely elongated, almost Pompeiian, cast-iron columns. The glazing bars of the windows are also of iron and form charming classical or Adamish patterns. In the roof three glazed domes, two small, the middle one bigger.

w of the church and alongside the river are two MOATED AREAS of rectangular form, of which the more southerly appears to be the site of a castle.

BENEFIELD

9080

There are two sections: Upper and Lower Benefield. Both have nice stone houses, though nothing of great quality.

ST MARY. 1847 by *John Macduff Derick*, paid for by the Watts-Russell family of Biggin Hall (*see* below). 'An important specimen of the sumptuous Tractarian church' (Goodhart-Rendel). w tower with broach spire, interior with much sculpture. Encaustic tiles on the floor throughout, doubtless by *Mintons*, especially fine in the body of the church. The N chapel has a painted ceiling. – STALLS by *Derick*, with MISERICORDS said to have come from Fotheringhay. These have a lion, a green man and a foliage sprig. – ROOD SCREEN by *Comper*, 1897, with loft and rood also by Comper, added in 1904. – REREDOS. 1897. Small, also by *Comper*. – NORTH SCREEN. Assembled in 1926, by the Hon. *Charles Yorke* with a splendidly carved open-work centre of *c.* 1700 with the Russell coat of arms, from Biggin Hall. – STAINED GLASS. E window of *c.* 1847, in a pre-

Pugin style by *D. Evans* of Shrewsbury, with painted panels of St John Baptist and the Evangelists. – s aisle, a window with medallions, *c.* 1849 reputedly by *M. & A. O'Connor*, and a pair of windows dated 1935 by *J. Powell & Sons*. – Tower window also by *O'Connor*. – N chapel two windows 1851 by *Ward & Nixon*.

RECTORY FARM, N of the church. 1877–8. Tall and gabled. In CAUSIN WAY, which runs E–W through the village, a number of C17 houses with mullioned windows, notably on the N side BANHAW FARM, and E on the road to Glapthorn, BROOK FARM. Elsewhere much evidence of the tidying up by the Watts-Russells of Biggin in the middle of the C19 with single houses and rows in solid Tudor manner.

CASTLE. Of the castle, licensed in 1208, only the moated platform is left, immediately W of the church. It had gone by 1315.

BIGGIN HALL

0080

1½ m. NE of Benefield

The origins of the house are a medieval grange of Peterborough Abbey, and a deer park had been formed by the early C14. On the Dissolution the estate became the property of John Russell, 1st Earl of Bedford. From the Russells it passed to the Herberts, Marquises of Powis, from whom in 1724 it was purchased by James Joye, and it is probable that he built the core of the present house. It then seems to have been tenanted and by the 1730s was in the occupation of Maurice Berkeley, bailiff to the Earls of Westmorland. The Berkeleys sold in 1822 to Jesse Watts-Russell of Ilam, Staffs., and it remains with his descendants.

The core of the house is of *c.* 1720: five bays and two storeys. It shows in the middle of the W front and is partly hidden behind the fine portico of *c.* 1750 on the E front. The alterations of *c.* 1750 have been attributed to *Hiorne* of Warwick, who designed similar but unexecuted alterations to Stanford Hall, Leics. This is the show side. Basement and two storeys. Portico reached by a wide open staircase. Four giant columns and pediment slightly in front of the rest of the façade. Behind each of the two outer columns another column and, outside these, pilasters to make up the width of the old house. Then three-bay one-storeyed connecting links and three-storeyed end pavilions in the tradition of Houghton, Holkham, Hagley, etc. The end pavilions have Venetian windows on the ground floor, tripartite windows with pediment over the middle part on the first floor. The W side has an entrance with a shell-hood typical of *c.* 1700 and a three-bay pediment. The end pavilions also have pediments to the W. Some changes were made in 1876 by *J. P. St Aubyn*, notably the change of the roof into a mansard form. Further changes were undertaken by *C. H. Biddulph-Pinchard* in 1911. To this date belong the raising of the connecting links to two storeys, the central pediment and shell-hooded doorway on the entrance front and the subdivision of the dining room to create a new staircase. Much C20 work also in the interior, all in the appropriate style; partly of *c.* 1911 with the creation of the LIBRARY and the STAIRCASE and partly of *c.* 1938 by the Hon. *Charles Yorke* when a DINING ROOM was formed in the r. pavilion. The DRAWING ROOM has a fine mid-C18 stucco ceiling and a chimneypiece attributed to *J. F. Moore*. It has pastoral reliefs and central panel. The SALOON has another good fireplace, this time late C18 and attributed to *Thomas Banks*.

6050

BLAKESLEY

ST MARY. Chiefly of ironstone, but the W tower of rough grey blocks. The tower is of *c.* 1300. Tower arch with triple responds, the main one with a fillet. Bell-openings of two pointed-tre-foiled lights. Three-bay Dec arcades of two continuous sunk quadrant mouldings, an unusual sight. Dec also the chancel arch with C19 foliage capitals. Perp clerestory and battlements. The roof is supported on corbels of angels making music. Above the tower arch a distinct roof-line and a blocked opening with a shouldered lintel. Late Perp S chapel. Money for its building was left in 1500. Continuous mouldings to the arches to W and N. Typical Tudor straight-headed windows. There was a general restoration by *Law & Son* in 1874 and the chancel was rebuilt in 1897 by *Edmund Law*, in both cases funded by the Bartholomew family of Blakesley Hall. – FONT. 1844 with lots of Gothic decoration (cf. Adstone). – REREDOS. 1915, but looking Victorian. Alabaster with Dec style arcading designed by *Law & Harris*; the central relief, the Last Supper, a fine piece of carving by *Harry Hems & Sons*. – Rich sanctuary TILES. – STAINED GLASS. Several Bartholomew memorials, notably the chancel E, N and S windows, 1897, all by *J. Powell & Sons*. – Tower window of 1924, a fine design again by *Powells*. – S aisle. 2004 by *Caroline Benyon*. – SCULPTURE. Pelican, medieval, of wood (over the tower arch). – MONUMENTS. Brass to Matthew Swetenham, bowbearer to Henry IV, †1416. The figure is 3 ft 2 in. (97 cm) long. – William Wattes †1614. Hanging monument with four kneeling figures in two tiers. They are headless.

GLEBE FARMHOUSE, opposite the church to the W. A C15 hall house, though considerably altered and extended in the C17. On the N side an original window of two lights with a quat-refoil and to its r. a doorway with a four-centred head. To the l. of the window is a blocked opening containing a square-headed two-light window with a hoodmould. The three-bay arched, braced collar-trussed roof survives as do some fire-

places. In the SE corner of the churchyard is WALNUT FARM-
HOUSE, dated 1689. Upright two-light mullioned windows.
Circular window in the gable. Moving S along CHURCH
STREET, on the E side is the OLD VICARAGE, 1839 by *G. G.
Scott*. A large ironstone house, Tudor style. A little further S
comes SYCAMORE FARM. Dated 1672. Symmetrical front
with four-light mullioned windows, those on the ground floor
higher in proportion to width than they would have been
earlier. No. 8 THE CROFT is solid C18 with Victorian bays and
a canopied doorway. THE WALNUTS is mid C19 of three bays
and two storeys with a pilastered doorcase with a somewhat
oversize dentil cornice. The street opens out into THE GREEN,
with the SCHOOL on its S side. Founded 1669 by William
Foxley. Enlarged 1876 with an elaborate half-timbered central
section and big stone wing on the r. Additions by *Law & Harris*
in 1911. On the E side is No. 7, late C17 with a gabled wing of
two storeys and on the N side an ironstone house *c.*1800 of
three storeys with a pilastered doorcase with fanlight. Ball
finials to its roof.

BLAKESLEY HALL. Demolished in 1957–8. It stood immediately
S of the village. Two simple early C20 LODGES with timber
portals and Victorian gatepiers are all that survives.

At WOODEND, 1 m. S, several fine houses, some with banded
stonework, and the former BAPTIST CHAPEL of 1813. Stone
with two shallow recesses containing windows with red
brick voussoirs. Larger central window over the canopied
doorcase.

SOUTHFIELDS, 1½ m. SE. Formerly a C17 farmhouse but greatly
altered and extended in 1921 for Major Pomeroy. Two C17
wings with mullioned windows and a three-bay infilling on the
garden side of banded stone with a central doorcase. Hipped
roof and dormers. Tall porch on the W wing. A date of 1660 is
recorded.

SEAWELL FARM (1½ m. N). One of the Grafton Estate farms of
c. 1840; *see* Introduction, p. 53.

BLATHERWYCKE

9090

HOLY TRINITY (Churches Conservation Trust). Away from the
village in the park. Norman W tower with unmoulded arch
towards the nave and small window at the top on E side. The
upper stages entirely rebuilt C17. W doorway also looks C17.
Norman S doorway with one order of shafts; simple. E.E. N
arcade of two bays with minimum capitals and slightly chamfered round arches. The E respond has a stiff-leaf capital. Of
c. 1300 the fine arcade towards the N chapel. Three bays.
Quatrefoil piers, double-chamfered arches. Of about the same
time the S side. The chancel follows, with its windows with
reticulated tracery and the two niches l. and r. of the E window,

in the Dec style, but in its present form 1854 rebuilding by
W. Slater. It had already been rebuilt in 1819. The whole E end
was shortened then, so a doorway in the chancel is no longer
viable, and a piscina in the N chapel is almost within the E wall.
Much of the N side is also C19. – PULPIT. Late Georgian.
Another in the N aisle brought from Skidbrooke, Lincs. A curiosity made up with Elizabethan and Jacobean carved panels and
sounding-board. – STAINED GLASS. N chapel E window by
Clayton & Bell, 1858. Quite good, with medallions in the C13
style and clear colours. The window with the Corporal Works
of Mercy is from a cartoon by *J. R. Clayton* himself. – N chapel
N, 1938 by *Heaton, Butler & Bayne*. – N aisle W, 1865 by *A.
Gibbs*. – Chancel E reputedly by *Clayton & Bell*. – Chancel S,
1921 by *Kempe & Co.* – Another good window with figures of
Faith, Hope and Charity, 1939 by *Heaton, Butler & Bayne*. –
MONUMENTS. Humphrey Stafford †1548 and wife. Brasses
set in a coarse architectural surround. – John Stafford †1595
and his wife. The C19 inscription is wrong. The shields are
identifiable as Stafford and Clopton. Two upright panels
framed with egg-and-dart. In the panels in relief the kneeling
figures of Sir John, his wife and children. Surround with
columns, top with strapwork and achievement. It at first sight
appears rather crude, but the quality of detail carving, notably
of the figures, is fine. It is very probably a late work of the
Thorpe workshop. – Thomas Randolph, poet, †1635. By *Nicholas Stone*, 1640. A very simple, completely classical marble
tablet with a frame with ears at top and bottom. Poem in an
oval laurel wreath. The monument was commissioned by Sir
Christopher Hatton, *musarum amator*. The poem reads as
follows:

> Here sleepe thirteene together in one tombe
> And all these greate, yet quarrell not for roome.
> The Muses and ye Graces teares did meete.
> And grav'd these letters on ye churlish sheete;
> Who having wept, their fountaines drye,
> Through the Conduit of the eye,
> For their freind who here does lye,
> Crept into his grave and dyed,
> And soe the Riddle is untyed,
> For which this Church, proud that the Fates bequeath
> Unto her ever-honour'd trust,
> Soe much and that soe precious dust,
> Hath crown'd her Temples with an Ivye wreath;
> Which should have Laurell been,
> But yt the greived Plant to se him dead
> Tooke pet and withered.

BLATHERWYCKE HALL, by *Thomas Ripley*, 1720, was demolished in 1948. The contract for building it exists (NRO). NE of
the church a large STABLE building survives, with the inscription D. OB 1770 (for Donatus O'Brien). Extensive C18 kitchen
garden walls. Parkland with extensive lake. Plans drawn up in

2008 by *Craig Hamilton*, for a very grand Neoclassical house with Ionic porticos on both N and S fronts and a central galleried hall, are yet to be realized (2013).

Several houses with Gothick glazing in the village dated 1826–31, including the former SCHOOL and SCHOOL HOUSE (No. 23) with triangular-headed windows.

BRIDGE. Built 1656, but with O'Brien dates of 1726 and 1826. Widened by *Law & Harris* in 1905. On the road to Kingscliffe the buildings of a former WATERMILL with similar Gothic windows.

BLISWORTH

7050

ST JOHN BAPTIST. Perp W tower. The chancel S windows are late C13, the E window of a very strange Dec design (renewed, but correctly), the N window Perp. The arcades are both of the C13, the N one partly earlier. Five bays, octagonal piers, double-chamfered arches. There is an evident difference between the E and W parts. The earlier work is the E bays. The S arcade is shorter and also not of one build. The E bays and the arch across the aisle are earlier, the W pier with its rare quatrefoil and trefoil frieze looks C15. The church was restored in 1856 by *E. F. Law* and the S aisle rebuilt 1926 by *Matthew Holding*. – SCREEN. Tall, of one-light divisions, Perp, but only partially original. – REREDOS. C15 style, early C20. *Temple Moore* took a commission at Blisworth in 1910 costing £150, and this may be it, although *W. Talbot Brown* is also recorded working here. – COMMUNION RAIL. Later C17; dumb-bell balusters. – STAINED GLASS. In the tracery heads of chancel N windows some C15 figures of Apostles and some canopy work. – Chancel S: C14 and C15 fragments. – Chancel E window 1885 by *J. Hardman & Co.*, and a S window of 1852 by *Ward & Nixon*. – S aisle, 1873 by *J. Hardman & Co.* – S chapel E, 1939 by *Sidney Meteyard*. – MONUMENT. Tomb-chest with shields in quatrefoils, linked by knob-pattern and the Wake knot. On the lid good brasses to Roger Wake †1504 and wife. The figures are 2 ft 4 in. (90 cm.) long. Close by is an ogee-headed recess.

BLISWORTH HOUSE, E of the church, dated 1702. Seven bays, two and a half storeys, the windows in flat frames. Considerably altered and added to in the early C19.

Former RECTORY, W of the church. Symmetrical Tudor, 1841. Elegant curved staircase of Late Georgian character.

VILLAGE HALL, Stoke Road. The school of 1861, of stone with Gothic window.

BAPTIST CHAPEL, Chapel Lane. 1885 by *T.H. Vernon*.

The village has a remarkably good number of stone and thatched cottages. Many display the use of the local sand and ironstones in bands. STONEACRES in High Street, C17, is certainly one of the best in the district. THACKSTONE COTTAGE, Stoke

Road, has on the ground floor and the first floor of its gable end three-light stepped mullioned windows.

STEAM MILL, at the W end of the village. Built 1879 for Joseph Westley & Sons. Red and blue brick. Converted. Opposite, GRAFTON HOUSE was a coaching inn of the 1790s when the main road ran through the village. Early C19 door case and dormers.

RAILWAY BRIDGE across the Northampton Road. 1837–8 under the direction of *Robert Stephenson*. A big elegant stone arch. A viaduct was intended. Alongside GRAFTON VILLAS of the same period. Both were built by *Richard Dunkley*, an enterprising Blisworth builder. STONEWORKS FARMHOUSE, Stoke Road, with a columned porch, small pediment and outbuildings also with columns, was opened in 1821 by the Grafton Estate and later taken over by Dunkley.

CANALS. The Grand Union Canal near Blisworth enters a TUNNEL to Stoke Bruerne (q.v.), 3,076 yds (2,813 metres) long, the longest canal tunnel in use in the country. Constructed 1793–1805 by *William Jessop & James Barnes*, engineers. The VENTS, circular, of vitrified bricks, are beacons by the road. N portal rebuilt 1902–3 in blue brick. While the tunnel was under construction, a tramway ran over the hill to convey freight (sections of the rails and some sleepers are in the Stoke Bruerne Waterways Museum). The Northampton Branch Canal has seventeen locks between Blisworth and Northampton.

BOUGHTON

Boughton just survives as a village on the northern edge of Northampton. Its outer fringes have already become suburbia.

ST JOHN BAPTIST. In the village, along the road, without a new churchyard – i.e. an urban position. In existence by 1546, according to Baker. The church began as a chantry. The W tower is Late Perp. Repairs are recorded to it in 1599 and 1653. The body was rebuilt and enlarged in 1806 by *Luke Kirshaw*, and enlarged by two extra E bays in 1846 (date on the E gable). Tall two-light C17 windows (three lights at the E end) with arched lights and hoodmoulds. No structural division between nave and chancel; no aisles. – STAINED GLASS. Chancel E, 1848 by *Webb & Nixon* (hidden by the organ). – W window by *Kempe*, 1897. – MONUMENT. Mary Tillemont †1706. Tablet with curly open pediment. Two cherubs' heads at the foot.

Former SCHOOL, N of the church tower. 1841, with tall pointed windows and doorway.

OLD CHURCH, 1 m. E. In 1719 Bridges records that the church lay in ruins with no part of the roof remaining. It then had a spire, which with the tower collapsed *c.* 1785. What remains is almost smothered in ivy. Just a few broken walls and shattered window openings. A tall C15 niche is the only architectural item. The blocking of a large NE window is amusing as it is a patchwork of mullion sections.

The old village centre has a number of attractive stone and thatched houses and a small green with topiary gardens. MEREWATER, facing towards it, is dated 1639.

BOUGHTON PARK, between the village and the A308. Boughton had been a possession of the Greene family in medieval times and a house of some substance had been built there. The estate was acquired by Thomas Wentworth, who became 1st Earl of Strafford (second creation) in 1717. He created around the house a formal landscape, ably recorded in an engraving by Thomas Badeslade in 1732. When the Earl died in 1739 the estate came to his son, William (1722–91), then only seventeen. Following a grand tour and a marriage in 1741 to the daughter of the Duke of Argyll, he embarked on redesigning the landscapes of his various estates, Wentworth Castle, Yorkshire, and here at Boughton. William was a dilettante architect of ability, a close friend of Horace Walpole and a confirmed Gothicist. At Boughton the old rambling house (*see* Boughton Hall, below) was adorned by castellations and towers, a theme much used on his buildings in the landscape.

The earliest excursion in this vein of Gothick was a gate lodge on the Market Harborough road (A509), a castellated tower known as the HAWKING TOWER. This is first mentioned in a letter from Walpole in 1756, and may have been new then. It looks like a church tower of three storeys, two light ogee-headed Gothick windows and a large quatrefoil in the top stage, all topped by pointed pinnacles. The wall rises S to support an outer staircase to the top floor. Its design was to be used again on the Wentworth Estate in the 1770s at Stainborough Castle, where it looks even more churchlike. The Earl's main activities took place c. 1770. He had already erected S of the park an OBELISK to his idol William Cavendish, 4th Duke of Devonshire. (It still stands but now engulfed in the middle of a housing estate. *See* under Kingsthorpe, Outer Northampton, p. 498) N of the park is NEW PARK BARN (now called Fox Covert Hall). It originally had a date of 1770 and two castellated towers. These were largely removed c. 1929, so it now looks rather stark and is converted into a residence. On the E side of the park is THE SPECTACLE, also c. 1770, a large Gothick arch, castellated with tall hollow side turrets and mock ruined wall supports. Nearby to the S is HOLLY LODGE, whose outer walls bear carved plaques with cherub's heads. Behind is a Gothic mansion built for the chemist Philadelphus Jeyes in 1857–61 by *Alexander Milne* of Northampton. Grand conservatory. An amusing cast iron GATE using agricultural implements in its design.

To the N of the park is the most elaborate of Wentworth's buildings, BUNKERS HILL FARM, securely dated 1775 and named of course after the famous American War of Independence battle. The house is rectangular, all castellated, of two storeys, with a central wide tower and a projecting bay. The upper floors have the familiar quatrefoil shapes. While windows have been replaced the pattern of the façades has been retained. A round castellated archway is alongside. A further castellated ARCHWAY stood near Boughton Hall, but only its piers remain topped by heraldic beasts. One final landscape feature needs to be noted: a GROTTO, to the N of the house in a spinney. Just a simple rustic stone alcove and a spring. The whole landscape is a remarkable survival.

BOUGHTON HALL fell into decay in the early C19 and was replaced by an essay in the Tudor manner by *William Burn* in 1844. Inside the porch splendid large ROYAL ARMS of Elizabeth I, of stone, re-coloured. It was found in the middle of the C19 amongst the ruins of the old hall. It may have been rescued from Holdenby House. In the garden is a heraldic flying horse with cartouche bearing the arms of Martha Baroness Wentworth, that is *c.* 1725. It was mounted on a plinth in 1968. It once topped one of the piers of the gateway by the Hawking Tower.

BARROWS. One lies just S of Bunkers Hill Farm, and a second in the angle of the lane to Boughton Grange.

BOUGHTON HOUSE

9080

Boughton House is beautifully set in an expansive park, and in recent years its surroundings have been greatly enhanced by the recreation of some of its water features. The house may be chiefly remembered for its noble N façade and the other work done by the 1st Duke of Montagu. But there are in fact behind that façade substantial remains of a house of the C16. Boughton was purchased from Robert Burden in 1528 by Sir Edward Montagu. He became a leading lawyer and one of Henry VIII's executors. The main changes were wrought, as noted, by Ralph, 1st Duke of Montagu, who inherited the estate in 1684 and died in 1709. His son John, as 2nd Duke, was more active outside, extending his father's layout to a design by *Bridgeman* and planting vast avenues of limes around the edge of the park, still a memorable part of the landscape. His daughter Mary married George, 4th Earl of Cardigan of Deene, who in 1766 was allowed to call himself the 3rd Duke. Their daughter Elizabeth married the 3rd Duke of Buccleuch, who had extensive estates in Scotland, so little was done to the house after the middle of the C18, and it is the extraordinary preservation of the C17 State Rooms at Boughton which makes it such a remarkable house.

EXTERIOR. Externally the effect is due to the 1st Duke. The NORTH FAÇADE is perhaps the most French-looking C17 building in England. It has such French motifs as banded rustication on the ground floor, a mansard roof and a complete absence of all ornament. Recessed nine-bay centre, projecting wings of four by three bays. The plainly framed upper windows have sashes, some of the earliest in England,* and are separated by short Doric pilasters, coupled at the corner of the wings. The ground floor of the centre is opened in an arched arcade from l. to r. In the roof are dormer windows with alternating triangular and segmental pediments. The strikingly French climate of this façade can be explained by the fact that the Duke had been ambassador in Paris from 1669 to 1672 and again in 1678–9. His London house, Montagu House, where the British Museum now stands, was built in 1674–80 by *Robert Hooke* and called by Evelyn 'after the French pavilion way'. It was burnt in 1686 and rebuilt, according to *Vitruvius Britannicus*, 'in the French manner' by the otherwise unknown French architect, *Pierre Pouget*. John Cornforth suggested that Pouget may be the architect *Bouget* known from drawings in the Smithson Collection at the RIBA. Dr Whinney also pointed to the similarity of the Boughton façade to a plate in the so-called *Petit Marot*. It should be remembered that this façade was not intended as the entrance front, but a garden front. It is thought that a grand entrance front was intended for the E side. So there is no majestic front door and behind the façade a rather uncomfortable space where the alignment of the façade and the Hall, at a different angle, join.

The rest of the work of the 1st Duke appears curiously bitty after this restrained grandeur. Behind the loggia on the ground floor runs the front line of the time before the N front was erected. It continues to the E and is there exposed. Its front is of ashlar, but its back is of exposed brick with rubbed brick dressings. To the front seven bays, two storeys, still with cross-windows. Pedimented dormers in the roof. Further E a continuation somewhat set back: eleven bays, two storeys, and the same windows and dormers. No string course. This branch merges into the outbuildings (see below). The STABLES almost join up. They are a fine composition, stone to the W front, brick to the E back. The centre is a tunnel-vaulted archway, with a pediment to the W with an attic over crowned by a very squat four-sided lead dome. The pediment has heraldic carving by *Duchesne*, completed in 1704. The windows are of the cross-type, the quoins of even length, to go with the banded rustication round the archway and in the N façade. S of the stables are more outbuildings including three different late C17 brick houses. The E side of the house proper needs no comment. It contains among other things the kitchens. One storey, hipped roof with dormer windows.

Nor does the irregular SOUTH SIDE call for study. The WEST FRONT also, though evidently taken more seriously, was not regularized. It starts from the N with the four bays of the wing of the N façade, recedes and continues with three bays, changes its direction slightly and runs on with six bays and a top bal-

---

* Those there now are modern copies of the originals.

ustrade instead of the mansard roof, and then settles down to an eight-bay front which is a little higher, also finishes on top in a balustrade, and has on the ground floor in the middle a four-bay loggia on arches. This is now glazed.

INTERIOR. The STATE ROOMS should be looked at first. They begin at the NE corner with the LOW and HIGH PAVILIONS, both lined with panelling by *Roger Davis*. The ascent is by the spectacular STONE STAIRCASE with scrolly wrought-iron balustrade, *trompe-l'œil* wall paintings in gilt paint, and a ceiling, all painted by *Louis Cheron*, who decorated the rest of the state sequence together with the Great Hall. The State Rooms are on the first floor facing N. They all have their original panelling still with its original drab paintwork. They also have painted ceilings by *Cheron*. Most have simple bolection fireplaces, often with mirrors set above. The rooms also have parquet de Versailles floors. Alas, their extraordinary furnishings, tapestries and rare early carpets are not within the scope of this book. The Fifth State Room is different, having no parquet since the space was

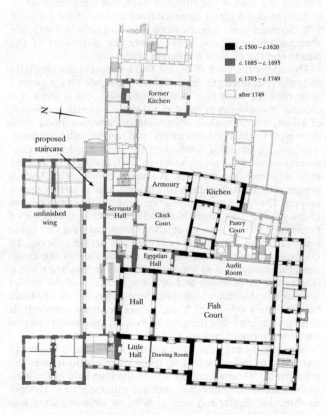

Boughton House.
Plan

originally intended to hold a staircase. At the E end of the State
Suite is the LIME STAIRCASE, an original 1690s creation, with
turned balusters running through all floors. The balusters were
largely renewed with limewood from the estate in the 1950s.
This leads down to the UNFINISHED WING, another extraordinary interior. Just an open shell with its beams and floor joists
in place. Some painted panels thought to be made for this wing
survive. It now houses a curious example of Chinoiserie: a port-
able tent of oilskin, made in 1745 for the garden terrace of
Montagu House on the Thames. On the ground floor it is worth
noting the ARMOURY, the original servants' hall, for the rare
sequence of late C17 imaginary portraits of Montagu ancestors
(cf. those in the King's Dining Room at Drayton).

It remains to consider the other interior rooms. First, beginning at the W end of the house is the LITTLE HALL, notable
for its fireplace with the elaborate heraldic display in carved
stone, inserted by the 2nd Duke. Then the GREAT HALL,
where an elaborate C16 roof, with five curved tie-beams, four
cusped collar-beams with queenposts, and cusped and quatrefoiled wind-braces, is hidden by a vaulted ceiling on which in
1706 *Cheron* painted the Apotheosis of Hercules. The 1st Duke
remodelled the S front of the C16 Hall giving it five tall two-
light windows with two transoms. The panelling and fireplace
were put in by *A. W. Blomfield* in 1911. Prior to this it had tall
Ionic pilasters dividing its walls, very like those at Drayton. Of
the early hall is an elaborate doorway with decorated spandrels
and a gadrooned frieze which makes a date *c.* 1550–60 probable. Its S façade opens into the FISH COURT, where, on the
upper floor on the r.-hand side, can be seen windows of the
Tudor house. Above that wing also a Tudor roof survives, now
hidden by later ceilings. Then at the E the EGYPTIAN HALL,
taking its title not from its style but from a society founded by
the 2nd Duke's cousin, Lord Sandwich. It has original painted
panelling and an interesting architectural model of a mid-C18
Gothick bridge which *William Stukeley* devised for the park but
never built. It is known that the model was made by the builder
and clockmaker, *Thomas Eayre* of Kettering. The 2nd Duke
was an early dabbler in Gothic design (a set of chairs exists at
Beaulieu Abbey, for example). Both these two rooms have ceilings by *Cheron*. The AUDIT ROOM in a wing added in 1742–3
has its original panelling. The fireplace is important. It is
carved from clunch, dates from *c.* 1550–60 and has pilasters
with pretty foliage arabesques in its sunk panels. There are also
two inscriptions and, as one of them is a motto of Sir Edward
and as he died in 1557, this fireplace must be earlier. It is
among the incunabula of the Elizabethan style in England with
intriguing classical inspired details, and can be compared with
similar work at Apethorpe (q.v.), and almost certainly linked
to the workshop of the mason *Thomas Thorpe* of Kingscliffe.
However, here the detail is finer, and several elements, notably
the small carved heads, have a very Continental feel and are
reminiscent of decoration found in the Loire chateaux. As the
room was only created in the middle of the C18, it must have

been brought from elsewhere, perhaps from another early Montagu house. There is a further example of work of this period in the fireplace in the DRAWING ROOM. This can be linked directly to the Griffin monument at Braybrooke *c.* 1565–70, where there are almost the same groups of sturdy tapered Ionic and Corinthian columns. Once again the work can be ascribed to the *Thorpes* of Kingscliffe. This fireplace is known to originate from the former Montagu house at Hemington (q.v.) in 1910.[*] At the end of the s range the CHINESE STAIRCASE with a shield with the family coat of arms on each tread, probably of *c.* 1740.

This interior progression has followed around a series of enclosed courts. There are four in all, and it is from these that can be glimpsed further evidence of the Tudor and Elizabethan house with several gables and some windows.

The elaborate formal GARDENS were laid out by the 1st Duke, who employed a Dutch gardener, *Van der Meulen* from 1685. They were still in progress by 1694 when Charles Hatton of Kirby wrote: 'Here is great talk of vast gardens at Boughton but I heard my Lord Montagu is very much concerned that ye water with which he had hoped to make so fine fountains hath failed his expectations.' This did not prevent him from laying out a network of canals and pools to the w of the house, covering most of the park between it and Weekley. Since 2000, several canals and pool have been recovered and water is once again a feature of the park. In 2007 the 10th Duke commissioned *Kim Wilkie* to design a feature alongside the recreated pyramidal mount. This feature, entitled 'Orpheus', takes the form of an inverted pyramid with shallow spiral descent to a further pool: an Orpheus Hades to complement the Olympian Mount.

In 2013 a further sculpture called 'Lifeflow' by *Angela Connor* was installed by the Lily Pond above the Rose Garden. A flow of red material issues from the ground, goes below and issues forth again, weaving its way through a large white marble disc and back into the ground once more, and so along the banks of the pool. It is splendid to see this brave introduction of Modern pieces into the historic landscape.

9050

BOZEAT

ST MARY. Of the local grey sandstone. The whole building, despite work done under *William Slater* 1867–9, was recorded as being in a bad state by the mid 1870s. The spire collapsed in 1877 but drawings had been done and it was eventually rebuilt in 1880–3 by *R. H. Carpenter*. The w tower is basically Late Norman. Original is the arch towards the nave, round, single-stepped on simple imposts and the shafted s window. In

---

[*] The 2nd Duke had already imported other armorial overmantels from Barnwell, now in rooms on the first floor.

the rebuilt section, twin bell-openings with a separating polygonal shaft and a round hoodmould with nailhead decoration.
The spire has broaches and two tiers of lucarnes. The w
doorway and w window are Perp. Late C13 s doorway. Two
orders but missing shafts, foliage capitals, deep arch mouldings. Late C13 also the chancel partly blocked lowside lancet
and priest's doorway. Otherwise the chancel is Dec with reticulated tracery in the E window. Dec also the small quatrefoil s
aisle w window, and the pretty N aisle E window with the figure
of a four-petalled flower in the tracery head. Perp the side
windows of the chancel and the other windows of the aisles,
straight-headed with ogee lights. Dec arcades of three bays.
Octagonal piers, double-chamfered arches, the N capitals
looking a little earlier. The arches die into the w and E imposts
so no responds. E end of each aisle have remains of image
niches or brackets. Sizeable stair-turret N aisle for the rood loft
stair. – SCREEN. Perp, unusually ambitious, four-light divisions, with the main mullion running into the apex of the
four-centred arch. Each two lights taken together under an
ogee arch. Busy minor tracery. Clear evidence of a lost canopy.
On the dado panels PAINTINGS illustrating the Expulsion, the
Annunciation, the Adoration of the Magi, and the Baptism. It
was restored by *W. Talbot Brown* of Wellingborough *c.* 1914. –
BENCHES. Simple, low, square-topped with thin buttress
shafts, C16. – CHANDELIER. Brass, Georgian, small (chancel).
– ROYAL ARMS. Fine, painted, for George III, said to date from
1770. – STAINED GLASS. E window by *W. Holland* of Warwick,
1869. – N aisle 1919 by *Geoffrey Webb.* – s aisle a Millennium
window showing village scenes, designed by *Chris Fiddes* and
made by *Nicholas Bechgaard,* 2000.

In the centre of the village, the former SCHOOL of 1873,
quietly Gothic with a small octagonal turret above the infants'
entrance. The local sandstone has weathered giving it a rocky
appearance.

The village has considerable signs of C19 rebuilding, largely due
to the establishment by John Drage in 1861 of a FOOTWEAR
FACTORY. Its early C20 premises (Hope Court) survive. The
Drage shoe sign painted on its end wall in 1932 was repainted
in 2000.

BOZEAT GRANGE, 1½ m. s. Fine farm complex by the same
builder as several village houses, using the local sandstone and
red brick dressings. Dated 1862. On the road side a pair of
labourers' cottages like lodges to a formal estate.

BRACKLEY

5030

Brackley is now happily bypassed by the busy A43. The centre is
the Market Place and running N the High Street, the medieval
route from Northampton to Oxford. In early days, however, the

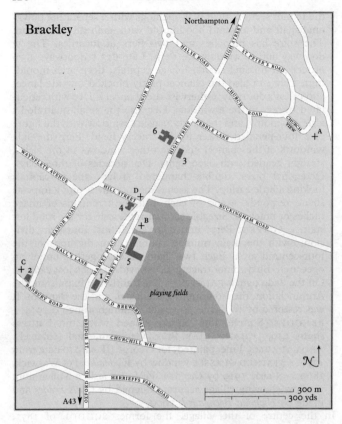

Brackley

Northampton

A St Peter
B St John
C Former Congregational Chapel
D Methodist Church

1 Town Hall
2 Police Station (former)
3 Fire Station (former)
4 Bell Tower (former School)
5 Magdalen College School
6 Winchester House School

centre lay to the E around the church already referred to by the C13, presumably to distinguish it from the settlement which had grown up around the castle to the S. The castle itself was destroyed in 1173 but its motte survives off Hinton Road. There were, in fact, two parishes and two churches, St Peter's in the Old Town and St James's at the lower end, and while the building has long since disappeared, its small graveyard, at the corner of Oxford Road and St James's Road, still exists. The market and the new town were granted a charter in 1260 and gradually both settlements became linked by buildings. Wool was a staple trade in early medieval times but this collapsed with the rise of the Cotswold industry. In the C17 Brackley was described as decayed and in 1649 a major fire around the market began at the Crown Inn. The town had some rise in reputation in the C18 because of its lords of the manor, the Egertons, Earls and later Dukes of Bridgewater, and after the expiration of the dukedom in 1803, Earls of Ellesmere. The Ellesmeres built and altered a number of buildings in the town in the later C19 using the Shrewsbury architect *Charles Bather*. The basic layout of the town has changed little* and the properties on the w side of High Street and the Market Place still have long burgage plots of medieval origin running to a back lane, Manor Road, several with passages linking the two roads.

St Peter, Old Town. The Norman church is represented only by the s doorway, with one order of shafts, decorated capitals, zigzag in the arch and hoodmould of a motif like flattened dogtooth, and in addition by the impost of the NW arch of a transept which exists no longer. To this church a fine w tower was added in the C13. It has a doorway with shafts with stiff-leaf capitals, a lancet w window with cusped niches to the l. and r. in which are still original C13 seated figures (St Peter on the l. and St Hugh of Lincoln on the r.), bell-openings of two lights with a shaft between and blank arches to their l. and r., a pointed-trefoiled top frieze, and later battlements. Weather-vane in the shape of a key. To the C13 also belongs the s arcade of four bays. This has w and e responds with stiff-leaf capitals and three piers (the e respond partly shaved off), of which the first two have circular capitals of the style corresponding to the responds and water-holding moulded bases, but the third has an octagonal one which corresponds to the third pier and must be a later addition, dating from the time when the arches were renewed and the N arcade was built. Four bays with octagonal pillars. That time was probably the early C14, to which the s and N aisle windows belong. They have ogee heads. The easternmost window of the aisle has a very unusual tracery pattern. That to its w is Victorian but before then the chancel had been rebuilt and connected with the nave and aisles by a short, low arch. The mouldings around here are late C13 and very good. The same moulding also characterizes a respond at the NE end of the s aisle, meant to carry an arch across the aisle and open into the former transept. When the N aisle was built such a respond was also provided in the cor-responding N position. A Dec chapel was added to the chancel in the early C14. The tracery of part of the N aisle windows is identical with that of the s chapel. The nave is ceiled with three circle motif, probably early C19. There was a main restoration in 1873 by *Charles Bather* of Shrewsbury and the chancel was restored and enlarged by *J. Oldrid Scott* in 1886 and the N arcade rebuilt. The rich SEDILIA in the Dec style with marble pillars, the *Minton* TILES and the STALLS, SCREENS and

---

* The population in the 1960s was some 3,000. It is now around 15,000, with the inevitable spread of housing and industrial estates on the town's perimeter.

PULPIT are presumably all part of the Scott work. – FONT. Square, on a big base, with chamfered corners and filleted shafts in these corners. Gables with ballflower stops. Below the top an oak frieze. Early C14. – TILED FLOOR, S chapel, probably C18. – ROYAL ARMS. George III. – STAINED GLASS. The best windows are as follows. N wall, E end two by *M & A. O'Connor*, 1868 and 1869. – Chancel E, 1886 by *Burlison & Grylls*. – S chapel, three by the *Kempe* firm: one S of 1901 by *Kempe* himself; the E window and a S window by *Kempe & Co.* – Fine S aisle window with three bishops, 1900 by *J. Hardman & Co.* – MONUMENTS. Defaced effigy of a priest in the churchyard (at the W door of the church turn l. and pass through a gap in the hedge; the effigy is then immediately to the r.). – A curious little plaque near the pulpit: Elnor Lewis and a shield, C17. – Edward Yates †1864 by *M. W. Johnson.* – CHURCH HALL. 1998.

ST JOHN, E side of High Street. Built as the chapel of the Hospital of St James and St John, founded *c.* 1150 by the Earl of Leicester. It was originally for resident brothers, was refounded in 1423 for travellers, and was sold in 1484 to William of Waynflete, who handed it on to his Oxford foundation, Magdalen College. In 1869–70 it was restored by *Charles Buckeridge* for the use of Magdalen College School (*see* Perambulation, below). It is difficult to follow the evidence of the building in its present state. The W front has a Late Norman doorway with zigzag, also at right angles to the wall, with foliage in the resulting lozenges. Above it is a late C13 window of three stepped lancet lights with dogtooth decoration. To its l. and r. are niches with C14 statues (cf. St Peter, above). Recessed on the N side is a short tower. The bell-openings are plain single lancets. Only on the W side is there a blank arch to the l. of the lancet. The S side of the chapel has much disturbed masonry, including doorways, leading presumably to the hospital localities. The windows are lancets, and in the chancel stepped three-light lancets. On the N side there was a short aisle and a long chapel, the former of one bay, W of the tower, the latter of four to its E. Of the aisle the tall quatrefoil pier still exists and the springing of the arch; of the latter the quatrefoil piers with fillets and in addition thin shafts in the diagonals. Some little nailhead decoration. In the S wall SEDILIA and DOUBLE PISCINA with pointed-trefoiled arches and dogtooth decoration. To their W a big recess with many shafts and mouldings. There is in all this no evidence later than the early C14, though how much the C19 has done is not certain. – FONT. Circular, Norman, with intersected arches and below them a band of long barbaric trail. – PULPIT. By *E. P. Warren*, *c.* 1890. – REREDOS. 1922, designed by *Henderson* and sculpted by *Reynolds*. – STAINED GLASS. E window of 1897 by *Bucknall & Comper*.

Former CONGREGATIONAL CHAPEL, Banbury Road. Now a shop. 1856. Three bays with Doric pilasters and a pediment. Graveyard still behind.

METHODIST CHURCH, High Street. Typical Nonconformist
   Gothic of 1905 by *Ewen Harper* of Birmingham, with an asymmetrically placed short tower with a cross. Earlier church
   building behind.
TOWN HALL. Built by the 1st Duke of Bridgewater in 1704–7.   84
   The architect is unknown but the mason was *John Wootton* of
   Brackley. Not only very distinguished but superbly set at the S
   end of the Market Place. Two bays to the S, five to the E and
   W. To the N blank except for a middle projection and a broken
   pediment. In the projection a Victorian doorway and a window
   over with a curly open pediment. Two storeys throughout,
   hipped roof and splendid cupola. Arched ground-floor
   windows, originally an open arcade. Slim iron pillars on the
   ground floor with intertwined Es for Egerton, the Bridgewater
   family name.
Former POLICE STATION and COURT, Banbury Road. 1851.
   Stone in the Tudor style with decorative cast-iron windows. It
   looks exactly like a school.
Former FIRE STATION, High Street. 1887. A gabled stone front
   with a vacant bellcote. Brick hose tower behind.
Former GREAT CENTRAL RAILWAY STATION, on the N edge
   of town. 1899. Closed 1966. Red brick with arched openings,
   partly created when it changed use as an auto business.
PERAMBULATION. The starting point has to be the Town Hall
   in the Market Place. S of it at the corner of Banbury Road is
   a half-timbered Victorian row, part of development put in hand
   by the Earl of Ellesmere and the Rev. Thicknesse using *Charles
   Bather*. On the E side of Market Place at this end, some altered
   Georgian survivals, including just below the Town Hall a wide
   house with a Venetian window below a pediment with a lunette.
   W of the Town Hall the CROWN HOTEL. Regency frontage,
   stuccoed with pilasters, a Venetian window and a pretty ironwork balcony. Older work at the rear. Its former central
   entrance now blocked. Then LLOYDS TSB, of ironstone, late
   C19 Neo-Jacobean, with a porch and a corner bay. Set back is
   OLD HALL. Late Georgian front of five bays and three storeys,
   brick and stone. Heavy keystones and a canopied doorway.
   Again older work below. Further N is BRACKLEY HOUSE of
   1875, built by a branch of the Cartwrights of Aynho, hence the
   coat of arms. Rough stone Jacobethan with shaped gables and
   canted bays. Next to it, BRACKLEY LODGE is mid-C18 and of
   five bays also with Doric pilasters. Doorway with Gibbs surround interrupted by a canopy. Framed windows with keystones, those on the first floor with bracketed sills. The adjoining
   late C19 block is of ironstone, a mixed façade of Jacobean and
   Georgian elements. A central shaped gable with sections of
   Doric frieze. An open pedimented doorcase. Rounded bay on
   the r. It amounts to a rather bizarre effect. Next, set back and
   on a higher level, the BELL TOWER, the former Church School
   of 1871 by *Bather*. Mostly half-timbered above a stone ground
   floor. One gable inscribed 'Feed my lambs'. Porch and a
   square tower with blue brick bands and a turret with a spirelet.

Additions of 1896 by *Henry Hopkins* of Banbury and in 1946–7
by *Walter Rosser* of Northampton. The sides of HIGH STREET,
called here The Avenue, have wide grass verges and trees and
an early C18 house on the E side, No. 7, with a good doorway
with an open scrolly pediment. The house formerly belonged
to MAGDALEN COLLEGE SCHOOL, whose chapel is St John
(*see* above) and whose own buildings begin here. The school
was founded in 1548. The buildings are largely Victorian, but
there is evidence of the medieval hospital of St James and John
in the house lying back from the street to the s of the chapel
and of the later C16 in the chimney-breast, the masonry and a
two-light window of the main building.

The street now narrows with some nice stone houses such
as No. 20 (w side) dated 1737. Its Victorian cast-iron trellis
porch was brought here in 1924 when it became the Conservative Club. Opposite, the thatched PLOUGH INN. Nothing then
of great merit on the w side until WINCHESTER HOUSE
SCHOOL, at one time a Woodard School. This is the Egerton
manor house much rebuilt and enlarged. The Earls of Ellesmeres left Brackley in 1917. The manor house was a one-
storeyed dormered C17 house of which only the doorway and
the mullioned window to its l. survive (now chapel). The
rebuilding was done for the Earl of Ellesmere in 1875–8 by
Charles Bather. It is also in the Jacobean style and has gables
and mullioned-and-transomed windows. The upper quadrangle was originally stables with an impressive arched entrance
and cupola above. Elaborate ironwork gates with cartwheel
type designs and Es for Egerton or Ellesmere by local blacksmith *Harry Mobbs*. Opposite is BRACKLEY PARK (National
Trust), a survival of one of the many gardens and orchards
which surrounded large properties. Ironwork gates like those
at Winchester House with more Es. A little further on the
CREWE ALMSHOUSES. They were founded by Sir Thomas
Crewe in 1633. The six dwellings have been ingeniously turned
into four flats. The conversion was done by *Blackwell, Storry
& Scott*, 1969–70. The range has one storey and dormers, three
pairs of two, above the windows not the doorways of the
dwellings.

OLD TOWN lies to the NE of the Market Place and High
Street and is a huddle of old buildings around the parish
church. Coming from High Street along CHURCH ROAD a
small green, a remnant of the larger Brackley Green, is near
the GOLDEN SPRING, in medieval times regarded as a holy
site. Its head has a reset C13 arch above its brick bowl. The
general character of the area is vernacular and largely still of
stone with an occasional row still thatched. Other than the
church the only building of any pretension is the modest
gabled former COTTAGE HOSPITAL, built in 1876, looking
very much like a school.

MISSION CHURCH, Halse, 2 m. NW. A Gothic 'iron church' of
1900, built for railway workers originally, then bought by the
Earl of Ellesmere and moved here as a mission church.

BRADDEN

ST MICHAEL. As is all too obvious the church had a thorough Victorian restoration. This happened in 1858–9 by *William White*. Of the medieval building survive the short, broad, unbuttressed C13 W tower – see lancet window and the bell-openings – although Bridges records it was rebuilt *c.* 1700. Internally the medieval arcades also survive. The N arcade is a little puzzling. The two E bays are of C14 date and very similar to the three bays of the S arcade. Octagonal piers, double-chamfered arches. There is, however, a pier of masonry from which a further W bay, of limestone, extends, which appears to be C15. This would suggest that there was probably a C12 building whose W wall ended on the line of the masonry pier, to which a N aisle was added. In the C13 the tower was built a little further W, then linked to the earlier church. In the C14 both arcades were replaced and finally in the C15 a new arch replaced whatever existed at the W end on the N side. – PULPIT. 1858 but the back panel is Jacobean and has provided the inspiration for further panels on the pulpit, so an odd mixture of Gothic and Jacobean designs. – STAINED GLASS. N window, 1889 by *William Pearce*. S aisle W window, St George by *J. Hardman & Co.*, 1961. – MONUMENT. Large tablet for the Ives family, 1888 by *Belton* of Northampton.

Former RECTORY, E of the church. 1860–1, also by *William White*. The usual rectory type architecture. Somewhere between Gothic and Tudor. Many gables.

BRADDEN HOUSE. There was a pre-Reformation house here, and it had the projecting wings which the present house has. The present house is almost entirely 1819, although the W front looks earlier Georgian. The two wings have pediments. Ground-floor windows altered in the 1960s.

MANOR FARMHOUSE, Main Street. A large late C17 wing with three-light mullioned windows on two floors, two-light in the gable, to which is attached a three-storey early C19 wing of three bays of sandstone with ironstone dressings, the floors divided by platbands.

BRAFIELD-ON-THE-GREEN

A most attractive green with a pond and some pleasant stone houses around.

ST LAWRENCE. Norman W tower. Small S doorway. One upper S window. Arch towards the nave C19. The bell-stage is Perp. Three big but impressive buttresses, made larger to reinforce the tower in order to allow bellringing. Two-light transomed bell-openings, battlements, pinnacles. Chancel rebuilt 1848 by *J. M. Derick* (stencilled patterning restored 1992), N aisle and arcade 1850 when the church generally was restored. The aisle had been removed in 1808. The s porch is of 1911. The s arcade is interesting. It must date partly from the late C12 and partly from the early C13. The first pier has a highly unusual square section. Big keeled shafts in the diagonals, fine coupled shafts in the cardinal directions. The capital has stiff-leaf and faces at the corners. On the E side a serpent and a cat. It is clearly much restored but seems basically original – of the early C13. The second pier is earlier: circular with a square abacus whose angles are cut off. The capital has waterleaf but is less trust-worthy. The E respond has, again much re-cut, upright leaves. Facility addition of 1999. – FONT. Big, rich Norman style, but C19. – FURNISHINGS. Elaborate panelling with medallion carvings and reredos with painted Crucifixion, all a memorial to the Sargeant family 1946, the carving by *Faith-Craft*. – STAINED GLASS. Most unusual soft sepia grisaille windows in the chancel, *c.* 1840 by *Smith & Drury* of Sheffield. – N chapel two windows by *T. D. Randall* of *Faith-Craft*, 1947.

SCHOOL, by the church. Main part of 1842 by *E. F. Law*, described by Whellan in 1849 when it was thatched as 'pictur-esque Swiss'. All that has gone since it was enlarged in 1885. The s front is Tudor with a central gabled entrance and three rectangular windows to each side.

No. 25 CHURCH LANE is partly C15 with timbers of its original roof. It was possibly a priest's house. Its Tudor wall paintings no longer exist.

BRAMPTON ASH

ST MARY. Chancel of the late C13 with an interesting E window of four lights (two plus two lights, in the spandrels tiny encir-cled trefoils, in the main spandrel a bigger encircled trefoil), contemporary N windows, SEDILIA and PISCINA, and a chancel arch on triple shafts. The rest Perp, especially the W tower and the arcades inside. The former has clasping buttresses, a big top frieze of cusped lozenges, and a broach spire with two tiers of lucarnes. There is evidence that the tower was originally vaulted inside. The arcades have slender piers with a long hollow-chamfered projection to nave and aisles and shafts with capitals to the arch openings. Perp also the N porch with side windows and the two handsome niches to the l. and r. of the E window. The details of the nave are very similar to Islip, and Simon Norwich inherited Brampton Ash and a manor at Islip in 1427. He died in 1468 and is buried in the church. Fine series of C15 gargoyles, notably a bearded man at the E corner of the N aisle. There was a restoration in 1849 by *J. G. Bland* of Market Har-borough. – COMMUNION RAIL. Fine C18 balusters. – Fine carved Stuart ROYAL ARMS above the chancel arch. – GALLERY and other woodwork introduced following a bequest in 1992.

– STAINED GLASS. Roundel of a rose within a Collar of SS, C15 (S aisle). – MONUMENTS. There were BRASSES to Sir John Holt †1418 and his wife standing under canopies on the floor in front of the chancel. Vandalized in 1984 when the male figure and the head of the female were stolen. Now reset, with restored missing parts, in a large stone slab. – Charles Norwich †1605. Two kneeling figures under an arch. Fine quality, good enough for *Hollemans*. – George Bosworth †1804. Tablet. Two weeping willows bending over an urn.

W of the church the OLD RECTORY with a five-bay Georgian front, and in HERMITAGE ROAD, E of the church, pairs of Althorp Estate COTTAGES. Ironstone with date plaques 1842, 1843 and 1845. The manor had been acquired in the early C18 by Sarah, Duchess of Marlborough, and thence it passed to the Hon. John Spencer of Althorp.

BRAUNSTON

5060

ALL SAINTS. Built 1848–9 by *R. C. Hussey* of Birmingham, and a real credit to him. A faculty dated 1843 shows the design was already drawn. An impressive, prosperous-looking church in the Dec style with a heavily crocketed spire and plenty of pinnacles and pierced quatrefoil parapets. All in pink sandstone with limestone dressings. Some original Perp work in the S chapel. Tall, open interior, made lighter by the roofs having ceilings. – FONT and PULPIT. Both in rich marbles and alabaster, the font with inlay. Both part of a restoration of 1874–81 by *William Butterfield*. Some further work was done by *Caroe & Passmore*, 1934–8. – FONT. Circular, Norman, with an almost defaced rope moulding at the top. – LECTERN with 'Celtic' figures. By *Trevor Cox*, 1956. Also by him the panelling with engraved figures in the N aisle. – SCULPTURE. Cross-head of a churchyard cross with the Crucifixus and three other figures, badly defaced. – STAINED GLASS. A wealth of Victorian windows of which the best are: S chapel E by *Wailes*, 1849; chancel N by *Ward & Hughes*, 1863; and chancel E, by *A. Gibbs*, 1872. N aisle W of 1883 also by *Gibbs*, and N aisle a fine window of 1898 by *Heaton, Butler & Bayne*. – MONUMENTS. Excessively cross-legged knight of *c.* 1300, a gabled flat trefoiled canopy above his head, a big shield by his side.

Former RECTORY (Merryhill House), S of the church. 1839, by *H. J. Underwood* of Oxford. Cement-rendered, with a colonnade of Tuscan columns and square piers around its garden façade. W is BRAUNSTON MANOR, of C17 origin, ironstone, some mullions but many windows reframed with hoodmoulds early C19.

E of the church in HIGH STREET on the N side, a tall TOWER MILL of brick, *c.* 1800, now converted into a residence. Also on the same side, No. 101 has an exposed cruck construction on its end wall. Further on, on the s side, a COTTAGE with heavy timber framing and the head of a cusped two-light window, pre-Reformation, and perhaps C14.

The Grand Union Canal reached Braunston by 1793 and was joined to the Oxford Canal, just W of the village, in 1796. The triangular junction was remade in 1829–34. Passing over it a fine pair of BRIDGES, 1834, of the hump type, with sweeping approaches. Balustrade of cast iron, signed by the *Horseley Iron Works*. Just s of the village by the canal a PUMPING HOUSE, 1896, brick, the building with arched windows and a tall square chimney with letters GJCC. A flight of six locks follows, with bridges and a pub, then ¾ m. SE is the entrance to the BRAUN-STON CANAL TUNNEL of 1793–6 by *James Barnes and William Jessop*. Brick-lined, 2,042 yds (1,867 metres) long. Several of these buildings form part of BRAUNSTON MARINA (by *Peter Rainbow* of *The Architectural Design Group*, 1995).

BRAGBOROUGH HALL, 1½ m. E, in parkland. Early C19, centre of three bays with small linked windows under round heads and slightly projecting wings with tripartite windows. Doric portico of two pillars (plans of 1841 are signed by the builder, *William Thomson*; the architect is unknown). ENTRANCE HALL with two Tuscan columns, and a C19 carved wooden fireplace with figures of musicians, leading to an ante-room with an open circle in the centre. On its r. the staircase, ascending in one arm and returning in two. Very simple iron balustrade. Other rooms have fireplace surrounds, mostly brought in, including a fine late C18 fireplace said to be from a house at Twickenham. The panelled LIBRARY also has a carved surround with a central tablet carved with hunting trophies. Two LODGES, one original with slender detached columns and wide eaves.

BRAYBROOKE

ALL SAINTS. Mostly of *c.* 1300 and Perp, but incorporating remains of the C13 cruciform church. Arcades of three bays with octagonal piers and double-chamfered arches and in the E bay solid piers either side of the nave with on the N side capitals with stiff-leaf foliage and another similar on the s. Chancel E window with intersected tracery. Of *c.* 1300 also the s doorway. Perp the big long panel with crenellations forming the REREDOS of the chancel. Perp also the ambitious s chapel of three bays with four-light and five-light windows. There are similarities between the chapel and work at Whiston church, suggesting a date of *c.* 1520–30 or later. Perp also the slender W tower. Top frieze of cusped lozenges, broach spire with two tiers of lucarnes. Similar to nearby Brampton Ash.

FONT. Square, Norman, with rosettes, beaded intertwined monsters, and on one side the incongruous combination of a cross and by its side a figure holding two fishes and placed horizontally, not vertically. How can such a thing be explained? A fine piece, reminiscent of the carved capitals in St Peter's, Northampton. – SCREEN. To the s chapel, Perp, coarse, of one-light divisions. – PULPIT remade in 1894.* – Panels from C18 box pews line the aisle walls. – LECTERN. A spirited eagle carving of 1884. – ROYAL ARMS. Painted, for George III. – SCULPTURE. Big, somewhat Rabelaisian medallion containing the head of a military man, reminiscent of the early C16 terracotta medallions at Hampton Court, and with a similar Renaissance frame. More than life-size. He has a walrus moustache, a goatee and a wreath across his forehead. It is *c.* 1550–70 and traditionally from Braybrooke Castle, which belonged to the Griffins. It also has much in common with carved work at Dingley (q.v.). Brian Giggins has pointed out that the proportion suggests it was meant to be seen from below. – WALL PAINTINGS. Barely visible (s aisle). St Anthony with his pig(?). A knight to the l. – STAINED GLASS. Nave s, C14 Trinity shield. Griffin Chapel: fragments, late C15–early C16. N chapel window by *Alan Younger,* 1967, made by *Goddard & Gibbs.* – MONUMENTS. Cross-legged knight, thought to be Sir Thomas le Latymer †1333, of oak. – Splendid Elizabethan monument to members of the Griffin family, *c.* 1570. A classic Renaissance piece. Base with short pilasters with roundels and a cartouche with scrolls. Main tier with four bulgy Ionic balusters, the outer ones trebled and set out in front of the others. Their bases are shorter balusters, and they carry another set of short balusters. Centre panel with shield in a gadrooned frame. Further shields l. and r. Top with urns and finials, and a semicircular centrepiece containing a shell and crowned by another urn finial. No figures at all. It is without doubt a product of the *Thorpes* of Kingscliffe and relates especially to a chimneypiece at Boughton House (q.v.), formerly at Hemington. The heraldry suggests it is a monument for Sir Thomas Griffin †1566 and his wife. – FUNERAL HELMET. It hung near the Griffin monument.†

p. 136

BRIDGE, to the SE. Begun by Sir Thomas Latimer *c.* 1400, completed in 1402–3. Of brown stone. Three pointed chamfered arches. Two massive cutwaters on the E side. Low stone parapets.

CASTLE. To the E of the village, on the N side of the Desborough road, extends the complex of moated and banked platforms of the castle. The ditches are dry almost everywhere, but were once supplied from a wide artificial pool covering the N of the position. The whole area is about ¼ m. long, and many of the enclosures are very weak; in fact it is unlikely that there was any intention of defending anything except the castle proper against a serious attack. Some of the earthworks may in fact be the remains of fishponds. This part of the area is occupied by a farm, whose business has inevitably done a good deal of

---

* The C18 communion rail noted in 1961 disappeared in reordering in 1968.
† The VAMPING HORN, 5 ft 6 in. (1.7 metres) long, to rouse the village choir to more fervent singing (cf. Harrington), is now at Harborough Museum.

Braybrooke, All Saints, Griffin Monument.
Lithograph, *c.* 1830

damage to the earthworks; but the central island appears to have been double-moated, with a strong bank between the moats. Its stone defences have vanished.

BRIGSTOCK

ST ANDREW. The Anglo-Saxon tower is of course the chief object of interest at Brigstock. It has long-and-short quoins and a rounded stair-turret. Long-and-short quoins also indi-

cate the width and height of the Saxon nave. They are visible
outside at the NW and SW end and inside at the SE end. It was
a Saxon church of substantial size. The tower top is Dec. So
is the spire. Low broaches, three tiers of lucarnes. Mighty
Saxon tower arch, remarkably tall, with the same cyclopic
unmoulded blocks representing capital and abacus as at Wittering in the Soke of Peterborough, and with the familiar raised
band running up parallel with the jambs and round the arch
at a distance which excludes any thought of structural expression. Inside the tower, in the side walls, other splayed windows
with radiating voussoirs. Small triangular-headed entry to the
staircase. Holes in the wall inside the turret suggest an original
stair of wood. Another similar blocked window appears over
the N arcade, visible on both sides. Further Saxon windows in
the upper stage of the tower, one blocked on the S side, partly
hidden by the clock. Saxon masonry over both arcades. This
would all fit with a late pre-Conquest date, late C10 or into
C11. The unmoulded N tower arch must be a Norman insertion. During the Late Norman decades a N aisle was added to
the Saxon nave.

The arcade consists of two bays. Circular pier, flat capital with
broad flat crocketed leaves, square abacus, round, single-stepped
arches. The details point to c. 1190. Somewhat later the S
doorway with thin shafts, and a round finely moulded arch. C13
also the columns of the SEDILIA in the chancel with their
mature stiff-leaf capitals, though not making sense any more,
being set partly within what is left of a trefoil arch. Also C13
the N chapel arcade with its slim quatrefoil pier and double-
chamfered arches. Of c. 1300 the low tomb-recess outside the
S aisle. Dec the S arcade (octagonal piers, double-chamfered
arches) and the E extension of the N arcade. This and the E
arch of the S arcade, being wider, seem to take into consideration some early, possibly Saxon, feature, such as a central
space, of which there is no other evidence. Dec the chancel E
window (four lights, reticulated tracery). Perp in conclusion a
number of features: the elegant tall chancel arch (of the four-
shafts-four-hollows type), the exterior of the N side with a
stair-turret halfway down the N chapel to allow access to a
screen, within the chapel a big, damaged niche alongside the
E window, the exterior of the S side, a single flying buttress over
the S chapel, and the two-storeyed porch, with its picturesque
turret at the NW angle. Its entrance has pierced traceried spandrels with a small shallow niche and sundial above. There are
restoration drawings by *Carpenter & Ingelow*, 1877–8. – SCREEN
to the N chapel, a fine piece, but surely partly made up. The
traceried base panels look C14, but the top C15. It is said to
have come originally from Pipewell Abbey. – MONUMENT. 1st
Lord Lyveden. By *Matthew Noble*, 1876. Recumbent white
marble effigy on a sumptuous alabaster tomb-chest. – REREDOS.
A painted and gilded scheme, 1927, by *Hubert Adderley*, a pupil
of Comper. – STAINED GLASS. Several windows by *Ward &
Hughes* including N chapel N, Vernon memorial, 1884 and

another of 1877. – S aisle E, 1892 also theirs. – Chancel E, 1885 by *Ward & Hughes*. – Chancel S, 1901 by *Heaton, Butler & Bayne*.

MANOR HOUSE, W of the church. The core is a hall range of before the Reformation. The hall itself has always been one-storeyed and there was a chamber over it. The windows have four-centred heads and are of two lights with a transom, the lights two-centred and cusped, also below the transom. A drawing by George Clarke of 1846 shows hoodmoulds over the windows and the porch doorway, but these have been removed. On the garden side is the original buttressed porch, heightened in the C17. The porch on the opposite side is not original. Jacobean extensions to the N, of three floors including the porch heightening, and S of two. In addition a larger S extension by *Gotch & Saunders*, 1890. Inside a Jacobean staircase (vertically symmetrical balusters), a fireplace of c. 1750, and a room with Adamish decoration. The house was surrounded by a moat.

MARKET CROSS. In the square to the N of the church. Square, set on steps, bevelled shaft, head, created 1586 but altered at various times. There are dates 1705, 1778 and 1887. Near the church, in THE SYKE, a row of Victorian stone and brick cottages with decorative cast-iron windows.

In SCHOOL LANE the CONGREGATIONAL CHAPEL of 1798, simple with arched windows, but some C19 alteration, and LATHAM'S SCHOOL and SCHOOL HOUSE, rebuilt by *A. W. Blomfield* in 1873. Below the school a former WATERMILL, with in its large end wall a round-arched window and restored iron wheel.

A number of good stone houses in HIGH STREET. At the top of the Square a gable end with a plaque of an animal (a sheep?) dated 1588, together with the date 1730. To the W FOTHER-INGHAY HOUSE, in well-coursed stone, with gables and mullioned windows.

On the road to Corby the imposing former FACTORY built for the clothing firm of Wallis & Linnell in 1873–4, converted for use as offices by the *John Whyte Partnership* in 1982. Still in the early C19 tradition. Of stone, thirteen bays long by only two wide, four storeys, all windows arched, so designed to allow full use of light for the workers. In the middle a pedimental gable with a bell.

BRIXWORTH

Brixworth is too close to Northampton to have escaped the commuter housing estates. These have proliferated since the village was bypassed, especially on the S side, and show little respect for the character of the old village. On the N side the inevitable industrial estates. However, the centre of the old village below the church is still a haven of old buildings.

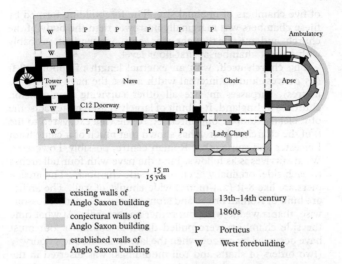

existing walls of
Anglo Saxon building

conjectural walls of
Anglo Saxon building

established walls of
Anglo Saxon building

13th–14th century

1860s

P Porticus

W West forebuilding

Brixworth, All Saints.
Plan

ALL SAINTS.* An outstanding church. One of the grandest examples of Anglo-Saxon architecture in England – one might even say Europe. Much research and excavation over recent years has led to a reassessment of the building and there is doubtless much more still to be learnt, and it remains, to a degree, a building of which we still do not understand its true significance. Whatever its problems the church cannot fail to impress the visitor.

A C12 text claiming that Brixworth was a monastery is highly suspect, but if the church did serve a community (as its scale might suggest) it is not known how long it continued as such and by *c.* 1200, at the latest, it had been reduced in size, presumably to adapt it to more conventional parochial use.

The church is predominantly Anglo-Saxon, but not of the C7 date claimed by Clapham. Excavations in 1981–2 showed that the foundations of the NW corner of the original building (later demolished) were dug into a ditch containing C8 material, so a date in the latter part of that century or early C9 is likely. It was altered again later in the Anglo-Saxon period. The first Anglo-Saxon phase consisted of a wide and tall nave with a clerestory and N and S side chambers or *porticus* that, according to most recent excavations, were conceived as separate chambers, and a spacious choir, as wide as the nave, and a narrower, probably semicircular, apse, surrounded by a half-sunk ambulatory or outer ring crypt. Across the W end of the nave excavations have revealed another set of *porticus*, made up

6, 7

* For the account of the Anglo-Saxon church I am totally indebted to Dr David Parsons.

of five chambers of unequal size. The forebuilding formed by
these chambers was marginally narrower than the body of the
church, and must be thought of as semi-independent, probably
with a great chamber at first-floor level.

The church itself, with an external length of about 148 ft
(45 metres) and an internal width across the nave of 30 ft (9
metres), surpasses in size all other surviving Anglo-Saxon
churches in England. It is built of largely reused material, some
of it clearly Roman, but unrelated to the villa excavated to the
N of the church; research has shown that much of it came from
Leicester and some other Roman centre, possibly Towcester.
What survives is as follows. First the nave with four tall arches
to each side, originally open to the side chambers. The arcade
piers are like 8-ft (2.4-metre) wide chunks of wall. The arches
are built of Roman bricks and stones not used strictly voussoir-
wise, that is wedge-wise, but rather haphazardly. At what time
the side chambers were pulled down is unknown, but must
have occurred by *c.* 1200 when the late Romanesque S doorway
(two orders of shafts and roll mouldings) was inserted in the
most westerly arcade arch. Above are the clerestory windows,
also with Roman brick arches. They are placed above the
spandrels and not the apexes of the arches. The choir was
divided from the nave by a central arch, possibly flanked by
smaller arches or doorways as at Bradwell-juxta-Mare, Essex,
of *c.* 655 and at Reculver, Kent, of *c.* 670 – see the springers
of arches visible on either side of the present (late medieval)
chancel arch. The main body of the original church may
therefore be regarded as a variant of a basilica in the Early
Christian sense, that is an arcaded nave (there are Late Antique
and early medieval parallels for piers rather than columns supporting arches) with a clerestory and an apse at the E end; the
subdivision of the side chambers is the principal non-classical
feature.

Of the W *porticus*, those to the l. and r. of what is now the
tower can be recognized from the bits of wall running N from
its NW and S from its SW angle. The N and S doorways from
the middle compartment also survive, with Roman brick
arches. This compartment was the entrance porch and the
outline of its great W doorway can still be seen inside. This
went out of use later in the Anglo-Saxon period when the tower
was raised over this bay of the demolished forebuilding and
given the big W stair attachment (cf. Brigstock). The masonry
of the tower and stair-turret includes herringbone courses.
Above the doorway from the former porch into the nave is
another doorway. Both have arches of Roman brick. The upper
doorway served either as access to the first floor of the forebuilding from a staircase in the nave or as a way through from
the forebuilding to a gallery in the nave. This might have been
either full width (as at Wing, Bucks.) or a small platform (for
which there is evidence at Bosham, West Sussex). It is now
blocked and had gone out of use when the triple opening into
the nave with its baluster shafts was inserted above, probably

at the same time as the tower was built. It cuts into the arch
of the earlier doorway below.

The choir had a low N doorway, again with Roman brick
voussoirs, to the most easterly of the N range of *porticus*. The
apse is narrower and has an arch of Roman brick flanked l.
and r. by windows, below the r. one an image niche. At ground
level are rough arches cut in the plaster to crudely represent
the entries which led to a half-sunk ambulatory or an outer
ring crypt that surrounded the apse. A ring – or semicircular
– crypt inside and below the apse is found at St Peter's, Rome,
c. 590; outer crypts or ambulatories inside the apse are characteristic of Carolingian and Ottonian architecture in France
and especially Germany. They begin in the mid C8 and culminate in the C10 and C11. At St Emmeram in Regensburg,
Germany, there is a rare example of a ring crypt lying outside
the apse, as at Brixworth, with which it is roughly contemporary (documentary reference to the crypt in 791). The ambulatory was entered by oblique stairs l. and r. of the apse arch and
had a tunnel vault, of which traces can be seen all round and
especially on the N side where the steps are. The apse, originally
a stilted semicircle, has been reconstructed more than once,
on the first occasion later in the Anglo-Saxon period, possibly
at the same time as the tower (both use tufa). It was then
rebuilt with a square E end in the Late Middle Ages and later
in sandstone in its present form. Original are the two bays on
the N side adjacent to the choir, framed by projecting pilaster
strips. There is evidence against the choir wall that the strips
were joined by semicircular arches, as at Wing. Part of an
original N window survives in the second bay. The apse was
restored to its original form in 1864–6 under the direction of
William Slater, based on evidence which had been uncovered
by the vicar, the Rev. Charles Watkins, a keen antiquarian.
Slater was assisted by *William Smith* although the faculty plan
is signed *Slater & Carpenter*.

The handsome two-bay SE chapel is of *c*. 1300. One bay has
semi-octagonal responds, the other keeled semicircular ones.
There are two tomb-recesses in the S wall. Its third, W, bay was
removed in the 1860s to reveal more of the early nave wall. In
the C14 the Anglo-Saxon tower was refashioned and heightened. Bell-stage with two-light openings with ogee heads, surmounted by ashlar pinnacles, broaches and a spire with two
tiers of lucarnes. Some repairs were carried out in 1904–6 by
Matthew Holding under the direction of *W. D. Caroe*.

FURNISHINGS. RELIQUARY. Small, of stone, with on each
side a cusped arch under a crocketed gable on each side. It
was found in the wall of the SE chapel containing a wooden
box with a relic inside. The date of the piece is probably
c. 1300. A replica is now exhibited in the nearby Heritage
Centre. – SCREEN. To the S chapel, but formerly rood screen.
Much restored. With tall one-light divisions and panel tracery
above. – FONT. C17 with Georgian ogee top. – SCULPTURE.
Inside the W jamb of the S doorway an eagle in relief, possibly

the evangelist symbol of St John; Anglo-Saxon and perhaps the top arm of a cross. The suggested date is late C8. – Also part of a Saxon cross-shaft with a combat, almost entirely defaced. – STAINED GLASS. On the S side, three windows of 1888 by *A. O. Hemming.* – On the N side windows of 1913 and 1915 by *Burlison & Grylls.* – MONUMENTS. Cross-legged knight, *c.* 1300 (S chapel). – A good many fine engraved slate headstones such as those immediately alongside the gate: Elizabeth Bates, 1787 signed by *Thomas Holt,* and Mary Green, 1790 signed by *Hind,* both local carvers.

METHODIST CHAPEL. 1811, enlarged 1860, mottled blue and red brick. Still entirely of the Georgian type with pedimented gable and arched windows. Now adapted as a house.

Just below the church the base of MARKET CROSS, four rounded steps and just the stump of the shaft. Opposite THE GRANARY, once a farmhouse with outbuildings beyond, all now converted. Late C17 with some mullioned windows and a projecting porch, originally entered by a round archway at street level, now blocked.

MANOR HOUSE, Harborough Road, E of the church. Late C16/C17, now L-shape but perhaps missing a wing. Ironstone and limestone. Two storeys and attic with three- and four-light mullioned windows. Several C17 four-centred stone fireplaces. Winder stair with splat balusters.

BRIXWORTH HALL PARK. The simple square Georgian house of the Saunders family was demolished in 1954. It was refronted in 1743 by *William Smith II.* Presumably he did the stables, which survive as LAKE HOUSE. Ironstone, nine bays with a three-bay projection, low, square windows and oval windows over, the centre raised and in the middle of this raised portion a vertically placed bigger oval window.* At the E entrance to the estate THE LODGE, a good small house of 1957 by *J. C. C. Warren.* Opposite a good ironstone house *c.* 1800 with pedimented doorcase and wood mullion-transom casements. Pretty, early C18 ironwork gateway.

Former RURAL DISTRICT OFFICES, Spratton Road. Now a commercial building, incorporating parts of the former workhouse by *James Milne,* 1836. This was enlarged in 1897 by a forward pedimented bay on square pillars, rather like a porte cochère, which is now glazed. Next to it the LIBRARY and COMMUNITY CENTRE built 1999. Ironstone and glass with a sweeping curved roof with heavy projecting beams.

NE of the A508 the large impressive complex of MERCEDES BENZ, by *Oculus Building Construction,* opened 2007, sweeping curves and blue glass.

CHESHAM MEMORIAL CROSS. ½ m. S on the A508. Erected following the death of Charles, 3rd Baron Chesham, while hunting with the Pytchley Hunt. A mock medieval market cross on the verge.

---

* The ORANGERY was moved to Kelmarsh Hall (q.v.).

BROCKHALL

ST PETER AND ST PAUL. Small, close to the Hall, with village houses the other side. An interior of considerable charm. Of *c*. 1200 the S doorway and the two bays of the S arcade with circular piers, simply moulded capitals, square abaci, and round arches with a slight chamfer. The C14 W bay was added when the W tower was built, and a further bay to embrace the tower. Within, the tower is supported on two further chamfered arch supports on the N and S sides. The tower itself is small and low, and has a W lancet window in a projection, and in the S aisle is also a window with two lancets under one hoodmould. The chancel arch corresponds. The chancel was rebuilt in 1873–4 by *E. F. Law* but replacing one already rebuilt *c*. 1840, of which the Gothic roof survives. In the S aisle the big splendid cusped arch of a tomb-recess, decorated with much ballflower, i.e. early C14. Two light Perp windows in the nave. – FONT. Plain, octagonal, Perp. On the underside of the bowl fleurons. – DOOR SURROUNDS of the N and S doorways inside. Strawberry Hill Gothic, probably *c*. 1800. – REREDOS of 1890 in the Perp style. – ROYAL ARMS. Painted, George III. – STAINED GLASS. Nave N. Two late C14 roundels. Chancel E, 1869, Christ the Good Shepherd by *Heaton, Butler & Bayne*, 1890. – MONUMENTS. Many tablets to Thorntons, e.g. Thomas †1783 by *William Cox*. Another in the S aisle †1737 by *John Hunt* and doubtless by him too, in the nave, William Lee †1728. A heraldic surround for William Thornton †1782 and a large urn memorial for Thomas Lee Thornton †1799, whose grey marble base fits over the C14 ballflower recess.

BROCKHALL HALL. An impressive if somewhat forbidding Elizabethan S front. Originally it had two gables and three dormers instead of the straight top it has now, and was recorded thus by Peter Tillemans in 1721. Three storeys, half-H shape, with short wings and bay windows in the re-entrant angles. Three- and four-light windows, transomed on the ground floor. The windows all have arched lights. The principal doorway is not original. It leads into the middle of the hall. Originally it would have led into its end. The Hall bay window survives, and its opposite number. In the HALL a fine fireplace of *c*. 1740 when other work was done, probably by *William Smith* of Warwick. Several original fireplaces remain, with four-centred openings, not all *in situ*. The E side continues the Elizabethan house. Part of it was a tower. The N front is late C18 Gothick with pointed windows, including pointed Venetian windows. The W front had the same character, but was adjusted about 1900 to fit the Elizabethan façades. Inside, several fine late C18 interiors, especially the STAIRCASE with a very elegant and unusual iron balustrade of single unconnected fern-like stems. The DINING ROOM has a classical stucco ceiling, but a Gothick frieze below the ceiling. The staircase and the Gothick alterations were designed by the owner, *Thomas Reeve Thornton*, *c*. 1799. The

DRAWING ROOM has a good ceiling in the Adam style, by
C. Wood, 1889. Some additions by *E. F. Law* in 1863.

STABLES to the E, C18, three sides of a courtyard, with
cupola, 1799. The garden was replanned at the same time on
picturesque principles. Some later landscaping was done for
Thomas Reeve Thornton (†1862) by the Staffordshire landscape architect *John Webb*. Both house and stables have been
coverted into apartments.

MANOR HOUSE, E of the stables. A small but fine, regular house,
dated 1677. Half-H shape, mullioned windows. The central
section has a wooden dentil cornice. Good outbuildings with
a barn in whose W gable is a circle with three mouchettes. A
medieval fragment?

MUSCOTT. *See* p. 420.

BROUGHTON

A number of good stone houses in the village, thankfully now
bypassed.

ST ANDREW. Informally placed. Of ironstone. Mostly early C14,
except for the SW angle of a former Norman aisleless church
and the S doorway, which is also Norman. One order of colonnettes with primitive scallop capitals. Arch with zigzags on,
and at right angles to, the wall surface, making lozenges. One
moulding has beads in the lozenges. Norman also the SW buttress and the E quoins. The W tower has in the W window, as
well as the bell-openings, forms of the late C13 but with ogee
arches. Broach spire with two tiers of lucarnes. N aisle W
window and doorway, blocked S aisle S lancet and both arcades
(octagonal piers, double-chamfered arches, differing details)
are of the early C14. The chancel is earlier, but was rebuilt in
1828. E window of five lights with intersected tracery leaving
the top out to fit a circle in. The chancel arch corresponds in
date. It is set forward from the arcades allowing walls with
access for the rood loft on both sides. Further restoration
1854–5 by *E. F. Law*. – FONT. Octagonal, with panelled stem
and rich nodding ogee arches against the bowl; C14? – STAINED
GLASS. S aisle E, coats of arms, *c.* 1400–50; three heads,
c. 1420–50. – Chancel E window by *J. Powell & Sons*, 1855;
mainly grisaille, still in the tradition of the early C19. – S aisle,
central window, a war memorial, *Morris & Co.*, 1919. – MONU-
MENTS. Two of 1631, one in a tradition of certain monuments
of divines, the other in a more recent, more courtly fashion.
Robert Bolton, rector. Painted stone. Frontal demi-figure,
praying, his hands on the Bible, the Bible on a pillow. The
figure is in a shallow arched niche. – Harold Kynnesman,
attributed to *Edward Marshall* (GF). Bust in an oval medallion
surrounded by fleshy, curly ornament no longer indebted to

the strapwork convention. Also painted stone. Over N arcade Elizabeth Henchman †1772, by *William Cox*.

BAPTIST UNION CHURCH, High Street. 1868, by *Habershon, Brock & Webb*. Small, of ironstone with red, yellow and blue brick dressings. Two Gothic windows in the street façade.

BROUGHTON PRIMARY SCHOOL, Cransley Road. 1931–2 by *J. T. Blackwell*. Addition of 1935 by *Gotch, Saunders & Surridge*. Typical of its time. A long one-storey brick range with end projecting wings, all under a tiled roof. The long section originally opening from the classrooms with French windows. Extended forwards in 1985, but with care. Taller buildings behind including the master's house.

THE GABLES, SW of the church. A manor house built for the Else family 1620. The front with its two wings and central section with its two gables has a datestone of 1685, but still in the Jacobean style. Mid-C19 rear additions and the front porch.

YEOMAN'S HOUSE, NW of the church, on the edge of the Green. Jacobean. Tall, of ironstone. Steep gable to the street, smaller gable at right angles to it, to the S. Barn S of the house.

Nos. 9–11 CHURCH STREET. Quite distinguished semi-detached pair of neo-Queen Anne houses by *Blackwell & Thomson*, 1902–3. Red brick and white render with bays, dentil cornice; both house linked under a single pediment with a small lunette.

BUGBROOKE

ST MICHAEL. Fine early C13 S arcade of four bays. Circular piers, capitals of which two have stiff-leaf foliage (one, it seems, only set out and not completed), pointed arches with one slight chamfer. The N arcade (octagonal piers and double-chamfered arches) is somewhat later, but still C13, the one-bay N chapel perhaps of the same date as the N arcade. Lancets at the W ends of both aisles, also a pair of lancets in the N wall of the N aisle. Perp three-light clerestory windows. There was a partial restoration in 1881 by *Law & Harris*. The chancel was rebuilt and a S chapel added to the S aisle by *Matthew Holding* in 1890–1. Dec W tower with recessed spire (two tiers of lucarnes). N porch extension 1996–8 by *Stimpson & Walton*. – FONT. Octagonal, Perp. – SCREEN. Perp, good and still with its vaulted cove, with two-light divisions, the mullions reaching up into the apex of the arches. – STAINED GLASS. Several good windows. Chancel E, 1902 by *Burlison & Grylls*. N aisle, 1906 by *Burlison & Grylls* and 1953 by *Celtic Studios*. S aisle, St Michael 1902 and 1914–18 painted design. 1926 window by *J. Powell & Sons* and 1920 Christ with children by *Burlison & Grylls*. – MONUMENTS. Two good memorials to the Whitfield family, alas rather cramped, either side the altar. Especially fine is that on the N side for Jane Whitfield †1711. A beautifully carved cartouche with floral garlands. An urn at the top.

Attributed to *William Woodman* the elder (GF). On the S side, a simpler tablet, rectangular, with a marble frame for Alice Whitfield †1697. Samuel Keynton †1753, by *Henry Cox*, of the familiar pyramidal design, as is another to James Warren †1707. Hickman Rose †1850, a low Gothic tomb.

Former RECTORY, W of the church. Completed 1815, yellow brick. Porch with fluted Doric columns. Much of its interior survives.

PRIMARY SCHOOL, High Street. 1872 by *T. H. Vernon*, red brick with lancet windows and a central gable on a stem.

A number of good houses at the SE end of the village in HIGH STREET, e.g. one of 1706 with blocked framed openings with odd scrolled lintels; one of the late C17 still with mullioned windows but symmetrically placed; and a Georgian ten-bay group canted twice round a corner. The BAPTIST CHURCH is of 1808. Front with two doorways and segment-headed windows. The yellow brick cottages E of the church, beyond the brook, were built in the Gothic style in 1844 by *E. F. Law*. They were the NATIONAL SCHOOL with dwellings for the master and, it is said, the policeman. Just E on the S side of the road is ORCHARD HOUSE, c. 1905 by *Alexander Anderson*, a neat Art Nouveau house of the kind Anderson was building in Northampton (*see* Christchurch Road, Northampton p. 476). At the NE end of the village the MANOR HOUSE, basically C17 but considerably renewed during a restoration by *E. F. Law* in 1881. A wide arched entrance to its yard.

CAMPION SCHOOL, Kislingbury Road. By the *County Architect's Department* (*A. N. Harris*), 1966–8, extensions (by *John Goff*) 1971–2. The first purpose-built comprehensive school in the county. A large, powerful composition in brick and concrete, with effective black mullioned staircase windows. Much added to since.

BUGBROOKE MILL (Heygates Ltd), ¾ m. N. A massive tower complex for flour milling. Built in the 1940s, much extended since and refurbished in 2005. It incorporates the stone-built mill building of 1784.

CLAPPER BRIDGE. C16. Damaged by river widening.

9090

BULWICK

ST NICHOLAS. Tall Perp W tower with clasping buttresses. Two tall two-light bell-openings with transom. Quatrefoil frieze below the battlements. Recessed spire with roll mouldings up the edges and two tiers of lucarnes in alternating directions. Late C13 chancel. The E window of five lights is specially characteristic. Intersected tracery cusped, but with a circle at the top to break the regularity of the intersections. The window is shafted inside. Late C13 also probably the doorway into the N aisle. Two orders of stone shafts with shaft-rings;

moulded arch. The principal aisle windows are Perp and remarkably big.

On entering the church it is seen that it was originally provided with transepts (see the pieces of wall after the first two orders of the arcades). The N arcade is earlier than the rest, say of *c*. 1200. Two wide bays with a short octagonal pier. Capital with short upright stiff-leaves. Pointed double-chamfered arch. RCHME postulate it started with round arches, hence the somewhat uncomfortable shaped arches, but there are also considerable signs of movement. Even the central pillar is leaning outwards. The S arcade is Dec. Both arcades were lengthened by incorporating the former transept arches. The heights and details of these and the chancel arch differ, the latter probably C15 on plinths. – SEDILIA and PISCINA, Early Dec, crocketed gables with detached columns. The church was restored by *Slater & Carpenter*, 1870, which is doubtless the date of the alabaster and coloured marble REREDOS. – FONT. Just a simple round bowl on a stem, perhaps C13. – BENCH-ENDS. Carved by the rector of 1862–92, the Rev. *J. H. Holdich*. All the pews have them, foliage squares and figures below, except ten in N aisle, which were removed due to base rot, their ends created into a cupboard in 2010. – STAINED GLASS. Nave N, C14 and C15 canopies and grisaille work. – Chancel E window of 1877 by *Heaton, Butler & Bayne*. – N aisle, memorial for Rev. J. H. Holdich †1892, by *F. C. Eden*, 1938. Tryon memorials in S aisle, one of 1871 by *Heaton, Butler & Bayne* and two others of 1902 by *J. Powell & Sons*. Also by them the N aisle centre 1940 window. – N aisle W of 1932 by *F. C. Eden*, designed by *G. Daniels*. – MONUMENTS. Jane Fowkes †1609 and her husband Henry (date not filled in, but 1612). With kneeling figures facing one another across a prayer-desk. Good quality figures of Southwark type. Surround much rebuilt and damaged. – Vice Admiral Sir George Tryon †1893. Bronze plaque with portrait medallion. In mock C17 stone frame.

BULWICK HALL, ½ m. SW of the village. In medieval times the estate belonged to the Zouche family. By the early C17 it was in the ownership of the Tryon family of Harringworth and in 1888 passed by marriage to the Conant family. The present house is assumed to be the remains of a courtyard house of 1676, the date on the handsome arcade with a balustraded balcony which forms the N entrance into the courtyard. Rusticated segmental arches and niches under. The house itself has cross-windows to the E which go with its date. The S range, however, which is also basically 1676, was largely refaced in the C18 (*c*. 1730?) and sashed. Two storeys, twelve bays with a small doorway with Gibbs surround. No other enrichment. The Gibbs surround doorcase gives onto a staircase with an ornamental, slightly Rococo ceiling for which *John Tillson* of Stamford was paid in 1809. A S wing had already gone by the 1720s and the W end of the house is 1805, when additions and alterations were made by *W. D. Legg* of Stamford. It has a large double-floor bow window and a large DRAWING ROOM with a reeded fireplace surround. In the GARDEN ROOM, at the S end of the arcade, a fireplace almost certainly made up, but which in essence must be Early Elizabethan, say *c.* 1550–60. Very tapering columns with foliate capitals and bases, the shafts richly decorated with the pattern of connected circles and squares familiar e.g. from the Tresham buildings; one is tempted to suggest a connection with the *Thorpes* of Kingscliffe, though it is more crude in design if not in workmanship than one might expect. It appears to be Kingscliffe stone, and was once coloured. The shelf is a gadrooned cornice and the central lintel has horizontal fruit and wreath with the Tryon lion crest in the centre, but this looks more like *c.* 1650. Additional service rooms were added in 1838. Two fine wrought-iron GATES into the park: the first, simple vertical railed gates with spray points on its curved head, probably late C17; the second much more elaborate with scrollwork, points and a pretty overthrow with the Tryon crest and initials JM, early 1700s. Very much in *Thomas Warren*'s manner.

On the road into the village from the W, on the S side, is BULWICK HOUSE, early C19 of brick but rendered and quite handsome. Three bays with windows with low segmental lintels. Double-arched doorcase. Behind the church the former RECTORY of 1827, extended in 1862 for the Rev. J. H. Holdich. Partly remodelled 2010–11 and a Tudor style doorway and porch added. S of the church the QUEEN'S HEAD INN. Mullioned windows with two datestones RE (Ralf Exton), 1675 and 1683. A double-fronted property which was originally more formal than it now appears. The l.-hand section had windows either side the blocked C18 framed doorway surround. Just the infill mark of its former ground-floor window to the r. The r.-hand section has the replaced doorway and again signs of window adjustment.

FINESHADE ABBEY. *See* p. 277.

9070

BURTON LATIMER

ST MARY. Set in a leafy churchyard. Considerable signs of Victorian restoration, especially the chancel. It was begun by *William Slater* 1864–8, with further work by *R. H. Carpenter* 1879–82. We start inside, however, with evidence of the transepts of a cruciform Norman church. In the centre of each arcade are two round arches, the S with chevron ornament, and in both cases, despite later rebuilding, their Norman imposts remain. On the N side a masonry pier marks the beginning of the transept. To this church, of which no actual feature remains, a S arcade was added, still in the C12, and of that we have two and a half arches from the W. Circular piers, square capitals with many scallops and one with upright leaves, the arches (from the W) unmoulded, then with a thin angle roll, similar to the N transept arch. The N arcade, also with a half-arch, follows in the early C13. One pier is circular with a circular stiff-leaf capital, the next is square with four demi-shafts (cf. Rothwell) and stiff-leaf. Also with stiff-leaf, the surviving respond to the N of the transverse arch into the transept. The C13 arches are pointed and single-stepped. The S doorway also is of the early C13. The arch is still round, but complexly moulded, and the shafts have stiff-leaf capitals. Next came the tower, cutting off half the first arcade arches. To the N and S and, at a lower level, to the W, the tower has blank arcading of three large arches on each side. The tower arch towards the nave has clustered shafts as responds and is triple-chamfered. The bell-openings are of two lights and heavily shafted. They are of after 1310. Battlements, recessed spire with two tiers of lucarnes. The spire was rebuilt in 1864. About 1280 or 1290 the former chancel was taken into the nave, and the arcades were correspondingly lengthened. Three bays, quatrefoil piers, double-chamfered arches. At the same time a new chancel was built. The E window, remade in 1867, is of five lights with a central circle with four octofoils. The side windows are late C13, having Y-tracery with foiled circles. Perp most of the other windows, and Perp the N porch with a niche over the entrance. The aisle would appear to have been heightened also in the C15. The Victorian VESTRY was extended with a chapter-house-like addition in 1984.

SCREEN. Perp, much restored and the canopy added. Of two-light divisions with good, clear tracery. – REREDOS, ALTAR and PANELLING. 1897 by *Dunstan Powell*. – NORTH DOOR. Studded, dated 1510 and carved with its donor's names: 'JHON CAMPYON AND JHONE HYS WYF'. – CHESTS. One Jacobean with arcaded front, and another with iron binding dated 1629. – POOR BOX. Jacobean, on a decorated pillar. – WALL PAINTINGS. On the N aisle wall fragments of a cycle of St Catherine, C14, restored by *Tristram* in 1933–5 and with a set of his watercolours showing more detail than now is visible, though they were revived by *Eve Baker* in 1972. Near the W end Martyrdom of the Saint; further E St Catherine led away from the judge. In the spandrels of the nave arches, figures representing the Twelve Tribes of Israel or the Twelve Patriarchs, in scrolled cartouches. Late C16 and rare to find painting of this period. Anthony Wells-Cole has identified the source as engravings in *De testamenten der twalf patriachen Jacobs kinderen*, published by Joos Lambrecht of Ghent in 1552, although the strapwork borders are an invention. – STAINED GLASS. E window, 1896 by *J. Hardman & Co.* Chancel N and S, 1915 and S aisle E of 1922 also *Hardman*. – N aisle E by *Capronnier*, 1874. – S aisle, heraldic panel of the Bevan family c. 1850. – Tower window by *Clayton & Bell*. – MONUMENTS. Boyvill brass (E end of nave). Only a group of children remains. The parents were in shrouds. Probably early C16. – Brass for Edward Bacon †1626 (chancel). Only part survives. – Margaret Bacon †1626 (S aisle). Brass in a large, tall stone frame with fluted pilasters, a fluted frieze, and a top with a shell motif and three obelisks. Almost certainly the frame from the *Thorpes* of Kingscliffe workshop. Samuel Barwick †1820 (chancel), with an inscription and urn framed by weeping foliage in the manner of *John Bacon* Jun.

BAPTIST CHURCH, Meeting Lane. A plain ironstone building with Gothic windows. Perp style doorway. Simple brick pedimented school alongside, 1889–90 by *Gotch*.

ST MARY'S PRIMARY SCHOOL, High Street. 1885 and 1898–9 by *Gotch*, but mundane Jacobean.

WAR MEMORIAL, set at the junction of High Street and Church Street. Once more *Gotch c.* 1920. Gothic column on steps with a statue of St George on its summit.

Next to the church the MANOR HOUSE with a gabled S front dated 1704. Just W of the church is the JACOBEAN HOUSE, really the Old School, 1622, converted *c.* 1972. Oblong, one-storeyed, with two three-light mullioned windows on each side of a doorway which has a four-centred head and flanking pilasters. Above it a big ogee-sided gable with finials. Inscription over the door and donor inscriptions on the window lintels. Original oak roof. E of the church other stone houses, notably No. 24 which has heavy dark ironstone quoins and window frames. At the S end of HIGH STREET on the E side is a group of buildings which were established as a Cottage Home for the Kettering Workhouse. No. 159, originally a farmhouse of *c.* 1700 of ironstone with an early C19 limestone ashlar front, was the first building to be used in 1896. Then a new set of buildings of brick were built in 1901–2 by *Gotch & Saunders* to the S, Nos. 163–165. All are now residences.

BURTON LATIMER HALL. Jacobean. Originally of half-H shape. Cross-windows and mullioned-and-transomed windows; gables. The original staircase remains with balusters with Ionic heads. The doorways by the staircase with their carved frames look rather later C17. So does the large Hall fireplace. Also of the later C17 the two windows in the E wing opening S. The upper one has the typical arch inserted in the middle part of a tripartite window below the lintel. The W wing was lengthened in 1873. Behind it, the W front towards the road received a new face some time early in the C18. Five bays, two storeys, pedimented doorway.

The WEETABIX complex lies on the N side of the village. Large indeed but of no architectural merit.'

BYFIELD

21 HOLY CROSS. Essentially Dec, and an ambitious building. Tall chancel with fine, slender two-light windows. The tracery is of the intersected type fully cusped, but the heads of the windows are segmental – quite a piquant effect. The flowing tracery of

the E window is 1870–1 when the church was restored by *Albert Hartshorne* using the builder *Cornish* of North Walsham (cf. Arthingworth). The aisle windows, simpler intersecting tracery and doorways are also Dec. The S transept window a little more intricate. The W tower has a sumptuous portal with ballflower in a continuous moulding, a crocketed ogee hoodmould and pinnacles, a two-light window above, and niches with nodding ogee arches to its l. and r. A third niche above it. The upper part of the tower is Perp. Two widely set, tall bell-openings linked by an arch of the basket or *anse de panier* type. Battlements and a recessed spire. The spire is not tall, but has two tiers of lucarnes in alternating directions. The big S porch entrance repeats the design of the W portal. The sides of the porch have small two-light windows. Dec again the arcades of four bays (octagonal piers, double-chamfered arches) of Hornton stone. The C14 clerestory had circular windows, of which evidence exists, but which were replaced by two-light windows in the C15. – BENCHES. Mostly 1870 but some reused tracery panels on fronts, backs and ends. – REREDOS. 1884–5 by *Edmund Law*. C13 style of stone with some alabaster and marble pillars. The SEDILIA also probably *Law*. – STAINED GLASS. Several windows by the *Kempe* firm: S transept E, 1897 (especially fine with Kempe's wheatsheaf skilfully used as decoration on the pot of lilies), chancel S, 1902, the N aisle of 1921 and the tower window of 1893. – Chancel E, 1884 by *Burlison & Grylls*. – S transept, 1884 by *J. Hardman & Co.* – N aisle, 1942 by *J. Powell & Sons*.

CHURCH END HOUSE, E of the church. The former Rectory. C17 work at the back, the front early C18. Later alterations. Icehouse in the grounds.

Nos. 19–21 HIGH STREET, although looking largely C18, have the bones of a C15 cruck-framed hall house, still with smoke-blackened timbers. The hall was subdivided in the C16.

MANOR HOUSE, ¼ m. NW, at the main crossing. Five bays, two storeys, quoins. *c.* 1700. Doorway with an open segmental pediment. A small cherub's head in the opening. Stone window frames with wooden cross mullion/transom casements.

CANONS ASHBY

A truly rewarding place now totally in the care of the National Trust.

ST MARY. A fragment of the church of an Augustinian priory founded *c.* 1150. What remains is two bays of the nave and N aisle, the big NW tower added to the aisle in the mid C14 and one of the most impressive church façades in the county. The tower has tall two-light bell-openings, still Dec, ballflower strings on its corners, and battlements and pinnacles, though these are probably later in date and probably 1709–10. A further row of ballflower on a horizontal string course across the aisle and above some unusual trefoil cresting. The tower base, which fronts the aisle, has blank arcading typical of the late C13 (pointed-trefoiled arches) and the shafts of the window above look *c.* 1310. The nave front is distinguished by a splendid portal, richly shafted and with a richly moulded arch. To its l. and its r. are two bays of blank arcading. Rounded trefoil heads under richly moulded arches. The shafts have stiff-leaf capitals. All this must be of *c.* 1230–40. The big window above is Perp, of five lights under a four-centred head with ogee top. The nave s windows and the E window are post-Reformation. Those in the s wall are set between wide classical pilasters so probably *c.* 1710 when other remains of the monastic buildings were removed. The arcade inside does not contradict the C13 dating although it may have been remodelled when the tower was built. Very tall and substantial piers. The first has clustered octagonal shafts, the second is free-standing, circular with circular abacus and water-holding moulded base, the third octagonal with octagonal abacus. The arches have three hollow chamfers, and there are conical foot-pieces on the second and third piers. Doorway to the tower with the typical Dec moulding of two sunk quadrants. Another late C13 moulded doorway with shafts, externally on the N side, in the angle between the tower and the aisle. The church never had a s aisle. The cloister was attached immediately to the nave. It was surrounded by the usual buildings, including a long oblong chapter house. On the N side however an aisle existed, erected probably a little after the nave and its w end. The nave was originally 96 ft (29 metres) long and was followed by a long aisleless chancel.

FONT. Octagonal, with patterns of window tracery as if from a pattern book. They are both Dec and Perp. – READER'S DESK. With Jacobean panels. – COMMUNION RAIL. Probably also *c.* 1710. – WALL PAINTING. Around the E window are crimson curtains being held back by cherubs. This is attributed to *Elizabeth Creed*, Edward Dryden's cousin, so again *c.* 1710. More of her decoration is to be seen in the house. – HATCH-MENTS. A fine series of eleven dating from 1708 to 1851. – ARMOUR of Sir Robert Dryden †1708, the most elaborate funeral achievement in the county. Large banner, two pennons, helmet and crest, wreath and mantling, tabard, shield, gauntlets, spurs, sword. – STAINED GLASS. Fine E window of 1912 by *J. Powell & Co.* – MONUMENTS. Brass to John Dryden †1584; the 23-in. 58-cm. figure is a replica of 1998. – A splendid marble ledger stone for Sir Robert Dryden †1708. – John Turner Dryden †1797. By *Rossi*. In the Bacon style, with a large female figure seated at the base of an urn. – John Edward Turner Dryden, 1818 by *Rossi* (Murray). Standing, mourning Grecian woman holding a garland to lay on an altar. – Several lesser tablets including one for Gervase Jackson-Stops †1995, who when working for the National Trust was instrumental in saving the house for the nation. – In the churchyard a tall Celtic cross memorial for Sir Henry Dryden †1899.

WELL-HOUSE, NNE of the church and E of the house, in an orchard. Small, with a pitched roof and an arched entrance. Tunnel-vaulted inside. It dates from the time of the priory.

CANONS ASHBY. After the Dissolution a house, which has now gone, was made by Sir John Cope out of the buildings of the priory. It stood just E of the church. Another house was created in the mid C16, by John Dryden, who married a Cope daughter in 1551, incorporating portions of an already existing and substantial structure called Wylkyns Farm, although what survives of it suggests it was a building of higher status, and probably had some connection with the priory. The Cope house stood till the late C17, when it was demolished. The mid-C16 Dryden house stands immediately by the road and is built round a smallish courtyard with a hall range on the W, kitchens etc. on the NE and state rooms on the S. It is of ironstone but with much brick, especially on the N side. The house had a sequence of alterations, notably the building of a new hall and service range c. 1570–80. Then when John's son Erasmus succeeded in 1584, the house was enlarged and altered. He was created baronet in 1619. Further minor changes occurred during the C17 but the next major alteration did not happen till the property was inherited by a cousin, Edward Dryden, in 1708–10, principally refronting the S side, with sash windows arranged as regularly as could be managed with the presence of a big tower of the C16 building in its centre. The work has much in common with that of the *Smiths* of Warwick, and within the house there are a number of chimneypieces in different marbles of the type they made. Edward Dryden also created the terraced gardens which are one of Canons Ashby's finest features. Little was done to the house after this time. Sir Henry Dryden, who lived here from 1837 to 1899, was a considerable antiquarian and did careful conservation work on a number of local churches. He built a stable court on the E side of the house but did little inside. The house remained in Dryden possession, with a series of not very successful leases, untill 1980, when, since the building was in some decay, it was offered to the National Trust. The gift was established largely through funds from the National Heritage Memorial Fund and following extensive restoration work the house opened to the public in 1984.

The approach to the house is from the S on the line of an early road. This account basically follows the visitor's route, and exteriors are dealt with later. Nothing much need be said about the E side. This is irregular, its only ornament a C16 oriel window near the r. end under the gable. The mullioned window below was opened up by *Sir Henry Dryden* in the C19 and two C18 sash openings were blocked in. The S range also had an oriel or a bay of which evidence can be seen. Between the gabled wings is a lower two-storey range with an archway

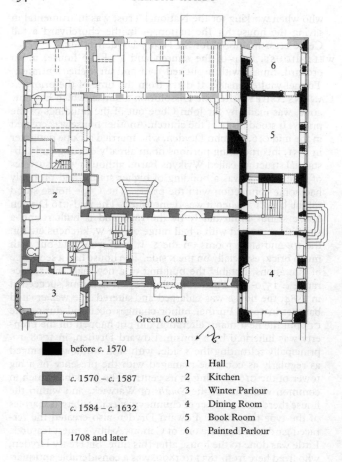

Green Court

before *c.* 1570

c. 1570 – *c.* 1587

c. 1584 – *c.* 1632

1708 and later

1 Hall
2 Kitchen
3 Winter Parlour
4 Dining Room
5 Book Room
6 Painted Parlour

Canons Ashby House.
Plan

which gives access into the COURTYARD. Ahead is the hall range of two storeys above a basement. It has two tall late C16 three-light mullion-and-transom windows. Simple wooden casement windows light the floor above which served as a gallery. The four-centred arched doorway is approached by a short flight of steps. On the r. are the kitchen and other services. The end of the Tudor house is marked by a broad buttress. These additions created a broad H-shaped house, with the earlier structure surviving as an extended cross-wing. This house in its turn was extended E in the 1590s, creating the courtyard that exists today. The E addition on the r. contained the bakehouse and laundry. Wooden cross-mullion-transom windows. Beside a doorway a circular window with three triangles inside, probably a remnant of the priory. On the l. is the tall tower, whose straight joint marks the junction of the earlier Tudor house with that of the 1590s. Two-light arched-headed window at the base, square three-light mullions above. Conspicuous is the huge chimneystack. The E side of the court contained further service rooms.

Moving into the house one enters the HALL through what was originally the screens passage. It is ascribed to c. 1570. Its two original doorways to the service rooms survive. In the W wall a recess marks the original W entrance, which will be considered later. The outer walls are of the 1590s with similar windows in the W wall to those already noticed in the E. The ceiling is of the same period though its plasterwork decoration is C18 and originally there was a dais at the S end. The floor was inserted by Sir Edward Dryden c. 1708–10 when the dais was removed, and is made of two local stones: the pale stone from Culworth, the dark from Byfield, both just a few miles away. Large military painted panel, c. 1715, almost certainly by *Elizabeth Creed*. A passage at the N end of the room leads, via parts of a Jacobean staircase with flat pierced balusters and a finial, to the KITCHEN, a remarkable survival containing many early fitments. The big masonry pier now embedded in the wall supports a partition in the room above. A large segmental arch of c. 1710 covers the main ovens etc. with smaller arched openings on either side, one a cupboard, the other access to the bakehouse. A narrow back stair W of the kitchen gives access to the WINTER PARLOUR in the NW corner of the house. This became the Servants' Hall in the C18. The fireplace dates from the 1570s, but the panelling is of the 1590s and remarkable for the painted decoration. This dates from the time of Sir Erasmus Dryden who inherited in 1584 and died in 1632. The decoration includes several shields of local families: the Copes, the Knightleys of Fawsley, the Fermors of Easton Neston, the Spencers of Badby and just l. of the fireplace the Saunders (with an elephant's head). There are also moral inscriptions in Latin and some Masonic elements. It is all rather reminiscent of the symbolism used by Sir Thomas Tresham at the same time at Rushton (q.v.). An interesting feature is the small buffet recess.

Returning across the hall one reaches on the r. the DINING ROOM, a room with Queen Anne panelling divided by Corinthian pilasters and including a curious and amply curved original mirror above the fireplace. Crossing the Staircase Hall is the BOOKROOM, in the 1590s addition. Of this date is the fireplace with Doric pilasters below and columns above, either side of wooden heraldic panels. There are traces of original colour and marbling, and behind the wooden panels evidence of earlier plasterwork. The heraldry is puzzling since it refers to the Copes, so it may have been rescued from the Cope mansion when that was demolished in the late C17. During the restoration a large beam was found above the windows indicating that originally there had been a projecting bay overlooking the garden. The oak bookcases were designed by Sir Henry Dryden *c.* 1840–50. The last room on the ground floor is the PAINTED PARLOUR, now called Sir Henry's Museum Room, as it was so used in the C19. This is the latest of Edward Dryden's interiors and a charming example of the talents of *Elizabeth Creed*, all the panelling and the Corinthian pilasters being painted in *trompe l'œil*. The fireplace of a pale purplish marble is of a type often supplied by the *Smiths* of Warwick Marble Yard.

Moving back to the STAIRCASE we return to the 1550s part of the house. As originally built this had a spiral stair in one corner, portions of which survive at the top of the house. The present stair dates from the 1630s. It has been partly rebuilt at ground-floor level, since it is clear from other evidence that when the s ground-floor rooms were formed 1708–10, the floor level was dropped several inches. This probably results from the fact that before then it matched the level of the dais in the hall. Once that was removed it became necessary to match the reduced level in the wing.* There is further adjustment at first-floor level with a landing lined by a detached section of balustrading. The stair has double baluster shapes and square newels with grenade caps. On the first floor, on the l. is the DRAWING ROOM, one of the most spectacular interiors in the county. It is more complicated than initially appears. Originally the room had a barrel ceiling, the frame for which still largely exists above the present ceiling. It has a very grand fireplace of the 1590s, with Ionic columns flanking the opening and three pairs of Corinthian columns in the overmantel. The marbling and painted decoration of the chimneypiece are original, and a rare survival, while the painted panels in the overmantel are for Edward Dryden (i.e. *c.* 1710). The splendid domed ceiling was inserted by Sir John soon after inheriting in 1632. It is gorgeous, highly coved, decorated with plasterwork with the patterns of broad bands usual in the early C17, and culminating in a big openwork pendant with four demifigures of women like galleons' heads. The patterns are chiefly foliage, a few heads and arabesque. There is very little strapwork. The style looks decidedly Elizabethan, in spite of the arms of Sir John. Plaster ceilings at Hardwick Hall (Derbys.) and Dorton House, Bucks. (1626), have some of the same motifs.† The walls of the room were thickened on the fireplace wall in order to support the weight of the new ceiling. The old-fashioned design may be due to it having been designed to match that of the earlier ceiling which would have projected

---

* There is similar evidence of floor levels being lowered in the early C18 when a dais was removed at Deene (q.v.).
† I am grateful to Claire Gapper for this reference.

on the s, in the lost bay (portions of the plasterwork from that are preserved in the house). It should be noted that several pieces of furniture in this room are those mentioned in a 1717 inventory. The final room on the s front at this level is the SPENSER ROOM, so called for the association of the poet Edmund Spenser, cousin by marriage to Sir Erasmus Dryden. It has extraordinary murals illustrating episodes from the Old Testament story of King Jeroboam, which were discovered in the 1980s. The interpretation is not exactly clear, but they would again seem to date from the time of Sir Erasmus, so 1585–1632. Architecturally the most significant feature here is the timber internal stud wall. This is a survival of the Early Tudor house acquired by John Dryden in the 1550s. Clearly visible are a blocked earlier doorway and its threshold, above the level of the present floor. Cambered angled beam with remains of its moulded edge and painted decoration. Interesting geometrical patterns in black on yellow and red panels. The Rococo ceiling is also interesting, being c. 1750 and of papier mâché rather than plaster. At the w end of the wing is the TAPESTRY ROOM which retains early decoration on the shutters at the end of the room.* To the N of the stair is the GALLERY. This originally covered the width of the hall, but was subdivided in the C17 to allow for bedrooms on its w side. The arrangement was reversed c. 1710 but the scars of the partitions are visible in the floor. At the end of the gallery is a room, above the Winter Parlour, repeating the heraldic theme with parts of a painted ceiling surviving, again of the 1590s. Black and yellow geometric designs only, no other colour. Suggestions of heraldry. Was it finished? Also a large monochrome panel showing a family group in a room, in a manner similar to the Spenser Room paintings. Another room at the E end of the range has c. 1700 panelling with Ionic pilasters.

It remains to consider the external façades of the house, beginning on the w side in the GREEN COURT. This was the main parade approach to the house in the C16. It is not apparent initially but this is built of brick, rendered. The front is symmetrical with projecting ends, that to the s with the C16 windows, that to the N with the square-topped mullioned-and-transomed windows of Sir John. Just off centre is the blocked four-centred doorway of the screens passage. On either side in the centre are the Jacobean windows of the hall, but otherwise the façade is as revised by Edward Dryden c. 1710. Sash windows in the wings on the ground floor, but above them the rise in the centre of the string course betrays the position of the earlier mullioned window. Segmental pedimented doorcase with Tuscan pilasters. Most interestingly this has a central achievement of arms for Edward Dryden, not of stone but of lead. It was supplied by *John Nost c.* 1710, as was the STATUE of the shepherd boy with his dog and pipes, standing now in the court (it was originally sited further w in the park). The

---

* These are usually covered by tapestry.

cone yews are also of C18 origin, as are the splendid GATES
AND PIERS, both in the court and on the Preston Road
(restored in the 1980s). The SOUTH FRONT, overlooking the
terraced garden, is an uneasy combination of Tudor tower and
Georgian sashes. The tower has mullioned windows with
arched lights, and so have all John Dryden's windows. In this
and, it seems, all other important respects, the building begun
in the 1550s and continued into the 1570s was still entirely
pre-Renaissance. Although largely of stone it rested on decayed
timber framing. Its windows originally formed a descending
line, but *c.* 1710 the ground-floor window was moved to the E
to allow the insertion of a new garden doorway. The NORTH
FRONT overlooking the road, largely of *c.* 1570, is again of
brick, the E portion chequered, but incorporating various portions of the house built of stone. At either end are canted bays,
but in between irregular fenestration due to the kitchen alterations of 1710.

The GARDEN LAYOUT is an important survival from the
early C18. It takes the form of a sequence of terraces with a
central path axis, each of different pattern, parterres near the
house and less formal planting lower down. Fine stone walls,
several topped by early C18 round urns. The vista originally
extended beyond a gateway with piers topped by the lions, the
Dryden crest, into a long double avenue of elms which extended
across the valley towards Eydon.

BARROW, ¼ m. due N of the church. A Late Bronze Age spear-
head was found in it.

CASTLE ASHBY

ST MARY MAGDALENE. The church lies immediately next to the
balustrade of the terrace of the E garden of the house (*see*
below) and with its other side even nearer to the Orangery.
Rarely is a church made so much part of the private garden
furnishings of a mansion. The church is entered from the
terrace by the N porch, which has a re-set Late Norman or
earliest E.E. doorway, very sumptuous and very much restored.
It has as the elements of the decoration of its arch zigzag and
lozenges (i.e. two zigzags meeting) as well as fully developed
dogtooth, a rare (and historically instructive) combination. The
zigzag and lozenges are set parallel to the wall surface as well
as at right angles to it. Door into the church probably C17. The
church has a Dec N aisle with flowing tracery and a one-bay N
chapel. Otherwise the building is entirely Perp with consistently designed windows. W tower (doorway with traceried
spandrels, tall three-light W window, tall tower arch, battlements), a chancel with large windows (E window of five lights),
and S aisle. Inside, Perp arcades of three tall bays. Octagonal
piers, double-chamfered arches. The fine ogee-headed niche in

the s aisle, which is clearly Dec, is not *in situ*; it came from
Grendon church. It contains a statue of St Mary Magdalene
by *Clare Abbatt*, 1995. The restoration in 1870 was controlled
by *G. E. Street*. His are the STALLS with tall poppyhead standards topped by angels, the REREDOS and the alabaster ALTAR
RAIL. Several drawings show how the church looked when full
of box pews. Of the same time the TILES by *Minton*, to designs
by *Lord Alwyne Compton* (†1906), whose memorial, a stone
Gothic surround, is in the chancel. – PULPIT. A very sumptuous early C17 (*c.* 1630?) piece with pedimented, vivaciously
framed panels and a tall tester with a kind of lantern. – SCREEN
(vestry). Of the same style, and indeed made up of the parts
of the reader's desk. – STAINED GLASS. N chapel E made by
Ward & Hughes to a design by *Lady Marian Alford*, *c.* 1873. –
Splendid windows in the chancel all by *Burlison & Grylls*: E
window, Choirs of Angels, 1879, the three s windows depicting
Old Testament figures, apostles and martyrs, 1880s. – MONU-
MENTS. Effigy of Purbeck marble on a tapering coffin-lid.
Knight, cross-legged, supposed to be Sir David de Esseby †
before 1268. – Brass to William Ermyn †1401, rector. The
figure is 5 ft 3 in. (1.6 metres) long. Small figures of saints on
the orphreys. – 1st Marquess of Northampton †1828. Designed
by *Edward Blore*. A stone reredos in rich Gothic forms, at the
E end of the N aisle, in harmony with the window above it. –
2nd Marchioness †1830. Made in 1836 by *Pietro Tenerani*,
sculptor of the monument to Pope Pius VIII at St Peter's in
Rome. Relief of Charity: a fully draped elderly woman gives
money to a young woman with children. Bust portrait of the
marchioness in shell-like canopy at the top. – 2nd Marquess
†1851. Also by *Tenerani*, 1866. Seated angel, much above life-
size and somewhat overpowering, with a trumpet in his lap.
– Lady Margaret Leveson-Gower †1858, the architectural
setting a thickly detailed Gothic recess by *William Gillett* of
Leicester, the sculpture by *Marochetti*. Recumbent effigy with
a white angel in shallow relief against the back wall. – In the
churchyard wall an aedicule and in its niche a large white angel.
This is the monument to the 4th Marchioness, †1877, by *J. E.
Boehm*. The aedicule is within the back wall of what was an
Orangery designed by *William Talman* (*see* below). – 5th Marchioness †1902. Also in the churchyard. Surrounded by four
life-size praying angels. – To the SE of the porch a grave slab
for the important early C18 wrought-iron smith *Thomas Warren*
(1675–1735), 'fam'd for his skill in Mechanicks and Ironwork',
whose forge was in the village.

Good example of an estate village with neat and tidy houses.
SCHOOL in the village. By *G. E. Street*. The plans approved in
1856. Picturesque Tudor, banded and with steep roof and a big
chimney-breast on the front. Next to it a row of cottages of
1874 by *E. F. Law*. The HOME FARM is also by *Law*. A number
of red brick rows with half-timbering dated 1921–2.

CASTLE ASHBY. The mansion stands across from the church but
also at the end of a 3½-mile-long avenue, four-square and 63

self-confident as only Elizabethan and Jacobean houses can be. It is indeed essentially Elizabethan and Jacobean, of 1574 etc. and of about 1600 etc., with inset between the Elizabethan wings a screen of 1625–35, traditionally by Inigo Jones. The arms of the 1st Earl of Northampton, who died in 1630, are above the entrance. The later contributions are important inside but not outside. The house is almost entirely of Weldon stone, with some ironstone used in the earliest phases.

Castle Ashby had been a castle from the C11, but when Leland saw the place in the 1530s he wrote that it was 'now clean down'. By then the estate had been bought by Sir William Compton, a personal friend of Henry VIII and hence a very rich man. But Sir William did not at once do anything to the building, for in a survey of 1565 it is still called an 'old ruined castle'. Work was started by the first Lord Compton in 1574 when a long-drawn-out litigation was settled, but no doubt before his wife, whom he had married only in 1572, had died in the same year (1574). Her and his arms still appear together on the spandrel of the doorway to the SW tower. Lord Compton's house occupied three sides of a long courtyard. Externally it is a little wider than it is deep, but the sides of the wings to the courtyard are longer than the recessed middle range, a type familiar from such mid-C16 houses in East Anglia as Long Melford and Rushbrooke. In common with them also is the placing of polygonal staircase turrets near the ends, but not quite at the ends, of the courtyard fronts of the wings. Of this Elizabethan work, the S ends of the wings meet one as one approaches the house. They were heightened later.

But the principal impression of the S side is the SCREEN. The attribution to *Inigo Jones* comes from Bridges' *History* (information collected *c.* 1720, finally published in 1791) and from Campbell's *Vitruvius Britannicus* vol. 3 (1725). However, this can now with some certainty be laid to rest. In the 1980s Gervase Jackson-Stops did extensive work on the house archives and found a payment in 1631 to 'Cartor surveyor'. He plausibly suggested that this referred to Jones's deputy surveyor *Edward Carter** and the attribution is now accepted in the literature (e.g. Colvin, Worsley, etc.). The S front is of two storeys, i.e. lower than the rest of the house, and ashlar-faced. It is nine bays wide with a wide tripartite and pedimented centre and the end bays a little projecting. All along the façade there is articulation by pilasters or attached columns, Tuscan with three bands of rocky rustication below, slender unfluted Ionic above. The centre has in addition an archway with segmental head and the same bands of rocky rustication, niches to its l. and r., and, on the first floor, a Venetian window also with niches l. and r. Another Venetian window in the E wall of the chapel at the SE corner. The Venetian window was an innovation in England at that time. Inigo Jones had used it for the first time in the Queen's Chapel in London in 1623. The

---

Country Life, 30 January 1986.

foot-line of the top pediment recedes slightly above the Venetian window. To the l. and r. of the pediment balustrade with
lettering. It reads 'Dominus custodiat introitum tuum'. On the
inside of the screen building the text is 'Dominus custodiat
exitum tuum'. This balustrade lettering is a speciality of Castle
Ashby, and more will be said of it later.

The internal front of the building is identical with the external except that it is only seven bays wide, because the last bays
disappear behind the stair-turrets of *c.* 1574, and that it has
attached columns throughout, also where the s façade has
pilasters. Campbell illustrates a scheme for the whole s front
according to which it was to have been extended with a system
of pilasters to the faces of the E and W wings and to have
replaced the – still brand-new – balustrade with its quaint lettering by a plain balustrade and a plain parapet. It should be
noted that the 2nd Earl of Northampton, who succeeded in
1630 and died in 1643, was closely attached to the Court,
having accompanied Charles on his adventurous trip to Spain
in 1623. The ground floor of the screen range is filled by a
loggia open to the courtyard. The s wall has niches with pediments on Tuscan pilasters.

The motif of a screen wall across the entrance side of a
COURTYARD is French in origin (Bury), but had been adopted
by the Elizabethans and Jacobeans and occurs in Northamp-
tonshire also at Rushton and, long before Castle Ashby, at
Kirby. Again in the usual way the hall range of the Elizabethan
Castle Ashby was the range facing the screen, i.e. the N range.
The three ranges were originally two-storeyed, except for the
Hall, which rises through both. The windows are mullioned
and transomed. Those in the ground floor in the hall range
have two transoms, all others one. The first window from the
W is smaller, and there is a small doorway below it with a four-
centred head. There are six bays on the W, five on the E side.
On the W side in the centre is a later C17 doorway with an oval
opening above, placed vertically. Shortly before 1624 a third
storey was added with windows of a different design, in a different rhythm and with a top balustrade on which one can read
these lines from Psalm 127: 'Nisi dominus custos custodiverit
domum frustra vigilat qui custodit eam. Nisi dominus aedifi-
caverit domum in vanum laboraverunt qui aedificant eam
1624'. The idea of openwork inscriptions on parapets is probably French. It occurs in the apse of the church of La Ferté-
Bernard in 1535–44. In England other examples are Felbrigg
Hall in Norfolk (*c.* 1600), Temple Newsam (*c.* 1630) and,
somewhat later, the gatehouse at Skipton Castle in Yorkshire
(*c.* 1660). It is worth noting that at Skipton the work was put
in hand by Lady Anne Clifford, whose second daughter was
the wife of the 3rd Earl of Northampton. The SE and SW stair-
turrets were also heightened between 1624 and 1635, and one
of them has the last date at the top.

Now for the external faces of the three wings. The EAST
FAÇADE is a composite job. It is ashlar-faced, while the rest of

the façade is of rubble. Starting with the Elizabethan work near the N end, the two big bay windows here correspond in their two-transomed upper parts with the Elizabethan Great Chamber. There follows to the S a ten-bay part, 1624–35, which had on the ground floor originally an open loggia like Burghley, Longford Castle, Cranborne, Audley End and other Elizabethan and Jacobean houses. The loggia was of five wide bays, the arches separated by coupled diamond-banded pilasters with a niche between. The motif of the niches repeats on the upper floors, separating pairs of windows from each other. The whole of this part of the façade is stylistically a transition from the Jacobean to the Jonesian. The loggia was infilled in 1691 to create further rooms on the ground floor. The NORTH FAÇADE, i.e. the N side of the hall range, originally had a recessed centre corresponding to the N wall of the hall and offices, and projecting wings. *William Talman* provided a scheme in 1695, but that was not accepted and the centre was filled in in 1719–22. The former E wing remains, with a bay window and the large, six-light, two-transomed N window of the Great Chamber. The corresponding W bay window is an addition made for symmetry's sake in 1719–22. The new centre has five bays. Open stairs to the doorway. All windows segment-headed, but curiously enough still with mullion-and-transom crosses. Below the parapet horizontal oval openings, another conservative motif. No designer is recorded, just a mason, *Nixon*. The thin, plain pilasters either side of the central bay and the slightly ungainly effect show similarities with *John Lumley*'s contemporary Westmorland Building façade at Cambridge. The lettered parapets here and on the W range were added in 1827.

The Elizabethan WEST SIDE must have been quite informal. Only the N and S ends are part of it. The rest was recessed and filled in about 1630–5. The fenestration is conservative and irregular because of the W staircase behind. The two small single-storey wings projecting from the N and S corners were built at the same time as the N front (1719–22), the N wing providing extra kitchen accommodation. A RIDING SCHOOL (now the estate office) and extensive stables form the courtyard. All are Late Jacobean with mullion-and-transom windows.

The INTERIOR must be described chronologically. All that remains of Elizabethan interiors is the rib-vaulted UNDERCROFT of the hall and the Great Chamber (N range centre and NE corner). It looks decidedly older than 1574. Of *c.* 1630–6 is first of all the splendid plaster ceiling of the Great Chamber (first floor, NE corner), known as THE KING WILLIAM ROOM. The plasterer was *James Leigh*, master plasterer to the Office of Works, who also worked at Hatfield. It is no longer strictly Jacobean: that is, the main division is panels with frames in strong relief, though the cartouches etc. in the panels still exhibit strapwork. Pretty coving with allegorical figures in cartouches. The tremendously elaborate chimneypiece is of about the same time but comes from Canonbury House, London.

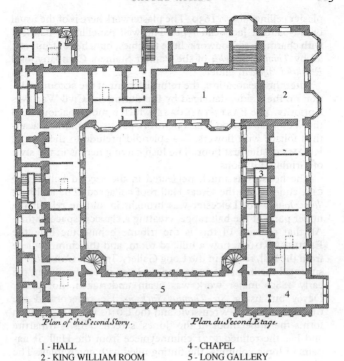

Plan of the Second Story.   Plan du Second Etage.

1 - HALL	4 - CHAPEL
2 - KING WILLIAM ROOM	5 - LONG GALLERY
3 - EAST STAIRCASE	6 - WEST STAIRCASE

Castle Ashby House.
First floor plan as shown by Colen Campbell

There are six small allegorical figures in the overmantel and
two larger caryatids l. and r. of the fireplace opening. Everything ornamental is overcrowded. Nothing here strikes one as
post-Jacobean. The date of the chimneypiece is indeed 1601.
The panelling and door frames of the room are later C17. Of
c. 1630 the OLD LIBRARY, in the SE corner on the second
floor. This has a plaster ceiling by *Leigh*, in the same style as
the Great Chamber, though, in accordance with the lower
proportion of the room, the relief is less bold. But the combination of semi-classical framing with strapwork continues. Again
of similar date the WEST STAIRCASE. It runs through all
storeys. Its style harmonizes with that of the other two rooms.
It has openwork panels, a motif more characteristic of the
second than the first half of the century; they are not yet filled
with acanthus foliage (*see* East Staircase, below), but with
strapwork. This motif occurs at Radclive, Bucks., in 1621, and
at Cromwell House, Highgate, London, in 1637–8. The posts
are square and end in Jacobean pendants below but in plain
balls above. On the ground floor in the W range at its S end is
the BOWER, a charming cabinet with panelled walls and a

plaster ceiling, also *c.* 1630. The plasterwork here is of the usual broad-banded Jacobean type. The wall panelling is painted, with charming ribbonwork, little trophies, bunches of fruit, etc. all by *Thomas Knight*, of the Painter Stainers Company, and *Rowland Buckett*, gilder.

After the Restoration, the refurbishment of the accommodation on the E side, damaged by fire during the Civil War, was a priority. The EAST STAIRCASE, which is more spacious than the West Staircase and has openwork panels of luxuriant acanthus foliage with flowers, is a splendid prelude to the STATE ROOMS on the first floor. The lush carving here is in the style of Grinling Gibbons.

The house was much neglected in the second half of the C18, and in 1771 the Great Hall roof collapsed. The architect *John Johnson* of Leicester was brought in and he rebuilt the upper parts of the hall range, creating a classical space within. All that remains of this is the tribune behind the hall, the FIGURES ROOM, now a billiard room, and the chimneypiece from the hall, resited in the Long Gallery. In 1876 *George Devey* surveyed the hall roof again and declared it unsafe, and in the early 1880s major work was again undertaken, not under Devey but using *Sir Thomas Jackson*. He redecorated the CHAPEL in a Neo-Wren style and the LONG GALLERY which forms the upper floor of the 'Jones' screen. This is tripartite and has the refined 1771 chimneypiece from the Hall. It has pairs of Ionic columns, the fluting filled with green inlay. The HALL was redecorated in Jacobean manner in 1884 by *Gabriel Wade*. Genuine only the chimneypiece, dated 1599, brought from Canonbury like that in the King William Room (*see* above). One further room should be noted, THE CHINESE BEDROOM, on the W side, redecorated *c.* 1870 by *E. W. Godwin*, and still intact with green lacquered woodwork and a ceramic fireplace with fish dragons.

Much is to be seen in the gardens and outbuildings. Close by the Jacobean stables an imperious Victorian WATER TOWER, built in 1865, designed by *Sir Matthew Digby Wyatt*, who had known the Comptons since the 1840s. The great avenues in the grounds were laid out immediately after the visit of William III, which took place in 1695. Specially spectacular the wide and long SOUTH AVENUE, which ends towards the house with wide GATES. They were designed by *Digby Wyatt* and are dated 1865. The spectacular piers are of terracotta from *J. M. Blashfield*, a material much favoured by Digby Wyatt. The style is derived from the Certosa of Pavia or similar Lombard work. The elaborate iron gates are said to have come from Italy.

On the E side of the house are elaborate TERRACES. The layout was originally created in 1695 by *George London*, and his ornamental parterre appears on a view of the front drawn by Peter Tillemans in 1719. Their form today is that of the 1860s designed by *Digby* W*yatt*, using the garden designer *W. B. Thomas*, with *Blashfield* terracotta forming the balustrade to the E and N. This has inscriptions on the pattern of the

Jacobean inscriptions of the house. One of them says 'The grass withereth and the flower fadeth but the word of God standeth for ever', the other 'Consider the lilies of the field how they grow they toil not neither do they spin but yet I say unto you that Solomon in all his glory was not arrayed like one of these'. Theodosia, 3rd Marchioness, died in November 1864 while the work was under way and the balustrade touchingly records 'begun in hope, finished in despair'. There is further terracotta work in the form of urns, basins, etc. (The lettered balustrades have been largely removed for safety reasons and are in store awaiting restoration at the time of writing.)

To the s of the churchyard is the ITALIAN GARDEN, formed in the early 1870s. At its entrance the tall brick façade of *Talman*'s Orangery of 1695, topped by *Coade* stone pineapples. The large free-Italianate ORANGERY by *Digby Wyatt*, 1870–2. It is thirteen bays long with raised arched centre and end bays. Balustrading throughout. Above the three middle bays a *Blashfield* terracotta frieze. The centre represents the sacrifice of Iphigenia, the two ends Bacchanalian, and the circles contain figures representing the Elements. Aisled interior. The pool surround was designed by *William Burges*, 1875. Facing the Orangery to the s at some distance a SCREEN or gloriette of nine arched bays with the centre arch raised and fronted on the s by glasshouses by *Clarke and Hope* of Birmingham 1868–9. Beyond again the walls of the very large KITCHEN GARDEN by *E. W. Godwin*, who worked on the garden 1868–70. In the walls an unusual BEE HOUSE having alcoves ready for bee-boles. There is also an early C19 CAMELIA HOUSE.

As for the wider landscape, *Robert Adam* provided a plan in 1760, but the work was finally entrusted to *Capability Brown* who worked here from 1761 till 1774. Of his time remain the DAIRY, immediately NW of the house, with a wooden veranda and a horizontally placed oval in the parapet; the BRIDGE, with a terracotta balustrade of *c.* 1868; and the pretty MENAGERIE TEMPLE on the far side of the park to the NE, with a semicircular centre, four columns and a semi-dome. There is also a well-preserved ICE HOUSE of the Brown period in the park. Then to the w of the village in their own valley are the ENGINE POND and ENGINE HOUSE. Built of courses of limestone and ironstone with a simple front with two oval window recesses and the date 1737. Its origin is earlier, from when *Samuel* and *Thomas Warren* first constructed an engine to carry water up to the house (*see* Introduction p. 49).

It remains to record four lodges. One *c.* 1820 at the w edge of the village, at the head of the Grendon Road lakes which, although proposed by Brown, were actually dug during the Napoleonic Wars. It is called the BRICKYARD LODGE, since it was opposite the estate brickmaking works. On the s edge of the park, on the A428, an ENTRANCE SCREEN (1868) across the South Avenue, by *E. W. Godwin*, in his best French Renaissance manner, and also by him, on the N side of the park, at the end of a carriage drive, facing the road to Earls Barton and the former railway station, the picturesque STATION LODGE (1869), with a tall wide-arched entrance and a small circular turret. Finally on the E boundary of the Brown landscape is NEVITT'S LODGE, a charming *cottage orné*, with a very twiggy veranda, which marks the start of a carriage drive laid out by the 1st Marquess after he had purchased the neighbouring Easton Maudit Estate in 1801 (*see also* Easton Maudit for another *cottage orné*). Associated with this drive is the nearby KNUCKLEBONE ARBOUR, a small, rustic, thatched rotunda with bark-covered columns, whose floor is made up partly with pebbles and partly sheep knucklebones.

CATESBY

LOWER CATESBY was the site of a small Cistercian priory founded *c.* 1175. It was dissolved in 1536, and the remains of its buildings were purchased by John Onley whose son converted parts of them into a a sizeable Jacobean mansion with its own chapel. It was demolished in 1860.

ST MARY, close to the site of the priory church. 1861–2 by *W. Gillett* of Leicester. The style is C17 with three-light arched square-headed windows. Elaborate timber porch and tiny dormers instead of a clerestory. Arch-braced roof inside. The SEDILIA and PISCINA with crocketed gables and pinnacles are original and of *c.* 1300. – C17 furnishings from the chapel of

Catesby Priory.
Drawing by G. Clarke, *c.* 1850

the house: big Jacobean PULPIT with tester. – Also Jacobean
panels in the PEWS and the READER'S DESK. – COMMUNION
RAIL. with strong twisted balusters; late C17. – STAINED GLASS.
Mixed C14–C15 fragments in the W window (the Virgin and
Saints). The 1862 glass by *W. Holland* of Warwick now some-
what faded. Nave S window of 1897 by *J. Powell & Sons*.

COTTAGES, N of the church. A C17 row of four which looks as if
it had been built as almshouses. Mullioned windows with
arched lights.

Former STABLES, SE of the church. Large, red brick, 1890s. Striking if somewhat bizarre. Three-bay central section with arched
glazed doors, gables above with the central one having a clock.
Tall pyramidal roof with a pointed turret on top. Lower side
wings with dormers. They belonged to CATESBY HOUSE,
which is wonderfully set on a terrace overlooking the valley.
Mock Elizabethan mansion with shaped gables, built in 1863
and extended in 1894. From the C17 house comes the fine
staircase with strong twisted balusters and the panelling in one
room. Linenfold panelling in the staircase hall may have come
from the priory itself.

OLD CHURCHYARD, Upper Catesby. Obelisk Monument with
a bulbous base to John Parkhurst, 1765. The ball on top
was originally gilt. STONE HOUSE, E of the churchyard, Victorian ironstone with some decorative brickwork. Its doorway
is a reused C13 piece. Two orders of shafts and three roll
mouldings.

Running under Catesby is the former TUNNEL of the Great
Central Railway, opened in 1899. Of a mile, the longest on the
line. Closed in 1966 but its portals are visible. About ½ m. N
is a VIADUCT over the River Leam of twelve blue brick arches.

CHACOMBE   4040

ST PETER AND ST PAUL. Essentially Dec, but over-restored in
1856. The arcades are original and interesting. They are low,
of three bays, and although their piers are octagonal, the capitals are quatrefoil and typically Dec. Double-chamfered arches.
Slight differences between the two arcades. Again, though the
windows are all renewed outside, the continuous filleted
moulding of the jambs inside accredits them and gives them
status. Their forms are of *c.* 1300–30 (cusped lights and a
cinquefoiled niche, reticulation, etc. and nearly all with ogee
tops externally). C14 chancel arch with continuous chamfers.
Mortice marks for a tympanum. C14 opening above the arch
giving light before the chancel was heightened. The S porch,
whose entrance arch is clearly Dec, has its stone roof supported on two big single-chamfered transverse arches (cf. Middleton Cheney). The W tower is C15. A post-medieval blocked
doorway at the W end of the N aisle may have given access to

an early vestry or school room. – SEDILIA and PISCINA. Just a low seat in the window embrasure on both sides of the chancel. The piscina with a trefoil head. – FONT. Circular, Norman, with intersected arches. – SOUTH DOOR. Battened and with ironwork, ascribed as c. 1300–25. – PEWS, mid-C19. Not original to the church but brought in from Holy Trinity church, Cambridge. They replaced decayed box pews. – WALL PAINTING. Late medieval. Martyrdom of St Peter, on the splay of a square-headed window at the E end of the N aisle. Discovered and conserved 1982–3. – STAINED GLASS. Chancel E by *Clayton & Bell*, 1920–5. – BRASS. Michael Fox †1567. Inscription plate not completed, so the date not fully filled in. Another plate representing the Trinity and two shields, one the arms of the City of London, the other the Grocer's Company (chancel, N side, in the floor, c. 8 in. (20 cm.) in size).

WESLEYAN CHAPEL, Wesley Place. 1873, Geometric Gothic in brick and stone with a large window with a quatrefoil head in its W wall and smaller windows either side of the central doorway. Two light windows in the side walls.

There was a PRIORY of Augustinian canons at Chacombe, founded in the mid C12. Nothing is known about its exact site, but the house called The Priory has, to the N of its E end, a short building known as the Chapel which is medieval. It has on its ground floor a plain doorway and a two-light window, both apparently late C13, and on its upper floor a two-light window with cusped ogee lights. The house otherwise has a big Elizabethan porch with a balustrade of vertically symmetrical balusters near the top, interrupted at the corners by spiral-fluted shafts, and a top cresting of a pair of S-curves. To the l. and r. four bays and an outer bay all apparently Georgian. The staircase is late C17. It is reached past two wooden Corinthian pilasters and has massive twisted balusters. There was a fire c. 1910 and restoration and some new work was done by *F. B. Ward*. Ponds to the N may be of medieval origin. The moat is probably C18 landscaping. The site was acquired by Michael Fox following the Dissolution and the manor remained with that family till 1810.

CHAPEL BRAMPTON

Attractive ironstone village, with Althorp Estate MODEL COTTAGES of 1848 by *Edward Blore* (*see also* Church Brampton) on the A5199. Also two distinctive houses (Nos. 30–31 Welford Road) c. 1860–70, with free-hanging timber gable trusses, possibly part of the work that *Devey & Williams* were doing on the estate at that time. CEDAR HYTHE is a small housing estate by *R. H. Stobbs*, 1967–71. Nicely grouped monopitch roofs, still looking fresh and interesting. Just by the cross-roads a good ironstone house with a large arched opening within its gable and workshop window alongside which was once the blacksmith's forge.

CHARLTON

INDEPENDENT CHAPEL, Main Street. 1827. Simple, with arched windows and pedimental gable.

THE COTTAGE, opposite. The name derives from the first house which F. E. Smith (later Earl of Birkenhead) acquired in 1907. This was enlarged over the next two years and then in 1911–12 the building was redrafted following the acquisition of the adjoining cottage, and the infilling of the gap between the two with a tall block containing a grand library. The front façade was created and the garden side revised by *Alan James*. The façade has a three-bay centre with giant angle pilasters and a pedimented doorway, the whole in a revived late C17 style. The doorway was blocked and a new entrance porch formed on the r. in 1960. The garden side is more irregular with three gables at the N end and two at the S and a veranda. There are dates for 1911 and 1929. F. E. Smith was a central figure in the legal world of the early C20 and rose to be Lord Chancellor. He was created Earl of Birkenhead in 1919. The visitor list at Charlton contains many of the leading figures of the political, literary and artistic circles of the day, including figures like George VI (when Duke of York), Churchill, Cecil Beaton and Munnings. In the garden a charming seat resting on two elephants as a memorial to Robin Birkenhead (*see* below).

CHARLTON LODGE, at the S end of Main Street on the E side. Victorian Gothic; gabled, asymmetrical around a tower and spirelet. Just SW of the Lodge is HOLLY HOUSE, a Georgian farmhouse with a good S front of c. 1790, the date on a water pipe. Rendered of three bays and two storeys, central round-arched doorway and window above. Pediment with a circle.

CEMETERY. Tiny Gothic CHAPEL of 1903. – F. E. Smith, Earl of Birkenhead, †1930. Altar tomb by *Lutyens*, carved by *Broadbent*. Similar to the Wimborne tomb at Ashby St Ledgers. Chest with circles set on a coved base. – Robin, Earl of Birkenhead †1985. Obelisk cenotaph, incised decoration with at the sides a lion and a griffin.

CHARWELTON

HOLY TRINITY. Remote in the fields, far E of the village. Big Dec ashlar W tower. Chancel mostly of 1901–4. Good Dec N arcade of three bays with tall piers continued straight into the arches. Two piers have wave-chamfered projections to the four sides. Lower and rather coarse s arcade with octagonal piers and double-chamfered arches. Perp s porch, two-storeyed, the lower coarsely rib-vaulted. But the s aisle w window of three steeply stepped lancet lights seems to be of *c.* 1300. Internally there are marks of two arches, one nearer the E end and the other above the doorway to the porch upper room. RCHME suggest that the easternmost opened into a s chapel, or are they signs of previous windows? Prior to 1900 the church had box pews and a w gallery (photographs in the church) but in 1901–4 the CHANCEL was rebuilt by *George C. Carter* and the interior refitted and this makes it rather special. Externally the rebuilding is clear, with brick tile relieving arches over the reshaped windows, that at the E end having carved reliefs with angels and insignia. Fine foliate scroll guttering. Internally the chancel was panelled and the E end lettered by *Eric Gill*. Darkening of the wood makes it difficult now to see. The altar, with carved panels of grapes, and the two brass chandeliers are 1904. A lectern was added, both given and carved by the *Rev. A. Hemsted c.* 1920, in memory of his son killed in the First World War. The whole ensemble is excellent. – PEWS. Brought in in 1973 from Emscote Lawn church, Leamington, Warks. (dem.). A forest of poppyheads and pierced backs. They were designed by *G. F. Bodley*. – FONT. Octagonal, with square stem. On bowl and stem closely scattered individual leaves and flowers. Is this C15 work or C17? – PULPIT. With Jacobean parts. – COMMUNION RAIL. With slender dumb-bell balusters, *c.* 1700. – MONUMENTS. Brasses to Thomas Andrewe †1496 and wife, good 4-ft (1.2-metres) figures; to the wife of Thomas Andrewe †1490 (he died *c.* 1530; 3 ft (0.9-metres) figure); and to Thomas Andrewes †1541 and wife (2 ft 1 in.; 0.6-metres). – Sir Thomas Andrew †1564 and two wives attributed to *Thomas Parker* of Burton upon Trent. His first wife Katharine was a Cave of Stanford, so compare the Parker monument there. A splendid tomb of alabaster with some remains of colour. Free-standing tomb-chest with shields, some in roundels, separated by pilasters with flat baluster decoration, typical of Parker's workshop. At the foot end shield with kneeling children l. and r. Three good recumbent effigies. He is shown bearded and wearing an SS collar with a rose pendant. The two ladies look remarkably alike, but they have different cushions. The tomb was conserved in 2001 by *Carol Galvin*. – Sir Thomas Andrew and family. An outstanding relief of fine white stone. The centre is a relief with twelve figures, mostly kneeling. The attitudes are well rendered, especially sensitively in the standing smaller children on the l. side. Tapering caryatids l. and r. Inscription below and, to its l. and r., roundels with profiles. The whole monument looks rather more 1570–80 than 1590, which is the date on it. It is one of a series of very similar mural monuments attributable to the *Hollemans* workshop (cf. Harrington, Nether Heyford, Welford and Thorpe Mandeville).

MANOR HOUSE, s of the church. A most attractive fine house of five bays and two storeys; ironstone; hipped roof. The façade probably early C18. Two ranges of outbuildings in front at right angles, so looking rather Palladian in effect. Inside much early C16 panelling with the initials and coat of arms of Sir Thomas Andrew and his wife Katharine (†1555) and other ornamentation like various animals. It is very similar to the panelling at Abington Abbey, Northampton (q.v.). Also a fireplace of c. 1620, and a fine late C17 baluster staircase. Behind a stone SUMMERHOUSE with a pyramid roof. Both house and church were originally surrounded by a village which had been depopulated to allow the breeding of sheep by the late C15. Some platforms and a hollow way can be traced.

PACKHORSE BRIDGE, on the W side of the A361. Only 3 ft (0.9 metres) wide. Medieval with two pointed arches; one cutwater.

CHARWELTON HALL (on the A361). C18 with framed windows, altered in C19. Good baluster staircase.

CHAPEL OF THE GOOD SHEPHERD, Church Street. Former Wesleyan chapel, 1887. Extended 1931. – MURAL. Nativity by *Henry Bird*, 1985.

MANOR FARM NURSERIES, ½ m. W. In the grounds, three corrugated iron SHEDS formerly used by the Park Gate Iron & Steel Co. for the transport of iron stone from nearby quarries to the Great Central Railway. It operated between 1919 and 1963.

CHELVESTON

ST JOHN THE BAPTIST. Mostly C13. The tower stands on the N side. It has blank arcading at ground level to the N and double lancet bell-openings under a single semicircular arch. They are a little cramped under the battlements, so the top of the tower was probably rebuilt and lowered slightly at some post-medieval date. The buttress arrangement, with set-back, then clasping, is worth noting. S doorway also C13 with shafts. The porch, with its simple round-arch opening, was rebuilt 1685. Open light, limewashed interior, made more open by a reordering in the late 1970s when the chancel furnishings were removed. The arcades have C14 four bays with octagonal piers and double-chamfered arches. The detailing suggests that the S arcade is slightly later than the N. S aisle windows of three lights with intersecting tracery. The N aisle was reinstated in 1849–50 by *E. F. Law*, having been removed at some unknown date, though the arcade remained within the wall. The last bay of the S aisle has a transverse arch into the aisle, creating a transept-like chapel. The C13 arch opening into the base of the tower remains, so there is a similar effect on the N side. The clerestory, a series of lancets, though restored, is also C13. The E and W windows are large Perp, that at the W having externally evidence of a trio of lancets on either side. The chancel E wall was rebuilt and the chancel shortened, and when the church was restored in 1909 (by *Talbot Brown & Fisher*) a double PISCINA was found. The lancet immediately above it was also reinstated at the same time. The N wall rather oddly has no windows. The two front BENCHES with traceried ends must be of 1909. – STAINED GLASS. Nave N window by *Shrigley & Hunt*, 1894.

VILLAGE HALL (former SCHOOL and SCHOOL HOUSE). Gothic, 1864–5 by *E. F. Law*.

CHIPPING WARDEN

ST PETER AND ST PAUL. One of the finest churches in the county. Mostly Dec and Perp. The chancel is early C14, with its three-light windows with richly detailed intersected tracery. The E window of four lights is Early Perp (two-centred arch, ogee details). Lowside window of before 1300. It is of two lights separated by a shaft and has pointed-trefoiled lights and a quatrefoil pierced through the spandrel. In all probability it is re-set. Dec S aisle windows of strange varieties of tracery developed from reticulation set rather widely. The N aisle windows are again different, but equally unusual. They culminate in a large circle with a wheel of four mouchettes. The E window is ogee-shaped and a version of reticulated, but the shapes in the tracery are subdivided by horizontal bars. Externally the N aisle has a frieze of heads and ball-flowers. The most interesting element however is the arcades inside. They are probably of the same date as the E window, i.e. Early Perp, but still with memories of the Dec, although they could be as late as the W tower, which is definitely Perp. They are tall and wide, of four bays, separating a wide nave from wide aisles. The piers consist of four main shafts and four subsidiary shafts, all with such broad fillets that they are more than fillets. The arches are many-moulded, and the bases and capitals are overloaded with mouldings. W tower, fully Perp. Its doorway has one order of fleurons and a crocketed ogee hoodmould. Damaged stoup on its N side. Niches with tiny vaults either side of the window. Battlements and pinnacles. In the S aisle SEDILIA and PISCINA with shafts with fillets and a hollow moulding with fragments of dogtooth. The chancel poses a further problem. On the S side of the chancel, outside, the wall is very disturbed, and one can recognize traces of a small C12 round-headed doorway. On the N side are two tall blocked round arches, one of them cut into by the chancel arch, probably rear arches of windows of the C12, so indicating that at that time the chancel extended further W. Behind this wall a vestry consisting of two rooms, one E of the other, but with W walls to both which may possibly not be medieval. In the W room is a Perp window and in the

s wall a PISCINA set on a moulded stem, and in the E room a
Dec E window. The division of the two rooms is not axial with
the blank arches inside. Corbels on the s wall of the w room
show that it originally had a separate gabled roof.

– FONT. Octagonal, carved with a rose, a thistle and a
fleur-de-lys, probably of the 1660s. – PULPIT with back panel
and tester, open BENCHES, and BOX PEWS in raised tiers at
the w end facing E. They would appear to be C18, but the pulpit
has clearly been rearranged and its stair has distinctive metal
ornaments, so there is clear evidence of some tidying up, and
work is recorded here 1902–4 by *G. Christopher Carter* and
Owen Little. In 1909 Little returned and did some rearranging
of the seating. – CHANCEL PANELLING. Made of C18 pew
ends, so again indicating some later rearrangement of the furnishings. – The REREDOS appears to have a stone frame of the
C15, but this is inset with a wooden shelf supported on pillars
with geometric inlay of 1901. – RAILS. Early C18. – SCREENS
at the back of the aisles, C18 with spiked rail. – NAVE ROOF.
Of C15 date, though much repaired. – SHELF, of stone, N of
the altar, embattled, on a good head corbel of a king, C14. –
AUMBRY with a door dated 1627. – Some excellent Art
Nouveau metalwork, e.g bronze eagle LECTERN of 1902, in the
style of Henry Wilson, and Celtic ALTAR CROSS, CANDLE-
STICKS and VASES, brass, all by *John Williams*, 1901. – WALL
PAINTING. Part of a late C16 text surround in the N aisle. –
ROYAL ARMS. Stuart period. – STAINED GLASS. Very fine E
window of 1903 by *Christopher Whall*. – BRASS to William
Smarte, Rector, †1468, chancel floor, a 13 in. (33 cm.) figure.
Near the church a green, which holds the base of a MARKET
CROSS on five steps. COURT HOUSE, Mill Lane. A good stone
house of four bays with a C19 Tudor style porch. Remains of
mullioned windows in its E gable end. The interior has C18
panelling and a staircase with turned balusters. Mill Lane ends
with a small LODGE with bargeboards and ball-topped GATE-
PIERS on the field road to Edgcote House.

MANOR HOUSE, E of the church. An intriguing house whose
development is not fully understood. It is basically a double
pile with service wings at the rear. A thick spine wall suggests
early origins and there is a surviving Tudor four-centred arched
fireplace on the first floor. There are two dates known: 1659
and 1668, and decoration inside the house fits well within
these. The main front, formerly entrance and now garden, was
on the s side through a square porch. The house is two storeys
of dark local ironstone but the porch is asymmetrically placed
with two bays on the l. and three on the r. Cross-mullion-
transom windows and a flat parapet. The w side has two later
canted bays. The E side is irregular with a lower later tower-like
projection. The porch leads into the original hall, now the
drawing room, which has panelling with slightly odd details
but of a kind associated with those sequence of houses built
in the Cromwellian period of which Thorpe Hall, Peterborough is the obvious example. The r. section of the front houses

Chipping Warden, Manor House.
Drawing by G. Clarke, *c.* 1850

a parlour with a fine plaster ceiling divided into compartments each with a wreath of fruit, again typical of the Thorpe Hall series. Simple panelling with moulded edges. Behind is the staircase of some magnificence. Newels with pierced ogival finials and decoratively carved splat balustrades. It rises right to the top of the house into what are now attics but it must have gone to something of more importance, possibly a roof-walk. Bridges records there were good gardens and there is still a small water canal to the SE of the house. In one bedroom there is a wooden fireplace totally in the Thorpe Hall tradition with side scrolls to both fireplace and overmantel and heavy garlands. Another room has an original mid-C17 landscape overmantel painting. The first floor otherwise is odd as it has what appears to be original plasterwork but of a form suggesting that what is now a sequence of rooms was one long room, though hardly a gallery. There are also throughout the house a number of changes of floor level which add to the intricacies of the layout. The kitchen was originally the room behind the hall. The rear service wings are now of two storeys but their stone mullioned windows on the ground floor suggest they started as single-storey ranges, being heightened in the C18. Although they have an Elizabethan air they are almost certainly mid-C17. Their roofs have the same little finials as appear on the main block.

The mid-C17 house must have been built for Richard Saltonstall (†1688). His great-grandfather was Sir Richard Saltonstall of Essex who was Lord Mayor of London in 1598, but nothing is known about Richard himself. His father (†1649) was knighted but is also a mystery figure. The Saltonstalls held the manor till the early C18 when a daughter married George

Montagu, later 2nd Earl of Halifax, and their daughter married
Frederic, 3rd Baron North of Wroxton Abbey, near Banbury,
and the house was then let, being finally sold in the 1920s.

ARBURY BANKS. Just S of the village, on the W side of the road
to Wardington (Oxon), lies an extensive ditch and bank. The
monument is roughly circular and measures *c.* 600 ft (183
metres) in diameter, with an entrance to the SE. It is presumed
to be an Iron Age hillfort.

CHURCH BRAMPTON 7060

ST BOTOLPH. An attractive-looking church, but less important
due to over-restoration in 1861 and considerable renewing of
the reticulated window tracery in recent years. The S porch
entrance with shafts and waterleaf capitals looks early C13,
otherwise the church, including the W tower, is mostly Dec.
Four-bay arcades inside with octagonal piers and double-
chamfered arches. The chancel arch has triple shafts and sunk
quadrant mouldings but the chancel was rebuilt in 1859–60 by
E. F. Law. Organ chamber also by Law, 1882. – ROYAL ARMS.
Over the S doorway, of Edward III, genuine C14, carved stone,
found during the restoration. – CHEST. Fine with decorative
ironwork, scrolls etc. *c.* 1325–50. – STAINED GLASS. Nave N.
Much decayed mythical beast, C15 or C16. – Chancel E, 1880
possibly by *Ward & Hughes.* – S aisle SE and N aisle NE by
J. Hardman & Co., 1876. – CROSS. Part of shaft and trefoil-
headed finial, C14.

Former RECTORY, just below the church. 1854 by *G. E. Pritchett*
of Bishop's Stortford. Ironstone of irregular form with two
gabled wings and tall chimneystacks.

ALMSHOUSES. 1858, built for Earl Spencer by his estate builder,
John Wykes. Neo-Tudor, gabled. The much more substantial
gabled Neo-Tudor Althorp ESTATE COTTAGES are dated 1848
but built 1844–51, the designs by *Edward Blore* (cf. Chapel
Brampton).

THE COTTAGE, Church Lane. Fine late C16 house with mullioned windows with arched heads. Sensitive C19 additions in
the same manner. Between Church and Chapel Brampton
HALFWAY THORN COTTAGES. Brick, designed by *Josiah
Mander*, surveyor for Lord Spencer, 1870s.

CHURCH STOWE 6050
Stowe-Nine-Churches

ST MICHAEL. Tall Saxon W tower. The early date is recognizable
externally by the lesenes on the bell-stage to the W and E and

one W window, inside by the arch towards the nave with its unmistakable blocks standing for both capitals and abaci of the responds and the remains of the equally unmistakable band along the arch and the jambs running at a distance from the opening. Above is a blocked round-headed Saxon opening, visible from inside the tower. In the W wall a blocked square-headed doorway. The piece of Saxon interlace at the NW corner externally is not *in situ*. It is rendered externally with a date in pebbles of 1775. Small Norman N doorway. E.E. S doorway with dogtooth in the hoodmould. The aisle windows survive from a partial rebuilding in 1639. Square headed of three lights. The E end was rebuilt in 1860 by *P. C. Hardwick* and the rest heavily restored by *Edmund Law* in 1895 producing a rather stark interior. – SCREEN. Jacobean, to the S chapel. With arches on balusters. – REREDOS. Made up in 1971 of Early Renaissance(?) domestic panelling. – MONUMENTS. Effigy of a cross-legged knight on a slab tapering like a coffin-lid. Purbeck marble; extremely fine quality. The effigy unusual in that he has closed eyes and he holds one arm across his chest, while the other holds his shield. His sword is hung behind him so that only its tip appears. Said to represent Sir Gerard de l'Isle †*c*. 1287. – Elizabeth Lady Carey, by *Nicholas Stone*, 1617–20. An extremely early case of the post-Jacobean style, and carved as beautifully as the best Dutch monuments of the time. Free-standing tomb-chest. Black-and-white marble. The white effigy is very realistic, yet not lacking in dignity. Lady Carey lies as if asleep, her dress beautifully represented and one of her slippers peeping from beneath it. For almost the first time in English sculpture she is represented as an old lady not in the prime of life. The monument was put up in her lifetime. She died in 1630. It is one of the greatest masterpieces of its age. – Dr Thomas Turner, President of Corpus Christi College, Oxford, †1714. Signed by *Thomas Stayner*. Huge standing monument. Inscription, long, Latin, and laudatory, in the middle, below a baldacchino with opened draperies. The lettering engraved across the folds. Big segmental pediment on fluted pilasters. To the l. and r. two life-size figures, the President and Fides. He stands on a terrestrial globe, she on a celestial. He is not buried here but the memorial records the fact that his fortune purchased the manor as funding for the Corporation of the Sons of the Clergy charity. This monument had originally been placed on the N side of the chancel and was moved to the chapel in 1860, which accounts for its cramped situation. – John Daye †1757 by *John Middleton* of Towcester. Architectural tablet with curly open pediment. Corinthian pilasters and cherubs at the base.

Former SCHOOL and SCHOOL HOUSE S of the church in Main Street. 1867 by *E. F. Law*. Gothic with different patterns of stone decoration and the usual bellcote.

MANOR FARMHOUSE, formerly Manor House, NE of the church. C16, altered later. A long irregular S front with central projection with arched windows. C18 N front. Evidence of an open

hall house with early timbers in the roof. DOVECOTE, CI7 or
CI8.
WYNDHAM HOUSE, former rectory, SW of the church. Described
as new in 1735, but of CI6 origin, of which a mullioned window
survives. The Georgian entrance front was refenestrated in the
early CI9 when two two-storey bay windows were added on
both N and S elevations. The upper storey of the S bow is later
and of yellow brick. Attractive Gothic glazing. Fine Georgian
staircase with slender turned balusters. W addition of 2010 in
keeping by *Paul Holland*.
Just S of the church the fine CI7 DOWER HOUSE of sandstone
and ironstone. Widely spaced façade with two canted bays.
Their upper windows alone light the first floor. Four-light
mullioned windows below and a four-centred doorway in the
middle. At OAKTREEHILL FARM, ½ m. NE, a BARN of *c.* 1860
with entertaining polychrome patterning of stone and brick.
EARTHWORK. A triple-ditched linear earthwork extends 100
metres up Church Stowe lane from the intersection with
Upper Stowe road. Excavations in 1972 and 2001 failed to
recover any dating evidence, but parallels elsewhere suggest
Late Bronze Age to Early Iron Age is the likely date.

CLAYCOTON

5070

ST ANDREW. Converted into a house in 2001–2, but the exterior
can still be enjoyed in its garden setting. Dec W tower, unbuttressed; very short recessed spire with one tier of lucarnes. Fine
tall Dec chancel windows with reticulated tracery. The rest
mostly a restoration of 1866 by *E. F. Law*.

CLIPSTON

7080

ALL SAINTS. Except for the priest's doorway, which may be of
c. 1200, there is nothing earlier here than the arcades. They
belong to the early CI3.* Three bays, circular piers, moulded
capitals, circular abaci, keeled responds, double-chamfered
pointed arches. The tomb-recesses in the N and S walls are
somewhat later. Dec the S aisle with its doorway and the
(rebuilt) W tower. The W window is ogee-headed. Spire with
low broaches and two tiers of lucarnes. The church was heavily
restored between 1884 and 1885 when the tower and the
chancel E wall were rebuilt and roofs and a good many windows,
such as the clerestorey, renewed. The STALLS with their poppyheads are part of this, as must be the Gothic LECTERN with

* Mrs E. Fisher in *Clipston*, 1923, gives the date as 1245 but does not say why.

pierced tracery. Chapter house type, ironstone and glass extension of 1981 by *Millwood, Gotch, Pearson & Kightley*. – FONTS. A simple stone tub (N aisle), probably C13. A mock Perp one of the 1880s (S aisle). – SCREENS. Across the tower arch and to the S chapel. Both of the same design and perhaps from something larger like a manorial pew. Very good Elizabethan pieces with rows of open low arches. Strapwork panels. There is a stone, high up above the chancel arch dated 1588, and this could easily be the date of the screens. – ALTAR CROSS and CANDLESTICKS, the former 1905, the latter 1907, the cross given by the Wartnaby family and equally interesting in design as their churchyard memorial (*see* below). Vaguely Celtic and both in a style which is perhaps best described as 'Libertys'. – STAINED GLASS. Chancel E, 1886 by *F. Holt* for *Holland* of Warwick. – Two S windows of *c*. 1885 by *Heaton, Butler & Bayne* and 1886 by *Clayton & Bell*. – MONUMENTS. Many of the Buswell family, a family of London merchants. George †1632. Frontal demi-figure, his hands on an upright book. Tapering pilasters with garlands l. and r. – Elizabeth †1636. Tomb-chest (N aisle E) with a fine frieze of macabre symbols. Brass inscription with indent of a demi-figure. – John †1659. White marble bust, hand on heart, in an oval, wreathed niche. Open pediment. Long Latin inscription. Attributed to *Thomas Cartwright the elder* (GF). – Sir George †1667. Alabaster. Cherubs at the foot. Open segmental top, and a fine portrait bust in it. Attributed to *Jasper Latham* (GF). – Hester †1706. Urn and two standing putti. Inscription with drapery and two putto heads at the top. – Eusebius †1730. Purely architectural. – Wooden filigree carved cross memorial for James Cobley †1944. – In the churchyard a good many slate headstones and to the N of the church a tall fluted column for Cecilia Hogg †1837. Big pedestal with claw feet. Alongside the S path memorials for the Wartnaby family including a Celtic type cross with a wreath of roses at the top for William Wartnaby †1910, and a simpler shorter cenotaph for another William †1925. Both are considerably stylish in design.

BAPTIST CHAPEL, Chapel Lane. 1803, with a gross and townish front of 1864 by *E. F. Law*.

VICARAGE, E of the church. Tudor Gothic by *James Milne*, 1841.

SCHOOL AND HOSPITAL, High Street. 1667–73, founded under the terms of the will of Sir George Buswell. Designed and built by *Matthew Cole* of Clipston. The frontage is in its original state; the interior and back were completely altered in 1926. E front with short wings and a broad flat central projection. Three straight gables. Two storeys with a third in the gables. The three doorways have four-centred heads. The windows are of broad cross-type, except for the one above the central entrance, which is of four lights and has a transom. Originally the centre had the headmaster's lodging on the ground floor, the schoolroom on the first, and the hospital, which was for twelve men, occupied the two wings. The central staircase has fine strong balusters.

Opposite the School, the MANOR HOUSE, Georgian, ironstone, of five bays and two storeys.

Small green at the top of High Street with WAR MEMORIAL, a simple obelisk and a long curved seat, and a *c.* 1900 iron PUMP. CLIPSTON HOUSE, opposite, is rather blank Regency with a wide curved bay in front. A drawing by George Clarke, probably 1830s, shows it with castellations and two Gothic castellated porches on either side. Another drawing dated 1849 shows it more or less as it is, save that the bow windows have arched heads.

GOLD STREET, a little to the NW of the green, has an entertaining selection. On the corner, THE CHESTNUTS, former farmhouse with a good series of outbuildings behind, many of chequer brick. Good quality red brick, in an early C18 manner, but one of its bricks has a neatly engraved date of 1758 and the initials WW for William Wartnaby. Five bays and two storeys, the windows with stone keystones and sills. Double pile with an elegant staircase. Beyond, No. 9 is a delightful three-bay brick house with a central gable, its walls having bands of inset terracotta leaves and flowers, late C19. Opposite, No. 6 is rich Victorian Gothic in blue and red brick.

CLOPTON

0080

ST PETER. 1863 by *Richard Armstrong*. In the late C13 style, w tower with saddleback roof. The N arcade survives with one pier of C13 quatrefoil plan and stiff-leaf capitals. The other arches are C14, octagonal with nailhead. – STAINED GLASS. Several windows with grisaille type patterns of 1863 and the E and W windows all by *Lavers & Barraud*. – MONUMENTS. At the E end of the N aisle a fragment of Anglo-Saxon interlace and an elaborate C13 coffin-lid. The top with a staff with on either side interlaced trails with animals, a lion and unicorn fighting and a winged serpent. Dogtooth along the edge and small arcading under. – Two weatherworn life-size stone recumbent figures. All that is left of an elaborate monument, recorded by Bridges, for Edward Dudley †1632 and his wife. – William Breton, rector †1658. Alabaster with pilasters with emblems of mortality. – Dame Judith and Mary Williams, *c.* 1750–60. Two very fine portrait medallions, reminiscent of *Cheere* or *Taylor*. Simple surround. – Tablet for Frederick Gilbert Mitchell †1962, 'Engineer and Builder of Great Public Works throughout the World'.

CLOPTON HALL. The present stone-built house dates from 1906–7 and is by *Gotch & Saunders*. Stables added in 1907–9. It replaced a rather plain house with a three-bay centre and one-bay wings, three storeys and castellated (recorded by George Clarke in 1846). Today it is quite imposing. The style is Renaissance with big mullion-and-transom windows all in ashlar. The entrance front has a central doorcase with two pilasters and a segmental pediment, set under a curved bay. Service wing on the r. The garden front has three storeys and five bays, two-bay centre and curved bays on either side and a single bay to the l. The bays have pediments and corner pilasters. Central top-lit hall. The staircase with a very Arts and Crafts patterned pierced balustrade. Some C18 panelling inside. In the grounds a roofless, five-bay wing of the manor house of the Dudleys, apparently of the late C17, and probably built by Sir Matthew Dudley, who succeeded in 1670 and died in 1721. There is also a rather earlier square, roofless GATEHOUSE of two storeys, with coats of arms including that of the Dudleys (who owned the property from the C14 until 1764). C18 gatepiers.

COGENHOE

ST PETER. The S and N doorways are a late C12 survival. The N doorway is plain, the S doorway shafted. Scalloped capitals. Round, slightly chamfered N arch, pointed, single-step S arch. The S doorway has a damaged stoup. The chancel belongs to the early C13. Paired side lancets, and at the E end a C19 replacement with three lancets, stepped and under one hoodmould. Inside, the chancel has tall, deep blank arcading. The shafts are triple, the middle one with a fillet. Simplest moulded capitals. The arches have only a slight chamfer. The shafting of the E window is interfered with. Two aumbries and a pointed-trefoiled niche above them in the N wall. C13 also, but a little later, the N chapel arch. One bay, cutting into the arcading. Arch on moulded corbels. The chapel, which had been founded as a chantry chapel by William de Cogenhoe c. 1340, was replaced by a vestry when the church was restored by *Charles Buckeridge*, 1868–9, but its W arch with a filleted shaft is also original. Also early are the nave arcades but they are both rather splendid and rather odd. The arcades of three bays have double-chamfered ironstone arches which fits with a C14 date, but they stand on oolite piers which are extremely curious and fascinating. The arches don't fit the piers at all. The piers are thought to date from the middle to late C13 on the evidence of heraldic shields for the de Cogenhoe family (*see* below). They belong to the four-shaft-four-hollow type, with the early wide hollow, but they are set diagonally, with the main shafts in the diagonals and the hollows frontal. The responds go with them and are of ironstone, especially in the charming motif common to them all of heads and shields at capital level. Only the shafts have moulded capitals proper; the hollows are terminated by the heads and shields. In one S pier a half-broken-off bracket for an image, carried on a small standing figure. The chancel arch corresponds to the arcade. Dec a S aisle window and the S porch. The S aisle E window was also probably Dec, but it was cut down and its mullions reused and as it stands it is probably C17. Tall Perp w tower with thin diagonal buttresses, w doorway with square head and shields in its spandrels, tall tower arch, two-light bell-openings with transom. – FONT. A C12 tub on a round base. – GABLE FINIAL (S aisle). Carved on all sides, one with a crucifix, C14? – STAINED GLASS. Chancel N 1864 and S 1887 by *Clayton & Bell*. – MONUMENT. Knight, cross-legged, late C13 (thought to be Sir Nicholas de Cogenhoe †1281: he carries a shield with the de Cogenhoe arms; cf. the arcade shields). The window jambs have been lengthened to contain the effigy. To the l. a tiny blocked opening which may have been used to hold a light.

THE GRANGE, E of the church. The former rectory. C17 with two wings with mullioned windows. Heavily restored; only the E wing is original, the centre with its two gables and the other wing are renewed.

Lots of good stone houses in the old part of the village including the MANOR HOUSE, Church Street, of C17 origin with mullioned windows and two gables, though much renewed in the C19. Alongside it a charming Edwardian addition with three casement windows perched on brackets, set around with pebbledash. On Station Road, S side, a good set of Victorian villas (Nos. 1–17) of red brick with some yellow stripes. Bracketed eaves and wooden porches at the sides. Some have square bays, others triangular. Opposite, BAPTIST CHAPEL of 1910 by *H. H. Dyer*. Brick and stone, Dec style. A little w, at the road junction, the former SCHOOL of 1895, red and blue brick, Gothic, also by *Dyer*.

COLD ASHBY   6070

ST DENYS. The access to the church is by a large High Victorian Ancaster stone LYCHGATE, built 1883, by *John A. Hanley* of Chester. Simple, w tower, nave and chancel. No aisles, but a clerestory. Norman the inner arch of the N doorway. Perp the tower and the S doorway with traceried spandrels and the fine roof. Chancel side windows of the C17. A drawing by George Clarke shows that the E window was once of the same date. The present window is, of course, C19 and part of the restoration by *Hanley*, 1881–2. The S porch usefully has the date of 1696. – WEST GALLERY of 1789 holding a small pipe organ of 1840. – FONT. Octagonal, Perp. Panelled stem. Fleurons against the underside of the bowl. Top battlements. – ROYAL ARMS. Painted and dated 1778. – STAINED GLASS. – Nave window of 1882, showing the interior when it had box pews and a plain E window, and another of 1884, both by *Frederick Preedy*.

Former SCHOOL and SCHOOL HOUSE, E of the church. 1867 in the Gothic style of red brick with the window arches using yellow and blue bricks.

THE OLD BAKEHOUSE, Crabtree Lane. Three bays and two storeys, of chequer brick with ironstone base and quoins. Mid-C18, and like many houses at Welford (q.v.).

COLD HIGHAM

St Luke. The base of the w tower is C13 with a saddleback stage added in the C14. The tower arch was originally narrower than it is now. The arch is too wide for the imposts. The chancel has a Dec tomb-recess in the s wall outside. The s chapel has a small lancet type lowside window with a wooden shutter. It is blocked inside by the only important piece in the church, a Dec MONUMENT, and the window may have been intended to show a light from the tomb. The monument consists of an oaken effigy of a slender cross-legged knight, said to be Sir John de Pateshull †1350. The effigy looks earlier, but the surround may well be so late. Tomb-chest with ten ogee-headed panels containing shields. Big ogee arch with ballflower decoration. Chancel rebuilt 1880–2 by *E. F. Law & Son*. – FONT. 1880, octagonal on marble pillars. STAINED GLASS. s aisle, 1880 by *Heaton, Butler & Bayne*. – s chapel, two by *Mayer* of Munich, 1894.

Former SCHOOL, w of the church. 1871–2, Gothic, with bellcote by *T. H. Vernon*.

COLLINGTREE

St Columba. A C12 church, according to the evidence of the chancel s doorway, the low round-arched recess to its e with an arch, only slightly chamfered, and the e parts of the n and s arcades with a circular pier with square abacus and corresponding e responds. The arcades were then extended to the w in the C13 (circular piers, circular abaci) and then or yet later received their double-chamfered arches. The n aisle was pulled down in 1808 and there was a fairly rigorous restoration 1871–4 by *E. F. Law*. Dec chancel windows and SEDILIA with very thin shafting and ogee arches. Perp w tower and five-light e window. – FONT. Circular; against the underside of the bowl a king's head, a monster, a winged figure, and a quite unrecognizable motif. The suggested date is C13. – Fine *Walker* ORGAN of 1891 with decorated setting and pipes. – LECTERN of brass. A standing female figure on a stand, given 1916. – STAINED GLASS. N lancet by *O'Connor*, 1871. Also an attractive diamond red, gold and blue design of 1857. – Chancel E window of 1892, Pickering Phipps memorial by *Clayton & Bell*. – In the chancel, N and s, two windows by *A. Stoddart* of Nottingham, dated 1916 but made 1922. – N aisle, St Hugh, 1922 and tower of 1871 by *J. Powell & Sons*. – s aisle Sears memorial 1952 by *F. Cole* of *Morris & Co*. s aisle w window, also Sears memorial by *Jane Cummings*, 1983. John Sears (†1981) was keen on pigeons and fishing, hence the motifs. – MONUMENT. A brass inscription for Horatio Woodhouse †1679 with shield and two skulls and crossed bones.

SCHOOL, SE of the church, 1861 of red brick with a turret and spirelet.

No. 43 HIGH STREET is a fine example of banded sandstone and ironstone, mainly late C17 (illegible datestone but a 1680s date suggested). Three bays with a central gabled attic storey. Mullioned windows with hoodmoulds.

THE GRANGE, Ash Lane. Dated 1631 but largely a 1960–8 rebuilding by *F. H. Allen*. It was the Sears family home. Symmetrical three-bay composition of three-light mullioned windows and a central dormer. Larger early C20 range behind. Italian Renaissance well-head. On the A508, Edwardian half-timbered entrance lodges and gateway for COLLINGTREE GRANGE (1875 by *E. F. Law* for Pickering Phipps, the Northampton brewer, dem.).

COLLYWESTON

One of the most attractive villages in N Northamptonshire and famous locally for the former production of stone tiles, known as Collyweston Slates. The industry was already in existence in Roman times but the pits are no longer worked. Part of the site, called The Deeps, is now a nature reserve.

ST ANDREW. The church originates from an C11 building with nave and chancel. A good deal of large block masonry from this exists, in a rebuilt state in the lower courses of the S wall of the nave and especially in the N wall of the chancel. The chancel was rebuilt in the C13: see the blocked lancet window in the S wall, now within the S chapel. Dec chancel arch and a window with Y-tracery on the S side. Externally this had a double lowside window at its base. Otherwise mostly Perp. Good W tower similar to Easton-on-the-Hill and St John's Stamford: ashlar, clasping buttresses, big pinnacles, peppered with tiny crockets, probably early C16. Tower arch with battlemented capitals. Perp N arcade of two bays. Perp also the most handsome feature of the church, the S doorway with an ogee-arched head, big fleurons in a broad moulding, and a crocketed top with finial and thin pinnacles. A shield with three bells, the arms of the Porter family who were here in the 1440s. S chapel, built *c.* 1490 when Lady Margaret Beaufort held the manor. Three-light Perp E window; the other two windows appear to be later, perhaps C17 when the chapel was taken over by the Tryon family, who raised the floor to create a burial vault. A restoration is recorded 1857–8, largely reseating, and in 1929 *Traylen & Lenton* converted the S chapel into a vestry. – MONUMENT. N aisle. Elizabeth Follett †1508. Brass, the figure 18 in. (46 cm) long. – FURNISHINGS. A fine complete series of poppyheaded pews, pulpit and lectern, all dating from the restoration of 1857. – STAINED GLASS. Chancel E and tower, both 1857 and by *Lavers & Barraud.* – N aisle W, 1906 by *Jones & Willis.* – S aisle two unidentified Early Victorian windows said to have been brought from a church in York. – N aisle E, memorial window of 1919 by *A. K. Nicholson.*

W of the church lay the mansion or Palace. It belonged to Ralph, Lord Cromwell, Henry VI's treasurer (of South Wingfield and Tattershall), and then to the Lady Margaret Beaufort. It survived till 1640. All that remains is some terracing, below the site, a BARN (now converted to residential) with attached DOVECOTE dated 1578, and in a garden, a very handsome SUNDIAL, C18, set in a large alcove in its wall. Ashlar, with a segmental-apsed top.

A good many houses with C17 mullioned windows. The best and most attractive houses are in HIGH STREET as it runs downhill. On the N side set back in its own grounds is BEAUFORT HOUSE, formerly the rectory, built 1832–3 by *James Richardson* of Stamford. Five bays, two storeys with a Regency doorcase. Good staircase. Some older work incorporated where an ironstone/limestone mix appears. No. 8 is a simple house with a gabled canted bay and a sundial. The gable set on kneelers, which is a characteristic of the area. Lower down another, No. 20, with gabled mullioned bay and the date 1637 in an adjoining rendered gable. Set back behind this row is the former SCHOOL (village hall) of 1876–7 built by *Perkins & Son.* Stone gabled end with three-light transomed window. Restored in 2000. Towards the bottom of the High Street, THE STEWARDS HOUSE with two canted mullioned bays with gables on kneelers and a four-centred arched doorway, linked into the bays with a string course. Plaque on the l. gable but does not seem to have a date. In Back Lane, opposite the sundial, MANOR FARM, also C17, again retaining mullioned windows on the first floor.

MANOR HOUSE, ¼ m. SW on the A43 at the approach to the village. Moved in 1912 from the middle of the High Street, using materials from a house dated 1696. Simple, already classical. Five bays, two storeys. Cross-windows.

BRIDGE, ½ m. NW across the Welland. Medieval origin. Three pointed arches and three segmental arches of which one is dated 1620. Triangular cutwaters.

CORBY

Corby owes its status to the discovery of rich ironstone deposits in the 1870s. These were exploited originally by the Cardigan Estate and later by Lloyds Ironstone. Then in 1932 the Glasgow firm Stewarts & Lloyds arrived and set up a major steel manufacturing plant. Exploration was first to the NE of the village and the first blast furnace was created in 1934. Housing was constructed near the village in 1934 and subsequently larger estates

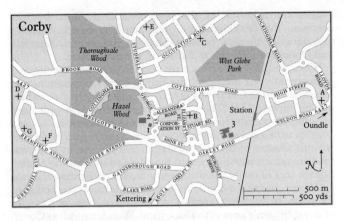

A St John the Baptist
B The Epiphany
C Our Lady of Walsingham
   (R.C.)
D St Brendan (R.C.)
E St Columba

F St Peter and St Andrew
G St Ninian

1 Corby Cube
2 Corby International Pool
3 Tresham College

were built to the N, either side of Rockingham Road, with over 2,000 homes by 1939. In the same year the Corby Urban District Council (UDC) was established and following the Second World War a further burst of building with government support took place to the NW of the previous sites. Even this did not keep up with the demands of Stewarts & Lloyds who were continuing to expand production. The result was that in 1950 Corby was designated a New Town and under the Corby Development Corporation the aim was to increase the population from 14,000 to 40,000. A Master Plan was drawn up in 1951 by *Holford & Wright* which suggested a new civic centre designed by *Denis Harper*, to the W of the old village but linking the earlier developments. This remains the centre of Corby.

Construction began in 1953 and continued till 1958. By 1960 Corby's population was nearly 35,000 with over 5,000 houses having been built. The following year Stewarts & Lloyds announced a further expansion of their plant and this produced a second phase of development. In 1961 a new designated area had been added to the W taking in all available land as far as the Uppingham Road and stretching S and enveloping Oakley, and to the N towards Rockingham. The Master Plan for this was devised by *John H. D. Madin & Partners*. Meanwhile the town centre was under review. The UDC had already had built a technical college and library in 1955–60 but there was a need for a set of municipal offices. A national competition was launched and this was won by *Enrico De Pierro & Partners*. The plans were for a building complex, including a swimming pool at the E end of the new centre. It was opened in 1965. It coincided with a further expansion of the shopping precinct designed by *John Stedman*, the Development Corporation's architect. Stedman also designed the new housing estates at Kingswood, Beanfield and Danesholme to the w and sw of the new centre.

When, in 1967, the government decided to nationalize the steel industry into one amalgam, the British Steel Corporation, iron ore extraction at Corby was quickly overtaken by that elsewhere and by imported ore. The Corby plant closed in 1979 with a loss of some 6,000 jobs immediately which eventually rose to over 10,000, with a devastating effect on the town. A further disaster was the closure of the railway station in 1966. An attempt was made to attract new business to the area and in 1984 the Market Square area of the centre was given a facelift by *Bradshaw, Rowse & Harker*, but this did little to dispel the gloom which pervaded the town. In 1982 help seemed at hand when there was an idea of siting Britain's answer to Disneyland, Wonderworld, at Corby. It was a false hope and with the inevitable problems over planning the scheme never materialized.

Corby's revival began in 2001 when an urban regeneration company, Corby Catalyst, was set up. One of the first objectives was to reopen the rail link and revitalize the central area. Regeneration was also aided by an improved road network with links to the already well-established A14 and the realization that Corby, being in the middle of England, was an ideal centre for distribution. There followed considerable business relocation with the expansion of the industrial estates to the N and E of the town. A number of major companies moved to Corby and unemployment began to ease. Aided by the North Northants Development Company schemes were put in place for more housing and regeneration of older estates, including those which Stedman had devised. The central area was enhanced by a new shopping complex, Willow Place, completed in 2007. De Pierro's civic buildings have gone, a new civic hub, the 'Corby Cube', was opened in 2009, and in the same year a new railway station opened. The following year saw the addition of an Olympic-standard swimming pool and leisure centre. Educational facilities have also been upgraded together with major additions, such as the Corby Business Academy (2008) and a new Tresham College (2011).

The population of Corby was 15,000 in 1951, in 1960 it was *c.* 35,000 and by 1970 it had risen to some 49,000. In the 2001 census it was over 53,000.

CHURCHES

ST JOHN BAPTIST, Church Walk. The church for the original village. s arcade of two bays built *c.* 1200. Octagonal pier, tall capitals with upright stiff-leaf. Pointed double-chamfered arches. About 1300 the w bay was added. Of *c.* 1300 the s aisle windows with cusped and uncusped intersected tracery, the s doorway, and the s porch. The porch is remarkable inside. It has later (see the former roof-line) chamfered transverse stone ribs rising right up to the roof and standing on chamfered stone posts along the w and e walls. In addition the ribs are connected, as if they were of timber, by a ridge rib and stone purlins. Much in the church is Dec, namely the w tower (tower arch with continuous mouldings, quatrefoil frieze below the spire, spire with low broaches – the charming pairs of little heads should be noticed – and two tiers of lucarnes), and the chancel (bar tracery with a spherical triangle in the head, reticulated and flowing tracery, SEDILIA and PISCINA with ogee arches). As Richard Marks has deduced from C17 records of heraldic glass formerly in the windows, the tower was built shortly after 1337 and the chancel between 1340 and 1350. The w face of the tower has shields either side of the doorway, though these are much weathered and appear to be blank. Perhaps the heraldry was painted. In the chancel a large tomb-recess without an arch, just with a big crocketed triangular gable on short columns with fillets. A panel infill in its centre perhaps suggests it was an Easter sepulchre (cf. not dissimilar recess at Irthlingborough). N arcade and N aisle of 1902 by *J. C. Traylen* of Stamford. This is probably the date of the elaborate mosaic floor in the chancel. Its panelling dates from 1922–9, as does the vestry. – FONT. Circular, with six low dogtooth arches at the bottom of the bowl; C13. – STAINED GLASS. Fragments of canopies etc. in the chancel N and S windows and nave s aisle. Also a small panel of St Christopher. All *c.* 1340–50. – Several windows by *Morris & Co.*, *c.* 1920, i.e. long after the deaths of Morris and Burne-Jones, chancel s and s aisle w. – The N aisle N wall window by *J. Powell & Sons*, 1902. – A chancel s window of 1904 and the N aisle W window of 1902 are both by *Hardman & Co.* – s aisle E window by *Pearce & Cutler*, 1938. – MONUMENT. Perp tomb-chest with coped roof and quatrefoil and shield decoration. In the churchyard, s of the church.

THE EPIPHANY, Elizabeth Street. 1961–2 by *D. F. Martin-Smith*. Greek-cross plan. High gables over the arms, a folded star roof with clerestory lighting over the centre, slender spirelet above.

OUR LADY OF WALSINGHAM (R.C.), Occupation Road. 1938, brick with rather plain entrance front with one tall window. Canopied portal and low pediment. Tall tower on r. with slender vertical slit-windows, the bell-stage with three stronger slit-openings. Body with narrow aisles and five long double windows. – STAINED GLASS. A window of *c.* 1940 by *Pearce & Cutler*.

ST ANDREW (Church of Scotland), Occupation Road. 1938 by *Bowmans* of Stamford in a pared-down Romanesque style. Triple windows at each end. Round-arched arcades and arcaded reredos.

ST BRENDAN (R.C.), Beanfield Avenue. Brick. Central section rising up to a squat pedimented tower. The body with clerestory. – STAINED GLASS. A window of 1962 by *Theodore Kern*.

ST COLUMBA, Studfall Avenue. 1957 by *S. Dodson & Sons*. A miniature version of Coventry Cathedral with angled side windows. Green copper roof. Tall rectangular tower with long cross-slits. Hall and rooms at right angles to the church.

St Peter & St Andrew, Beanfield Avenue. 1966–7 by *Dodson, Gillatt & Partners*. A Latin cross with pointed arms, the church hall occupying the 'nave'. Tall pitched roofs reaching nearly to the ground. Large triangular gables jazzily echoed by other triangular motifs; even the bell-tower is a triangle. Was Rushton Lodge the inspiration?

St Ninian (Scottish Church), Beanfield Avenue. 1968 by *Gotch, Saunders & Surridge*. More restrained, and consequently more successful. Hexagonal church with split-pitched roof, linked by a vestry to a hall at 45 degrees to the church. In front a freestanding brick bell-tower.

Corby Baptist Church, at the corner of Rowlett Road and Darley Dale Road. 1967 by *Reynolds* of Oxford. Trapezoid form.

PUBLIC BUILDINGS

126 The Corby Cube, George Street. 2008–10 by *Hawkins Brown*. This splendid statement of the 'new' Corby rises a blue-glazed, striped, monolithic structure demanding to be noticed. Horizontal slots reveal that there is a garden with trees at roof level. It contains council offices, a library, a theatre and studios. Its entrance projects as a low annex and begins a rising series of levels, initially giving access to the library with a long ramp. The theatre is below, a horseshoe-shaped auditorium with flexible seating and proscenium arrangements. Fine use of wood and colour. There are wide corridors, red carpets and much light. The council chamber has walnut-lined walls and spectacular views over the town. At the top of the building is an open roof garden. In front is a large mounded patterned paved piazza with STATUE of a steelworker, 1989 by *Michael Grevatte*. The surrounding area is currently (2012) under review.

Corby International Pool, George Street, w of the Cube. *S & P Architects*, 2008–9. A huge hangar-like steel-framed structure under a low curved roof. Much wood cladding. Pool of Olympic standard with multi-use leisure facilities.

124 Corby Business Academy, on the e edge of Corby on the Priors Hall Estate. 2007 by *Sir Norman Foster & Partners*. A fine building, set well back. Big columned atrium and ranks of teaching spaces facing playing fields. Much use of glass. Open central space with sweeping staircase.

Corby Enterprise Centre, adjacent to the Academy at Priors Hall. 2010–11 by *Bela Partnership*. Angled form with central low rotunda with glazed entrance screen.

Tresham College, Oakley Road. 2009–11 by *Bond Bryan* of Sheffield. A long three-floor construction with a curved frontage using an abstract design of glass and green and blue panels. At the rear of the site is Corby House (or the Manor House), built in 1904–5 for James Pain by *J. A. Gotch*. Queen

Anne style in ironstone and limestone with central porch
feature and prominent chimneystacks.

There have been a number of new SCHOOLS of which the fol-
lowing are a selection: BROOKE WESTON ACADEMY, 1992 by
Design Team Partnership with additions of 2001 by *Gotch, Saun-
ders & Surridge.* – KINGSWOOD, 2010 by *Aedas Architects
Ltd.* – LITTLE STANION to be completed 2012–13 by *GHM
Rock Townsend.* – MAPLEFIELDS, 2011 by *Gotch, Saunders
& Surrridge.* – OAKLEY VALE, 2008 by *Ellis Williams
Partnership.*

MATERNITY HOSPITAL, Cottingham Road. By *R. Llewelyn
Davies & Weeks*, 1959–61. Small, of brick, adjoining the
NUFFIELD DIAGNOSTIC CENTRE. The roofs are treated with
unusual variety because one looks down on the hospital from
the road. Later additions.

RAILWAY STATION, Station Road. *North Northants Development
Corporation & English Partnership*, 2008–9. Glazed booking hall
with wide overhang roof.

ROCKINGHAM MOTOR SPEEDWAY, 1 m. N of the Weldon
Industrial Estate. Opened 2001. The first purpose-built race-
track in the United Kingdom since Brooklands in 1907. Its
main stand all too obvious on the E approach to Kirby Hall
(q.v.).

PERAMBULATION

To the w of St John the Baptist a little of the original VILLAGE
remains with a few nice stone houses. On the corner of
MEETING LANE a handsome house with gable end and E front
Georgian, but its w side wall still with late C16 mullions. On
the other corner a pair of early C19 cottages like those Lord
Cardigan erected at Deene and Deenethorpe. The Cardigans
were lords of the manor at that time. Further w a short row
of shops with stone parapet marked 'KICS rebuilt 1925' (i.e.
the Kettering Industrial Cooperative Society) and Nos. 77–79,
a thatched row, once Manor Farm, with a central gable dated
1609. The former RECTORY, N of the church, is 1874 by
H. Goddard of Leicester but nothing special.

The TOWN CENTRE is dominated by the Cube (*see* Public
Buildings) which sits majestically on its w edge with the curved
outline of the International Pool beyond it.* If only what
was facing it to the E was as inspiring. The central area begins
with the wide piazza of CORPORATION STREET. Originally
designed for traffic but later pedestrianized, it is the predictable
arrangement of shops with flats above and exactly what one
would expect of the post-war decades. A southern expansion,
WILLOW PLACE by *H. G. B. Construction*, was opened in 2007
but it is equally predictable and uninspiring. Its wavy patterned

---

* The TRESHAM COLLEGE building of 1955–8 by *A. N. Harris* which stood a little
further N was demolished 2012. It is to be replaced by an Odeon Cinema by
Mulberry Developments.

paving does little to alleviate the mundane architecture. Looming over both is the CORBY COUNCIL OFFICES building of the 1960s, originally a hotel. An irregular jagged five-storey block with an incredible amount of metalwork on its roof. The E end of the complex was the MARKET SQUARE, but this has been almost totally built over. Tucked away a small space with a SCULPTURE, the 'Spirit of Corby', a twist of steel of 1974 with alongside the PEDIMENT of the former Stewarts & Lloyds office building of concrete with the date 1933. Both re-erected here in 2004. The E edge of the area is ELIZABETH STREET, an unintegrated miscellany: CROWN HOUSE by the Department of the Environment (Architect: *I. J. Pennycook*), 1967–70, large eight storeys of aggregate panels on a brick base (empty 2012). Further N the indifferent POLICE STATION (1954–6) and COURT HOUSE (1957–8) by the *County Architect's Department* (*A. N. Harris*).

TATA STEEL, Weldon Road. The former headquarters offices of the British Steel Corporation, by *J. Douglas Matthews & Partners*, 1960–2. Two powerful blocks, one of eight storeys, one of four. Heavy brutalist details; projecting floors, shuttered concrete bands on top. Inside a wall made from a Roman MOSAIC PAVEMENT with a chequerboard design of red and purple squares. Discovered in 1960 at Thistleton, Rutland.

OUTER CORBY

Corby well demonstrates the changing fashions in housing development from the 1960s onwards. All that can be attempted here is to summarize some of the various types of housing which appeared over the years.*

The earliest housing estates were built by Stewarts & Lloyds to the N and E of the old village on either side of ROCKINGHAM ROAD. They were planned 1934–5 on a modified garden suburb arrangement, largely using their architect *L. M. Gotch* and still with a faint air of the Arts and Crafts movement in the brick houses, most of which are semi-detached, interspersed with some lower cottage-style houses. Many groups are laid out as culs de sac with small grass greens. The whole area has survived extremely well, even with the inevitable changes of fenestration and the sacrificing of some gardens for car park spaces. The estates were served by a shopping precinct, with flats above (1934), the SAMUEL LLOYD SCHOOL of 1937 (now the Pen Green Centre) and the ODEON CINEMA (1936 by *L. M. Gotch*, now A6 Furniture and somewhat shaved of its Art Deco decoration, though its outline form survives), all on Rockingham Road. By the end of 1935 nearly 800 houses had been built.

---

*A comprehensive study of the development of Corby has been conducted by Matthew Bristow, published as *The Physical Development of Corby: Steel Town to New Town 1930–1950*, 2007, and the account here relies extensively on this.

NW of these, the FOREST GATE, STUDFALL and WILLOW-BROOK ESTATES, developed post-war by Corby UDC with some 1,500 houses of the prefabricated type known as BISF, a form designed for the British Iron & Steel Federation by *Frederick Gibberd* and *Donovan Lee*. Examples exist in DOVE-DALE ROAD. The UDC also built a number of concrete houses of a type known as 'Easiform' (examples in CLYDESDALE ROAD). To serve this increased housing stock a shopping precinct was designed in Studfall Avenue in 1952 by *Blackwell, Storry & Scott* of Kettering and two presentable pubs of similar date, THE OPEN HEARTH and THE ROCKINGHAM ARMS. Alongside the construction of the new town centre further housing estates were being built to the S and SW of the new town centre (either side of GAINSBOROUGH ROAD), largely of the terraced form, Messrs Wimpey having the largest contract. To the E of the town centre a development which included maisonettes and flats was created.

With the creation of the Corby Development Corporation further major estates were created to the W and SW of the centre under the direction of the Corporation's architect, *John Stedman*. KINGSWOOD, created 1965–72, was regarded as a model development with careful use of linked green spaces and footpath access to community facilities and a shopping area, CANADA SQUARE. There was a mixture of two- and three-storey dwellings with garages at ground level as well as smaller units. Stedman also used existing woodland to give the area a feeling of tradition. Inspiring though it seemed to be at the time, Kingswood has not survived well and both houses and Canada Square are now largely derelict and under review for regeneration. Another of Stedman's estates, DANESHOLME (1971–4), being further away from the town centre, needed more individual facilities, with two schools and community facilities linked again with open spaces. In this case, rather than being built solely by the Development Corporation, private developers were encouraged to invest in the estate. This was a significant change and altered the future way that housing would be built in Corby. The OAKLEY VALE estate was begun in 1975 on the reclaimed land of the Oakley Quarry but the major development in this area was not undertaken until 2006–11. A further estate, PRIORS HALL,* on the E side of the conurbation on the A43 close to Weldon, on the site once intended for Wonderworld, was begun at the same time and continues to expand. As well as housing, there is an INDUS-TRIAL ESTATE with the impressive reflective glazed block of the 1960s R.S. COMPONENTS building, the Academy (*see* above) and the Enterprise Centre.

---

* The name is a misinterpretation of the medieval Priors Haw.

COSGROVE

ST PETER AND ST PAUL. Very over-restored. The result of *E. F. Law* in 1864–5 trying to re-Gothicize what had been made Georgian in the later 1770s (a lead plaque is dated 1778) by the efforts of the then rector, Pulter Forester (*see* below). The chancel E wall has clear evidence of the C12 church with a decorative string course and the edges of two round-headed windows. The inserted Dec window has reticulated tracery. The N doorway and the N aisle are original early C13 work. The arcade has five bays. The piers are quatrefoil. The arches are double-chamfered and have hoodmoulds with small zigzag at right angles to the wall surface. At first sight it appears to be nailhead. The same motif in the simple, blocked, N doorway. W two bays of the arcade filled in 2000 to create facilities in the N aisle. The tower arch is even more tampered with. In its present form it looks as if it might have been C14 work. The tower itself is Perp. The chancel arch was apparently rebuilt in 1586 following a fire; a datestone removed from it is now at the W end of the nave. The chancel itself has two rather bizarre windows, interpretations of the lancet style, of 1864. *Law* could be very wayward when he chose. There is an equally bizarre interpretation of the C12 on the N side of the chancel outside. – NAVE ROOF. Exposed in 1935 having been ceiled in the late C18. A wonderfully wavy set of tie-beams with braces and kingposts, probably C15 or C16. – COMMUNION RAIL. With twisted balusters, late C17. – ROYAL ARMS. A painted oval for George III. – Gilded copper WEATHERCOCK. It 'may well be medieval'. – STAINED GLASS. Nave S. Three shields, C15–C16. Not original to the church, probably brought in by Rev. Pulter Forester. – Chancel E of 1873 by *Clayton & Bell*. – Two chancel S windows of 1891 by the same maker, attributed to *F. Holt* of Warwick. – Nave window with heraldic designs for the Atkinson family by *M. C. Farrar-Bell*, 1973. – MONUMENTS. Rev. Pulter Forester †1778. With an open book in front of the familiar obelisk. By *William Cox Sen.* 'He was possessed of every amiable virtue' and the inscription also records his work in improving and adorning the church. Other Cox memorials elsewhere. Big Gothic memorial over the pulpit for the Mansel family, *c.* 1840 by *Bedford* of London.

COSGROVE HALL, SE of the church. Originally a half-H plan. Early C18. It has been attributed to *John Lumley* of Northampton. Seven bays, two storeys. The garden side has Doric pilasters in two orders, the entrance side Corinthian ones. On this side the centre was later filled in. The interior was much altered soon after 1800. One room has late C16 or early C17 panelling. STABLE BLOCK and square DOVECOTE with pyramidal roof, both C18. At its entrance is a charming thatched early C19 *cottage orné* LODGE.

THE PRIORY, ½ m. SE. C17 origins, but largely C19 Tudor manner. Inside a most sumptuous SCREEN of the time of Henry VIII. It is supposed to have been bought in Devon. Two archways. In the spandrels leaves, also a man lying on his back. The panels to one side normal linenfold, to the other a very uncommon variety with cusping and little grapes.

In 1800 the two halves of the GRAND JUNCTION CANAL met here. It had been started at Braunston (q.v.) and Brentford in Middlesex. SOLOMAN'S BRIDGE, ¼ m. SE of the church, is Gothick and very charming, and designed so because it could be seen from The Priory, the home of the lord of the manor, George Biggin. The arch has nice blank cusping. The cutwaters end in little half-cupolas as do projections on the banks. There are also ogee-headed niches and blank arches and quatrefoils and it all looks much more like Strawberry Hill than 1800. Restored in 1972. Another BRIDGE, of conventional design, is probably by *William Jessop*, 1793–1800. There are other canal features, including a short cast-iron AQUEDUCT, SE of the village, of 1809–11, by *Benjamin Bevan*, and a cattle tunnel.

Former BREWERY and MALTINGS, on the edge of the canal. Three and two storeys, the lower stages stone, the upper brick, with a tower block, built 1858 and enlarged later.

COTON MANOR

½ m. s of Guilsborough

An attractive house set in a beautiful garden. Of ironstone with a curious mix of grey oolite. It is used rather randomly, the front gable almost having banding, but not quite. Elsewhere it appears in patches and odd blocks. The mullioned windows are also limestone. The whole effect is very much more Elizabethan than 1662, which is the date on a stone with the initial H and W E. The significance of this datestone, which is oddly placed, is unclear.

In a room on the first floor, as the lintel to the fireplace, a section of a large Doric frieze. Just two metope panels and triglyphs. In one panel a bucranium and in the other a rosette pattera. Beautifully carved. The scale and size of the mouldings makes it clear that the frieze came from a very large building and the tradition that it came from Holdenby House (q.v.) is perfectly credible. It certainly dates from *c.* 1570–80. The jambs of the fireplace also appear to be from something larger. One begins to wonder whether all the limestone used in the house might have come from Holdenby. The rear extensions date from 1903.

COTTERSTOCK

ST ANDREW. The thrill of the church is its Dec chancel, tall, wide, airy, and with large windows with flowing tracery, only marred by the savage restoration by *G. E. Street* in 1877, which stripped the walls and gave them obtrusive pointing. The E window, of five lights, is especially sensational. The side windows are of three lights and simpler. ROOD STAIR entered from the chancel. Top opening ogee-headed. The chancel looks out towards the River Nene. It is higher than the rest of the church. SEDILIA and PISCINA inside with ogee arches and crocketed gables. This chancel was built in connection with the foundation of a college at Cotterstock in 1338. The founder was John Gifford, canon of York and rector of the church. It was a large establishment: a provost and twelve chaplains. The next piece to be admired is the C15 S porch. Elaborate entrance, battlemented with animal finials, tierceron vault with ridge ribs and fine bosses. Central boss for the Trinity and surrounded by others for the Evangelists. The Dec S doorway is disappointing by contrast. After that one will pause by the W doorway, a Late Norman piece with one order of scalloped capitals and a round arch with much zigzag, also at right angles to the wall surface. The C12 tower base has blocked openings on its S wall and, apparently also, hidden, on its N, and there are signs of a possible lean-to roof above them. What does this mean? The bell-openings of the tower are C13 (two lights with a shaft); the parapet is Perp.

Now for the interior. Tower arch a little later than the tower doorway. Nailhead decoration, double-chamfered pointed arch. Roof-line above showing early church had no clerestory. Early C13 arcades of two bays with circular shafts, octagonal capitals and double-chamfered pointed arches. The detail on the S side (angle spurs of the bases) is a little earlier. Central capital has etched fleur-de-lys leaves. – FONT. Octagonal, Perp, with panelled stem and elaborately cusped quatrefoils etc. against the bowl. – TILES in the chancel. C19. Reminiscent of *Lord Alwyne Compton*'s at Castle Ashby – ROOF. Chancel, with grotesque heads and the Gifford arms, so partially original. – WOODWORK. Screen, stalls and pew ends of the 1870s, but interesting carved ends in the nave. – STAINED GLASS. Nave N. C14 canopies and coat of arms. – S aisle, E window 1875 by *J. Hardman & Co.*, and S window 1892 by *Shrigley & Hunt*. – N aisle 1878 by *Heaton, Butler & Bayne*. – Tower window *c.* 1870 by *Hardman & Co.* – Another N aisle window, the Adoration, unidentified. – MONUMENTS. Fine brass to Robert Wintringham, canon of Lincoln and provost of the College, †1420 chancel. The figure is 3 ft 1 in. 94 cm. long and stands in a fragile architectural frame with a concave-sided gable on thin shafts and tall pinnacles. The whole of this is balanced on a shaft as if it were a monstrance. – Defaced stone effigy of a canon(?), C13 (under the tower). – John Simcoe †1760. By *Edward Bingham* of Peterborough; also under the tower. Inscription between strongly tapered pilasters, almost as if they were Elizabethan. At the top an obelisk with, at its foot, what Rupert Gunnis called a 'naval still-life'. Simcoe died at the siege of Quebec, and this is illustrated in the base relief.

– s aisle. Lt. Kenneth Dundas †1915, erected 1919. With scenic reliefs, angels and foliage. Cast rather than carved and possibly by *Mary Seton Watts* (cf. Courteenhall).

MANOR HOUSE (former rectory), w of the church. Dated 1720. Six bays, two storeys, classical, but completely unadorned. Fenestration altered.

SCHOOL (Village Hall). 1875–6 by *A. Sykes* of Peterborough. Tudor style windows in the façade and three tall round-arched windows at either end.

Opposite, COTTERSTOCK HOUSE, Regency with pretty later iron verandas, and a little to the w the OLD VICARAGE. Gable end on the road with the date 1651. Long range to the N restored and extended early C19 by *James Richardson* of Stamford. A slightly later extra wing on the w side. A number of 1864 COTTAGES. s of the church a MILL, badly damaged by fire in 1968 but restored in 1972. Three- and four-storeyed, with the handsome miller's house, 1803, close at hand.

COTTERSTOCK HALL. Built 1656–8 for John Norton. The earlier date appears reset in a C19 wing, the later date is on the gable of the porch. It remained in Norton hands until 1693, then had a succession of owners coming into Fane (Westmorland) hands *c.* 1840. Col. H. Fane began alterations in 1856 but died the next year; his cousin, Henry Viscount Melville, completed the work. The house is E-shape. Straight gables l. and r., the gable behind the porch with ogee-volutes and flat strapwork. The porch has two floors and a balcony. Semicircular pediment with thick foliage on the big volutes. Mullioned and transomed windows, except for four large Georgian windows on the w front. Several 1658 fine stone fireplaces inside including one of the local fossilferous limestone (cf. Drayton House). One in particular with big volutes is much of the type of Thorpe Hall, Peterborough. Entrance hall with early C18 arcading l. and r. Three arches on Roman Doric columns of wood. They are presumed to have been open into the principal rooms originally. Big 1856–7 staircase projection at the back with windows with two transoms housing the C19 staircase. The subsidiary staircase is original. An attic room has reset early C17 panelling reputedly brought from Fotheringhay.

COTTESBROOKE

ALL SAINTS. A long, cruciform church – only the N transept is pulled down – and all of *c.* 1300. Beautifully restored in 1959–60 by *Lord Mottistone* (of *Seely & Paget*). The big windows with Geometrical tracery cannot be trusted with certainty. They may have been foliated originally, with the foliations cut away when reglazed in C18. In a trustworthy state the s and N doorways, the w tower with its beautiful pairs of two-light bell-openings with Y-tracery (circular mullions), the shafting of the

windows inside, their capitals (some left undetailed), and some
of the small headstops outside. The s transept still has its
c. 1300 cornice with carved heads, flowers and the occasional
dogtooth. The battlements of the tower have shields of arms
of the Butvileyns, patrons of the church in the C13–C14. Bridges
records a slab in the chancel for William Butvileyn, rector
†1305. The two E broad lancet windows are Early Victorian
(called 'recent' in Whellan's Directory of 1849).

Inside is one of the best Georgian interiors in the county.
The nave roof is ceiled and has, in the coving, a painted frieze
of acanthus scrolls, in imitation of plasterwork. During the
1959–60 restoration the plaster ceilings were removed from the
chancel and s transept, revealing the C15 roof timbers. At
the same time painting of theatrical swags of curtains was
discovered over the s window of the transept, but this was not
sufficiently intact to be left uncovered. – BOX PEWS all down
the nave – Fine three-decker PULPIT, with elegant staircase
and star-design inlaid sounding-board, and another staircase
opposite to the raised FAMILY PEW in the s transept, all mid
Georgian, oak and excellent joinery, and very probably by
craftsmen associated with the *Smith* of Warwick yard, c. 1750.
The pew has a fireplace of dark purple fossilized marble of a
type much used by the Smiths (notably in Cottesbrooke Hall's
former entrance hall). – REREDOS and COMMUNION TABLE
by *Lord Mottistone*, Wrenian, set halfway down the chancel (so
that a vestry is formed behind). – FONT and FONT COVER. Of
wood, C18. (The font designed by *Street*, who did some restoration 1852–3, is now in Uppingham parish church.) – STAINED
GLASS. Chancel windows 1857–65 by *J. Powell & Sons*. – MON-
UMENTS. John Rede †1604 (s transept). Alabaster and marble
recumbent effigy on a half-rolled-up mat. Flat arch between
two columns. Big strapwork inscription tablet under the arch.
On the ground ten kneeling children. All a bit battered.
Hollemans type. – Sir John Langham †1671 and wife (s transept). The Langhams bought the estate in 1637. It had previously belonged to the Saunders family. Sir John Langham was
a London Turkey merchant. A splendid monument by *Thomas
Cartwright Sen.* He was paid £290 for it in 1676. Free-standing.
Of white and grey marble. Tomb-chest with good fleshy cartouches with flowers and fruit. Recumbent effigies, lively
carving, he in his Alderman of London robes. Surrounded by
its original ironwork grille with corner standards of twisted
columns with fleur-de-lys finials. – Mrs Mary Langham †1773
(chancel). With a classical urn. By *J. F. Moore.* – Sir James
†1795 and his children who both died young (nave). Long
inscription; standing female figure by an urn. Probably also by
Moore, or by *Richard Hayward* (GF). – The following four (nave)
by *John Bacon Jun.* Lady Langham †1807. Standing figure of
Faith. – Marianne †1809 (made in 1810), simple, with a draped
urn. – Lady Langham †1810. With columns and the rock of
Golgotha. – Sir William †1812 (made in 1815). Free-standing
in the nave. A large urn on pedestal with marble inscription

plaques inset. It must be *Coade* stone and is signed *Bacon*. Fine churchyard with rows of tubbed yews and a magnificent cedar tree by the E gate.

COTTESBROOKE HALL. Built for Sir John Langham in 1702–13. The builder was *Francis Smith* of Warwick. The house belongs to the type of the former Buckingham House, London, and Cound in Shropshire, both of almost exactly the same years as Cottesbrooke. The type is continued in the later houses designed by the Smiths. It is characterized by the use of brick, beautifully laid here, with Ketton stone dressings, articulation by giant pilasters, stressing the angles as well as the centre bays, and a top balustrade. The original entrance side faces towards the E, its vista aligned on the spire of Brixworth church. When the house was acquired by the Macdonald-Buchanans in 1937 they reversed the use of the fronts, so what was the entrance front is now the garden side, and vice versa. The width of the former entrance front is seven bays, the height two storeys. The centre is three bays wide; the pilasters are Corinthian. The only other emphasis is on the doorways, to the garden with a plain pediment, to the entrance with an open curly pediment on Corinthian columns. The circular motif in the broken pediment, deriving from Borromini, can be compared to a similar feature at Chicheley Hall, Bucks., also by *Smith*. The detail is exquisitely carved. It is in addition given more prominence by blank quadrant walls leading to one-storeyed pavilions with hipped roofs. They have segment-headed windows, large doorways to the forecourt (open segmental pediments on Doric pilasters), and central broken pediments reaching up into the roof on the sides facing the approach. About 1770–80 a bow window was added on either of the short sides. This made the doubling of the giant pilasters on the garden front necessary. The work of *c.* 1770–80 is by *Robert Mitchell*.

Beautiful interior, kept in perfect condition. Three-bay ENTRANCE HALL, with mid-C18 stucco work and a fireplace of *c.* 1770–80. To its l. and r. the DINING ROOM and DRAWING ROOM, both redecorated when the bows were added. The PINE ROOM, originally the entrance hall, still with panelling and a bolection chimneypiece of the same purple mottled marble as in the family pew in the church. Charming corridor to the wing with little domes. Library with a good mid-C18 fireplace and overmantel (brought in). Finally the STAIRCASE, the most 92 beautiful ensemble in the house. Rococo papier mâché decoration of *c.* 1750 on walls and ceiling attributed to the *Woolstons* of Northampton. Fine wrought-iron handrail with addorsed S-curves. There are payments to the ironsmith *William Marshall*, who worked at Chatsworth. In one of the wings a BALL-ROOM was contrived between the wars (by *Gerald Wellesley*). Its fine fireplace of *c.* 1740 came from Woburn Abbey. In the OAK SITTING ROOM, Elizabethan panelling from Pytchley Hall. This had been moved to Sulby Hall when Pytchley was demolished in 1828. The fine furniture collection and the famous

Woolavington collection of sporting pictures are outside the terms of this volume.

In the early 1990s the N service wing was adapted as a smaller living area under the direction of *Francis Johnson*. This provided a new entrance hall and circular ante-room, a sitting room and a dining room. Especially striking are the floors of the first two rooms using basically Ancaster stone, one floor with traditional black diamonds and the other a circular pattern.

Very fine GARDENS, incorporating parts of a pergola designed by *Robert Weir Schultz*. The Baroque style parterre in front of the house dates from the 1930s. The wall and steps by *Sir Geoffrey Jellicoe*. In the Yew Walk s of the house four statues by *Peter Scheemakers*, of Homer, Lycurgus, Epaminondas and Socrates. They were formerly in the Temple of Ancient Virtue at Stowe, Buckinghamshire, and casts have been placed there.

In 1770–80 *Robert Mitchell* also provided the one-storeyed square LODGES and SCREEN with decorative *Coade* details. (They were originally on the Leicester Road and were moved to their present place, as a W entrance from the village, and enlarged by *Wellesley & Wills* in 1938.) Mitchell also provided a handsome BRIDGE. A copy of this was built on the old drive from the E in the 1930s.

Cottesbrooke Hall is one of the candidates for being the pattern of Jane Austen's Mansfield Park.

OLD RECTORY. Alongside the church. Built *c.* 1735–40, perhaps by *William Smith II*. Five bays, two storeys, with hipped roof. Stone, with a Gibbs doorcase. Good pine staircase with twisted balusters. Drawing room with Regency features (cf. Lamport Rectory) and marble chimneypiece, perhaps by *John Whiting*. Some C19 additions and modern C18-style windows.

THE GRANGE. Opposite the church. Ironstone and handsome, with four big chimneystacks. Of late C17 origin but now almost entirely C19.

LANGHAM'S HOSPITAL AND SCHOOL. On the road to Brixworth. Built in 1651. A long series of almshouses. One-storeyed. Three-light mullioned windows. Just E the C18 entrance to the park with two tall GATEPIERS with ball finials. The pre-C18 house was sited between here and the river.

Many attractive stone houses, several thatched, all speaking of the care which one associates with an estate village.

CALLENDER FARM, 1 m. W on the road towards Thornby. Some earthworks remain from the Premonstratensian cell of Kayland founded *c.* 1155.

COTTINGHAM

ST MARY MAGDALENE. Of ironstone. The story begins with the W wall inside. This has a Norman window and traces of a former roof-line. The two need not be contemporary. Then follows the N arcade, which will be remembered by any visitor to the county. It is of a mid-C13 date, and has the unique feature of capitals decorated with human figures placed without qualms horizontally: two ladies, in opposite directions, their wimples meeting, two knights with characteristic helmets, a bishop, etc. In addition the responds have stiff-leaf foliage, very damaged in the E respond. One respond has typically E.E. grotesques. But the existence of this respond poses a problem. The first arch is separated from the second by a piece of wall, always a sign of a former cross wall. What can that wall have been, if the Norman W wall ran one bay further W? The only answer which suggests itself, and it is a doubtful answer, is that it was the E wall of a Norman tower. If so, the C13 aisle embraced the tower, until it was replaced by the present tower. RCHME suggest that the block of wall may represent the line of an earlier W wall of the nave, possibly of Saxon origin. The tower was begun in the late C13. It is a very fine piece indeed, with angle buttresses, tall, shafted two-light bell-openings with quatrefoiled circles, and a spire with low broaches on which stand short pinnacles and two tiers of lucarnes in alternating directions. The S arcade is of *c.* 1300: three bays with quatrefoil piers and double-chamfered arches (but the E window has flowing tracery). The chancel, again of *c.* 1300, has a very interesting, if only copied, E window of four cusped lights, consisting of two plus two with Y-tracery and a big quatrefoiled circle in the spandrel between the two super-arches. Big, low, shafted recess inside the N wall (keeled mouldings). The church was restored 1878–80 by *Albert Hartshorne*. Plans show that he added the N chapel and the S vestry. There is evidence that the arch into the vestry was originally on the N side of the chancel and the shafted recess was moved eastwards. – STAINED GLASS. Chancel E, Life of Christ and saints, 1901 by *Burlison & Grylls*. – Chancel S, 1882 by *F. W. Dixon* and 1916 by *A. L. & C. E. Moore*. – S aisle W end, Trevor memorial 1974 by *G. Maile* of Canterbury.

METHODIST CHAPEL (former Wesleyan), Corby Road. 1878 in red brick with yellow and blue brick dressings. Round-arched windows. The original Methodist chapel alongside of 1808.

Former CONGREGATIONAL CHAPEL, Main Street. 1844, of stone. Three bays under a pediment with round-arched windows above and square below.

COTTINGHAM HALL (also called Bury House), High Street. The main front early C18, of seven bays, the two at each end slightly projecting. Three storeys (the top one blind). At the rear a gabled block of three storeys, C17 and later. Simple mid-C17 staircase inside. Alterations are recorded by *William Parsons* in 1835. Its STABLE BLOCK is now part of the Hunting Lodge Hotel.

Former WALLIS'S CLOTHING FACTORY (Burghley House), Rockingham Road. Built 1872. Three storeys of brick, its courses decorated with amusing carved heads. Now apartments.

The ROYAL GEORGE pub, Blind Lane, incorporates in its S portion the earliest cruck structure surviving in the county, and indeed the area. Dendrochronology has dated the timbers to 1262 and a reasonable amount survives, notably two trusses, one with a collar, and a ridge-beam.*

At MIDDLETON, W of Cottingham, COTTINGHAM HOUSE is stately Georgian of five bays and two and a half storeys with a graceful doorway; late C18. Elegant cast-iron rails in front c. 1840. Several other solid Late Georgian houses including the MANOR HOUSE, dated 1785, with a limestone ashlar front. Three bays with rusticated windows and doorway. Dormers with alternating triangular and segmental pediments. At the W end of Main Street a pair of ironstone ALMSHOUSES, Tudor style, of 1862.

7050

COURTEENHALL

ST PETER AND ST PAUL. There is evidence of a late C12 church. The most obvious feature is the E pier of the three-bay N arcade (circular, capital with leaf ornament and square abacus). To this can probably be added the responds of the S arcade with simple impost mouldings. The strange S doorway with a trefoiled head under a blank round arch, though entirely rebuilt, may have been part of this building. There is also a curious round-headed blocked opening high up above the roof on the E face of the tower. Can this really be C12, as has been suggested? Of the C14 the fine S arcade (single-chamfered arches, octagonal piers) but noticeable is the wider arch at its E end, presumably marking an earlier S transeptal chapel. Of the same time the W continuation of the N arcade (double-chamfered arches) to make it even with its opposite number. The chancel and its N chapel all part of the C14 rebuilding. The SEDILIA and PISCINA have ogee heads, diapered jambs and knobbly crocketing. The piscina also a pretty piece of blank flowing tracery. Squint through to the S aisle. The W tower is Dec with a Perp parapet. The aisle windows c. 1680 following a bequest left in the will of Sir Samuel Jones (†1672). The church had a particularly harsh restoration in 1882–3 under *J. P. St Aubyn* (the 10th Lady Wake was a St Aubyn). Before that the interior had a three-decker pulpit, box pews and flat plaster ceilings. The pointing of the walls is especially to be deplored. Further work was done in 1897 by *William Hull*. – FONT. C12. – WALL PAINTING. Upper halves of female figures against the W side of the W pier of the S arcade. – HATCHMENTS. Four for the

*I am grateful to Nick Hill for alerting me to this and for use of his researches.

Wakes, 1823, 1846, 1864 and 1963. – STAINED GLASS. Two fine windows in the chancel of 1897 by *Heaton, Butler & Bayne*. – MONUMENTS. Tomb-chest with black marble lid. On it indents of brasses to Richard Ouseley †1599 and family. Rhyming inscription. – Sir Samuel Jones †1672 and wife. Black-and-white marble. Ionic columns with big open segmental pediment. Large kneeling figures in an attitude nearly facing one another – that is the convention of Elizabethan and Jacobean monuments. But the figures are now much more at ease. Behind, black panel with a putto head and garlands l. and r. The monument is attributed to *William Stanton*. – Sir Charles Wake Jones †1769. By *William Cox Sen*. A large, well-accomplished architectural tablet. Corinthian pilasters. Above the inscription a winged skull surmounted by a baldacchino with draperies. – Iola Campbell †1852. Porcelain baby, her mouth open, about 18 in. (46 cm.) long, in a niche. Numerous other memorials to the Wake family, especially notable the more recent (1960s–70s) floor slabs in the N aisle with excellent lettering by *Michael Royde-Smith*, a pupil of Eric Gill.

RECTORY, S of the church. Built *c*. 1805. Front with a canted bay window and pointed windows.

Former FREE GRAMMAR SCHOOL (village hall), ¼ m. w in the grounds of the house, and just NW of it. Built *c*. 1680 under the will of Sir Samuel Jones (†1672). Oblong, with a fine big eared doorway with open segmental pediment enclosing a shield in the N wall. Hipped roof. The w side with three windows, tall, of the wooden cross-type. On the E side at right angles the school house adjoins. This is of three bays and two storeys. Inside the schoolroom forms and desks are preserved. They run along the walls, and at the foot of the desks run lower benches for smaller children. Raised seat with desk for the master. Rear addition of 1935. The Master's House was extended in 1658 and heightened in the 1980s.

COURTEENHALL HALL. Built in 1791–3 for Sir William Wake. The architect was *Samuel Saxon*, a pupil of Chambers, who was recommended by *Humphry Repton*. Saxon was at the time providing designs for a new infirmary in Northampton (q.v.). It replaced a C17 house which was on a lower site to the SE of the present building. This had been largely rebuilt in 1572 by Richard Ouseley, whose family had acquired the estate following the Dissolution, it having been a property of St James's Abbey in Northampton. The Wakes did not acquire Courteenhall till the mid C18. The house is of moderate size and treated architecturally and internally with great restraint but great sensitivity. The entrance side is almost forbidding. Seven bays, two and a half storeys. The ground-floor windows in blank segment-headed panels. The tripartite doorway (with Tuscan columns) is treated in the same way, so that it seems slightly recessed. The garden side has a three-bay pediment, and the principal windows below it on the ground floor are treated again slightly recessed with Ionic columns and segmental

Courteenhall Hall.
Engraving by Saxon, 1810

arches. The E façade is as fully treated architecturally with a garden doorway and top pediment. In the ENTRANCE HALL a screen of two tall Roman Doric columns at the back. Frieze with fine, slender garlands. A cross corridor linking the three rooms on the S front. The DINING ROOM has a frieze of vine garlands and at the back a screen of Corinthian columns with a fitted sideboard. Superbly carved Corinthian capitals. The DRAWING ROOM very chaste with just a frieze with honeysuckle and palmettes. Pretty chimneypiece. In the LIBRARY the end is a segmental apse with two curved niches set out with columns; palm-frond capitals. This end of the room beautifully contrived with doors curved to fit the apses. Bookcases, built into the walls, with slender decorative borders. Delicate frieze with a flowing wave pattern. The ceiling is in the Adam fashion. Finally the STAIRCASE with a very reticently designed cast-iron balustrade with honeysuckle motifs and a glazed oval dome. The marbled walls are a rare survival being part of the original decoration. On the first floor the centre of the house is a corridor reached by a door from the staircase and lit by another glazed oval dome. Simple marble fireplaces in the ground-floor rooms. Elegant wooden surrounds on the first floor.

On the SW end of the house a service court, flat facing the garden but curved on the drive side.

STABLES. Palladian, *c.* 1780, attributed to *John Carr* with characteristic raised towers with pyramid roofs. Arched lower windows. Three-bay pediment. The main range runs N–S. Behind it not a complete courtyard, but lower individual ranges.

The GROUNDS were laid out by *Repton* and his Red Book dated 1791 is still in the house. The garden is especially notable for its trees.

CRANFORD ST ANDREW

9070

ST ANDREW (Churches Conservation Trust). On the edge of the lawn of Cranford Hall. N arcade of *c.* 1200. Three bays. Very plain circular piers. Round single-stepped arches. Late C13 W tower. Shafted, finely moulded doorway. Two-light bell-openings with quatrefoiled circles. Lively tower arch. Battlements. The clerestory with pointed-trefoiled spherical triangles must be of *c.* 1300 or a little later. Big Perp windows in E wall. Clumsy turret in N aisle with steps for rood loft. The S chapel was remodelled 1674, so the Perp window and flat ogee-headed doorcase probably of that period. The C19 restoration, including the pews, some with poppyheads, and the addition of the N transept, all of 1847 by *E. F. Law.* – PULPIT. With late C16 Flemish panels with biblical stories (cf. Cranford St John). – SCREEN. 1893, somewhere between Gothic and Art Nouveau. – STALLS of same period. – STAINED GLASS. E window: an assortment of Netherlandish bits collected together by Sir George Robinson *c.* 1841 (cf. Cranford St John); also one kneeling English late C15 figure. More fragments at the top, partly C14. – Chancel S, 1860 and the tower window by *Lavers & Barraud.* – MONUMENTS. Brasses, wall-mounted N aisle: to John Fossebrok †1418 and his wife, nurse to Henry VI; 20-in. (50-cm.) figures, and to John Fosbroke †1602 and wife. – Bernard Walcot †1671. Attributed to *Joshua Marshall* (GF). Alabaster surround with swags and cherub's head. – Sir William Robinson †1679. Tablet with twisted columns. Bust at the top in an open segmental pediment. Attributed to *Jasper Latham* (GF). The pattern was later much used by his pupil *James Hardy*, to whom Gunnis attributed it. The Robinsons did not acquire Cranford till 1715 and this monument was apparently brought from Nuneham Courtney, Oxon. Several beautifully inscribed slabs, 1727–65.

CRANFORD HALL. Early Georgian with later alterations. Rather plain, of Weldon stone, seven bays and two and a half storeys. Dated 1769 on a lead pipe. On the entrance side an early C19 one-storeyed porch with two pairs of Tuscan columns. Towards the garden the same motif, but in attached columns. Pedimented central window. Terrace. Converted into flats in 1946. Original drawing room. Early C19 STABLES to the E, Tudor style.

To the W, DAIRY FARM. Said to date from 1610, but much beautified mid C19 and given gables with shields (several other houses in the village have the same features). At the corner of the garden a circular DOVECOTE, probably C15.

Several thatched cottage rows, notably Nos. 6–18 on Grafton Road. READING AND RECREATION ROOM built 1896 by *Blackwell & Thomson* of Kettering. Vernacular ironstone. A little altered since, having lost its chimneystacks.

CRANFORD ST JOHN

9070

ST JOHN. No solution has yet been offered for the earliest piece of architecture in the church, the Norman W arch of the N arcade, round with one step only, on the simplest imposts and made of ironstone. It is followed by a stretch of wall and then the late C12 arcade of two bigger arches with rich, rather wild stiff-leaf capitals and round arches with one step and one slight chamfer. A stretch of wall in an arcade usually means the position of a former cross wall and thus a lengthening beyond this previous wall, and the VCH does indeed explain the arch as a lengthening of the existing arcade to the W. But it is in style emphatically earlier than the arcade. How can that be so? The only answer seems to be that the Early Norman arch is a reused piece. A reason for this procedure can perhaps be given. The W tower of the church was begun in the C13 (see the ironstone lancets in the lower part), the chancel at the end of the C13 (see the window of three lights with cusped intersected tracery and the two-bay arcade to the N chapel with its octagonal pier). The Early Norman arch in question might either have been the arch of a preceding Norman W tower which fell and whose ironstone materials were reused in the new W tower in other places, or the chancel arch. It does in fact not quite fit its present position. The S aisle is almost entirely of 1842, especially the heavy leafy arcade capitals. Its E extension is 1880. The pier shapes, the first a square with four demi-shafts, the second round, are probably correct and of the same date as the N arcade, and the arches may also be old. Dec the upper part of the W tower and the triple-chamfered arch towards the nave. Two-light transomed bell-openings. Frieze of wheels of three mouchettes. Blocked W doorway with depressed ogee-headed clerestory like Cranford St Andrew with trefoil openings, but circular with mouchettes in the centre. – PULPIT. With two Flemish C16 panels with religious stories (cf. Cranford St Andrew). – SCREEN. Low across the chancel. Made up of Jacobean bits. – STAINED GLASS. Three early C14 shields, England and two for the Bassingbourne family.* Small head of Christ *c.* 1310–40, similar to the glass at Lowick. Many C16 or C17 Netherlandish bits; also figures of Christ and two saints of 1841, when the window was assembled by Sir George

---

* There is no known connection of this with Cranford, but they owned the manor of Abington, near Northampton, and shields with these charges which are recorded being there disappeared when that church was damaged in a storm in 1821.

Robinson. – Chancel E, 1847 by *William Wailes*. – Tower window by *Clayton & Bell*, *c.* 1860.

MANOR HOUSE. E of the church. C18 front of three bays, but inside fine Jacobean staircase through two storeys. Flat open-work balusters. Newel posts with, at the top, openwork arches. String with carrot-like gadrooning. A date of 1629 by the W doorway.

TOP HOUSE, to the W, at the corner of Grafton Road. C17 with later alterations. Inside a large pre-Reformation fireplace. Cas-tellated beam, castellated side supports. Opposite a pair of COTTAGES, 1849. Sandstone with heavy golden ironstone lancet windows, transomed on ground floor.

CRANSLEY   8070

ST ANDREW. Big Perp W tower, ashlar-faced. Clasping but-tresses. Pairs of two-light bell-openings with transom. Quatre-foil frieze, battlements, pinnacles. Recessed spire with two tiers of lucarnes. Most of the body of the church of *c.* 1300–30, i.e. the S aisle, S doorway, windows l. and r. of it, E window of three lights with a quatrefoiled circle, low tomb-recess, the chancel arch (triple shafts), the SEDILIA in the chancel, with detached pillars, the tomb-recess opposite, the chancel doorway (the E window tracery is C19, part of the restoration, 1870, by *Slater & Carpenter*) and the arcades with their octagonal piers carry-ing capitals, which in the N arcade have ballflower enrichments. Perp clerestory and roofs (low pitch, tie-beams on arched braces, wall-plate decorated with quatrefoils, and longitudinal arched braces above the clerestory windows). Angel supports. – FONT. Baluster type, early C18. Spiral-strigillated stem, Corinthian capital, the bowl marked no more than if it were the abacus. – STAINED GLASS. C14–C15 fragments (Cranes for Cransley), S aisle W window. – E window designed by *J. Wimbolt* and made by *H. Bryans*, 1900. – Tower, window gifted by American servicemen who worshipped here during the Second World War, 1945 by *A. J. Davies*. – S aisle SE window, 1944, is also by *Davies*. – S aisle E window is by *J. Hardman & Co.*, 1909. – BRASS to Edward Dallyson †1515 and wife (S aisle E), 25-in. (63.5-cm.) figures. – Another within a mural monument for Edward Dallyson †1589, and his wife, with kneeling figures. Incised slab to Edward Barnwell †1557 and wife; a skeleton.

CRANSLEY HALL. An elegant Georgian-looking house, whose unified exterior belies a more complicated story. There is evi-dence of a house of late C16 date when the manor was owned by Sir Thomas Cecil, son and heir of Lord Burghley. His coat of arms on a carved plaque is on the W front and limestone ashlar blocks within the wall may also date from this period. Cecil sold the manor in 1595 and it passed into the Robinson family. Henry Robinson embarked on rebuilding soon after

inheriting in 1677 and his coat of arms is in the pediment of
the doorcase within a limestone frontispiece on the E side. The
exact form of the early house is not easy to establish but the E
range is probably an early cross-wing with the hall on its W
side, represented today by a large room on the S side of an
internal courtyard. The hall originally extended across the
passage which now runs across the room's S side. The S and E
façades were then rebuilt 1708–9 using the local ironstone, of
two colours, and limestone for the dressings, the E side first
then the S. The house is basically five by five bays, though the
E and W fronts were extended later. Hipped roof with pedimented dormers. No architect is recorded but the name of
John Lumley of Northampton has been suggested (cf. Cosgrove
Hall). The W front was extended in 1750 to create a new dining
room and a canted bay was added in the middle of the S front.
Inside the DINING ROOM and BOW DRAWING ROOM have
good plasterwork. The dining room especially has splendid
floral garlands, a grand fireplace and overmantel and a pretty
ceiling. Accounts at Hoare's Bank reveal the architect to have
been *David Hiorne* of Warwick, and the plasterers *Thomas
Roberts* of Oxford and *John Woolston* of Northampton. About
1800 or shortly after, when the property had passed by marriage to the Rose family, a central E–W cross-corridor was
inserted with a wide shallow alcove on the W side, fitted with
a sweeping staircase. The service area was also modernized. In
1905 the estate was sold to Major Arthur Thurburn and the
service area completely changed to create further reception
rooms with a billiard room and music room at the NE corner.
Both are lined with impressive oak panelling. At the same
time the exterior was given its overall unified Georgian
appearance.

To the W is a 1708–9 STABLE BLOCK, converted to housing in
the 1990s, but still retaining its arched entranceway beneath a
squat square tower with angle pilasters topped by urns.

Former reservoir PUMP HOUSE, ¾ m. NW. Three linked brick
buildings, now rendered white, with tall transomed cast-iron
windows, *c.* 1900.

CREATON

ST MICHAEL. A modest church but having rather special Victorian altar fittings. Short Dec W tower with later parapet and
pinnacles. Late C12 N doorway. One order of shafts, one waterleaf capital, the arch steeply pointed. Windows lancet, Dec, and
Perp, mostly renewed. Rood loft opening to l. of chancel arch.
Re-set in the N vestry a transomed C13 lowside lancet window.
The surround of another in the chancel S wall. The S aisle and
its arcade added in 1857 by *William Smith*. An organ chamber
was added in 1888 and there was a further restoration by *A. W.*

Blomfield in 1898. – PULPIT. Jacobean. – RAILS (under the tower). Late C17 balusters. – REREDOS, ALTAR, STALLS etc. Also 1898. The side walls with fine paintings of St Peter and St Paul. The painted and gilded altar with its pierced Gothic front is surmounted by a gilded triptych bearing symbols of the Evangelists. A splendid array. – STAINED GLASS. Chancel E window of the Resurrection by *Powell Bros* of Leeds. Fine. – S aisle two windows of 1905 and 1910 by *Mayer* of Munich. Fragments in a nave window (a dove and two cherubs), *c.* 1905 also by *Mayer.* – MONUMENTS. A simple Tudor arched tablet for Mary Crow †1858 by *Reeves* of Bath. – Bob Wroughton †1914. A grey stone Gothic surround enclosing an alabaster relief of a young knight with a horse.

UNITED REFORMED CHURCH (formerly Congregational), High Street. Rebuilt early C19. Two large round-arched windows and a pyramidal roof.

Pleasant village green with nice stone houses around, notably at the SW end the MANOR HOUSE, dated 1603 with mullioned windows in an ashlar façade. On the E side ALMSHOUSES. Founded 1825, but totally rebuilt 1897. Six gables, the central four timber-framed.

HIGHGATE HOUSE, ¾ m. S on the main road. A simple iron-stone C18 inn turned into quite an impressive mock Tudor residence *c.* 1900, although it looks earlier, by Major Charles Eyre-Coote. Front with two bays whose lower windows have cusped arched heads. Central porch with four-centred arched doorway. The interior fitted up in a Jacobethan manner. The so called 'baronial hall' has linenfold panelling but this, the staircase and other woodwork all *c.* 1900, save some arcaded panels above one fireplace which do seem to be genuine Jacobean. Now a conference centre and much extended. Good Italian wrought-iron gates.

CRICK

ST MARGARET. A fine Dec church with little restoration and little that is earlier or later. Its problem is, being on the War-wickshire border, many windows are of the pink and grey-green Warwickshire stones, and these are very adversely affected by the weather. It is the window tracery which makes the church so attractive, and which is the most vulnerable (two windows dismantled 2011). The aisle and chancel windows are splendid. The culmination is the five-light E window and the crazy S aisle E window with very low lights and an oversized circle at the top. The S aisle windows have mostly a large five-petalled flower as their principal motif. Of earlier date, the first two bays of the S arcade and the reused E respond. These are E.E. circular piers, stiff-leaf capitals, circular abaci. When the W tower was built the S arcade was linked up with it and a N

Crick, St Margaret.
Engraving, 1849

arcade built. Octagonal piers, double-chamfered arches. Its
respond is also earlier. The tower has Y-tracery and a broach
spire. Three tiers of lucarnes. The lowest of the lucarnes have
ballflower decoration. The lucarnes are curiously arranged, the
lowest in the cardinal directions, the two upper in the diagonals. The chancel inside is very fine being built at the cost of
the Astley family in the second half of the C14. SEDILIA and
PISCINA with ogee arches, the N doorway with an ogee arch
on two head corbels, large beasts, monsters, and heads on stops
to the window arches. The chancel arch also rests on head

corbels. Evidence of an earlier church is the clear roof-line above the tower arch. There was a restoration in 1840 by *R. C. Hussey* and there are sections of plain Gothic panelling from his time. – FONT. Circular, Norman. The foot is three kneeling figures, an Italian motif. On the bowl vertical chains of big beads, three or four in a chain, and top border of zigzag. – BOX PEWS, again of 1840, a little altered. – REREDOS (s aisle) made from sections of Jacobean panelling, probably parts of former pews. More along the walls. The 1840 reredos is now mounted as part of the vestry screen in the N aisle. – ORGAN. Of 1819 by *Thomas Elliot* of Tottenham Court Road, London, and originally intended for the Chapel Royal, St James's Palace. Presented in 1841. Gilded pipes in an impressive case, mounted in the w gallery. – CURIOSUM. A sentrybox-like shelter for the priest at funerals. Also two large *Gurney* cast-iron STOVES. Splendid things with ribbed sides and mounted by a crown. – STAINED GLASS. Flemish bits in a N window. Chancel E of 1863 by *John Milner Allen* for *Lavers & Barraud*. – MONU-MENT. Stone effigy of *c.* 1300, a slender lady.

Former SCHOOL (Crick Club), s of the churchyard. Victorian Gothic of 1845–7 by *D. G. Squirhill* of Leamington. Purple diapered brick, with a turret. Opposite, VYNTNER'S MANOR. It dates from 1652, but much altered in a picturesque manner in 1925. Many thatched dormers. Vaulted cellars said to be medieval. E of the church is a late C17 HOUSE, six bays, three storeys, with cross-windows.

RUGBY RADIO STATION, 2 m. N. Main building brick, by the *Ministry of Works*, 1955. In addition dozens of masts, mostly in Warwickshire.

GRAND UNION CANAL TUNNEL, SE of the village. 1,528 yds (1,397 metres) long, opened in 1814.

CROUGHTON

ALL SAINTS. Some minor Norman evidence in the chip-carved stones with saltire crosses etc. to the s of the tower arch inside. The N arcade is of three bays and must date from the later C12. It is continued to the E by one half of a round arch with a slight chamfer. Its date is uncertain and so is the reason why it is here. It may represent the transept of the Norman church but there is no clear evidence. The arcade itself has circular piers, flat capitals with trumpet scalloping and one with flat leaves, square abaci, and single-step arches which are pointed. The unbuttressed w tower seems to belong to the same time. Its E arch is unmoulded but pointed. The s arcade is E.E., with circular piers and circular abaci. The E respond has small, early, upright stiff-leaves. The windows are mostly renewed, but point to work of *c.* 1300 etc. This included the clerestory, which is more decorative on the s side than the N. Late medieval nave

roof with tie-beams. Tracery above the arched braces. Rood
stair in the s aisle probably c16. A beam across the chancel
arch suggests a rood or tympanum, there being no chancel
arch. The top stage of the w tower is c16 or c17. The chancel
was rebuilt *c.* 1830, carefully it is said, by the *Rev. H. L. Bennett*
(rector 1819–48), who did a good deal of tidying of the interior
during his incumbency. The body of the church was restored
by *William Weir* of *Micklethwaite & Weir* in 1919–20. – FONT.
Circular, c13, but re-carved in the c15 and by the Rev. Bennett
c. 1830. Friezes of dogtooth, pointed arches, naturalistic leaves,
and also tiny medallions with figures, symbols and animals. –
ROOFS, especially the aisles, late medieval with wall-plates with
flowers and in the s aisle, castellations. – PULPIT, c17, simple.
– SCREEN. Perp, of one-light divisions. Largely remade. –
COMMUNION RAIL. Mid-c18. – BENCHES. They are a mixed
lot and appear to be largely a make-up. They are square-topped
but inset with varied tracery panels, one with a hat, another
with a chalice and wafer, and another with a shield within a
wreath. The tracery looks c16. In the N aisle one seat has
curious open tracery sides. Are they more of the Rev. Bennett's
work? – PANELLING, N and s aisles, with bits from a c15 screen
or bench fronts. Georgian panelling around the sanctuary.

WALL PAINTINGS. Discovered *c.* 1921 by Tristram and
restored again *c.* 1960 but already many scenes have faded. It
is, however, a memorable series of the early c14 in the style
more familiar from illuminated manuscripts, and it covers
most of the walls of the body of the church. In essence the s
aisle has the life of the Virgin, and the N aisle the Passion of
Christ. The pictures represent the following scenes. s wall from
E, upper zone: the Rejection of Joachim's Offering, the Meeting
at the Golden Gate, the Birth of the Virgin, the Presentation
of the Virgin, the Virgin leaving her House, the Espousals of
Mary and Joseph; lower zone: the Visitation, the Nativity, the
Angel and the Shepherds; then over the arch of the door: the
Magi before Herod and the Adoration of the Magi; then
the Massacre of the Innocents, the Flight into Egypt (two
specially well-preserved scenes), the Presentation of Christ;
and after that the Angel giving the palm to the Virgin, the
Virgin giving the palm to St John, the Arrival of the Apostles,
the Death of the Virgin, the Funeral of the Virgin and the
Miracle of the Jews, Christ and the Apostles at the Tomb of
the Virgin, and the Assumption. N wall from w, upper zone:
the Entry into Jerusalem, the Last Supper (well preserved), the
Betrayal, Christ before the High Priest, the Mocking (not
recognizable), the Scourging, Christ carrying the Cross, the
Crucifixion; lower zone: the Deposition, the Entombment, the
Harrowing of Hell, the Resurrection, the Angel and the Virgin,
the Annunciation. Finally, of the c15, the Last Judgment either
side of the chancel opening with the Weighing of the Souls and
the Descent into Hell. – REREDOS. *E. W. Tristram*'s record of
the Last Supper wall painting. – STAINED GLASS. Chancel E
window of 1934 by *Sir Ninian Comper*, incorporating, in its

central spandrel, a shield with the arms of England, pre-1340.
S aisle E of 1855, unidentified maker, but incorporating some
C14 fragments in roundels. – MONUMENTS. John Clarke
†1603, with the inscription in a bold cartouche of three-dimen-
sional strapwork. Steep pediment. – Rev. William Freind †1689.
Good tablet, which must date from *c.* 1720. Odd shape with
angled sides. Urn at the top and a pile of books and papers on
either side of it. Attributed to *Francis Bird* (GF). His signed
Spratt monument in Westminster Abbey was erected by
Freind's brother. – Rev. John de l' Angle †1719. Marble tablet
with scroll sides and a shaped base.

READING ROOM, N of the church on High Street. 1903 of sandstone and red brick, incorporating a building of 1842. Its
windows have coloured glass diamonds in their upper lights.
The attached house of three bays is of similar build but much
tidied up and looking now rather Georgian.

SCHOOL, further W along High Street. The earliest part with
Gothick wooden windows is 1842 and converted from cottages.
The later section with bellcote is 1866. Both parts are thatched.

BARN, NW of the church. Good stone barn, 68 ft (21 metres)
long, converted into a house.

CULWORTH

ST MARY. Externally entirely new looking except for the unbuttressed W tower, in its lower parts probably late C13, in its
upper Perp. What in the body of the church can be trusted
points to *c.* 1300 or a little later, but inside, both arcades (of
three bays) are of *c.* 1200, lengthened in the C13. The earlier
part has on the N side an octagonal pier with a many-scalloped
capital on the S side with flat broad single leaves. The abaci are
octagonal too. The continuation has round piers with round
abaci and double-chamfered arches. In the S aisle a large tomb-
recess with ballflower decoration. The shafts have nobbly or
still naturalistic foliate capitals, i.e. again *c.* 1300 or a little later.
Chancel with its transverse arches is a rebuilding of 1840; other
alterations and refitting *c.* 1880–1 by *E. F. Law.* – FONT. Small,
octagonal, dated 1662, mostly with simple fleur-de-lys panels.
– PULPIT. Jacobean with the usual scroll arcading. – BENCHES.
C15 with tracery on ends, fronts and backs. – Chancel REREDOS,
1884, Gothic with inset painted panels. – N aisle REREDOS,
c. 1900, painted. – STAINED GLASS. Chancel S of 1849 and
1852 both by *J. Hardman & Co.* to designs by *Pugin.* Chancel
E and S aisle E, both 1898, and N aisle, 1901, all by *Lavers &
Westlake.* Two others of 1863 and 1880 by *William Wailes.* –
Tower window 1880 by *A. L. Moore.* – MONUMENTS. Judeth
Rye †1698. An oval inscription panel topped by an elegantly
carved garland of fruit and flowers. Winged cherubs at the side
and a winged skull at the base. – To members of the D'Anvers

family, erected 1790. By *Thomas Burnell & Sons* of London.
White, brown and grey marble. Short sarcophagus with an urn
standing on it. Two standing cherubs. Big obelisk on top. A
fine design. – Rev. James Harding †1837 by *M. W. Johnson*, with
a relief of a poppy and a broken lily.

Former RECTORY, E of the church. 1854, with additions and
alterations of 1869 by *E. F. Law*. Very elaborately Gothic. A low
tower over its entrance and a big gabled wing on the r. with
triple windows. Big chimneys on the l.

PRIMARY SCHOOL, NW of the church. The earliest part is the
DANVERS FREE SCHOOL, described as 'lately erected' in
1794. Ironstone of five bays with four upper windows and a
cupola. Enlarged in 1887 and 1902, the latter by *Law & Harris*.

DANVERS HOUSE. High Street, near the W end of the village.
Incorporating parts of the large mansion of Sir John Danvers
(succeeded 1712, †1744). The street façade somewhat confusing with two recessed two-bay sections with wide segmental
pediments and projecting wings of four bays with framed
windows, the r. bay slightly grander than the l. The window
frames with the pendant pieces and the giant angle pilasters
with unmoulded blocks instead of capitals might indeed be of
c. 1700 or a little later. At both E and W ends a big barn with
curved walling. A brick stable court on the W. There is a
sundial dated 1732 and a staircase with turned balusters. Now
subdivided.

The village is most attractive and has many good houses, several
of C17 date with banded stonework. Inside WESTHILL HOUSE,
High Street, good panelling, and a Jacobean overmantel with
Doric columns. A gable end by THE FORGE has a distinguished blacksmith-made six-hour Jubilee clock, unveiled
2012. In the centre a small green with the four-stepped base
of the MARKET CROSS, holding the war memorial in the form
of a medieval cross. N of the green THE OLD MANOR, an
L-shaped house of banded limestone and ironstone, mostly C17
with mainly wooden casement windows but a few stone mullions. Tall chimneystack on the W front. On the S side is MOR-
AVIAN COTTAGE (former chapel), 1810. Red brick, very simple
three-bay front.

CASTLE. Behind the church is the ringwork of a small castle
about 80 ft (25 metres) across with parts of its surrounding
ditch up to 20 ft (6 metres) wide. Of Anglo-Saxon or Norman
period, but its history is unclear.

DALLINGTON *see* OUTER NORTHAMPTON

DAVENTRY

Daventry was a small market town which in the C18 benefited
from the coach traffic that diverted through it from Watling

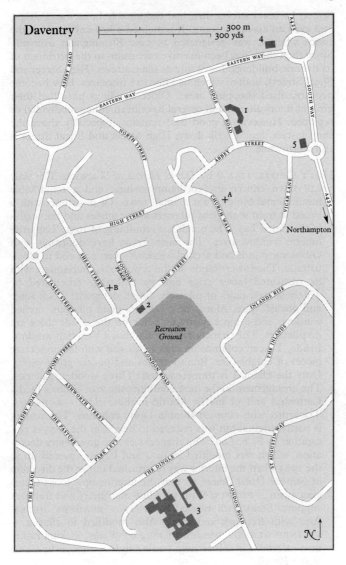

A Holy Cross
B United Reformed Church

1 District Council Offices
2 Police Station and Court House
3 Danetre Hospital
4 Icon Building
5 Working Mens Club

Street. Its main streets then had fashionable houses and shops, and even an assembly room. It remained a low-key town till the 1960s when it was designated to take Birmingham overspill. Since then there has been massive expansion to the detriment of its historic buildings. Inevitably its main streets (High Street and Sheaf Street), both of which had fine c18 frontages, have become pedestrianized shopping areas. Older buildings have had their ground floors altered and several have been either subdivided or replaced. However, a good deal remains, especially above the shop fascias, and a walk down High Street and Sheaf Street is still worthwhile.

76 HOLY CROSS. 1752–8 by *David Hiorne* of Warwick. The only c18 town church in Northamptonshire, and a remarkably monumental building for a small town. Of ironstone, with a broad W front with giant pilasters at the angles and the angles of the centre bay. The porch is a rebuilding of 1951. Tripartite lunette window over. The aisle fronts have doorways with Gibbs surrounds and arched windows over, and end in a balustrade. The tower stands on the centre bay, four-square with its rusticated lower stage and its bell-stage articulated by widely spaced pairs of pilasters. Small octagonal clock stage and obelisk spire. Along the S side are giant pilasters, arched windows and a top balustrade, while on the N side there are no pilasters. The chancel projects and has a Venetian window. Inside, Tuscan columns on high bases and with far-projecting pieces of entablature. Round arches and plaster groin-vaults. Only the chancel is tunnel-vaulted. Three wooden galleries. The arrangement in the nave combines those of Gibbs's Derby Cathedral and of his St Martin-in-the-Fields. – REREDOS. Tripartite, with coupled Roman Doric columns. The seating is partly original but was reduced in height in the 1873–4 restoration by *E. F. Law*. The chancel was also given extra decoration, which was modified in 1921 and largely covered up in the 1963 when the interior was refurbished under the direction of *Stephen Dykes Bower*, so that the interior now looks Georgian again. – PULPIT. With very fine marquetry and fretwork support. Stairs with twisted balusters. – READERS' DESKS. Also with fretwork and inlay. Also modified in 1873–4. – STAINED GLASS. E window of 1872 by *Wailes*, looking rather uncomfortable in this setting. S aisle window, 1930, is by *Christopher Powell*.

CHURCH (R.C.), London Road. 1971 by the *Ellis Williams Partnership* of Manchester.

UNITED REFORMED CHURCH. *See* Perambulation.

DAVENTRY DISTRICT COUNCIL OFFICES, Lodge Road. 1986–7 by *Hutchison, Locke & Monk* of Richmond, Surrey. An awkward angular site has been taken full advantage of, with multi-angled buildings in light and dark brown brick. A pyramidal roofed corner block houses the council chamber. Well-planted entrance with much red metalwork.

POLICE STATION and COURT HOUSE, New Street. The former a nondescript brick block. It replaces a police station of 1860. The court house with some late C17 allusions: an ironstone wall along the street, strongly projecting eaves, a hipped roof, and a cupola of 1982. Later extensions.

DANETRE HOSPITAL, London Road. Street frontage formed by the former WORKHOUSE. Red brick, of 1836–7, still classical and with a central pediment. At the side a simple brick Gothic CHAPEL, with a small apse. Interior with an ornamental iron roof and decoration of 1956 by *Henry Bird*. Some work by *E. F. Law* in 1880. Behind is the new hospital of 2004–6 by *AEDAS Architects* of Huddersfield. A fine complex with canopied entrance of glass and tubular metal. Two large segmental-arched wings, with another beyond. The low reception area gives way to a tall galleried hall. Large canvases of Morris dancing also by *Henry Bird*.

ICON BUILDING, on the roundabout of Eastern Way and Northern Way. 2009–11 by *Consarc*. A combined business and conference facility built by a consortium which includes the Daventry District Council, the West Northants Development Corporation and the University of Northampton, who now own the site. Expansive curved frontage with timber slats hiding the main building. Much glass. The structure was designed to be eco-friendly.

DANETRE SCHOOL, Hawke Road. Alterations and extensions 2001–2 by *PDD Architects* of Milton Keynes.

RECREATION GROUND, London Road. 1916 by *Arthur Harrison & George Cox*, architects. Ornamental ironstone gateway, classical, with two piers topped by floral drops, and a segmental-arched entrance, the spandrels of which are carved with people exercising dogs.

WORKING MENS CLUB, Abbey Street. 2009–10 by *Webb Gray & Partners* of Birmingham. An impressive building with metal cage turrets filled with ironstone chunks. It is sliced through by a big red wedge-shaped wall.

PERAMBULATION. The MARKET PLACE, with the church at its N end, is the place to start. S of the church the former RECTORY, early C19 stucco with a Doric porch. Next to the church, ABBEY BUILDINGS, the former National School. Ironstone in the Gothic style. Built in 1826, with additions of 1870. Big Gothic windows, marred by inappropriate glazing. It is on the site of a Cluniac priory, founded in 1090 at Preston Capes and moved to Daventry in 1107–8. It depended on La Charité-sur-Loire. Alongside a row of three-storey mock Georgian town houses, 2007–8, replacing a more modest row.

On the square's W side the MOOT HALL, 1769. Ironstone, three bays, two and a half storeys, the ground-floor windows arched. Pedimental gable right across; cupola. The adjoining house is of 1806 and contains the main entrance, with a porch. (The staircase of the Moot Hall is now at Welton Manor House.)

HIGH STREET starts with the BURTON MEMORIAL, a Gothic cross of 1908. Several houses of ironstone, especially No. 17 with a Gibbs surround to its doorway; then No. 27, late C17, with a porch (alas now a glazed box) and low, broad windows on three storeys; No. 29, a three-storeyed higher and plainer house of seven bays, Early Georgian, restored 1984 by *Sursham Tompkins & Partners*. On the r. into NORTH STREET to see two buildings once connected with a former school: first, to the l. is BISHOP CREWE HOUSE, *c.* 1840 Gothic, and further w, on the r. is WARDENS LODGE, 1887–8, by *N. M. Brown*, architect. Red brick Jacobean style with Ionic pilasters and many decorative panels. The main school buildings date from 1938, by *Bosworth & Wakeford*. The hall is now the Daventry Library. Lower in North Street is a small Neo-Georgian lodge and the charming little early C19 Gothick BEEHIVE HOUSE. Back to HIGH STREET for two banks: LLOYDS, late C19 red brick and stone Jacobean, and NATWEST, 1929 by *Law & Harris*. Three-bay Italianate top, having absorbed another Victorian building with much decoration alongside. Then the CONSERVATIVE CLUB, Early Victorian with Ionic pilasters and columns framing its doorway. Then a weak repeat of a façade which had canted bays and three gables, 1968 by *A. W. Walker & Partners*. Again on the former side Nos. 57–59, statelier than the others. Seven bays, two storeys, with quoins and a three-bay pedimented centre with quoins. Doorway, not in the centre, with Gibbs surround. Facing the end of the High Street, i.e. at the corner of Tavern Lane and Sheaf Street, No. 2, an Early Victorian Tudor fantasy, castellated and extending in a rambling fashion along Tavern Lane. Opposite, on the corner of Brook Street, the SARACEN'S HEAD, dated 1769, with a slightly squeezed courtyard of that date, including Venetian windows and a Venetian doorway. This was the Assembly Room and still has panelling and Georgian fireplaces at each end of the main room. Pretty staircase with three slender turned balusters to each tread and carved tread-ends.

Into SHEAF STREET, on the r. Nos. 20–22, KNIGHTLEYS, supposedly the town house of the Knightleys of Fawsley. A credible suggestion since it retains inside several fine C16 four-centred arched stone surrounds, that in the rear ground-floor room being wider and having remains of ovens. C17 splat baluster staircase. No. 24 was also originally part of the same property and has an inglenook fireplace. At the top of the street, on the l., Nos. 47–49, an eight-bay frontage of chequered brick with the archway which leads to the UNITED REFORMED CHURCH (former Congregational chapel) dated 1722. Four-square ironstone, stucco on entrance side with two doorways and two ranges of windows, some with delicate Gothick glazing. The house was Doddridge's Academy, 1752–5, where the scientist Joseph Priestley was a pupil. The street ends in a small square with a modern brick kiosk with pyramidal roof. At the corner of Sheaf Street, the WHEATSHEAF HOTEL, whitewashed, long, with irregular fenestration, but held together by the fine large Ionic lettering. C17 origin (traditionally where Charles I stayed on the night before Naseby) but C19 stucco externally. C17 staircase.

Turning N into NEW STREET, first the police station and court house (*see* above). Then, bypassing the inevitable supermarkets which have replaced old buildings, first JESSON'S WELL pub (the former Wesleyan chapel), 1824. Neoclassical, stucco. Then on the r. several red and blue late C18 chequer brick houses, No. 9 with pretty Late Georgian doorway and No. 5 the Master's House for the early GRAMMAR SCHOOL, dated 1600. No. 3 (Daventry Town Council) has a good late C18 baluster staircase (and currently houses a small museum). Ironstone with two ranges of four-light arched mullioned windows in its side wall. The house also has remains of mullions. Other chequer brick houses follow. So back to the Market Square.

The main INDUSTRIAL AREAS lie to the SE and to the NW (on the ROYAL OAK ESTATE), e.g. the former Ingersoll factory (CUMMINS) by *H. Sheppard Fidler & Associates*, 1967–8; and the FORD MOTOR CO. of 1966–72. To the SE on the edge of Borough Hill is the pleasantly laid out SOUTHBROOK ESTATE, designed by *J. A. Maudsley* (City of Birmingham Architect's Department). This was the first comprehensive neighbourhood unit designed for the town expansion, and was begun in 1966. The houses are grouped in short terraces, mostly in culs de sac. On the N side of the town, off the A425 above the Drayton Reservoir, is MIDDLEMORE, a modern estate by various developers but keeping a Neo-Georgian town house manner, amusingly with street names taken from National Trust properties. On its N edge MIDDLEMORE FARMHOUSE, late C18 brick, now a public house and restaurant, incorporating the fine long brick barn with its old timbers.

The hamlet of DRAYTON, W of centre, still has several stone cottages, a MANOR HOUSE of C17 date with mullioned windows, and a pretty Victorian former SCHOOL, red brick, Tudor style with diamond glazing, and a bellcote.

BOROUGH HILL. An Iron Age hillfort of at least two periods. On top of the hill there was a group of round barrows that were probably of Bronze Age origin, but investigations in C19 also recovered both Roman cremation burials and Early Saxon metalwork, indicating two periods of secondary use. The barrows are now levelled. A bank and ditch along the 180-metre contour line encloses some 150 acres (60 ha), and this is best observed on the W, close to the golf course. A small hillfort at the N end of the hill was probably a later addition, but the sequence has not been established by excavation. An impressive bank and ditch, with counterscarp bank, encloses an area of 4½ acres (1.8 ha), with the S side protected by a double bank and ditch, with a possible original entrance to the SE. Trial trenches excavated within the hillfort in the 1980s and 1990s recovered finds of the Late Bronze Age and the Early to middle Iron Age, and evidence for roundhouses within the hillfort. A Roman villa within the smaller hillfort was extensively excavated in C19. Now an open area save for several buildings of the former BBC TRANSMITTING STATION, dating from 1925, and others of 1932 and 1935.

BURNT WALLS, S of Borough Hill, between the railway and the main road. A ditch and banked enclosure is roughly triangular, measuring 180 metres by 90 metres, with a central entrance strengthened by a counterscarp bank. It is undated, but its low-lying position and well-preserved earthworks may suggest a medieval date.

7040

DEANSHANGER

HOLY TRINITY. By *B. Ferrey*, 1853–4. Nave, N aisle, chancel. Lancet windows and windows with plate tracery. Good W wall with tall blank arch inset with two lancets and a sexfoil circle above and triple bellcote. Alterations to the building are recorded in 1896–7 by *E. Swinfen Harris*. – PULPIT. A rich piece with three statues in niches and red marble columns. – STAINED GLASS. Chancel E, 1906 and nave S window of 1915 both by *Jones & Willis*. – Another with the Good Shepherd, 1950, probably by *G. Maile*.

METHODIST CHAPEL, just E of the church, of 1892, built by *C. Coker* of Wolverton. Gothic red brick, with gabled school behind.

A wide GREEN at the S entrance to the village, with, on its S side, the SCHOOL, 1858, stone in the Tudor manner. On the N side CARPENTER'S CHARITY HOMES, built in 1823. Eight bays in a 2–4–2 rhythm. The ground-floor windows have hoodmoulds, the upper windows are lunette-shaped. To the N in High Street the CONSERVATIVE CLUB, 1889, red brick and stone, and further W the remaining buildings of E. & H. ROBERTS ENGINEERING business. Red brick of five bays of *c.* 1860. The business was established in 1847 and closed in 1999. Conversion into apartments proposed in 2012.

9090

DEENE

ST PETER (Churches Conservation Trust). Mostly the work of *Thomas Henry Wyatt*, who in 1868–9 restored the church and completely rebuilt the E portions. The whole conception of a church of unified design, placed entirely on its own like a model on a table, is highly Victorian. Original work the W tower. It is of the C13. W doorway with stiff-leaf capitals and dogtooth. Two-light bell-openings with shafts and quatrefoils over. Parapet. Recessed broach spire with ribbed edges, and one of the earliest recessed spires in the country. The lower lucarnes are very tall and have two tiers of windows, the lower trefoil-headed with cusps, the upper of two lights with a shaft and a trefoil over. Very small second lucarnes higher up in the diagonals. C13 arcades with tall circular piers, circular abaci and double-chamfered arches. Dec aisle windows. Wyatt extended the nave to the E and added his extremely ornate E.E. chancel and chapels. Much use of rich foliage carving and different coloured marbles for pillars. Splendid array of *Maw*'s tiles on the chancel floor. The stencilling and other decoration of the chancel is of 1890 by *Bodley*. Not the most unified effect with large panels of damask patterns in red and green and areas of more open stencilled designs. SEDILIA and PISCINA all coloured and gilded. – FONT. 1868–9. – REREDOS, Brudenell Chapel. 1635, i.e. of the time when the Brudenells were Roman Catholic, and probably originally in the chapel of the house. Three oval medallions, corn-ears and paten, the Sacred Heart, and vines and chalice. – STAINED GLASS. E window by *Lavers, Barraud & Westlake*, 1869, and the armorials in the S chapel are also by them, as is the tower window. N aisle two windows of 1897 by *Burlison & Grylls*. A fine S aisle window by *R. Anning Bell*, 1919. – MONUMENTS. The monuments of the Brudenells fill the S chancel chapel. They are, in approximately chronological order: Sir Robert †1531 and two wives, alabaster effigies of fine quality on a sarcophagus with coarse Renaissance balusters and still Gothic quatrefoil panels between. Attributed to *Richard Parker* of Burton upon Trent. – Brasses of *c*. 1580 (Edmund †1585), 1586 (Sir Thomas †1549), and *c*. 1606 (John †1606). – Plain blank arches without figures: Agnes Lady Brudenell †1583 with Ionic pilasters and a top with cartouches, arms in a wreath, and obelisks. On the base simple geometrical shapes connected by bands. – With Doric pilasters John †1606 and Edmund †1652. – Robert †1599. Tomb-chest, used as an altar. With three shields connected by coarse arabesques. The inscription still in black letter. – Thomas, 1st Earl of Cardigan, †1663. Odd, fragmentary-looking monument, made from a fossily stone from near Raunds, known locally as 'Rance'. Front one open arch with Ionic pilasters. Sides two half-arches. No figures. – Anne, Duchess of Richmond, †1722. Bust by *Guelfi* (terracotta study for the bust in the V&A). On an inscribed base surrounded by an exquisitely designed and detailed frame with egg-and-dart and two young caryatids outside it in profile. Metope frieze and pediment. The frame is taken from the frontispiece of *Kent*'s Palladio edition of 1730. The frame was carved and signed by *John Bossom*. – Countess of Cardigan †1826. By *Sievier*. Tablet with lush, somewhat French, Grecian decoration. – 7th Earl of Cardigan †1868. By *Sir J. E. Boehm*. Recumbent white marble effigies of him and his second wife on a big sarcophagus of alabaster and coloured marbles (models for the two heads by Boehm are preserved in the house). Bronze reliefs on this and bronze seahorses, the Brudenell crest, at the bottom corners. – Coloured wooden

102

memorial, enclosing an early medieval stone crucifix found
near the coach house, for Lord Robert Brudenell Bruce †1912
and Lady Emma †1921, erected 1923 and very much of its
time. – George Brudenell †1962 and his wife †1972, two finely
lettered plaques by *David Kindersley*. The churchyard has a
good assembly of carved headstones and table tombs.

DEENE PARK. The Brudenells had lived for at least 250 years in
Northamptonshire when in 1514 Sir Robert acquired Deene
Park. The house is still in the family. Most of what we see now
was done by the Brudenells and first of all by the two owners
after Sir Robert: Sir Thomas, who married a Fitzwilliam of
Milton, took over Deene Park in 1520, and died in 1549, and
Sir Edmund, who entertained Queen Elizabeth I at Deene in
1566 and died in 1585. While it is this C16 work which makes
the house architecturally important and enjoyable, it is the
remains of the pre-Brudenell house which make the layout
interesting. The architectural story is, however, not without its
problems.

The house is large and built round a spacious courtyard. It
is approached from the N, and the NORTH RANGE is of the
second half of the C17, with cross-windows and castellated. The
tall four-storeyed tower at the NE angle belongs to the E rather
than the N side and this should be looked at first. The EAST
FRONT is the most interesting and the most unexpected. It is
also the most picturesque, as it appears across the lake or
foreshortened from the fine C18 bridge. The front is completely
asymmetrical, demonstrating almost every period of the architectural history of the house, and it has a complicated sequence.
The centre is the pre-Brudenell chamber range, with its solar/
undercroft proportion, now only evident in the corner where
we have a large window on the first floor and a smaller below.
This feeling of proportion is essential to understand what has
happened here. Already noted is the work of Sir Robert and
Sir Thomas Brudenell in the early C16. So one has to visualize
an L-shaped range, with the stem of the L as the chamber range
and the foot of the L the added SE range, and all this just one
room thick. Only the southern half of the SE range is Tudor,
so the chimneys mark the original back wall of the wing.
Immediately behind the Hall, whose gable, with its diamond-
shaped opening, rears above the range at the corner of the L,
was a two storey chamber. To this was added around 1550–60
a large ornamental bay window. All this time formal gardens
were on this side of the house. Around 1620 Sir Thomas
Brudenell decided to add a new block onto the back of the SE
range, and this had a library above and an open loggia below.
The arches of the loggia were filled in in the C18 but are still
traceable in the N wall. This addition meant the removal of the
1550–60 bay; rather than being discarded, it was rebuilt against
the chimneystack further N along the wing, and it is this which
is the showpiece of the E front. It is an extraordinary thing to
have done, and the clue to it being a rebuilding is that its
storeys are in reverse: the smaller windows, formerly of the low

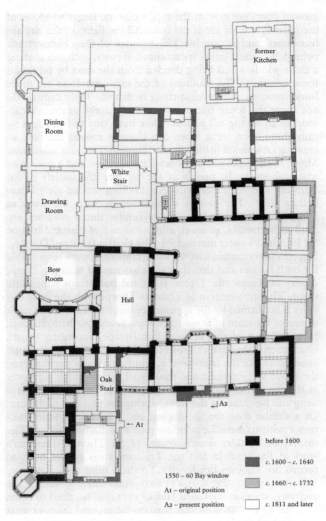

**Deene Park.
Plan**

former
Kitchen

Dining
Room

White
Stair

Drawing
Room

Bow
Room

Hall

Oak
Stair

A2

A1

before 1600

c. 1600 – c. 1640

c. 1660 – c. 1732

c. 1811 and later

1550 – 60 Bay window
A1 – original position
A2 – present position

ground floor, are now at the top, while the larger windows of
the taller first floor are at the base. All the lights of the bay are
transomed and all are blocked because of the chimneystack
behind. The eight lights are arranged in pairs, each pair making
a cross-window and being divided from the next by fat fluted
Ionic columns. The mullions of the cross-windows are more
Ionic columns. The oddest thing is that the Ionic capitals do
not carry the frieze but are part of it. Lively strapwork cartouches in all the sill panels. They have tiny trefoil edges so
must have been recut when Sir Thomas moved the bay, so
creating an allusion to his wife, Sir Thomas Tresham's daughter
Mary. In the ogee gable a three-light window and a rosette or
wheel above it. In panels at the top are the initials of Sir
Edmund and Agnes his wife. All this supports an early Elizabethan date. The closest comparison is with the work at
Dingley of the late 1550s, where similar fluted columns are
used as buttresses, so an equally naïve use of classical motifs.
Sir Edmund's sister married into the Griffin family of Dingley.
It seems fairly certain that the same craftsmen were responsible
for both houses and that they were associated with the *Thorpe*
quarry at Kingscliffe. Deene is indeed built from Kingscliffe
stone. The involvement of Thomas Thorpe with the early C17
work is confirmed by the appearance on stonework of the mark
of one of his team of masons, *Samson Frisby* (*see* Introduction,
p. 36). Just s of this curious frontispiece, according to C18
illustrations, the chapel projected. This also had a truncated
ogee gable like the frontispiece, and there was a gap between
the broad SE projection and the chapel. The dominating tower
at the NE corner was formed by reducing the length of the N
wing and heightening the walls, during the first half of the C17.
Of a similar date are the gables, and the curious little stair-
turret with its heraldic window piercings halfway along. The
display of heraldry is reminiscent of Sir Thomas Tresham's
work at Rushton. In fact the Tresham arms appear here, to
record Sir Thomas Brudenell's Tresham marriage.

Returning to the COURTYARD and entering under the
archway, ahead is the Great Hall of 1571, but we need to begin
with the EAST WING. Within this, on the ground floor, in what
is now the billiard room, are the earliest visible remains from
pre-Brudenell days, the jamb of an archway of C13 or C14 date,
which originally went through to a chapel. This range was the
chamber range of the early house and it still has the proportion
of a solar/undercroft arrangement with the larger rooms on the
first floor. Unusually it is lit from the courtyard by what
appears to be a large bay window, the work probably by Sir
Thomas Brudenell in the early C16, but it is clear that what
appear to be blocked lights were in fact built in this way to
disguise the floor level. The top lights only have four-centred
arches. There is also a small doorway with four-centred head
and hoodmould. The attic gables are an early C17 addition (see
also the E front and the NE tower).

The Elizabethan GREAT HALL on the s side of the courtyard is the work of Sir Edmund and has on the porch his arms
and those of his first wife, who died in 1583. A note by Sir
Edmund states that he began the Hall in 1571. The composition is still entirely asymmetrical, the porch to the r. of the
centre, the hall bay window in the angle between this side and
the E side of the courtyard. Inside, this links the new Hall with
the older house. The bay window has two transoms, the other
windows one. All have lights with four-centred heads, also
below the transoms. Parapet with semicircular merlons instead
of the normal battlements. This motif had appeared at Dingley
already in the 1550s. This is so far the only faint sign of Italian
influence. The PORCH on the other hand is almost wholly
Italian. The doorway has a round arch and busy foliage in the
spandrels. To the l. and r. are pilasters with a decoration by
vertically linked oblongs and ovals which is specially characteristic of Northamptonshire at this moment. Ionic capitals.
Frieze with handsome foliage scrolls and little naked figures
holding the coat of arms. The pilasters on the upper floor have
guilloche decoration and Corinthian capitals. The pilasters
repeat singly on the sides of the porch. All is crisply carved and
very probably by the same carvers who were working a few
miles away at Kirby Hall, so once again associated with the
Thorpes of Kingscliffe.

Now, the INTERIOR. The largest room inside is the GREAT
HALL of the 1570s. It has a splendid open timber roof of sweet
chestnut with alternating single and double hammerbeams,
pendants, and ogee wind-braces. Fine wall panelling of the dais
wall, the lower tier with Doric pilasters, the upper with caryatids and volutes and small panels with inlay patterns. The
splendid chimneypiece of Kingscliffe stone with the date 1571   42
was moved back here in 1966 from the ground floor of the E
wing where it had been resited in the early C18. The fireplace
frame is still in the Perp tradition of mouldings, but it is flanked
by pilasters with sunk panels and roundels and lunettes in the
Venetian fashion. These repeat in the overmantel. The centre
here is a coat of arms within an elegantly detailed frame. The
workmanship compares with a chimneypiece at Apethorpe
dated 1562 and the Yorkist tombs at Fotheringhay of 1573, all
like the E front feature linked with the *Thorpes* of Kingscliffe.

The early house lay to the E and NE of this hall. The present
BILLIARD ROOM takes up most of the ground-floor area of
the early chamber range. Within it is the early C14 arch already
mentioned,* and also the sill and base of the C16 courtyard
bay window. The curious internal arrangement behind the E
front bay window centrepiece was revealed when the fireplace
was moved, and shows considerable signs of not being in its
original form, with some misplaced corbels. Simple moulded

---

* There is another possible medieval arched doorway leading into the North Room
at the base of the tower.

beamed ceiling of Tudor date overlaid with early C18 plasterwork.

The OAK STAIRCASE, E of the Great Hall, was prior to the C19 the principal stair. It was inserted into a two-storey chamber, lit originally by the 1550–60 bay window. The wall which divides the space from what was the loggia room of the C17 marks its former position. (In 1971 a chapel was formed in that room.) The stair has large vertical supports of late C16 date and at ground level there are remains of stud partitions between the uprights. When Sir Thomas made his alterations c. 1620 and the bay window was removed, the space must have been very dark, so partitions were cut away and the simple, somewhat coarse geometrical openwork balustrade panels were inserted. The two geometrically decorated posts at the base of the stair may have been part of the first floor arrangement. Their form is reminiscent of the supports for the table and bench in the hall, original from 1571. To create extra light an octagonal skylight was added c. 1720. At the top of the stairs the TAPESTRY and TOWER ROOMS, with splendid Jacobean plaster ceilings. The pattern in the Tapestry Room is especially attractive, with short pendants. The pendants here are the hub of large circles divided into four quarters with framed strap-work cartouches, a pattern derived from Serlio. Above the Tapestry Room are the remains of an early C16 flat timber ceiling with heavily moulded beams. Above this, rebuilt within the attic, is the original C15 open timber roof of the range, with collar-beams on arched braces.

The rooms in the SE wing are still basically early C16 in layout, and many have contemporary fireplaces with four-centred heads. The very thick spine wall running E–W through this wing was originally the outside N wall. On the upper floor in KING HENRY'S ROOM is fine but rearranged early C16 linenfold panelling of unusual pattern. Sir Thomas Brudenell, later Lord Brudenell and yet later the 1st Earl of Cardigan, who died in 1663, was so convinced that Henry VII had slept here that he set up Henry's arms in the room. In SIR EDMUND'S ROOM is part of a timber-framed partition wall of the early C16.

Back on the ground floor, from E to W along the S range. First a small lobby (called the Void), thought to be the site of the early medieval or Tudor staircase; then a panelled room with a fine early C18 moulded plaster ceiling, probably the work of *Joshua Needham*;* then the OAK PARLOUR with good mid-C17 panelling brought from Howley on the former Brudenell Estate on Yorkshire, with frieze ornament almost identical to that in St John's church in Leeds. There follows a

---

* Needham was a plasterer frequently employed by *Francis Smith* of Warwick and there is documentary evidence that Smith was advising on creating a new staircase to the S of the Hall. To gain access a large arch was cut through the S wall of the Hall, and this is when the fireplace was moved in to what is now the Billiard Room (*see* above). These changes are recorded on a fine plan of 1746 by *Brasier* in the house.

suite of large rooms of *c.* 1800–10, with simple Regency decoration, the BOW ROOM, DRAWING ROOM and DINING ROOM, the last with a good late C18 chimneypiece brought down from upstairs *c.* 1970. Then the WHITE HALL, also *c.* 1800, with an open-well staircase with cast-iron balustrade and an octagonal glazed dome, and the ANTE-HALL, the family dining room, with an elegant *c.* 1770 chimneypiece.

Finally, the other external fronts. In the courtyard the WEST RANGE is an Elizabethan refacing of the earlier range, with some later remodelling, including C17 gables. The SOUTH FRONT, overlooking the terrace and park, consists of three parts: the E third is buttressed work of the early C16, but with sash windows of *c.* 1725; the centre third is of *c.* 1800 in a Neo-Tudor style, a slightly larger edition of its earlier neighbour; and the remaining third contained the ballroom added in 1865, but this was demolished in 1984 and only its base courses now stand. The W side of the house is totally irregular, and since the demolition of the mid-C18 laundry block in 1968 has no features of note. The laundry was a two-storeyed, seven-bay building with a one-bay pediment.

Something needs to be said about STAINED GLASS. The earliest are the quarries in the window at the top of the Oak Stair with heraldic animals and shields; this may have originally been in the 1550–60 bay window. Of *c.* 1620 is the extensive heraldic glass in the Great Hall windows with a display of heraldic alliances of the family, with notably shields for Tresham and Fitzwilliam. Of early C17 date are painted figures of saints, a pair of windows high up at either end of the hall, and a further pair of figures in a window by the North Room. In the Conservatory at the W end of the house are several panels with heraldry from the Victorian ballroom. The excellent mock late C17 glass panels in the chapel were made in 2008 by *Alan Younger.*

The GARDEN retains a brick-walled kitchen garden, already in existence by 1715 (plan in the house), and a Tudor style SUMMERHOUSE built by the 6th Earl. A parterre was created along the S front in 1991 using designs by *David Hicks*, deriving from Elizabethan patterns within the house. The water below the house incorporates the length of an C18 formal CANAL created by *Van der Meulen.*

STABLE BLOCK. C18/19 with attached circular RIDING SCHOOL.

ENTRANCE LODGE on the A43. *John Crake* exhibited a design for a lodge in 1841, but this does not seem to have been built, since *T. H. Wyatt* exhibited another design in 1850 and that must surely be what stands today. Tudor style, with a tall archway, turrets and battlements.

The village has some pretty thatched cottages and a number of *c.* 1800 ESTATE COTTAGES of a consistent style with deep overhanging eaves. Former SCHOOL of 1872 by *George Vialls*. Stone in Tudor style. The earlier building of 1825 to the l. Opposite the kitchen garden walls is the former SEAHORSE

INN, now two houses. Originally built as the dower house and called 'Little Deene'. Two three-bay wings on either side of a central projection. The W wing is C17 (mullioned windows), altered when the rest was built *c.* 1720. E wing with mullion-and-transom-cross windows. In the centre a Venetian window with pointed centre arch. Dormer windows with alternating segment-headed and triangular pediments. Interiors of unusually high quality. In the W wing a panelled room with arched recess, in the E wing a room with plaster panels and two arched recesses.

On the other side of the main road to the SW the estate hamlet of DEENETHORPE with further early C19 cottages. Many new houses built in sympathetic style 2005–8, others added in 2011–12.

DELAPRÉ *see* NORTHAMPTON

DENFORD

9070

HOLY TRINITY. Close to the River Nene. Fine C13 W tower with lancets, tall two-light bell-openings with spherical triangles over, a blank arch l. and r. of them, and a tall spire with two tiers of lucarnes. The spire is both broached and recessed behind a parapet with pinnacles. C13 chancel of bands of iron-stone and grey stone. The windows are renewed but represent the late C13. Late C13 also the N aisle NE and the S aisle SE windows, equally typical in their tracery, the S porch (entrance with nailhead decoration), the simple S and N doorways, and the arcades of four bays with quatrefoil piers and double-chamfered arches. The details differ with only the S still having its bases. Inside the original SEDILIA and PISCINA, and, on the N side, blind arcading of the same design. Doorway to former N chapel. Moulded arches with large cusps and the columns miniature versions of the nave arcades. Above this a mysterious relieving arch with small holes in the tympanum made for acoustic jars. One of these survives. Only the E window of four lights is Perp but its jambs show that it may have originally been a series of lancets or a large window with bar tracery like those on the S side. Good Late Dec windows in the S aisle, straight-headed with reticulation units, the one to the E of the porch almost Perp. Two very large Perp windows in the N aisle. The restoration was 1864–5 by *Wadmore & Baker*. Further work was done in 1925–7 by *H. F. Traylen*, when much of the interior, including the arcades, was limewashed and the Perp style stone PULPIT introduced. A rather jolly series of grimacing gargoyle heads. – CURIOSITY. A wonderful painted piano decorated on the front with Apollo with his lyre charming the animals. The sides have trees with birds. – STAINED

GLASS. S aisle E. C16 and C17 Flemish roundels. Brought here in 1969.

Nice selection of stone cottages some with datestones such as the pub clearly declaring 1593 and to its r. a gable end of 1622 with carved finial.

DENTON

ST MARGARET. Unbuttressed C13 W tower. The body of the church rebuilt in 1827–8 by *Charles Squirhill* and similar in pattern to his rebuilding of Abington church, Northampton (q.v.). Aisleless with pointed windows. Flat ceiling and W gallery. However, the W responds of the former aisles have been allowed to remain, and so have the C13 chancel and two C13 lancet windows, re-set in the vestry. – FONT. Circular with bold, coarse, large cross patterns. Probably 1629, which is the date on a stone in the chancel. The building was until 1975 just a plain box but then a scheme of MURAL DECORATION was begun by the Northampton artist *Henry Bird*. This has transformed the interior with a delightful colourful programme. There are ten murals beginning on the N side: the Garden of Gethsemane; St Dorothea; St Margaret of Antioch; Moses and the Burning Bush; the Conversion of St Paul; the Flight into Egypt; Joseph of Arimathea; St Werberg and St Chad; the Three Wise Men; the Shepherds. Under the gallery panels with historical figures connected with Denton. In addition a three-arched SCREEN, painted with architectural tracery, was inserted across the chancel. This is the least satisfactory part of the scheme, more so since 2011 as it cuts across the STAINED GLASS E window designed by *Susan Brownridge* and made by *Nicholas Bechgaard*.*

BAPTIST CHAPEL, just S of the church. 1878 with a red brick pedimented front, pilasters with two round-arched windows and a doorway.

Below the church a pretty GREEN with some pleasant stone houses, some thatched, others with pantiles. A house near the church has a Georgian Ionic porch but mullioned windows in three storeys. In a field a little more to the W a circular DOVE-COTE with a C17 lantern. Elsewhere considerable evidence of the Compton Estate of Castle Ashby with several neat rows of stone cottages. Especially good ones in Bedford Road.

COMPTON HOUSE, Vicarage Lane. Built for the son of the 5th Marquess of Northampton by *Fairfax B. Wade* in 1893, in elaborate brick and stone Jacobean.

DENTON WOOD LODGE, SW of the village. Brick and rendered farmhouse containing fragments of timber framing believed to be part of a Tudor hunting lodge.

*A proposal for reordering the interior which includes the possible removal of the screen is under consideration (2013).

DESBOROUGH

Desborough has suffered by ill planning since the C19, and is split by the main road. Except for the parish church and a small number of ironstone buildings in the High Street it has little to offer.

ST GILES. Arcades of two bays, but in reality one-bay nave and wide transept. Originally probably two bays and no transept. Of that date the C13 quatrefoil pier on the N side with a curious stiff-leaf capital, the leaves emanating from diagonally placed long, bare stalks. Then the transept was formed, the second N arch reused over a wider distance, and the S bays were built (octagonal pier). The short, wide plan is due to the peculiar site of the church. The N doorway belongs to the quatrefoil pier or may be yet earlier. The date of the transepts can be read from the windows. They have Y-tracery cusped, three-light cusped intersected tracery, and also two lights and a trefoiled circle. Those in the E wall of the S transept rather more elaborate than the rest. The chancel SEDILIA and PISCINA again clearly late C13, with renewed trefoil arches. The church was restored by *Edmund Law*, 1870–2. Ashlar-faced Perp W tower. It looks C15, but a donation to its building is recorded for 1529. Clasping buttresses. Pairs of two-light transomed bell-openings under one big ogee arch (cf. Arthingworth). Frieze of cusped lozenges. The battlements fade into broaches, the pinnacles do the same. Spire with two tiers of lucarnes. Perp clerestory. Very pretty stone roof above the rood stair, with a four-centred arch, battlements and a double frieze of quatrefoils, probably Late Perp like the tower. – SCREEN. C15 across the S transept, but originally across the chancel. – STAINED GLASS. A number of good windows, including chancel S, 1921 by *Curtis, Ward & Hughes*. – N aisle, W, 1907 by *Percy Bacon*. – In the S transept two windows, one the Annunciation, 1955 by *M. Davis* for *Leonard Matthews Studios*, the other, 1948 by *G. R. Smith* for *A. K. Nicholson Studios*. – SCULPTURE. Part of a Saxon cross-shaft with two addorsed beasts and interlace. Also two other Saxon fragments. – MONUMENT. Mrs Pulton †1779, of *Coade* stone, and very fine. A sarcophagus at the top with two putti holding a drape with a coat of arms. Below an inscription tablet recording the Pulton family. At the base a delightful cherub head amidst palm branches.

UNITED REFORMED CHURCH, Union Street, an extension of Victoria Street. Of 1912 by *Sharman & Archer* of Wellingborough. An extraordinarily fine building. Basically cruciform but each wing given very individual treatment using red brick and here and there some chequer tiling. The style is somewhere between Romanesque and classical, with most interesting roof levels, recesses, shallow buttresses and corbelling. The interior is one large space but simply treated. – STAINED GLASS. E window, 1949 by *Barton, Kinder & Alderson*. – W window, 1967 by *Abbot & Co.*, Lancaster.

HOLY TRINITY (R.C.), Victoria Street. Formerly a Wesleyan chapel of 1894 *by J. A. Gotch.*

HAVELOCK JUNIOR SCHOOL, Victoria Street. 1891, also *Gotch.* Ironstone with projecting gabled bays and the usual large mullion-transom windows.

N of the church is CHURCH HOUSE. Five bays, of *c.* 1700. The original wooden cross-windows have been replaced by sashes. A little further NE, in Paddock Lane, a former FACTORY, five storeys, ten windows wide, very shallow. Late C19, though the date is uncertain. At the corner of the HIGH STREET, SERVICES CLUB, an elegant stuccoed C19 house. Porch with Doric columns in antis. Further N, HAZELAND, old people's flatlets, by the County Architect, *John Goff,* 1970–1, in brown brick and wood, with split pitched roof, nicely in scale with what still remains of the town centre. By the N end of the High Street the MARKET CROSS, a rusticated C18 pillar with a ball finial. On the s side '81 miles from London'. Further N, on the w side of HARBOROUGH ROAD (A576), are the former garages of the UNITED COUNTIES OMNIBUS CO., built in 1925, now a commercial unit. Brown and red brick with an entrance between two wide pedimented wings divided by pilasters into three bays with two windows in each, except on the r. which has a further opening.

Former CO-OPERATIVE SOCIETY CORSET FACTORY, s on the Rothwell Road. 1905 by *L. G. Ekins* of the Wholesale Co-operative Society and ingeniously laid out behind in 1919, also by Ekins, to take in the sloping site of Federation Avenue. The gentle Neo-Georgian office building *c.* 1930 alongside is probably his too (cf. Christchurch Road Co-op premises, Abington, Northampton).

DINGLEY

7080

ALL SAINTS. On the edge of the lawn of Dingley Hall. The church originates from a C12 building of which the responds of the s arcade are the only clear remnants. The arcade otherwise is C14 (octagonal piers, double-chamfered arches). The N arcade is odd. All the arches are round suggesting C12, with a pier of masonry for the westernmost pillar. This presumably marks the w end of the C12 nave. But are the arcades C12? The s chapel was either added or rebuilt under the terms of the will of Edward Griffin *c.* 1571 and most of the windows are four-light arched mullion type of a late C16 form. The N arcade looks suspiciously like a reworking at the same time and if this is so it is a useful indication of that period. The w tower is Perp. There was a restoration of the chancel in 1885–7 by *John T. Lee,* and some work was done in 1926 by *Talbot Brown & Fisher.* The interior has been reordered and of the old furnishings remains panelling in the aisles and chancel, made from the former box pews. – PULPIT. Georgian, adjusted, so that its star inlaid panel instead of being on the front is near the back. – RAILS. Wrought-iron scroll shapes, *c.* 1950–60. – STAINED GLASS. N aisle of 1934 by *A. K. Nicholson.* – BRASSES. Anne Boroeghe †1577, a former nun who settled at Dingley. Kneeling figure and interesting inscription. – Countess Beatty †1932, also a kneeling figure. – MONUMENTS. Many, but few of note. The best is for Thomas Peach †1770 by *Joseph Evans* of Derby. – In the churchyard, by the gate, the grand tomb of the Jutland hero, Admiral David Lord Beatty †1936. – A number of nice slate headstones, with a pretty one on the wall S of the church with an ogee engraved surround of 1776 and nearby a touching one for Joseph Tapfield †1783, aged twenty-three, footman to J. P. Hungerford, erected by 'His grateful Master in memory of his FIDELITY, HONESTY and SOBRIETY' and at the bottom: 'Servants – follow his Example'!

DINGLEY HALL. The years between 1550 and 1560 are rare years in English domestic architecture. The style is no longer Henry VIII and not yet Elizabethan. What it is can be learned in few places as interestingly as at Dingley.

There was a preceptory of the Knights Hospitallers of St John here which was dissolved at the Reformation. It is possible that parts are incorporated or reused. The house in the form in which it survived up to 1961 is due to Edward Griffin and Sir Edward Griffin, the one dating work in 1558 and 1560, the other building in the 1680s and, according to Sir Gyles Isham's suggestion, using as his architect *Hugh May*, who was a relation of his wife. Marcus Binney, however, has suggested that *William Winde* might be responsible. The house was a courtyard house. The W wing was pulled down in 1780–2. The E wing was partly demolished in 1972. Nothing is now left of the original interiors, which had already been altered in the 1930s. There was panelling of 1560 on the first floor of the S range, and a fine chimneypiece with monkeys and garlands, of *c.* 1730, was in a first-floor room projecting to the E of the S range. There was also a good late C17 staircase. The house became derelict after it was sold in 1961. The C16 parts and the 1680s house were converted into residences in 1978 by *Kit Martin*.

The approach is from the S through a gateway still flanked by polygonal towers, although these towers are not made into a showpiece as was usual under Henry VII and VIII and Queen Elizabeth. The archway has a four-centred head, the spandrels a little foliage decoration. Round the arch run two lines of writing. Edward Griffin was Attorney General to Edward VI and Queen Mary and demonstrates by the inscriptions on his building that he was a fanatic Catholic – a forerunner of Sir Thomas Tresham in the architectural demonstration of his faith. The inscriptions read as follows:

What thing so fair but Time will pare. Anno 1560. Sorte tua contentus abi. Ne sutor ultra crepidam. Emeri pro virtutem proesta quam per dedus vivere. That that thou doest do it wisely and mark the end and so forth. Invigilate viri, tacito nam tempora grassu / Diffu-giunt, melloque sono convertitur annus / Si Deus nobiscum quis contra nos. God save the King 1560

– that is King Philip of Spain. So that could still be written in stone so publicly two years after the accession of the Virgin Queen. The window above the archway is of three lights, transomed, and has no arched lights, although many windows in the rest of the house have. Above the window a characteristically steep pediment. To the l. and r. of the archway are pilasters, and they carry corbels instead of capitals. On the corbels stand strips, and pilasters which are set diagonally, as if they were buttresses. All such details are eloquent of the fancifulness, the lack of discipline, and the brimming-over inventiveness which precede the Elizabethan Settlement. The gatehouse and the wing to its l. which linked up with the w wing have instead of battlements round, or rather more than semicircular merlons.

After passing through the archway one is in what is left of the courtyard and, turning round, sees that the archway went through the last of four arches of a short arcade or cloister placed rather inorganically. It occupies only the l. half of this façade; the r. half is closed, and ends in a polygonal tower, again with the rounded merlons. The arcade arches are four-

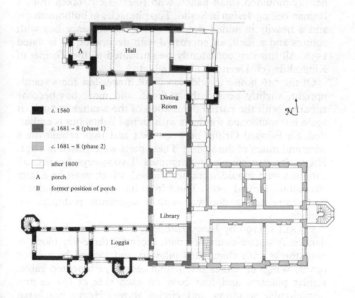

Dingley Hall.
Plan

centred, not round. The windows here have mullions and arched lights, and the cresting is not merlons but elongated half-decagons with concave sides and shell or arms infillings. The arcade arches are separated by elongated Ionic columns with an excessive entasis, clearly derived from the baluster and candelabra shapes so popular in the 1530s and 1540s. On the upper floor the columns are indeed balusters. Foliage grows up their bulbous lowest parts. It is all redolent of Northamptonshire masons getting to grips with ideas of the Renaissance.

What the E and W sides were like we cannot now say, and the present appearance of the N side, which contains the Great Hall, is also mute. However, the entrance to the Hall exists; it has been re-set against the W end of the Hall and converted into a porch. Drawings by George Clarke show that the porch originally was opposite the arcade. When it was rebuilt many details were misplaced. It is a showpiece which one is not likely to forget. The doorway has a four-centred head and scrolly carving in the spandrels. To the l. and r. are coupled fluted Corinthian columns. Turning round the corner single columns flank a window (cf. Kirby Hall). On the capitals stand semicircular projections, and they carry thin fluted shafts. The upper window is altered, but has its original steep pediment. At the foot of this a cornice runs to continue along front and side, projecting in a curve above the shafts. Above it the shafts continue. To the l. and r. of the window and the pediment heavily moulded small panels with rosettes etc. taken from a Roman ceiling design in Serlio. Top pinnacles of bulbous shape and a heavily moulded flourish above the entrance bay with volutes and a shell, all encrusted with decoration. It is dated 1558. All this can confidently be attributed to the *Thorpes* of Kingscliffe (cf. Deene, Kirby Hall, etc.).

Of the C16 house in addition a tall, tower-like mass stands upright, slightly behind the N front, and more has become apparent with the partial demolition of the E range in 1972. It again has mullioned windows with arched lights, but is embattled. Sir Edward Griffin between 1681 and 1688 rebuilt the E wing and much of the S wing. These parts were gutted in 1972. His work is very simple, but dignified. Two storeys, quoins, tall windows with moulded frames (sashed, which must be a later alteration), hipped roofs. The S front has a pedimented three-bay centre and a doorway with a segmental pediment on corbels.

STABLES. 1790 by *Henry Hakewill*, also converted into residences. A square courtyard with a central three-bay block of two storeys with channelled pilasters and topped by a clock turret. Wings on either side with a central pedimented gable, similar pilasters and four bays on each side of the centre. Semicircular windows and circles above. Heavy bracketed eaves throughout. Fine decorative railings.

OLD PARSONAGE, E of the church. Part late C17 but refronted 1703 with a large painted sundial of that date. It was extended in 1841–3 by *Henry Goddard* of Leicester and has some chimneystacks typical of that firm.

DITCHFORD *see* RUSHDEN

DODFORD

St Mary. The s wall is Norman. Two windows remain, one of them visible only inside, elements of a blocked doorway in the s aisle and a quantity of herringbone masonry. C13 w tower, see e.g. the bell-openings of two lancets under one arch, C13 n aisle with an arcade of four bays (octagonal piers, double-hollow-chamfered arches) and lancet windows (the one in the w wall is unrestored). Dec s windows with transom. Perp s porch, two-storeyed, the lower storey heavily rib-vaulted. Chancel 1850 by *Philip Hardwick*, replacing a Georgian chancel of 1747. *E. F. Law* provided designs for the roof. The body of the church was restored by *Butterfield* in 1878–80. – FONT. Circular, Norman, with lunettes upright and upside down, their outlines beaded. They are linked up, and the links are beaded too. Foliage in the lunettes. – SCREEN. Of one-light divisions. Said to have been given in 1440 by Sir John Cressy. – PULPIT. Jacobean panels. – STAINED GLASS. E window by *Clutterbuck*, in the style of the German or Dutch C16, rather faded in parts. – N aisle E window by *J. Powell & Sons*, 1863. – Tower window, 1883 by *William Wailes*. – MONUMENTS. Brasses to John Cressy †1414 and wife, 19-in. (48-cm.) figures; William Wylde †1422 and wife, 80-in. (46-cm.) figures; and Bridget Wyrley †1637, 19 in. (48-cm.) – Beautiful Purbeck marble effigy of a cross-legged knight (Sir Robert de Keynes †1305?), the slab on which he lies still with tapering sides like a coffin-lid. The effigy shows well the lacing of his surcoat at the side. – Early C14 tomb-recess (N aisle) and in it oak effigy of a lady thought to be Hawise de Keynes †c. 1280. Pushed in front of it a stone tomb-chest with five small figures of mourners against it. On the tomb-chest effigy of a lady with angels by her pillow, said to be Wentiliana de Keynes †1376. In the arch, PAINTING of a soul taken to heaven by angels, and the hand of God. – Sir John Cressy †1444. Free-standing alabaster monument with recumbent effigy. Against the tomb-chest at the head-end two kneeling angels holding a shield, against the sides stiffly frontal angels with shields and between them smaller mourners in arched panels. The angels have hooked wings, just like those on the 1420 Greene tomb at Lowick by *Prentys* and *Sutton* of Chellaston. – John Wyrley †1655. Alabaster mural monument with figures holding chains of shields. Attributed to *C. G. Cibber* (GF). – Henry Benson family. Architectural monument erected after 1730. Probably from the yard of the *Smiths* of Warwick.

To the s of the church a fine late C18 MANOR FARM of red brick.
Five bays with platband, the windows with stone keystones. To
the N at the foot of the hill, DODFORD HOUSE (former vicarage, and for a vicarage quite grand), mid Georgian, five bays,
two storeys, with parapet. Central pediment with circle. Below
it a Venetian window and the doorcase and side windows
reflecting the same pattern. The ground-floor windows have
segmental heads and lighter stones alternating as voussoirs.
Two-bay addition on the l. The existence in the church of a
monument associated with the *Smiths* of Warwick suggests a
connection, though this house is more likely to be by the
Hiornes rather than the Smiths. To the r. PORCH HOUSE, with
a two-storeyed Jacobean porch. Considerably rebuilt 1788 and
again in 1911.

GLOBE FARM, SE on the A45. Plain late C17. Seven bays, two
storeys, stone.

DRAUGHTON

ST CATHERINE. W tower late C12, still with a small round-arched
w window, or is it just pointed? Also an arch towards the nave
which is pointed though unmoulded and stands on imposts
with nailhead. The top must be C17. C14 arcades, both with
octagonal piers and double-chamfered arches, but otherwise
differing. The s side capitals have a little nailhead enrichment,
and are of a different harder stone. It could be that quarried
N of Oundle, one of the Blisworth limestones, used later at
Lilford and Lyveden. The simple s doorway with slender
columns and two windows of the s aisle also in the C13 style.
The N aisle also has a lancet at its w end; other windows are
C19, when it had to be propped up with large buttresses. It still
has an alarming lean outwards. C14 Dec windows in the s aisle
(E and S) which served as models for those in the chancel when
that was largely rebuilt in 1892 under the direction of *J. P. St
Aubyn*. At the same time it was give multi-flights of steps and
an array of *Minton* tiles in the sanctuary. Prior to that it was
Georgian, with two round-arched windows in the s wall and
the large Gothick window, now in the N transept, at its E end.
This work dates from *c.* 1780, by *John Wing* of Leicester (cf.
East Carlton).[*] – FONT. C18. Baluster with a serpent winding
round the stem. It was removed from Maidwell church in 1781,
and recorded as having been brought here by Wing. – BENCHES.
Late C14, with uncommonly inventive tracery panels, to some
degree remade in the 1880s. – PULPIT, CHOIR STALLS and
NAVE BENCHES. All paid for by the Loders of Maidwell, who

---

[*] Wing's involvement is confirmed by entries in the C18 diary of John Corby, parish
clerk. The diary actually refers to 'Mr. Wing (jun) and his men from Hallaton', so
this is John Wing the younger, who would have been twenty-five at the time and
before his removal to Bedford. I owe this reference to Paul Sanders-Hewett.

were patrons. Pulpit and stalls part of the 1892 restoration. At the W end a canopied pew of the same design as two at Maidwell, the Loders' other church. In both aisles open benches in a C17 manner like those at Maidwell. – LECTERN. Mid-C19; rather Puginesque in style. – PULPIT TESTER. At the W end of the S aisle. A very fine thing with an elaborate inlaid star in its centre. It could easily be the work of *Joseph Daniel* who made the altar table at Lamport, which has similar inlay, so probably *c.* 1740. – ROYAL ARMS for George III, painted. – STAINED GLASS. S aisle E window by *Kempe*, 1894. – Chancel E, 1933 by *C. E. Moore*. Refreshing use of pale colours.

THOR MISSILE SITE, RAF Harrington, 1m NW. Harrington airfield was built 1942–4. Part of the site, having largely been returned to farmland, was refitted in 1959 as a satellite Thor Missile launch pad and is now the best preserved example surviving. A number of reinforced concreate blast walls and other structures remain. The site is on the W side of the Lamport/Harrington road, where there is an American servicemen's memorial, and access is from a track by the A14 road bridge. There is also a Carpetbagger Aviation Museum.

DRAYTON HOUSE 9070

Drayton House, secluded in its park, S of Lowick, has an intricate 36 descent. It begins with the de Draytons, then to the Greenes, the Mordaunts, who became Earls of Peterborough, the Germaines, the Sackvilles, and today the Stopford-Sackvilles. Yet this descent has always been through some family relationship and the house has never been let or sold. Substantial portions of the de Drayton house of the late C13 still survive. The Greenes made the early house grander and their entrance porch, on the W side, still exists. The 3rd Lord Mordaunt around 1580 added wings down each side of the medieval house, and his tall three-storey state wing forms the major part of the N range. It has very tall and pillar-shaped chimneyshafts, very like those at Kirby Hall, and a tall staircase tower with polygonal turret and battlements. Several mullioned windows survive, although many were replaced initially by sashes in the C18, and then again by new mullions in the early 1900s by *J. A. Gotch*. The second Earl of Peterborough, a staunch Royalist and personal friend of James II, moved the entrance from the W side to the E in the early 1650s, and made other alterations using the architect *John Webb*. Lord Peterborough's daughter Mary and her second husband, Sir John Germaine, then called in *William Talman c.* 1700, and he refronted the hall range and built a second set of towers on the S side, copying the earlier N set, to hide a new kitchen. It was Talman's masterstroke to top both towers with a cupola. Since then, save for some internal redecoration, the architecture of the house has hardly changed.

R.ᵗ Hon.ᵇˡᵉ the Lady ELIZABETH Germain
This Prospect is humbly Inscrib'd by:

Drayton House.
Engraving by N. Buck, 1731

The approach is from the SE, which for simplicity we will call
E. Standing in the GRAVEL COURT one is faced with a tall battlemented wall, dating back to the 1300s, the original rear wall
of the early house. Simon de Drayton was granted licence to
crenellate in 1328. In the centre is the battlemented GATE-
TOWER, with coat of arms over the arch, inserted by Lord Peterborough in the early 1650s. He also built the STABLE BLOCK on
the r. and the GARDEN GATE on the l. This work of the 1650s
is convincingly attributed to *John Webb*. Inside the gate-tower a
fine pendentive-domed stone ceiling, unparalleled at this date.
The splendid GATEPIERS and ironwork, at the entrance of the
court, are part of the work of *c.* 1700 by *Talman*. The ironwork
is by the *Tijou* workshop, as is that within the Garden Gate.

73   Entering the COURTYARD, ahead is *Talman*'s Baroque façade,
a refacing of the 1300 wall of Simon de Drayton's Hall range. A
contract of 1702 exists between Sir John Germaine and *Benjamin
Jackson*, the master mason, working to designs by Talman. Jackson
was eventually replaced by the mason *John Woodall*. The façade
is very lively and very characteristic of Talman. As John Harris
has pointed out, it has parallels with Talman's designs for a
Trianon for William III and for Welbeck. It has six tall windows
with alternating pediments, and a doorway with detached Corinthian columns and a trophy over. The capitals of the columns,
instead of the front volute, have a hawk, Germaine's crest. Above
is a large military trophy, he having served alongside Marlborough. The windows immediately l. and r. of the doorway are also
more playful than the others. Instead of pediments proper they
have delightful scrolly foliage pediments with small heads. Talman
may have seen similar pediments on Henry Bell's work at Kimbolton. Above the windows runs an attic divided by blank panels,

in the same rhythm as the windows, and against each a bust on a bracket. Finally there is a top balustrade, rising in the middle into an open pediment, carried by caryatid girls and holding a large cartouche of the Germaine arms. The ultimate source of the forms is no doubt the Italy of Borromini.

The sides of the courtyard have colonnades of Roman Doric columns reminiscent of those by Wren at Hampton Court, where of course Talman was similarly employed. They bear the arms of Germaine and his second wife, Lady Elizabeth (Betty) Berkeley, and were built in 1710, also by *Woodall*. The CHAPEL in the E range, to the N of the gate-tower, was originally created by Lord Peterborough in 1676 to designs of *Isaac Rowe*, and then redecorated for Lady Betty Germaine in 1725, following advice from *Thomas Coke* of Melbourne. It still has the Peterboroughs' Wren style reredos with plasterwork of Lady Betty's time by *George Worrall*.

The usual entrance is by the UNDERCROFT of the original solar, with its two naves separated by short octagonal pillars and with a rib-vault with chamfered ribs, suggesting a late C13 or early C14 date.

The HALL is structurally that of the 1300s, but refurbished by Germaine with its giant Ionic pilasters and coved ceiling. The decoration, marbled panelling and painted ceiling, was done around 1850 for Caroline Harriet Sackville and her husband William Bruce Stopford, and has their initials in the design. The decorator was *Alexander Roos*. The large veined marble chimneypiece dates from 1703, the work of the carver *William Woodman*. He also provided the marble urns in the window embrasures, originally part of a Buffet Room, dismantled in the 1790s.

To the W of the Hall is the DINING ROOM, one of two rooms changed when Drayton became the property of Lord George Sackville in 1770. It has fine plasterwork with pretty Adamish motifs by *William Rhodes*, 1771–4. The chimneypiece is original to the room as is its garniture of basalt Wedgwood and the two splendid side tables.

To the NE of the Hall is the STONE STAIRCASE, described as new in 1710. It has more *Tijou* ironwork and paintings by *Gerard Lanscroon* filling the walls and, without any caesura, the coving and the ceiling. People are agitating and tumbling over the whole space, a scheme favoured in England at that moment (cf. Burghley House and Hampton Court). The painting was done in 1712 and represents a Heaven and Hell theme. Only children are eligible for Heaven, where Diana and Mercury give them lessons. On the other wall figures representing Malice, Envy and Strife are being expelled by Justice. More classical allusion appears on the ceiling with a figure representing Victory or Fame, sitting on a cloud, with a remarkable similarity to Queen Anne! The staircase leads to the noblest room on the first floor, the KING'S DINING ROOM, situated above the C13 undercroft so originally the medieval Great Chamber. It has big panelling of pine, painted and grained to look like walnut. The ceiling has a large circular wreath of oak and bay leaves, part of *Webb*'s work of the 1650s.

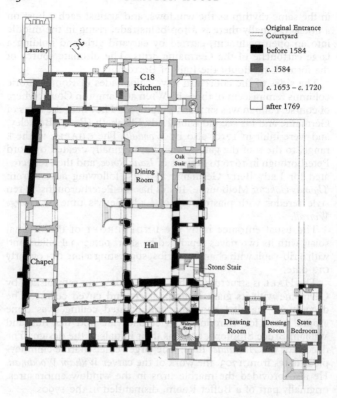

Drayton House.
Plan

Big fireplace surround carved from a stone quarried in the park, known as Drayton Marble. It is worth noting the series of imaginary portraits of the ancestral Lords Mordaunt all painted in the middle of the C17 and probably originally inset within the panelling (cf. Boughton House).

Moving into the N range, originally built by Lord Mordaunt in the 1580s, the only original interior is a large CELLAR, curiously medieval-looking with its short octagonal piers and chamfered ribs. It has an interesting series of carved heraldic bosses. The tower is now filled with one of the most remarkable features of the house, the WALNUT STAIR, built c. 1700. It is of wood, but constructed on the principle of Inigo Jones's Tulip Staircase at Greenwich and Wren's Geometrical Staircase at St Paul's, that is as a flying staircase. It is more or less contemporary with Wren's staircase, that is c. 1707, but then Wren's is in stone. No other timber staircase of this date and form survives anywhere else. At the top is the Elizabethan LONG GALLERY, structurally intact, but adapted as a library in the 1790s; the Georgian

Venetian window at the w end was altered *c.* 1905 by *Gotch* when he also replaced the barrel ceiling with a canted design. On its s side a rare survival, a CLOSET with its marquetry floor *in situ,* bearing the cypher of Mary Mordaunt, Duchess of Norfolk, so before 1705.

Back on the ground floor is the DRAWING ROOM, with a ceiling whose design is taken from Robert Wood's *Ruins of Palmyra,* that is a coffered surround with a circular centrepiece within a square. This is part of Lord George Sackville's work of the 1770s, also using the plasterer *William Rhodes.* The chimney-piece also of that date. Beyond is the STATE DRESSING ROOM with doorcases of the 1650s and next the STATE BEDROOM, where the overmantel designed by *John Webb* survives. It has characteristically heavy classical forms with an open scrolly pediment and thick hanging garlands of fruit, all reminiscent of Webb's work in the Double Cube Room at Wilton. The State Bed of 1700 and Mortlake tapestries complete the ensemble. A small LACQUER CLOSET, *c.* 1700, with inset Coromandel type panels with garden scenes and china cupboards, gives access into the garden.

Two more rooms need to be noted on the w side, the BREAKFAST ROOM and the NORTH SITTING ROOM, both created in the late 1790s, under the direction of *William Stephens,* both with wooden Neoclassical chimneypieces, and the sitting room having glazed china cabinets either side the fireplace.

The GARDEN terraces derive from Lord Mordaunt's time and the two BANQUETING HOUSES still have stonework of the 1580s. They were, however, rebuilt and enlarged by Lord Peterborough, again using *Webb,* and have fine doorcases with his usual heavy garlands either side a coat of arms. The gardens were much enhanced by Germaine who purchased statues and urns from *John Nost* in 1718. On the N side of the garden a simple brick ORANGERY built *c.* 1710. There are more good ironwork gates to the w, another set by the E banqueting house, and yet another at the E end of the garden with the date 1699.

To the s of the house further buildings, with the GARDENER'S HOUSE contrived within the structure of a barn with a C16 gable end, and a DOVECOTE probably dating from the 1650s.

DUDDINGTON*

9000

ST MARY. The oldest part of the church is the N arcade. It must date from *c.* 1150–75. Two bays, circular pier, scalloped capitals, big square abaci, big round arches with roll and zigzag mouldings, the zigzag being placed on the wall surface as well

*Information gleaned from 'Duddington in the Past', a typescript by Peter Hawkins (2007–8) of a manuscript collected by Frank Goddard Jackson. I am grateful to Christopher Young for alerting me to this.

as at right angles to it. The s arcade has two bays, circular piers, waterleaf capitals, circular abaci, double-chamfered round arches: i.e. late C12. The s doorway into the church must again be of *c.* 1190–1200. The capitals still have waterleaf, but the finely moulded arch is pointed. The third w bay of the arcades on the N and s was added as a later enlargement, *c.* 1225. The arches are still round. The tower is also late C12. It stands in an unusual position: at the E end of the s arcade, probably because of the falling ground w of the nave. The ground floor of the tower has round-headed slit-windows and a simple N doorway. The arch to the aisle has a little nailhead decoration and is double-chamfered and pointed; that to the nave is similar. Higher up the tower is clearly C13. Two-light bell-openings with a shaft between the lights. Spire not high, with very low broaches and two tiers of C13 lucarnes. C14 s porch and clerestory. The chancel is totally Victorian and a little unhappy in appearance externally with large lancets with nail-head. This is due to the over-restoration by *Edward Browning* of Stamford in 1844–5. Tactful vestry of 1937 by *H. F. Traylen.* – DOOR. The s door, with its remarkable ironwork, could well be of the time of the s arcade. – COMMUNION RAIL. Looks mid-C17, with vertically symmetrical balusters and delightful fluted finials, but there is record of *Thompson* of Peterborough making new rails in 1921. – REREDOS. Gothic of 1933 by *Traylen & Lenton.* – BOX PEWS. Largely 1844 in nave and aisles. Later at the back of the church. There was adjustment to the interior woodwork in 1906. – MONUMENTS. Many in the chancel to the Jackson family who held the manor from the C17, though none of special merit. The Jacksons are the family of the architect *T. G. Jackson,* and the monument to William Goddard Jackson (†1906) with a foliate wreath was designed by him. He also restored the tower in 1911–13. – STAINED GLASS. E window, Jackson memorial, by *T. Baillie,* 1852.

Former SCHOOL, High Street. 1892–3 by *J. B. Corby* of Stamford, and built by the Jackson family. Large central gable with four-light mullion-transom window with Jackson shield above. Two one-storey stone-tiled rooms l. and r.

An attractive village, thankfully bypassed, and subject of a conservation scheme so there are no overhead wires or cables. Many good stone houses. Just s of the church the VILLAGE HALL, barnlike and vernacular, of 1931 by *F. G. Lenton* of *Traylen & Lenton.* In the centre of the village an attractive GREEN and on its E side the finest house in the village, STOCKS HILL HOUSE. It had an open hall of late C15 date of which the roof survives. The s gable end still has two two-light late C15 windows and others survive on the E façade. Above a two-light mullioned window and the date 1601. There are still other C17 mullioned windows, but otherwise the house has been much altered, notably in 1858, and in 1973 by *Kelham & Hart* of Stamford, when the former blank w side was given new mullioned windows and gabled dormers. In MILL STREET, w of the green, is CHURCH FARM, an amalgam of buildings. A rear block has two- and three-light C17 mullions. The street range altered in the C19 but mullions in its end wall. Attractive early C20 veranda. On the s side of the Green, perched above the street, BEAUMONT, a fine 1828 villa of three bays, two storeys with a Doric fluted pillared porch. Fine cast-iron balustrade to steps. To the w in HIGH STREET, on the s side, the MANOR HOUSE, with a date 1633 in one gable and the initials of Nicholas Jackson. Much Tudor Gothic of the C19, and with a relief of St Hubert above a fireplace. DOVECOTE and BARN late C16. A little further on the N side BRADDAN HOUSE, of three bays with three-light mullioned windows and a pretty latticed porch. Then ROSE COTTAGE, dated 1830, three bays again with two canted bays and even prettier latticed porch with pyramidal roof. Opposite the beautifully thatched PEARTREE COTTAGE. At the A43 junction the ROYAL OAK INN, simple vernacular by *F. G. Lenton*, 1931.

BRIDGE, over the Welland w of the church. Four arches and cutwaters, probably C14, but much altered, notably in 1919 when it was widened. By the bridge a picturesque WATERMILL of 1664, rebuilt 1793 and altered since. Tall wing with mansard roof. Nicely converted for offices. The MILL HOUSE opposite *c.* 1775 of four bays, the windows with flat labels and the ground floor with early C20 canted bays.

DUSTON *see* OUTER NORTHAMPTON

EARLS BARTON

The village centre with the church, a green and several old cottages is most attractive. The shoe industry led to the establishment of a number of factories and the inevitable red brick housing associated with it. Since then there has been considerable development around the village.

ALL SAINTS. The prime interest is of course Saxon, the secondary is Norman. The Late Anglo-Saxon w tower is a mighty piece, unbuttressed, but with three set-backs. The angles have long-and-short work and, as this appears at all four angles, it seems that the tower was originally not followed by a nave, i.e. a wider vessel, but by a chancel, i.e. a narrower vessel. The tower has its main entrance on the w. As usual the capitals and abaci of the responds are one block, entirely unmoulded. However, at Earls Barton they are decorated with blank arcading. Also the arch of the doorway is moulded, competently enough to be Norman. The jambs and arch are, however, accompanied in the accepted Saxon way by a raised flat band. The same raised flat bands become lesenes up the walls of the tower. The walls are very thoroughly decorated in that manner, and the same bands run diagonally and form triangles and even combine to form X-patterns. The whole taste may well be derived from timber customs. There are three external doorways, and there are windows in many irregular positions. The most interesting ones are on the first floor, complete to the s, incomplete to the w. They have very short turned balusters and shallow arches decorated with a cross. On the s side these windows are filled by mid-wall slabs, each pierced by a cross-shaped opening. The bell-openings, a most unusual enrichment, have five narrow arches, each again on turned balusters. There is no indication of any w attachment. The plan can therefore not have been like Barton-on-Humber with the tower in the middle of a tripartite plan. There is no known parallel to a tower nave with narrower chancel.

The Normans enlarged the church in two campaigns, in the early and the late C12. Of the former time the w quoins of the nave and responds of the chancel arch with shafts carrying one-scallop capitals; of the latter the remodelling of the tower arch with responds with many-scalloped capitals and a curious arch displaying a surfeit of billet work. This arch was reused and made pointed later. Of the later C12 also the s doorway. Two orders of shafts with horizontal zigzags and spiral decoration. The inner moulding is continuous zigzag. One arch moulding has beakhead, the other zigzag. In addition the chancel received some very ornate blank arcading with rich zigzag. It includes the stepped SEDILIA.

The arcades of three bays are of the late C13 (s, octagonal piers, double-chamfered arches) and the early C14 (N, piers with four shafts and four thinner shafts in the diagonals, arches with two sunk quadrants). The chancel E end is C13. Three stepped individual lancets, shafted. There were originally three lowside lancets. The SEDILIA and PISCINA also C13. The aisles have Dec windows with reticulation. – PULPIT, late C16 or early C17, heavily moulded panels, and more Elizabethan than Jacobean. – SCREEN. Tall, of two-light divisions, much restored in 1892. The painted panels are by *Henry Bird*, 1935. – TILES. (Chancel) 1875 by *Minton, Hollis & Co.* to designs of *Lord Alwyne Compton* (*see* Castle Ashby). – BRASS. John Muscote †1512 and wife. The figures are 2 ft (60 cm.) long. – STAINED GLASS. A good selection and some fine pieces including chancel E, 1872 by *Bell & Almond*. – Chancel S, 1994 by *Michael Stokes*. – Chancel N, 1902 by *W. J. Dixon* for *Mayer & Co.* – N aisle E, 1960 by *Christopher Webb*. – N aisle NE, memorial to Canon Ewart, 1980 by *Francis Skeat*. – S aisle E, 1931 designed by *F. E. Howard* and made by *Jones & Willis*. – S aisle, a 1923 window by *Morris & Co.*, the central window 1983 by *Francis Skeat*, and S aisle, two W windows by *Heaton, Butler & Bayne*, 1890 and 1910.

The churchyard forms the point of a fairly well-marked ridge. To the N, towards the higher ground, stands a conspicuous and quite unmistakable Norman CASTLE MOTTE. It is so close to the church that it stands partly in the churchyard; on this side it appears to have been cut back to make more room. To the N it is protected by an unusually fine ditch. As a result of its position, the motte is completely overlooked by the Saxon church tower. From this it has been argued that the motte itself (contrary to the received opinion on these earthworks) must be older than the church; in all probability, however, the castle was founded at the Conquest or soon after, and its builder ignored the existing church – which from its position must have been in his bailey – intending to take it down at his leisure, an operation which he never carried out. The rounded shape of the motte suggests that it was disused at an early date.

BAPTIST CHURCH, The Square. 1874 by *Edward Sharman* of Wellingborough. Ironstone with a large triple lancet window with cinquefoil above. Lancets either side.

WESLEYAN CHURCH, Broad Street. 1870–1 of red and yellow brick. Three-bay façade with pilasters under a pediment. Round-arched windows.

Former NATIONAL SCHOOL (Village Hall), on the SE edge of the churchyard. Ironstone, Tudor style. 1843–4 by *William Hull*. To its N, SAXON LODGE (former vicarage), ironstone of a lighter shade of two storeys with canted bay topped by mock timber framing, *c.* 1885, when a faculty was granted for the site. Good enough for *Pearson*, who restored the church in 1884.

SCHOOL, Broad Street. Two quite large buildings of brick. One, 1867–8 by *Edward Sharman* of Wellingborough; the other, 1893 by *E. F. Law*. Later additions.

The shoe industry is still very much in evidence with, especially, BARKER'S FACTORY complex in Station Road; the former WARD & SHEFFIELD FACTORY, on Harcourt Square, *c.* 1900, a familiar pattern of red brick of three storeys; another FACTORY NE of the village centre, just beyond the point where High Street becomes Wellingborough Road; and on the w side BROOKES MEWS, the former factory of W. J. Brookes. Three-storey brick of the standard form 1889. In SUNNYSIDE, on the SW edge of the village, behind a terrace of brick houses of 1886–1900, is an interesting series of one-storey outworkers' workshops. Most have survived, but altered. Where Dodding-ton Road becomes BROAD STREET Nos. 82–86 a set of Early Victorian ironstone cottages with odd pointed windows and recess with red brick surrounds. Bargeboarded gables. In HIGH STREET, the MANOR HOUSE (No. 76) of ironstone. Four bays with simple renewed wooden casements and two gabled dormers. Thatched. Dates of 1714 and 1737 recorded.

EAST CARLTON   *8080*

ST PETER. 1788 by the younger *John Wing* (cf. King's Norton, Leics.). In the Decorated Gothic style, handled remarkably seriously, with a real attempt to reproduce medieval tracery patterns. A broad T-plan, with Palmer chapel and vestry forming the arms of the T. w tower and E end ashlar, the tower with the quatrefoils so beloved of the C18 gothicists. Quatrefoil frieze below the battlements, and frieze of cusped lozenges below the top of the other parts of the church. Flat ceiling on tie-beams with quatrefoil tracery. Pointed arches inside with the fluted capitals typical of the late C18. – Original furnishings including a two-decker PULPIT, BOX PEWS and COMMUNION RAIL with attenuated balusters. – Sanctuary DADO with typical late C18 frieze. – FONT. 1860 by *Kirk* of Sleaford. – STAINED GLASS. In the s chapel heraldic panels, one dated 1659. – s chapel window of 1895 by *Heaton, Butler & Bayne*. – Chancel E window of 1869 by *Clayton & Bell*. – s aisle two of 1862 by *H. Hughes* of *Ward & Hughes*. – MONUMENTS. Sir Geoffrey Palmer †1673 and Lady Palmer. An extraordinary memorial. Two standing figures of alabaster in their shrouds in a black cupboard-like shrine with open arched doors. Segmental pediment. Attributed to *Joshua Marshall* on the strength of the close similarity to the Noel monument of 1664 at Chipping Campden (Glos.). – Thomas Palmer and wife, erected *c.* 1660, attributed to *Joshua Marshall*. – Jeffrey Palmer †1661, attributed to *Edward Marshall*. – Many minor tablets. Lady Palmer †1783, attributed to *Richard Hayward* (GF).

EAST CARLTON HALL. The Palmer family were at East Carlton from the mid C15 till the 1930s. The present house is of 1870 by *E. F. Law* (replacing a Late Palladian house by *John Johnson* of Leicester, 1778). A huge, rather monstrous affair of red brick and ironstone. Symmetrical façades. Italian detail but tall French pavilion roofs topped with ironwork rails. All rather heavy in its handling, but wonderfully situated with a superb view across the Welland valley. Now apartments. STABLE BLOCK of red brick, six bays each side of a round-arched entrance below a triangular pediment enclosing a coat of arms. Part of Johnson's 1778 work.

ALMSHOUSES, near the church. Rebuilt in the Tudor style in 1866 by *E. F. Law*. A pair of COTTAGES w of the church of 1873 doubtless also by *Law* as is a nearby house dated 1870. They all follow the Tudor manner. The former RECTORY of 1873, a little further on, is also by *Law*.

EAST FARNDON

ST JOHN BAPTIST. Dec and Perp. Perp chiefly the upper part of the w tower, slender, with battlements and pinnacles and with an arch towards the nave which has capitals decorated with fleurons. Similar motifs on the capitals of the two-bay s chapel. Dec the ogee N doorway, the chancel arch with moulded capitals, the s doorway, a tall niche to the r. of the E window and the s arcade with piers of the type of Stanford and Leicestershire, i.e. a slender chamfered projection to nave and aisle, a broader one to each arch opening, and continuous mouldings throughout. It all seems quite simple – but is it? There is reference in a survey of 1631 to a ruinous N aisle and the N wall of the nave does seem somewhat stark. Also the clerestory is very odd. Looking at it externally, the w window is clearly a C17 two-light mullioned opening. The next one appears to be a bit of a make-up, with a sensible two-light opening with ogee heads, but its r.-hand light is rather clumsy and its head is a simple V-point. The third window is equally curious: three lights with decorative tracery. All this supports the notion that there may have been a partial early C17 rebuilding, so perhaps one should not place too much reliance on some of the other features, even the arcade. Confusing also, the double-arched recess to N of the chancel arch, partly in the nave wall. The obvious answer is that it is probably some remnant of a rood loft. Tall vestry which, although rebuilt, probably has origins as a medieval two-storey structure. Small opening in its N wall. There were restorations in 1872 and 1879, the latter by *William Taylor* of Coventry, and this is doubtless the date of the painted decoration of the nave roof. The eastern portions of the chancel have all the signs of being rebuilt by Taylor and the tiled floor and stepped form is doubtless also his. – SEDILIA. C14 with cinquefoil heads. – SCREEN. Across the tower arch, made locally in 1991 when the bells were recast, and decorated with images of the original bells, with their inscriptions. – MONUMENTS. Daniel Halford, rector, †1622. Brass plate with standing figure in gown. Hourglass and skull at the side. – Two engraved brass plates with Rococo decoration to members of the Saunders family, signed *Parry*. – Slate slab to commemorate a whole family tree of the Lee family, from one who died in 1693 to one who died in 1804. – STAINED GLASS. Chancel E, 1876 by *Camm Bros* of Smethwick, Birmingham. – N aisle NE by *Percy Bacon*, c. 1915.

Former SCHOOL, by the church. 1883 by *H. W. Chattaway* of Coventry. Brick, in Tudor manner with adjoining school house. The front wing is a sensitive addition.

MANOR HOUSE, Back Lane. Part ironstone, part infilled with brick. Two canted bays with mullioned windows. Straight joint halfway along the façade by the brick infill. The impression is of part of something bigger. It was the home of the Lee family (*see* above). Armorial tablet dated 1664 with the initials TL for Thomas Lee (†1693).

EAST FARNDON HALL, Back Lane. Large, brick, late C17 or early C18 but fully rendered in the C19 when an extra storey was added, making it look rather stark. The EARTHWORKS near the Hall are of uncertain date and may be related to earlier settlement.

ORCHARD HOUSE, N of the church. A very asymmetrical L-shaped house of c. 1900. Gables, irregular fenestration, timber balconies at either end of its ranges. Curved hooded doorcase with tapered pilasters, bulging forward at their base. Some decorative glass. Much stylish woodwork inside. Built for F. G. Cox, chairman of Symingtons, corset manufacturers, of Market Harborough. KILNYARD HOUSE, Marston Lane, was built for his son c. 1935. Outstanding Art Deco house, thought to be by *Clement Stretton*, of rendered brick in a Modern marine style. Two storeys with a tower having an additional solarium prospect room. Curved staircase bay with row of windows at its top. Several interior features survive.

EAST HADDON

St Mary. Of the Norman church the responds of the chancel arch remain, double-nook-shafted, with little leaves and water-leaf in the capitals. The chancel arch and the rest of the chancel probably remodelled in the C14. But the windows are over-restored. The restorations were by *Mackesey*, 1872–4, and *E. F. Law*, 1877–8. Further work 1901 by *J. C. Traylen* of Stamford. Perp the big N windows and the later S aisle windows. The Dec four-bay S arcade has octagonal piers and double-chamfered arches. PISCINA with ogee arch. The basin stands on a half-projecting pillar. Dec base to W tower (see doorway), but otherwise mostly of 1673, when it was rebuilt, including the bell-openings and battlements. There are C17 windows at the ends of the aisle, so presumably more work was done then than is apparent now. – TILES. Chancel pavement by *Maw*'s, 1878. – FONT. Circular, C13. With a frieze of intersected arches and one of foliage trails with a man holding two affronted dragons (cf. Brackley). – STAINED GLASS. Chancel N and S by *M. & A. O'Connor*, 1861. – Chancel S, one by *C. A. Gibbs*, 1873, the other by *Kempe*, 1883. – S aisle E, 1891 probably by *Shrigley & Hunt*, and another by *Kempe & Co.*, 1912. – MONUMENTS. Several nice tablets, e.g. Clarke Adams †1776, by *William Cox*.

East Haddon Hall, N of the church. Built in 1780–1 for the Sawbridge family. The contract signed by the builder, *John Wagstaff Jun.* of Daventry, survives. The design has been attributed to *John Johnson* of Leicester. Of five bays and two and a half storeys with a rusticated ground floor, a centre pediment, and, beneath it, a tripartite window with a blank segmental lunette decorated with thin garlands. The original doorway, which survives inside the porch added 1912 by *Law & Harris* when they also added a wing, is similar to one that existed at Johnson's Kingsthorpe Hall. Inside, a fine staircase with wrought-iron balusters, top-lit; good fireplaces and plaster-work. The C19 servants' wing has been removed, and the vaulted cellars ingeniously converted into a garage. Fine C18 ironwork ENTRANCE GATES from Stoke Doyle Manor, later at The Berrystead, Oundle. At the entrance STABLES of 1663, on an E-plan, with three gables. The porch entrance has a round arch, and there is a big, vertically placed oval window above it. The GARDENS were laid out by *Gertrude Jekyll* and *Lutyens* in 1897, but only a fragment of the formal rose garden survives (with metal reliefs on the sundial of 1905).

Primary School, Church Lane. Of golden ironstone and built in 1851. Gothic with a three-light Perp window in the large wing. Extensions of 2001 by *Stimpson & Walton*.

The MANOR HOUSE, Church Lane, is a good stone building of C17 date with some mullioned windows. It is the headquarters of Haddonstone.

VILLAGE PUMP. Under a thatched roof.

EASTON MAUDIT

8050

ST PETER AND ST PAUL. Of grey stone, and quite grand. Almost entirely Dec. Fine tower with graceful spire. In the tower a small quatrefoil and a small pointed trefoil opening. Perp bell-openings. The spire is connected with the tower pinnacles by flying buttresses of openwork quatrefoils. Also parapet with openwork quatrefoils in lozenges. Three tiers of lucarnes. The body of the church has all its windows renewed, but they represent the Dec style too (some straight-headed with ogee lights). Dec N doorway and doorway into the N chapel. Arcades of four bays, quatrefoil piers, arches with sunk quadrant mouldings. The chancel arch has the same mouldings. Tower arch with Dec capitals and a triple-chamfered arch. N chapel of one bay. The arch to the chancel dies into the imposts. To the N aisle instead a strainer arch of openwork quatrefoils etc., of exactly the same type as at Rushden and Finedon, i.e. with upcurved top and downcurved bottom. The church was restored by *W. Slater*, 1859–61, with *Lord Alwyne Compton* involved, hence the array of *Minton* tiles and the elaborate REREDOS and alabaster ALTAR RAILS (cf. Castle Ashby). – FONT. Beautiful gadrooned bowl of stone on a square base; C18. – PULPIT. 1860. With panels carved with elaborate naturalistic foliage; more on the CHOIR STALLS. – COMMUNION TABLE. Elizabethan with heavy bulbous baluster legs. – DOORS. Both with ironwork, probably C15. The woodwork with its latticed pattern of the N door original. – PEWS. Those at the back of the church with much old work, again probably C15. – STAINED GLASS. Fine E window by *Clayton & Bell*, 1906. MONUMENTS. Two big, self-confident Yelverton monuments. Sir Christopher †1612 and wife attributed to *William Cure II* (GF). Six-poster of alabaster. Very plain, uncouth pillars. Sir Christopher Yelverton (†1654) directed that his grandfather's tomb was 'to be hansomely repaired and set up', the repairs being made from the local fossily stone known as 'Rance'. They carry a pair of coffered cross-arches. Strapwork and vases at the top. Recumbent effigies, the children in relief, kneeling along the base. – Sir Henry Yelverton †1631 and wife. The effigies semi-reclining on their elbows, he above and behind her. He was Solicitor General, hence the legal dress. The back wall behind him a pattern of books standing upright with their edges, not their backs, showing (cf. Dr Bodley's Monument at Merton College, Oxford, 1615, and the Catesby Monument of 1636 at Hardmead, Bucks.). Above this, ribbonwork round the

49

Easton Maudit.
Drawing by P. Tillemans, 1721

inscription with a skull, a shield and other emblems. To the l.
and r. the surprising motif of two nearly life-size standing
statues of hooded and bearded bedesmen carrying cushions,
and on these the superstructure – a mixture of a Sluter and a
Floris motif. Arch and five small allegorical figures at the top.
The children again kneel against the base. It was re-coloured
by *Ingar Norholt* in 1972. – Thomas, Bishop Morton, †1659.
Shields surviving from this destroyed monument are in the N
chapel. – A wooden achievement of the Yelverton (Grey de
Ruthvin) arms above the S doorway of the chancel. – At the
NE end of the churchyard, Derek Nimmo †1999. Inscribed
'Actor, wit, life enhancer'.

Former VICARAGE, SW of the church. Thomas Percy, vicar from
1753 to 1782, published the *Reliques* in 1765 and entertained
numerous literary figures of the day such as Garrick. The house
was much altered in the C19. S wing of 1852. Good C18 staircase, possibly from the Yelverton mansion (dem. 1801) which
stood to the N of the church.

In the lane opposite, rows of COTTAGES show the attention of
the Castle Ashby Estate. At the end of a long row, on the l., a
charming *cottage orné* with thatched roof and very twiggy
veranda, built *c.* 1812 as a feature on a carriage drive from
Castle Ashby.

EASTON NESTON

ST MARY. In the park, S of the house. Perp W tower, Perp S side,
except for the fine S aisle W window, which is of the late C13

and has bar tracery of three stepped lights and three foiled circles over, all daintily detailed with bars, circular in section. The chancel has a blocked priest's doorway in the middle of a broad, buttress-like projection. C13 SEDILIA and PISCINA with trefoil heads, much renewed. Perp arcades of three bays. Octagonal piers, double-chamfered arches. N chapel of 1713. Chancel restored by *E. F. Law* in 1863. – FONT. Octagonal, with a band of fleurs-de-lys leaning forward and treated in a stiff-leaf manner. Is it C13? – COMMUNION RAIL. Of *c.* 1700, with twisted balusters. – FURNISHINGS. One of the best collections of C18 fittings in the county. PULPIT, a two-decker, with a little marquetry, BOX PEWS, and a raised platform at the W end. All of the best quality. Probably *c.* 1780 when it is recorded that the interior was painted. – REREDOS. 1950s, but with a superb tapestry of *c.* 1500 with scenes of the Passion of Our Lord. – WALL PAINTINGS. N aisle, around a blocked window above the N chapel arch. Architectural, perhaps the Holy City? C15 or C16. – ALABASTER PANEL. Chancel, under S window. A typical C15 altarpiece panel, still with some colour. – STAINED GLASS. The E window and others, with heraldic labels and decoration, 1840s, it is said, designed by *Sir F. Shuckburgh* and made by *F. & C. Crace*. – Chancel S, Fermor Hesketh memorial, 1961, by *M. C. Farrer-Bell* 1968. – MONUMENTS. Richard Fermor †1552 (chancel S). He bought the manor early in the C16. Tomb-chest with brasses, the figures 2 ft 3 in. (69 cm.) long. The brasses are a palimpsest of brasses of *c.* 1480–1525. – Sir John Fermor †1571 (chancel S). Small with two kneeling figures, facing one another. – Sir George Fermor †1628 (chancel N). Alabaster. Two fine recumbent effigies. Children kneeling in relief against the front of the tomb-chest (some renewed). Arch behind and a splendid peacock's tail of ornamental panels separated by sixteen pennons. Columns, obelisks, achievements. Attributed to *Jasper Hollemans*. – Sir Hatton Fermor, erected in 1662 (chancel S). A hanging monument of alabaster, but very large. Two standing figures, he in a very mannered attitude, and a bust between them. Columns and cornice. On it three frontally praying demi-figures. Obelisks l. and r. The monument can be firmly attributed to *Pierre Besnier* on the strength of a comparison with his signed monument of 1656 at Shuckburgh in Warwickshire. Sir Hatton's daughter Catherine married a Shuckburgh. – 2nd Earl Pomfret, erected in 1819 (S aisle). Grecian relief, a scene of bidding farewell. Unsigned, but by *Chantrey* (payments in his ledgers). It is paired on the other side of the doorway for Peter Denys †1816 and Lady Denys †1835, signed by *E. H. Baily*. Relief with urn and two sarcophagi. Three female genii above. At the top acroteria and an urn. – 3rd Earl Pomfret †1830 (chancel N). By *E. H. Baily*. Life-size relief figure of a man seated comfortably by an urn. – 1st Lord Hesketh †1944 (N chapel). Large white marble Neo-Georgian aedicule. – 2nd Lord Hesketh †1956 (N aisle). A classical sarcophagus of alabaster.

61

72 EASTON NESTON. Without doubt, architecturally the finest and grandest house in Northamptonshire, with more controversy and discussion attached to it than any other house in the county. One of the main problems is that there is scarcely any documentation. There are no full building accounts but a brief summary with some names is attached to an estate rental of 1708.* The estate came into the possession of the Fermor family in the 1530s. They rose through the peerage to become baronets in 1641, barons (Lempster, i.e. Leominster) in 1692 and finally earls (Pomfret, i.e. Pontefract) in 1725. In 1885 the succession passed to the Heskeths of Rufford, Lancashire, and the Fermor-Hesketh title became Lord Hesketh in 1935. Easton Neston remained with the family till 2005 when it was sold, but it remains in private hands.

The early house was s of the present one, closer to Towcester. The new house site was carefully chosen so that looking w the spire of Green's Norton church acts as an eyecatcher, and indeed it was rebuilt in the early C18 like an obelisk with urns at its base (*see* Green's Norton). Plans for a new house were instigated by Sir William Fermor in the early 1680s. Through his wife's family he was a cousin of Sir Christopher Wren and in a letter of 1682 Wren is giving general advice about building, but in terms which suggest he is not personally closely involved. One of the earliest statements about the house is in John Bridges's *History of Northamptonshire*, for which material was being collected *c.* 1720. Bridges says: 'The wings are of brick and were built by Sir Christopher Wren, the body . . . was built by Hawksmoor, who hath very much departed from the first design.' Bridges was fairly careful about his statements so this should not be quickly set aside. Wren was clearly involved at some level, but could the reference really refer to the office, that is the Office of Works, rather than to the man himself? Another complication is the survival of a model made at an early stage of the house's development. This has almost exactly the same dimensions and room layout as the house as built, but the façades differ considerably and it is not quite as tall as the final building. Giles Worsley presented a very plausible case that the model emanated from designs by *William Talman*, and Talman was, of course, in Wren's office. In a letter of 1731 Hawksmoor calls the wings 'good for nothing'. Would he have been so derogatory if they were by Wren? What is clear is that two wings and most of the basement was built by the mid 1680s.

Hawksmoor was also involved already by this time, as a memorandum of his survives dated 1686, and the final form of the exterior appears to be his own independent work. It differs from the model in that the model has two superimposed orders instead of the consistent giant order which endows the house with its unparalleled nobility. Hawksmoor's

---

* This (NRO) is summarized in VCH *Northamptonshire*, vol. 5, p. 98–126. I am grateful to Brian Giggins for alerting me to this.

design combines grandeur with urbanity to a degree rare in England and perhaps only matched at Chatsworth. Yet Hawksmoor's is very different from Talman's style. The source of Hawksmoor's is no doubt Wren's office about 1700. But there is no executed work of Wren's that could be compared with Easton Neston. Hawksmoor's own style in addition changed towards a more Baroque ideal immediately after Easton Neston, and indeed inside Easton Neston. This change is often attributed to the influence of Vanbrugh, under whom he worked and with whom he collaborated at Castle Howard from 1699 onwards. But the particularly Vanbrughian conceits inside Easton Neston are earlier than any comparable ones in Vanbrugh's *œuvre*. So the credit for them must go entirely to Hawksmoor and to Wren. Hawksmoor left ninety-five drawings for the house when he died. However, Howard Colvin refers to a letter of 1708 which mentions that the staircase was designed by Wren and Hawksmoor, and Sir Gyles Isham discovered a document of *c.* 1766 in the Duke of Northumberland's collection which states that Wren built the Hall. So the interior may have been worked out jointly by Wren and Hawksmoor – unless it is by Talman!

The house is entirely faced with ashlar from the Helmdon quarries. Morton in 1712 calls the stone 'the finest building stone I have seen in England'. One is tempted to agree. It is nine bays wide and two storeys high above a basement. A balustrade finishes the composition at the top. The middle bay projects a little as against the rest and the third, fourth, sixth and seventh bays project again a little, as against the outer pairs of bays. The windows are simply framed and have slightly projecting hoods on the ground floor. The basement has banded rustication and the windows are segment-headed. Above the basement on both fronts, W and E, rises the giant order, of Corinthian pilasters all along, except that on the entrance side (w) the middle bay projects slightly and has attached columns instead of pilasters – the only Baroque motif of the exterior. Here the balustrade is replaced by a segment-headed piece of attic too, with a coat of arms – a late Wren motif. In the frieze the Latin motto of the Fermors, *Hora e sempre*. A late C18 curved two-arm staircase with a fine iron railing rises to the arched entrance, and there is an arched window of the same size above it. The garden side (E) is identical, but has pilasters flanking the central bay as well. In the frieze is the date 1702, and there is no attic achievement. The S side is of five bays, the N side of seven. The S side is regular and has giant pilasters only to flank the whole side and the middle bay. Also there is an extra storey tucked in between the first floor and the balustrade. The N side is curiously restless, of two storeys in bays one, four and seven, of one and a half plus one and a half, i.e. with two mezzanines or one mezzanine and an attic, in the other bays, so creating two corner towers of smaller rooms inside. Broken pediment over the middle bay, in which is the large, tall arched staircase window.

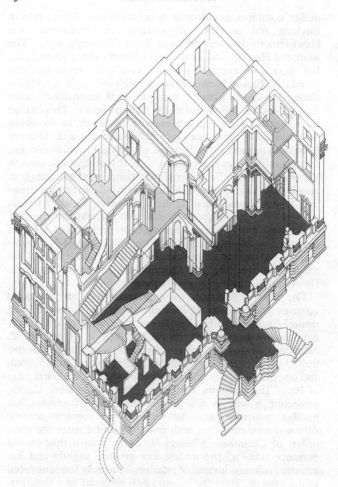

Easton Neston, axonometric view.
Drawing

The INTERIOR was originally designed to house the sculptures of the Arundel Marbles which had been purchased by Sir William Fermor in 1691, so there are numerous niches which formerly housed them. The HALL has been altered. It was originally tripartite with screens of columns to separate the parts. The centre went up through two storeys, an excessive height in comparison with width and breadth. The effect as one entered from the half-lit lower entrance ante-hall, rather like a medieval screens passage, must have been wonderfully dramatic, with light pouring down from the upper windows. It is an idea which Hawksmoor revived in the early stages of his designs for St Mary Woolnough in London. It is still dramatic today with its tall, stone-faced walls and beautifully carved Corinthian columns. Photographs, taken before the ceiling was inserted, show that the central part of the hall had large niches, with statuary, divided by Corinthian pilasters, either side of the fireplace. The central niche was also drawn by Peter Tillemans in 1719 and he shows the chimneypiece surmounted by a sculpture of Hercules, supported by huge carved scroll consols laden with garlands of grapes. It was horizontally subdivided at some time at the end of the C19, and an entrance hall was created out of an adjoining room and the N section of the Hall. Only the S screen and S quarter of the original hall remain. In the centre part, a large grey marble and stone chimneypiece with alternating blocking of the flanking pilasters in their lower halves. The late C19 entrance hall had an arcade of three arches, but this was removed in 1920 and Corinthian columns inserted at the sides of the opening. *J. A. Gotch* was consulted, but it is unclear if he was responsible.

The STAIRCASE is a splendid, spacious composition rising with an intermediate landing straight on from the centre of the house to the centre of the N side and there reaching the main landing, from which it returns and, again with an intermediate landing, arrives at the first floor. 'Flying' steps. Noble wrought-iron balustrade, chiefly with lyre-shaped patterns. At the top landing however a cypher and leaves instead. This must be by the *Tijou* workshop in association with *John Gurdom*, for whom some small payments are recorded. Gurdom worked with Tijou at Chatsworth but also at Kiveton, the home of Sir William Fermor's second wife, Sophia Osborne. Tunnel-vault with rich plasterwork which is probably as late as *c.* 1708, when payments for that work were still being made. There are also payments to *Davis* the carver for work in the hall and staircase. This is probably *Thomas Davis* or *Davies* who also worked at Chatsworth. Monochrome wall paintings from the life of Cyrus; by *Thornhill*, between 1709 and 1711. (Sir Justinian Isham says in his diary in 1708 that the staircase wall 'is to be painted'.) This is an arrangement infinitely more satisfactory than the coloured wall and ceiling paintings of Hampton Court, Burghley, Boughton and Drayton.

The other most ornate room is the former DINING ROOM in the SE corner. The decoration here dates from *c.* 1730–40. The house is indeed called 'not quite finished' in 1731. Baker mentions *William Kent* for certain work done for the then owner, the 1st Earl of Pomfret, and this may well refer to the Dining Room. Ceiling with lively stucco work. The centre is a large oval panel with Venus and Adonis. On the walls stucco panels with freely double-curved frames, though strictly symmetrical. But while they are in themselves symmetrical, they differ in size according to the size of the hunting pictures framed by them, and with size position also was made to differ. One for instance is an overdoor panel, another partly over a door, but carried to the l. of the door so that a hunting trophy had to be fitted below this overhanging l. part of the frame to restore balance. The total effect is gay but curiously restless. The ceiling has been attributed to *Charles Stanley*, but it is more likely that the wall panels are by the *Woolstons* of Northampton. Noble, very classical chimneypiece of black-and-white marble with slender volutes up the sides of the opening and a pulvinated frieze. This could easily be by *Kent*.

The staircase leads into the GALLERY with a change of axis, as one enters in its centre with opposite a grand alcove. It is again tunnel-vaulted. There is more vaulting downstairs, in the small room between the staircase and the garden door, here a groin-vault. The delight in vaulting inside private houses is also something one connects primarily with Vanbrugh, although its appearance at Easton Neston ante-dates that in any of Vanbrugh's buildings. A small drawing room on the E side was redesigned as a LIBRARY in 1967 by *R. Gradidge* and *D. Hicks*. It has heavy projecting piers, and is derived from Hawksmoor's Codrington Library at All Souls, Oxford. In the room is a late C18 chimneypiece with, above, a fine marble plaque of *c.* 1730, formerly in the Hall, showing putti playing with a donkey, after a design by *Duquesnoy*. It is good enough for *Rysbrack*. One other space ought to be mentioned, the basement, and especially the kitchen under the Hall, a splendid room bridged by wide shallow segmental stone arches. These, of course, support the Hall. There is a similar wide stone arch under the staircase and here it was inserted across an already built vaulted undercroft, an indication of a change of plan at an early stage in the development.

Only one of the 1680s WINGS now exists, on the N side of the forecourt. Its partner was demolished in the late C18. The wing is of nine bays, built of brick with stone dressings, and has a hipped roof. The middle bay is ashlar-faced and pedimented. Doorway with segmental pediment on brackets. Tall windows in stone frames and with two transoms. More building of the same type behind towards the stables. The wing was severely damaged by fire in 2003 but was sensitively restored under the direction of *Ptolemy Dean*, 2008–10, when the many dormers were inserted based on evidence found. They are shown on a drawing by Peter Tillemans of 1719.[*]

The S forecourt with its brick wall, niches and balustrade is all part of the *c.* 1920 phase. The STATUES in the niches are early C19 and formerly adorned the niches of the S portico at Stowe.

To the NE of the house a TEMPLE with rainwater heads dated 1641. Three bays with two broad windows and a broad doorway with segmental pediment. Between the windows Tuscan capitals, but no pilasters. Pronounced quoins. Tall one-bay attic with pediment on wildly Jacobean, rather Dietterlin-like pilasters. The side bays have quarter-circle curves leading up to the attic. Behind this façade a room two

---

[*] See Ptolemy Dean's article about the wing in *The Georgian Group Journal*, vol. 20 (2012), pp. 33–50.

windows deep. Except for the fanciful upper pilasters, the façade is in the Inigo Jones style, and ought to be compared with the summerhouse at Ecton, and also with Lamport. But could it be a later pastiche made up of pieces from the old house? Late C17 GATEPIERS W of the W façade. They are of a strange Baroque composition. Alternating bands of rocky rustication. Niches towards the house. Fragments of segmental pediments at the top. Tillemans shows them on the N side of the E parterre in 1719. They would have acted as entrance gates until the road was moved away from the house in the late C18. In the gardens much STATUARY, some from Stowe. The canal, pool and avenue E of the house belong to the original layout, but the formal gardens were made in the early C20. Plain c. 1795 STABLES to the N of the house.

The NW and SW LODGES on the road to Towcester are late C18. There is another of the same date near Hulcote together with POMFRET LODGE, a charming early C19 *cottage orné*. In 1822, *John Raffield* designed the more extensive and handsome GATE SCREEN as a SW entrance to the park. It is now the entrance to Towcester Racecourse. This is signed by *William Croggon*,* 1822, and has decorations made of *Coade* stone, of whose works he was manager. Archway with Corinthian columns. Lower screen of five bays. Urns on it. One-storeyed, one-bay lodges.

TOWCESTER RACECOURSE. Started in 1876 by Sir Thomas Fermor-Hesketh for the entertainment of Elizabeth, Empress of Austria, who had taken Easton Neston for the hunting season. It was such a success that it was formally established in 1928 when the first stand was erected. The GRACE GRANDSTAND was built 1997–8 by *Francis Roberts*. Somewhere between Georgian and Colonial. Rendered brick and timber. Two storeys with Chippendale fret balconies supported on fluted wooden Doric columns. Red tiled roof with central turret. Tower with pyramidal roof at its S end. Round-arched Arts and Crafts type entrance in red brick. The MAIN GRANDSTAND by *Armstrong Burton*, 2005–7, has less of a period feel. Tall seven-storey tower and long façade, again with fret design balconies.

122

EASTON-ON-THE-HILL

0000

A perfect hill village of the oolite band, picturesquely sited, with signs of care and restoration. It has been part of the Exeter (Burghley) Estate since the late C16. The church stands at the N end amongst trees.

ALL SAINTS. Norman one nave window on the S side, exposed inside. In the late C12 a S aisle was built. The arcade is of three

---

*It is in fact signed Croggan rather than, correctly, Croggon.

bays. Circular piers, octagonal abaci, double-chamfered round arches. The S doorway is also round-arched, but has many deep mouldings. In the early C13 a vestry was added on the S side of the chancel. It had a tall shafted E window and an arch to the S which is less easily explained. The trefoiled PISCINA is probably not *in situ*. The S chapel is also early C13, see e.g. the nailhead decoration of the arch. Below the S window is a slab with an inscription in French commemorating Richard de Lindon, who died *c.* 1255, and his wife. Good straight-headed Dec window in the chancel N wall. It has unusual tracery with a central quatrefoil and circles with mouchettes on either side (the same tracery copied in a S aisle window). In the same wall an inscription recording Henry Sampson and his wife as founders of a chantry, and Robert Senkel, rector, who in 1411 registers this foundation. Dec N chapel. Fine Perp W tower, ashlar-faced, with clasping buttresses, a quatrefoil frieze below the battlements, and tall crocketed pinnacles. The model is St John Stamford. Its arch inside has battlemented capitals (cf. Collyweston). Chancel also Perp with a battlemented E gable and three clerestory windows. S aisle rebuilt 1786, doubtless the date of the two square-headed windows at the W end and to an extent the vestry beyond. The N chapel E window with intersecting tracery is probably C18 also. Porch sundial dated 1791. N aisle rebuilt 1856. – FONT. Octagonal, Perp, with shields and tracery. Charming crested wooden cover by *Martyn Barratt*, 2000. – SCREENS. Two stone screens, different in design, to the N and S chapels. The former apparently made up from parts of window tracery from the N aisle. A faculty of 1888 records that the screen was rebuilt a few feet back from its previous position to accommodate stalls. The S, C14 with cusped openings and ogee-headed doorway. – Many BOX PEWS. C18 or early C19, incorporating BENCH-ENDS. Simple, straight-headed. One in the nave dated 1631. – Two-decker PULPIT for which a date of 1759 is recorded. Sounding board renewed 1975. – ORGAN. 1849, by *G. M. Holditch* in a Gothic frame. – REREDOS. C15 style, by *H. F. Traylen* of Stamford, 1910–13. – ROYAL ARMS. George IV, 1826. Painted and very fine. – SCULPTURE. A finely detailed piece of a Perp stone frieze, perhaps from a reredos or a monument (s aisle). – STAINED GLASS. Chancel N. Head of Christ and foliage fragments; C14. – MONUMENTS. Incised slab to a lady, upper part lost; *c.* 1340. – Many finely carved Georgian headstones, especially on the S side of the church. On the N side a large sarcophagus for the Perkins family (mid-C19 to 1929).

PRIEST'S HOUSE, West Street. Built by Thomas Stokes, rector from 1456 until his death in 1495 and probably intended as a chantry house, he having left a bequest for a foundation in his will. Dendrochronology has dated the timbers *c.* 1474–99. Two storeys, windows with arched lights. A projection contains a stone newel stair which leads to the upper room. This has a fireplace and an open timber roof (restored). The ceiling of the ground-floor room has moulded beams. Converted to a cow house in 1868 by *T. G. Jackson*, who was born in nearby Duddington (q.v.). Fortunately Jackson showed great respect. It was almost demolished in 1963 but saved by the energies of the Peterborough Society and passed to the National Trust who opened it to the public in 1967.* It is now a meeting room and museum.

GLEBE HOUSE, former rectory, at the N end of West Street. 86 Handsome early C18, of five bays, two storeys, but the basement still with mullioned windows. Ashlar limestone with framed windows. Dentil cornice.

VILLAGE HALL, High Street. Former school of 1867–8, probably by *J. B. Corby* who did much work for the estate at this period. Large Gothic window of three lights with one large and two smaller circles in its head. Tall Gothic clock tower and a bell turret. Three-light windows with trefoil heads in the side wall and similar in School House. Exeter of Burghley coat of arms.

The village has a good many stone houses, of which the following are some of the most interesting.† Starting at the E end of HIGH STREET, Nos. 54–56, now a single house, with C17 two- and three-light mullioned windows, doorway in l. section. The datestone of 1832 probably refers to heightening. Roof with dormers. Opposite, the school, THE FIRS, a very neat Late Georgian square house, three bays with quoins, its central windows blind. Two C19 canted bays to the ground floor. To the W some pleasant cottage rows. Nos. 30–32, probably C18. Single-storey with dormers and stone stacks. No. 11, N side, has a datestone of 1607 but another for 1792, and is similar to the previous row. On the S side, No. 26 has a Victorian gable end with a projecting chimneystack on its upper floor ending in an ivy leaf stop. No. 20 of three bays and two canted bays with stone tiled roofs below and two-light mullions above. Just w of the Church Street junction the BLUEBELL INN, late C17 but much renewed in the C19 when the street façade was refenestrated.

Up CHURCH STREET, at the corner of The Lane, EASTON HALL, elegant, *c.* 1820–30 and attributed to *J. Richardson* of Stamford. Five bays, three storeys. Tudor style. In the centre bay a pretty Gothic window below a curved gable. Tall Gothic pinnacles and frieze. Long later C19 wing behind with more shaped gables on the courtyard side and a diamond quatrefoil balustrade. On the E side below The Lane No. 24 has two- and three-light mullions with the date 1688, and opposite, No. 23 is good Late Georgian dated 1830. No. 19 appears to be two properties joined together, the l.-hand end the older portion using some ironstone bands and its end gable dated 1686. Its now raised blocked doorway shows how the street level has changed. Just below, on the r., GLENVILLE, slightly eccentric

---

*I am grateful to Nick Hill of English Heritage for sight of his detailed report on the building (2011).
†A full inventory of the village can be found in the RCHME volume *An Inventory of Architectural Monuments in North Northamptonshire*, HMSO (1984).

mock Jacobean dated 1839 and 1902. Northamptonshire Jacobean-style central gable, its side windows interrupting a heavy dentil cornice. At the end of Church Street EASTON HOUSE, a typical 1870 house, much extended, has its former STABLE BLOCK fronting the road. Three bays (Clock House) and on the other side of the former arched carriageway two bays (Archway House). Open timberwork in the gable above. 1870 datestone in N gable which also records its restoration in 1992.

Less good buildings in WEST STREET where houses have been much tidied up in recent times, although here and there are mullioned windows. On the corner of the Lane the former WHITE HORSE, a solid C19 stone house in classical mode, with quoins and rusticated windows, its former doorway now a round-headed window. At the S end of the street, set back on the E side is PRIORY COURT, a fine former granary of the Burghley Estate dated 1878. Recessed façades N and S with yellow brick segmental-arched windows with yellow brick lintels. The centre of the S side has a pediment and Jacobean finials.

Former GIRLS' SCHOOL, on the A43 at the E end of the village at the corner of Racecourse Road. 1830. Small, rather classical in appearance, set back with gabled centre with round-arched doorway and plaque above. Side walls have single windows and quoins. Mistresses' house at right angles, end on to the road. Rear wing by *Bryan Browning*, 1849.

Former GRANDSTAND, Racecourse Road, nearly 1 m. SE. Built for the C18 Stamford racecourse. A building lease was granted to John Terrament, a Stamford innkeeper, in 1766. The upper room served to some extent as an assembly room. The building has a long five-bay arcaded S elevation with five semicircular lunettes above. The end façades also have arcading and lunettes in two bays. The building was repaired and enlarged 1818–20. Races continued until 1873 when the building fell into decay. In 1994 it was converted into a residence with the upper viewing platform restored.

ECTON

ST MARY MAGDALENE. Of ironstone, large, and away from the street. Built in the C13 to early C14. The W tower is prominent and out of the ordinary. Cusped almond-shaped window above the W doorway. Dec bell-openings, their bases blocked, then a sloped section and on it, ashlar-faced, another storey with bell-openings. They are Perp, pairs of two lights each, with a transom. Quatrefoil frieze, battlements, pinnacles of an odd form, like fluted chimney pots. The low arcades of the aisles are of four bays, i.e. three plus a fourth different one, so C13 but altered in the C14. The first three bays on the N change from octagonal to round piers; on the S they are octagonal, and very rough. The fourth bay represents the former transepts and has continuous chamfers. Late C13 a recess in the chancel. Ogee niche to r. of chancel arch. Blocked doorway on s side of chancel, partly hidden by the Palmer monument. Late C13 to early C14 the s porch and the doorway. The N porch is unusual since it has a dated inscription for 1456. The chancel was lengthened in the C17, but later rebuilt, partly in 1889 and partly in 1903–8 by *Matthew Holding*. Prior to that the church had a much more Georgian-looking interior, of which survives its flat ceiling and the PULPIT and BOX PEWS of shortly before 1825 (Cole). The pews, which may have been lowered, have rounded corners at the front with fluted pilasters. The pulpit was formerly a three-decker. – FONT. Circular, defaced; the raw tracery may indicate the C14. It has all the appearance of having been rescued from outside.* – ROOD STAIR. In the s aisle, its top section of wood panels. – COMMUNION RAIL. Later C17. – REREDOS (chancel). Dec style with painted scenes by *J. C. Tancred* (s chapel). All refurbished as a Sotheby memorial, 1908–9. – FAMILY TREES of the Palmer and Whalley families, built up from slabs of marble and fitted into the spaces of pointed arches. The Palmer one was moved from the N side of the chancel in 1889. – ROYAL ARMS, painted, of George III. – STAINED GLASS. Chancel N by *Morris & Co.*, but as late as 1924. – Chancel E of 1912 by *Percy Bacon*. Two more by him in the s chapel, 1915 and 1918. – N aisle, 1915 by *Burlison & Grylls*. – MONUMENTS. Samuel Freeman †1707, Dean of Peterborough (chancel W wall). Elaborate cartouche, urn at the top, two cherubs' heads above, two below. Rather fine, but too high up to be appreciated. – In the chancel: John Palmer. Erected in 1732. By *Rysbrack*. With an excellent bust at the top and very fine architectural detail. – John Palmer †1761, with another bust by *Rysbrack*. The surround was carved by *Henry Cox* of Northampton after the pattern of the Rysbrack opposite, but with a bit more Rococo flourish. Books l. and r. of the bust. It stands against a banded obelisk. – Catherine Whalley †1817. By *Rossi*. Oddly Victorian in its Quattrocento inspiration. Two kneeling angels holding a circular medallion. – In the s chapel: Ann Isted †1763. A splendid design using coloured marbles. An urn above a tablet flanked by two standing putti. Rococo decoration and almost certainly by *Sir Henry Cheere*. – N aisle. Bronze plaque with portrait roundel to commemorate the American connection with Benjamin Franklin, whose ancestors were from Ecton and which he visited in 1758. It was made by *Fritz Roselieb* in 1910.

ECTON HALL. The front is very much in the style of, and very likely inspired by, *Sanderson Miller*, and the foremost example of the Early Gothic Revival in the county. The designs are signed by *William Hiorne* of Warwick. Built 1755–6, with the s front being dated 1756. The scheme with the canted bays in

* There is a record of an early C19 font made by *John Whiting* of Northampton, but this has disappeared.

the gabled wings and a porch in the middle is traditional Tudor and not specially Gothic. The gables in fact are self-consciously in what Horace Walpole once called 'King James' Gothic'. The porch on the other hand is pure Gothick, small, with an ogee head and with prettily shafted niches inside with little rib-vaults. The front also displays the large blank quatrefoils which were so popular at the beginning of the Gothic Revival. It is, needless to say, castellated. The windows on the other hand are sashed and simply Georgian. Sizeable additions were made at the back in 1888–91 by *J. B. Everard* of Leicester (his plans for an extended s front with an ornamental tower were rejected), of which portions were removed in the 1960s and the rest, and unfortunately most of the interior, was destroyed in the late 1980s when the building was converted into apartments. Stable block converted in 1989.

In the grounds to the NE a SUMMERHOUSE worth a careful look. Its style places it in the second third of the C17, and quite probably the 1630s. An attribution to *Inigo Jones* cannot be substantiated. It is purely classical and built on an oval plan, which is remarkable for its date. Tuscan pilasters and Ionic pilasters over. On the ground floor opened in three bays by means of Tuscan columns. The third bays have upright oval windows. Access to the room on the upper floor by an outer staircase. The upper windows have ears. They are partly framed by close laurel garlands, partly given some oak foliage above the lintel. It has much in common with the summerhouse built by *William Hiorne* in the 1750s at Farnborough, Warks. If it is of his time it probably incorporates some earlier work.

ECTON HOUSE (former rectory), N of the church, built by Thomas Palmer in 1693. Seven bays, two storeys, hipped roof. The windows have odd winged lintel stones of which the central one is carved with acanthus scrolls (cf. *Henry Bell*'s Sessions House in Northampton). Lower two-bay attachments. Along the front an early C19 trellis veranda. Additions by *Talbot Brown, Panter & Partners*, 1966–8. On the staircase heraldic glass by *William Price*, 1742.

SCHOOL, Northampton Road, 1876, by *E. Sharman*. Gothic with big gable. SCHOOL HOUSE, contemporary, with openwork timber gables.

Many good ironstone houses in the HIGH STREET. On the E side, set back, the former SCHOOL, built by John Palmer. The inscription has the foundation date 1752 in black letter. Further s on the w side the MANOR HOUSE, 1694. Still with mullioned-and-transomed windows, but they are now completely symmetrically arranged. Three-bay front, two storeys. Steep pediment above the doorway which has a curious strapwork surround. There is a tradition that it was saved from Catesby manor house (*see* p. 166). Some Sotheby ESTATE COTTAGES. Three pairs dated 1896 by *Matthew Holding*. Ironstone with red brick dressings. Two sets have verandas. Further s is the READING AND RECREATION ROOM of 1897–8, the gift of the Sothebys. Probably by *Everard* of Leicester (*see* the Hall above).

EDGCOTE

ST JAMES. The church, surrounded uncommonly closely by trees, and the house form a delightful picture. The oldest features are the simple S doorway and the S arcade of three bays. They are C13. The arcade has circular piers with circular abaci and pointed double-chamfered arches. One capital is decorated by rather timid crockets and small heads, one held by an outstretched arm. Dec the N side, Perp the W tower, though its doorway with crocketed ogee hoodmould and pinnacled buttresses is a Dec design. Perp W window, transomed bell-openings and battlements. Perp also the big S windows of the chancel and the NE vestry, originally two-storeyed. Fireplace inside. Its doorway with original door, Tudor four-centred arch. The S aisle E window, three lights with mullions, probably late C17. – PULPIT and BOX PEWS, C18. – FAMILY PEW on the N side of the chancel, a separate small room originally accessed externally from the house. – REREDOS. Gothic, of wood, c. 1900. Above on the l. a small statue of St James. – STAINED GLASS. S aisle windows with C16 or C17 heraldic panels, one dated 1596. – The later glass is all by *J. Hardman & Co.*, some c. 1860 (E window), the rest mostly c. 1890, the chancel S window the best. The latest window N aisle W is dated 1927. – MONUMENTS. A remarkable series of monuments of the Chauncy family, including four by *Rysbrack*, though three of them are mundane architectural tablets for which the family might just as well have gone to a less distinguished artist. The series starts with William †1585 and Sir Toby †1607 and two wives. Both are of the same form, free-standing, of alabaster, with effigies on tomb-chests. The N side of Toby's has nine children in relief, several daughters in swaddling clothes. The decoration of the chest fronts with flat balusters and especially a series of spiral gadrooned balusters, all typical of the *Roiley* workshop of Burton upon Trent. They may very well both have been made at the same time. Wonderful lion at Toby's feet, whose tail is divided against the soles of his feet. – The architectural tablets begin with another Toby †1662, attributed to *Joshua Marshall* (GF). – Toby Chauncy †1724. Architectural tablet of variegated marbles attributable to the *Smiths* of Warwick (cf. Lamport and Fawsley). – In 1760 *Rysbrack* made the ambitious memorial for the builder Richard Chauncy. This has an excellent bust, though it is perhaps not perfectly connected with the architectural background. Under the terms of his will Richard Chauncy gave instructions for memorials for his ancestors. These, also by *Rysbrack*, are for William †1644 (E end S wall), the children of yet another Toby (W end S wall) and Richard †1734 (W of S door). – Mary Chauncy †1779 and others. Pretty Neoclassical surround with coloured marbles. – Julia Cartwright †1856. Gothic triptych with two allegorical figures. Unsigned. – Aubrey Cartwright †1904. Slab with a brass inscription over a cross with scroll supports. – Several other memorials and a good set of ledger stones.

87   EDGCOTE HOUSE. Built in 1747–52 for Richard Chauncy and
      impressive with its dark Hornton stone walls with lighter Cub-
      lington stone dressings. The commission for its building origin-
      ated with *William Smith II* of Warwick and he built the stables
      just before his death in 1747. They stand to the l. of the
      entrance side and are, in a very Age of Reason manner, bal-
      anced by the church. It is likely that he designed the house as
      well. The job was then taken over by *William Jones*, best known
      for designing the Rotunda in Ranelagh Gardens. He brought
      in *Abraham Swan* to mastermind the interior decoration. The
      names of the craftsmen are all known: *Swan* for the woodwork,
      John Gilbert (woodcarver at the Mansion House, London,
      1749–51), *Benjamin King* (one of Smith's craftsmen) and
      Richard Newman for fireplaces, *J. Whitehead* for the plasterwork,
      and *John Cobb* for furniture. The house is nine bays in width
      and two storeys plus a basement in height. Hipped roof. Three-
      bay pediment with a shield in a cartouche. Open staircase in
      two flights, in the Kentian manner, originally with ironwork
      balustrade replaced in the C19 by stone balustrade. On the
      principal floor the three-bay side parts have a pediment over
      the middle window. The doorway pediment is stressed by
      corbels. The arrangement on the garden side, which overlooks
      a lake, is essentially the same. The plan is basically a double
      pile with the entrance hall and the saloon in axis with it.
          The ENTRANCE HALL is relatively simple with a decorative
      beamed ceiling and deep Doric frieze. Two niches in the end
      wall. Stone fireplace probably by *King*. To the r. the BILLIARD
      ROOM with a fine wood Rococo fireplace inset with a late C16
      stone panel of the Chauncy arms saved from the earlier house.
      The STAIRCASE, provided by *Swan* is deep plum red mahog-
      any with turned balusters bulbous at the foot, and a carved
      string instead of carved tread-ends – a conservative feature.
      Very tall lantern high up with a ceiling divided by frames into
      panels. The SALOON has the most sumptuous ceiling, in
      Rococo forms. Splendid wooden Rococo fireplace again and
      columned overmantel. DINING ROOM with another good fire-
      place and overmantel. All the ground-floor rooms have decora-
      tive plasterwork friezes and rich doorcases. On the first floor
      two good bedrooms. The SCREEN ROOM with curved alcove
      screen of two Ionic columns, and the more orthodox ALCOVE
      ROOM, with bed set between two dressing room wings. The
      attic rooms have a considerable amount of plain C16 panelling
      from the old house, for which a date of 1598 is recorded. The
      old house is endearinglyly recorded in the local poet Mary
      Leapor's work as 'Crumble Hall'.
      KITCHEN GARDEN, s on the opposite side of the Culworth road,
      across a small pool, with two COTTAGES, their temple façades
      contemporary with the house.
      ESTATE COTTAGES (once called Snobs Row and Rags Row),
      ¼ m. sw on the Wardington Road. Stone with pedimented
      centres, *c.* 1790–1800, built by William Chauncy.

VICARAGE, s of the church. Simple Georgian, of five bays and two storeys.

TRAFFORD BRIDGE FARMHOUSE. Late C18. Stone shield inside, late C16, with the Chauncy arms.

EVENLEY

ST GEORGE. A rebuilding of 1864–5 by H. *Woodyer* and of some merit, with a number of the eccentricities which one expects from him. It is basically in the Late E.E. style and the transept plan derives from the medieval church. w tower with shingled broach spire and stair-turret. The windows double lancets, most with rounded tops. The easternmost s window of the chancel has three doubles with small quatrefoils above, grouped together under an arcade set on pointed corbels. Inside in the N aisle is a group of four doubles, again linked together, but this time with a detached arcade in front. Most of the other windows have shafted embrasures. Everywhere there is luxurious foliage carving of the stiff-leaf type. It is all leaves save two stops on the N arcade hoodmould, one of which has a bird as a pendant, and the other a tiny dragon. The clerestory windows are quatrefoils set within circles. The interior fittings pulpit, font, reredos, tiles, roofs, etc. have survived almost intact. The REREDOS has arcading with diaper decoration, an alabaster and marble centrepiece with statues of angels. The porch doorways have spider's web ironwork. – STAINED GLASS. E window, probably *c.* 1865, N transept window 1864 and s transept window 1874, all by *J. Hardman & Co.* – MONUMENTS (sadly gathered under the tower). Sir Creswell Levinz †1700, attributed to *Nost*. Only the statue, its plinth and a cartouche survive, skied in a corner. There was originally an arched architectural background, and to the l. and r. of his feet putti on the arms of an open scrolly pediment. The statue is a fine piece, dressed in judge's robes and sporting a full wig. – H. Gwynne Browne †1803. By *R. Blore Jun.* Mourning woman by an urn. – Pearne family, big sarcophagus with large urn, in the churchyard. Erected before 1757.

The large square green has nice rows of two-storeyed *c.* 1870 COTTAGES, all part of a tidying up by the squire, the Hon. Philip Pierrepont. Most have roofs with stripes of blue and red slates. On the SE corner the RED LION pub. Mid-C19 Tudor style with two canted bays and pretty glazing.

OLD MANOR HOUSE, Church Lane. C17. Symmetrical, of three bays with four-light mullioned windows. Central porch with gable.

EVENLEY HALL, ½ m. N. The present house was built *c.* 1740 by Francis Bassett. It is a four-square block of the Palladian villa type, with its original main façade on the N side, overlooking expansive parkland towards Brackley. It has five bays with a three-bay centrepiece with attached unfluted Ionic columns on the upper storey. Windows with alternating triangular and segmental pediments. At the back, unusually, two semicircular staircase turrets and a plain Venetian window, somewhat Vanbrughian. There were also two detached pavilions. Facing the house on this side a simple stable block, half-H in plan with cupola and a central triangular pediment. In 1872 *Alfred Waterhouse* was called in to alter the interior, but his work was almost totally lost in 1897 in a disastrous fire. On rebuilding, somewhat bizarrely, the interior was made Jacobethan and a new grand hall created in the centre of the house with a wide sweeping stair. A school between 1947 and 2001 and since then happily returned to its Georgian appearance under the direction of *Stephen Oliver*. The pavilion blocks, which had been Victorianized, have been reduced to their original footprints and given more appropriate roofs, a new entrance has been made connecting these to the main block and Victorian plate-glass windows have been replaced by sashes.

EVERDON

ST MARY. A big grand church with an especially spacious interior. Mostly early C14, namely the W tower the N aisle E window, the S aisle windows, and the N and S doorways. That on the S especially sumptuous. Three orders of shafts with nobbly leaf capitals, three orders of voussoirs with foliage trail, ballflower and fleurons, crocketed ogee hoodmould with finial. They are of a finer, lighter stone than the ironstone used elsewhere. The S aisle E window is an interesting example of the transition between Dec and Perp (cf. Kislingbury), curvilinear with vertical lines. There are other Perp windows. The chancel windows date from a restoration by *G. G. Scott* in 1862–3. The arcades probably also Dec. The arches have one sunk quadrant moulding, and that moulding is reproduced on the moulding of the piers. They are thus circular with very wide fillets. The E capitals octagonal but the W pair round. The nave is wide, and the arcade is tall. The chancel arch is the same, only with a wave rather than a quadrant moulding, again taken up by the responds. In the chancel SEDILIA with ogee arches and crocketed gables, and opposite a low tomb-recess, also ogee-headed. – FONT. Octagonal, C13, of Purbeck marble, of a familiar, often supplied type with two flat, blank, pointed arches to each side. – SCREEN. Dec, wide one-light divisions corresponding to two panels of the base. Ogee arches and fine tracery above them. A good piece, as Northamptonshire screens go. – Fine CHOIR STALLS by *Bodley & Garner*, 1891–2. – ORGAN CASE in keeping, of 1906. – LECTERN. Also *Bodley & Garner* with stem supported by pinnacled buttresses. – PULPIT. Made 1808 on a stand of 1892. – BALCONY. High up at the W end above the tower arch, giving access to roofs. C17 balustrade. – REREDOS of 1946. – ROYAL ARMS. Painted panel for George III. – STAINED GLASS. Fragments in several windows, including a C14 Pelican in her Piety (nave N) and two shields of the Lovell family, *c.* 1400. Chancel E of 1906, S aisle of 1921 and 1892, all by *Burlison & Grylls.* – MONUMENTS. Purbeck slab (N aisle) with a foliate cross. The now illegible inscription is recorded as for Henricus de Everdone †1330. Thomas Spencer, 1606. Tablet with Corinthian columns, many shields but without figures. Fine quality and doubtless by *Jasper Hollemans,* who made the Spencer tombs at Great Brington.

Former SCHOOL, on the Green. 1877 by *E. F. Law.* Rather charming in red brick and stone building with with a pretty bell-turret at the E end. Another wing behind.

Amongst the many stone houses on the S side of HIGH STREET, set back, the OLD RECTORY is a substantial C17 and Late Georgian house. Seven-bay front with central two-storey porch with oculus at the head. Simple Gothick glazing in the l. wing. Two more gabled wings on the r.

EVERDON HALL, Little Everdon. A beautifully set early C19 stone house with a rather severe three-storey double-gabled entrance front with a shallow pilastered porch. The garden front has the addition of a two-storey canted bay on its l. gable and in the centre a wide, curved two-storey bay, both topped by balustrades. Inner hall with Doric columns and a stone cantilever staircase. Extensively altered inside *c.* 1900. Several rooms have plasterwork cornices and ceilings and pretty fire-place surrounds.

OLD HOUSE, Little Everdon. 1690. Mullioned windows and one blocked vertical oval window by the doorway. Inside, staircase with a balustrade of splat balusters of twisted form.

EYDON

ST NICHOLAS. Much of the church is the work of *R. C. Hussey,* 1864–5. The S aisle and S porch were added at this time. The history starts with the N arcade. Its first two bays are original work of the early C13. Circular pier, square abacus, double-chamfered arches. The rest is C19. Early C14 W tower – see the doorway with two continuous sunk-quadrant mouldings and the arch towards the nave with three chamfers. Chancel arch chamfered on foliate corbels. Details of the chancel and the N aisle are also Dec. Rather slender reticulated windows. – FONT. Norman. The base is like an octagonal scalloped capital reversed (cf. Buckinghamshire fonts). Big leaf in the scallops. The bowl is circular and fluted with a band of foliage at the top. Foot and bowl are joined by a rope moulding. – STAINED

GLASS. Two heraldic windows in the N aisle by *J. Russell* of Oxford, *c.* 1830. Chancel E and side windows, 1865 and later by *Ward & Hughes* and S aisle window 1882 also by them. – S aisle E window 1878 by *Heaton, Butler & Bayne*. Several other Victorian windows. – MONUMENTS. Effigy of a lady, *c.* 1340. – Rev. Francis Annesley †1811, by *Bacon Jun.* Very simple tablet above the S door. – Two Lewis sons killed in the First World War. Alabaster surround with inscription inset with two white marble portrait plaques.

EYDON HALL. A most attractive house, built for the Rev. Francis Annesley, 1789–91. Designed by *James Lewis* and illustrated in his *Original Designs* (1797). It is of moderate size and great, if reticent, elegance in a beautiful setting. Only five bays, and only a basement and two storeys, but refined in proportions and details. Dark ironstone ashlar from the local quarries. The garden side has a four-column portico of attenuated Ionic columns and a pediment. The entrance side has no portico, but also a three-bay pediment. Above the doorway a frieze of thin garlands. The first and fifth ground-floor windows are set in blank arches. Parapet partly balustraded. The W side has a projecting curved bay running over the two main floors and also the basement, here revealed. The interiors are again delicately decorated. No display is made anywhere, not even in the ample staircase hall with its simple cast-iron stair balustrade and its oval glazed dome. Charming oval room behind the staircase. Several fine Neoclassical marble chimneypieces. Service rooms are all in the basement. ORANGERY of four bays, the upper parts by *Sir Herbert Baker*.

STABLES. A successful design of 1923–4 by *C. H. Biddulph-Pinchard*. Curved buildings in the stable court were converted to create further stables and an estate office 1983–5 by *Erith*

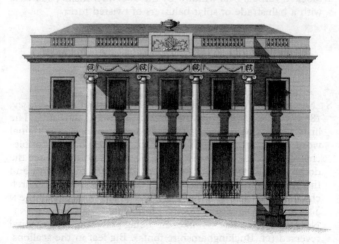

Eydon Hall.
Engraving by James Lewis

& Terry. They also renovated the Orangery 1985–7. The gently landscaped grounds have many fine trees.

At the village entrance late C18-style GATEPIERS and a gabled early C19 romantic LODGE with an odd tower ending in four pointed gables.

Outside the Hall gates a small green with the STOCKS, well preserved. The village has an excellent supply of good ironstone houses, many with mullions, not surprising since there were extensive quarries here. On the opposite corner of the green a C17 HOUSE with a two-storeyed gabled porch and mullioned windows. To the N in School Lane an outbuilding with a blocked two-light C15 window which appears to be *in situ*. It is part of RECTORY FARMHOUSE, which is otherwise largely C17 with a big carriage entrance. Opposite THE OLD SCHOOL, a two-storey late C17 house with a porch and mullions. Also two houses in the vernacular manner by *Erith & Terry* (1986–8) in High Street, by the entrance to the Hall, and another on Hollow Way (1988–90).

The village plan is an interesting and rare survival from early medieval times with two parallel streets (High Street and Lime Avenue) linked at the N and S ends, creating a long roughly rectangular shape, the original land plots then laying across the rectangle.

FARTHINGHOE

5030

ST MICHAEL. Norman the lower part of the tower – see the W doorway and the arch towards the nave, which is round, unmoulded, quite wide, and stands on the simplest imposts. Of the early C13 the S doorway and the fine S arcade. This is three bays long and has circular piers and circular abaci. One capital and the bits of decoration by the E respond are stiff-leaf. Double-chamfered pointed arches. The N arcade is different but roughly contemporary. One capital has stiff-leaf too, but the capital is flatter. Dec the N aisle, the pretty pairs of small two-light windows in the S porch, itself Victorian, and the chancel (E window with reticulated tracery). The S aisle is Perp including a tomb-recess with a four-centred arch and a brass indent. Perp also the head corbels in the clerestory. Rood-loft stair in the N aisle with a turret externally. The top part of the tower has an inscription referring to 1654 and a coat of arms framed by columns. Attached to the S aisle is a building which appears to be C17. It was certainly used as a schoolroom by the early C19 and may well have been built for this purpose. It was originally totally separate from the church, being entered by a doorway on the splay of its SW corner. It is now accessible from the aisle. There was a fairly heavy restoration of the church in 1871. – STAINED GLASS. E window 1851 by *William Wailes*. – MONUMENTS.

Cartouche tablets of 1684, 1694 and others. – A pretty tablet, broken into two parts, having been on the E wall of the aisle and dismantled when access was made into the vestry, to the Misses Henrietta and Catherine Rush †1801. With a young woman by an urn. – George Rush †1806. By *Charles Regnart* of Cleveland Street, Fitzroy Square, and reckoned his masterpiece. The conception is still one of the C18. Comfortably reclining figure on a sarcophagus, completely free-standing. The old gentleman wears night-cap and slippers and an ample kind of toga. He has been reading and is now looking up. It is a pity the monument's present position has him facing the wall, since it is a fine piece of sculpture.

ABBEY LODGE, W of the church. The remains of a C15 hall house. Subdivided in the C16. Though the datestone 1581 is Victorian, it is probably reliable. What survives is the archway formerly leading into the front garden, the doorway, back doorway and a doorway to the r. into the Hall, all three with four-centred heads, and the fireplace in the Hall, placed, against all local custom, against the screens passage. The surround has lozenge-shaped medallions. There are blackened arch-braced collars in the roof.

SCHOOL, just E of the church. 1877 of sandstone and ironstone. Two gabled bays with large windows and a porch in the centre.

FARTHINGHOE LODGE (1 m. SW). Dem.

6050

FARTHINGSTONE

ST MARY. Simple N doorway of *c.* 1200. Late C13 chancel – see the S windows and the doorway; also the SEDILIA with rough pointed arches. To their W – an unusual position – a tomb-recess with low segmental arch. Dec (but altered) the arch on the N side of the nave, with a free-standing octagonal pier, i.e. the arch did not lead to a transept proper but to a bay of a N aisle, which presumably was never completed. C13 W tower, unbuttressed. Narrow triple-chamfered arch towards the nave. Perp windows in the nave. A forest of poppyhead PEWS and further poppyheads on the chancel STALLS. These have delightful carvings, some with amusing animals playing musical instruments. They date from a restoration in 1852. A further tactful restoration was conducted by *W. Talbot Brown* 1924–8. – FONT. A rough octagonal bowl, C14? – STAINED GLASS. Chancel E window, Grant memorial 1882 by *Swaine & Bourne* of Birmingham. – Chancel S window, an 1896 memorial but made 1927 by *Morris & Co.* – Nave S of 1927 also by *Morris & Co.* Especially grand design of Flora standing amidst a rose bush. – Others in the nave of 1930 and 1943 by *J. Powell & Sons.*

KING'S ARMS, opposite the church. Picturesque Neo-Tudor. Built before 1845. Reconstructed after a fire *c.* 1870. Pieces of old carving incorporated. Big H on the front gable for the Hurley family of builders.

SCHOOL (Village Hall), Maidford Road. 1875. Ironstone with blue brick dressings. T-shaped with a front gable inset with three lancets and a bellcote above. Set behind it, PENSION ROW, two odd cottages with brick door and window frames and giant arches round them. The walling is faced with old crocks and plaster. The sort of thing one finds at the seaside.

LITTLECOURT YARD. The intact stable block of Littlecourt House (dem.). Half-H plan. The s-facing courtyard has stalls all round and cottages at each end. Littlecourt itself was a grand Arts and Crafts mansion built in 1905 by *Walter Cave* for Philip Agnew, proprietor of *Punch* magazine. It was demolished after Mrs Agnew's death in 1957. The successor house of 1961–2 by and for *A. E. Henson* of *Brown & Henson* has also gone. E of the church in High Street is JOYMEAD, a garden created in 1922 by the Agnews in memory of their daughter who died from tuberculosis. Columned SHELTER by *Frank L. Pearson*. The CLOISTER on the W side is by *W. Talbot Brown*, 1930, and contains a memorial to the Agnews' son who died that year.

CASTLE DYKES, 1 m. N of the church. A large medieval castle earthwork of unusual type. The narrow main bailey is cut virtually in two by the ringwork which forms the inner stronghold, and there is a large outer bailey.

CASTLE YARD, a little s of Castle Dykes, is a double ditch and banked rectangular enclosure beside the Stowe road. In poor condition, only readily visible from the N and W. Excavation in the 1950s has indicated that this is an Iron Age hillfort with a box rampart.

FAWSLEY

One of the most picturesque and atmospheric groupings in the county, with the church sitting alone on the site of a deserted village looking across to the mansion, and surrounded by the remnants of a majestic deer park. This was made more picturesque by *Capability Brown* in the 1760s, who created a lovely curving double lake.

ST MARY. The earliest feature is the two C13 bays of the arcades, with octagonal piers and double-chamfered arches. They may be contemporary with the intersected tracery of the chancel E and s aisle E windows, but are earlier than the Dec W tower, with which they were linked by a new bay. The tower has an ogee-hooded niche and cusped Y-tracery in the bell-openings. Dec also the reused arch of the N doorway. The clerestory is C16 and Bridges records an inscription of 1518 referring to 'fenestras'. It should be compared with that of the same time at Great Brington, possibly by the same masons. Much of the building appears to be a reworking in the C17, with the chancel dated 1690. – FONT. Originally probably C13, but the big heads certainly reworked. – WOODWORK. Late Perp and Early Renaissance panels, many ornamented, some with heads in medallions or with grotesques; reused in the early C19 box pews. – STAINED GLASS. Many imported Flemish roundels; also Knightley heraldic glass of C16, much rearranged, probably in the early C19 and reglazed and reset by *E. W. Twining* of Northampton in 1929–30. – Chancel E, *J. Hardman & Co.*, 1861.

MONUMENTS. The church is a veritable mausoleum to the Knightleys. Thirteen are worth attention. They follow each other roughly chronologically like this: Brass of Thomas †1516 (nave) 18 in. (46-cm.) figure. – Sir Richard †1534 and wife, by *Richard Parker* of Burton upon Trent. Alabaster; free-standing. An outstandingly fine monument, especially in the small figures of the mourners standing against the tomb-chest under broad, flat ogee arches, four daughters to the N, eight sons arranged in pairs to the S. They are delicately characterized and move with ease. At the head end two praying angels and a shield. The effigies beautifully carved and detailed with much original colour. They have heraldic dress. – Brasses to Sir Edmund †1542 and wife. The figures are 3 ft (91 cm.) long. His head lies on a helmet, hers on a pillow. – Sir Valentine †1566, Mary Knightley †1573, Sir Richard †1615, and Sir Valentine †1619. Standing monument, broad, with a big sarcophagus high up, supported by two praying caryatids. Between them, lower down, small recumbent effigy on a slab supported by tall brackets. Two putti by the sarcophagus, probably not original. The surround of the Doric order with metope frieze and pediment. It is made of clunch and was coloured in 1930. It is one of a number of monuments which can be associated with the *Thorpes* of Kingscliffe (*see* Introduction, p. 34). – In the chancel, two white marble tablets with columns for Sir Richard †1661 (but erected 1683) and Essex †1670, both attributed to *Abraham Storey* (GF). Three large architectural tablets, recording deaths of Knightleys, 1728 and 1738 (nearly identical), and 1731, all three attributed to *Francis Smith* of Warwick, with characteristic mottled marbles. They make interesting stylistic comparisons. Only the one of 1731 (Jane Grey Knightley) has a figural element, a small bust on top. Another has a trophy of arms, of which the holster of the gun is labelled 'Warwick'. – Devereux †1681, also attributed to Storey (GF), and Elizabeth †1715 (N aisle). Two very similar large standing urns on tall pedestals. Again a comparison is enlightening. The later monument is richer, and the skill in the carving of the four garlands deserves notice. – In the S aisle, Lucy †1805, by *Richard Westmacott Sen.* Architectural, without any figures. Very finely detailed and still entirely pre-Grecian. – Selina †1856. By *John Gibson* of Rome. She is being received into Heaven by an angel.

FAWSLEY HALL. Home of the Knightleys from 1415 till 1913. It then remained unoccupied and became increasingly derelict after the Second World War. In 1966, on the excuse of repairing the Hall roof, its ancient timbers were removed, but fortunately the house was rescued in 1975 by Mr E. A. Saunders, an antique dealer. Since the late 1990s it has been a hotel.

The Tudor house was begun by Richard Knightley (†1534) and completed by his son Edmund (†1542). It consisted of a Great Hall facing E with a cross-wing containing chambers together with services at its S end. A further range of service buildings lay behind the hall to the W. It is uncertain what existed at the N end of the hall. Little was done in the C16 and C17, although a long wing of lodgings was built out to the SE (demolished early C19). In 1732 the N rooms were replaced by a large brick-built block by *Francis Smith* of Warwick. This was remodelled in 1815 in a Gothic castellated fashion by *Thomas Cundy*, and remodelled again, substantially, in 1866–8 by *Anthony Salvin*, who added a further large block at the SE corner. It is Salvin's wings which dominate the E front today, rather overpowering the Tudor hall between them.

Externally the HALL has five bays separated by buttresses. The first three and the fifth have a three-light window with arched lights high up. The walls were rebuilt in the 1860s since another row of windows had been inserted below, probably by Cundy, and recorded by George Clarke drawings of 1843. The fourth bay is the splendid tall oriel window. Its base is decorated by shields in lozenges or quatrefoils. The window itself has two embattled transoms, and there is an embattled upper storey above it, reaching above the eaves of the roof. What can it have contained, and how can it have been entered? Finials on the end gables. Access to the Hall was in the first bay, where there was originally a porch. The exit into the courtyard behind still exists. The Hall remains a splendid apartment, not least due to Mr Saunders's brave reconstruction of its roof, using what was left of surviving old timbers that he rescued from the grounds and tactfully leaving the old timbers dark and the new light. It has large arch-braced collars and tiers of curved windbraces. Very similar roofs exist at Upton (another Knightley house) and Boughton. Huge stone fireplace, about 12 ft (3.7 metres) wide, with a big quatrefoil frieze with shields over, then a foliage frieze as fine as in any wooden rood screen, and finally a cresting. Pretty four-centred arched doorway on the r. which may have led to a staircase. There are windows high up to the courtyard as well as the outer world, and one of them, originally open, stands right above the fireplace. The flues were conducted to its l. and r. The oriel window has panelled jambs and a fan-vault. The spandrels of the panelling and of all window lights are prettily decorated. The STAINED GLASS armorials are all copies of originals now in the Burrell Collection, Glasgow, made by *Chapel Studios* and *Monastery Glass*.

To the C16 building also belong the PARLOUR, facing S with a buttressed front and a two-storeyed oriel window, the

KITCHEN and BAKEHOUSE, W of the parlour, i.e. at an angle to the Hall, with their big fireplaces, those of the kitchen back-to-back, and the long range known as the BREWHOUSE, which runs N parallel with the Hall range, from the bakehouse. At its N end is a large transomed oriel window on a big corbel. This and the other windows of this range also have arched lights. The three ranges so far mentioned enclose an inner court. Several fine rooms on the upper floors in the S tower block, some with original timber roofs and timber stud partitions. Another has a barrel ceiling. The S façade is more irregular but includes the projecting three-floor tower block with a canted oriel of two upper floors and a garderobe in its l. corner, as well as the bays of the Salvin wing to the E. Tactful partly glazed additions at the NW corner of the building when the conversion to a hotel took place.

To the N, STABLES, C18, of red brick, three sides of a court, with a cupola by *Smith* of Warwick.

DOWER HOUSE, ¾ m. NE. A small Tudor house, in the middle of the park, already in ruins *c.* 1710, and the more romantic for being so. Largely brick but with some ironstone. Brick the tower (with dark blue diapering) and what remains of a wonderful series of twisted shaped chimneys, which now only partially survive. The windows with arched lights. Also later straightforward mullioned windows. The house seems to belong to the same time as the Hall, and may even be a little earlier, that is, it is the earliest example of brick construction in the county.*

FAXTON

Now deserted. The village had declined after C18 enclosures. Excavations have produced evidence of settlement from the late C12 onwards. The church of ST DENIS was demolished in 1958.†

FERMYN WOODS HALL
2 m. SW of Benefield

The epitome of the Rockingham Forest hunting lodge, beautifully set in wooded parkland. It appears Elizabethan but this is largely the result of the work of *Edward Browning* in the 1840s. The core of the house was built for John Robinson, keeper of

---

*Although medieval bricks have been excavated at Lyveden.

† The FONT is at All Saints, Kettering. A mural tablet to Mrs Raynsford †1763 by *William Cox* is at Lamport. The MONUMENT of Judge Nichols (†1616), a tablet by *John Hunt* and another by *John Bacon Jun.* are in the Victoria and Albert Museum.

Farming Woods between 1650 and 1656. His nephew, James, was the owner of Cranford Hall (q.v.). Originally of H shape, of which the porch and a portion of its r. façade remains. By marriage it passed in the early C18 into the Fitzpatrick family, subsequently Barons Gowran and in 1751 Earls of Upper Ossory. Additions were made in 1777 and 1788. In 1841 it was inherited by Emma Fitzpatrick who was married to Robert Vernon Smith, created Baron Lyveden in 1859. It was they who called in Browning, who redrafted the C18 additions and added a large wing on the W side, demolished in 1968. Some interior work was done 1919–20 by *Blackwell & Riddey* of Kettering, including Dining Room panelling with Ionic pilasters (now the Drawing Room). The Entrance Hall has an elaborate tiled centrepiece with the arms of Lord Lyveden, and it is his shield, held by lions, which tops the newels of the staircase. The staircase is said to be a copy of that formerly in Lyveden Old Bield.

STABLE BLOCK. Originally built in 1740, but again much altered in the C19. Its S entrance has as its centrepiece the GATEWAY from Lyveden Old Bield (*see* p. 404). Archway with paired niches l. and r. Three shields above each pair. Crowning with openwork geometrical motifs, volutes and arms.

In the PARK, a short distance W of the house, is a pretty small Gothic WATER PUMP erected 1829. Worthy of Pugin. Octagonal turret with traceried sides and an ogival crown.

Opposite the house, on the S side of Benefield Road, is the tall former WATER TOWER built in 1900 with its attached former workshops now converted as a residence. The tower originally had an internal spiral staircase but this was removed in 2011 and a new external stair tower designed by *Adrian Baynes* was attached to the N side of the tower, allowing its rooms to be used as accommodation.

FINEDON

9070

Finedon lays between two main roads: the A6 and A510. On neither of these approaches does Finedon have much to show, but there is a great deal of interest in the older part of the village NW of the road junction. The church is one of the finest C14 churches in the county and the village is made singularly interesting by the Victorian Gothic excursions of its squire, William Mackworth-Dolben (†1872), and his architect *E. F. Law*.

ST MARY. An exceptionally beautiful, large church in a fine situation. Rich dark ironstone from a quarry just N of the village, with ample grey stone dressings and battlements. All Dec, and built quickly. The joint between tower and nave shows that a start was made from the E as well as the tower and that the latter work met the former when the tower was already standing to a certain height. The W tower has a doorway with an ogee sur-

round flanked by pinnacles, pairs of tall bell-openings, a quatrefoil and an ogee frieze, battlements, and a very fine recessed
spire with two tiers of lucarnes. The S porch is two-storeyed,
with big gargoyles (which also pop out from other parts of the
building). Its lower floor is vaulted (a quadripartite vault) and
leads to an unusually tall doorway. The body of the church is
embattled, the windows are mostly Dec, mostly with reticulated tracery of a tall, elongated variety, and unusually in this
region, uncusped (assuming this is an original feature).* Others
have three steeply stepped lancet lights under one arch. Many
are shafted inside. The chancel E window has five instead of
three of the stepped lancet lights. The chancel may have been
first intended to have a different fenestration as the priest's
doorway and the shafted lowside window are cut into by the
present windows. The latter, however, shows signs of having
been tampered with both in the C18 and during the C19 restoration (see below under SEDILIA). Also, the chancel was intended
to be vaulted, as the interior proves – a great rarity in English
C14 parish churches. The two W springers stand on head
corbels. The arcades are of three wide bays, the N side with
quatrefoil piers and arches with two sunk mouldings; the central
pair on the S side had to be replaced in 1957 somewhat glaringly
in limestone and of a slightly different design from the rest.
Oddly the pillars of the arcades have pale limewash on their
lower sections, producing a bizarre effect. This was probably
done between 1778 and 1787 when the E portions of the church
were considerably replastered. It was already there when the
Rev. Aliffe Poole compiled his description in 1849 for *Churches
of the Archdeaconry*. There is an irregularity at the transept,
where the N pier has six shafts and six hollows, and the S pier a
cluster of six shafts which gives them an odd oblong shape. The
S pier and the triple-shafted responds of the chancel arch have
big leaves in the capitals. The clerestory is also Dec. Across the
nave runs a strainer arch very similar to that at Rushden, curved
top and bottom, and with the sinking top curve incongruously
embattled. In the spandrels circles with the motif of the four-
petalled flower inscribed. At the foot of the arch l. and r. angel
busts facing W as well as E. This may well be as late as *c.* 1400.
Another feature worth noting is that the whole building has a
running string course with hoodmoulds over the doorways. In
the chancel a handsome though badly mutilated SEDILIA. It is
recorded that the chancel was refurbished *c.* 1710. Its floor of
Ketton stone with black marble insets survives and the rise of
steps at the E end is the result of a Dolben family vault being
constructed below. The walls were lined with panelling, and
this is when the sedilia was shaved of its canopy. The two
columns are just jammed into the recess and were part of the

---

* There is a record of the E window of Kettering church having cusps removed in
the early C19 and the E window of Raunds church had no foliations till Scott put
them back in 1873–4 (see illustration in *Churches of the Archdeaconry of Northanpton*,
1849, p. 57). Here it could well have been done in the C18. It had certainly happened
by 1847.

supporting structure. It must have been a grand feature with tipped-up vaults on shafts with leaf capitals. – NAVE ROOF. C14 with tie-beams and bosses, including coloured Green Men. – SCREEN. Of stone, mostly of 1858 when there was a partial restoration by *William Slater*, but a small section is original. Prior to that there was an original simple stone screen. – FONT. C12, reworked probably in the 1830s, octagonal. On one side of the bowl a group of the Annunciation. – BENCH-ENDS. C14, simple, straight-topped, with traceried sides, the rest redone in 1858. – ORGAN CASE. Brought here in 1717. The case bears the royal arms of 1702–7. It is a very fine, sumptuous, famous piece, with both leaf carving and open segmental pediments by *Shrider*. It may have been in one of the royal chapels originally. – IRON GATE. Early C18, in the S porch entrance, probably by *Thomas Warren*. – STAINED GLASS. Chancel E, Mackworth-Dolben memorial window 1879 by *Heaton, Butler & Bayne*. – Chancel S, 1912 and N, 1880s, both by *Heaton, Butler & Bayne*. Chancel S of 1847 by *Wailes*. – Transept windows, S, 1918 and N, 1921, both by *Kempe & Co.* – MONUMENTS. N transept. Rev. James Affleck †1784 by *J. F. Moore*. – N aisle. Lt. William Roberts †1747 by *John Hunt*. Naval trophy. – In the Dolben vault at the E end of the church, visible from the E outside, with many others: Mary Dolben †1710, Elizabeth Dolben †1736, with busts by *John Hunt*.

FINEDON HALL. The manor of Finedon was with the Mulso family from the C15 until 1682, when it passed to the Dolbens. Something of the Elizabethan house is said to remain on the NW side. In the early C18 Sir Gilbert Dolben rebuilt and enlarged the house roughly to its present size. It had a five-bay S front paired by two projecting matching wings of two bays, the whole of two storeys. At some date towards the end of the C18 this was castellated and a tall two-storey porch was added in the centre. The architect *John Johnson* of Leicester did some work here in 1780. Everything changed in the middle of the C19 following the marriage of William Mackworth to Frances Dolben. Mackworth-Dolben (†1872) was ably assisted by his architect, *E. F. Law* of Northampton, who worked on the house from 1835 till 1859 (dates recorded on the building). He is usually a conservative designer, but here, given the opportunity, he launches into a fantasy style which might best be described as 'Gothic Tudorbethan'. The effect is amusing and bizarre. There are several big Gothic inscriptions, many gables, straight, Jacobean and otherwise, decorative friezes, bay windows and a porch with a small circular turret.

Behind the main block are STABLES with a tower sporting gables and a pyramid roof. The latter was originally more elaborate and had more decorative gables and a short spire. It was reduced in scale after 1972. The house is now separate apartments. The grounds were landscaped by *Repton* and are mentioned in his *Sketches* (1794), but most of the garden has been developed for housing. Within this, on Mackworth Drive, is THE OLD CHAPEL. Really a cloister arcade in the C14 style, converted into a house in 1981 by *Maurice Walton*. On Holly Walk, a house incorporates a miniature round tower in the Norman style which stood over the vaulted ICE HOUSE.

PERAMBULATION. What is worth seeing is a little scattered but worth the effort even if there is some rather mundane C20 infilling. The main accent remains that of Mackworth-Dolben and his architect *E. F. Law*. The churchyard is a good place to start. On its N side is the OLD SCHOOL. A central gabled range of three storeys, mullioned windows and at the top a plaque with the arms of Elizabeth I and the initials ER. It was a boys' school founded in 1595. An E wing was added in 1858 and extended in 1874, by *Law*. Both wings have been modernized since, but tactfully. On the W side of the yard is the former VICARAGE, dated 1688, of ironstone, seven bays, with wooden cross-windows. On the N side of the church driveway is an almshouse, reserved for spinsters, with 'HAMPTON CELL ANNO DOM 1742' on the doorway lintel. A short diversion N into STATION ROAD reveals on the W side EXMILL COTTAGE, the remains of a windmill built in 1818 and given battlements in 1858 by *Law*. Moving S, at the corner of CHURCH STREET a handsome group including the GIRLS' SCHOOL of 1712, with its seven bays and doorway with a big segmental pediment. On its l. MULSO COTTAGE, C18, with wooden casements and a cartouche with the Mulso arms over the doorway. Below on Stocks Hill, THINGDON COTTAGE, built 1862 by *Law*. Gothic Tudor, not quite as playful as the Hall. Modern extension respecting the earlier part. S into Bell Hill the frontage of the BELL INN of 1872, doubtless by *Law*. A most fanciful essay with an eccentric porch labelled 'ER 1042 THINGDENE HOSTELRIE VR 1872'. The earlier date refers to the accession of Edward the Confessor, whose queen, Edith, owned the manor of Finedon, and whose statue stands in a niche. In fact, the building does have an ancient history, though not as an inn, and there are older sections behind and a datestone for 1598. A little to the E in REGENT STREET next to the tall Vale Cottage, No. 19 of two storeys has in its E gable end the remains of a C15 wooden window.

There are other Mackworth-Dolben buildings elsewhere. Along HIGH STREET is PYTCHLEY ROW, eight gabled houses looking remarkably like a set of almshouses, 1847 also by *Law*. Opposite a pair of mid-C19 houses, with conjoined doorcases and a slight wavy bargeboard. Beyond again, in Berry Green, the TOWN HALL. 1868 by *R. W. Johnson*, built as a temperance hall. Two storeys, rather bald Gothic, with trefoil-headed first-floor windows. Further again, on r., on AFFLECK BRIDGE, so named since it crosses the culverted town brook, the WES-LEYAN CHAPEL, 1874, mildly classical, red and yellow brick, with an extension of 1900 at the back. S from here is DOLBEN SQUARE where, on the S side behind railings, there is a PRE-HISTORIC STONE, now recumbent but presumably formerly standing and probably a waymarker. Just W is WHITSUNDALE FARM. The one surviving thatched building in the village, of C17 origin but largely C18. Leading S from the Square is LAWS

LANE. The 1853 house on the corner was built as a coffee house with a former institute next door with double lancet windows on the first floor. Next an 1898 meeting room, STAR HALL by *Mosley & Anderson*, of red and yellow brick with pilasters between its six main windows. Opposite is MACK-WORTH GREEN. A little square of ironstone houses round a small green, dated 1840, Mackworth-Dolben's first exercise in tidying the village. Back in HIGH STREET, No. 49, an elegant ironstone house of 1711. Its dormers still have horizontal sliding sashes. Further E, No. 55 of three bays has an ashlar front and under the eaves an inscription recording the destruction of the centre of the village by fire in 1739. Beyond this the earliest QUAKER MEETING HOUSE in the county, 1690. Just a simple ironstone building with later windows and porch. Its interior no longer survives. The INFANT SCHOOL beyond is typical of its date, 1930–1, long and low in scale.

The main WELLINGBOROUGH ROAD (A510) bypasses the old village and was not generally built on till towards 1900. It has another scatter worth looking at. Starting at the E end, on the corner of the A6, is a stumpy OBELISK, erected as a way-marker by Sir English Dolben in 1789 as a thanksgiving for George III's recovery from insanity. W of the junction on the N side a sizeable two-bay gabled property with pargetting decoration (cross-keys and a wheatsheaf), built 1902 for the Finedon Industrial Co-operative Society by *Sharman & Archer*. On the l. MULSO JUNIOR SCHOOL of 1900 by *Talbot Brown & Fisher*, Renaissance style. Later even more Renaissance wings of 1934. W again the large former METHODIST CHURCH (Community Centre) of 1904 by *T. Dyer* of *H. H. Dyer & Son*, Decorated Gothic style, and W again, on the r., the WAR MEMORIAL, 1920 by *J. A. Gotch*. An unusual Renaissance style design: a square pillar with an ogee-domed top. Just W of this ARTHUR NUTT COURT, the converted former Arthur Nutt Shoe Factory, 1893, red brick with yellow and blue brick dressings, three storeys with arched windows. Sympathetically converted and added to in 2009–10 as apartments by *Spire Homes*. Opposite THE GLADSTONE, 1896 by *Mosley & Anderson*, the former Working Mens Club, faintly Renaissance. On the corner of Ivy Lane, ELM GRANGE, 1739 but refronted by Mack-worth-Dolben in Tudor style in 1868.

WATER TOWER, S on E side of the A6. Like a castle keep. Octagonal, five storeys, of red, yellow and blue brick, in a freely adapted Norman style, built 1904 by *Mosley & Scivener* of Northampton. The contractor was *O. P. Drever* of Kettering. Now a residence.

FINESHADE ABBEY

2¼ m. NNE of Bulwick

The remains of the Augustinian priory were destroyed in 1749. Only a fragment survives of the Georgian mansion, mostly

Fineshade Abbey.
Drawing by G. Clarke, *c.* 1850

demolished in 1956. It had especially fine mid-C18 decoration,
notably plasterwork in the saloon, with sumptuous hanging garlands of flowers and fruit, very like those at Cransley Hall (q.v.)
and also very probably by *Thomas Roberts* of Oxford.

STABLES. 1848, with a cupola above the entrance. Converted
into a house, 1988. At various points around the site of the house,
and particularly on the SW, are visible the remains of the earthworks of the CASTLE of Hely or Hymel, deserted before the
foundation of the monastery in the early C13.

TOP LODGE, 1 m. NE. Mid-C18 house of three bays, two
storeys and attics, considerably altered in the C19. 1761 and 1771
datestones on the S gable. Original turned baluster staircase.
Good C19 farm buildings.

FLORE

A large village with a good many stone houses of various dates.

ALL SAINTS. Mainly C13, i.e. the exquisite arcades of three wide
bays, with triple shafts to the four sides, twelve in all. One pier
and one respond have stiff-leaf capitals. Of the C13 also the S
doorway with two orders of shafts with stiff-leaf capitals and
the chancel piscina, with two arches and quatrefoil in the head
under a depressed arch. About 1300 may be the date when the
W tower was begun and the aisles continued to embrace it.
Of the same date the N aisle windows and doorway. Dec the
continuation of the W tower, the S aisle windows, and also
the N aisle E window. The chancel has a late C13 W part with
a heavily dogtooth-decorated doorway and windows with

intersected tracery, and a Perp E end. Fine E window and one on either side. Light, open interior with especially wide nave and plaster ceilings from the restoration by *James Milne* of 1831. Chancel ROOF painted to designs of *Stephen Dykes Bower* in 1960–3 when the interior was plastered and whitewashed and the sanctuary refitted. – SCREEN. Perp, of three divisions. – STALLS. 1876, incorporating Jacobean carved panels. Glazed TOWER SCREEN, with simple coronet designs, 2005. – ROYAL ARMS. George III. – COMMANDMENT BOARDS. Dated 1754, on either side of the W vestibule. – STAINED GLASS. Chancel E, 1903 by *H. Salisbury*. – N aisle E, very fine by *Fricker & Co.*, 1920. – S aisle E, 1923 by *Kelly & Co.* – BRASSES. Thomas Knaresburghe †1450 and wife †1498. 23-in. (58-cm.) figures. Henry Michell †1510 and wife. 26-in. (46-cm.) figures. Alyce Wyrley †1537. Of the cross which was the centre of the composition only the foot remains.

UNITED REFORMED CHURCH. 1889 by *E. R. Hewitt* of Camden. Red brick with three tall arched windows and a circle with a quatrefoil above. Original chapel of 1840, serving as a school, with a hooded doorway and two small lunettes.

FLORE HOUSE, N of the church. Partly Jacobean with a datestone of 1612, but much altered and added to when it passed into the Pack family *c.* 1830. The oldest windows are mullioned with arched lights. A billiard room was added in the early 1900s and the interior has been much refurbished since.

OLD MANOR, NE of the churchyard. Late C17. Ironstone. Five bays, two storeys, hipped roof, cross-windows on the first floor, sashes below. Rusticated quoins.

THE GRANGE. On the main road. The E range dates from 1695, but was much restored when the W block was built in 1931.

WAR MEMORIAL. A tall ironstone triangular obelisk of 1923, on a small green on the side of the main road. Its setting enhanced 2010.

FOTHERINGHAY

A neat village of stone houses built along a single street, dominated by its splendid church. We cannot now easily visualize Fotheringhay as it must have looked in the C15 when the castle towered over the village and the college buildings stretched to the S of the church.

FOTHERINGHAY CASTLE was built probably by Simon de St Liz, 1st Earl of Huntingdon and Northampton, *c.* 1100. It was largely rebuilt by Edmund Langley, 1st Duke of York and son of Edward III. It is remembered chiefly as the place where Mary Queen of Scots was held prisoner from 1586 to her execution on 8 February 1587. Little remains but the powerful motte-and-bailey on which it was rebuilt in the late C14; the earthworks themselves are almost certainly of the C12. There is an outer bailey which was probably never walled. Leland still called it 'fair and meately strong with double ditches and a kepe very anncient and strong'. He also mentions 'fair lodgyns'. Stukeley, writing in the early C18, says that the castle is 'mostly demolished', and it is recorded that it was already ruinous in 1635 and much was destroyed shortly after. All that now remains are the mounds and a block of masonry on the bank of the river.

26 ST MARY AND ALL SAINTS. Edmund Langley, 1st Duke of York, conceived the idea of a college attached to Fotheringhay Castle about 1377, but he died in 1402 and his son Edward of York, the 2nd Duke, made preparations to transfer the college to the church in 1411, although it was not confirmed till 1415, the year that Edward fell at Agincourt. The college consisted of a master, twelve fellows, eight clerks and thirteen choristers. Shortly after 1411 it was decided to rebuild the chancel of the church in a grand and ambitious manner, and Edward's body was laid to rest in the newly built chancel. It must have been largely complete by about 1430, for in 1434 his nephew Richard, the 3rd Duke, made a contract with *William Horwood*, a free-mason 'dwellyng in Foderinghay', to rebuild the nave. It is assumed that Horwood, clearly a metropolitan craftsman, had already been responsible for the chancel. The contract is detailed and specific, and it makes clear that the architecture of the nave was to match exactly that of the chancel, in height, width and style. The only difference is that the contract speci-fies the aisle arcades to be of 'six mighty arches', when in fact there are only four (there are also some variations in the size of the clerestory windows). This change may be due to the fact that by about 1450 Edward, heir to the dukedom, but soon to succeed as King Edward IV, was already thinking of establish-ing a York, i.e. royal, mausoleum at Windsor. However, his father, the 3rd Duke, who was killed at Wakefield in 1460, was also buried in the chancel. The church was completed around 1440, though glazing continued till the 1460s. Between 1480 and 1483 a cloister was added on the s side of the church. The college survived till 1548 when it was dissolved and its build-ings granted to Dudley, Duke of Northumberland, by Edward VI; he immediately removed the roof of the chancel and some of buildings for the lead. The sad state of the Yorkist mauso-leum was observed by Queen Elizabeth I on her progress in 1566 and in 1573 letters patent were sent to Sir Edmund Brudenell of Deene with orders to demolish the chancel and move the York tombs into the church.

What remains now is this: the stately w tower with broad w doorway. Eight-light w window with ample Perp tracery. Four-light bell-openings. Polygonal turret-pinnacles. The tower then topped by an octagonal lantern with another set of eight tall three-light bell-openings with a transom. Battlements, pinna-cles, no spire. The aisles, as the contract lays down, embrace the tower. On the N side in addition a two-storeyed porch at the w end. Four-light aisle windows, of a consistent design and beautifully executed. Four-light clerestory windows. Bold slender flying buttresses curved not only below but also above. From the E end of the s aisle disturbed walling with signs of openings marks the two-storey porch which gave access to the college cloister. Heavily buttressed E wall where the chancel started. This contains some of the oldest masonry in the building, having been part of the earlier church. The wide arch into the nave is clear, ending, lower down, at the height of the solid pulpitum. The chancel was the same height as the nave, so the large window in the E gable was an internal feature. The archways into the aisles also clear. The three-light window at the E end of the s aisle is a later insertion.

The interior is wide and airy, decidedly East Anglian in character. The arch towards the nave is exceptionally tall. Behind it appears a beautiful fan-vault, dated 1529, of a design very close to the fan-vaulting in the retrochoir at Peterborough Cathedral. Piers of a complicated Perp section. The shafts towards the arch openings are the only ones which have capitals. The shafts towards the nave run right up to the roof. The roof has curved braces and curved collars continuing the same curve. The whole is a noble conception, and a fine tribute to *Horwood* and his masons. There was a restoration 1911–13 by *Temple Moore*, but you would not know he had been there. – FONT. Octagonal, Perp, mounted on three steps. Panelled stem, bowl with quatrefoils and big leaf motifs alternating with animal faces on the underside. Cover made from two misericords from the chancel – REREDOS. A large plain triple arcade of Gothick arches with gold lettering, *c.* 1810. – ROYAL ARMS. An especially fine example, for George III, painted by *J. Everard* of Stamford and dated 1807. He could well be the artist of the lettering on the reredos. – BOX PEWS. Also *c.* 1810. – PULPIT. A very good Perp piece, repainted using evidence of original colouring, with a Perp rib-vaulted tester slightly tipped and a larger Jacobean tester above. – PEW ENDS (N aisle). C15, returned to Fotheringhay from Hemington whence they had been removed following the Dissolution. – STAINED GLASS. Alas, the rich programme of glass which originally existed no longer survives* but in 1992 a charnel house under the porch was excavated and a quantity of fragments was discovered. These were assembled by the *Barley Studios* and in 1994 placed in a window in the room above the N porch. The s aisle window, formerly blocked, was opened in 1975 and given heraldic glass of the Yorks by the Richard III Society. It is by *Harry Harvey* of York. – MONUMENTS. Either side of the altar, two identical, grand Elizabethan memorials to Edward, 2nd Duke of York, and Richard, 3rd Duke of York, erected in 1573 by Sir Edmund Brudenell following orders from Queen Elizabeth. Panelled base with the Yorkist badges, falcons and fetter locks. Coupled

30

*It is fully discussed in Richard Marks, 'The glazing of Fotheringhay Church and College', *Journal of the British Archaeological Association*, vol. 131 (1978), pp. 79–109.

Corinthian columns at the sides and a central heraldic panel surrounded by intricate strapwork decoration with masks (cf. Little Oakley). Attic with more Yorkist badges and a central semicircular merlon. A change of design may have occurred as there is another projecting column base in the centre below the panel. No figures at all. That these memorials were erected by Sir Edmund Brudenell is significant, since the carving of the central panel compares directly with that on the Hall chimneypiece at Deene. Architecturally these monuments fall into a line which starts at Deene in the 1550s, thence to Dingley in the late 1550s, Kirby Hall in the 1570s, and so here by 1573. This chain of works can all be associated with the masons and carvers of the *Thorpe* quarry at Kingscliffe – and indeed these monuments are of Kingscliffe stone (*see* Introduction, p. 34). The slabs beneath the tombs are almost certainly from the original memorials, and that on the s side has the indent of a brass.*

OLD INN, E end of the main street, on the s side. Transformed into cottages. In the middle, the jambs of a passageway with, to the l., an original four-centred timber doorway, flanked by a large room on either side. On the w side a large fireplace and a blocked doorway. Originally ranges extended back on either side of a courtyard. On the upper floor of the front range on the l., large room with arch-braced roof of two bays. A coat of arms recorded in 1821 may date the building to the reign of Edward IV.

GARDEN FARMHOUSE, opposite the Old Inn. Formerly the NEW INN, built shortly after 1460. Good C15 gateway with heraldry relating to Edward IV. A four-centred arch and traceried spandrels, and quatrefoil frieze. Two-light window above. Two buttresses. On the r. the parlour wing with C19 renewed C15 windows, and inside, on the ground floor, a cross-moulded beamed ceiling and an original fireplace. The l. projecting wing with blocked windows and doorway is presumed to be part of the lodgings. The l. wing has the remains of the open hall with arched braced timbers. It was altered, subdivided and extended to the N to form a large barn in the early C19. The inn had a courtyard at the rear. The rear of the entrance archway has half-timbering on its upper floor, probably of C17 date. Behind the E range a farmhouse built in 1863, the designs by *Josiah Mander*, Lord Overstone's surveyor.

The estate was purchased in 1806 by William and Thomas Belsey who then rebuilt a number of COTTAGES (e.g. Nos. 21/23 and 24/25 Main Street), easily distinguished by their Gothic tracery or cast-iron latticed windows. In 1842 the estate was acquired by Lord Overstone who did further rebuilding, mainly around *c.* 1850–60.

* The monuments are discussed in detail by Sofija Matich and Jennifer Alexander in 'Creating and Recreating the Yorkist tombs in Fotheringhay Church', *Church Monuments: Journal of the Church Monuments Society*, vol. 26 (2011), pp. 82–103.

OLD SCHOOL, W of the church in Main Street. 1876 by *Josiah Mander*, Gothic with a central gable and three lancets. On conversion into a house a porch was added.

BRIDGE over the River Nene. Of medieval origin, rebuilt in 1573 by *William Grumbold* and *Thomas Hayward*. Rebuilt again in 1722 by *George Portwood* of Stamford. Four arches and cutwaters.

FURTHO

7040

ST BARTHOLOMEW (Churches Conservation Trust). Remote, by a farm. Stocky W tower looking remarkably castle-like, perhaps because of the rather high battlemented top. Chancel largely C14, E window with elongated reticulated tracery. Blocked lowside windows on the N and S sides. The traceried side windows decapitated following rebuilding *c.* 1620, to which belong the straight-headed windows of the nave and the round tower arch and chancel arch and, of course, the tower itself. Blocked N doorway. One or two fittings deriving from a restoration by *E. Swinfen Harris*, 1870.

DOVECOTE. Probably late C15 (cf. Harlestone). Circular, with a bold string course at the top of the bottom stage. Conical roof later. Top stages renewed in 1990. The Manor House stood immediately W of the church but the remains were finally demolished early in the C19. There are some embankments of a formal garden to the N. The present farmhouse is 1907.

GAYTON

7050

ST MARY. Norman the W tower base but its W doorway perhaps Late Saxon. The upper stages were Georgian; George James De Wilde in his *Rambles* (1872) records a date of 1725 above the W doorway, the date of a faculty for heightening the tower, but they were rebuilt in 1883 using a different stone. A lancet above the doorway and another opening at a higher level, possibly of Norman origin. The arch towards the nave is pointed and has one step and one slight chamfer, C13. Conspicuous roof-line of the earlier nave. The rest of the church is Dec externally. The windows are much renewed. Sumptuous E window with flowing tracery. N chapel with a curious external W entrance squeezed into the wall behind a broad buttress. C13 to C14 arcades inside. Three bays, octagonal piers, arches of one chamfer and one hollow chamfer. The details differ between N and S. The S arcade is probably earlier. The N arcade, of a finer stone, was built more closely to the tower and out of symmetry with the W wall. Dec chancel chapels. Odd slender trefoil-headed opening with a transom on the S side of the chancel next to the arch. The S chapel of two bays has a quatre-foil pier with fillets on the projections and an arch with one chamfer and one wave, the N chapel of one bay has responds with fillets and an arch like the other. The church was restored in 1874 by *E. F. Law* and again in 1881–3 by *Matthew Holding*. Small N extension of 2010 by *Dennis Pearson*. – FONT. Circular with intersected arches – that is seemingly Norman. But the resulting pointed arches are cusped. Is it a C13 remodelling of a Norman font, or an example of archaism? – REREDOS. Early C19 Gothic top and base with linenfold panels, early C16. A made-up piece. – ROOD SCREEN. Only a stone base survives. – STALLS. Perp, with six MISERICORDS. They represent the Mother of Mercy (i.e. Mater Misericordia), a lion and a dragon, a seraph astride two figures (posssibly a warning to gossips), three seated female figures, Christ in Majesty, Christ's Entry into Jerusalem, and a small praying figure. – PULPIT. Jacobean, with two tiers of the familiar short, broad blank arches. – TOWER SCREEN. 1985 by *Leonard Goff*. Gothic. – STAINED GLASS. In the N chapel a single shield of the De Gayton family *c.* 1300–20. In the N chapel E window assembled glass, including some that is heraldic and a number of Neth-erlandish roundels. – Other windows have grisaille type glass by *J. Powell & Sons*, 1846–8. – Chancel E and tower, both 1885 by *A. O. Hemming*. – MONUMENTS. In the N chapel a very fine C13 coffin-lid with an uncommonly lush foliated cross. – Between the chancel and the N chapel an ogee arch with but-tresses and finial and beneath it a tomb-chest with six ogee-headed crocketed panels. In the N chapel, under an ogee-headed recess, on the tomb-chest an effigy of oak, a cross-legged knight, supposed to be Sir Philip de Gayton †1316. – N chapel, N recess. Effigy of a lady on a plain tomb-chest. Above her on corbels a tiny effigy with an inscription beneath. The large effigy is supposed to be Scholastica de Gayton †1354; the small effigy is Mabila de Murdak, early C14. – In the chancel S wall Perp tomb-recess with an almost flat arch, traceried inside, and battlements. Stone with a Purbeck marble slab. Probably *c.* 1500. – Francis Tanfield †1558 and wife (N chapel). Tomb-chest with shields in lozenges. Incised alabaster slab, attributed to the *Roileys* of Burton upon Trent. Restored 1998–2000 by the *Skillington Workshop*. Other C18 tablets including in the N aisle a charming oval tablet with a shield and scroll for Richard Kent †1753, by *William Cox*. – Lockwood family by *Robert Blore*, the latest date 1759. Architectural frame, long inscription.

MANOR HOUSE. Built by the Tanfield family. A very interesting house, probably of the third quarter of the C16. The shape is roughly that of a Greek cross and the building is three-storeyed, including the gables. All windows with arched lights. To the S, E and W there are canted bay windows in the middle of the ends of the cross. To the N a flat staircase projection.

The E and W bays are of four lights plus the one-light canting, but they taper at the gable level to three lights only. The bay window gable is placed in front of the gable of the cross-arm, slightly lower and narrower. On the S side the bay window has three lights and tapers to two. Small subsidiary bays in the corners of the S wing. Compact interior, well preserved with panelling and some decorative carving. Several original stone fireplaces. Staircase with busily detailed vertically symmetrical balusters. Odd series of levels on the ground floor. The upper floor was originally an open gallery with two round pillars dividing off the S bay.*

GAYTON HOUSE was demolished in 1972. It was probably early C18, but with a SE front with two-storey porch and bay windows added by Roger Eykyn, who acquired the property in 1874. Only its GATEPIERS survive and they are thought to have been designed in the early 1900s by *Clough Williams-Ellis*, a friend of the Eykyn family. They have brackets with Chinese lanterns.

Former SCHOOL, Deans Row. 1844–5 by *S. S. Teulon*, Tudor style. It was altered by *Edmund Law* in 1873 and has been much modified since and rendered. Also in Deans Row on the corner of High Street, the former DOWER HOUSE, later called the Deanery, with alterations and additions of a similar date also by Teulon. Street façade with two small canted oriels, a barge-boarded gable with inscription and on the garden side a staircase turret with small spire typical of Teulon.†

THE WEIR, High Street, at the SW end of the village. C17. A small house of two storeys. In the S front four-light mullioned windows and a massive double buttress disguised as a porch, complete with fine doorway. Nearby a big Victorian stone house with a gable with a Northamptonshire Jacobean top.

KILNYARD, Park Lane. A house built using traditional methods and incorporating old materials. Begun in the 1980s by its owner *Bob Price* and continuing (2012).

GEDDINGTON

8080

A most attractive village with ensembles of stone-built cottages, many thatched, interspersed with the occasional brick house. All of gentle scale with hardly a disruptive element.

ST MARY MAGDALENE. Interesting evidence of an Anglo-Saxon nave, *c.* 950. A frieze of triangle-headed arcading ran along the outer walls and is now visible from the aisles. Also a window embrasure and long-and-short quoins at the E end of the nave. The window on the N side cuts into the arcading, and therefore

---

*I am grateful to the late Andor Gomme for his thoughts on this house.
†Information from Alan Teulon.

could be a later insertion unless its position is due to adjustment when the arcade was cut through. This nave was enlarged
by a N aisle in the late C12. The arcade consists oddly enough
of two and a half bays, and it must be assumed that the intention was to pull down the Saxon E wall and to continue the
arch, but that this was given up. Circular piers, volute and
waterleaf capitals. Square abaci. Single-stepped round arches.
The next part of the church is the C13 S aisle. It has three full
bays, which shows that by then the position of the Saxon
chancel arch was accepted. The arcade has quatrefoil piers and
double-chamfered arches. To this aisle belong the S doorway
(two orders of shafts with renewed rings). After the S arcade
the chancel. N window with two lights and a spherical triangle
which looks late C13, but S window with ogee-headed lights in
spite of intersected cusped tracery. The splendid five-light E
window also has ogee-headed lights. It culminates in a big
circle filled with three pointed trefoils without ogee arches.
Good headstops l. and r. of the E window head corbels. Clerestory windows, below the main Perp ones, in the form of
alternating quatrefoils and spherical triangles. All this might
well be called c. 1300, but the ogees in the lights make it necessary to add another ten or twenty years. One would not be
tempted to add more. Yet in an inscription in Lombardic lettering along the foot of the chancel walls the date 1369 is
explicitly quoted. It refers to the death of 'Wilhelmus Glovere
de Geytyngton Capellanus', who 'fecit scabella eius are et
pavimentare istum cancellum' and who 'obiit in festo Corpus
Christi anno domini MCCCLXIX'. The inscription continues
without a break into the S chapel, and there records 'Robertus
Launcelyn de Geytingtoune', who 'fecit istum cancellum'. The
S chapel to which the second inscription refers looks, just like
the chancel, c. 1300, and certainly not later than c. 1320. Two
bays, quatrefoil piers, double-chamfered arches, one big S
lancet window. The E window is Perp, but its internal shafting
looks c. 1300 too. How is one to explain this? Did the two men
do their good deeds fifty years before the death of one of them?
That seems unlikely. If they left the money, one would have to
assume that forms which for the whole of England one has
every reason to call c. 1310–20 were used in Northamptonshire
fifty years later, which is just as unlikely. Does the truth lie in
the middle? There is evidence in other places of conservatism
in tracery. The chancel arch with its thin responds belongs in
any case to the rest of the chancel. Clear roof line above and
rood loft entrance on S side. The rather blank N wall of the
chancel is partly due to the C19 vestry but projecting here was
a chapel for the Maydwell family which had already been
removed when Tillemans drew the church in 1719, although
he shows its blocked arch. The vestry, N chapel and S porch
are part of the restoration by *G. G. Scott*, 1854–7, and this
probably included some of the window tracery.

The ashlar W tower is Perp and has clasping buttresses, two
pairs of two-light bell-openings with transom, a quatrefoil

frieze, and a recessed spire with three tiers of lucarnes in alternating directions. – REREDOS. In the chancel, stone, Perp, with a quatrefoil frieze, thirteen blank arches, the middle one much wider, and crenellation. – SEDILIA and PISCINA, C14 with simple moulded arches. – SCREENS. The western portion, between chancel and S chapel, of the early C14 (or c. 1370?), cusped pointed arches and shafts with a ring. It still has its central door and was formerly across the S chapel arch. – Screen between S aisle and S chapel, formerly the rood screen. Dated 1618, the gift of Maurice Tresham of nearby Newton. A most interesting piece of Early Gothic Revival. The carver has faithfully repeated the tracery of the chancel E window, only filling all the spaces with small scrollwork of his own. The Tresham trefoils obvious. – Chancel screen 1906 designed by *Sidney Gambier-Parry*, who had previously worked for the Dukes of Buccleuch at Dalkeith. Full Gothic with ironwork grilles. The stalls of the same period with linenfold fronts. – WARDROBE, in the vestry. Made of BENCH-ENDS, one dated 1602. – CHARITY BREAD BOX. In the porch because of the 1636 will of Sir Robert Dallington, born here in 1561. The charity is still active. – STAINED GLASS. Chancel N and S by *Clayton & Bell*, 1860; chancel E by *Ninian Comper*, 1893, still entirely in the Victorian tradition and the Lady Chapel E of 1950 also by him; S aisle, 1957 by the *Rev. E. S. H. Homer* of Mells in Somerset. Very much in the Comper/Webb tradition. Another with figures of Samuel and David, 1925 by *Hubert Blandford*. – MONUMENTS. Effigy of a priest, C13, the lower part of his body covered by a shield. – Brass of Henry Jarmon and wife, c. 1480, 18-in. (46-cm.) figures partly damaged. In the N aisle, memorials brought from Newton church when it was closed in 1972. – Especially fine brass to John Mulsho †1400 and wife. A very attractive composition with small kneeling figures looking up to a large cross and throwing up, as it were, inscribed scrolls which issue from their mouths. In the cross-head a figure of St Faith. The kneeling figures are only 13 in. (33 cm.) long. – Richard Tresham †1433 and wife. The date may be an error: 1533 would seem more correct for the style. Large incised alabaster slab with their effigies. – Two large stone slabs for Maurice Tresham †1646 and his wife with armorials.

There was a royal hunting lodge at Geddington. It stood NE of the church. The centre of the village is the small square dominated by the ELEANOR CROSS (cf. the cross at Hardingstone, Northampton p. 480). Erected shortly after 1294. Of the three surviving Eleanor Crosses, this is the most modest and the best preserved. Its shape heralds the end of the classic Gothic moment and the coming of Dec capriciousness. Triangular and carrying on at the top, by means of six pinnacles, to a recessed hexagonal star with more pinnacles. Close diapering in the lower parts. The three figures in the three niches characteristic also of the end of the crisp and sharp carving of up to 1275–80 and the heavier flow and broader masses of 1290 etc. At the foot of the cross a stone CONDUIT HOUSE built 1769.

Running s is QUEEN STREET which begins with the BRIDGE. C13, with large cutwaters on one side. Two pointed arches, the round one of 1784. Much repaired. E from the square is GRAFTON ROAD with on the N side the OLD SCHOOL, mildly Gothic, of 1847. Its replacement is in WOOD STREET, 1894 by *Gotch & Saunders*, brick and stone in their typical style. Back in Grafton Road is a pair of Tudor-style Victorian cottages with bargeboards. Further on and r. is the PRIORY, L-shaped, with a projecting wing dated 1588 (mullioned windows), the main house late C17 with early sash windows, but some blocked, detracting from the effect. The garden façade is more regular with a five-bay centre, two storeys with sash windows. The ends of the lateral wings on each side, two bays, with the windows blocked on the s wing. Later additions and interior.

GLEBE HOUSE, West Street, was built by the 5th Duke of Buccleuch as a vicarage. Tudor style, 1847, the N front having the Buccleuch shield. Opposite a Late Georgian house with three bays, three storeys, the windows having fluted keystones, and another on its doorway lintel.

GLAPTHORN

ST LEONARD. A slightly confusing building until it is realized that its earliest phase has almost disappeared. While it is mostly a C13 church, it takes its form from a mid-C12 structure with nave, chancel and one if not two aisles. The w end of the Norman nave is marked by the piers of masonry dividing the arcades on each side. The building was then extended to the w with the late C12 s aisle of two bays surviving. Low circular pier, octagonal capitals, round, double-chamfered arches. The w wall is very thick and high up there is evidence of two small openings which, together with evidence within the roof, suggests the existence of a bellcote. Early in the C13 comes the replacement of the Norman arcades, on the N side at the w end by one with round pier, round abacus and pointed double-chamfered arches. The base of the pier includes two reversed scalloped Norman responds of the preceding aisle. The C13 eastern arcades are of two bays, that on the s having some reused voussoirs with chevron ornament. Later C13 chancel and N chapel. The chancel windows with bar tracery, Y-tracery and cusped intersected tracery at the E end. The central window on the s side has a slim central shaft internally and also shafts on the jambs. Stone bench along the s wall. Also a PISCINA with dogtooth. The chapel opens towards the chancel with an arch. One demi-shaft and one continuous chamfer. E window, two lancets with circle in the head. In the Dec period the s aisle was widened and given reticulated tracery windows. Two unusual windows at the w end of each aisle, of C13 form, tall, square-headed with shouldered tops.

The tower butts up against the W wall and is post-medieval, with a resited C14 window. Post-medieval also the clerestory. – FONT. Octagonal, Perp, with panelled stem and quatrefoiled bowl. – FONT COVER with a reused Perp finial. – PULPIT. With Jacobean panels. – READING DESKS. With some reused linen-fold panels and a Perp band. – COMMUNION RAIL. Jacobean or a little later. – PEWS. One or two C15 bench-ends, but otherwise, with the rest of the woodwork, from the restoration 1895–6 by *J. C. Traylen* of Stamford. – WALL PAINTINGS. Many traces, mostly foliage trails. Most clearly discernible the large St Christopher on the N wall of the N aisle. Over the chancel arch, a red chequer pattern, probably the background for a rood cross. – STAINED GLASS. N aisle, the Good Centurion, 1916 by *Alfred Bell.*

MANOR FARM. Dates from 1530s when the manor belonged to Thomas, Lord Cromwell. It was acquired by the Brudenells of Deene in 1574, and the house largely rebuilt in 1599. The oldest parts are at the back. The front range is C18.

SCHOOL. At the corner of the yard of the present school. Tiny, Gothic, built 1847 for the Countess of Cardigan. Extensions by *J. A. Gotch*, 1912.

GLENDON HALL

2½ m E of Rothwell

The house consists of two parts, with a third not originally belonging to it. This third component is chronologically the first. It is the porch from Pytchley Hall, which was pulled down in 1828. It is a very noble piece of Elizabethan design, probably begun *c.* 1578 (*see* also Pytchley, p. 536). Arched doorway. Roman Doric columns to the l. and r., frieze of very wide metopes, fluted Ionic columns on the upper floor with two small beaded bands across. Cross-windows, also one on each of the sides of the porch. Balustrade of vertically symmetrical balusters. The porch is set in front of the Georgian part of the house. To the E is an earlier part which looks Jacobean. On the N side a doorway with four-centred head. Cross-windows on the ground floor, large mullioned-and-transomed windows on the first floor. A shallow canted bay. On the S side one wide semicircular bay window like those at Kirby Hall. The later part of the house was probably built after 1758. Plasterers are recorded in 1761 and there is a reference in estate accounts of that year to 'ye new Building'. Red brick, two and a half storeys, with on the N side a three-bay pediment now partly hidden by the Pytchley porch. Towards the S also a big canted bay window, mediating between the new and old parts. Inside the Georgian portion there is a fine mid-C18 cantilever staircase with a delicate wrought-iron scroll design balustrade and one or two good doorcases. Some pieces of Flemish STAINED GLASS in an upper room from the demolished church at Glendon. They are dated 1563 and four of them represent the story of David and Abigail. They were all drawn by Peter Tillemans in 1719. The house is now subdivided.

STABLES. Late C17. Gabled sides, pedimented centre with cupola.

In the garden by the pond two STATUES from Boughton (Aeneas and Anchises, Samson and the Philistine), attributed by Gunnis to *Andreas Kearne*. Fine pedestals with garlands.

7040

GRAFTON REGIS

ST MARY. Mostly Dec. However, the N arcade, excepting its responds, is early C13 work. Four bays, low, with circular piers and circular abaci. Hoodmoulds with small zigzag at right angles to the wall surface. Dec tomb-recesses in both the S wall and the N aisle wall. W tower completed, according to the inscription on his monument (*see* below), by Sir John Woodville ('campanile peregit'), so *c.* 1400. The chancel windows are Perp. It is clear externally that they were originally longer, and in between is a slimmer blocked window. Internally their jambs fall to floor level, then between them and the doorway are two deep, tall rectangular recesses; all three, like the doorway outside, have flat ogee heads. Presumably these form the SEDILIA, which must have had moveable wooden seats. The PISCINA, also ogee-topped, is fitted into the E jamb of the easternmost window. It is an interesting and rather sophisticated composition. Although normally considered to be Dec could it be that they fit with the Perp windows? If the tracery in them can be trusted, that is. A watercolour of the church by Thomas Trotter dated 1789 shows them even shorter and there is no tracery at all in the easternmost window. There was a restoration in 1870 by *E. Swinfen Harris*. – SCREEN. A panel of the former rood screen now above the vestry door. – FONT. Of tub shape, Norman. With intersected arches. – PAINTING. Betrayal of Christ. Probably part of the former rood screen (above chancel S doorway). – STAINED GLASS. All by *Mayer* of Munich. – MONUMENTS. Tomb-chest with panels and three semi-octagonal piers. – Tomb-chest with seven ogee-headed panels and on it the incised alabaster slab to Sir John Wydevyl, *c.* 1415 (both N aisle, W end). – Charlotte, Countess of Euston, †1808. By *Flaxman*. Grecian tablet with figures of Faith and Hope at the corners, placed diagonally – which a pure Grecian would not have done. – Lord James Henry Fitzroy †1834. By *William Behnes*. Tablet with a draped urn. – Vice Admiral Robert Fitzroy †1865, a simple memorial erected 2011. He was Captain of the *Beagle*, designer of the Fitzroy Barometer and pioneer of the science of weather forecasting.

MANOR HOUSE, near the church. Now a care home. An oblong
outbuilding has a buttress to the street and some mullioned
windows with arched lights, i.e. is of pre-Reformation date. It
is a relic of a large royal house built by Henry VIII. This was
destroyed in 1643 and the house now on the site is largely C19
but incorporates parts of the late C17 house. It retains some
stone four-centred arched fireplaces and a C17 staircase with
turned balusters.

SCHOOL (now Village Hall), at the entry into the village, in The
Lane. Early C19 origin, but as it stands a rebuilding of 1870 by
E. Swinfen Harris.

The supposed WOODVILLE MANOR HOUSE site, w of the A508,
was excavated in 1964–5 revealing medieval buildings, apparently monastic in origin, arranged round a cloister, with a small
church on the s side. They were converted to secular use in
the C15. In the E end of the church were tiles with the Woodville arms (some of these are displayed in the parish church).

The GRAND UNION CANAL cuts through the parish and there
are two BRIDGES (NE and SW of the village) of 1793–1800,
probably by *William Jessop.* Standard design, brick with elliptical arches.

For the Grafton Estate model farms, *see* Introduction, p. 53.

GRAFTON UNDERWOOD   9080

ST JAMES. Of C12 origin. The lowest stages of the tower have
herringbone masonry and a rough blocked doorway on the s
side. Late C12 N arcade of three bays, round arches with circular piers carrying square capitals with leaf volutes and crockets, square abaci, and single-stepped round arches. Still later
C12 s arcade, also round arches with circular elementary stiff-
leaf capitals, circular abaci, and round arches of one step and
one chamfer. C13 chancel arch (pointed, double-chamfered,
some nailhead on corbel supports) and C13 w tower (arch
towards the nave single-stepped but pointed, lancet windows,
twin bell-openings under a round arch). N aisle also retains C13
doorway. Recessed Perp spire with two tiers of lucarnes.
Chancel higher than the nave, in its E part Dec. The four-light
E window is odd but possible, though the mullions are suspicious. Flowing tracery. At the top the motif of the four-petalled
flower, each petal quatrefoiled and the whole in a depressed
circle. On the s side another Dec window with flowing tracery
and one later C13 with normal bar tracery. Big niche inside to
the N of the E window with ogee arch, thick finials, heads and
ballflower frieze. Smaller, similar niche to the s, but lit by its
own tiny two-light window. Perp windows in N aisle and chapel.
Fine ogee-arched and cusped SEDILIA and PISCINA. – PULPIT.
Simple and nice, with inlay dated 1728. – FONT. Octagon,

probably C17 like its cover, with ball finial. – SCREENS. Chancel, Perp, base only. N chapel, another base c. 1500. Restoration 1896–7 by J. C. Traylen, who is presumably responsible for the elaborate roofs, especially in the chancel. – STAINED GLASS. E window, 1884, signed by E. R. Suffling of London. – S aisle E, American 384th Bombardment Group Memorial, by Brian Thomas, 1977, with a bomber aircraft across the window. – MONUMENTS. Family of Lord Gowran to the 2nd Earl of Upper Ossory †1818. By Richard Westmacott R. A. Two kneeling women bending over and holding a medallion with a portrait of the Earl. – Lady Anne Fitzpatrick †1841. By Westmacott Jun. Large relief with a charitable lady offering bread to a child, a kneeling mother, and a vieillard. Gothic arch, but the relief in a sentimental classical style. – Lady Gertrude Fitzpatrick †1841, made by J. Hardman & Co. to a design of A. W. N. Pugin. Black marble slab on low tomb with a brass in medieval style with canopy above kneeling figure.

Former RECTORY, W of the church. 1869. A large stone house in Renaissance style.

Picturesque village with good stone houses, thatch etc. as befits one owing much to the Boughton Estate. Several have shields with the Montagu arms. THE MANOR HOUSE is dated 1653 although considerably rebuilt in the C19. Stepped three-light mullioned windows in the gables. Former SCHOOL of 1866, Gothic. Bridges over a stream which is known for its ducks.

AMERICAN AIRFORCE MEMORIAL, ½ m. NW on road to Geddington. Commemorating 384th Bombardment Group who flew from the adjoining airfield 1943–5. Small stocky obelisk of brown granite.

GREAT ADDINGTON

ALL SAINTS. Mostly late C13 to early C14. Arcades with octagonal piers, except for the E pier on the N side, C13 style and quatrefoil. The arches, with ironstone and grey stone voussoirs, are double-chamfered. The W pair are wider and the clerestory matches the rhythm of the others, so a W extension when the tower was built? Contemporary chancel arch and one-bay N chapel. In the S aisle a tall tomb-recess with Dec mouldings. The chancel is Dec too (see the ANGLE PISCINA and the N doorway), but was rebuilt in C15, hence its Perp windows. It was heavily restored and partly rebuilt in 1891 by W. Talbot Brown. The tower is Dec and built of a soft chalky stone. Above the W doorway a niche with vaulting beneath a nodding ogee arch. Strange lozenge-shaped windows to W and S, with mouchette tracery and cusping respectively. Bell-openings of two lights. Pretty frieze of little ogee arches with quatrefoils in the spandrels. Battlements with cross-slits (why?). Arch towards the nave with three continuous chamfers. The entrance to the s porch has not yet been mentioned. This must be re-set and belong to the predecessor of the present building. Round arch with zigzag, former shafts whose leaf-crocket capitals survive: i.e. *c.* 1190–1200. Like the aisle walls, of sandstone and ironstone. – FONT. Of tub shape, on five supports. At the corners projecting heads. C13. – PULPIT. Late C17; simple. – SCREEN to the N chapel; C15 one-light divisions. Unusual tracery, based on two crossed diagonals. – CHANCEL STALLS and ROOF. 1891, with a decorative barrel ceiling and elegant stalls in a mild Arts and Crafts manner. – STAINED GLASS. N chapel: two shields for Wake and Vere, *c.* 1490, and an assembly of fragments with a female head, late C14. Nave: C14 grisaille fragments. Chancel E, Christ in Majesty, 1900 by *Burlison & Grylls*. S aisle E, Lane and Downe memorial. Presentation of Jesus in Temple, by *J. G. Hunt*. – MONUMENTS. In the chancel but formerly in the N chapel: John Bloxham, *c.* 1519. A 2-ft (61-cm.) brass figure with a scroll emanating from his head. On a plain low slab. – N chapel, in remade recess: Sir Henry Vere †1493. Alabaster effigy of Nottingham workshop. SS collar. He had founded a chantry in the church, the chaplain of which was Bloxham, and he willed that his 'towmbe be made in oure lady chapell . . . of alabaster'.

Former RECTORY, behind the church. 1857, in typical rectory style by *Walter Parker*, builder of Thrapston.

ADDINGTON MANOR, S of the church. A gabled Jacobean house with extensive Neo-Jacobean additions. On the S side the old centre has an E-shaped front with very little space between porch and wings. Dated 1610 over the doorway, with the initials of Christopher Curteys and his wife, Dorothy. The top central gable having some diamond diaper panels. Two further big wings either side added at some time following the acquisition of the house in 1863 by Sidney Leveson Lane and his wife, Viscountess Downe, probably 1870–80. Plaques on N side with his initials and hers with coronet and a big D. Considerable additions at the back of the house. The low two-storey wing on the S side was already there when George Clarke drew the house in 1848.

GREAT BILLING *see* OUTER NORTHAMPTON

GREAT BRINGTON   6060

ST MARY. What endows the church with a far higher than regional importance is the Spencer Chapel, one of the great storehouses of costly and self-confident monuments of the C16, C17 and C18. The church itself is, however, not without its own qualities. It is approached by GATEPIERS of 1840 from the W as well as the E. The W gatepiers have handsome cast-iron GATES. The church is large, of ironstone, and has a C13 W tower. The bell-openings are two lancets under one arch. Late Perp doorway and large w window. The s doorway is of c. 1300, and not far from it in the s wall is a gabled outer tomb-recess with dogtooth decoration which must be of about the same time. It contains a worn stone effigy of a priest. Dec reticulated traceried windows in both N and s aisles. Perp s chapel window, chancel and N chapel. The chancel is known to have been rebuilt at Sir John Spencer's expense. He died in 1522. The N chapel, which was to be the family chapel, was begun by him and completed by his son, Sir William; an inscription recorded in the C17, formerly in a window, had the date 1526. Fine six-bay arcades with octagonal piers. The N arcade has simple octagonal piers and double-chamfered arches and is clearly Dec, but the s arcade is taller and finer, with double hollow-chamfered arches; the piers have concave sides, reminiscent of those chimneystacks often seen on Tudor houses. Is it also Dec or could it be part of Sir John Spencer's rebuilding? The clere-story with its range of square-headed windows is clearly his. The s porch is a rebuilding of 1832 by *Edward Blore*. – FONT. C13, circular bowl of Purbeck marble, with flat, blank pointed arches and in the spandrels crosses and flowers. Stone base with dogtooth. – BENCHES. A wonderful array of poppyhead finials. Most are presumably of Sir John's time, but some others date from 1606. They were all restored in 1846 but many still have traces of red stencilled patterns. – POOR BOX on baluster column; C17. – COMMUNION RAIL. C17. – SOUTH DOOR. Studded, probably the original door of c. 1520. – REREDOS, MARBLE FLOOR and PULPIT. 1903–4 when the church was restored under the direction of *Matthew Holding*. – STAINED GLASS. Chancel s, w window. St John Baptist, some Spencer shields and the other remains, c. 1522–6. – Chancel s, E window, dated 1855 by *Ward & Winston*. – E window by *Morris & Co.*, 1912. – s aisle, E window, 2000 to mark the Millennium by *David Pilkington*. – MONUMENTS in the chancel. John de Clipston †1344. Brass with demi-figure of priest. – Laurence Washington †1616. Tombstone with shield in relief.

The design of the SPENCER CHAPEL has been attributed to *Thomas Heritage*, who was rector of Great Brington and later Surveyor of the King's Works. He had been given the living by Sir John in 1513. However, as he only became involved in the King's Works c. 1530 the attribution remains speculative. The chapel is three bays long. The exterior was rebuilt in 1846 by *Edward Blore* and it was he who added the pretty polygonal bay window to the N. The design was suggested by the then rector, the *Rev. H. Rose*. It has a fan-vault in imitation of that of Henry VII's Chapel at Westminster. The chapel has its original STAINED GLASS by *Ward*, who was advised by *Charles Winston*. The N wall w window by *Morris & Co.*, 1909.

In the chapel the SPENCER MONUMENTS, superbly restored by the 7th Earl Spencer in 1946. The IRON RAILS are probably

C17. The monuments are described here in chronological order.

Sir John Spencer †1522 and wife (E arch of the chapel). Two effigies, he in armour, she in heraldic mantle, at her feet two tiny lapdogs. They are finely carved from alabaster and similar to the effigies on the Knightley tomb at Fawsley, dated 1534, which is attributed to *Richard Parker* of Burton upon Trent. Sir John's son William married a Knightley. No work is known by Parker before 1530, so the tomb is probably of that period. The effigies lie on a tall tomb-chest with three quatrefoils with shields. The monument is placed under an elaborate canopy with a broad four-centred arch panelled inside, all carved from clunch. Big attic with quatrefoil etc. friezes. Against its apex, almost detached, the beautiful figure of an angel in the Doric peplos worn by the angels on Torrigiano's tomb of Henry VII – the only indication of the Renaissance here.

33

Sir William Spencer †1532 (below the E window). Low, long tomb-chest with quatrefoils. No effigies left. The inscription tablet is Elizabethan or Jacobean and belongs to a general labelling which must then have taken place.

Sir John Spencer †1586 and wife (W of Sir John). By *Jasper Hollemans* of Burton upon Trent. Tall tomb-chest with shields separated by very curious, coarsely ornamented strips. Effigies recumbent, she with an excessively heavy hood. To the l. and r. big obelisks covered with strapwork. Round arch and pediment over.

Robert, 1st Baron Spencer, and wife (W of the above). Erected in 1599 and also made by *Hollemans*. He is in armour, she wears an even bigger and heavier hood. The lower half of her body is covered by a heraldic coverlet, denoting that she died in childbirth. It is a most uncommon, if not unique, feature. They lie on a sarcophagus painted with strapwork. To the l. and r. fluted Corinthian columns. Depressed round arch. At the top three obelisks continued downwards as pendants hanging into the arch.

Sir John Spencer †1599 and wife (NE corner). Also by *Hollemans*. Although now standing against the wall, before 1846 this was a detached monument. It is the tallest in the chapel. Four-poster on thin square pillars covered with close and dainty arabesques. Diagonally outside the pillars, four tall detached black columns with Corinthian capitals carrying supporters. The centre of the monument carries openwork strapwork and small obelisks. The lady wears the same curious hood as the others. Inscription plate against the E wall of the chapel. A receipt exists from *Hollemans* dated 1601 and this could well mean that all three monuments are of the same date. They all have splendid heraldic displays.

William Lord Spencer †1636 (NW part of the chapel). By *Nicholas Stone*. Completed in 1638. He received £600 for it (including apparently the materials) and paid £14 of this to *John Hargrave* for carving the effigy of the lord, £15 to *Richard*

White for the effigy of the lady – not a very generous apportioning (but probably these were only extra gratuities). Noble detached eight-poster. Black marble columns with white marble capitals, connected along the long sides by small arches. The canopy similar in style to Stone's monument for the Lucy family at Charlecote, Warwick. Tomb-chest of black-and-white marble. Very fine white marble effigies on a black moulded lid. Lady Spencer's head especially beautiful.

Sir Edward Spencer †1655 (in the SE corner). 1656 by *John Stone*. Very curious indeed. Demi-figure rising out of the Urn of the Resurrection. To his r. the square pillar of the Word of God, to his l. the column of Truth. On it rests the Bible. Sir Gyles Isham irreverently but memorably christened this memorial 'The Potted Earl', forgivable even if he was not an earl!

83 John, 1st Earl Spencer, †1783 (w of the bay). By *Nollekens*. The design is by *Cipriani*. (The drawing is at Spencer House.) A large hanging monument. Female figure of Plenty standing on clouds and holding a medallion with the profile of the Earl, also on clouds. Big cornucopia at her feet. The poem ought to be read.

Georgiana, Countess Spencer, †1814 (w wall). By *Flaxman*, originally designed as a base to the Nollekens monument. Big oblong tablet. Architecturally extremely simple. The inscription in the middle. To the l. Faith, to the r. a noble and lovable figure of Charity. The two monuments were originally set one above the other on the E wall of the chapel before the window was opened up in 1846.

Captain Sir Robert Cavendish Spencer (E of the bay). 1833 by *Chantrey*. White marble bust on plinth. A copy of one in the house.

In addition numerous small brass coffin plates let into the floor of the bay window, and many HELMS, CORONETS, SWORDS, GAUNTLETS and HATCHMENTS together with inscriptions for later generations of the family. C19 memorials for the family are in a plot at the E end of the churchyard, alongside the lychgate of 1887 by *Edmund Law*.

CROSS on a small green, w of the churchyard. A concave-sided shaft mounted on steps. It was moved from a site elsewhere in 1938 and the top was replaced in 1947 having been found in the vicarage garden.

OLD RECTORY, s of the church. By *Blore*, *c.* 1825, picturesque Tudor with a polygonal tower and spire at the back. It was built for the Hon. and Rev. George Spencer who was appointed 1825 but converted to Rome in 1830 when he resigned the living.

Both Great and Little Brington owe much to the influence of the Althorp Estate, most notably since the C19. In each case there was much tidying up of village properties and building of model ESTATE COTTAGES. The earliest wave of these date from the middle years of the C19. Before about 1880 the firm of *Devey & Williams* (i.e. *George Devey*) acted for the estate and then later into the early 1900s *Josiah Mander*, a surveyor who

Great Brington, Old Rectory.
Drawing by George Clarke, *c.* 1850

worked for both Lord Spencer and Lord Overstone, also provided designs. It is not easy now to be sure who did what since
both Devey and Mander had a liking for timber-framed gables.
In GREAT BRINGTON, opposite the church in WHILTON
ROAD, there is ample evidence of their efforts. One house is
dated 1890. Then s from the church past a delightful ironstone
thatched row, on the r. are two pairs of cottages, ironstone but
with brick and stone façades, with a central gabled section, a
three-light Gothic window with a castellated bay below. The
datestone is rather weathered but 1862 would fit. A little
further on the l. is the WAR MEMORIAL, 1921, designed by *Sir
John Brown* of Northampton. It is a reduced version of the
famous Cenotaph. Beyond, again on the l. is HAMILTON
LANE where, beyond a discreet modern development, is the
ALMSHOUSE of 1851. Gothic, and probably by *Philip Hardwick*
(*see* below).
In LITTLE BRINGTON, ½ m. s. Immediately on the r. is the
SCHOOL, also 1851 and known to be by *Hardwick*. A fine
Gothic brick and stone structure with an elaborate traceried
window in its bay. Additions 1892–3 and more recent. At the
bottom of the hill, on the r. the former BAPTIST CHAPEL of
1835. Neat brick. Then a little further on the l. is CARRIAGE
DRIVE, an avenue drive from Althorp, with a pretty Gothic
LODGE, 1852, with timber porch and bargeboards. Opposite
into MAIN STREET further rows of brick and stone cottages
dated 1848. Further s on the l. is WASHINGTON COTTAGE, a
reconstruction of 1960 following a fire. There is no concrete
evidence that it was the Washington home. On the brow of the
hill the remains of ST JOHN'S CHURCH. Just the tower and
spire of a building by *Hardwick*, 1851. The rest was demolished
in 1949.

GREAT CRANSLEY *see* CRANSLEY

GREAT CREATON *see* CREATON

GREAT DODDINGTON

St Nicholas. The lower part of the tower is of the C12, with a round-headed window to the W as well as into the nave and clear roof-line. The fine double-shafted W doorway was inserted about 1200, at the same time perhaps that the thin E buttresses were provided which are now cut into by the nave arcades. The top stage of the tower top has the date 1737, which doubtless refers to its rebuilding with the rather feeble bell-stage windows. The rest of the church mostly early C14, except for a Norman scallop capital just inside the S doorway (not *in situ*). Windows with cusped intersected and with reticulated tracery. Chancel SEDILIA of *c.* 1300. There are three lowside lancets and a priest's doorway. The upper windows are straight-headed and Dec. The E window is C19, but a correct restoration: four lights, with a top circle with three spherical triangles in it. Shafted inside. Tall S doorway with many fine continuous mouldings. Arcades of four bays dating from *c.* 1300. Octagonal piers, double-chamfered arches. On the S side one pier is earlier and probably reused. It has a little nailhead. On the N side a pier before the last arch, perhaps denoting a Norman transept angle. Triple-chamfered tower arch of *c.* 1300. There was a restoration in 1870 masterminded by, to quote the *Northampton Mercury*, 'the excellent vicar of the parish', the *Rev. Maze W. Gregory* using *Goodridge* of Roade as contractor. Chancel roof redone by *Law & Son.* – FONT COVER. C15, but much redone. – PEWS. A series of C15 buttressed seats (S aisle). – SCREEN. Minor parts, reused in various ways in the chancel stalls. – PULPIT. Jacobean, with two tiers of the usual short, broad, flat arches. – HOURGLASS STAND. Also Jacobean. – STALLS. Four with poppyheads and MISERICORDS with leaves etc. and a carver at work. – COMMUNION RAIL. With twisted balusters; late C17. – DOOR. The S door is of the C15; traceried and with original ironwork. – PORCH GATES. Delightful with spiked balusters and scroll finials, perhaps the same date as the tower top, 1737? – WALL PAINTING. Crucifixus with the Virgin and St John, a large head of Christ above; only a few outlines survive (S of the chancel arch). – SCULPTURE. In the vestry. Satan and the apple of Eden. Supposed to be late C12. – STAINED GLASS. Nave N: C14 coat of arms; nave S: C15 roundel.

MEMORIAL CROSS, in the churchyard. For Bishop Spencer Leeson of Peterborough, 1956. Carved by the rector, *Rev. R. Cromwell*. Attractive, with carved string incorporating the signs of the Evangelists.

MANOR HOUSE. Just S of the church. C17, small, of half-H shape and well preserved with nearly all its mullioned windows. In the recessed part the doorway with a four-centred head and the Hall window to its l. The projecting wings are gabled. The staircase (with vertically symmetrical balusters) is original but not *in situ*. On the house is a now illegible datestone, but 1610 is recorded.

TOP FARM. The main range possibly of 1588, with a reused C14 window. In a wing with the date 1661 is an upper room with C17 panelling.

GREAT EVERDON *see* EVERDON

GREAT HARROWDEN

ALL SAINTS. Of ironstone, except for the tower of grey ashlar limestone. In the W wall of the nave the remains of a Norman window and the responds of the Norman tower arch. The tower was rebuilt in 1821–2 by *F. Gibbins* of Wellingborough. It had had a spire which, however, had collapsed in the C18. Inset inside in its N wall a grimacing head which would appear to be the missing gargoyle from the S aisle. The rest is of the C13 and C14. The arcades are specially interesting, that on the S side having been blocked when the S aisle was demolished *c.* 1700. Both arcades have the four-shafts-and-four-hollows section which is so familiar from the Perp style but the S arcade is clearly earlier. The suggested date is very late C13. The shafts are very fine, the hollows wide, and the capitals round. Interestingly the inner pier of the arcade would appear to be ironstone with the detached shafts in limestone. The intersected tracery of the S windows and the doorway, which were re-set when the aisles were pulled down, bear out a date of about 1300. In the limestone N arcade the shafts are stronger and the capitals polygonal and more what one expects from Perp. Dec chancel with beautifully slender two-light windows with ogival heads externally and a very grand five-light E window, shafted jambs internally. The tracery in both cases is reticulated. A sill moulding runs all round. SEDILIA and PISCINA with continuous mouldings and trefoil heads. Blocked lowside window. The chancel was reconstructed in 1845 (though there is a loose datestone in the chancel dated 1848) but it would seem correctly though the sedilia arches cut into the sill moulding. The REREDOS arcading is part of the 1840s rebuilding. The chancel is closed off from the nave and no longer used for worship. The NE vestry is also of late C13 origin (cf. the stone at the base of the chancel and that of the vestry) but remodelled in the C14. An external low arch in its W wall refers to a charnel crypt beneath. There was a restoration in 1896 by *Talbot Brown & Fisher* and the pews with their crisp tracery carving will be theirs. – FONT. Perp manner, also 1896, with nicely carved details. – SCREENS. Chancel, fine, Perp, of two-light divisions, the mullions reaching up into the apexes of the arches. Crocketed ogee gables. The loft is a restoration. – Tower, Maddock memorial, 1940, carved by *Robert Thompson*, the 'mouse man'. – WALL PAINTING. Above the chancel arch. Doom, only partially recognizable. It was uncovered in 1896 and restored in 1963 by *Eve Baker*. – HATCHMENT. Alice Watson-Wentworth †1743. – STAINED GLASS. Chancel s. Early C14 grisaille glass. – Nave, the Burning Bush by *Lisa Thompson*, 1993. – BRASSES to William Harrowden †1423 and wife (Chancel). Fine large figures, 3 ft 7 in. long. The architectural surround has not survived. – MONUMENTS. N aisle two Purbeck marble slabs with remains of inscriptions. That in the middle of the aisle coffin shaped and recorded by Bridges as being in the chancel. The stone coffin at the end of the N aisle may well be related to it having been removed hence when the chancel was rebuilt. – Mary Millbanke †1786, Neo-classical surround. – Rev. William Wright †1843, a simple tablet signed by *W. Henson* of Kettering.

HARROWDEN HALL. In the C15 the manor of Harrowden was held by the Vaux family, another important ownership by a Roman Catholic family in Northamptonshire. They were here till 1662 when it passed to Charles Knollys, Earl of Banbury. He seems to have established a sizeable mansion here of which there are some remains in the basement and outbuildings, and these remains, largely C17 but with some indication of medieval, determined the plan of the present house. In 1693 Knollys's son sold Harrowden to Thomas Watson, son of the 3rd Baron Rockingham. As in 1694 he inherited the Wentworth Woodhouse Estate in Yorkshire, it is unlikely anything was done at Harrowden until he passed the Wentworth Estate over to his son in 1716. In fact the dating is well documented. The house is not mentioned by Morton in 1712. Bridges about 1720 calls it 'new built', and rainwater heads proclaim 1719. There are however certain features which may have been incorporated from the earlier house. These might include some of the panelling and two very boldly and largely detailed fireplaces look like 1690 at the latest. There is also a fireplace with the date 1667. The property remained with the Watsons till 1782 when it passed by marriage into the Fitzwilliam family, and they held it till 1895. It was then purchased by Lord Vaux, descendant of the C15 owners, who built the Catholic chapel in the grounds. In 1966 Harrowden was bought by the Macdonald-Buchanans of Cottesbrooke, who conducted a major restoration of the interior, and they sold in 1975 to the Wellingborough Golf Club.

The exterior is completely plain with a five-bay centre of two and a half storeys with three-bay two-storey attachments l. and r., equally plain. Entrance hall with a splendid scroll stone fireplace. It seems to be made of the local stone known as Rance, quarried in the area. Fine staircase of *c.* 1719 with three fluted balusters to the treads and carved tread-ends. This is very like the staircases which are known to have been created by *Joseph Daniel*, a joiner who worked for *Francis Smith* of

Warwick at Lamport and Dallington. The suggestion is, therefore, that Harrowden is by Smith, though it does not fit exactly
with his manner. Could it be by another hand like *Lumley*? The
staircase was decorated with large canvases attributed to *Gerard
Lanscroon*. They were in a poor state in 1966 when they were
restored in a cut-down form. They are thought to illustrate the
story of Psyche. Some later C18 chimneypieces elsewhere.

Very beautiful GARDENS which retain an almost perfect early
C18 formal layout with a series of brick walls and gatepiers. On
the front GATEPIERS and the fine wrought-iron GATES the
Watson arms, almost certainly by *Thomas Warren*. They were
partly remade in 1869. Also in the gardens three groups
of LEAD STATUARY probably contemporary with the house,
one of them a copy of Giovanni da Bologna's Samson and
the Philistine, now in the Victoria and Albert Museum, but
formerly at Hovingham Hall, Yorkshire, and originally in
Florence. They will have come from the *Nost* yard.

In the grounds, s of the house, a CHAPEL (R.C.) built by
the Lord Vaux in 1905–7. It is a copy of the C15 school at
Higham Ferrers and was built by *E. Brown* of Wellingborough,
who supplied an estimate in 1905 and records in a letter of
1906 that he had been to Higham to measure parts of the
building. In the Vaux papers there are a number of unsigned
drawings presumably by him. Simple interior fitted up by
J. Hardman & Co.; carving by *R. L. Boulton* of Cheltenham,
with panelling and a timber ceiling supported on carved
corbels. In 1924 a small mortuary chapel was added with an
altarpiece of alabaster and marble, again by Hardman. Four
STAINED GLASS windows also by Hardman, 1905–36.

MANOR HOUSE, w of the house, at the beginning of Orlingbury
Road. L-shaped. Originates from the C16 house of the Char-
nocks. An early C17 wing was added and a new porch in 1648.
Considerably altered in the late C19 when the garden front was
refaced.

GREAT HOUGHTON

ST MARY. Built in 1754–5 by *David Hiorne*, and alas restored by
John Henry Hakewill in 1875–8, when the Georgian windows
received their unfortunate Norman two-light subdivision. One
original Georgian window in the w wall of the tower. Fine w
tower, strong and square, with an octagonal peripteral order
of Tuscan columns at the top, each carrying a volute and a
strange projecting piece of entablature, each of which originally
carried an urn. The volutes lead up to a spire. Aisleless body
of three bays, the middle bays stressed by pediments. Projecting chancel with an undetailed Venetian E window. The side
panels were filled in 1910–11. Flat plaster ceiling with dentil
cornice. – FURNISHINGS. Good quality Georgian style altar,

panelling and rails, all set on a diamond-pattern slab floor.
Does this too date from 1910–11? – MONUMENTS. Two pyramidal tablets, 1778 and 1782 by *William Cox Sen.*; and two
identical tablets, †1825 and 1833, with inscriptions on flat urns.
STAINED GLASS. Fine Chancel E window of 1911 designed by
A. J. Dix of *J. Hardman & Co.* – N window 1884, also by
Hardman. – S aisle window for the Queen's Jubilee, celebrating
achievements of her reign (an oil rig, Concorde aircraft and
science), designed by *Ray Coomber*, painted by *Sydney Endacott*
and made by *Wippell* of Exeter, 1981.
BARROW, W of a moated enclosure.

8080

GREAT OAKLEY

Great Oakley is now almost a part of the expanding Corby, but
its house and park mean that the old village centre survives, and
it is still very much a village. The church stands within the park
S of the house.

ST MICHAEL. Much evidence of late rebuilding and a considerable overhaul in the C17. Small ashlar W tower of 1618 with
arched lights and battlements. Huge catslide nave roof of Collyweston stone slates, reaching on the S side right down to the
eaves of the low aisle wall. E walls of both nave and chancel
have stepped battlements, probably an early C19 conceit but
could be C17. Interior plastered with a barrel ceiling. S arcade
originally of three bays, then – soon after – lengthened to the
W by another three, an odd enterprise. Both parts have
octagonal piers and double-chamfered arches with foot-pieces.
The earlier E part has one capital with a little nailhead, i.e. is
C13; the later may be of the C14, assuming it is medieval. The
only original early window is in the N wall of the nave. Two
lights and a lozenge over, i.e. late C13. Below, interrupting the
base of the window, low wide tomb-recess, probably C14. On
the porch roof medieval ridge tiles. The church was restored
in 1857–8 by *W. Slater.* – Chancel SCREEN. Perp portions but
mainly *c.* 1840, and remains of another reused in the vestry
partition, but only two stall-fronts C15 and some later linenfold
panelling. – STALLS. C19, but looking later than the 1857 restoration. Four with little heads on the arm-ends and MISERI-
CORDS of Father Time with the Scythe and Hour Glass, a
head, an angel and a pelican. – PULPIT. Georgian, and probably part of a two-decker arrangement. The brass plaque on
its platform, dated 1777, may be relevant. – COMMUNION
RAIL. Jacobean, with vertically symmetrical balusters. – TILES.
Medieval, red clay, some stamped with shields and others
incised with patterns and animals. From Pipewell Abbey. –
STAINED GLASS. Chancel N. Two angels' heads, early C16.
Flemish or German? – MONUMENTS. Arthur Brooke †1620.

Stone surround with pilasters and strapwork above. Modern colouring. – Mary Supple †1782. A stone inscription on a carved base, reusing some C17 scroll brackets, as on the 1620 monument. – Sir Richard Brooke de Capell Brooke †1829, with a draped urn. By *Francis* of London.

GREAT OAKLEY HALL has been in the ownership of the Brooke family since the C15. In 1762 the property was inherited by a daughter who had married into the Supple, or as it had been, the de Capell family. Her son Richard assumed by royal licence the name de Capell, which is still held by the family. Sir Arthur de Capell Brooke (†1858) wrote many important foreign travel books.

The original house was L-shaped, with the Hall in the recessed wing. Bridges gives the date as 1555, a credible date, but one gable has the date 1575. The original work has all mullioned windows with arched lights and hoodmoulds. The recessed centre has five bays in three storeys, all windows on the ground floor and the first floor of four lights. The centre is divided by a slight step back, the front wall of the section to the l. of the porch having been brought forward, probably in the C18, to improve circulation. To the l. of it ashlar, to the r. rendered. To the l. the top storey has three-light, to the r. four-light windows. The Hall was evidently single-storeyed from the beginning. Four gables connected each time by one semicircular merlon (cf. Dingley). The merlons have inscriptions: VIRESSCIT VULNERE VIRTUS (Virtue flourishes by trial) and INVIDUS ALTERIUS MARCRESCIT REBUS OPIMES (The curious man grows lean in [the sight of] another's prosperity). Finial on each gable. Elaborate early C17 porch with coupled, bulgy, fluted Doric pilasters, a round-headed entrance, shields to its l. and r., and a heavy balcony (cf. Rushton). Large S additions of 1893 when the S wing was replaced. These alterations were directed by Bishop Trollope, father of Lady de Capell Brooke; he placed verses from the Bible wherever he could and added much highly Elizabethan detail. The interior much revised at the same time. Jacobean parts of overmantels. Some pretty C18 plasterwork (*c.* 1750) and fireplaces. Late C17 staircase with twisted balusters Jacobethaned in 1893. Attached to the N wing a small GAZEBO of C18 date. To the E a range of STABLES of mid C18 date with a small cupola. In the garden, W of the front, is a Victorian FOUNTAIN from Market Harborough, which had been donated to the town in 1891 by the de Capell Brookes and was brought back in 1965.

The small village has just a few old cottages and a Gothic former SCHOOL of 1857.

At OAKLEY HAY, just W of the village on A6104, THE SPREAD EAGLE pub. A handsome red brick house of five bays with large cross casements and a raised brick string dividing the two storeys, mid C18. An earlier stone wing to the l. with a later large canted bay window.

Former GEDDINGTON STATION, 1 m. SE on the road to Little Oakley. Built 1879 on the Midland Railway line from Kettering to Manton. Brick with plain bargeboarded gables. The line closed in 1948 and the buildings were converted into houses.

GREAT OXENDON

St Helen. Isolated on the brow of a hill ¼ m. N of the village. Oddly proportioned W tower. Buttresses only below, upper parts receding in four stages. The base probably C14 with two pretty traceried panels above the W window, but heightened in the late C15 when the bell-stage, battlements and pinnacles were added. The tower arch, also late C15, has tall bases with crenellations and capitals with flowers. Odd how the tower floor is at a higher level than the nave. Exterior of the rest of the church varied, with both medieval and later (C17) windows, but no feature of individual interest. Inside, C13 S arcade, although the responds probably C15, early C14 N arcade, with circular piers, circular capitals and abaci, and double-chamfered arches, the latter with quatrefoil piers with ballflower enrichment. Half-arches are thrown across the N aisle. Early C14 chancel arch, renewed. – FONT. Of tub shape; Norman, with raw vertical zigzag. – STAINED GLASS. Chancel E window, 1870 by *J. Powell & Sons*. The single figures in the tracery lights deserve notice. – Chancel S window of 1863 by *Lavers & Barraud*. – Tower window, 1870 also by *Powells*. – Fine 1914 war memorial window in the S aisle by *Daniels & Fricker*, 1920. – Nice rows of SLATE TOMBSTONES line the path.

GREAT WELDON *see* WELDON

GREATWORTH

St Peter. A small church, W tower, nave and chancel, but with some charm. The lower part of the W tower is of *c.* 1300 (see the arch towards the nave). The chancel is of the C13 (see the pointed window). The nave was rebuilt in 1750 and of that date its coved eaves survive, but otherwise it was totally refurbished by *H. R. Gough* in 1881–4. S porch added 1894 by *J. Timms* of Banbury. Of the 1880s the TILED FLOOR, in carpet-like patterns, and the GLAZING, which is unusual. It has gentle colours with geometric patterns. Photographs in the church show the church when it had box pews and a gallery. – MONUMENTS. Sir William Pargitter †1678. A circular wreath within a draped surround, held up by three ploughboy cherubs. Clearly local work. – Elinor Howe †1696. Simple but good quality. Urn at the top and a shield and two cherubs at the base. – Charles Howe †1741. A most Rococo conceit and of good quality.

Asymmetrical cartouche and asymmetrical surround, as if to
fit into the spandrel between an arch and a straight wall. The
carver must have enjoyed this restriction. The composition is
not unique, cf. e.g. Norwich, St Giles and Melton Constable,
Norfolk. – Rev. Henry Dyke †1873. A white sarcophagus on a
black surround by *R. Mander* of Banbury.

The Manor House was destroyed by fire in 1793. It was built by
Charles Howe within the first two decades of the C18. He
purchased a marble chimneypiece from 'Mr. Townsend', who
may be *William Townsend* of Oxford, or another member of that
mason family. The house was fortunately recorded by Peter
Tillemans in 1721. He shows it in dark wash so it was almost
certainly built of the local dark ironstone, probably from the
Eydon quarries. It was of two and a half storeys and five bays
wide. Some GATEPIERS remain, and the inner ones especially,
of limestone, with their beautifully carved, wondrously large
pineapple finials sprouting from scrolly leaves, are splendid
things.

METHODIST CHAPEL, Chapel Road. 1860, of stone in the Dec
style, with two windows and a doorway edged with the naming
inscription. 1878 lancet style school attached.

GREEN'S NORTON   *6050*

ST BARTHOLOMEW. Interesting Anglo-Saxon remains, in effect
the body of the early church. The main evidence is the long-
and-short work of the external NW and SW quoins (of Barnack
rag) of the tall and wide nave and the jambs of a window now
high up in the E wall of the nave above the chancel arch. (This
has a triangular head, although it is not visible from below.)
There are further quoins visible, high up, behind the SE pier
of the S arcade, and also faint traces of blocked windows above
the N arcade. The C14 arcades are inserted within the Saxon
walls, the first two bays being separated from the third by
pieces of wall where the W arch of the crossing (i.e. the Saxon
wall) ran. The third bays represent a central space, a recognized
feature of Late Saxon churches, and they may originally have
opened into transepts. The arch within the E Saxon wall, which
is in effect the chancel arch, although that structurally begins
further E, without an arch, has sockets in its soffit showing
there was a tympanum for the rood screen. The arcades have
octagonal piers and double-chamfered arches. Flowing tracery
in windows of the N and S aisles. The chancel was C13 with
pairs of double lancets in each wall, but only one pair on each
side are now open. It was totally rebuilt in 1890–2, by *Edmund
Law*, when the E lancet windows were created. The large dark
ironstone W tower is part of the C14 rebuilding but the upper
parts were Georgianized under the direction of *John Lumley* of
Northampton after its partial collapse in 1718. Pointed bell-

openings with Gibbs rusticated surrounds and angle pilasters. It had urns at each corner in the C18 and served as an eye-catcher for Easton Neston house. The spire was rebuilt in 1807 and again in 1957. Vestry on the N side, added 1923. It is interesting that while the interior is all light stone, the whole of the exterior is clad in dark ironstone, and that goes back to medieval times. – FONT. Circular, Norman, decorated with beaded lozenges filled with flowers. – PULPIT. With Jacobean panels. – Large iron bound CHEST, C17? – STAINED GLASS. E window by *Kempe*, 1896. – Two more, later *Kempe & Co.* windows, 1914 and 1922 in S aisle. – N aisle, 1891 by *Jones & Willis*. – Another S aisle window of 1961 by *Francis Spear*. – MONUMENTS. The Greene monuments were gathered together in the N aisle during a drastic reordering of the interior in 1826. They were put together in a totally unhistorical manner, but have since been rearranged in a sensible fashion. – The big recess with four-centred arch has the memorial for Sir Thomas Greene †1462. Brasses of good quality, 3 ft 6 in. (1.1 metres) long. The tomb-chest has shields in pointed quatrefoils. – In front to the l. the broken alabaster effigies of Sir Thomas Greene †1457 and wife, mounted on a modern support. Panels from the tomb-chest on the wall behind. Nottingham alabaster school, still, despite the damage, with elements of colour. (S aisle) brass to Lady Greene (part of monument for Sir Thomas †1417). The figure is 20 in. (51 cm.) long. – (Chancel) William Hicklinge †1606, but the monument must be of *c.* 1620–30. It is attributed to *Maximilian Colt* (GF). Very fine quality. Small kneeling figures below a baldacchino which curves forward and has a shell motif ceiling. The draperies are lifted up by two fine large standing angels, in the best Netherlandish Mannerist tradition (cf. Colt's Mildmay monument at Apethorpe). At the foot two small corbels in the shape of female heads under Ionic capitals. – LYCHGATE by *Edmund Law*, 1897.

SCHOOL (Village Hall). 1874 by *E. Swinfen Harris*. Rough stone with red brick dressings. Front gable with three lancets and a porch with bellcote above. Extensions of 1891.

OLD RECTORY, N of the church. C17 core with an C18 wing. One Tudor arched fireplace and C18 panelling and staircase.

BENGAL MANOR. 1698. The elegant doorway is of 1934, but the windows and the four oval windows in the W gable are original. Is the spiked frieze of brick original too? Good gatepiers.

KINGTHORN MILL, ½ m. SW on the Bradden road. A substantial 1930s house with a half-timbered central gabled feature.

Near Green's Norton are CASWELL and FIELD BURCOTE, two of the farms built by the Grafton Estate about 1840.

GRENDON

ST MARY. The story of the church begins inside. The first three bays on both sides are Late Norman, W imposts with many scallops, circular piers with many slightly enriched scallops, circular abaci – an early case (but cf. Holy Sepulchre, Northampton) – and unmoulded round arches. Next in order of time the late C12 S doorway with one order of shafts carrying simple moulded capitals and an arch with a thick roll moulding and a flat face decorated with saltire crosses and palmette leaf. Early C13 the simple N doorway close to a pair of lancets. The E bays of the arcade come after that, Dec presumably. Much taller with octagonal piers and double-chamfered arches. The pointed trefoil-headed PISCINA in the S aisle wall must be earlier, but the chancel may well be contemporary – see the chancel arch resting on corbel heads, the crocketed ogee-arched SEDILIA, the simple EASTER SEPULCHRE, and the tall (much renewed) straight-headed two-light windows. Two of them are of the lowside type. Tomb-recess in chancel. C14 S porch. Perp W tower, of banded brown and grey stone. Ashlar at the top. Original door with tracery. Money was left to the fabric of the campanile in 1453. Tall arch towards the nave. Slim diagonal buttresses. Big doorway and W window. Battlements, pinnacles. There were restorations in 1848 by R. C. Hussey, and also in 1880–1 by H. M. Townsend and in 1898. – REREDOS. Elaborate Gothic c. 1910. – MARBLE FLOOR of the sanctuary, black-and-white designs, 1914. – STAINED GLASS. Chancel E, 1911 by Heaton, Butler & Bayne. – BRASS. Lady and two knights, late C15.

GRENDON HALL (Northants County Council). Fine ashlar E front, early C18. Three-bay centre and two-bay projections, restrained detail, doorway with segmental pediment on brackets containing a cypher 'HC' (for General Hatton Compton), quoins, hipped roof. The S side of four bays corresponds. The designer is thought to be John Lumley of Northampton. The N side is older, probably later C17. Mullioned windows with straight architraves (no longer hoodmoulds). The transomed staircase windows create a break in their pattern. Pedimented dormers. Inside, some rooms with early C18 panelling. Staircase with twisted balusters, rather late C17 than early C18. Simple IRONWORK GATE, early C18 and presumably by Thomas Warren. Stables to the N of the house, and oblong DOVECOTE to their N, both C18. The STABLES were converted into a residential block by the County Architect's Department (A. N. Harris), 1964.

NOS. 8–10 CHURCH WAY, NW of the church. Part of a single house with a garden porch created from an archway from Holdenby. Archway flanked by Ionic pilasters. Round arch with circles in the spandrels. A large Jacobethan gable on the W front, part of alterations of 1859. On the street façade a carved achievement of the Compton arms, early C18. The house was for many years the home of the Northamptonshire historian Christopher Markham. Next to it facing the church a pretty COTTAGE with bargeboards and patterned glazing, c. 1840 and very sensitively extended.

THE GRANGE (former rectory), SW of the church. 1850–1 by S. S. Teulon, picturesque Tudor and for Teulon surprisingly calm in manner. A lantern with cupola since the building also for a time served as a school. Some alterations by *H. M. Townsend* in 1878–9. Further on MANOR FARM HOUSE, C17, handsome, gabled, with mullioned windows.

GRETTON

ST JAMES. The story starts with an aisleless Early Norman church of which two blocked windows remain in a fragmentary state above the nave arcades. There follows soon, about 1130, the W part of the N arcade, with a circular pier, capitals with three and four scallops, a square abacus, and arches with fat rolls. The W part of the S arcade follows after that, a little later, but still Norman. The difference in time can be measured by the development at Peterborough Cathedral. The difference in form is that the scallops are livelier. In the C13 both aisles were extended to the E and a new chancel and new transepts built. Evidence of the C13 chancel is the blocked lancet windows on the S side. Evidence too of lowside windows on both sides. The chancel was raised by four steps in the C18, when the Hatton family vault was established, and this is doubtless the period of the large rectangular windows. The puzzling thing about the transepts is that they are not in line with the E bay of the arcades. Does that indicate that they were a rebuilding of Norman transepts? But they can hardly have been in line with the Norman nave, to which the W bays of the arcade were added. They both have bridging arches from the aisles. In detail the new E bay has on the N side a round pier and round abacus, on the S an octagonal pier. The E respond has nailhead decoration here. Both arcade extensions have pointed double-chamfered arches. In the N transept are one E lancet window and three stepped (renewed) single N lancets. In the S transept are an E lancet, remains of a W lancet visible from inside, and, inside also, some sumptuous and baffling arcading. One arch, trefoiled with a pointed moulding to the N. Stiff-leaf capitals and dogtooth. A second at right angles to it, to the E, was probably a squint. It has dogtooth decoration too, but the arch-head is simply a curved line rising to the l. to join up with the arch round the corner. Next in order of time the chancel E window of four lights with reticulated tracery, i.e. of a Dec date, and the equally Dec clerestory. The clerestory windows are foiled circles and at the W end cusped spherical triangles. Finally the W tower, which is of ironstone and Perp, and the short ironstone arches which connect the arcades with it. The golden stone comes from the Welland valley from quarries near Caldecote, where most houses are built of it. The tower is tall and has slender clasping buttresses. Two-light bell-openings with transom. Ashlar battlements and pinnacles. A moderate restoration was undertaken by *Talbot Brown & Fisher* of

Wellingborough in 1893, when the roof was renewed and several windows were replaced. The s porch appears to have been moved to the w, probably to allow for revision of the seating arrangements inside (*see* below). – FONT. Octagonal, Perp, with shields and panelling. – SCREEN. Jacobean, with vertically symmetrical balusters. Now in the tower arch. Also some resited Jacobean baluster rails. – C18 chancel PANELLING and COMMUNION RAIL. Of *c.* 1700, with strong balusters. All painted. – PULPIT, wine-glass form, mid-C18 with sunburst inlay, and later, low BOX PEWS, handsomely receding in a curve to the l. and r. to leave space for a central three-decker pulpit arrangement, in front of the chancel. Such arrangements rarely survive, but there is one not far away at Kings Norton, Leicestershire. – Some Jacobean PANELLING in the N transept. – MONUMENTS. The Ladies Hatton, 1684 by *William Stanton*. Two identical tablets with draperies and a cherub's head at the foot. – Viscount Hatton †1706. Grey sarcophagus. Two cherubs, looking a little uncomfortable, perched on white volutes. White obelisk, heraldry and inscription. Attributed to *Chevalier Claude David* (GF).

BAPTIST CHURCH, High Street. 1824 with a three bay brick façade and later porch in front. Schoolroom to r.

PRIMARY SCHOOL, Kirby Road. 1908 by *J. A. Gotch*. In Gotch's typical style, of red brick and stone with one of his very distinctive campanile-like towers.

The village has a good many fine stone houses,* of which the best are in HIGH STREET. BARN HOUSE (No. 74) is *c.* 1635 and has an unusual plan with a central entrance hall flanked by a kitchen and parlour, both with large inglenook fireplaces. A slightly later wing has a good quality bedchamber with a garderobe. Good masonry, mullioned windows and chimney-stacks. GRETTON HOUSE (care home) in the High Street is Georgian (five bays, two storeys) but has large irregular Neo-Jacobean additions of 1905–6 by *J. A. Gotch*. Fine façade with stone-framed windows and platband. Three dormers in the stone-tiled roof, of which the central one is made a little grander. The C18 staircase with turned balusters survives. Opposite is MANOR FARMHOUSE, L-shaped with mullioned windows and bands of ironstone and sandstone, dated 1675. Central stair hall and stairs with turned balusters. Some original stone fireplace surrounds. Just beyond to w another banded house, THE YEWS, *c.* 1700, but of earlier origin, with a stair-turret, moulded doorcase and square windows. A small green near the church has a WAR MEMORIAL by *Gotch*, *c.* 1920. Squat obelisk with ball top and low curved side walls. Also STOCKS and WHIPPING POST. Also on the Green the former NATIONAL SCHOOL, 1853. Five bays with porch. Originally one storey; now with dormers. s of the church in High Street PAGES ROW, Victorian sandstone and ironstone cottages with a little red brick added for effect. Just w of the church in

*I am grateful to Nick Hill for his notes on several houses.

Station Road the OLD VICARAGE with mullioned windows and one horizontal oval window, late C17, and beyond, STONE-CROFT, again with mullions and a stair-turret, also late C17. An inset panel contains miscellaneous architectural fragments including some C12 chevron. No. 16 contains a cruck truss of C15–C16 date, though much of the house is later.

There are a number of other good houses and rows within the somewhat complex street plan. Notably, s of the Green, by the corner of School Road, THE MALTINGS, late C16, mullions and four-centred doorway, and opposite a Late Georgian house (No. 78) with a Tuscan porch.

Former STATION, Hatton Lane. On the Midland Railway Kettering to Manton line. A charming example unusually in sandstone and ironstone. Just a small, square one-storey building under a pyramidal roof held on multi-bracketed eaves. Built with a basement below.

HARBOROUGH HILL HOUSE, ¼ m. N. 1858, built for the agent to the Winchelsea Estate, whose coat of arms is on the front. An arch from Kirby Hall is built into the w side. Rusticated pilasters and spandrels. Archway with ears and volutes. Shield in cartouche with swags – i.e. the 1640 phase of Kirby.

GUILSBOROUGH

An attractive village with a good selection of houses and cottages and much green space.

ST ETHELREDA. Conspicuously set on the brow of the hill on the easternmost edge of the village. w tower and spire E.E. in style, but the spire dated 1618, and the complete structure probably all of this date. The bell-openings are two lancets. (Double-lancet bell-openings appear also at St Giles Northampton, 1619, and Wicken, 1617.) Low broaches, spire with two tiers of lucarnes. The rest of the building Dec. Arcades of four bays with octagonal piers and double-chamfered arches with cone-shaped foot-pieces. Capitals are of a different and harder stone. The chancel arch is later, with fleurons in the capitals and double-hollow-chamfered arches (cf. Great Brington). The nave roof has the low pitch usual in the county, tie-beams, and carved corbels and bosses, mainly with big heads. The structure is basically C17 but the bosses probably early C19. – REREDOS and ALTAR SURROUND of 1846. Really elaborate, with much cresting of gables and pinnacles. The corners of the sanctuary treated as seats. The PEWS of 1815 with thin Gothic arcading, including some in rising tiers at the w end of the aisles. – TILES of 1868. – FONT of terracotta, Perp style. Dated 1823. According to Wetton's Guide, by *Grimes*, 'an amateur'. – STAINED GLASS. The chancel windows are by *Morris* and *Burne-Jones*, 1879. They commemorate Adelaide Countess Spencer †1877.

Much transparent glass with dainty Gothic patterns. In the E and N windows the figures stand isolated against these patterned quarries; in the S window they have a pale brown background panel. The subject of the E window is Christ crucified, with the Virgin and St John. – S aisle SE and S of 1901 and 1909 by *Morris & Co.* (Morris and Burne-Jones were dead and the original inspiration had left the firm). – N aisle E by *Burlison & Grylls*, 1894. Two others in N aisle of 1908 and 1918 by *J. Powell & Sons*. – MONUMENTS. Several mural monuments by the *Cox* family. The earliest is a draped curtain inscription attached to a pier of the S arcade, by *Samuel Cox Sen.* (†1741). Thomas Lucas †1756. Obelisk with inscription in a medallion on it. Signed by *Henry Cox.* – Others, with and without the familiar obelisks, by *William Cox Sen.* and *Henry Cox.*

GUILSBOROUGH SCHOOL, West Haddon Road. 1955–9 by the County Architect's Department (County Architect *A. N. Harris*). Very different from the normal architectural character of mid-C20 schools in England. An oblong two-storeyed block, faced in its upper storey with stone from the demolished Guilsborough Hall,* with a tower in a notched-out corner crowned by an odd top, one-storeyed attachments for laboratories, kitchens, library etc., and with formal fenestration in pairs of upright windows. Large extension by *John Goff,* 1967–8. Three storeys, curtain walling and brown concrete panels.

GRAMMAR SCHOOL, High Street. Converted into flats in 1972. Founded by Sir John Langham of Cottesbrooke in 1668. It was a most generous foundation as C17 schools went – for fifty boys, a master, and an usher – and the building is correspondingly large. It is of ironstone, seven bays wide, with a middle porch of four storeys and to the l. of it one storey, plus another behind the dormers, and on the r. two plus one. The part to the l. of the porch was the master's house, that to the r. was the schoolroom, with bedrooms above. The windows are mullioned in the dormers, mullioned-and-transomed otherwise. The porch doorway is round-headed. The sides of the porch on the ground floor have vertically placed oval openings. The porch leads to a passage at whose end was the projecting staircase, going up square in a narrow well through all floors. Square, tapering balusters. The style of the building is decidedly conservative. No echo can yet be heard from Lamport Hall, or even semi-classical mid-century endeavours.

In the village several Late Georgian brick houses which deserve a glance, e.g. the SUN INN and RED HOUSE, facing the GREEN, both of which have the Midland motif of the middle bay being stressed by a blank giant arch. The form is best seen at Rothwell (q.v.), but it compares with work in Leicestershire. Round the corner in Nortoft Road a three-storey Victorian house with heavy stone-framed windows. Red brick with four sections of brick cogging as a diamond pattern. The central first-floor room has a balcony whose railway platform fringe acts as a

*Demolished 1959. Only its entrance gatepiers and a bit of walling survive.

canopy to the front door. Opposite on a rise a simple Victorian red brick house has an extraordinary water tower with a big octagon pattern on its side. On the Green the former LOCK-UP with part cob walling. There are other sections of cob elsewhere. In HIGH STREET, GUILSBOROUGH HOUSE, with an C18 part of two storeys and five bays with a later E addition. Just beyond the Post Office, on the l. is, set back, OLD HOUSE. The core is a red brick house of two storeys dated 1687 to which was added *c.* 1800 a wing with a bowed end. Other later extensions. On the r. the OLD MANSE. Brick, of two storeys, five bays with the centre bay recessed. Nice doorcase.

ROSE MANOR, at the NE end of the village. 1686. Of ironstone. A very handsome five-bay front of two storeys. Two-light, upright, mullioned wooden windows. Doorway broad, with a pediment. In the frieze below it the date and horizontal laurel leaves l. and r.

GUILSBOROUGH GRANGE, 1 m. NW. A house of Georgian origins but the main block is early C19, three storeys and three-bay front with larger windows in the lateral bays. Columned porch and two ground-floor bays added *c.* 1850. Stable block with turret.

HANGING HOUGHTON

SCHOOL HOUSE. Built in 1775 according to the will of Sir Edmund Isham. Seven bays, two storeys.

THE LODGE. Dated 1856.

HANNINGTON

ST PETER AND ST PAUL. A two-naved late C13 church, as such a great rarity in England, and here there was no later enlargement. But cf. Stretford in Herefordshire of the early or mid-C13, Wootton Bassett, Wiltshire, also C13, and Caythorpe, Lincolnshire, early C14. On the Continent occasional examples can be found in Germany (St Nicholas Soest, St Eucharius Nuremberg), and the Blackfriars had not infrequently adopted the two-naved plan (e.g. Paris, Toulouse, Frankfurt, Pirna) which may derive from monastic rather than church buildings. At Hannington, which at the time was in the gift of Sempringham, the Gilbertine mother house, the two-naved plan is specially interestingly handled. There are two tall circular piers with circular abaci and double-chamfered arches. The E arch runs against the wall above the chancel arch, the W arch against the projection in the W wall which corresponds to the slender W tower. When this received its bell-openings the Dec style had arrived. The tower is overlapped by the aisles and its W doorway forms an impressive portal. The windows of the rest of the church have consistently intersected tracery, i.e. on the N and s sides and in the chancel, except at the w ends of the aisles where there are C13 lancets. The SEDILIA in the chancel have dogtooth decoration and there are lowside windows on each side. Only the s doorway with its round arch with two slight chamfers and its simple foliate capitals is evidence of a predecessor of the present church. It must be of *c.* 1180–90. The church was restored by *Slater & Carpenter* 1868–9. – PULPIT and SCREEN. Perp, with the same dainty tracery. Probably by the same carver. – PRAYER DESK. Two C15 poppyhead pewends. – The STALLS continue the theme but they are Victorian. – The EAGLE LECTERN is also of the same period, but rather fine. – TILES. In the chancel, also Victorian and by *Mintons*, some with *Pugin* designs. The nave tiles look earlier, early C19? – STAINED GLASS. Chancel E, 1890, possibly *A. Gibbs.*

HANNINGTON HOUSE, the former rectory. 1867–8, by *E. F. Law.* Former SCHOOL and SCHOOL HOUSE, School Lane, 1870–1, also by *Law.* Stone building, altered but still with bellcote.

HARDWICK

8060

ST LEONARD. Unbuttressed C13 w tower. Lancet in the w wall. Two-light bell-openings with double lancets under a single head enclosing a carved quatrefoil. Battlements. C13 also the s arcade of four bays. Circular piers, circular abaci, double-chamfered arches. C13 the original chancel too, see the lowside lancet, the priest's doorway and the chancel arch. Dec windows (mostly renewed), also in the clerestory. The s aisle and the porch are by *Slater & Carpenter*, 1867. The aisle had been removed in 1795. – FONT. Looks C13. – PULPIT. 1860s, of Derbyshire spa, not alabaster, with mosaic panels. – Painted REREDOS and *Minton* TILES also 1860s. – ROYAL ARMS. Painted, Late Stuart. – STAINED GLASS. In the lowside window, St John the Baptist, a damaged figure, *c.* 1280–1310. – Some nice 1860s grisaille type windows. – MONUMENT. Francis Nicholls †1604 and a later inscription for Sir Francis †1642. Slate panel with kneeling figures in an alabaster surround. Attributed to *Francis Griggs* (GF).

MANOR HOUSE, s of the church. In the NE gable a two-light C14 window. In the s and E gables a Jacobean bow window, shallow and heavily detailed. The top floor of the s bay recedes slightly. Inside a late C16 wooden overmantel with Ionic pilasters and painted shields for the Nicholls family. The elements of the C14 hall survive, including some roof timbers, but it was subdivided probably during the time of Francis Nicholls (1557–1604). The last Nicholls to live there was Sir Edward †1717 and parts of the house were subsequently demolished. A carved stone inscription says: 'Restored 1775. Repaired 1887.'

SCHOOL and SCHOOL HOUSE, N of the church. 1870 by *E. F. Law.* Ironstone. The school with Gothic s gable and bellcote, the house more Tudorish.

Former RECTORY, NE of the church. 1867–8, Gothic manner, red and blue brick decoration.

0070

HARGRAVE

ALL HALLOWS. The bones of the building are early C13 but the appearance of the church, certainly internally, owes as much to the restoration of 1868–70 conducted by the rector, the Rev. *Robert Sibley Baker*, himself a talented carver, and his architect brother, *William Lewis Baker*, as it does to the medieval period. The doorways are the clearest survivals. The finest is the S doorway, shafted prettily with one order in front of two others, and with half-dogtooth, dogtooth, and heavy horizontal chevrons in two orders in the arch. The hoodmould rests on twisted corbels. To this can be added the N doorway and the chancel S doorway. Then the arcades with original round columns and bases, but the rest rebuilt in the C14 with octagonal piers. Double-chamfered arches. The C13 E responds run together with the chancel arch. In the chancel a low arched tomb-recess and a squint to the N transept. On the N side of the nave is a shallow transept with a large Perp window similar to those in the chancel. Some of the other windows are also C13, e.g. N aisle W, S aisle E, and one S. The S aisle is very narrow. The tower and spire were totally rebuilt with a larger S stair-turret 1868–70.* It has an excessively tall lancet window, two-light shafted bell-openings, and a broach spire with two tiers of lucarnes in the cardinal directions and the third in the diagonals. The S porch likewise is *c.* 1870 and is a memorial to the Rev. William Lake Baker †1865, father of the Rev. R. S. Baker, who executed all the lettering here (*see also* below). – FONT. Octagonal, probably C13, with small faces on two sides. Its tall pedestal later, perhaps C17. – SCREEN. Perp, one-light divisions. Colour restored *c.* 1870 based on remnants found. – BENCHES, early C16, with tracery on the ends and the fronts and backs of whole blocks. Linenfold panelling on some ends. – POOR BOX. Of pillar form, inscribed and dated 1597. – WALL PAINTING. A dark and badly faded St Christopher on the N wall of the nave. – TILES (N aisle behind the pulpit steps). Early medieval with incised patterns. Also a nice display of Victorian tiles. – ROYAL ARMS. Charles II repainted by *S. Turner* of Market Harborough in 1776. – The CHANCEL FURNISHINGS are largely due to the *Bakers*. The CHOIR STALLS were devised by them and both the REREDOS and the ALTAR TABLE (made up from some mid-C17 pieces, turned legs and Jacobean frieze pieces) have carving by the rector. The lettering around the altar step is also by him. – STAINED GLASS. Nave. C14 and C15

---

*A watercolour in the church shows the building in the course of restoration and there is nothing standing beyond the W end of the nave.

fragments. – Chancel E window of 1883, a memorial to Baker's mother, and S aisle E of 1879, both by *A. O. Hemming*. – MONU-MENTS. Lettered slabs in the sanctuary to the Baker family including the architect W. L. Baker (†1908). – In the church-yard, behind the N aisle a large Roman COFFIN discovered 1893 by the Rev. R. S. Baker, a keen antiquarian, whose grave (†1897) is alongside.

CHURCHLANDS (former rectory), w of the church. Early C17 front with central porch projection. Mullioned windows with hoodmoulds. Exposed timber-framed wing at rear. Earlier roof timbers.

VILLAGE HALL (former school). 1856–7 by *W. L. Baker*. Pat-terned brick, mainly red but lines with yellow, blue etc.

Former NAG'S HEAD pub. Picturesque long thatched cottage, partly of cob. C17 to C18 with C19 additions. Impressive addi-tions behind of 2005 by *Toby Pateman* of Wellingborough with a large thatched barn-like wing and a linking canopied passage.

HARGRAVE HALL. 1903 by *W. L. Baker* for himself, then already in his eighties. Red brick with a central tower with Baker's initials in a panel over the entrance. Dutch gable at the S end and the style broadly *c.* 1700. When Baker died in 1908, the house was bought by Charles Kenneth Murchison (later Sir Kenneth Murchison, M.P.) and his wife, Evelyn, a relative of the Bakers. In 1913 Evelyn, who had some artistic talent, designed a wing at the rear to contain her husband's library, built in 1914 by *Charles Pettit* of Thrapston. It is in the same style as the main house. Minor alterations since.*

HARLESTONE

In two parts, Lower Harlestone on the main road (A428) but Upper Harlestone, confusingly, about a mile to the S in a valley. Both are full of good golden ironstone cottages and houses, not surprising since this was quarried from medieval times and between the two villages the hills and hollows of stone working are evident. The Harlestone Estate, owned by the Andrew family since 1530, was acquired by the Althorp Estate in 1831.

ST ANDREW. The church is all Dec – with the exception of the w tower, the Late Perp clerestory and the E window, which is in the style of 1275 and was designed by *G. G. Scott*, who restored the church in 1853. The tower is largely C13 with a single lancet in its W wall. It is unbuttressed. The bell-openings are two pointed-trefoiled arches under one arch. Henry de Bray records in fact the purchase of the bell-rope in 1294. The tower arch is quadruple-chamfered and above it is an opening which gives access onto a C17 balcony, thence to the roofs of

*Information from Mr & Mrs Brotherton.

the aisles. Above this is the clear roof-line of the early church.
The Dec work has the privilege, rare in parish churches, of
being dateable. In his estate book, Henry de Bray, who owned
the manor in the early C14, writes: 'Magister Ricardus de Het
[the rector] ipse de novo fecit cancellam A.D. 1320.' He adds
that 'tota ecclesia facta fuit', A.D. 1325, he himself providing
the stone and timber and *Johannes Dyve* the carpenter's work.
The aisles with their windows with reticulated tracery slightly
overlap the chancel at their E ends. The chancel has two transomed lowside lancets, that on the N better preserved. Internally all the chancel windows have side-shafts, their tracery
dating from 1853. Internal walls are also ashlar rather than
rough masonry, and there is a continuous sill moulding running
around the building. Dec the tall S doorway with its continuous
mouldings and the reticulated tracery of the S windows, Dec
the more restored N windows, and also the N doorway. SEDILIA
with cusped arches and crocketed gables, linked to a PISCINA
in the SE angle, which rests on a big head corbel. Arcades of
two bays with octagonal piers and double-hollow-chamfered
arches. The responds are concave-sided (cf. Great Brington).
Below the chancel a CRYPT of two bays with chamfered ribs
in the vault. Further restoration by *E. F. Law* in 1883 with the
organ loft of 1888. – FONT. Circular, plain, but from the foot
project four heads, probably early C13. – PULPIT. Made in 1891
by *Edmund Law*, incorporating some fine Flemish panels of
c. 1500. – COMMUNION RAIL. Mid-C17, with vertically symmetrical balusters. – ALTAR, REREDOS and CHAIR, 1938 by
Caroe & Passmore. – Two HATCHMENTS for the Andrew family
1807 and 1832. – STAINED GLASS. Chancel E window by *Burlison & Grylls*, 1897. – Other chancel windows by *Ward &
Hughes*. – N aisle E, Faith, Hope and Charity, by *J. Powell &
Sons*, 1896. – S aisle W of 1903 by *H. A. Hymers*. The tower
window of 1897 is also his. – MONUMENTS. (N aisle window
sill) Portrait bust of a man with flowing hair, part of a lost
memorial to Robert Andrew †1667, recorded by Baker.
Attributed to *Jasper Latham* (GF). – Many tablets, including
Sir Salathiel Lovell †1713 by *Edward Stanton*, with Ionic
columns and an urn. – Robert Andrew †1739, coloured marble,
probably by *Smith* of Warwick (*see* Lamport). – Lady Lovell
†1718 with Corinthian pilasters and baldacchino probably also
by *Stanton*, and Maria Townsend †1743, a copy of the former
monument.

The churchyard has a good assembly of stones and tombs.
By the path to the porch some stones for the Lumley family,
several of whom were masons, and some of their stones have
the masons' arms (three castles and a chevron), for example
Tubalcain Lumley †1729. *John Lumley*, the C18 Northampton
architect, was from this family. An elaborate Gothic tomb SE
of the chancel for the Wright family, 1869, with extraordinary
lettering.

Former RECTORY. Of *c.* 1700 but largely rebuilt 1812. Two gabled
parts and a slightly recessed centre. Quoins. Finely framed

Harlestone House.
Drawing by G. Clarke, *c.* 1850

doorway. The window above it connected with it and distinguished by leaf volutes. Small stable block, half-H-shaped with
a central low tower with pyramidal roof, now converted into a
house, as are other outbuildings.

HARLESTONE HOUSE is one candidate for Jane Austen's Mansfield Park. The house, demolished in 1939, was almost certainly
originally built to designs by *Francis Smith* of Warwick, hence
the Andrew monument in the church. At its demolition, a
carved board dated 1728 was found. The big Palladian STABLES
remain, just above the church. They were designed 1808–11 by
Humphry and *John Adey Repton*, who also altered the house.
The grounds are indeed referred to in Humphry Repton's
Fragments of 1816. The lake and a bridge survive but the rest
has been turned into a golf course. The CLUBHOUSE (1990,
Peter Haddon & Partners) stands on the platform of the house.
The stables have the familiar quadrangle with corner pavilions
with pyramid roofs (cf. e.g. Courteenhall). Impressive entrance
archway with Tuscan columns and a pediment. Restored and
partly converted into residential by *Colin Clayson*, 1990s, with
Peter Haddon & Partners.

SCHOOL, near the church. 1885 by *George Devey*. It was burnt
down in 1978 but rebuilt exactly. Later extensions including
1911 by *Law & Harris*. Also some good stone COTTAGES with
thatched roofs, partly C17 but considerably rebuilt. The half-
timbered gable *c.* 1880, when *Devey & Williams* were working
for the Althorp Estate.

In LOWER HARLESTONE, on the main road five pairs of ESTATE
COTTAGES, built 1844–51 after a design by *Edward Blore* and
bearing date plaques of a type found on many cottages built
by the estate. Opposite, the former entrance to Harlestone

House and tucked inside the gateway a tiny rustic LODGE, with apsidal end with tree-trunk pillars. It was once thatched but is now tiled. A remnant of the Repton landscaping. Lower down is the FOX AND HOUNDS, Late Georgian, five bays. The OLD MALTING HOUSE opposite was converted from outbuildings in 1972. A little further on the l. a short lane with an early C19 three-storey row fronted in mottled brick. Lower still, THE OLD HOUSE, also Late Georgian, with two painted sundials. A little further on the s side a monumental stone HORSE TROUGH erected in 1904 as a memorial to Charlotte Countess Spencer (†1903) for 'God's dumb creatures' as the inscription states.

UPPER HARLESTONE has an intricate pattern of roads and lanes. Everywhere delightful ironstone houses and cottages, many thatched and many with signs of earlier periods such as mullioned windows, but also showing much evidence of C19 tidying. At the centre is the weatherboarded VILLAGE INSTITUTE of 1924 designed by *Austin Durst*. Nearby is GRAFTON HOUSE, L-shaped with cross mullion-transom windows, early C18. Elsewhere will be found: two rows of houses of note in a lane at the E end of the village off Port Road, Nos. 76–83 a red and blue brick row of 1872, and on another lane three pairs of Swedish design weatherboarded houses of 1949 and alongside the former BAPTIST CHAPEL of 1873–4 by *J. Ingman* converted into a house in 1950. At the W end of the village on Port Road are PARK FARM HOUSE, of five bays and two storeys, ironstone with quoins, C18 and just beyond to the W the former DOVECOTE LAUNDRY, with a dovecote in front, probably of the C15. Circular, of two stages separated by a bold string-course. Conical roof.

HARPOLE

ALL SAINTS. Norman the s doorway (decorated imposts and capitals, single-step arch), the s chancel doorway (waterleaf capitals, single-step arch), and the chancel arch (scalloped capitals). Of *c.* 1200 the N doorway (moulded capitals, pointed arch with one step and one slight chamfer) and the N aisle W lancet. Of the C13 the W tower (quadruple-chamfered arch on the W front above the doorway three blank arches, bell-openings of two lancets, corbel table, later battlements and pinnacles), the chancel arch and the N chapel. The N chapel arches each with grimacing head corbels. In this twin tomb-recesses with pretty leaf capitals of *c.* 1300. Dec arcades of three wide bays, short octagonal piers, double-chamfered arches. The detail of the N arcade of three bays is more primitive. The s arcade of four bays has different, harder stone for capitals, which are more carefully moulded. Perp chancel windows. Restorations are recorded in 1867 by *E. F. Law* and

1903–8 by *Matthew Holding*, which included reseating. – ALTAR
SLAB. Mounted on plinth on N side of sanctuary. – ALTAR
RAILS. Portions of early C18 rails in S aisle. – DOOR. C12
perhaps, studded (from priest's doorway), mounted in S aisle
with sections of C17 beams. – FONT. Norman, circular, very
closely entwined leaf trails and dragons; a remarkable tangle.
– STAINED GLASS. Chancel E, fine, 1905 by *H. A. Hymers*. –
Chancel SE 1895 by *J. Hardman & Co.* – Chancel SW 1870 by
C. A. Gibbs. – S aisle S 1870 also by *Gibbs*. – N aisle, 1905 by
Hymers.

HARPOLE HALL. Early C19 with massive Doric porch.

Former SCHOOL (now village hall), School Lane. 1835 of ironstone with brick addition of 1916 by *Law & Harris*.

HOUSES. At the SE end of the village a sequence of good houses.
One (No. 35) has a porch on primitive pillars. Mullioned
windows are continued into the C18; but a house of 1731 has
them no longer.

ROMAN REMAINS. *See* Introduction.

HARRINGTON

ST PETER AND ST PAUL. At the E end of the village in a tree-
embowered churchyard full of wild flowers. Impressive, light
and airy interior. The building dates from the C13, though there
is little evidence now save possibly the bases of the nave
arcades, the narrowness of the aisles and the transeptal plan,
which probably originated then. The external W elevation has
lines of earlier roofs, again probably of this time. There was a
substantial rebuilding in the C14. Arcades of four bays. Quatrefoil piers, the foils connected in a single curve by a deep hollow.
At the W corner of the transept sexfoil piers instead. The
quatrefoil piers have fine capitals with big leaves, standing or
lying, unusual in Northamptonshire. The W responds have oak
on the S and vine leaves on the N. The sexfoiled piers have
moulded capitals instead. The arcade arches have two hollow
chamfers, and the chancel and transept arches the same, the
latter running into the walls on the E side without responds.
All this fits a date of *c.* 1300–50. The W walls of the transepts
were partly caught on corbels when the aisles were built. The
N corbel is of simple but playful shape. The transept W walls
do not quite line up with the nave arcade, again suggesting an
early origin for the plan. Major refenestration took place in the
early C16, and while the style is basically Perp, changes in
design suggest a late date, say, *c.* 1530–40. Windows are largely
of three lights, the earliest with cusped heads, then some
without cusps, slightly later perhaps. Externally parts of the
ironstone walling were refaced with limestone ashlar at the
same time. Nice N doorway of the chancel of the same period,
four-centred arch with beautifully carved foliage spandrels,

though one side broken. Internally in the N transept a stair-turret for the rood loft, also entered by a four-centred arched doorway. Attached to the S transept is a tower of 1809 with round-arched bell-openings, all in grey ashlar. It replaced an earlier tower which collapsed in 1802. It is rather a bald piece of work and architecturally, compared with the rest of the church, a bit of a let-down. – SCREEN. Also early C16. Tall, of two-light divisions, each with a middle mullion reaching up into the apex of the arch. Much fine tracery with pinnacles and crocketing. – PEWS and STALLS. Victorian but their fronts have pieces of Perp tracery. They may well date from 1859 when some work was done by *E. F. Law.* – TILES. In the chancel of the C14 to C16. – VAMPING HORN, C17 or C18 (cf. Braybrooke). 5 ft (1.52 metres) long. – MONUMENTS. Laurence Saunders †1545. Grey Purbeck marble. Tomb-chest with three shields in lozenges, which housed brasses. The arch of the recess almost a lintel, jambs and soffit panelled. Back wall with kneeling brass figures, 15 in. (38 cm.) tall. – Saunders monument, dated 1588, confidently attributed to *Garrett Hollemans.** Of very fine quality. The family in relief is represented kneeling on two panels facing each other. Two allegorical figures called Spes and Fides in shallow niches to the l. and r. Fine scroll foliage frieze at the top. Very little strapwork is used. There is only a verse inscription but the monument is almost certainly for Sir Edward Saunders †1576 and his two wives, the second of whom died in 1588. – Rev. William Wilson †1831, a simple white marble plaque by *Peter Hollins* of Birmingham.

THE FALLS, High Street. The terraces of the gardens of Har-rington Manor House, originally with the house (dem. 1740) at the base in the valley and five majestic terraces descending the slope. The name may derive from the water cascade which flowed from a pool on the top terrace. There is evidence of other pools on other terraces. On the E side of the garden a walk where tree-root holes are still apparent. The exact date of the gardens is unclear. The house derived from a preceptory of the Hospitallers of St John, which after the Dissolution came into the ownership of the Saunders family. In 1582 the estate was acquired by the Stanhope family, and then in 1675 it passed by marriage to Lionel Tollemache, 3rd Earl of Dysart. Bridges attributes the gardens to him, but Tim Mowl has sug-gested they could be earlier and from the Stanhope period, that is 1620–75. The platform of the house is clear. In its way as remarkable a survival as the garden layout at Lyveden.

THORPE UNDERWOOD HOUSE, 1 m. NE. A grand villa built *c.* 1850–60. Golden local ironstone with lighter dressings. Tall round-arched windows on the ground floor, quoins, porch and strange chimneys with gabled hats. Much more what one might expect in a town rather than in a remote hamlet. It seems to have been built for Mary Hall, daughter of the Rev. John Keene Hall (†1829), a Baptist minister who succeeded Andrew

---

*Pevsner in 1961 said 'Not in its original state', but there is no reason to think it has been altered (cf. similar monuments at Nether Heyford and Charwelton).

Fuller in Kettering. Her mother was a Fry from Bristol and the house would not look out of place on the Downs at Clifton.

HARRINGWORTH   *9090*

ST JOHN BAPTIST. The W tower must have been begun before 1200 – see the waterleaf capitals and the pointed arch with two steps and one chamfer towards the nave. It is of limestone and ironstone mixed. Clasping buttresses, lancets below, twin bell-openings of two lights separated by a shaft. Spire with low broaches. Big heads above the broaches. Three tiers of lucarnes. They look early C14. A change in masonry at the base shows the division of the rebuilding. Wide nave and chancel. The chancel arch and doorway are of *c.* 1300, but the rest of the chancel is Perp. Big five-light E window and buttresses with big creatures perched on top. Early C14 S aisle, S porch, and N aisle and arcades. The S aisle especially fine, in ashlar, with gabled but-tresses. The windows range from two lights with a circle, spherical triangle or pointed quatrefoil to reticulated tracery. The entrance to the S porch a resited C13 doorway of ironstone with dogtooth. The S doorway also early C14, but partly blocked when a smaller C16 Tudor type doorway was set in, with big leaves in the spandrels. Handsome early C14 N doorway with shafting inside as well as outside. The nave is wide, and the C14 four-bay arcades have low octagonal piers and double-cham-fered arches. Finely moulded arched Dec SEDILIA and PISCINA in the S aisle below a straight-headed Dec window. A range of clerestory windows of C15 or early C16 date. A restoration is recorded in 1891 by *H. M. Townsend & F. C. Tomlinson* of Peterborough. – FONT. Square, with two shallow ogee arches on each side, *c.* 1300. – PULPIT. Dated 1605, of the usual type with broad blank arches in the panels. Brought from Bar-rowden, Rutland. – SCREENS. Perp, tall, with one-light divi-sions and ribbed coving. Traces of colour. – An C18 screen with baluster rail for the vestry in the N aisle. – PANELLING. Some of Jacobean date. – Iron circular CHANDELIERS of an attractive design of *c.* 1990. – BENCH-ENDS. Some square-headed Perp bench-ends with tracery, loose. – Former early C18 ALTAR RAILS in the S aisle. – HELMET. In the N aisle. From the monu-ment to Lord George Zouche †1569 in the former family chapel between church and manor house. – STAINED GLASS. Chancel. C14 fragments and C15 angel's head. – Chancel E (1919) and S aisle E, both by *Burlison & Grylls*. – MONUMENTS. In the N aisle, sunk by some steps, the family vault of the Tryons, the platform on top raised by four steps. The vault was built *c.* 1650. Excellent wrought-iron RAILINGS screening off the vault. Standards with elaborate finials and spiral twists, *c.* 1700. One hanging monument to four generations of Tryons, probably *c.* 1710. Two standing cherubs, two cherubs' heads at the foot. Garlands and a shield at the top. Attributed to *William Stanton*.

MANOR HOUSE, N of the White Swan Inn and S of the church. Handsome late C17, five bays, two storeys, cross-windows, hipped roof, flat quoins, rusticated door surround. Coarsed rubble walls with quoins and dressings of limestone. Original staircase with turned balusters. Nice run of Victorian cast-iron rails. No. 25 Station Road, W of the church, a simple thatched cottage, has the remains of a C13 hermitage with its cross wall still holding the moulded chancel arch and just a few remains of early stonework in the side walls of the E portion.

On the corner of Seaton Road, the WHITE SWAN INN. Early C16 but much renewed. Its main façade with a central gable and an original four-light mullioned window. Otherwise rebuilt in C19. Tudor style windows with arched lights. Mark of a former central doorway. To the r. a blocked two-centred archway. A long cottage forms its r. extension. At the junction of the Gretton and Wakerley roads, a VILLAGE CROSS. Possibly erected in 1387. Shaft of eight clustered shafts of alternating girth. Capital and square abacus. The top of 1837. On one side, CROSS FARM, mid-C19 of three bays; Tudor style windows and a pedimented porch. Its ironstone end gable reveals it is a refronting of an older structure. Opposite, THE OLD SMITHY. Cottage, with a C14 or C15 chimney in the form of an arcaded pyramid. OLD MANOR HOUSE, NE of the church. Of the much larger medieval manor house of the Zouches, there survives on the first floor of the S range one two-light window with cusped ogee heads. Behind is a shorter parallel range with mullioned windows. C17 staircase inside. Further E along Wakerley Road, several pleasant houses, notably LIMES FARMHOUSE, late C17 of three bays of ashlar with three-light mullioned windows on each floor. The rear elevation also with mullions.

WELLAND VIADUCT, W of the village and dominating the countryside. Built for the Midland Railway, Kettering to Manton line, 1874–9 by *John Underwood*. Blue brick, of eighty-two arches, about 1,275 yds (1,166 metres) long, the longest on Britain's railways. It rises to some 60 ft (18 metres).

HARRINGWORTH LODGE, 1 m. S on the W side of the road to Deene. In the centre of a former medieval deer park. It dates from the Zouche period, that is the C15. One window of that time exists now as an internal feature. Upper floors of the main range were timber-framed. Extended and refaced in the early C17 and further added to in the C19.

HARTWELL

ST JOHN THE BAPTIST. The medieval chapel was about 1 m. SW on what is now a deserted village site. Because the village had moved to what was then Hartwell Green the present building was built 1851 by *Charles Vickers* of *Vickers & Hugall*. Very simple but extremely neat. Neo-Norman nave and bellcote with a lower Neo-E.E. chancel. Ornately carved s doorway in a slightly projecting gabled portal. The arcade inside is original work of the latest C12 from the old building. Four bays. Circular piers, square abaci. Capitals with leaves and dragons, stiff-leaf crockets, and less foliate crockets. Unmoulded round arches. Very much what is described as Transitional. The Victorian chancel interior is more elaborate E.E. style with dogtooth string course and a charming triple arcade in its N wall leading into the stone pulpit, which has foliage carvings on its tapered base. – FONT. 1851 with E.E. arcading. – REREDOS. N aisle. Gothic surround and a splendid painting of Christ resurrected by *E. W. Twining*, 1912. Twining lived in the thatched cottage just s of the church. – STAINED GLASS. E window centre by *F. C. Eden*, 1937, the sidelights of 1953 by *Geoffrey Webb*. w window of 1946 by *J. Powell & Sons*.

OLD MANOR, No. 38 Forest Road. Dated 1681. Heavy mullioned windows with hoodmoulds and pulvinated frieze, all renewed.

HASELBECH

ST MICHAEL. The w tower is Perp and probably quite late, say *c.* 1500 (cf. Arthingworth and Desborough). It has pairs of two-light bell-openings with an ogee super-arch. Quatrefoil frieze, battlements, of the pinnacles only the stumps. Most windows are C19 but the w windows of the aisles seem original C13 work. The arcades inside are low, of three bays. They both have quatrefoil piers, but the N arcade, where the four foils are more like independent shafts, is C13, the s arcade C14. The capitals are not consistent. Both arcades have double-chamfered arches. The eastern parts are all C19. The church restored and the N aisle rebuilt by *W. Slater*,* 1859–60, and the chancel further elaborated by *F. Butler*, 1881. Very ornate French Gothic decoration. The exquisite carving of all the details, with stiff-leaf, animals, birds and portrait heads, was done by *J. Forsyth*, at the expense of Elizabeth Pym, and is well worth examining. The doorway into the s chapel, for example, has all sorts of creatures appearing within its foliage trails. The carving of the capitals of the sanctuary arcades is beautifully done, as are the ornaments between the arches. Equally ornate s chapel. With arms surrounded by Gothic ornament in the gable outside and a SE entrance. N chapel 1872 by *Salvin*, built for *Viscountess Milton*, who painted the windows herself. They are rather poor quality and somewhat faded, which is odd since they are recorded as being made by *Heaton, Butler & Bayne*. – PULPIT. Late Elizabethan and Jacobean, complete with back

* William Slater was born in Haselbech and is buried here, which accounts for why he was employed so much locally.

panel and tester. – BENCH-ENDS (at the front of the nave). Perp. With two tracery panels to each end and framing buttresses. – TOWER SCREEN. Elaborate; Continental Gothic at the top and linenfold at the base. It was erected as a memorial to C. Bower Ismay †1924. – CHANCEL GATE. Tall. Of wrought iron, early C18 and probably by *Thomas Warren*. It was given to the church by William Wykes (*see* below). It has been adjusted in more recent times with open panels at each side. – STAINED GLASS. E window by *Alan Younger*, 1966. A memorial for Mrs Ismay. – MONUMENTS. Several by *John Hunt* of Northampton including that for William Wykes †1721 (to r. of S doorway), which records in Latin his donations to the church (in translation: By his dutiful goodwill this sanctuary was beautifully endowed with work wrought in wood, and skilfully adorned with iron gates). – George Ashby †1802. By *Benjamin Button*. Also by him Mary Alcock †1798. Pretty with black border ad gold ornamentation. – Albert Pell †1907 (S aisle). A Gothic alabaster inscription with delightful ironwork at the base of a spider in his web. – Charles Bower Ismay †1924. A plaque in the S aisle, partly ceramic, part mosaic. – His grave in the churchyard, N of the tower. A remarkable memorial. Block-like sarcophagus with an incised frieze of animals, rather Egyptian in inspiration. By *A. H. Gerrard*, 1926.

HASELBECH HALL. N front of three bays and three storeys, with Jacobean gables and a projecting two-storey central porch. The original house was built just before 1678 by *Henry Jones* for Randolph Wykes, but the present building is the result of alterations made in 1855–6 for Lady Milton by *Ambrose Poynter* when it was turned Jacobean with Northamptonshire gables. Gutted by fire in 1917, and rebuilt for Captain Bower Ismay by *G. Crawley*. E side pulled down in the 1960s. STABLES, E of the house. Of 1856. *Henry Goddard* of Leicester, Poynter's builder, seems to have been largely responsible. Brown stone with brick facings (converted into a house in 1971). In the same style as the SCHOOL in the village, built by Viscountess Milton in 1872, which may well also be by *Goddard*. Converted into a house in 1999.

ESTATE COTTAGES opposite the Hall. Tudor manner with latticed glazing, 1853. On the road to Naseby, past the school, some other cottages, originally red brick with blue brick patterns, 1861, but refronted in a Neo-Georgian style in 1920.

HASELBECH HILL, ½ m. S. In its own grounds. Built 1908 in a C17 manner. Of two storeys, ironstone, with two castellated bays and a central gable. Mullioned windows.

HELLIDON

ST JOHN BAPTIST. Dec, but much redone by *Butterfield* in 1846–7. N aisle added by him in 1867–8, the organ chamber and vestry in 1897 by *Matthew Holding*. Somewhat severe interior, largely because of the odd N arcade. The piers are square with a slight chamfer, and the chamfered arches die into them. It looks more like late C19 than mid. The W tower is C13 in origin with a Dec upper stage. Very curious S doorway, clearly dated 1591 but looking earlier in its heavily moulded arch. Perhaps a recutting? – REREDOS and TILES. From the 1867–8 Butterfield era. Gabled centrepiece with simple inlay. The wall tiles form a mass of chevrons. The STALLS, with fleur-de-lys poppyheads, are also his. – STAINED GLASS. Chancel E of 1863 by *F. Preedy*. – Chancel S, two windows of 1880 by *A. Gibbs*. – S aisle window of 1919–20 by *Daniels & Fricker*. – S aisle window of 1922, unidentified. – Tower window by *A. Gibbs*, 1860s. – MONUMENT. Rev. C. S. Holthouse †1881, who commissioned Butterfield. Just a shaped plaque with edging.

THE GRANGE, S end of the village. The former parsonage by *Butterfield*, 1852, and a school wing added by him in 1867. A rather extraordinary house. Basically L-shaped. The street view is into the angle of the L. The house, a big gabled wing on the l., vaguely Gothic, and the lower school wing on the r. also gabled but this time with half-timbering. A large Gothic gable in the corner lights a large gallery type room, designed as the schoolroom, accessed by an outside staircase into the tall timbered gable on the r. The garden front on the E side is more orthodox but equally variable. Two projecting wings from the main house of stone, one with canted bay and the other a flat gabled wing with a half-timbered top. Many original interior features such as panelling etc. The gallery has a typical Butterfield fireplace with inlaid circles and a striped fireplace surround.

LATCHETTS (HELLIDON HOUSE), E of the church. Late C18 front of five bays. Porch of pairs of unfluted Doric columns. In the S gable a mullioned window.

WINDMILL, ½ m. SE. Red brick tower mill built 1842, three storeys. Converted into a residence in 1975 and given an aluminium cap.

HELMDON

ST MARY MAGDALENE. W tower rebuilt in 1823. Dec chancel, long and tall. The E window earlier than the rest with intersecting tracery, while the rest have reticulated tracery, all ogee-capped externally. Lowside windows to the S and N. SEDILIA and PISCINA with leaf capitals and crocketed ogee arches. Shafts with fillets. N doorway with ogee top, aumbry with ogee top. Nave arcades of standard elements. Three bays, octagonal piers, double-chamfered arches. The details vary. The N arcade is taller. In the S wall a tomb-recess with a Purbeck coffin-lid.

A trefoil-headed PISCINA in the external N wall of the chancel, partly covered by the N aisle wall, suggests an earlier N chapel. There was a general restoration by *E. F. Law & Son*, 1875–6. – In the sanctuary the BRESSUMER of a wooden fireplace with a carved dragon, a date 1533 (or 1535), and initials, removed from the rectory. – REREDOS, 1882, with four painted panels of angels. – STAINED GLASS. Original fragments in the heads of the Y-tracery including an early C14 stonemason donor figure, William Campion, in the N aisle dateable to 1313 (restored 1976–7 but the original leading preserved). A Lancaster shield is the same date. Otherwise there are parts of borders and a roundel with a leaf design, all C14. – Chancel E window, Wonnacott memorial 1917, fine but unidentified.

HELMDON HOUSE (former rectory). A heavy stone house of 1856–8 by *Manners & Gill* of Bath. Why did the commission for a relatively plain house go all the way to Bath?

PRIMARY SCHOOL, Station Road. 1852–3 by *Connell & Gill*. Chequer brick but considerably altered. Additions of 1900 and later.

READING ROOM. A Farebrother memorial built 1887 in the Tudor style, by *James Brown* of Wappenham. Big wing with a four-light mullion-transom window. Inscription panel above.

The Helmdon quarries, largely N of the village, produced some of the county's finest building stones in the C17 and C18, famously for Easton Neston House and considerable amounts at Stowe. There are rather fewer good stone houses than one might expect in a quarrying village.

OLD CROSS, Cross Lane. A former inn, with C17 mullions and a doorcase with moulded surround and Doric columns.

HEMINGTON

ST PETER AND ST PAUL, ½ m. S of village. Late Perp (that is C16) W tower with the Montagu arms over the doorway. The rest was 1667, but was entirely Gothicized in the Decorated style in 1873 by *Carpenter & Ingelow*. Just a nave and chancel. – REREDOS. Triple-arched with foliage carvings and painted panels of the Crucifixion. – FONT. Square, with chamfered corners. On the chamfers four faces. Short circular foot with nailhead, like a section from a pier; C13. – STALLS. From Fotheringhay College, so mid-C15. With splendid ends, their tops forming a swan's-neck curve. Tracery and leaves below on the ends. Misericords including the hawk in fetterlock (the device of Edward IV), a publican with a jug, a mermaid, an owl, a tumbler. – PULPIT. Incorporating fragments from a screen. – STAINED GLASS. E window by *Heaton, Butler & Bayne*, 1873. – BRASS. Thomas Montagu †1517 and wife. The figures 18 in. (46 cm.) long (in front of the pulpit).

HEMINGTON MANOR, s of the church. Former vicarage, built 1849 at the expense of the 5th Duke of Buccleuch. Tudor brick and stone.

In the village some mid-C19 ESTATE COTTAGES in yellow and red brick with patterns.

MANOR HOUSE, on the village's E edge. Late Elizabethan. One wing of a larger mansion. Gable, mullioned-and-transomed windows. An elaborate carved stone chimneypiece attributed to the *Thorpes* of Kingscliffe is now in the Drawing Room at Boughton House (q.v.).

HIGHAM FERRERS

9060

One of the most rewarding places in the county with a good assembly of interesting buildings, several surviving from medieval times. Higham Ferrers Castle stood N of the church but only a few embankments survive. It was built in the late C11 by a Peverel, then came into the hands of the Ferrers, and in 1266 was granted by Henry III to his son Edmund Crouchback, Earl of Lancaster. The castle, town and manor remained with the Lancasters and shared their vicissitudes, until under Henry IV, son of John of Gaunt, Duke of Lancaster, they went to the Crown. Higham Ferrers is still part of the Duchy of Lancaster. While this connection with the house of Lancaster accounts for the early greatness of Higham Ferrers, its later architectural achievements are connected with Archbishop Chichele, who was born at Higham Ferrers about 1362. He founded a college in 1422, and built a bede house in 1423; a school is also attributed to him. The college was for a master, seven chaplains, four clerks and six choristers. Two of the chaplains or clerks were to teach grammar and singing.

ST MARY. A very grand and interesting church, spacious with its two naves and dominant with its superb spire. Two periods chiefly contributed, the C13 – *c.* 1220–80 – and the second quarter of the C14. Rebuilding apparently began at the E end, but of the C13 chancel there is no more evidence than the nook-shafts of the E window and the priest's doorway. The s arcade is mid-C13, of four bays, with ironstone detail, quatrefoil piers and double-chamfered arches. The s doorway has four orders of colonnettes, the capitals with upright leaves, the arch containing two hollow chamfers. The W tower followed. However, as it stands it little resembles what was originally built. In 1631 the spire and a good deal of the tower collapsed. A local mason, *Richard Atkins*, was brought in and set about rebuilding, and it has to be admitted he did a spectacular job. It is only when one examines closely that one realizes that over three-quarters of what we see is C17. So what does survive? The N side of the tower is the most revealing. Here there is still a row of C13 arcading, slender columns with amulets, but above this evidence of the rebuild. The two-light window is probably a C17 invention. It incorporates a charming little medieval figure of a man making music. The NW buttresses are largely intact, and so, thankfully, is the W portal. The SW buttresses are clearly C17, and on the S side all that is left of the C13 are two half shafts and some damaged column bases. The whole thing must have collapsed across this SW corner. Back to the W front, the two Gothic nodding niches, the W window with the curious supports and everything above has to be C17. Two square plaques with now barely legible inscriptions record the 1631–2 catastrophe. Pretty round opening with dogtooth surround, then the bell-openings of two lights, transomed and richly shafted. At the sides various pieces of sculpture salvaged from the original building. A triangular tympanum with a figure of Christ in Majesty, and some large pieces of leaf carving. The top parts are perfectly credible as Dec building period: an openwork frieze, pinnacles, and the beautifully slender, recessed, crocketed spire with three tiers of lucarnes. The pinnacles are connected with the spire by flying buttresses with openwork quatrefoils. Atkins, and his masons and the people of Higham must have realized that their spire was almost the same as that at nearby Rushden. Well done Richard Atkins!

Now back to the medieval work. The whole is the work of one generation: *c.* 1220–80. The style is closely connected with Westminster Abbey, especially in the sculpture. The W portal is recessed, with two bays of cusped blank arcading with leaf capitals and a pointed tunnel-vault with a chamfered arch across and floral diapering. There are two W doorways with a trumeau between. The doorways have segmental arches (cf. Sainte Chapelle Paris and the early work at Westminster Abbey), and jambs and arches are decorated with small figures in the way of the French cathedral voussoirs. In the middle of the tympanum is a modern image of the Virgin on a leaf corbel. The rest of the tympanum has roundels with sacred stories, including some of an inorganically fragmentary shape doubtless due to the C17 rebuilding (N: the Meeting at the Golden Gate, the Annunciation, the Three Magi, Christ among the Doctors, the Baptism of Christ; S: Joachim and his flock, the Crucifixion, the Annunciation to Joachim, the three Maries at the Sepulchre, the Harrowing of Hell). The motif of such roundels derives no doubt from illuminated manuscripts and stained glass. Towards the nave, inside the church, the arch has to W and E seven shafts in the responds. The moulding with a hollow between the shafts heralds that which became popular in the Perp style.

The church was spacious in this form, and its tower ambitious, but the volume of enlargements which was embarked upon some time after 1327 was much more so. This may be owed to the 3rd Earl of Lancaster (†1345) or to Laurence St Maur, rector of Higham Ferrers (†1337; *see* below). What was

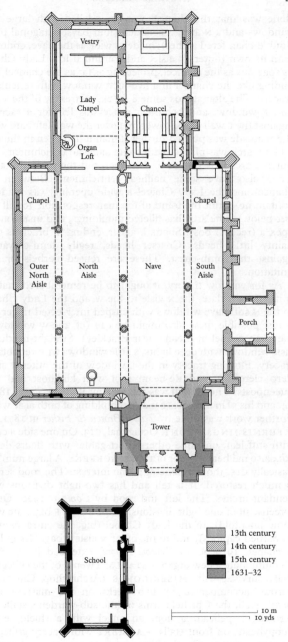

Vestry

Lady Chapel

Chancel

Organ Loft

Chapel

Chapel

Outer North Aisle

North Aisle

Nave

South Aisle

Porch

Tower

School

	13th century
	14th century
	15th century
	1631–32

10 m

10 yds

Higham Ferrers, St Mary.
Plan

done was that the chancel was remodelled with large Dec windows and a N aisle was added (four bays, octagonal piers, double-chamfered arches), made as wide as the nave, endowed with its own (outer) N aisle, and continued in a Lady Chapel as spacious as the chancel, projecting as far as the chancel, and ending like the chancel in a five-light window with reticulated tracery. The altar stands some 8 ft (2.4 metres) W of the E wall and E window, and behind it space was left for a sacristy. Against the E wall of the tower, to cover the wall left bare when the N arcade was pushed further N than it had been in the C13, a blank arch was placed, with some nailhead enrichment. The outer N arcade is similar to the inner, but the piers are taller. They also have some nailhead enrichment. Between the chancel and the Lady Chapel a wide opening was made to contain no doubt the tomb of the man responsible for all this (*see* below). The arch has filleted mouldings, and inside at the apex a (recent) boss. Shafts l. and r. ending in brackets with dainty little heads. Coarser heads, really demi-caryatids, against the tomb-chest. These are reused corbels or C17 imitation.

As for window tracery, it ought to be remembered that, in spite of their date, the N aisle to the W and the Lady Chapel to the N still have windows with cusped intersected tracery. It is just possible these also might be C17 (cf. the W window of the 1620 chapel at Steane near Brackley). Straight-headed N aisle windows with ogee lights, S aisle windows with reticulated tracery. Flowing tracery in the E window of the outer N aisle. Perp clerestory and tie-beam roof with kingpost and two queenposts. The church was restored by *William Slater*, 1857–64, and his plan indicates a major rebuilding of both aisle walls. Further work was done by *Talbot Brown & Fisher* in 1871.

FURNISHINGS. – FONT. Octagonal, C13. On one side a cross with stiff-leaf, on three others short gables with fleurs-de-lys etc., also nailhead. Cover of 1966. – SCREENS. A large number, basically C15, though none of prime interest. The rood screen is much restored. It is tall and has two-light divisions with pendant arches. The loft and rood by *Comper*, 1920. Other screens, all of one-light divisions, to the S aisle E bay (late with some linenfold), to the Lady Chapel (big, the entrance with embattled capitals), and to the outer N aisle E bay. Organ loft, N chapel, 1919–20 by *Temple Moore*, extended in 2008 to accommodate a new organ. – STALLS. Twenty of the collegiate stalls survive, with MISERICORDS (Archbishop Chichele's portrait accompanied by two clerks on the master's and vicar's stall, the Chichele arms on the sub-warden's stall, the vernicle, a pelican, a lion, an angel with a shield, etc.). Poppyheads on front stalls. – AUMBRY with tracery grille, by *Comper*. – TILES. On the altar steps; of *c.* 1330. – STAINED GLASS. A good selection. Chancel E, 1884 by *Clayton & Bell*. – Chancel side windows, 1897 and 1899 by *Shrigley & Hunt*. They also made the 1909 (memorial †1899) window in the S aisle. In the S aisle also figures of St Alban and St Columba by

Morris & Co. Three windows by *Kempe & Co.*, the splendid N chapel Tree of Jesse window of 1932 and the N and S chapel E windows of 1914. N chapel N window, 2003 by *Christine Boyce.* Glazed screen and W doors by *John Hayward*, 1969. By him also the window at the W end with the descending dove. – ARMOUR, outer N aisle wall. Several pieces of *c.* 1600. – MONU- MENTS. Tomb-chest between chancel and Lady Chapel. Four panels with shields; buttresses with small heads at the top. No doubt the most important monument in the church. But whose was it? The brass now on it does not belong to it. It is of Laurence St Maur, †1337, a priest. It is one of the finest English brasses. The side shafts have saints, and of the canopy there remains a strip of five arches, the middle one with the deceased's soul held in a napkin by angels. The figure is 5 ft 4 in. (1.63 metres) long and lies under an ogee arch. – In the Lady Chapel many more brasses, the best that of Archbishop Chichele's brother †1425 and his wife, under ogee gables; 4 ft 3 in. (1.30-metre) figures. – Also Archbishop Chichele's father †1400 and mother, a foliated cross with Christ in the centre and the symbols of the Evangelists in the ends. – William Thorpe †1504, wife and children (near the Chicheles), 2 ft 1 in. (104-cm.) figures. – Also three brasses without any inscriptions: two civilians of *c.* 1540 and Edith Chancellor, *c.* 1435, headless; 12½-in. (32-cm.), 17-in. (43-cm.) and 26-in. (66-cm.) figures. – To the N and S of the high altar brasses of Richard Walleys, Warden of the College, *c.* 1500, 3 ft 6 in. (106 cm.) and a civilian, dated 1501, 22 in. (56 cm.). – In the S aisle E bay Henry Denton †1498, priest, 19½ in. (50 cm.). – In the N aisle E chapel Thomas Rudd †1656, Charles I's chief engineer, with several epitaphs by himself ('Always looking up to Christ's only merit/Hopes new Jerusalem to inherit'). – CHURCHYARD CROSS, early C14, on steps, the shaft with oak- leaves, ballflower, etc., the head with triangular ornament on the four faces.

ARCHBISHOP CHICHELE'S SCHOOL, NW of the church. Built after his death (†1443) for a school established in 1391. A beautiful three-bay Perp building in limestone ashlar, with three-light side windows and five-light end windows. Below the W window a tier of small single windows. Openwork bat- tlements and pinnacles. Roof with cambered beams. Panelled interior, with a wooden doorway dated 1636. Reredos with a few pieces of C15 tracery. Restored by *Temple Moore*, 1915.

ARCHBISHOP CHICHELE'S BEDE HOUSE, S of the church. Founded in 1423 for twelve old men and a woman attendant. Oblong block, bands of ironstone and grey stone on the N and W sides, W side with a doorway with crocketed ogee arch and a bellcote. More crocketing over the window. The building consisted of the living quarters and the raised square CHAPEL at the E end. This has two- and three-light windows, much restored, especially the E window. Niches l. and r. of the E window. The living space was divided into cubicles for beds and lockers. Some of the lockers have been reconstructed. In the middle of the s side a very large fireplace. Two-light windows with transom. – STAINED GLASS. Some coats of arms by *John Hayward*, 1969.

METHODIST CHURCH, High Street. 1902–3 by *H. H. Dyer* of Northampton, brick and stone, double-fronted with large Geometrical Decorated windows and a trefoil-headed portal.

HIGHAM FERRERS JUNIOR SCHOOL, Wharf Road. Brick and stone Gothic of 1873 by *E. Sharman* of Wellingborough, with an addition by him, 1886–7. Neoclassical with turret. Infants' school added in 1897.

PERAMBULATION. The MARKET PLACE, so close to the church, is an added attraction, and a worthy preparation. It is triangular, with the MARKET CROSS as its pivot (C14, tall shaft, ball-flower capital; the conical base replaces original steps) and a Georgian house at the N end, a good focal point (Venetian windows on two floors, pedimental gable, but the top dated 1802). The TOWN HALL lies at the s end, 1809, of three bays, with a Venetian window in the centre. The WAR MEMORIAL, *c.* 1920, a rectangular rusticated column, is by *W. Talbot Brown* of Wellingborough. The best houses are on the w side: No. 5 late C16 with two canted bays and mullioned windows, and Nos. 6–8, mid Georgian, of eight bays with a pedimented two-bay centre with a decorative shield. On the E side No. 11 with mullioned windows and No. 12 of seven bays, C18, altered later. From the s end of the Market Place to the E into WOOD STREET, with at the corner of Midland Road the MANOR HOUSE, L-shaped, C17 with a three-storeyed, gabled, mullioned bay window. E of the church the LIBRARY (former Parish Rooms) by *Talbot Brown*, in an attractive Northants vernacular Jacobean manner and dated on the chimney 1904. Then the former office of JOHN WHITE FOOTWEAR, undoubtedly by *Alexander Anderson* of Northampton, 1906, originally a factory for Charles Parker. Classical porch with garlanded Ionic columns and his characteristic lettering and heraldic shields. Next a sizeable Neo-Georgian block, again for John White, by *Sir Albert Richardson* 1936. Richardson also designed the retirement home complex opposite in his usual simple but attractive Neo-Georgian manner (*see* also the John White factory at Rushden, p. 563).

Back to the Market Place and N into COLLEGE STREET, so called after Archbishop CHICHELE'S COLLEGE, founded 1422. On r. the GREEN DRAGON, two C18 buildings joined together and given rusticated window surrounds in the mid C19. Of the College, what remains is as follows. First the s range. The E part of this is called the chapel and is single-storeyed; the E window is apparently reduced in size. The w part is horizontally subdivided into two storeys, of which the upper oversails into the chapel – if it was a chapel. Excavations in 1966 indicated that as first planned, the N range was to have been much larger. When the plans were reduced in scale, it is possible that part of the domestic s range was converted into the chapel. Secondly the gatehouse and a lodging to its E. The gateway has a four-centred arch and three niches over. Thirdly part of the W range, which seems to have contained the hall. Opposite the entrance to the College is COLLEGE HOUSE, consisting of one part, dated 1633, with a gabled porch and a canted, dormered bay window, much infilled at the base, and another of the late C17, with wooden cross-windows in four bays and two storeys. Some way beyond, on r. a small row of ALMSHOUSES for the Newman Charity, ironstone and lime-stone, Gothic, six in pairs with timber X-roofed porches, 1855 by *E. F. Law.*

s of the Market Place gentle rows of stone houses on each side of HIGH STREET and THE GARAGE, W side, of *c.* 1930.

HIGHAM PARK
2 m. SE of Rushden

9060

HIGHAM OLD HALL is a farmhouse of C16 or C17 origin. It stands just outside a former moated enclosure on the N side of a former medieval deer park whose outline can still be traced. The enclosure was probably the site of the Great Lodge, a building of some status with a hall, chambers and a chapel. In 1672 the park was sold to Sir Robert Long and it would appear that the Lodge was demolished not long after. The present building retains one four-light mullioned window with arched lights; probably early C16.

HINTON-IN-THE-HEDGES

5030

HOLY TRINITY. Norman W tower, the arch towards the nave with rough voussoirs. Early C13 upper parts. Two-light bell-openings with a shaft under a round arch. Corbel table. Late C12 or early C13 N aisle. A small area of herringbone masonry externally in the W wall. The arcade of two bays has a circular pier with a multi-scalloped capital and a later, probably C14, pointed double-chamfered arch. Early C14 N doorway. The chancel arch also C14 with its arch resting on corbels with grinning faces. In the jambs of the S doorway nice, dainty, very small pieces of C16(?) carving. The external evidence of the church is disturbed by the restoration by *William White* 1868–9. – FONT. Tub-shaped, C13. With friezes of stiff-leaf, intersected arches, and dogtooth. – SCREEN. Perp, with one-light divisions but much remade. – ROOD STAIRS with a timber surround. – PULPIT. Jacobean, an unusual arrangement of usual motifs. – A fine ROYAL ARMS. For Queen Anne, dated 1707 and signed by *Thomas Hinton* of Lincoln. Restored 2007. – REREDOS and STALLS. The former in C15 style with cresting and two side candleholders, the latter with square foliate poppyheads. They look later than the 1860s and may be of 1884 when some work was done. – STAINED GLASS. Chancel S. Two finely drawn fragments from a Coronation of the Virgin. The Virgin as Queen of Heaven and Christ the King, c. 1400–30. They do not fit any of the tracery in the church today. At the top of the window, a small shield with a lion rampant of a similar date. They were all conserved by the York Glaziers Trust in 1973. – MONUMENTS. Sir William Hinton(?) and wife. Later C14 of stone and good quality. Tomb-chest with quatrefoil frieze. His head still on the pillows usual in the C13. By her pillow two angels. The effigies are now separated. – Reynold Braye †1582. Slate inscription plate. Good architectural surround with Corinthian demi-columns and entablature. Top achievement. – Salathiell Crewe †1686. Tablet with open scrolly pediment. Attributed to *William Stanton*. – Hon. Herman Ryland †1838. A shaped tablet by *W. T. Hale*.

OLD RECTORY. 1678, gabled and symmetrical. The windows are altered.

HOLCOT

ST MARY AND ALL SAINTS. Much restored: 1845, and 1861 by *E. F. Law*, notably the chancel with its E window and 1888–9 by *Law & Harris*. N aisle, Dec windows (Y-tracery cusped, also reticulated – see the well-preserved window at the end of the N aisle now inside the church). Dec arcades of three bays. Very short piers with four shafts and four subsidiary shafts in the diagonals. The capitals on the N side look earlier than those on the S side. The chancel arch is of the same period and again a little different. Other windows Perp, three lights, square-headed. Tower arch also Perp. Two-light bell-openings with transom. Battlements. – FONT. A C12 or early C13 bowl on a C13 stem. Base of 1889. – WALL PAINTINGS. All C14 but not much to see now. S aisle W end: Ascension, Pentecost, Coronation of the Virgin(?), and adjoining these Incredulity of St Thomas(?). Near the S door, Resurrection. N aisle: Martyrdom of St Thomas Becket, St Catherine before the Emperor, etc. In window splays single saints, in the window arches scrolls. A representation of the Descent of the Holy Ghost, unique in English wall painting, has totally faded away. More in the N aisle but no longer visible. – ROYAL ARMS. Painted, Queen Victoria, but early. – STAINED GLASS. Quite a good collection. Chancel E window, a leaf and circle design 1878 by *J. Powell & Sons*. – S wall, two windows dated 1914, both by *Heaton, Butler & Bayne*. – S aisle, E window by *E. R. Frampton* 1932, his only work in the county. – S wall, 1937 by *C. E. Moore*. – W end, 1885 by *Ward & Hughes*. – Tower *A. L. & C. E. Moore* 1927.

THE GRANGE. A substantial stone house in the Tudor style
c. 1890.

HOLDENBY

ALL SAINTS (Churches Conservation Trust). The church belongs
to the house more than to the village, i.e. the village was
removed when the house was built. It stands about ¼ m. S of
the village and can only be reached by footpaths. All is green
around it. Chancel rebuilt in 1843–5 to the design of *Sir Henry
Dryden* of Canons Ashby. Restoration by *G. G. Scott*, 1868.
Organ chamber and lychgate by *E. F. Law* in 1873. So the
church now appears mostly C19. Dec however the arcades of
three bays, the S side with octagonal piers and double-hollow-
chamfered arches, the N side with taller piers and normal
double-chamfered arches. The S aisle is remarkably wide and
has a tall PISCINA with vaulted interior. The low recess once
contained a wooden effigy. The window tracery owes more to
Scott than the medieval masons. Small clerestory windows on
the N side but now inside the church, the N aisle roof having
been raised in the C15. – FONT. Perp, style octagonal, of 1873
designed by *E. F. Law*. – STALLS. C15, the ends by the screen
traceried. Simple MISERICORDS partly replaced in 1845. A
separate stall is apparently French of *c.* 1720, with dainty ribbonwork. – SCREEN. The rood screen is almost certainly part
of the woodwork of Holdenby House and this would seem to
be confirmed by the measurements of the Hall screen shown
on John Thorpe's plan. It is a splendid and remarkable piece
and, as Mark Girouard has proposed, was without doubt
designed by *Garrett Hollemans*. Roman Doric columns, metope
frieze, slender columns to fill the sections above the dados. The
top with a middle arch with tapering pilasters flanked by two
splendid foliage volutes with openwork. The latter are especially distinctive and with the Doric frieze relate to a series of
monuments in the area, and most notably to that at Harrington
to Hatton's relatives, the Saunders, where it is dated 1588.
These scrolly volutes do not at first sight look Elizabethan
which is why Pevsner in 1961, thinking the work must be C17,
stated: 'They especially make an earlier date impossible' – but
there is no doubt they are just that. The middle section at the
top with its two Roman soldiers must be a made-up arrangement. Part of the screen had formerly been across the tower
arch but they were reunited in 1986. – TILES. Chancel, by
Minton to designs of *Lord Alwyne Compton*. – WALL PAINT-
INGS. Handsome long inscription panels with strapwork surrounds. They date from *c.* 1600 but were repainted in 1862.
Two metal panels with the Creed, Lord's Prayer and Commandments are C19. The chancel walls also painted, though
now in some decay with stencilled floral patterns and mock

masonry. All done 1868 by *Lea* of Lutterworth. – REREDOS. Made from Late Elizabethan panelling. Behind it is a painted panel of the four Evangelists also 1868 by the Rev. *Frederick Sutton*. – PULPIT. Large panelled form, C18. – ROYAL ARMS of George I. – STAINED GLASS. Chancel S, Coronation of the Virgin, *c.* 1290–1300. – Chancel E by *Clayton & Bell*, uncertain date. – S aisle SE 1887, S aisle W 1871 and N aisle E 1870, all by *Clayton & Bell*. – W window by *J. Powell & Sons* to a design by *Wooldridge*, 1871. – N aisle N window by an unidentified maker. – MONUMENT. Coffin-lid (S aisle) late C13 with the usual cross relief. – Incised alabaster slab rather crudely carved to William Holdenby †1490 and wife (S aisle E). – Several small BRASS inscriptions. – Several memorials to the White family (S aisle) including a large marble plaque with flags and a fur helmet for Lt. Col. the Hon. R. F. White †1903. – In the churchyard, on the N side of the chancel a series of graves for the Hartshorne family including the archaeologist, historian and architect Albert Hartshorne †1910. – A big ponderous grey granite tomb surrounded by decorative rails and chains is for the 2nd, 3rd and 4th Viscounts Clifden †1836, 1866 and 1895 respectively.

Former SCHOOL, 1876 by *R. H. Carpenter*. Gothic with a bellcote.

Former RECTORY, ¼ m. E. 1854 by *Anthony Salvin*. Large, of red brick and irregular in form. A curious tall stack on the front facing the road. It has windows so not a chimney.

HOLDENBY HOUSE. That so little survives of Holdenby is one of the tragedies of English architecture. Even standing on the site one gets no idea of its scale. One has to rely on the survey plan by John Thorpe to get some feeling of this prodigious house. It was built by Sir Christopher Hatton, who became Lord Chancellor at the age of forty-seven in 1587. The work was begun after 1570, Lord Burghley visited in 1579, and the garden layout was established by 1580. By 1583 it must have been more or less complete, since this is the date on the two surviving archways which led into the Green or Base Court. W from this, the mansion had two principal courts in addition and was 350 ft by 225 ft (107 by 69 metres) in size. This compares with the *c.* 475 (or *c.* 320) ft by *c.* 165 ft (145/98 by 50 metres) of Theobalds and the *c.* 475 ft by *c.* 300 ft (145 by 91 metres) of Audley End. The principal ranges were of three storeys, symmetrically arranged, with mullioned-and-transomed windows. The hall range, which lay between the two courts, had an open loggia or arcading with coupled Roman Doric columns, and the hall frontispiece had a tall tower-like porch with the ascending orders of classical architecture (cf. Burghley House, Lincs.). Portions of this were still standing when Sir James Thornhill visited the site.* Inside the hall, instead of a screen, stood two large obelisks decorated with

* His drawing is illustrated in Mark Girouard, *Elizabethan Architecture*, 2009, p. 192, fig. 215.

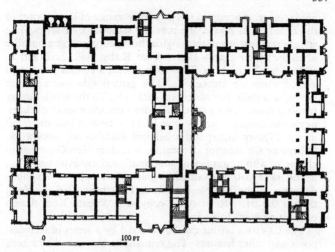

Holdenby House.
Plan after C17 plan by John Thorpe

coats of arms of Hatton's neighbours, just as at Sir Thomas
Tresham's Market House at Rothwell. There were numerous
large bay windows. The ruins as they stood in the early C18
are recorded also by drawings by Peter Tillemans (c. 1720) and
an engraving by Samuel and Nathaniel Buck (1729).*

James I bought Holdenby in 1607, as he had bought, or
rather exchanged, Theobalds in the same year. In 1650 it was
purchased by Captain Adam Baynes, a Roundhead soldier and
M.P. for Leeds, and demolished except for part of the offices
which were adapted to form a new, smaller house. The only
important architectural remains of Hatton's palace are the two
archways already mentioned. There is a third archway, almost
identical, to the N of the house. This has the date 1659, and a
defaced coat of arms. It must have been erected by Baynes,
when he had completed his destruction, to give access to the
small house he had made in place of the palace. The original
arches now stand on an ornamental lawn. They are tripartite,
with two orders of lesenes dividing the tall main arch from the
blank outer bays with arched niches. Top achievement of
clumsy outline.[†]

The new house of 1873–5 by *Slater & Carpenter* is approached
through the 1659 archway. About one-eighth the size of its

---

*A detailed analysis of the probable arrangement of the various rooms at Holdenby
can be found in RCHME, *The Country Houses of Northamptonshire*, 1996, pp. 235–8.
[†]Part of an external Doric frieze is at Coton Manor (*see* p. 193). Other fragments
are at Grendon (p. 307) and possibly a fine carved royal arms at Boughton (p. 120).
A number of other features are recorded as having been added to properties in
Northampton, but all these disappeared in Victorian rebuilding.

predecessor, it occupies roughly the N range of the W court of the Elizabethan house, the part left standing by Baynes. The style is reminiscent of the original but incorporating a number of ideas which clearly derive from Kirby Hall. Enlarged in 1887–8 by *W. E. Mills*. Two storeys with a central porch and gabled wings on either side. The garden side has a similar porch, and three-bay ranges on each side. To the W is a further two-bay range. There are regular dormers and a series of chimneystacks copied from those at Kirby. One fireplace surround in the Library incorporates original Elizabethan woodwork. Otherwise the interior decoration is mainly Neo-Georgian in character with a number of good marble chimneypieces. That in the BALLROOM, swathed in grapes, is a copy of the chimneypiece in the Marble Parlour at Houghton Hall, Norfolk; that in the DINING ROOM a copy of a William Kent design originating from Inigo Jones.

The GARDEN layout can be detected by a series of terraces, pools and other features. The remains lie between the present garden and the church. Immediately S of the present ha-ha is the mark of the main terrace which had knot gardens and a small central mound, and on either side wide stepped terraces. Below the W series is a long rectangular pond which is shown on a map of 1587 by Ralph Tresswell. This map also shows the series of ponds which lay E of the church, with at the SE corner a mount. The map indicates that this area was the site of the original manor house. It also shows that to the E of the Green Court there was a further enclosure with, as it were, a processional approach from the E.

HOLLOWELL

A pleasant hillside village with several mid-C19 brick cottage rows but rather overwhelmed by housing development since the 1970s.

ST JAMES. 1840 by *Sampson Kempthorne*. An extremely neat job in golden ironstone, well sited on the hillside at the top of the village. Lancet style with a polygonal apse and a bellcote. Quite ambitious triple-shafted W portal. Wheel window over. The apse arch is shafted and has nailhead decoration and the apse has vaulting and arcading, all decorated white, pink and red – almost Georgian Gothick. Gristly carved poppyheads on the stalls. Hammerbeam roof carried on foliate corbels. – FONT. Rounded octagonal with foliage panels. Is it original? It looks cast rather than carved. Most unusual. – STAINED GLASS. All by *J. Powell & Sons*. The wheel window has intricate patterns designed by *Moberley* and the apse windows have panels and grisaille designed by *H. Holiday*, 1863. – MONUMENT. R. M. Dukes, some time curate of Hollowell, †1843.

Brass on the floor, a foliate cross surrounded by an inscription border.

On the miniscule green a BUS SHELTER erected 2000, not only thatched but with a clock and a weathervane, whose ornament is a steam engine. Hollowell is famous for its steam rally. Two good houses: BEECH HOUSE, former vicarage, just below the church. 1698, of ironstone. Elegant front of two storeys, five bays, but the centre bay having narrow windows l. and r. (cf. Stone House, Lilbourne). Framed windows with sills and keystones. Quoins. The interior with several original features, notably the staircase with twisted turned balusters, panelled doors and two ground-floor rooms with grand stone bolection surrounds. In the garden the former SCHOOL and MASTER'S HOUSE (now village hall) of 1847 and part 1855 by *J. W. Hugall*, which may well refer to the low square clock tower.

THE MANOR HOUSE, Guilsborough Hill. Dated 1665. Mullioned windows. Georgian doorway, pilasters and pediment. Extended at the rear in 1869 and some work done by *J. A. Gotch* in 1925. A circular DOVECOTE, partly of cob, in the stable yard. Other sections of cob walling in the village.

HORTON

ST MARY (closed). C13 W tower – see the pointed, very slightly chamfered arch towards the nave. The upper parts of the early C18 (pre-1720). The splendid tall curly weathervane noted in 1961 has now alas gone. It is recorded on George Clarke drawings and may well have been the work of *Thomas Warren*. The rest of the church almost rebuilt, somewhat severely, in 1862–3 by *E. F. Law*. Clarke shows the tower with distinct quoins so it was probably rendered. S arcade of three bays, probably of *c.* 1300. Octagonal piers, double-chamfered arches. (Elaborate Victorian marble panelling around the altar with coloured inlay patterns by *Messrs Poole*. – STAINED GLASS. Chancel E, Gunning memorial by *M. & A. O'Connor* 1862. S aisle 1903 by *H. Hymers* and 1916 by *Sylvester Sparrow*.)* – MONUMENTS. Brass to Roger Salisbury †1491 and two wives; 2-ft (61-cm.) figures. – Lord Parr †1546, Catherine Parr's uncle, and wife by *Richard Parker* of Burton upon Trent: a good example of his work, the detailing of the effigies excellent. Free-standing tomb-chest. At the foot a foliage frieze with hunting dogs. Five flat niches with balusters between them. Mourners in the niches, male, including beadsmen, under him and female under her. Shields under canopies, at the short ends. Two recumbent effigies. – Sir William Lane and family, *c.* 1580. Small alabaster tablet with kneeling figures. The quality is good and it might just be from the *Hollemans* workshop.

---

* The panelling is dismantled and several of the windows in store in 2012.

– Edward and Henrietta Montagu, 1756, by *James Lovell* to a design by *Horace Walpole*. Walpole wrote to Frederick Montagu in August 1756: 'I saw Lovell today, he is very far advanced, and executes to perfection; you will be quite satisfied; I am not discontent with my design, now I see how well it succeeds.' It is indeed a handsome piece. Architectural tablet, with two chaste urns in arched niches and just a touch of Rococo in its decoration.

HORTON HALL is one of Northamptonshire's tragedy houses, sadly pulled down after its sale in 1936 to a developer. It was a grand house of Tudor origins in the ownership of the Parr family, including Queen Catherine Parr's uncle, Sir William, later Lord Parr (*see* below). It then passed into the Lane family and thence in the C18 to the Montagus, Earls of Halifax. Work is recorded by *Daniel Garrett* and *Thomas Wright*. It was sold to the Gunning family in 1781 and some work was done to the interior in the 1890s, after purchase by G. Winterbottom who *c.* 1910 employed *W. Courtney le Maitre* to revamp the entrance hall (some of the fittings are now at Overstone Manor, q.v.). What remains at Horton is the two LODGES, two-storeyed with giant pilasters, one original C18 the other a copy of *c.* 1910, and the stables (CAPTAIN'S COURT), chequered red brick, early C18, of two storeys with a raised centre of three bays and an archway in the middle, which, like the six doorways in the lower wings, has rustication of alternating sizes. Urns on the parapet. The grounds between the lodges and the stables were built upon in the 1960s.

At the end of the drive, near the site of the hall, and next to a splendid cedar, HORTON ROUNDS, a striking house by *A. A. J. Marshman*, built for himself from 1966. The dominating features are the broad curving eaves of the shingled roofs, and the taller circular service cores and chimney of local yellow stone. In plan the house is a comma, with a full stop linked by a bridge. The tail of the comma, open on the ground floor, with bedrooms above, shelters a paved garden. The broad end has service rooms and entrances below, and a circular living area above, which has views in all directions.

Further afield are some of the garden furnishings of the old house. The MENAGERIE lies to the SE, a one-storey ashlar building facing N. It has a raised centre which has a semi-domed canted bay containing the entrance and a broken top pediment. The windows to the l. and r. of the bay have Gibbs surrounds and pediments. Above them lean-to roofs in the manner of Palladio's church façades. The whole is quite a dynamic composition, reminiscent of Kent. On either side screen walls with gateways with rustication and a squat pavilion at each end. It is firmly attributed to *Thomas Wright* working in the 1750s. Inside a splendid banqueting room with a fine plaster ceiling, with Father Time, the four winds, with under them plaques representing the Continents, and the signs of the Zodiac in medallions surrounded by plants of the seasons, firmly attributed to *Thomas Roberts* of Oxford. Summer plants in the bay and winter plants around the fireplace. Alcoves at either end with Doric pillars and frieze. Niches with urns. The building was rescued from dereliction in 1972 by the architectural historian *Gervase Jackson-Stops* who converted it into a residence, 1974–6. The damaged plasterwork of the main room was restored by *Christopher Hobbs*. The s front, which is brick and has a simple portico, was extended by doubling the corner towers and creating rooms between them and the main block. On the s side a romantic garden was created by *Ian Kirby* and an amazing Shell Grotto created in the vaulted basement, again by *Christopher Hobbs*, finished in 1995. It has a figure of Apollo charming animals. In the garden are two thatched arbours, inspired by Wright's designs, one classical and rustic and the other Gothic, both devised by *Charles Morris*. Further work was done in the gardens by *Vernon Russell-Smith* in 1989 and *Ginny Blom* 2004–5.

To the E, THE ARCHES, a tripartite triumphal arch with Ionic pilasters. The arches and the frames of the medallions above the side arches are rusticated. Also to the NE, THE TEMPLE, with a fine Ionic portico carrying a pulvinated frieze and a pediment. Probably Early Georgian. A c19 brick former farmhouse to its l.

HOTHORPE HALL
½ m. s of Theddingworth

6080

Now a Christian Conference Centre. Built in 1799–1801 for William Cooke. Six-bay front with two-bay pediment. A square and round bay on the ground floor. Round the corner five bays with a one-bay pediment and a porch of coupled columns. The apsed CHAPEL by *A. E. Purdie* was built by the Roman Catholic Sir Humphrey de Trafford shortly after his arrival in 1891. Stuccoed brick. Coffered tunnel-vault and coffering in the apse. The angelic faces in the apse represent the de Trafford children. The house was used by the Lutheran church 1955–84. Extension of 1992.

HULCOTE

7040

The estate village to Easton Neston. Along two sides of a green eight very lovable and a little funny HOUSES. Largish, two storeys with a third in the gable, chequered brick and with pointed Gothick windows, some just false and painted. Four on the E side are simply gabled, four on the s have lower one-bay wings with half-pediments reaching up to the main block. Built for the 3rd Earl of Pomfret, *c.* 1817–20, by the local builders *William Johnson* and *William Inns*. Payments to them occur in estate accounts together with a payment to *John Raffield* who may have been responsible for their design – he subsequently designed the w gate screen at Easton Neston (*see* p. 255). Pair of C18 ironstone LODGES to the park with polygonal ends. By them the tiny former SCHOOL of 1816, simple chequer brick with pedimented porch and pedimented side gable. Just within the park, on the l. another late C18 LODGE and, a little SW, POMFRET LODGE, a very attractive early C19 *cottage orné*. Gothic windows and bargeboards. Built as the vicarage.

9060

IRCHESTER

Irchester, as its name implies, is the site of a Roman town (*see* below). There is otherwise little in the village though there are many stone houses and a little thatch.

ST KATHARINE. Mainly C13 to early C14. The only older pieces are the w responds of the nave arcade, both late C12 with leaf crockets in the capitals, a nook-shaft in the w wall of the N aisle, probably of a former doorway, and the bases of the first two N piers. So there were clearly aisles at that time. The s aisle w wall has an early C13 pair of lancets. The arcades are early C14. The piers are octagonal and have double-hollow-chamfered arches. C13 also the chancel – see the chancel arch, the very low SEDILIA with leaf capitals, the trefoiled N doorway, the surprising small niche to its r. It has a chimneyshaft, and is thought to have been used as an oven for baking altar breads. The otherwise rather blank wall is due to the fact that there was a vestry on the N side of the chancel, of which there is evidence externally. The chancel floor was raised in the 1886–9 restoration by *J. L. Pearson*. Externally the chancel E window has remains of shafts on its jambs and there is an elegant priest's doorway on the s side, trefoil-headed with foliate cusps and shafts. A little later the N chapel with odd, very complex responds to the chancel, a low tomb-recess in the N wall, and the shafted s and N aisle doorways. The N aisle must be C14 since over its doorway and on its w buttress is a shield of the Lovel arms: they were lords of the manor from about the 1340s. Fully Dec the w tower. Bands of ironstone and yellow oolite. Pairs of two-light bell-openings. Spire with low broaches and three tiers of lucarnes. Perp chancel windows and s porch with entrance framed by buttress shafts and side windows. – FONT. Octagonal, with flat trefoiled arches. In them barbaric demi-figures, faces, and stiff-leaf; C13. – SCREEN. Rood screen, much restored. Work by *H. F. Traylen* is also recorded in 1932. Wide one-light divisions with ogee arches. – Parclose screen to the s chapel, after 1500. With tall linenfold panels and decorative circles instead of tracery. – PULPIT. Early C17, with coupled little balusters at the angles. There is record of it being a replacement in 1611. – BENCH-ENDS. C15, straight-topped, each with two traceried panels and angle buttresses. – ROYAL ARMS. Large, painted, George I. – BREAD SHELF. Very pretty. Jacobean or a little later. With small, vertically symmetrical balusters (N aisle). – WALL PAINTING. There is a record of traces of a C15 Doom above the chancel arch, but this is no longer visible. – STAINED GLASS. Several windows with fragments in their heads of *c.* 1340 and of the C15. Chancel E window 1890 by *Mayer* of Munich. – N aisle, a splendid St Katherine window of 1926 by *Veronica Whall* and a window showing Tischendorf saving the Scrolls by *J. E. Nuttgens*, 1966. – S aisle, 1925 by *Edward Woore*. – MONUMENTS. Brasses to John Glynton †1510 and wife, 19-in. (48-cm.) figures (N side of tower arch). – Thomas Jenyson †1681. Double inscription tablet flanked by Corinthian columns. The pediment is consequently wide. At the foot shield and leafy branches. Attributed to *Thomas Cartwright* the elder (GF). Jenyson ledger stones on the floor below. Several minor tablets.

METHODIST CHURCH, High Street. 1869 by *C. Day* of Bedford, red and yellow brick, pilastered three bays, three arched windows in the central section.

LIBRARY, High Street. A Carnegie library by *Sharman & Archer*, 1909. Brick with two gabled blocks and arched doorcase between.

Former SCHOOL, No. 14 School Road. 1848 by *J. G. Bland*. Stone Tudor manner. Much altered as a residence. Later brick building with some banding in lighter colour on the l. The SCHOOL of 1906–8 by *Talbot Brown & Fisher*, again with later additions, is behind in School Lane.

MANOR HOUSE, s of the church, is of medieval origin but much altered. Towards the church a gable wall with a large ogee-headed window. E front rendered three-bay façade with Edwardian veranda. A large buttressed barn alongside. In HIGH STREET, No. 53, with rustic stonework and arched windows in its gabled house, *c.* 1850 originally built as a post office. The former FORGE next door with its wide arched entrance.

CRADDOCK COURT, East Street. The former Irchester Boot & Shoe Co. of 1892, a standard three-storey brick factory building, now flats.

CHESTER HOUSE, ½ m. N. An L-plan quite grand farmhouse, which by the middle of the C18 had a formal garden. The main block C17 with mullioned windows and a Georgian wing with sashed windows. Gutted by fire 2010. It is situated on the E edge of the site of a walled Roman town (*see* below), and E of the farm are the remains of a deserted medieval village.

STATION HOUSE, Station Road, ¼ m. E of the village. 1857, quite simple. Red brick with pedimented wings. 1883 goods shed.

RAILWAY VIADUCT, ½ m. N. 1857, *Charles Liddell* surveyor, *John Crossley* engineer. Fourteen arches across the Nene. Additional viaduct alongside of 1883.

KNUSTON HALL, 1 m. NE. The history of the house is not totally clear. There was already a substantial house here by the late C17, and the S façade has some courses of ironstone which suggest an early house. The lower E wing, although altered, is probably C17 with a canted bay, and the N wing, of limestone ashlar, although probably Georgianized, has a dated stone in its pediment of 1666. About 1775 Knuston was acquired by Benjamin Kidney who is said to have spent some £10,000 on it. It is probably this house, a tall Georgian block, with N and W fronts of three bays and three storeys, which is recorded in drawings dated 1840 by George Clarke. On the N side is a Late Georgian limestone ashlar stable block with C19 ironstone and brick outbuildings on each side. There are survey plans by *J. B. Papworth* in 1817 but it is not clear if he did any work on the building. In 1865 the estate was bought by Robert Arkwright, great grandson of the famous Sir Richard, and he put in hand extensive alterations, including an added N wing and this and its new W front were given Jacobethan style gables. The W front section also included a new entrance and the ground floor of the earlier house was given bay windows and everywhere new fenestration of a rigid and not altogether pleasant form. The S front is especially unattractive. The general effect now there-fore is of a Victorian house. The interior was also revamped and there are elaborate ceilings incorporating some genuine C18 work, some resited Jacobean panelling and a new staircase. Since 1949 the house has been owned by Northamptonshire County Council and is used as an adult education centre. FOX COTTAGE, former lodge of 1866 with banded stone. Another decorative stone and brick cottage of similar date with Gothic windows a little E on the main road.

KNUSTON LODGE FARMHOUSE, NE of Knuston Hall. One of a number of farms built in 1769 following enclosure. Ironstone with limestone dressings. Various ancillary buildings now mostly converted to commercial uses.

ARKWRIGHT SCHOOL, NE of Knuston Hall, pleasantly sited on a slope, among trees. A residential school for girls by the County Architect, *John Goff* (Architect in Charge *J. R. Woolmer*), 1968–70. A series of self-contained three-storey units, linked in an informal range, with lower buildings at right angles. Tile-clad slightly projecting upper walls and monopitch roofs. The total impression not at all institutional.

ROMAN TOWNSHIP. The site of this unidentified settlement lies N of the village, immediately N of the A45. The rectangular ditch and bank cover an area *c.* 220 by 275 metres, enclosing *c.* 20 acres (8 ha). Only parts of the N side are still visible on the ground. The defences date to the later C2, and were imposed on an existing more extensive town, retaining the earlier road system. Camden mentions the site and C18 accounts refer to walls still standing. Excavations in C19 examined buildings in the centre of the settlement, and foundations in the sw corner that supported a bastion. Excavations in the 1960s and 1970s located middle to Late Iron Age settlement s of the town and excavation in the 2000s to the w examined further Iron Age settlement and part of the w suburb. The area including the walled town is owned by Northamptonshire County Council with plans to create a heritage resource centre. Geophysical survey has provided a detailed plan of the towns' buildings, which range from simple strip buildings to temples/ shrines, bath houses and two courtyard arrangements of either wealthy town houses or perhaps a government *mansio*. To the NE a cemetery of at least 300 graves was discovered in the late C19 during quarrying.

IRTHLINGBOROUGH

A large village, almost a small town, with a busy but not especially appealing High Street. Its former centre to the E, above the church, now feels a somewhat lost space. It is the view of its extraordinary church tower which brings one here.

St Peter. A quite remarkable sight, lying as it does between the village and the river. The church is large and at first seems quite incongruous. What appears to be incongruous is however the survival of not only the church, but also the very tall and dominant tower to the w of the church which belonged to the college founded by the widow of John Pyel, a mercer of London, in 1388. The manor had been conveyed to John Pyel in 1354 and he had obtained licence in 1375 to make the church collegiate. The tower, which was rebuilt correctly in 1887–93 under the direction of *J. L. Pearson* but with the work done by *W. Talbot Brown* of Wellingborough, was probably begun shortly after 1354. It is of ironstone and grey stone. Recessed buttresses, turning clasping higher up. Lancet openings, one a doorway to college buildings to the N. Two Dec bell-openings with tracery on each side, a niche between them. The tower top battlemented with polygonal turrets at the corners, their battlements a restoration of the 1880s. Then two octagonal storeys, the upper one with straight-headed three-light windows with reticulation motifs, and battlements again. Each face has a shield of the Pyel arms. One has to assume that many of the now blocked openings were originally open and if not glazed then fitted with some kind of louvre fitment. The tower is accessed by a normal spiral staircase but the octagon is more sophisticated with its stairs running in the thickness of the walls. Also, very puzzlingly, there appear to be two square fireplaces suggesting the space was fitted with subdividing floors, but for what purpose, at such a high level? What remains of the buildings of the college is sandwiched between the

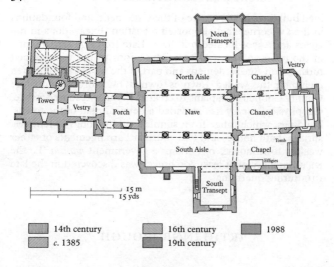

Irthlingborough, St Peter.
Plan

church and the tower and it is only a fragment and difficult to make much sense of now. To the N of the tower there only remain two undercrofts, with rib-vaults, one of two quadripartite bays, the other with ridge ribs as well. The bosses are carved, one with a rose, the other with the Pyel arms, so meant for some domestic purpose, although today hardly enough height to admit such use. The former are in line with a room to the E of the tower which has two storeys and connects directly with the church porch, that is a room with entrances from the N, the S, the W, and of course also the church to the E. The openings are again lancets, looking decidedly earlier than 1300, but the doorway to the E has sunk rounded mouldings and a sunk chamfer, the same details exactly as in the N, S and W doorways.

The church is very wide for its length and very tall, made so by the addition of the large Perp clerestory windows above both nave and chancel presumably resulting from it becoming a collegiate foundation. It was built in two phases, in the C13 and c. 1300–50. The arcades come first, mid C13, with quatrefoil piers and double-chamfered arches in voussoirs of ironstone and sandstone. The N piers are stronger, the S piers slenderer. Transepts independent of the arcades. In the S aisle and the W wall of the S transept contemporary lancets. Two-bay chancel chapels, again quatrefoil piers and again different details, the capitals, for instance, somewhat larger. Late C13 the E end of the chancel, with a low cusped recess on the N side (naturalistic leaves in the capitals and sheltering a coffin slab carved with a cross) and indications of the existence of the SEDILIA opposite with a fragmented capital. Typical late

C13 chancel E window (five steeply stepped lancet lights under one arch), N transept N window, S aisle W, and others with bar tracery, not all of which may be medieval. Above the chancel arch a blocked lancet and signs of a roof-line. Another roof-line above the chancel E window and yet another visible over the W window externally. Of *c.* 1300 the strange large, triple-shafted arch formerly filling the E wall of the N transept, the shafts small and raised above the floor level. What was its purpose? It is surely too big for a reredos. It was opened to provide access to new facility rooms in 1988. Dec windows with reticulated tracery in the S transept on the S side and a straight-headed one in the S aisle; Dec window with fine flowing tracery at the W end of the nave. The W doorway under the porch is flanked by two niches on each side, the top ones with canopies. Remains of a stoup on each side of the doorway. Dec also an elaborate aumbry in the N chapel. It had been discovered elsewhere in 1880 and was fitted here then. The VCH calls all this Dec work in church and tower *c.* 1385. Stylistically such a date must appear too late. Shortly after 1354 would be more convincing, but do the documents allow this? There was a restoration in 1872 by *Talbot Brown & Fisher.*

FURNISHINGS – FONT. Perp, octagonal, with traceried panels, embattled. – STALLS. Late C15, eight survive, the fronts with poppyheads. They have MISERICORDS but only one with a carved emblem, a shield held by an angel. – PULPIT. Incorporating some elements of C15 woodwork. – GLASS SCREEN. N transept, with etched figures of Christ washing the Disciples' feet, 1988 by *Jennifer Conway.* – STAINED GLASS. Chancel E window, 1920 by *Kempe & Co.* – N aisle, a window of 1962 by *A. K. Nicholson Studios.* – N chapel, another of 1930 by *Morris & Co.* and by them also a window of 1937 in the S aisle. – S chapel, memorial window 1947 by *A. K. Nicholson Studios.* – N annex, 1920 by *A. J. Davies* of Bromsgrove (formerly in the N chapel). – S transept tracery glass by *Helen Whitaker* 2011. – MONUMENTS. All in S chapel. Alabaster effigies of a civilian and a lady, *c.* 1390 traditionally for John Pyel †1378 and his wife. Tomb-chest with quatrefoils containing shields. At the head end angels holding a shield. – Alabaster effigy of a lady, *c.* 1490. Both alabaster tombs are in some decay and have the appearance of having been outside for a period. – Two brass indents. – A monument of grey marble, supposedly the tomb of Sir Thomas Cheney †1513 whose will gives directions for its construction. Tomb-chest and recess with pendant arches (the colonnettes are C19 replacements). Panelling and remains of pendants inside. One end solid, the other open, so clearly moved from elsewhere. Indents of brasses of kneeling figures on the back wall. An interesting example of Gothic just becoming Renaissance, with the decorative columns (cf. Marholm, near Peterborough). – N chapel has several memorials to the Wyckley family, C17 or C18.

ALL SAINTS. In ruins already in the C16. Excavations in 1965 revealed that the earliest building, possibly mid-C12, had a nave, chancel and apse. In the C14 the chancel was lengthened and aisles and a w tower were added. Nothing now remains.

METHODIST CHURCH, College Street. 1897 by *John Wills*, of red brick and stone, Gothic with a large Geometric-style window above its porch, and lancets on either side. Two storeys of lancets on the side walls. Galleried interior reordered in 2009 by *Gotch, Saunders & Surridge* for better community space, regrettably destroying the fine original woodwork of the pulpit platform.

Other than the churches, Irthlingborough has little to offer architecturally.* On the square N of St Peter, a CROSS-SHAFT, thought to be of religious significance. A tapered shaft with crockets and a trefoiled foliage capital, and raised on polygonal steps. It seems to be late C13, though was resited and rebuilt in 1966–7. On the s side a former BANK, four bays, its upper windows with Gibbs surrounds. It is a refronting of an earlier building with the date 1713 in its E gable. Further E in Station Road, MANOR HOUSE, a stone C17 house, half-H-shape with some mullioned windows. It was given a new entrance façade on the E side in the early C19. s of Station Road towards the river in Nene View is HALL FARMHOUSE, still a working farm. Another C17 house with several mullioned windows. E of it, at the bottom of LIME STREET, a row of six Victorian cottages, probably built for the farm's labourers. Stone with varied gabled roofs and and arranged in pairs with shared porches. Of distinct charm.

HIGH STREET runs w from the square and has a number of rows of stone houses of varied dates. On the s side is the former WESLEYAN CHAPEL of 1865. Brick and stone façade with Gothic window. Nearly opposite is the former TRIGG ENDOWED SCHOOL. The original foundation of 1760 but the buildings of 1867–8 by *Joseph Peacock*. School with master's house on l. Stone with Gothic windows and shaped gables. Now all converted to housing. Parallel to High Street, in College Street, is IRTHLINGBOROUGH JUNIOR SCHOOL, with the original 1879 brick and stone building with Gothic details, alongside the five-pedimented extension of 1886–7 by *Sharman* of Wellingborough. More recent buildings behind. A little further down is the former EXCELSIOR BOOT & SHOE FACTORY of 1893, now flats. Five-bay, three storeys, with a side pediment bearing the name and date. Some way further on the corner of Queen Street, the former premises of HOBBS & CO. A rather quirky 1900 façade of brick and stone which must be by *Alexander Anderson* of Northampton. The former office entrance has a one-and-a-half bay façade with canopied entrance, and circular windows on either side whose keystones extend upwards to meet the aprons of the first-floor windows. Big name plaque with a pretty garland of flowers beneath.

---

* The impressive former Shortland's Express Works of 1899 by *Alexander Anderson* of Northampton, latterly Woolnough's Bookbinding, which stood opposite the church, was demolished 2009–10.

Rusticated lunette at the top. The façade divided by pilasters with limestone panels at their heads. The half bay has a large curve-headed window for the ground floor, and the factory extension on the l. of one storey has five bays with similar windows.

BRIDGE across the River Nene. Of ten arches, mostly pointed all with chamfered ribs; C14. Cutwaters. Stone carved with crossed keys for the Abbey of Peterborough. Widened in 1922. The big concrete VIADUCT dates from 1936 to designs by *Gotch, Saunders & Surridge*.

NENE PARK INDUSTRIAL ESTATE, E of the A6. A striking ensemble by *Gotch, Saunders & Surridge*, 1996, notably WATERSIDE HOUSE with its balconied façade.

ISHAM

8070

ST PETER. The first two bays of the arcades are Late Norman. Circular piers, N with many scallops, S with a scrolly leaf trail and heads at the corners. Square abaci. Unmoulded N, single-stepped S arches. The third bays belong to the same period as the chancel and the openings into the chapels, i.e. the C13. Dec a number of windows and the ambitious recess in the N aisle. Ogee arch containing small ballflowers and tall pinnacles, a quatrefoil frieze at the back. Finally the W tower, Dec to Perp, with a top frieze of cusped lozenges and battlements. – CHANCEL SCREEN. Perp; only the base remains. – TOWER SCREEN. Made in 1966 with some pieces of C16 or C17 carvings. – STALLS. Also with sections of Perp panels for their backs and one misericord. – PULPIT. Late Elizabethan, with its back wall and a small ogee tester. Primitive angels and figure carving. – CHANDELIER. 1816. – COMMUNION RAIL. Jacobean, with vertically symmetrical balusters. – STAINED GLASS. A good sequence. Chancel E, 1882 by *Burlison & Grylls*. – N aisle, St Francis, 1961 by *Abbot & Co*. of Lancaster. – S aisle, Virgin & Child, 1939 also by them. – N aisle E window, Scopes memorial, 1973 by *K. Barton Studios*, Rottingdean. – N aisle W window, Ellerby memorial, made 2010 by *Michael Stokes*.

WESLEYAN CHAPEL, Church Street. 1861, of yellow brick with red brick dressings. Three bays under a pediment with chequered pilasters and round-arched windows.

Remains of Pytchley Hall, demolished in 1828, are worked into a façade of a three-bay house N of the church (No. 1 Church Street) and a cottage next to it. Doorway with three fat vases. The door surround also made up of pieces. The first floor windows have curved sections of some archway. In MIDDLE STREET, at the corner of South Street, MANOR HOUSE FARM. Intriguing house with a large blocked carriage archway with semicircular top with dripmould and a blocked smaller arch slightly pointed on its l. Although the building appears now to be largely C17 and C18 it may well have medieval origins. Further in Middle Street, on the s side, ALL SAINTS HOUSE (No. 26) is of deep-coloured coursed ironstone with ashlar course between its floors and ashlar keystones to its windows. Range on r. of lighter stone with entranceway. There is a date-stone of 1763.

Former WATER TOWER, Orlingbury Road, ½ m. w. Early 1900s. An impressive square red brick tower with two rows of three round arches on its ground and first floors.

ISLIP

ST NICHOLAS. A complete and fine Perp church. Simple windows, mainly three lights, with five at the E end. The w tower is the only ornate piece. It is similar to Lowick next door, but has a spire instead of the octagon. w doorway with traceried spandrels. Clasping buttresses. Top frieze of cusped lozenges. Tall, square, panelled pinnacles. The spire is recessed and crocketed. Two tiers of lucarnes in alternate directions. The body of the church with an entertaining series of gargoyle heads. Interior with arcades of four tall arches. Piers with a deeply hollow-chamfered projection without capital to nave and aisles and slim shafts with capitals to the openings. Ogee hoodmoulds. Angel corbels for the roof, also in the chancel. – FONT. Octagonal on a shafted base. Ogee cover *c.* 1840. – STOUP. By s doorway. A vaulted niche. – SCREEN, ROOD and REREDOS. All by *Temple Moore,* 1911 with the rood added 1920, and the gift of the Nicoll family of New York to celebrate their ancestor (*see* below). Other woodwork is of the time of the restoration by *William Slater,* 1854–5. – STAINED GLASS. E window by *Kempe,* 1886 (with C15 Pelican in her Piety). – Chancel s, three saints by *H. V. Milner* 1909. – N aisle E, in medieval style, by *Clayton & Bell,* 1878. – s aisle E, 1864 by *William Wailes.* – MONUMENTS. The big and fine-looking brasses on the chancel floor for John Nicoll and his wife, 1467, are a re-creation of 1911 by the *Rev. H. Macklin,* author of one of the standard books on brasses. – Dame Mary Washington †1624 and Catherine Curtis †1626. Stone tablets with brief inscription between two coarse columns. – FIRST WORLD WAR MEMORIAL. N aisle. Painted by *J. Bayes.*

NICHOLAS HOUSE. Just NE of the church. Mainly C16 or C17 but of medieval origin. Part timber-framed.

Former SCHOOL, s of church, 1861–2 by *William Slater.* Banded sandstone and ironstone. SCHOOL HOUSE dated 1877. Later building alongside of 1905.

In the main street, to the N, WAR MEMORIAL by *J. A. Gotch,* 1921. Like two Georgian gatepiers. A little further on r. MANOR HOUSE, L-shaped, partly C17 with additions by *Gotch,* 1905. Porch from the early C19 toll house. SE of the church the long

Neo-Georgian façade of ISLIP GRANGE, 1913 by *Coales &
Johnson* of Market Harborough, to a building of C17 origin.
CLANFIELD (care home), Tollbar Road. Large red brick villa of
1898 by *Blackwell & Thomson*. Some additions since.
ISLIP HOUSE, by Thrapston Bridge. Georgian, of seven bays and
two and a half storeys. Built for the manager of the wharf.
KING EDWARD COTTAGES, Thrapston Road. A red brick row,
1900–3 by *Blackwell & Thomson* for the workers at the Islip
Iron Co. (begun in 1867 by W. B. Stopford of Drayton, continued by Stewarts & Lloyds of Corby until 1955). ½ m. N on
the Drayton estate is a brick VENT SHAFT 16 ft (5 metres) high
which ventilated mines some 100 ft (30 metres) below. The
shaft is built purely using headers.

KELMARSH   7070

ST DIONYSIUS. The tone of this church is set as you walk up
the path, passing on the l. the gigantic grave of Richard Naylor
†1899. A pink granite enclosure with huge plain cone finials at
each corner. It comes as no surprise to be met with more
Aberdeen granite inside, and all due to Naylor's rebuilding of
the old church in 1874. His architect was *J. K. Colling* and he
produced one of the most lavish High Victorian interiors in the
county. Aisle arcade with circular piers of pink Aberdeen
granite. Exuberant foliage capitals and foliage corbels above
supporting an elaborate hammerbeam roof. The chancel is
particularly rich. Blind arcading all round with panels of alabaster and antique marble, said to have been brought from
Rome by Naylor. Emblems of the Passion in the spandrels.
Cosmati design ceramic floor, a rare example of the work of
J. M. Blashfield of Stamford. The wall decoration is by *Powell's*
to designs by *H. E. Wooldridge*. Above are ceramic panels of the
Evangelists and Saints Denys, Peter and Paul. There is more
foliage carving in the nave on the rich array of seating. The
seats have panels of different plants on their backs, sides and
arm-rests. There is a veritable horticultural catalogue. It is
almost as if Naylor knew that a future owner of Kelmarsh Hall
would be the great garden designer Nancy Lancaster. The
whole interior boasts of the brashness of Victorian money.
What a contrast with the refinement of the chancel in the next-
door village of Haselbech. In its way also extraordinary is the
N chapel. It was clearly built to contain the monument of Sir
John Hanbury †1639, and built probably a few years earlier.
The N window is quasi-Perp, with wide lights and a transom,
but the E window has the most extraordinary Carolean tracery,
consisting of lozenges and circles. Jacobean Geometric. The
top frieze and pinnacles are at once recognizable for their
period. Little survives of the medieval church save the W tower,
Perp, with clasping buttresses, pairs of bell-openings with a

transom, and broach spire with two tiers of lucarnes in the cardinal directions, and some sections of the s wall of the chancel. – FRONTAL and ALTAR RUG by *Morris & Co.* – SCREEN in the tower arch. With late C16 or early C17 panels of Netherlandish (story of Esther) and German origin. They apparently came from the Hall, so remnants from the Jacobean house. – STAINED GLASS. Chancel E by *Lavers, Barraud & Westlake*, 1874, and N and s by *William Pepper*, also 1874. Cicely Lancaster †1946 memorial window by *Hugh Easton*, 1947. Gentle colours and much clear glass. The other s window is thought to be by *Morris* of Westminster, but no documentation has yet been found. – MONUMENTS. Brass to Morrys Osberne †1534, the figure in its headless state 23 in. (58 cm.) long. – Sir John Hanbury †1639. Big standing monument with two figures kneeling and facing one another across a prayer-desk. Drapery opened above them, baldacchino-like. Open pediment. Rustic rather than metropolitan in quality. – William Hanbury †1768. Very tall inscription base, *c.* 9 ft (2.7 metres) high. Strigillated sarcophagus above; no figures. – William Hanbury †1807, by *Chantrey*. No figures. Grecian altar with drapery and two inter-locked wreaths. – Outside the church, E of the chancel. William Hanbury, 1st Lord Bateman †1845, by *Samuel Cundy*. Coped tomb-chest with low 'basket' arches of the shape the French call *anse de panier*. – The big pink granite affair for Richard Naylor †1899 has already been noted.

KELMARSH HALL. An important Georgian house but especially interesting as an early example of the work of the interior and garden designer *Nancy Lancaster*. The estate came into the ownership of the Hanbury family in 1618, but the present house was built, on a different site, *c.* 1730–6, to the designs of *James Gibbs*, using *Francis Smith* of Warwick as builder, hence the beautiful brickwork. In 1842 *Edward Haycock* of Shrewsbury added an extension on the s side. The Hanburys were here till 1865 when it was purchased by R. C. Naylor, of the Liverpool banking family, a devotee of hunting. He employed *J. K. Colling* to make additions, notably a ballroom. Following Naylor's death in 1899 the estate was bought by G. G. Lancaster and in 1907 inherited by his son Claude ('Jubie'). In 1927 he leased the house to Ronald Tree and his wife, Nancy. They too loved hunting. Nancy Tree had already acquired a reputation for interior design, and above all comfort. She stripped away much of the C19 décor and having been alerted to the existence of Gibbs's original designs she returned the house to its Georgian effect. Her innovation was to estab-lish bedrooms with their own hot and cold facilities, so that Kelmarsh became 'the most inviting hunting box in England'. Their own bedrooms were actually fitted up en suite, then unknown in the country. Nancy Tree brought in her architect uncle, *Paul Phipps*, a pupil of Lutyens, to oversee the work. The Trees wanted to buy Kelmarsh but Colonel Lancaster, as he had become, declined, and in 1937 the Trees moved to Ditch-ley, Oxfordshire. After their divorce, in 1948 Nancy returned to Kelmarsh, this time as 'Mrs Lancaster'. The marriage was short-lived and in 1953 they separated. She had however already suggested the removal of Haycock's 1842 extension and in 1953 *Sir Albert Richardson* was employed to do this and return the s elevation to the Gibbs design. Colonel Lancaster died in 1977 leaving the estate to his sister, on whose death in 1996 it passed into the hands of the Kelmarsh Trust.

The house is red brick, and more Home Counties than Northamptonshire in looks. A perfect, extremely reticent design. Seven-bay centre of two storeys connected by one-storeyed quadrant wings with two-storeyed pavilions of five by four bays. The centre has a three-bay pediment, ground-floor windows with triangular and segmental pediments, a doorway with a segmental pediment on fluted Corinthian columns, and a parapet at stretches replaced by balustrading. The garden side (w) is more or less like the front, except that the three-bay centre projects and the doorway receives less stress. The quadrant arches have Ionic pilasters and a pedimented doorway. The pavilions also have pedimented doorways. Their roofs are visible, having been heightened into mansard shape *c.* 1820 for William Hanbury III. The whole is done in an impeccable taste which also applies to the original interiors, i.e. the staircase, and especially the ENTRANCE HALL. This is one and a half storeys high. The back wall here is an arcade of three arches, and above it there are corridor windows as if they were in an outside wall. Very restrained stucco work with decorative pan-elled ceiling and garlands of flowers, attributed to Gibbs's favourite plasterers *Artari & Bagutti*. The mid-floor frieze and the swags are thought to be Naylor period. The stucco work is somewhat richer in the STAIRCASE, but this is largely because Richardson replaced most of the end wall. The large frames at first-floor level may be original, but the panelled effect is 1950s. The wrought-iron balustrade with lyre-shaped units must be by *Thomas Wagg*, who worked on Hanbury's London house in 1736; the design is also very similar to his documented work at Wolterton, Norfolk. The SE DRAWING ROOM has splendid C18 Chinese wallpaper which Nancy acquired from Kimberley Hall, Norfolk. SW is the LIBRARY, designed by *W. Delano* in 1928, with its end wall recreated by Richardson following the w addition removal. It has a fine early C20 Kentian chimney-piece in yellow Sienna marble. Gibbs's designs for the other rooms are recorded, but very little survives, save for one good bedroom. The SALOON, in the centre of the w front, is the work of *James Wyatt, c.* 1778. It is higher than the other ground-floor rooms with a coved ceiling. Plasterwork roundels and frieze. Exquisite marble chimneypiece good enough for *van Gelder*. Wyatt's DINING ROOM, with its alcove, was redecor-ated by *Saxon Snell*, also in the 1920s. The BALLROOM at the NW end was added in 1873 by *Colling*. It originally had a wide alcove at its N end, but this was removed by the Trees and the room brought back to Georgian effect with fine new doorcases etc. The marquetry of the alcove now floors a passage.

The first floor has unusual levels due to the heightening of the Saloon below. Several bedrooms still have Nancy's en suite fittings, with black marble tops and mirrors. The surviving Gibbs period BEDROOM has been noted. It has an introduced fine early C18 marble chimneypiece with a head beneath drapery. The original service staircase with slender balusters is still intact.

Great efforts have been made since the 1990s to revive Nancy Tree's GARDENS. These date largely from the 1930s when she had much help from *Norah Lindsay* and the involvement of *Geoffrey Jellicoe*, and then she revived them later. Borders, rose gardens and hedges are all now in fine shape. The kitchen garden is surrounded by C18 brick walls ornamented with *Coade* plaques of a classical female head. They house restored glasshouses by *Foster & Pearson*.

ORANGERY, S of the house. Of stone. Late C18. Five arched openings. The building was brought from the demolished Brixworth Hall (q.v.).

SOUTHLODGES and GATES. Built in 1965–6 to *James Wyatt*'s design of 1778 which was discovered in Northampton Public Library. Each lodge has a pedimental gable, and a window framed by an arch. Rusticated gatepiers with urns. NORTH LODGE of the Naylor period.

ESTATE BUILDINGS. In 1949 Colonel Lancaster began remodelling and renewing many of the farmhouses. The earliest, RECTORY FARM, was designed in Neo-Georgian manner by *Peter Dunham* of Dunstable, a Richardson pupil. Several others were built in a similar way during the 1950s (notably Bassetts Lodge, Hill Farm and Grasslands). The last and grandest, SE off the A508, is Scotland Wood Farm, similar but by *R. J. Beswick* of Swindon, 1962.

WILDERNESS FARM, N of the church, in the park. This includes an attractive house, dated 1778. It has a deep culvert at its rear and was probably originally a building associated with providing water for the main house. It was lived in and altered by the Trees while work was being done at the Hall and still has *Nancy Tree*'s doorcase, much of the interior and garden. Alongside is a complex of wood-clad barns built under the direction of *Paul Phipps* in the 1930s.

KETTERING

Kettering was, until the early C19, a relatively small market town, clustered mainly around its medieval church and manor house. It was large enough to be granted a market charter in 1227. By the C14 it had already begun to expand E into the area still called Newland. A grammar school was founded in 1577. The manor, which had been in Crown hands in the C16, was granted in 1585–6 to Sir Christopher Hatton, whose family sold it in 1596

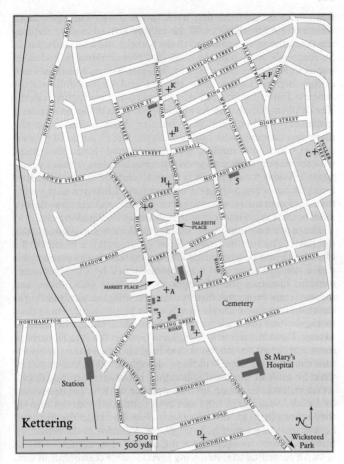

Kettering

500 m
500 yds

A   St Peter and St Paul
B   St Andrew
C   St Mary
D   St Michael and All Angels
E   St Edward (R.C.)
F   Carey Memorial Baptist Church
G   Fuller Baptist Church
H   Toller Congregational Church
J   United Reformed Church
K   Salvation Army Citadel

1   Municipal Offices
2   Library
3   Alfred East Art Gallery
4   Police Station and Magistrates
    Court
5   William Knibb Centre
6   Business Exchange
    (formerly Rockingham Road
    School)

to Edmund Sawyer. The Sawyers then held it for some one
hundred and thirty years. In the mid C18 the town had a reputation for woollen manufacture, although this had declined by the
end of that century. There were serious fires in 1744 and 1766.
In 1778 Thomas Gotch established a shoemaking enterprise and
this soon became the main industry of the town. The Gotch

family also created the first bank in the town. The town lands were enclosed in 1804–5 and the railway arrived in 1857. During the 1860s the town expanded to the N and E and a second church, St Andrew's, was built in 1868–70. Nonconformity had been strong in Kettering since the C17. Thomas Toller, a pupil of Doddridge, arrived in the town in 1775 and he was followed by Andrew Fuller in 1783. In the early C19 the key figure was the Rev. William Knibb, slavery abolitionist. With the introduction of machinery the boot and shoe industry became dominant and many fine factories were built during the late C19, a good proportion of which still survive, mostly converted. Since the 1960s, with the import of foreign goods, shoemaking has virtually disappeared. Today the emphasis is on retail and social activities. Kettering is not a town of great architecture. Little remains earlier than Victorian times, save the parish church, and the main flavour reflects the Late Victorian and Edwardian shoemaking era.

There are two important architectural names associated with the town. The first is *Thomas Eayre* (1691–1758), a member of a blacksmith and bell-founding family who was also a surveyor. He was a talented artist and was commissioned by the Northamptonshire historian John Bridges to help with illustrations and maps for his projected history. Eayre's only certain building is the church at Stoke Doyle (q.v.), but it is sufficiently competent to suggest that there are more buildings which should be credited to him. The other name is *John Alfred Gotch* (1852–1942), perhaps more important for his books on English Renaissance architecture than for his own buildings, though the fact that much of what he built in the town still stands is testament to his ability. As an architect he set up his own practice in 1879. He was joined by *Charles Saunders* in 1887 and both continued with the firm till they retired in 1937. In 1899 *Henry Surridge* joined the firm and he was made a partner in 1930. *Gotch, Saunders & Surridge* continues as a firm recognized for the quality of its commissions. It is worth recording that following J. A. Gotch's collaboration with Lutyens on the Midland Bank, Poultry, in London, between 1924 and 1930, the firm was commissioned to design some 140 branch bank buildings across England.*

CHURCHES

34   ST PETER & ST PAUL. Wonderfully tall tower and spire, some 179 ft (54.6 metres), dominating the skyline, especially when approached from the w. The siting at a distance from the main modern street of the town and along an avenue of trees gives the church a curiously ungenuine look, as if it were an imitation or re-erected. Yet the tower is indeed seen in this way to its best advantage and is one of the finest of its type certainly in the county if not in the country. Perp, with a spire not too

---

*For a full discussion of J. A. Gotch's work see Dr Roy Hargrave, *The Life and Works of John Alfred Gotch*, PhD thesis, Royal Holloway, University of London, 2005.

short and not too long. Set-back buttresses. Four stages with altogether five friezes of quatrefoils or cusped lozenges, w doorway with tracery in the spandrels, a crocketed gable, and pinnacles, framed by a quatrefoil frieze. Five-light window with transom. Then a tall all-panelled stage. Bell-stage with three fine, slender bell-openings with transom. Battlements, polygonal turret pinnacles. Recessed spire with crockets and three tiers of lucarnes. It is thought to date from *c.* 1450 and has a good deal in common with the tower and spire at Oundle (traceried panels, polygonal turrets etc.). The tower must have been built before the nave, as its buttresses, fully decorated, appear inside. This suggests the rest of the church is Perp of *c.* 1500, with the exception of the early C14 N doorway and the Dec E parts of the chancel with the odd E window. Its basic forms are Geometrical (unfoiled circles due to early C19 reglazing), but the lights have ogee arches. That may seem the fault of the drastic restoration of 1868 by *W. Slater*, but Billings in 1843 shows it such. Indeed the chancel seems rather mean and somehow lets down the scale of the interior. Perp aisle windows of three lights with embattled transoms, doorways in the first bay, and on the N side in addition a two-storeyed porch. Entrance with traceried spandrels. Three niches above it with statues by *J. L. Carr*, 1984–8. The aisle E of the doorways has five windows, i.e. the arcades inside are of six bays. Tall, elegant piers with the usual four-shafts-and-four-hollows section. Arches with two sunk quadrant mouldings. The same details in the chancel chapels. They have five-light E windows. The S chapel is ashlar-faced but this may be partly due to *Sir Arthur Blomfield* who added the vestry to it in 1893. Perp clerestory. – SCREENS. Lady Chapel, classical, not Gothic, 1926 by *Martin Travers*; tower lobby screens, 1997 by *Brian Austin*. – Wrought-iron GATES (towards the road) of 1963 by *W. F. Knight*. – WALL PAINTINGS. Two large angels either side the chancel arch, so part of a rood arrangement of which there are other traces such as openings. N aisle. St Roch, now unrecognizable. – READING DESK, for chained books. C17. – STAINED GLASS. In the S chapel assembled original bits. Chancel E, 1848 by *Ward & Hughes*. S chapel E, 1854 by *Webb & Nixon*. The tracery lights in both N and S aisles are also theirs. – N chapel N window, Roughton memorial, 1855 by *Francis Oliphant*. – N chapel E by *Comper*, 1937. – Tower w window by *Kempe*, 1893. – N chapel N window, (†1959) by *King & Sons*, designed by *A. L. Wilkinson*, 1963. – Head of St Faith by *Clayton & Bell* saved from Newton-in-the-Willows church as a memorial to the writer *J. L. Carr* of Kettering (†1994). – MILLENNIUM STONE. 1999 by *Gotch Pearson*. – MONUMENT. Bronze plaque for John Nettleship, animal painter, †1902, with Art Nouveau trees and a central lion panel. Rather fine.

ALL SAINTS, William Street. 1926–8 by *E. Turner & E. J. May*. Red brick with blue dressings in a lancet style. Reduced in size in 1981 with a plain, low, brick addition at the w end. – FONT. From Faxton (*see* p. 272).

St Andrew, Rockingham Road. 1869 by *G. E. Street*. Ironstone, in the Late Geometrical style. A polygonal bell-turret over the nave. Wide nave. Arcades with octagonal piers carrying arches which die into them. Roof with arched braces and collar-beams. Vestry added 1899 by *Blackwell & Thomson* and N aisle added 1925 by *Blackwell & Riddey*. – PULPIT. 1929 by *Leslie T. Moore*. – SCREEN. S aisle, painted 1960 by *Henry Bird* with a panel showing the young Christ in the carpenter's shop. – STAINED GLASS. E (1893) and S (1906) by *Kempe*. – N aisle, two windows of 1925 and 1930 by *Morris & Co*. of Westminster. – Fine W window 1979 by *Graham Pentelow* and also by him the 2000 Millennium glazed screen below the organ in the chancel.

St Mary, Fuller Street. 1893–5 by *Gotch & Saunders*. Ironstone, in the C14 Gothic style, with a charming bell-turret on the vestry. Good interior lit by the extensive clerestory. Arcades with low moulded arches topped by ogee curves die into their piers. No capitals but a band of carved decoration picked out in gold and red. Tall screen and mock rood beam. Large TRIPTYCH PAINTING of the Last Supper in the chancel. Gilded baldacchino. – PULPIT with pierced panels. – STAINED GLASS. Some good windows. Chancel E, 1901 and baptistery, 1915–33 by *Percy Bacon*. – W window, 1927 by *Martin Travers*, very fine. – S chapel, 1961–84, a series by *K. Barton Studios* of Rottingdean. – Narthex, 1930s series by *Pearce & Cutler*.

St Michael and All Angels, Roundhill Road. 1907 of corrugated iron and remarkable as it survives intact. Timber gables and windows with Gothic glazing and a small turret. It has distinct charm.

St Edward (R.C.), London Road. Brick, with broad W tower inset with round arches. By *E. Bower Norris* of Stafford. Opened in 1940. The interior simple with round-arched arcades. The aisles have transverse arches creating the illusion of vaulting. The church is sited W to E so the reredos is at the W end. Some nice GLASS by *Pearce & Cutler* of Birmingham. The door glazing is by *Rachael Aldridge*, 2005. The former church of 1893 is behind, serving as its hall.

Carey Memorial Baptist Church, King Street. A quite grand essay in quasi-Perp Gothic manner of 1911 by *Cooper & Williams*. Cantilever construction of the galleries so the interior is open without pillars. Tie-beam timber roof. Original coloured patterned glass including a STAINED GLASS portrait of William Carey in the vestibule. The original 1891–2 church in Nelson Street serves as the hall.

Fuller Baptist Church, Gold Street. 1861–2 by *E. Sharman* of Wellingborough. Lombardic classical façade of ashlar with a big pediment, but the details such as the round-arched one-storeyed portico and the small round-arched windows above it, and especially the bits of mosaic friezes, are Victorian. – STAINED GLASS. A portrait medallion of Andrew Fuller, co-founder of the Baptist Mission.

ROCKINGHAM ROAD BAPTIST CHURCH. 1926–7 by *R. J. Williams*. Originally designed as the Sunday School with space for the intended church in front, never built. Brick with a central hall and lateral small rooms. The interior space with transverse round arches. Refurbished 1996 by *Jonathan Davies & Alan Bruton*. – STAINED GLASS. E window of 1950 by *A. E. Buss* for *Goddard & Gibbs*.

TOLLER CONGREGATIONAL CHURCH, Gold Street. 1723, but little recognizable of that date. The side with the ironstone facing and the arched windows on two floors looks Late Georgian; the rather brutal red-brick façade with two short towers is of 1875. Up Meeting Lane TOLLER CHAPEL SUNDAY SCHOOLS, 1883 by *R. W. Johnson*. Also of red brick with two towers. Behind the church, the BURIAL GROUND. A slab records the foundation of the 'Great Meeting', Kettering's first Independent chapel in 1736. Several nice slate stones and the Gothic tomb of Rev. Toller and another memorial for the printer, publisher and collector Thomas Dash †1841, whose Northamptonshire collections are in the British Library.

UNITED REFORMED CHURCH (formerly Congregational), London Road. 1898, by *Cooper & Williams*. Red brick with two short polygonal turrets and details typical of a Neo-Gothic Nonconformist chapel of *c.* 1900, somewhere between Perp and Art Nouveau. Wide interior opening into two shallow transepts from whose rear angled walls two arches support tall fluted pillars, which in turn support the wooden barrel ceiling, with small Jacobean pendants at each side. Sunday School of the same period in St Peter's Avenue. – STAINED GLASS. Three windows on the S side, 1930–3 by *Abbot & Co.* of Lancaster. – N side, a fine window of 1946 by *A. J. Davies* of Bromsgrove.

SALVATION ARMY CITADEL (former Wesleyan church), Rockingham Road. Brick and stone, large Renaissance style with big arched windows with cinquefoiled heads, 1906, with the former Sunday School block of similar style in Regent Street. An earlier 1892 school sandwiched in between. All by the *Gotch* firm.

CEMETERY, London Road. The CHAPELS are of 1861 by *R. W. Johnson* of Melton Mowbray. They are separated by a spire.

PUBLIC BUILDINGS

MUNICIPAL OFFICES, Bowling Green Road. Built by *Gotch & Saunders* in 1913 as the Grammar School. Large of red brick, Neo-Georgian.

PUBLIC LIBRARY, Sheep Street. 1904 by *Goddard & Co.* of Leicester whose design was chosen by Gotch. Half-H-plan, red brick, gabled wings and a pretty little cupola in the centre.

ALFRED EAST ART GALLERY, just W of the parish church. 1913 by *J. A. Gotch*. Although small, quite monumental. Portland stone with solid walls and pairs of Doric columns.

POLICE STATION AND MAGISTRATES' COURT, London Road. By the *County Architect's Department* (*A. N. Harris* and *John Goff*), 1968–71. A large, quite formal composition. Low central block with steps in front, with one-storey links to the two-storey magistrates' court on the r., and to the more elaborately detailed three-storey police station on the l. This has a porch, and the motif of beam-ends slightly projecting beyond the brick walls.

BUCCLEUCH ACADEMY, Laburnham Crescent. To be completed 2013, *Nicholas Hare Architects*.

KETTERING SCIENCE ACADEMY, Deeble Road. To be completed 2013, *Nicholas Hare Architects*.*

TRESHAM COLLEGE, Windmill Road. Opened 2007, replacing the former grammar school building of 1960–2. Broadly cruciform in plan with a T-shaped façade facing the road. Basically four storeys, the projecting wing of terracotta panels and the side wings of yellow brick panels. Long rows of windows. Central clear-glazed reception and circular staircase. Four-storey main block with cream spandrel panels; various lower ranges. The ceramic MURAL of 1960 by *Kenneth Budd* (†1995) which decorated the entrance to the grammar school has been dismantled and is to be resited elsewhere.

BOARD SCHOOLS. Kettering was late adopting the Act of 1870, the new schools dating from the 1890s. *Gotch & Saunders* cornered the market, building three out of the four best. Each has a tall campanile-like chimney tower and each one manages to be quite different. The finest is STAMFORD ROAD SCHOOL (William Knibb Centre), E of Montagu Street. Red brick, Tudor, with gables, 1892. Tall, asymmetrically placed tower with odd, original circular tracery patterns, one set pierced through and a top with four gables. Later additions behind. Further out is PARK STREET SCHOOL, Jacobean style of three bays with large mullion-transom windows. Tall octagonal campanile behind. HAWTHORN SCHOOL comes within the Perambulation (*see* below). The former ROCKINGHAM ROAD SCHOOL (now Business Exchange) is of 1893–4 by *H. A. Cooper* of Kettering. Rather grand in a red brick and stone Flemish Renaissance style. Central tower feature with pedimented double-window wings on each side. The side elevations in Dryden Street have similar double-window wings and an elaborate centrepiece with the school name plaque.

ST MARY'S HOSPITAL, London Road. The old part was the former WORKHOUSE, 1837, latest classical. The characteristic raised octagon in the centre was taken down in 1971, when the building was altered by *Gotch, Saunders & Surridge*. The front has been reduced to one storey throughout, and the three-bay central pediment lowered.

GENERAL HOSPITAL, Rothwell Road. The original hospital, 1897, consists of a one-storey outpatient department and a

*The Technical College in St Mary's Road was demolished in 2011 and replaced by a housing development by *William Davies Ltd*.

three-storey wing. Ironstone. Hugely expanded since the
1960s. The CHAPEL has a fine STAINED GLASS window by
A. J. Davies of Bromsgrove.

CREMATORIUM, Warren Hill. An impressive 1940 essay of grey
brick and Portland stone with some Art Deco features designed
by *James Haugh*, Borough Surveyor, and chief assistant
C. Gingell. Church-like in form with a tower and cloisters and
well set in wide lawns. Extensions and some modernization
also in brick by the borough architectural staff in 1978 with an
additional chapel and a Chapel of Remembrance.

STATION. Originally 1857 by *C. H. Driver*, but the present buildings date from 1895. Small, red brick and light brown terracotta with big Midland Railway plaques. Shaped gables.
Attractive ironwork canopy supports.

PERAMBULATION

A good place to start is with *J. A. Gotch*, at the Alfred East Art
Gallery (*see* Public Buildings) in SHEEP STREET. Outside to
s his FIRST WORLD WAR MEMORIAL, a square tapering
stone column with carved wreaths, *c.* 1920. Alongside the
gallery to the N, inset, is a BUST of Sir Alfred East, 1911 by
George Frampton. On the roadside, once more by *Gotch*, the
DRYLAND MEMORIAL (John W. Dryland 1834–1906, Kettering's influential Medical Officer of Health), another square
column on scrolled base, with carved rose garlands and a horse
trough on each side, of 1907. Opposite are *Gotch*'s PICCA-
DILLY BUILDINGS, 1926, typical of many commercial rows
he built elsewhere in the town. Long ten bays with two triangular pediments and at first floor pairs of projecting oriels.
Behind the library (*see* Public Buildings), the MANOR HOUSE
(now MUSEUM), once owned by the Sawyer family. Small
evidence of C17 but largely Georgian with a plain four-bay
façade of two storeys. Later additions following conversion to
a museum in 1987. Beyond the library is the small MARKET
PLACE. This was redesigned 2009–10 and given a semicircular
paved amphitheatre with stepped seats and the now almost
mandatory water spurts on its edge. The w end was given a
new set of buildings designed by the *Stephen George & Partners*.
A three-block arrangement, faintly Georgian, of brick with
some rendering and its s block given wide stone rusticated
arches, holding balconies and a canopy. It has the unfortunate
appearance of being of the 1970s New Town style rather than
of the 2000s and is, alas, a lost opportunity. What it does do
is to make the former CORN EXCHANGE, 1853 by *E. F. Law*,
on the E side, look rather grand. It is red brick, two storeys,
three bays with giant blank arches. The first floor was designed
to be used as the town hall. Much altered below. It later
became a cinema and housed the first moving picture show in
1909. Its Hippodrome poster still painted on its end wall.
Opposite on the s side the ROYAL HOTEL, 1878 by *Gotch*.
Brick and stone in the Jacobean manner and typical of the way

he turns the corner. Ionic doorcase. Rear and side additons 1925–6 by *J. T. Blackwell* in association with *Gotch & Saunders*. Running alongside the Royal Hotel is WEST STREET with some early C19 stone and brick terraces and at the bottom WESTFIELD, a large gabled stone house of mid C19 date with a pretty veranda.

Leading off E is MARKET STREET, quite impressive in its way with its rows of Renaissance-style façades: first, MARKET STREET CHAMBERS with adjoining on the r. what was the Sun Hotel, dated 1894, by *Gotch*, the site belonging to the Kettering Grammar School, hence the plaque; then another set of chambers; and ending in a five-bay brick angled corner with triangular gables and splendid tall chimneystacks, also *Gotch*. Returning to HIGH STREET, on the corner the former LLOYDS BANK, now a restaurant, a typical mixture of Victorian Gothic and Renaissance, especially the decorative pilasters on the rounded bay. Then on the W side comes HSBC, 1903 by *Gotch* for the Midland Bank, the first of a series of designs by his firm for the bank. Five bays, classical with rounded windows at ground floor and triangular pediments at first. Double Tuscan-columned entrance. Almost next the former Regal (later Granada) Cinema, now GALA BINGO, 1936 by *George Coles*. Rather a fine brick façade, with a wide concave arc and a central round glazed turret with a mushroom top. Back on the E side a nice double-fronted brick and stone building of 1902 with tiny shell motifs, built for Barclays Bank. Then NATWEST, 1901 by *Blackwell & Thomson* of Kettering. Stone, four bays with rustication and much banded double Ionic columns at first-floor level. A little further on the W side, MARKS & SPENCER. 1930s brick Neo-Georgian, three-bay centre with a flat pediment, and fluted brickwork at the sides. Opposite comes another of *Gotch*'s 1880s rows, six bays and the usual assembly of windows, bays etc. Plaque with a rearing horse denoting the Old White Horse Inn which used to stand here.

The street now opens out into a triangular space, in the centre of which is the pointed metal ROTARY CLOCK by *Terry Eaton Associates*, 2006. Leading off to the W is LOWER STREET, and worth the diversion for two interesting Georgian survivals. But first the 1950s POST OFFICE, five bays, Neo-Georgian brick, with decorative masks over the windows. Then on the r. the former MALTINGS for Elworthy's Brewery, 1904, brick, three floors with pilasters and still with its conical turreted roof. On the N side DEENE HOUSE, ironstone with a pretty timber Victorian Gothic porch. Beyond on the same side, set back, CAREY MISSION HOUSE. Georgian, rendered, seven bays with a Doric doorcase. This was the home of J. A. Gotch's brother, Thomas Cooper Gotch (1864–1931), a talented artist. In its front wall a classical plaque recording that it was here in 1792 that Andrew Fuller and William Carey founded the Baptist Missionary Society. Opposite, also set back, another Georgian survival, CHESHAM HOUSE, built 1762. Three bays and three floors. Pretty columned doorcase with Adamish decoration. Former outbuildings to E. This was the Gotch family home from where Thomas Gotch (1748–1806) set up his shoemaking business in 1778, and where J. A. Gotch was born. Beyond, on the other side, the THREE COCKS, 1894 by *Gotch*, brick, four bays, two of them gabled.

Back to HIGH STREET, which now turns E and becomes GOLD STREET. On the corner the conspicuous brick towers of the Toller Church (*see* above). Further on the NEWLANDS shopping arcade of 1975–7 by *Shingler Risdon Associates*. It was later extended northwards in the 1980s. A big gabled entrance on columns with a carved relief of a shoemaker in the pediment and shoemaking tool reliefs either side. Opposite a nice Jacobean brick façade of 1888, and beyond the Fuller Baptist Church (*see* above) with its Lombardic arcade. In NEWLANDS itself the imposing façade of the Kettering Industrial Cooperative Society's building of 1896–9, again by *Gotch*. At the busy junction of Gold Street with Montagu and Silver Street, some sensible 1930s façades, and on the corner of Montagu Street, MONTAGU BUILDINGS, 1898 by *Gotch*, three floors in the Jacobean mode, with big arched windows on the first floor. In MONTAGU STREET, on the l. the CONSERVATIVE CLUB, 1888 by *S. Perkins-Pick* of Leicester. A large red brick Jacobean-style block with a gabled wing of three bays, central entrance with foliate panel and a mask and another single bay beyond. A half-timbered gable with decorative supports. Back and along SILVER STREET, nothing of note till the street narrows (it had been widened in 1933), with on the r. and prominent, the former LIBERAL CLUB (now XTRA), 1888 by *Gotch*. Double-fronted with canted bays connected by a triple arcade and a big gable with a stepped window. Opposite a nice red and yellow brick building with decorative panels, built 1880 by *R. W. Johnson* as the Cross Keys Coffee Tavern and Temperance Hall, now ironically a pub. Then a further space, HORSE MARKET, a small green, re-landscaped in 2011, with a cast-iron WATER FOUNTAIN of 1894, formerly in North Park. One or two ironstone buildings around, remnants of earlier periods, the S end building being a conversion of the former National Infants' School. Just beyond on the E side is GREEN LANE with STAPLES BUILDING, a converted shoe factory of 1873 built for Abbott & Bird. Brick and stone, Italianate with round-arched windows. Former offices alongside with arcaded cornices, added in 1890s.

Moving along LONDON ROAD, on the l. on the corner of ST PETER'S AVENUE, the Tudor Gothic façade of the United Reformed church (*see* above). In the avenue a row of expensive villas dating between 1896 and 1899 with amusing sequence of names, the first in honour of the explorer H. M. Stanley: Stanley, Rhodesia, Durban and Pretoria. Round the corner in TENNYSON ROAD everything becomes literary with further villas: Tennyson, Carlyle, Wordsworth and Ivanhoe. Back in London Road, on the r. the CORN EXCHANGE HALL and on the corner of BOWLING GREEN ROAD, opposite the cemetery, DROVERS HALL, an ironstone corner block of 1880 by *R. W. Johnson* which was the offices of the former cattle market.

HEADLANDS contains some of the most impressive Late Victorian and Edwardian houses. The development dates from the early 1880s with more villas built in the 1890s. Nearly all are brick, but there is one ironstone and limestone house, LONSDALE (Headlands Surgery), Tudor style of 1881. Further on the r., QUEENSBERRY ROAD with two double-fronted blocks, one typical Edwardian Queen Anne with small side towers topped by cupolas and half-timbered gables, and next door one with big gables, pebbledash, pilasters and a wide foliate frieze. On the corner of THE CRESCENT is SUNNY-LANDS, a big Jacobean-style brick house with tall chimneys and decorative porch which *Gotch* built for William Timpson, the shoe manufacturer, in 1894 (now a school). Opposite is HAWTHORN ROAD with some entertaining rows *c.* 1900, and the frontage and tower of *Gotch & Saunders*'s Hawthorn School of 1893–4. Returning to Bowling Green Road, it remains to glance at the SAWYER ALMSHOUSES of 1688. Ironstone with mullions on the ground floor and casements above. Armorial doorcase. Round the corner in Northampton Road, at its junction with Station Road, just worth noting is NORTHAMPTON HOUSE. Brick and stone, built 1910 by *J. T. Blackwell* for James Pain, whose investment in iron ore extraction began the Corby industry. The BUS GARAGE opposite was built in 1935 and still looks the part.

OUTER KETTERING

Following the arrival of the railway in 1857 and the establishment of industry, Kettering expanded to the N and E of the centre with terraces of working-class housing and factories. A good deal of this still survives, notably in the area between Rocking-ham Road and Montagu Street. In a number of streets there are at the back of properties, at the end of their gardens, small brick workshop buildings (called barns) for the boot and shoe outworkers. Off Montagu Street is WELLINGTON STREET with on its corner one of the largest and most elaborate factor-ies, built for H. HANGER (later F. S. Bryant), of 1887–91. It is by *Gotch* and typical of the form to be adopted elsewhere. Three storeys of brick and stone with a curved corner entrance and above an oriel, here canted and of two floors. Seven bays fronting Montagu Street with pedimented bays at either end. Similar façade in Wellington Street. Just beyond in Wellington Street, on the l. is the former WORKING MEN'S CLUB, 1887 by *H. A. Cooper*. Further down the hill in Montagu Street, on the corner of BATH ROAD, is TIMSON'S 1990s factory. Brick with oversailing lead roofs. In Bath Road the original office building proudly stating 'Perfecta Works'. The former METH-ODIST CHAPEL of 1890 opposite also became part of the Timson complex. It is rather fine, red brick with round-arched

windows. Along Bath Road at the corner of Digby Street is the
former T. BIRD factory of 1890–1 also by *Gotch*, similar in effect   108
to the Hanger factory and almost as grand. Pedimented gables
with bands of brick and stone, two in Digby Street and four in
Bath Road. Gotch's familiar corner feature. Parallel streets N of
Montagu Street are REGENT STREET and HAVELOCK STREET.
In Regent Street the former HALES & JOWETT factory of 1890.
Eight bays with brick pilasters, three storeys with iron windows.
Four pedimented gables. At the W end of the same street is
CROWN STREET and the former CO-OPERATIVE MODEL
BAKERY building of 1900. Three floors, the ground floor taller.
Between each window KCS cyphers. In Havelock Street the
former KETTERING CO-OP factory, 1890 by *H. A. Cooper*.
Angled bay with roundel and their 'Hand in hand' motif. In
WOOD STREET, the next N, one of the most decorative factor-
ies, LOAKE'S, still in operation. 1894 by *Mosley & Anderson*.
Red brick with a large scrolled Dutch gable in the centre and
smaller similar gables on the side elevation. On the W side of
Rockingham Road is FIELD STREET with another very decorative factory of 1878. Round-arched façades of red, yellow and
blue brick. Opposite, on the corner of Dryden Street, the
former factory of the KETTERING CLOTHING MANUFAC-
TURING CO-OPERATIVE SOCIETY, 1895 by *H. A. Cooper*, four
somewhat gaunt storeys, but a nice Neo-Georgian doorcase on
its corner. Then either side of Field Street other factories in a
more typical *c.* 1900 fashion. Four storeys with masses of large
windows. One other building in the area deserves mention. In
ESKDAILL STREET, on the E side, remains of the 1920 façade
of the former EMPIRE CINEMA. Big round arch and garlanded pilasters.

ROCKINGHAM ROAD, running N from the centre, also has
several quite grand Victorian and Edwardian villas and some
brick and half-timbered terraces, including No. 113 on the W
side, EASTON HOUSE, an amusing example of 1885 timbering
with lots of gables and a crinkly porch.

ELM BANK, Northampton Road. *c.* 1890 by *Gotch*, converted to
a residential complex 2010–11. Broad Elizabethan with two
canted bays on the garden side. New blocks added on conversion. Round the corner in HALL LANE two further *Gotch*
houses: the first 1898 red brick Neo-Queen Anne and beyond
another four-bay house built 1898 for Charles Wicksteed. Both
were acquired by a convent which closed in 2008. Their future
is uncertain (2012).

WICKSTEED PARK, on the SE edge of town. The brainchild of
Charles Wicksteed (1847–1931), engineer and inventor, who set
up his business in Kettering in 1876. The company began
making steam ploughing engines, then by 1898 bicycles. His
most important invention was a form of automatic gear box in
1907, the forerunner of that used in cars today. Following an
initial purchase of land in 1913, a plan for a public park and a
housing development was drawn up by *Gotch & Saunders*.
Work began in 1918–21 when a LODGE to Gotch's design was

built at the then entrance to the park, at the junction of Barton Road and Pytchley Road, where it still stands. One of the innovations was the Railway opened in 1931 which still takes visitors round the park. In 1921 *Gotch* designed a PAVILION with a clock tower. The bones of this survive, though engulfed by extra wings added 1927–35, largely by *Gotch, Saunders & Surridge*. There have inevitably been changes to the interior since then. Below the pavilion is a flower garden which contains a MEMORIAL designed by *Gotch* for Wicksteed, an octagonal obelisk with reliefs of running winged children at the top. There are two *c.* 1930 STATUES near a memorial to Wicksteed's dog: one a boy with a sailing boat, the other a girl feeding a bird.

In the early 1930s it was decided to develop a housing scheme in PARADISE LANE. A number of designs in the 'Modern' idiom were created by *J. & N. Brandon-Jones* between 1934 and 1937 and several pairs and single houses were built. These still exist. They are remarkably good examples of the period, rendered concrete, with curved ends, balconies and sweeping lines. Those in Paradise Lane have largely lost their original Crittall type metal windows but another pair, on the other side of Pytchley Road on the corner of LEWIS ROAD, are almost untouched. This pair was built by the Kettering builder *A. P. Lewis & Son*, from whom the road takes its name. They, a little later, built more semi-detached houses further along, more orthodox in manner but still with balconies, several of which have since been filled in. The Paradise Lane scheme never reached full fruition and the other properties are of various later dates. Just NE on London Road is THE WAYFARERS, built as a club and institute 1930 by *Gotch & Saunders* in their Neo-Georgian manner with two floors of sash windows, though those below now altered.

KETTERING BUSINESS PARK, S of the town by the A14. It includes at its lower level, alongside the A509, the dramatic VELUX HEADQUARTERS, by *White Associates*, 2001. An extraordinary curved structure, largely of timber, rather like one side of a vast ship. On the apex of the slope the huge and innovative RCI HEADQUARTERS, 1990–1 by *Lister Drew Haines Barrow*. Red and yellow brick with a tall white-columned entrance. A segmental canopy above, and segmental-topped pavilions at each end. At the rear between its wings a tall glazed staircase tower.

KILSBY

ST FAITH. Unbuttressed C13 W tower with single lancet window. C14 belfry stage with battlements and a small recessed spire. One tier of lucarnes. The body of the church was somewhat over-restored in 1868–9 by *Ewan Christian*, and further work was done in 1895, which reduces its architectural interest. Inside tall Dec arcades of four bays with octagonal piers and

. Eydon, South Northamptonshire sandstone village (p. 5)
. Easton-on-the-Hill, North Northamptonshire limestone village (p. 5)

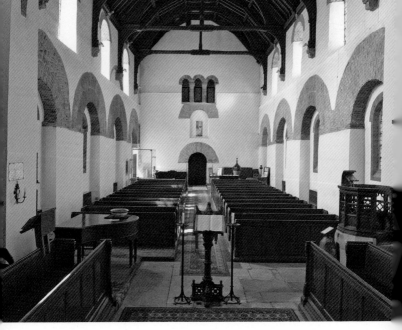

10. Northampton, St Peter, nave and tower arch, *c.* 1140 (p. 437)
11. Northampton, St Peter, detail of capital, C12 (p. 437)
12. West Haddon, All Saints, font detail, *c.* 1120 (p. 666)

3. Castle Ashby,
   St Mary
   Magdalene,
   N doorway, C12
   (p. 158)
4. Crick, St
   Margaret, font,
   C12 (p. 209)

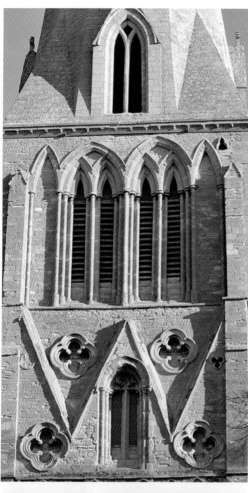

15 | 17
16 | 18

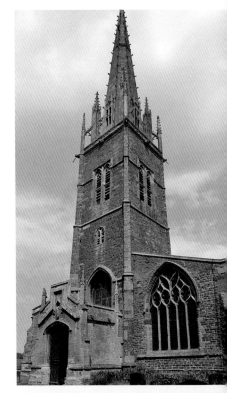

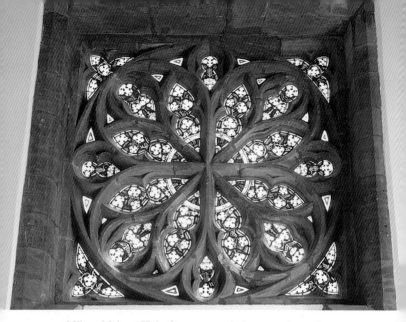

✠ S MA ꞇ ꝩ Iꜳ꞉

6. Fotheringhay, St Mary and All Saints, 1430 (p. 280)
7. Lowick, St Peter, largely C15 (p. 399)
8. Ashby St Ledgers, St Leodegarius, screen, C15 (p. 91)
9. Slapton, St Botolph, interior, wall painting of St Christopher, late C14–C15 (p. 574)
0. Fotheringhay, St Mary and All Saints, pulpit, C15 (p. 281)

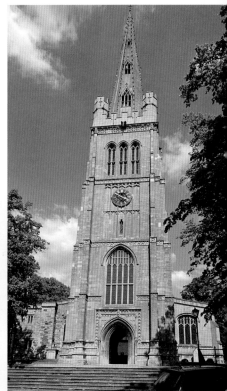

43 | 44
   | 45

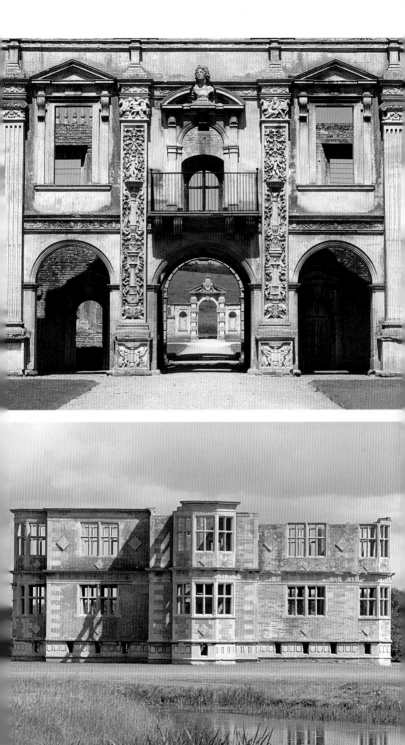

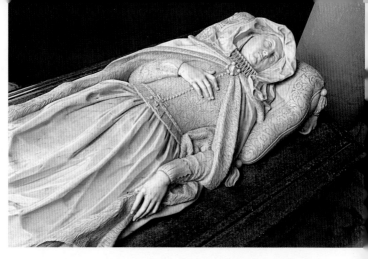

62	65
63	66
64	

67. Northampton, All Saints, interior, rebuilt by Henry Bell, 1676–80 (p. 433)
68. Northampton, Sessions House, by Henry Bell, 1676–8 (p. 442)
69. Norhtampton, All Saints, sw exterior, portico, 1701 (p. 434)
70. Northampton, Sessions House, Crown Court ceiling, by Edward Goudge, 1684–8 (p. 442)

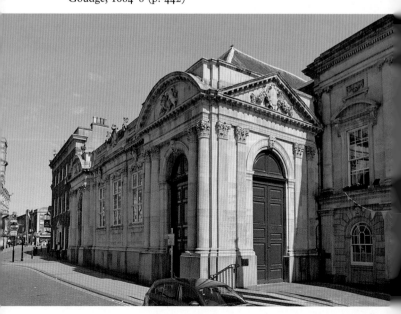

84 | 86
85 | 87

92. Cottesbrooke Hall, staircase plasterwork, mid c18 (p. 197)
93. Drayton House, Dining Room ceiling, by William Rhodes, 1771–4 (p. 237)
94. Laxton Hall, entrance hall, by George Dance, *c.* 1812 (p. 387)

95. Braunston, canal bridges, 1834 (p. 134)
96. Weedon Barracks, Royal Ordnance Depot, begun 1804 (p. 645)

107	109
108	110

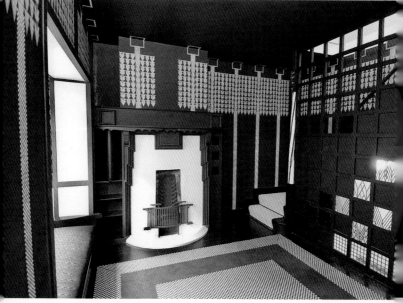

114. Northampton, All Saints, war memorial, by Lutyens, 1926 (p. 435)
115. Northampton, Christchurch Rd, Co op building, by L.G. Ekins, 1920 (p. 475)
116. Kettering, Wicksteed houses, Lewis Rd, by J. & N. Brandon-Jones, 1934–7 (p. 366)

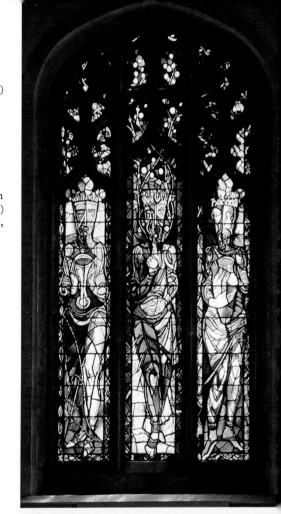

| 117 | 119 |
| 118 | 120 |

121. Northampton, Express Lifts Tower, by Maurice Walton, 1980–82 (p. 483)
122. Towcester, The Grace Grandstand, by Francis Roberts, 1997–8 (p. 255)
123. Northampton, Eastern District housing, c. 1970 (p. 489)

124. Corby, Business Academy, by Sir Norman Foster & Partners, 2007 (p. 188)
125. Upton Park, housing, by H.T.A. Architects, 2007–8 (p. 629)
126. Corby Cube, George Street, by Hawkins Brown, 2008–10 (p. 188)

Kilsby, St Faith.
Drawing by G. Clarke, c. 1850

double-chamfered arches. Drawings by George Clarke show that the s aisle had two rectangular plain-glazed windows and the clerestory had two lunettes with bars, so much of the present tracery is due to the restoration. – BOX PEWS but of late date, probably 1816 according to Wetton's Guide. – STAINED GLASS. Chancel e window by *W. Holland* of Warwick, designed by *Frank Holt*, 1877. Chancel s also theirs. – Another s window has a Resurrection, designed by *J. Doyle* for *J. Powell & Sons*, 1869. – s aisle, Lucas memorial 1928 by *Burlison & Grylls*. – Tower window by *T. Cox & Sons*, 1874.

UNITED REFORMED CHURCH (formerly Congregational), Chapel Street. Said to be of 1764. The façade of the stone building with the pedimental gable and what was a tripartite lunette window in it. Inside a canopied PULPIT and GALLERY on Tuscan columns. Memorial for Thomas Strange †1784 who 'this house erected'.

OLD VICARAGE, set back on the e side of Watling Street. A large brick house built 1867–8 by *Ewan Christian*.

RAILWAY TUNNEL. 2,400 yds (2,195 metres) long. By *Robert Stephenson*. Part of the work of the London–Birmingham Railway, opened in 1838. Limestone arch to tunnel opening and on the s approach to the village a brick castellated ventilation shaft.

KINGS SUTTON

ST PETER AND ST PAUL. Kings Sutton has one of the finest, if not the finest, spires in this county of spires. The w tower is tall. To its W is a porch built of limestone with its own pinnacles and three niches above the entrance. The inner W doorway has tracery panels, and the porch a tierceron vault with the tracery pattern of the four-petalled flower as its central motif. The bell-openings are of two lights with a straight hoodmould and Dec tracery. So while the porch is Perp, the tower is Dec. Below the battlements runs a frieze of cusped lozenges. At the top corners thin, tall pinnacles connected by thin, short flying buttresses with more substantial and taller pinnacles which keep close to the spire. This is crocketed, and the tall, sturdier lower lucarnes are transomed. High up a tracery band and yet higher another set of tiny lucarnes. The spire is probably of the late C14. It had to be partly rebuilt in 1883–4 by *H. M. Townsend* of Peterborough, and in 1968 was repaired again. Beasley in 1848 says that the greatest thickness of its walls is 9½ in. (24 cm.) The total height of the steeple is 198 ft (60 metres). As for the body of the church it is mostly Dec as is, although rebuilt in the 1880s, probably the N two-storeyed vestry. Only the chancel E window, the N aisle W window (alas, decapitated), and the S porch entrance are Perp, but interestingly the frame of the S doorway still has ballflowers in it, so only just Perp. Dec are the chancel side windows, the S aisle windows culminating in the fantastic tracery of the E window, which has at the top a circle with a trefoil of three segments, and the N aisle.

Internally the picture is different. The greater part of the chancel turns out to be Norman, and this is borne out by the corbel table outside. Inside there is blank arcading along both walls. The shafts are original; the arches with their zigzag are part of the restoration in 1866 by *G. G. Scott*. As for the nave and aisles, their grandeur and airiness, it is true, are due to the early C14, but the S arcade is considerably earlier. It makes a strange impression. Its piers and arches are earlier than is its general character. This can only be explained by the reuse of the piers and arches, and indeed the outer hoodmould of nailhead. The piers are circular, the abaci square. One capital has many scallops, the E respond waterleaf. The arches are unmoulded. This points to the late C12. But the proportions are the same as those of the N arcade, with soft quatrefoil, almost drumlike piers and arches with a moulding of two slight chamfers – which is C13 work. Actually the moment when the S arcade was readjusted can be determined by the fact that the one capital which is not late C12 in style has some ballflower decoration, an unmistakable sign of the early C14. Rood stair access in the S aisle. The clerestory is probably C16. SEDILIA and PISCINA in the Dec style are also part of the restoration by *Scott* and conjectural. The fine TILES also 1866. There was further restoration work in 1897. – PEWS. A fine series throughout the church, all with poppyheads and from a restoration 1841–2 by *D. G. Squirhill* of Leamington. – SCREEN. Also by *Scott*. – FONT. Rough, plain, created in 1923 with advice from *Leslie Moore*. The stone was found under a mound in the churchyard and the base is a millstone. The lead-lined bowl

measures 2 ft 8 in. (81 cm.) internally. – REREDOS (N aisle) in
the E.E. style with painted panels, formerly at the E end of the
chancel, and part of *Scott*'s restoration. The painted panels
replace statues and are of *c.* 1950 by *E. W. Tristram*. – STAINED
GLASS. Chancel E, 1866 by *William Wailes*. – Chancel S, 1869
and 1872 (Samuel), both by *Burlison & Grylls*. – S aisle E, 1871
also by *Wailes*. – S aisle, 1877 by *Frederick Preedy*. – N aisle NE
by *J. Powell & Sons* 1858. – MONUMENT. Thomas Langton
Freke †1769. Most unusually of plaster. Attributed to *John
Bacon*, but much in the Roubiliac tradition. At the bottom rocks,
on them Christ triumphing over a recumbent skeleton, the
hollow chest with the ribs hideously exposed, the more so since
some of the plaster has come away. To the r. a kneeling angel.

BAPTIST CHAPEL, Wales Street. Small ironstone of 1866 with
sharply pointed windows.

Former METHODIST CHAPEL, Richmond Street. 1936 of brick
with a wide low gable and three-light window. Narthex porch
with central doorway and rooms either side. Typical 1930s
gable key blocks.

PRIMARY SCHOOL, Richmond Road. 1907 by *J. T. Blackwell* of
Kettering in his usual brick manner. A central projecting pedi-
mented block with three windows with relieving arches.
Entrances and further wings on each side. Hall behind.

MANOR HOUSE, on the S side of the Green. A classic Jacobean
house. Largely early C17 with gables and mullioned windows.
W front E shape with a central gabled projection. Original
staircase with turned balusters. Some later additions.

The STOCKS are between the Manor House and the Bell Inn.

COURT HOUSE, a little further E. Half stone and half timber-
framed with an oversailing upper floor of *c.* 1500, altered in
the C16 and C18. Great chamber on the first floor, probably
used as the courtroom, with heavily moulded tie-beams and
large fireplace. Late C16 wooden window surrounds and
staircase.

KINGSCLIFFE

0090

Kingscliffe was famous in the later Middle Ages and the C16 and
C17 for its stone quarries. There are still considerable signs of
workings to the NE of the village. In the later C16 and early C17
the quarries were worked by the *Thorpe* family of masons (*see*
below and Introduction, p. 34). Kingscliffe stone was especially
regarded as a fine stone for carved work and notable C16 examples are the two Yorkist tombs at Fotheringhay, an architectural
monument at Little Oakley and the Hall fireplace at Deene. It
was also used at Burghley.

ALL SAINTS. Norman crossing tower – see the twin windows
with dividing shaft and round arch. The upper parts, includ-

ing the broach spire, are of the late C13. Two tiers of lucarnes, the lower starting below the broaches. Two lights, Y-tracery, dogtooth. The nave w window is Dec and has flowing tracery. Above it appears the sharp-pointed roof-line of before the addition of the Perp clerestory. Mostly Late Perp the rest of the exterior, with windows under triangular heads. Inside, the w and E crossing arches are a C13 remodelling, the N and S arches are Perp. At the w end of the chancel on the N side sign of a former N chapel. Triple responds with fillet. C15 aisle arcades with octagonal piers and moulded arches. Embattled abaci. Perp roof on good corbels. The chancel also Perp with windows with almost triangular tops. The E gable has patching and a date of 1648. There were restorations in 1862–3 by *Edward Browning* of Stamford, and another in 1898 by *J. C. Traylen* of Stamford. – FONT. C14. Rounded with four plain raised medallions and four with quatrefoils. – BENCH-ENDS. From Fotheringhay; C15. – PULPIT. Made up in 1818 using some C15 tracery panels from Fotheringhay. – SCREENS. N chapel of 1929 by *Traylen & Lenton*, the S of 1895. – CHOIR STALLS, with poppyheads. Nicely carved, part of Traylen's restoration of 1898. – STAINED GLASS. N aisle w end. Some C15 fragments from Fotheringhay, including angels with musical instruments, fetlocks and roses. Brought here by the then rector, the Rev. H. K. Bonney, who researched Fotheringhay and published a history in 1821. – Nave N windows with early C16 fragments thought to be from Barnack Manor House. – Chancel E window of 1863 by *W. Wailes*. – S aisle windows by *Kempe*, 1904 and *Kempe & Co.*, 1911. – MONUMENT. *Thorpe* family, 1623. This is the family of masons whose only famous member is John Thorpe, born *c.* 1566 and living till 1655, whose sketchbook is at Sir John Soane's Museum and has led to the erroneous attribution of many Elizabethan houses to him. Very simple architectural frame with Doric pilasters and an open pediment and obelisk at the top. At the foot 'Thomas, Thomas, Thomas', recording three generations, proavus, avus, pater. Of the proavus nothing is known, the avus died in 1558, the pater in 1596, the famous John being one of his sons. – W. Pyemont †1759. Floor stone, recording him tellingly as a 'Faithfull Diligent and Always Resident Rector'. – In the churchyard William Law †1761, in the form of a writing-desk.

Former WESLEYAN CHAPEL, Bridge Street. Original simple stone chapel of 1823 on the r. and the 1909 chapel on the l. by *William Hinson* of Stamford. This has an elaborate Geometric Gothic window, central in its façade, and slender lancets either side the porch. The 1909 pattern of glazing was also used for the windows of the earlier building.

Former CONGREGATIONAL CHAPEL, West Street. 1846. Three bays, two storeys with rusticated windows and doorcase and big triangular pediment, looking rather Georgian. *Joseph Slingsby* of Kingscliffe was the mason.

The village has numerous good stone houses, though many were altered and added to in the C18 and C19, and there is less evidence of earlier periods than one might expect. It is impossible here to chart more than some of the highlights.*

Immediately E of the church HALL FARMHOUSE, with fine set of Victorian cast-iron rails and gates in front. Originally a late medieval hall house, now of courtyard plan. Irregular Georgianized façade with a 1603 datestone above its four-centred arched doorway. The former hall was in the N range and some smoke-blackened timbers survive, but it was largely rebuilt during the C17. S of the 1603 range a large music room created c. 1790 when much of the interior was refitted. It has an elaborate ceiling in a late Adam pattern. Big fluted circle in the centre surrounded by a looped garland. At either end intersecting circles of a Palmyra pattern. Deep cove. Home of the C18 divine William Law between 1744 and 1761 and remained with the Law family till the late C19. S is the RECTORY, the former Mill House, mid-C18 with a good ashlar S front with three sash windows, platband and early C19 porch. Square C18 DOVECOTE to W. S is the former WATERMILL, early C19 T-plan of three storeys and three bays with a wide round-arched mill race. It was already here in the C17.

In BRIDGE STREET, rear of No. 4, is LAW'S CHAPEL, C18 but much altered, originally with three open arches on the S. Pediment on the S side. At the further E end of CHURCH STREET are several charitable and educational buildings established by the Rev. William Law and his disciple Mrs Elizabeth Hutcheson. To the N in SCHOOL HILL, Nos. 27–29, ELIZABETH HUTCHESON'S SCHOOL AND SCHOOLHOUSE. This is a house of c. 1700, converted into a master's house in 1745. Law's books were kept here from 1752. Over the door the inscription: 'Books of piety are here lent to any persons of this or ye neighbouring towns'. Symmetrical three-bay front. Upright mullioned windows. Adjoining the house the BOYS' SCHOOL, 1749. Single storey with two wooden mullion-transom windows. Inside the master's seat and some of the childrens' seats survive. To the E, WIDOWS' ALMSHOUSES, dated 1749. S of Bridge Street, No. 18 is the former WILLIAM LAW SCHOOL for girls, a building of 1752, with rooms for the mistress on the ground floor and a schoolroom above. Wooden cross-mullion-transom windows. The original staircase, and panelling in the schoolroom (now divided), survive. To the W, SPINSTERS' ALMSHOUSES, 1754, with a rather grim tall stone wall on the road side. Further E are Nos. 26–32, CORNFORTH HOMES, built 1891–2 by *J. B. Corby* of Stamford. Reset dedication plaque from the 1668 Thorpe Almshouses in Park Street (*see* below).

---

*A full detailed inventory of the buildings of Kingscliffe is in RCHME, *Inventory of Architectural Monuments of North Northamptonshire*, 1984.

N of the church in PARK STREET, other good houses. No. 2 is fine Late Georgian, originally three bays with an extra bay added on the l. Ashlar coarses with thin rubble bands between. Shutters to all the windows and a canopied doorcase. Further on the E side KINGSCLIFFE ENDOWED PRIMARY SCHOOL, of C17 origin, the original building of two storeys, L-shaped with mullioned windows, surviving at the rear, the central section turned into the hall in the C19. The building was much altered initially in 1873 when the house was converted into a school and then extended in 1881 with two gabled wings in a sympathetic style. Curious metal ventilator turrets on two roofs. On the W side on the cusp of the bend the former JOHN THORPE ALMSHOUSES, founded in 1668. One-storeyed. Mullioned windows with straight hoods. Considerably altered in 1937. Further out, on the l. ROCKBOURNE, dated 1900 by *J. B. Corby* with bays and a porch, all with wavy parapets and ball finials, in the Jacobethan manner. Opposite is ROSARY FARMHOUSE, three-bay ashlar house with narrow thin rubble courses (like No. 2 above), late C18 or early C19 with an additional wing on the r. Regency doorcase. Windows with keystones. Outbuildings behind.

WEST STREET on the N side has the CROSS KEYS, C17 or C18 with a two-storey canted bay with mullions having the Cross Keys plaque. A little further on this side, Nos. 8–12, a good Georgian refacing of an older row with platband. On the S side, No. 19 is of C16 date with a large chimneystack and to its r. a doorway, with a single-light window above with a pointed head. Set back in FOREST APPROACH on the N side is WELLINGTON HOUSE, two storeys with three- and four-light mullioned windows. Framed doorcase with pulvinated frieze. Back in West Street on the N side, the unassuming façade of No. 22 shelters a wing behind with remains of a late medieval hall house, much altered but still with smoke-blackened cruck timbers. Further still on the same side Nos. 40–42, Late Georgian of three floors with C19 pilastered shop fronts below. On the S side Nos. 41–43, four bays, three storeys with platband, Late Georgian. Regency doorcase. Beyond the Congregational chapel (*see* above), still on the S, THE MANOR HOUSE, a well-constructed late C17 house with wide banded ashlar façade and two canted bays with mullion-transom windows. Lower two-storey addition on r. Inside, a graceful early C19 staircase. In the garden a stone screen and a good circular DOVECOTE. Early C19 garden front. Much further on, on the S side, is No. 63, a neat early C17 house of three bays, two storeys with three-light mullioned windows at the sides, a central four-centred arched doorway with a two-light window above.

KINGSCLIFFE SPA, I m. SW. A chalybeate spring was first promoted in 1670 by the Kingscliffe physician Dr Brown. Morton in 1712 records 'a fit cistern of stone' and this seems to be what still exists. It is a rectangular tank, with a paved surround and ashlar walls, entered by a short flight of steps.

KINGSTHORPE *see* OUTER NORTHAMPTON

KIRBY HALL

9090

Kirby* is one of the most important and interesting houses of its date in England. It is also a wonderfully visually rewarding house, despite being part a ruin – indeed this adds to its magic. The estate was acquired by Sir Humphrey Stafford in 1542 which then passed to his son, also Humphrey, in 1548. There was already a house here of which some slight remains exist under the SE corner of the present building. In 1566 Stafford served as sheriff for Northamptonshire, and it was in that year that Queen Elizabeth conducted a Progress passing through Northamptonshire. It must have rankled Stafford that she visited his neighbours the Brudenells at Deene but did not come to Kirby. Was it this omission that prompted him to embark on building a new house? In 1570 work began but the house was incomplete when he died in 1575.

The estate was then purchased by Sir Christopher Hatton, one of the Queen's handsome young men, already building his vast palace at Holdenby (q.v.). All that seems to have been done is the finishing of the state wing at the SW corner of the house. It remained in Hatton ownership till 1706 when Sir Christopher Hatton IV died, having created a remarkable garden. It then passed by marriage into the line of the Earls of Winchelsea, who assumed the name of Hatton, becoming the Finch-Hatton line. They had London property and the Eastwell Estate in Kent, which they favoured. There was a considerable refitting in the 1790s but eventually there was a sale of contents in 1824 and subsequently Kirby gradually fell into decay. It was occasionally used in the early C19 but by the early 1900s many roofs had collapsed and it was already partially a ruin. In 1930 it was taken into guardianship by the Ministry of Works, and it remains with their successor English Heritage today. Since the 1990s there has been an attempt to recreate a garden layout and reinstate some of the interiors.

The house is built of Weldon stone. The master mason was *Thomas Thorpe* of Kingscliffe. His son, John, became an important London surveyor and it is his collection of plans and drawings now in the Soane Museum which has gained him fame. It was on one of these plans, of Kirby, that he inscribed 'Kerby whereof I layd ye first stone AD 1570'. At that date he was just seven years old, so a good luck charm to have a child lay the foundation stone. However, it is clear that while Thorpe was the builder, the sophistication and innovation of the building's design are far beyond a Northamptonshire mason. It is the authorship of the design of Kirby which is its chief enigma. While some decoration derives directly from Serlio the derivation of much else remains a mystery. What is clear is that

*I am most grateful to Nick Hill of English Heritage for his observations.

whoever designed Kirby had an immediate knowledge of what was happening in France.

The principal range of Kirby, with porch, hall and parlour on one side, and kitchen etc. on the other, is the s range. The hall is one-storeyed, the kitchen range two with a basement. To its N is the courtyard with E and W ranges of two storeys containing sets of lodgings. The N range is occupied with a loggia with originally a gallery over and the main entrance from the N. Both N and S ranges were altered in 1638–40 and it is this confusing interaction of the 1570s with the 1630s which adds to the intrigue of the building.

To appreciate the complexity of Kirby's architecture, the COURTYARD should be the starting point. Looking s we have the principal range: a central porch, the hall to the r. and services to the l. The form of the PORCH, setting aside its lavish decoration, is what one might expect from 1570. It is divided into two storeys, and each storey has its own order of columns or pilasters – Ionic below and Corinthian above. It carries the date 1572 as well as 1638 on an inserted later window, which has a round arch and open pediment. The doorway into the porch is also round-headed and is framed by coupled Ionic pilasters. A third pilaster is set round the corner to the E and W, but has no counterpart close to the wall of the range, as one would expect. A foliage frieze follows made up of elements which occur right round the courtyard but here are, surprisingly, curiously unbalanced. Then, on the upper floor, instead of Corinthian pilasters, which there should be, pairs of Corinthian columns perched on brackets. They cause a projecting and receding of the frieze above which prepares for the fun and games of the attic gable. It is this frieze which contains the 1572 date and the Stafford motto: *je seray loyal*. The whole surface of the gable is decorated with designs, a curious pattern of tiny circles and odd curved scrolls like wings, and all this set between seven Corinthian colonettes, also perched on brackets, and again one to the E and W around the corner. At the top two concave curves contain a vase backed by a peacock's tail design. Finally a semicircular gable with a shell motif. Fanciful it is, yet there is a sense of proportion which shows an astute mind. There is one curious thing about the courtyard at Kirby: it is not a rectangle, though it may appear one. The only 90 degree corner is that at the SE; all the others are variants and the N side of the court is narrower than the S. It is thought these anomalies are due to some portions of the pre-1570 house being incorporated in the new. Both at the E and W ends of the hall there are odd thick walls and the retention of these may have contributed to this unusual effect.

To the r. of the porch is the HALL. It has two large double eight-light mullion- and transom-windows and another of ten lights with a lower sill and at its r. end, as one would expect, a projecting bay window. It looks as if this lights the dais end of the hall, but it does not – it lights the ante-room beyond. It

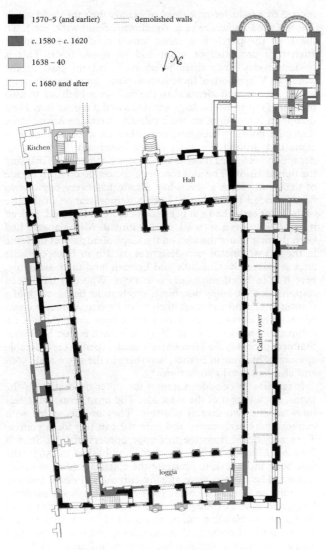

- ■ 1570–5 (and earlier)
- ▨ c. 1580 – c. 1620
- ▨ 1638 – 40
- □ c. 1680 and after

······ demolished walls

Kitchen

Hall

Gallery over

loggia

Kirby Hall.
Plan

is the ten-light window which lights the dais. Applied to the
façade, between the windows, are two tall Ionic pilasters,
almost too elongated. They rise through the whole height since
the designer is treating this block as a single storey. Above their
capitals, within the parapet, are two panels which bear the
names of its builder: 'HUMFRE' 'STAFARD'. Each is then

topped by a baluster-type finial of exactly the same kind which Thorpe used elsewhere (e.g. Apethorpe, Southwick, etc.). To the l. of the porch is a range which contains a basement kitchen, a ground-floor room and an upper floor. This is obvious today since there is no roof and no glass in the windows. When both of these were in place, however, this range would have looked identical to the hall since both are treated the same: tall pilasters, large windows and a corner bay. Here then is an innovation: an Ionic pilaster stretching across more than one floor. It becomes more obvious when the motif is continued around the sides of the courtyard. There is no deception here since those ranges have a distinct frieze marking the floor division. The idea reaches a crescendo on the N façade of the court. Here a seven-bay arcade has every bay of two floors divided by a pilaster. Such a demonstration of the use of the giant order had not been seen before in England. Indeed it had hardly been seen on the Continent. Michelangelo had been the first to use the idea on the Capitoline palaces in Rome in the 1530s. One or two designers used it in France a little later at places like Chantilly and Ecouen, and then, suddenly, here it is in Northamptonshire in 1570. Who can have been responsible? We know not, but it surely must be the work of a Continental hand and most likely from France. Whoever it was seems only to have been here a short time since there is no comparable work elsewhere. What is known is that Sir Roger Stafford, probably Sir Humphrey's uncle, spent a considerable amount of his time in France, was there in the 1550s and 1560s and also had royal connections.*

It remains to consider some of the other decoration of the 1570s, notably that of the N façade. The most remarkable features are the two central pilasters. They are decorated with extraordinary arabesques and here we can provide a source. They are copied from the title-page borders of John Shute's *First and Chief Grounds of Architecture*, published in 1563 – the first book in English to illustrate the classical orders of architecture. The designs were already current in France and can be found in books of hours. John Shute remains a shadowy figure and as yet, although he describes himself as 'Painter and Architect', no building can be ascribed to him. Of course there is yet another Continental feature here, and that is the open loggia. The nearest comparable loggia is in France at Charleval, but it can hardly be the inspiration since the chateau there was being built at exactly the same time as Kirby. The façade has lost its original glazing and its superstructure is a later addition, to be discussed below, so that the horizontal running frieze of Vitruvian scroll marks its original height. The same frieze runs right round the other sides of the court and across the hall range.

---

* For Sir Roger's Continental dealings see Mark Girouard, *Elizabethan Architecture*, 2009, p. 181. His exact relationship to Sir Humphrey has not so far been established. I am grateful to Mark Girouard for other comments.

As for the lodgings, they are also innovative. We are familiar with this arrangement today as it is a feature of Oxbridge colleges, but in country house terms, it was a new idea here. Ionic pilasters divide up the ranges and then each lodging has its own doorway, some with the initials of Stafford's parents, 'HS' and 'MS', others with the Stafford knot and heraldic crests. They were on two floors on the E and W. In the early C17 the Long Gallery was moved from its original position above the loggia of the N range to the upper floor of the W range.

The N façade of the courtyard was altered 1638–40 during the time of Sir Christopher Hatton III (†1670). He introduced new fenestration with alternating triangular and segmental pediments and heightened it by the addition of a clock tower. In the centre another window with a balcony was made. This has an open pediment containing a bust of Apollo. It is similar to the window of 1638 on the S porch already noted. Across the house many of the chimneystacks were renewed, the only 1570 stacks being the tall set on the S side of the Hall.* All this work was done by *Nicholas Stone* and payments are recorded in his account book.

With the purchase of the house by Sir Christopher Hatton some work was done to complete the house as left by Stafford. It is thought the SW wing had only just been started and this was partially completed. The Thorpe plan only shows a single state room at this corner and it is uncertain whether it was Sir Christopher I (†1591) or Sir Christopher II (†1619), his son, who added a second space. What is known is that it was Sir Christopher II who entertained Queen Anne of Denmark at Kirby in 1605 and James I in 1612, 1616 and 1619. It was very likely he who completed this suite and added the remarkable twin bay windows which complete the southern aspect. Thorpe's plan shows a square end to which has been added later a curved bay and it is possible that he was involved in this phase of work. Looking at these windows from the garden terrace one can appreciate Sacheverell Sitwell's description: 'Like two huge galleons tied up at anchor'.[†] They are fully glazed, of ten lights (in groups of two), with two transoms to the ground floor, one to the upper floor. The added transom on the ground floor is due to them having been lengthened in the late C18. The roof dormers are also bent semicircularly, in a stepped form, so the centre light has a transom. A touch of magic is added by the pinnacles and the curly strapwork volutes on either side. These are taken up in the other contemporary parts of the W side. Within the wing, but projecting from it, is the Great Stair, with huge timber baulks and a deep moulded stone handrail.

It remains to describe the N OUTER COURT. It is entered E and W by two large archways. These have details very similar

---

* There are in fact three types: the tall 1570s Stafford ones, later C16 Hatton period, with twin columns, and those of 1638–40 with panelled sides.
† Sacheverell Sitwell, *British Architects and Craftsmen*, 1944.

to the archways of Hatton's Holdenby and are therefore likely to be of that period. They can safely be attributed to *Thomas Thorpe*'s workshop since one has the mark of his known workman, *Samson Frisby*.* In the N wall there is a delightful gateway with rusticated sides and an open pediment with the Hatton arms. This is clearly of the 1638–40 period. It is thought to have been resited here from the W garden (*see* below). To its N there is now a grassed slope but this is the result of landscaping after deep open-cast ironstone mining. There was formerly an avenue and a carriageway to Gretton. The walls are topped by an arcaded balustrade and again some of this may have come from the garden.

As for the N front of the house, this had in 1570 two projecting bays either side of the entrance arch and two further projecting bays at either end. The original entrance archway still exists as an inner arch today. The E and W gaps between the bays were filled in after 1575 by Hatton, and then finally in 1638–40 the whole front was revamped, the centre infilled and heightened to form the clock tower and new fenestration and gables added.

Of the INTERIOR only fragments of fittings survive. The S porch has plaster ceilings with garlands of flowers of *c.* 1670. The hall has a beautiful canted ceiling of the 1570s with double curved wind-braces, all the timbers carved with foliage. Its gallery is thought to be part of the 1670s work. The Great Stair leads up to the end of the Long Gallery where a short section of the plaster tunnel-vault remains, with broad ribs and large circles. Probably *c.* 1620. Elsewhere there is some evidence of refitting at the end of the C18, notably in the ground-floor SE room which has a curved internal bay matching the window shape, and on the first floor, in the former Great Chamber, with a screen of columns. There is also a further staircase tower built of brick of the 1638–40 period, which was added to the S of the service range. This still contains parts of a cantilever stair, but this is probably late C17, replacing a wooden staircase.

The GARDEN has to some extent been recreated in a style which Christopher Hatton IV (†1706) would recognize. It consists of a large rectangular parterre bordered on the N and W by raised terraces. Documentary evidence dates the formation to 1684–6. Some changes were made in 1693–4 when gateways at both S and W sides were removed and rebuilt, one on the N side and one resited in the outer courtyard. Despite an archaeological excavation (1987–8) no clear evidence was found of the C17 pattern. The evidence for this seems to have been destroyed when the Ministry of Works took over the site in 1930. The present pattern was laid down in 1994–7 based on a design in the archive at Longleat. A plan at Deene shows that in the C17 the garden layout stretched S, across the stream and up the slope to the line of the present road.

* *See* Introduction p. 36.

It should finally be noted that in the C16 and C17 the approach to Kirby was from the SE where originally a small village was sited. A slight depression can still be detected in the field where the village street ran. Also on the E side of the house a stable block was built, but this has totally vanished.

KISLINGBURY

6050

ST PETER AND ST PAUL. Mostly Late Dec and very fine, especially the chancel, and built at that moment when Dec is changing into Perp. The chancel has a splendid five-light E window with interesting tracery based on intersected ogee arches and lots of little verticals. The same principle is used for three-light windows on the N and S sides of the chancel. A fleuron frieze runs all along the S side below the eaves. Inside the chancel the N doorway is a piece of unusual and very attractive design. Two continuous orders, one of leaves with knotty branches and one of flowers with the same kind of branches (cf. the capitals at Radstone). Hoodmould on headstops of a bishop and a king, probably renewed. SEDILIA and PISCINA are ogee-cusped and have crocketed triangular gables. The foliate finials reach above the window sill, these partly renewed 1829–30 when the church was 'thoroughly repaired'. Elaborate canopies of former statues l. and r. of the E window. Late Dec also the aisle reticulated W windows, the N doorway and the S porch with its side windows, and the pretty S doorway with one continuous order of fleurons and ballflower and a hoodmould on headstops. Dec finally also the arcades of four bays. Octagonal piers, double-chamfered arches. Responds with head corbels. The tower, although sporting Y-tracery, is almost certainly a total rebuilding of 1717, but judging from the spire, faithfully. The straight-headed aisle windows might well also be as late as that, although the ones with arched lights look earlier. Open light interior with plastered walls and flat Georgian ceilings. These perhaps as late as 1829–30 when the Gothick vestry was added. The fittings, STALLS, REREDOS and PEWS of a most elegant design are 1903 by *Edmund Law*. – FONT. Octagonal, Perp but probably the same date as the rest of the building. Shields in quatrefoils and a panelled stem. – CHEST. Of *c*. 1500, with blind arcading and many big rosettes. – CHANDELIER. Of brass, two tiers; C18, it could well be 1717 too.* – STAINED GLASS. Chancel E window of 1945 by *Basil Bayne*, a Resurrection war memorial window with delicate colours and lots of service personnel. – MONUMENTS. Several tablets. John Perkins †1728. Alabaster surround signed by *John Hunt*. John Jephcott †1743 but erected *c*. 1776, and Catharina Jephcott †1798, both clearly from the *Cox* yard.

---

* The collection of leather fire buckets of 1743 was, alas, stolen in the 1970s.

RECTORY. One of the finest in the county. Attributed to *Francis Smith* (cf. Cottesbrooke Hall, Lamport Rectory); built probably *c.* 1710–20. Ironstone. Five by three bays, two storeys, quoins, hipped roof. The windows in finely moulded frames, the doorway with an open curly pediment. Staircase with twisted balusters and carved tread-ends. A fireplace of *c.* 1740 with a sun-face. The interior adjusted when the chimneystacks were rebuilt in the C19. Good wrought-iron garden gate undoubtedly by *Thomas Warren*. The rectory BARN has a cupola, and in it are over 1,300 nesting-places for pigeons.

Many good ironstone houses in the village. Several small greens, and on that at the SE corner of the village THE ELMES, 1886, with canted bays and an ogee doorcase. Just E, LEEDONS COTTAGE, with mullioned windows.

7070   LAMPORT

ALL SAINTS. Close to the Hall, but across the road. Externally a medieval tower with a classical C17 and C18 church (with, alas, a Gothic S vestry of 1879 – alas, even though it is by *Bodley* and does have lively animal stops to its window). Internally a medieval nave and aisles under an C18 ceiling and leading to an C18 chancel. The low W tower is Late Norman and was buttressed later. The arch towards the nave has keeled responds. The bell-openings of two lights are C13. Of the C13 also the three-bay arcades. Octagonal piers, double-chamfered arches. To this church Sir Justinian Isham added a N chapel in 1672. The chapel, which was built probably by *Henry Jones* of Walgrave, who later lived at Lamport, opens towards the chancel in three arches. The E window is still in its original state. It is of cross-type, with the transom remarkably high up. Segmental pediment on corbels. This is clearly influenced by John Webb's work at the Hall. It is even possible that *Webb*, who died only in 1672, designed the chapel, since he designed a circular, domed family mausoleum in 1654, but this was not carried out. Then, after 1737 (completion 1743), *William Smith* of Warwick rebuilt the outer walls of the aisles and nave and most of the chancel, placing at the E end a fine Venetian window with Doric pilasters. His other windows are round-headed, heavily and bluntly framed, and have that Y-tracery which was the C18 favourite of all Gothic tracery. By Smith also the S porch, rusticated and pedimented. The plasterwork inside is by *John Woolston*, alderman of Northampton. It is simple in the nave – three circles with emblems, that in the middle circle being the eye of God surrounded by cherubs – and richly Rococo in the chancel. Especially happy the cartouches above the spandrels of the arches to the chapel and the ROYAL ARMS of George II over the chancel arch. – FONT and FONT COVER, tall, designed by *Bodley*, 1869. – COMMUNION RAIL. Of wood, no doubt of *c.* 1745. – IRON SCREEN, between chapel and chancel. 1965 by *W. F. Knight.** – STAINED GLASS. E window, Resurrection, by *Warrington*, 1847, very strong, in dark colours and with heavy figures. – Other glass *c.* 1865, designed probably by *Sir Charles Isham*, who was certainly capable of this, as he also illustrated books. – MONUMENTS. All of Ishams and an important collection, not least since every member of the *Stanton* family of Holborn is represented. Chancel N wall, Mrs Jane †1638. Slab with, at the top, in bas relief, three putti with three wreaths. By *Thomas Stanton*, according to a drawing in the Isham archives. – In the chapel, Sir Justinian by *William Stanton*, paid for in 1699–1700. Fine tablet with twisted columns. The price was £64. – Elizabeth †1713. By *Edward Stanton*. Tall tablet with fluted pilasters and at the top two putti l. and r. of a coat of arms in a scrolly surround. The price was £55. – Sir Justinian †1730. A fine architectural tablet, making use of variegated marbles, known from documentary sources to be by *Francis Smith*, allowing similar monuments e.g. at Harlestone, Fawsley, Edgcote, Dodford, to be attributed to the Smiths. – Sir Justinian †1737. There is a long-standing tradition that this is by *Scheemakers*. However, the powerful bust and the volutes to the l. and r. of the inscription plate make it almost certainly the work of *Michael Rysbrack*. The large arched surround might well be the work of the *Smiths*. – John †1811 by *Henry Westmacott*. – Mrs Raynsford †1763 by *W. Cox* (from Faxton church). – In the churchyard, just by the gate is a memorial stone, like a Greek stele, with a bas relief of figures for George Jenkinson †1907 which according to Gyles Isham was from the *Gleichen* studio.

OLD RECTORY, E of the church. Built in 1727–30 for the then rector, Dr Euseby Isham, by *Francis Smith*. Handsome five-bay front of two storeys. Doorway pedimented. Good staircase inside with three slender turned balusters to the tread and carved tread-ends. Ground- and first-floor rooms panelled. The library (formerly the drawing room) was altered in 1819, when the panelling was covered up and a coved ceiling and new fireplace (by *John Whiting*) were added. The original fireplaces are of red Derbyshire marble.

LAMPORT HALL. The Ishams lived at Lamport from 1560 until 1976. Sir Gyles Isham died in that year having set up a Preservation Trust, which continues to maintain the house and the estate. Lamport was only one of the Isham houses; Pytchley was the other. The Elizabethan house had its front, with its great hall, E of the present large porch and facing NW towards the church. The builder was John Isham who died in 1595 and had been three times warden of the Mercers in London. The core of the present building, however, is in the centre of the W front. It was built for Sir Justinian Isham, who succeeded his father in 1651 and married in 1653. The designer of the house was *John Webb*. Enough correspondence is preserved to be sure

64

*A processional cross, dated to *c.* 1475, is now at the Victoria and Albert Museum.

Lamport Hall.
Drawing by J. Blackemore, 1761

of many details for which one is in the dark in the case of most Stuart houses. The letters start in 1654 and end in 1657. Webb signs himself 'your assured ffreind', which shows that he and his client considered one another as of equal social status.

Webb's house is only five bays wide and two storeys high, that is a villa in the sense in which the Queen's House at Greenwich by Inigo Jones, Webb's master and his relative by marriage, is a villa. Villa is indeed the term since it needs to be remembered that when built it had three external walls, and was only attached to the old house at the back. The form of the side façades is not clear, but there must have been some windows, probably on the S side. Webb wanted first to give it a portico, a feature he liked, but that suggestion was not accepted. He then suggested a porch, but that also was not built. Webb's front was ashlar-rusticated throughout, with raised quoins and a top balustrade, so that it was infinitely purer in its Italianism than e.g. the exactly contemporary Thorpe Hall near Peterborough. Actually a small dormer-like pediment was added as early as 1657. This was hidden by another bigger pediment about 1730–40. The present pediment is of 1829 and stands rather awkwardly behind the balustrade. Webb's doorway has an open segmental pediment, with shield carved by *Peter Besnier*, and the windows to the l. and r. are given pediments of alternatingly segmental and triangular shape. The windows themselves are now sashed but originally in all probability had mullion-and-transom crosses similar to those of the N chapel in the church. On the top frieze below the balustrade the inscription: In things transitory resteth no glory, added by Sir Charles Isham, the tenth baronet, *c.* 1850. The front of this block was intended as a garden façade, being screened from the old house by hedges.

The ENTRANCE HALL, now called the High Room, is structurally Webb's work, though almost entirely redecorated. It is noteworthy that with all his Italianism Webb still allowed this hall to be entered not in the middle but close to one end, that is in the medieval and Elizabethan way. The chimneypiece was designed by Webb and made by 'Mr Keyes', probably *Caius G. Cibber*, who is known to have designed other items for Lamport in 1670. Webb's drawing for it exists. He would, he writes, have preferred 'to employ our own countrimen'. It is a splendid piece, with big, powerful forms, grand though somewhat restless in the same way in which the details at Thorpe Hall are so much more restless, that is e.g. an open segmental pediment and in it a smaller triangular one, or the mantelshelf projecting in three places and fruit panels squeezed into the parts of the frieze of the shelf where it does not project. The decoration has thick, compact fruit and leaf garlands so typical of Webb, and also two swans, the heraldic badge of the Ishams. Only the lower part incidentally is of stone; the overmantel is of wood. The simple door frames are also designed by Webb. The panelling of the walls was redone in 1686. Originally the walls had straight-headed niches with wax figures by *Andrew Kearne*, Nicholas Stone's brother-in-law. He was a German, and therefore probably Kern. He may well be a member of the Kern family of Würzburg and Württemberg. Of Webb's time also several carved panels from the former STAIRCASE. They have, like those of Thorpe Hall and others of about 1660 and after, openwork foliage scrolls. At Lamport these scrolls are a little flatter and more formalized than at Thorpe. Portions of this at first-floor level are still in their original position. By the window wall are two newels with ball tops, with an inserted carved piece. This was the opening for the descent of the stair, which fell along the wall to a half-landing, then turned alongside itself to the ground. The openwork balustrade stood in a single plane between the flights. Nearly all the pieces of it survive.

The Elizabethan house remained independent of the new one, which faced SW, and the emphasis till the C18 remained on the N side. The first addition was the STABLES. They date from 1680. There were originally two ranges forming a generous forecourt to the NW. The W range, which had a small cupola, was pulled down in 1829. The E range consists of two parts, that nearer the house structurally Elizabethan – see the windows at the back – the other of 1680. Seven bays, two storeys, cross-windows, large round-headed archway. The archway in the Elizabethan part is re-set and comes in all probability from the W range. The stable quadrangle behind was built in 1907 when the house was let to Lord and Lady Ludlow.

The next addition was more momentous. In 1732 a N wing and in 1741 a S wing were begun to widen Webb's W façade from its original five bays to thirteen, to create a new entrance front, thereby totally altering its character. Yet the *Smiths* of Warwick, *Francis* on the N, *William* on the S, kept very tactfully to the style of their Palladian, Jonesian predecessor. Only the window details and the balustrade details differ. At the back of the surprisingly shallow s wing William Smith made an open arched garden hall. The work of the Smiths inside is more spectacular. It culminates in the splendid redecoration of the HIGH ROOM, i.e. the former entrance hall. This dates from 1738. The stucco work was done by *John Woolston*. Attic with beautiful lettering and above it panels containing 'trophies' of musical instruments alternating with profile busts in roundels, on the s wall being Inigo Jones and Palladio. The lettering is Victorian, added by *Sir Charles Isham*. Big coving and flat ceiling with three large plaster panels. The middle one is circular, and has a bold wreath of foliage and fruit and three frolicking cherubs in the centre. On the l. and r. panels mermaids. The style of the wreath is only superficially similar to Webb's. The foliage is in fact much looser and more deeply undercut.

Of the time of the Smiths also the STAIRCASE. Slim turned balusters, two to the tread, and carved tread-ends. It is a rebuild, 1825, replacing the Webb staircase, and formerly occupied the inner hall to the N, where the long round-arched window which lit it still survives. The rebuilding unfortunately curtailed its base so an elegant Smith scrolled finish now ends rather abruptly. Elegant plaster ceiling. Stained glass from Pytchley Hall, dated 1596. Similar ceilings in the adjoining corridors. The OAK ROOM is Neo-Jacobean, though it has an original mid-C17 fireplace with overmantel and panelling. It was introduced by the Ludlows *c*. 1910. It was brought from Bayhall House, Pembury, Kent following its demolition in 1908. Again part of the Smith work is the LIBRARY in the N wing. The fireplace and the flanking giant pilasters are of 1732, the rest is a remodelling of 1819, by *Henry Hakewill*. At the same time Hakewill built a new Neo-Tudor N front which was replaced later, the quadrant porch at the back of William Smith's s wing with Tuscan columns, and the pediment above Webb's façade. He was followed by *Henry Goddard* of Leicester, who in 1842 added the mildly Jacobean lower part of the s front, and Goddard was followed by *William Burn*. Burn's is the Italianate N front. He wanted to go Jacobean, but was prevented by Sir Charles, who thus succeeded in keeping the original character of Lamport safe through the dangerous Victorian decades. Burn in 1861–2 added the massive Tuscan porch, the low, rather weak square tower, and the lower range beyond. Inside is Burn's dining room.

The GARDEN probably has remnants of its earliest periods, notably the raised bank on the w side. At its end is a fine IRONWORK GATE, between two stone piers, *c*. 1700 and possibly by *Warren*. The Italian garden near the house with its fountain is Victorian as is the planting of Irish yews. The circular stone structure in the centre of the lawn is thought to have been a cockpit. The part C18 and early C19 brick KITCHEN GARDEN WALLS have an attractive Regency ironwork gate. The Lily Pond marks the site of a former conservatory. Most impressive is the ROCKERY, SE of the house, created by *Sir Charles Isham*, 1847. Looking from the garden like a ruin; behind is the cascade of the rockery. It was populated shortly after with small ceramic gnomes. These were removed after Sir Charles's death, save for one little fellow who was discovered by Sir Gyles when he took over the house after the war. It is celebrated as the earliest garden gnome in England. The rockery faces the DAIRY with its canted projection, part of *Hakewill*'s work in 1824.

LODGE, on the Northampton Road, probably by *J. G. Bland* of Market Harborough, 1849–50, who designed LAMPORT MANOR (Home Farm) in 1848 in a similar Tudor style. The GATES, with their cast-iron swan tops, had already been built by *Hakewill* in 1824.

SWAN INN, on the Northampton Road. Large Late Georgian ironstone of three bays with canted bays on the ground floor. Much altered and extended in recent times.

In the village a number of ESTATE COTTAGES, some of red brick dated 1854 with elaborate polychrome geometric patterns, others of stone with less elaborate decoration dated 1869, both typical of the taste of Sir Charles Isham; and a former DOVE-COTE of 1735, converted by Sir Charles into a bakehouse (hence its inscription 'Where pigeons once did sport and fly, you now may bake a pigeon pie'). A pair of houses and four others, ISHAM TERRACE, were designed by the *Lamport Estate* and *Tad Dobraszczyk* in the early 2000s. Both are of stone in the vernacular manner.

Former RAILWAY STATION, ¼ m. NW on the A508 on Brampton Valley Way. It served the Northampton–Market Harborough line which opened in 1859 and is the only station building to survive. Stone, rendered with decorative gables, faintly Tudor style.

LAXTON

9090

ALL SAINTS. Exterior much restored, largely by *William Evans-Freke*, 8th Baron Carbery (†1894), who was a talented amateur carver. His memorial in the chancel tells all: 'He designed the stonework of the windows, rebuilt the Chancel, added the North Aisle and himself carved the Pulpit and the exterior gable cross and the bull's head above the Chancel.' So his are the archaeologically inaccurate E windows with their combination of Dec and Perp motifs. No doubt also the bronze WATER-SPOUTS in the shape of dragons. There is indeed a large bull's head on the chancel gable! This all happened 1867–8. Left from the medieval church are Norman parts of the S doorway, i.e. the two shafts with weird volute capitals. Late C13 the W tower with bell-openings of two lights separated by a shaft and with a blank cinquefoil over. Short spire with low broaches and two tiers of lucarnes. Double-chamfered arch on head corbels to the nave. Late C13 also the three-bay S arcade with quatrefoil piers and double-chamfered arches. – PULPIT. Victorian Gothic open-traceried top, with a base carved by *Lord Carbery* in the style of 1700. – MONUMENTS. A memorial to the 8th Lord Carbery †1894 recording the restoration of the church. Other Carbery memorials. A good selection of carved gravestones in the churchyard.

LAXTON HALL. Now a Polish residential home. The Laxton Estate was in the hands of the Staffords of Blatherwycke in the C16, but early in the C18 it went to a daughter who married George Evans, who in 1715 became Baron Carbery. A house was built between 1778 and 1783 for George Evans, 3rd Lord Carbery, and the S front of this survives with its two projecting wings and central bow window, which originally lit an oval drawing room. The 4th Lord Carbery's widow married her cousin, George Evans-Freke, and they began the transformation of the Georgian house. *Humphry Repton* was consulted in (1806), when he was working at Harlestone (q.v.), and the STABLES were built 1807–8 (though their bell is dated 1805). A quadrangular block with tall arched entrance topped by a pediment with deep eaves. Similar pediments l. and r. However, the relationship between Repton and Evans-Freke collapsed and the project was taken over by a surveyor, *William Carter*. He finished the N side about 1811 (rainwater head). Originally there was an entrance staircase hall with a portico or porte cochère. The columns of this were infilled after 1845 and the N front now looks rather bleak, with its excessively broad Doric pilasters and the tacked-on pediment of the doorway. In 1811

Laxton Hall.
Engraving by J. P. Neale, 1824

George Dance Jun. was called in to redesign the ENTRANCE 94
HALL. The result is a spectacular space: square, with, facing
one as one enters, four Ionic columns in a row on the upper
floor, inset with pretty cast-iron balustrades with honeysuckle
motifs by *John Baker* (partly glazed and infilled because of the
use of the house). Segmental arches, pendentives, and a circular dome on a glazed lantern. Very restrained plasterwork by
Francis Bernasconi, done as horizontal rustication on the
ground floor. To the l. an ample staircase hall. Oblong staircase
with open well. More honeysuckle ironwork. Oblong glazed
lantern. Also in 1811 *Richard Westmacott* the elder supplied
several marble chimneypieces which are still extant in the
former library and music room. The Carbery Estate held the
estate until 1924. The house then became a Roman Catholic
school till 1968 when it was converted to a residential home.
– CHAPEL (formerly orangery). Built *c.* 1845. Portico with four
columns. (This is now closed and a chapel has been contrived
in the former drawing room.) – ICE HOUSE, partly infilled but
still with its brick domed top. – GATES on the E side of the
estate, on the main A43. Two pedimented lodges and a tripartite archway with attic. Built *c.* 1824 after designs by *Repton*
c. 1806. The ironwork by *John Parker* of Knightsbridge.
The VILLAGE is one of those charming ESTATE COTTAGE ensembles, owing to the Evans family, Lords Carbery. The general
effect looks *c.* 1840–50, but this is misleading and largely results
from thatched roofs being changed to stone slates in the early
1900s. In fact the village was started much earlier, a pair of
cottages (Nos. 9 and 10) in the village street having a datestone
of 1804. The *Beauties of England and Wales* (1810) says that
George Evans-Freke had 'erected several new and comfortable
cottages', and this refers to the employment in 1806 of *Humphry*
Repton and his son *John Adey Repton* who supplied designs for
further cottages, a school and a parsonage. The cottages are
built of stone, gabled, many with the later bargeboards, mostly
in pairs, and prettily arranged around a green. One of the pret-
tiest is a house which was formerly an inn, THE STAFFORD
KNOT. Large central gable and smaller ones on each side. The
OLD VICARAGE is set back S of the street, towards the church.
It has two gables with finials and a tall buttressed porch with
pinnacles. There is a datestone for 1806. Just within the park
at the E end of the village, WOODLAND COTTAGE still has its
thatch and a rounded end with wooden columns. A little
further E the former SCHOOL, originally just a simple rectangular building with crow-stepped end gables, that to the N
having a mock Perp window. It was designed in 1806 and built
1807–8. In 1833 a cottage was added for the schoolmistress.
Both school and cottage were considerably altered when they
were joined together to form a larger residence in 1925.
HOME FARMHOUSE, on the W side of A43. Probably C18 but
remodelled *c.* 1830 as a model farm complex with associated
barns, dovecote, etc.

LILBOURNE

ALL SAINTS, ½ m. N of the village. Unbuttressed w tower with
Perp arch towards the nave. The tower base could be C12 and
there is a blocked doorway in the chancel which may also be
of that date, but it is somehow a little rough. Considerable
work was done here in the late C17 (*see* below) so one needs
to be cautious. Dec chancel. The windows have ogee-headed
lights under a fine segmental arch. Hoodmoulds on small
heads outside as well as inside. They are a splendid set and in
some ways seem too grand for such a modest church. They
have a domestic character and one wonders whether they
might have been brought in. The arcades are interesting. The
first one and a half bays on the S side come first. They have a
circular pier with circular abacus and double-chamfered
arches. They date from the C13, and the first arch was cut into
when the tower was built. The rest of the S arcade comes next,
with the piers and arches in a continuous moulding of the
Stanford and Leicestershire type (cf. North Kilworth), i.e. with
piers with continuous slender chamfered projections to nave
and aisle and broader ones to the arch openings. That is Dec.
The N arcade, with octagonal piers and double-chamfered
arches, is part of a rebuilding of the N aisle in 1683 when the
church appears to have had a serious make-over. It is instructive to compare the C17 capitals with their medieval neighbours. The aisle retains two C13 double lancet windows. Nave
roof of low pitch with tie-beams and carved bosses, certainly
late, and could easily be also 1683. During the C18 many of
the windows had their tracery removed and filled with clear
glass. Other windows replaced totally. The church suffers, like
so many on the Warwickshire border, having windows made
from the soft sandstones of the area (cf. Crick). S porch, brick,
C18. The church had a partial restoration in 1878 by *E. F. Law*
(chancel roof) and more sensitively in 1906 by *R. Weir Schultz.*
– PULPIT. Mid-C18, with its tester. Fine star inlay. – SCREEN.
Perp; only parts of the base survive with a few bits of tracery.
It is said to have been brought from Lutterworth church in
1611. Odd frieze of horizontal sections of linenfold. – COM-
MUNION RAIL. C18. – PEWS. Made from the former box pews,
many still with the marks of their numbers. Other sections
within the chancel stalls. – ROYAL ARMS. A very fine large one
for George II. – COMMANDMENT BOARDS. A nice C18 set. –
STAINED GLASS. Chancel E window. A C15 circular Glory set
within leaves. – MONUMENT. In the yard, just by the porch, a
fine SLATE HEADSTONE with a central relief of Father Time
with a tiny hourglass. On the l. a relief with a small skeleton,
and on the r. a globe inscribed 'Time how short, Eternity how
long'.
EVANGELICAL CHAPEL (former Wesleyan), on the Green. 1868.
Red brick with blue and yellow brick patterns, two lancet
windows and a quatrefoil above the porch.

OLD RECTORY, by the church. 1852 by *Edward Browning*. Red and blue brick with diaper patterning. Relieving arches over the windows and a tall angled chimneystack.

STONE HOUSE FARMHOUSE, S of the Green. Of the late C17 (cf. Beech House, Hollowell of 1698). Five bays, two storeys, hipped roof. Three bays are widely spaced, but the middle one has flanking, much narrower windows. Doorway with heavy pulvinated frieze. Staircase with dumb-bell balusters.

CASTLE. Site of a motte-and-bailey castle, N of the village and immediately E of the church, close to the river. A second smaller bailey was to the NE of the motte. It was a small but well-protected castle. To the E is a ditch, measuring 84 ft (25.6 metres) across. Another small motte with a single, rather feeble bailey lies ½ m. w. Its history is unclear.

LILFORD

ST PETER. Demolished 1777 and the village removed to Thorpe Achurch (q.v.). Part of a medieval arcade was sited as a landscape feature by the river.

LILFORD HALL. The Lilford Estate was owned by the wealthy Stamford merchant William Browne at the end of the C15 and it then passed by marriage to the Elmes family. William Elmes inherited in 1632 and embarked on building the present house. A date of 1635 presumably marks the completion of the main block. The Elmes family sold in 1699 to the eminent lawyer and later Solicitor General Sir Thomas Powys who *c.* 1711 made substantial additions. His grandson, Thomas, employed *Henry Flitcroft* 1740–50 to redecorate the interior and build a new stable block. The Powys family were created barons in 1797. The 4th Lord Lilford, a renowned ornithologist, brought in *W. G. Habershon*, who produced lavish plans 1847–50, though little was done to the house, except in the S wing. But there are several Jacobethan garden gates and balustrades from his time. It was not until 1909 when the 5th Lord Lilford employed *Dunn & Watson* that a modified version of Habershon's plans was executed, resulting in major E extensions to the wings. The house was requisitioned in 1947 and after the war passed through a succession of owners who only used parts of the building and it became severely decayed. It came into new ownership in 1995 and since then is slowly being brought back into condition.

The approach is from the W, between two small Jacobethan lodges of *c.* 1850 by *Habershon*. The house is a large U-shaped plan and the 1635 house had its main block on the W with two symmetrical wings projecting back to the E. Both have huge chimneystacks on their internal faces, dated 1635. Especially fine WEST FRONT, immaculately built of a grey limestone found in the Oundle area and used to equally superb effect by

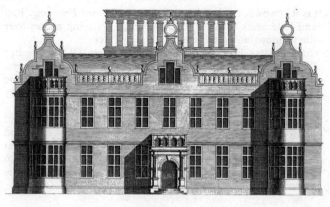

Lilford Hall,
Engraving, 1791

Sir Thomas Tresham at Lyveden some forty years earlier. The
dressings are the paler Weldon stone. The front is nine bays
wide, of which the first and the last are generous bow windows,
of two storeys and topped by balconies. Their balustrades are
an unusual design with arches from which stalactites hang
down. It was a pattern adopted by *Habershon* for his garden
walls. The windows between are tall and slender with a central
mullion and two transoms. Leaded lights. Exactly the same
forms are used in the bows where four windows are linked
around the semicircle. Three big gables with convex and
concave parts and an open ring as a finial. They have three-
light stepped windows, with those over the bows changed by
Flitcroft into Venetian form to give access to the balconies. The
central entrance is a one-storeyed porch with Roman Doric
columns and a balcony, largely an C18 addition. One of the
most striking features of the front is the line of thirteen chimneys linked by arches on the roof. This is probably an original
feature, though rebuilt later. While on this front, it is worth
considering how the house worked inside when originally built.
On the ground floor to the r. was the hall, on the l. an ante-
room, and in the bay the parlour. On the first floor to the r.
the great chamber and on the l. main bedrooms. Then at the
top, running the full width of the house, a Long Gallery. So
all the main rooms overlook this front, so one might expect a
garden rather than a gravel entrance court.

The NORTH and SOUTH FRONTS, while of equal length
originally, were not symmetrical. That on the N begins with a
gabled wing, of the same design as the main façade. Here there
are four floors with mezzanine levels at the base for kitchens.
The fenestration is more orthodox and the range is topped by
three pyramidal gables. On the S side the extent of the original
house is detectable by a change of masonry. It likewise had a

gabled wing at the W end, as on the N, but there were just two
gables. The fenestration of the façade is much altered, partly
by *Flitcroft*, with Venetian openings, but much more so in the
C19. At the E end is a gabled extension created by *Habershon*,
initially replacing an early C19 music room, then finally
reshaped by *Dunn & Watson c.* 1910.

At the back of the house, on the E side, the central block has
even fenestration with smaller cross-windows, an addition by
Powys *c.* 1711. Seven bays, two storeys, with a simple entrance
doorway and small pediment in the centre. The attic storey is
a C19 addition. There was originally a prospect platform here
accessible from the Long Gallery. There is still a flat roof platform. Here can be seen the two huge chimneystacks with their
date 1635, and the C19 extensions to both wings with the date
1858. A parterre garden looks E to the two STABLE BLOCKS
built by *Flitcroft*. A very handsome composition, surprisingly
formal. Both broad U-shaped with pretty cupolas. The IRON-
WORK SCREEN linking the stables was made by *Edward Prid-
more* in 1751.

Inside fine ENTRANCE HALL of *c.* 1740 by *Flitcroft*. The
triple arcade is shown on a plan acting as a screen to the hall,
so creating a kind of screens passage. The original hall was
turned into a DINING ROOM in the early C19 then refurbished
c. 1910 with excellent oak panelling and sideboard recesses at
either end. It still has its stone fireplace by Flitcroft and an
overmantel comprised of a circular relief and some resited
Grinling Gibbons-type garlands. The corresponding room on
the N side, with the bow, is a PARLOUR with early C17 panelling
and overmantel. Very fine STAIRCASE by Flitcroft with stucco
panels, garlands, etc. Two Ionic columns on the ground floor,
two Corinthian ones on the first. The plasterwork augmented
by extra decoration *c.* 1910, especially on the landing. On the
first floor above the dining room a BALLROOM created *c.* 1910
with exuberant decoration by *Cowtan & Son*. The mirror compartments were designed to have bird paintings by *Wolf*. The
ceiling is however Flitcroft's, for which the design exists. Other
rooms have remains of Flitcroft fireplaces and further plasterwork, though much enhanced either in the C19 or
c. 1910. The LONG GALLERY on the top floor was subdivided
in the C19 but still has C17 stone four-centred arched doorcases. Within the first-floor rooms there are also some C17
stone fireplaces, notably in the S wing, now in a passage,
topped by a C17 stone-carved achievement of the Elmes arms,
discovered in the courtyard in 1909 and resited here. In the N
wing is a four-centred stone fireplace surround bearing a
mason's mark which has been found on other buildings associated with the *Thorpes* of Kingscliffe.

LILFORD HAMLET. 1 mile SE. An assembly of estate cottages.
Several pairs with central gables, 1880 by *J. B. Corby* of Stamford, and another cottage with some timber-framing and The
Bothy, opposite the entrance to the estate yard, 1902, both by
the estate surveyor *R. W. Collier*.

WIGSTHORPE, 2 m. SE. A small hamlet. Hall Farm in mock Tudor style *c.* 1880 probably also by *J. B. Corby* and built by the estate builder *Halliday*.

LITCHBOROUGH

ST MARTIN. Dec almost throughout: W tower, chancel with reticulated tracery in the N and S windows (the E window is Perp), clerestory with quatrefoil windows, N doorway and S doorway, and S arcade of four bays with octagonal piers and double-chamfered arches. Lowside windows on both sides of the chancel. Above the S arcade remains of a C12 window. An intriguing puzzle attached to the church was highlighted by research by Hugh Richmond of the RCHME. Bridges's *History* (published 1791) says the church has both N and S aisles, but now it only has one on the S. However, the dimensions in Bridges are those of the church as it stands. Yet the N wall externally does have a change of masonry and weathering line just where a N aisle roof would come. Was it that *c.* 1720 when Bridges was collecting information there was a N aisle, but by 1790 when it was being edited for publication it had gone, so the dimensions are as today, but the editors omitted to correct the description? A nice enigma for future research. The restoration of the chancel is recorded in 1881. – SEDILIA with rounded trefoil heads. – RECTOR'S PEW and elsewhere low pews of box form. – PULPIT. Some fluted Jacobean panels. – FONT. Probably C13 with a Jacobean pyramidal cap. – STAINED GLASS. Nave windows with early C14 Annunciation and Trinity Shield. Chancel N: C14 foliage work. Chancel S, at the top of the window, a rare sundial, probably C17. Chancel E of 1888–9 designed by *Christopher Whall*, made by *J. Powell & Sons*. Less vibrant than some of Whall's work. S aisle E, 1849 by *Ward & Hughes*. The other S aisle S windows also by *Ward & Hughes*, except that at the W end of 1911 by *Burlison & Grylls*. Tower window also by *J. Powell & Sons* 1883. – MONUMENTS. Sir John Needham. Erected in 1633. Noble alabaster effigy on a very large, rather plain tomb-chest. The figure of metropolitan rather than provincial quality. The VCH says this has the latest 'military pillow' in the county. Behind the monument, on the wall, inscription tablet with two columns and some foliage decoration of a much more rustic provincial quality. – Frances Simpson Grant †1907. White marble angel with raised arm, like a monument in a churchyard.

WAR MEMORIAL, on the Green, 1920 by *J. A. Gotch*.

BAPTIST CHAPEL, Towcester Road. Small stone building of 1862 with round-arched windows.

Former SCHOOL at the corner of Northampton and Farthing-stone roads. Ironstone Gothic of 1870 by *T. H. Vernon*.

LITCHBOROUGH HALL, slightly w of the church. C17 house embedded in Neo-Tudor work of 1838 by *George Moore*. The garden front has two wings with ground-floor bay windows. The r. wing is an addition of 1889. Centre of four bays, two storeys with curved gable attics. Good staircase. A separate C17 ironstone service cottage to the SW with mullioned windows. Broad avenue vista to the S bisected by the village road.

ORIGINS OF RADAR MEMORIAL, I m. E on a sharp corner of Northampton Road, just before A5. Erected 2001, a stone block with an inscription recording the first experiments in radar here in 1935.

LITTLE ADDINGTON
9070

ST MARY. Of the late C13 to mid C14. Of the latter date the W tower, embraced by the aisles. Sumptuous doorway with figures up the jambs and a crocketed ogee gable with flanking pinnacles. The bell-stage is treated as a recessed panel. On the N side is a shield with the Pyel arm (*see* Irthlingborough). The family had land here at the end of the C14. Quatrefoil frieze, battlements, recessed spire, not high, with two tiers of lucarnes. Of the windows the chancel E window has a reticulation motif, and the lowside window has tracery below the transom. The S wall however overlaps a blocked doorway from the aisle and there are signs of a blocked window, with a small section of the l. jamb *in situ*. Then above, over the nave, is a decapitated huge gable roof-line. In its present form the whole chancel is suspect. *Churches of the Archdeaconry* (1849) describes it as 'sadly curtailed in height and length'. Of late C13 date the arcades, similar but not identical. Four shafts (or quatrefoil) with thin keeled shafts in the diagonals. The proportions differ, and the slenderer S arcade has fillets on the main shafts, while the N arcade has not. Fine S doorway with two orders of shafts and a many-moulded arch. Heavily vaulted N porch with room above. Late C13 tracery in the windows of the W parts of the aisles, Geometric on the N, and bar tracery on the S. The E end of the S aisle has evidence of a much grander effect and windows have reticulated tracery and a charming piscina with a traceried front. The church was restored by *E. F. Law*, 1857 and further in 1882–3 when the vestry was added. – PULPIT and SCREEN. Both show signs of being made up, the screen especially, though both have parts of old woodwork. The pulpit partly Perp, with traceried panels, and the screen with C14 tracery of two-light divisions, based on the Y-type of arrangement. – STAINED GLASS. Nave N. C14 fragments. Chancel E window by *A. O. Hemming* 1880s.

ADDINGTON HOUSE. Former vicarage, 1858 in the Tudor manner by *E. F. Law*.

LITTLE BILLING *see* OUTER NORTHAMPTON

LITTLE BRINGTON *see* GREAT BRINGTON

8070

LITTLE HARROWDEN

St Mary. Late Norman s doorway with three orders of shafts carrying volute capitals. Three roll mouldings and an outer zigzag moulding. Chronologically there follows the third bay of the s arcade. This is of ironstone and must have been a transept arch. Then, late C13 to early C14, the other s bays and the three N bays, the s aisle windows, the grand chancel E window of four lights consisting of pairs with cusped Y-tracery and a sexfoiled circle in the head. Intersecting Y-tracery in other windows. Conspicuous date of 1601 above the s doorway suggesting some alteration. Perhaps just the projection in which the doorway sits, or could the w end of the s aisle also be partly rebuilt? The window tracery, whilst seemingly just like that of the s chapel, is just a bit different and under a rounder form of head. It could easily be early C17. The N aisle is 1850 by *E. F. Law*, when the church was restored. The Dec w tower collapsed in 1967 and was then demolished (the spire had fallen in 1703). A small vestry is on its site with a bellcote above. The tower had two-light bell-openings and a quatrefoil frieze below the battlements, sections of which are on the w side of the churchyard. – SCREEN. Perp, of one-light divisions. – COMMUNION RAIL. Jacobean. – STAINED GLASS. A memorial screen for both World Wars with a window built into the former tower arch. The window forms the apex of the arch with a design of lilies and poppies by *Meg Lawrence* installed in 2010.

SCHOOL, NE of the church. Partly of the 1850s in ironstone in the Tudor manner, by *E. F. Law*, and extended in 1876. The SCHOOL HOUSE is also by Law.

WESLEYAN CHAPEL, High Street. 1882 in the lancet style, of yellow brick with red brick dressings.

8050

LITTLE HOUGHTON

St Mary. s doorway of *c.* 1200. One order of shafts with leaf-crocket capitals, round arch with two flat steps. C13 w tower. What was the bell-stage then has five blank arches with two lancet windows. The Perp top stage has two-light bell-openings, a quatrefoil frieze and battlements. The rest of the church was almost rebuilt in 1873–4 by *Charles Buckeridge*. The windows were all renewed, the N aisle was built, and the s arcade restored at that date. Three-bay arcade with octagonal piers and double-chamfered arches. One-bay chancel chapels to the N and S. Lots of C19 corbel heads. – FONT. Circular, with flat shafts carrying rough single-scallop capitals. The bowl looks C13, but the support later, perhaps C15. – STAINED GLASS. Chancel E window by *Ward & Hughes*, 1873. – Chancel N, 1897 and S, 1868, both by *Clayton & Bell*. – N aisle E, by *Clayton & Bell*, 1905, and W, by *A. K. Nicholson*, 1932. – S chapel E, 1995 by *George Wigley* incorporating in the centre of each light panels *c.* 1870 by *Heaton, Butler & Bayne* (brought from the chapel of King's School, Ely). – MONUMENT. Pretty tablet to William Ward and family, erected in 1775. By *William Cox Sen.*

STOCKS, SE of the church on the S side of the road to Bedford.

LITTLE HOUGHTON HOUSE, on Bedford Road, at the E side of the village. Built probably *c.* 1777–80 (the old manor house was demolished in 1777). At the rear are portions of an older house of *c.* 1720. The newer part is built of white Kingsthorpe stone, of three storeys, with five bays on the E front, four on the S front, with a pediment added in the 1950s, but based on C19 drawings, made up of stone from the demolished Horton Hall. The entrance was originally on the S side and is recorded thus in a drawing by George Clarke. It was moved to the W side in 1848. A drawing survives signed *Talbot Bury*. The interior was further altered 1865–6 by *E. F. Law*. The original staircase survives, rising in a sweeping curve. It is this feature and the proportions of the exterior and the use of Kingsthorpe stone which suggest the hand of *John Johnson* of Leicester, although there is no documentary evidence.

A village with a good selection of dated stone houses and cottages, mainly owing to the local availability of two stones, a dark ironstone and a buff sandstone, often used to striking effect with banded courses. The best example is at the E end of the village, on the N side of Bedford Road, RANDOLPH HOUSE. It is firmly dated 1601 and has excellent banded courses and mullioned windows, with those on the ground floor having relieving arches over them. A small attic gable. A choice example. Still in Bedford Road, but W of the church on the S side, LODGE FARMHOUSE. The main block of the house is C17 with a stair-turret with a vertically placed oval window. The front wing is dated 1702 with framed windows. Further W, THE MERE. Built as the dower house for Little Houghton House *c.* 1838. Stuccoed, five bays, two storeys, with parapet. On the E side of the churchyard in Meadow Lane, CHURCH FARMHOUSE, mid-C18. Opposite a little square house dated 1685, once the summerhouse for the Ward manor house, which was demolished in 1777. It has Latin verses commemorating the Ward family's support of James II. Round the corner to the W, THE OLD HOUSE, dated 1689 on the big datestone on its W gable, and on the end of the N platband another date, 1689, and the initials 'KC' – could this be the builder? Finally in Station Road the former VICARAGE, C18 brick, and THE GRANGE, dated 1687.

CLIFFORD HILL, *c.* ½ m. N of the village, on the banks of the Nene. A large MOTTE, which is remarkable in several ways: first for its size, as it is one of the largest mottes in the country; secondly because it appears that there is no historical record of the castle which stood upon it; and finally because with any considerable motte it is reasonable to expect a bailey. Clifford Hill has nothing but a counterscarp bank, well marked to N and S, destroyed or vague on the other two sides. A disturbed area on the W may mark the position of some sort of dependency, but certainly not that of a bailey worthy of so splendid a mount. Part of the S side of the motte appears to have collapsed at some date (not recent), and it is possible that this may have led to the early abandonment of the castle.

8080

LITTLE OAKLEY

ST PETER. Fine early C13 chancel. Lancet windows, the group of three stepped ones at the E end shafted inside, the shafts with stiff-leaf capitals. Lowside window. C13 S arcade of quatre-foil piers, broadly detailed, and double-chamfered arches. The N arcade of the same elements, but with more mouldings in the capitals, a little later. Single window at the W end of the N aisle and roof-line of C13 aisle. Aisles heightened and given new square-headed windows in the C14, except the E window of the S aisle, which has curvilinear tracery. Perp W tower with clasping buttresses, tall bell-openings, and battlements. The church was restored by *Slater & Carpenter*, 1867, and given some splendidly carved corbel heads and a PULPIT. Further work by *Carpenter & Ingelow* in 1882. – SCULPTURE. In the vestry a fragment of a C12 capital set in the wall. – MONUMENTS. Figure of an archer with arrow in his belt under a trefoil-headed canopy, C13. It is very weatherworn. – William Markham †1571, erected probably a little later. Markham was the second husband of Elizabeth Montagu (†1569), eldest sister of Sir Edward Montagu of Boughton. An uncommonly fine and noble design without any figures or inscriptions and superbly carved. Three pairs of coupled Roman Doric columns on high bases with garlands and grotesques. Between the columns strapwork cartouches and shields. Simple roof-like top storey with a shield between pilasters. Scallop shell at the top. Two dragons' legs act as supporters l. and r. The monument is without doubt a product of the *Thorpe* workshop at Kingscliffe and carved from that stone, and relates to the monuments at Fotheringhay and the hall chimneypiece at Deene. – William Montagu, †1619. With a big kneeling figure between columns. In the foot-piece lies a putto with an hourglass. Inscription: Hodie mini eras tibi. – STAINED GLASS. Chancel E, 1867 by *Clayton & Bell*. – Chancel S and N, both 1874 by *Ward & Hughes*. – S aisle E, 1874 by *Clayton & Bell*.

46

MANOR HOUSE, W of the church. Similar in its windows to Great Oakley Hall and so also probably of *c.* 1550–60. Gabled, with mullioned windows with arched lights. Also a date of 1721.

Several nice cottages in the small village, some thatched. Some estate cottages *c.* 1850 and former SCHOOL, Tudor style, 1852.

LODDINGTON

ST LEONARD. Of ironstone. C13 W tower. Bold W doorway with a tall gable, representing in relief the end of a stone-tiled roof. The portal beneath has three orders of shafts, two of them with shaft-rings. Later (grey stone) frieze of cusped lozenges, big gargoyles, and broach spire with two tiers of lucarnes. C13 also the S aisle – see the SW lancet and the arcade of three bays with one octagonal and one quatrefoil pier. C13 again the S chapel of two bays and its elegant little doorway. The chapel arcade has a circular pier with four attached shafts (cf. Rothwell). The arches have two hollow chamfers and an inner roll with a fillet. The chancel is of *c.* 1300, see the intersected tracery in the E window, the S window of two lights with a circle, and perhaps the SEDILIA. The latter are either severely restored or C19 work (there was a restoration in 1859 by *Ewan Christian*). Tomb-recesses in the S chapel and S aisle. Niches l. and r. of the S aisle E window. S aisle parapet, limestone with date 1578. Tudor type doorway within the N porch, probably C16. Perp clerestory, with a narrow frieze with small shields. – FONT. C12, tub-shaped with patterned rim. – SCREENS. Perp. Of the rood screen only the base remains, but the parclose screens to the S chapel are intact. The simpler side, on r. looks C14, and the other part C15. – PEWS. At the end of S aisle three C15 or C16 (a bequest for fittings by the Kinnesman family is recorded in 1532) with traceried ends. – STAINED GLASS. S aisle W, shield for Kinnesman, C15. Chancel, S window by *Morris & Co.*, designed by *G. F. Campfield*, 1893. Chancel E, 1859 by *J. Powell & Sons*. Quarries in other windows also *Powells*.

LODDINGTON HALL. The building originates from a C13 hall house of the Le Baud family, and a good deal of the roof structure of that house survives. It had a cross-wing at its N end. Work in 1989 in the Hall revealed some evidence of windows and a doorway. In the early C17, after acquisition by the Syers family, the Hall was subdivided and the SW front given a porch and new windows, creating the present Jacobean E-plan effect. In the late C19 the estate had passed to the Brookes of Great Oakley and was much added to and altered *c.* 1890 (N wing dated 1893), partly under the direction of *J. A. Gotch*. The C17 work has mullioned and mullioned-and-transomed windows and many gables. The doorway into the Hall is original; the porch may be a later addition. In the Hall fireplace with strapwork. The fireplace in the kitchen (to the w of the hall) has the date 1615. Big early C20 wrought-iron GATES in C18 manner. The Hall was for several years a school but is now flats. The former educational building by *John Goff*, the County Architect, 1970–1, has been converted to commercial use. It is faced with simulated ironstone with vertical hanneling. Thick mullions on the ground floor, and some boxed-out windows. Irregular roof, because of the top lighting.

Attractive village with good stone houses. LODDINGTON HOUSE, large mid-C19 stucco, later N extension, mildly Italianate.

VILLAGE HALL, Main Street, 1928 by *F. H. Allen*, Tudor style with half-timbered gable.

SCHOOL, Main Street, 1860–3, with to r. the original ironstone building. A charity inscription in the church has a bequest in 1705.

LONG BUCKBY

ST LAWRENCE. Of ironstone. The w tower is of the C13. Very flat, thin, set-back buttresses with a shaft at the exposed angle, w lancet in a projection. Two-light bell-openings separated by a shaft. Pointed-arched top frieze. Battlements. Dec arcade of four bays. Octagonal piers, double-chamfered arches. Dec probably also the aisle walls and the chancel. The chancel E window still has its side shafts, but otherwise the windows are too renewed to be of use. The aisles had in fact been made Georgian in 1774 (restoration by *G. G. Scott*, 1862–3, and by *W. Bassett-Smith*, 1883–7). Dec cinquefoiled clerestory windows. On the N side an arch resting on corbels with fleurons. There

Long Buckby, St Lawrence.
Drawing by G. Clarke, *c.* 1850

was no doubt originally a monument here. In the chancel SEDILIA, the backs of the seats deepened into little niches. – STAINED GLASS. Chancel E window by *D. Evans* of Shrewsbury, 1863. The window commemorates the daughter of a Shropshire vicar (†1858). – MONUMENT. Cilena I'Anson Bradley †1726. By *John Hunt*. With a small but charming marble bust. – John King †1816. Large Neoclassical monument with sarcophagus against a pyramid. Urns alongside.

UNITED REFORMED CHURCH (formerly Congregational), SW of the Market Place. Dated 1771. Three-bay front with arched windows and doorways, segment-headed below, round-headed above. Two-storeyed fenestration also along the sides. Three galleries internally and a blank arch behind the pulpit of 1859. Sunday School of 1880. The MANSE to the l. is of three bays and two and a half storeys.

BAPTIST CHAPEL, Brington Road. Dated 1846, but still in the same classical tradition.

SCHOOL, High Street. 1873 of brick with two wings in gentle Queen Anne revival manner. Additions by *Law & Harris* in 1906.

In the MARKET PLACE a fine Victorian brick house with a wide cast-iron balcony, and N, on the corner of Church Street, just the remnant of the terracotta gable of the 1910 CO-OPERATIVE shop. In King Street, on the way from the Market Place to the church, SIBLEY HOUSE, a handsome L-shaped group of two houses, dated 1734. Extended N in the same style but with C19 brick gable end. Shoemaking was an extensive trade largely done by outworkers and there are several examples of workshops at the end of gardens behind houses. Two of the best are behind houses in HOLYOAK TERRACE off the N side of East Street. The former CASTLE SHOE FACTORY, *c.* 1890, still stands, converted to offices, on the N side of King Street.

CASTLE. In the middle of the village, a little distance to the SW of the church, is a rather curious earthwork consisting of an oval ringwork in the middle of a triangular bailey. Excavations have indicated that the ringwork is of mid-C12 date, partly overlying an earlier enclosure. A stone wall around the bailey was added later.

BUCKBY WHARF, 1½ m. SW on the Grand Union Canal. MISSION CHURCH of 1874–5 by *T. H. Vernon*, now a residence.

BUCKBY LION, on the A428, 1¾ m. NE. Large, Neo-Georgian, with pediment on its rear façade and two bays on the S. Designed by *Tad Dobraszczyk* in 2009.

LOWICK   *9080*

ST PETER. A very good Perp church, built chiefly at the expense   27
of members of the Greene family of Drayton, namely Sir

Henry who succeeded at Drayton in 1369 and died in 1399, Ralph who died in 1417, and Henry who died in 1467–8. Ralph is buried between the chancel and the N chapel, Henry in the southern transeptal chapel. The nave and aisles probably came first. The E end probably complete by 1394. The tower was probably built only after 1470 (bequest for bells 1479). Earlier than the Greene period the early C14 S doorway (hoodmould on angels with shields) and probably the SEDILIA in the chancel and a blank arch at the E end of the N aisle, which must originally have formed part of it. They have the ogee arches and crocketed gables with elongated pointed trefoils characteristic of c. 1330–40. In the N aisle a cusped segment-headed tomb-recess, also a remnant from the C14 church. The rest then is all C15. The nave is divided from the aisles by four bays of tall octagonal piers with double-chamfered arches (tall vertical pieces at the springing of the arches). The chancel arch is of the same design. The aisles have tall transomed windows of three and four lights with embattled transom and four-centred arches to the individual lights. The same windows in the S transept, except that the two-light S window has two transoms. Its E window however is quite different and much prettier. It has nice cusping below the transom, and in the top the motif of the four-petalled flower. The chancel even has panel tracery below the transoms of the windows, and the same motif is used in the N chapel. And so to the W tower, a beautifully erect and vigorous piece, not too much opened up, and of a type found elsewhere in NE Northamptonshire. Clasping buttresses. Big W doorway with tracery in the spandrels. Three tiers of quatrefoil or cusped-lozenge friezes. Big two-light upper windows. Battlements with tall square-panelled pinnacles. Then an added lantern top storey between the pinnacles, octagonal and with its own eight pinnacles, doubtless inspired by Fotheringhay, but here treated more decoratively. This and the new wide, three-light, transomed bell-openings provide a splendid finale to the church. The church was restored 1867–73 by *Slater & Carpenter*. The faculty plan dated 1869 shows seating across the tower arch, which accounts for the sloping marks on each side of the archway.

FURNISHINGS. – BENCH-ENDS, S aisle, c. 1520. With fleur-de-lys poppyheads. Some have heads instead of the two side pieces. One has in addition two mitred heads as the top piece. – STALLS, PULPIT and PEWS. All date from 1867–73. The carving is by *J. Forsyth*, with especially fine details on the stalls. – REREDOS. 1929. Designed by *W. H. Randoll Blacking* with painted work by *Christopher Webb*. – ROYAL ARMS. 1718, painted, over the chancel arch. Fine. – SCREEN (S transept), c. 1850, stone, of Perp design by *Thompson* of Peterborough. – STAINED GLASS. Sixteen beautiful figures in the N aisle windows. They come from a Jesse window of c. 1310–30. Excellent quality. The figures are four kings and eleven prophets, the kings seated and in the first window from the W. The sequence is: the kings

Rehoboam; David; Solomon; Asa; then the prophets Jacob; Isaiah; Habakkuk; Daniel; Ezekiel; Jeremiah; Isaac; Joseph; Zachariah; Micah. Finally a donor knight, thought to be Simon de Drayton. More C14 figures from other windows at the tops of each. In the spandrels of the chancel windows C15 coats of arms. The other windows with Victorian and Edwardian glass are: chancel and N chapel E windows both by *Clayton & Bell*. – Chancel S windows by *Heaton, Butler & Bayne*. N chapel heraldic window by *Lavers & Westlake* 1888. – S aisle window by *J. Powell & Sons*. – S aisle w by *A. K. Nicholson*. – Tower window by *Ward & Nixon*.

MONUMENTS. John Heton, rector 1406–15, large Purbeck slab in centre of chancel. Ralph Greene †1417. The contract of 1419 for the monument exists. It pledges '*Thomas Prentys* and *Robert Sutton*, kervers of Chellaston' (the village in Derbyshire with the famous alabaster quarries) to make two images, a counterfeit of an esquire and a lady in her open surcoat with two dogs at her feet and two angels by her pillow. Husband and wife were to hold hands, and there were to be angels along the sides and an alabaster arch above, the whole to be gilded and painted. The delivery date was Easter 1420, and the price £40, to be paid in five equal instalments. The arch has gone, but the tomb-chest has indeed six by three angels. They stand stiffly frontal in an identical attitude, each holding a shield. Excellent effigies. Over their heads canopies with lierne vaults, with traces of colour. He is in armour with excellent detail, notably the straps holding the pieces together. A jewelled band around his helmet. Tilting helm with the Greene crest, a stag's head. One antler missing. She has a wonderful winged hairpiece with jewelled circlet. At their feet a mastiff and a puppy. – Henry Greene †1467. Tomb-chest with shields in quatrefoils. On the lid good brasses, in heraldic garb, 3 ft (91 cm.) long. – Edward Stafford, 2nd Earl of Wiltshire, †1499. Alabaster effigy on a tall tomb-chest with lozenge panels inside cusped square panels. Finely carved, again with traces of colour. Also in heraldic surcoat. Under the soles of his feet two tiny clerics with rosaries, denoting the chantry founded under the terms of his will. The inscription especially beautifully done with raised letters and leaf trails. Good Nottingham school work. – William, son of the 1st Earl of Peterborough, †1625, eighty-two days old. Two columns with very unorthodox capitals. Short inscription done with initial letters only. No figures. – Lady Mary Mordaunt, Duchess of Norfolk, †1705. Semi-reclining white figure in contemporary dress. No background. – Sir John Germaine †1718. Young-looking, semi-reclining, in armour. Three semi-reclining figures of children. No background. Both monuments probably from the yard of *William Woodman* the elder, who provided marble work at Drayton. – 5th Duke of Dorset †1843. By *R. Westmacott Jun.* White tomb-chest. The Duke's mantle lies and hangs over it, his shield leans against it, his coronet stands on the ground. At the foot of the tomb-chest a big, white, life-size but lifeless seated angel. – Good Georgian headstones line the path.

The village has an attractive collection of stone houses, many with roofs of thatch and pantiles. THE SNOOTY FOX was, until it became an inn *c.* 1700, known as the Great House and was used for some time as a dower house for Drayton. It dates from the first half of the C16 and inside has fine moulded beam ceilings of that date. It was extended *c.* 1580 with further beamed ceilings and upstairs stone fireplaces of the same design of those of the same date at Drayton.

THE OLD RECTORY. Large Elizabethan design of 1855–6 by *Edward Browning* of Stamford. Big barn rebuilt in 1786. The Rev. Lucas Collins entertained Trollope and George Eliot here.

GERMAIN ROOMS, at the corner of Drayton Road. The former CHARITY SCHOOL and SCHOOL HOUSE. Founded in 1718 by Sir John and re-augmented in 1725 by Lady Elizabeth Germaine for twenty poor children. The long mullioned windows, although replacements, are an original feature. Coat of arms over the door. The school house has a beamed fireplace with battlement cresting of late C16 date.

J. A. Gotch did much work for the estate. In Drayton Road is a pair of cottages (Nos. 10–12) built to his designs by *Charles Pettit* of Thrapton, and in Drayton Park are another pair similarly dated 1908, and also, of the same date, a LODGE on Kettering Road.

For Drayton House *see* p. 235.

LUDDINGTON-IN-THE-BROOK

ST MARGARET. Hidden from the road, in a garden churchyard. C13 W tower with clasping buttresses, bell-openings with Y-tracery, and a short broach spire with one tier of lucarnes. The spire dates from 1874, a completion of one only partially finished. The body of the church all very Late Perp, probably into the C16, except the C13 W wall of the aisle with its buttress. The exterior remarkable for the delightful collection of gargoyles and creatures clinging to parapets. S aisle with piers of a characteristic section. Long chamfered projections to nave and aisle without capitals, attached shafts with capitals to the aisle openings. S porch, whose inner doorway is almost Tudor; two big Perp N windows. Victorian chancel, appearing somewhat incongruous. It is a rebuilding by *R. H. Carpenter* of 1874–5, following the C13 original. – BENCHES. C16; straightheaded, with linenfold type panels. – SCULPTURE. In the chancel N wall some C13 diapering. – STAINED GLASS. S aisle E, remains of original canopy work.

LUDDINGTON HALL, 1½ m. SW on the Thurning/Winwick road. 2009–10 by the *Whyte Holland Partnership*. Georgian style of stone with three bay centre with porch and two bay wings all under a hipped roof with four dormers.

LUTTON

A village somewhat remote on the very edge of Huntingdonshire.

St Peter. Perp w tower with clasping buttresses, four-light bell-openings with transom, and battlements. Big buttresses inside so it was probably built as a separate structure. Of the same time considerable remodelling of the structure – see parapets etc. In 1447 Lutton was united with Washingley, Hunts, and was given permission to utilize material from that church. Late C13 chancel with an interesting four-light window with one trefoiled and one quatrefoiled circle and a spherical triangle above them. N arcade of three low bays, also C13. Circular piers with octagonal abaci, nailhead enrichment, double-chamfered pointed arches. In the aisle w wall one lancet. The C14 s arcade with piers of quatrefoil section. Responds on head corbels, a stylish female head at the E end. Hoodmoulds with small headstops. Another grimacing head at the w end rather engulfed by the tower buttress. A restoration of 1880–1 by *Alfred Sykes* of Milton, Peterborough, of which date is the remodelling of the chancel arch. – NAVE ROOF. Partly C16 with figures holding emblems supporting the beams. The central one on the N side holds a chalice and wafer. The aisle roofs also of the same date. – EASTER SEP- ULCHRE. C15, four-centred arch above six blank panels. The two middle ones stop halfway down to allow for a blank tablet to be set in them. – ALTAR RAILS. Thin balusters, *c.* 1700. – SCULPTURE. In the tower N wall some Anglo-Saxon inter- lace and a single piece of dogtooth. – MONUMENTS. Robert, William and Robert Apreece of Washingley, 1633. Three fron- tally kneeling figures, their hind-parts left out. Somewhat squeezed into their setting. Thin Corinthian columns and arms above. – Adlard Apreece †1608. Small figure kneeling in profile, as usual. Heraldic pilasters, skull at base. Of fine quality and attributed to *Maximilian Colt* (GF). Some fine late C17 ledger stones in sanctuary. A small brass inscription with shield for John Loftus, 1657.

Former SCHOOL, School Lane, SW of the church (now village hall). Incorporated is the original building of 1872 in mottled brick by *A. Sykes* of Peterborough. Crow-stepped gables.

MANOR FARM HOUSE (W of the church). Late C16 and C17, L-shaped, altered later. Two storeys, with mullioned windows. Thought to have been built during the ownership of John Loftus who held the manor 1572–1615.

LYVEDEN

9080

Lyveden* is a very special place – unique in Northamptonshire and a rarity in the rest of England: a late C16 garden layout which has remained almost untouched since it was abandoned in 1605. Just how untouched it is became apparent when in 2006 in America an aerial reconnaissance photograph taken in 1944 by a Luftwaffe pilot came to light. This remarkable view showed that even the plant holes for the orchard trees were still there, as were the concentric circles of a garden.

Lyveden was already in the ownership of the Tresham family by the middle of the C15, and Prior Sir Thomas Tresham (†1559) was granted licence to empark in 1540. However, what we see today represents the work of his grandson, Sir Thomas Tresham of Rushton (†1605), in the last decade of the C16. Sir Thomas's fervent preoccupation with religious symbolism is most vividly demonstrated in the Triangular Lodge, at Rushton (q.v.), but here also at Lyveden it is a dominating theme. Following Sir Thomas's death his widow, Muriel, lived on at Lyveden till her death in 1615, but she was so encumbered by settling his debts it is unlikely that she did other than maintain the garden. In 1609 she offered Lord Burghley fifty trees for Hatfield. The later history of Lyveden only becomes clear in the C18 when in 1732 it was acquired by Lady Gowran. She was the daughter of Sir John Robinson, the owner of the adjoining Farming or Fermyn Woods Estate. In the 1740s her husband commissioned designs by *Dougal Campbell* to Palladianize the unfinished building by completing the walls, adding another floor and topping the building with a large dome and cupola.† Thus Lyveden was annexed to the Farming Woods Estate which by descent came to the Lords Lyveden. The estate was sold in the early 1900s and the Lyveden buildings became a cause for concern. Mainly due to the energies of the Kettering architect *J. A. Gotch*, a fund was raised for their purchase and in 1922 they passed into the ownership of the National Trust. There are three sections to the site: first what may be called the Old Bield, which includes the former manor house site (in private ownership), then the garden terraces and water garden, and finally the New Bield (both in the care of the National Trust).

To understand the impact of the garden layout a start should be made in the valley at the OLD BIELD. The 1944 aerial view shows a central axis path running from the site of the old manor house, largely demolished following the death of Sir Thomas in 1605 and the sale of the Rushton Estate. There was certainly some work being done on the old house in 1604, but the present house, which stands slightly to the W of the former manor house, is almost entirely the work of Sir Thomas's son, Sir Lewis, so Jacobean rather than Elizabethan. It is basically

---

*I am grateful to Mark Bradshaw for comments and ideas.
† The designs are in the Northamptonshire Libraries collection.

an L-shaped structure with mullioned-and-transomed windows. The windows in the upper storey had two transoms; one window in a lower annex is older and still has arched lights. It has been considerably altered since and the interior almost completely redrafted. A large, impressive staircase was removed c. 1900 and is now in America, with a copy having been created in the late 1990s in the present house. An ornamental gateway was also removed and this is now at Fermyn Woods Hall (q.v.).

The GARDEN rises S from the Old Bield, up a gentle slope. Beyond the confines of what would have been formal gardens in front of the old manor house is the ORCHARD. A letter of 1597 survives from Tresham to his gardener John Slynne in which he lists the varieties of apple, pear, damson, plum and cherry trees, and in 2000 the National Trust in collaboration with the Brogdale National Collection of fruit trees embarked on replanting with as near varieties as could be obtained. The central axis walk was lined with walnuts and in total the orchard contained over three hundred trees. Moving up the slope the visitor then meets a wide TERRACE with small pyramidal mounts at each corner, and now the view changes, for one overlooks a large square plot bounded by water canals, THE MOATED GARDEN. Tresham envisaged this as a moated orchard. The 1944 photograph shows clear evidence of a concentric ringed design which Tresham planned to be planted with roses, raspberries and junipers. The moats or canals run round each side of the square. On the W side the line is interrupted at the N end and it may never have been completed. On the S side of the square the canals encircle two SPIRAL MOUNTS. Mounts such as these, known then as 'snail mounts', were to be found in many C16 and C17 gardens, and here they have spiral walkways around them.

It is from the SE mount that one gets one of the most entrancing views of the main building of the garden, the lodge or NEW BIELD. This was a large summerhouse, banqueting house and hunting lodge rather than a house proper. It is an exquisite building, immaculately built using two local stones: Weldon for the quoins and dressings and a darker slightly purple-grey stone, quarried N of Oundle,* part of a series of limestones generally known as the Blisworth limestones. Work was being carried out by Tresham's own masons, the *Grumbolds* doing the chief work and the *Tyrells*, who built the Triangular Lodge, the rest. Carved work was in the hands of a mason called *Parris* and there was some involvement of a surveyor, *Robert Stickels*. In 1596 Tresham is writing to Parris about 'The dooryk freeze of passion work', and there is a letter to Stickels, undated, referring to the Doric architrave, frieze and cornice. Much of the time it was being built Tresham was imprisoned at Ely and a series of letters survives illuminating the building's progress.[†] The building was begun in 1594, but was unfinished

45

---

* Pilton is mentioned in the Tresham manuscripts as a source for stone.
[†] They were discovered in a recess at Rushton Hall in 1832 and are now in the British Library.

when Sir Thomas died in 1605. The plan is drawn in John Thorpe's famous book of plans and elevations of houses and has therefore wrongly been assigned to him; there is little doubt that it derives solely from Tresham's own ideas. The rigid symmetry of the plan and the symbolism of the details are equally characteristic both of the date when it was built and the man for whom it was built. The plan is a Greek cross with, at each end, a canted bay window rising to full height. Two storeys above a high basement. Mullioned-and-transomed windows. The entrance with a round arch was approached by an open flight of steps into the N bay. There are three rooms on each floor with a staircase in the S arm. The joist holes for its construction are clear. The two rooms in the W–E axis are larger than the others. They are the hall and parlour on the raised ground floor, and the Great Chamber and probably a bedroom on the upper floor. The kitchen and buttery were in the basement below hall and parlour, and bakehouse ovens are to be found in the W bay, cut off from the main space. Indeed, rather curiously, nearly all the bay windows are divided from the main rooms by a partition wall, that of the parlour being the only one open. On the ground floor three arches on piers connect the staircase with the hall and the parlour. The central archway from the entrance hall bears Tresham's shield. In the entrance hall at the NW corner there is a corbelled bracket made either for a statue or perhaps a lantern.

The cross-shape of the building is an allusion to Christ's Passion. The metope frieze above the ground floor and the frieze above the upper floor are Catholic demonstrations, referring in particular to the Passion and to the Mater Dolorosa. In the metopes the X sign, the IHS sign, the Instruments of the Passion, and Judas's money-bag. In the upper frieze the following inscription partly remains:

Iesus mundi Salus – Gaude Mater Virgo Maria – Verbum autem Crucis pereuntibus quidem Stultitia est. – Iesus. Beams Venter qui te portavit. – Maria Virgo Sponsa innupta. – T. earn. alt. – Bene-dixit te Deus in aeternum Maria. – Mihi autem absit gloriari nisi in Cruce Domini XP.*

Some kind of roof may have been completed as timbers in the house survived until the 1650s when they were removed by Major General William Boteler, Cromwell's Lord Chamberlain, to be used in his new house in Oundle, Cobthorne (see p. 512). There are still small sections of joists in many sockets. It is also thought that the building may have been intended to have a further storey containing a viewing gallery, so that it would have been an even more conspicuous object than it is today (cf. Gayton Manor House). A design for a glazed cupola by Robert Stickels, normally associated with this building, is

---

* For further details of the symbolism see Sir Gyles Isham, *Sir Thomas Tresham and His Buildings*, Northants. Ant. Soc. Reports and Papers, 65, 1966, and the National Trust guidebook by Mark Bradshaw, 2004.

Lyveden New Bield.
Frieze, details, 1883

now thought to have been intended for the Hawkfield Lodge at Rushton, which no longer exists. It is worth remembering that Tresham's other buildings at Rushton and Rothwell are only two storeys high. There were further formal gardens intended around the lodge, and one with transverse lines appears on the N side of the building in the 1944 photograph. Doubtless more were intended. The hunting aspect needs to be considered, for the views over the landscape are extensive and one of the rewards of a visit. It should also be remembered that the trees of Fermyn Woods and the rest of Rockingham Forest are now at a distance from the building, but in the C16 they would have been much closer and would have encircled the southern aspect.

What does all this amount to? Not just a pretty garden and summerhouse surely? Is this Tresham creating his own Garden of Gethsemane, ending with his own allusion to the Crucifixion on the ridge? If only we could conjure up the mind which created this place.

MAIDFORD

6050

St PETER AND St PAUL. The imposts of a blocked doorway in the N aisle may be late C12. Base of W tower C13, heightened in the C14 with its original saddleback roof. C13 also the S aisle, see the W lancet, but rebuilt and enlarged C14. Dec three-bay arcade. Octagonal piers, double-chamfered arches. Most of the window tracery dates from a restoration of 1879. Odd chancel arch, just a flat rounded shape, early C19? Clerestory windows simple square openings, probably C18. The S porch is dated 1883. – Sanctuary PANELLING partly Jacobean. – SCREEN. The tops of two lights attached to the responds of the chancel arch. – STALLS. They are plain Perp benches from Eydon church. – COMMUNION RAIL. Early C18 with slim balusters. – FONT. C19 in the E.E. style. – ROYAL ARMS. Dated 1813 by *James Collins*. – STAINED GLASS. Chancel E window of 1879 by *Ward & Hughes*. – S aisle E window of 1880 by *J. Hardman & Co*. – MONUMENTS. Rev. Samsom White †1825, a white marble Gothic tablet by *Whiting* of Northampton. John White, M.D. †1821, also by *Whiting*. Worth reading the epitaph.

Former SCHOOL, N of the church (now village hall). 1872 by *T. H. Vernon*. Simple red brick Gothic with three tall lancets.

MANOR FARM, S of the church. In the gable towards the street a large, blocked medieval window with a two-centred arch. The house largely C17 with later alterations. A C15 window survives. BARN alongside the churchyard with a C16 four-centred arch.

MAIDWELL

St Mary. A simply planned church with just a nave, chancel and w tower. The first items chronologically are the s and n doorways, with plain single-stepped round arches and no responds: that is c12. Then follows the lower part of the w tower, which must be of the c13. The first stage has conspicuous shafts at each corner. One upper lancet window. It has diagonal buttresses with chamfered edges which must be a c14 addition. Over the w window is a worn carved plaque of c16 date. It has damaged animal supporters and a shield with the letters TC and what looks like a barrel (tun) below; this presumably relates to the Seyton family who were here in the c15 and early c16 centuries. The bell-openings are of 1705. c13 single lancets and two-light windows with a quatrefoiled circle also in the nave n and s walls, shafted inside with heavy moulded heads. Curious arrangement of the tower arch, with inside the tower further shafts and the beginnings of an arch (s side) suggesting arcading. A masonry joint on the n side of the nave externally and a scar on the s would suggest that the tower was originally built separately, then joined to the nave. The chancel was rebuilt in c13 style in 1890–1 at the cost of Sir Robert Loder by *St Aubyn, Son & Walding*. George Clarke drawings show that before 1891 there was just a short rectangular aedicule with one round-arched opening attached to the e end of the nave. A faculty records the rebuilding of the chancel and forming of a recess for the broken Gorges monument in 1775. An c18 diary records the involvement of *John Wing (Jun.)* of Leicester in the 1780s so he was doubtless responsible. St Aubyn resited the Gorges monument in the chancel recess, removed the clerestory and put on the rather grand roofs. – PULPIT. c18 on a c19 stone base. Also panelling from c18 BOX PEWS reused against the nave walls. N and s doors also c18. – CANOPIED PEWS of 1891; the BENCHES are in a c17 style and one or two appear to have old woodwork, but in general they look more like early 1900s (*see also* Draughton). – FONT. c18, of baluster type. – STAINED GLASS. All by the *Kempe* firm, 1892 (e) to 1906. – MONUMENTS. Katherine, Lady Gorges, erected in 1634 by her husband, Edward Gorges, Lord Dundalk. Quite a grand standing monument in stone. Two recumbent effigies, she a little higher than him and behind him. Two kneeling figures of children not *in situ*. Shallow coffered arch. Cartouche with strapwork. Open broken pediment above, framed by halves of an open broken pediment. Provincial rather than London work, although it has similarities to the monument to Sir Thomas Gorges, 1635, in Salisbury Cathedral. – Haselwood family. Elaborate marble cartouche. Erected in 1695 by Elizabeth, Viscountess Hatton. Attributed to *William Woodman* the elder (GF). – Rev. Thomas Holdich †1866, father of G. M. Holditch the organ builder, who was born here. Simple marble plaque.

SCHOOL, opposite the church. 1875 of ironstone with bands of blue brick. A single building with a s aisle. Timbered portal. Fine extension on N side 2000.

WYATTS, Draughton Road. A late C16 gateway with framed square-headed eared archway. Entablature topped by open pediment with three obelisk finials. Rebuilt here in 1914, presumably from the Hall.

MAIDWELL HALL (Maidwell Hall School). A rather curious-looking house with four corner towers topped by ogee caps. In the C16 the owners were the Seton family but in 1526 it was sold to the Haselwood family. The core of the house seems to be early C17, with possible earlier work at the back. The entrance side faces E with a limestone ashlar faced porch which manages to look very out of place since the house is otherwise of ironstone. It bears the date 1637. Two storeys, with a balcony on top. Shaped limestone gable behind. Balustraded parapets. At the back of the house a staircase tower has two shields for the Haselwood and Wilmer families, referring to Sir Anthony Haselwood whose wife was a Wilmer of Sywell which would fit the 1637 date. The house was bought by Sir Robert Loder in 1884 and much altered and extended the following year by *J. A. Gotch*, and it would seem he is responsible for the general exterior façades and fenestration and the corner towers, as these are not shown on early C19 drawings by George Clarke. There are here and there faint traces of earlier windows. In 1895 it was gutted by fire and what stands today owes most to *Matthew Holding* who rebuilt it 1901–2. Splendid cast-iron dragon waterspouts. A former detached service wing to the E with mullioned windows but much rebuilt. Attached behind the OLIVER WYATT HALL by *Gotch, Saunders & Surridge*

Maidwell Hall.
Drawing by G. Clarke, *c.* 1850

1982–3, recording Maidwell's first Headmaster, Oliver Wyatt (†1973) who purchased the house from the Loders in 1933 and set up the school. He was also a renowned horticulturalist. There is a further block with a colonnade, a remodelling of 1999. Fine grounds.

MARSTON ST LAWRENCE

5040

St Lawrence. Spacious interior. The s arcade is of the C13. Four bays, circular piers, circular abaci, double-hollow-chamfered arches. Much else is Dec: the N arcade of two continuous chamfers, i.e. no break between piers and arches, the N aisle and doorway, the chancel arch (two continuous sunk chamfers), the SEDILIA, EASTER SEPULCHRE (of soft pink sandstone and very worn), niches l. and r. of the E window, all with pretty little vaults behind the arches, and also the chancel windows, although the E window is clearly of the later C14, i.e. has passed the frontier to the Perp. The N and s windows are tall, of two lights, with cusped Y-tracery, and transoms. Sections of wall between the arcades and the chancel arch, the s side pierced by a rood stair. Perp w tower and Late Perp aisle. There was a partial restoration in 1849, though this was mainly seating, and a fuller one in 1877–8 by *H. R. Gough*. The s aisle wall was reinforced 1968–9 by *Donald Insall & Associates* (directed by *Alan J. Frost*). – FONT. Octagonal, with crocketed blank arches, Dec or Perp. The tall crested canopy was designed by *Donald Insall* in 1994. – SCREENS. Those to the N chapel are Late Perp and simple, but the tower screen, dated 1610, made up from a reredos, is an uncommonly good example of Jacobean carving. Four columns with ornament and diamond studding. Four figures and cartouches at the top. More Georgian and Jacobean in the vestry. – STAINED GLASS. Chancel E window of 1878 (faded), and N aisle windows 1881 and 1898 are all by *Burlison & Grylls*. – s aisle window of 1888 (painterly) is by *J. Hardman & Co.* – MONUMENTS. Sir John Blencowe †1726. Signed by *Edward Stanton & Christopher Horsnaile*. Architectural tablet. Sir John was a Baron of the Exchequer and 'as a just reward had his salary continued to him during his life'. – John Botry †1728 (N chapel). Yet still with the cartouche form, the drapery, and the putto head at the foot, as had been customary thirty years before. – John Blencowe †1777, by *Thomas Burnell & Sons* of London. – William Wellesley †1809. Signed by *R. Westmacott* (later Sir Richard), very Neoclassical and still in the style of his father. – John Jackson Blencowe †1852. Signed by *M. W. Johnson*. A scroll with books and a branch of willow. – Many other lesser tablets of the C18 and C19.

Marston House. A large house on a strangely irregular plan. The plan is specially puzzling because the principal features on the entrance and garden sides are of about the same date – sometime between 1700 and 1730 – but do not connect in plan. One is the doorway on the entrance side, with a characteristic open curly pediment, the other the doorway on the garden side, which has a Gibbs surround. The garden side is on a half-H plan, and this is certainly of medieval origin as there are C14 arched-braced timbers of the original hall in the roof. Much rebuilt in Elizabethan or Jacobean period for in one of the wings is a panelled room apparently *in situ*, with one very rich overmantel which carries the date 1611 and the coat of arms of John Blencowe, owner 1609–43. A similar shield of the same date in panelling in a room upstairs. Georgian staircase with slim turned balusters, three to the tread, and carved tread-ends, partially damaged in a fire in 1923, which destroyed a NW wing. Fine grounds with lakes and a mid-C18 Gothick ORANGERY.

GLEBE HOUSE, W of the church. The former vicarage. Georgian, the N side earlier than the S side. The latter is of three bays and two storeys, with the outer windows tripartite. The N side has a bay of c. 1800. Handsome oval dining room.

MARSTON TRUSSELL

ST NICHOLAS. Tall Perp W tower with clasping buttresses, ironstone and ashlar. Pairs of two-light bell-openings with transom. Battlements and pinnacles. Tall arch towards the nave. The nave arcades differ. The S arcade is of 1300 at the latest. Quatrefoil piers, double-chamfered arches. The N arcade (octagonal piers) is later. The chancel encroaches on the S arcade, see the last pier, now half embedded in the chancel wall, and the S aisle was shortened at the E end, so forming an uncomfortable junction with a small window in its wall next to the chancel arch. In its present form the aisle is probably late C16. Externally there is a large diagonal buttress from the E end of the nave. These odd changes seem to have been done either in the C17 or C18. There is a tie-beam in the chancel dated 1763. Otherwise the windows and doorways are mainly of the late C13 to early C14. SEDILIA with two seats, ogee tops with trefoil arches, C14. Under the sill a row of dogtooth. The N porch is timber-framed. Its entrance is of extremely heavy timbers and the general construction of the porch looks post-Reformation. Its entrance beam has a wide ogee arch, but this could be C19. – FONT. Octagonal, Perp, with quatrefoils. – STAINED GLASS. S clerestory. Parts of figures, C14; Trussell arms, C14–C15. The Victorian and Edwardian windows are all by *Lavers, Barraud & Westlake* except the N aisle NE and S aisle, 1918, which have not been identified. – PULPIT. Late Georgian, formed of simple panels, and a tester above. Until

Matthew Holding's restoration of 1907 there was an assembly of box pews in the nave, and some parts of these were utilized in creating the present benches. – ALTAR RAILS. Slender C18 balusters. – CHEST. Of the dug-out type; C14. – MONUMENT. Mark Brewster †1612, a London merchant who died 'in the city of Mosco in Russia'. Big kneeling figure.

THE CEDARS (former rectory, next to the church). A grand 1901 house of brick with tall chimneys and tile-hung gables by *W. H. Ward*. Prior to this the rectory was on the far E side of the parish just N of Sibbertoft (q.v.).

In the village a row of houses built 1905 by the Ewins-Barwell-Ewins family of the Hall.

MARSTON TRUSSELL HALL, at the W end of the village. Lavish Gothic front with two canted bays and a porch. Heraldic shields in the gables, a date of 1869 and plenty of quatrefoil friezes. Initials BEB for Barwell Ewins Bennett. The building seems externally all Victorian. Kelly (1894) mentions alterations to the W side in 1847. At the back some late C17 windows. The staircase with twisted balusters goes with them. Exceedingly fine *c.* 1700 gatepiers, topped by slender garlanded urns, and large wrought-iron gates brought from Brampton Ash Hall when that was demolished *c.* 1735. They probably date from *c.* 1705, the year when Sir Erasmus Norwich of Brampton Ash served as high sheriff. They were reset here *c.* 1830–40, which is the date of the two rather fine cast-iron side gates.

MEARS ASHBY

ALL SAINTS. S doorway (round single-stepped arch) and chancel S doorway of *c.* 1200, the rest mostly C13 to early C14. Low W tower. The two bell-openings on each side are placed in three blank arches. Of *c.* 1300 the S aisle windows (Y-tracery), the blocked outer recess and the low arcades of four bays. Octagonal piers, double-chamfered arches. The details differ. Restoration 1859–60 by *Charles Buckeridge*. – FONT. Norman, octagonal. With rosettes, interlace, etc. The carving is detailed and so sharp that it appears to be re-tooled. – SCULPTURE. Saxon wheel cross-head. – POOR BOX. A standing pillar type, probably C16 or C17. – WALL PAINTING. Doom, above the chancel arch. Christ sitting on a rainbow. Hell to the r. is very clear but Heaven on the l. is unrecognizable. – STAINED GLASS. Chancel E 1859 and S aisle E, 1875, both by *Clayton & Bell*. – Chancel S by *A. Lusson*, 1859. – W window by *Clayton & Bell*, 1860. S aisle, two windows by *Lawrence Lee*, 1970. Some nice carved HEADSTONES in the yard, especially on the S side.

Immediately S of the church, facing the churchyard, with a doorway with four-centred head, is an oblong HOUSE with mullioned windows.

Former VICARAGE (SE of the church). Steeply gabled with Gothic windows. This is of 1859–60, by *Charles Buckeridge*, following his restoration of the church.

MEARS ASHBY HALL. Fine front of 1637. E-shaped, but with very little space between the wings and the porch. The wings have big straight gables, the recessed pieces little ones, the porch an ogee-sided gable into which an ogee-sided three-light window is squeezed. The other windows are of three and four lights. No transoms. The doorway has coupled Roman Doric columns. Large added Tudor wing of 1859–60, by *Salvin*. Adjoining to the W STABLES dated 1647, a square SUMMER-HOUSE with a pyramid roof, and a DOVECOTE.

MANOR HOUSE, W of the church. Early C18. Three widely spaced bays, two storeys, hipped roof.

MIDDLETON CHENEY

ALL SAINTS. A fine-looking church with much restoration work by *G. G. Scott* in 1865. The building is almost entirely the local (S Northants and Oxon) Marlstone, and a fine example of its use, though the arcade pillars are limestone, almost certainly from the Helmdon quarries. Tall Perp W tower with a doorway with the two figures of the Annunciation and tracery in the spandrels, a moulding enriched with fleurons and a top frieze of angel busts. Three-light W window. Tall panelled battlements, pinnacles, recessed spire with a band of pointed quatrefoils and two tiers of lucarnes. The total height is *c.* 150 ft (46 metres), and the proportions are exceptionally good. Most of the windows in the body of the church are Geometrical or in the style of *c.* 1300, but they are renewed. Original S doorway of *c.* 1300. The steep stone roof of the S porch is supported by a transverse arch with a sunk quadrant moulding and big bold tracery motifs above it. Four-bay Dec arcades with piers of quatrefoil section, but with separate narrow hollows in the diagonals. The arches have one chamfer and one hollow chamfer. While the chancel owes much to Scott, it appears to be basically C14 as is the vestry on its N side. Above the chancel arch a blocked window and a circular trefoiled window above that. The Dec contributions have been assigned to the years when William of Edington, the future Bishop of Winchester, was rector, 1327–35. Fine Perp clerestory. – FONT. Perp, octagonal with four-leaved flowers on each face. – PULPIT. Perp, with simple panels repainted 1865. – SCREEN. Perp; but the canopy by *G. G. Scott*. – STALLS. Poppyhead finials by the screen, angels with spread wings at the E end, by *Scott*, of course. – RAILS. Incorporating C18 balusters. – BENCHES. Perp, plain, with buttresses. – DOOR. The S door is medieval and has its original wicket. – MONUMENT. Gothic shrine in the churchyard to the Horton family, designed by *William Wilkinson* of Oxford, made by *Earp*, 1866–7.

All this is interesting enough, but what makes Middleton Cheney a place of pilgrimage and of unforgettable enjoyment is the STAINED GLASS by the *William Morris* firm. It was put in during the incumbency of the Rev. W. C. Buckley, a personal friend of Burne-Jones. It is so beautiful and so important that it deserves a detailed record.*

The E window was designed in 1864 and fitted in 1865 as a memorial to William Croome, who died in that year. Starting at the top of the window is the Adoration of the Lamb by *Burne-Jones*, then Angels and Seraph with folded wings by *Philip Webb*. Then come the Symbols of the Evangelists (four Beasts) also by *Webb*. The Flags of the Tribes of Israel are again by *Webb*, but the figures of the Tribes are by *Simeon Solomon*, who rarely worked in stained glass. In the next row are Adam and Noah by *Ford Madox Brown*; David and Isaiah by *Solomon*; St Peter by *William Morris* and St Paul by *Madox Brown*; and St Augustine and St Catherine by *Morris*. The bottom row has: Abraham and Moses by *Solomon*; Eve, the Virgin and Mary Magdalene by *Morris*; St John by *Madox Brown*; St Alban by *Burne-Jones* and St Agnes by *Morris*. The backgrounds are all by *Morris* and the borders by *Webb*. – In a chancel S window, of 1868–70, are panels from the Old Testament (Cain and Abel, and Melchizedek and Abraham, both by *Ford Madox Brown*, with tracery glass of shields and emblems of the Passion by *Webb*). – In two chancel N windows are scenes from the Life of Christ. These are a memorial to the Rev. Buckley (†1892) and designed by *Burne-Jones* in consultation with Buckley himself. – In the N aisle E window, a memorial to the Horton family of 1880, are: St Mary by *Burne-Jones*; St Anne and St Elizabeth by *Madox Brown*; the Annunciation by *Morris*, and shields etc. probably by *Webb*. – In the N aisle NE window, also of 1880, Samuel by *Burne-Jones* and Elijah by *Morris*. – The Dove in the E gable window is by *Webb*, 1870. – Finally the tower W window of 1870 is the most striking of the series and indeed one of the most dramatic windows ever produced by the firm, with the three young men in the fiery furnace by *Burne-Jones*. – Not by the Morris firm but by *J. Powell & Sons* are two S aisle windows of 1877 and 1885 with figures of Apostles designed by *J. W. Brown*.

ROOFS. All designed by *William Morris* in 1865, the work done by *George Cottam* of Banbury. Fine corbel heads. – MOSAICS made by *J. Powell & Sons*, the circular one (S aisle) designed by *Holiday*.

CHENEY HOUSE (care home), NE of the church. The former vicarage. C17 stone, altered by *George Wyatt* of Oxford in 1858 and further altered by *Scott*.

* This account is based on information from the Rev. Glynne Jones, A. C. Sewter and Martin Harrison.

TENLANDS (SW of the church off Queen Street) is the site of THE HOLT, a large stone manor house built for the Horton family by *Wilkinson* in 1864, which was demolished in 1973 and its grounds built over. Its COACH HOUSE partly survives, incorporated in a modern house at the entrance to Tenlands. A LODGE also survives.

BAPTIST CHAPEL, Queen Street. 1806. Quite large, of stone, with pedimental gable and arched windows.

METHODIST CHAPEL, Queen Street. 1867, of red brick and stone in the lancet style. Extended S in 1907.

SCHOOL, High Street. 1856–7 by *G. E. Street*. Coursed stone with Gothic windows, especially the W side with triple trefoiled lancets and circles above. N extension later. The SCHOOL HOUSE is simpler, but in the same mode.

HORTON ALMSHOUSES, SE in High Street. 1869, in red brick and stone. Two sharp gables and a large roof.

The village has a number of good stone houses, many C17 with mullioned windows. A good example is THE GABLES just SW of the church in Church Lane. L-shaped with its gabled end having at the top two single openings, two two-light windows below, and a three-light window on the ground floor. The side elevations a mixture of two and three lights. In the same street just N of the church another cottage of three bays with three-light mullioned windows, beautifully restored.

7050

MILTON MALSOR

HOLY CROSS. Of the C13 the bases of the N arcade piers, the lower courses (limestone) of two of them and probably the lower parts of the unbuttressed W tower with a doorway with three continuous chamfers. Later battlements and pinnacles. Then a short recessed Dec octagonal stage and a short crocketed spire with two tiers of small lucarnes. The rest seems to be of the late C13 to mid C14. Late C13 are the aisle W walls with their windows The principal windows in the aisles and the chancel are all Dec, specially noteworthy being the square one at the E end of the S aisle with an inscribed wheel of radially set two-light arches. Internally a stone frame below indicates a former reredos position. The similar window in the N chapel is an 1874 copy. The N chapel has a good N window. The E window in the chancel is of five lights with reticulated tracery. The arcades are of the late C13. Four bays with tall slender circular piers carrying octagonal abaci and double-chamfered arches. The same details in the tall chancel arch and the lower N and S chapel arches. The chancel was restored in 1874 and the rest 1876–8, in both cases by *E. F. Law*. – STAINED GLASS. Chancel E 1895 by *H. A. Hymers* (restored 2000). N aisle NE 1977 by *Jane Cummings*. – MONUMENTS. Mrs Sapcoates Harington †1619. Tablet with some strapwork. – Richard Dodwell

†1726. With garlands down the volutes l. and r. of the inscription and two cherubs' heads at the foot. Attributed to *Thomas Cartwright III* (GF).

BAPTIST CHAPEL, Green Street. W of the church, set back in a small yard. 1827, of stone, the usual three-bay front. The interior with box pews, gallery etc. still intact, although partly refitted in 1976.

METHODIST CHAPEL, 1865. Simple round-arched doorway and two windows under a pediment, red and blue brick with double blue brick arches over doorway and windows.

SCHOOL, Green Street. Originally built 1848 in a mild Gothic manner, the old building behind with two wings and a small flèche; extended 1893 with further forward wings including a broad pedimented entrance with an inscription plaque. Additions were made by *J. T. Blackwell* in 1905.

MILTON HOUSE, Rectory Lane, SW of the church. Mid-C18, extended in 1777. Five bays, two storeys, doorway with Tuscan columns and a broken pediment. A little further E the MANOR HOUSE of C16 origin, the W entrance side with canted bay and mullioned windows. Later E front of chequer brick and curiously unbalanced. It has an off-centre giant pilaster with brick and stone bands, and the same motif is used on the N quoin. The house was for some years the home of James Harrington (1611–77), political theorist and author of *Oceana* (1656).

MANOR HOUSE, W of the church, in Malsor Lane. Handsome, with five-bay, two-storeyed front of the early C18. This façade was stuccoed, but has since been removed. The windows are in flat frames. Inside an uncommonly fine mid- or later C17 staircase with openwork acanthus scrolls, comparable with the C17 work at Lamport Hall and Castle Ashby. It runs through two storeys.

Just N of The Greyhound pub on the main road is the former HOPE BREWERY of 1888, now converted.

CREMATORIUM, N of the village on Towcester Road. A large domed Renaissance building with a central chapel and wings of 1937–9 by *J. P. Chaplin*. Impressively situated.

MORETON PINKNEY

5040

ST MARY. Delightful airy plastered interior owing something to the careful restoration by *Sir Henry Dryden* in 1846. Further work was done by *E. F. Law* 1891–3, mainly on the tower. Of c. 1200 the simple N doorway and the N arcade. This is of three bays and has circular piers with square abaci. The arches are pointed but unchamfered, one capital having small leaves at its corners. C13 the S arcade (rebuilt correctly). Circular piers with octagonal abaci, single-chamfered arches. The PISCINA inside cannot be much before 1300. Also C13 the W tower. Lancet windows and bell-openings. To the N two blank arches l. and r., both trefoiled, but one rounded, the other pointed. The chancel was rebuilt in 1846, but probably also correctly. Its elegant style is again that of the C13, as is proved by the single lancets to the N and S, the three tall stepped lancets to the E, shafted inside, and the DOUBLE PISCINA inside. Late C13 foliage capitals and foliage hoodmould stops. Rood loft entrance on S side of the chancel arch. – STALLS. Fleur-de-lys poppyhead of the Dryden period. – CHARITY PANEL. Painted on the S aisle wall. The last date is 1779 and its decorative borders fit that. – Three lozenge-painted INSCRIPTION PANELS which could also be 1770s. – STAINED GLASS. N aisle E window by *J. Hardman & Co.* 1925. – SCULPTURE. Fragment of an Anglo-Saxon cross-shaft with some simple decoration, now in the SE corner of the churchyard.

MORETON PINKNEY MANOR. Mainly of 1859 by *E. F. Law* and extended in 1870. Elizabethan style. At the turning to Weston, turreted LODGE and impressive entrance arch, of 1859 with a rope-work surround and heraldry of the Barons Sempill.

An attractive village, the cottages a mixture of brown and grey stone, some of them with banded patterns. Wide verges and two greens. Facing the N one, a chequered brick BAPTIST CHAPEL of 1837; by the southern one, near the church, the former SCHOOL dated 1822 (enlarged 1876). The older part on the r. and the more recent on the l., still with its tall many-paned windows overlooking the green.

MOULTON

Moulton is too close to Northampton not to have escaped the addition of housing estates. These are largely on the S and E sides between the village and the Kettering Road (A43).

ST PETER AND ST PAUL. Of ironstone. There was an aisleless C11 Norman nave, of which the arch of one window has been exposed inside. To this about the end of the C12 was added a N aisle. This has low square piers with four demi-shafts and one-step round arches (but *see* below). About 1300 much was done to alter and enlarge the church. Witness of this is the S arcade, with octagonal piers and double-chamfered arches. Of *c.* 1300 also a number of windows (intersected tracery, Y-tracery) and the arches to the N and S chapels. Dec W tower with Perp, ashlar-faced top storey. Pairs of two-light bell-openings with transom. Quatrefoil frieze. Battlements. Perp also the windows in the S aisle. Rood loft openings on both sides of the nave. There was quite a harsh restoration 1884–9 by *Law & Son.*

But we must return to the N arcade, with its two tall masonry plinths of the first and second piers from the W – the puzzle of the church. The usual explanations are that these plinths refer either to the original arcade and that there was a change of plan during rebuilding, or that they refer to a scheme to rebuild the arcade which was never finished. Neither of these seems satisfactory. Why is one circular and the other octagonal? Why are they so crude and at different heights? The upper sections of the piers do seem to be supported by the plinths, not encased by them. Is it conceivable that they are the remnants of masonry infilling when there were box pews in the nave, and were just tidied up in 1884? The whole arcade looks a bit sharp and its capitals somehow do not look quite right for the late C12. The pier of the chancel s arcade also looks a little odd and its capital looks possibly post-medieval. It is very similar to the capitals of the nave arcade at St Giles's church in Northampton, which are known to be early C17. The spire was taken down or fell down in the C17, and this must make one wonder whether there might have been damage to the arcade. There seems no easy explanation and it remains one of the county's church puzzles. – FONT (N chapel). C18. Plain baluster, small alabaster gadrooned bowl. – COMMUNION RAIL. C18. – SCULPTURE. Fragment of a Saxon cross-shaft. A beast biting its tail. Interlace below. – STAINED GLASS. Chancel E, 1899, the Last Supper by *E. R. Suffling*. N chapel, memorial to Philadelphus Jeyes, the chemist (i.e. Jeyes Fluid), 1931 by *Percy Bacon*. s aisle w, two panels of St Peter and St Paul by *Heaton, Butler & Bayne*. – MONUMENT. Slab in N aisle for Saunderson, 1689 with painted shield. Curious mural tablet in s aisle for Edward Gee †1799, but very Rococo in concept.

METHODIST CHAPEL, Cross Street. 1835. With steeply pointed windows and doorway and a steep gable. Very pretty glazing bars.

CAREY BAPTIST CHURCH, West Street. Rebuilt during the ministry of William Carey (1761–1834), orientalist and missionary, between 1786 and 1789. Stone with brick dressings. Round-headed windows. Enlarged and altered 1870. His cottage, with an inscription, is in West Street.

MOULTON SCHOOL & SCIENCE COLLEGE, Pound Lane. 1952–4 by *A. N. Harris* (County Architect) and *John Goff*. Three-storeyed classroom with curtain walling all round. The horizontal bands between the window bands faced with vertical wood slatting. To the w and E assembly hall and gymnasium, the former connected with the classroom block by a concourse, the latter by a one-storey service and workshop range. – SIXTH FORM CENTRE, 1992 by *Aldington Craig & Collinge*. Brick walls with curved spine entrance and low angled wings. Built into a rising site, so deep glazed façade on the E.

MOULTON COLLEGE OF AGRICULTURE. The main building (West Street) of ironstone, in the vernacular manner, is of the 1930s by the then County Architect, *G. H. Lewin*. Administrative and teaching block 1964, hostels 1967–8, conference hall and library 1968, and other buildings, by the County Architect's Department (*A. N. Harris* and *John Goff*). The site much extended since, and on the road to Pitsford a new block, rectangular with wide gables, 2011 by *Gotch, Saunders & Surridge*. Alongside this a farmhouse and outbuildings with two pyramidal roofs from the Overstone period, *c.* 1840 (*see* Overstone). The village is large and within its slightly intricate street plan there are many good stone houses. In Church Hill, THE ARTICHOKE pub, for example, has some mullion windows and the date 1680. Other good houses in Cross Street and West Street.

MUSCOTT

1 m. N of Brockhall

6060

Very fragmentary remains of the GATEWAY to Muscott House, reduced to farm buildings following the acquisition by the Spencers of Althorp in the C16, the main house probably demolished in the C18 and the gateway reduced to the entrance to a farmyard. Ironstone and presumably late medieval. Just the side walls, low buttresses and a newel staircase to an upper floor which retains a C16 fireplace. The upper sections rebuilt in brick in the C19.

NASEBY

6070

ALL SAINTS. The finest part of the church is the S arcade, as far as it is early C13. It is of three bays and has quatrefoil piers, stiff-leaf capitals and double-chamfered arches. The responds are Dec and have naturalistic foliage. The N arcade is of the C14. Four bays, also quatrefoil piers and double-chamfered arches. The lower parts were encased in the C17 or C18, perhaps when box pews were introduced. The fact that the W bay on the S side is later, but on the N side is not, dates the beginning of the W tower, with which the S arcade was to be connected. Its ground floor is indeed Dec. The upper parts are Perp. Pairs of tall two-light bell-openings with transom. Battlements, and a recessed spire (rebuilt by *W. Slater* in 1859–60, when the church was restored) with crockets and three tiers of lucarnes. The chancel arch is of the same date as the N arcade, the chancel E and N windows have intersected tracery. There is evidence that the chancel was reconstructed and shortened in length in 1830 (faculty) so its details cannot be trusted. – FONT. Circular, Late Norman, with blank arcading and, below the arches, individual flowers. – RAILS. (N aisle). Thin balusters, *c.* 1700. – TABLE. Called Cromwell's Table. Perhaps from Shuckburgh House, the manor house which was partly pulled down in 1773. What remains of it is now Shuckburgh Farm (completely altered). The story of the table is that the King's Life Guards supped at it the evening before the battle. –

STAINED GLASS. Tower window by *Clayton & Bell* 1860. – Chancel S, 1874, by *Lavers, Barraud & Westlake*. – S aisle window, 1924 by *Morris & Co*. The 1947 date was added later. – BRASS. To John Oliver †1446 and wife, the figures 2 ft 2 in. (66 cm.) long. Another inscription and shield for John Shuckburgh †1576. – MONUMENT. Richard Herbert †1790, unsigned but the familiar *Cox* obelisk type. – CURIOSITY. N aisle, a big copper BALL. It is said that it was originally brought from Boulogne in 1544 (Kelly) and that it holds sixty gallons of ale. It was added to the stump of the spire about 1780, and then removed when the spire was rebuilt.

METHODIST CHAPEL, Church Street. Originally 1825 but rebuilt in red and blue brick with three circular windows in 1871. Next to it the SUNDAY SCHOOL, mild Gothic of 1905. In the village a number of rows of cottages also of red and blue brick, and recent (1990s) housing has kept the tradition of the same effects.

SHUCKBURGH HOUSE. Opposite the church on the w. Part late C17 with a mid-C18 front of chequered red and blue brick and a platband.

MANOR FARM, formerly New Hall. Georgian. The spring which is the source of the River Avon is in the garden.

ROYAL OAK, Church Street. Quite a decent essay of 1935 by the *Northampton Brewery Co*.

NASEBY HALL (also known as Woolleys), ½ m. NW. The house altered by *E. F. Law* in 1859 was largely gutted by fire in 1948. It was drastically reduced in size and a surviving wing was used to create a new house by *R. J. Page* of Colchester, though his original quite grand Neo-Georgian designs were simplified on building.

NASEBY BATTLEFIELD MEMORIALS. – OBELISK, Clipston Road. Put up in 1823 by the squire John Fitzgerald, but as an eyecatcher rather than to mark the site of the battlefield. On the supposed site ¾ m. N is a MEMORIAL with a shafted column topped by a ball, designed by *J. A. Gotch*, 1936.

NASSINGTON

ALL SAINTS. Saxon nave, see inside the SW angle (in the S aisle room behind its 2001 glazed screen) and the nave w wall with the mark of a round-headed and a triangle-headed opening high up above. Then followed the w tower; for the tower arch is Late Norman with a demi-shaft, capitals with some leaf details, and a double-chamfered round arch, and there are straight joints outside between the tower and the aisles. The (re-set) N doorway is late C12 too, see the waterleaf capitals and the hoodmould with small flowers. The w doorway into the tower would be a little later, say early C13. It has dogtooth mouldings and is pointed. Later small quatrefoil window above it. The upper parts of the tower are Perp. The top storey turns octagonal halfway up the bell-openings. These are of two lights with an embattled transom. The octagonal part has big pinnacles in the diagonals and battlements. Behind these rises a recessed spire with big leaf crockets up the edges. Two tiers of lucarnes. The spire is dated 1640. Aisles were started in the C13, at about the time when the w doorway was made. The tower is embraced by slightly narrower chambers w of the aisles – see the dogtooth moulding in the w part of the s aisle including its transverse arch with nailhead, the w lancets, and the s porch, also with much dogtooth. The rest of the aisle is early C14. Arcades with octagonal piers, triple-chamfered arches, but slightly different in treatment where the arches rest on the capitals. The N windows with late C13 or early C14 Y-tracery, intersected tracery, and further E, three C13 stepped lancets under one arch. The s windows are Dec (reticulated tracery). Perp chancel (with early C14 chancel arch) and clerestory. Marks of a former vestry on the N side, and its four-centred doorway inside. Tactful restoration 1885 by *J. C. Traylen* of Stamford. He had hoped to do a more elaborate job with a new screen and pews. – FONT. Octagonal, early C14, with two tiers of small, flat arch-heads and big ballflowers on its base. – PULPIT. Late Elizabethan or Jacobean with arched panels and strapwork. – ROOFS. C16 panelled over the nave and similar over aisles. – CROSS-SHAFT. A fine Anglo-Saxon fragment. Crucifixion with sun, moon and soldiers. Also a cut-off figure, and much interlace. – COFFIN-LIDS. Quite a collection, mostly broken but an especially fine one with the usual cross in the N aisle. – SCREEN FRAGMENTS. Two sections of damaged tracery of C15 date. – WALL PAINTINGS. All rather faded. Last Judgment above the chancel arch. – N arcade and N aisle figures and scenes, e.g. the Weighing of the Souls, with a bearded kneeling donor; St Katherine and the Wheel; St Martin or St George (N arcade). All *c.* 1350. – STAINED GLASS. Roundels and fragments in the s aisle windows, C14. – s aisle w of 1894–5 by *Lavers & Westlake*.

PREBENDAL MANOR HOUSE, SW of the church. This has the reputation of being the oldest occupied house in the county. The prebend of Nassington was established in Lincoln Cathedral in the early C12. The house was built in the early C13 and was lived in by the prebend or his tenants until the prebend was dissolved in 1836. The endowment included the church and all its lands. What survives is the hall of three bays, later subdivided, and to the s the rebuilt service wing. A narrower N range, which probably contained the solar, was demolished *c.* 1800 but its foundations have been uncovered, and it is thought there was a detached kitchen beyond the s wing. There is also documentary evidence for a gatehouse which stood E of the house, a little N of the present gate. The whole building had a substantial refurbishment in the C15 and the s wing was largely rebuilt then and altered again in the C16. It then became a farmhouse and there are considerable C19 and C20 altera-

tions, especially windows (post-1943). The approach from the
E shows more sign of the later phases of the building than
anything early, save for an original buttress and faint marks of
a blocked window (*see* later).

The house is entered by a porch, probably of the C15. It has
a timber-framed gable. The large *c.* 1300 heads by the entrance
are not *in situ*. The early C13 HALL is entered by a screens
passage, its wall and openings into the hall dating from the
C15. Its W doorway has externally a round head with a single
chamfer of C13 date, while the E doorway is C15 with a pointed
arch and mouldings. Although the hall was subdivided portions of the floor have been removed to create a gallery, so
revealing the full height of the hall and the full scale of the two
tall windows in its W wall. They are of C13 outline though their
traceried heads are C15, and the N window is largely a modern
replacement. There is evidence of another window in the E
wall, noted above. The cross wall of the screens passage is a
C15 replacement with later timber surrounds to its openings.
Within the subdivision at the N end of the hall is evidence for
a projecting bay of full height on the E side of the hall. It probably dates from the C15 phase and is interesting in having
squints looking towards the porch in its S corners at both
ground- and first-floor level. So the subdivision of the hall
must already have occurred by the C15. The present infill is
probably C18. Externally the N gable wall has a series of blocked
openings and scars. There are marks of blocked doorways, two
on the first floor and one at ground level, all of C13 date. The
scar of the W wall of the lost N range is also clear. The roof,
though largely reconstructed in the C19, has C15 moulded tie-
beams, collars with twin struts, though these only exist at the
S end. The S RANGE, projecting to the W to form an L with the
hall, is largely a C16 and later reconstruction with some re-set
medieval pieces, such as two carved heads in its S end wall. It
is entered from the screens passage through a series of round-
headed openings with chamfered edges, probably post-medieval. A first-floor room has C16 moulded beams. There are also
a group of STABLES of C17 date, a large BARN of nine bays,
thought to have been built following the enclosure *c.* 1777, and
a DOVECOTE of late medieval date with an C18 roof.

MANOR HOUSE, N of the Prebendal Manor House. Of *c.* 1500.
To the E blocked arched entrance and windows with four-
centred arched lights. The N gable has a blocked window at
ground level which still has its label, a small four-light canted
oriel above and a two-light window in the gable. Both windows
with arched heads. The S gable has three blocked windows.
Considerable sections of roofs survive. The manor was owned
by Sir Guy Wolston of Apethorpe in the C16.

A number of other good houses in the village. At the beginning
of Church Street is the BLACK HORSE INN, rendered white.
Two storeys with canted bay and mullions, dated 1674. Four-
centred fireplace opening. Along CHURCH STREET, the
SCHOOL of 1862. Stone with four gables in centre and two

wings with tall five-light windows in C17 manner with stepped heads. Small square turret. Former WESLEYAN CHAPEL, 1875 and next to it yellow brick VILLAGE HALL, 1912, with 1998 annexe. The chapel has a pedimented façade divided by pilasters with two round-headed windows and a circular name plaque in the centre. Its pilasters have carved initials presumably for all those who paid for it. Further on No. 45, early C19 with rounded bays, shutters and a pedimented doorway. Past the church on the E side a row of COTTAGES, Nos. 56–60, c. 1900, of sandstone with ample red brick dressings and small bays on the ground floor.

CEMETERY. ¼ m. N 1882 by *J. C. Traylen*. Large LYCHGATE.

NETHER HEYFORD

6050

ST PETER AND ST PAUL. C13 the N aisle and the S doorway. The doorway has one order of shafts, a single-step arch and some dogtooth decoration. The Dec N aisle arcade of five bays has single-chamfered arches on octagonal piers. In the N wall a low C13 tomb-recess. The windows are lancets, one of two lights with a circle over. The S arcade is Dec (four wider bays, octagonal piers, arches with two sunk quadrant mouldings). Dec also the chancel windows and probably the clerestory windows in the shape of a pointed quatrefoil placed diagonally. Dec the W tower too. The S aisle has some renewed C16 or C17 windows. There was a restoration by *William Butterfield* in 1855. The chancel was restored by *E. F. Law & Son* 1878–9. – STAINED GLASS. Chancel E 1879 by *A. L. Moore*. – MONUMENTS. Brass for Sir Walter Mauntell †1467 and wife. Good figures, 4 ft (1.2 metres) long, holding hands. – Judge Francis Morgan †1558 (he was the judge who cast sentence on Lady Jane Grey in 1553 and is said to have gone mad as a result). Hanging monument. Kneeling figures facing each other. Family group in centre. To the l. and r. were allegorical figures of Faith and Hope in niches on elaborate brackets. Only the r. one, Spes, survives. Sumptuous foliage frieze beneath the relief. It has been moved and it lacks its superstructure which contained cresting and a shield of arms, recorded by Peter Tillemans in 1719. Somewhat crudely painted. It can be confidently attributed to the *Hollemans* workshop. Other memorials of this form are at Welford, Harrington, Thorpe Mandeville and Charwelton.

SCHOOL and SCHOOL HOUSE, Bugbrooke Road. Ironstone of 1878–9 by *E. F. Law*, basically Gothic, with large window with a circle in its head. Bellcote. Extended in 1913 by *Law & Harris*. Further extensions of 2009 by *Stimpson & Walton*.

HEYFORD LODGE, Church Street. The former RECTORY. Yellow and grey stone, Gothic, 1850 by *Raphael Brandon*.

MANOR HOUSE, NE of the church at the end of Manor Park. Early C18. Ironstone, five-bay front of two storeys, with framed windows with small keystones and quoins. Doorway on Doric pilasters set against rustication; metope frieze. Lower three-bay wings. In the r. wing, above the ground-floor windows, horizontally placed ovals. The garden side also with Doric doorcase. Staircase with turned balusters and carved tread-ends. The quality fine if provincial. Not quite up to the *Smith* of *Warwick* standard and another possible candidate for *John Lumley*.

Near the church a tall three-storey brick house row, Nos. 33–35 Church Street, dated 1859 in blue brick. In Middle Street THE OLD SUN INN, ironstone of the late C17 with several mullioned windows and just beyond an ironstone row dated 1635. Part banded and a mullioned window.

At UPPER HEYFORD, just off the A45, two brick COTTAGES, mid-C19, built by the Althorp Estate (cf. Harlestone and Chapel Brampton).

NEWBOTTLE

5030

The manor house and the church in the trees and a few houses – that is all that remains at Newbottle. The village has disappeared.

ST JAMES. C13 chancel but the E window and S wall are of 1865–6, when the church was restored. *George Hannaford*, who was working for G. G. Scott at Kings Sutton, advised. The builder was *Franklin* of Deddington. Prior to this the S wall had two small oval windows high up, presumably because the Cresswell monument filled the space inside. In its N wall externally a round-headed doorway with a keystone, C17 or C18. In its S wall the remains of a C13 PISCINA with dogtooth and a restored lowside window. Dec tower and Late Perp S aisle. Internally it becomes clear that the tower is basically of *c.* 1190–1210. The arch towards the nave has many-scalloped imposts and a pointed arch with two slight chamfers. Small window high up under the roof. Dec four-bay N arcade. Octagonal piers, arches with two sunk quadrants. The S arcade, probably a little earlier but still Dec, has double-chamfered arches. Somewhat oversize capitals compared with the pillars, also octagonal. Narrow aisles, so of early origin. Rood loft entrance above N arcade. – PULPIT. Simple, with little lozenges in inlay. Dated 1584. – SCREEN. With heavily detailed Perp type tracery, but probably still C14. Only the tracery is medieval, the rest clearly C19, with some odd tree trunk pieces at either side. – REREDOS. 1878, of mosaic patterns. – STAINED GLASS. E window by *Kempe*, 1895. Two windows in the chancel of 1896 and S aisle window of 1864 all by *Heaton, Butler & Bayne*. – MONUMENTS. Peter Dormer †1555. Brasses. He is 12 in. (30 cm.) long; to his l. and r. his two wives kneeling. The slab into which the brasses are set was the back panel of an elaborate monument with a vaulted canopy supported by pillars and with Tudor four-leaved flower cresting. Several portions of this are at the back of the church. – John and Elizabeth Cresswell. By *John Stone*, 1655 and one of his best works. Sarcophagus with a very Roman foliage scroll. On it the inscription base and on this two good free-standing busts. The architectural surround with a big arch and looped-up draperies, recorded in watercolours by Thomas Trotter, unfortunately disappeared when the monument was removed from the chancel in 1866. – Albert Pym †1897 with scroll leaves in brass, inset with an inscription plate redone when his wife died.

MANOR HOUSE. Centre and W wing only; the E wing no longer exists. The centre has mullioned windows with arched lights and probably dates from the time of Henry VIII. Doorway with four-centred head near the l. end and symmetrically grouped upper windows. The HALL has chamfered beams and its fireplace also survives. Some original fireplaces upstairs and one room has red and white striped painted decoration. The W wing is a C17 addition. Part was demolished *c.* 1800 and some windows on the W side renewed. Library panelling of *c.* 1730. Big square Georgian brick and stone GATEPIERS. DOVECOTE to the W. Stone, lined internally with brick. Octagonal, with an open lantern on eight oak posts.

RAINSBOROUGH CAMP. An oval Iron Age hillfort on the S edge of the parish, W of Camp Farm. Excavations in the 1960s revealed that the Early Iron Age fort had a three-tiered rampart faced with drystone or turf walls, a V-shaped ditch and a counterscarp. The W entrance was inturned and had guard-rooms set into the passage walls behind the gates. In the early C4 B.C. the fort was deliberately burnt, and in the late C2 B.C. it was re-fortified with a double bank of dump construction, U-shaped ditches, and simple entrances. In the C4 A.D. a 10ft (3.05 metre) square building was built over the deliberately filled-in ditch, and the entrance passage was remodelled. In the C18 the inner bank was heightened, the ditch was deepened, and beech trees were planted.

NEWNHAM

ST MICHAEL. The W tower is opened as a porch to N, S and W. Tall, wide, double-chamfered arches. Pink and brown stone. Rib-vault inside with ridge ribs and a large bell-hole. Decorative cross-patterned pavement created in 1977. To the E an arch into the church and in addition a smaller doorway to the tower stairs. It looks almost like the arrangement usual for medieval

domestic archways into courtyards. A niche with a nodding
ogee arch to the w. Set-back buttresses. Recessed spire with
two tiers of lucarnes in alternating directions. Perp s doorway
with two orders of fleurons. Fine chancel of *c.* 1300 with a large
five-light E window. Cusped intersected tracery interrupted to
allow for a trefoiled circle at the top. Internally a hoodmould
and sill mould runs along the walls. The side windows simpler
but also intersecting with trefoils. The arcades differ in date,
though both are slim. On the N side two quatrefoil piers of
c. 1300. The third bay and the whole s arcade Perp. The NE
respond is a bust of an angel. Chancel arch of two continuous
sunk quadrant mouldings. Unusually a step down into the
chancel. Perp aisle E windows. s porch classical with round-
arched doorway, C17 or C18. The church was restored 1885–6.
– SEDILIA. Under the easternmost window of the chancel with
just trefoil shapes carved into the jambs. – PISCINA with trefoil
head. – ROOFS. The chancel has moulded beams, probably
C16, and the nave tie-beams of the C17. – BOX PEWS at the rear
of the nave and in the aisles. A seating plan dated 1825 in the
church suggests these may be late in date. – FONT. Perp style
with rich tracery. Octagonal but sloping down into a wine-glass
stem. Early C19? – ROYAL ARMS. Large, painted for Queen
Anne. – STAINED GLASS. The glass is all by *W. Holland* of
Warwick. Several windows with mid-C19 coloured grisaille
glass. That at the E end of the s aisle with some unusual monochrome panels. N aisle W end, two figures, and s aisle s window
with Apostles and angels in its tracery. – MONUMENTS. Brass
to Letitia Catesby. Her husband died in 1467. Also a defaced
shield in a scroll surround. The figure is 2 ft (61 cm.) long.
Thomas Thornton †1632. Alabaster tablet with side pilasters
with mortality symbols and shield at the top. Fine quality and
good enough for *Hollemans.* – Two simple decorative alabaster
surrounds for members of the Blacklock family: Lt John †1912,
who died 'The result of an accident while pigsticking' at
Lucknow in India; the other for Captain William †1894. – To
the l. of the altar, set into a panelled REREDOS of 1933, a stone
inscription, now illegible, with two putti standing on skulls l.
and r. and two praying angels above. Another cartouche type
with a date of 1762 on the other side. These came from the
churchyard.

Former CONGREGATIONAL CHAPEL, School Hill. 1909, of red
brick and stone with a large Gothic window and contemporary
patterned glazing.

PRIMARY SCHOOL, School Hill. The large wooden-clad building
was designed by *J. T. Blackwell* of Kettering, 1910–14.

MANOR HOUSE, s of the church. Gabled, with mullioned
windows.

VILLAGE HALL, N of the church. The former school of 1871,
enlarged 1894. Tudor style with half-timbered porch.

Several good ironstone houses attractively set on a sequence of
greens. Near the church THE COTTAGE, 1857 of pale yellow
brick with bargeboarded wings and a central shaped gable and

porch between them. Opposite is DUNGLASS HOUSE, late C19 of brick with a façade inset with five terracotta plaques with classical heads. A little S, in Perkins Way, three COTTAGES *c.* 1880, vaguely Tudor style with square-headed windows with hoodmoulds, all of banded herringbone patterned stone and red and blue brick ornaments. There are others of the same design in Manor Lane and off Weedon Road. Also in Manor Lane MEADOW COTTAGE with two- and three-light mullioned windows. Four-centred stone fireplace inside.

NEWNHAM HALL, ¼ m. NE. Whitewashed Regency house *c.* 1820 with bow windows to the S and W sides. On the N side a Greek Doric porch. Forecourt with brick curved walls with blank Gothic arches, the W side containing rooms, the E sheltering a stable block with clock turret. Several original marble fireplaces and a staircase with slender balusters. Grand topiary walk runs NW. To the N an EYECATCHER of *c.* 1850.

Former WINDMILL, ½ m. N on the road to Daventry. A round brick tower built *c.* 1820. The pyramidal roof and viewing gallery are a restoration of 1990. Now a house.

NEWTON BROMSWOLD

ST PETER. Small but of some charm, set in a garden churchyard. Largely Dec and Perp. Probably mid-C13 the base of the W tower. Internally also mid-C13 the SEDILIA and PISCINA in the chancel, part of a simple scheme of blank arcading, and the recess opposite. The recess seems too tall for a tomb-recess. Was it an Easter sepulchre perhaps? Dec the tower top with its spire, the chancel five-light E window with reticulated tracery and the N doorway. The N arcade however is Perp, of the four-shafts-four-hollows type. One capital with upright oak leaves. The arches are low and four-centred. Richard Marks dates the *in situ* glass in the N aisle window to 1425–50, yet the character of the arcade with its flat arches is more Tudor in manner, as is that of the S doorway. There was a restoration in 1878 by the *Rev. Robert Baker* (*see* Hargrave). – BENCH-ENDS. Remade into seats, one at the front and two at the back of the nave. Plain, straight-topped, with little buttresses, C15. – FONT. Perp with a plain octagonal bowl, but its base inscribed with traceried patterns. Most unusual. Its COVER is a simple crocketed pyramid, probably early C19. – PULPIT. Contains a few pieces of C15 tracery and a Jacobean panel at its rear. – SCREEN. Broadly Perp style, a 1914–18 memorial by *Talbot Brown & Fisher*. – ORGAN GALLERY of 1936. – STAINED GLASS. N aisle N, head of a bishop and some canopy fragments, *c.* 1425–50. N aisle E, two seaweed grisaille panels, early C15. Chancel N, heads of Apostles, *c.* 1400–30. – Chancel E, 1900 by *A. L. Moore*. – BRASSES. William Hewet †1426, rector, 14-in. (36-cm.) figure, and Roger Hewet †1487, chaplain, 2-ft (61-cm.)

figure. – MONUMENTS. Henry Lambe †1727. A simple tablet with nice decoration by *John Hunt*. Two good early C19 slate stones under the E window outside.

NEWTON-IN-THE-WILLOWS

ST FAITH. Now a field centre. All alone in the meadows. Short Perp W tower. Pretty circular traceried window in W wall, two-light transomed bell-openings, deeply recessed broach spire. Dec to the N and S, reticulated tracery, but much renewed when *W. Slater* rebuilt the chancel in 1858. The chancel arch on corbels with naturalistic vine and oak.*

DOVECOTE. NE of the church. The only relic of a mansion of a cadet line of the Treshams (see Rushton). The Tresham trefoil is on it. A large oblong building nearly 60 ft (18.3 metres) long. With two compartments each with its own lantern. There are nests inside for 2,000 pairs of pigeons. The date must be Late Elizabethan as it has the name of Maurice Tresham. Below the dovecote was the house. Traces of the terraced gardens survive.

NORTHAMPTON

*Fittings all removed. *See* Geddington for Mulsho brass of 1400 and the Tresham slab. Windows by *Clayton & Bell*, 1858 were vandalized.

INTRODUCTION

Northampton was an important town in the Middle Ages. Traces of pre-Conquest settlements have been found on the site of the castle. In the castle, of which hardly anything remains (*see* p. 444), the trial of Thomas Becket took place, and many councils and parliaments were held at Northampton. The town had a large Cluniac priory colonized from La Charité-sur-Loire at the end of the CII, near the present Priory Street, the Augustinian abbey of St James established *c*. 1105, and houses of the Greyfriars (N of Greyfriars Street, founded in 1225), Blackfriars (NE of the castle, before 1233), Whitefriars (between Abington Street and Princes Street, 1271), and Austin Friars (NW of St John's Hospital, before 1275), and short-lived houses of the Friars of the Sack and the Poor Clares. The first extant charter dates from 1189. The medieval town was largely destroyed in the fire of September 1675. Rebuilding began immediately, and an Act of Parliament of December 1675 established a body of Commissioners to draw up regulations and carry out planning improvements. It is clear that *Henry Bell* of King's Lynn was involved in this work together with a London surveyor, *Edward Edwards*. An anonymous biographical essay published in 1728, referring to his interest in architecture, states that 'the town of Northampton, which was Re-built agreeable to his Plan, and pursuant to his own Direction, is a Testimony sufficient to evince his Masterly Hand in that Noble Science to succeeding Ages'.*

Defoe calls post-fire Northampton the 'handsomest and best built town in all this part of England'. All Saints and the Sessions House are the finest buildings of those years. The medieval town plan survived the rebuilding, but has largely disappeared since the 1970s. The curving line of Bath Street–Silver Street–College Street and Kingswell Street probably indicates the site of pre-Conquest defences. The town expanded E, and the line of the medieval walls can be traced along St George's Street, Campbell Street, Upper and Lower Mounts, Cheyne Walk and Victoria Promenade. Excavations in 1971 confirmed that there was a pre-Conquest ditch, which was filled in when the town expanded in the CI2–CI3.

*See H. M. Colvin and L. M. Wodehouse, *Architectural History*, 4–5 (1961–2).

Already in 1712 Morton says that 'the Principal Manufacturie is that of shoes whereof mighty Numbers are, and have been, sent to Foreign Plantations, and to the Army in Flanders'. But the trade remained small until the Grand Junction Canal reached Northampton in 1815. In 1801 the town had only 7,000 inhabitants, in 1821 10,000, in 1831 15,000. Even that is only a moderate size. The London–Birmingham railway touched a point 5 m. s of Northampton (Blisworth) in 1838, and the town received its own railway station at last in 1845. The line went to Peterborough. Law's very informative map of Northampton was issued in 1847. Growth speeded up so that in 1861 the figure of 33,000 inhabitants was reached. The shoe trade differs from most others in that for a long time it did not encourage either the introduction of machinery or the creation of large units of production. Machinery began to appear only in the 1860s and 1870s, and large units are a yet younger phenomenon. There are still considerable areas of the town, mostly on the E and N sides of the old town, where remain terraces of houses interspersed with former shoe factories, schools and churches. The full prosperity of the boot and shoe industry is reflected in streets with grand terraces and villas, such as Billing Road, Barrack Road and the eastern parts of Wellingborough Road. A number of good architects appear, such as *E. F. Law* (early to mid C19), *Matthew Holding* and *Charles Dorman* later on, and around the turn of the century *Alexander Anderson*, one of a more personal and eccentric manner. The influence of W. J. Bassett-Lowke is also notable, not only for commissioning *Charles Rennie Mackintosh* to design the interior of his house in Derngate, but also for his involvement in the 1930s civic buildings on the Mounts.

Things began to change in the mid 1940s and with the 1947 Town and Country Planning Act the then Borough Architect, *J. Lewis Womersley*, proposed a redevelopment of the central areas of the town. Although Womersley left the town to move to Sheffield and create his greatest legacy, he had already designed the Kings Heath estate on the w side of the town. This resulted in a drastic redevelopment of the area w of the centre around Horsemarket and Marefair with the first high-rise block, St Katherine's House, of ten storeys, in 1952.

In the 1960s Northampton was still characterized by the many small factory buildings of brick scattered amongst the houses in many parts of the town. Then in 1968 Northampton was designated as a new town, which led to the establishment of a New Town Development Corporation working alongside the Borough Council. A Master Plan was drawn up in 1969–70 by *Hugh Wilson* and *Lewis Womersley*, who returned as a consultant. The main accent was on the development of areas E and S of the town, Weston Favell and Billing, and Hunsbury and Brackmills. Linked with these was a disastrous and badly thought out development of the central area with the Market Square, until then one of the finest in England, suffering most devastatingly. The E side was robbed of the Peacock Hotel, which dated from the post-fire period, and the N side saw the removal of the tall Art Nouveau

Emporium Arcade and the 1930s Chronicle & Echo offices. The former was replaced by a nondescript supermarket, which has already been replaced, and the latter by the Grosvenor Centre shopping arcade, with as a sop to the local population the restoration at its entrance of Welsh House, the one house which had survived the 1675 fire. Further old buildings on the Square were also to disappear, so that now only the s and w sides bear any of the character of the original. Since the 1990s efforts have been made to rescue the central area, notably from All Saints church along St Giles' Street, Derngate and Guildhall Road, and there are now moves to replace some of the more disastrous buildings such as the ugly 1976 bus station by *Arup Associates* N of the Square. The eastern district continues to expand overtaking the Billings and Moulton, and to the sw Upton has seen the most dramatic change with open meadows being replaced (2011–13) with an almost outer city housing complex, mostly of three storeys, which has received commendation, not least by the Prince of Wales. On all sides of the town there are the inevitable industrial parks which spread their tentacles ever onward into the landscape. That to the s of the town, Brackmills, does have one of the finest recent buildings, the Barclaycard Headquarters of 2000 by *Fitzroy Robinson*.

However, one should celebrate some outstanding renovations and restorations, most notably that of the *Mackintosh* house, 78 Derngate, in 1998–2003 by *John McAslan & Partners*, and of the Guildhall, for the refurbishment of its interiors by *Roderick Gradidge* (1991–2) and its extension of 1992 by *Stimpson Walton Bond*. And if nothing else, travellers on the M1 cannot pass Northampton without seeing the 400-ft (122-metre) 'Northampton Lighthouse', the Express Lifts Tower by *Maurice Walton* (1980–2).

TOWN CENTRE

The area circumscribed by, and including, the mainline S–N railway, Grafton Street, Campbell Street, Upper and Lower Mounts, York Road, Cheyne Walk, Victoria Promenade and St Peter's Way. This corresponds roughly with the walled medieval town.

CHURCHES*

ALL SAINTS. The medieval church was burnt in the fire of 1675, except for the w tower and the crypt below the chancel. The lower parts of the masonry of the tower may go back to the C12; the crypt could be of the C13. In 1232 an indulgence was granted to contributors to the building of the church. The

---

*St Andrew, 1841–7 by *E. F. Law*, was demolished in the late 1960s.

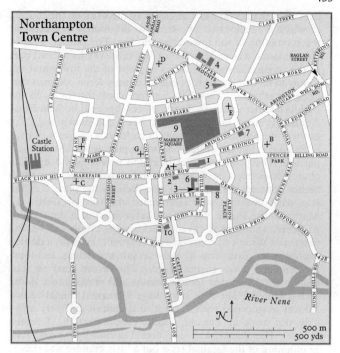

Northampton
Town Centre

River Nene

𝒩

500 m
500 yds

A	All Saints		I	Guildhall (Town Hall)
B	St Giles		2	Sessions House
C	St Peter		3	Council Offices
D	Holy Sepulchre		4	Police, Fire Station and Public Baths
E	Quaker Meeting House		5	Crown Courts
F	United Reformed Church		6	Museum and Art Gallery
G	Baptist Church		7	Library
			8	Royal and Derngate Theatres
			9	Grosvenor Centre
			10	St John's Hospital (former)

crypt lies below the W part of the present chancel and has a
central octagonal pier and four compartments with simply
chamfered rib-vaults. The tower is mostly of the C14 including
the triple-chamfered arches to the N and S, dying into the
imposts, though these are remarkably similar to those at St
Giles's church and may be C17 infilling of the earlier C12
arches, whose outlines can still be seen. The tower was originally a central tower. The upper part was repaired in 1617 and
received its balustrade probably in the late C17. The pretty
cupola is of 1704, the details of the bell-openings of the C19.
The rest of the church was rebuilt in 1676–80. The architect 67
was almost certainly *Henry Bell* of King's Lynn. Henry Bell
was certainly associated with the rebuilding work, as a document of 1676 records the appointment of Mr Henry Bell and
Mr Edward Edwards, 'two experienced Surveyors now residing

in . . . Northampton', as 'managers' of the work on the church, to which was allocated one-tenth of the money collected for the rebuilding of the town after the fire. The portico built of Ketton stone was added in 1701 but may well have been part of the original design. This lies in front of the tower and the rooms to its l. and r. It is of eight unfluted Ionic columns carrying an entablature with inscription along the frieze. In the middle a rather undersized STATUE of Charles II by *John Hunt*. Amusingly he is in state armour but a full-blown wig. The motif of the portico comes from Inigo Jones's former w portico of St Paul's, but the scale at Northampton is modest by comparsion. The portico at Northampton is two bays deep. The church is entered by three arched doorways with two small niches between. The w tower rises behind the portico in the somewhat awkward way later made the rule by Gibbs (St Martin-in-the-Fields etc.). The church itself is in the form of a square, about 70 ft (21 metres) across, composed on the pattern of Wren's St Mary-at-Hill (1670–6), i.e. with a domed central space, four arms of equal length and height, and four-flat-ceilinged lower corner pieces. The centre rests on four monumental unfluted Ionic columns and opens into a dome with a lantern. The four arms have segmental tunnel-vaults. All this is stuccoed with decorative spandrels and very probably the work of *Edward Goudge*'s team (*see* the Sessions House). The chancel was redecorated in 1888 by *Edmund Law* in imitation of the original style but a little grander and richer. The extra decoration is by *Jacksons*. The moulded arch on Ionic columns in the chancel and the giant pilasters at the E end of the nave are also his additions.

The N and S sides of the church are externally symmetrical, of five bays with an oval window under a segmental pediment above the centre. The same motif repeats above the E end of the nave. The windows have curious tracery throughout, with pointed lights and circles in a kind of plate tracery which occurs in some Dutch churches of the period. It is worth remembering that Bell's father traded with Holland. The glazing with moulded circles is like that at Lamport (q.v.) so probably *c.* 1860. The late C17 church was highly admired at the time, and is indeed one of the stateliest of its date outside London. Morton in 1712 called the most eminent 'Public Structures' in the county Peterborough Minster for the 'Greatness and Beauty of Gothic Architecture' and All Saints for 'the Conveniences and Ornaments of the modern Improvement of that Art with relation to Buildings of this kind'. The WAR MEMORIAL CHAPEL is an addition of 1920 by *Sir A. Blomfield & Sons & A. J. Driver*.

The DOORCASES of the three w doorways into the body of the church are of *c.* 1680 and very fine, especially the middle one with open segmental pediment. The wooden GALLERIES spoil the interior, partly because they introduce a longitudinal motif in a central plan and partly because they were cut back in 1865. Originally they came forward to the four giant columns.

ORGAN CASE. 1706 by *Thomas Swarbrick*. – FONT. Of marble, given in 1680. – PULPIT. Wood, of *c*. 1680. Originally attached to one of the N columns and then in the C19 in front of the chancel arch. The stand is of 1888. – The former SCREEN was removed a long time ago. – MAYOR'S CHAIR. A splendid piece, dated 1680. – COMMUNION RAIL. Of *c*. 1680. Turned balusters. Halfway up each baluster an openwork bulbous motif. – The REREDOS is of 1888 by *Edmund Law* with carving by *Harry Hems* of Exeter and *S. L. Reynolds* of Northampton. PAINTING of the Crucifixion by *Heaton, Butler & Bayne* (*P. H. Newman*). The original reredos with the PAINTINGS of Moses and Aaron, split apart, is now above the W gallery and the Commandment section above the N gallery. – THRONE with coat of arms above (E end of N aisle). Formerly in a consistory court in the SW vestibule of the church. – ORGAN CASE. By Thomas Swarbrick, 1706. – STAINED GLASS. S chapel E by *Percy Bacon*, 1927. – S chapel S by *A. L. Wilkinson*, 1958. – MONUMENTS. Many, all minor, e.g. Mrs Beckett and Mrs Sargeant †1747 and 1738 by *S. Cox* (with a charity child standing against an obelisk), and Richard Backwell, 1771 by *William Cox* (with some rocaille ornament). – In the churchyard to the E, WAR MEMORIAL by *Lutyens*, 1926. Two widely spaced obelisks and an altar between them. They have stone flags, which is what Lutyens originally wanted for the Cenotaph in Whitehall.

ST GILES, St Giles' Street. Grand setting in a tree-embowered churchyard. The dominant element is the tall crossing tower. This is Norman, but its upper parts fell in 1613 and were rebuilt in 1616. The top was again renewed in 1914. The church is long, with a nave of five bays, of which the two W bays are an addition of 1853–5 by *E. F. Law*. It has aisles, a clerestory of the C17, and an outer aisle rebuilt also in the 1850s. The aisles extend to where the Norman transepts were. The chancel has N and S chapels. The earliest remaining parts are the Norman arches of the crossing. The tall W and E arches were unblocked in 1854 and reconstructed on the basis of remains of the original E arch. They have two orders of shafts and capitals with leaf volutes. Traces of the Norman N arch survive. The W doorway is of the same time, but even more restored. It was re-set when the church was lengthened. It has a continuous inner order of zigzag and two outer orders with shafts and more zigzag. To the N of the tower is a stair-turret. The simple late C12 doorway of this survives inside the N aisle. The staircase itself has a rotating tunnel-vault. With the turret doorway goes another doorway, on the S side of the chancel, close to its E end. That proves the chancel to be to its full length of a date earlier than the present early C13 lancet windows, assuming that the doorway is in its original position, though there is the mark of a similar blocked doorway by the transept wall. The difference in masonry is indeed clearly visible outside. The two flat buttresses on the S wall and one on the N should also be noted. They break off where the masonry changes. The big E window has C19 tracery. Of the chancel lancets one remains

114

to the s, close to the C14 s transept, and one and part of a second on the N side can be seen inside. It will be noticed that the N wall of the C13 chancel was slightly pushed N as against the Norman one, whose position can be guessed from the relation to the chancel arch. The N crossing arch was reduced in size about 1300. The other crossing arches were blocked in the C17. The present arch to the N is triple-chamfered and dies into the imposts, while the inner order of the double-chamfered s arch rests on two head corbels. Of about the same time is the s arcade, as far as it is medieval, i.e. in its three E bays. Octagonal piers, double-chamfered arches. The old parts of the N arcade were damaged when the tower fell, and coarsely renewed in 1616. Of the C14 the arches to the N and s chapels, that of the N chapel triple-chamfered and dying against the imposts, that to the s chapel very tall and of three hollow chamfers. A blocked ogee-arched lowside window in the s wall of the s transept. The N chapel windows were redone in 1512. They have four-centred arches and simple panel tracery. The C19 work by *E. F. Law* was based on a report made in the 1840s by *G. G. Scott*, whose brother was curate of the church. – FONT. C15 with blank Perp windows as motifs of the panels. Much re-cut. – REREDOS. Stone, alabaster and mosaic by *Edmund Law*, 1883 and carved by *H. Hems* of Exeter. The mosaic marble floor of the same date, and tiles by *Maws*. – PULPIT. Richly panelled Jacobean. – CHAIR. One of those curiosity items. Dated 1641 but its Jacobean carving owing more to, say, 1841 than 1641. – CHANDELIER (N chapel). Brass, 1745. – STAINED GLASS. Chancel E window by *Clayton & Bell*, 1876. Chancel s side all by *J. Powell & Sons*. – N aisle NW by *J. Hardman & Co.*, 1886. – N aisle W window by *Heaton, Butler & Bayne*, 1884. Other figures in N aisle by *Clayton & Bell* 1890. – s aisle W also by *Powells*, 1873. – MONUMENT. Alabaster tomb-chest of the C15 with figures under shallow tripartite cusping and separated by thin buttresses. They are alternatingly angels and bedesmen (N aisle E end). – Many wall monuments, several by *Hunt* and the *Coxes*.

ST PETER, Marefair (Churches Conservation Trust). The most interesting Norman church in Northamptonshire and indeed one of the most exceptional Norman churches in the country. It is relatively large and has a number of unusual features. Its origins are Anglo-Saxon when it may have had almost minster status and had an important shrine, probably that of the Anglo-Saxon prince St Ragener, nephew of St Edmund, slain in battle in 870. At that time the church was part of a large complex which was partially excavated in 1980–2. To the E of the church were uncovered the foundations of a large timber hall, later replaced in stone, suggesting a palace-like collection of buildings. The present church was built on the site of its predecessor *c.* 1130–40. The exterior appears long in relation to the relatively stumpy w tower. This was rebuilt in the early C17, several feet E of its original position cutting into the internal arcade arrangement as will be seen. Its upper stages clearly C17 but the lower stages would appear to be largely of the original form, containing much reused Norman work. In the W wall an elaborate flatly carved arch containing saltire crosses, knots, etc. which would have originally surrounded the head of a W doorway. Above, blank arcading to the N and S in two tiers. Scalloped capitals. The curious thing about the tower is the angle buttresses. They are semicircular in plan and have on either side a semicircular companion. Along the N and the S of the church the most remarkable fact is the absence of any structural division between nave and chancel and the emphasis on this fact by an uninterrupted row of blank arcading all along the clerestory. Every so often a Norman window under one of these blank arches. N and S doorways Norman and simple. The E end was rebuilt by *G. G. Scott* in 1850, but it is affirmed that he had sufficient evidence for the semicircular buttress in the middle of the E wall. Most of the windows are of the C17, save one Perp window in the N chancel aisle.

Internally, before being sidetracked by the lavish carvings, one needs to consider the plan and internal arrangement. It is highly unusual and without parallel at the time. The building is a basilica, that is a rectangular compartment with continual arcades from W to E and without any break – so no chancel arch. The nave had originally three bays of two arches between tall half-round supports for the roof beams, a motif familiar in cathedrals and abbeys (Jumièges, Durham, Peterborough transept, etc.) but highly unusual in parish churches. The piers of the bays are quatrefoil clusters of columns. At the W end now there is only half a bay owing to the building having been shortened when the tower was rebuilt in the C17. The two arches of the bays are then supported on a single round column, but most unusually with an amulet or shaft-ring at mid-point. The capitals are of cushion form except the responds which have volutes. The chancel is of three single-arched bays and here the capitals are volutes but the responds cushions. Again columns with shaft-rings. This sophisticated pattern is rare indeed. Is the ambitious conception of St Peter connected with its situation close to the castle? Surely so and conceived by a mind not native. Extremely elaborate tower arch, obviously reconstructed. Three orders of shafts, some uncomfortably supporting their capitals, decorated with lozenges, zigzag and fluting. Decorated abaci, arches with much zigzag. As for the other carved work, it is also exceptional. All arches with zigzags. The capitals are of many types, with thin curly trails, with broader bands, with volutes, palmette leaves and occasionally animal heads. Just one capital, with volutes, in the S aisle has on its inner face a tiny human figure. The abaci equally elaborately carved in the same manner with more beasts and scroll leaf work. This luxurious carving was preserved since it was plastered over in the C18 and was then patiently unpicked by Anne Elizabeth Baker, sister of the historian George Baker, in the early C19. The bases of the columns are of a more standard form with moulded circles and beak forms at their corners.

Northampton, St Peter, frieze.
Engraving, 1880

The aisles had transverse arches from each of the quatrefoil
piers. Interesting use of limestone and ironstone. The w arches
may have been neatened with alternating courses during the
C17 rebuild. The clerestory also has odd spacing with the
central bay having two windows while the lateral bays have only
one in the centre, the w one cut in half during the C17 rebuilding. In the s aisle an early C14 tomb-recess.

FURNISHINGS. – FONT. Octagonal, Dec. Stem and bowl in
one. Blank windows with tracery as decoration. Cover designed
and painted by *Scott* 1850. – REREDOS. By *J. Oldrid Scott*,
1875–9, with central painting of Crucifixion by *Burlison &
Grylls*. The painted decoration of the E wall is of the same time.
It was painted over in 1914, but has been uncovered and
restored. – SCULPTURE. In the s aisle, E end, a remarkable
Anglo-Saxon tomb-slab, C10 or C11, and reputedly the grave
slab of St Ragener. A 'Green Man' form of head from which
issue foliage scrolls inhabited with beasts and birds. In the
tomb-recess alongside more fragments with two Anglo-Saxon
carvings with interlace decoration, one a cross-shaft of the C9,
reused as Norman bases, together with other Norman pieces.
– STAINED GLASS. Chancel E by *Clayton & Bell*, 1864–5. –
Chancel N by *Clayton & Bell*, 1883. – s aisle SE and SW both

by *J. Powell & Sons*, 1892, designed by *Henry Holiday*, 1892. – N aisle by *H. A. Hymers*, 1899. – Tower also by *Powells* and *Holiday* 1892. – MONUMENTS. Rev. William Lockwood †1802 by *R. Blore*. Large marble inscription in Gothic frame. – William Smith, the creator of modern geology, †1839, bust of marble by *M. Noble*. Smith was a friend of the historian George Baker and was staying with him when he died, hence his burial here. – John Smith, the mezzotint engraver, †1742, by *John Hunt*. – George Baker †1851, the historian, and his sister Anne Elizabeth. A simple tablet also by *Noble*. – Many other minor tablets by *Hunt* and the *Coxes*.

HOLY SEPULCHRE, Sheep Street. A Norman round church with a C14 W tower and a long C13 chancel. Round churches are a rarity in any country. They were favoured by the Knights Templar and Knights Hospitaller in memory of the rotunda which formed part of the church of the Holy Sepulchre in Jerusalem. In Britain a round Templars' church survives in London, and remains or records tell us of more: in London on the first site of the Templars, in Holborn; in Bristol; at Dover; at Asleckby and Temple Bruerne in Lincolnshire; and at Garway in Herefordshire. There are also remains of St John at Clerkenwell, London, belonging to the Hospitallers, of St Giles Hereford, a hospital dependent on the Hospitallers, and also the C14 church of the same order at Little Maplestead in Essex. But the round church at Northampton, just like that at Cambridge, though called Holy Sepulchre, is a parish church and always has been one. A circular nave also exists at the chapel of Ludlow Castle and another has been excavated beneath the parish church of West Thurrock in Essex.

Holy Sepulchre at Northampton was founded about 1110 by Simon de Senlis, Earl of Northampton, who had taken part in the First Crusade. The church then consisted of an oblong chancel in addition to the round nave. Of this chancel windows can still be traced inside the present chancel aisles, and long stretches of the corbel table, partly re-set, also remain. The nave has a circular central space and a circular ambulatory. They are separated by eight strong round piers with circular, many-scalloped capitals. The two to the E have square abaci, the next two square ones with the corners notched back, the four to the W circular abaci, perhaps the earliest ones in England. The arches and the octagonal upper storey were remodelled in the C14. The arches are tall and single-chamfered. The elaborate ROOF of the rotunda dates from 1868, that of the ambulatory from 1879. The ambulatory is said to have been originally two-storeyed with a vaulted lower floor. The springing of the vault is still in places visible against the outer wall, but it is difficult to visualize how the vault would have met the circular piers. There are, however, remains of Norman ambulatory windows on a lower and an upper level. There is also a mysterious built-in Norman shaft, just N of the W entrance into the ambulatory. It is taller than the springing points of the surmised vaults. Externally the only Norman feature apart from the windows is some remaining flat buttresses.

The chancel was gradually rebuilt and enlarged by aisles and an outer N aisle from *c.* 1180 to *c.* 1330. The N arcade comes first. Two bays are original. The responds have three shafts separated by right angles and leaf capitals. The pier is circular with four thin tripartite groups of shafts in the cardinal directions and moulded capitals. The difference in style has made Professor Bony suggest that the pier was replaced about the middle of the C13. The arches are pointed and have two slight chamfers. Two splendid image brackets from the E wall are set in the present E wall. They are big leaf capitals on the heads of a king and a Bishop. An outer aisle was added in the late C13 (rebuilt by *Scott*). It consists of three instead of two bays, and has quatrefoil piers with slenderer subsidiary shafts in the diagonals, moulded capitals and double-chamfered arches. A PILLAR PISCINA in the E respond. Renewed Purbeck shaft and a little nailhead decoration. The S aisle is assigned to the C14, but cannot be in its original state. The arches are earlier than the clumsy square piers, and their mouldings do not go with the shapes of the piers. The ambulatory is connected with the chancel aisles by triple-chamfered arches. Of the C15 roof of the chancel 'nave' the CORBELS remain, carved with figures playing musical instruments (bagpipes, portative organ, hurdy-gurdy, kettle-drum, etc.). The whole E end of the church, including the semicircular apse, is by *Scott* and dates from 1860–4. It is a typically High Victorian attempt at improving on the Middle Ages. Scott introduced polished shafts and a greater variety of flora in the capitals. Finally the W tower, a very impressive piece of the early C14. Very big diagonal buttresses with five set-offs. Recessed spire with three tiers of lucarnes. Deeply moulded doorway with continuous mouldings. Also moulded frames of the W window and the bell-openings.

FURNISHINGS. – BANNER-STAFF LOCKER. C14? In the ambulatory S of the chancel arch. Such lockers were usual in East Anglia, but are rare otherwise. They are simply very tall recesses. The one at Holy Sepulchre is 11 ft (3.4 metres) high. – SCULPTURE. Norman trefoiled tympanum with the bust of a man between a small human figure and a dragon. Early C12 (ambulatory, W wall). – In the S wall of the churchyard, near the SW corner, head of a churchyard cross, C15, with Crucifixus on either side. – CHANCEL SCREENS. By *J. Oldrid Scott*, 1880. – Victorian TILES in the rotunda by *Lord Alwyne Compton*, 1861. – STAINED GLASS. A large selection. Chancel E, six figures by *J. Powell & Sons*, 1921. – S chapel E, *Burlison & Grylls*, 1887. – S chapel S, two by *Powells*, 1919 and 1921. – S aisle SE, *A. J. Dix*, 1903. – S aisle, SW, *Mayer & Co.* of Munich, 1899. – N aisle E, *C. E. Kempe*, 1887. – Outer N aisle W, Richard Coeur-de-Lyon at the Battle of Joppa by *Mayer & Co.* of Munich 1883. In the same aisle, E and NW are two windows by *Morris & Co.* designed by *Dearle*, 1919 and 1920. – Tower w window by *Hardman*, 1878. – BRASS to George Coles †1640 and two wives, all modishly dressed. Still cut-out figures, as in the Middle Ages.

FRIENDS MEETING HOUSE, Wellington Street. Early C19, altered, red brick, hipped roof, with a single-storey porch on the N side. Inside there is a monument to *John Hunt*, the sculptor (†1754).

NONCONFORMIST CHAPELS. A good many of the C19 chapels have been demolished and several that do remain have been converted to other uses (*see* Perambulations). Of those that remain in the central area the following are important. First, the UNITED REFORMED (formerly Congregational) CHURCH, Chalk Lane, where Philip Doddridge preached for twenty-two years. Square, secular-looking stone building of 1695, enlarged in 1862 and largely rebuilt 1875–80. Pyramid roof. Two-storeyed. Three by six bays. Interior with galleries and box pews. School building added 1919. – MONUMENT. Philip Doddridge †1751. An asymmetrical pyramid of the *Cox* type, although signed by *John Hunt*. Much grander is the COLLEGE STREET BAPTIST CHURCH (now New Testament Church of God), 1862–3, by *William Hull*, where the pediment rests on detached giant columns. The builder was *Richard Dunkley* of Blisworth. It has one STAINED GLASS window of 1930 attributed to *Percy Bacon*. The outer parts of Northampton have a similar assortment of chapels and churches.

PUBLIC BUILDINGS

GUILDHALL (or TOWN HALL), St Giles' Square. Without doubt one of Northampton's 'great' buildings. The assertively Gothic façade consists of two parts, the seven E bays with the symmetrically placed tower by *Edward Godwin*, 1861–4, begun when he was only twenty-eight, and the additional w bays with the big gable by *Matthew Holding*, with assistance on the interior from *A. W. Jeffery*, 1889–92. The style is Gothic of the late C12, and in general Franco-English, but with allusions to Italian Gothic as well. (The *Illustrated London News* called it 'Continental Gothic'.) Godwin himself stated afterwards that he was strongly influenced by Ruskin's *Stones of Venice*, which he read just before the competition (see *The British Architect*, 1878, vol. 2, p. 210). Rich texture, with plenty of reliefs and statues illustrating various events in the town's history and at ground level various trades and industries (the reliefs in the porch by *T. Nicholls*, the statues by *R. L. Boulton* of Cheltenham). Inside, a corridor leads through the building from the entrance. All the main interiors were restored and refurbished in splendid style in 1991–2 under the direction of *Roderick Gradidge*. Some of Godwin's tiled floor designs were recreated from his designs in the V&A. The interiors are amongst the best Victorian civic interiors in the country and while Manchester may lay claim to having the finest town hall in England, Northampton ought to claim the second. The most impressive room is

107

the GREAT HALL on the r. Walls with arcading below, large
circular windows above. The panels under arches decorated in
1925 by *Colin Gill* with paintings of famous men connected
with Northampton. The columns of the blind arcading are of
cast iron and have elaborate capitals of foliage. They carry
cast-iron brackets also with foliage, and on these rest the
wooden arches for the roof. Arched recesses at both ends of
the hall. Much stencilled decoration and renewed colour on
the arches producing a spectacular interior. On the l. of the
corridor a small winding staircase (stained glass on the landing
by *Lavers & Barraud,* 1863) leads up to the GODWIN ROOM,
the former council chamber, in the centre of Godwin's building. This has its original table and chairs and two fireplaces,
all by *Godwin*, in a heavy style reminiscent of Burges. The
painted decoration was devised by Gradidge. A corridor lined
with *Doulton* tiles leads w to the present COUNCIL CHAMBER
in Holding's extension, a fine room richly decorated on all four
sides with French Gothic arcading in white and brown stone,
sculptured frieze and naturalistic capitals. At this end of the
building a strange, cramped Gothic staircase (which divides in
two despite its size) leads to the ground floor. Here also much
carving, the capitals illustrating trades and industries, etc.
Godwin's building has a rear façade to Dychurch Lane which
originally housed a fire station, reading room and museum.
Large extension on the E side of the building designed in a
sympathetic style, using patterned stone and Gothic arches,
built 1991 by *Maurice Walton* of *Stimpson & Walton* and very
successful. Within the entrance area has been placed the
STATUE of Spencer Perceval, M.P. for Northampton, 1817 by
Chantrey. One of his more static creations. It stood originally
in All Saints Church.

68 SESSIONS HOUSE, George Row. 1676–8 by *Henry Bell* of King's
Lynn and *Edward Edwards*, surveyor. There was also input by
Sir Roger Norwich, head of the Committee of Justices of the
Peace, who 'contrived and layd out' the plan. An extremely fine
building, beautifully built of Ketton stone. Five-bay N front,
the l. and r. bays stressed by attached unfluted Corinthian
columns and segmental pediments. The three bays between
have large windows with carved scroll surrounds and flat
wooden mullion-and-two-transom crosses. The scrolled surrounds are almost identical to those Bell designed for the
courtyard of Kimbolton Castle and for the Duke's Head Inn
in King's Lynn. Hipped roof, originally with a cupola and
pedimented dormers with oval windows. To the w one bay
treated like the first and last bays to the N, but with coupled
pilasters. Finely carved heraldry. This forms an excellent
picture with All Saints as one approaches from the w. Inside,
70 splendid plaster ceilings by *Edward Goudge*, 1684–8. First the
WEST ANTE-ROOM with a wreath of flowers and fruit. Partitioned off to the E is the NISI PRIUS COURT, to the S is the
CROWN COURT. The partitions between the courts are later
additions and both were partially refitted in 1964 by *Rattee &*

Kett. They both have especially fine ceilings with central wreaths with deeply undercut leaves, and even more daringly undercut flowers etc. in the spandrels. At the end of each ceiling a fat boy Justice between cornucopia, and also an angel's head and a devil's head.* Goudge did equally prodigious work at Cambridge and at Belton House, Lincs, but this is as good as he gets. Behind the Sessions House was the GAOL, built in 1791–4 by *Brettingham.* Enlarged in 1846 by *James Milne.* Largely pulled down in 1930. What remains is a big range, almost entirely re-windowed, which stretches s to Angel Street and ends in a broken pediment with a lunette.

To the w of the Sessions House the COUNTY HALL, an extension in a remarkably ornate Palladian style. Of five big bays. Rusticated ground floor with short pilasters. Upper floor with attached unfluted Ionic columns and heavily pedimented windows. The building was originally a post-fire town house for Sir William Haselwood of Maidwell. It was entirely rebuilt in 1845 by *James Milne,* remodelled in 1890 by *Edmund Law,* who designed the half-oval Council Chamber, and altered again *c.* 1900 by *Aston Webb,* who redesigned the entrance, vestibule, octagonal antechamber and staircase.

COUNCIL OFFICES, Guildhall Road. Designed in 1934 by *G. H. Lewin,* then County Architect, and *J. A. Gotch*; plain neo-1700 details.

POLICE STATION, FIRE STATION and PUBLIC BATHS, Upper Mounts. An impressive group of 1938–41 by *J. C. Prestwich & Sons* who won a competition in 1931. Ashlar stone, not in any period style save that of its own, severely block-shaped, especially the l. and r. buildings, i.e. the police and bath. The fire station is a tall block with floors of flats above the station arches. The swimming bath, opened in 1936, is one of the most important of its period and still almost totally intact. It has big parabolic concrete arches and side windows in three diminishing tiers. Not surprisingly W. J. Bassett-Lowke was Chairman of the Baths Committee. If only Northampton had had the courage to proceed in this same way.

CROWN COURTS, Upper Mounts. Designed in the mid 1980s by *Kit Allsop Architects* but not built till 1992. It gives a certain tone to the area, though its asymmetric rear façade is rather bald. The main entrance of more pleasing form, with a glazed atrium, is in Ladys Lane.

MUSEUM AND ART GALLERY, Guildhall Road. 1883, 1889 (remodelling) and 1934. Extension of 1987–9 (*Borough Architect's Dept*) with glazed staircase and refurbishment of entrance etc. in 2012. The museum houses the national collection of footwear. Fine engraved glass screen of St Crispin and Crispianus by *John Hutton.*

CENTRAL LIBRARY, Abington Street. 1910 by *Herbert Norman.* Excellent Palladian interpretation. Statues of Northamptonshire worthies. The interior remodelled in 1969–70 by

---

*It is said to wag its tongue when a prisoner is committed.

the Borough Architect, *Leonard Howarth*, and further altered since.

ROYAL AND DERNGATE THEATRES, Guildhall Road. The Royal was formerly the Opera, by *C. J. Phipps*, 1884. The splendid original auditorium survives, small but lavish. The Guildhall Road façade is by *Charles Dorman*. The theatre is now linked into the DERNGATE entertainment centre, created in the 1980s by *Renton Howard Wood Levin* and refurbished 2003–5 by *RHWL Arts Team*. The atrium entrance is tucked back from the street. Large theatre seating 1500 and foyer etc.

TELEPHONE EXCHANGE, Spring Gardens. The large, unexciting extensions of 1971–2 are by *F. L. Mason* of the Department of the Environment, consultant architects *Leonard J. Multon & Partners*.

CASTLE STATION. Rebuilt in 1963–4* by *R. L. Moorcroft* of the London Midland Region's Architect's Department. An attractive glass-walled gabled range with booking office etc. at right angles to the track. A small courtyard behind. Other stations have been demolished: St John's Station was of 1872 by *Alexander Milne* of Northampton; porte cochère with excessively fat pillars and columns; Bridge Street Station was of 1845 by *J. Livock*; brick, Jacobean, symmetrical. It started the line to Peterborough (*see* also Barnwell and Oundle stations).

CASTLE

A royal castle, one of the most famous Norman castles in England, founded in the early C12. An inner bailey was walled in stone, with semicircular earthworks covering the N gate and an outer bailey to the S. Leland mentions its 'large kepe'. It was the location of Becket's trial in 1164, besieged in 1215 and last saw military action in the Civil War as a Parliamentary garrison. Charles II ordered it to be slighted and the site was used as an orchard attached to Hazelrigg House (*see* Marefair p. 458). What remained was obliterated with the creation of the LNWR station in the 1880s, although a postern gate with continuous chamfers was dismantled and re-erected on the Black Lion Hill approach to the station. Excavations in the early 1960s on the E revealed a ditch nearly 98 ft (30 metres) wide and 29 ft (9 metres) deep, and a bank 20 ft (6 metres) high, which partly survives behind houses on Chalk Lane. Remains of an undercroft were also found, containing masonry and window glass collapsed from the rooms above, which were part of the royal apartments of Henry III. Excavations in the 1970s located Late Saxon buildings beneath a levelled length of the bailey bank on the E. Excavation beneath the station concourse car park in 2012 and 2013, prior to the rebuilding of the present station, located a building of C12, above Late Saxon deposits, at the W end of the outer bailey, which stood above the W bridge.

---

*Due to be rebuilt again (2013).

TOWN DEFENCES. Excavation in the 1990s at Green Street, s of the castle, located a length of clay bank with a timber revetment from the C10 defences, replaced by a stone revetment in C11 and with a broader wall placed on top of the bank c. C12.

PERAMBULATIONS

1. Central area around All Saints

The centre of Northampton is All Saints church. It dominates the centre even though it is surrounded by milling traffic. It deserves a rather grander piazza than it has, but in the early 2000s it was given a paved area which has done much to enhance the space and create a true town centre feature.

We start on the s side of the church in GEORGE ROW. Immediately s of the portico is LLOYDS BANK, a grand classical façade of 1922–4 by *F. W. Dorman*. A little E is WHITWORTH CHAMBERS, quite an amusing classical essay of 1897. Three storeys and attic. Interesting variety of windows: first floor *à la* Michelangelo (cf. the courtyard of Kirby Hall), the second with broken pediments and the attic with Doric columns. Next comes the COUNTY CLUB. Seven bays, dentil cornice, porch with banded pillars, tiny central pediment. It dates from after the 1675 fire and is associated with Henry Bell's activities. It was built as a town house and later used as a gaol. Between 1743 and 1792 it became an infirmary, the precursor of the General Infirmary in Billing Road. Inside a fine late C17 staircase with cylindrical balusters survives, the stairwell ceiling of c. 1740 having Rococo designs and a splendid acanthus rose: it must be by the *Woolstons* (cf. Lamport church and Hall). Cellar with fine late medieval vaulting; octagonal piers, quadripartite rib-vaults. Work in the building to the r., Whitworth Chambers, in 2003 revealed on the second floor the remains of a small C14 two-light window with reticulated tracery and some courses of stonework in the wall alongside. The window had been revealed in 1897 when Whitworth Chambers was being built and it was recorded by Sir Henry Dryden. It would seem, therefore, that this wall largely survived the 1675 fire. Wing at the rear of ironstone dated on the central window keystone 1753 and behind that a fine brick wing of 1878 by *William Hull*. Extraordinary toothed horseshoe arcading. Inside a billiard room of the same date, hardly changed. Next l. of the Club are the Northamptonshire County Council offices and the Sessions House (*see* Public Buildings). E of the Sessions House the JUDGE'S LODGING, a dignified flat-fronted Late Georgian house of ironstone and of five bays. N of the Judge's Lodging and E of All Saints churchyard is WOOD HILL, and more aware of its surroundings is the former MIDLAND BANK, 1963–7 by *Whinney, Son & Austen Hall* (now Nandos and Prezzo). A slightly concave front faced with yellow Casterton stone. Ground floor with arched windows, top floor set back. The pilastered block which corners Abington Street is by *Hillier, Parker, May & Rowden*, 1935. On the N side of the church MERCER'S ROW, another amalgam of styles. It begins at the E end with the 1911 ceramic façade of BEWLEY HOUSE by *Alexander Anderson*, backing on rather incongruously to the 1960s Waterloo House (*see* below). Rather fine with two canted bays between rusticated panels with circular garlands and attractive rounded corners. Further on is TOWN CENTRE HOUSE of 1909 with another ceramic façade. Three broad bays divided by thin moulded pilasters. Then a tiny remnant of post-fire building, just two bays with the distinctive deep cornice of the period. In the centre of the row a tall brick Renaissance façade built for wine merchants Lankester & Wells in 1901 by *Herbert Norman*. Simple Georgian façades follow and then on the corner of Drapery the fine classical façade of the former WESTMINSTER BANK (Nationwide) of 1926 by *Campbell Jones & Son*. A bowed corner with Ionic columns and a small attic feature topped by a dome.

Turning r. we come into DRAPERY. This really begins opposite All Saints with COUNTY CHAMBERS, on the corner of Gold Street, an elaborate classical frontage in a sort of Jacobethan manner of 1902 by *J. P. Sharp* of Birmingham. Then a curious façade with an arched balcony on its top floor, built 1902 by *W. Shaw*. No. 6 was for a long time the base for Philadelphus Jeyes, the chemists of Jeyes Fluid fame, who set up here in 1810. It is an interesting example of the C18 white Kingsthorpe stone, inevitably in some decay and now repaired with another stone. Still at the S end, on the E side one delightful survivor, No. 12 (W. & R. SHIPMAN), early C18 and later. Only one bay wide. Good C19 shopfront with square bay window above. Back to the W side a progression of mixed façades including Nos. 15–17, a grand 1904 French Renaissance façade of stone by *Matthew Holding*, four storeys with elegant decorative pilasters. It is followed by a narrow ironstone façade with a pretty pink sandstone French Gothic bay. Next No. 21, a good four-bay Italianate building, brick and stone, with arched windows, built for Marks, Booksellers, in 1901 by *Herbert Norman*. A little further on the same side are two post-fire façades, one having broad eared surrounds to its windows and lurking behind the drainpipe remains of Ionic pilasters. On the E side opposite other post-fire or Georgian façades just survive. Further N on the same side, several reasonably discreet 1960s buildings, e.g. No. 50, built for SKIPTON BUILDING SOCIETY, 1968–9 by *Sir John Brown, Henson & Partners*, brown brick with hipped roof, and No. 48, originally GLYN MILLS BANK, 1965–6 by *John & Michael Chaplin*. On the W side, built for ADNITT'S (now Debenhams), 1958–62 by *Deacon & Laing*, Northampton's first large store in the Modern idiom. Next door one of the town's most remarkable and finest façades, the NATWEST BANK, 1841 by *E. F. Law*, restrained, majestic and pure. Palladian, with upper giant columns and a pediment holding a carved phoenix, the badge of the former

103

Northamptonshire Union Bank. The interior still has Victorian plaster ceilings with glazed skylights. The row finishes with a long Italianate façade of 1894 (Nos. 43–49) with first-floor pedimented windows with balconies.

Moving N, past the access to the Market Square with some C19 Jacobethan in ironstone facing one, SHEEP STREET begins. It is worth now just taking in its s end, before it is interrupted by the Inner Ringroad. On the l. side is BRADSHAW STREET, with on the corner the former FISH MARKET of 1939* and at the w end the CRITERION pub of 1934 by *H. J. Ingman*. In Sheep Street, next to the Fish Market, No. 5 is the last remaining two bays of what was in the C17 the Red Lion Inn. The top windows have eared surrounds and their aprons connect with the keystones of the first-floor windows. Quoins survive which mark the r.-hand end of the earlier building, which was nine bays wide, with a central pedimented three bays with garlands (cf. Market Square), so again post-fire building.† Just N THE BEAR pub, a rather good example of Edwardian half-timbering. On the r. side, past quite a nice white brick and stone Victorian façade with a rusticated archway having a bunch of grapes on its keystone, are Nos. 18–20, late C17 of ironstone. Heavily tapered Ionic pilasters on the first floor. The main motif, l. of the centre, is the niches flanking a window (altered). This was once an inn, then the town house of the Earls of Halifax, and, after 1740, the seat of Dr Doddridge's Academy for Dissenting Ministers.

Now back to the top of Drapery and l. into MARKET SQUARE. One of the largest in England, it is just sufficiently linked with All Saints not to be a backwater, and yet sufficiently isolated to retain an unmistakable identity, something of the character of market places in Holland or Belgium – Defoe thought it one of the handsomest in England. Another reason

Northampton, Market Square.
Engraving, *c.* 1850

---

* Demolished 2013 to make way for a replacement bus station.
† I am grateful to Brian Giggins for alerting me to the relevance of this building.

for giving that impression is that only two streets (and three passages) enter it, and that the streets enter it at the corners. Also no building is too dominant – if the Town Hall had been placed here, the square would have become its forecourt – nor any too awful. That was the impression in 1960. But since then several good buildings have been demolished. The replacements have so far been, to say the least, mediocre: on the N side of the square THE PARADE has been grossly mismanaged. It begins at the W corner with No. 3, *c.* 1900 with jolly Dutch gables. Beyond it is the former CORN EXCHANGE, later the Gaumont Cinema, by *Alexander & Hull*, 1850, classical, but stuccoed and with a giant Ionian order *in antis* above a rusticated ground floor. The iron gates from the Corn Exchange are at the Museum at Abington. There then was an elegant Victorian Italianate bank by *Law* followed by its centrepiece, the EMPORIUM ARCADE. This was of 1901 by *Mosley & Scrivener*. A grand archway decorated with *Doulton*'s tiles led to an engagingly off-centre octagonal space with a glass dome. The whole could have been rehabilitated as a shopping precinct leading to the bus station planned in Lady's Lane. Instead it was replaced in 1972, as part of the Grosvenor Centre development, with a boring block with a central flat clock tower, built using the local golden ironstone, giving access to a depressing gloomy passage from the Square to the GREYFRI-ARS BUS STATION, the ugliest building in the town. A ghastly trapezoid block of 1976 by *Arup Associates*, happily due for removal (2013). The Square deserves something better than this.

The Parade ends with the enormous, overpowering GROS-VENOR CENTRE, *Stone, Toms & Partners*; consultants: *Percy Thomas Partnership* 1972–3. Its predictable interior, refurbished in 2009, extends N to Lady's Lane and E to Wood Street, with pedestrian shopping malls on two levels, and a car park and ten-storey office block behind. Excavations in 1972 when the Grosvenor Centre was being erected revealed remains of medieval buildings which must have been part of Greyfriars. They included a double-vaulted structure, *c.* 30 ft by 120 ft (9 metres by 37 metres), which was probably a N–S claustral range, and floor areas with glazed tiles, no doubt part of the church. The sop to the town was the recreating in the mid 1970s, using dispersed elements, of WELSH HOUSE, one of the few houses on the Square to escape the 1675 fire. It had been savagely altered in the C18 and C19 but was rebuilt and restored to its original form based on surviving records and drawings, notably that by George Clarke. The house is dated 1595 and has above the bay window some Elizabethan decoration and an inscription in Welsh. A broad doorcase with fluted Doric pilasters, and a pediment. Good rebuilt post-1675 staircase with twisted balusters inside. The bay with a Late Georgian Gothick window replaces a projecting porch, whose top gable and balustrade, when it was removed, was rebuilt into the façade. The porch was still there in 1768. The building stands at the bottom of the former street called Newland which disappeared when the Grosvenor Centre was built.

The E side of the Square has been similarly ravaged, but first we have BEETHOVEN HOUSE, given this name as it was the home of a former organist at All Saints. Ironstone, handsome mid-C18 Georgian, of four windows and two and a half storeys. In the middle a pretty later C18 Gothick oriel. Inside its grand staircase with tough balusters shows that the building is basically post-fire in date. Then the site of the most drastic loss, the PEACOCK HOTEL, built immediately after the 1675 fire and which dominated the E side of the Square. It was eleven bays wide with an off-centre carriageway and above it openings with fine details of the kind now associated with the work of *Bell* of Lynn. It has been replaced by a sadly nondescript block with shops, originally of 1960–1 by *Leslie Cook*, but given a jazzy façade and revamped in the 1990s, depressing evidence of late C20 aesthetic standards compared with the efforts made in the town after the fire. A through passage, PEACOCK PLACE, leads via the shopping precinct to Abington Street. On the S side of Peacock Place the top of a building of the mid 1930s of some style and No. 24, respectable 1930s brick Neo-Georgian.

On the Square's S side the corner is occupied by WATERLOO HOUSE, 1962–5 by *A. W. Walker & Partners*. Five storeys, much too large and clumsy for its site. It replaced a simple building of *c.* 1840, stuccoed, with giant pilasters. No. 19 is early C19, stuccoed, with a pleasant C19 ground-floor window. Its neighbour, No. 18, is much humbler, but much more genuine. Later C17, with pilasters through the upper storeys. The Ionic capitals have garlands connecting the volutes. Thick garlands also below the upper windows. Broad proportions of the windows. It may well be by *Bell* himself. At the W corner is DRURY CHAMBERS, stately, post-fire, but refaced and grandified in the mid C19. Five bays, three storeys, giant upper pilasters. Two windows on the first floor with curly open pediments. These façades make one realize what has been lost elsewhere in the Square.

The W side has some pleasant façades, a mix of remnants of post-fire building, Georgian, Victorian refacing and the occasional 1930s Neo-Georgian. It ends at the NW corner with VICTORIA HOUSE, probably of *c.* 1840, stuccoed too, and with a giant order too, but here pilasters, very elongated, through two and a half storeys.

The centre of the Square had a splendid tall FOUNTAIN of cast iron, erected in 1863 and somewhat like a green candelabrum. It was designed by *Mr Atkinson*. The commemorative panels have been preserved, and are at Abington Museum. There are still buildings to admire here but it is a sad memorial to the development of the 1970s and 1980s. But for that, Northampton's Market Square would be hailed as one of the finest in the land.

2. East of All Saints to Derngate

From George Row we move E into ST GILES' SQUARE. Immediately to the l. of the Guildhall a gabled four-bay office building in the so-called Queen Anne style as made fashionable by
Sir Ernest George. Brick and rubbed brick. Superimposed
pilasters. By *Matthew Holding*, 1886. Opposite, the former
BARCLAYS BANK (now Old Bank restaurant), originally for
the Stamford & Spalding Bank, 1888 by *Charles Dorman*, in a
classical manner with Ionic pilasters, round-arched windows
and two Palladian doorways; three-bay extension by *Rex Bryan
& Pennock*, 1971. Part ironstone with three aggregate arches to
its ground floor. The Square was to a degree recreated in 1992
by removal of shops on the S street frontage which has much
enhanced the effect of the Guildhall. Exposed is the façade of
No. 10, called MR GRANT'S HOUSE, looking Georgian but
probably post-fire. Its ground floor is a conjectural restoration.
Alongside the mildly Gothic former POLICE STATION and
HOUSE of 1873. The junction of St Giles' Street and Derngate
has the upper storeys of PRUDENTIAL BUILDINGS, an acceptable brick and stone 1930s Neo-Georgian block.

Now off E into ST GILES' STREET past on the S side the
POST OFFICE by *A. R. Myers* of the *Office of Works*, 1915–16,
suitably grand in stone in a Palladian mode. On the other side
the rather charming 1872 Gothic brick former WEIGHTS &
MEASURES DEPARTMENT by *E. F. Law*. Then on the N side
is FISH STREET, where there are some rewarding buildings.
They stand either side of The Ridings which bisects the street.
On the r. by far the most outstanding is the five-storey CITY
BUILDINGS with its elaborately sculptured rounded portal. As
its inscriptions still proclaim it was designed for the Glasgow
leather factors Malcolm Inglis & Co. There are labels for all
their trading contacts, big bulls' heads and over the doorway a
sunburst relief. The designs of 1900, appropriately, are by *Alexander Anderson*, who came from Glasgow. The sculpture is by
Abraham Broadbent. Opposite, a block of former NORTHAMP-
TON CORPORATION OFFICES of 1895, also by *Anderson* and
bearing his distinctive lettering and rose patterae. Worth a
glance is THE FISH, quite a nice essay in the pub vernacular
manner of 1896–7 by *Charles Dorman* with gables and a round
turret on its corner. Just worth a glance, opposite, in DYCHURCH
LANE is a former small MISSION CHURCH of 1868 (now
Buddies), Gothic with blue brick decoration. It was built by
Henry Holding, doubtless in collaboration with his son, *Matthew*,
then only in his early twenties. Back in St Giles' Street, on the
N side, a block built for the MASSINGBERD CHARITY in 1864
with some good if disturbed Victorian shopfronts, and to the S,
in CASTILIAN STREET, the MEMORIAL HALL by *Alexander
Anderson*, 1919 (formerly YWCA, built by the Taylor family in
memory of a son killed in the First World War). A fun building,
Scottish Baronial in miniature. Doorway with curly pediment
between two turrets; on the l. a corbelled-out, stepped gable.

On the corner of Castilian Street running along the s side of St Giles' Street, the upper floors were built as a Liberal Club, 1897–8 by *Mosley & Anderson*. Further in St Giles' Street, on the N side the entrance to the Co-operative Store and Arcade (see Abington Street, p. 455), and next to it the WELFARE CENTRE of 1936. Simple brick of one storey. Opposite, at the corner of Hazelwood Road, the MANNA HOUSE (built as St Giles's Parochial Buildings) by *S. J. Newman*, quite grand, 1888–9 Renaissance style with big windows on the first floor. Then ST THOMAS'S HOSPITAL, that is 'hospital' as in 'almshouses'. Built 1834, castellated and stuccoed, of five bays with a central doorway and window above with pointed arches. Opposite a fine terrace of houses in the Ernest George style by *Holding* (Nos. 81–87, also 73) of two tones of red brick, shaped gables with cast-iron railed basement areas. Round the corner to the N into ST GILES' TERRACE, the former ST GILES'S SCHOOL, very Gothic, stone with brick dressings, with some banding and herringbone decoration by *E. F. Law*, 1858–61. It originally had a tall flèche spire but this was reduced in size when the building was refurbished by *Stimpson & Walton* in 1984. Just N on the r. a nice Victorian brick terrace, Nos. 1–8, well landscaped with railings and brick patterned paving.

Back in St Giles' Street on the s side, on the corner of Spring Gardens, the former VICARAGE of 1884, again by *S. J. Newman*. Continuing E, in SPENCER PARADE, s of the churchyard, an especially good sequence of Regency façades of the 1840s by *William Hull*. First castellated (Nos. 1–3, being built 1841) then gabled Tudor (Nos. 4–5), and then Neo-Jacobean houses (Nos. 6–7). E of the churchyard *c.* 1838, the angle bays with giant pilasters, the centre house with a Greek Doric porch *in antis*, the end houses with thickly ornamented Victorian cast-iron porches.

At the busy junction with York Road it is worth noting on the E corner of CHEYNE WALK the EDWARD VII MEMORIAL with a bronze bust by *G. Frampton*, 1913. Typical Frampton bronze St George on the parapet of the exedra wall. Now s down CHEYNE WALK. Here the houses are detached villas. The northernmost is High Victorian Gothic in patterned brick of 1868, by *Law*.* The elegant pair further s probably of *c.* 1845. On the E side the BARRATT MATERNITY HOME, 1936 by *Sir John Brown & Henson*. Brick with horizontal forms and some Art Deco details around its entrance, but still looking fresh although it has lost its lawn to car parking. At the corner facing SE is EASTGATE HOUSE. Late Regency, stuccoed, a grand composition but trailing off in the l. third. Worth a note, just a little to the E along BEDFORD ROAD, is ST THOMAS'S WELL, a gabled Gothic recess in the C13 style; 1843. Often known as Becket's Well, though the idea of it being associated with Thomas Becket is highly suspect.

Two more recent buildings to the SE deserve mention: AVON COSMETICS headquarters building, in Nunn Mills Road, on

---

* The YMCA by *Nicholls & Moodie* of 1957–8 was demolished 2013.

the river bank, 2007–8 by *Ryder HKS*, two huge rectangular ranges linked in a horseshoe plan, with two long glazed sections lighting the five floors; and on the N side of Bedford Road, RIVERSIDE HOUSE (partly Northants County Council), another vast block with pre-cast concrete and aggregate window panels ranged in five floors and at the top end a tall staircase tower. It is by *Stone, Toms & Partners*, 1976. Just beyond on the S side, a curiosity, a round, tapered, fluted COLUMN built in 1862. It was in fact a chimney for a steam engine which served the town's sewage disposal.

Back to the centre NW along DERNGATE, with at the SW corner of the junction with Victoria Promenade No. 82, BECKET HOUSE. Plain Regency with a prettily ornamented cast-iron porch, converted in 2007 into the Visitors' Centre for NO. 78 DERNGATE, one of Northampton's most important buildings, being a rare example of the work of *Charles Rennie Mackintosh* outside Glasgow and important in his œuvre as his last architectural work. No. 78, which forms part of an early C19 terrace, was acquired by W. J. Bassett-Lowke in 1916. Ideas for remodelling the house were drawn up probably by *Bassett-Lowke* himself in collaboration with the Northampton architect *Alexander Anderson* together with ideas from Mackintosh, though his contribution was mainly concerned with interior decoration and furnishings. The tiny tiled front bay is almost certainly owed to Anderson, though the rear façade with its much more functional appearance may owe as much to Bassett-Lowke as to Mackintosh. Restoration plans were drawn up by *John McAslan & Partners* in 1998 and the house was finally opened to the public in 2004. The interior of this tiny house is highly intriguing. The remodelling in 1916 involved moving the staircase as well as adding bays to the front and rear of the building. The most dramatic interior is the hall where Mackintosh's decoration has been recreated using his original designs and stencils held by the Hunterian Museum in Glasgow. With its black walls, vivid yellow triangular patterned frieze and black-and-white chequer standards it is as remarkable today as it must have been in 1916. Further drama is created by the stair screen with its square panels, several pierced through with glazed designs using more triangles and yellow shapes. Extraordinary spiral-shaped newel at the bottom. To the rear is the dining room. Finely orchestrated fireplace wall with central fireplace with ingenious curved lantern lights and on each side glazed cupboards. The woodwork all walnut veneered. The other walls have speckled wallpaper arranged in a sequence of tall panels. On the top floor another extraordinary room, the guest bedroom. Striped designs flow from the recreated pair of beds onto the back wall and across the ceiling.* Expansive views across Beckett's Park

---

*George Bernard Shaw, a friend of Bassett-Lowke, slept in this room and was greeted on the doorstep the next morning by the local press and asked whether the striped ceiling worried him. 'No', he replied, 'I always sleep with my eyes shut.'

and the Nene valley which are now alas less rural than they would have been in 1916, but still welcomingly leafy. Kitchen in the ground floor basement still with its tiled walls and patterned floor. The rear façade is rigid in form with a projecting rectangular bay of three floors. Glazed windows to the kitchen, a long window with an unusual and original large glass panel for its centre, and for the bedroom an open balcony – the Bassett-Lowkes were keen on fresh air. It is easy to overlook the front door on Derngate, its Regency proportion decorated with a central lantern and almost oriental stepped angle pieces with dentil pendants, a design Mackintosh had used at the Glasgow School of Art.

Opposite, BEDFORD MANSIONS, a four-floor block of flats of 1934–6 by *Sir John Brown & Henson*, and typical of its date with long horizontal lines, curved ends and balconies. No. 70 has some good decorative glass. It was for many years the home of the architect *Keightley Cobb* and was altered with a rear staircase addition by him 1914–15 together with his master, *Anderson*. No. 66, TOWERFIELD, mid-C19, has a tall (altered) doorcase with fanlight. The rear façade with two canted bays. The S side of Derngate is split apart by SCHOLAR'S COURT, a housing development of 1996 which covers grounds of the former Derngate High School for Girls. The apartment blocks nicely designed in a style somewhere between Georgian and Regency with pediments, arched doorways and balconies here and there. Three storeys in yellow brick with rendered ground floors. Opposite, Nos. 59–69 are offices redeveloped for Sun Alliance by *Leach, Rhodes & Walker*, 1972. No. 44 was built *c.* 1826 and used by 1845 as the vicarage of All Saints church (now English Heritage offices). Large curved bays at the rear. Good late C19 terraced row beyond, then S in ALBION PLACE a brick terrace of *c.* 1830. Halfway down an unfortunate gap where stood the VICTORIA DISPENSARY, built as a public bath, 1844–5 by *George H. Willox*, which had an elegant central bow with Doric pilasters. Another brick terrace of *c.* 1835 leads down to Victoria Promenade. Cast-iron porches and an unusually beautiful cast-iron first-floor veranda with big honeysuckle motifs (Nos. 17–18). Beyond this, a 1964–6 office building, ALBION HOUSE, by *A. W. Walker & Partners*. Four storeys, with a projecting wing neatly containing the porch. White mosaic panels, black mullions.

So back to Derngate. On the S side the rear of the Derngate theatre complex (*see* Public Buildings) and on the N side NEW-ILTON HOUSE by *R. A. Barker* of *Wilson Properties*, 1961–3. Just before St Giles' Square a good mid-C19 brick house in the Italianate manner.

Now S from St Giles' Square and the Guildhall into GUILD-HALL ROAD. On the E corner an ironstone office building, Gothic, *c.* 1860 by *Law*. Moving downhill on the r. the Museum & Art Gallery and on the l. a good brick façade, No. 9, built as Franklin's Hotel in 1872–3 by *E. F. Law*. Four floors of ten bays. Brick and stone in the Gothic style. Pointed windows on the first and second floors with patterned brick infill. The ground floor altered. Further on the l. the Royal & Derngate Theatres. The Derngate frontage is building of *c.* 1870, originally for Phipps, the brewers. Twelve tall bays with red, blue and yellow brick arcading. Six gables with interlaced Gothic arches. The s corner and below is occupied by a former Co-operative building of 1932 by *L. G. Ekins*, chief architect of the Co-operative Wholesale Society, of beige faience; with a wondrously stylish staircase in its entrance; now apartments. The large panels containing windows edged with wave designs. A grand building of its period. In ANGEL STREET, on the w side, views of the rear of County Hall with the former tall blocks of the early C19 gaol building, part ironstone, part brick, still obvious. Adjoining them on the w the former COUNTY CONSTABULARY building of 1901. Rather good Neo-Georgian in brick and stone with excellent detailing. Guildhall Road ends, on the w side, with a row of tall faintly Italianate houses of three storeys, 1881 by *Alexander Milne*.

3. North of the central area

SHEEP STREET is interrupted by a major inner ring road traffic complex (Greyfriars and Lady's Lane) with the multi-storey CAR PARK, by the *Borough Architect's Department* (Borough Architect *Leonard Howarth*), 1972–3. Northwards beyond this is a good, even flow of Georgian town houses, with quite a number of nice doorcases, several built of ironstone and having platbands. Of special note is No. 52 on the e side. Five bays in dark ironstone with arched windows, a projecting oriel. Its ground floor rendered. Alas a rather feeble attempt at a Georgian doorcase. Even finer is, further, on the w side, No. 55, mid-C18, of five bays and three storeys, with a pair of doorcases with coupled Roman Doric pilasters. Above, a Venetian oriel and above this a Venetian window. Behind No. 47, the ROADMENDER CLUB, a rear extension by *Rex Bryan & Pennock*, 1972 and internal refurbishment 1999–2000 by *Gotch, Saunders & Surridge*. Past Holy Sepulchre church the street opens out into what was REGENT SQUARE, cut through by the ring road system. On the e side still a mix of Victorian façades, two with shaped gables and trios of round-arched windows by *Alexander Milne*, 1881. Beyond a nice simple Regency façade with tall flat Ionic pilasters. Worth a glance, w along GRAFTON STREET, and just surviving, the upper parts of the façade of a former CHINESE LAUNDRY, Early Modern of the 1930s, by the local architect *Lawson Carter*. Jazzy Art Deco cresting. Running NW from the junction in ST GEORGE'S STREET, Nos. 10–14, a pleasant early C19 stuccoed group, and some humbler C18 houses on the other side.

We now move se uphill onto CAMPBELL SQUARE and the MOUNTS. The loss here is on the s side where stood the finest of Northampton's shoe factories, MANFIELDS. It was large, of

three tall storeys and impressive with Italianate details and a
campanile, built 1857–9 to designs of *William Hull*. Its replacement is the horror of the Greyfriars Bus Station (*see* p. 448)
and blocks of flats dating from 1988–9 – but to better things.
UPPER MOUNTS is graced by one of the most impressive of
Northampton's 1930s groups, originating from an attempt to
create a civic centre and ring road sequence designed by the
landscape architect *Thomas Mawson* in 1926. All that materialized were a police station, fire station and public baths (*see*
Public Buildings, p. 443). One regrets that the space was not
further developed at the time. A little SW a more recent public
building, the Crown Courts. Set back on the St Michael's
Road junction with the Mounts the CHRONICLE & ECHO
building of the 1980s (threatened 2012). A little further down
Lower Mounts the striking, multicoloured and difficult to
describe NORTHAMPTON COLLEGE town centre site of 2008
by *Pick Everard* of Leicester. A series of graded blocks and
towers with a sweeping curved end in ochre, red and black.
Below, and forming the E corner, is the former SAVOY CINEMA
(now Jesus Centre) of 1936 by *W. R. Glen*, with one of those
typical upstanding façades with fins. Considered one of the
finest surviving examples of Glen's work, it was sensitively
conserved and restored 1999–2000 by *Gotch, Saunders & Surridge*, when the interior, which retained most of its original
features, was revived. On the corner of Abington Street
GOODYEAR CHAMBERS, the former offices of the Anglia
Building Society (now Radio Northampton) with original parts
by *Mosley & Anderson*, 1891–3, in Renaissance brick manner,
extended 1930, and with portions on the Mounts 1962–5 by
Rolf Hellberg & Maurice Harris. Five storeys with marble-faced
spandrel panels and a brick staircase tower. Standing forward
from the main block is a tall glass-walled lobby. Inside, a
double-height hall with gallery. Opposite its S façade, on the
corner of York Road, the former *c.* 1860 MISSION CHURCH
(Food Centre). Yellow and black brick, three bays with big
round-arched sets of windows.

Turning W we come into ABINGTON STREET, the main
shopping street of the town. There is much variety but little of
quality. On the S side, on the corner of St Giles' Terrace,
EASTGATE has a quite good 1930s upper section. Further on
the appalling blank PRIMARK façade replaced the NEW
THEATRE, an agreeable Palladian essay with a triple-arcaded
front by *W. Sprague*, 1925. In the centre of the street 'DISCOV-
ERY', a double curved metal arch ending in flying figures,
designed by *Lucy Glendinning* and erected 2005. It is a memorial to Sir Francis Crick, the co-discoverer of DNA, who was
born in Northampton in 1916. On the N side a pleasant brick
Neo-Georgian essay dated 1928, adjoining VICTORIA BUILD-
INGS of 1897. Brick and half-timbering with bays and oriels.
Opposite, the Neoclassical Public Library (*see* Public Buildings) and the frontage of the CO-OPERATIVE STORE &
ARCADE. Long, angled ceramic frontage of 1938 and extended

in the same manner in 1950, partly intact though much mangled. An arcade, originally created in 1935–8, runs through to St Giles' Street. It is cut through by a cross-access street called THE RIDINGS which survives from the medieval street plan. On the opposite side a short detour into WELLINGTON STREET with first WELLINGTON HOUSE of 1935 and, tucked away, the Quaker Meeting House. Back in Abington Street, a little further on the S side the ceramic 1930s façade built for WOOLWORTHS (now Tesco Express) and opposite two predictable 1960s stores, BRITISH HOME STORES, extended by *Beecroft, Bidmead & Partners*, 1967–70, and MARKS & SPENCER by *Monro & Partners*, 1968–9.* Then an open space forming a broad crossroads, on the r. leading into the Grosvenor Centre and on the l. into Fish Street (*see* p. 450). The focus here is another SCULPTURE, this time of a boot repairer's last with children prancing on its top (1986 by *Graham Ibbeson*), then a return to the standard 1960s–70s shopfronts relieved on the N side by a tall double-fronted Victorian brick and stone Gothic building with carved heads. Its façade cruelly cut into by the entrance to Peacock Place. Next a long ceramic façade of 1936 by *Hillier, Parker, May & Rowden*, and a more classical stone façade on the S, dated 1940 and built for KINGHAMS STORE by *Law, Harris & Croft*. These are followed on the N side by one of those inevitable 1920s essays in half-timbering, and eventually, on the r.-hand corner, No. 1, which despite having a modern shopfront still has on its first floor a plaque dating the building originally to 1677, the windows embellished with stucco garlands added by *Alexander Anderson* in 1910. So back to the Market Square and All Saints.

4. South and west around the centre

To the S from the piazza of All Saints runs BRIDGE STREET, with buildings of varied periods and varied quality. At the E corner Lloyds Bank (*see* above, p. 445). Opposite, No. 4 has a fine deep cornice with Art and Crafts decoration. Further S No. 7, a one-bay C18 house with two early C19 storeys of bow windows. Some good C19 upper façades in an Italianate manner with framed windows, quoins, etc., notably Nos. 20–24. No. 36 is quite grand Late Regency with Tuscan pilasters and framed windows. On the W side, at the bottom, the former BLUE COAT SCHOOL and ORANGE SCHOOL. Two houses, of brick, both dated 1811 on prettily lettered nameplates over the doors. The S part higher, three bays, three storeys, stucco quoins and lintels. The N part lower, with big windows on the upper floor separated by niches. Two statues of charity children in the niches.

---

* Rearing up behind Abington Street to the N is the mediocre bulk of NORTHAMPTON HOUSE, 1971–2 by *Stone, Toms & Partners*, which for many years held the offices of the County Council and was subsequently converted into flats.

A little further s, almost beyond reach on its traffic island, but with thankfully a patch of grass and some trees, is ST JOHN'S HOSPITAL, now a restaurant. Part of the medieval Hospital of St John, founded *c.* 1137. The hospital had probably at first an infirmary hall and aisles for the beds and an aisleless chapel to the E. The chapel was allowed to remain but, when the infirmary became an almshouse, the domestic quarters were built on the site of the former s aisle. It is for this reason that the NE angle of the former almshouse just touches the SW angle of the chapel. The almshouse building was in 1955 converted into a R.C. church, with a new chancel, and the old chapel, which had been restored in 1881–2 by *S. J. Nicholl*, thus became a side chapel. It ceased to be a church in 1985. The master's house lay further to the N and was destroyed when the (now demolished) railway station was built. The former chapel has a Perp five-light w window and doorway (traceried spandrels) and an early C14 E window (three lights, intersected, cusped). The s wall was rebuilt in 1853. In it a simple original early C14 doorway, now connecting what was the chapel with the former almshouse. Good traceried WEST DOOR. The almshouse portion has an early C14 front to the street, with a tall blank arch on shafts with moulded capitals and a smaller doorway set into it. This has a re-set arch with deep mouldings. Above the blank arch a handsome rose window filled by a saltire cross of pairs of pointed arches. The building before conversion consisted of a two-storeyed w part, a two-storeyed E part and a one-storeyed centre. The latter must have been the Hall. It has Late Perp windows. The other windows are Elizabethan or later. Roof with tie-beams and queenposts. The w gallery incorporates the balusters from the former staircase. – STAINED GLASS. Upper part of a C15 figure. – St John (nave s window). It comes from the chapel of Ashby St Ledgers. – Three complete figures of *c.* 1845 by *William Wailes*, SS Thomas Becket and Felix and the Virgin; good. From *Pugin*'s original church of St Felix, now R.C. cathedral (*see* p. 459). – In the former chapel the Crucifixion by *J. Hardman & Co.* 1919.

s of the hospital, at the s ring road junction with Victoria Promenade, on the l. is the PLOUGH HOTEL of 1877, in the 'Olde English' manner by *S. J. Newman*, a combination of stone, panelled chimneystacks and half-timbering. Just round the corner to the E, in VICTORIA GARDENS, a charming Swiss Cottage type house *c.* 1860, complete with fretwork, a balcony and a tiny tower. It was built as a refreshment kiosk when there were indeed gardens in this area. The gardens gave way to houses in the 1890s and in 1892 this house was remodelled. On the other side of the inner ring road was the CATTLE MARKET of 1873. Its two Lodge Houses with banded brickwork, somewhat French in style, survive with MORRISON'S supermarket behind (*Watson & Batty* 1995–6). An extraordinary attempt to pick up some echo of earlier buildings with two towers with openwork pointed tops and big Gothic arches below.

The area sw of Bridge Street has become a complex of commercial properties and car parks. (For the area s from here see p. 478). On the s side of the complex road junction of St Peter's Way and Towcester Road is the former GAS COMPANY OFFICES of 1880. Substantial, of two storeys in red brick with decorative detailing. Two C19 GASHOLDERS still stand on the other side of St Peter's Way. There is then nothing to detain us till we reach, on rising ground to the NW, St Peter's church (*see* p. 436). Across another traffic complex NW is Castle Station (for this and the medieval castle *see* p. 444 and for the area w of the station *see* p. 482). It is a relief to return E into MAREFAIR with just beyond the churchyard HAZELRIGG HOUSE. Coursed rubble, three big dormers with the semicircular gables typical of the late C16. Tall mullioned windows. Irregular fenestration. Doorway with flat classical surround. A photograph exists showing that the present three-gabled façade was just the central portion of a much larger house having a further gable on each side. Its r.-hand wing, altered later, partially surviving. Staircase with twisted balusters, late C17 but an original late C16 section at the top. There is record of a moulded beamed ceiling of C16 date formerly in No. 31. Behind, a series of linked courts designed by *Marshman, Warren & Taylor* begun in the mid-1970s. The N side of Marefair was formerly dominated by Barclaycard House, by the London firm of *R. Seifert & Partners*, 1969–72, but this has been demolished and replaced by the rather grotesque mass of the IBIS HOTEL. The area of HORSEMARKET, running N, has likewise been drastically redeveloped since the 1970s. On the E side further N is the SAXON INN HOTEL, 1971–2 by *Ivan Nellist & Ian Blundell*. It has a distinctive roof-line formed by a series of canopy-like arches. To the NW is an area of council housing. ST MARY'S COURT, the point block of ten storeys (the first in the town), is by the then Borough Architect, *J. L. Womersley*, 1952. More blocks since.

Moving eastwards into GOLD STREET, another street with a variety of façades somewhat marred by modern intrusions. On the N side No. 42, late 1930s brick, Neo-Georgian with a Venetian window design on its first floor, and next the former WOOLWORTHS has quite a good 1934 ceramic frontage by the Woolworth's architect. Typical fluted pilaster forms and three shallow canted bays with a deep gadrooned frieze. Opposite Nos. 47–49 of 1892, brick and stone with fanciful Jacobean gables and a fine row of fanlighted *c.* 1900 shop windows on its first floor. Higher up No. 39 has a fanciful *c.* 1900 façade with Ionic pilasters and garlanded circular windows. All rather theatrical. Towards All Saints is the former GRAND HOTEL (Travelodge), by *Charles Dorman*, 1889–92, of no architectural merit. Just s into KINGSWELL STREET the BECKET AND SARGEANT CHARITY SCHOOL, 1862 by *E. F. Law*, brick and stone, five bays, symmetrical Gothic, and back on the s side of Gold Street a tall block, YORKSHIRE BANK, with two pedimented gables and pointed arched recesses, equally

Gothic. It is also by *Law*, 1875–6. Opposite just into COLLEGE STREET rather a grand mid Victorian Gothic building on the r. with carved heads. Finally on the N side of Gold Street the former offices of PHIPPS'S BREWERY, built in 1881 by *S. J. Newman*. A really splendid façade. Three bays, brick and stone, tall, three tall upper bay windows with round corners. Its entrance façade, with its shell-hooded doorcase and the Borough shield, acting as an arcaded walk. The elaborate style is a mixed Dutch and French C17. The piazza of All Saints now opens up.

INNER NORTHAMPTON

NORTH*

ST LAWRENCE AND ST STANISLAW, Duke Street. By *Burder & Baker*, 1877–8, in the Pearson style and notably good and progressive. Tall, of red brick, with nave and chancel under one roof. No tower. Lancet windows. The brick is exposed inside. Wide nave with low aisle passages and very tall clerestory. Tall s chancel chapel of two double bays, the subsidiary piers octagonal and as slender as in Pearson's St Augustine, Kilburn. The arcade repeats on the N side for the organ chamber. Straight E end with lancets in groups but more elaborate W end with Geometric-style windows. – STAINED GLASS. SS Hilda and Etheldreda, by *A. Stoddart* of Nottingham, 1915. – Weiss glass with Polish saints by *Francis Skeat*, 1978. – Other windows 1926–30 are by *William Lawson* of *Faith-Craft*.

Former VICARAGE, to the SE, 1887 by *Matthew Holding* in a domestic Gothic manner, red brick and stone, half C14 and half C15 with mullioned-and-transomed windows and a Perp porch. Tall chimneystacks. The former CHURCH BUILDINGS (Polish Club), Craven Street are by *Matthew Holding* 1909 in his lancet style.

ST MARY AND ST THOMAS (R.C.) CATHEDRAL, Kingsthorpe Road. A small church of St Felix was built by *A. W. N. Pugin* in 1844. This was enlarged to three times its size by *E. W. Pugin* in 1863. The enlargement consists of a nave and aisles with a polygonal apse to the W. The original E end was replaced in 1948–55 by a straight E end, transepts and a crossing tower, all of pale brick and by *Albert Herbert*. The old parts have lowish arcades with rich leaf capitals, a tall clerestory with Geometrical tracery, and a very curious roof with a first stage of stone panels carrying a second stage of timber. The E end was extended and the interior refurbished in 1999 by *Greenhalgh & Williams*. – PAINTINGS. Resurrection and Assumption by *Heinrich Hess*, large, now stored. – STAINED GLASS. Except for

*St Paul's, Semilong Road, 1890 by *Holding* was demolished 1984–5 because of structural failing.

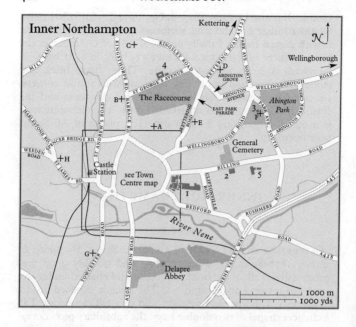

Inner Northampton

Kettering

Wellingborough

N

MILT LANE

KINGSLEY ROAD

KINGSTHORPE RD.

KETTERING ROAD NORTH

PARK AVE. NORTH

c+

4
ST GEORGE'S AVENUE

+D
ABINGTON GROVE

ABINGTON AVENUE

WELLINGBOROUGH ROAD

B+
The Racecourse

EAST PARK PARADE

Abington Park

ABINGTON PARK CRES.

KETTERING ROAD

+E

3
F+

HARLESTONE RD.

SPENCER BRIDGE RD.

BARRACK ROAD

ST ANDREW'S ROAD

+A

WELLINGBOROUGH ROAD

PARK AVE. SOUTH

A45

WEEDEN ROAD

ST JAMES' RD.

+H

Castle Station

see Town Centre map

General Cemetery

BILLING ROAD

2
5

CLIFTONVILLE ROAD

I

RUSHMERE ROAD

ROAD

TOWCESTER ROAD

LONDON ROAD

A508

BEDFORD

River Nene

ROAD

A428

G+

Delapre Abbey

NENE VALLEY WAY

1000 m
1000 yds

the S chapel E window, which is by *J. E. Nuttgens*, 1999, all the other glass is by *J. Hardman & Co.* The S, W and N windows all date from 1866–7. The chancel and S chapel figures date from 1923 but were reinserted in the extended cathedral in 1959. The two S transept windows are also 1959.

To the r. of the cathedral a small, older church, then a narrow gabled front with an original C14 two-light window reused, then a three-bay Georgian house. Down Marriott Street the BISHOP'S HOUSE, Tudor, by *S. J. Nicholl*, 1884. It has armorial STAINED GLASS by *Lavers, Barraud & Westlake*. NAZARETH HOUSE (now Bosworth Tutorts), Kingsthorpe Road, is part of the same complex. 1876–7 by *F. W. Tasker*. Elizabethan with some Gothic details. Incorporated within it the former chapel with lancet windows and a flèche.

HOLY TRINITY, Balmoral Road. 1909 by *Holding*, completed by *E. de W. Holding*. A big, dominant church with several fine features. Perp in style. Big transeptal tower on the S side balanced by a N transept. Higher stair-turret. Closely set, spec-

tacularly large clerestory windows, two to the bay. Seven-light
W and E windows. Low Perp arcades with ogee arches. –
STAINED GLASS. Chancel E by *Christopher Webb* and *Francis
Skeat* 1946. – Other windows are all by *H. A. Hymers* 1909.

Former PRIMROSE HILL CONGREGATIONAL CHURCH. By
Alexander Anderson, 1901–3. Brick, octagonal, with a pedimented forebuilding and a semicircular portico of Tuscan
columns. Sculptured pediment by *Abraham Broadbent*. Former
hall behind of 1922. Converted into housing 2009.

NORTHAMPTON UNIVERSITY (MAIDWELL AND NEWTON
BUILDINGS), St George's Avenue. Maidwell incorporates the
1932 buildings by *Keightley Cobb*, built as a College of Technol-
ogy and a School of Art. The plan was a half H and its two
original entrances in a Neo-Georgian manner with Ionic
columns still survive at either end. The centre was then infilled
in 1960 by *Brian Bunch*. Next is the Newton Building, formerly
the Northampton School for Girls, built in 1915 by *Sharman
& Archer*. Symmetrical, Neo-Georgian, with a turret. Brick,
but the centre, including a segmental pediment, stone-faced.
Both buildings have been refurbished internally and substantial new blocks have been built to the rear. The complete site
is under review following the appointment in 2009 of *Alison
Brooks Architects* as advisers. The Maidwell building is to be a
central 'Forum' and most of the earlier buildings behind the
frontage will be replaced. (For the main campus see Kingsthorpe, p. 496.)

MALCOLM ARNOLD ACADEMY, Trinity Avenue. On the site of
the 1956–8 Trinity High School, which was demolished to
make way for Unity College. This was refurbished and reopened
as the Malcolm Arnold Academy in 2010, to honour the
Northampton composer.*

Former DRILL HALL (Territorial Army Centre), Clare Street.
1859. Brick with round towers and lancet windows, entirely
like an American armoury. Central gatehouse with entrance
somewhat squeezed between its towers. Lateral wings also
ending in round towers. Almost opposite ALBANY HOUSE, a
good example of a factory conversion by *Tad Dobraszczyk*
2007–9.

PERAMBULATION. The early C19 development of the town can
be followed starting from Regent Square and moving N along
BARRACK ROAD. The array of houses and terraces is an interesting sequence showing differing tastes in design from
mundane to highly decorative buildings. First on the W side
ROYAL TERRACE, three storeys, stuccoed, begun 1827.
REGENT HOUSE, set back, follows, three storeys, three bays,
with central two-storey porch. Part of the former ST SEPUL-
CHRE'S PAROCHIAL SCHOOL of 1845 follows. Ironstone in
the Perp style, though considerably altered as commercial
premises. Then a small section of oldest part of the 1796 BAR-

---

*Military Road School, 1885 by *Gorman* and *Talbot Brown*, one of the more decorative Board Schools in a Renaissance manner, was sadly demolished in the 1980s.

RACKS, ashlar-built, converted into residential. Further on is LEICESTER TERRACE and, a little grander, ADELAIDE TERRACE, 1830–40 with some later alterations. Nos. 1–3 Adelaide Terrace are treated as one composition with a recessed centre with triple-arcaded balcony. Then follows LEICESTER PARADE with Nos. 1–4 in the Neo-Jacobean style of the early 1880s and No. 5 Italianate, c. 1875. The most impressive is the QUEEN'S BUILDING, built 1900 by *Charles Dorman & Son* for the Town & County Nursing Association. Five bays and three storeys in the English Renaissance manner. Opposite on the E side THE POPLARS, c. 1865, with a porch with Ionic columns and a pretty veranda at the side. It replaced a charming *cottage orné* house named 'La Belle Alliance' of c. 1820. Opposite on the W side is Hester Street which leads down to SEMILONG ROAD, with on the corner a good example of *Alexander Anderson*'s CO-OPERATIVE SOCIETY shops. This one 1908, red brick with banded pilasters with circular paterae, two gables with dentil cornice sheltering large arched windows. Big panels with lettering. The shopfront inevitably altered but still the Co-op.

Further N on Barrack Road the quite grand LANGHAM PLACE, begun in the 1840s and completed in the 1860s, three-bay houses with projecting porches and cast-iron balconies. The uniform houses built 1861–4 by *O. S. Pratt*. Running E from the end of Langham Place is ST GEORGE'S AVENUE, overlooking the Racecourse (*see* p. 467) on which are the Newton and Maidwell buildings of the University (*see* above). On the W side of Barrack Road are the buildings of the Roman Catholic Cathedral (*see* above), followed in KINGSTHORPE ROAD by a succession of terraces with progressively fussier details. The sloping road is called PRIMROSE HILL and there is on the W side a mixture of houses, including some using ironstone, some as early as the mid 1850s, while some infill was still going on in 1901 (No. 15). ST PAUL'S TERRACE with its houses with their odd mixture of stone and timbered gables dates from 1884. The raised terraces on the E side, ST GEORGE'S PLACE, were begun in 1855 but not finally completed till the early 1880s. Then comes the former Primrose Hill Congregational Church (see above) with opposite the tall impressive former BARRATT FOOTSHAPE BOOT WORKS. This is of 1913, and one of the finest examples of the work of *Alexander Anderson*. Red brick and stone, nine bays and three storeys, with many Baroque motifs in terracotta by *Gibbs & Canning*. Central entrance doorway with Ionic columns and good details, narrow bays with semicircular tops either side, and similar bays at each end of the long façade. Typical Anderson lettering in the parapet and decorations, especially in the curved gables. It was converted into apartments in 1979 by *Ellis Williams Partnership*.

Nothing of note below in Kingsthorpe Hollow save, just worth a glance, on the E side, tucked into a wall, a ceramic gable with the date 1919. This was saved when the Coliseum

Picture House was demolished. It was also by *Anderson*. Mention should also be made of two excellent factories to the E, just off Balfour Road: the former WEBB factory with a grand nine-and-a-half bay frontage of 1896–7 in Bunting Street by *Mosley & Anderson*, topped by Dutch gables, the façade divided by stone-faced rusticated pilasters with paterae, including the familiar rose of Anderson, with wide segmental arches between them and the centre, and a large carved stone plaque with shields and the coat of arms of the firm and the Borough of Northampton; and in Arthur Street, opposite, the former MILLER LAST CO. factory (Rushton Ablett), originally three storeys and a basement, built 1896. It has a tall, rather stark Neoclassical tower by *Alexander Anderson* with the date 1903 within circular motifs at the top and clasping buttresses ending in flat-topped turrets. Later additions 1905 and 1910 by *Brown & Mayor*.

NORTH-EAST

ST MATTHEW, Kettering Road. 1891–3 by *Matthew Holding*. Big and prosperous and as good an example of Late Victorian as one could wish to see; when seen from the E with apse and spire the church looks good enough for Pearson, with whom Holding had recently been working (*see also* St Mary Far Cotton, p. 478). Brown Kingsthorpe stone, cut into small regular blocks, a manner much used by Holding, with Bath stone dressings. Asymmetrically placed NW tower with a stone spire 170 ft (52 metres) high added in 1895. Transepts, flèche, polygonal apse. Tall proportions, lancet windows and windows with plate tracery. The S porch continues the W front. The fine spacious interior is all in white Bath stone. Stone-vaulted chancel and apse. The nave not vaulted but with a timber roof on big diaphragm arches pierced with quatrefoils. Many contemporary furnishings which are as much a memorial to Holding as to Pickering Phipps in that Holding began his architectural career under Charles Buckeridge and on Buckeridge's death in 1873 was taken into the practice of J. L. Pearson just at the point when Pearson was working on Truro Cathedral. – PULPIT and FONT, of alabaster, by *W. Aumonier*. – REREDOS. Added 1895 by *Nathaniel Hitch* with the structure by *Robert Davison*. In 1887 Hitch had provided the reredos for Truro Cathedral for Pearson and one wonders whether Holding had seen Hitch's work while in Pearson's office. – FONT RAIL and CHANCEL SCREEN, ironwork by *G. R. de Wilde*. Also added in 1895. The font rail especially fine with lily finials. – TRIPTYCH, N chapel, by *C. E. Buckeridge*. – The church is a veritable gallery of STAINED GLASS and all of fine quality. It is arranged in a deliberate pattern and was gradually inserted up to the early C20. The apse windows with Apostles are by *Clayton & Bell*, 1890. – W window with Old Testament figures is by *Burlison & Grylls*, 1910. – S transept two windows forming a Jesse window by *Kempe*, 1911. – N chapel (Lady Chapel) and

N and S aisle windows by *Alexander Hymers*, 1899. – Baptistery windows, appropriately with children, by *Pownall*, 1908. – A N transept window by *Percy Bacon*, 1913. – In the porch four figures also by *Hymers*, 1902. But much more important the contributions of the late C20 and C21. – SCULPTURE. *Henry Moore*'s famous Northampton Madonna. Made of Hornton stone in 1944 for Dean Walter Hussey, then vicar of St Matthew. Dean Hussey shortly after commissioned a PAINTING as well: *Graham Sutherland*'s Crucifixion. This was unveiled in 1946. The Moore is in the N transept, the large Sutherland in the S transept. The Moore is as peaceful as the Sutherland is violent. Sutherland must have been deeply impressed by Grünewald's Isenheim Altar. Background mauve, squarish shapes, to the l. and r. of the feet of Christ brick-colour. As for Moore's Madonna, the subtle way should be observed in which the colour variations and the veining of the stone have been used. In May 1944 Eric Newton wrote in the *Architectural Review* about the Madonna: 'She is not part of an art-revival but a stage in evolution. Therefore, a century hence, whatever may have happened to Christianity, she will have lost none of her potency. She will be seen as an example not of Henry Moore's sculpture but of a deep seriousness somehow inherent in the mid-twentieth century.' His statement holds good.* To these two impressive works have been added: the STATIONS OF THE CROSS, terracotta by *David Thomas*; a hanging CHRIST figure by *Malcolm Pollard*; and a bronze almost life-size STATUE OF ST MATTHEW, 2009 by *Ian Rank-Broadley*, a worthy addition to the collection. The VICARAGE is also by *Holding*, built 1903.

ST MICHAEL, St Michael's Mount. 1882 by *George Vialls*, who was born in Northampton. Brick, in the lancet style. Only a thin SW turret but wide lower transepts (two bays wide), with two groups of stepped lancets and a rose window over. The brickwork shows inside as well. Open interior without pillars. The roof part coved and part wagon vaulted. – STAINED GLASS. Chancel E, upper part, *Percy Bacon*, 1919. Lower part, Choirs of Angels, *Heaton, Butler & Bayne* (design by *H. Lonsdale*), 1882. – CHURCH BUILDINGS behind are 1891 by *Charles Dorman*.

Former MANFIELD HOSPITAL, Kettering Road. Now subdivided into apartments. A substantial mansion begun for the shoe manufacturer Sir Philip Manfield by *Charles Dorman*, 1899–1902. Jacobean, with a large r. gable. Porch with heavy strapwork above. Inside, a staircase with lavish screen and large stained glass window. On the frontage the CYNTHIA SPENCER HOME of 1976, extended 1985. The grounds now built over with housing.

PERAMBULATION. The starting point is ABINGTON SQUARE with the WAR MEMORIAL. 1937–8 by *Sir John Brown & Henson*. Memorial loggia. Light brick, the slim circular piers faced with

---

*I am grateful to Tim Llewellyn for alerting me to this quotation.

gold mosaic. Long seat against the back wall and above this inscriptions. Set within the garden the MOBBS MEMORIAL, 1921 by *Sir Alfred Turner*, removed here from the Market Square in 1937. Edgar Mobbs (1882–1917) was a rugby football player who captained Northampton and England. He was initially turned down to fight in the First World War and formed his own 'sportsman's battalion' (known as Mobbs Own) for the Northamptonshire Regiment. The memorial is in the form of a stone cenotaph topped by a standing figure of Fame with a bust of Mobbs below. On each side are plaques showing a rugby match and soldiers fighting, all these in bronze. At the front of the garden the *Doulton* terracotta STATUE of Charles Bradlaugh, M.P., by *Tinworth*, 1894. On the S side of the Square the tall range built for Yardes, seed producers, 1901 by *Alexander Anderson* with plant forms above the second-floor windows, and the former ABINGTON SQUARE MISSION CHURCH (now Urban Tiger) of 1878 by *H. H. Dyer*, and not in his usual Gothic manner but classical. Big pediment with a large round arch below, under which are three round-headed arched windows. Side features with lower arches and two-light windows. The entrance altered.

KETTERING ROAD runs NE with on the S side rather stranded on a traffic island the former UNITARIAN CHURCH, 1896 by *Charles Dorman*. Geometric Gothic with an asymmetrically placed turret topped by a spire. Brick with stone dressings. Hall attached on the r. A typical Nonconformist design. On the W side, just beyond the junction, is ST MICHAEL'S ROAD, one of a series of streets in this area developed in the 1870s and 1880s where terraces of houses are interspersed with the occasional shoe factory. Of special note here are, at the W end at the junction of Overstone Road, the former G. T. HAWKINS FACTORY of 1886, and about halfway along on the S side, the 1902 factory of R. E. TRICKER, still in production. The brown ceramic brick frontage with large windows on two floors with attractive glazing and small coloured foliate shapes was added in 1924 by *E. R. Baretrop*. On the same side the elaborate rusticated brick façade of the former UNION CHURCH (Jen Yen Temple) of 1886 by *S. J. Newman*. Continuing in Kettering Road there follows, on the W side, QUEENS GROVE METHODIST CHURCH of 1879. Reactionary. Red and yellow brick. Arched, i.e. Italian or Romanesque, windows. Sides with two tiers. Front with triple doorways and five arched windows above under a pediment. At the side two rather starved towers with pyramidal roofs. Just above in GROVE ROAD the remains of the façade of a cinema, 1912 by *F. H. Allen*. On the next corner, the former QUEENS ROAD METHODIST CHURCH of 1887 by *H. H. Dyer & Son*, whose façade was savagely maltreated when the premises were converted into a shop (Jones Furnishers). The side elevation still has its Geometrical Gothic windows. Considerably further, on the W side, the former KETTERING ROAD SCHOOL (Northamptonshire Music & Performing Arts Centre). The original school of 1878 is by *Bland & Cossins* of Birmingham (that is *J. G. Bland*) and basically Gothic with some 1890s additions at either end in a more typical Board School manner. Subsidiary entrance with Jacobethan wooden arcading. Further along, still on the W side, is MOUNT PLEASANT CHURCH of 1887 by *H. H. Dyer & Son* in a Late Perp style. Elaborate doorway and large six-light window above. On the E side, set back in St Michael's Mount, behind St Michael's church (*see* above), in Perry Street, the factory of one of Northampton's most important shoe manufacturers, CROCKETT & JONES. 1889, in a broad Renaissance manner by *Charles Dorman*.* Attached to it the main factory of 1910, Northampton's first steel frame factory.

Back in Kettering Road we arrive shortly at the RACE-COURSE, one of Northampton's fine open spaces. Some races were held here in the C17 but the course did not become official till 1737. The last race was held in 1910. The park held army camps in the First and Second World Wars and was finally brought back as a public space in 1953. The original STAND building survives, having been reconditioned and extended in 1930 by *Law & Harris*. On the E side of Kettering Road, just S of Abington Avenue, the remains of the façade of the 1912 PICTUREDROME cinema (now a café) by *F. H. Allen*, the dreamchild of a local stonemason, *Charles Robinson*, who built it. A detour to the E into ABINGTON AVENUE past the NEW JERUSALEM CHURCH (built for the Swedenborgian faction) of 1890, again by *H. H. Dyer & Son*, in Perp style, to the corner with HOLLY ROAD, for the intriguing No. 19 by *Mosley & Anderson*, 1895, with a rounded front and a pyramid roof. Side elevations with decorative entrance and gables. In HOLLY ROAD, a nice example of an 1890s street with houses all having canted bays, is a curiosity, HOLLY COTTAGE, 1892, halfway along on the E side. The humble terrace house given sculptured ornamentation by its builder and owner, *John Brown*, who worked on the Guildhall. The Prodigal Son over the doorway. Back in Kettering Road and heading N the E side is EAST PARK PARADE, quite a fine terrace of tall three-storey houses begun in the mid 1860s but mostly after 1880. The styles vary and get more varied as one moves N. In the centre, for example, Nos. 36–41 are a group of stone-fronted houses with pillared porches, then others have half-timbered gables and others have balconies. An especially grand stone-built house at the end, on the corner of Abington Grove (No. 58), with two bays under arches beneath a shaped gable.

Opposite, on the corner of Kettering Road and Kingsley Road, THE WHITE ELEPHANT pub, of 1883 (originally the

*A little SE of St Michael's church, at the corner of Whitworth Road and Adnitt Road, the CONSERVATIVE CLUB of 1892–4 by *Charles Dorman*, celebrated in the 1973 edition of this guide as 'one of the best examples of the early Norman Shaw style in Northampton'. Alas, it has been revamped and reglazed in a totally banal way and reduced to a travesty of its former self.

Kingsley Park Hotel but because of its site nobody believed it would prosper, hence its nickname). On the opposite corner of the RACECOURSE a former TRAM SHELTER, which, though looking Victorian, is of 1923–4 by *David Rowell & Co.* To the NW along KINGSLEY ROAD some good Late Victorian and Edwardian villas, even more mixed in manner than East Park Parade. The row includes No. 32, a grand red brick Renaissance façade dated 1884; No. 34, Neo-Georgian of two storeys, five bays and a bay window; and a nice group, Nos. 36–40, with Gothic details and cast-iron porches. To the SW, on the N side of the Racecourse, runs ST GEORGE'S AVENUE which begins with another grand terrace of 1880s houses (Nos. 106–128). Further W are Maidwell and Newton, part of the campus of the UNIVERSITY (*see* p. 461). Parallel with the E section of St George's Avenue is HOMESTEAD WAY with the BETHANY HOMESTEAD, a series of almshouses founded in 1924 with plans by *F. H. Allen* 1925–7. Later buildings by the same in the 1930s. The style is domestic, mildly Neo-Georgian, with rows with verandas, bays and some half-timbered gables.

Back on Kettering Road, to the NE is PHIPPSVILLE, a spacious well-to-do suburb built up slowly from the 1880s in a variety of styles and an appropriate setting for St Matthew's church (*see* above). Good examples in COLLINGWOOD ROAD and in THE DRIVE. On the corner of The Drive, facing St Matthew's, a good *c.* 1920 Arts and Crafts type house, brick, tall chimney and tiled roof, and No. 11, WESTBROOK, handsome formal brick Neo-Georgian with a slightly asymmetric façade, 1905 by *Walter Shaw.* Nos. 1–3 The Drive are probably by *Holding.* No. 5 was *c.* 1920 the home of W. J. Bassett-Lowke's brother-in-law, Frank Jones, and he commissioned a copy of the *Mackintosh* 78 Derngate dining room décor for the sitting room of this house. It survives, a slightly larger room than the Derngate room but with the same glazed cupboards, fireplace and wall lanterns. Opposite St Matthew's church in Kettering Road is KINGSLEY PARK METHODIST CHURCH of 1886 by *H. H. Dyer* in a mixed Gothic manner. Big circular Perp traceried window in the façade, otherwise some lancets and some Geometric windows. S transept window, a memorial to H. H. Dyer, moved from Queens Road Methodist church when that was closed.

There is now little to detain the viewer until after the junction with Park Avenue. Just SE of this, on the corner of BROADMEAD AVENUE, BAPTIST CHURCH, of 1932–4 by *F. H. Allen.* The present building was designed as the church hall and the church itself was never built. Plans in hand for a new church (2012). Beyond this, in Kettering Road, on the E side of the hill, is the SPINNEY HILL HOTEL, a good mid-1930s essay. Central block with small pavilions all with green tiled roofs. Probably by *Lawson Carter.* Again very little of note until the former Manfield Hospital complex (*see* above). Nearby on the main road one or two pleasant houses of *c.* 1900 with half-timbering.

EAST

ST PETER AND ST PAUL, Abington Park. Of *c.* 1200 the lower parts of the W tower, the S doorway and the chancel. The tower is stone and unbuttressed. Some blocked original windows. Plain one-step tower arch. The bell-stage is Perp (two-light bell-openings with transom). Simple S doorway, the arch with two flat steps. In the chancel N wall small lancet. The nave had aisles, but these were ripped out in 1821 after a storm had damaged the church, and a wide ceiled nave was created. Large windows with pointed arches and bar tracery. The rebuilding 1824–6 was done by *Charles Squirhill*. The aisles formerly continued into side chapels. They survive, with their W arches in line with the arch of the chancel, which survives in its medieval form with tall square-headed Dec windows on its side walls. The E window must be 1820s. A faculty of 1874 records some adjustment of furnishings, such as the lowering of the height of the sounding board of the pulpit. *Matthew Holding* did a partial restoration in 1897 when the baptistery was created at the base of the tower. The churchyard walls and ironwork are almost certainly his. VESTRY added in 1938 by *L. T. Moore*. – Perp SEDILIA (damaged). – FONT. Octagonal, Perp, the stem with blank tracery panelling, the bowl with quatrefoils, a rosette, a large leaf, etc. – FONT COVER. Octagonal, spire-shaped, with crockets up the angles. – PULPIT. A splendid piece of *c.* 1700, as richly carved in the Gibbons style and with as large a tester as that of any Wren church in the City of London. – COMMUNION RAIL. Of *c.* 1700, with dumb-bell balusters. – WEST GALLERY. Of *c.* 1938. – Splendid carved ROYAL ARMS above, of *c.* 1660. – STAINED GLASS. Chancel E, 1860 by *Heaton & Butler*. – S aisle, 1990 by *Monastery Glass*. – N chapel E window by *Patrick Reyntiens & John Piper*, 1982. More pictorial than much of their other work and therefore less remarkable. – MONUMENTS. Brass to William Mayle †1536. Only the piece with the daughters survives (chancel floor). – Two tomb-chests with black marble tops, to Sir Edmund Hampden †1627 and Dame Elinor Hampden †1634 (N chapel). – Sir Robert Bernard †1666, attributed to *Joshua Marshall* (GF). – William Thursby, 1730 by *Samuel Cox* (S chapel). Stiffly standing in barrister's robes below a bald-acchino; Ionic pilasters l. and r. – Downhall Thursby, 1733, also by *Samuel Cox*. Tablet with bust at the top in an open pediment. – Several other tablets to the Bernards and Thursbys, including the familiar pyramid type by the *Coxes*.

CHRIST CHURCH, Wellingborough Road. Begun in 1904–6 by *Matthew Holding*, completed by *E. de W. Holding*. Designs produced 1913 but only finished in 1925 because of the war, under the direction of *Charles Dorman*. Of small, regularly cut ironstone blocks. The style is the lavish Decorated of *c.* 1300. E end with transepts two bays wide. Chancel with S chapel. The W end was never completed. It was to have one more bay and a big W tower. – STAINED GLASS. All the glass is by *A. K. Nicholson* notably the E window of 1930.

ST ALBAN, Broadmead Avenue. By *William Randoll Blacking*, one of his last buildings, consecrated in 1938. Brick, mildly Tudor, with a s tower close to the w end. Whitewashed inside. Square piers and unmoulded arches, no capitals or other moulding between pier and arch. – SCREEN. With classical columns, wide open.

ST GREGORY (R.C.), Park Avenue North. Incomplete. 1952–4 by *J. S. Comper*. Brick, Neo-Byzantine. Entered by a triple arcade with rose window above. Basilica plan with arcades of five round arches on stone Corinthian chamfered columns. Simple limewashed interior with a wide apse. – STATIONS OF THE CROSS. *Anthony Foster*, acquired 1957. STATUE OF THE VIRGIN. By *J. S. Comper* based on a medieval French original. – STATUE OF ST GREGORY. *Michael Royde-Smith* 1959. (Interestingly both Foster and Royde-Smith were pupils of Eric Gill.) The original plan was a larger church with nine bay arcades and sacristy etc. The present SACRISTY is 1980–81 by *Seely & Paget*.

CONGREGATIONAL CHURCH, Victoria Road. 1888 by *Matthew Holding*. Large façade of brick and stone with Decorated Gothic windows set within an enclosing arch. Spired turrets on either side. STAINED GLASS. In the transepts two large windows by *Percy Bacon*, 1919 and 1929. Porch windows by *H. A. Hymers*, 1906–7.

UNITED REFORMED CHURCH (former Congregational), Abington Avenue. 1910 by *E. R. Sutton & F. W. C. Gregory* of Nottingham. Entirely C. of E. in style. Ironstone, the same small regular blocks which Holding used. SW tower. The STAINED GLASS in the E window is by *Sir Frank Brangwyn*, 1921 and made by *P. Turpin & Co*. It illustrates the removal of Christ's body from the Cross. Crossley Davis in the *Architectural Review*, August 1921, fittingly says: 'There is a strength about the memorial window which compels attention . . . It is an epic in stained glass.' The interior, which has Bath stone arcades and a hammerbeam roof, was handsomely reordered into auditorium form by *SDS Designs (Jane Stapleton)* in 2003–4. The SCHOOL alongside is by *C. Dorman*, 1900.

METHODIST CHURCH, Park Avenue. 1923–4 by *George Baines & Son*, brick, in a free fancy Gothic, typical of Baines. Asymmetrically placed tower, flèche, lively skyline. The same firm added church rooms in 1932.

BAPTIST CHURCH, Adnitt Road. 1898–9 by *Mosley & Anderson*. Quite small, Gothic of brick but now rendered. SCHOOL of 1936 by *F. H. Allen* in Lea Road.

GENERAL CEMETERY, Billing Road. Planned 1846–7 by *Marnock* of Regents Park Gardens. It originally had a mock Norman chapel but this has been demolished and the site largely cleared. Close to where it stood is the one remarkable MEMORIAL, a sorrowing horse sculpture by *Charles Robinson* of Kettering to the memory of Sir Robert Fossett †1922, circus owner, erected 1923. The inscription states 'He has pulled in for his last rest'.

GENERAL HOSPITAL, Billing Road. The original main building, plain Neoclassical, is of 1793. The architect was *Samuel Saxon*. Nineteen bays and three storeys, ashlar-faced. The rhythm is 3–5–3–5–3, with a three-bay pediment over the centre. Below this on the first and second floors are arched windows on short columns. Wing to the r. 1887–9, to the l. 1891–2. Amongst the later additions are the Barratt Maternity Home 1936 (*see* p. 451), Nurses' Home 1939, Outpatients Department 1959, all by *Sir John Brown & Henson*, in brick in the Modern style. The Pathology Laboratory by the *Oxford Regional Hospital Board's Architect's Department*, 1968, the Cripps Medical Centre by *Cartwright, Woollatt & Partners*, 1969. Nurses' Home, Cliftonville, by the *Oxford Regional Hospital Board*, 1971. A new main building complex was built in Cliftonville in 1979.

ST ANDREW'S HOSPITAL, Billing Road. The first part, by *James Milne*, 1837, is of Bath stone, nearly a quadrangle and utilitarian in its details. Corridor 14 ft (4.3 metres) wide and 60 ft (18.3 metres) long. Impressive *c.* 1900 staircase and hall on the first floor. Separate CHAPEL to the r., Gothic, by *G. G. Scott*, completed in 1863. STAINED GLASS. Two windows by *Burlison & Grylls* 1895, 1897. Beyond the chapel first ISHAM HOUSE by *Gotch, Saunders & Surridge*, 1971–2, an attractive long range, of two storeys, broken up by projecting windows, stairs and a lift tower. Broad horizontal stone bands. Aluminium-covered roof, slightly sloping, with excrescences of various shapes. Then CHAPLAIN'S HOUSE (behind Isham House), a thatched Regency *cottage orné*; WANTAGE HOUSE, 1924–7 by *Law, Harris & Croft*, who also designed at the same time the E pair of LODGES on Billing Road; and GLOUCESTER HOUSE (Recreational Centre), 1962 by *Saxon Snell & Phillips*. To this is added, approached by a covered way, a social centre, TOMPKINS HOUSE, by *Gotch, Saunders & Surridge*, 1972. A further block also by *Gotch, Saunders & Surridge*, 1983. The site spreads S and in 2010 absorbed a former school site in Cliftonville Road and this now (2011) has a vast Neo-Georgian building, WILLIAM WAKE HOUSE by *Robert Adam Architects*. It is best described as a huge country house montage using elements deriving from C18, Adam, Soane, etc. which, though symmetrically arranged, somehow end up in a rather confusing array. It is splendidly built and fitted out and once landscaped with its gatepiers and entrance will be as impressive as Castle Howard.

Former ST EDMUND'S HOSPITAL, Wellingborough Road. The workhouse of 1837 by *G. G. Scott*. Brick, classical, cruciform plan, with pedimented façade (derelict 2013). Rear portions already partly demolished and replaced by flats.

THREE SHIRES HOSPITAL, Cliftonville. 1981 by *Gotch, Saunders & Surridge*.

NORTHAMPTON SCHOOL FOR BOYS, former Grammar School, Billing Road. 1911 by *H. Norman* and *A. McKewan*. Its original building still very much in evidence. Two-storeyed, of brick, symmetrical with central block and canted wings. Grammar school Renaissance style. Impressive recent buildings. To the l. the Cripps Centre, with theatre and teaching rooms. A handsome essay in varied brick of 1999 by *Peter Haddon & Partners*. Behind the original block and linked to it by an atrium is the Concourse & Teaching Block, 2005–7, also by Peter Haddon & Partners. Most impressive two-storey interior with a series of interlinking spaces and much use of American red oak cladding. Sports hall of 2003 by *Stimpson Walton Bond*. Opposite the School for Boys, the half-timbered gabled former SCHOOL HOUSE. It was originally built in 1901 by *Josiah Mander*, surveyor to the Overstone Estate. In the 1970s it was converted and extended to form apartments.

Three tolerable examples of BOARD SCHOOLS off Wellingborough Road are: SE off St Edmund's Road and Stockley Street, VERNON TERRACE PRIMARY SCHOOL, 1874 by *G. E. Bland* of Birmingham, and 1887, 1894; lancet Gothic and a tiny bellcote; further E, on the N side, STIMPSON AVENUE SCHOOL, 1893–4 and 1899 by *Charles Dorman*; brick and stone in a broad Jacobean style, quite large with lots of gables and an elegant cupola; and on the S side, further E, BARRY ROAD SCHOOL, 1902 by *Sidney Harris* of *Law & Harris*. Brick in a rather plain Renaissance manner. Rather charming, at each end of the blocks, half-octagonal low turrets with hexagonal tops. Its SWIMMING POOL, Covington Street, is of 1904 by *Edmund Law* with an Italianate gable.

ABINGTON ABBEY (now MUSEUM). Formerly the manor house and still, despite being in a public park, having something of a country air. The estate had belonged to the Bernards since the C15. The hall survives from John Bernard's time, and he had inherited in 1496 and died in 1508. The Bernards sold in 1669 to William Thursby, a lawyer of Middle Temple, and he in the later 1670s rebuilt the W cross-wing and added a further suite of rooms onto the S side. In 1736, by marriage, it went to the Harveys of Warwickshire, who assumed the extra name of Thursby. It was the first John Harvey Thursby who in the late 1730s refashioned the S range and rebuilt that to the E using the *Smiths* of Warwick as architects. In 1841 the estate was bought by Lewis Loyd of Overstone who let it for a period to the progressive medic Thomas Prichard for use as a mental institution, when it was rechristened 'Abbey'. Loyd's granddaughter, Lady Wantage, presented the park and the house to the town of Northampton in 1897, when the house became a museum.

The S range is of before the Reformation. Hall with thin hammerbeam roof (some timbers renewed in 1951). To the courtyard tall four-light mullioned windows, one in the hall proper, one in the big square bay, part of the alterations of the 1670s. In the windows fragments of early C16 heraldic glass relating to the Bernard family, which therefore dates from the building of the Hall. A blocked doorway with its four-centred head, visible in the courtyard, marks the axis of the screens passage, and openings to the service rooms to the E are still in the wall, Gothicized in the C19. Good stone fireplace of *c.* 1740. At the same time the S façade, built by Thursby, was given new fenestration and the E range rebuilt. There are dates of 1738 (S) and 1743 (E). The architect was *Francis Smith* of Warwick together with his brother *William.* The S front has square projections in the middle and at the ends. Broad arched doorway with rusticated surround and rusticated pilasters, all of the 1670s. The lobby between the façade and the Hall Gothic with a plaster vault. Another vault in the bay window. These date from *c.* 1760–70 and attributed to *Hiorne* of Warwick. In the spandrels of the entrance screen, two glass roundels with Labours of the Months, of *c.* 1500. The E front of eleven bays with three-bay pediment and typical of the Smiths. As for the other rooms, the staircase with turned balusters is of the 1670s, and the Oak Room has plenty of panelling, of *c.* 1500. Mostly linenfold panels with many rustic scenes and heraldry. One especially fine shield of the Bernards. Probably all from the Hall screen.

The essence of the PARK still survives, though bisected by the busy Park Avenue. Some humps and hollows, immediately across the road to the SE of the church, mark the site of the village, removed by Thursby. Below to the E a series of former terraced fishponds have been variously landscaped. To the N, a TOWER, recorded as being dated 1678. A dovecote above, and a well below, which was served by a waterwheel, and originally supplied water for the house. It was contrived almost certainly by *Samuel Warren* of Weston Favell, who had a considerable reputation at the time for such mechanics (*see* Introduction, p. 49). Remains of an eyecatcher ARCHWAY towards Weston Favell, *c.* 1820. KEEPER'S COTTAGE (once the Rectory) to the W of the house, C17, thatched, altered later, and to its N a Victorian cast-iron BANDSTAND.

PERAMBULATIONS

1. Wellingborough Road to Billing Road

WELLINGBOROUGH ROAD has little to offer until it arrives at the former St Edmund's Hospital. Worth a glance in PALMERSTON ROAD, on the W side of the churchyard of the former St Edmund's church,* PALMERSTON COURT, a respectable 1990s housing development of red brick with blue and yellow brick dressings picking up ideas from the former SHOE FACTORY opposite. Three storeys and seven bays, red brick with yellow brick pilasters and window lintels. Just below and doubtless by the same builder, two charming houses with Gothic doorways and pedimented windows, again all in red, yellow and blue brick, with a band of black-and-white diamonds. The fenestration sadly altered in one of them.

---

*ST EDMUND, 1850–1 by *Vickers & Hugall,* additions by *Holding,* 1882 was demolished in 1980.

Back in Wellingborough Road, further E on the N side is the former ST EDMUND'S MISSION HALL of 1886 by *Matthew Holding* in his best Tudor vernacular manner. Stone built with half-timbered gables and bargeboards. Some way further E is STIMPSON AVENUE. As well as the school (*see* above), opposite, a small fragment, just the porch, left from the former FACTORY of Green & Co. originally built 1897 by *Alexander Anderson* and added to and altered by him 1911–13, now converted to residential; and on its N side, in ADNITT ROAD, is the former SEARS SHOE FACTORY of 1891, extended 1912–13 also by *Anderson*. Quite grand with nine bays in three floors divided by brick pilasters. Doorway with Ionic pilasters, banded pilasters at the sides and an ornamental gable above. Nearby a curiosity in MONKS PARK ROAD: on the corner of Florence Road a charming vernacular house of stone, render and half-timbered gable, with a fragment of high stone wall and an ironwork gate. This was the LODGE of Monks Park Hall, built 1895 by *Charles Dorman*. The Hall, an 1830s house with later additions, stood to the N in Monks Hall Road, but has been demolished. Returning to Wellingborough Road, in BARRY ROAD, opposite the school (*see* above), the remains of the former CO-OPERATIVE FACTORY and Steam Bakery of 1912 by *Alexander Anderson*. Just the tall factory façade with brick and stone pilasters with scrolled tops. Projecting sections of cornice. Canopied doorway and a big name plaque at the S end. Further E in Wellingborough Road, on the S side, is DEVON PARADE, a long elegant terrace dated 1900. Uniform houses of three storeys, canted bays and small pediments on the bays and over the doorways. A little E and we have arrived at the Christchurch area, which is much better explored as part of Abington (see Perambulation 2).

As a small addendum, one of Northampton's early footpaths, doubtless of medieval origin, ran from St Giles's churchyard to Abington, along what became ST EDMUND'S ROAD, then across the series of streets from Vernon Street through to Collins Street. Its route is still partly preserved by a series of passages (jitties) cut through the terraces. From there it disappears although Christchurch Road more or less picks up the route.

Between Wellingborough Road and Billing Road to the S an area of streets with housing of the late C19 and early C20 which now has some of the best examples of terraces interspersed with factories and the occasional chapel or school, reflecting the expansion of the town during the flourishing years of the boot and shoe industry.

BILLING ROAD is one of the most rewarding roads in the town with a rich variety of Victorian terraces of an almost consistently good quality. While only an occasional building is of great note the general effect is highly enjoyable. At the junction with York Road, a good example of a brick house of *c.* 1890 almost certainly by *Matthew Holding*. Holding's father built *c.* 1880 the red brick row which forms the E side of YORK ROAD, N of the junction, and Matthew is credited with the charming carved heads decorating the bays. Opposite, backing onto St Giles's churchyard, a pretty Regency and Victorian cottage type row, some houses with later alterations. Back in Billing Road, the main terraces are now all on the N side. Some (Nos. 2–7) of mixed designs, then the other side of Denmark Road Nos. 10–13 red brick and stone Gothic dated 1871, an early pair. There follows a long three-storey row of yellow brick, all 1880s. The General Hospital complex on the S side includes the c. 1870 Dispensary jutting onto the pavement edge.

CLIFTONVILLE, S of Billing Road, was designed as an expensive suburb and built up from c. 1845 but only partially completed. At the corner of Cliftonville on the E side NINE SPRINGS (now called Oxford House), 1864 Neoclassical, and on the W, BEAUMONT, a large c. 1860 Italianate mansion with a tower by *William Hull*, now part of the Hospital and shorn of some of its decoration. Further S, SUNNYSIDE, dated 1865, Tudor Gothic, with elaborate conservatory at the side and four less inspiring villas. No. 43 Cliftonville Road is by *Holding*. Some good houses in the tile-hung Norman Shaw manner E of this in THE AVENUE, laid out by *Holding*, 1880–2. Back on Billing Road, on the N side No. 30, originally named Ivy Tower, is elaborate Gothic of 1863, with a tower over the porch. Gothic details inside as well. It was built for William Shoosmith, the Town Clerk. ADDISON VILLAS (Nos. 34–35 and 36–38) are by *Holding*, 1880. Three storeys with projecting bays and balconies with stucco garlands, Neo-Queen Anne. No. 39 is striped polychrome yellow and red brick, and No. 40, dated 1869, more polychrome brick with two projecting bays which squash its pointed roof turret between them. No. 41 in dour Gothic was designed as the vicarage for St Edmund's church. Then, past the crossroads, come ST MARTIN'S VILLAS, brick with stone dressings, Gothic, of 1865, and important as the work of *E. W. Godwin*. Sculptured panels over the doorways and odd rectangular windows on the top floor. Opposite was Godwin's RHEINFELDEN, a formidable, rather Germanic Gothic red brick villa of 1876–7, now replaced by 1970s flats. Other good Victorian rows follow, notably Nos. 45–49 of yellow brick, once known as Lyveden Terrace, all two storeys, some with bays, and dating from c. 1850–60. On the opposite side the main gates of St Andrew's Hospital (*see* Churches and Public Buildings).

2. *Abington*

The Perambulation proceeds anticlockwise around Abington Park (*see* Abington Abbey, above). At the NW corner of the park ARCHWAY COTTAGES, two symmetrical sets of late 1670s cottages with dormers and mullioned windows connected by an arch which now leads down to a courtyard with other later cottages. It was originally designed as the entrance to Thurs-

by's park. W of the cottages, in ABINGTON AVENUE, tucked
in behind on the S side, LOYD ALMSHOUSES, 1846 by *E. F.
Law*, Tudor style, symmetrical, yellow and grey stone, with
gables and dormers. The E extension of Abington Avenue, just
before it unites with the Wellingborough Road, on the corner
of Woodland Avenue, THANET, a splendid example of *Alexander Anderson*'s work. Built *c.* 1910 it has three gables, two held
by large S scrolls. Pretty hooded doorcase with string garlands.
At the end of the garden a fine motor house with a lavish half-
timbered gable and a veranda, added in 1912. Back along
Abington Avenue to the W is the COUNTY GROUND, home
since 1885 of the County Cricket Club. Impressive Indoor
Cricket School, 1997–8 by *Gotch, Saunders & Surridge*. White
and silver, the curved roof held by eleven steel columns. N in
PARK AVENUE NORTH, above the Methodist church (*see* p.
469), on the corner of Ashburnham Road, STONEHENGE,
1906, by *Alexander Anderson*, with a rounded corner decorated
with Ionic columns topped by urns. Deep cornice and a porch
on the side elevation with a large sundial.

Back to WELLINGBOROUGH ROAD and moving SW, a
rather good early C20 terrace of houses opposite the park with
half timbered gables and canopied porches, No. 425 at the
corner of Wantage Road having a charming octagonal bay
topped by a pyramid. At the corner of Roseholm Road, THE
ABINGTON (formerly Abington Park Hotel), 1898 by *Matthew
Holding*, brick and stone with lavish French Renaissance detail
and especially fine gabled skyline, *à la* Waddesdon. Then opposite Christ Church the MANFIELD FACTORY, 1890–2 by
Charles Dorman, long, low and symmetrical, one to two storeys,
brick, Tudor style, with mullioned-and-transomed windows
and gables with Dutch C17 decoration. The works were all on
one floor, an advanced system of production for its date. Now
converted into residential and a restaurant.

Back to Abington Park along CHRISTCHURCH ROAD, with
on the S side the long classical ranges of the former CO-
OPERATIVE FACTORY, 1920 by *L. G. Ekins* of the Co-operative Wholesale Society. Quite a grand conception in pale
and purple brick. Eleven bays with a central entrance
with coupled Doric columns and a sort of Venetian window
feature above. Original walls with brick pillars and rails.
Another façade in Ardington Road with rusticated pilasters
with odd drop features at the top. Two storeys with three in
the centre with bracketed windows supporting the next foor
windows and those above with carved aprons. Just below in
ARDINGTON ROAD, on the corner of King Edward Road, a
doctor's SURGERY and PHARMACY complex, 1994 by *Bundie
& Rogers*. An interesting group. The main building has a
tower on the corner with a flat mortar-board cap and four
small square openings. The upper floor fully glazed. Yellow
brick ground floor with angled sides. Another building behind
has two similar towers with a big curved glazed bow between
them.

Back in Christchurch Road and moving E, opposite the park, a garden suburb was planned in the early 1900s. The architect was *Alexander Anderson*. Only a few houses were built at the time. In Sandringham Road two of the most delightful, THE COTTAGE and THE BUNGALOW, descriptions which if one is honest fit neither! They were both built 1905–6. In Christchurch Road are No. 38, THE NOOK, and occupying a corner site, HILLCREST, both with Anderson's distinctive lettering and on Hillcrest his favourite rose patera. Anderson himself lived in this house for some years. There are other small remnants of the project along Christchurch Road (Nos. 50 and 52) and also a house on PARK AVENUE SOUTH (No. 55). A little S on the E side is No. 10, ARMIDALE, a splendid example of 1928 by *John Brown*. Gabled with a canted bay, delightful coloured glass and grapevine-bordered name plaque and sundial. Other typical 1920s and 1930s houses follow, No. 6 being a timbered and tiled essay in the Grimms' *Fairy Tales* mode. Massive timber porch.

From Park Avenue South, the route moves NE round ABINGTON PARK CRESCENT. Set back behind the houses, ST CHRISTOPHER'S (care home), the former rectory, is by *E. F. Law*, 1846, yellow and white stone, Italianate, with low-pitched roofs. More recent extensions. Abington Park Crescent received its houses mostly in the first quarter of the C20. A number of them are pleasant to look at, notably Nos. 22 by *W. W. Webster*, 1932, a typical essay in white rendered horizontal shapes. It originally had a flat roof. There is an instructive variety of styles in this area. A short detour into WESTON WAY reveals some cottagey and half-timbered essays of the early C20. Just E, THE HOMESTEAD (No. 6) is a joyous example, thatched with a nice use of ironstone and timbering. It was designed in 1924 by *E. de W. Holding* and made the pages of the *Ideal Home* magazine. Back on the corner of Abington Park Crescent, No. 61 is a nice example of the mid-1930s Arts and Crafts manner with its varied roofs and small spire over the porch. Bays with decorative panels, good brick detailing, and a tall chimneystack which bisects the front façade. It was built by the Northampton builder *H. A. Glenn* for himself. Following Abington Park Crescent N into WELLINGBOROUGH ROAD, and moving W, is ADELAIDE HOUSE, careful Neo-Georgian by *Brown & Henson*, 1937–8. Two tones of red brick, angle pilasters, three bays and two storeys with an attic in a mansard roof. Pretty fanlight doorcase. On the N side of the road, set back off Norman Road in Taylor Avenue, is ABINGTON LODGE, *c.* 1840, ironstone, faintly Tudor, formerly a farmhouse of the Wantage (Overstone) Estate.

A number of sensible Edwardian houses follow but by far the most important house is NEW WAYS, No. 508 Wellingborough Road, designed by *Peter Behrens* in 1925 for W. J. Bassett-Lowke, the first house in England in the International Style and among the first to appear anywhere. Bassett-Lowke would have liked *Charles Rennie Mackintosh* to design his new house,

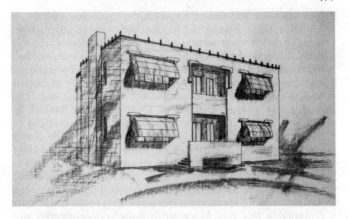

Northampton, New Ways, perspective of garden front.
Drawing by P. Behrens, 1925

but had lost contact with him when he moved to the South
of France. One does not know what to admire more, Mr
Bassett-Lowke's discrimination in engaging Mackintosh at a
time when his genius was no longer given adequate opportunities to express itself, or his courage in engaging Behrens,
one of the earliest leaders of a completely new style of architecture then entirely untried in Britain and only just beginning to be publicized by one journal, the *Architectural Review*,
which duly illustrated New Ways in 1926. How revolutionary
this style must have appeared at the time is obvious, whether
one looks at the house from the entrance or garden side; how
prophetic it was of the future style of the mid C20 can only
be seen on the garden side. Here the two-storeyed façade is
divided into three parts, with the centre recessed with open
balconies, an echo from No. 78 Derngate. The side parts have
on each floor just one large horizontal window without any
surround or mouldings. There is in fact no more than an odd
little hoodmould above the upper loggia to remind one of the
early date of the house. It is different on the entrance side.
Here the house is decidedly dated. That façade belongs to the
passing phase of Expressionism in German architecture
which comes between the earliest pioneer work of Behrens
himself, Gropius and others, and the mature, settled Modern
style which began in the mid 1920s. Behrens himself sacri-
ficed to the idol of Expressionism in his headquarters for the
German Dye Trust at Hanau, built in 1920–4. The Expressionist (or as some would say jazzy) motif at New Ways is the
triangularly projecting staircase window which cuts the front
in half. This was topped by pylons with illuminated tops, and
the white front has a curious top cresting 'redolent of Paris
in 1925' (i.e. the Paris Exhibition of 1925), as the *Architectural
Review* put it. The house has a practical and symmetrical plan:

hall, staircase and dining room on the main axis with living rooms on the one hand and service rooms on the other. Basements provide more service and storage. The construction is brick rendered. Inside the house the floor of the entrance hall has an irregular geometrical pattern, designed by Behrens, and this is also very typical of the mid 1920s, say of carpets and such-like work which came out of the Bauhaus. The lounge has a wide fireplace of stone and tile, flanked by windows admitting light by day and artificially illuminated by night, and having special tinted glass from Berlin. The dining room also has a special ceiling light composed of walnut strips and opal glass. One room inside was reinstalled from Bassett-Lowke's preceding house, 78 Derngate, which had been altered and decorated by Mackintosh. The room blended well with these Expressionist features owing to the historically remarkable fact that Mackintosh quite independently, and indeed prophetically, turned from his exquisite Art Nouveau of about 1900 to a private Expressionism, with cubistic and sometimes a little jazzy shapes, as early as 1907. The colour scheme of the rooms was black furniture and walls with orange, grey, blue and yellow stencilling. Behrens, of course, never came to Northampton and one has to admire the tenacity of Bassett-Lowke and his builder, *Henry Green*, in transferring Behrens's somewhat sketchy drawings into full architectural designs.

SOUTH AND DELAPRÉ

ST MARY, Towcester Road, Far Cotton. 1884–5 by *Holding* using a combination of local and Bath stone, cut in small brick-like blocks much favoured by Holding. Prominent E view with tall NE tower crowned by a spire (added 1901–2) and tall semicircular apse with lancet windows only high up. The other windows also lancets or with plate tracery. The interior is stone-vaulted throughout, as will be expected by anyone who knows that Holding was for a time a pupil of Pearson. No structural division between nave and chancel. STAINED GLASS. Chancel E of 1933 but unidentified artist. – Tower window 1908 by *H. A. Hymers*. – Two on the N side by *Jane Cummings*, 1977.

The VICARAGE and buildings alongside of 1886–7 also by *Holding*.

METHODIST CHURCH, Towcester Road. Red brick and stone in an attractive Decorated Gothic style, 1923–4 by *George Baines & Son*. Church buildings 1956, in a more angular Gothic manner.

Former BAPTIST CHURCH (Chapel House Flats), Abbey Road. Built 1893–5, in a very correct Perp style. Converted to housing 1986. A new chapel on the corner of Southampton Road was built 1989.

BRIAR HILL NURSERY SCHOOL, Hunsbarrow Road. 2003–4 by *Peter Haddon & Partners*. Central cube with a pyramidal roof.

Subsidiary blocks of varied heights. Copper shingle cladding and colour.

DELAPRÉ ABBEY. The house stands in its own park effectively joining Northampton to the village of Hardingstone. It is on the site of one of the only two Cluniac nunneries in England (the other was Arthington in the West Riding). Delapré Abbey was founded c. 1125 by Simon, the son of Simon of St Liz (or Senlis) who had founded the Cluniac priory of St Andrew, Northampton, about fifty years before. It was dissolved in 1538 and the estate was acquired by the Tate family of London. A house was created using portions of the monastic buildings. It was in Tate possession till 1764 when it was sold to the Bouverie family; it remained with their descendants until 1964 when it was acquired by the Borough of Northampton and served for many years as the County Record Office. Since 1981 it has remained unoccupied and its future is uncertain.

The house is of four ranges round a nearly square courtyard. This in all probability represents the cloister, and the passage around the N, W and E sides the cloister walks. The thick walls of the N range in that case represent the wall of the aisleless nunnery church. But no medieval feature survives, except perhaps two rectangular recesses in the cloister walk which may have served to keep lights in at night. Of the mid C16 three doorways, one from the courtyard to the E corridor, the other two in the N corridor. One of them leads to a spiral stair. They have four-centred arches or heads. Near in time comes the remodelling of the W range, due to Zouch Tate, who was in possession from 1617 to 1651. His is the most conspicuous contribution to the house, the W front. This is of ironstone, E-shaped with the central section little more than a screen with a passage behind. The wings had big shaped gables of which only the l. one survives. The r. one was awkwardly replaced by a library added between 1820 and 1840, higher than the rest, stuccoed, and with thin Tudor detail. The l. wing is an C18 extension of the N range when large sash windows were inserted into the front. Porch with arched entrance between fluted and banded Roman Doric columns. In the side walls blank, horizontally placed ovals in oblong frames. Embattled top. The rest of the roof is also embattled and the side wall of the original S wing, still with its battlements, remains somewhat uncomfortably within the wall of the library wing. Mullioned-and-transomed windows of two, three and four lights. The E side of the house is irregular but was also remodelled by Zouch Tate. The N side is even more irregular. The jamb of one blocked window has been explained by W. A. Pantin as belonging to the nunnery church. The S range was made in the mid C18 with its rooms at a higher level than the rest of the house. The S front was of twelve bays and two storeys. The two l. bays were replaced by the library addition already referred to. The two r. bays project, and the angles of this projection have rusticated Doric pilasters. There are plans of the 1750s signed by *Francis Smith* and *William Hiorne* with a survey plan dated

1755 (NRO). At the same time a circular staircase was added within the courtyard, later replaced, and a corridor system with alcoves, steps and domed ceilings devised leading from the entrance passage up to the s rooms.

No specially interesting interiors. In one of the s rooms two columns separate the back part of the room. Most of the rooms were redecorated in a Raphaelesque mood, probably c. 1860–70. In the w range a minor re-set early C17 staircase with vertically symmetrical balusters and the kitchen of similar date. The STABLES to the N with cupola are also of c. 1750. They were called new in 1756. They were renovated by *John Goff*, the County Architect, in 1971. Mock Jacobean LODGE, part of the c. 1820–40 work. In the walled garden *Frank Dobson*'s 1951 sculpture 'Woman with Fish'. In concrete and regarded as one of his most successful works.

ELEANOR CROSS, London Road, on the edge of Delapré Park. Queen Eleanor had died at Harby in Nottinghamshire in November 1290. Edward I decided to set up crosses on lavishly decorated substructures at the places where the funeral cortège had halted overnight. The same had been done in France for the body of King Louis IX in 1271. The stopping places were Lincoln, Grantham, Stamford, Geddington, Hardingstone, Stony Stratford, Dunstable, St Albans, Waltham, Cheapside, and finally Charing Cross. Most of the places chosen had royal castles or monastic houses of distinction. Hardingstone really meant Delapré Abbey (*see* above). Of all these crosses only the three of Hardingstone, Geddington (*see* p. 285), and Waltham in Hertfordshire survive. The Hardingstone Cross was begun in 1291 by *John of Battle, caementarius*, and, as far as the statues of the queen were concerned, *William of Ireland, imaginatar* and *caementarius*, both artists in the employ of the king. William received £3/6/8 a figure. The Hardingstone (or Northampton) cross is octagonal. It stands high on (renewed) steps. It is in three tiers with a crowning terminal which does not exist any longer and whose original form is not known. It may have been a Crucifixus. The lowest tier has panelled buttresses at the angles and two-light panels with blank cusped Y-tracery between. Each light has a small flat ogee arch – a complete innovation in the 1290s – and below this a suspended shield with a coat of arms. On every second side there is an open book on a lectern against the two-light panel. Originally there was no doubt a painted text in the book, as the whole monument was painted. Above each panel is a crocketed gable, fantastically and quite illogically cusped. Above the gable is a frieze of big flowers, and then a piece of cresting again quite fantastic. It consists of concave curves. The second stage has four canopies containing four images of the queen. They differ in composition of the draperies but are all less crisp, with less sharpness of folds and clarity of distinction between body and mantle than statuary had possessed at Westminster Abbey some forty years before and at Lincoln some twenty or thirty. The canopies have thin buttresses instead of shafts, and crocketed gables with decoration by means of naturalistic foliage. Several kinds of leaf can easily be recognized. The arches below the gables have ogee heads and are ogee-cusped. Behind the gables appears the crocketed pyramid roof of the canopy. The third stage is square and retracted behind the canopies. It has a blank four-light panel on each side, made up of the units of Y-tracery. There are again buttresses, gables and finial to link up with the missing terminal. The present broken column was placed on top by *E. Blore*, who removed various c18 accretions in 1840. The whole structure is memorable as the beginning of that development which was to lead to such superb excesses as the canopy of the monument to Edward II at Gloucester.

PERAMBULATION. Bridge Street continues beyond the inner ring road with on the r. the extensive premises of the former PHIPPS'S BREWERY, redeveloped from 1971 for CARLSBERG. The architect was *Knud Munk* of Copenhagen. The brewhouse itself is a massive pile with a jagged roof-line. Long low storage buildings running N–S. The original buildings of the 1860s and 1870s have gone. At the N end of the Bridge Street front a building with an inset of curtain walling. 1956–7 by *F. C. J. Smith*. New buildings projected 2012.

SOUTH BRIDGE was originally built 1816–18 and widened in 1912. Classical rusticated arches. The NENE RIVER FRONTAGE is currently (2013) under review for development, of which a small section from South Bridge to Beckett's Park has been undertaken. Blocks of standard brick flats of not especially inspiring design. The river frontage deserved something better.

To the SE of the bridge is an area of housing of the early c21 with three- and four-storey ranges of flats, all rather angular. One of the main streets through the area is HENRY BIRD WAY. Henry Bird was a local artist (†2000) who had an especially caustic approach to much modern art and one can imagine what he might have said about this development. On the main road the OLD WHITE HART INN, 1899 by *C. Dorman*, neo-*c*. 1700 with a hooded doorway, gables and large chimney-stacks. A splendid band of lettering across the façade. After a dismal gap where the former railway crossing ran through we arrive on the r. in FAR COTTON. Here a series of four streets, parallel to St Leonard's Road, to the w of London Road, derives from an 1852 Freehold Land Society scheme with *Alexander Milne* as architect. By 1854 thirty houses had been erected and by 1861 over two hundred. The scheme was completed in the early 1870s. Some single houses, some double-fronted. To the s along TOWCESTER ROAD, Nos. 162–182 are the beginnings of the DELAPRÉ GARDEN VILLAGE, 1911 through to *c*. 1920. All the houses were designed by *Gibson, Skipworth & Gordon* except for Nos. 172–174 which are by *H. M. Scrivenor* of Northampton, who lived in one himself. The houses are usually in pairs. Of red brick and some with Dutch style gables and casement windows.

WEST

ST JAMES, St James' Road. 1868–70 by *Robert Wheeler* of Ton-
bridge. Red brick, in the lancet style with enrichment in black
bricks and ironstone in a typical High Victorian fashion.
Extended 10 yds (9 metres) to the w by *Matthew Holding*,
1899–1900, faithful to the original detail but with an apsidal
baptistery. Tower 1924 by *G. H. Stevenson*. The brick is exposed
inside. Arcades with low circular piers of polished pink granite.
Foliage capitals, square abaci. Low aisles. w half partitioned
off as a hall and rooms in 1982. – STAINED GLASS. Chancel E
by *Burlison & Grylls*, 1901. N aisle window by *Francis Skeat*,
1968. The other windows by *William Pearce* 1907–15.

DODDRIDGE MEMORIAL CHAPEL, St James' Road. 1895 by
Mosley & Anderson. Brick and stone in a debased Perp manner.
Large gable with inscription and a window of six lights with
transoms. The Schools and Institute buildings were added in
1913 by *F. H. Allen*.

PERAMBULATION. ST JAMES' ROAD starts at West Bridge and
the station. On the S side are the former MALTINGS of Thomas
Manning & Co., 1887–8 by *J. Ingman & Son*, on a T-plan with
the maltings pyramidal roofs still at the end. There is nothing
of consequence till the Doddridge Memorial Chapel. Opposite
is the factory of one of Northampton's important surviving
shoe manufacturers, CHURCH'S. The frontage is 1905 by
Mosley & Anderson, brick and stone. Three-floor entrance
feature with curved glazed two-storey oriel above a doorway
with characteristic Anderson lettering and two roundels with
American Red Indian heads, the motif of Padmore & Barnes
for whom the factory was originally built. The factory less
ornate, its side elevation in Sharman Road with eight gabled
ranges. Anderson added to the original building variously
between 1907 and 1914. Across Sharman Road, the former
garages of NORTHAMPTON CORPORATION TRANSPORT
originally built 1904. First the office building. A nice Neoclassical essay of two storeys, upper windows with aprons and
X-pattern glazing. Set back the former tram and later bus
sheds. Shaped gables with circular ventilation openings and
originally with three round-arched openings below. The format
still apparent in the l. block. St James's church follows on the
r. The road then opens up into ST JAMES' SQUARE, a junction
of Weedon and Harlestone roads. On the NE side the NAT WEST
BANK building, originally built in 1882 as a café. It was altered
in 1926 by *F. H. Allen* but still has canted oriels on the first
floor and a corner turret with a pyramidal roof. To the NE runs
SPENCER BRIDGE ROAD. The area immediately on the E side
was planned as a housing estate in the late 1870s by the Althorp
Estate. It was part of the Dallington Estate which they had
bought in 1863. In 1880–1 *Devey & Williams*, who were
working for the estate, designed groups of houses. Only a few
were built and, although altered, those on the corner of St
James' Park Road survive from the scheme. An intriguing
example of George Devey's late career. On the opposite corner

the former St James's CHURCH INSTITUTE of 1904–7 by *Stevenson & Dorman.*

Now along WEEDON ROAD with on the l. side the SAINTS RUGBY FOOTBALL CLUB. The front office is the former FRANKLIN'S GARDEN HOTEL, 1921 by *Law & Harris*, pseudo *c.* 1700 style. Brick with hipped roof, quoins and cross-windows on the first floor. Projecting porch. Conspicuous to the l. the Tetley Stand. The Bingo Hall next door needs no comment. Behind but rising above both is the former EXPRESS LIFTS TOWER, locally known as 'The Northampton Light-house'. It was built as a lift testing tower in 1980–2 and designed by *Maurice Walton* of *Stimpson & Walton*. The Express Lift Company was taken over by Otis in 1997 and the factory was closed in 1999. The factory was demolished and replaced by a housing development, THE APPROACH, and its arms of blocks of apartments.

HARLESTONE ROAD begins on the l. with SCOTT FOWLER, a nice conversion and extension of the former Harlestone Road Methodist church of 1899 by *Tad Dobraszczyk*, 1998–90 and 2009. Further W on the r. ST JAMES' PRIMARY SCHOOL, an interesting complex of linked blocks each with a low pedimented roof and square turret. After a while the houses get grander as we approach Dallington Park. Opposite is THE AVENUE, a long crescent with a number of grand villas. At the s end, on the westernmost arm of the road, is the most eccentric of them, built in 1896 by *Alexander Anderson* for A. E. Marlow, the shoe manufacturer, and originally called Skitterdene. An almost normal villa with central gable and wings has attached on the l. a billiard room extension, semi-octagonal, and a shaped turret with a large oval window. It originally had a loggia in front. It is now divided into two residences with the inevitable changes to the exterior and only parts of the interior now survive. This brings us to Dallington (*see* below).

For UPTON PARK housing development *see* Upton (p. 629).

OUTER NORTHAMPTON

DALLINGTON AND KINGS HEATH

ST MARY. Late C12 s doorway with one order of shafts carrying early leaf capitals and a round, only slightly stepped arch. C13 the N aisle, see the pair of lancets and the simple doorway. N arcade with simple octagonal piers and double-chamfered arches, s arcade similar, though differing in details but both Dec as is the chancel arch. Circular opening above, now blocked, but drawings by George Clarke show it with tracery. Odd tall narrow openings at either E end of the arcades. Are they medieval or later? The W arches of each are shorter than the rest suggesting the tower is a late addition, though it has double lancet bell-stage windows. The ground-floor lancet dates from the restoration of 1883 when many of the other windows of the church were renewed. The N or Raynsford Chapel was built in 1679 but its E window is C19. There is much evidence of Victorian restoration. The S aisle was rebuilt in 1877 probably by *E. F. Law*, there was a general restoration 1880–1 by *E. F. Law & Son* and the chancel was rebuilt in 1882–3 by *Edmund Law*, finally completing his father's restoration in 1889. Prior to that the chancel had a Georgian E window (Clarke drawing). – FONT. Octagonal, Perp, with quatrefoil panels. The three standing putti around it are part of the 1678 Raynsford monument (*see* below). – BENCHES. Some, with fleur-de-lys poppyheads, at the W end of the nave. Early C19? – REREDOS. 1883, with statues by *Harry Hems* and mosaic. – PULPIT. Jacobean. – SCULPTURE. A curious small Saxon fragment in the inner N wall to r. of the middle window. Small human figure like an embryo, small quadruped below. The stone has a triangular head. – STAINED GLASS. A nice selction of *c.* 1900 glass. – E window by *Kempe*, 1892. – S aisle S Annunciation, 1893 by *Clayton & Bell*. – Another S window by *Morris & Co.*, but 1907, i.e. after the deaths of both Morris and Burne-Jones. – S aisle W and N aisle W and tower window, all by *Lavers & Barraud*. – S aisle W SS George and Cecilia, 1936, designed by *G. Daniels* for *F. C. Eden*. – N aisle W end, 1931 by *J. E. Nuttgens* and *Nathaniel Dearle*. – Another of 1911 by *Charles Steel* of Leeds. – TAPESTRY PANEL. *Morris & Co.* of the Virgin and two angels. – MONUMENTS. Sir Richard Raynsford †1678. Big base with, in the middle, oval inscription surrounded by splendidly carved flower garland. Big urn on top, with garlands. There were putti at the top, but they have been removed and stand by the font (*see* above). The tomb may be by *William Stanton*, who made the ledger stone to Dame Catherine Raynsford †1698, although it has also been attributed to *Latham* (GF). – Three Raynsford daughters †1657, 1662, 1664. Inscription framed by black columns. Open segmental pediment. Attributed to *Cibber* (GF). – Two fine large tablets with urns before obelisks and some coloured marbles, the earlier Rococo and attributed to *Cheere*, the later just a little chaster and probably by *Sir Robert Taylor*. Joseph Jekyll †1752, Lady Anne Jekyll †1766. – S aisle a wooden memorial plaque with the Virgin and Child, Arts and Crafts manner but 1923.

DALLINGTON HALL, immediately W of the church. Built by Sir Joseph Jekyll, Master of the Rolls, who bought the estate from the Raynsfords in 1720 and died in 1738. An attribution to *Francis Smith* is accepted. The entrance side five bays and two storeys with basement. Giant angle pilasters, parapet, hipped roof, doorway with pediment on brackets. The garden side seven bays, with giant pilasters at the angles as well as the angles of the three middle bays. Similar doorway. The three windows above have pilasters and arches. Fine staircase behind the middle of the garden side. Three balusters to the tread, two twisted, one columned; carved tread-ends very similar to those at Lamport Hall and Rectory and therefore probably by *Joseph*

Daniel. To the N of the house the STABLES, their S end concealed by a pedimented front with a doorway flanked by two niches. The stables incorporate masonry from the C17 house of the Raynsfords. In the gardens a DOVECOTE, octagonal with ogee cupola, probably *c.* 1720.

Dallington retains its village centre and atmosphere even though it is now well within the borough boundary. The church and other nice ironstone buildings are grouped around a small green and its pretty stream. Immediately N of the church is the former SCHOOL of *c.* 1840 with one large gable and a lower wing to the l. Vernacular C17 with mullioned windows. Adjoining to the w, the RAYNSFORD ALMSHOUSES, a row of cottages dating from 1673. Four dwellings, middle gable also in the same manner. To the r. of the school, drive to the former VICARAGE. This is dated 1741. Three bays wide, on the ground floor either side the fine bracketed doorcase two Venetian windows which are probably part of alterations in 1771.

A few pleasant ironstone houses in RAYNSFORD ROAD, both w and E of the Green, e.g. THE WHEATSHEAF pub, THE BARTONS and DALLINGTON WEIR. Along the main HARLESTONE ROAD many prosperous Victorian and Edwardian houses, e.g. GREENWOOD SHIPMAN HOME at the corner of Bants Lane, Tudor and Renaissance, *c.* 1880 by *Charles Dorman*, and further w, on the N side, ELMLEIGH, by *Godwin*, 1885, but nothing special. *Law & Harris* made some alterations in 1925.

KINGS HEATH ESTATE. Designed by *J. L. Womersley*, then Borough Architect, in 1950. Planned for 5,000 inhabitants. The plan is completely symmetrical, a kidney shape being the basic motif. The centre is a green. To its N a SCHOOL. Yet further N on the r. a HOME FOR OLD PEOPLE, and at the N end the former CHURCH HALL of St Augustine. At the other end ST MARGARET'S CHURCH (R.C.) of 1960. 'The very successful pedestrian SHOPPING CENTRE . . . in the middle axis to the s of the Green' that Bridget Cherry described in 1973 is now a dismal, bleak boarded-up affair. Its success was, alas, short-lived. It is flanked along the green by flats, and these carry on along the curved ends of the green as well as s of the shopping centre to form the main approach from the s. These nicely designed three-storey terraces of pale and dark red brick with balconies and moderately pitched roofs give the estate its character, which, though looking a bit worn, still survives. The fact that Womersley's houses and blocks stand almost without alteration says something for his concept of the estate.

To the s an industrial area. In Gladstone Road the first tall office block of the town, for BARCLAYS, by *Green, Lloyd & Adams*, 1970–1. Ten storeys high.

DUSTON

ST LUKE, Main Road. Evidence of a late C12 building is the s doorway and the w respond of the s arcade. The latter is semicircular with a many-scalloped capital, the former has two orders of shafts with leaf capitals and a deeply moulded round arch, including keeling. Of the early C13 the fenestration of the C12 W wall. Three big lancets and a small one above. Conspicuous roof-line. The aisles were added in the late C13, see the change of masonry in the W wall from mixed brown and grey rubble to bands of brown and grey; see also the aisle windows: three lancet lights under one arch, three intersected lights, Y-tracery, i.e. all late C13 motifs. The arcades of three bays probably of the same date: octagonal piers and double-chamfered arches. Clerestory with small windows of three different shapes, including quatrefoils. The E end of the arcades has no responds. Corbels on pairs of heads instead. The crossing tower is probably basically Norman, but the arches are again late C13. The E arch has the same corbels on pairs of heads. The narrow N and S arches are double-chamfered and die against their imposts. There is no trace of transepts. One-bay N and S chapels. Dec chancel and tower top. Of the former chancel roof the supporting C14 figures of musicians remain. There were a number of Victorian restorations, notably 1862–3 by *E. F. Law* and 1902 by *Edmund Law*. – FONT. Norman. The lower half of the bowl fluted. – SCULPTURE. Dancing Madonna and Child, 1977 by *Maureen Coatment* of Monks Risborough. – TILES. *c.* 1860–70 and a fine series, to designs by *Lord Alwyne Compton*. – STAINED GLASS. Chancel E, 1877 by *Heaton, Butler & Bayne*. – MONUMENTS. Rev. John Woodford †1706, but the tablet probably *c.* 1750. By *John Hunt* and typical with delicate carved scrollwork. – In the yard a massive granite block surmounted by a bronze anchor for William Butlin †1923. The Butlin family were ironmasters and created several ironworks in the middle of the C19.

Former VICARAGE, to E of the church. 1840–1 by *E. F. Law* in his usual vicarage Tudor Gothic manner. Some additions by the same in 1863.

UNITED REFORMED CHURCH, Main Road (formerly Congregational). With an attractive church hall with three gables to the street, by *A. W. Walker*, 1967–8.

Former SCHOOL, prominent on Main Road. The original building in the centre, 1856 by *E. F. Law*, red brick, Tudor style. Side extensions r. of 1893 and l. of 1898–1900. Behind, additions of 1933–7 and more recent (sadly derelict 2011).

DUSTON SCHOOL, Berrywood Road. The main building Neo-Georgian. Extensions of 1971.

Former ST CRISPIN'S HOSPITAL. Built as the BERRYWOOD ASYLUM in 1873–6 by *Robert Griffiths* of Stafford. A large red brick building with a prominent tower, vaguely Rhineland Romanesque in inspiration. Many later additions. Separate CHAPEL (now St Neophyte's Greek church) *c.* 1880, Early Gothic, four bays with aisles, redecorated in 1954 by *Henry Bird* and *G. H. B. Holland* with large panels depicting the Arthurian legend. The hospital closed in 1995 and since the early 2000s partly converted for residential use with some new housing also built. The main central buildings and the tower remain derelict and partly fire damaged (2013). The site is best seen from St Crispin Drive which passes a large white rendered building of 1934–5 (former Pendered block) by *Gotch, Saunders & Surridge*, of three and four storeys, five-bay centre with small towers and small pedimented sections, now apartments. A little further E is KEYSTONE HOUSE, the first of the converted older buildings, of red brick with bands of yellow brick and some blue for ornamentation. It is a two-storey range with five bays in the centre and two at each end. The model is repeated in an adjoining block. Further N is BERRY WOOD CLOSE with a small green and trees with on its W side an interesting building with a small central tower with spirelet, and wings of red brick with yellow bands as before, with either end of the wings little angled square projections with pyramidal roofs. A new BERRYWOOD HOSPITAL was built 2009–10 by *Balfour Beatty Construction*. The original complex should be contrasted with the PRINCESS MARINA HOSPITAL, further SE, by *Stillman & Eastwick-Field*, 1964–72. This was the first hospital in the country to be designed specially for psychiatric patients with severe mental impairment. The buildings are arranged in clusters, each group catering for patients with different needs. There is also a community centre with a shop, and staff housing (the buildings with pitched roofs).

PERAMBULATION. Several nice houses in MAIN ROAD. In MELBOURNE LANE pairs of ironstone estate-like cottages 1876–8. THE SQUIRRELS pub, probably C17 and C18 and still thatched. At the corner of Saxon Rise DUSTON HOUSE, large, early C19, stuccoed. Porch with paired Corinthian columns. Originally built 1822 for a member of the Samwell family of Upton but Italianized 1872–3 by *E. F. Law*, when a billiard room was added. It was then the Butlin family home. On the opposite corner a brisk ironstone house *c*. 1890. One or two thatched one-storey cottages still survive. A little further on the E side is OAK LODGE (care home), 1899 ironstone in the Elizabethan style. Nos. 72–74 of red brick Neo-Queen Anne of *c*. 1900. To the E of the village stood the large factory of BRITISH TIMKEN (established 1941) which was a main employer of the area till it closed in 2002. The main building was demolished in 2005 and only a pair of brick gatepiers stand to mark its presence. The site has been built over with housing since.

SIXFIELDS STADIUM (Northampton Town F.C.), Weedon Road/Upton Way. 1993–4 by *Ballast Nedam Construction Ltd*, with the architects *Taylor Tulip & Hunter*.

EASTERN DISTRICT

The initial development of the Eastern District began in the 1950s under the then Borough Architect, *J. L. Womersley*, with the Eastfield Estate and shortly afterwards Thorplands. However, the major development occurred following the New Towns Act of 1965 when Northampton was so designated. The Northampton Development Corporation was set up in 1968 with a Master

Plan created in 1969. Some new houses were built in Little Billing, but the very early 1970s concentrated on the development of the town centre. By 1972 attention then focused on the Eastern District with the construction of the dual-carriageway Lumbertubs Way and industrial sites at Round Spinney and Moulton Park. By the middle of the same year over 2,000 dwellings were under construction, with the Thorplands and Arbours areas largely finished. Through the later 1970s there then followed a sequence with on the N side Southfields, and, to the S, Goldings and Blackthorn, to the E, Rectory Farm, and further S, the development of housing around the Billings, Bellinge and Ecton Brook. Most of these areas were largely complete by 1980. The earlier estates show the controlling hand of the Development Corporation and two of its leading architects, *Gordon Redfern* and *Gerald Callaghan*. The later housing is of a more standard form that has continued since. Nearly all the schools have been either replaced or revamped since the 1970s and do not merit special mention.

SACRED HEART (R.C.), Pyramid Close, on the E side of the Weston Favell Shopping Centre. 1974 by *Williams & Mathers* of Cheltenham. It is indeed of pyramid form. Impressive painted Stations of the Cross by *Matthew Hughes*.

NORTHAMPTON COLLEGE, Booth Lane/St Gregory's Road. The original building of 1972 was replaced 2010–11 by a large diamond plan complex by *Pick Everard* of Leicester. The sides of the diamond are formed of long three-storey ranges, somewhat warehouse looking, which meet at the diagonal corner, SW and NE, with large circular glazed units. The NE is the entrance suite with a slender pillared canopy and open well, and the SW the cafeteria and library, again with a central atrium.

NORTHAMPTON ACADEMY, Wellingborough Road. 2005–6 by *Feilden Clegg Bradley*. A series of linked blocks, trapezoid in plan. Timber-clad in a varied pattern of panels with some glass inter-sections and rather more informal smaller openings.

WESTON FAVELL SCHOOL, S of the College, was redesigned 2007 by *Ellis Williams Partnership* and converted into an Academy 2011.

ST GREGORY'S (R.C.) PRIMARY SCHOOL, Booth Lane. 2004–5 by *Gotch, Saunders & Surridge*. An interesting design with a central entrance with curved canopy on slender pillars. Lower, stepped wings set at angles. Good use of materials and colour.

THOMAS BECKET (R.C.) SCHOOL, Becket Way. 2005–6 by *Gotch, Saunders & Surridge*. An unusual sequence of angled blocks, in outline like broken apart pediments with canopied roofs on slender pillars.

WESTON FAVELL SHOPPING CENTRE. Opened in 1974 and designed by *Gordon Redfern*, Development Corporation. A huge complex which includes community facilities and Emmanuel Church. The malls are set beneath a high triple-arched coffered ceiling, but despite the height the interior seems cramped and overcrowded.

PERAMBULATION. The earliest development of 1953 by *Womersley* is the EASTFIELD ESTATE (1 m. N of Phippsville either side of the E end of Broadmead Avenue). It is in what was then described as 'the New-Town style', with low-pitched roofs, terraces of houses and occasional three-storeyed flats. 'Pleasant if uneventful architecture' is how it was described in 1973. It now looks rather dull, and is considered below standard. A regeneration plan was drawn up in September 2010. Across Lumbertubs Way, NE, is the THORPLANDS ESTATE, of a little later date. It has a more open plan than Eastfield, though its housing is more tightly packed. It also is now looking tired and is likewise the subject of plans for regeneration. THORPLANDS FARM, among housing N of Billing Brook Road, is a fine Overstone Estate farm complex, built in 1848 but extended in 1862. It comprises a long range of brick buildings with ironstone dressings, formerly stables, sheds etc. to which are attached three modern ranges forming an E-plan. At the end of the ranges are original hexagonal buildings, one of which was a dairy. The farm became well known in agricultural circles during the period of Lord Overstone's agent John Beasley for his progressive methods. Converted to housing in the early 1980s when the entrance archway with its clock was built. The original farmhouse, almost unrecognizable save for the rear portion with carriageway, is N on the other side of Talavera Way (now a Toby Inn).

There now follows the main eastern development under the Northampton Development Corporation (NDC) built from 1972 onwards and still in progress in the 1980s. The area is broken up into a series of estates: ARBOURS, BILLING BROOK, SOUTHFIELDS, GOLDINGS, BLACKTHORN, ECTON BROOK and BELLINGE. The N–S eastern edge of the whole area is bounded by a brook with sections of woodland and this has been used to advantage in creating a number of open spaces and green areas linked in a linear park. The NDC housing is often only apparent on the edges of these while later housing is of a more standard and varied type. There is considerable use of monopitch roof forms, these deriving from designs of the NDC architect, *Gerald Callaghan*, and further interpreted by *Neil Richie* and *D. Colin James*. A detailed exploration of these estates is neither practical nor justified. All that can be done is to highlight one or two places where the NDC style is most easily appreciated or where there are any buildings of distinction. In SOUTHFIELDS, for example, Farmhill Road has wide verges with trees and a series of monopitch two- and three-storey dwellings, some of brick, some rendered with cladding. BILLING BROOK has further good examples of monopitch housing in, for example, Crestwood Road and Midfield Court. Where possible areas of mature trees have been retained. GOLDINGS ROAD is a good example of this, as is

BARLEY HILL ROAD in Southfields. In BILLING BROOK ROAD the advantage of a stream and tree planting has allowed housing to be set back and also provided a setting for a school, shops etc. Close to this is one of the more distinctive housing complexes, BROOKVIEW (*Muir Housing Group*), a range of three-storey flats, brick with some timber cladding, a moving façade with angled bays, some with overhanging sections. In RECTORY FARM, old farm buildings serve as a community centre. The farmhouse of the 1880s survives. Stone with red brick dressings. On the same estate, in ERMINE ROAD an unusual range of flats. They are built on a slope with a stepped formation, the levels revealed but enclosed at the sides by long sloping sections of roof. Here also, in Olden Road, is another of the more distinctive buildings of the area, THE BARN OWL pub, 1987 by *David Byrne Associates*. Roughly cruciform in plan with a big half-timbered gable facing the green and its side elevation an open split pediment held on tall square pillars. It was gaily coloured red and blue originally but has since sadly been given a white overall wash. The less satisfactory areas are those where car parking has been given priority over landscaping. A single example is Dryleys Court in Goldings, where the cars dominate the streetscape. The southern estates of ECTON BROOK and BELLINGE, which surround the former villages of Great and Little Billing, are 1980s housing of a type now found in almost every town in the country. Travelling through these estates there is, on the whole, a feeling of care, the presence of people and also the integration of open spaces, community services and shopping facilities which seems to work. The rather dead atmosphere which now hangs over *Womersley*'s Kings Heath Estate (see p. 485) is thankfully not here.

GREAT BILLING

Despite being engulfed by outer Northampton the village survives and has numerous nice ironstone houses and here and there still some thatch.

ST ANDREW. The church is attractively sited, a little away from the old centre, still overlooking green fields. It was near the Hall (*see* below). The church parapets include C16 balustrading from the pre-1776 mansion.

The story starts with a Norman nave to which a two-bay N aisle was added in the late C12. Circular pier, capital with flat, elementary leaves, square abacus. This aisle was extended to the W to meet a tower and to the E to meet a new chancel. The extensions have circular piers with circular abaci and double-chamfered arches. At the same time or a little later a S aisle was built with piers of an unusual and handsome type: triple shafts to each of the four sides. One arch has a nailhead hood-mould. All this is of the late C13 to early C14. It is perhaps significant that the same light veined stone is used for the W piers of both arcades. Does this mean that the s one is carved out of an earlier pier? The tower is also of this date, but the upper part was rebuilt after the spire was shattered by lightning in 1759. Much of the body of the church had to be renewed after this disaster (see the Georgian quoining at the ends of the N aisle). Late Perp s doorway with heavy hoodmould and a bust of an angel at the apex. Porch of after 1759. In the s aisle a very fine Dec tripartite REREDOS with wider and higher centre and ogee heads. The N chapel is dated 1687. In the E wall a tall blind opening with an open segmental pediment. The chancel is largely a rebuilding of 1866–7 by *E. F. Law* and of this period the Y-tracery of the windows, which had all been removed in the Georgianization of the building. Two C15 square-headed two-light windows were revealed in the N wall when the church was restored. The C19 work with richly carved foliage capitals and corbels. The E window has side shafts which probably survive from the C13 building. The chancel TILES also of 1867. – FONT. Octagonal, Perp. Tall panelled stem, moulded top; no separate bowl. – SCREEN. C19 but with some pieces of C15 tracery. – STAINED GLASS. Chancel E window of 1913 by *J. Hardman & Co.* – Chancel s of 1959 by *Christopher Webb* (inscription of 1960 added). – W window by *J. Powell & Sons*, 1870. – MONUMENTS. Henry, Earl of Thomond †1691. By *John Bushnell*, according to Vertue. It was erected in 1700 and is shockingly inept. *The Beauties of England and Wales* (1810) describes it as 'more distinguished for its bulk than its elegance'. However, it is important since it was probably Bushnell's last work and is a fine Baroque composition. He died, insane, in 1701 and this no doubt accounts for its rather crude workmanship. The Earl and Countess kneel at a prayer-desk on which lies a baby. They have not enough room to kneel, and the foreshortening which would have been necessary to make the full-round heads and shoulders and the absence of the legs credible was not now at Bushnell's command. Two kneeling children behind the parents and more children kneeling in relief along the front of the desk. At the top draperies and what Mrs Esdaile calls 'two exquisite flying cherubs' – viewers may not agree! The whole group supported on an enormous Baroque tomb-chest with big black marble corner stones and gadrooned side supports. – Caroline Elwes †1812 by *Flaxman* and Robert Elwes †1852 by *Weekes*, both with women by urns, and neither specially memorable. – The rear part of the churchyard is reserved as a Roman Catholic burial place and has the Elwes memorials on its E side. One a tomb-chest carved with a crozier and a mitre for Bishop Dudley Cary-Elwes †1932, who was bishop of the Northampton Roman Catholic diocese, and another for the famous singer Gervase Elwes †1921 (*see* below).

OUR LADY OF PERPETUAL SUCCOUR (R.C.). Incorporates the former school building of 1845, but extended in 1878–9 as a church following the conversion of Valentine Cary-Elwes to the Roman Catholic faith (*see* below). The slim brick tower with

Northampton, Billing Hall.
Drawing by G. Clarke, *c.* 1850

tall slits and the aisles were added in 1926. No architect seems to be recorded but the obvious candidate is *Guy Elwes* (also *see* below).

BILLING HALL was the home of the O'Briens, Earls of Thomond, in the C17. In 1776 it was bought by Lord John Cavendish who called in *John Carr*. The house had a plain nine-bay frontage, that is 3–3–3, of three storeys with a pediment over the centre. In 1796 the estate was bought by the Elwes family who resided there till 1931. After then it was tenanted, but finally demolished in 1956. The interior had been much altered by *E. F. Law* in the 1860s and by *Law & Harris* in 1924. The Elwes family are interesting. Valentine Cary-Elwes (†1909) converted to the Roman Catholic faith in 1874 and was responsible for the creation of the Roman Catholic church in Billing (*see* above). His eldest son, Gervase, who dropped the Cary name, became famous as a singer in the early C20, being one of Elgar's favourite tenor soloists. He died by a tragic railway accident in 1921. He married Lady Winefride Feilding and three of their sons became important artistic figures, notably Rudolph, an actor; Guy, an architect, and Simon, a fashionable portrait painter. Guy Elwes (†1966) does not seem to have had a professional practice but designed fluently in the Neo-Georgian manner for friends and relations. His most ambitious work is Warwick Hall, Cumbria, 1934–5, built for his sister-in-law.

In CHURCH WALK Nos. 6 and 8, THE CHANTRY, are converted from remains of the late C17 stable block of the Thomond mansion. Mullioned windows and on the rear façade some oval openings. To the s runs ELWES WAY with, on the l., THE OLD RECTORY, partly of 1678 with some mullioned windows and refronted in the mid C18 with ashlar. Five bays and two storeys with central doorcase. Just further on, beyond the bend on the s side is HEREWYTE HOUSE, built for Gervase Elwes's sister Maud and designed by *Guy Elwes* in 1935–6. A neat example of the Colonial Georgian fashion with a weatherboarded façade ending in two brick pilasters which are the sides of tall chimneystacks. Wide pedimented doorcase.The village centre has a number of good stone houses, notably the OLD POST OFFICE, a building of 1703. Interesting for its date. Five bays, two storeys, quoins, doorway with straight entablature, but the windows still two-light mullioned. In a wall alongside, bronze MEMORIAL to Gervase Elwes by *Arthur E. Vokes*. A number of 1866 stone COTTAGES for which *E. F. Law* was largely responsible.

Former W. PEARCE & CO. TANNERY, ½ m. NW just off the A45001. 1939 by *Lawson Carter*. An excellent example of Early Modern, the details quite functional, but with a formal entrance in the angle of the L-shaped office block. Houses built in the grounds during the 1990s. (Future use under consideration 2012.)

BILLING MILL, 1 m. S. Former watermill with medieval origins, but the present attractive buildings mostly early C19 and later. Now a restaurant but some machinery existing.

HARDINGSTONE

ST EDMUND. Much embowered with trees. Unbuttressed C13 tower. In its N side the arch of a former Georgian doorway (recorded by George Clarke) and its Victorian replacement. Broad, squat, double-stepped arch towards the nave. Bell-openings with cusped Y-tracery and battlements with obelisk pinnacles. Although looking Dec the whole of the top of the tower could be C17. The body of the church over-restored. The chancel was Georgian, *c.* 1760, and still has its rusticated quoins. The windows mostly Late Perp. C14 five-bay arcades with octagonal piers and double-chamfered arches. The SEDILIA is made from an Elizabethan tomb-recess – a segmental arch with some foliage decoration round it and on the supporting pilasters. Below is the tomb-front with shields, upside down. At the apex of the arch an angel on clouds and an armed fist above. This is the heraldic crest of the Tate family of Delapré, and the tomb is probably for Bartholomew Tate †1572. The church was restored by *R. Palgrave* 1868–9. – FONT. 1869, Gothic, the gift of Palgrave. – PULPIT. 1913 with pierced floral borders. The church was reordered in 1969 and new RAILS were made in 1984 with floral borders by *Gerald Burton* of Hardingstone. – STAINED GLASS. Only the top of the chancel E window survives, its panels having been removed in 1914 and then lost. It was by *Wailes*, 1869. – N aisle E by *Heaton, Butler & Bayne* but not their usual standard. – S aisle, SS Edmund and Dorothea, *c.* 1920 by *E. W. Twining* of Northampton. Sadly partly broken (2011). – HATCHMENTS. The two in the chancel are Bouverie family, 1858 and 1871.

That at the rear of the church for Rev. Vade †1820. – MONU-MENTS. Stephen Harvey †1606. Alabaster. Kneeling figures in two tiers, two facing one another at the top, three more below, the central and r. figures placed frontally. Good quality. – Sir Stephen Harvey †1630. Recumbent effigy. Simple back architecture. Also good. – Bartholomew Clarke †1746. By *Rysbrack*. Quite superb, with two oval medallions with busts in profile in front of an obelisk. Rococo surrounds. Fine architectural detail below of typical Rysbrack form (cf. Ecton). At the foot a third medallion was added by *Rysbrack* to commemorate Mrs Clarke's brother Hitch Younge †1759. – Also a large number of identical oval commemorative plaques to members of the Bouverie family of Delapré Abbey, eleven on the l., four on the r. of the altar. They go down to the 1870s. Thomas Peach †1732 signed by *John Hunt*, who was doubtless responsible for the adjoining monument to John Vinter †1747.

The village, despite the advancement of outer Northampton, is still very much a village, and has a number of good ironstone houses, many with Late Georgian fronts and doorcases. At the w entrance to the village Nos. 80–84 are an attractive stone row, still thatched. Opposite the church is the fine BLUE BARNS FARM YARD complex (Collins Pet Foods) which is older than it first appears. It was attached to a farmhouse, which may not have been built, and erected as part of the Bouverie of Delapré Estate in 1769 by *John Wagstaff* of Daventry. Two barns joined by lower section with an impressive arched gateway with a pediment, all in dark chequered brick with red brick and stone dressings. Later alterations of 1883 and 1900. Just beyond the VILLAGE HALL (former Board School, 1866 with pyramidal roofs) is Back Lane with CORFE HOUSE and THE HEIGHTS (Nos. 28 and 30), a pair of Regency villas. Four bays wide, two storeys high, white. In the first and last bays doorways with Greek Doric columns *in antis*. On the first floor lesenes with Soanian incised ornament. No. 24 is late C18 with a nice doorcase, but much added to with bays etc. probably early C20. Back Lane returns to High Street with a GREEN where there are other attractive stone houses.

BRACKMILLS INDUSTRIAL ESTATE, N and NE of the village. Developed since the 1970s with the usual array of warehouses and office blocks. Of outstanding quality the BARCLAYCARD HEADQUARTERS, Pavilion Road/Caswell Road. A huge double rank of buildings of concrete construction, too complicated in format to try to describe, and designed for energy efficiency by *Fitzroy Robinson*, 2000–6. It is elaborately landscaped with considerable tree planting and water.

N of Brackmills, straddling the Bedford Road (A428) is THE LAKES. A pleasant development of the 1990s with a group of individual block, all designed in the same format – red brick with some yellow brick decoration, hipped roofs and glazed upper storeys, some two, some three, and some with low towers. Especially nice are those occupied by HSBC, Bidwells, Ricoh and MacIntyre Hudson. Another more varied building is a branch headquarters of the County Council. The whole area enhanced by some good landscaping. For those who look for something more adventurous, just to the w is the NENE WHITEWATER CENTRE.

KINGSTHORPE

A visitor to Northamptonshire if asking for Kingsthorpe will undoubtedly be directed to a main road junction of the A508 colloquially known as 'The Cock Hotel'. Old Kingsthorpe lies about ½ m. w of this. It is worth seeking out as it is still an old village centre, with a good selection of ironstone houses, an interesting church and a green with an ancient well. In the late C18 Kingsthorpe had a considerable reputation for its fine white sandstone. It was much used locally by the Leicester architect *John Johnson*, not only for Kingsthorpe Hall but also at Pitsford Hall, and if one accepts the attribution, at Little Houghton House – all built between 1770 and 1800. Unfortunately it suffers from frost exposure and, not only in Kingsthorpe but in the surrounding villages, has almost disappeared. A more creamy limestone, which became available in the latter years of the C19, was much used by *Matthew Holding* for his churches.

ST JOHN BAPTIST. The church stands well above the extensive green and with its surroundings forms a welcome oasis from the main roads and supermarket complex nearby. It has an interesting and unusual interior. An aisleless Early Norman church is recognizable by its windows above the arcades in the nave as well as the chancel. About 1170–80 aisles were added, first, it seems, to the chancel on the N side, then to the nave on both sides. The chancel aisle has two bays, circular pier with square abacus, many-scalloped capitals, and unmoulded round arches with a hoodmould decorated by nailhead. The same arches continue in the three-bay nave arcades. The piers are circular too and the abaci square, but the capitals are very shallow and have leaf motifs. They both have big nailhead hoodmoulds. The chancel was lengthened after 1300 – see the one ogee-headed lancet in the N chapel and the central pier of clustered columns in its S arcade. A rib-vaulted CRYPT with a central octagonal pier lies below the E end (cf. All Saints Northampton). The ribs are chamfered. The wide one-bay chancel chapels are of the early C14. ROOD LOFT entrances either side of the chancel and in the S aisle so presumably a continuous screen across the church. Externally the most noteworthy feature is the two square-headed S windows of the S chapel. They are Dec. The lights have ogee heads, and the windows are framed on three sides by fleuron friezes. Dec but simpler the aisle windows, those of the N aisle having ogee heads, and the N doorway. Fine w tower of the C14, refaced in its upper parts in ashlar, but when? Perhaps in the C15? Doorway with continuous mouldings, tall tower arch. Tall two-light bell-openings. Recessed spire with lucarnes in three tiers.

The church had a severe restoration by *William Slater* in 1862–3 when a good deal of the exterior walls was largely rebuilt and the windows renewed. A new elaborate chancel arch was also inserted where the C12 arch would have been. – PULPIT. Jacobean. – STALLS. Four in the chancel, with carved poppyheads, are original C14 or early C15. – RAILS. Mid-C18 with elegant balusters on ball supports. – REREDOS of 1891. Memorial (†1881) of alabaster and splendidly carved. Two statues and a central panel of Christ resurrected by the tomb. Vine canopy. – STAINED GLASS. Nave N. Early C14 grisaille and border fragments. – Much later glass. Chancel E window 1884 by *J. Hardman & Co.* – S chapel by *Herbert Bryans*. 1901. – S aisle E window by *Clayton & Bell* 1904. – S aisle S window 2000 and a Joyce memorial 2010 by *Sue Brownridge & Nicholas Bechgaard*. – N aisle two windows also by *Bryans*. – MONUMENT. Edward Reynolds †1698. Oval cartouche surrounded by excellently carved flowers etc. Two putti at the top. Attributed to *William Woodman* the elder (GF).

ST AIDAN (R.C.), Manor Road. 1963–4 by *J. S. Comper*. The exterior red brick, the interior whitewashed, aisleless, in a minimal Gothic. Spatially quite effective. Domed Lady Chapel in the SE corner.

BAPTIST CHAPEL, High Street. 1835. Still classical and of the familiar three-bay form with round-arched windows. The interior and porch of 1892 by *Ingman & Shaw*. Sunday School of 1881 on the l. similarly with round-arched windows on the first floor.

NORTHAMPTON UNIVERSITY, Moulton Park, Boughton Green Road. This originates from a College of Education opened in 1972. In 1975 it was redesignated as Nene College. During the 1990s it absorbed a number of other institutions, notably the Leathersellers' College in London. In 1999 it was renamed University College and finally achieved full university status in 2005. It has a further campus in St George's Avenue, Northampton (*see* p. 461). The Park campus has been much enhanced since the 1970s with a number of new buildings by *Gotch, Saunders & Surridge*. These include the Business School in 1991–2, a restaurant in 1994–5, the Leather Conservation Centre (1997) and the Senate building (1997–8).

KINGSTHORPE COMMUNITY COLLEGE, Boughton Green Road. 2007–8.

KINGSTHORPE GROVE SCHOOL, ¼ m. SE from the junction in Kingsthorpe Grove. One of the finest Board Schools in Northampton by *Law & Harris*, 1905–8. A large single-storey building decorated with bright red terracotta. Art Nouveau drainpipes and patterned glass within its large central gabled projection.

KINGSTHORPE PRIMARY SCHOOL, Knights Lane. By *A. W. Walker & Partners*, 1962.

PERAMBULATION. The old village centres around the green and the church. N of the church in VICARAGE LANE is WELL YARD HOUSE, with a gable to the road, of two storeys with C17 mullioned windows. GRIFFIN COTTAGE, behind and once part of the house, has a stone door surround with fluted sides. Other simpler stone houses further on. s of the church a pleasant group around the GREEN. At the NE corner KINGSWELL with its stream, now mostly culverted, which supplied water to the Hall. Just by it is KINGSWELL COTTAGE, C17 ironstone with one remaining two-light mullioned window and the lintel marks below of others. To its r. is THE OLD RECTORY, an impressive c. 1900 house with big tile-hung gables, bracketed oriels and a timber porch, and original glass in its front door. It has all the marks of being the work of *Matthew Holding*. To the w runs GREEN END with another Edwardian Queen Anne row, FREMEAUX TERRACE. Three big rendered gables and canted bays below. Opposite the KING WILLIAM IV pub. A nice essay in sandstone and red brick with bands of herringbone decoration, c. 1890.

N from the green is HIGH STREET with on the corner of Knights Lane the former SCHOOL of 1840 by *H. J. Underwood* in respectable Tudor mullioned window style. Just round the corner in MANOR ROAD is an exceptional pair (No. 45A and B) built for himself by *Tad Dobraszczyk*, 1991. The style is best described as Arts and Crafts Romanesque. The two houses of ironstone and brick have sequences of tall round-arched windows with, in between, lower timber-framed sections and porches. No. 45A has its plaster panels painted with a copy Arts and Crafts floral design and its glazing, with its triangles, is inspired by Mackintosh's 78 Derngate. It is an exciting addition to an otherwise standard brick terrace street.

Off High Street, in KINGSWELL ROAD, close to the entrance to Kingsthorpe Hall, the HOME FARM, old buildings including an oblong DOVECOTE. KINGSTHORPE HALL, s of Mill Lane, in its own small park, is by *John Johnson* of Leicester, for James Fremeaux, 1773–5. White Kingsthorpe stone, five by five bays, two and a half storeys. In the main façade the ground-floor windows in blank arcading. Simple plan with basically two rooms on either side of the central entrance-cum-staircase. Vaulted entrance passage with shallow central dome. Very handsome spiral stair behind going all the way up and lit by a dome. Wrought-iron balustrade. Pedimented STABLES behind the house. From the Fremeaux family the estate passed to the Thorntons of Brockhall and on the death of Hugh Thornton in 1938 the house and park were purchased by Northampton Borough Council. The stable area has been redeveloped for housing but the main house still (2011) waits a certain use and restoration.

Further w, N of Mill Lane, an impressive 1990s development centring on KINGSMOOR HOUSE, a two-storey Neo-Georgian house of brick with a three-bay centre under a pediment and two bays on each side. Sash windows and a pilastered and canopied doorcase. Rusticated quoins. Impressively done, but unfortunately completely hemmed in by later obstructing ranges. From here Mill Lane leads E to the main HARBOR-

OUGH ROAD. At the junction, THE COCK HOTEL, extremely competent gabled Tudor of 1893 by *G. H. Stevenson*, and opposite, ST DAVID'S. This is on the site of the Hospital of Holy Trinity, of which the last minor remains were demolished in 1928. The house was built for the Robinson family and dates from 1882. It was for many years used as a Roman Catholic school and has since been added to, notably with a large gymnasium of 1984 by the *Ellis Williams Partnership*. A small green in the centre of the road junction has a cast-iron TRAM SHELTER of *c.* 1920 with rounded ends and a WAR MEMORIAL which formerly had a bronze statue of a crusader by *Sir Alfred Turner*. This was stolen in 1999 and replaced with an approximate replica by *Olive Wootten* (2002). Further N on the W side of Harborough Road the ASDA store, built for Presto in 1988 by *Seymour Harris Partnership*. Interesting pyramidal core with triangular side openings. A little further on the same side a ceramic gable of the former CO-OP store of 1904 by *Alexander Anderson*. ¼ m. N of this, No. 12A HARBOROUGH ROAD NORTH is a decent flat-roofed brick bungalow by *Alan J. Ede*, 1968, for himself.

OBELISK, 1 m. NW, off Holly Lodge Road. It once stood on an open hilltop within view of Boughton Hall (q.v.) and was one of the various structures within what was its landscape park, but now surrounded by modern housing. Erected in 1764 by William Wentworth to the memory of his friend William Cavendish, 4th Duke of Devonshire, who died that year. Cavendish served briefly as Prime Minister 1756–7 but spent some of his youth at Boughton. It is built of Kingsthorpe stone, though some of this has been replaced during restoration in the early 1980s.

LITTLE BILLING

The tiny village has all but disappeared and is now totally engulfed by housing estates.

ALL SAINTS, Manorfield Road. The church had a N aisle, but the arcade was removed *c.* 1500, when the W half of the building was rebuilt as a wide hall. Several windows and doorways derive from this early C16 building. According to *Wetton's Guide* the arcade consisted of wooden posts on stone bases. C15 windows in the chancel and N chapel, the latter a total restoration copying that in the chancel. A 1838 drawing by George Clarke shows the jambs infilled with masonry and a three-light C17 window. *Lewis Loyd* of Overstone rebuilt the N chapel in 1849, and *E. F. Law* restored the church in 1852–4. The N tower, with its pyramidal spire, built on an old base, owes its somewhat starved appearance to Law. The N chapel and the chancel both open now into the nave. Between the two arches is a tall C15 niche which holds a STATUE of the Virgin carved by Sister *Mirabel* of Wantage Convent 1925. – REREDOS of 1852–4 with very Victorian colourful painted lettering. –

STALLS in the chancel with poppyheads of 1852, and a
PRAYER-DESK, late C19 with finials of an angel and a bull for
SS Matthew and Luke from Cookham Dean, Berks. This may
well be part of the furnishing there which *Temple Moore*
designed in 1889. – FONT. Big plain, Saxon, of tub shape, but   8
of great interest because of its inscription: 'Wigberhtus artifex
atq cementarius hunc fabricavit / Quisquis suum venit mergere
corpus procul dubio capit.' Professor Talbot Rice drew attention to fonts with comparable Latin inscriptions at Potterne,
Wilts., and Patrishaw, Brecon.

MANOR HOUSE, N of the church. The fragment of a larger
mansion of the Longuevilles. One circular quatrefoil window
in the E wall, one four-light window with arched lights in the
s wall. Large C17 mullion-transom windows on the first floor
on both s and E sides.

OLD RECTORY. Mainly an enlargement of *c.* 1820 of an older
building. Handsome panelled entrance hall and a pretty
staircase.

A good thatched COTTAGE to the w of the church.

SOUTHERN DISTRICT AND HUNSBURY DISTRICT

DIVISIONAL POLICE HEADQUARTERS, Mereway. By the
County Architect's Department (*A. N. Harris*), 1963.

WOOTTON HALL PARK. At the entrance, the COUNTY
RECORDS OFFICE, a prestigious pyramidal building of 1991.
Further s is WOOTTON HALL (County Police Headquarters
since 1947). Red brick, Neo-Georgian, built soon after 1913–14
by *J. Brown* following the destruction by fire of an earlier house.
A long red brick frontage of two storeys, mildly Georgian in
manner. Small four-columned portico. Mid-1970s extensions
by *John Goff*, County Architect, and more since. In the grounds
some temporary single-storey offices of the 1960s for the
County Council.

The area s and w of the London Road and Mereway forms part
of the SOUTHERN DISTRICT of the expanded town with
immediately s the estates of Merefield and Blacky More, predictable 1980s–90s housing. On the s edge Collingtree Park
with 1990s housing of a more executive kind. To the w is the
HUNSBURY DISTRICT, named after the Iron Age hillfort
which occupies a central open space within the development.
Impressive in the centre of the development is ST BENEDICT'S
CHURCH of 1982 by *Brian Austin* of the *Featherstone Austin
Partnership*. Trapezoid form with a slender tower. Lofty interior with heavy beam structures. – FURNISHINGS. Several
brought from elsewhere, such as the STALLS from Upton and
the FONT from Normanton, Rutland. The HUNSBURY HILL
CENTRE is based around a farm complex which dates from
the mid C18.

HUNSBURY CAMP, SW of Danes Camp Way. This is an Iron Age
hillfort consisting of a bank, ditch, and counterscarp bank
running round the 90-metre contour line and enclosing an area

of *c.* 4 acres (1.6 ha). Of the three breaks in the defences, that to the NW was created in the C19, the entrance to the NNE was at least widened in C19, while the entrance to the SE seems to be original. Excavation of the bank in the 1950s and 1980s has shown that the original rampart, probably constructed in the late C6 or C5 B.C. had a timber revetment and probably timber box construction. This rampart was burnt and later reconstructed, probably as a glacis form. The reconstruction may have coincided with the intensive use of the interior in the Late Iron Age, C2–C1 B.C. The ironstone working of the 1880s removed much of the interior and revealed numerous storage pits containing an important assemblage of Iron Age domestic finds, including late Iron Age pottery with curvilinear decoration and some 150 beehive-shaped rotary querns. Traces of an outer ditch system, found 75 metres to the N, is of uncertain date. Following abandonment in the early C1 A.D., a number of extended inhumations, possibly Saxon in date, were deposited on top of the glacis rampart. Geophysical survey and trial excavation in the 2000s has shown that slightly more of the interior inside the SE entrance has survived than previously thought, with the area containing further pits and at least one roundhouse.

WESTON FAVELL

ST PETER. Of the C11 or early C12 the lower part of the originally unbuttressed W tower with a rough blocked W doorway, the N doorway (shafts with scalloped capitals, segmental arch), and the S priest's doorway (one slight step in the arch) – i.e. the bones of the church. Of the C13 the chancel (good stepped lancets under one arch in the S wall) and most of the W tower (double-stepped tower arch, pair of lancets in the W wall, lancets in twos as bell-openings). S doorway C16 with four-centred arch. Evidence of a stoup on its r. side. In 1725 the spire on the tower was struck by lightning and collapsed on to the N aisle; it was decided not to rebuild either. In 1881–2 *Matthew Holding* put in hand a major restoration, replacing the N aisle and its arcade, rebuilding the chancel arch, adding the N transeptal chapel and replacing several S and N windows. Interestingly drawings exist for these changes signed by the Stamford architect *J. C. Traylen* but newspaper reports of the opening give the credit totally to Holding. The TILES are 1881 copying some found during the restoration. The STALLS with their poppyheads are of 1894–5, designed by *Holding* and carved by *S. L. Reynolds* of Northampton. – FONT. Octagonal, Late Perp, that is early C16, with motifs such as rosette, shield, large leaves. – PULPIT. Jacobean. – BELFRY SCREEN by *Frank Webber*, 1971. – HOURGLASS. C17 in a Victorian wrought-iron holder. – EMBROIDERY. A delightfully naïve Last Supper, dated 1698, said to have been worked by *Lady Holman*. It was in all probability a dorsal. It is notable for the use, at that time, of tiny glass beads as a general background. Restored 1990. –

STAINED GLASS. Chancel E window of 1881 by *Heaton, Butler & Bayne*. – Chancel S 1896 and N aisle 1893, both by *H. Hymers* and a panel in the N transept. – N aisle engraved windows with figures of saints of 1977 and 1981, two by *John Hutton*, one by *Jennifer Conway*. Tower window also by *Jenny Conway c.* 1973. – MONUMENTS. Gertrude Ekins †1689, but probably erected 1704. White marble with arched inscription and lush acanthus at the base. – Mary Greene †1725. An impressive marble mural monument with a small black sarcophagus above the inscription tablet and a gadrooned base on console brackets. Good quality. Large slab by entrance to the vestry for Rev. James Hervey †1758. He was famous in the mid C18 for his writings, notably 'Meditations among the tombs', published in 1748. – Elizabeth Halford †1769. The familiar pyramidal *Cox* family type. This one with yellow marble background and a Rococo cartouche.

Excellent VESTRY on the N side of the chancel, 1969–71 by *Frank Webber* (of *Marshman, Warren & Taylor*). In a yellow stone which tones well with the church. Low hipped roof with a prominent projecting drainpipe.

VILLAGE HALL, Wellingborough Road. A small brick building mildly Colonial in manner, 1929–31 by *John Brown*.

Weston Favell still has its old village centre around the church. Immediately W of the church, three pairs of stone houses with tiled roofs and bays, 1920 by *Law & Harris*. Some nice houses S of the church. First PRIORY HOUSE, with an early C19 Gothic front to the garden. In the garden an octagonal GAZEBO. Tucked away behind, No. 111, by *Stimpson & Walton*, 1967–9. One-storeyed. Brick facing panels projecting above the roof-line. Just E are DEVONSHIRE COTTAGES, a brick row of 1887 built for the workers at the MOORE FACTORY whose building, converted into a residence, still stands behind them. To the N in HIGH STREET the 1930s BOLD DRAGOON pub, in a C17 manner, and further on the WESLEYAN CHAPEL of 1853 with Gothic windows. To the W of the church, across the road, the RECTORY, stone, partly faced with a red brick façade of five bays built 1758 by the Rev. James Hervey, who died before it was complete. Additions of 1777 which probably include the castellated wing on the l. More stone houses further S.

(For Weston Way *see* Abington, p. 476 and for the Eastern District *see* p. 487.)

NORTON

ALL SAINTS. C13 W tower with Perp top. Otherwise the church is mostly Dec. The S doorway has small capitals to its shafts decorated with faces. S arcade of six bays, an impressive sight. Quatrefoil piers, arches of one chamfer and one sunk quadrant. The N arcade with octagonal piers is also Dec, but a little later.

The clerestory is late c16 or early c17. Restoration of 1894 by
R. Armstrong. – FONTS. One c18, of baluster type of grey
marble. – The other circular, with four faces sticking out. Probably a c13 piece, completely re-cut. – WEST SCREEN. A fine
ensemble. Three-storeyed. As high as the nave; with pilasters
and arches. The lower part is of 1810, the upper is of the c18
and has the usual commandment boards; it presumably formed
the reredos. Now much hidden by the w gallery and organ. –
PULPIT, c17. – STAINED GLASS. E window signed by *Willement*
and dated 1847. With three large figures in somewhat gaudy
colours. – Grisaille type glass with figures and shields *c.* 1850
is also by *Willement*. – ROYAL ARMS (in the tower), painted and
dated 1709. – HATCHMENTS. A display of six; three are for the
Breton family, 1764, 1785 and 1798, and three for the Botfield
family, 1813, 1825 and 1863.

MONUMENTS. An uncommonly large number. Brass to
William Knyght †1501 and wife, 23-in. (58-cm.) figures. – Lady
Elizabeth Knightly †1602. Large standing monument of alabaster. Recumbent effigy. Arch with rows of coffering and
much ribbon work on the back panel. Black columns, outer
obelisks. The surround of better quality than the effigy, but
almost certainly from the *Hollemans* workshop. – Nicholas
Breton †1624. Tablet with two cherubs; very quiet, not really
Jacobean in style. – Ann Breton †1635 – Tablet. Banded obelisks l. and r. A skull in the open segmental pediment. – Elizabeth Verney †1633. Large kneeling figure. On the broad piers
l. and r. two allegorical figures. Also attributed to *Hollemans*.
– Nicholas Breton †1658 and wife. Large standing monument,
progressive for its date. The centre has two busts of white
marble. Big surround of pink and white marble. Open segmental pediment with shield and heavy garlands. Attributed to
C. G. Cibber (GF). – Mrs Botfield †1825. By *William Behnes*. A
strange conceit. The only figure is her son, life-size, mourning
her. Does this show filial piety, or also a wish to appear himself,
close to the altar? Grecian style.

NORTON HALL was blown up in 1945. It was originally built by
the Knightleys of Fawsley in the c16 but was much added to
by the Botfield family, who acquired the manor in 1800. In
1809 *Humphry Repton* advised and may have made some slight
alterations. He certainly did some work on the landscape. By
1840 the house had become a romantic castellated Gothic
affair owing to alterations and enlargement done for Beriah
Botfield (†1863), the bibliophile.

ALMSHOUSES, Daventry Road. A row of six built 1853 by *E. F.
Law*.

CANAL JUNCTION, ½ m. N, just W of the A5. The junction of the
Grand Union and Grand Junction canals created in 1814.
BRIDGES with horse ramps and former TOLL HOUSE built
1914.

BANNAVENTA. At Whilton Lodge on Watling Street is the site of
a Roman settlement, extending on both sides of the main road
and into Whilton parish, and covering at least 30 acres (12 ha).

Finds of pottery and coins have been made since C18. Excavation in the 1970s showed that the defences consisted of a ditch with earth rampart. In the early C4 the ditch was filled, and a stone wall and further ditches beyond were constructed. In the 2010s there is an ongoing programme of geophysical survey across the town and its hinterland.

OLD

St Andrew. Ironstone and limestone. Perp W tower with pairs of two-light transomed bell-openings, a quatrefoil frieze and battlements. Very ornate Late Perp N doorway with leaf spandrels, a Tudor rose and a portcullis, flanking buttresses with pinnacles, and ten fleuron motifs all along the hoodmould. The DOOR would seem to be original. Responds, doorway and windows of the S aisle, with Y-tracery, are late C13, as is the piscina with dogtooth arch. Fine Perp arcade of four bays, wide arches, piers with four shafts and four hollows. The arcade could be later than the tower, its details reminiscent of the arcades at Whiston, so a date after 1500 likely. Nave roof with good angel corbels of stone, single and in pairs, holding shields with the Instruments of the Passion. The C14 chancel, which has a recess with a four-centred head, perhaps an Easter sepulchre, now containing a memorial inscription of 1606, was totally rebuilt in the C19. Its gable is dated 1671. The restoration was by *C. Bather* of Shrewsbury 1874–5. Good TILES of that time. – FONT. Perp, octagonal with quatrefoils and roses. Shields under some bearing a fret design. – PULPIT. C19 but incorporating some tracery and a ribbon frieze of Perp character, again probably early C16. – STAINED GLASS. In a S aisle window medieval fragments (including a man with the devil on his back, *c.* 1520, indistinct label probably a warning about chattering in church). – MONUMENTS. Some simple C17 or C18 tablets under the tower by *John Hunt* and the *Coxes*. – In the churchyard some good SLATE HEADSTONES, including several for the Palmer family between 1793 and 1839, all with verses, and one for William Wright of Scaldwell †1769 with a figure of Faith leaning on a tomb, clouds, cherubs and a crown.

The Old Rectory. Thought to have been built by the Rev. Robert Townsen in the early C17. A beam in the dining room is dated 1616. Extended W in the mid C18 when a canted bay was added. There were later alterations, which probably included the graceful staircase, between 1835 and 1850. Hipped roof.

The Manor House, NE of the church. A relatively simple two-storey ironstone house but having a fine two-storey limestone ashlar porch with the date 1607 and the initials G I. which has the appearance of not belonging. The proximity to Lamport (q.v.) suggests the I is for Isham.

N of the church in HARRINGTON ROAD, two handsome, excellently built stone farmhouses, WOLD FARMHOUSE dated 1758 and its neighbour, BREWERY HOUSE, dated 1759 and 1760. Both would appear to be by the same builder, with coursed stonework and limestone platbands. Window frames are original but the fenestration is later: C19 in Wold Farmhouse, and later wooden transomed leaded casement windows in Brewery House.

ORLINGBURY

8070

ST MARY. 1843 by *R. C. Hussey* of Birmingham. An impressive and remarkably serious, substantial job. Tall crossing tower with filigree battlements and very tall pinnacles, in 1970–1 lowered by 10 ft (3 metres). At the E end a large rose window. The crossing arches chamfered but dying into the walls. The style is Dec throughout. Paid for partly by the rector and partly by A. A. Young of the Hall; wall inscriptions of commemoration in Gothic framing are to the l. and r. of the S transept E window. Fittings largely intact. – FONT. Sumptuous, and of ogee form. Richly traceried. – BENCHES with fleur-de-lys heads. – ALTAR SURROUND. Metal standards topped by gilded angels, 1970s, made by *Frank Knight*. – STAINED GLASS. Chancel E, 1922 by *J. Hardman & Co*. – Other chancel windows by *A. Gibbs*, 1863. – Nave N window, St Christopher, 1928, also by *Hardman*. – Nave S window, Ormerod memorial. Very pictorial, showing the village, countryside and sheep, designed by *Chris Fiddes*, 1994 and made by *Nicholas Bechgaard*, 1995. – MONUMENTS. Alabaster effigy of a knight, *c*. 1375 (chancel N). – Brasses to William Lane †1502 and wife (S transept), 18-in. (46-cm.) figures. – Sophia Bridges †1853. By *Hussey*.

ORLINGBURY HALL. Bought by Richard Young in 1706 and rebuilt apparently immediately after. No architect is known. While it fits the *Smith* of Warwick type an equally suited candidate would be *John Lumley* of Northampton. Justinian Isham mentions the house in 1709. Ironstone with Weldon stone dressings. The entrance side is original. Nine bays divided into three threes by giant Doric pilasters. Each pilaster carries one metope. Tall windows in flat frames. Pedimented dormers and tall chimneys. The other sides and the interior are altered. The garden side has a large canted bay and a W addition, both of the C19. C19 service wing.

Small rectangular DOVECOTE on the E side of the village. Probably C18.

Former SCHOOL and SCHOOL HOUSE. 1843 in the Tudor style with a tall three-light transomed window in its end wall.

RECTORY. On the green, the entry close to that of the Hall. Dated 1703. Five bays, two storeys.

An attractive small village, made the more so due to its leafy green. In the village a number of ESTATE HOUSES built by Mr Young 'after his own plans'. His architect was *R. C. Hussey*. THE OLD FORGE at the SE corner of the green is typical with light sandstone and dark ironstone dressings. It has a castellated bay window.

ORTON

8070

ALL SAINTS. Closed in 1964, now a stonemasons' training centre. Short, unbuttressed Norman W tower. Later medieval top with battlements and pinnacles. Norman arch towards the nave, pointed. Norman also the chancel arch. The rest all over-restored in 1887 by *H. A. Cooper*. The original work points to the late C13, see the S arcade, the S aisle E lancet, and the S doorway. – FONT. Circular, with four faces – human and animal – like knobs. Is it C13? – COMMUNION RAIL. C18. – STAINED GLASS. All by *J. Hardman & Co*.

OUNDLE

0080

Oundle is the most rewarding stone-built town in Northamptonshire. In this area it comes a close second to Stamford, with which it has much in common; neither was ever an industrial town. There was leather in the C16 and brewing in the later C18 and C19, but neither of these produced major buildings. Oundle has always been a market town and social centre, and it remains so today, but equally it has a reputation nationally for its public school. The problem of the public school in the small town can be solved in several ways. At Harrow or Uppingham the school is the *Stadtkrone*, at Eton it is the great surprise at the far end of an undisturbed little town. At Oundle it is nowhere in prominence except in one place outside the main circulation; and the small, beautiful, stone-built town with its dominating church in the centre has it all its own way. Indeed the school has been one of Oundle's architectural benefactors, not only for its own set of buildings, but because over the centuries it has acquired some of the finest and most interesting properties in the town, so ensuring their preservation and conservation. The finest house in the town, Cobthorne, for example, is the home of the school's headmaster.

Oundle has an ancient history. The Abbey of Peterborough established a minster here, already in existence by the C8, although it was rebuilt at the end of the C10. Its exact site is uncertain but the parish church probably occupies part of it, there being portions of Saxon carving preserved there. There was already a market in Oundle by 1086. In medieval times the whole space between the churchyard and the present Market Place was in use. Gradually at first temporary stalls and shops were erected on its northern flank, these becoming permanent by the C17. Not immediately apparent but obvious when one explores is the layout of properties along the streets. It is most obvious in West Street. On each side the main property is on the street frontage, then stretching back, both N and S, are long rectangular plots of varying width. These long plots with yards and gardens run back on each side to back lanes: South Road and Milton Road. In many cases there were passages or alleys between the plots running back to the lanes and several of these also survive. One or two of the most fashionable properties erected gazebos over-

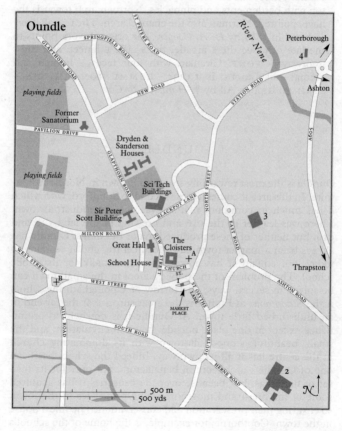

Oundle

River Nene

Peterborough

Ashton

Thrapston

playing fields

Former Sanatorium

Dryden & Sanderson Houses

Sci Tech Buildings

Sir Peter Scott Building

Great Hall

School House

The Cloisters

MARKET PLACE

500 m
500 yds

SPRINGFIELD ROAD · ST PETERS ROAD · NEW ROAD · STATION ROAD · GLAPTHORN ROAD · PAVILION DRIVE · BLACKPOT LANE · NORTH STREET · EAST ROAD · MILTON ROAD · NEW STREET · CHURCH ST. · ST OSYTHS LANE · WEST STREET · MILL ROAD · SOUTH ROAD · SOUTH ROAD · HERNE ROAD · ASHTON ROAD · A605

A St Peter	1 Town Hall (former)
B Church of the Holy Name (R.C.)	2 Prince William School
	3 Laxton Junior School
	4 Railway Station (former)

looking the countryside beyond their gardens, and two survive, almost inevitably divorced now from their original properties. Over the centuries some building has taken place within these plots, but they are still very clear today.

The main effect of Oundle, again like Stamford, is 'Georgian', but this is a broad classification since it covers properties dating from the middle of the C17 right through to the C19, and even into the early C20. The façades should not delude the visitor since in a good many cases there is plenty of evidence of earlier structures behind. There are in any case many properties with C16 or C17 mullioned windows, often in projecting bays.

CHURCHES AND PUBLIC BUILDINGS

ST PETER. A fine church in a fine setting, much enhanced by the surrounding buildings of Oundle School and a wealth of Georgian tombstones, many with pretty decoration. The finest feature is the tower and spire, a feature which still dominates the skyline on the approaches to the town. It belongs to the specially happy variety with a really tall slender tower and a not too excessively tall recessed needle spire. The style is Late Dec, but at that moment when Perp is on the horizon. W doorway with cusped ogee arch and gable. Niches l. and r. Small panelled tunnel-vault inside the entrance (cf. Higham Ferrers). Two-light window above this with identical blank windows l. and r. The S and N sides have tall blank arcading with ogee forms instead and a blank storey over this. Then a shorter blank arcading. Beautifully tall and elegant bell-openings. Three very slim two-light openings with transom and identical blank windows l. and r. Quatrefoil frieze, fleuron frieze, battlements, and short, polygonal embattled turret pinnacles. Battlements and pinnacles have decorative cross-shaped arrowslits. The tower was built independent of the body of the church initially, as is clear from buttresses visible inside either side of the tower arch. The spire is crocketed up the angles and has three tiers of lucarnes all in the cardinal directions, but its form is a little suspect since at its base is a large plaque with the date 1634. So another example of a spire which fell, probably because of a lightning strike (cf. Raunds and Higham Ferrers, amongst others). The nave clerestory downpipes likewise have a date on elaborate hoppers of 1637, so this early C17 period needs to be borne in mind.

The church owes its origin to a Saxon monastery, and a piece of Saxon carving is set into the inside W wall of the tower. This was followed by a Norman church of which there is equally scant evidence. One chancel window with roll moulding visible from the N chapel and some pieces of zigzag from an arch and a small capital with similar moulding. The cruciform plan originates from this church and it was retained when the body of the building was rebuilt in the C13. Early the S arcade with circular piers and circular capitals and abaci and pointed double-chamfered arches. A little nailhead decoration.* Both chancel chapels of about the same time, see their arches. The arch from the N chapel to the chancel is segmental. The N arcade is of the later C13. Responds with fillets. Nailhead in the arch to the N transept. Much of the outside is also C13. Window tracery throughout the church is instructive, even bearing in mind some rather harsh C19 restoration. It begins with the W window of the S aisle: a group of five lancets under a single arched head. Then at the W end of the N aisle four lancets of equal height with, within the arched head, circles with a sexfoil at the top and two smaller quatrefoils below. There is evidence that before its restoration there were small eyelet insets between the circles. The slender chancel windows come next together with the side windows of the S transept. Those in the chancel (N and S) are of two lights and a quatrefoiled circle in their heads. They were lengthened when the chancel was heightened in the C15. Its original height clearly defined externally on the S side. Geometrical tracery also in the S chapel where there are now three circles with quatrefoils. Much more elaborate is the S window of the S transept, but this is largely due to the restoration by *G. G. Scott* in 1864 and may not be reliable. The Dec style begins with some simple windows with intersecting tracery (N transept W and larger on N). The E window of the N transept is unusual. It has basically Geometrical tracery for its three lights but in the head of a sharply pointed arch is a large trefoil with ball-flower ornament. The best of the Dec windows is the E window of the N chapel, five lights with intricate patterning above. Less complex is the window in the S aisle to the E of the porch. Five lights with the side pairs with reticulated tracery. The head, however, is odd and flattened and this could easily be the result of tactful reforming in the 1630s. The furthest E windows of the clerestory also have reticulated tracery but the others are different and simpler, and again one might remember the 1637 date. Finally the large E window of the S chapel, again five lights with somewhat uncomfortable flowing tracery but clear indications that Perp is on the way.

Returning to architectural features, when the tower was rebuilt it prompted the rebuilding of the arches N, S and E of the crossing. They have the same mouldings and angular capitals as the tower arch. The Perp period is well represented by two fine windows, the chancel E and one in the N aisle. Not quite orthodox but clearly from the same workshop. However, the finest feature of this period is the S porch. It is a dramatic piece, paid for by a rich merchant, Robert Wyatt, and his wife, and built *c.* 1485. Two storeys with battlements and pinnacles. Tierceron vault with ridge ribs and a pendant. Foliated bosses. S doorway with slanting reveals decorated with panelling. The two-storey vestry on the N side of the chancel also C15. It is

---

* Amusing carved heads as stops on the first arches of each arcade, put up in 1996–7. They are of the former vicar Canon Caddick and Bishop Westwood of Peterborough, wearing glasses.

worth recording the reordering of the interior of the church in 1991–2. This has revealed the full scale of the arcades and opened up the chancel. *Scott*'s choir stalls etc. remain. – Ornate Dec SEDILIA with crocketed ogee arches A similar but more highly ornate PISCINA in the S transept. – FONT. Unusual, like the plinth of a monument. Usually called early C18 but could it be as early as the 1630s? Of oblong form with small fluted shafts at either end. The edges of the bowl have cherubs' heads. It looks a different stone and might be older and reused – PULPIT. Perp, repainted in original colours in 1965. – SCREENS. Two Perp parclose screens and remains of the base of the Perp chancel screen. – REREDOS. 1864 with much fine foliage carving and a central incised panel of the Last Supper, by *Clayton & Bell*, the carving by *Cox & Sons*. – S DOOR. Outer portions Perp, with tracery panels. – LECTERN. Fine C15 brass eagle, the same as at Urbino Cathedral, Southwell Minster, Newcastle Cathedral, Long Sutton, Lincolnshire, Oxburgh, Norfolk, etc. – AUMBRY (S chapel) with gilt canopy. By *L. H. Bond*, 1971. – CHANDELIER. Of brass, two tiers. Dated 1687. The smaller chandeliers are the work of *Frank Knight* of Wellingborough, 1970s. – STAINED GLASS. Chancel E, 1864 by *Clayton & Bell* and S, Smith memorial, 1918 by *Sir Ninian Comper*. – N transept, 1868 by *Clayton & Bell*. – Tower, 1875 also *Clayton & Bell*. – S aisle W, 1934 by *Margaret Chilton*. – MONUMENTS. Some impressive medieval brass indents in the chancel, one with a floriated cross for the rector John de Oundle †1278, others for priests. – Martha Kirkham †1616 (chancel). Made of stone. Back arch with cartouche no longer with strapwork. A draped curtain below. Achievement with two putti. On the l. and r. detached Ionic columns carrying obelisks. – William Loringe †1628 (nave W end). Small, of alabaster, with black marble columns and a broken pediment with arms. Ten children praying beneath. – Sophia Whitwell †1707 (E wall, exterior). Brass plate on a fully moulded sarcophagus base. – Mary Kirkham †1754 (S chapel). Standing monument largely of stone with obelisk and pretty carved Rococo floral pendants. Probably by *Bingham* of Peterborough. – William Walcot †1827 (chancel). Tablet with draped urn by *Francis* of London. – Rev. John Shillibeer †1841 (S aisle W end) by *John Thompson* of Peterborough. Elaborately Gothic. In the yard, opposite the S transept, a large Gothic table tomb for William Bodger †1856, parish clerk for fifty-seven years.

CHURCH OF THE HOLY NAME (R.C.), West Street. Originally the Jesus Church. 1878–9 by *Sir Arthur Blomfield*. Byzantine 'quincunx' or inscribed cross plan. Square centre with octagonal tower on squinches. The piers carrying the tower are clustered and of red stone. The four low corner spaces have pointed arches. C13 style fenestration. Matching vestry added in the SW corner, 1971.

TOWN HALL. 1826 in the Tudor style, paid for by the Watts-Russells of Biggin. Cruciform with open glazed arches and an oriel on the S side. Watts-Russell coat of arms at the top. Handsomely placed in the Market Place and skilfully adapted for commercial use in 1984 by *Paul Bancroft*.

COURT HOUSE (Oundle Town Council and Museum), Mill Road. 1876–7, stone in Renaissance manner partly by *E. F. Law*.

Former ISOLATION HOSPITAL, Woodlands, ½ m. w. Several buildings of 1903–4 *by J. A. Gotch*, incorporated within housing.

PRINCE WILLIAM SCHOOL, Herne Road. By the County Architect, *John Goff*, 1970–2. Some extensions since.

LAXTON JUNIOR SCHOOL, East Road. Opened 2002. By *Gotch, Saunders & Surridge*. A long low building of two storeys, brick at base and mainly windows on the upper floor. The hall section rises above the curved roof-line. Exposed metalwork canopies give interesting shadows.

Former RAILWAY STATION, NE edge of the town. Now converted into a residence. In the Old English style. By *J. Livock*, 1845 to serve the Northampton–Peterborough line. The former Station Hotel, on the junction, is also by *Livock*.

CEMETERY, ¼ m. w. Opened 1860. Lodge and chapel by *Edward Browning* of Stamford. The usual cemetery Gothic, the chapel in the Early Dec style, lancet windows and a thin pretty crocketed spire.

PERAMBULATIONS

An exploration of Oundle falls into two parts: the town (that is S, E and W from the church) and the rest, largely the school site (N of the Market Place). There are overlaps inevitably, mainly with the school's ownership of town properties.

1. *The town*

While it would be natural to begin in the Market Place, to get a feeling of what Oundle is all about it is much better to start at the far (W) end of WEST STREET by the R.C. church (*see* above), which sits on an island, the site of a medieval chapel. NW is BENEFIELD ROAD and just along on the S side are Nos. 2–4, PALMER COURT by the *Whyte Holland Partnership*, a tasteful infill of three houses of 1988. Brick, with varying roofs, gables and dormers. To the SW in STOKE HILL, NEW HOUSE (Oundle School), another house with two two-storeyed bay windows. It is dated 1640. MILL ROAD turns down to the S. Nos. 1–14 are a terrace of one-storeyed cottages, largely of the C18. At the end of Mill Road the former premises of the ANCHOR BREWERY of the 1870s.

Now into WEST STREET. On the l. a passage leads N and gives a view of the end gable of the former BRITISH SCHOOL, 1843, with an arched bellcote. Just N, into INKERMAN WAY, tucked back on the r. at the back of Queen Anne's House, are two splendid early C18 gatepiers topped by urns which formerly had ironwork gates. These were re-sited by the School next to the Talbot Inn in New Street. Back in West Street, past some not very inspiring C20 houses is the façade of the former ZION CHAPEL (now a residence) of 1852, but still with a classical front with arched doorway and windows and pediment. Solid row opposite with the date 1877, and on the l. VICTORIA YARD, one of the cut-through passages. Still on that side DYSONS (No. 51), with shop and house. Nice shopfront of *c*. 1900. On the s side a small house with late C16 mullions in its two-storey bays (called for no good reason THE MANOR HOUSE). Further on the N side QUEEN ANNE'S HOUSE, with an ashlar stone façade of 1824, but older behind with a double-gabled façade on the passageway, a huge chimneystack in the second bay and a five-light C17 mullioned window facing the yard. At the end of its former garden (in Milton Road; *see* below), an example of a surviving GAZEBO. Opposite another house with mullioned bays of the C17. Then on the N side the first Gothic intrusion: the STAHL THEATRE (former Congregational church) of 1864, by *W. F. Poulton* of Reading. Rough stone in the Early Dec style with two porches and a large four-light traceried window. Very sensitively adapted as a theatre for Oundle School by *Robert Weighton* of Cambridge, 1980. Then on the r. is DANFORDS. An early C19 impressive façade with a large central arch into its yard. Four Tuscan pilasters and balustrade at the top. Opposite is one of the most interesting buildings in the town: PAINE'S COTTAGES. What exists now are two wings of a large hall house, presenting their end gables with canted bays to the street, and in between a wall with a delightful early C17 doorway topped by a curved pediment and obelisk finials balanced on small balls. The l. wing was rebuilt when it was incorporated into the adjoining property, but the r. one is still intact and has beams and a fireplace of medieval origin, probably C15. It is unclear when the hall range between the wings was demolished. It was left as almshouses in 1801 by a Nonconformist, John Paine. Next, No. 43, a substantial two-storey early C19 house with shallow curved bays and carriage entrance. Opposite, No. 44 is another substantial detached stone house, double fronted with bays, two storeys topped by triangular gables. Framed doorcase with pediment holding a shield. Probably *c*. 1870. On the N side quite a nice shop façade of the early 1900s (OXFAM) with a triangular gable with slit inset pattern.

On the other side one of the most impressive C19 houses in the town, TOWNLEY HOUSE. Built *c*. 1840 as offices for the Oundle Union Brewery. The brewery was short-lived and the premises were taken over by a school for young ladies. Colvin records work for a school in 1841 by *Christopher Davy*, and this may well be the property. Two storeys and attic. Triple windows on the street, those of the first floor round-arched with a balcony. Small lunette in the attic gable. Back on the N side a big four-bay yellow brick house of the early C19 again with carriage entrance. Simple rusticated doorway. A little further on the r. one of the earliest Georgian façades, dated 1715 on its lead pipe. Long façade in two sections, three plus two bays of three storeys. Framed windows with small keystones. An access passage reveals a fine hooded doorcase with carved brackets on its s façade. Then back on the N side a further Gothic chapel, now converted into shops (THE BAZAAR), the former METHODIST CHURCH of 1842, again in the Early Dec style. Pairs of lancets either side of its doorcase and a big octofoil wheel window above. Then another detached piece of Victorian, VICTORIA HALL (Oundle Town Council), in the Renaissance manner, by *J. B. Corby* 1902–3. The hall inside has an open timber roof with pierced honeysuckle patterns.

66　　Opposite is the most exciting house in the town, COB-THORNE. Beautifully set back for effect. Built 1658 for Major General William Boteler, Cromwell's lord chamberlain, who is said to have removed wooden beams from Tresham's Lyveden New Bield (q.v.) to use in its construction. It is five bays with square-framed windows, now sashed but which must have been cross-mullion-transom casements originally. The first-floor windows have aprons. Fine doorcase with round-arched doorway having a circle in its pediment. Slim pilasters. The window above joins it and has scroll supports on its jambs. Deep coved cornice breaking forward slightly over the central feature. Four dormers and panelled chimneystacks on its end gables. The house has its own stable block dated 1728 and entrance. The garden façade is similar to the entrance façade, but the side elevations are interesting. Double gables with their stacks, two oval openings in each, then two sets of small rectangular openings, blocked on the r. The interior has been much altered but the original staircase with turned balusters and ball-topped newels survives. It rises the full height of the building. Behind the house is a magnificent garden, running right down to South Road, where there is a gateway. The plot is huge and fans out each side behind adjoining properties. Architecturally the house has a good deal in common with *Peter Mills*'s Thorpe Hall, near Peterborough, of similar date, but perhaps more with the work of the Peterborough mason-builder *John Lovin* who built Thorney Abbey House in 1660 and the Market House in Peterborough in 1671. The lower block on the l. was originally built as a bank in the early C19. Still on the s side, next comes a fine double-fronted property with a most elegant late C18 double-bayed shopfront. Then a mid-C19 three-bay house, Neo-Georgian with rusticated quoins, arched windows with keystones and a Tuscan pilastered doorcase.

Next the delightful BUTCHER'S SHOP with its painted tile decorations, and then facing up New Street a late C18 five-bay house (VINCENT SYKES), sash windows on first floor, the ground floor altered but still with doorway with fanlight. Returning to the N side of West Street, nearly opposite Cobthorne and running the whole of the rest of the street and turning into New Street is a sizeable property, now but a shadow of its former self. Its extent now is only obvious by

noting the C17 mullioned windows on its first floor. At its w
end a shop has a small C18 doorway with a Gibbs surround
and its final section has three instead of two storeys with a
gabled top, admittedly rebuilt. It is very probable that the
whole West Street façade originally had further gables and
an upper floor. A datestone for 1626 existed in the West
Street gable, with the initials WW for William Whitwell, a
leading figure in the town at the time, but this is now
indecipherable.

A short diversion into NEW STREET, with at the centre of
its entrance the 1914–18 WAR MEMORIAL. Next to the altered
C17 property on the corner comes the POST OFFICE, 1903,
Renaissance manner with two dormers with squat Ionic pilasters. Then the TALBOT INN, another of Oundle's fine buildings. It is dated 1626, but is an older foundation of the 1550s
called 'The Tabret'. Two canted bay windows of two storeys,
mullioned and, on the first floor, mullioned-and-transomed
windows. Three dormers irregularly placed. Ball finials. Central
archway. Inside a fine big staircase, which is clearly integral
with the building, so the tradition that it was brought from
Fotheringhay Castle can be discounted. Its window to the back
is of six lights with the sill running down diagonally to follow
the staircase. So it has partly one, partly two transoms. Deep
archway entrance with just on the l. side in the yard, much
rebuilt, a remnant of its former galleried courtyard. On the E
side of New Street, BARCLAYS BANK, a fine Victorian Gothic
essay. Five bays with round-arched windows and a doorcase
with garlands. The adjoining property on the l. also Victorian
with flat hoodmoulds to its windows with foliage stops. (For
buildings beyond to the N see the School Perambulation.)

Back to the MARKET PLACE. The centre is taken up by the   4
former town hall (see Churches and Public Buildings). On the
N side Nos. 7–9, Late Georgian, ashlar-faced. On part of the
ground floor the High Victorian Gothic NATWEST BANK.
Marble columns with foliate capitals. A little further THE
ROSE & CROWN, a quite nice Edwardian pub front. Three
bays with a continuous hood for its two bays and central
doorway. OUNDLE BOOKSHOP, opposite the Town Hall, is
late C17. It has a colonnade on the ground floor with heavy
Roman Tuscan columns. Broadly framed windows. Under the
colonnade a Georgian shopfront. On the Market Place s side
Nos. 4–6, an ambitious double-fronted house of ten bays with,
in the middle, an arched doorway with rusticated surround.
The dormers with alternating triangular and segmental pediments. The date could be before 1700, although the façade
details look later, mid-C18. Nice Georgian shopfront. Opposite
the Town Hall No. 26, early C18, four bays with platband and
aprons to the first-floor windows; No. 28, late C17, with broad,
eared doorway and an oval plaque; and finally BRAMSTON
HOUSE (Oundle School), early C18, stately, of five bays and
three storeys with giant Doric end pilasters, dentil cornice and
a balustrade. It originally had a large cupola on its roof, which

Tillemans recorded in his drawing of 1721. At the E end of the square, tucked back, is JERICHO, a sizeable house of C16 origin, mullioned windows in its N gable end and a four-centred doorway under its Georgian porch.

From here NORTH STREET winds N. On the r. first the WHITE LION, dated 1641, with three canted bay windows, the r. one one-storeyed, the other two of two storeys. They end in gables, above the r. bay a dormer in the roof. Bulgy finials. Then comes THE BERRYSTEAD (Oundle School), early C18 front, set back from the road, seven bays (2–3–2) and two storeys, quoins, all to stress the three-bay centre. Tall, slender windows in broad frames. Staircase with twisted balusters. The building is older and there survives a datestone of 1670. The basement with mullioned windows perhaps survives from then, as does probably the long range of outbuildings on the N side of the garden. Extensive grounds behind with at their far end, but visible from East Road (*see* below), another of Oundle's garden GAZEBOS. The Berrystead's fine ironwork gates are now at East Haddon Hall (q.v.). No. 22, LAUNDIMER HOUSE (Oundle School), early C19, ashlar-faced, of five bays. Behind, a REFECTORY by *Pick, Everard, Keay & Gimson*, 1961. Then LATHAM'S HOSPITAL, founded in 1611. The N court is original, the S court a continuation of 1837 by *J. W. Smith* of Oundle, in the same Jacobean style with mullioned windows and gables. Wall to the street and in each court an archway in Early Victorian medievalizing forms. Main doorway in the old court with strapwork volutes. No. 34 has a curious doorway with an open pediment on tapering half-fluted pilasters. Is that a mixture of C17 and C18 parts? On the W side No. 47 is again of the early C18. Windows with lintels curved on their underside. Other pleasant Georgian houses follow and at the corner of East Road is FOTHERINGHAY MEWS, a former maltings converted to housing.

Further to the N is the long BRIDGE which Leland describes as having some thirty arches. It was largely rebuilt after a flood in 1571 and widened 1912–14. Just before the bridge is RIVERSIDE MALTINGS, with more converted maltings and a fine 1990s housing complex with dark brick houses of varying heights and levels, with wooden gables, porches etc.

For those wishing to explore further, E of the square is EAST ROAD and a little N, beyond Laxton Junior School (*see* Public Buildings), on the l. is HAVELOCK TERRACE, a charming mid-C19 terrace of ten cottages, beautifully reconditioned in 1986 by *Chapman & Dawson*. Running SE from East Road is ASHTON ROAD which gives access to NENE BUSINESS PARK, where are two excellent examples of commercial design: FAIRLINE BOATS office development, two storeys with rendered wings and a central stone-glazed canopied entrance, large panels with glazing all round, built 2008–9 by *PDG Architects* of Peterborough; and nearby PGR CONSTRUCTION, built by the same firm 2004–5. It is worth comparing these with the other boring standard warehouse units in the park.

2. *The School and North Oundle*

The route moves northwards keeping to the w side of Glapthorn Road, and then returns along the e side.

OUNDLE SCHOOL was founded under the terms of the will of Sir William Laxton, grocer of London, in 1556. He left property in London to the Grocers' Company on condition that they supported the school which he had himself attended in Oundle. The original foundation was a modest grammar school which dated back to the later C15 and was still extant in the mid C16. The school rose to having about 60–70 boys in the mid C16, but was hit hard by the Fire of London and the misfortunes which befell the Grocers' Company. It remained a small school in the C18 going through many vicissitudes and occasionally being almost in abeyance, until the mid C19, when, as in so many public schools, conditions and reputation changed rapidly. There were 26 boys in 1848, 132 fifteen years later, 217 in 1882. Then numbers went down again (1891: 104), but by 1909 there were 323. Currently there are over 1,100 pupils, both boys and girls.

An exploration of the site, taking in some outlying areas attached to the town, should begin on the s side of the churchyard with what was LAXTON GRAMMAR SCHOOL. What stands today is a replica built in 1855 by *Joseph Gwilt*. Gwilt and his son, John Sebastian, were architects to the Grocers' Company. The building had a schoolroom on the first floor, and there is still one single room with an arch-braced roof. The ground floor was originally the almshouse but after that was removed to Church Street, and the building rebuilt, an open arcade was formed, now glazed. Further buildings were added on its e end when it was rebuilt. They are in a Tudor style. The block to its w was added in 1933. The two Georgian houses on the w side of the churchyard were the first additions to the original school. The s one is 1763 and the n one 1799 by *W. D. Legg* of Stamford. They are relatively plain two-storeyed houses. The rusticated opening in the second is mid-C20. To the n an extension of 1899. Moving into Church Street are the former ALMSHOUSES, one of the earliest C19 buildings, 1855 by *Joseph Gwilt*.

The centre of Oundle School is NEW STREET with THE CLOISTERS on one side and SCHOOL HOUSE on the other. The Cloisters is by *John Sebastian Gwilt* and dates from 1880. It is Tudor with a big gatehouse, asymmetrical, and with turrets at the s end. Through the gatehouse one enters a courtyard with a cloister. Above this classrooms have been added. These and the ART SCHOOL in the SE corner of the courtyard are by *Green, Lloyd & Son*, 1960. The n extension is by *A. C. Blomfield*, 1934–5. Half-length bronze statue of Sir William Laxton by *Jeremy Oddie*, 2006. SCHOOL HOUSE on the opposite side of New Street is also Tudor and also asymmetrical and of 1887 by *H. C. Boyes*. To the s is TALBOT STUDIES, an informal range with two timber-framed gables of 1909, by

A. C. Blomfield, by this time architect to the Grocers' Company. Fine ironwork gates, partly C18 though reworked, and from the garden of Queen Anne's House, West Street. Just above the Cloisters, on the r., the three-bay Regency house is the VICARAGE. To the N of School House is one of the most impressive buildings, the GREAT HALL. Perp with a large end window and corner turrets. Inside it has a mock hammerbean roof and a Wrenish s gallery on columns. It is also by *A. C. Blomfield*, 1907–8. A small garden forms the corner of Milton Road and contains a charming bronze SCULPTURE of a boy reading, 2005 by *Jeremy Oddie*, as a memorial to former pupil Elliot Viney (†2002).

On the l. is MILTON ROAD, and just along on the s side is the former NATIONAL SCHOOL of 1855 by *George Bevan* of Oundle. Three gabled wings, the centre set back. Tudor style with three-light mullion-and-transom windows. It used to have a bargeboarded centre and because of changes does look a little bleak, but it is basically all still there. Extended and altered by *Traylen & Lenton* in 1936. Further also on the s side the little, square, early C18 GAZEBO, which was formerly at the end of the long garden plot from Queen Anne's House in West Street. In its grounds, opposite the chapel, is ST ANTHONY HOUSE, 1925–8 by *A. C. Blomfield*. Nine bays with a centre tower with four-sided copper dome. The window with segmental head and foot is a motif familiar e.g. from Herbert Baker. Further back standing proudly on its green lawn is one of the star buildings of the school, the CHAPEL of 1922–3. This is *Blomfield* at his best. It is large and long with low aisles, an apse and an ambulatory. The style is Perp with a row of large windows. The outstanding feature is the STAINED GLASS, a veritable gallery of C20 and C21 art. In the apse are three windows designed by *John Piper* and made by *Patrick Reyntiens*, 1955–6. Nine large single figures, not realistic, but recognizable, and in their entangled forms and deep colours emotionally potent without being too exacting. The nearest parallel is the German and Dutch Expressionism of the 1920s, but the style is undoubtedly quite independent. Clerestory s, 1924 probably *Clayton & Bell*. – The windows running around the ambulatory illustrating the Seven Ages of Man are all by *Hugh Easton*, 1949. – N chapel window of 1997 by *Paul Quail*. To mark the Millennium the school commissioned a series of windows along the aisles, by *Mark Angus* and *Katharina Eisch*. The CROSS and CANDLESTICKS, good simple designs by *Paul Morris*, 1966, are of bronze, finished to look like steel. In the ambulatory a memorial to Oundle's famous headmaster Frederick Sanderson (†1922). It and the accompanying war memorial are by a former pupil, *Clough Williams-Ellis*. To the w of the chapel SIDNEY and GRAFTON HOUSES, 1905 and 1902 by *Blomfield*, symmetrical, with a steep gable and a semicircular porch hood, and FISHER and CROSBY, also by *Blomfield*, c. 1900 and 1907. Tudor, with five gables and mullioned-and-transomed windows. w of these, SWIMMING POOL and games complex by *Cartwright, Woollatt & Partners*, 1969–71.

Back in GLAPTHORN ROAD, the pattern gets looser and greener, especially on the W side. First comes the fine Neo-Tudor SIR PETER SCOTT BUILDING, built as a science block. Once again by *A. C. Blomfield*, 1914. It looks like a small country house with its mullioned-and-transomed windows, projecting wings with straight gables and curved Northamptonshire middle gable. To its N, much smaller, the YARROW GALLERY, also Tudor but simpler, 1918 also by *Blomfield*. Charming interior with good use of woodwork. A gallery to the upper floor on sturdy columns. The walls panelled with discreet lockers – an idea Blomfield uses elsewhere. Bronze STATUE of a standing boy by *Kathleen Scott* ('Here am I, Send me'). Returning to Glapthorn Road a short diversion l. onto the site of *G. G. Scott*'s 1837 workhouse, of which only the CHAPEL survives, behind Fletton House. It is stone, Gothic with two flights of small windows in the Dec style. It is by *Comper*, 1889 and his first work in England. Inside the painted ceiling of the sanctuary survives. The building has been converted into a residence. FLETTON HOUSE, the former infirmary, is a large red brick Neo-Jacobean building of 1900 by *Gotch & Saunders*. Its coach house has been converted into the PUBLIC LIBRARY. On the l. along Pavilion Drive are KIRKEBY and WYATT, two girls' boarding houses and a new sanatorium of 1989–90 by *Roger Hampson* of *Berry Bros* of Northampton. They are yellow brick with a band of blue bricks linking the ground-floor windows. Wings with large canted bays and big almost pyramidal sloping roofs with tiny gabled ridges. An impressive set. Further N, the Cricket Fields with a PAVILION by *Peter Bicknell*, 1957, two-storeyed with a lantern and cupola and a one-storeyed curved attachment. Changing rooms etc. below, a large room above, and N again, alongside Glapthorn Road the former SANATORIUM of 1931–2 by *Joseph Dorey* of Brentwood. An angled building of two floors with columned balconies, now houses.

Moving now to the E side of Glapthorn Road, at the N end of the playing field, DRYDEN and SANDERSON, two well-designed identical big houses of 1932–8 with tall hipped roofs of dark tiles above the light brick walls. They are by *W. A. Forsyth*. On the s side of the field, its long angled columnar-like stone façade reflected in water, is the SCI TEC block by *Feilden Clegg Bradley Studios*, 2005–7. The s side white with much glass. An outstanding addition to the school's campus. Appropriately to the SW of Sci Tec is a 1930s WORKSHOP. Brick, part rendered. Very much of its period in its shape and the big arched window in its s wall. Headmaster Sanderson was one of the first heads to ensure that the boys had a taste of mechanical engineering, a tradition that has continued at Oundle. In front of it and replacing another 1930s block is THE PATRICK CENTRE built 1998. The road s of these is BLACKPOT LANE and on the corner, set back from New Street, is GREENWAYS, built 2007 by *Paul Bancroft*. A majestic mock mid-Georgian town house with pillared porch. A path s leads to the GASCOIGNE BUILDING. The s core of this is the former manor house of the rectory of Peterborough Abbey. It was leased 1673 to the Walcot family and the building would seem to date from then. It had a Gothic extension and new E entrance porch added by *W. J. Donthorn* in 1845. The S front is still just recognizable, even with Donthorn's bay. Coursed stone, some oval windows and nice arched chimneystacks. Similarities to Bramston House on the Market Square. Internally everything has been altered. It is just a step or two now and we are back in the churchyard by the Laxton building, where we began.

OVERSTONE

ST NICHOLAS. Simple little Gothic estate church, in white ashlar, built in 1807. Remodelled in 1902–3 by *Josiah Mander*, when the S aisle and porch were added. All very elegant with a W tower. – STAINED GLASS. E window, French early C16 glass; good, arranged by *Egington* of Birmingham. – Splendid armorial glass of 1903 by *J. Powell & Sons* in the N window for the Loyds, Barons Wantage. – MONUMENTS. Frances Stretford †1717 and Edward Stretford †1720, both by *John Hunt*. On the later monument curly open pediment with two putti blowing trumpets.

OVERSTONE PARK. Tragically gutted by fire in 2001, the house is an open shell. Designed about 1860 for S. Jones Loyd, 1st Lord Overstone, the son of the Manchester banker Lewis Loyd. Described in 1865 as 'one of the wealthiest subjects in the world', he had a fortune estimated at £5 million. *The Builder* guardedly writes (1862) that 'the style adopted is claimed to be that, in a simple form, of the age of Francis I'. It can safely be said, however, that it is neither simple nor Francis I. The architect was *W. M. Teulon*, brother of the more famous, and some would say more notorious, S. S. Teulon. The front is done *asymmetricalissime*, with bays, gables, a tall tower, motifs from the Italian Trecento, Italian Cinquecento and French C16, and Jacobean strapwork. The architect was careful to avoid the reappearance of any major motif. The big S tower has an open top storey with coupled columns. A second tower on the E side further back was reduced in height some time ago. The house had double outer walls throughout, tied together by iron clamps. The large stables are no less ornate. The girls' school which was at Overstone Park had a dining hall added, simple with arched windows. This was done by *Sir Guy Dawber* in 1935. Of the Stretford house of the C18 no more than parts of outbuildings remain.

TOWER COURT, to the S, is the former STABLE BLOCK of 1862 with central carriageway and a short tower with a cupola. Of ashlar ironstone and limestone in a somewhat bizarre style vaguely Jacobean with scrolly gables and double windows with

Overstone Park.
Engraving, 1862

circular motifs in their heads. Converted into residential in the 1980s.

GATEWAY, at the NW corner of the grounds. From Pytchley Hall when this was pulled down in 1828, and therefore of *c.* 1590. Three arches of which only the middle one is original. This is flanked by attenuated Roman Doric columns. Frieze with wide metopes. Gable of two S-curves. A total of five obelisks at the top. Severely damaged in 1973 but restored.

The village was moved in 1821 from near the house (earthworks survive) to the road outside the park. Estate cottages of the 1830s following the acquisition of the estate by Lewis Loyd. Others, *c.* 1900 with timber-framed gables, are by *Josiah Mander*, Lord Overstone's surveyor. SCHOOL of 1877 and SCHOOL HOUSE of 1895 likewise typical of *Mander*.

OVERSTONE MANOR, Ecton Lane, 1 m. s. Built as a club house for a solarium in 1937–8 by *G. Alan Burnett* of Leeds for Francis Gandy. Georgian style. Colonnaded veranda on the w side. Some fittings are from Horton Hall (q.v.), mostly from the revamping of the entrance hall there by *W. Courtney le Maitre*, 1910. Partly subdivided inside on conversion into a restaurant.

For THORPLANDS FARM, one of the Overstone Estate farm complexes of the 1840s, *see* p. 489.

PASSENHAM

7030

ST GUTHLAC. A remarkable church and especially important for work of the C17. Base of the W tower C14. Doorway with fine

continuous mouldings. The three niches above it have later
ogee heads. The upper stages rebuilt in the early C17. Pairs
of lancets as bell-openings, almost identical to the tower at
Wicken which is dated 1617. Parapet and pinnacles later. C13
nave, see the lancets on the N side. The fabric is perhaps earlier,
as a string course on the N wall is interrupted by the windows.
In the E wall of the nave, S of the chancel arch, an odd lancet-
headed opening was revealed during work in the 1960s. The S
windows are C19. The chancel was rebuilt in 1626 by Sir
Robert Banastre in what can only be described as a bastardized
version of Perp, the E window sheltering under a rounded
gable. The priest's doorway has a depressed arch of the type
which the French call *anse de panier* and an inscription above.
The whole is a fascinating example of Gothic survival. Inside,
the wagon roof of the chancel is also of Sir Robert's time, gaily
painted blue with gold stars (restored in the 1960s based on
original remains; *see* below). The nave roof is also partially C17,
one corbel dated 1621. – Very remarkable furnishings of
c. 1626, especially the STALLS with MISERICORDS of 1628 – a
lion, a unicorn, a monster, heads, etc., no doubt a self-
conscious archaism. Vibrant frieze of dragon-like creatures and
at the chancel entrance two mermaids. Above the stalls are
niches with the names of the apostles. They are very shallow
so perhaps intended to have painted insets rather than statues.
Also part of the original scheme of decoration are the WALL
PAINTINGS, large single figures in shell-arched niches divided
by pilasters. They are in the style of the Venetian late Cinquecento. Restored in 1962–6 by *E. Clive Rouse*; the backgrounds
repainted by *Ann Ballantyne*. On the N wall Isaiah, Jeremiah,
Ezekiel, Daniel, on the S wall the Evangelists (St Mark obscured
by the monument to Sir Robert), on the E wall Nicodemus
and Joseph of Arimathaea. The WEST GALLERY has more
carved woodwork of the Banastre period. Fluted Ionic columns
and a frieze with affronted sirens, if that description be permitted. It was once part of a chancel screen, or what Morton in
1712 calls 'the Wainscoted Partition betwixt the Chancel and
Body of the Church'. An inscription under the tower records
that Charles Viscount Maynard 'substantially repaired and
beautified this fair chancel' in 1772, and the last date on the
painted charity panels on the gallery front is dated 1766, so
presumably made up during that period. It is probable that the
BOX PEWS and the PULPIT, in its present form, although basically Jacobean, also date from then. – ROYAL ARMS. Small, of
cast iron, between 1816 and 1837. – FONT. Elegant tapered
column with marble bowl, designed by *Lawrence Bond*, 1976.
– STAINED GLASS. Chancel S, figures of SS Peter and Paul,
probably German C16. Nave N, St Elizabeth of Hungary of the
same vintage. The chancel E had poor quality glass of 1867 but
this has been removed except for some sections in the upper
tracery. – In the nave N and chancel S, canopies of *c.* 1350. –
MONUMENTS. Sir Robert Banastre †1649, attributed to
Thomas Cartwright the elder (GF). Demi-figure in an oval niche

surrounded by a wreath. Volutes with compact garlands to the
l. and r. Steep open pediment. – Rev. Richard Forester †1769.
Charming Rococo cartouche by one of the *Coxes*, no doubt.

The MANOR HOUSE is likely to contain evidence of the time of
Sir Robert. The front with gables l. and r. and a slightly recessed
centre looks C17. The SE side of five bays is Georgian. Much
C19 remodelling; attic nursery and re-roofing by *Lutyens*, 1935.
By the manor house two grand BARNS at right angles. The
larger one is of pre-Reformation date. It is 110 ft (33.5 metres)
long and has three collar-beams one on top of the other. The
smaller is dated 1626. The roof structures of both suggest
considerable reworking by Banastre.

Former RECTORY. Late C17 and later. Five-bay front. Central
window with moulded architrave. Central shallow gable.

PATTISHALL*

6050

HOLY CROSS. The Anglo-Saxon nave can still be recognized
externally in both its NW and NE angle. Both are quoined in
the unmistakable long-and-short work. Although no quoins are
visible, the width of the s wall of the nave suggests it is also
Anglo-Saxon. The Saxon chancel was replaced by a Norman
chancel whose arch remains. It has simple imposts and probably dates from the C11. There is also a doorway of the same
date in the N aisle. The church then had a N aisle and a N
transeptal chapel. The N chancel chapel has respond mouldings
which repeat in a respond in the N aisle, so it must mark the
arch from the aisle into the transept, which became useless
when the present arcades were built without regard to a transept. The arcades differ. The s arcade is C13 of ironstone, the
N arcade C14 of grey oolite. Both have three bays, octagonal
piers and double-chamfered arches. Above the s arcade in the
aisle are remains of two C13 lancets. The transeptal chapel was
also rebuilt in the C13. Rood loft doorways survive on both
sides of the nave, with remains of stairs on the N side. C13
TOMB-RECESS in the chancel and a trefoil-headed AUMBRY
with above it a name plaque for John Gylling, a rector appointed
in 1317 and who probably died 1349. s windows and w tower
of *c.* 1300 with the usual tracery forms based on the Y-motif.
The tower was rebuilt in 1663 and there is other post-
Reformation stonework on the exterior of the chancel. The s
porch is probably 1683 when a sundial is recorded as being set
up. – TILES. A fine array by *Maws* in the chancel and N chapel,
all dating from the restoration of 1870–1 by *E. F. Law & Son*.
Some PAINTED DECORATION to the s aisle roof of the same

---

* The former George Inn (now a restaurant) in Butcher's Lane is dated 1637 but
extensively altered, and the pargetting noted by Pevsner in 1961, a rarity in the
county, had disappeared by 1972.

period. – FONT. Also of 1870–2 and rather good of its type. A rounded bowl with decorative bands and quatrefoil plaques for the Evangelists. – ROYAL ARMS. George II. – STAINED GLASS. Some faded Victorian panels (chancel E by *Heaton, Butler & Bayne*; a S window not identified, and N aisle probably by *Powells*). – Nice window in the vestry of 1913 by *J. Hardman & Co.* – MONUMENT. Simple Grecian sarcophagus tablet for William Drayson †1840 signed by *Joseph Stephens* of Worcester.

METHODIST CHAPEL, Astcote, ½ m. S. 1874 of red and yellow brick in the lancet style.

At EASTCOTE, I m. SE, BARTON HEAD, in The Close, is a basically an early C17 ironstone house. But in its end gable, at the top, a two-light window with arched heads, which could be older; beneath a two-light mullioned window with a hood-mould; and above, under another hoodmould, panels with worn inscriptions, one with the names of John Barton and Richard Barton. On the main front a datestone of 1674. Inside an original four-centred arched fireplace and beams. The house was extended in 1926.

CORNHILL, I m. N on the road to Bugbrooke. A large house and stables by *Alan L. Goodwin & Harold O. Tarbolton*, 1910. Brick with two wings, one flat, one rounded, a veranda between and three dormers in the roof.

PAULERSPURY

ST JAMES. The medieval church was basically Dec, but the body of the church was rebuilt with old materials in 1843–4 by *Eginton Harvey* of Worcester, and the chancel restored in 1850 by *R. C. Hussey*. The mural decoration is 1885–6 by *E. Swinfen Harris* when he added the vestry. The nave arcades are of five bays, with the same elements, except that in the N arcade circular alternate with octagonal piers. In the chancel the splendid SEDILIA and DOUBLE PISCINA are original early C14 work. Little vaults inside. Much crocketing. The top is a foliage frieze, then an ogee-arch frieze, and then battlements. The piscina has a six-pointed star in the spandrel (cf. the chancel stalls at Winchester Cathedral). The chancel must however be older than the sedilia; for the N chapel is of before 1300. Pairs of lancet windows provided with beautiful detached shafts inside. A little dogtooth and nailhead decoration. The arcade to the chancel has an octagonal pier and double-chamfered arches. Perp W tower. Stair to the tower in the form of a very large buttress; unusual and effective. – FONT. Circular, Norman, with lunettes upside down, their outlines beaded. Leaf capitals inside the lunettes and in the spandrels below (cf. Tiffield). – STAINED GLASS. The E window of 1873 is by *Clayton & Bell*. – The chancel S window of 1880 was designed by *Daniel Bell* and made by *Lavers, Barraud & Westlake*. W window of 1894 by *J. Hardman & Co.* – TILES by *Mintons*. – REREDOS of 1898 designed by *E. Swinfen Harris* and painted by *N. F. Westlake*. – HATCHMENTS. Three for members of the Sheddon family, 1826–7. – MONUMENTS. Oaken effigies, knight and lady, mid-C14. He is no longer cross-legged. Her pillow is supported by angels. Supposed to be Sir Laurence de Pavely, alive in 1329. – Sir Arthur Throckmorton †1626 and wife. A most unusual and slightly ludicrous monument, looking more so as it stands in front of a C19 pierced Gothic opening. Large, long base, and on it the two effigies *accubantes*, i.e. comfortably reclining on their elbows and so placed that their faces face each other and their elbows touch. He has a decidedly humorous, rather jowly face. The effigies are of alabaster. It has been attributed to *Nicholas Stone* (GF) but lacks the refinement of much of his work (cf. Church Stowe, for example). Some funeral ARMOUR belongs to this monument. – Benjamin Bathurst †1704 and his wife †1727, tablet of good workmanship, hidden behind the organ. – Joseph Spinnall †1726 by *Hunt*. – Robert Sheddon †1826 by *Theakston*. There is a modern plaque recording the missionary William Carey (1761–1834), who had connections here.

SCHOOL. 1861–2 by *John Haits* of Southsea, Hants – an extraordinary choice, but the rector, Rev. J. B. Harrison, had relatives in Southampton. Wildly Gothic, four-gabled façade with in the centre a little spirelet standing on a highly unconventional flying buttress. A pillar supports a clock and two child busts reading. It is inscribed: 'Bring up a child in the way he should go.'

A COTTAGE ROW on the green near the school, clearly Grafton building mid-C19. Two three-bay blocks with a gabled centre having an oriel over its arched entrance.

STABLE HOUSE, one of the Grafton farms. Three bays, two and a half storeys. Grey stone with ironstone dressings. Doorway with Ionic pilasters.

PIDDINGTON

8050

ST JOHN BAPTIST. Strange and unsatisfactory W tower of the C13 to C14. The strangeness is the spire, which starts with tall broaches and one tier of tall lucarnes (with Y-tracery), all in grey stone and dating from the C13, and then carries on with a big collar like a parapet. The second tier of lucarnes is small and set in the diagonals, both these of dark ironstone and a later repair of 1847. The outlines of the collar look from a distance as if repairs were carried on with a suspended scaffolding. This may well be yet another case of a spire being struck by lightning. The body of the church is much rebuilt, mainly in 1877–8 by *E. F. Law* and in 1900–2 by *Edmund Law*. Again the nave and chancel of the grey stone but the aisles of the dark. All windows, except those of the Perp clerestory, are renewed. The probability is that the church was of *c.* 1300. Arcades of four bays with octagonal piers and double-chamfered arches. – GLAZED DOORS in the tower arch, with etched design, *c.* 1970. – ORGAN. 1854 by *G. M. Holditch*, in a tall gabled Gothic case. – STAINED GLASS. Chancel E, Sansome memorial by *Francis Spear*, 1970. – MONUMENTS. Many C18 tablets, by such local carvers as the *Coxes* of North-ampton and *James Andrews* of Olney, mostly hung in the span-drels of the arcades – a slightly uncomfortable arrangement. Joseph Swayn †1720, apothecary, pretty, with three heads at the top (chancel).

BAPTIST CHAPEL (Carey Memorial), at Hackleton on the main road. Gothic of 1887–8 by *S. J. Newman*, brick and stone.

ROMAN VILLA. The Upper Nene Archaeological Society (UNAS) have been excavating this large and complex villa since 1979. Occupation began in the Late Iron Age, and a timber hall preceded the construction of a stone-built cottage-type villa at the end of C1. This building went through a complex sequence of development, and became a large winged-corridor-type villa with two phases of detached bath house, and a courtyard. The sequence of development and occupation continued well into C5, and there was also some Saxon occupation, including a small cemetery. The site is backfilled outside of the digging season, but a small museum has been made in the village's redundant Wesleyan chapel.

PILTON

ST MARY AND ALL SAINTS. The church forms a fine group with the old manor house. The exterior mostly late C13. But the s doorway is of the late C12. Waterleaf capitals, arch with zigzags meeting at right angles. Hoodmould with early dogtooth. Late C13 first of all the w tower. Doorway with filleted shafts and arch mouldings, shafted bell-openings with Y-tracery, corbel frieze of small heads, spire with low broaches, two tiers of lucarnes. The lower has two lights with continuous roll mould-ings and a quatrefoiled circle. Late C13 the s aisle, see the E window with three quatrefoiled circles in the tracery, and the corresponding two-light s window. The s porch entrance is a little uncomfortable and probably made up. It has a late C13 surround with heavy nailhead on the arch and stones at the sides with two shields one of which is reputedly Tresham and is accepted as such by VCH. However if the shield is late C13 can it really be Tresham, since the family was not in North-amptonshire till the beginning of the C15? Heraldically the charges are oddly disposed on the shield and do not fit the normal layout of the Tresham arms and the saltire cross on the upper shield adds further to the mystery. The N aisle has a three-light window with intersected tracery and a w lancet, i.e. is late C13 too. Dec clerestory. Inside, C13 arcades of three bays with octagonal piers and double-chamfered arches. At their springing little corner motifs like halved dogtooth. Nailhead on one S pier. C13 chancel arch with stiff-leaf. Late C14 clerestory with two mouchettes under a square head. The chancel is of 1862–4 and probably also the S door with its mock Norman wooden arcading. *Thomas Littleton Selby*, agent for the Lilford Estate, was, as his memorial in the N aisle states, 'sole architect for the restoration' of the rest of the church 1874. – FONT. Octagonal, with leaf decoration on the foot. Somewhat worn but probably C14. – STALLS, 1860s with finely carved poppyheads with birds and animals. – TILES. A fine display throughout the church, especially in the chancel of the 1860s, with very attractive leaf designs which may well be designs by *Lord Alwyne Compton*. More orthodox those in the nave, of 1874 and probably *Mintons*. – STAINED GLASS. E window of 1866. Scenes of Adam and Eve at base, by *J. Hardman & Co*. They also made the other chancel windows in 1868 and they make a good set. MONUMENT. In the churchyard, N side, a table tomb with a large slab bearing a roundel with a heraldic achievement, clearly Tresham. The boar's head crest is still legible and on the shield the Tresham trefoils are represented by three drilled holes but slightly oddly dispersed with other charges. The inscription is too worn to read. It would appear to be late C17 or early C18 and Pilton remained in Tresham hands until 1715 when Sir Thomas Powys of Lilford bought it. The tomb deserves more investigation.

MANOR HOUSE. Built by the Treshams of Newton in C16. The external appearance Jacobean and picturesque. The SE part is the earliest, probably dating from the 1560s (cf. the dovecote at Newton). The SW part contains a good Jacobean staircase with vertically symmetrical balusters, and on the first floor a panelled room with an overmantel over the fireplace. This has handsome groups of three detached little columns, one standing in front of the other two. This part of the house was added *c*. 1620 during the Tresham period. The house was altered and improved by *Edward Browning* of Stamford in 1847 when many mullioned windows were replaced and the small bay was added. It was at that time the rectory.

THE BEDE HOUSE (also known as the Old Watch House). With medieval fragments around the upper windows, such as a ballflower frieze and two shafts on headstops, traditionally from the demolished chapel at Thorpe Waterville. A curious lookout of Tudor brick, like a large chimney with a pyramid roof, at one end. The upper room has remains of a dovecote and was originally only accessible by an external stone staircase. Considerably altered in the C19.

ELMES HOUSE. Late C17 with an early C18 ashlar front. Five bays with leaded casements, cross-mullion on the ground floor and two-light on the first. Three dormers. Canopied doorcase.

PIPEWELL
1½ m. N of Rushton

Of the Cistercian abbey nothing is preserved. It was founded in
1143 from Newminster in Northumberland, which was founded
in 1137 from Fountains Abbey, which was founded in 1133 from
Clairvaux – so rapid was the spread of the Cistercian order in
these early years. Earthworks survive, possibly of a dam or fishponds; some may be remains of the village destroyed in 1143: the
earliest deserted medieval village in the county. The abbey was
dissolved in 1538. The plan of the abbey was recovered in an
excavation, 1908–9 by Harold Brakspear. The site is S of the
present church, behind the rows of cottages.

CHURCH. Small, cruciform and rustic rough stone. Erected in
   1881–2 for £600 in what was then called the 'Norman' style,
   apparently the inspiration of its designer the Hon. *Mrs
   Holden-Hamborough*. Wooden bell-turret over the centre. It
   manages to look more like early C19, with its rusticated
   windows and wide battlements, and the style like a country
   house park folly.
PIPEWELL HALL. Of C17 origin, three bay centre and two bay
   projecting wings and with a canted Georgian bay on the rear
   façade between the two wings. A date of 1675 is recorded.
   Around 1850 the whole house was refaced in a Tudor manner
   and a little later the canted bay was removed and the central
   section of the rear façade given a flat front. Minor alterations
   by *L. M. Gotch c.* 1920 and at the same period also by *Blackwell
   & Riddey*. There is a Tudor Gothic LODGE of the same period,
   and COTTAGES in the village have similar bargeboarded
   dormers.

PITSFORD

ALL SAINTS. Dec style as one approaches, all in yellow sandstone and golden ironstone dressings. The restoration of 1866–7
by *Slater & Carpenter* almost amounts to a total rebuilding.
Norman S doorway. Shafts with zigzag and two kinds of trellis,
one of them beaded. Perhaps re-assembled wrongly. Outer
arch moulding with beakhead, inner with zigzag. The tympanum represents either St Michael slaying a dragon, or more
likely Faith fighting Evil. The figure is not mounted but standing. The carver is always ready to lose himself in interlace. Thus
e.g. there is a cock in the bottom l. corner, and his tail is interlace. Dec W tower. The ample buttresses have a nook-shaft all
up the re-entrant angle, an unusual and successful motif. The
bell-openings are of two lights, but to the N and S there is an
extra cusped lancet asymmetrically at its side. N aisle E window

with reticulated tracery. The arcades with their intricate foliage capitals are of 1867, when the chancel was rebuilt too. The carver, *Gillett* of Leicester, added in the corbels in the nave, which support the roof, symbols representing the twelve apostles. – DOOR. The s door contains old woodwork, perhaps C17, but more importantly some remnants of ironwork which could be C12. – FONT. Octagonal, C14. With flat gables. – SCREEN. Base only in the N aisle, *c.* 1500. – STAINED GLASS. Chancel E of 1867 by *Heaton, Butler & Bayne.* – MONUMENT. A tablet of pink marble with a roundel inscription for Eustace Garden †1897, who lost his life in the shipwreck of S.S. *Aden*, by *Pullen & Son* of Northampton.

VILLAGE HALL. Tudor. By *Morley Horder*, early C20.

PRIMARY SCHOOL. Incorporating a building of 1846 to which a SCHOOL HOUSE was added by *E. F. Law*, 1850.

Many stone houses, including the GRIFFIN ARMS, interesting since instead of the local ironstone its street façade is faced with ashlar white Kingsthorpe stone.

PITSFORD HALL (Northamptonshire Grammar School since 1989). By *John Johnson* of Leicester, before 1785. Originally a centre and two wings, but much altered since the Second World War. An additional storey was added and the garden side was changed sweepingly. There had already been work by *Law & Son* in 1887 and an enlargement in 1898 by *Law & Harris*. Good staircase with wrought-iron balustrade. The house has been used as a school since the 1950s and a dormitory block was added by *Walker & Sturgess*, 1966.

MOULTON GRANGE, ¾ m. E. Built just before 1830. Bald Regency classical, the s front Italianized *c.* 1850, the E parts extended 1911–12.

SEDGEBROOK GRANGE, ½ m. SW on the Chapel Brampton Road. A very distinguished red brick Neo-Georgian house by *Sir John Brown & Henson*, 1930–1, for John Douglas Houison Crauford.* Entrance side with three central bays and projecting wings of two bays with quoins. Stone doorcase with segmental pediment and Ionic columns. Hipped roof with deep wooden cornice and dormers and two chimneystacks. The garden side has a central canted bay. The interior has some fine carved fireplaces. Single storey E wing, 1988.

SEDGEBROOK HALL (Hotel), 1 m. SW on the Chapel Brampton Road. Gyles Isham maintained the house was by a London architect. Dated 1861. Façade with central pediment, and a grand porch with Ionic columns on the l. Garden façade with large canted bay. Work was done by *Law & Harris* in 1921.

LONG BARROW on Lymans Hill, 100 metres up the lane to the village, off the main Northampton road. Possibly Neolithic. The site is much damaged, leaving its true form and date uncertain.

*I am grateful to Mr J. A. Houison Crauford for identification of the architect.

5040

PLUMPTON

St John Baptist. Small and perfectly charming: like a model church on top of a wedding cake. Mostly a rebuilding of 1822; the tower arch and chancel arch seem reused. – FONT. Could be of the 1660s. – Complete set of original fittings: BOX PEWS, BENCHES at the rear, and COMMANDMENT BOARDS. – REREDOS incorporating Jacobean carving with a date of 1617. – MONUMENT. Anne Moore †1683. A fine marble tablet with drapery and a cherub at the foot. Attributed to *C. G. Cibber* (GF).

Manor House. A most attractive house, set behind a series of enclosing walls with rusticated gatepiers. Early C17 but extended and altered for Sir Roger Wilbraham in the late C17. Ironstone and limestone with some banding. Two-storeyed, with a gabled porch and three- and two-light mullioned windows. Gables with ball finials. Several simple C17 fireplaces and original staircase.

Former PARSONAGE, E of the church. 1858 by *John Davies* of Banbury.

0080

POLEBROOK

All Saints. An interesting rather than a beautiful church, dating mostly from *c.* 1175–*c.* 1250, odd in shape, short, with far-projecting transept and a tower at the SW end. Viewed from the S a lot of wall but few windows. Indeed neither the S or N walls of the body of the church have any, nor is there a clerestory. The development unravels within. The earliest evidence is Early Norman. The church had a nave, a central space, perhaps with a tower, with or without a transept (see the piece of wall interrupting the N arcade), and a chancel. To this were added *c.* 1175 a N transept and a N aisle. The chancel, or only the chancel arch, was also rebuilt. The chancel arch, the transept arch and the aisle arcade exhibit circular, or in the responds semicircular, shafts, waterleaf capitals, square abaci notched at the corners, and round, double-chamfered arches. In the arcade there are also capitals with foliage, like Norman volutes but not quite stiff-leaf. Next followed the tower. It has round-headed W and S windows decorated with dogtooth. The arches to the nave and S aisle are triple-chamfered, round, and have simple moulded capitals. So a S aisle was by then also planned. In its execution it is a little later. The circular pier and responds are much taller and slimmer, and the setting out takes no account of transepts. Stiff-leaf capitals. Double-chamfered round arches. Simple round-headed S doorway, placed in the first bay E of the tower. The chancel and the transepts in their present form must date from about the same time. The priest's doorway still has a round, only slightly chamfered arch. The

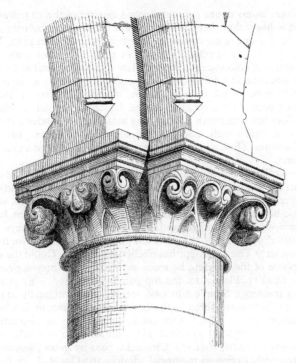

Polebrook, All Saints.
Engraving of capital, 1880

chancel windows are lancets, including two lowside lancets and a fine group of three stepped separate lancets at the E end. They are splendidly double-shafted inside with shaft-rings. The chancel PISCINA is even more splendid, if a little barbarically so. Two very odd decorative sub-arches rise above the pointed lights from the middle in a single curve outward to meet the super-arch. Much dogtooth enrichment. Externally the profile of the S aisle is clear with its single small lancet window, and a similar lancet in the N transept W wall. Inside the N transept a startlingly sumptuous display of blank arcading, covering the W wall and part of the N wall. Detached shafts, plain capitals with dogtooth behind, deeply moulded arches, and leaf and rosette stops. The shafts were not there when Bridges was collecting for his history, *c.* 1720, and there is something odd about the way the arcading of the N wall meets that on the W. Yet the double capital in the corner, carved from a single block, suggests a turn here (but would the C13 masons have made such a clumsy join?). The same rosette or patera as here occurs also in the hoodmould of the vestry doorway in the chancel and the chancel piscina. Eaves courses with small heads in the chancel and N transept. The work in the chancel and transepts takes us no doubt into the second quarter of the C13, and so it is likely that there is a connexion between this activity and the granting of the church to Peterborough Abbey in 1232. The N porch is a spectacular mid-C13 piece. Entrance with two orders of colonnettes with lively late stiff-leaf capitals and three vertical bands of dogtooth. The arch must have been intended still to be round. It has many fine mouldings. Eaves course of dogtooth. The tower now reached the stage of its bell-openings. They are twins with a separating shaft and still under a round arch. Spire with medium-high broaches and three tiers of lucarnes. The S porch entrance is also shafted, but has a pointed arch.

Of later contributions no more needs mention than the two C14 E windows of the N transept with flowing tracery, and the Perp N transept N window. – NAVE ROOF, dated 1636, with tie-beams and collar-beams on queenposts. The purlins have strapwork patterning, and one tie-beam the cross-keys for Peterborough. (Do the other low pitched roofs also derive from the C17? The S transept has obelisk-type finials. Could the C17 phase of the building be more significant than now appears?) – PULPIT. Plain, C17, the top panels gadrooned. – BENCHES (S transept). Simple and raw, scrolled tops, originally C13 or C14, but reassembled in the C17, hence the obvious Jacobean pillars etc. – FONT. Octagonal, with flat pointed-trefoiled arches; c. 1300. – SCREEN. Perp, minor, with one-light divisions. – STAINED GLASS. Chancel S, 1982 by *Brian Thomas*. – S transept, Ferguson memorial window 1929 by *A. L. & C. E. Moore*. Two other windows here, 1896 and 1912, are by *A. L. Moore*. – N transept window, 1918 also by *Moore*, and that of 1863 is by *Webb & Nixon*. – MONUMENT. Captain John Orme †1764. Coloured marbles, almost certainly by *Bingham* of Peterborough.

POLEBROOK HALL. Jacobean (1626 in the panelling of a room on the upper floor) but much restored and remodelled. The N front has two slightly projecting gabled wings. Inside was an oblong courtyard, now glazed. The S front looks all Victorian and a date of 1881 is recorded, except for the two-bay piece dated 1719, which is under a Jacobean gable. Mullioned windows. Much panelling, the finest in the ground-floor room behind the front of 1719. This has strongly moulded panels and a coved ceiling with stucco patterns of thin ribs. Many wooden chimneypieces, all with flat carving. C18 staircase. C18 iron gates to the N and E. GARDEN recast by *Sir Reginald Blomfield.*

A very pleasant village with many nice stone houses and some thatch. The OLD POST OFFICE, W of the church, has one big fireplace with a four-centred head. In the front garden two fragments, probably from the church. THE OLD DUKE'S HEAD, a former inn, has moulded beams and a fireplace bressumer dated 1595. THE GABLES, Main Street, N of the Hall. Dated 1698, but with a C16 doorway. The work of 1698 is purely classical.

POTTERSPURY

ST NICHOLAS. Perp W tower with a very elaborately moulded doorway. The rest of the exterior is all Victorian, first in 1847–8 by *R. C. Hussey*, and secondly in 1860–1 by *E. F. Law*. It is the first restoration which gives the interior its most striking effect, the tripartite chancel arch with two tall octagonal piers and a wide middle arch. The side arches die into the imposts. It is visually most dramatic, especially since 1991 the interior has been reordered and cleared of pews. It is a great credit to Hussey, who had a full understanding of medieval architecture (cf. Orlingbury and Braunston). The arcades are interesting. They are of three bays. That on the N side has its E pier clearly of the C12. It is circular and has a square abacus. The capital is flat and decorated with many scallops. The abacus has some dogtooth. The W pier is octagonal and belongs to the C13. The arches date from the time of this. The S arcade is slenderer and has octagonal piers and arch mouldings indicating a Perp date, though it may well owe something to Hussey. C13 N chapel of two bays. The chancel arch cuts across its first bay. Several fine Perp windows, those of the N aisle having blocked bases externally. SEDILIA and PISCINA. Revealed in 1991. Early C14 with stiff-leaf foliage capitals. Somewhat damaged. The piscina has dogtooth and was altered in the C14. – FONT. Octagonal, Perp. Panelled stem, bowl with shields and pointed quatrefoils. – BOX PEWS but late, i.e. 1848. – STAINED GLASS. A fine ensemble, notably for several fine windows by *C. E. Moore*. They are the chancel E of 1951 and three in the N aisle of 1920. – S aisle E window of 1919 by *Jones & Willis*. – S aisle window of 1997 by *Chris Fiddes* and *Nicholas Bechgaard*, showing village trades, and one by the same team for the Millennium. – MONUMENTS. Gabriel Clarke †1624, Cuthbert Ogle †1633. Both with black inscription plates and both without figures. The first with alabaster surround, the latter stone. A simple tablet for John Meal †1742, 'late gardiner to His Grace the Duke of Grafton', a trade he carried out for sixteen years.

UNITED REFORMED CHURCH (formerly Congregational). Two-storeyed brick range with dark chequer pattern, looking like a farmhouse, dating from 1780. The first three bays are the manse and have a middle canopied doorway, the next three were the chapel and have two storeys of segment-headed windows. School and manse added 1846.

Just NW of the church is the former MILL of *c.* 1850–60. Three storeys and five bays of rubble with red brick dressings and still with its roof hoist projection. In the village, GRAFTON TERRACE or Duchess Row, or also Factory Row, because it was at one time a lace factory. Terrace of eight houses. Another group of four houses is no doubt a little later. This is rock-faced, gabled and bargeboarded, and has leaded lights.

POTTERSPURY LODGE (Steiner School), 1 m. NW on the A5. Of limestone with ironstone dressings, with platband and quoins. 1664 with additions of 1899 and the 1920s. *Lutyens* is said to have been involved with the 1899 additions. The central range could be 1664 but the appearance is more Georgian, although this is probably owed to the 1920s alterations. It has a slightly projecting three-bay section in the middle topped by a parapet with segmental-arched top. Large projecting canted porch to ground floor. Cupola above also 1920s. Two bays to r. and one to l. On the l. a taller and grander wing with two sash windows on the first floor and a Venetian window below, all with keystones. One room on the upper floor has Jacobean panelling. The staircase runs up in an open well. Twisted balusters with bulbous feet. Considerable outbuildings, some adapted in 1976 by *Gotch, Saunders & Surridge*. The Steiner School was set up here in 1956.

90 WAKEFIELD LODGE, 1½ m. WSW. Designed by *Kent c.* 1745 for the 2nd Duke of Grafton, for whom he also built at Euston in Suffolk, although Wakefield was not completed till after Kent's death in 1748. The property remained in Grafton hands till 1921, and since then has had a number of owners. Much has been done since the 1990s to bring the original character of the house back. Wakefield is a lodge indeed, a hunting lodge in Whittlewood Forest of which the Duke was ranger, but a cyclopean lodge. It is not actually large, only five bays wide, but the motifs used are all somehow over-sized. They are not beautiful in themselves, nor is the whole beautiful, but the effect has power and a strange primeval attraction. Kent, Lord Burlington's protégé, is customarily regarded as the apostle of strict Palladianism. In fact he was nearer in spirit to Vanbrugh than to Palladio. The front has a recessed centre, which was two-storeyed originally, and the end bays are raised by a half-storey and covered with flat pyramid roofs. The centre was raised by a further floor in the late C19. On the ground floor a three-bay portico of Tuscan columns with exaggerated entasis and a flat top. The windows are of the Venetian type, but they have depressed, segmental arches, and the same arches above all three parts. The upper floor has tripartite lunette windows, but they also have this squashed, segmental shape. Big and unmoulded dentil frieze between ground floor and first floor.

Inside there is one all-dominant room, the Saloon, filling the centre on both floors and surrounded by a balcony on brackets like the entrance hall in Inigo Jones's Queen's House at Greenwich. Kent was the editor of Inigo's works, and he has obviously taken his inspiration here from the Queen's House. That is equally clear in the very restrained panels of the stucco ceiling and in the circular, flying or geometrical, staircase with an iron railing – an echo of Inigo's tulip staircase at Greenwich. The ceiling centre has the Duke's Garter star. Big stone chimneypiece with hunting motifs. Richard Garnier has suggested that the later phases of Wakefield *c.* 1750 were undertaken by *Sir Robert Taylor*, who was working in London and elsewhere for the Graftons. He also suggests that the staircase may owe more to Taylor than Kent and Inigo Jones. The DINING ROOM,

on the s side of the house and formerly between later s wings
which were demolished in 1948, is part of additions made in
the 1770s.

STABLES of mottled red and purple brick, fifteen bays wide,
with a three-bay pediment with a Rococo cartouche. A little
later than the house. Probably 1759 and either by *Matthew
Brettingham* or *Taylor*.

The AVENUES to the w and s can still be traced. The park
was landscaped by *Brown* 1750–5 when lake was created.

PRESTON CAPES

ST PETER. The chancel appears to be *c.* 1300 although it has a
lancet in its N wall and signs of another to its E. Several aisle
windows of *c.* 1300–50 with intersecting cusped tracery. The N
aisle two Dec windows with reticulated tracery. Perp windows
in both aisles. Perp also the W tower with two-light transomed
bell-openings and battlements. The s doorway looks Late Perp,
probably C16, and has its original door, and the clerestory
could be the same period. C17 three-light square-headed
windows on the s side of both chancel and s aisle. Inside, the
s arcade is of the early C13, two and a half bays, circular piers
and octagonal abaci, pointed arches and one slight chamfer.
The N arcade is later (octagonal piers, double-chamfered
arches) but also has a half-arch at the w end. The half-bays are
the result of the tower having been inserted within the existing
building, necessary since there is a deep slope W of the churchyard. – FONT. Perp, with panels illustrating window tracery as
if taken from a pattern book. – BENCHES. They have traceried
panels and buttresses. Some may be original, but most, with
nicely carved poppyheads, are owed to the restoration in 1853,
funded by the Knightleys of Fawsley, whose shield is on one
of the heads. – STALLS. Similarly part old, made up with C18
panelling. – COMMANDMENT BOARDS. Probably *c.* 1800, with
marbled borders and small gilded urns at the top. Nicely
restored. – CHARITY BOARD. Pretty borders with garlands and
cherubs, dated 1736. – ROYAL ARMS. Stuart period. Fine. –
STAINED GLASS. Several windows by *William Wailes*, 1853,
some with diamond coloured patterns, N aisle E window with
heraldry. Chancel E window with fragments in its tracery but
largely filled with etched designs, 1974 by *Annabel Rathbone*. A
complex design with trees, birds (a prominent peacock), figures
etc. It is a memorial to ten-year-old George St John Raven-
shear. His face appears as St George.

Former SCHOOL by the church gate. Gothic, dated 1845, but
more Regency than Victorian with pretty glazing. Top-lit by a
charming square skylight.

OLD RECTORY, next to the church. Said to contain part of a
medieval priest's house. Some C17 windows, but much rebuilt

in the C18. Late Georgian wing. Gothick glazing, like the school.

THE FOLLY, Old Forge Lane, W of the church. Built as a castellated farmhouse and designed as an eyecatcher for Fawsley Hall. Baker calls it 'modern' in 1822 and it is most likely to have been built following *Cundy*'s Gothicizing at Fawsley Hall in 1815. Red brick, and originally two cottages facing each other, either side of a castellated archway, their N aspect in the form of castellated towers. The cottage rows originally had lean-to roofs but have been heightened.

CASTLE. A short distance to the E of the church are the remains of a motte-and-bailey castle already in existence by 1090. The motte has a flat top some 80 ft (24 metres) in diameter. Parts of its ditch on the N side. The site is largely covered by trees.

MANOR FARM, on the SE side of the castle, set back from the road. The side facing towards the road has a C17 façade, but at the back are mullioned windows and a C17 corbelled-out bay window. Hipped roof with dormers.

PRESTON DEANERY

ST PETER & ST PAUL (Churches Conservation Trust). Impressive tall Norman W tower of rough stone. Shallow buttresses, like pilasters, up the middle of the sides. Two round-headed windows on the W side and similar opening on N and S. The belfry stage added in the C14 or C15. Narrow round tower arch. The chancel arch is Norman too, round-headed and unmoulded. Inset are some pieces of interlaced design but these may not be in their original positions. The chancel has a round-headed doorway of *c.* 1200 and a blocked lowside window of *c.* 1300. In the Elizabethan period part of the body of the medieval church was pulled down and this presumably accounts for the damaged site of a sedilia and piscina in the chancel. The building was restored by Charles Edmonds after 1620, the date of the two-light windows with square hoodmoulds. There was a restoration in 1901 by *G. H. Birch*, curator of the Soane Museum. – COMMANDMENT BOARDS. Gothic-arched, early C19. – Two HATCHMENTS. – STAINED GLASS. Chancel E window of 1878 by *M. & A. O'Connor*. – MONUMENT. Mrs Langham, 1773. By *Henry Cox*. Standing architectural memorial with Doric pilasters and coloured marbles. – Gothic stone memorial to the Christie family, 1866. Pretty frieze of Passion flowers. – Stone slab with a brass Gothic cross for Rev. Samuel Parkins †1853 by *Waller Bros*, 1855.

PRESTON HALL. There was a large Victorian red brick and stone house of which portions of garden walls line the road. Probably by *E. F. Law*, who designed the main gate and other estate buildings. Demolished in 1934. The present building, converted from part of a subsidiary building, dates from after this. Beautiful setting.

THE ROOKERY. A sizeable brick house in the Georgian style *c.* 1900. The front has a central gable enclosing a circular opening; doorway with two windows above. On each side canted bays. Most windows stone-framed with keystones, but the ground-floor windows of the bays having triangular pediments.

PURSTON

5030

1¼ m. w of Farthinghoe

An impressive and handsome house. The s front is *c.* 1700, built probably for Richard Cresswell.* Three-bay centre of Hornton ashlar with two-bay projections to the l. and r. Two storeys, hipped roof with two dormers. Stone cross-windows. Doorway with a frame with ears and a steep open segmental pediment. The E wing, the fireplace in the hall in the middle of the s range, and the staircase, are, however, Late Elizabethan or Jacobean (a fireback in the house has a date of 1591 which may be significant). Hall fireplace of grey stone with Doric fluted pilasters and a strapwork frieze. Staircase with vertically symmetrical balusters and short flights within a tight well. Extensively restored. A long low two-storey w wing was added in 1931 in a Late Arts and Crafts manner with wooden casement windows and stocky chimneystacks. N wing also extended with a new entrance doorway with swan-necked pediment. Grand stone-tiled roofs also of 1931.

PYTCHLEY

8070

ALL SAINTS. To record the history of the building one must start inside. Nave and aisles are comfortably wide. The arcades are not high. The first two bays of the N arcade are Late Norman (circular pier, capitals with horizontal foliage scrolls and heads at the corners, square abacus, single-stepped arch with remains of painted decoration). Then follows the s aisle. Its arcade has three bays. Quatrefoil piers with stiff-leaf capitals and double-chamfered pointed arches. That is C13. So are the s doorway and the arch of the chapel (now vestry) in the N aisle with keeled mouldings. The chancel followed at the end of the C13, but was over-restored in 1861. The windows still have Geometrical tracery, but the sedilia and piscina are Dec, all with

---

* There is unfortunately no clear pedigree of the Cresswells after 1697, but the initials RC on a stone in the garden wall, with the name Cresswell House, presumably refer to him. The two previous Cresswells were both John.

ogee arches. A little earlier the E continuation of the N arcade
to link up with the chancel. Quatrefoil piers, one with a
moulded capital, the other with big upright oakleaves. –
PISCINA. N aisle, C13 but only partially surviving. Vertical
marks above the nave arcades show the position of earlier roof
supports. Drawings by George Clarke show that before 1861
most of the windows were either without tracery or of C17
mullioned form, and there is no sign of the handsome S aisle
windows E of the porch: three steeply stepped lancet lights
under an ogee arch, so these must be C19. Essentially C13 the
tall, unbuttressed W tower. Blocked arcading in its upper stage.
Perp the transomed two-light bell-openings, battlements, pinnacles. There was a gentle restoration in 1903–4 by *Matthew
Holding*. – WOODWORK. Much of various dates. The earliest
pieces are C15 fragments of SCREEN PANELS incorporated in
the chancel stalls. Jacobean the SCREEN in the N aisle, COM-
MUNION RAIL with vertically symmetrical balusters, and the
PULPIT. The SEAT in the chancel is made up from C16 or C17
pieces. The REREDOS dates from 1913. – FONT. Of very odd
design, semi-castellated. It was apparently restored in 1838. –
COFFIN-LIDS. Medieval. Two portions in the N aisle. – COM-
MUNION TABLE. Probably the one recorded as made in 1704.
– The curious internal PORCHES were introduced during a
restoration of 1844–5. The N one is Carpenter's Romanesque
and the S one Gothick with an ogee top. A beam in the N aisle
is inscribed *Thomas Westbury* 1845, and he is very likely the
carpenter. – ROYAL ARMS. Part of a painted 'tympanum',
originally over the chancel screen, but moved over the tower
arch in 1844. It is painted on lath and plaster. Intriguing since
it is dated 1661, but has the Prince of Wales Feathers and CP.
This suggests it was originally painted before the Civil War,
then amended in 1661, perhaps following the founding of the
school in that year (*see* below). The church had BOX PEWS, but
these were cleared because of decay in 1973–4. – STAINED
GLASS. S aisle W, Lane memorial (†1941) by *Christopher Powell*,
1948. – S aisle S, a window with a floral wreath set in plain glass
by *Chapel Studios*, 1985.

PYTCHLEY HALL stood immediately E of the church. Demolished in 1828–9. It was a grand Elizabethan mansion, built by
Sir Euseby Isham about 1580–90, of two storeys and attics with
projecting wings.* A small square GATEHOUSE with pyramid
roof survives E of the church. It existed in 1820.

PYTCHLEY MANOR HOUSE. Dates 1633 and 1665, with good
chimneys, gables and mullioned windows.

SCHOOL HOUSE. Red brick with stone dressings, *c.* 1770. Five
bays, two storeys. On the garden side a central doorcase with
pulvinated frieze, and a Gibbsian window above. The school

---

*Some stained glass preserved at Lamport Hall (p. 384) has the date 1596. A
gateway went to Overstone (p. 519), the porch is at Glendon (p. 289), minor fragments at Isham (p. 349), panelling from a room at Cottesbrooke (p. 197), and a
Vanbrughian fireplace at Shortwood Lodge (p. 571).

was founded by William Aylworth in 1661, and his charity still operates today. The SCHOOL behind was enlarged in 1852 and 1870 by *E. F. Law & Son*, and has been further added to.

QUINTON

ST JOHN BAPTIST. Before the church received its W tower in the C13, the nave ended to the W without a tower, as is testified by the Late Norman pointed lancet in the W wall and the SW quoin. The tower has two-light C13 bell-openings and above them Perp bell-openings and battlements. Early C13 S arcade of three bays with circular piers and circular abaci. Keeled responds. Double-chamfered arches. The blank N arch indicates a former N transept which was removed in 1800. The chancel arch seems C13. Dec clerestory. The E part of the chancel and the S porch were remodelled in 1801. The rounded corners of the chancel and the porch and the similarly rounded chancel windows are unusual. Gyles Isham suggested that this work may have been designed by *Samuel Saxon* when he was working at nearby Courteenhall. Refreshing clear glass and plaster. – FONT. C18; of baluster type. – MONUMENTS. Two curious plaques, early C20 but recording Baggison deaths in the 1700s. In the churchyard, Eleanor McCollum †1909. Of terracotta, with two angels at head and miniature ones at the foot. By her sister, *Mary Seton Watts*. – STAINED GLASS. War memorial window of Renaissance design *c.* 1950 by *Harry Stammers*.

FOXFIELD, ¼ m. NW. 1934 by *Charles Riddey* of Kettering for Arthur Gawthropp, a Quinton farmer. A three-bay rectilinear house, rendered white, its centre slightly projecting. Two storeys with horizontal metal windows and flat roofs. Beautifully preserved. The only change is that the r. wing has had an extra floor added.

RADSTONE

Strangely remote despite being close to Brackley and the dual-carriageway A43.

ST LAWRENCE. Just a W tower, nave, chancel and S aisle, surrounded by trees. The W tower is somewhere between Late Anglo-Saxon and Norman and probably C11, see the unmoulded round arch towards the nave and the blocked W window. The upper stages are early C13, and the later bell-openings Dec. Early C13 also the chancel, see the S doorway with the small zigzag at right angles to the wall surface and the two-lancet window, largely rebuilt by *C. Buckeridge*, 1853–8 (stencilled wall decoration at the E end and tiles of the period). Early C14 S aisle and N aisle. Arcades of three bays, tall, with octagonal piers and double-chamfered arches. The SE respond and one S pier have very fine capitals decorated not only with oakleaves and acorns but also with knotty branches (cf. the doorway at Kislingbury). – FONT. Probably Norman. Circular, with two tiers of flat round arches, the upper standing on the apexes of the lower. STAINED GLASS. Chancel E, *c.* 1860 by *Clayton & Bell*. – S aisle window of 1898 by *Curtis, Ward & Hughes*. – Tower, 1890 by *Holland* of Warwick.

RAUNDS

A somewhat disparate and spread place which owes the beginning of its expansion to the shoe industry. The Square, which ought to be its centre, hardly functions as such. The church stands at the town's N end, while most of the activity is a good ¼ m. S in Brook Street. Whatever else is looked at, the church should not be missed.

ST MARY. This is without doubt one of the finest medieval churches in the county, not only for its architecture but for decoration. Although the basic development is quite clear, there are enough problems to keep architectural historians puzzling.

The description must start from the ornate E.E. W tower, standing high above the street across a green slope. Its proportions are exceptionally satisfying. Set-back buttresses. Shafted W portal set back behind an outer entrance, also shafted, a little higher than the portal proper and flush with the W wall of the tower; l. and r. small blank trefoil-headed arches. On the next stage two lancets in blank, nicely shafted arches and blank arches l. and r. set out with a quatrefoil – a curious arrangement. The question becomes more pressing on the stage above, where to the W there is a two-light trefoil-headed window placed under a gable filling nearly the whole height. To the l. and r. of it corresponding rising diagonals or half-gables towards the angles so that the whole stage has a letter W inscribed, as it were. Moreover, blank quatrefoils are set in the surfaces, one in each of the four side triangles. The N and S sides are simpler. They have no quatrefoils, just noble blank arcading, on the N subdivided Y-fashion by pendant arches on heads. The bell-stage has two pairs of shafted lancets and blank lancet arches l. and r., again subdivided Y-fashion. Broach spire with broaches reaching up about as high as the very tall tier of lucarnes. There are two more, and they are placed in alternate directions. The spire was rebuilt in 1826 by *Charles Squirhill* after being struck by lightning. Internally the tower

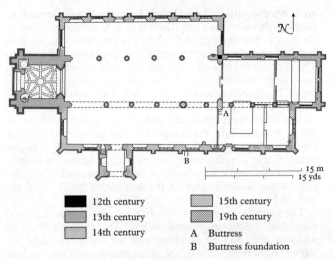

■ 12th century	▨ 15th century
▨ 13th century	▨ 19th century
▨ 14th century	A Buttress
	B Buttress foundation

Raunds, St Mary.
Plan

arch has inset an exceptionally rare early C15 CLOCK DIAL, stone-faced with twenty-four discs of the hours. The dial is held by two angels, and behind them kneel the donors, John Elen and his wife. The whole in colour, which slides onto the capitals of the tower arch. Above is a series of roof-lines which help one to deduce the various phases of development of the building.

The interior is intricate and this is where the puzzles lie. It clearly represents a development in stages, but the differences in detail are such that reuse or retention of older parts has occurred. The story certainly starts with the remains of a window above the S arcade, evidence of an unaisled Norman nave, and the shape of the last S pier but one and the quoin edge above, evidence of walls at that place which probably mark the angle of a Norman S transept. There are foundations of earlier buttresses externally at the easternmost end of the S aisle and S chapel, which also refer to the earlier plan. The church may have been cruciform, but there is no evidence now surviving on the N side. There followed, begun c. 1225, the tower and the two semicircular W responds of the nave, evidence of the intention of E.E. aisling. But the Norman W wall must have been further E, so that the first bay of the S arcade is wider than the others, bridging the distance between new tower and old nave. At the same time, or before, a new chancel was begun. A blank window arch in the S wall shows that its wall had gone up to a certain height before a S chapel was added. The chapel arcade was originally of three bays with a circular piers with circular abacus and double-chamfered arches. The third bay is now interrupted by the C14 chancel arch. So the earlier chancel arch must have been further w, roughly where, on the s side, there is now an octagonal column. Of the C13 also the external s doorway into the s chapel, with stiff-leaf capitals, and the N and s aisle doorways and s porch. The N doorway, resited when the aisle was rebuilt in the C14, has a slight chamfer, the s doorway is normally double-chamfered. Its details otherwise, especially the capitals, and the details of the s porch including its shafted entrance and the corner shafts for a rib-vault, correspond closely to those of the w doorway into the tower. The last glory of the C13 at Raunds is the splendid six-light E window, hardly possible before *c.* 1275, with cusped trefoil-headed lights, six quatrefoiled circles, and a big octofoiled circle in the head. The foliation of the circles is part of the restoration by *G. G. Scott*, 1873–4.*

The s arcade was reshaped probably *c.* 1300. It has octagonal piers and double-chamfered arches. The irregularity of its wider w arch and its junction with the earlier transept has already been noted. There are other irregularities too, such as the reuse of ironstone voussoirs from an earlier phase in the westernmost arches. What then seems to have happened is the rebuilding of a grander N aisle and its arcade. Its details are full C14, and it has no irregularities worth speaking of. The N windows, fitting the rhythm of the arcade, have flowing tracery. Alongside this comes the insertion of a new chancel arch, further E than the earlier one and cutting in two the w bay of the earlier chancel arcade. It has finely moulded responds, thin imposts rather than capitals and ballflower in the arch, and to support it a buttress within the s aisle. To resolve the junction of the s aisle and the removal of the earlier transept, the s arcade was extended and given a further octagonal column and a half-arch to join it to the new chancel arch. It was presumably the intention to rebuild the s aisle and arcade, but that never happened, so we are left with the odd effect of half-arches either side the chancel arch. The s wall of the s aisle, the E portions of the s chapel and the chancel s wall were rebuilt in the C15 and given large Perp windows, several with embattled transoms. In the s wall of the s chapel are the jambs of a former window and another jamb remnant on the N side of the E window. In the chancel this meant the unhappy reduction of the E bay of the s chancel arcade. The C13 PISCINA survives together with SEDILIA and another PISCINA of C14 or C15 date. The nave was also heightened and given a new Perp clerestory. Fine late medieval ROOFS, the one over the nave with tracery in the spandrels. There was further restoration work done *c.* 1900 by *H. M. Townsend*.

FURNISHINGS. – FONT. Circular, with one very realistic ram's head sticking out. Can this be C13? – SCREENS. The s chapel screen seems to have a C13 beam decorated with trefoil

---

* *Churches of the Archdeaconry* (1849) shows the window and describes it as having plain circles.

arcading. In the next arch the capital is cut away to suggest a further beam existed originally there too. The lower section columns, with their rings, would also appear to be C13, but they were given C14 ogee tracery above. A very rare survival. – The base of the rood screen, C15, survives. – REREDOS (chancel). All part of the 1906 refitting. A splendid Perp-style affair all coloured and gilded, set into plainer panelling. (N aisle.) Wooden panels with flamboyant tracery. – BENCHES. Parts of late medieval benches are incorporated in the choir stalls of 1894. – PULPIT. The polygonal C18 TABLE (N aisle) was originally the tester of the pulpit. The present pulpit is of the 1860s by *William Gillett* of Leicester. – COMMUNION RAIL. Jacobean, with vertically symmetrical balusters. – WALL PAINTINGS. Especially well preserved in the nave, though fragmentary in the N aisle. Nave N wall, Pride and her Six Children, St Christopher, the Three Quick and the Three Dead. Over the N doorway St George; on the N aisle wall fragments of a Legend of St Catherine. Over the chancel arch, angels with the instruments of the Passion with silhouettes of the rood cross and statues on either side. Rood stairs partially preserved in the S aisle, so a screen across both aisle and nave originally. All C15. – CHANDELIER. Brass, given in 1762. – ARMOUR (S chapel). Parts of two sets of the time of Charles I. – STAINED GLASS. – Chancel N, St Elizabeth, C15. Late C14 fragments in a window in the S aisle. – E window by *Kempe & Co.*, 1907. – S aisle windows of 1908 by *E. R. Suffling*, and 1954 by *Francis Skeat*. – Two windows in the N aisle, 1978 and 1981 also by *Skeat*. – MONUMENTS. Brasses to John Tawyer †1470 and wife, 18-in. (46-cm.) figures, and to a lady of *c.* 1500, also an 18-in. figure. – John Wales, vicar, †1496. Tomb-chest with shields in trefoil-headed panels. The shields are suspended from roses. No effigy.

CHURCHYARD CROSS (SE of the S porch). On one of the steps a quatrefoil frieze. Part of the shaft, C15.

ST THOMAS MORE (R.C.), Marshall's Road. Former Primitive Methodist chapel of 1870. Red brick and stone frontage of 1899. Windows with Y-tracery: large ones either side the doorway and a smaller one in the gable. Large gabled yellow brick Gothic building alongside built as a Temperance Hall in 1859, now converted.

METHODIST CHURCH, Brook Street. 1873–4, designed 1869 by *William Streather*. Rearing above the street with three tall round arches and round-headed windows. Rusticated pilasters. Triangular pediment. Galleried interior. Behind its former SCHOOL (Wesley Court) of 1860 by *T. Y. Littlewood* of St Neots and enlarged in 1896 by *Sharman & Archer*. The master's house survives more or less as built in a mild Tudor style, but the school behind was considerably altered when converted into a residence. Its curious metal conical ventilation turrets remain.

MANOR SCHOOL and RAUNDS PARK INFANTS SCHOOL, Park Road and Mountbatten Way. Now a large complex. The original school of 1869 was by *Walter E. MacCarthy* with extensions of 1874 and 1897, both by *Talbot Brown & Fisher*. Further rear extensions were added by *Beazley & Burrows* in 1910–11. Only portions of these older buildings survive incorporated into the new Manor School. Infants School, fronting Park Road, 1912–13 by *J. T. Blackwell* of Kettering, is brick with a central pedimented bay and wings on either side.*

PERAMBULATION. In BERRISTER PLACE, immediately E of the church, two Georgian-looking houses. BERRISTER HOUSE of five bays, two storeys and with a wooden doorcase with fanlight is as late as 1855 and built as the vicarage. It is by *Henry Goddard* of Leicester but a remarkably plain example of his work. No. 4 alongside, with an irregular façade, central large window and Doric columned porch on the r. To the s is MANOR STREET with on the junction the former CHAMBERS HEEL FACTORY. Victorian white Whittlesey brick with big windows. Fun cresting with ball finials. In Manor Street on the N side the MANOR HOUSE. C17, T-shaped with some remaining mullions and a nice stone gateway to the garden with a pediment and four-centred opening. Opposite the CONSERVATIVE CLUB. 1902 by *Kettering Co-operative Builders Society* red brick in Queen Anne style with dentil cornice over its five bays, a central segmental pediment, long window below with ironwork balcony and a stone-framed doorcase. Just w is HILL STREET, with on the N side, sandwiched between later houses, HILL END HOUSE, with its 1627 stone gable, much renewed in the C19. W again to BROOK STREET. Beside the Methodist church (*see* above), the former COFFEE TAVERN, 1883–4 by *Talbot Brown & Fisher*. Three bays, brick, with two large segmental-arched windows either side the entrance. Behind, at the s end of COLEMAN STREET, a rather choice villa, ROSEDENE, of 1905. Faintly chequered red brick, and two gables, one above a large lunette window with square bay beneath, the other with a timbered top and canted bay below. Timber-tiled porch between them.

On the other side of Brook Street, the long stone façade of the FRIENDLY SOCIETY, 1851. Four-centred arched doorcase. Forming the corner of Thorpe Road, with a large Jacobethan archway, is THE HALL (Raunds Town Council), 1871. Classical, very debased, with its main façade facing the street. Two storeys, five-bay central section with tall, slender Ionic-columned portico. Two wings with canted bays. On the rear façade the Ionic columns are even more elongated. Opposite a large CO-OPERATIVE SOCIETY store. 1901, red brick and stone, with a hall on the first floor and a small tower with pyramidal roof. Additions to the building are recorded by *Talbot Brown & Fisher*, so the whole is probably their work.

---

* The former National School and House of 1859 by *G. E. Street* have sadly been demolished.

SW, just beyond the roundabout in WELLINGTON ROAD, on the N side WELLINGTON WORKS, a classical archway with either side a pair of yellow brick houses *c.* 1880. Formerley a tannery, hence the standing Wellington boot on the top of the archway.

In THORPE ROAD some pleasant stone houses, including WARWICK HOUSE, Late Georgian of three bays, rusticated quoins, and beyond, THORPE HOUSE, late C16 with projecting porch on the E side, two big chimneystacks on the W, and many three-light arched mullioned windows. Original staircase. Traditionally the birthplace of *Robert Grumbold* (†1720), the master mason who did much work in Cambridge. If so then the building is likely to be the work of the Grumbolds, who were much used by Sir Thomas Tresham at Rushton (q.v.). The Grumbolds worked the extensive quarries at Raunds.

RAVENSTHORPE 6070

ST DENYS. Much of the C13, and in particular the W tower and the arcades. The tower (partly rebuilt in 1810) has two shafted lancets as bell-openings. The buttresses, battlements and pinnacles are later. The tower arch towards the nave is triple-chamfered. The arcades of three bays have double-chamfered arches on octagonal piers. Concave-sided responds. In the S aisle Dec doorway and W window. Also a low tomb-recess inside. The chancel by *W. Bassett-Smith* dates from 1865–7. – BENCH-ENDS. Largely *c.* 1500 – PULPIT. Jacobean. Painted panel on back and coat of arms of John Breton of Teeton, dated April 23 1619. – SCREEN. Parts of the screen are Perp. – ROOD-LOFT STAIR. At SE corner of N aisle. – CHEST. Magnificent, nearly 8 ft (2.4 metres) long, iron-bound. – ARMOUR. A few pieces. Said to have been found at Naseby. – HATCHMENTS. Two for the Langton family, probably for Thomas †1762 and his wife also †1762, whose mural monument by one of the *Coxes* is close by. – STAINED GLASS. Chancel E (Dykyns family memorial), 1937 by *Christopher Webb*.

In the village several COTTAGES built of cob.

RAVENSTHORPE RESERVOIR, Teeton Road. Formed in 1886, opened 1890. The engineers were *T. & C. Hawksley* of Westminster. Original brick buildings in Tudor style.

RINGSTEAD 9070

ST MARY. Good C13 W tower; not high. Unbuttressed with tall W lancet with stiff-leaf cusps. Shortish broach spire with high broaches and three tiers of lucarnes, the lowest very tall and with Y-tracery. Otherwise the exterior mostly Dec, i.e. the N porch entrance with ballflower decoration and an ogee gable, the simple doorways, the fine tall chancel windows (E five lights) with flowing tracery, the SEDILIA with ogee arches, also the S windows as tall as those of the chancel and with flowing tracery too, and the S porch with a quadripartite vault with ridge ribs. The ribs are round, not pointed. The N arcade inside is earlier. It belongs to the time of the tower. Five bays, quatrefoil piers, double-chamfered arches. The N chapel is of the same time again (circular piers and circular abaci, double-chamfered arches). Several large Perp windows on N side. – FONT. Octagonal, plain, with a stem with attached keeled shafts; c. 1300 perhaps. – SCREEN. Plain low stone base, also to the N chapel. Said to be partly original, but with the PULPIT largely the result of the restoration by *W. Slater* of 1862–3. – STALL-ENDS. Incorporated in the C19 choir stalls, carved by *S. Poole* of London, are two C15 ends, one with fleur-de-lys, the other foliate with a shield with a cross on the back. – MONUMENTS. Grouped on the walls of the tower. Several signed by *Coles* of Thrapston. The best is for Rev. Parris, no date, but signed by *Henry Cox*. Usual obelisk shape with a shelf with marble books.

SCHOOL. Next to the church. 1865–7 by *Wadmore & Baker*, much extended since.

MANOR HOUSE. W of the church. Handsome five-bay house with nice doorcase. 1765.

At the corner of Denford Road an especially good COTTAGE with banded ironstone and sandstone, immaculately done. Pantile roof and datestone for 1711. In Denford Road a tall former FACTORY, c. 1900, three floors, five bays, yellow brick with red used as ornamentation. Roundel for Ringstead Britannic Cooperative Society, and a boot marked 'Solid Reliable'.

7050
ROADE

ST MARY.* A small church, structurally Norman with nave, chancel and a central tower. Norman two chancel windows and the S doorway. Two orders of shafts, scalloped capitals. One arch moulding with a motif of two horns, the other with the beakhead motif. In the W wall a window of c. 1300 (three stepped lancet lights under one arch). The central tower C13 in its present form. Lancet to the N, lancet to the S, arch inside with dogtooth. On the upper stage lancet in three spacious blank arches. Perp top with transomed bell-openings. The N aisle and arcade of 1850 by *E. F. Law*, and the tower and chancel restored again by Law 1855–7. Church hall, N, 1972. – PULPIT. 1950 by *Paul Panter*, in a Gothic manner, of elegant wine-glass form. – STAINED GLASS. Chancel E, 1957 by *Christopher Webb*. – Nave W, Cripps memorial, 1985–6 by *Francis Skeat*, very much in tune with the Webb window.

* The vicarage by *S. S. Teulon* was demolished in the 1950s.

Former BAPTIST CHAPEL, E end of High Street. Founded in the
C17. New building 1736, rebuilt 1802. Altered inside 1871–2.
Limestone rubble, with two doorways and sash windows, those
above having a circular clock between them. Closed 1994, now
a residence.

METHODIST CHAPEL, Hartwell Road. 1907–8 by *Brown &
Mayor* of Northampton. Brick and stone, a large single gable
end divided by four pilasters with a Gothic window stretched
across them and porch below. Behind is the previous chapel of
1875 by *S. J. Newman*, converted into a Sunday School. Patterned brick.

ROADE PRIMARY SCHOOL, Hartwell Road. 1876 by *T. H.
Vernon*, of red brick with yellow and blue brick dressings. Big
Gothic window to the schoolroom and bellcote over. Two
former porches for boys and infants, the latter in a small tower
with pyramidal roof, both now incorporated into the main
building. Teacher's house on l.

CANDIDA COTTAGE, No. 39 High Street. Plain stone exterior.
The interior, however, preserves several features from when
W. J. Bassett-Lowke owned it from 1914. The original cottage
was altered 1914–18. *Charles Rennie Mackintosh* was involved
but this may only have been for interior decoration and furnishings. There is a possibility that Bassett-Lowke's neighbour
in Northampton, *Alexander Anderson*, who was certainly
involved at No. 78 Derngate, may have played a part. The result
is in a very chaste vernacular manner with rough stone and
some wood. The most original addition was a loggia with
square pillars and balcony above. If Mackintosh were not associated with it, it would not qualify for comment.

TYLECOTE HOUSE, No. 33 Hartwell Road. 1894–6 by *Edward
Swinfen Harris*. Built for the local doctor and originally incorporating the surgery. Large, of brick with the upper floors
tile-hung. The main block three bays with central porch and
tall roof with metal finials. Projecting wing with Gothic trefoil-
patterned windows and a half-timbered gable.

HYDE FARM HOUSE, at the end of Hyde Road. Externally a
simple farmhouse. The unimpressive exterior hides the bones
of a C14 hall house with a two-bay hall and two-bay solar/
parlour. Porch entrance with round arch of C17. Newel staircase. Timbers of roof in the form of arched braces with a collar.
Its circular DOVECOTE is now in the grounds of the adjoining
property, Dovecote Farm.

ROADE CUTTING, one of the most ambitious works on *Robert
Stephenson*'s London & Birmingham Railway. Opened in 1838,
it has an AQUEDUCT *c.* 1837 to carry a stream. Ironstone piers
and cast iron channel.

ROCKINGHAM

8090

CASTLE. Rockingham was a royal castle. Its position, commanding the valley of the Welland, was naturally well protected

p. 548

with a steep fall to N and W. Excavations around the keep have revealed traces of Roman and pre-Roman occupation. However, Domesday Book states that Rockingham 'was waste when King William ordered a castle to be made'. William's castle consisted of a motte with a double bailey (cf. Windsor), with curtain walls, gatehouse, great hall, and chapel largely of timber. The chapel (which has disappeared) and the hall were the venue for the Council of Rockingham of 1095. The motte was later given a keep and a gate and barbican of its own.

Of the early kings John was the most frequent visitor to the castle; he came fourteen times between 1204 and 1216. Although building work was carried out by him and by Henry III, the castle was in a sad state of repair after a siege in 1220, as recorded in a survey of 1250, and a major reconstruction was undertaken by Edward I in 1276–91. When Leland visited in the mid C16 it was already largely in ruins. It remained in royal possession until 1544 when Edward Watson was granted its lease. Much of what survives today derives from his work between 1550 and 1585. His son, also Edward, entertained James I in 1604 and his son, Lewis, did likewise in 1619. In 1645 Sir Lewis Watson was created Baron Rockingham. Being a Royalist house, the castle fortifications, such as the keep, were almost totally slighted by orders of Parliament in 1646. The church and a good deal of the village were also destroyed. Edward, 2nd Baron Rockingham, succeeded in 1653 and put in hand repairs and added some new buildings. His son Lewis married into the Sondes family of Lees Court, Kent, and was in 1714 created 1st Earl of Rockingham, a title which lapsed in 1746. However, through the Sondes family other estates were inherited and throughout the C18 Rockingham was treated as a secondary home and to a degree neglected. It did not become a family home again till 1836 when it was inherited by the Hon. Richard Watson, a close friend of Charles Dickens to whom he dedicated first *David Copperfield*. He brought in first *Edward Blore* in 1837, but his schemes were not carried out, and for reasons not clear he was replaced in 1838 by *Anthony Salvin*, who during the 1840s and 1850s brought the castle to its present appearance. In the 1960s extensive reconstruction work was undertaken, including an overhaul of the whole roof structure. At the same time various internal alterations for C20 domestic convenience were made by *K. J. Allsop* of *Gotch, Saunders & Surridge*. Rockingham remains with the Watson – now Saunders Watson – family.

Of the late C13 there survive the additions to the gatehouse, some of the E wall to its S, and remains of the reconstructed hall, which lies at right angles to them, with its main entrance on the N. The GATEHOUSE is of Weldon stone. It has two strong semicircular towers with cross-slits. These semicircular parts were almost certainly added by Edward I to earlier towers, although the building accounts do not survive to prove this. The history of the gatehouse appears to have been as follows: first, two square towers flanking a gateway (see the round-headed arches at the back); secondly, a square centre projection; thirdly, the rounded fronts added to the two towers. Their crenellations are C19. The arches of the gateway are two-centred and have fine mouldings. The portcullis groove ought to be noted. Doorways to the l. and r. Another window of Edward I's time, visible externally, survives on the W side of the adjoining E wall, towards the S end. The gatehouse gives access to a large COURTYARD with the main block of the house on the l., ahead a long Elizabethan range and a walled terrace on the r. from which there are panoramic views of the Welland valley.

An exploration of the EXTERIOR serves to unravel the main sequences of development. First the MAIN BLOCK of the house. This has first, on the l., the Elizabethan living apartments dated 1584 within the pediment of the central gable. This work has three gables and its two floors with four-light mullioned-and-transomed windows. Smaller windows in the attic gables. Although appearing uniform it is in fact a welding together of two formerly independent structures: one against the medieval curtain wall and another E of the hall. The first of these has evidence of being partially an older structure with windows looking out from the medieval wall. The r.-hand gable is in fact the end of a cross-wing with kitchen and service rooms behind its mixed ironstone walling denoting older structure. The central section of the house embodies the remains of the medieval HALL, only apparent now by its doorway and the large projecting chimneystack. The doorway has elaborate mouldings, rolls with keels and fillets and very weathered stiff-leaf capitals. The C13 S doorway also survives. Stylistically the doorways look later than 1216 but earlier than 1276. But that does not fit with the documented major building periods. The curious projecting canopy was originally a first-floor balcony, one of the few C18 alterations. Its opening above was infilled and given shields in the C19. Strange iron knocker in the form of a hammer. The stack may be an early feature but its present form is due to Edward Watson subdividing the hall to create a state apartment on the first floor, obvious by its four-light mullioned-and-transomed windows. The narrow block to the l. of the doorway was also remodelled. The last gable in the range and the small one-storey C19 addition mark the position of the Great Parlour, immediately W of the hall.

Running at right angles to the main block is the long two-storeyed LODGINGS wing, originally built in 1553 but remodelled in 1631 when the first floor was turned into a Long Gallery, an inscription recording this across the chimneystack. Two symmetrical sections with their own doorways and windows on either side, and the stack dividing them. Before moving on the buildings around the gatehouse need to be looked at. The rear of the gatehouse was rebuilt following Civil War damage c. 1660. To its N is a three-bay one-storey block with cellar and attic dormers. This is WALKER'S HOUSE, built in 1665, and named after the C18 house steward. It is still in

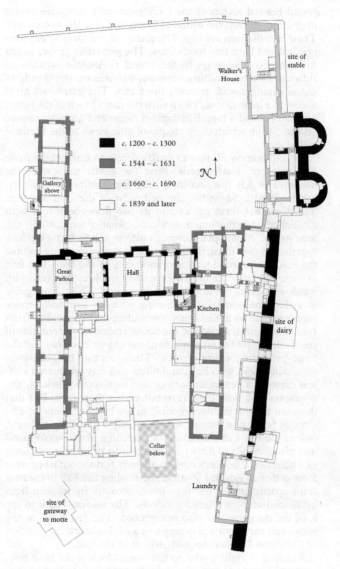

c. 1200 – c. 1300

c. 1544 – c. 1631

c. 1660 – c. 1690

c. 1839 and later

site of
stable

Walker's
House

Gallery
above

Great
Parlour

Hall

Kitchen

site of
dairy

Cellar
below

Laundry

site of
gateway
to motte

Rockingham Castle.
Plan

the vernacular tradition of the C16. Its staircase with turned balusters and newels topped by pierced ovoid finials looks late C16 (one side only; the other is a copy) and is probably resited from the main house. Now to the WEST FRONT. This is where *Salvin*'s work now makes its impact. His is the embattled TOWER of two storeys with its staircase turret built 1849–51.

It adds a touch of majesty to the front which is very welcome. The range is otherwise of the 1550s with the wide gable marking the end of the Great Parlour and State Apartment above. At the S end of the range another gable marks a block added onto the house by Salvin to create further family rooms with bedrooms above. Its rear square turret is the staircase.

The INTERIOR is entered by a doorway close to the gate-house and this gives access into the former SERVANTS' HALL, alongside the medieval curtain wall, of which the stonework with herringbone pattern has been exposed to the r. of its Tudor fireplace. This leads to an extraordinary medieval sur-vival, THE STREET. Really a service passage to the laundry block, but wonderfully evocative with its cobbles and mixture of buildings – just like a medieval street indeed. On either side a miscellany of smaller buildings comprising a dairy, brew-house, bakehouse etc. At its S end the LAUNDRY, dated 1669 on its stack and one of the handsomest parts of the house. Two storeys with cross mullioned-transomed windows and a tall bellcote on its N end. The internal arrangement is less regular than its façades would suggest. Splendid lead cistern dated 1783. The Street gives access to the KITCHEN, still with its Victorian ranges by *Briffault* of Paris and London, installed by *Fosters* of Uppingham. Scullery and larder beyond. The HALL is noteworthy for its beams dated 1579 with their inscription: 'THE HOWSE SHAL BE PRESERVED AND NEVER WILL DECAYE WHEARE THE ALMIGHTIE GOD IS HONORED AND SERVED DAYE BY DAYE' and the Watson family motto 'MEA GLORIA FIDES'. The panelling is refitted from other parts of the house and appears to be largely C17. A rise in the paving beyond the hall marks the height of the former hall dais, and leads into the PANEL ROOM (formerly the Great Parlour) where are the jambs of two tall shafted C13 windows. The panelling dates from *c.* 1680 with shields for the Watsons and various alliances. The heraldry was redone in 1838 by *Thomas Willement*. The chunky STAIRCASE is part of Salvin's first phase of work in 1838–9 and by his standards very restrained. The ground floor of the S range was given a side corridor and the rooms joined by a central opening to form a LIBRARY. Its Adam-style ceilings and decoration were added in 1904–5 by *Smith Bros* of Northampton. On the first floor of the N range is the LONG GALLERY. This remains a complete *Salvin* interior, much enhanced by the large bay within his tower. The white and gold patterned wallpaper was supplied by *Cowtan & Son* in 1850 and the room retains its splendid red damask curtains. The three spectacular *c.* 1780 Venetian glass chandeliers are also original. Charles Dickens visited Rockingham on five occasions and the Gallery was the inspiration for Chesney Wold, the melancholy Dedlock house, in *Bleak House* – it is far from melancholy today.

The GARDEN to the W of the house is bisected by the ELEPHANT HEDGE, a wondrous heaving mass of yew dating from the C17. To the S is the Norman MOTTE, surmounted by a rose garden. Above all it is the situation and the views which will remain in the memory, as much as, if not more, than the architecture. Outside the curtilage and just E of the church is an early CI9 ICE HOUSE.

ST LEONARD. Immediately below the N courtyard of the castle and in no connexion with the present village. The earlier village which surrounded the church was, like the medieval church, largely destroyed during the Civil War when a Parliamentary garrison was set up. The church was partly rebuilt *c.* 1660–70. However, the building today is small and irregular and almost entirely CI9. Small NE tower with octagonal pyramid roof of 1845–6 which is also the date of the Gothic tracery of the nave. The E portions 1868, including the S chapel, and the rest 1873, in both cases by *Edward Browning* of Stamford and for him a little disappointing. Internally also nothing of architectural interest. – FONT. Dated 1669. Of the oddly bleak kind of so many of the fonts of the 1660s. Big volutes, a heart, etc. – PULPIT. Jacobean manner, of the usual type but probably post-1660. – COMMUNION RAIL. Of wrought iron and fine; the gift of Lady Pelham *c.* 1730. – CARVED FRAGMENT. A medieval female head within a broken quatrefoil. – STAINED GLASS. A good selection. S chapel E by *G. Hedgeland,* 1853, very pictorial. – N aisle E looks like *Kempe* but is in fact by *H. W. Bryans,* 1905. – The two other windows in the N aisle are by *Percy Bacon c.* 1925. – N aisle W window by *Heaton, Butler & Bayne,* as is the chancel E window of 1868. – Other glass with pressed quarries is by *J. Powell & Sons.* – Small rose window presented by F. H. Sutton in 1868 and made by *M. & A. O'Connor.* – MONUMENTS. Many, and some of outstanding quality. It should be recorded that until 1873 all the monuments were in the chancel and only when the S chapel had been built were they moved, leaving just the two in the sanctuary. The Montagus of Boughton were more discriminating in their choice of sculptors. – Sir Edward Watson †1584 and †1616. (S chapel) Fragments of two monuments, reassembled and jumbled up no doubt after the Civil War. Two recumbent effigies, the children kneeling against the tombchest. The effigies are of *c.* 1616, and have been attributed to *Garrett Hollemans,* though the woman, Sir Edward's mother, wears the dress that belongs to her time. – Anne Lady Rockingham †1695 (chancel N), by *John Nost.* Heavy gesticulating standing figure. Roman Doric columns l. and r. Big Baroque pedimented top. Black draperies behind the whole monument. – Hon. Margaret Watson †1713, by *William Palmer* (S chapel). Also with a standing figure, but this one slender, in a serpentine posture with fluttering draperies. She originally had a skull entwined with a serpent at her feet, but, alas, this has been stolen. Big drapery canopy or baldacchino. Fluted Corinthian pilasters l. and r. An outstanding Baroque conception. – 1st Earl of Rockingham †1724 (chancel S). By *Delvaux.* Figures by *Scheemakers.* Big sarcophagus and standing figures to the l. and r., he in Roman dress, his wife wearing an ermine mantle.

Dancing putto on the sarcophagus carrying a wreath and a toy trumpet. Broad architectural background. – Lady Arabella Oxenden †1734 (s chapel). Free-standing figure on a pedestal, like a piece of Roman statuary in a museum. No architectural background. Of excellent quality, unsigned but it must surely be by *Rysbrack*. – Lady Sondes †1777 (s chapel N wall). Signed by *William Paine*. Almost too large for its position. No figures, only a base and a sarcophagus with domed top, all in flat relief and with very restrained decoration. – Various members of the Sondes family. Lewis Lord Sondes †1795 (s chapel s wall). Inscription plate with draped urn on top. – Also s chapel s wall Lewis Lord Sondes †1806, same composition, and Lady Sondes †1818. Hanging monument, woman by an urn. Several late C19 tablets but fashioned in the Jacobean manner. Inscription tablet for Lavinia, daughter of the Hon. Richard Watson, wife of Baron von Roeder †1933, the lettering by *Eric Gill*. Another finely lettered plaque for Sir Michael Culme-Seymour †1999.

The VILLAGE lies to the N, at the foot of the hill along a main road. It is one of the most picturesque villages in the county. C17–C18 houses and cottages, many thatched, the earliest date 1663 on the SONDES ARMS, the latest 1795 on a farmhouse. The best house is CASTLE FARMHOUSE, at the bottom of the hill. Half-H-plan, looking like a manor house. Two-light upright mullioned windows. Doorway broad, classical, with ears. The date is 1674. Of the rest, No. 6 on the E side, of red brick with blue diaper patterns, may be one of the cottages known to have been built by *J. G. Bland c.* 1850. On the other hand it may be the work of *R. C. Hussey*, who is also known to have improved several cottages in the mid 1840s. The former SCHOOL on the W side was originally built in 1843 but refashioned in 1858. Timber gable decoration. SCHOOL HOUSE, which is part of a row, is dated 1865.

ROTHERSTHORPE

ST PETER & ST PAUL. Of the C13 the W tower and the arcades. The tower has bell-openings with Y-tracery, a saddleback roof, and an arch towards the nave with semicircular responds and a hoodmould with headstops. A refreshingly limewashed interior. The arcades have piers with the rare form of a circular core with four triple shafts, i.e. altogether twelve shafts (cf. Flore). Arches with two slight chamfers. The arches into the chancel N and s chapels are probably Dec as is the TOMB-RECESS in the s aisle, with its wide crocketed ogee canopy. The windows partly of *c.* 1300 (s aisle), partly Dec (N chapel N), partly Perp (chancel E). s doorway of *c.* 1300; good. – SEDILIA and PISCINA. Dec with plain ogee heads. – PULPIT. With tall, plain, unadorned panels. One panel is inscribed FS1579 – an important date, as one would not expect such simplicity in the mid-Elizabethan decades. FS is for Francis Samwell of Upton. Small tester. Its panels have signs of grained patterns. Original? – COMMUNION RAIL. In a late C17 style, of 1954. – STALLS. Simple with vertical paneling and cross indents, of 1972. – COMMANDMENT BOARDS. C18, under the tower. – PAINTED TEXTS. C17, four in the nave, one each in the aisles. – SCULP-TURE. Cross-head with a crude figure of the Crucifixus and much stiff-leaf decoration. An E.E. cross-head is a great rarity.

BAPTIST CHAPEL, Church Street. Originally 1844, rebuilt 1892. Façade with three broad red brick arches inset with windows. Canopied doorway.

A number of good houses including, in North Street, the MANOR HOUSE, C17 five-bay façade with gables, the N end with two oval openings, and mullioned windows, and THE POPLARS of c. 1700. L-shaped, a wing with quoins and also two oval open-ings in another gable end. Signs of mullioned windows but now wooden casements. Behind the Manor House a C17 DOVE-COTE, circular, 20 ft (6 metre) diameter, with over 900 nesting places.

THE BERRY. NE of the church. A roughly triangular embankment of which nothing is known. It is said to be Anglo-Saxon or C12.

CANAL LOCKS, E of the village, alongside the A43. A flight of thirteen locks on the Grand Union Canal with alongside the fifth lock a wooden lifting bridge with massive overhead balance beams. A much altered LOCK HOUSE of 1815 at the upper end of the flight.

8080

ROTHWELL

Rothwell is one of the most attractive towns in Northampton-shire, a small town but decidedly a town. It has a splendid church, and a few houses of special note. The ensemble is however what matters most.

HOLY TRINITY. A large church of ironstone, remarkably long in particular (at 173 ft (53 metres) the longest parish church in the county). It has an intriguing development and a number of puzzles for the architectural archaeologist. There are unmis-takable marks of yet larger size originally with blocked arches along the fronts of the transepts and the chancel chapels indi-cate a wholesale cutting-down. In the case of the transepts it took place in 1673; for the chapels no date is known. It is also known that its tower once had a spire, but that was struck by lightning in 1660 and fell onto the body of the building demol-ishing sections of the nave arcades. So all this has to be taken into account when exploring the architecture.

The Norman church which preceded the present one must already have been unusually long; for there remain on the S side of the chancel the corbel table and five windows high up, three visible outside, the other two only inside. This cruciform Norman church also had a crossing tower. It ought to be noted however that the outer string course round the Norman windows is continued above the transept N arch, evidence, it seems, of no transept when the Norman windows were put in. Evidence for the Norman tower is in the bulk and the irregular shape of the E piers of the aisle arcades, which were built about 1200. Both aisles were in fact added at the same time and to the same design. The interior resulting from this and a later alteration, to be described presently, is singularly beautiful in its tawny colour. The arcades look very imposing in their erectness, more so in fact than they did when they were first built; for the suggestion is convincing that they were heightened when the aisles were widened. What height they originally had is not at all certain. Possible evidence is (a) the fillets on the piers which (with the exception of the E imposts) end halfway down, (b) a respond with a stiff-leaf capital of slightly later date between the N aisle and the N transept, (c) a shaft with a damaged circular capital in the S crossing pier. Andor Gomme pointed out that on the third pier from the W in the S arcade, the masonry changes colour two-thirds of the way up. On the other hand the collapse of the spire might also account for these inconsistencies. The arcade piers alternate in shape between a circular and a square core with four demi-shafts attached. The shafts are divided by rings. The capitals are of a very early stiff-leaf variety with small leaves; the arches are pointed and double-stepped. The aisles were originally narrower than they are now, although the original width cannot be taken from that of the CRYPT or charnel house below part of the S aisle, an early C13 room. The room is 30 ft (9 metres) long and only 15 ft (4.6 metres) wide, but it is its S wall that corresponds to the S wall above, whereas its N wall lies to the S of the S arcade. The crypt has two bays and is rib-vaulted. Single-chamfered ribs and transverse arch. When the arcades of the church were heightened we do not know. The only *terminus ante quem* is the splendid tower arch with the naturalistic foliage of its ample filleted shafts. This cannot be later than *c.* 1280–90. But that arch itself is a surprise, for the tower was started a good deal earlier. This is shown by the W doorway, although it should be said at once that the arch of this doorway is a re-set piece. It is Late Norman, say of *c.* 1170, and may originally have had a round arch. It has rich zigzag and crenellation motifs. The doorway itself has five orders of shafts with shaft-rings and fully developed stiff-leaf capitals, say of *c.* 1225. The tower is sturdy and rather short, though it would look less so if its spire still crowned it. There is much evidence of damage and alterations within the tower, even at base level. On the N side, for example, on the first upper stage there is a blank pointed arch and a second with trefoiling inside the arch, with a lancet window sitting inorganically under one of them. Internally there was a window, now blocked, on the S side and there are further fragmental marks elsewhere. Then there are the strange flat relieving arches on the S and W sides. The upper parts of the tower are certainly later, with the pairs of transomed two-light bell-openings with tracery below the transoms. The whole structure looks as if it was tidied up, and probably refaced following the spire's collapse.

After this digression the building history must be resumed. The Norman chancel, at the time when the aisles were built, received a S and shortly afterwards a N chapel. They had four bays. The first pier on either side is quatrefoil, the second bay has two demi-shafts instead of one towards the central vessel, and the third, only partly surviving on the S side, had the same. The chapels themselves are altered now and partly demolished on the S side. The arches of the arcade are pointed and have one step and another with a thin roll moulding.

To the chapels and the nave arcade, or to a slightly later date, the resited S porch entrance seems to belong. It has shafts with rings, a round arch and dogtooth decoration. Later C13 the rather damaged SEDILIA and PISCINA in the chancel with their handsome little quadripartite vaults inside the canopies. Unusually the sedilia has four seats and the piscina three drains. The dividing shafts are probably Alwalton marble.

The next problem is the widening of the aisles decided upon probably at the same time as the heightening. There is in fact one detail which would tell a date if it could be dated precisely: the N respond of the N aisle E arch. The S respond was (*see* above) early C13; this N respond looks later in the same century. In addition we have the windows. The S aisle windows have three steeply stepped lancet lights under an arch, again a sign of the late C13. The S transept and S chapel correspond in date too. But they pose their own problem. They originally extended further S than they do now, and they all, save for one at the W end of the S aisle, have clumsy segmental heads. Are these also the result of C17 changes when the aisle walls were lowered? The Perp style cusped heads may well be C19 restoration (1893–4 by *A. W. Blomfield* with further work begun by *Sir A. Blomfield* 1902–3). In all cases the mullions are shafted and some jambs are shafted also. In the present S wall is a formerly free-standing pier. Its section is four major and four minor shafts. The S arches are now blocked, but the windows must have been moved back when the demolition took place for they are genuine late C13 work, two lights with a spherical triangle over. One still has its cusps, but the other not, again probably because of the C17 rebuild. The simple S doorway fits with the C13 work, as do the details higher up in the crossing, and that spectacular piece, the E window of the N chapel. This has three lights with intersection and much cusping, including a diagonally set cusped quatrefoil.

Of the fully grown Dec style there is no example at Rothwell. Perp and quite grand the chancel E end with a five-light E window and the excellent N windows of the N chapel with embattled transoms, but the shafts inside the E window are

C13, and probably mid-C13 the clerestory, the clumsy square pinnacles on the two shallow porches, and the tierceron vault with a large bell-hole under the tower, assuming this is medieval.

FURNISHINGS. FONT. Hexagonal and probably not in its original shape. A larger, higher and a recessed lower piece. Angle shafts with rings. Dogtooth decoration. It could be C13 but it is a very odd piece and could well be post-1660. – SCREEN, N chapel. Made up from inlaid panels from the C18 pulpit. – STALLS. C15, with poppyheads in the shape of figures and heads. Traceried fronts. MISERICORDS with angels, heads and a winged lion. – COMMUNION RAIL. C18. – CANDELA-BRUM. 1733; of brass; two tiers. – STAINED GLASS. Two windows by *J. Powell & Sons*, one in the N chapel dated 1933 and one on the S side of the chancel dated 1914. – S aisle window, 2009 by *Helen Whitaker*. – MONUMENTS. William de Williamsport †1309, vicar. In the S porch. Incised slab, the lower part not preserved. – William de Rothwell †1361, arch-deacon, brass, a 3-ft 5-in. (104-cm.) figure, angels by his pillow (chancel floor). – Edward Saunders †1514 and wife, also brasses, the figures 1 ft 10 in. (56 cm.) long (S transept floor). – Owen Ragsdale (*see* below), †1591. Plain big tomb-chest with a shield in a strapwork surround. Small brass plate with kneel-ing figure above. – Andrew Lane †1694. Architectural. Ionic columns, cherubs and garlands. – Magdalene Lane †1694. Elaborate hanging cartouche. Panel below with symbols of the Resurrection. Both attributed to *William Woodman* the elder (GF).

ROTHWELL METHODIST CHURCH, Market Square. 1899 by *Gotch & Saunders*. An odd composition, stone-fronted with a large cinquefoiled window in the centre and two small canted corner bays with mullions. Open interior with rear gallery and arched braced roof.

ROTHWELL UNITED REFORMED CHURCH (on the S side of Fox Street off the southern part of High Street), set back with the large ironstone façade of the former Congregational chapel, founded in 1655, the main building built 1735 and partially rebuilt 1826. It was extended and refronted in 1852 with Ital-ianate windows. There are also dates of 1893 and 1991. – STAINED GLASS. Two good windows of the Sower and the Reaper, 1930s by *A. Stoddart* of Nottingham. S of the church is the former SUNDAY SCHOOL of 1885.

JESUS HOSPITAL, SE of the church. Founded by Owen Ragsdale in 1591. He was a schoolmaster and fellow of Magdalen College. The two two-storeyed buildings at the entrance date from the C18 (r.) and 1840 (l.). Between them the original archway, four-centred, and with three finials at the top. The main buildings are a long S range and two L-shaped wings dated 1833 coming forward to the N, but not from the ends of the S range. The rest original. To the S front three gables, one above the archway (with the date 1593), the others oddly at the head of the chimney-breasts. Even the two-light windows under the gable are repeated. In the two halves l. and r. on each floor are a common-room and four sleeping cubicles. In the parts of 1833, a common-room and two cubicles. In the connecting bars of the L the staircase. The whole foundation was originally for twenty-six old men.

MOUNTSAYE COMMUNITY COLLEGE, Greening Road. Teaching block, 1990 by *Stimpson Walton Bond*. Swimming pool, 2004, also by them.

The MARKET SQUARE, E of the church, is dominated by Sir Thomas Tresham's MARKET HOUSE. The agreement of 1578 exists with *William Grumbold* (Grumball) 'for certain buildings at Rothwell Cross' to be executed to the 'plot' drawn by Grumbold. Oblong with four oblong projections, i.e. a cruciform shape with extruded angles. The symmetry disturbed only by the big spiral staircase in one angle. Two storeys with pilasters in two orders. They are decorated with the trefoils of the Treshams or with bands of oblongs and ovals linked together (cf. Rushton). Inscription frieze above the ground floor, frieze of heraldic shields above the first. The ninety coats of arms are those of landowners of Rothwell Hundred, and of some other Northamptonshire families. The ground floor was originally open. Mullioned-and-transomed windows above. The building remained incomplete for more than three hundred years. It was finally roofed in 1894–5 by *J. A. Gotch*.

On the S side in HOSPITAL HILL, a former factory converted into residences. Ironstone with blue brick voussoirs and part dated 1877. To its E another converted block adjoining ROSEWELL HOUSE, which was built in 1902 for Samuel Sargeant, a shoe manufacturer. Above the Methodist church (*see* above), on the E side of the Square, is a good double-fronted ironstone house dated 1701 with a central projection, which must originally have been the entrance. At the top of the Square the CONSERVATIVE CLUB with a Doric and Ionic centrepiece with a balcony, by *Gotch*. BRIDGE STREET runs W. ROTHWELL HOUSE (once the vicarage) is quite grand late C18. Red brick, three bays, three storeys. The centre windows (one round-headed, one circular) framed by a giant arch. Undoubtedly by a Leicestershire architect, the designer of Church Langton Hall and a house at Mountsorrell, which all have the giant arched façades. Edward Saunders suggested the architect was *William Henderson* of Leicester. There is another house of the form at Guilsborough (q.v.). Then the WORKING MEN'S CLUB, 1931, also by the *Gotch* firm, but this time in brick. Finally on the corner of DESBOROUGH ROAD a former bank (London Joint City & Midland) again by *Gotch*, 1919. Two-bay centre with double Doric pillars and big scrolled keystones, all under a triangular pediment. This is in stone, while its single wings are brick. N along Desborough Road an ironstone house with a narrow projecting porch with a four-centred doorhead and an upper window of three stepped lights. It is dated 1660, but considerably altered.

MANOR HOUSE, in the pretty tree-lined street leading to the church. An uncommonly fine mid-C18 house. Five bays, two storeys, a pitched rather than a hipped roof. The ground-floor windows have Gibbs surrounds. The doorway has Roman Doric pilasters and the window above is of the Venetian type, with Ionic pilasters.

RUSHDEN

9060

A small town with little left of its medieval origins save for its parish church, and owing much of its present appearance to the boot and shoe trade. Until the later C19 it was just a village with a large green below the church and a straggle of houses along what is now High Street South and to a lesser extent N along what is High Street today. The first shoe factory was built in High Street South in 1874 and there then followed the expansion of the place to the N and E with the railway arriving in 1893. This resulted in the centre moving eastwards with new civic buildings and the development of High Street in the early 1900s. Inevitably most of the old stone cottages were replaced and today the general effect is very much of a red brick town of the late C19 and early C20. A number of the grander boot and shoe factories have been demolished and others converted into residential.

CHURCHES

ST MARY. A fine medieval church with a handsome interior. Nothing visible earlier than *c.* 1300, but sufficient to define a church almost the same size as present with w tower, aisles, transepts and chancel, the bones of which survive. Otherwise the building is essentially Perp, and a very grand Perp parish church. The early evidence is one chancel s window, the fine SEDILIA and PISCINA beneath it (trefoil-headed, gabled with small trefoils and heads at the junctions), the N transept E and w windows (the unusual level doubtless due to C15 rebuilding), the N transept N window with intersected tracery and six tre-foiled circles in its head, the s transept window, the delightful little top frieze of the s transept with tendrils, flowers and heads (or is this a little later?), and the s porch entrance and s doorway. The N doorway with a trefoiled head looks earlier than anything else. The base of the w tower is also clearly early. Now the Perp contributions. The superb w tower will be described a little later. The s chapel is also a very fine piece. It was given by Hugh Bocher and Julian his wife, as can be read inside the w arch. This arch is very handsome. It has capitals with small heads and, as supporters of the hoodmould, two standing angels. The chapel has windows with crocketed, almost trian-gular, headed windows (as the chancel E window also has) of

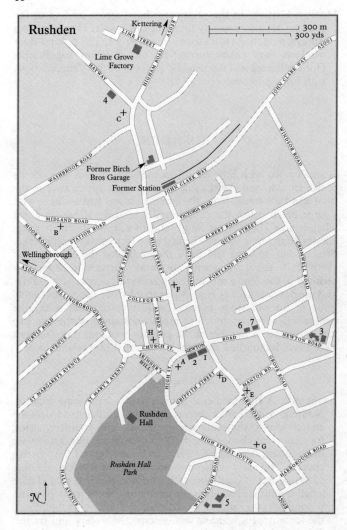

Rushden

Kettering

Lime Street
A6028
Highham Road
Hayway
300 m
300 yds
A6001
Lime Grove Factory
John Clark Way
A6001
4
C
Windsor Road
Washbrook Road
Former Birch Bros Garage
Former Station
John Clark Way
Midland Road
Victoria Road
Moor Road
Station Road
Albert Road
B
Queen Street
Wellingborough
A6001
Rectory Road
Portland Road
Cromwell Road
Duck Street
High Street
Wellingborough Road
College St.
Alfred St.
F
Purvis Road
Park Avenue
H
Newton Road
3
Church St.
6 7
Road
St Margaret's Avenue
Skinner's Hill
A 2 I
St Mary's Avenue
Newton
Griffith Street
Manton Rd.
Grove Road
D
E
Park Road
Rushden Hall
Rushden Hall Park
High Street South
G
Wymington Road
Harborough Road
A6
A6
N
5

A	St Mary	I	Council Buildings
B	St Peter	2	Carnegie Library
C	St Peter the Apostle (R.C.)	3	Newton Road Schools
D	Hope Methodist Church	4	Hayway Infant and Nursery School
E	Baptist Church		
F	Independent Wesleyan Chapel	5	Rushden Hospital (former)
G	Baptist Chapel (former)	6	Fire Station (former)
H	Salvation Army Hall	7	Athletic Club and Institute

a design found nearby at Higham Ferrers on the Bede House which dates from the 1420s. The N chapel is Perp too with its polygonal stair-turret. So are the two-bay arcades of both chapels with four shafts and four hollows as the pier section, the much simpler nave arcades (two bays, octagonal piers), the narrow vestry behind the former altar of the N chapel, the clerestory and the panelled nave roof on angel corbels and with bosses, several windows, and the N porch, which has one open side with a three-light window, ogee gable, a niche over it, and a vault with ridge ribs and tiercerons. The porch is two-storeyed. On the upper floor a fireplace. Perp moreover the most memorable item at Rushden, the strainer arch across the nave. This has a curved top as well as bottom, which has curious results. The bottom is of course an arch. At its springing there are demi-figures of angels to the W and E. The spandrels are made into complicated tracery with, as its principal motif, circles enclosing wheel-wise six mouchettes. Along the upper curve run a quatrefoil frieze and battlements. The details are all Dec rather than Perp – an alarming fact for the historian eager to date. The strainer arch under the tower arch is of the restoration by *Gordon Hills*, 1873–5. Finally the W tower. Set-back buttresses. Doorway with gabled porch, playfully connected with the buttresses by tiny flying buttresses. Small quadripartite rib-vault with ridge ribs inside. Pairs of two-light bell-openings, quatrefoil frieze, frieze of little ogee arches over, battlements and shafted pinnacles. Recessed, tall, crocketed spire connected by small openwork flying buttresses with the pinnacles. The crockets are uncommonly big. Three tiers of lucarnes. Total height 164 ft (50 metres).

FURNISHINGS. – FONT. Octagonal. The bowl C13 (big stiff-leaf groups), the stem C14 (various tracery motifs). – REREDOS in the N chapel. Stone with a row of embattled ogee arches. – PULPIT. Perp, small on a thin stem. – SCREENS. Of different details, but all with single-light divisions: rood screen, parclose screens to the S chapel from the W, to the N and S chapels from the chancel, to the N transept and S transept. – ROOFS. S chapel C15. Nave likewise, with big angel supports. Panelled with flower bosses. N aisle, similar but with niches for statues at each corner. – STAINED GLASS. Considerable amount of C15 glass. Good Tree of Jesse figures in the tracery lights of the E window, blue backgrounds. – Figures of apostles in the tracery lights of the N chapel E window, white and yellow. – Figures of apostles with creed scrolls in one N aisle window. – Several *Kempe & Co.* windows (N and S aisle W 1931 and S transept windows 1933). – Chancel E, a Tree of Jesse window of 1874 by *Lavers, Barraud & Westlake*. – N chapel, tracery lights by *Lavers, Barraud & Westlake*. – DOORS. With medieval ironwork. – MONUMENTS. Perp tomb-chest with quatrefoiled circles in the churchyard E of the chancel. To the Pecke family. – Robert Pemberton †1608 and wife. Standing monument. Two large kneeling figures facing one another across a prayer-desk. The children kneel below in the base. – Sir Goddard

Pemberton †1616. Standing monument. Effigy semi-reclining under a flat coffered arch. Both good quality, and both restored by *Ingar Norholt*, 1972. – John Ekins †1677. Ionic columns. Drapery base.

To the NE of the church is a building which is also medieval and has a Perp window.

ST PETER, Midland Road. 1906–7 by *Talbot Brown & Fisher*. Large, brick and stone in a free version of Transitional Decorated/Perpendicular Gothic. Arcades of four bays with a half bay at the W end. Simple stone FONT with a Comperish canopy, all coloured and gilded and made by the local builders *Marriotts*. The eastmost column of the N arcade has a carved Memorial Inscription for the builder Robert Marriott †1948. – STAINED GLASS. In the N chapel, E 1924 by *F. C. Eden*, and a Nativity 1938 also by *Eden* designed by *G. Daniels*; St Anne 1946 by *Shrigley & Hunt*. The former church of 1894–5, yellow sandstone, is behind and was converted as the Church Hall in 1935, also by *Talbot Brown & Fisher*.

ST PETER THE APOSTLE (R.C.), Higham Road. Brick Romanesque, 1955–6 by *J. S. Comper*, but unremarkable.

HOPE METHODIST CHURCH, Park Road/Griffith Street. 1903–4 by *J. Jameson Green* of Liverpool. Free Perp with an asymmetrically placed tower. Brick with stone dressings. Minister's house attached, 1904–5 by *Thomas Watson*.

BAPTIST CHURCH, Park Road/Manton Road. 1900–1 by *H. H. Dyer* of Northampton. Large, brick and stone in the Geometric Gothic style. Big double-arched doorway and two large three-light windows with octavo circles. – ORGAN. Built by *John T. Austin* of Detroit, and the only example known in this country of work by this American firm.

Former BAPTIST CHURCH, Little Street. The old chapel, originally early C18, but enlarged 1868 and 1873, the date of its yellow brick façade with pediment, three round-arched windows under an arched head and two doorways. Converted into residences in 2003.

SALVATION ARMY HALL, Church Street. Former Congregational chapel of 1894 by *E. Sharman* of Wellingborough. Brick gable with diaper decoration above a big triple-lancet window. Modernized ground floor.

PUBLIC BUILDINGS

COUNCIL BUILDINGS, Newton Road. 1904–6 by *W. D. Madin*, the Council Surveyor. Northern Renaissance with an Ionic-columned entrance with arched balcony. Next door the CARNEGIE LIBRARY of 1905 also by *Madin*. Italianate Renaissance with many triangular-pedimented windows. Tuscan-columned entrance and swan-necked pedimented name plaque.

NEWTON ROAD SCHOOLS. 1894 by *E. Sharman* of Wellingborough, a typical and fine example of his Renaissance style with diaper brickwork gables. Additions 1928 and 1931 and later. (It provided educational tutelage for the novelist H. E. Bates.)

HAYWAY INFANT AND NURSERY SCHOOL, Hayway. Originally built 1902–3 by *Sharman & Archer* as a mixed school, as the labels over its doorways demonstrate. Red brick with an interesting sequence of large pedimented wings and smaller pedimented dormers in between.

Former HOSPITAL BUILDINGS, Wymington Road. Of special interest is the former RUSHDEN HOUSE, built 1869–70 for E. Currie (†1901) by *Walter E. MacCarthy* and extended 1903–7 for E. C. Browning in the same style. Rough sandstone with ironstone dressings in a broad Tudor manner. Castellated bays and simple bargeboards. (Under threat 2012.)

Former FIRE STATION, Newton Road. 1903–4 by *J. W. Lloyd*, Council Surveyor's Department, with oval window and pyramidal tower. It formerly had two round-arched openings on the ground floor. Next to it the ATHLETIC CLUB of 1897 with canted bays.

PERAMBULATION

Just on the SW corner of the churchyard the WHEATSHEAF HOTEL, 1880s Jacobean, stone with mullioned-transomed windows and timber gables. Its central bay has big volutes either side the first-floor windows. To the S runs HIGH STREET SOUTH where there is a scatter of older buildings. Notably on the S side, just beyond the entrance to Rushden Hall Park, No. 22 a cottage row of probably C17 origin, the last surviving thatched house in the town. Further on the same side is the former WAGGON & HORSES (now Teza). 1892 Queen Anne Revival with a big segmental rusticated arched frontage, and a little further on the CONSERVATIVE CLUB of 1888 by *W. Talbot Brown*. Yellow brick with red and brown brick dressings. Two gables and a first-floor oriel bay on the l. Then further S the Elizabethan style former NATIONAL SCHOOL (Gospel Church) of 1870 by *Walter E. MacCarthy*. Almost opposite, facing Wymington Road, No. 83, the former WILLIAM GREEN FACTORY of 1874, the first shoe factory built in the town. Tall and narrow of three storeys, yellow brick with red bands and a round plaque with the date and shoemaker's tools.

Back to the church with to the SW, on its small green (a tiny remnant of its medieval predecessor), the WAR MEMORIAL, 1921 by *J. A. Gotch*. Renaissance style, octagonal in stages with statues, garlands and a conical top. Just W in WELLINGBOROUGH ROAD, the SARTORIS ALMSHOUSES of 1883. Two stone-built houses, which have been modernized, and two single-storey Tudorish stone cottages. Opposite on the corner of St Margaret's Avenue the MASONIC HALL of 1930 by the local builder *H. Adnitt*. Simple brick of three bays with wide angle pilasters.

Now back to the church and below it to the N, in CHURCH STREET, at the corner of Alfred Street, a good Victorian brick building with decorative patterns. In ALFRED STREET Nos. 4–6 with arched doorways and slim wooden balconies. Back in

Church Street, No. 10 (Spoors), a charming yellow and red brick cottage, pretty wooden porch and bargeboards. Then N into HIGH STREET, with the first of the banks, NATWEST. 1889 by *Matthew Holding* in French Renaissance style. Rich decoration with pilasters and a carved phoenix (the badge of the Northamptonshire Union Bank) in the gable pediment. Adjoining are the remains of an Art Deco frontage with jazzy turrets and pillars of brown tiles. Into COLLEGE STREET for the former Ritz Cinema (now a bingo hall). 1935–6 by *Paul Panter* of *Talbot Brown & Fisher*. Three-bay brick with central projection framed in mini-fluted frame. Centre has large rectangular four-light window. Blank openings on the wings. The interior largely survives. Just below two 1930s Neo-Georgian blocks, the larger one formerly the Post Office. Back on the corner of High Street, HSBC (built 1903–5 as a combined Post Office and bank by *Alexander Anderson* of Northampton; the Midland Bank later took over the whole building). Elaborate Renaissance with Ionic pillars, banded at their bases. Double-arched windows, and on its rounded corner a clock between garlands and a big shell-hood over the doorway. Almost opposite, remains of a Victorian row of yellow and chequer brick patterning with two bay windows and a plaque of a lion under a palm tree. Then the large former INDEPENDENT WESLEYAN CHAPEL, 1898–9 by *Preston & Wilson* of Rushden. Italianate, with broad pediment over arched window. At the corner of QUEEN STREET is CENTRAL BUILDINGS of 1895, a curious brick row with crow-stepped gables. On the other side THE FEATHERS, 1936–7 by *Usher & Anthony* of Bedford. Neo-Georgian with Art Deco central feature. Rounded doorcase topped by Prince of Wales feathers. Triple windows on ground floor. Then, after an interval, LLOYDS TSB, originally Capital & Counties Bank. 1889 by *Talbot Brown & Fisher*. Jacobean style of four bays, three storeys. Two large panelled gables, pilasters to each floor. Round arches on the ground floor to windows and doors.

Much further out, beyond the junction, conspicuous by its tall mansard roofs is QUEEN VICTORIA HOUSE (a former hotel) of 1899 by *F. W. Dorman* of Northampton. Eleven bays with two wings. Central projecting porch feature with classical columns and pilasters. On the same side further N a fine Art Deco block, built 1936–7 by *Riley & Glanfield* as a motor showroom and garage for BIRCH BROTHERS, with horizontal string courses, the garage entrance now filled in. Big rounded corner turret with helmet-like top.

Turning back to JOHN CLARK WAY the former RAILWAY STATION, 1893–4 built by *Parnell* of Rugby. Simple red and blue brick. Now restored as a Transport Museum with lots of metal trade signs. Opposite into RECTORY ROAD, off to the l. a number of good brick terrace rows built for shoe workers, such as BEACONSFIELD TERRACE and BEACONSFIELD PLACE of 1890. Behind the houses there are still several outworkers workshops. In VICTORIA ROAD another terrace, many gabled in the Edwardian Queen Anne style. At the corner of ALBERT ROAD the former factory of E. Claridge (Denbros Ltd) of 1894 by *Mosley & Anderson*, with shaped gable and pilaster ends. Worth noting at the top end of QUEEN STREET the 1895 factory of WILLIAM GREEN (still trading as Grenson Shoes Ltd). One of the largest factories still standing. Brick, four storeys with rows of arched windows. A canted bay corner with a short spire, though its original entrance doorway has been removed. At the bottom of the hill back in Rectory Road the large impressive Neo-Georgian frontage of the former CO-OPERATIVE WHOLESALE SOCIETY FACTORY by their architect *F. E. L. Harris*, 1901, now converted into flats. Fifteen bays with central columned doorcase and wings with large side doors topped by circular paterae. Next, behind its stone wall, THE CLOISTERS (former rectory). 1870 Gothic, in yellow sandstone with dark ironstone bands and voussoirs to its porch. Gabled wing with decorative oriel. Bargeboards. So to NEWTON ROAD with the impressive Newton Road Schools, the fire station and Athletic Club (*see* Public Buildings).

Former UNICORN INN, Grove Road. Now residential. Edwardian Queen Anne by *Talbot Brown & Fisher*, 1907, with a big pediment, dentil cornice and two hooded doorways. It still proudly boasts a letter frieze: 'Praeds Fine Ales & Stout'.

LIME GROVE, in Lime Street, ½ m. N. A large former FACTORY of the John White Co. 1937–8, interesting since it was designed by *Sir Albert Richardson* (*see* also Higham Ferrers, p. 332). Brick painted white. One floor off the street, but on the E side two deep floors overlooking a scooped-out garden. Big rows of metal windows. The centre projects with a large glazed bay. Steps down to the garden. It was converted into apartments in 2000.

FERRERS MERE, No. 142 Northampton Road, was John White's home. It is a reasonably standard Edwardian villa built in 1901, but in 1936 White asked *Richardson* to make additions, adding semicircular bay windows on the entrance side and revising the interior. The house remains completely as left in 1936, and even his delightful ironwork gates in a Georgian manner have survived. Other sizeable *c.* 1900 villas in the area.

RUSHDEN HALL, 1 m. S in a public park. The house originates from the C15 house of the Pembertons, although what stands today is early C17. It was probably rebuilt by Robert Pemberton (†1609) since a date of 1606 is recorded. After the mid C17 it changed hands several times, including in the 1820s when it was owned by Thomas Williams, who extensively revised the interior. In 1843 it was purchased by the Sartoris family who put in hand further considerable restoration and refurbishment, including the introduction of panelling etc. from elsewhere. In 1930 it was acquired by Rushden Town Council. The building was restored and converted by *Talbot Brown, Panter & Partners*, 1970 and is partly used as offices, as well as having public rooms.

The oldest part is to the W, where a first-floor room retains a wide C15 fireplace with corbelled lintel. Within the C17 main block the hall survives and at its former W end, now a staircase hall, the three arches from the screens passage to the original office quarters survive. They have four-centred heads and mouldings. The N front has wings with semicircular, two-storeyed embattled bays attached, and shaped gables, their tops open semicircles. An identical semicircular bay was added in the centre in the C19. Doorway to the r. of the middle bay; with a four-centred head. The E side was regularized with a porch and bays initially by Williams in the early C19, the date of the porch, and then again 1860–70 by the Sartoris family when the bays were added and the porch entrance redone. The rear of the house is a much altered long range with fine three-light transomed-mullioned windows, two now surviving, the third having been replaced in the early C19. It may have been a gallery or a set of lodgings. There is a small central courtyard. The interior owes more to the C19 than the C17 with an extraordinary display of carved woodwork brought in by the Sartorises: panelling, overmantels and an assembly of carvings. One staircase in the W range, although a C19 creation, has early C17 or even late C16 elements: Ionic tapered splat balusters and newels with shaped caps. The other staircase in the E range is almost totally a C19 creation, though its base newel is of a C16 date (the newels are similar to those on the 1580 staircase at Drayton House, q.v.).

DITCHFORD BRIDGE, 1 m. NW on the River Nene. Probably C14: the datestone states '1330/1927'. 14 ft (4.3 metres) wide, with six arches and massive cutwaters.

RUSHTON

ALL SAINTS. Of ironstone. A Norman survival the W wall of the nave with the deeply splayed window (now behind the organ). The rest of c. 1300–50 and of the restorations of 1853–4 and 1869 by E. F. Law. Of c. 1300 the W tower with the triple-chamfered arch towards the nave. Tall twin bell-openings with continuous mouldings. Perp battlements. Also of c. 1300 the N arcade and, a little later, the N chapel arcade, the former with circular, the latter with quatrefoil piers, and both with double-chamfered arches. The chapel is higher than the aisle and has Dec windows. Dec S side and S porch, all minor. But major indeed the splendid SEDILIA with robust nodding ogee canopies, two lions, a delightful little man, nobbly leaves, and very rich crocketing. Why such a grand piece in such a modest church? To the S of the chancel a vestry with pitched roof and, under it, a pointed tunnel-vault with a single-chamfered transverse rib. – The rather too large ORGAN CASE is by Gotch, Saunders & Surridge, 1966. – STAINED GLASS. Remarkably good and restful glass in the s windows, by *J. Powell & Sons* to designs of *Henry Holiday*, 1871–3. – N aisle, Good Shepherd by *A. L. Moore*, 1922. – Chancel windows by *Clayton & Bell*, 1860s. Theirs also N chapel E, 1887. – MONUMENT. Fine late C13 effigy of a knight, cross-legged, of Purbeck marble. Naturalistic foliage at his head. – Sir Thomas Tresham †1559. Alabaster effigy on a tomb-chest with shields in circular bands separated by twisted shafts. Bearded effigy in the dress of a Lord Prior of the Knights Hospitallers of St John of Jerusalem, the only one in England. He was given this honour by Queen Mary when she revived the order. He wears his mantle over armour. The monument was probably erected in 1562, and is clearly by the Derbyshire sculptors *Gabriel* and *Thomas Roiley*. It was moved here when St Peter's church by the Hall was demolished in 1799. Beautifully restored in 1968 by *Ingar Norholt* following damage to the church by fire in 1964. The stone slab carved with the Cockayne arms, on the wall nearby, also came from there. In the churchyard, on the N side of the tower, tomb in the Georgian manner by *J. A. Gotch*, erected to the memory of Mrs Breitmeyer †1917.

A number of nice stone houses and some sensitive modern cottage-style dwellings.

MANOR FARM HOUSE, NE of the church. L-shaped, mullioned windows. Doorway with four-centred arch.

MANOR HOUSE, ¼ m. SE of the church. Half-H-plan, mullioned windows. Dated 1694 with alterations 1856.

OLD RECTORY, N of the church. Late Georgian, of five bays and three storeys but older work behind. Said to date from *c.* 1690. There is a faculty concerning the Rectory in 1798.

SCHOOL, Station Road. 1892, extended 1904, each time by *Gotch & Saunders*. School Master's House also 1892. Alongside the school, and opposite, pairs of brick gabled cottages with painted quoins, also early 1900s.

STATION. 1857, coloured brickwork, and typical of the Midland line and probably, therefore, by *Driver*. (Derelict 2011.)

RUSHTON HALL (Hotel). The Treshams were a distinguished family in Northamptonshire more than a century before the time of Sir Thomas, who must principally engage our attention. William Tresham was Attorney General to Henry V and Speaker in the House of Commons. He bought the Rushton Estate in 1438. His son, Sir Thomas, lived at Rushton and was also Speaker. His younger son lived at Newton-in-the-Willows (*see* p. 429). Sir Thomas was beheaded after the Battle of Tewkesbury. His grandson, another Sir Thomas, is the one whose monument is mentioned above. He was succeeded by his grandson, the Thomas who interests us. This Thomas was born in 1534 and knighted in 1575. He was brought up a Protestant but turned Catholic in 1580. His Catholic zeal was exceptional. He was learned in divinity and a great believer in symbols and other conceits to demonstrate his faith. Among his books and papers there was, according to the calendar of the Rushton papers, 'A Roll . . . containing figures and signs

apparently working out a religious anagram upon his name and
that of his Patron Saint' and also 'Some mystical notes . . . on
the Trinity with a ridiculous account of a miracle which happened to him'. He was imprisoned as a Catholic in 1580 and
remained confined to the Fleet and other less rigorous places
till 1593. He was again in prison in 1596–7 and in 1599–1603
(or a little earlier). He died in 1605, in the same year in which
Francis, his son, died in the Tower after having been involved
in the Gunpowder Plot.

Rushton Hall was sold in 1619 to Sir William Cokayne,
skinner and Lord Mayor of London. In 1612 he had been the
first Governor of Ulster. He also founded Londonderry. The
Cokaynes (later Viscounts Cullen) sold the estate in 1828 to
W. W. Hope (of the family of Thomas Hope of Amsterdam,
London and Deepdene), and although he rarely visited the
place, he made many alterations and additions, notably a new
s front and extra bays. The interior was also refurbished in a
semi-French Renaissance manner. It was sold again in 1854 to
the Clarke-Thornhill family who leased it in 1904 to James Van
Alen, and he in 1907 brought in *T. G. Jackson* together with
J. A. Gotch to bring the house back to Jacobean. Gotch did
most of the work, and a good deal of the interior is essentially
his.

Rushton Hall is essentially a building of before and after our
Sir Thomas. It consists of three ranges round an oblong courtyard and a screen closing the courtyard to the E. The wings are
longer than the end (W) range. The screen and about one-third
of the wings date from the Cokayne years, the rest mostly from
the time of Henry VIII. Sir Thomas Tresham only made some
alterations. It is built almost entirely of Weldon stone, though
the C16 work on the W side is ironstone.

The building is approached from the E through the SCREEN
of *c.* 1630, which has a corridor behind. Broad middle entrance
with round arch and slender niches l. and r. containing figures
of rather picaresque-looking soldiers. Tapering fluted pilasters.
To the l. and r. of the entrance four bays with unfluted pilasters
and three-light windows. Top balustrade, over the centre with
the Gothic Revival motif of quatrefoils. On the centre of the
balustrade statue of a reclining youth with a cornucopia. The
N and S ranges of the house project, framing the screen. Broad,
two-storeyed, arched bay windows with a strapwork cresting.
Large shaped gables with thin obelisks. In each gable a double-
stepped six-light window, i.e. a window with two transoms, and
two lights above the top transom, four between the two transoms, and six below the lower one.

On entering the spacious COURTYARD one is faced with a
rich, stately picture, at first unified-looking but highly confusing in its details. What pulls the composition together is the
attic storey and the gables. The attic has short pilaster strips
with simple geometrical ornament, lozenges or vertical zigzags,
and a balustrade. The gables are straight-sided except for the
centre of the W range, where the gable and the window in it

correspond to the E ends of the W and S ranges. There is a date, 1595, i.e. of Sir Thomas Tresham's time, on one of the gables of the W range (and another on the outer, i.e. W side, of the same W range). From the Rushton papers it appears that Sir Thomas made a new gallery here, and added a bay window with a great chimney. The masons were the *Tyrell* family. So the system just described is of the Tresham time and was continued by the Cokaynes. They dated the central gable of the W range 1627 and the gable above the Hall bay window (*see below*) in the S range 1626. Sir Thomas's date of 1595 is in the gable between these two. The decorated pilasters are in fact similar to those of Tresham's Rothwell Market House.

However, Sir Thomas Tresham only heightened and modernized an older house. Its date is not certain. Gotch calls it on his plan late C15, in his text late C15 or early C16. The latter date seems more likely, and perhaps one should not go too early in the C16. The motif of the four-centred arches to the lights of the windows was established at that time. It remained in use with the Treshams but was discontinued by the Cokaynes. Its chief example is the bow window of the GREAT HALL in the S wing, overlooking the courtyard. This has a total of eight

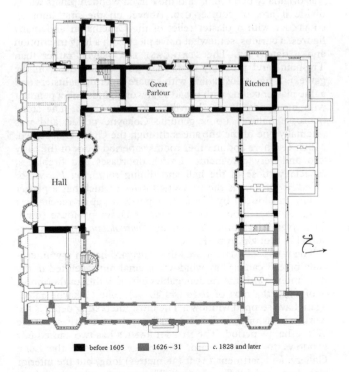

■ before 1605 ■ 1626 – 31 □ *c.* 1828 and later

Rushton Hall.
Plan

lights, little buttresses, two transoms and battlements. The interior of the hall is somewhat confused by the fact that its s side received two more bow windows in the C19 (*see* s front below). The bow window which corresponds to the original one on the courtyard side is also C19 work. To have even one bow window of so early a date is surprising enough. The semicircular plan for bay windows as against the oblong or canted plan came into use only at the end of the C16 (cf. e.g. Kirby Hall). The hall rises to the roof. It has hammerbeams with some tracery in the spandrels (restored) and four-light windows to the l. of the bow. There is only one tier of them, whereas the living quarters the other side of the bow must from the beginning have been two-storeyed. The original entrance into the hall must have been in line with the s E bow, and that makes it likely that the kitchen and offices of the C16 house extended further E in place of the Cokayne extension of the s wing. In the sw bay window some STAINED GLASS, largely Netherlandish and German roundels of the C16 and C17. Some later pieces.

At the sw corner is the LIBRARY, which has an original early C17 wooden overmantel with a Tresham shield, and an odd simple architectural stone fireplace which could be late C16. It was originally two rooms and the carved wooden pillars which divide it are, of course, C19. Above, on the first floor an ORATORY with a plaster relief of the Crucifixion and many figures, a curious, somewhat naïve piece with a long inscription and a date 1577. The STAIRCASE is Cokayne rather than Tresham, and probably of *c.* 1625–30 (see the dates in the gables). It has balustrading with square tapering balusters and a fine plaster ceiling with broad strapwork bands and a pendant with mermaids. It was heavily redone by *Gotch*. The stone doorcase halfway up is genuine Cokayne period and was originally one of the entrances through the Great Hall screen. Much else here and in other rooms is period work of the early C20 and very convincing. Lavish doorcases and fireplaces, especially those in the hall and dining room, by *Farmer & Brindley*. Of note is the DRAWING ROOM which has a plaster ceiling introduced by *Gotch*. It is partly a papier mâché cast from the 1771 dining room ceiling at Drayton House (q.v.). The splendid chimneypiece is by *Thorvaldsen*, and was presumably brought in by Hope.

The WEST RANGE towards the courtyard has an asymmetrically placed canted bay window, original but facelifted in the C19, and towards the garden, gables of which the southernmost is of 1595, the next of 1626 (*see* above). The Cokayne gables again have stepped windows. The most interesting detail is the work in ironstone which indicates the end of the earliest s range of Tresham's period. The NORTH RANGE has two canted bay windows to the courtyard. The range contained the Long Gallery, an apartment 125 ft (38 metres) long, but the interior was destroyed by fire in 1835. The SOUTH FRONT of the s range with its bays dates from 1848, and is part of Hope's remodelling. It is finely built of Weldon stone and suitably impressive.

Thomas Mawson was also brought to Rushton in 1909 to redesign the GARDEN. An elaborate scheme was drawn up but he and Van Alen did not agree and, apart from some terracing, little was done. To the S of the house the early C18 formal CANAL still survives, extended into less formal water to the W. A little SW is a delightful early C19 water cascade with a COLD BATH, probably dating from the C17, altered when Hope had the cascade pools created in the 1840s. It originally had inscriptions and sculptures.

EAST LODGES. Gothic, early C19. – GROOM'S HOUSE. Early C18, of five bays and two storeys with some original wooden cross-windows and some segment-headed windows. – STABLES of 1828. Three sides of a quadrangle. Much altered and extended. – DOVECOTE. Late C16, rectangular and gabled.

TRIANGULAR LODGE. An enchanting little building, at the NW corner of the estate. Built by Sir Thomas Tresham, using his own masons, the *Tyrells*. It was begun in 1594 and completed in 1597, although the dates on the building are 1593 (date on the iron anchors of the ground floor) and 1595 (date on the chimneyshaft). The most perfect example in architectural terms of the Elizabethan love of the conceit. Everything about the little building is directed by the number three, i.e. allegorizes the Trinity. It was also a pun on Tresham's own name. The Treshams' emblem was the trefoil, and so there are plenty of trefoils on the building. But the plan and most of the details are based on the equilateral triangle. The building is of alternating bands of light limestone and darker ironstone. Its sides are 33 ft 4 in. (10.2 metres) long, i.e. one-third of a hundred. There are three storeys, each with three windows in each of the three sides. The principal room on each floor is a hexagon. The corner spaces are triangular. One contains the newel staircase, the others small rooms. The basement windows are small trefoils on all sides with a smaller triangle in the centre of each. On the raised ground floor the SE side has a very narrow entrance which has the figures 5555 written on the lintel and a very odd steep gable consisting of short straight sides and two-thirds of a circle standing on them. The windows on this floor are on all three sides roughly lozenge-shaped and consist of a cross with, at the end of the arms, four groups of three circles arranged as a trefoil. Coats of arms to make the lozenge into a square. On the upper floor the windows are trefoils, each with triangles set in them, but each with a different pattern. Only one window has a circle instead with groups of three elongated leaf-like almond shapes branching off it on all three sides. Above the upper windows an inscription broken up into single letters and reading MENTES TUORUM VISITA. On the frieze above the upper storey the continuous inscription (of thirty-three letters!) reads on the SE: Aperiatur terra et germinet salvatorem; on the N: Quis separabit nos a charitate

43

Christi; and on the SW: Consideravi opera tua domine et expavi. On each side there are three gables with crockets, triangular top obelisks, emblems and inscriptions. Among the emblems are the seven-branched candelabra, the seven eyes of God, and the Pelican. There are also the dates 1580 (the year of Tresham's conversion), 1626 and 1641, and the unexplained figures 3509 and 3898. The inscriptions add up to: Respicite non mihi soli laboravi. Sir Gyles Isham pointed out that the building symbolizes the Mass as well as the Trinity. The triangular chimneyshaft has symbols of the Mass, e.g. IHS, the Lamb and Cross, and the Chalice. The initial letters near the gargoyles below the gables read: Sanctus Sanctus Sanctus Dominus Deus Sabaoth qui erat et qui est qui venturus est – i.e. quoting from the Preface to the Canon of the Mass. In addition, the chimney itself, mysteriously resting on no visible interior support, may represent the mystery of the Mass. Even the smoke holes are arranged in threes. What does all this amount to? A folly? A bauble? A pretty conceit? It cannot be treated so lightly. It is no more nor less than a profession of faith in stone – of a faith for which Tresham spent more than fifteen years in prison and confinement. So one should look at the Triangular Lodge with respect.

For Tresham's other principal buildings *see* Lyveden, p. 404, and Rothwell, p. 556.

SALCEY LAWN

2 m. SW of Horton

A hunting lodge situated in the middle of a forest lawn. Of Tudor origin, with two fireplaces of that period. Refronted towards the end of the C17. Five bays and two storeys, with quoins and a hipped roof with dormers. Nine-bay stable block, early C18 with wooden cross-mullion-transom windows. Platband and keystones to the openings. One room has a C17 decorative oak overmantel. Late C17 staircase with twisted balusters.

SCALDWELL

ST PETER AND ST PAUL. Unbuttressed Norman W tower, with C17 top stage. C13 N aisle windows, S arcade of the later C13. Two bays, very primitive octagonal piers, double-chamfered arches. The S doorway, if correctly rebuilt, could be contemporary in spite of its round arch, and the W lancet window certainly is. The N arcade is taller and later. The N chapel was built at the same time. Divers Perp windows. Extensive restoration with some additions in 1863 by *William Slater* and *William*

Gillett of Leicester. *Lord Alwyne Compton* was much involved and the *Minton* TILES are his design. – STAINED GLASS. Chancel E of 1863 by *A. O. Hemming*. – S aisle of 1946 by *A. K. Nicholson*.

Many nice houses, notably around the green. Attractive use of local ironstones, both light and dark, so many cottages almost have a mottled appearance. S is the former RECTORY. 1716. The porch is added. The doorway with its pretty cartouche was originally flush with the windows, that is, it was a normal five-bay front. Flat window frames, pedimented dormers. On the corner SCALDWELL HOUSE, a Georgian farmhouse refronted and a billiard room added by Captain Robert Soames 1894, with a huge datestone and initials on the W gable. SCALDWELL GRANGE, towards Brixworth. Charming Regency villa, just three bays and a Doric porch and lateral pilasters.

SHORTWOOD LODGE
7070
1 m. NE of Lamport

Almost certainly associated with Harrington Manor House (q.v.). An impressive and intriguing three-storeyed stone HAWKING TOWER of *c.* 1720 with later two-storeyed wings, their two storeys being as high as the ground storey of the tower. The top storey is canted and there is a top balustrade. The S front window on the third floor is surrounded by a strange piece, traditionally a chimneypiece from Pytchley Hall. If that is true, it was a chimneypiece of Vanbrughian dimensions. The jambs l. and r. must be at least 6 ft (1.8 metres) high. Unmoulded blocks instead of bases and instead of capitals. Depressed arch, big keystone. It looks more C18 than C16 and of service rather than state room origin, that is kitchen rather than drawing room. Other windows are flat Late Georgian with keystones, some of these clearly replacing earlier openings. Further evidence of blocked openings, such as two on either side at the base, where the ground level has been raised. At the back of the tower two openings with exceedingly heavy chunky rustication. C20 brick extensions somewhat unsympathetic. The building stands on one of the highest points of the neighbourhood and there are commanding views, especially to the S.

SHUTLANGER
7050

CHAPEL OF ST ANNE. 1886, attached to the former School Room of 1884, both by *Matthew Holding*. – STAINED GLASS. E window by *Kempe*, 1887. (Partly damaged.)

THE MONASTERY, SE of the chapel. John Bridges, writing early in the C18, mentions a chapel converted into a farmhouse. In the roof smoke-grimed late medieval timbers confirm this was, in fact, the substantial remains of a C14 hall house. The main block exists with a two-storey S porch and service bay to the l. and hall to the r. To the r. of the porch remains of two two-light windows with trefoil heads and a transom, the E one having a lower sill, marking the hall's high end. Both windows were altered when the hall was subdivided in the C17, but were restored to their original form in 1965. Inside the buttressed porch a vault with quadripartite single-chamfered ribs and a transverse ridge rib. Foliage boss apparently C14. In the side one low two-light window. The doorway seems to be *c.* 1300. It gives access to a cross-passage in a half bay, the hall itself being of two full bays. The hall has two original doorways in its cross wall, the larger giving access to the service bay and the smaller to a stone spiral staircase rising to the first floor of both the service bay and the porch. Another doorway at the E end of the hall is thought to have originally given access to a solar. There is a later newel stair at the other end of the cross-passage. Most remarkably the complete arch-braced collar roof structure survives. Despite C17 and later alterations and additions, the general air of the house is still very medieval.

GROVE FARMHOUSE, ¼ m. S. An especially grand example of an early C19 Grafton farmhouse. Ironstone with limestone dressings. Three-bay two-storey house with columned porch and two-bay lower wings. Quoins and platband.

SIBBERTOFT

ST HELEN. Mostly of 1862–3, especially the S aisle with its terrible plate tracery outside, surprising since the architect was *Edward Browning* of Stamford, who is usually perfectly responsible. Inside the S arcade also his with round pillars and a profusion of very good foliage carving. Unfortunate cramped spacing in the interior. The chancel was originally of *c.* 1300 (see e.g. the E window). The N aisle and chapel are Perp, but oddly joined with two separate arches leading into it. The N doorway outside four-centred arch with traceried spandrels. – SCREEN. In the chancel, over the S doorway, the top of the entrance part of the former rood screen, exceptionally richly decorated with twisted branches and top crocketing. C15 and looking Continental. – Everywhere TILED FLOORS, most elaborately in the N chapel with a heraldic panel and recognizable *Pugin* designs by *Mintons*. – STAINED GLASS. Chancel E of 1890 and S of 1869 are by *Clayton & Bell*. – Chancel S of 1865, the N aisle window and that in the tower are all by *Heaton, Butler & Bayne*.

Former SCHOOL and SCHOOL HOUSE, next to the church. 1847 by *E. F. Law*. Polychrome red and blue brick with diaper patterns.

SIBBERTOFT MANOR, Church Street. 1899 by *Sheppard & Harrison* of Newark. A sizeable mansion with half timbering and tile-hung façades. Now a care home.

THE COOMBES, ½ m. N. The large former rectory for Marston Trussell, of 1844 by *G. G. Scott & W. Moffatt*, again red and blue brick with diaper patterns. The builder was *Cooper* of Derby. Interestingly, it was built for the Rev. William Law, whose relations had property at Gawcott, near Buckingham, Scott's birthplace.

LOW FARM HOUSE, 1 m. SE. In the Carolean style, a double pile of two storeys, five bays of ironstone with the central bay faced with white stone, on the entrance side with a one-storey portico which links to two plain pilasters which rise into chimney-stacks. Low one-storey wings either side. The roof topped by four big stone chimneystacks. It was built 1998–2000 to designs of *Charles Morris*.

CASTLE YARD, in a wood *c.* ½ m. NE of the village. A motte-and-bailey with the motte on the uphill side. Late C11–mid C12.

SILVERSTONE

ST MICHAEL. 1884 by *J. P. St Aubyn* and paid for by the patron, Sir Robert Loder (cf. Whittlebury). Of yellow sandstone with golden ironstone dressings. Nave and aisles under one tiled roof. On the roof a little E of the W front a shingled wooden turret with a spirelet. All in the Dec style, and very correct and very precise. Internally the arcades are more E.E. than Dec. – REREDOS. E.E.-style arcading with a central painted ceramic and mosaic Crucifixion scene. – Good TILES. – STAINED GLASS. Chancel E, three figures in panels by *J. Hardman & Co.* (brought from St Edmund's Northampton, dem. 1980). Nave W with two panels, 1994 also by Hardman.

Remains of FISHPONDS N of the churchyard may indicate the site of a royal hunting lodge. It was ruinous by 1313.

METHODIST CHAPEL, Little London. 1811, of stone. Three bays with central porch and two very long windows.

LODGES, Nos. 29 and 31 Brackley Road. *c.* 1800, stone with panelled walls and doorways with hoods on consoles. Pictur-esque C19 roofs. They are on the very N tip of the C18 landscape of Stowe, Bucks.

SILVERSTONE RACING CIRCUIT, 1 m. S. Opened in 1948 by the RAC. Rearing up with a series of white planes and a zigzag roof-line is the PIT & PADDOCK COMPLEX by *HOK Sports Architects*, opened in 2011. Amongst other buildings are the BRITISH RACING DRIVERS' CLUBHOUSE of 1999 by *Ridge Architects*, with a curved two-storey balconied form and an overhanging canopy, and the PRESS FACILITY of 1989 by *Denton Scott*, long, angular with much glass.

6040

SLAPTON

 St Botolph. A memorably intimate, unspoiled church. The architecture is low key. Early to mid-C13 W tower, see the unmoulded pointed arch towards the nave and the blank arcading of the bell-stage to the S. Early C13 S arcade of two bays. Circular pier, square abacus. Unmoulded pointed arches. Later third bay. Interesting tripartite chancel arch, the side parts now blocked except for two small straight-headed two-light windows. Dec chancel E window, and Dec N and S windows, with elements of flowing tracery. In the chancel two wide recesses, one with its arch on shafts, the other with an ogee arch from the floor. There was a tactful restoration by *William White* 1875–83 when fittings were replaced. – SCREEN to the S chapel: Jacobean, panelled below and balustraded top. – WALL PAINTINGS. Restored 1971. They date from the later C14 and C15. Almost every wall has something. Nave N side a large St Christopher, with delightful mermaid and fishes, a Pieta to the l., another scene to the r. – Nave S side a St Francis receiving the stigmata, a St Michael weighing souls. Below and partly painted on top of this, barely visible, remains of a St George. – In the arcade W arch two figures, in the middle arch the Mass of St Gregory. – On the rear of the S arcade: to the E the Annunciation, to the W a Martyrdom or the Suicide of Judas and St Anne teaching the Virgin. On the S wall of the S aisle: to the E the rare subject of St Eloi, with a horse being shod, the figures incised with firm lines before being coloured. To the W, traces of the Three Living and the Three Dead. Only the latter visible. Under the W arcade arch two heads talking: a warning to gossips. – STAINED GLASS. E window. Lucy arms and grisaille; early C14. – S aisle, 1903 by *Jones & Willis*, designed by *P. H. Newman*.

Some good stone houses including BOXES FARM, a stone house with a re-set datestone of 1693. The front range, originally two storeys, was heightened and given a new façade *c.* 1846, rendered with Late Regency details. At the W end of the village, SLAPTON LODGE, broadly E-plan but altered considerably in the C19. Mullioned windows in parts and dates 1670 and 1719.

9070

SLIPTON

A village on the W side of the Drayton Estate.

St John Baptist. Little more than a chapel of ease, standing on its own in fields. Nave, chancel and bellcote. One Norman N window. Chancel arch probably originally C13 but rebuilt in the C15. A carved stone with interlaced decoration revealed on its N side, also C13. Lancet window N side of the chancel. Otherwise the building was rebuilt in the C15 or early C16

(windows and blocked N doorway). The chancel was length-
ened slightly and new E window, altar fittings and stalls
installed 1910–11 by *Temple Moore*. The STALLS have pointed
poppyhead finials, looking older than they are. – PULPIT.
Simple Georgian panels. – FONT. Octagonal, plain, probably
C14. – STAINED GLASS. Two rather good windows by *Heaton,
Butler & Bayne*, 1915 and 1918. – CHURCHYARD CROSS.
Medieval base, the cross a war memorial of 1920 by *W. Talbot
Brown*.

Several nice thatched cottages and a pair of Drayton Estate
model COTTAGES *c.* 1850.

DRAYTON HOME FARM, ¼ m. E. 1890 by *J. A. Gotch*. Quite
grand on the hill above the village. Brick and stone with Jacobean shaped gables. A little further E a pair of COTTAGES dated
1908 built by *Pettit* of Thrapston, based on Gotch designs (*see
also* under Lowick).

SOUTHWICK

ST MARY. C14 W tower with provision for a vault. Big head
bosses, like those in the Hall. Two-light bell-openings with
reticulation motifs and a transom. Recessed spire with crockets
up the edges. Two tiers of lucarnes. Carved shields on each
face, on the N for Knyvet and on the S for Bassett, then both
together on the W. Sir John Knyvet married Eleanor Bassett in
1381. The nave and chancel were rebuilt in 1760, but unfortunately in 1864 received Gothic fenestration. Although the
chancel arch remains of the C14, the interior is now rather
stark. – MONUMENT. George Lynn †1758. By *Roubiliac*. In a
tall niche in the chancel. Grey and white marble. Big base and
on it an obelisk in relief with the oval medallion of the deceased,
bust with lively drapery, and ample drapery hanging down
from the medallion. To the r. in front seated female figure in
contemporary dress, her arm resting on a remarkably restrained,
classical urn. Her slippers ought to be noted. Her figure is
identical to that on the Shannon monument at Walton-on-
Thames, upon which Roubiliac was working at the same time.
There the figure is subsidiary, here it is dominant. – STAINED
GLASS. Two windows by *Horwood Bros* of Mells, Somerset,
c. 1864.

SOUTHWICK HALL. The fascination of the Hall lies in the substantial remains of a C14 house. It owes its existence to the
Knyvet family who had been at Southwick since the C13. The
earliest portions are due either to John Knyvet (still alive in
1319) or his son Richard Knyvet, Keeper of the Forest of Cliffe,
who died in 1352. The latter added a tower to the S of the
original house and his son Sir John (†1381), a lawyer who rose
to become Lord Chancellor, extended this by a further bay.
The Knyvets sold, within a family link, *c.* 1440 to the Lynn

family and the house remained with them till 1840 when it was sold to a solicitor, George Capron, who carried out a partial restoration and added to the house 1848–50. It remains with that family still.

The approach is picturesque with the C14 Knyvet house on the l. and the C16 gabled wing of the Lynns to the r. The C14 tower is, and probably always was, almost detached from the main house. It has two floors and today is entered on the S by a doorway, but that only dates from 1909 when this became the entrance hall. It replaces a small window, but even that was a C19 insertion, as a drawing at Southwick by Moses Griffiths of the later 1770s shows a Gothick veranda-like attachment along the ground floor. On the lower floor, inside, a vault with single-chamfered ribs, both diagonal and along the ridges, and big carved heads as supports, two two-light transomed windows with a reticulation motif, and an original entrance towards what is now the Elizabethan part. On the upper floor, in the oriel, a square-headed E window with Dec tracery, but this again must be C19 as it is not shown on the Griffiths drawing. A piscina in the room suggests it may have been used as a chapel. There are in the windows two fine C14 shields of arms of Bohun and Montfort *in situ*. In the W wall is an original fireplace with two big re-tooled heads supporting its hood. The later C14 annex also has a vault with single-chamfered ribs. Several of the windows in the tower were replaced *c.* 1850 but there is an original chimneystack over the W gable with a pierced top. On the N side of the Hall is more C14 work, of the earliest phase, including a doorway to the former screens passage and further W a large round turret housing a spiral staircase which must have led to the upper solar. The anteroom to it again has single-chamfered ribs. Boss with a rose and corbels also with roses. Two doorways with shouldered lintels.

The Elizabethan rebuilding carries the dates 1571 and 1580. A further date cut on a roof parapet, with initials TW and probably done by one of the masons, carries the date 1594, so probably marking final completion. The Hall range is of two storeys, with two straight gables, the W wing of three storeys. Many finials with small fluted balusters set on pedestals with dentil cornice, some perched on a corbel with an acanthus scroll. These are almost identical to finials at Apethorpe, so an association with the *Thorpes* of Kingscliffe as builders is indicated. The upper floor has two large bedrooms with barrel ceilings, and one room still has C16 panelling. The interior of the house, on the ground floor especially, was Georgianized by the Lynns *c.* 1740. Several panelled rooms, remains of a staircase, rebuilt, and a fine wooden fireplace surround in the dining room with Apollo head tablet, worthy of Flitcroft. At the same time an addition was made NE and this was Gothicized in the early C19 with a wooden bay window with quatrefoil frieze and three openings above.

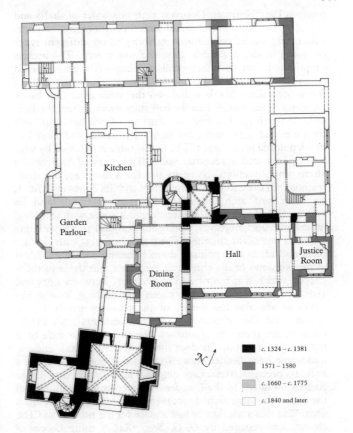

c. 1324 – c. 1381

1571 – 1580

c. 1660 – c. 1775

c. 1840 and later

Southwick Hall.
Plan

Behind the house is a long range of outbuildings, partly late
CI7 but at its E end an earlier block with cruck roof which may
have been the site of the kitchen. N of this a further range of
STABLES, mildly Gothic, designed by *W. G. & E. Habershon* in
1850.

LONGWOOD HOUSE, ½ mile NW. Set back from the road before
woodland. Designed by *SpaceLab* and completed in 2002, with
a side extension of 2005. The house is basically a timber-clad
cube of open-plan form with the S elevation largely of glass.

SPRATTON

ST ANDREW. Of an Early Norman church the W wall remains
with one (lengthened) window in the present tower. The ornate

tower is Late Norman. Doorway with one order of shafts and zigzag in the arch. Hoodmould with Saxon-looking interlace. Interesting use of polychrome masonry (three different types of stone) in the C12 work. Low C12 tower arch. The arch is unmoulded, but the many-scalloped imposts were reworked when the tower was built. On the next stage in the middle of the W side three blank arches, on the stage after that blank arcading all the way. When the bell-stage was reached, the E.E. style had arrived. The bell-openings are of two lights and still have a round super-arch, but they are pointed, and there is a blank pointed arch l. and r. The corbel table is followed by later battlements and a recessed spire. Two tiers of lucarnes in alternating directions. Norman also the S doorway, but over-restored. Of the ending C12 the N aisle with its doorway (round, single-stepped arch, capitals similar to waterleaf) and its arcade. Four bays, circular piers, capitals some with waterleaf others with upright leaves, square abaci, round arches with one step and one slight chamfer. The S arcade is C13, with circular piers and abaci and pointed double-chamfered arches. Most of the windows of the church are renewed, but those of the N chapel, which was built by John Chambre between 1495 and 1505, stand out, Perp but without any cusping, coarse but virile, as are also the details of the two-bay arcade to the chancel. Of Dec details the SEDILIA and PISCINA in the chancel, the three tomb-recesses (the two in the S aisle have ballflower decoration, as does the sill of the piscina), and the handsome ogee-headed REREDOS niche at the E end of the S aisle. Its pretty buttresses are diapered in its lower parts. Large corbels on heads to the l. and r. An interesting detail, also of the C14, is the large arched recess in the nave above the chancel arch. Was this a window or just a place for the rood cross? The church was restored by *G. G. Scott* 1846–7 using *Cooper* of Derby as a builder. Cooper is also credited with seating, which will not only mean the CHOIR STALLS with poppyhead finials, one with a piper and another a winged angel, but also the restoration and rearrangement of the BENCHES. Mostly of the early 1500s (see Chambre chapel, above) but some clearly C19. The ends have traceried panels and buttresses. Also prettily traceried fronts and backs. It is an interesting speculation as to which are C16 and which by Cooper. – FONT. Octagonal, C13. Plain, with three blank trefoiled arches. – STAINED GLASS. Fragments in the E window of the N chapel, *c.* 1500, part of a shield of arms for Ardern and an Arma Christi shield. – Chancel windows by *J. Powell & Sons*, E 1899 and S 1906. – Two windows (chancel and S aisle) by *Mayer* of Munich, 1906. – A N aisle window 1863 by *Clayton & Bell*. – MONUMENTS. Brass to Robert Parnell †1464 and family (under the organ; the figures are *c.* 2 ft 3 in. (69 cm.) long). – Tomb-chest with quatrefoils in panels. (On it formerly a wooden effigy. VCH) – Sir John Swinford †1371. Alabaster, well preserved and of good quality, metropolitan rather than provincial. The jupon is laced at the side. The SS collar is said to be the earliest on any monument. Charming lion at his feet, whose tail encircles the sword scabbard. His initials are on the plaques of his sword belt. The iron GRILLE, partly dismantled, may be original but is more likely C17. – Many tablets, the best among them the two identical ones to Francis and Elizabeth Beynon †1778 and †1770 by *William Cox*. They both have a cherub's head set against an obelisk. – CROSS. Just part of the shaft on steps, probably C14. – In the yard, by the N porch a large MONUMENT for the Lansbury family 1821. Small sarcophagus, with cast-iron feet, mounted on a large tomb-chest.

SPRATTON HALL (Spratton School). Dated 1773 for Francis Beynon. The house is of Kingsthorpe stone ashlar, five bays, two and a half storeys. Between entrance hall and staircase a wide segmental arch with a pretty Adamish fanlight. The staircase has three slender turned balusters to the tread and carved tread-ends. Later additions and much altered inside.

Several good stone houses in the village, some with distinctive datestones with a cloverleaf pattern, e.g. NW of the churchyard, on the corner of Yew Tree Lane, one dated 1684. Opposite the church W end, a fine late C18 chequer-brick fronted house.

BROOMHILL, 1 m. W. 1869–71 by *Goddard & Son* of Leicester, for Colonel Henry Tessier. Red brick, semi-Gothic, and with Goddard's typical tall chimneystacks. Some later alterations inside. The carved staircase, introduced by Sir Mervyn Manningham-Buller *c*. 1902, is said to come from Burlington House, London.

SPRATTON GRANGE. 1 m. SW. The mock Tudor brick house built in 1847 for the Dowager Lady St John of Bletsoe had half-timbered gables and at the back a Gothic arcade with a small octagonal turret with an ogival roof. The estate was bought by William Henry Foster of Apley Park, Salop. and in 1878 he added further half-timbered gables and bays on the W end and refurbished the interior. Practically the whole of the extension was demolished after 1946 by Dr Tom Starkie who employed *Jean Jackson-Stops* to reduce the house to manageable size. The S front is now symmetrical with paired half-timbered gabled wings and the W side simply brought together by a plain brick façade but incorporating some earlier features. The arcade and the octagonal turret survive. Spectacularly sited on a hillside looking S over a wide valley towards the Bramptons over a lake created in 1988.

STANFORD*

5070

ST NICHOLAS. An imposing church, mostly of *c*. 1300–50 and hence unified in its external and internal appearance. In

---

*Stanford Hall is in Leicestershire. See *Leicestershire and Rutland* in this series, 1984.

addition a veritable gallery of stained glass and statuary. The exterior is determined by the very tall chancel windows of three and, at the E end, five lights, all with intersected tracery. The same motif recurs in the S aisle and in the simpler Y-form in the bell-openings of the tower. Reticulation instead in the N aisle windows and the S aisle E and two S windows. The S and N aisle E windows are of four lights. Inside, the arcades are of five bays, with tall, very white piers and arches – an attractive contrast to the pale rose and grey of the chancel exterior. The piers have a slender chamfered projection to the nave and aisles and a broader one to each arch opening. There are no capitals at all; all mouldings are continuous. The type is not uncommon in Leicestershire (cf. Kibworth and North Kilworth; also Lilbourne, Northants). In the S aisle PISCINA with crocketed gable, and next to it a low stone bench below the window with a quatrefoiled front. Good roofs in nave and aisles with carved bosses. The nave roof has tie-beams with tracery over, and the tie-beams are supported on thin wall-shafts which rest on carved brackets. Externally there is one more motif which deserves mention: the little square pinnacles at the corners of the E wall. The pinnacles on the W tower in contrast are coarse and may be C16 or C17. – FONT. C14 with simple tracery patterns. – PULPIT. Incorporating part of the rood screen. – SCREENS. The base of the rood screen is original; the upper parts come from Lutterworth in Leicestershire. – Under the tower arch a smaller Perp screen, with one-light divisions. – STALLS. With panelled fronts and simple poppyheads. One MISERICORD with a flower. – CHOIR PANELLING. C16, with linenfold. – COMMUNION RAIL. Fine, of wrought iron; early C18, by *Thomas Paris* of Warwick. – WEST GALLERY. On Tuscan columns. On it the rightly famous ORGAN CASE. The tradition that it comes from the Royal Chapel at Whitehall is false. It was in fact built in 1630 by *Thomas and Robert Dallam* for Magdalen College, Oxford where it stood until replaced in 1736 when it was acquired by Sir Thomas Cave.[*] Excellent, very dainty scrollwork. – FRONTAL. Embroidered by Lady Eleanor Rowe, *née* Cave, it is said in 1613.

STAINED GLASS.[†] There are four main periods: c. 1324–30, c. 1330–50, late C15 or early C16 and c. 1553–60. The first two are associated with two incumbents: Alan of Aslackby (†1337), a kinsman of the Abbot of Selby, Yorks., which held the advowson, and John of Winwick, rector 1341–52. Both held high offices. The late C15 glass records numerous anonymous donors, their figures set in panels with roundels above their heads. The 1550s phase is associated with the Cave family, already at Stanford by the 1430s, eventually acquiring the freehold of the manor after the Dissolution. It includes a large display of heraldic shields. A major rearrangement of the glass

---

[*] Information Dominic Gwynn.
[†] This account relies exclusively on Professor Richard Marks's detailed catalogue in *Corpus Vitrearum Medii Aevi*, 1998.

was undertaken *c.* 1720 when much Cave heraldic glass, formerly in the old manor house, was introduced, and it is this arrangement which largely survives. A major restoration between 1987 and 1997 allowed for a number of adjustments in order to reunite items which had become separated.

The description here can only pick out the highlights. It begins in the CHANCEL and the most complex arrangement, the EAST WINDOW. Starting at the bottom are five panels installed in 1932 when they were found at Stanford Hall. The designs derive from Holbein's Whitehall Palace mural of Henry VIII and his family, 1536–7. All that is here are Henry VII and Elizabeth of York, with, on either side, royal supporters with banners (a red dragon holding a portcullis banner, and a greyhound holding one with the Tudor rose). In the centre is a shield of the royal arms. The panels would appear to be the same date as the mural and may indeed have come from Whitehall. Above these, across the middle of the window, a narrow strip of canopy work which would have sheltered figures. Then above is Cave glass of the 1550s, somewhat rearranged, from the l. the three sons of Sir Thomas Cave, Cave himself, the Cave shield (centre), Lady Elizabeth Cave, and various Cave fragments. What survives *in situ* from *c.* 1324–30 is at the top of the window, within the tracery. At the top of the four tall lancet lights, from the l. shields for Wake and Warenne; a Virgin and Child; and on the r. shields for Bohun and Hastings. Then above four further shields, from l. to r. Lancaster, France ancient, England (either for Edward II or III) and another England (for Edward the Black Prince). In the top openings are two bishops and right at the apex is the head of a young king, perhaps Edward III.

Next the two chancel N and S WINDOWS. These have a common pattern, with across the centre three panels *c.* 1324–30 with figures of apostles. They are set within Georgian glass with various other fragments, notably some pretty canopy spires. On the N side, the first window has figures of, from the l., St Peter, St Paul and one other uncertain apostle. In the two top lozenges, on the l. a roundel with Death shooting an arrow at a tiny figure of a cleric (Henry Williams), who left directions in his will in 1500 for this to be made. On the r. the arms of the Grocers' Company. In the apex a panel of three women being taunted by devils, a warning about idle gossip (the only recorded example of this subject in medieval glass). The second N window has figures of St Barnabas, another apostle and St Philip. Above the apostles, centre, a kneeling female donor *c.* 1470–1500 between two shields, that on the r. of the Goldsmiths' Company, early C16. At the top of the lights two abbots and above them on the l. an angel representing St Matthew *c.* 1330 and on the r. a roundel representing dyeing (the Cave family were involved in the cloth trade). In the apex the head of St Veronica. On the S side, from E, the first window has again apostles, one uncertain, St John and St Andrew. Above them two Cave shields and in the centre the arms of Westminster

Abbey. The next window has St James the Great, St Matthias and another apostle, and similar Cave shields below. Original C14 grisaille border work with roundels in each window.

Moving to the nave and to the NORTH AISLE E window. This has almost entirely C14 glass. The two figures are St Barbara and a bishop. Above rich canopy work. Within the reticulated tracery are centre a Crucifixion, l. the Virgin, r. St John and above two censing angels, and at the top Christ in Majesty. Moving along the aisle, the first window is partially blocked by the Cave monument of 1568. It has panels with two C16 Cave shields and a panel of the Stuart royal arms. The next window has more Cave shields. In the very apex of the centre light is a perky little rabbit. The quatrefoils have roundels with remnants of the Symbols of the Evangelists (SS Luke and John), with in the centre the Lamb of God. The final N window has further Cave heraldry. In the central light, an elongated diamond panel with the arms of the Mercers' Company. Higher up a Virgin and an Evangelist roundel for St Mark.

Finally the S AISLE, starting from the E, a window very similar to that in the N aisle. Original C14 glass with figures of St Anne teaching the Virgin to read, a female saint, St Agnes and another female saint. Rich canopy work above. The first line of quatrefoils has a Crucifixion centre, with the Virgin and St John. Above two angels and at the top Christ in Majesty. Delightful eyelets with birds and fish. The side windows again similar to the N aisle. The first has Cave shields and above c. 1500 kneeling donor figures and roundels with the Virgin and Child and St John, and above two angels. At the top a roundel with a barrel (perhaps denoting Thomas Morton, vicar of Stanford 1472–86). The next window has more Cave shields and donor figures. The tracery has a pair of C14 panels for the Coronation of the Virgin. The next window is similar with a central panel with quarries of Cave crests, a greyhound and the motto 'Gardes'. Diamond panel with the Stuart royal arms and garter motto. Right at the top a C19 roundel of the Holy Spirit. The tower WEST WINDOW has miscellaneous fragments.

MONUMENTS. There are fifteen in the church worth discussing. They are in chronological order as follows. In the S aisle, under an arch which belongs in date to the time when the church was building, a priest, defaced. The effigy lies on a low tomb-chest with quatrefoils on its front. To the l. and r. buttresses and finials. The top is Perp. Upper quatrefoil friezes. – Sir Thomas Cave †1558, undoubtedly by the *Roileys* of Burton upon Trent. Alabaster, free-standing between N aisle and nave. Recumbent effigies on a tomb-chest with shields in roundels. Twisted shafts separate them. At the head-end two putti hold the roundel, at the foot-end small kneeling figures in relief in two rows. – Sir Ambrose Cave †1568 (N aisle). Fine and quiet, of moderate size and without any figures. Broad panel with shield, flanked by two Corinthian columns which carry a wide pediment. Three roundels on the tomb-chest. No strapwork or any other ornamental display. – Henry Knollys and his wife Margaret Cave, c. 1600 (N aisle). She lies stiffly on her side, he lies behind and above her on a half-rolled-up mat. Two young daughters kneel to the l. and r. Simple, but big background with a flat arch. – Sir Thomas Cave †1613 (chancel N), attributed to *Maximilian Colt*. Alabaster. A splendid piece.Two recumbent effigies on a mat. Kneeling children in profile against the tomb-chest. Two columns of touch support a coffered lintel. Coffered arch between and big strapwork cartouche against the back wall. – Richard Cave †1606 at Padua. He kneels frontally inside an arched canopy placed on a tall pedestal. Obelisk on top. – Dorothy St John †1630 (chancel N). Small tomb-chest. Against it three shields in lozenge panels. Garlands between them. Black top. No effigy. Decidedly post-Jacobean. – Sir Thomas Cave †1733 (chancel s). Attributed to *Smith* of Warwick (cf. Lamport). Of coloured marbles and purely architectural. – Sir Verney Cave †1734 (chancel s). Good bust in front of an obelisk. – James Callcutt †1751 (s aisle). Standing monument. Small grey sarcophagus, white Rococo volutes l. and r. Obelisk above. – Sir Thomas Cave †1778 (chancel s), but the monument must be early C19. Profile in oval medallion. Otherwise inscription only. – Thomas Otway Cave †1830 (chancel N). Said to be by *Kessells*, a Dutch pupil of Thorwaldsen. With a fine relief of the dying man, an amply cloaked woman seated at his couch, and a genius with an extinguished torch standing by his head. – Robert Otway Cave †1844, by *Westmacott Jun.* (N aisle w). Large monument. Background a Gothic arch. The deceased lies asleep on a couch. An afflicted young woman kneels on the l. Books lean on the r. On one it says 'Scriptores Graec et Rom'. Also some leaves by the books. – 3rd Lady Braye †1862, daughter of Sir Thomas Cave, by *Mary Thornycroft* (s aisle w). As large as the previous monument. Gothic background with a steeper arch. She lies asleep on a half-rolled-up mattress. Behind, a kneeling young woman with a cross and book. Three angels in relief above. These are by *John Gibson*. These two C19 monuments take up much more space than any other; they occupy positions not customary for such ambitious monuments, and go to the expense of white marble. – Edmund Verney. By *Felix Joubert*, 1896. It is surprising to find a Baroque scheme carried on or revived at that date. Obelisk with portrait in an oval medallion. In front to the l. an all-round figure of a lancer. To the r. military still-life. It is modelled in terracotta.

STANFORD HOUSE, E of the church. Formerly the Dower House. Georgian brick. Four-bay centre and two canted bay windows. Two storeys. Doorcase with Ionic pilasters and pediment.

Just s on the Yelvertoft Road paired and single COTTAGES of 1929. Picturesque ironstone, mullioned windows and thatched. Built by the Stanford Estate and apparently designed by the 6th *Lord Braye*.* Others of a similar style have been built in recent years but not by the estate.

*According to Lady Braye.

PARISH BOUNDARY MARKERS. On each road into the parish.
Fine piers with finials. Especially fine the ones on the Yelvertoft
Road, erected after 1839.

STANION

ST PETER. The dominant style of the church is late C13, most
obvious at the E end of both chancel and N chapel and especially in their windows with pretty tracery. That of the N chapel,
three lights, trefoil-headed, with three quatrefoiled circles. The
chancel E window has been altered and what appears to be a
circle in its head can be seen externally to have been more
elaborate. Inside it has side-shafts and string courses to mark
its altar. The S aisle windows are likewise cusped intersected
or at the W end with a big circle surrounding three small
spherical triangles. Along the top of the S wall an engaging
frieze with numerous tiny heads. The chancel arch, the SEDILIA
(a double seat with trefoil headed arches) and PISCINA,
the blocked lowside window, the N chapel arcade (two bays,
quatrefoil pier, double-chamfered arches) and the N chapel
SEDILIA, if this is what it is (a double arcade with trefoil heads
and single arch beyond, but no piscina), bear out this dating.
The chapel also has remains of a large image bracket, part of
a figure with an arm support and framing for the altar. Late
C13 also the S doorway and the chancel S windows of double
lancet form, though these were altered externally and given
square heads and a running string course. The building was
considerably altered in the C15 when the tower and spire and
the nave arcades were rebuilt. The tower is a commanding
piece. Set-back buttresses. Doorway with traceried spandrels.
Two two-light bell-openings with transom. Slender broach
spire with two tiers of lucarnes. The arcades of four bays and
distinctive Perp design. The piers have a long chamfer towards
nave and aisles with a hollow in its centre and shafts towards
the arch openings which alone carry capitals. The simple
straight-headed N aisle windows are of the same time. The
chancel was restored by *J. C. Traylen* in 1899. – FONT. Perp,
octagonal, very generously decorated. The most interesting
thing is that the stem is switched by 22½ degrees against the
bowl so that all the quatrefoiling, lozenging, etc. appears
broken at the corners, and the little buttresses support the sides
and not the angles of the bowl. – COMMUNION RAIL. Late
C17, with vertically symmetrical balusters. – There is no record
of a Victorian restoration so the church has very complete late
C18 WOODWORK in the nave, i.e. an especially elegant wine-
glass shaped PULPIT and two-decker READER'S DESK, with a
matching pair of pews on the N side, and BOX PEWS in the
aisles set longitudinally and rising in tiers as in an auditorium.
All of oak and of fine quality, probably owing to the patronage

of the lord of the manor, the Earl of Cardigan of Deene. The
nave benches are simpler and of pine, and could be an early
C19 alteration. – WALL PAINTING. S aisle. A delightful and
iconographically mysterious piece of the late C15, with a kneeling stag and a kneeling unicorn worshipping the place where
originally a sculptured image must have stood. In the nave,
above the S arcade, another faded figure, probably St Michael
weighing the Souls. – STAINED GLASS. Nave N. Zouche arms
and grisaille fragments, early C14. – CURIOSITY. A large whale-
bone which led to a romantic legend that it was the rib of an
enormous dun cow.

LITTLE STANION, 1 m. W. Housing complex begun 2008 with
a mixture of houses and apartment blocks of varying sizes and
designs by various firms under the directorship of *Bela Partnership Ltd*. Competent and sufficiently varied to be interesting.
It adjoins EUROHUB, which is the expected complex of huge
boring warehouses.

STANWICK

ST LAWRENCE. The essential parts are C13, i.e. the W tower, the
chancel and the arcades. The tower is the most interesting
piece. It is octagonal from the ground, and has a triple-
chamfered W lancet with a pretty, heavily framed pointed octofoil above it, clasping buttresses, a triple-chamfered arch
towards the nave, shafted twin bell-openings under a round
arch in the cardinal directions and tall blank arcading of the
same type in the diagonals, a pointed trefoiled top frieze, and
battlements dying into the spire. This of course has no broaches.
Three tiers of lucarnes, again in the cardinal directions. C13
also a double piscina in the S aisle, the S doorway and the (later)
S porch. The doorway has a stiff-leaf capital. Inside, the arcade
is of three bays with quatrefoil piers and double-chamfered
arches. The chancel is at a much higher level than the nave,
and this seems to be an original form. The chancel arch has a
hoodmould to the W with nailhead, and to the E some zigzag
at right angles to the wall surface. To the N of the arch facing
into the chancel a beautiful trefoiled niche, either a doorway
or some sort of seat, but for whom? Its position is odd and it
looks as if it has been moved here from elsewhere. The outer
moulding is continuous, the inner has stiff-leaf capitals. Most
of the windows are Perp. Those in the N wall a debased form
of Perp and there is externally a small shield and the date 1664,
so they could be of that date. It is also worth noting that,
externally, the roof-line against the tower runs beyond the wall
line and at the E end the chancel steps forward from the same
line. Could this mean that this whole wall is a C17 rebuild following the removal of a N aisle? Would this also account for
the big flat buttress on the N side of the tower, which seems to

have a masonry joint? Somehow the grandeur of the church deserves a N aisle, and internally it seems odd not to have one. The church was restored by *W. Slater* in 1856, with further work by *J. C. Traylen* in 1896. – FONT. Perp, octagonal, richly panelled. The stem is missing. On the foot a real foot. – CURIOSITY. Under the tower, two firehooks for pulling down burning thatch. – STAINED GLASS. Chancel E, 1897 and S aisle, 1884, both by *Heaton, Butler & Bayne*. Tower window by *Clayton & Ward*, 1856. – MONUMENT. John Atkins †1668 with his wife and her 'isheu'. Inscription tablet and arms over.

OLD RECTORY, W of the church. By *Sir James Burrough* of Cambridge. Dated 1717 over the porch. Five bays, two storeys. Remnants of a good staircase. Elegant but nothing special.

STANWICK HALL, ¼ m. SW. A simple Georgian house, five bays, two storeys. Rusticated quoins and platband, from which big keystones hang for the ground-floor windows. It was built in 1740 by *William Smith* of Warwick. The interior was largely destroyed by a fire in 1931, but one or two features survive, including some panelling in an upstairs room of the early C17.

STANWICK LAKES, 1 m. W. A country park, created since 2004 from former gravel pits, with an impressive VISITOR CENTRE, by *Laurie Wood Architects* opened 2009. Wide sweeping curved slate roof with tall pointed glazed viewing suite overlooking the lake. Near this is a surviving Bronze Age ROUND BARROW with a Neolithic long barrow and further round barrows excavated in advance of gravel extraction in the 1980s. Excavations have also revealed an extensive Iron Age settlement, Roman settlement and villa, and to the N, in Raunds parish, the deserted medieval hamlet of West Cotton. There is a small display of finds in the visitor centre, a small reconstructed Iron Age roundhouse and a heritage walk, with marker stones, links the barrow, the roundhouse and the excavated sites.

STAVERTON

ST MARY. Mostly early C14 and Perp. Earlier only the round-arched simple N doorway. Especially grand the Perp W tower, dark ashlar, with pairs of two-light transomed bell-openings and battlements. Also a S aisle window with a double set of panel tracery filling the whole upper half, and the chancel E window, although renewed. Of *c.* 1300 the unusually long N arcade of seven low and narrow bays with octagonal piers and arches with one hollow chamfer and one sunk quadrant. The W respond a face stop and the E a corbel. Of *c.* 1300 also the N aisle E window and a S window. The N chapel is Dec with reticulated tracery in the E window. The arcade to the chancel is of three bays with octagonal piers and double-hollow-chamfered arches with signs of a further arch at the E end. Conical foot-pieces. Big ogee-arched SEDILIA and PISCINA in the chapel and two image brackets, one with oakleaves the other ballflower. A squint through to the chancel. There was a restoration by *H. M. Townsend* of Peterborough 1884–5. – PULPIT. A striking piece of 1910. Very much in the Cotswold Arts and Crafts manner. Octagonal on a pillared stand. Carving of Christ blessing children. – CHOIR STALLS also 1910. – TOWER SCREEN. 1897 by *Townsend*. – STAINED GLASS. Chancel E window of 1902 by *F. C. Eden*. – Chancel s window with roundels including the arms of Christchurch College Oxford (i.e. the former Cardinal College, hence the cardinal's hat). – s aisle windows of 1882, 1892 by *Heaton, Butler & Bayne* and 1855 by *J. Hardman & Co.* – MONUMENTS. Thomas Wylmer †1580. Standing monument of freestone. Two short Ionic columns but set under a Doric frieze. Brass plate with kneeling figures set into a Purbeck-type stone. A skied monument over the s doorway with Ionic pilasters, an arched inscription and Rococo base panel. Of a type associated with the *Smith* of Warwick Marble Yard (cf. Whilton). – Rev. John Bull †1838. Gothic ogee surround and a bust medallion.

The village is most attractive and has a fine variety of good houses. In CHURCH STREET a small cottage dated 1699, with casement windows in stone surrounds. STAVERTON COURT was formerly the vicarage. C18 brick with a Tuscan porch. One of the finest houses is GODFREES (Manor Road), late C17, its long façade having two-light mullioned windows and a wide canted oriel on corbels. The house was considerably enhanced *c.* 1900 with some brought in features. Nearby THE MANOR, C17, seems originally to have been part of its outbuildings with a big chimneystack. Another house on the Green also has a canted oriel. Also on the Green HALL FARMHOUSE (once The Crown pub and the village bakehouse), early C18, part banded stonework. Bread ovens made by *David Ogg* of Northampton survive.

THE CROFT, Croft Lane. Dated 1700. w front three bays, two storeys, with later three-light mullioned windows and central door. Staircase with twisted balusters.

THE OLD HOUSE, The Orchard. Dated 1694 but remodelled in the early C19. Its rear façade, of brick, is rendered and has an ornamental cast-iron veranda.

TOLLGATE COTTAGE, 1 m. NE on the edge of A425. A charming Victorian brick toll house.

STEANE

One of the most intriguing and delightful places in Northamptonshire.

STEANE PARK. Much of the house, the mansion of the Crewe family from 1583, was demolished after it was inherited by the

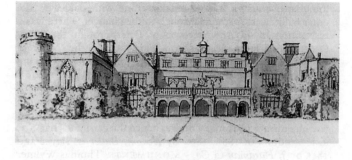

Steane Park.
Drawing by P. Tillemans, 1719

Hon. John Spencer of Althorp in 1744. Tillemans recorded it in 1719 showing the centre containing the hall, fronted with a loggia. At either end were curious wings with round battlemented towers and Gothic windows. What remained was a portion of the w wing which contained the services, and was then converted into a farmhouse. It was refurbished in 1882–5 by *Josiah Mander*, surveyor to the Althorp Estate, probably working alongside *George Devey*, who was also then working for the estate and rebuilt other properties at Steane. It is gabled and has on the s side some mullioned-and-transomed windows, but is otherwise entirely Victorian.

Behind the house a STABLE BLOCK, again largely 1884–6. s alongside the main road is a former TOLL HOUSE which was rebuilt in a new position, set back from the road, at the same period.

54 St Peter. In a lovely garden setting. The chapel of Sir Thomas Crewe, built in 1620 using the local, probably Helmdon, limestone, is one of the most interesting examples of Gothic survival in England. Some parts, such as the w window, are so convincing that they could be seen as genuine medieval work reused. There is, however, little doubt that what stands here is totally C17. It makes one wonder about many windows one sees in medieval churches. The w window is entirely in a C14 manner. Other windows are more what one would expect in the Late Perp period, some square-headed. Obelisks on the corners of the nave, front and back. A small w doorway of 1620. The s doorway on the other hand, with unfluted Ionic columns and a big, open segmental pediment, must be later and probably *c.* 1630, perhaps added by Nathaniel, Lord Crewe when he was Bishop of Oxford. The chapel is only two bays long and has a s aisle, nearly as wide as the nave, and a N chapel, a mortuary chapel for the Crewes. The pier and responds of the arcade have a strange section with four wave-chamfered projections. E respond on a corbel with grapes. Charming INTERIOR with C18, probably 1720, BOX PEWS and PULPIT. – RAILS. Twisted balusters, late C17. – SCREEN. Prob-

ably *c.* 1630, although missing some of its decoration. – COM-
MUNION TABLE. Of marble, given by Bishop Crewe in 1720.
– ARMOUR. Banners, helmets, crests, spurs, swords. – MONU-
MENTS. A very fine array. – Sir Thomas Crewe, Speaker of the
House of Commons, †1633 and wife. Alabaster and grey
marble. She is recumbent, he behind her resting on his elbow.
Two columns, arch, obelisks and achievement. Geoffrey Fisher
has suggested it is of two periods: first *c.* 1619 the background,
then *c.* 1633 the effigies and tomb. – Temperance Browne
†1634. Signed by *John and Matthias Christmas* and dated 1635.
Hanging monument. She is sitting up in her coffin, still in her
shroud. Two columns, two pendant arches. Under them two
small arched niches with allegorical figures. In the spandrel the
angel blowing the last trumpet. Top square with arms of an
open segmental pediment. On them cherubs. In the 'predella'
'Disce mori' and 'Mors mini corona'. – John Crewe †1669,
attributed to *Thomas Burman* by Geoffrey Fisher, an attribution not accepted by Adam White. – John, 1st Lord Crewe,
†1679. Simple tablet, attributed to *Jasper Latham* (GF). –
Thomas, 2nd Lord Crewe, †1697. Attributed to *Catterns* by
Mrs Esdaile, but it could equally well be from the workshop
of *Edward Stanton.* Very pretty standing monument, with
cherubs' heads, cypher, two standing putti, garlands, etc. –
Nathaniel Lord Crewe, Bishop of Durham, †1721. Architectural tablet. At the head two coronets and a mitre, at the foot
a grape. This was originally a skull, but as the monument was
put up before the bishop's death, and as he disliked the skull,
the change was made (*Gentleman's Magazine,* 1786). It is good
to see the tradition of black painted shadows around the monuments preserved, much enhancing their effect.

N of the chapel remains of a formal water garden with a short
CANAL.

STOKE ALBANY

ST BOTOLPH. Mostly of *c.* 1300, i.e. the W tower with a window
of three steeply stepped lights under a steep arch, a window in
the form of a spherical triangle higher up and pairs of transomed two-light bell-openings; chancel with an E window with
intersected tracery, and quite a variety of two-light windows
with quatrefoils, quatrefoiled circles, round and pointed trefoils, and also two lowside lancets; S aisle with similar windows
(a little later, see the one window with reticulated tracery), a
shafted doorway, and an interesting W window with a five-
cornered star in a spherical quadrangle; N aisle with an E
window with Y-tracery. On the S side of the tower parapet is
a shield with the Roos arms, supporting the *c.* 1300 date. Inside
a wide nave and a wide S aisle. Both arcades are also of *c.* 1300
(octagonal piers, double-chamfered pointed arches, but differ-

ing details). The N aisle windows curious. Their outer arches suggest they were larger and have been decapitated, though the head tracery seems to be solid. In the chancel a low tomb-recess with a trefoil-cusped arch and SEDILIA and PISCINA. All this again of *c.* 1300. Perp especially the S aisle E window of five lights with much panel tracery. S porch has an C18 look, but a charity tablet inside dated 1683 might be nearer the mark. Restoration by *W. Slater* 1856–7, and his, presumably, the rather fine arch-braced roof with curved wind-braces above the S aisle. Just a restoration? He presented further plans 1871–3. – Unusual painted REREDOS with panels painted with spider's web designs, 1916. – FONT. A bowl on a fluted baluster, dated 1681. – STAINED GLASS. Chancel. Roos arms and grisaille, *c.* 1295. Several good later windows. – Chancel E and S, of 1878 and 1885 both by *J. Hardman & Co.* – Three N side windows, 1878, 1902 and 1906, also by Hardman. – Chancel windows of 1908 and 1913 are both by *J. Powell & Sons.* – MONUMENT. N aisle, Gothic tablet for John Lefevre †1844.

WAR MEMORIAL, on the green outside the churchyard. By *J. A. Gotch*, 1921. An elegant tapered cross on an octagonal stepped base.

OLD HOUSE, former Manor House. W of the church. Dating from the C14 with the solar wing incorporated in the later house. Window with Y-tracery in the N end of the E wing and on the ground floor inside two arched doorways leading into what was the hall. Much altered in the C17 (datestone of 1619) when the hall was largely removed, but a big buttress remains on the S side. Newel stair. Further alterations late C17. There were tactful alterations and additions by *Gotch*, 1893 and 1907.

MANOR HOUSE, Ashley Road, on the way to the A road. Oblong, the l. half of before the Reformation, the r. of 1682. The l. half has buttresses, a doorway with two-centred head and two shields over (one for Roos), a window of two-plus-two lights and two-centred cusped heads at ground-floor level. As with the Old House, gentle alterations by *Gotch*, 1903.

STOKE HOUSE, ¼ m. S on Desborough Road. Set back in its own grounds, a sizeable brick house of 1835 with a two-storey five-bay front with two bay recessed wings. Regency details such as doorway and staircase with cast iron balustrade. Some alterations by *Henry Littler* in 1858. Stable block etc. of the same date.

STOKE BRUERNE

ST MARY. Norman W tower, see the two windows and the pointed but single-stepped arch towards the nave. The upper parts are Perp. Perp also the chancel E window. The side windows of the chancel do not seem in their original state and may be due to the restoration of 1881–2 by *E. Swinfen Harris* of Stony Stratford, who also added the organ chamber and vestry. What is trustworthy of the aisle windows is Dec, reticulated tracery. Tall arcades of five bays of unusual design with just a simple moulded impost rather than capitals. Clerestory of circular windows, probably due to the restoration of 1849. In the N aisle a cusped tomb-recess. Further work was done 1900–1 by *Matthew Holding*. – FONT. Octagonal, part C15, set within an ironwork compartment made in 1901. – SCREEN. Tall, Perp, one-light divisions, ogee arches, and panel tracery over. – COMMUNION RAIL. With dumb-bell balusters, C17, now used as stall fronts. – STALLS. On the S side of the chancel a stall with two C15 poppyhead bench-ends. Then running up to the screen what appear to be stalls with misericords with bench-ends with fleur-de-lys finials. Difficult to date, and some appear to be older than others. There is however a similar set of stall-ends at nearby Alderton, and it is clear that they date from the 1840s. They have a frieze of Gothic traceried panels of the 1840s above them. The painted inscription panel above the pulpit, recording a bequest by Mary Arundell in 1676 'for beautifying and repairing of this church', might be relevant. – REREDOS. 1878–81 by *E. Swinfen Harris* and *N. F. Westlake*. Panelled wall with stencil decorations, the central section with painted and gilded figures. Christ in Majesty etc. Tiled floor of same period. – HATCHMENT. A painted lozenge for Jane Nailour †1655/6, and although strictly speaking not a hatchment, as such it is the oldest in the county. Another for Elizabeth daughter of Francis Arundel, †1731. – MONUMENT. Richard Lightfoot †1625. A small brass with kneeling figure in a stone surround with pilasters and strapwork. John Smith †1768. Large stone tablet with acanthus scroll supports signed by *John Middleton* of Towcester. Many fine ledger slabs especially in the S aisle. – STAINED GLASS. S aisle E window of 1877 by *Wailes*. – S aisle W of 1946 by *A. J. Davies* (repaired twice, 1997 and 2011). – S aisle window, Fisher memorial (†1987), designed by *Chris Fiddes* and *Barbara Bowden*, made by *George Wigley* 1988. It has Northamptonshire roses and Chinese fish, denoting the deceased's interest in oriental porcelain.

The village centres around the GRAND JUNCTION CANAL, with locks, early C19 cottages, an inn and the CANAL MUSEUM, converted in 1963 from a C19 grain warehouse. Alongside the Museum is a barge-weighing machine of 1836, brought from the Glamorganshire Canal. The exceptionally attractive CANAL BRIDGE, with two arches and robust curving brick and stone walls, which carries the road through the village, was strengthened with commendable care in 1972 by British Waterways, in collaboration with the County Surveyor, by the insertion of a reinforced concrete structure invisible from the outside. The bridge probably dates from *c.* 1835–40, when the canal was widened and a double set of locks constructed. NE of the village is the TUNNEL between here and Blisworth (q.v.). There are also rows of Grafton ESTATE COTTAGES in the village, some with bargeboarded gables (Nos. 1–5 for example), of the same period as well as one or two thatched cottages.

Also due to the Grafton Estates are several buildings, notably farm complexes, in the area, all *c.* 1840. Examples are ROOKERY FARM on the E edge and STOKE PLAIN, just N of the village on the road to Blisworth, built of stone, three bays, with lower wings in line but recessed, and STOKE GAP LODGE, ½ m. E of the village on the E side of the A508. This is of the form of a farmhouse with a quadrangle of outbuildings behind.

62   STOKE PARK, ½ m. SW. The house has had a long tradition of an attribution to *Inigo Jones*. It was built in 1629–35 by Sir Francis Crane, founder of the Mortlake Tapestry Works, who had acquired the estate in 1629. Crane was, of course, an intimate Court figure and entertained the King at his new house in 1635. John Bridges's *History*, which was in preparation in the 1720s, says that Crane had 'brought the design from Italy and in the execution of it received the assistance of Inigo Jones'. Both statements are credible. Stoke Park is the earliest house in England on the plan of Palladio's villas with a central

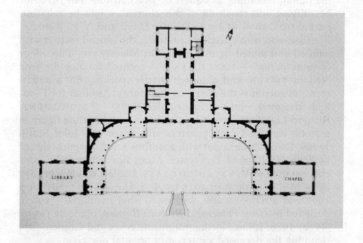

Stoke Park.
Plan by Colen Campbell, 1725, and drawing by P. Tillemans

corps-de-logis connected by quadrant colonnades to end pavilions, a plan form which was to become *de rigueur* in the early
C18. Crane could just as well have brought this idea from an
Italian journey as Inigo Jones might have brought it after he
had been in 1613–14 and studied Palladio with unprecedented
intensity and zest. The elevations on the other hand pose some
problems. The main building was of H-shape with the front
serif larger than that at the back. It is possible that the house
was an older building which was altered when the pavilions
were added. Old photographs show that the back parts had
very plain mullion and cross-windows. The end walls of the
front serif had curved Jacobean gables. This building was burnt
down in 1886 and what we know of it – it is e.g. illustrated in
Campbell's *Vitruvius Britannicus*, vol. III, 1725 – does not tally
with Jones's style. Campbell says indeed that it was designed
by 'another architect'. Yet it had the motif which is also the
hallmark of the end pavilions and which was going to be a
favourite motif in the Jones connexion and the circle of architects of 1700 and after: the giant pilaster. This was a motif used
in the Cinquecento by Michelangelo (Capitol) and Palladio
(Palazzo Valmarana) but with more enthusiasm in France
(St Maur, then the Long Gallery between the Louvre and
Tuileries, etc.), from where it migrated to Holland. In Dutch
classicism it became popular at nearly the same moment as it
appears at Stoke Park. The s front of Stoke Park was of five
bays, grouped by giant Ionic pilasters in three parts with one,
three, one windows. There was an attic storey above the giant
pilasters and a cupola or belvedere on the roof. The windows
had frames of rustication in alternating sizes and were vertically laced together. Campbell only says that the Civil War
interrupted work on the house. The main house was refronted
between 1790 and 1800 in a more conventional Neoclassical
form with pilasters and a pediment, and the w pavilion was
given a tall Venetian window and its interior refurbished.

After the fire of 1886 a new house in an ornate heavy Jacobean style was built in varying local ironstones, attached in a
most unfortunate way to the E pavilion, which had an equally
unfortunate bay window added to its front. The whole future
of Stoke Park hung in the balance in the 1950s, it never having
been used again after the war. It was rescued in 1954 by Robin
Chancellor, saving it from demolition. The Victorian house was
removed and the C17 pavilions were restored, with the E pavilion being converted into a house. The directing architect was
Marshall Sisson. They are faced with cream oolite and dark
brown ironstone, both from local quarries. The columns of the
colonnade are of a golden ironstone, probably brought from
the Duston or Harlestone quarries near Northampton. The
combination adds greatly to the beauty of the pavilions. (It is
worth remembering that Jones's Banqueting House in Whitehall was also originally built using Northamptonshire stones.)
They are of one and a half storeys, oblong, with a slightly narrower projection to the forecourt. The oblong part is of three

bays with a one-bay pediment to the s. The façade of the E pavilion was restored according to the illustration in *Vitruvius Britannicus*. The giant pilasters carry an entablature with a pulvinated frieze. To the forecourt, i.e. the side where the two pavilions face one another, the middle projection has a loggia on the ground floor with Ionic columns carrying a straight lintel and set fairly close to the framing giant pilasters, a motif familiar from Michelangelo's Capitoline palaces, not a likely source for Inigo Jones. Above this, on the upper floor a large arched window. The roof above is now hipped, but it formerly had a small pediment on this side, and another on the s side of the projecting part of the pavilion. To the l. and r. of the projection a one-bay, one-storey loggia. Those facing N mark the start of the quadrant colonnades. In the W pavilion, according to Campbell, was the Library, in the E pavilion the chapel. The roof structure of the pavilions uses an ingenious kingpost structure which is only found in buildings associated with Jones. So is the Jones attribution to be accepted? Giles Worsley presented cogent arguments for it in 2005 (*Country Life*, 29 Sept). If it is not Jones, then who is it? A tailpiece of evidence is a mason's mark on the doorway of the W pavilion which also occurs at Kirby Hall on the work of 1638–40. That is known to be the work of *Nicholas Stone*, Jones's master mason in Whitehall. But could Stone have been this Italian?*

STOKE DOYLE

75 ST RUMBALD. St Rumbald is a rare dedication (but cf. Astrop). The date of the church is 1722–5, and that is a rare date in Northamptonshire. Designs exist for the body of the building by *Thomas Eayre* of Kettering and it is likely that the whole building is his. The mason was *Charles Drew*. Tower with angle pilasters at the top, a balustrade and obelisk pinnacles. Arched W doorway with pilasters, arched bell-openings with pilasters. On the s side a doorway close to the W end with a rusticated surround and an open segmental pediment on Doric pilasters. Then four round-arched windows and a Venetian E window. Plain coved ceiling inside. In other words a simple but quite sophisticated little building and internally still totally Georgian in atmosphere. There was some redecoration of the church between 1842 and 1844 under the direction of *James Morris* of London, when the reredos was regilded and a new E window with stained glass was suggested but not carried out. – FONT. On baluster stem. – REREDOS and COMMUNION RAIL original. – PULPIT and BENCHES original. – ORGAN. *c.* 1845, Gothic. – SCULPTURE. Two large, beautifully carved angels above the sides of the E window. They were brought in in 1844, look

---

* The garden statue of Sir George Cooke by *Henry Cheere* is now in the V&A.

totally at home and could well be C18. – CROSS BASE outside
the S door. Square with corner spurs of a bulbous indeterminate form to carry over into an octagon. The date can hardly
be guessed. – MONUMENTS. Outside the church, to the E.
Priest, C13, the head under a trefoiled canopy. – Mrs Frances
Palmer †1628. Hanging monument with columns, obelisks and
an achievement. She lies stiffly on her side, head on hand and
elbow propping up the arm. Her husband kneels in front of
her in profile – an unusual composition. Unfortunate colouring. – Sir Edward Ward †1714, made soon after his arrival in 79
England by that young and brilliant sculptor *J. M. Rysbrack*.
He had arrived in 1720. Not signed but a model recorded. It
stands serene in the transept made for it. White and grey
marble. Reredos with Ionic columns and a pediment, very
much in the Gibbs mode. Exquisitely carved elegant semi-
reclining figure with wig. The detailing is as good as Rysbrack
ever gets: the wig, the folds of the gown, the fur and the beautifully carved hands. Certainly the best early C18 carving in the
county and some of the best in England. – Mrs Roberts †1819.
By *Chantrey*. Quite small. An instructive comparison with the
monument to Mrs Palmer. The subject is almost the same, but
taste and sensibility have changed. She lies on a Grecian couch.
He bends mournfully over her hand. She died in childbirth. A
larger version of the design was used by Chantrey again for the
Greaves (†1821) monument at Waterperry, Oxon. – Other early
C19 tablets including Thomas Capron †1829 by *H. Hopper*.

STOKE DOYLE MANOR. The Ward house survived until 1800
when it was demolished. The C18 gates were removed to The
Berrystead in Oundle and from there to East Haddon Hall. It
stood close to the present Manor Farm, S of the church.

OLD RECTORY, E of the church. L-shaped. The entrance front
with two canted bays, the N bay of two storeys, the S one
with the date 1633. The S wing perhaps built as a hall range.
Datestones of 1731 and 1790 must refer to alterations. C19
additions.

Former SCHOOL of 1872, Gothic. Opposite a long row of COT-
TAGES, vaguely Tudor with hoodmoulded windows built
1842–4.

MILL HOUSE, ¼ m. SW of the church. 1865 in the Tudor manner
with a fine set of stone piers and cast-iron rails.

STOWE-NINE-CHURCHES *see* CHURCH STOWE
and UPPER STOWE

STRIXTON 9060

ST ROMWALD. A C13 church rebuilt in 1873 except for the W
wall, but with old materials and, it is said, correctly. There are
restoration drawings of 1869 by *Slater & Carpenter*. The W wall

has a triple-chamfered doorway on two orders of shafts and a sexfoil window over with a wavy frame. Tiny cusped lancet to the r. Carpenter produced a design for a tall saddleback campanile with pairs of lancets topped by quatrefoils in circles, set on a large arch across the nave wall, unfortunately not done. The windows of the church are mostly pairs of lancets. At the E end three stepped separate lancets with a quatrefoiled circle in the gable, and, also in the gable, three blank quatrefoils placed diagonally. S doorway with a double-hollow-chamfered arch. Inside, PISCINA with some dogtooth. – SCREEN. Perp. Simple, with one-light divisions. – COMMUNION RAIL. With heavy twisted balusters; c. 1700. – STAINED GLASS. One small quatrefoil with Virgin and Child, unidentified.

The Strixton Estate was acquired by Sarah, Duchess of Marlborough, in 1737 and after her death it passed to the Hon. John Spencer of Althorp. It remained part of the Althorp Estate until 1945 and the small village shows evidence of their tidying.

CHURCH FARMHOUSE, next to the church, although of late C17 origins is largely c. 1850 with pretty cast-iron diamond glazing. A little further W is MANOR FARM, which has some C17 mullioned windows, shows similar evidence.

GREENFIELD LODGE FARM, ¼ m. SE, off the A509. A new building in 1848.

9080

SUDBOROUGH

ALL SAINTS. An attractive and very interesting church. Mostly of the late C13, at that point where the pure E.E. is giving way to Dec. Here we have a mixture of both but it seems to be an almost a single build, though perhaps in more than one phase. Internally wide, light and spacious. Three-bay arcades with circular piers and circular capitals and abaci. The first piers N and S are sturdier and may be older than the others. Pointed arches of one chamfer and one hollow chamfer. Most unusually cross-arches in the aisles from each pillar with responds against the outer walls. Arches into the transepts too. Both transepts have a wide arch recess in the E wall with a shelf. The S transept S window is specially fine and typical of its date. Four lights arranged as two-plus-two with cusped Y-tracery, and above a large spherical triangle with three small ones inscribed. Steeply pointed arch. The N transept window is C19 but probably a copy of what was there before. Stone bench along the S aisle wall. The chancel also E.E. in character, notably the SEDILIA with triple shafts, fillets and headstops, just two arches, with the piscina in the E arch. The windows are tall with cusped lights and straight-headed. A single one at the W end, that on the N with a lowside window, and judging from internal blocking, that on the S had one too. Then a two-light window and finally one with three lights. And finally the

E window with four lights. Late C13 W tower. It has lancets on the N and S, bell-openings of two lights with, above them, a spherical triangle or a circle with four inscribed circles or cusped Y-tracery, a corbel table with dogtooth and heads, and four thin (later) pinnacles. The lower half in dressed stone with a curious opening (cf. All Saints, Stamford, Lincs). A blocked circular opening is almost certainly the remains of a medieval clock face.* Tower arch with semi-octagonal responds with concave sides and abaci and hollow-chamfered arches – i.e. Dec rather than late C13. The chancel buttresses have tiny gables inset with trefoils on the top offset. Extraordinary pinnacles with clusters of shafts and cresting. The N doorway is also of *c.* 1300. There was a partial restoration by *E. F. Law* in 1850 and some work on the chancel in 1872 by the same. – FURNISHINGS. Excellent woodwork pews, stalls and pulpit in Arts and Crafts manner, all the result of *J. C. Traylen*'s restoration 1890–1. – STAINED GLASS. S transept, crown in the centre of the S window, and two roundels with a monogram 'MR' in the E. – Chancel E window by *Kempe*, 1892. – Chancel N, two panels of angels, by *J. Powell & Sons*, 1912. – S aisle W, Harvey memorial 1904 is also by them. – N chapel E Annunciation, by *A. O. Hemming.* – MONUMENTS. Tomb-recess with a near-segmental arch in the chancel with stone effigy of a cross-legged knight, slender, late C13. Thought to be Sir Robert de Vere, who was killed while on crusade in 1249. – N transept, brass to William West †1390 and wife, 18-in. (46-cm.) figures. Stone in yard, W of tower, to Anne Martin †1997, 'mother, artist and teacher', with an artist's palette carved on the reverse.

Many delightful thatched cottages, especially the row W of the church.

OLD RECTORY, adjacent to the church. Largely *c.* 1825 by *William Abbott* of St Neots. He built the four-bay block of the main house. In 1846 *John Eaton* of Titchmarsh added the l. wing and the bay.

GRANGE FARMHOUSE, further W, set back, is handsome late C18 brick.

SUDBOROUGH MANOR. C17 origin. *Thomas Farnolls Pritchard* did some work here 1775–6 and the house he designed forms the r. section of the S front. It was three bays with a Serlian front door, two storeys with dormers. A good deal was done for Captain Charles Harvey 1904 by *J. A. Gotch* and this presumably includes almost doubling the length of the façade and adding another Serlian window and round-headed first-floor windows at a higher level than the earlier part of the house, so they cut into the roof-space.

ROUNDHOUSE, former Toll House, on the A road, but now bypassed. Circular with conical roof. With a datestone of 1660, but largely late C18. It was for many years the home of the naturalist and writer Denys Watkins-Pitchford who worked under the pseudonym 'BB'.

---

* Information from John Smith of Stamford.

Sulby Hall.
Drawing by G. Clarke, *c.* 1850

₆₀₈₀ ## SULBY

Rene Payne purchased land in Sulby in the early 1780s, and in
1792 he asked *Sir John Soane* to provide designs for SULBY
HALL. It was more a hunting lodge than a grand house, with
a large dining room filling one wing. In 1824 Soane was again
consulted about enlarging it, though it is unclear whether he
was finally responsible for the additions, which, in effect,
doubled the size of the house. A new N entrance front was built
with a large bow with Corinthian columns and extra wings
were added on the sides of the building. Payne's grandson
George lived an extravagant lifestyle, and in 1847 had to sell.
The house was demolished in 1948–9. PARK FARMHOUSE
built *c.* 1795 was also designed by *Soane*. It is a simple brick
house with a hipped roof and a series of outbuildings. In the
park is a large crescent-shaped LAKE. An ICE HOUSE survives
on the E side of the site. There was a Premonstratensian abbey
at Sulby but only a collection of mounds survives around
ABBEY FARM, itself late C18 brick.

₅₀₄₀ ## SULGRAVE

ST JAMES. In the w tower a triangle-headed doorway, i.e. a Saxon
relic, possibly not *in situ* although the lower parts of the tower
may incorporate early masonry. The upper parts of the tower
are E.E. Two-light bell-openings. Otherwise mostly C19 with

the main restoration in 1884–5 by *J. P. St Aubyn* which included the rebuilding of the N aisle. The S doorway is original Dec work but its porch is securely dated 1564 and the four-centred doorway, quatrefoils and initials supports this. Dec S arcade of four bays with octagonal piers and double-chamfered arches. Chancel arch Dec with continuous mouldings and mortices for a tympanum. Chancel S window Perp with a lowside window and a squint on the S side. Big corbel heads of a king and queen thought to be Edward III and Queen Philippa. The E end C19. – FONT. Octagonal, with leaf ornament, probably of the 1660s. – PEW. The Washington Pew is an open bench with front and back, of the C17, restored in 1924. – TOWER SCREEN of 1928 with pierced panels and a painted frieze. – Magnificent iron-bound CHEST, C16 or C17. – STAINED GLASS. In the S aisle E window, C16 or C17 Washington heraldic, brought in in 1943. – N aisle window of the Good Shepherd, 1884 by *Lavers, Barraud & Westlake.* – S aisle, St James the Less window of 2002 by *Nick Bayliss.* – MONUMENTS. Brass to Lawrence Washington †1584 and wife; 21-in. (53-cm.) figures. – John and Moses Hodges †1724; architectural tablet with Ionic pilasters. Of a type associated with the Marble Yard of the *Smiths* of Warwick.

An attractive open village with STOCKS on the village green. Opposite the church the tiny former CHARITY SCHOOL (now shop) built by the Hodges family in 1720. Ashlar with central doorway and sundial and two flat mullioned windows each side. Many good stone houses, mainly C17 to C18, several with thatch.

OLD VICARAGE. Part C17 but much enlarged *c.* 1850, possibly by *G. E. Street.*

SULGRAVE MANOR, E end of the village. The manor house was bought by Lawrence Washington, wool stapler and Mayor of Northampton, in 1540 and sold out of the Washington family in 1659. This mecca for American visitors owes its existence to US President Roosevelt who in 1911 suggested some form of commemoration of a hundred years of peace between Britain and America since 1812. The idea of acquiring Sulgrave Manor, with its Washington connection, was suggested and its owners readily agreed. An appeal on both sides of the Atlantic was launched and the manor purchased in 1914. A plan to restore the house and rebuild a wing which had been pulled down around 1780 was created with the architect *Sir Reginald Blomfield*, a rather mundane commission for such an eminent figure. Due to the First World War the scheme did not reach fruition until 1921. Blomfield also designed the formal garden layout. The house consists of a centre with porch and a N wing added at the time of Queen Anne. Of the centre only the r. half with the porch is original; the l. half being 1921. The date of the original work is later than 1558 (arms of Elizabeth I on the porch), but need not be much later. The whole front consists of no more than three very widely spaced bays. The porch doorway has a four-centred head. Inside the hall, the fireplace is original, the screen C20. Behind the hall pretty, late C17 staircase with twisted balusters. Armorial glass with Washington connections mostly 1915 but an earlier shield dated 1580.

CASTLE, W of the church. Excavations in 1967–76 revealed a remarkable timber hall of the early C11 beneath the Norman ringwork. The building was 80 ft (24 metres) long, with a service room, screen and opposed entrances at the screen end – a very early example of the standard later medieval arrangement. At the opposite end to the screen a cross-wing which was on stone footings and therefore possibly of two storeys. A detached timber kitchen lay beyond the service room. On one side of the hall stood a stone building, whose walls survive to a height of 7 ft (2.1 metres). After the Conquest the timber hall was replaced by a timber first-floor hall on a stone undercroft; the Saxon cross-wing was retained as a chamber block, and the free-standing stone building was used as a gatehouse in conjunction with the new earthwork defences. The site was abandoned c. 1125.

Former WINDMILL, ¾ m. NW. A tower mill and mill house, probably C18. In 1788 the mill-owner, John Brockhouse, ordered machinery, no longer in existence, from *Boulton & Watt*.

BARROW. Below Barrow Hill, 1 m. N of the village, on the S side of Banbury Lane.

SUTTON BASSETT

ALL SAINTS. Nicely situated on a small green. A chapel more than a church, just a nave, chancel and bellcote. The building originates from a small mid-C12 nave and chancel which was extended both to the W and E in the C13. In the N wall of the chancel a Norman window. The responds of the chancel arch are also Norman. The capitals have animals on the N and faces on the S. The chancel arch pointed of chamfered orders, C13. Norman the S doorway to the nave too. One order of columns with scallop capitals. Tympanum with relief diapering (cf. Peterborough Cathedral). On the S side two later C13 windows. The double bellcote also C13, projecting from the W wall, which has a small two-light Perp window. The building was largely rebuilt by *Henry Goddard & Son* of Leicester in 1861–2. From that date the interior, which, although simple, has a nice period feel. Simple pews, a small FONT, octagonal with quatrefoil decoration standing on a cluster of pillars. The REREDOS, which has painted panels, is by *Traylen & Lenton*, 1931. – STAINED GLASS. Chancel E of 1887 and nave S of 1905 are both by *Burlison & Grylls*.

MANOR HOUSE, an L-shaped house with a wing of alternating iron and sandstone, dated 1642, and its main block of dark

ashlar, mullioned windows and a low canted bay. A date of
1631 is also recorded. Opposite, SUTTON BASSETT HOUSE,
ironstone also with mullioned windows, but considerably
renewed in the C19.

SYRESHAM

ST JAMES. The chancel arch is of *c.* 1200. The corbels still have
the Late Norman trumpet capitals. The arch has one hollow
chamfer. Hoodmould with nutmeg decoration. C13 W tower.
Two-light bell-openings with separating shaft. Short recessed
shingled spire. N windows C17, S Dec style windows all renewed.
Dec arcades of four bays with octagonal piers and double-
chamfered arches. The church was restored by *William White*
1867–8 when the spire was rebuilt, with further work by *E. F.
Law* in 1874. – REREDOS of 1880. Of wood in an elaborate C15
manner with painted decoration. Rather fine. – FONT. Circular,
Norman, with a rope moulding at the top (from Turweston,
Bucks.). – WALL PAINTINGS. Several C17 texts and other frag-
mentary remains in the aisles. – CHARITY BOARDS. Mid-C18.
– STAINED GLASS. Chancel, E window of 1908 by *Burlison &
Grylls* and S window of 1881 by *Heaton, Butler & Bayne*. –
MONUMENT. 'Petri Andrewe generosi' †1612. Alabaster tablet
in an architectural frame with good details. Good enough for
Hollemans. (Cf. Welford, as it was erected by a member of the
Saunders family.) Opposite a fine alabaster lozenge with a
shield of the Saunders family, also probably *c.* 1600.

WESLEYAN CHAPEL, High Street. Refronted 1846. Red brick
with three recessed round-arched windows. Opposite the
former SUNDAY SCHOOL of 1926.

THE PRIORY, S side of the village between High Street and Main
Road. Externally C18 brick but inside considerable evidence of
its medieval origins. Service doorways of C15 or C16 date in
the former hall end wall.

GATE HOUSE, SW in Bell Lane. A particularly good Arts and
Crafts house by *C. H. Biddulph-Pinchard*, 1920–5. Partly of
stone with mullioned-and-transomed windows, and partly of
timber from old barns, with brick infilling. Carriage arch
leading to a raised courtyard. Long curved garden wall.

CROWFIELD CHAPEL, 1 m. W on the B4525. 1890. Stone with
two big lancet windows.

SYWELL

ST PETER AND ST PAUL. Short late C13 W tower. Bell-openings
of two lights with a shaft between. The same motif repeated in

the windows on the s side below. The picturesque stair projection in the middle of the w side is not medieval. The interior is odd indeed. When the s arcade was rebuilt in 1870, the e wall of the tower must also have been interfered with. The tower arch now has a triple-shafted n respond, but instead of a s respond a whole quatrefoil pier with thin diagonal shafts which cannot have been there originally. No medieval architect would have placed the corner of his tower on a pier. Nor did *Josiah Mander*, surveyor to the Overstone Estate, the architect of 1870. He reinforced the corner by setting close to the quatrefoil pier two round ones with square abaci, one of original late c12 work (waterleaf and leaf crockets in the capital) and one imitated. The arcade then goes on with such imitated piers. Could the original late c12 arcade have been of two bays with one more added in the late c13? Original the s doorway, late c12, pointed, with one slight step. Original also the c14 tomb-recess in the n transept. Chancel rebuilt in 1862 by *E. F. Law*. – STAINED GLASS. e window by *Willement*, 1839, a very handsome and civilized composition made up of heraldic glass dated 1580. Nave, a superb First World War memorial window (Joshua) by *Christopher Whall* 1920.

SYWELL HALL. Quite a long front, straight, with two small and one central larger gable, irregular mullioned windows. To the l., at the end of the front, three-storeyed porch. The four-centred doorhead is not shown on drawings by George Clarke so a later c19 alteration. Above the first-floor window a frieze of linked squares and circles (cf. Rushton Hall). The front might have gone on to the l. of the porch. The house seems to be Elizabethan and this fits with the grant by Queen Elizabeth I of land to 'her dear and faithfull servant, Anthony Jenkinson', a diplomat, in 1582–3. After his death it came into the ownership of the Wilmer family, and above the porch are the arms of William Wilmer, knighted in 1617. Sash windows were introduced on the s front in the c18 and there were alterations in the mid c19, probably after the acquisition of the estate by Lord Overstone.

The village was largely rebuilt by Lady Overstone between 1860 and 1864, so a good collection of ESTATE COTTAGES. A combination of simple double ironstone cottages and rows of more elaborate stone and brick. The former SCHOOL and SCHOOL HOUSE were rebuilt in 1861. sw of the church the OLD RECTORY, early c19 yellow brick. Three-bay front with pretty porch.

SYWELL AERODROME. A fine Art Deco building of 1928–30 by *Sir John Brown & A. E. Henson* of Northampton, still miraculously with much of its exterior and interior intact. Low white angled building with a glazed portal and glazed observation tower. The AVIATOR HOTEL opposite incorporates the original clubhouse of 1933–4. Hanger buildings were erected 1938–40. The interiors of both were skilfully restored to their Art Deco form 2001–8 by *Adrian Baynes*.

TANSOR

0090

St Mary. The history of this building is one of the most intricate in the county. It looks more complicated than it is, largely because at the various stages parts of the preceding structure were incorporated into the new building. The history starts with the w tower of the late C11. The body of the church, a nave and aisles, probably of four bays, and a chancel were then rebuilt in the mid C12. The chancel at that time occupied the E sections of the present nave, its division from the nave being marked by a step. A N chapel was added overlapping the chancel in the late C12. Then in the C13 the aisles were rebuilt and extended eastwards, which entailed adjustments to the arcades. The s aisle was especially wide and this seems to be connected with the division of the lordship including the advowson in 1215 (cf. Woodford). By the mid C13 this division was resolved and following the unification the chancel was extended E, and the building resumed a more normal pattern. The only changes then were the rebuilding of the s chapel in the C14 and some changes to roof levels and a new E window in the C15.

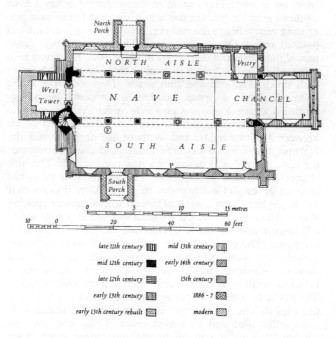

Tansor, St Mary.
Plan

Now for what we see. The W tower is basically CII with two small windows on its N and S sides. The recessed W side was rebuilt at some stage (RCHME say C19). The mid-C12 work is nearly all internal. It consists of the W bays of the arcades, all with round arches, three on the N and two on the S. The capitals all with scalloped decoration. The E respond reused when the arcades were lengthened in the C13. Of the C12 chancel short pieces of wall survive at the E end of the nave, on the S especially with pieces of carved string course with scallop and billet ornament and on the N where there are signs of early windows. Externally, on the N aisle a slim buttress marks the original extent of the building at that time. The tower arch also survives with, to its S, a stair-turret giving access to an upper chamber, whose window looking down into the nave is clear. What was this for? (cf. Brixworth). The late C12 N chapel or vestry is more apparent externally. It has a small lancet under a round arch. Late C12 the N doorway. Two orders, one with shaft-rings and stiff-leaf capitals. Round arch, with rich zigzag decoration, also at right angles to the wall surface. Then comes the C13 extension of the aisles. On the S first, then the N and the partial rebuilding and adjustment to the arcades. The S arcade has wider arches to reach the E line of the vestry, i.e. the link for a new chancel (which is however later; *see* below). The capital of the single pillar has a little nailhead enrichment. On the N side the arcade ran to a pre-existing vestry; hence the odd rhythm of the double-chamfered pointed arches. Of the same time the pairs of lancets in the W part of the S aisle and the lancets in the N aisle. The vestry arch was partly filled in by a wall, and in this is a pretty doorway with much dogtooth and thin shafts. Dogtooth is also the hallmark of the S doorway. In addition however it has a dog-tooth-like zigzag and so may be a little earlier. At the same time the W tower was continued – see the bell-openings with a shaft between the two lights; and as there are no buttresses the Norman tower was considered unsafe and the arch towards the nave was reduced in size by a new narrow arch. The new chancel dates from the later C13. The E window is Perp, but remains of the C13 window can be seen inside. It looks as if this might have been a series of lancets with a circular opening above. The side windows are typical of their date with single tall lancets and on the N intersecting tracery and on the S geometric. There is a DOUBLE PISCINA with openings under a single arch, within which is a tiny niche. The aisle walls also have C13 elements. Inside the S aisle a tomb-recess and a PISCINA halfway along the aisle, marking an altar position. The PISCINA in the S chapel is a made-up affair reusing a late C12 capital. The C14 S chapel is a fine piece of building with some ashlar used and a recessed series of base courses. The window tracery is an odd design, of three stepped lights under one arch, the outer ones with rounded trefoil cusping. It may not be authentic and RCHME suggest it is C19. The church was restored by *Ewan Christian* 1886–7 when some rebuilding of the N and S aisles is recorded. Could he be responsible? There was a further restoration by *Traylen & Lenton*, 1933–5.

FURNISHINGS. – FONT. Plain octagonal bowl supported on octagonal shafts with leaf capitals. On the diagonals, four monstrously big ballflowers, and smaller ballflowers on three edges of the bowl. Early C14. – SCREEN. Against the E wall of the S aisle part of the upper parts of the Perp rood screen with traces of colour. – STALLS. From Fotheringhay. With good MISERICORDS. Some have the fetterlock badge, others have birds and a lady with a horned head-dress. – PULPIT. Jacobean. – RAILS. Early C18. – CHANCEL ARCH, CHOIR STALLS and BENCHES, 1933–5 by *Traylen & Lenton*. The arch is a contrived timber affair with tall side pillars supporting traceried spandrels in the Perp fashion. – ALTAR. Partly made up from some pieces of C17 carving. – STAINED GLASS. Chancel E, 1887 and S chapel E, 1902, both by *Burlison & Grylls*. – BRASS. John Colt, Rector, †1440. The figure is 19 in. (48 cm.) long. Another for Rev. F. Wallis †1919. MONUMENT. John Cave †1821, in a stone frame with tapered fluted pilasters. Signed by *Harrison* of Oundle.

TANSOR COURT, N of the church. The former rectory built 1860–2 by *John Norton*. A large, lavish Gothic house with an elaborate entrance porch and doorway. The garden front has a delightful semicircular oriel with a pointed turret. Later additions in the Elizabethan style, and outbuildings converted into houses.

Pleasant village with many good stone houses, one dated 1651. A pair of Gothic COTTAGES of 1864 by *E. Browning* with Gothic porches (cf. Cotterstock).

Former SCHOOL (Village Hall), 1877 with a bellcote, by *Alfred Sykes* of Peterborough.

LINDEN HALL. On the E edge of the village. An impressive house with an intriguing history. It was originally built 1901–2 as a new rectory by *Talbot Brown & Fisher* in a loose Queen Anne style, a main block with an entrance projection at its r. hand end. This had a doorway with a gently curved canopy and a circular window on its l. side. To the l. of the entrance in the main range a tall window lit a staircase hall. In 1984, after its sale by the Diocese, the house was almost doubled in size by adding on to the r. end of the building by *Chris Fowler*. This was done by adding a further section onto the entrance projection to create what is now a central feature. A second circular window was added on the r. of the doorway and above the r.-hand window became a central window, made taller with a semicircular head, so forming almost a Venetian window effect. The frontispiece rises above the roof eaves with a shaped gable and has lateral pilasters topped by urns. The new r. wing is of two bays matching the rhythm of the earlier building. The present effect, therefore, is perfectly regular with a three-bay entrance frontispiece and two bays on each side. The whole facade has been rendered and the wings also given corner pilasters. Dormers in the deep roof. The result is hugely successful and has given the house a distinct Colonial air of the

kind that Clough Williams-Ellis was so fond. Just to confuse
later architectural historians the 1902 datestone has been reset
into the top of the new gable.

TEETON
1½ m. w of Spratton

TEETON HALL. The origins seem to be a mid-C18 house probably designed by *John Wagstaff* of Daventry for John Langton.*
The s garden side has a well-built quoined ironstone façade of
five bays, a three-bay centre and wide single bays each side,
while the entrance front is brick, chequered red and blue also
with quoins. It has three gables which are alterations or additions of 1879 created by a builder, *W. Smith*, although his
designs are dated 1868. There had been wings added to the
house in the early C19 but these were removed in 1879 and the
house extended E. The entrance front was given Tudor-form
windows at the same time. Inside the plan is odd as the front
door opens into a cross corridor with the rooms opening off
it. Was the house reduced in size perhaps, which would account
for why the two fronts are so dissimilar? Fine original staircase
with slender turned balusters, two twisted and one plain to the
tread. The simple plaster decoration of the stairwell and elsewhere fits with the mid-C18 date. Two good late C18 wooden
fireplace surrounds. There is a low quadrant wall to connect
the house to a range of STABLES, also of chequer brick. The
bell in the stables is dated 1702. There had been an earlier more
rambling house on the site of which there are drawings dated
1738 signed T. Wing.
OLD STONE HOUSE (formerly Teeton Hall Farmhouse). A C17
house with mullioned windows with a small but handsome
front façade added late in the C17. Ironstone, three bays, two
storeys. Stone cross-windows and quoins. Former doorway
with pediment. Fine mid-C17 gatepiers.

THENFORD

ST MARY. Perp w tower with tall transomed bell-openings and
battlements. The rest externally mostly of *c.* 1300. The s
doorway however and the s aisle w and E windows point to a
date of *c.* 1200, and this is borne out by the impressive s arcade.
Octagonal piers, a stiff-leaf capital and a stiff-leaf respond,

---

* The drawing by him at Northampton Record Office does not, however, seem to
relate to the present house, and is more likely a project for a new house of the
c. 1770s.

both with early upright leaves, double-chamfered, pointed arches. The s doorway has a round arch instead and, according to the blank arch visible inside to its w, has been re-set. The N arcade is of *c.* 1300. Octagonal piers and double-chamfered arches, but triple-shafted responds, the middle one with a fillet. The w and NW windows of the aisle have internally corbels with naturalistic foliage. The chancel appears to have been shorter originally (i.e. in the C13) and then was lengthened in the C14, as there is a distinct joint halfway along on the s side. The chancel arch is chamfered and dies into the side walls. There is a rood-loft entrance on the s side. The w tower is Perp. There was a restoration in 1877 of the nave and aisles by *F. Preedy*, and he returned in 1884 and partially rebuilt the chancel. The N porch is dated 1885. – FONT. *c.* 1200 on a C19 pillared base. – SCREEN. Perp; simple, the top renewed. – PEWS. Simple with moulded edges, probably C16. – PULPIT. A made-up piece with some C15 grapevine frieze carving and inset small Jacobean panels at the base. – ALTAR. Also with an inset Jacobean arched panel in the middle. – POOR BOX. A single pillar of wood, iron-bound on the top; of rough workmanship. – TILES. The E end of the s aisle has an old tiled floor, probably C18. There is a painted inscription panel in the N aisle which records the church being 'repaired and beautified' in 1701. Could they be as early as this? – RAILS. Of 1960 of wrought iron with delicately done lilies. They were designed by *G. Forsyth Lawson* and made by *F. Banks* of Westonbirt, Tetbury. – STAINED GLASS. In the N aisle E window some very good early C15 glass (St Christopher and St Anne with the Virgin). They are both beautifully drawn, damaged though they are. The St Christopher shows him wading the stream with fishes around his foot, and a tiny gold tree on the l. Crowns in the border. – A s aisle window has some border pieces, an IHC roundel, C15, and some fragments from a coat of arms, C16. – MONUMENT. Fulk Wodhull, 1613. Recumbent effigy in a recess with a depressed arch, with head within leaves in the spandrels. It is coffered underneath. Flanking coupled fluted columns of the Composite order. A frieze with bunches of fruit and more heads and strapwork along the base. The effigy has slight traces of colour and is carved from a soft chalky stone. The whole is quite impressive but rustic in quality. – In the churchyard, s of the chancel, a tall square memorial for the Rev. Edward Ellis †1823.

THENFORD LODGE (s of the church). Substantial stone house of 1885 with half-timbered gables. It was extended in 1911. It may be the work of *John Alder*, Preedy's assistant.

THENFORD HOUSE. Begun 1761, according to a handwritten inscription on an engraving of the bibliophile Michael Wodhull (†1816), who built the house and was twenty-one when he started. It was structurally complete in 1763, though more work went on until 1765, the date on a lead rainwater tank. The house is of fine quality, but decidedly conservative for its date, not only because its decoration is still Rococo without a touch of the new Adam style, but even more because of its strange twin hipped roofs with a cupola or belvedere in between, of the kind fashionable in 1650–80 or 90. The puzzle of Thenford is its designer. A surviving account book running from 1763 to the early 1770s has large payments to 'Mr *Barnard* on account in part for the building' but it is not clear just who Mr Barnard is. The two John Barnards recorded by Howard Colvin somehow do not seem to fit. It is quite likely that Wodhull himself contrived the design, hence its unorthodox appearance. What is clear is that the craftsmen involved in the building were all local, with the exception of the plasterer *Thomas Roberts* of Oxford. The house has several splendid wooden fireplaces with carved flowers and other decoration, all done in the manner of the designer *Abraham Swan*, who is known to have been involved nearby at Edgcote. The fitting up of the house went on into the late 1760s with the furnishers *Say & Kay* of London being used.

The house, built of Hornton stone with lighter limestone dressings, probably from Culworth, is two storeys high on a semi-sunk basement, with a quoined centre of seven bays, then one-storey three-bay linking walls, and then lower three-bay pavilions. Outside these another three bays of the same walls. The walls have blank arches and the pavilions a centre pediment and half-pediments leaning against the centre. The principal block has an open stair up to a doorway with Tuscan columns, a metope frieze, and a pediment, alternating pediments and balcony-like balustrades to the three middle windows on the first floor, and a three-bay pediment with a cartouche. The two hipped roofs looking a little odd to the l. and r. of this. The garden side is simpler, with two canted bay windows. No doorway here but stepped access from the bays.

Entrance hall and Saloon in the middle axis. In the entrance hall a beautiful stone fireplace with long slender brackets set frontally as well as in profile. In the Saloon the windows are accompanied inside by volutes. Good Rococo plaster cornice and fine wooden fireplace. The cornice in the drawing room with delicious flower garlands is an especially fine example of Roberts's work. Excellent wooden fireplace with carved details. The dining room was originally part of Wodhull's library and though its fireplace dates from the 1760s its ceiling cornice is later, either C19 or even early C20. The grand staircase has two slender turned balusters to the tread, starting in bulbous shapes at the bottom. The tread-ends are carved, and a running Greek frieze accompanies them diagonally. Set into the floor is a fine Roman mosaic with a centrepiece of Ceres, taken from the Roman villa site excavated E of the house in 1971–3. The building dated to *c.* A.D. 300 and had six rooms.

The first floor has been altered and partly subdivided. It has a central corridor with a large fitted cupboard. The room on the s side, referred to in the account book as 'my Wife's dressing room', has a fine plaster ceiling with a pretty Rococo centrepiece. The cupola lights a sizeable attic room which may have been for billiards. This and other attic rooms have late C16 or C17 panelling from the earlier house. There is further evidence of this in reused mullioned windows at the back of the wings. Their mouldings are apparently late C17. The right-hand pavilion was converted into a galleried library by *Quinlan Terry* in 1994.

The grounds have been much enhanced since the 1980s with lakes and a spectacular arboretum. To the E of the house a SUMMERHOUSE in the Palladian manner, 1981–2 by *Quinlan Terry*. Of Hornton and Clipsham stone, with a pedimented three-bay centre. Half-engaged Composite fluted columns and round-arched glazing. The wings have Corinthiam fluted pilasters and one bay has a further round-arched window while the end bay has a niche and rustication.

THORNBY

ST HELEN. Only of slight architectural interest. W tower, nave and chancel. The tower is unbuttressed, probably C14, with C15 battlements. Some Perp windows remain. N aisle added and chancel rebuilt by *E. F. Law* in 1870. Arcade arches with alternating courses of limestone and ironstone. Rather good TILES in the sanctuary and edging the steps. These and the REREDOS, ALTAR and ROOFS all of 1870. – FONT. Circular, Norman, with saltire crosses, interlace, and (re-cut) leaves. – STAINED GLASS. Chancel E of 1867 and S of 1884 by *Heaton, Butler & Bayne*. – N aisle window of 1904 by *J. Powell & Sons*.

THORNBY HALL, Naseby Road. A large house in a grand setting. Formerly Elizabethan and traditionally where Cromwell spent the night before Naseby. However, the house was transformed and enlarged between 1921 and 1925 for Captain A. S. Wills by *Charles S. Mordaunt* who acted as resident architect. Some additions had already been made around 1873 by *George Hart*. The house is built of ironstone in the Tudor style. It has irregular fronts, with many gables and bays. The entrance is into a small court through gatepiers between two square gazebos. It is a perfect example of its period with grounds to match.

THE MANOR HOUSE, Naseby Road. Mid-C18 chequer brick, with Regency period windows. Earlier work in the basement and behind built of ironstone.

STONE HOUSE, on the main road. Very attractive. Of *c.* 1700, with additions. The front is of five bays and two storeys with rusticated quoins and platband. Wooden cross-windows. Eared door surround with pediment converted into a window. Considerably tidied *c.* 1900.

THORNBY GRANGE, ¾ m. SW. Built 1911–12 for W. H. St John Mildmay by *J. A. Gotch*. Large, Neo-Stuart, of rendered brick. Seven-bay façade between two gabled wings. The interior, altered in 1920, also by Gotch, has been considerably changed.

THORPE ACHURCH

ST JOHN BAPTIST. Externally an almost total Victorian appearance, but much survives of the medieval church, which was of transept plan. Late C13 W steeple. Spire with broaches and two tiers of lucarnes. W doorway with finely moulded segmental arch. Lancet windows and quatrefoiled circular windows. Bell-openings with Y-tracery and a circle in the spandrel fitted with three cusped spherical triangles. Similar the S transept S window. Here the lights have in their heads pointed trefoils, but the circle is normally quatrefoiled – i.e. *c.* 1300. The chancel buttresses also seem to be of *c.* 1300. They have at their top tiny blank arches with the Y-motif. Inside, the tower arch is triple-chamfered with the inner chamfer on headstops. The N transept arch is also on head corbels. The E respond has good upright early stiff-leaf of *c.* 1200. The S transept arch also looks original. The rest, notably the arcade with its sturdy stiff-leaf capitals, is all of the restoration by *W. Slater* of 1862–3. He did more work in 1874. There was a further refitting in 1912 when the C15 style reredos and the choir stalls were installed. – STAINED GLASS. Three windows by *J. Powell & Sons*, all 1897: chancel E, chancel S and S transept, for the 4th Lord Lilford, a renowned ornithologist, with two angels and birds in the border. – N chapel, *c.* 1862 by *M. & A. O'Connor*. – MONUMENTS. Several including Arthur Elmes †1663 (under the tower). Large alabaster tablet. Inscription in big oval wreath. Skull and bones below, cherub's head above. – Sir Thomas Powys †1719 of Lilford Hall (S transept). By *Robert Hartshorne*. Big standing monument with detached Corinthian columns and an open segmental pediment. Big asymmetrical drapery falling over it, which a putto is desperately trying to hold. The deceased semi-reclining and wearing a wig. Religion on r. and Eloquence on l. standing outside the columns. (Both monuments from the demolished Lilford church – *see* below.) Fine series of ledger slabs in S transept, 1719–82. – Charles and Henry Powys †1804 and 1812. With a military still-life below the inscription. – Henrietta Maria Powys †1820. With a still-life of books, chalice and dish below the inscription. Thomas Lord Lilford †1800 by *Sir Richard Westmacott*. Nothing special. – Thomas Atherton Powys †1882 with a marble portrait medallion. – LYCHGATE of 1896.

Below the churchyard to the SW the re-erected remains of LILFORD CHURCH, which was demolished in 1778. They have been assembled picturesquely but hardly correctly, and show early C14 semi-quatrefoiled responds.

OLD RECTORY. The SE part is of 1633. In the centre a two-storeyed porch, at the ends two-storeyed bay windows. Mullioned windows. The NW part is C18. Some minor additions at the E end by *Lewis Vulliamy* in 1833. Mid-C19 alterations by *W. G. Habershon*.

Much evidence of the Lilford Estate. A former SCHOOL, 1868, with additions by the Estate Surveyor *R. W. Collier* in 1900. A row of seven identical estate cottages of *c.* 1830–40, but now somewhat altered. Opposite them a large WELL-HEAD, 1882–3 also by *Collier*. Like a lychgate, with timber frame whose supports have oakleaf carving and two angels. A memorial for Lord Lilford's son, Thomas Atherton Powys. It continued in use until 1950.

THORPE LUBENHAM HALL

7080

On the Leicestershire border, just S of Lubenham.

The core of the present house is brick and *c.* 1790–1800. The S front still has its two generous semicircular bows. After *c.* 1920 Sir Harold Wernher added the E wing and made other alterations but Viscount Kemsley bought it in the early 1960s and removed considerable portions of the E and W wings in the 1970s. Refurbished in 1985 under the direction of *Keith Cheng*. In 2008–9 the entrance front was given a Tuscan portico, balustrades were added to the parapet and the E wing was improved following designs by *Kavan Brook Shanahan*. Throughout these phases of alteration the Georgian character has been maintained.

On the N edge of the park is the site of the hamlet of Thorpe Lubenham and below it a large MOAT, still water-filled, which was until the late C18 the site of the earlier manor house. It was largely timber-framed and was still standing when Nichols published his *History of Leicestershire* in 1798.

THORPE MALSOR

8070

ST LEONARD. Of ironstone. Chiefly late C13 and early C14. A lavish restoration in 1877 by *Clapton Rolfe*; carving by *Harry Hems* for the Maunsell family. The N chapel was formed at this time, out of an older vault. Late C13 in style, but externally a later trefoil frieze at the top. The SEDILIA and PISCINA in the chancel are also late C13 in style, but over-restored. Late C13 W tower (clasping buttresses, pairs of lancets as bell-openings; later quatrefoil frieze and broach spire with two tiers of lucarnes). Dec chancel E window (of four lights consisting of

two two-light parts with cusped Y-tracery and a big quatrefoiled top circle – all lights being ogee-arched; cf. Geddington)
and N aisle windows. They are somewhat unusual: of two lights,
straight-headed, with reticulation at the top. One has ballflower
all along its frame – also internally – the other a hoodmould
with dogtooth. Much of this is renewed, but it seems correct.
The s side much altered and made more 'interesting' in 1877.
s porch, with a very E.E. interior, vaulted with much dogtooth.
Attached on the W a vestry and a picturesque turret, all again
in the E.E. style. Inside, the N arcade is of three bays and has
quatrefoil piers and double-chamfered arches. The s arcade,
also of three bays, has the usual octagonal piers and double-
chamfered arches. That goes with the ballflower windows. The
N chapel has two arches separated by a piece of wall and a W
arch on head corbels. The windows, though much renewed,
indicate again a date about 1300. – FONT. Octagonal, C14. With
crocketed ogee arches. C19 base. PULPIT. 1977, painted and
gilded with figures of four Evangelists and the Virgin. – ORGAN.
A splendid affair, by *Thomas Casson*, with much painting and
gilding. It was made for the s chapel, but found to be too big
and now fills the tower arch. – STAINED GLASS. All by *Ward
& Hughes*, between 1862 and 1892 and of varying quality. By
far the best is the chancel s window with angels, made by them
in 1889.

THORPE MALSOR HALL. Jacobean, on the E-plan, but with all
windows sashed in the C18. The garden (s) side of 1817, ashlar-
faced, with two storeys, a bow window and three bays to its l.
and r.

WELL, in the middle of the main street. Placed in 1589. The
inscription is in Greek.

THORPE MANDEVILLE

ST JOHN BAPTIST. Mostly early C14. Short W tower with pretty
recessed saddleback roof. A small figure high up on the E side.
There is record of *W. E. Mills* of Banbury partly rebuilding this
in 1898. s doorway with an ogee hoodmould on headstops. In
the chancel, windows of *c.* 1300 and a lowside lancet with a
transom. Dec N aisle windows, shafted inside. Three-bay Dec
N arcade with octagonal piers and double-chamfered arches.
The chancel restored by *A. Hartshorne*, 1872. Of this date and
made by *J. Powell & Sons* the REREDOS, designed by Hartshorne, with its painted ceramic and mosaic panels, and the
ceramic panel of St Nicholas on the s wall. Floor TILES also
of the period. The ALTAR is carved wood and was installed in
1899. Inset panels for the Evangelists. – WALL PAINTING. A
confused fragmentary panel in the N aisle, C14 or C15, incorporating a St Christopher. – STAINED GLASS. All the windows
by *Powell & Sons*. The chancel windows designed by *H. Burrow*,

1872, and the N aisle windows by *C. Hardgrave*, 1884. – MONU-
MENT. Thomas Kirton, Common Serjeant to the City of
London, †1601, and wife, †1597 (his date of death is added
later). Of freestone. Long relief with kneeling figures against a
background of six dainty arches. Frieze of light foliage scrolls
below. Tapering caryatids l. and r. Achievement in an open
scrolly pediment. On the pediment two reclining figures (cf.
Nether Heyford, Charwelton and Harrington). The quality is
good but not as fine as the alabaster memorial at Harrington,
but an attribution to the *Hollemans* workshop is appropriate.

MANOR HOUSE, E of the church. A very fine *c.* 1700 S front of
five bays and two storeys with quoins, also to the three-bay
centre. Over this an excessively large broken segmental pediment – an Archer-like motif. Doorway with open scrolly pediment. Handsome but provincial in quality. Large C19 extension
to the N. Good panelling inside, one room having Corinthian
pilasters, and a staircase with twisted balusters two to the tread
and carved tread-ends. The interior was modified *c.* 1936 by
Oliver Hill, when the pillared entrance hall was created. STABLE
BLOCK with rusticated archway under a pediment and two bay
wings. Both have quoins.

THORPE MANDEVILLE COURT. Formerly the rectory. The late
C17 house was grandified following its sale by the Ecclesiastical
Commissioners in 1923 giving it rather a Tudor effect. Wings
with square bays and mullioned windows with hoodmoulds.

THE HILL, 1 m. W. By *C. F. A. Voysey*, 1897–8. Built for Mr
Hope Brooke of the family of the Rajahs of Sarawak. Very
typical of Voysey with its pebbledash, its happily informal composition, its battered buttresses at the corners, its wooden
veranda on one side, and the way in which the screen wall on
the r., with its brick coping rising above arched entrances, cuts

Thorpe Mandeville, The Hill.
1898

off one bay of the house. The porch leads direct into the dining hall, which goes across the house. Adjoining to the s was the ladies' drawing room, to the N on the E side the study and then kitchen and offices.

THORPE WATERVILLE

THORPE CASTLE HOUSE. Licence to crenellate was given to the Bishop of Lichfield in 1301. The castle was, it seems, little more than a fortified manor house. The house now is partly C17 but considerably altered and added to in the C19 and later. One small lancet window reused. Big BARN with two chamfered circular windows in one end gable. In between them a chimneyshaft with octagonal top. Single-framed roof with tie-beams and kingposts with four-way struts. This may well be the hall of the C14 castle.

The hamlet, which was part of the Lilford Estate, has some attractive cottages. The FOX INN, on the main road, was rebuilt in 1895 by *S. F. Halliday* for the estate in the Tudor style.

BRIDGE over the Nene, w of the village. Early C14. With ribs under the arches, three straight across and two oblique. Widened on both sides.

THRAPSTON

ST JAMES. Dec w tower with doorway of continuous mouldings, frieze of cusped lozenges, battlements, and a recessed spire with three tiers of lucarnes. The nave and aisles rebuilt 1841–3 by *Bryan Browning* of Stamford. They are of nearly the same height. Dec chancel with two-light reticulated side windows, made longer and given transoms by Browning, and a five-light E window with reticulated tracery, also made higher in the 1840s. The round-headed priest's doorway and the string course which runs round it must belong to the early C13 predecessor of the present chancel. Inset into the N wall some fragments of chevron ornament which also come from the earlier building. Below the SE window SEDILIA with ogee arches, their tops cutting into the window. DOUBLE PISCINA with blank quatrefoil in a circle. Organ chamber and vestry, 1888 by *T. G. Jackson*. The interior open and broad and made lighter by some gentle reordering, notably the removal of pews. Arcades with tall quatrefoil piers with shaft-rings. Three wooden galleries supported on extra cast-iron pillars with amusing heads. – PULPIT with finely carved grapevine frieze. Dated 1910, given by *T. G. Jackson*. Elegant chancel FURNISHINGS by Jackson, 1902. Stalls with poppyheads. Black-and-white marble floor. The E end PANELLING is also by Jackson, 1920, with carved work by *Farmer & Brindley*. – Perp style SCREEN by *Leslie Moore*, 1929. – STAINED GLASS. Chancel E window by *Wailes*, 1863. – S window of 1872 by *Heaton, Butler & Bayne*. – WASHINGTON ARMS (by the tower arch). Carved stone, brought from Montague House (*see* below). – MONUMENTS. Elizabeth Darnell †1831. By *Physick*. Woman seated on the ground and holding a medallion. – In the churchyard, on the S side a C15 tomb with traceried sides and shields, possibly for a member of the De Vere family. A very pretty slate stone on the S wall for Sarah Adderley †1780.

BAPTIST CHAPEL, Huntingdon Road. The old front of 1787–91 still survives, in spite of mid-C19 additions. Red brick. Four bays, two storeys, arched openings. Doorways in bays one and four. The interior was modified by *Lawson Carter* in 1938.

METHODIST CHAPEL, Market Road. 1885 by *Charles Saunders* of Gotch & Saunders, of red brick with a large pediment supported by pilasters with fluted tops. Round-arched doorway.

EAST NORTHAMPTONSHIRE COUNCIL OFFICES. Incorporating the WORKHOUSE of 1836 by *Donthorn*. A long stone façade with wings and a central projecting block with a large first-floor window and a shafted gable – typical Donthorn. Behind, the former INFIRMARY block of red brick, quasi rather bland Queen Anne of 1897–1908 by *Blackwell & Thomson*. Complex enlarged with a new Council Chamber 1992–5 by *Pick Everard* of Leicester. Alongside, SWIMMING POOL by *Studio Bednarski*, 2002–6. Swooping roof-lines and blue glass. Eight timber columns which the firm describes as 'the Thrapston Order'.

KING JOHN SCHOOL, Market Road. Originally a National School of 1851 by local builder *Walter Parker*, enlarged 1881 and 1895. The present building is largely a reconstruction, first by *J. T. Blackwell* in 1906–7 and again in 1930. Much ornamentation has disappeared such as a bellcote which sat on the r. side of the large front wing.

PERAMBULATION. Thrapston at its centre is a modest market town with a largely Georgian air. A good deal has been done in recent years to revive the character of the streets. There are no houses of major interest, although the following are worth a look.

At the beginning of the HUNTINGDON ROAD, facing up Oundle Road, the former VICARAGE. The W wing of late C17 origin but the main house in the Tudor style is by *W. J. Donthorn*, 1836–7. Good carved figures in the cornice. E along Huntingdon Road, on the l. is THE COURT HOUSE INN, Tudor Gothic of 1870, built, as its plaque states, as a police station. Then THRAPSTON HOUSE, built it is said in 1805 but with a date of 1842 on the wing, which probably also fits the façade. Of three tripartite bays with a porch with fluted Ionic columns. Just beyond BELMONT HOUSE, a nice Early Georgian house, set back from the road. Now back in the HIGH STREET, on the N side where the road widens into an informal square, the entrance to the former CORN EXCHANGE, a conversion of a Georgian inn. Three bays and two storeys, with an open pedimented doorcase enclosing a wheatsheaf. Another entrance alongside with a heavy doorway with Tuscan columns inscribed 'erected in 1850'. Above it a wooden wheatsheaf and plough. Conversion by *Freeman Roe* of the Strand, London. Further on, on the s side of the Market Place, OAKLEIGH HOUSE, handsome C18, two storeys and dormers, red brick front, five bays. Windows with keystones, doorcase with fluted pilasters. Opposite in CHANCERY LANE several pleasant Georgian houses, some with bow windows, including MONTAGUE HOUSE. Reputedly the home in C17 of Sir John Washington. Pleasant Georgian interiors with some panelling and staircase. The Montague is nothing to do with Montagu of Boughton but an C18 Mrs Montague, a descendant of Washington (*see also* the church).

At the w end of town, the BRIDGE across the Ise brook. Of nine arches, largely medieval, widened later, and much altered with the arches rebuilt in brick. Some stone cutwaters remain. Just by the bridge HOUSING begun 2005 by *Westbury Homes* with a nice selection of stone and brick houses, even a mock warehouse by the bridge. Not quite Poundbury, but intelligent.

RAILWAY VIADUCT. 1920 for the Midland Railway. Nine arches of blue brick. The STATION, one of the most picturesque of *J. Livock*'s Neo-Tudor stations, was demolished in 2009.

THURNING

ST JAMES. Norman chancel arch, narrow, with short semicircular responds with four-scallop capitals. The arch has only one slight step. N arcade of two bays, *c.* 1200. Circular pier, circular capital and abacus. Double-chamfered round arch, the outer chamfer with an applied roll. A w bay was added a little later, beyond the line of the Norman w wall, but this was demolished at the time of the drastic restoration by *Carpenter & Ingelow* in 1880–1, when the church received its w face with a small spired bell-turret. The E respond of this added bay has nailhead. s aisle of *c.* 1300, see the E window (two pointed-trefoiled lights and two pointed trefoils over) and the arcade with a quatrefoil pier with fillets and double-hollow-chamfered arches. The w pillars of the arcades are now clumsily incorporated within the C19 wall. Of the C14 the chancel s windows with flowing tracery and the odd N chapel openings towards the chancel. They are a composition of two doorways of different size and an arch. All have continuous mouldings with one wide chamfer with a hollow set in it. Could the wide arch have been an Easter sepulchre perhaps? The SEDILIA are only two seats with a stone arm between, placed below the three-light s window. – PULPIT. Plain; Jacobean. – FURNISHINGS. The result of attempts by the Rev. H. B. Gottwaltz, inducted 1899, to introduce High Church liturgy. The nave has panelled pews, the chancel arch an odd screen, almost Eastern European in design, and behind it stalls like a college chapel. Most of the woodwork painted a dark, almost black, green, but the screen and chancel have much Morris type decoration. There are even Morris curtains. In the vestry more woodwork including a covered staircase giving access to the organ loft, which is inserted above the chancel arch. A date of 1902 is recorded with the architect *W. H. Fawcett* of Cambridge. It is a most unusual ensemble. – STAINED GLASS. Chancel E, 1874.

TIFFIELD
6050

ST JOHN. Small. Unbuttressed Dec w tower. The body of the church all renewed, the S aisle and porch in 1859 by *E. F. Law*, the rest in 1873 by *T. H. Vernon*. The original gable cross from the E end re-set in the S wall. Early C13 N arcade. Three bays. Circular piers with octagonal abaci and single-chamfered arches. – FONT. Circular, Norman, with upside-down lunettes beaded along the rim and filled with leaves. Leaves also in the spandrels below. The same design as at Paulerspury. – STAINED GLASS. Chancel, E 1873 and S 1893 both by *Jones & Willis*. – S aisle w, 1860s by *Clayton & Bell*. – Coats of arms by *Monastery Glass*.
PRIMARY SCHOOL, High Street South. 1860–70 by *T. H. Vernon*. Gothic, brick with schoolroom with two-light window with circle above and a porch with stepped gable. Some patterning. The school house simpler.
ST JOHN'S CENTRE (Northants County Council), ½ m. E. Founded as a reformatory in 1856. Some excellent buildings by *James Crabtree*, 1960–3, consisting of a series of two-storey brick pavilions with shallow hipped roofs, pleasantly grouped down a gentle slope. Those at the top near the road are entered at first-floor level. Extensions called THE GATEWAY SCHOOL, 2006–8 by *PDD Architects* of Milton Keynes. Steel frame construction with three curved wings of one storey converging on a two-storey administrative unit on a triple-looped plan.

TITCHMARSH
0070

A large village with a good selection of thatched stone cottages. A small green in the centre of the village and a large green space to the W of the church affording splendid views of the church tower.

ST MARY. There cannot be many churches in England whose churchyards have as their boundary a ha-ha. There certainly are not many churches either which can boast of a tower like

32   the tower of Titchmarsh. F. J. Allen calls it 'the finest parish
church tower in England outside Somerset' and it is indeed
very Somerset in manner, most notably the way the parapet is
done. Not the usual battlements but openwork pointed gables.
The best comparison is with Huish Episcopi, near Langport.
A bequest of stone in 1474 gives the date and the splendour is
doubtless due to the Lords Lovel, who owned the manor and
had a castle here, long since demolished. It has set-back buttresses. The base is decorated with three friezes of quatrefoils
one on top of the other, and there are two more higher up and
two friezes of cusped lozenges. On the w side the porch has
quatrefoils in the spandrels. Niches flank it, and there are two
more pairs of niches higher up. The arch towards the nave has
responds with castellated capitals. The bell-openings are pairs
of two-light windows with transom, and on the stage below, on
each side, is one more such window. The crown is sixteen pinnacles of which three on the middles of the sides are set
diagonally with the smaller openwork features in between. The
remaining exterior looks Perp too, with windows of three, four
and even five lights under depressed four-centred heads, but
certain details show that the structure is largely earlier. Of the
C13 are the long chancel with its string course, priest's doorway
and the porch s doorway. Of the C14 are a chancel N window,
the N doorway and the N aisle NW window. Earlier still is the
evidence of the interior. There is a Norman zigzag arch re-set
over the priest's doorway in the chancel. The N arcade and N
chapel arcade are C13 (circular piers and abaci, nailhead
enrichment); the s arcade belongs to the early to mid C14
(circular piers, two with capitals with big individual upright
leaves, naïve and clearly the work of a village mason). Shallow
N transept with a wide arch supported on corbels with foliate
stops. C14 and probably associated with the Lovels. In the s
aisle a low C14 tomb-recess with an elaborate cross coffin slab.
The porch has a chimneystack (Gothic top modern) as the
Pickering family adapted the upper chamber as a family pew.
– FONT. Octagonal, Perp, panelled. – SCREEN and PULPIT.
1926 by *Leslie T. Moore*. Roofs date from the restoration of
1841–2 by *Bryan Browning* of Stamford.* – REREDOS. Rich
alabaster of 1866 with unusual reliefs. Old Testament subjects
not easily identified. On the l. Melchizedek's offering of bread
and wine, and on the r. Abraham offering his son Isaac. –
PAINTED DECORATION in the chancel completed 1895 by
Agnes Saunders, sister-in-law of the Rev. Stopford. Now in
some decay. – STAINED GLASS. Chancel E, 1866 by *J. Hardman
& Co*. By them also the three s windows 1866, 1876, 1879. –
Two small panels by *Kempe* in the s aisle E window, 1890. – w
tower window, a memorial to the Rev. F. Stopford, who was
chaplain to Queen Victoria, 1904 by *J. Hardman & Co*. –
MONUMENTS. Two painted monuments by *Mrs Elizabeth*

* The pews of this date were removed in 2011.

Creed. In the N aisle the Rev. Theophilus Pickering †1710 (her brother). Painted bust on tall pedestal between pilasters and under an arch. Putti at the sides. – In the N transept John Dryden, the poet (her cousin), and his parents, just an inscription panel. Here the bust of the poet at the top is real. – N chapel, members of the Pickering family down to one who †1749. White, grey and pink marble. Column and a broken pediment. Pretty Rococo decoration, including two cherubs' heads. Also Pickering family erected 1698, tablet with floral garlands attributed to *William Woodman* the elder (GF). – S aisle, either side the E window, Major and Mrs Creed †1704 and †1705. Two very tall inscription tablets, l. and r. of the S aisle E window. They are the shape of Dec or Perp niches. Above an urn, below on his side a military trophy, on hers a flower basket. – Colonel John Creed †1751. Coloured marbles by *Edward Bingham* of Peterborough. – Mrs Creed, *c.* 1800. By *J. & J. Coles* of Thrapston. A plain white urn on a black base, set against the window. – WAR MEMORIAL. 1920 by *J. A. Gotch.*

OLD RECTORY, S of the wide green W of the church. 1861 by *Edward Browning.* Large, a mixture of Gothic and Tudor.

PICKERING ALMSHOUSES. On the S side of the church and the green. 1756. Of one storey with dormers. Extensions l. and r., 1857 and 1863.

Although plenty of stone houses only one or two of any quality. In HIGH STREET, TUDOR COTTAGE, one house now but originally three. Ashlar facade with fine four light stone Mullioned windows each with central king mullion. Thatched with evidence on the gables of original height. Beautifully restored stonework. BROOK FARM off High Street. Dated 1628, enlarged in the later C18. Traditionally the home of the Dryden family. In CHAPEL LANE the former WESLEYAN CHAPEL of 1871 of yellow brick with red brick bands and a large wooden Gothic window in its gable. On the same side at the E end YEOMAN'S COTTAGE with a datestone in the gable of 1712. Stone surrounds with hoodmould and king mullion inset with modern small sashes. The gable of the adjoining cottage on the r. has a nice carved obelisk shape finial. These both must be late C17 in essence, although the 1712 date makes one wonder.

CASTLE SITE. Lovel family from mid C13. Licence to crenellate was granted in 1304 but it was ruinous by 1363. A series of mounds and ditches on the SW side of the High Street is all that survives.

TOWCESTER 6040

Towcester is a relatively small town on the Watling Street. It first came into prominence in the Roman period under the name

Lactodorum (see p. 624) and elements of the circuit of the town walls are still traceable. In the time of Alfred the Great Towcester became a frontier town with Watling Street acting as the division between Wessex and the Danelaw. In the late C11 or C12 a large motte-and-bailey castle was established but this appears to have been short-lived. It was only in the C18 that Towcester became a fashionable place with the establishment of several coaching inns, the Saracen's Head, the Talbot and the White Horse. With the arrival of railways Towcester's fortunes declined and it became a simple market town. Today, with the bypass A43 and A5, it has resumed its quiet, gentle atmosphere.

The town has a selection of decent buildings ranked along Watling Street. While there are few outstanding examples, what survives is in scale and reflects the importance of the town as a stopping place for the coach trade. Towcester is also one of the few Northamptonshire towns where there is evidence of timber-framed buildings, albeit of minor importance and largely fragmented and hidden behind later shopfronts. Another feature is a number of alleys and passages between houses leading to yards and rows of cottages (Spring Gardens, for example).

ST LAWRENCE. Moderately large town church. Ironstone. Major rebuilding following a grant of stone from Whittlebury quarries by Edward IV in 1483. Proud Perp w tower with a doorway decorated with fleurons on the jambs and arch and a frieze of panelling above. Tall arch into the nave. The interior of the church over-restored following a series of C19 restorations (*D. G. Squirhill* 1835, *E. F. Law* 1848, but more obviously *J. L. Pearson* 1882–3). Of the 1480s period the aisle windows, not the normal Perp but three-light openings with cusped heads. At this period the arcades were heightened reusing C14 chamfered shafts and also three late C12 capitals, of which one (s) has the unmistakable waterleaf motif. Clerestories were also added to both nave and chancel. The chancel is, however, largely Dec, with its E end raised up to accommodate an unusual crypt. C14, like a small chapter house, with vaulted ceiling, central pier and seats round the walls. The church before 1883 had no chancel arch (engravings in the church) and Pearson introduced the C13-style arch which incorporates two thin Norman shafts with zigzag and lozenge decoration. The chancel chapels are both of two bays and both C13, that on the s with a circular pier with four circular shafts in the diagonals, that on the N with an octagonal pier. Dec also the s doorway with many fine continuous mouldings. ROOD-LOFT STAIRS in both N and S aisles, showing that originally the screen continued across the whole church. A type more familiar in the West Country but seldom seen in this region. A good deal was done in the C17 with a s aisle beam dated 1612 and the chancel roof, 1640, given by Sir Robert Banastre of Passenham (q.v.). There was also a w gallery put up in 1627 and panels from this were worked up in the C19 to create the PULPIT and s aisle reredos. The nave ROOF was rebuilt during the restoration of 1957 by *G. Forsyth Lawson*. It has heavy tie-beams whose ends are masked by bold feathery decorations suggestive of wings, which conceal lights. – FONT. C14 Restored stem with nodding ogee arches supporting the bowl, which has simple panelling.* – WALL PAINTING. Large pelican, probably C15, in an ogee-headed niche in the S chapel, and on the N wall a crowned female figure. – CHANCEL TILES. *Minton*, after designs by *Pugin*. – STAINED GLASS. Assembled old bits in the S aisle E window including C15 Sponne arms, brought from the Talbot Inn. – Chancel E window, 1898 by *H. Hymers*. – S chapel, Transfiguration, 1879 by *H. Hughes*. – S aisle, two windows by *Ward & Hughes*, 1875 and 1879, another of 1888 by *A. L. Moore*. – Another at W end by *H. Hymers*, 1895. – Tower W, 1968 by *Agnes Charles* of Condicote, Herts. Two other windows by her in the S porch. – MONUMENTS. Archdeacon Sponne, rector 1422–48. Of table type. On the ground, within an arcade a gisant or cadaver, on the top an effigy, much over-restored. Unusual in that he is dressed as a cathedral canon. The head and hands partly redone in wood. A bad C19 recolouring was removed in 1985. – Jerome Fermor (Hiero Farmore) †1602 and wife. Small, with kneeling figures, but of fine quality. Attributed to *Jasper Hollemans*, author of the big Fermor tomb at Easton Neston (q.v.). – Several other C18 wall monuments. Within the S chapel Mary Hodges †1759, its surround signed by *Middleton* of Towcester.

ST THOMAS MORE (R.C.), Meeting Lane. Former Congregational chapel of 1845 by *T. H. Vernon*. Ironstone and brick with an arcaded side façade and entrance front with stone doorcases and a later brick pediment.

WESLEYAN CHURCH, Brackley Road. 1893 by *H. H. Dyer*, of stone, in his Geometrical Decorated manner.

TOWN HALL, The Square. By *T. H. Vernon*, 1865. Italianate with a central tower and a spirelet on a leaded dome. It was restored by him following a fire in 1880.

p. 622

SOUTH NORTHAMPTONSHIRE COUNCIL OFFICES, off Brackley Road. 1982 by *D. F. Adams*, with opposite a LEISURE CENTRE by *Graham Lambert Partnership*, opened 1992.

SPONNE SCHOOL, Brackley Road. 1925–8 by *Blackwell & Riddey* of Kettering, replacing a building of 1890 destroyed by fire. Red brick with a central section with the entrance between pedimented wings. Reception block by *Gotch, Saunders & Surridge*, 1993–5.

POLICE STATION, Watling Street. 1936 by *G. H. Lewin*. Surprisingly large, and with its symmetry and Tudor style looking like a grammar school of between the wars.

MOORFIELDS (Sponne & Bickerstaffe Charities almshouses), Buckingham Way. 1985. A long low range in brick with a central water and clock tower and a two-storey house by the road.

---

* The splendid organ purchased by the 3rd Earl Pomfret from the Beckford sale in 1817 was damaged by fire in 1976 and has been placed in the Victoria and Albert Museum to await restoration.

Towcester, Town Hall.
Engraving

Former WORKHOUSE, Brackley Road, now residential. 1836 by
G. G. Scott. Ironstone, still late classical in composition and
detail. Quite unadorned.

BURY MOUNT, E of Watling Street. A large motte, remains of a
late CII or CI2 castle, built more to show power rather than
for defence. It was planted with pine trees in the CI8 to act as
an eyecatcher from Easton Neston. Restored by *Camlin Lons-*
dale, 2009–10, and given a spiral walkway with Towcester date-
line paving, and a stairway giving access via a quasi-Chinese
bridge to the water meadows of Easton Neston park. TOW-
CESTER MILL, a former watermill, dates from 1794, with later
extensions.

Excavations in the 2000s during restoration of the medieval
motte, Bury Mount, located a Roman building with a hypocaust, and a fragment of Roman pavement can be seen next
to the boiler room of St Lawrence's church.

PERAMBULATION. It is worth starting on WATLING STREET
about ¼ mile S of the Square, at the junction of Vernon Road,
by the former MISSION HALL of 1878. Rubble ironstone with
red brick surrounds, nicely converted so the arched windows
now form a glazed arcade. Further N on the E side the large
former BAPTIST CHAPEL (now flats), 1877 by *J. Ingman*, again
red and yellow brick, with a triple-arched façade. Just before
this, the quaint MONK & TIPSTER restaurant (in the CI9 Sun
Inn). Ironstone with a central turret dated 1650, later added
to on either side. Over the Silverstone Brook the road widens
and set back on r., on the site of a brewery, is MALTHOUSE
COURT. An English Courtyards Association development of
1988 by *Sidell Gibson Partnership*. Dark Hornton stone front-

age, with pediment centre and prominent dentil cornice. Through the arch an attractive wide grass plot lined with houses in the almshouse tradition. Some pleasant stone and brick houses follow, then an interesting example of an early 1900s GARAGE and workshop (Silverstone Recovery). Corrugated iron walls with large multi-pane windows. Timber façade with minuscule bargeboard. It needs to be preserved. The road now narrows with on the l. a fine Early Georgian house (No. 157). Ironstone, with three floors divided by platbands, arched windows with keystones, the centre projecting. The original door surround inset with a later door and fanlight. Next the long dark red brick façade of the former WHITE HORSE INN, said to date from *c.* 1770. Three floors with serrated brick storey-bands. Original fenestration. The carriage arch gives into a courtyard with two C19 stone stair-turrets with brick decorations, topped by a curious pierced parapet.

The street now opens up into a wide square with the Town Hall (*see* above) at the s end. On the l. the NATWEST BANK, a proud mid-C19 building of Italianate manner. Then at the SE corner CHANTRY HOUSE (Church Office), traditionally founded by Archdeacon Sponne in 1447 to house clergy. It remains a rare example of a medieval house of this type. The house is set behind a fine stone-coped wall, with an archway giving access. The house has a large room to the r. of the entrance, still with beamed ceiling and stone-arched fireplace (the wooden beam is an introduction). Long side façade with further stone-capped walls. Between the Square and the church, the VICARAGE. Stone, with on its front a small date-stone of 1613 with the initials of Sir Robert Banastre of Passenham, but it was largely rebuilt in 1695 and again in 1804. Rear extension of 1854 by *E. F. Law.* Back on the Square, on the E side is the handsome POST OFFICE. Red brick with dark blue chequer, of three storeys, dated 1799. The centre projects and has its own quoins and pediment. Opposite Elliots (No. 181), a minor example of a jettied shopfront. Dendrochronology suggests *c.* 1604. Further on the same side No. 185, brick painted, with a broad doorcase with coupled Doric pilasters and a metope frieze. This in the C15 was the Angel Inn and roof timbers still remain. Then the SPONNE SHOPPING CENTRE (formerly the Talbot Inn) of 1707. Five bays, two storeys, red brick. Central carriageway and heavy Venetian window of later date when the building was heightened. The windows on the r. still have original glazing. Through the arch the former inn outbuildings on the r. adapted as shops. In No. 8 a carved beam dated 1707 with a relief of a Talbot dog in the centre. Back in the Square, at the corner of Park Street, Nos. 191–193, a pair of shops inserted into a timber-framed façade, probably remains of the C15 Swan Inn. No. 193 still has the jetty beam. Now off to the w into PARK STREET, with some pleasant minor Georgian houses of brick and stone. No. 12 has fire insurance plaques and No. 16 is early C19 with columned doorcase. Further on the l. is OLD MINT HOUSE, a remnant of a large C16 house. Original door. Next, No. 23 has a fine dark ironstone façade, three bays wide, with a central one-bay projection and doorcase, both pedimented. Just on the corner on the r. the former YOUNG MEN'S INSTITUTE of 1903, ironstone rubble and red brick. On its W façade a plaque of 1932 when the fenestration was changed.

Watling Street N of the Square has HSBC (former London, City & Midland) of 1922 by *J. A. Gotch*. Pink Warwickshire stone. Georgian style, with Doric angle pilasters and a half-columned ground floor. It incorporates a building which housed Towcester's earliest bank, founded by John Jenkinson in 1781. Just beyond, No. 124, a small restored timber-framed house with an early C20 tiled overhang to the ground floor. Two large carved wooden animal heads above. Across the street THE SARACEN'S HEAD HOTEL, made famous by Dickens in the *Pickwick Papers*. Long ironstone front, seven bays, two storeys. Carriageway in the middle with arched window over. Two small niches with lead statues. Much atmosphere lost with alterations in recent years, especially in the yard behind.

Former WESLEYAN CHAPEL, Caldecote, 1 m. N. 1846. Charming, red brick on a stone base with two tall pointed windows with Gothic glazing. It now forms part of a cottage row (Chapel Cottage and Chapel House).

DUNCOTE HALL, 1 m. NW. Ironstone of 1902, of moderate size in the Elizabethan style.

TOWCESTER RACECOURSE. *See* Easton Neston, p. 255.

LACTODORUM. The site of a named Roman walled town, bounded on the E by the Tove. The fortifications extend *c.* 500 metres either side of Watling Street and enclosed an area of *c.* 28 acres (11 ha). Only a section to the N, behind the police station, is readily visible as an earthwork. Excavation in the NW corner in the 1950s, as well as more recent work, has shown that the rampart was constructed in the later C2 A.D. and overlay earlier buildings. The fortifications fell into disrepair in the C4. Excavation in the 1990s located the S defences along the N side of Richmond Road. Numerous sites have been examined prior to redevelopment around the town, providing disassociated fragments of the town plan and its extra-mural suburbs.

TWYWELL

ST NICHOLAS. A small church whose development is not totally clear. Essentially it is Norman, but probably of more than one phase. The earliest seems to be the basic structure of tower, nave and chancel. Small simple round-headed windows, two on each side. One window still in the N wall and its fellow to the E surviving as disturbed voussoirs above the later arch.

Then a later phase with two transept chapels being added. The
arch for the S still there. Scalloped capitals. The N arch now
only visible by its outline. Also of this phase the curious refacing of the central section of the nave with ashlar (why?) and
both N and S doorways. N doorway with tympanum on corbels.
In the tympanum diapering in relief (cf. Peterborough Cathedral). S doorway with one order of colonnettes with scalloped
capitals. Arch with zigzag, also set at right angles to the wall
surface (again as at Peterborough Cathedral). Professor Zarnecki compares the big impressive head in the apex and the
corbels of the N door with the Norman doorways at Ely Cathedral. Norman evidence also a window at the W end of the S
aisle (re-set), one chancel window and one window in the
tower. Unmoulded tower arch. The S aisle was added in the
early C13, and the transept arch thereby altered. The aisle is of
two bays and has octagonal piers. W respond with nailhead
enrichment. Double-chamfered round arches. In piers and
arches alternating blocks of ironstone. Much remodelling
c. 1300, i.e. the chancel arch and the chancel windows with
Y- and intersected tracery, the arch from the chancel into a
former S chapel (now vestry), and the S aisle with Y- and
intersected windows. It must be at this time that the N transept
was removed since a window with Y-tracery interrupts the
earlier opening. The S aisle E window is now internal and has
a crenellated transom, now open below. In the chancel a most
interesting EASTER SEPULCHRE consisting of a low segmental
arch on filleted shafts and above it two aumbry doors with a
pitched roof like that of a shrine, but in relief and hence only
half. There were originally pinnacles at the corners. They stand
on small headstops. C15 S porch and clerestory, and Perp tower
top with quatrefoil frieze and pinnacles. It had a spire till 1699,
when it fell, and this accounts for the mis-shaped bell-stage
windows and inset medieval fragments. The S aisle extended
to the W and the N wall of the chancel rebuilt during restoration
in 1867 by the builder *Stephen Brown* of Kettering. – FONT
COVER. Jacobean, very pretty. – STALLS. 1898 to designs of
J. C. Traylen and carved by *H. Hems & Son*, with elaborate
friezes of slaves on one side and African animals on the other.
A memorial to Rev. H. Waller (1835–96), one of the original
members of the Universities Mission to Central Africa founded
in 1859 and a friend of Livingstone whose last journals he
edited when they were brought back to England with Livingstone's body in 1874. – STAINED GLASS. S aisle W: a shield for
England, c. 1390–1415. The label suggests probably for Edward,
2nd Duke of York, killed at Agincourt 1415. All the later
windows, 1905–19, are by *Burlison & Grylls*.

Former RECTORY, SW of the church. Rather big. Dated 1760.
Five bays, two storeys. Centre an unmoulded Venetian window.
Rear façade with round-headed staircase window and two oval
lights either side the doorway.

MANOR HOUSE, W of the church. Dated 1591, but with a small
pre-Reformation chimney. This consists of two small polygons

of diminishing size. Little gabled smoke openings. Small green at the end of CHURCH LANE with house *c.* 1850, bargeboarded dormers, ogee window lintels. Fine cast-iron railings and a lamppost. HOME FARM HOUSE of 1663 is double-gabled. S side with small canted bay. Mullioned windows.

UPPER BODDINGTON

ST JOHN BAPTIST. Perp W tower, perhaps of the same date as the W doorway dated 1629. Inside, an older tower arch. Dec the slender chancel windows, the S transept S window with reticulated tracery, and probably the pretty, straight-headed S and N windows with their small encircled quatrefoils. Four-bay arcades with one round pillar and the others octagonal and double-chamfered arches. Very narrow S aisle. Two tomb-recesses, both of *c.* 1300, that in the N aisle with a cusped and sub-cusped arch, that in the S chapel with some dogtooth enrichment. Its back wall has the remains of two pointed-tre-foiled blank quadrant arches. In the S chapel the rood-loft entrance and two image brackets, but the E window is blocked. There was a restoration in 1874, architect unrecorded. – CHEST. A 'dug-out', iron-bound, on a projecting base with a quatrefoil frieze. Probably C16. – FONT. Octagonal. Probably C17. – STAINED GLASS. Chancel, E 1869 and S 1860s, both by *Heaton, Butler & Bayne.* – S aisle E of 1883 by *Burlison & Grylls.*

OLD RECTORY, N of the church. Of ironstone. Five bays. Quoins, rusticated doorway, central window with carved keystone; *c.* 1680. The third storey was added in the early C19.

DIAL HOUSE, Warwick Road, *c.* 1910. Red brick, partly rendered with a big curved painted sundial. The wing has a bay with a tiny terracotta ornamental opening in its head. Several windows have original glass patterns. Hooded doorway and looped brick garden walls.

MANOR HOUSE, a little S. Early C18 of five bays. Sash windows with keystones and a doorway with a triangular pediment.

UPPER STOWE
Stowe-Nine-Churches

ST JAMES. 1855 by *P. C. Hardwick.* Nave and chancel with extremely steeply pitched roofs. Bellcote at the W end. Lancet windows, five steeply stepped in the E wall. Timber porch. Stencilled decoration, painted roof and tiles in the chancel. – REREDOS painted with passion flowers. – STAINED GLASS. All by *J. Hardman & Co.* 1877–8.

Some COTTAGES of 1853 and 1879, rustic Tudor manner. Near the church CAVALIER COTTAGE, banded ironstone, dated 1653. OLD DAIRY FARMHOUSE opposite has dates of 1685 but was substantially rebuilt in the C19.

UPTON

7060

1½ m. W of Northampton but gradually being engulfed by development. The hall and the church remain separate in the hall park, but for how long?

ST MICHAEL. Just a simple long rectangle with tower, nave and chancel. Odd Norman windows survive in nave and chancel. Norman also the N and S doorways and the priest's doorway, all with shallow-stepped round arches. In the W wall two small lancets crushed by the W staircase projection of the tower. The tower was built into the nave in the C14 as was the chancel with its three-light window topped by a circle with trefoils. However, the side walls have two rather flat Late Perp windows, possibly as late as 1594, the date with Valentine Knightley's initials over the S porch. An interesting three-light Perp wooden window is re-set against the W wall (it came from the S wall of the nave). The church was restored by *Matthew Holding*, 1892–3, and the PULPIT and BENCH-ENDS with heraldic panels are of that date. – SCREEN. A part Perp re-set in the W wall. – REREDOS. 1907–8 but with a fine Art Nouveau plaster St Michael inset by *Jones & Willis*. – STAINED GLASS. Chancel E, 1871 by *O'Connor*, Crucifixion plus panels. – S aisle, Hudson memorial by *Walter J. Pearce*, 1936. – MONUMENTS. Sir Richard Knightley †1537 and wife. Made before his death. Rather battered alabaster effigies. Of the panels facing the tomb-chest only three shield-holding angels remain. – Many tablets, especially Sir Thomas Samwell †1757 by *Henry Cox* (the epitaph should be read), and Thomas Samwell Watson Samwell †1831, erected 1835 by *John Whiting*. Grecian with mourning female and trophies at the top. – Small plaque with an urn for Frances Samwell †1841 by *Austin & Seeley*. – An oval inscription erected 1810 to the memory of the author of *Oceana*, James Harrington †1677.

UPTON HALL (Quinton House School). The Samwells bought Upton in 1600 from the Knightleys of Fawsley, who had owned the house since 1419. The main E façade was built for Sir Thomas Samwell, who, as his memorial in the church states, had been on an extensive grand tour. It is an L-shaped front of three storeys, chequered brick with ironstone dressings of c. 1736–7, and is attributed to *Francis Smith* of Warwick. The main portion is seven bays wide and supposedly three storeys, but the attic, though glazed, is simply a parapet hiding the roof.

It may have been intended to replace the roof at a later date. The central bay, with a pedimented Tuscan doorway, projects slightly, as do the two southern bays. In addition there are niches dividing the first and second and fourth and fifth bays of the central five. These contain somewhat cold Neoclassical statues representing the seasons, of *c.* 1790. The long N wing also has niches, but here they are empty. Rainwater head with the date 1748 and the initials of Sir Thomas Samwell.

The entrance leads into a wide C18 groined vaulted passage running E–W. On the N two small sitting rooms, one with a pretty C18 plaster ceiling, and recesses with garlands below. On the S a tall room rising through two storeys which is clearly the original great hall of the early house. The entrance hall thus must be on the site of the screens passage. Above it is a gallery which looks down into the hall. The hall (now called the BALLROOM) is a splendid apartment with some of the finest Georgian plasterwork in the county. Its end walls are decorated with large Rococo medallions with portrait heads of Roman gods and goddesses, with console brackets below. In the long wall is a tall chimneypiece on whose pediment recline delightful putti holding wheat and grapes on either side of a benign bust of Ceres. Opposite, a tall niche with an elegant life-size statue of Apollo, also in stucco. This is signed by *Giuseppe Artari* and dated 1737, and all the work is indeed in the best manner of the Italian stuccatori. The ceiling, with Greek key borders, may be later. The gallery at the N end has a pretty gilded ironwork balustrade. The two doorcases flanking the fireplace, however, must be later C17 (cf. Webb's work at Lamport). The fireplace has some rather fine Victorian tiles. However, the major evidence for the early dating of the hall is the late medieval roof which survives above the hall ceiling. It is probably reconstructed and has two forms of support alternating: a simple arch-braced construction, and, probably later, a collar with screen-like arcading and curved braces which become quatrefoil shapes at the top of the roof. Dendrochronology has established the date between 1503 and 1529. In the S gable of the hall which survives within the roof-space of the S wing is a blocked four-light window with arched heads and moulded label. To the W another gallery chamber with a fireplace with four-centred head. This SW wing was perhaps added by the Samwells, *c.* 1600, to the earlier hall. The staircase was originally in the NE angle between the main block and the wing, and an early roof survives at the top of the turret space. Kitchens were almost certainly detached at the NW corner of the building where there are in the later block still some early beams.

The rest of the house has been altered at various times. The N front, of two storeys with dormers, is basically C17. Inside is a late C17 staircase with turned spiral balusters. To the W of the hall are some charming Gothick rooms, e.g. the DRAWING ROOM with a grey marble Gothick chimneypiece. Finally the S rooms, which date from *c.* 1808 (rainwater head), although some fitting up was still in process in the 1820s. Between the house and the church a fine series of early C19 Gothic cast-iron AVIARY structures.

UPTON PARK. An expensive-looking and dominant housing development on the rise of the river valley to the w of the w ring road, Upton Way (A5076) and s of the Weedon Road (A4500). The basic concept originates from the late 1990s with a broad master plan created in 2000 by *Quartet*. A number of separate developers are involved with the inclusion of *English Partnerships* and *The Prince's Trust* and from the outset the aim was to build housing which was eco-friendly. The streetscapes are made attractive by the use of SUDS (Sustainable Urban Drainage Systems) which run through the site between the rows of houses, a series of grass hollows and trees, and while some are dry others do hold water. They are crossed by attractive wooden bridges. Many of the houses have minuscule gardens with railings. While there are parking bays on the streets there are also more secure areas behind the blocks.

The earliest housing is at the NE corner of the site around BRUNEL DRIVE, but this pre-dates the master plan and is a predictable plot with detached and semi-detached houses mainly of brick with occasional half-timbered gables. It is from Upton Way that the impact of the more recent development is clear. It has the air of an outer city development with tall three-, four- and five-storey blocks, some glaringly painted white, others of mixed materials with much brick, arranged along a broad angled road, CLICKER'S DRIVE. A good deal of this by *BHC Architects*. The street behind becomes more homely with smaller and more domestic rows of brick terraces, many in a broad Neo-Georgian manner and others with half-timbering in an over-size Edwardian style. The linking green SUDS with their hollows and wooden bridges make a huge contribution to the effect. Clicker's Drive circles round to CLICKER'S PLACE, an open green area with trees and a children's play area. In Mill Pond Drive, SCRIBER'S MEWS has an impressive row with grid façades and a series of small circular wind turbines on the roof-line. Scriber's Drive ends in a central square (still largely empty 2012) which has on its E side UPTON MEADOWS PRIMARY SCHOOL, 2007 by *Johnson Design*. Big triangular centre with curved glazed entrance, lower wings radiating within the gated enclosure. More or less parallel to Scriber's Drive is HIGH STREET, forming at present the southern boundary of the development. It is not a high street in the commercial sense, just a main route. Off the SW corner is PARK VIEW with one of the most striking housing rows. Brick with big gables, many open like wide balconies, the apartments set back within them. They are by *HTA Architects* for *David Wilson Homes*. While there are some basic design effects, Neo-Georgian being the most dominant, the number of variations becomes almost confusing, well designed as they are, and because the population is almost entirely commuter and at present there are no shops, the streets often have an empty look, more like an architect's model rather than somewhere where people live. It is too early to say how successful this development will be. Perhaps once further community facilities are built it will become a more human place, but it feels very artificial at the moment. The main building phases are due for completion in 2013 although this seems optimistic.

WADENHOE

ST MICHAEL. Outside the village perched on a hill above the Nene, with a splendid view down the valley. Very Late Norman W tower, see the bell-openings to the E and a small round-headed window. Others are pointed. At the foot to the N three blank arches, round–pointed–round, with leaf capitals. Later saddleback roof. C13 chancel, see the fenestration and the chancel arch on head corbels – the one a green man, the other the type called in other places the man with a toothache. However, the outer casing is, or was, C18 when the interior was fitted up by Rev. Nathaniel Bridges before 1719, so the windows are suspect. C13 N arcade of three bays. Quatrefoil piers, one with nailhead decoration, the other a frieze of tiny flowers. Double-chamfered arches and water-holding moulded bases. Then of c. 1300 the S arcade. Quatrefoil piers with fillets. One of the capitals and the E respond have big upright leaves, looking almost Art Nouveau. Windows in both aisles C14, simple, of two lights with cusped heads. The N porch has early C19 plaster vault with foliate heads and another green man. A curious early C19 VESTRY on the S of the chancel with a Gothick façade. Two lancets and a niche. – FONT. Circular, C13. Top with a trail of stiff-leaf foliage. Below vertical pairs of flowers and dogtooth. – PULPIT. C18 on a modern stand. – BENCH-ENDS. In both aisles. Perp, simple, with traceried panels, and here and there some leaf carving. – WOODWORK. Portions of linenfold in the chancel and a panel dated 1595 in the S aisle. Otherwise the fittings derive from the restorations of 1844 and 1901. – STAINED GLASS. A few mid-C14 fragments in the S aisle. – N aisle E, memorial for George Ward Hunt, Chancellor of the Exchequer and First Lord of the Admiralty †1879, by *Clayton & Bell*. – All other windows c. 1912, by *Burlison & Grylls*. – MONUMENT. Brooke Bridges †1702. By *E. Stanton* according to Le Neve, but hardly characteristic. Simple pilastered surround and a segmental pediment. Three cherubs' heads at the foot.

A most attractive village with many stone and thatched houses and some sensitive reconditioning and new properties. At the N entrance to the village in Wadenhoe Lane, THE GREEN with a row of six cottages of mixed ironstone and sandstone dated 1865 and by *E. F. Law*. At the top of MAIN STREET, MANOR

FARM with dates 1593, 1653 and 1670. Inside two overmantels which look half a century earlier, one with plaster decoration of oakleaves and fleur-de-lys. C17 barn behind with ball finials on its gables. Just below on the r. THE THATCHED COTTAGE which has a blocked, possibly medieval window in its end wall. At the S end of the street HOME FARMHOUSE, also C17, with mullioned windows, though altered in the C19. At the corner of Mill Lane SOUTH LODGE, with pointed windows and just managing to be Gothic. A canted bay facing up the street. Its W side had a porch but this has been removed. An amusing building looking as if it were a toll house. It is just conceivable that this was designed by *Thomas Hunt* (1737–1816), son of the owner of Wadenhoe House, who had some talent as an amateur architect. Just into Pilton Road, on the S side, a circular DOVECOTE. Research by Brian Giggins suggests it is as late as *c.* 1800 (cf. Eaglethorpe House, Warmington). Further on the l. is the OLD RECTORY of C17 or C18 origin but remodelled by *Bryan Browning* of Stamford in 1834. On the S side, set back in its own grounds, is WADENHOE HOUSE. Slight remnants of a C17 house said to date from 1657 on the S side but now nearly all 1858. The Victorian parts on the W side creating a new entrance front. Neo-Jacobean with interlinked circle balustrading. A large square porch and to its l. a rounded bay. Inside two simple C17 overmantels. A charming LODGE with bargeboarded gables also of the 1850s. Still in Pilton Road, on the E edge of the village, LONGFIELD HOUSE. 1999 in a mixed Jacobean-cum-Georgian manner by the *John Whyte Partnership*. Extensions by the same 2005.

WAKERLEY

ST JOHN BAPTIST (Churches Conservation Trust) Outside the village on a hill. Excellent Norman chancel arch of the style and date of Castor, Peterborough. The bases of the responds have the same flat zigzag pattern and the capitals the same ornamentation with beaded interlace and figures. On the N respond a siege with a castle and knights on horseback, on the S respond foliage trails with monsters. The arch with roll mouldings and broad zigzag (not a Castor motif) has been made pointed but was originally no doubt round. The blind arches to the l. and r. were probably reredoses for side altars. Of the Norman church in addition the corbel table and frieze at the SE corner of the nave, re-set lozenge frieze inside the S chapel, and one shafted clerestory window can still be recognized inside. Good W tower, Dec below (see the tower arch and the W window) and Perp above. Tall two-light bell-openings with transom. Quatrefoil frieze below the battlements, tall recessed crocketed spire with two tiers of lucarnes in alternating directions. The aisles are in a transeptal position and only two bays long. The s arcade is C14, the N arcade C15. C14 N porch and N doorway, C15 chancel. Several two-light square-headed windows of C17 date. – NORTH DOOR. Iron-work, probably C13. – FONT. Late C13 with, on one side, a quatrefoil with leaf and flower motifs, on the second a pointed-trefoiled arch. The other two sides are not visible. – REREDOS. Lavish mosaic and tiles. 1875. – MONUMENT. Richard Cecil, second son of the 2nd Lord Burghley, †1633. No doubt made out of an existing C15 Easter sepulchre. Poor craftsmanship. Tomb-chest. Shallow four-centred arch with thin tracery.

At the E end of MAIN STREET on the s side KEEPERS COTTAGE, c. 1800 two storeys with two window front with Gothick glazing. Central Gothic arched doorway. Hipped roof. Further along the street, set back, is the MANOR HOUSE which also has a Gothick glazed front with a stone stating 'John Archer 1769'. Otherwise altered and added to in the C19. One Gothick fireplace surround inside.

Richard Cecil built for himself a large mansion between the church and the river. Of this house, demolished before 1700, there are some GARDEN REMAINS. A series of mounds, but clear enough to show a quartered parterre in front of the house site.

BRIDGE. Over the Welland, ¼ m. N. Medieval. Five pointed arches, double-chamfered ribs.

KILNS, W of village. Circular, brick. Built 1914–18 for calcining iron ore, but never completed.

WALGRAVE

The name derives from the Walgrave or, as they became, De Waldegrave family, who were to become more prominent later in Suffolk. Ralph Walgrave was granted licence to settle here in 1329.

ST PETER. A relatively simple early C14 church (Ralph Walgrave created a chantry in 1328), which on closer examination seems rather more sophisticated. Of local dark ironstone with lime-stone dressings, and constructed more or less at one period. The w tower was originally free-standing judging from internal buttresses. Three stages with at the top stage angle pilasters edged with slender shafts. Bell-openings of two lights with a quatrefoiled circle. Fine spire with small broaches and two tiers of lucarnes. The fenestration of the church is worth observing. The aisle windows are of two lights, cusped, with a quatrefoil in the head. This is consistent except that at the E end of the N aisle the easternmost window has three lights. The E wall is solid wall and inside it has a recess for an altar. The s aisle has the same arrangement but the E end has been lost because of a later s transeptal chapel. (Disturbed stonework in the s wall supports this theory.) The E wall survives externally, however, again without a window. The chancel is much grander with tall reticulated windows, especially the splendid five-light E window. On the S side a doorway with a flat ogee head and on the N side at the E end there was originally a vestry with a room above for the priest. Its scar is visibly externally and its doorway survives. The easternmost S window remained blocked till the C19 restoration, but one has to believe its tracery, again similar to the N chapel of three lights cusped, but here with trefoils above. The jambs of the E window with a lateral moulding run right down to the ground, again providing a recess at the base for an altar. Similarly below the easternmost window on the S side there is a recess where one would expect a sedilia and piscina. Might this suggest that in the C14 there was a series of wooden altarpieces and stalls? As it happens two tall stall-ends survive (in store) with huge carved foliate poppyhead tops; some panels from the base of two screens are set in the tower archway. Even more remarkable is the lowside window under the W window on the S side, with below the transom four lights with handsome tracery. It is rebated for shutters, and has a charming hooded recess alongside, presumably for a seat. To all this can be added the tall three-bay arcades with piers with four shafts and four small hollows between them – a type which, with different proportions, would become stand-ard in the C15. Their capitals look more C13 and C14, rounded in the arcade and angular in the responds. The tower and chancel arches are chamfered but have no shafts, just dying into their imposts. Roof-line of earlier roof above the chancel arch, which suggests that the clerestory of quatrefoil openings, with the central ones at a different angle from those either side, is later and probably C19. Another highly unusual feature for a small village church is that right round the building runs a string course, rather like a dado rail, and above all the open-ings, doorways, windows and arcades are hoodmoulds with small carved headstops.

It remains to consider the S transeptal chapel. This seems to be of 1778 when a faculty was obtained by Sir James Langham to 'take down Twenty one feet' of the S aisle and 'rebuild the same . . . to erect a Vault or Dormitory'. The Langhams of Cottesbrooke had acquired the manor in 1655. Its appearance with large blocks of masonry and no corner buttresses fits the idea. The vault was apparently 3 or 4 ft (0.9–1.2 metres) high, being finally removed in 1867. Yet the windows look early C14, although here out of pattern with the rest of the church, with just simple three-light bar tracery. Could they have been brought from elsewhere? It is worth recording that the restora-tion of the church and its reseating, in 1867–8, was done under the direction of *John Hayward* of Exeter, a curious choice since he worked almost entirely in the West Country. The restoration presumably responsible for the welcome clear glass in the windows. *Law & Harris* also did some work in 1911.

ROOF BOSSES. Exhibited in the chancel. They survive from a re-roofing of the chancel in 1633, done by the order of the rector Dr John Williams, who had been by this time translated as Bishop of Lincoln. The chancel parapet has the initials IL and the date. One of the larger bosses has a set of wings which are thought to denote the vicar Arthur Wingham (†1650). – The S aisle ROOF still has a good many old moulded beams, C16? – FLOOR TILES in the chancel, c. 1870 by *Goodwins*. – FONT. Rounded tub on a restored columned base, C13. – MONUMENTS. – In the chancel, Mountague Lane †1670, attributed to *Abraham Storey* (GF). Handsome tablet of alabaster with black marble tablet and columns. Interesting inscription stating he left money for a schoolmaster, but also £200 for the relief of the poor resulting from the Great Fire of London. – Nearby a large, flat alabaster slab, the remains of a larger tomb, with an inscription hardly legible today but which, although partly defaced then, was recorded by Bridges around 1720 as for John Lane †1557. – Huge slab of Purbeck marble in the centre of the chancel with an imprint of a large brass for a priest, c. 1300, the figure under a canopy. – MODEL of the church, in cork, made by *T. J. Hipwell*.

BAPTIST CHAPEL. 1786 of stone. Two storeyed with a façade of three bays with mullioned windows on the first floor and two entrances below. Hipped roof. Good interior. Mild Art Nouveau glass which is probably 1903 when *Cleaver & Sons* refurbished the chapel. Alongside Sunday School of 1899, also by *Cleaver & Sons*. Red brick with bands of yellow. Three tall round-arched windows under a pediment.

Former SCHOOL and SCHOOL HOUSE, Gold Street. T-shaped of ironstone with red brick dressing. Two storeys with low round-arched windows.

PRIMARY SCHOOL, Kettering Road. Simple red brick building of 1912–13 by *Law & Harris*. A hipped roof with three tall windows on each side of a two-storey centre under a dormer.

OLD RECTORY, E of the church. 1687. Ironstone. Two storeys, five bays, wooden cross-windows.

WALGRAVE HALL, on the SE edge of the village. The estate had belonged initially to the Walgrave family, then the Lanes, and was then sold in 1655 to John Langham. The Langhams owned it till 1911. What exists today is a fragment of a larger house which continued, according to old illustrations, on the l. with a tower and then a lower wing. The fragment is of ashlar and has a gable on the r. It contained the hall, now subdivided, but of which the plaster coat of arms of the Langhams with the date 1674 remains, together with the handsome staircase with an open well, balusters with Ionic heads with decoration of c. 1630, and openwork newel posts. Four-light mullioned-and-transomed windows. Good gatepiers.

On the N edge of the village, off Newland Road, is the site of the medieval NORTH HALL MANOR with remains of a moated site and fishponds.

Former STEPHEN WALKER SHOE FACTORY, Old Road. 1899–1900. Tall, three storeys of red brick with bands of yellow brick. The front of three round-arched bays under a pediment, the side elevations with broader double-windowed arched bays. Converted to residential 2003. The house adjoining, built of the same materials, has Walker's initials and the date 1899.

WAPPENHAM

6040

ST MARY. Chancel arch with stiff-leaf capital on the S respond. Its arch has housings for a tympanum. The chancel is wide, and its windows have Y-tracery. It may be connected with the foundation of an uncommonly large chantry in the church (warden and five priests) which took place in 1327. Externally it is rendered. The N arcade is C13. Three bays. Circular piers, circular abaci, double-chamfered arches, still round. The S arcade is standard C14 type (octagonal piers, double-chamfered arches) but the windows of the aisle are Late Perp, and the arcade could be of that period also. Large early C14 niche with a C19 top set diagonally in the angle between chancel arch and S arcade. Perp E window and Perp W tower probably of the same date as the S aisle. The N porch has a C17 round-arched doorway. The S porch also post-medieval. The triple arcade under the E window is a remnant from a REREDOS of 1833, when the Rev. Thomas Scott, father of G. G. Scott, was vicar and the chancel rebuilt. The PISCINA, CREDENCE and VESTRY DOORWAY are of the same period. Black-and-white sanctuary FLOOR of local stones, two with dates 1760 and 1766. – FONTS. One is Norman, circular, with two defaced knob-like heads. The other is octagonal with close patterns of honeysuckle-like leaves. The most likely date is the 1660s. – BRASSES. In the S aisle to Thomas Lovett (of Astwell Castle) †1492 and wife, 16-in. (41-cm.) figures, and to Constance Butler †1499, a 1-ft (30-cm.) figure. – S of the altar Thomas Lovett †1542 and wife, 16-in. (41-cm.) figures. – In front of the chancel steps a knight, c. 1460, 18 in. (46 cm.). – In the nave floor Sir Thomas Billing, Chief Justice, †1481 and wife. (From Biddelsden Abbey, Buckinghamshire.) The bottom parts are missing. The figures were c. 3 ft 5 in. (104 cm.) long. – STAINED GLASS. E and W windows: memorials to Rev. Thomas Scott †1880, by *Burlison & Grylls* 1883. Designed by his son? – MONUMENTS. Several rustic tablets in the N aisle for the Cockerill family, 1750s to early C19.

METHODIST CHAPEL. 1860, but still in the decent, modest Georgian tradition. Stone façade with arched windows.

OLD RECTORY, E of the church. Red brick, three bays, no adornment, and only remarkable for being *George Gilbert Scott*'s first building. Built in 1833 for his father and still in a Georgian tradition. The builder *James Wilmore* of Buckingham would have been known to the Rev. Scott since he had formerly been at Gawcott, near Buckingham, where G. G. was born.

Former SCHOOL, School Lane. Simple red brick of 1863 with a Gothic porch, presumably also by *Scott*. Altered and added to as a residence.

Attractive green N of the church, with on the w side THE MANOR, dated 1704. Six bays, two storeys. Still mullioned windows, but they are of two lights, upright and with flat frames. Moulded door surround. More modest wing at the rear. Several rooms have original fittings. BEECHES HOUSE, N of the church. Sandstone and ironstone, *c.* 1700. Wooden cross-windows on the first floor and three-light casements below.

THE LAURELS, NE in High Street. Five bays, two storeys, quoins. Doorway with steep open pediment and an oval in it with the date 1700. Windows in flat stone surrounds. One or two other houses in the village have similar windows, so a local builder.

WARKTON

ST EDMUND. Wonderfully positioned but not a specially attractive church, except for the fine Perp w tower. But Warkton is not visited for its architecture but for its monuments, the grandest C18 series in the Midlands.

The tower has clasping buttresses, a big doorway with tracery in the spandrels, a quatrefoil frieze above the doorway, a transomed three-light w window, transomed two-light bell-openings, a top quatrefoil frieze, battlements and pinnacles. The aisles are all of the 1868–9 restoration by *W. Slater*, except for the late C12 arcades of two bays (circular pier, square abacus, unmoulded round arches). Specially typical of the High Victorian restoration the chancel arch with its flowery capitals. It should be remembered that from about 1750 until 1867 the chancel arch was much smaller and Georgian classical. For a long time it was enclosed from the nave. The body of the church had also been Georgianized with plaster ceilings. The N and S aisles were sensitively extended and the interior was reordered by *Alan Foster* of Wellingborough 1996–7. – PULPIT and FONT, both 1868. The latter incorporates a medieval bowl. – STAINED GLASS. s aisle w window (in the 1997 extension) by *Capronnier*, 1875.

The story of the CHANCEL begins with the death of John, 2nd Duke of Montagu, in 1749. He left £1,000 to his widow for mourning. The idea of a mausoleum had already been considered and in 1742 William Stukeley had made sketches for one to be sited in the park at Boughton. The idea of a mausoleum in the church at Warkton may have been instigated by the Duke before his death. In the event it was masterminded by the antiquary Martin Folkes, but very soon after the Duke's death *L.-F. Roubiliac* had already been commissioned to prepare designs and was also involved with the design of the building itself.* It would seem that at an early stage it was decided to have four great alcoves to house further family memorials, and this is how the chancel was rebuilt. The huge alcoves have round arches supported on imposts decorated with the Vitruvian scroll. At dado level there are sections of a moulded rail, curiously broken apart: tiny sections between the alcoves and further sections at E and W ends of the chancel. The ceiling with a large rectangular panel edged by a diamond fret design. The large arched E window has its original small glass panes and is protected externally by iron railings. Also original is the black-and-white marble floor. In 1751 the Duchess died and so began the great series of memorials which fill the alcoves. Before the 1990s the chancel was filled by high Victorian stalls, but these, thankfully, save for two desks, have been removed.

Now the MONUMENTS themselves. They are placed in the large apsed niches to the l. and r., two on either side. The first two contain two of *Roubiliac*'s masterpieces, John Duke of 80 Montagu †1749, completed 1752, on the l. and Mary Duchess of Montagu †1751, completed 1753, on the r. By December 1749 the basic design of Duke John's monument, with Charity erecting a shrine to the Duke's memory, had been worked out and the terracotta and wood and plaster models now in the V&A show early stages. Also the concept of the grieving widow at the base. It has, as its centre, a big structure of indeterminate shape somewhat like a Rococo pottery stove. On its upper ledge lies a putto-boy, his hands busy hanging up an oval medallion with the profile of the Duke. To the r., on the base, stands Charity with two children, her arm stretched up to help him. One of the children is weeping and holding an extinguished torch. The other, endearingly, sits on her arm and is brilliantly captured. To the l., on the ground, that is yet lower down, the mourning Duchess with his coronet and shield of arms. The composition thus has the typical Rococo zigzag movement into space, a scheme equally characteristic of Boucher and of Tiepolo. Behind to the l. and r., projecting from the upper part of the structure, a gun barrel and cannon balls and a big flag and the trumpet of Fame.

The niche for Duchess Mary's memorial has sloping sides with cross-bars. Large urn with two putti draping a garland of flowers over it. Below, the three Fates, three beautiful young women, two seated, the third standing, and again in a zigzag composition into space. The composition is amplified specially piquantly by a little naked boy on the r., climbing onto the step.

Mary Duchess of Montagu, 1777–82 by *P. M. van Gelder*. 82 (The tradition that this was designed by *Robert Adam* cannot be substantiated and does not occur until the early C20. Even so there is indeed a marked difference between architecture

---

* Confirmed by agent's letters. I am grateful to Crispin Powell for alerting me to this reference.

and sculpture.) The architecture is exquisitely elegant and chaste. Coupled Ionic pilasters, coffered apse with bands of guilloche, in the wall panels three small figures in relief. The sculpture in comparison is grosser and obtrudes itself much more than Roubiliac's. In the middle of the stage a Neoclassical urn. To the l. stands a big angel in a distorted pointing attitude. To the r. the seated Duchess in despair, with two children, and an old woman who has pulled her big mantle over her head. The group seems to get the worst of both worlds. The figures are still excited, the gestures still flaming, but the illusionism of the group, the acting on a stage, as it were, introduces a *verismo* which the artistry of Roubiliac would have abhorred. The swirl of the angel's drape borders on Baroque. Yet Canova e.g. has the same *verismo*.

– Elizabeth Duchess of Buccleuch †1827 by *Thomas Campbell*. Centrally placed high plinth. On it a very straight, seated matron. Symmetrical figures l. and r., a young woman and a youth with an extinguished torch. How virtuous Campbell and his clients must have felt. Here is rectitude for you, and nobility. The vitality of the C18, however, has dried up. It is, however, a stately piece and it is a pity it has such brilliance alongside to contend with.

OLD RECTORY, NE of the church, 1865 by *E. F. Law*, in his familiar Tudor manner.

A typical Boughton Estate village. Stone cottages, many of them thatched and many showing C19 tidying. Nice pair of *c.* 1870 COTTAGES, just E of the church on Pipe Lane. Grey stone used between bands of yellow brick in an East Anglian flint manner. Attractive timber porches with side balustrades.

A ¼ m. W of the village on either side of the access road to the A43 are two residences. On the N side WEEKLEY RISE (now Country View care home), a mid-C19 modest stone house with timbered gables with tiny obelisk finials, was the home of *J. A. Gotch*. It shows no signs of his occupancy. Outbuildings much added to. On the S side ACRE HOUSE, pleasantly Art Deco of 1934. Rendered white with a central canted bay housing the front door and circular windows lighting the staircase. Two bays on either side. All openings with red brick voussoirs.

WARKWORTH

ST MARY. Out in the fields near Overthorpe and only approached by a rough track. Much restored and rebuilt in 1840–1 by *H. J. Underwood* of Bristol and in 1868–9 by *C. H. Driver*, who added the top parts of the tower, rebuilt the chancel and created the S arcade within the envelope of the medieval church. The tower was much shorter than at present, only just rising above the nave roof, and had a gabled, saddleback type top. Most of the original work is Dec, e.g. the S aisle windows,

Warkworth church.
Drawing by G. Clarke, *c.* 1850

the S transept E window (a fine design with ballflower externally), and the N arcade of three bays with octagonal piers,
capitals decorated with heads in the cardinal directions, and
double-chamfered arches. The transept S window is interesting,
being of Perp form with three ogee-headed lights with short
horizontal bridges joining the ogees to the vertical mullions.
Ogee-headed and crocketed PISCINA in the transept. – FONT.
Circular, with cusped arches, probably C14. – BENCH-ENDS.
Mostly with tracery, but one with the Annunciation and one
with a group of donors and the inscription 'Ora pro nobis'. –
REREDOS. Rich carvings of the Evangelists *c.* 1870. – TILES.
Victorian on the floor, some Pugin designs, and two Owen-
Jones-like panels either side on the E wall. – STAINED GLASS.
Chancel E and two side windows of *c.* 1860 and 1868. Further
windows in the S transept. All are from *Heaton, Butler & Bayne.*
   MONUMENTS. These make a visit to this church important
and memorable. A fine series of BRASSES: first the headless,
legless and upside down demi-figure of Sir John Chetwode
†1412 with praying hands (27-in. (69-cm.) figure, S transept).
Then Lady Chetwode †1430 (44 in. (112 cm.), S aisle), John
Chetwode †1420 (37 in. (94 cm.) N aisle), Margaret Brounyng
†1420 (35 in. (89 cm.), S transept), William Ludsthorp †1454
(33 in. (84 cm.), S transept). – Now for the monuments themselves. In the N aisle two C14 tomb-recesses containing stone   23
effigies thought to be of Sir John de Lyons †1312 and his wife.
– Free-standing is the unusually splendid tomb-chest with the
effigy of a knight, traditionally Sir John de Lyons *c.* 1350. It is
carved from clunch. The effigy is a very rich example of the
period. It is unusual in that he is wearing a cyclas, a garment
worn over armour, long at the back, like an apron, but shorter
in front. The details of his armour are finely shown, with a

baudric (belt) holding his sword and *genouillières* protecting his knees, both ornamented. His head rests on a helmet surmounted by his crest, a lion's head, and there is a rampant lion sculpted on his shield. Another lion under his feet. Against the tomb-chest three mourners in ogee panels with crocketed tops, and between them coupled panels with shields. On the w end a kneeling figure under a canopy. At the foot a quatrefoil frieze. The shields include Chetwode, a marriage link after 1350, and the weeper male figures are in armour of a slightly later date than the main effigy, so the usually ascribed date of *c.* 1350 may be too early. George Baker ascribes it to the Sir John who died in 1385. At its E end a canopy sheltering a Virgin and Child. Also of clunch, but probably nothing to do with the tomb, save it is clearly the same date. – Finally, in the s transept, William Holman †1740, signed by *R. Mottley* and purely architectural but on a grand scale. Corinthian columns beneath a broken pediment using variegated marbles. Nothing is known of Mottley and this is his only known work, yet it is clearly by a good London hand.

WARKWORTH CASTLE stood SE of the church. It was a mansion with a big gatehouse and semicircular towers, later converted into a spectacular Jacobean house and demolished in 1805.

In Warkworth, WARKWORTH FARMHOUSE is a finely preserved C17 ironstone house with coursed layers of large and smaller stonework. A sequence of three and four light mullioned windows, a central four-centred doorway and on the r. a shallow rectangular two storey bay. Dates of 1639 and 1658 are recorded.

The hamlet of OVERTHORPE, to the NW of the church, also has several more C17 good stone houses such as CHAPEL HOUSE with three and four light mullions and another house to the N with two and three light mullions, labels over the ground floor windows.

WARMINGTON

ST MARY. A large, noble and stylistically uncommonly unified church – built completely between *c.* 1200 and *c.* 1280. The story starts with the base of the w tower, and the arcades. Despite the variation of the capitals (waterleaf, very small scallops, or upright crockety leaves) and the difference in pier form (circular in the s aisle, octagonal in the N aisle) they appear to be of a single build. The fragment of a jamb of a N aisle w window shows the narrowness of the original aisles. A roof-line on the internal wall of the tower shows there was no clerestory. Two phases follow, curiously more elaborate at first and less later. Of the first is the s aisle with its triple-lancet windows, those to the E of the porch having dogtooth ornament, those to the w not. This difference is reflected internally since there were chapels on either side of the s doorway, marked in each

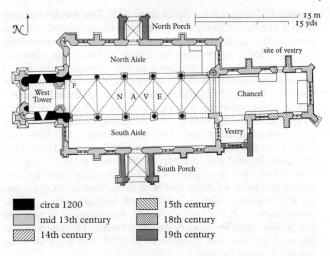

Warmington, St Mary.
Plan

case by a piscina and a tomb-recess. The form of the E window of the aisle is unclear since it is now internal and only its shafted jambs survive. The porch, sited in the middle between the two chapels, has a simple rib-vault, the outer doorway with many shafts with rings, the inner doorway with triple shafts. The walls are arcaded with three arches on detached shafts and fleur-de-lys stops. The outer arch mouldings run into the walls rather than on columns. At the same time the tower received its ashlar top stage with rich two-light bell-openings triple-shafted with shaft-rings, plate tracery and dogtooth. The shortish spire has low broaches and three tiers of lucarnes projecting rather much, so that from a distance it looks almost as if it were disfigured by warts. The base also had some alteration and a W doorway inserted. This has four orders of colonnettes, trefoiled arch with much dogtooth, and thin filleted mouldings. Outer arch moulding with alternating big dogtooth and big flowers. Above the W doorway one-light shafted window with dogtooth and flowers. Quatrefoiled circular window above this with stiff-leaf on the cusps. Contemporary tower arch, triple-chamfered.

The next phase includes the rebuilding of the chancel, the widening of the N aisle and, the most remarkable feature, the heightening of the nave with clerestory and its roofing with a vault. The vault is of timber, a great rarity, even if one might be disappointed it is not of stone. Single-chamfered ribs, quadripartite bays with ridge ribs. Bosses with five mitred bishops or abbots, a priest, a bearded man, grotesques. The vaulting shafts, so far as they have not been renewed into glorious Victorian foliage during restoration by *G. G. Scott* in 1876, are repeated as supports for the chancel arch. The window tracery is of a consistent design: two lancets with quatrefoil within a circle in the head, except the E window which has intersecting tracery. The N porch must be a later addition, but when? It cuts across one of the windows and the string course and is not bonded into the wall, yet it appears to be C13 with simple vaulting. Externally there are additional small round windows in the clerestory which gave light into the roof-space above the vault. Access to the roof is also intriguing, being gained from a stair-turret at the W end of the N aisle, then across the tower wall. The chancel has string courses both below and above the windows. Its end wall and part of the S were rebuilt in the C15 with a fine Perp five-light E window. Internally there are two image brackets: a simple one with crenellations on the S but on the N a most elaborate sculptural bracket with a female figure piercing herself with a sword, representing Wrath. On the N side outside marks of an early vestry. The chancel was restored by *Benjamin Ferrey* also in 1876 and he added the organ chamber in 1892.

FURNISHINGS. – ROOD SCREEN. Perp framework, but mostly 1876. Access was from a stair-turret in the N aisle. Battlemented top. – PULPIT. C15, but over-restored. – PARCLOSE SCREEN to the N aisle. Largely early C20 but including portions of C16 Early Renaissance woodwork with ogee-headed openings, but the ogees formed of Renaissance detail. Linenfold panelling side by side with pilasters with sunk panels with light Renaissance foliage. – REREDOS. Part of a screen which, with its rounded trefoils under pointed arches, looks remarkably early. – BENCH-ENDS. Nave at W end of N aisle. C16, high and low alternate. With coarse fleurs-de-lys. – ROOFS. N aisle panelled, dated 1650. – DOOR. In the S porch. C13 with iron hinges with chevron ornament. – STAINED GLASS. N chancel late C13 grisaille. Chancel E window 1876 by *Lavers, Barraud & Westlake*. – S aisle by *Curtis, Ward & Hughes*, 1902. – FONT. Stem of 1662 with small volutes. Bowl modern. – MONUMENTS. Very big plain tomb-chest (chancel N), *c.* 1500? – Tomb-chest with Purbeck top and richly panelled sides with indents for brass shields, early C16 (N chapel). – Thomas Elmes †1664. Hanging monument of alabaster and grey marble. Inscription surrounded by an oval wreath. Columns l. and r. and open scrolly segmental pediment. Attributed to *Thomas Cartwright* the elder (GF). – Sarah Cuthbert †1723. Small tablet with bust rising in an open segmental pediment.

SCHOOL, School Lane, NE of the church. Largely of 1872–3 by *Walter E. MacCarthy* with broad stone gable with one tall three-light window and smaller ones each side. SCHOOL HOUSE is mildly Tudor of brick and probably dates from the earlier phase of the building in 1848.

A number of good houses in the widespread village, including several C19 cottages with orange brickwork from a yard which operated in the 1870s. W of the church No. 22 CHURCH STREET, dated 1778. Two units joined: a four-window range with two bays on the l. in ironstone walling, the two r. bays of brick with timber studding. There is record that it was the home of *William Bullimore*, carpenter, and the brick stud section may have been a workshop. In Church Lane two ALMS-HOUSES of 1860 with timber porches and central gable with plaque. N again leads into Hautboy Lane with OLD HAUTBOY dated 1648 on a beam, single storey, thatched with two-light mullioned windows. Then into CHAPEL STREET. No. 35 is C17 and odd in that it is of two storeys with mullioned windows, but with only a single window on its first floor, whereas below there are four, somewhat irregular either side of the doorway. Further along the former WESLEYAN CHAPEL, red brick, 1881, and remarkably classical. Pediment above the façade with round-arched windows either side of a doorway linked to the windows by limestone platbands, then above a circular opening also linked to the windows. Then on the r. the very fine MANOR HOUSE. Jacobean but with a major ashlar refronting of 1677. Four-bay centre of two storeys and dormers, and wings of one bay of two storeys and attics in their gables. Broad framed cross-mullion-transom windows, heavily framed doorway, and oval opening above. Inside some panelling, turned staircase balusters, newels with ball finials, and stone fireplaces with heavy eared surrounds, all typical. Finely conserved 1972. Then a little to the N, on its separate green area, EAGLETHORPE HOUSE. A two-unit building of which the r. section is a symmetrical C17 front of three bays with mullioned-and-transomed windows. The l., more irregular section is early C19. Inside a door and wooden door surround said to come from Fotheringhay Castle. The door has linenfold panels, the spandrels of the surround are carved. Note the hawk in the fetterlock of Edward IV. To the W is EAGLETHORPE FARMHOUSE, largely a three-bay house of Late Georgian character, though it has a datestone of 1646. Just beyond is a circular DOVECOTE with a conical roof. Brian Giggins suggests it was built *c.* 1800 (cf. Wadenhoe).

WARMINGTON MILL, W of the bypass. Large fine three-storey, five-bay structure of *c.* 1835, well restored and converted as a commercial property.

WATFORD   6060

ST PETER AND ST PAUL. Partly of *c.* 1300 etc., partly Perp. Perp the W tower with the big four-light W window and the tall arch towards the nave, and Perp the chancel fenestration. Five-light E window, big three-light side windows. Of the window details of the earlier period the most interesting is the N chapel E window of five lights with two Y-groups l. and r. and above the middle light a big cinquefoiled circle. Other windows pairs of lancets (S), three stepped lancet lights (S), three-light intersected, uncusped (s) and cusped (N). Of the same time the arcades of three bays. Octagonal piers, double-chamfered arches. Long C14 N chapel opening to the chancel in one bay, with alongside a very richly detailed arch no doubt originally holding an important monument or possibly an Easter sepulchre. The N aisle and chapel have in their N wall three more tomb-recesses, so this must have been a family funerary chapel, probably for the Burnabys. – STALLS. Victorian with crocketed finials, but containing Jacobean panels. – BOX PEWS. In the aisles, but late, possibly even *c.* 1850. – STAINED GLASS. Chancel E, 1863, S, 1866, and S aisle, 1869, all windows by *Heaton, Butler & Bayne*. – MONUMENTS. Susanna Eyton †1631. Stone surround with strapwork but an inscription painted on a wooden panel. – Sir George Clerke †1648, attributed to the yard of *Edward & Joshua Marshall* (GF). Black-and-white marble. Uncommonly noble, very simple architectural tablet. No Jacobean exuberance left. Two black columns and an open segmental pediment. – George Clerke, probably the one who died in 1689 (to the l. of the former). A fine composition with Corinthian columns, a shaped inscription tablet, flower garlands and an elongated urn at the top. Attributed to *Edward Stanton*, and in the manner of his partnership with *Christopher Horsnaile* (cf. Marston St Lawrence). – Many lesser memorials to the Henley family.

WATFORD COURT. Sadly demolished in 1974. It had a fine N porch dated 1568, and two wings on the S front dated 1657 and 1659 which have been attributed to *John Webb*. Most of the rest was *c.* 1854 in a grand Elizabethan style. Only its gatepiers survive.

Former SCHOOL and SCHOOL HOUSE of 1855–7, S of the church in Station Road. Gothic, stone and brick, with a flèche. A pair of ESTATE COTTAGES of the same date alongside.

RAILWAY BRIDGE, ½ m. N of the church on the Jurassic Way footpath. 1881 with a segmental arch and on its pillars extraordinary cast-iron arched refuges. It was made ornamental to compensate Lord Henley for the intrusion of the railway.

CANAL LOCKS, W of the village between the M1 and the A5. A set of seven locks forming in part a staircase. Part of the 1814 Grand Union Canal system.

WEEDON

The village lies SW of the junction of the A5 and A45. It is a somewhat spread place, with the Weedon which most travellers see, Road Weedon, on the A45, the original village and the parish church, Lower Weedon, below in the river valley, and the hamlet of Upper Weedon to the SW. These separate districts have now become merged together by a mixture of C19 and C20 housing.

The Royal Ordnance Depot site lies between the A45 and Lower Weedon.

ST PETER, at the E end of Lower Weedon, is cut off from the village by the railway viaduct and from the E by the earth wall of the raised Grand Union Canal, with bridges on either side. Norman W tower – see the one W window, the large shafted bell-openings and the low unmoulded (but pointed) arch towards the nave. W doorway and window C16 Perp. The top stage of the tower is clearly a rebuild so the shafted bell-openings are a restoration. The body of the church 1825, except for the chancel, in what is best described as 'Churchwarden Gothic'. The chancel, in a richer and more correct Dec style, was rebuilt in 1863 by *E. F. Law*. Further work was done in 1886 by *Law & Son*. Interior with thin timber piers with thinner shafts and shallow Tudor-shaped arched braces to connect them longitudinally and also with the aisle walls, making a wide open auditorium. There was originally a gallery at the W end. Plans are signed by a surveyor, *Samuel Leeson*. Chapter house N extension of 1989. – ROYAL ARMS. 1825. – STAINED GLASS. Some coloured panels (E window and in each aisle) designed by *H. Holiday* and made by *J. Powell & Sons*. – S aisle window of 1965 (St Peter), another of 1982 (St Werburgh) and N aisle of 2009 (St Cecilia) all by *Anthony Macrae*. – SCULPTURE. Base of an octagonal shaft with monsters. C14 or C15.

UNITED REFORMED CHURCH (formerly Congregational), New Street, 1792. Three bays, segment-headed windows and two arched doorways with fanlights. Pyramid roof.

Former ROYAL ORDNANCE DEPOT, Bridge Street.* Begun in 1804 by the Board of Ordnance at a time when the fear of a French invasion was strong, and originally quite remarkably extensive. The construction was supervised and partly devised by *Captain Robert Pilkington*, Royal Engineers, and the clerk of works was *Thomas Lepard*. The site was chosen as being the farthest point from any coast and at the junction of two of the main turnpikes (Old Stratford to Dunchurch and Warwick to Northampton) and the Grand Union Canal, so giving good access to the Ordnance factories in Birmingham and London. The group consisted of, on the brow of the hill, three white brick buildings to house officials of the Depot, grand enough to earn the name of 'The Pavilion', and a set of barracks around a square; and below, within a walled enclosure, a series of storehouses and gunpowder magazines with a canal running between them. The idea that the Pavilion was built for George III to retire to when the feared invasion came is now discounted. The barracks on the northern portion of the site were pulled down in 1955–6 and the pavilions were demolished in 1970, and their site is now covered by housing.

96

---

*I am grateful to Mike Rumbold for comments and access to his researches.

Weedon, Depot.
Drawing by G. Clarke, *c.* 1850

Still within a walled enclosure with bastions are the store-houses with two gatehouses or lodges, and, running through the centre, the canal, 440 yards (402 metres) long. Beyond to the w are the five gunpowder magazines with blast houses set between each. The site is entered on the E side through THE LODGE, of white brick and built in 1812. The wharf is protected by means of a Traitor's Gate-like portcullis. It has a cupola with a clock face facing the complex. Behind it the wharf itself, flanked on either side by four pairs of red brick STOREHOUSES with ironstone plinths, built 1805–7. Each range has eleven bays with arched ground-floor windows and a central archway with Doric pilasters. The w gatehouse is similar to the E one and the canal formerly extended beyond it to the magazine enclosure. There were later additions to the site such as a clothing factory built in 1902. The complex continued in army use till 1965 and since then its future, despite a number of schemes, has remained uncertain. On the opposite side of Bridge Street, a long early C19 row, with cast-iron balconies and verandas, was built originally as flats for the firemen of the Depot.

In the village, NW of the church, Nos. 8–10 CHURCH STREET, despite having been drastically altered, is one of the most interesting buildings. It must once have been all one property, probably an inn, and dates from the mid C16. Sandstone façade with ironstone dressings, all somewhat weathered. Still three-light mullions on the first floor and a four-centred doorway at ground level. Inside there are four-centred arched stone fireplaces. Nos. 4–6 on the r., with its neat rendered façade, looks innocent enough, but behind the render the first floor is timber-framed with stud walls inside. On the first floor

another four-centred stone arched fireplace against the end
gable wall of No. 8, so again suggesting they were originally
linked.

BRIDGE STREET, leading N to the Depot (*see* above) has the
former WESLEYAN CHAPEL (now a nursery) with its brick and
stone frontage of 1890. Doorway and windows either side with
round arches, and a triple window similar above under the
pediment. It incorporates an earlier structure dating from 1811.
WEST STREET has a pleasant ironstone group around THE
MALSTERS ARMS, itself having an C18 front with windows
with wide lintels with rendered voussoirs and a Regency reeded
doorcase.

At UPPER WEEDON, THE OLD PRIORY, Oak Street, is not
monastic but a fragment of a large house, part C16 and part
C17. Buttresses and windows with arched lights to E and W.
Also THE FIRS, Queen Street. Dated 1692. On the street just
the end gable of banded ironstone and sandstone with three-
light mullioned windows and latticed glazing. Its five-bay front
of two storeys faces its yard. Upright two-light mullioned
windows. Above the doorway a horizontally placed oval
window. Some original fireplaces inside.

CROSSROADS HOTEL, on the A5/A45 junction. Incorporating a
pretty mid-C19 former toll house with two bargeboarded wings
and a porch between. Hotel additions and clock tower by
Stimpson & Walton, 1984. W, on HIGH STREET, Road Weedon,
the HEART OF ENGLAND pub, formerly the New Inn. Simple
C18 ironstone centre overpowered by two Edwardian wings,
that on the l. being multi-gabled with tile-hanging and timberwork. The r. wing less oppressive. Opposite a nice brick row,
early C19, each house with its own doorcase approached by
steps with rails and a window on each floor.

WEEDON LOIS   6040

ST MARY. Early Norman evidence the herringbone masonry in
the W wall and the lower part of the crossing tower. Cruciform
churches tend to be early anyway. The rest C14 to C15. Dec N
doorway – the N aisle rebuilt in 1849 by *W. Hurley* of Farthing-
stone – S porch and S doorway, S arcade, two tomb-recesses in
the S aisle, and ogee-headed PISCINA in the S aisle. The aisle
also has a sill moulding running along its wall. Several windows
with reticulated tracery. In the chancel one blocked lancet
window. Perp the upper parts of the crossing tower. The arches
of the crossing are identical to the W, N and S, but differ towards
the chancel, where the responds and the abaci are concave-
sided and Perp rather than Dec. Many head corbels and stops
in various places. Beneath the E window a Dec crocketed ogee-
arched recess. It has been suggested that this may have been a
shrine of St Lucien. There was a priory belonging to St Lucien

Beauvais in the village, and a mineral well dedicated to St Loys (or Lucien). – FONT. Circular, Norman. At the top hanging lunettes, beaded and with leaf inside (cf. Dodford). – PULPIT. 1849. Based on the octagonal font in Bloxham church, Oxfordshire. Stone, Perp, with ogee-headed panels. Pretty ogee-headed entrance to the pulpit through a crossing pier. – WALL PAINTINGS. Two seated figures above the E arch of the S aisle. – STAINED GLASS. Chancel E window of 1875, and S window of the same date, probably by *A. Gibbs*. – MONUMENTS. Rev. William Losse †1643. A Civil War casualty with an inscription worth reading.

In the CEMETERY, 100 yds E on the S side of High Street, memorials to the Sitwell family of Weston. That to Edith Sitwell †1964 is at the far end of the vista. It is by *Henry Moore*. A large tapering upright slab. Attached to it a square bronze plaque with two delicate hands in high relief, signifying Youth and Age. Other memorial stones in a country churchyard manner in a plot in the NE corner of the cemetery. They include the inspiring pioneer architectural writer Sir Sacheverell Sitwell †1988, who lived at Weston Hall (q.v.).

OLD VICARAGE, NE of the church. Stone. Built between 1696 and 1704. Pedimented doorcase. Altered later.

LOIS WEEDON HOUSE. On the E edge of the village, set back in beautiful grounds. A substantial red brick house built *c.* 1910. LODGE with half-timbered gable.

WEEKLEY

Small but beautifully maintained Boughton Estate village. A mixture of neat stone houses, many thatched.

ST MARY. Beautifully set in a green oasis on the N edge of the village, alongside the avenues of Boughton Park. Externally Perp, but for the following: S doorway of *c.* 1200. Two orders of shafts, round arch with roll mouldings, over-restored. In the N wall of the chancel one early lancet, now looking into the vestry. At the W end of each aisle, externally, are the voussoirs of two former openings. For what? They may not be medieval. Dec W tower with battlements and a short recessed spire. Two tiers of lucarnes. At the sill line of the lower tier a band. Triple-chamfered arch into the nave. For its size a very tall nave, though the interior a little disappointing due to over-restoration by *Arthur Blomfield* in 1872–3 and the windows being filled by rather mediocre Victorian glass. RCHME suggest that the tall proportions of the nave could indicate the Anglo-Saxon origins of the building. Fine Perp arcades of three bays with piers of the familiar section with four shafts and four hollows (cf. Kettering). The chancel arch of the same type. The E end is by Blomfield and has a good display of TILES by *Goodwins* and a tiled REREDOS with panels for the Evangelists. – SCULPTURE. In the E wall of the N aisle a fragment of a Norman slab with e.g. four rosettes. – ROYAL ARMS. Stuart period. – STAINED GLASS. Chancel E of 1873, as are the other windows in the aisles, all by *Clayton & Bell*. – MONUMENTS. Sir Edward Montagu of Boughton House, Chief Justice of the King's Bench, †1557. Recumbent alabaster effigy. Tomb-chest with a shield in the middle, flanked by twisted shafts and at the corners pilasters with mini-balusters, so just a hint of the Renaissance. The tomb can be confidently attributed to the *Roileys* of Burton upon Trent. – Sir Edward Montagu †1602. Of stone. Six-poster attached to the wall, with three columns and three pilasters covered with strapwork. The columns have broad shaft-rings. Tomb-chest with two recumbent effigies, he in armour and she with a gown tied with ribbons. The superstructure coffered on the underside. Top with obelisks and a pierced strapwork centrepiece around the arms. Fair quality but a provincial rather than London workshop. – Sir Edward Montagu †1644. Noble tablet. Marble inscription flanked by two pairs of columns placed one behind the other. They are carved from the local fossily stone known as Rance. Shield under the simple pediment. – Henry Baron Montagu †1842. A simple marble surround with Gothic arch enclosing a medallion portrait. – In the churchyard a group of Celtic cross memorials for the Montagu-Douglas-Scott family. Just S of them a tall stone with carved rose spandrels for the Kettering architect J. A. Gotch †1942.

WAR MEMORIAL cross on the green, by *Gotch*, c. 1920.

Former MONTAGU HOSPITAL on the edge of the green by the church. 1611. For a master and six brethren. Very pretty. Two storeys, widely spaced mullioned windows. Centre with a four-centred doorhead, an entablature on brackets, two obelisks on shells, and a bulbous gable with three obelisks perched on balls. Large painted sundial dated 1631. Now a private house.

Just S from this the former FREE SCHOOL, founded in 1624. Four-centred doorhead and inscription. Mullioned windows. Charming inscription: A FREE SCHOOLE FOR WEEKLEY AND WERCKTON FOUNDED BY NICOLAS LATHAM CLERKE PARSON OF BARNEWELL S. ANDREW TO TEACH THEIRE CHILDREN TO WRITE AND READ. C19 wing to the front and other additions.

Former VICARAGE, on the A43 junction. Tudor style, by *Blomfield*, 1873. Asymmetrical façade with a large gabled wing on the l. and a smaller gabled porch projection on the r. Mullioned-transomed windows.

BURDYKE, Weekley Wood Lane, ¼ m. N. Large brick and stone house dated 1902, by *Gotch*. Two storeys and attics. Two big gabled wings, the r. with a canted bay and the l. a smaller ground-floor bay. Mullioned-and-transomed windows. The rear elevations more irregular.

9080

WELDON

ST MARY. Internally older than externally. Later C13 S arcade of
three bays with quatrefoil piers, stiff-leaf capitals, and an arch
with one chamfer and two fine rolls, one with a fillet. In the
same style the arcade to the S chapel. In it SEDILIA with shafts
and filleted arches. The chancel SEDILIA are similar. Triple
shafts. At the E end of the S chapel a tall early C14 niche with
crocketed gable and finial, although its ringed shafts look C13.
The N arcade is Perp. Piers with a hollow chamfer towards nave
and aisle and shafts towards the arch openings. Only the latter
have capitals (cf. Lowick). It is a replacement of an earlier
arcade as the responds are C13. There is a crypt under the aisle.
The N chapel (organ chamber and vestry) was added in 1861–2
by *F. Preedy*, resiting in its E wall the former E window of the
aisle. At the same time both N and S aisles were extended
westwards. The C15 chancel arch is of two continuous chamfered orders with a decorative image bracket, and to its N are
the remains of the access to the rood loft, with a further
opening above the S arcade, so there must have been a screen
right across the church. The present openwork screen is C19.

Externally to the same period as the S arcade etc. belongs
the S porch. Entrance arch with filleted rolls. Wall arcading with
triple shafts. The external effect, however, is Perp. A S aisle
window points to *c.* 1300–20, i.e. it has cusped intersected
tracery; the other aisle window has reticulated tracery. Reticulated also the tracery of the chancel S window. Flowing tracery
in the N aisle W and E windows. The N windows are straight-
headed, but also Dec. Pretty frieze of tiny heads at the top of
the wall. Battlements, also on the S aisle, S porch and clerestory.
The base of the W tower is C12 with a round arch on imposts.
There are small lancets in the second stage, but otherwise it
was rebuilt at an unknown date. The bells are dated 1710, so
that could be the date, although it looks more like late C17.
Unbuttressed. Bell-openings round-arched with round-arched
lights and a circle over. Obelisk pinnacles. Handsome glazed,
wooden cupola with a scrolly iron weathercock. Designs were
published by *William Slater* in 1854 to restore the tower back
to its medieval appearance, topping it with a decorative lantern,
and for reseating, but the plan suggests the W extension to the
N aisle.

– ALTAR. Carved wood with the Lamb of God medallion,
1909, which is probably the date of the convincing Perp cresting of the E window sill. – FONT. A nice Perp piece. – REREDOS.
S aisle. Perp. A horizontal band of blank tracery. – BRACKET.
Fine Perp bracket against the N side of the chancel arch. –
STAINED GLASS. A good variety, in chronological order. N aisle
a window with a variety of medieval fragments, assembled in
1977, including several heads, *c.* 1340–50, some canopy work
and shields for the Basset family of the same date. – Chancel
E window, 1861 by *F. Preedy*. – S aisle a window of 1866 by
Lavers & Barraud. – In the W window a complete Flemish early
C16 representation of the Adoration of the Magi. An inscrip-

tion tablet below records it was a gift from Sir William Hamilton to Nelson. Its installation here in 1897 seems to have been due to the influence of Dr John Clark who as surgeon attended Nelson at Trafalgar (the E chancel window is his memorial as he is buried here). – Finch-Hatton memorial (S aisle E) 1911 by *J. Powell & Sons*. (Its many wheatsheafs are nothing to do with C. E. Kempe, whose signature it was, but an element from the Finch-Hatton heraldry.) – American War Memorial window (8th Air Force Bombardment Group; S aisle), 1944 by *Pope & Parr* of Nottingham. – Mason memorial (N aisle), 1992 by *Alan Younger*, representing the Holy Spirit. – In the vestry, heads of *c.* 1350 and an early C16 figure.

Weldon stone was one of the most widely used in the Middle Ages and later. The workings are to be seen on the N and W sides of the village. The quarries were reopened in the 1990s, and still produce enough limestone for some building and restoration work. There are, however, fewer good stone houses than might be expected here. HAUNT HILL HOUSE, Kettering Road, has datestones of 1636 and 1643. It was built by Humphrey Frisbey (†1648), one of a local family of masons.* The house might well be called a folly, if one sees it only from the S. Symmetrical front, of three bays, with low mullioned-and-transomed windows and a porch with an ogee-headed doorway over which is a shield bearing the masons' arms. The S façade is an extraordinary display. Three tiers of windows with fat volutes l. and r. of the ground-floor as well as the first-floor windows, and in the gable a stepped three-light window. Datestone for 1643 and Frisbey's initials and the arms of the Masons' Company. Dominant is the four-shafted chimney-stack with its ornate mouldings. High quality ashlar throughout. The plan has a central lobby with two equal-sized rooms on each floor. The S room on the ground floor has the staircase, most unusually in stone. The lobby has a blind arcade of round-headed arches. Fine stone doorcases with corbelled lintels. Several original fireplace surrounds. The whole would not surprise somewhere near Halifax or Huddersfield. Humphrey's brother, Samson Frisby, was also a mason and it has been possible to identify the mark used by him on stonework showing that he was one of Thomas Thorpe's workmen.†

A second sophisticated mason's house is No. 23 CORBY ROAD, again stone of two storeys with four-light mullioned windows and two four-centred arched doorways. Oval windows in the attic. A plaque is inscribed 'AG 1654', for Arthur Grumbold (†1670). The Grumbolds were one of the most productive families of masons from the C16 to the C18. The house is a two-unit plan, No. 23 being the larger and with two-room plan, while No. 25 is a one-room plan. The larger unit is similar in arrangement to Haunt Hill House with a cross-passage and hall on one side and parlour on the other. Winder stairs by the stack in the hall which continue up into the attic. It is thought

*I am grateful to Nick Hill for use of his research on the houses of the two masons.
†*See* Introduction, p. 36.

that Grumbold constructed the smaller unit to house his
widowed mother. A little further, on the same side, No. 31 is
a fine house with gables topped by ball finials. A mixture in
each bay of mullioned windows and oval openings and shield
plaques. It must be late C17. In HIGH STREET on the N side
No. 27, a C17 house with lateral Georgian additions and a
canted bay, but sadly its mullioned windows have been lengthened. Close by is ODDFELLOWS HALL, of stone, 1890 by
J. A. Gotch in the vernacular manner. Of three storeys, a big
gable with mullioned windows. Wide ground-floor window
with a central segmental gable. A little E is the GEORGE INN,
with two attractive mid-C18 curved bay windows. Its central
archway is now closed in. On the green, the circular LOCK-UP,
with a conical roof. Probably C18. Opposite the Green RANKIN
HOUSE, dated 1818, with an elaborate porch with honeysuckle
carved parapet, one wild large one and smaller ones on each
side. Then in Oundle Road are several further stone houses
with mullions and thatched roofs. Just E of the church in
CHURCH STREET an engaging timber house with cladding
and a large barn-like roof of 2011 by Solo Timber Frame.

Parallel to High Street to the N is CHAPEL ROAD with a number
of good houses, some with mullioned windows like THE OLD
FARMHOUSE at the E end probably around 1600 but possibly
older with some rough masonry and a buttress. Rear turret
with sundial. LORRAINE HOUSE (No. 6) is a brick house
c. 1900 with nice coloured glass, the upper window having a
peacock design. Moving W, THE SHOULDER OF MUTTON
pub, grey brick Tudor manner 1932 by the Gotch firm, and
just beyond Nos. 22–24 a tall red brick house with stone
quoins and decorations dated 1865. Then beyond the school
entrance, set back, the delightful CONGREGATIONAL
CHURCH of 1792. Diminutive in stone with round-arched
windows. Early C19 Sunday School in the same style. Restful
burial ground behind with a large table tomb for Rev. John
Philip †1837. Former manse on the street with a sundial over
its front door. On the N side No. 17 has a two-storey ashlar
front with platband. Beyond to the W are further low stone
cottages, some thatched with here and there a remaining mullioned window. No. 37 on the N side might well be older with
again some rough masonry and two buttresses.

MANOR HOUSE, E of the church in a beautiful setting. Late C17.
Symmetrical range of three bays with gabled porch. Mullioned
windows. Projecting wing on the r., also with mullioned
windows.

WELFORD

ST MARY. The best thing in the church is the E.E. S arcade, five
bays long and built all at one go. The first pier is circular, the

second circular with four attached shafts (cf. Rothwell), the third octagonal, the fourth again circular. Real crocket capitals of the French type. Double-chamfered arches. Perp W tower with a tall arch to the nave, clasping buttresses and battlements. Perp also the wide chancel arch. Late Perp S chapel of two bays, taller than the aisle. The details inside are coarse and include very large head corbels on the responds for the arcade and the arch into the aisle. The date is *c.* 1510. The N aisle and arcade are of 1872 (by *E. F. Law*), and only the arched tomb-recess is original. The tracery in the S aisle windows is also C19 (a drawing in the church by George Clarke show them as plain openings). Law had done a partial restoration in 1853. – FONT. Octagonal, with pointed-trefoiled arches and in the spandrels quatrefoils with pointed quatrefoils in them – probably late C13. – SCREENS. To the N and S chapels; Jacobean with arcaded tops. – BENCH-ENDS. Two, C14, reused for the reader's desk, are inscribed William Lovell. – REREDOS. Rich alabaster of 1888 by *A. Hill Parker* of Worcester, with central gabled canopy. A memorial to the Rev. George Ayliffe Poole †1883, rector here for thirty-three years. He was a considerable authority on church architecture and wrote several publications. – STAINED GLASS. S chapel, with some Netherlandish panels. – Chancel E, 1868 by *Alex Usher*. – S aisle, three windows 1897–1900, all by *A. L. & C. E. Moore*. – Another S aisle window by *A. Gibbs*. – N aisle windows of 1872 by *F. M. Drake*. – Chancel S, 1880s and Lady Chapel E, 1872 have not been identified. – MONUMENTS. Low C15 tomb-chest with shields and quatrefoils in panels. – Incised slab to a civilian and his wife, *c.* 1460, the female effigy effaced. – Francis Saunders, 1583. A fine mural tablet of alabaster with small allegorical figures (Charity and Peace) perched on a broken pediment either side of a roundel with a coat of arms. Splendid scroll frieze. Brass plate with kneeling figures. Originally the niches at either side contained figures. John Bridges records Faith on the l. but the r. figure, presumably Hope, had already gone. There is a similar monument at Harrington where the side figures survive, and as there, this can be confidently attributed to *Garrett Hollemans*.

CONGREGATIONAL CHAPEL, West End. 1793. Large and square with round-arched windows and an extraordinary metal turret. Altered 1893 by *Edward Sharman* of Wellingborough.

SCHOOL, West Street. 1859, by the rector *G. Ayliffe Poole*, with red and blue brick diaper patterns. Similar school house incorporated. Nos. 7–13 alongside also patterned.

MANOR HOUSE, N of the church. Stone, five bays, two storeys, with a porch carrying a broken pediment on Tuscan columns.

Former GEORGE HOTEL, at the N end of the village (actually in Leicestershire). Rendered brick, embattled and with an embattled porch. A CANAL WHARF adjoins the building.

Welford is altogether a brick village and there are several rows and cottages of Late Georgian character, often of chequered or mottled brick and with platbands. They include Nos. 20–28 High Street, with No. 28 having been heightened with blue brick diaper patterns, and others in West End, where they have timber-framed construction appearing. Most also have the use of ironstone for their base courses and often for quoins. In West End No. 36, one of the larger houses, is dated 1687, but its brick frontage must be later. In High Street other properties include SALFORD HOUSE, mid-C19 yellow brick with red brick dressings and a columned porch, and just below, Nos. 32–34, gentle Gothic of *c.* 1800, with pretty roof fringe.

8060

WELLINGBOROUGH

Wellingborough, before the end of the C19, was a relatively quiet and unassuming market town. Some evidence of Roman occupa-

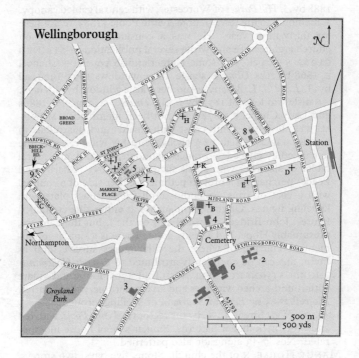

A	All Hallows	I	Police Station and Court
B	All Saints	2	Workhouse (former)
C	St Barnabas	3	Southwood House
D	St Mary		(former Cottage Hospital)
E	Our Lady of the Sacred Heart (R.C.)	4	Castle Theatre
F	United Reformed Church	5	Tresham College
G	Baptist Church	6	Wellingborough School
H	Wesleyan Chapel	7	Wrenn School
J	Friends' Meeting House	8	Victoria Schools
K	Hindu Temple	9	Freeman's Endowed School

tion has been found and the existence of Castle Street and Castle Road imply a castle, but no clear evidence has ever been discovered. The main medieval manor was owned by Crowland Abbey, Lincs. A barn and portions of their manor house survive. A market charter was granted in 1201 and the town had some reputation as a coaching stop. In 1738 a serious fire destroyed much of the centre. The railway arrived in 1845 and the boot and shoe industry had something of an impact on Wellingborough – it was the third largest supplier in the county in 1850 – but not as much as in Northampton and Kettering. Brewing was also important. The main expansion of the town began around 1870 with new estates on the E side of the town. The size of the town has hugely increased since the 1970s following its choice as a town to take London overspill and the involvement of the Greater London Council in building houses and the new library complex on the Market Place. Since the 1980s and the re-routing of the A45, Wellingborough has become a retail distribution centre with a major business park s of the town. Huge monolithic warehouses now dominate the approach from the A45.

CHURCHES

ALL HALLOWS. Well placed in a churchyard with old trees and away from the traffic of the town. The only Norman survival is the s doorway. The shafts are decorated with zigzag and the arch has a zigzag moulding at right angles to the wall surface. Otherwise there is much of the late C13 to early C14, and much that is Perp, the latter telling more outside, the former more inside. The w tower is of c. 1250–1300, its lower part in bands of ironstone and grey stone, the upper part grey. w doorway with three orders of shafts. A rose window above it with six arches radiating from a circle. Much-shafted pairs of two-light bell-openings, spire with low broaches and two tiers of lucarnes. Arcades of c. 1300, four bays, octagonal piers, double-hollow-chamfered arches. Dec chancel with a spectacular five-light E window. The lights are ogee-arched, but the top is still a circle with three inscribed cusped trefoils. Up the jambs and the arch little heads and flowers. Dec porches, both two-storeyed, that on the s side vaulted below with a tierceron star and curious details. Perp N and s chapels with stone piers of four-shafts-and-four-hollows section. Perp most windows and the copious battlements. There are several Perp roofs, the best being the panelled one of the s transept with angels and bosses and still with painting. The church was restored by E. F. Law in 1861 under the direction of G. G. Scott and further work was undertaken in the 1880s and between 1983 and 1991. – SCREENS. Perp. To both chancel chapels, with broad one-light divisions and much small tracery above the arches. The fine ROOD is by W. Talbot Brown and was added in 1917. – COMMUNION TABLE. A fine example dated 1633 with Ionic baluster legs. – STALLS. Late C14, with MISERICORDS. They represent a wood carver, an ale-wife with a customer, a mermaid, an eagle, two lions, a fox and a goose. – WALL PAINTING. S transept. Ascension by *Hans Feibusch*, 1952. – STAINED GLASS. The church has a fine array of windows and by far the best collection of C20 glass in the county. First the Victorian and early C20 glass. – E window by *Alexander Gibbs*, 1871. – S aisle: E window by *Drake* of Exeter (paid for by S. Gill of Tiverton, Devon, former resident), and two windows of saints, 1936 by *J. Powell & Sons*. – N aisle: Shatford memorial, 1949 by *G. Maile & Son*. – Jones memorial by *J. Powell & Sons*, 1910. – Lady Chapel: E window by *William Gill*, 1880. Sanders memorial by *F. C. Eden*, 1929. – S transept chapel, Davis memorial designed by *Carl Almquist* and made by *Shrigley & Hunt*, 1885. Now the later C20 stained glass. – S aisle W window by *Evie Hone*, 1955. Excellent, in a Continental Expressionism, with the Lamb, the flames of the Holy Ghost, the ark, the seven-branched candelabrum, loaves and fishes, etc. – Tower rose window by *Patrick Reyntiens* and designed by *John Piper*, 1964. – N aisle W window also by *Reyntiens*, to a design by *Piper*, 1961. Symbols of the Evangelists above emblems of the prophets. As impressive as the Evie Hone window. Also Expressionist, in brilliant colours. – S chapel W end, Chapman memorial by *Piper* and *Reyntiens*, 1969. Abstract, quieter in mood, the colours green, red, but mostly blue. – S chapel, second window from E, St Crispin and Crispinian, by *Jean Barillet*, 1962. – ROYAL ARMS. Stuart, carved wood. John Barker has pointed out that it is carved on both sides since it was originally part of the chancel screen. – MONUMENTS. Tablet dated 1570. Two tapering atlantes, the tapering pedestals with a vertical band of linked oblongs and ovals (cf. Rushton Hall). Shield with two supporting figures. Pediment at the top. – John Frederick †1773. Nice, with an urn before an obelisk. Coloured marbles. By *Nicholas Love*.

ALL SAINTS, Midland Road. 1867–8 by *Charles Buckeridge*. Enlarged 1889–90. Large, mixed ironstone, pale yellow with deep golden for dressings, with a vaulted apse, and a bellcote. Lancet clerestorey, otherwise Geometrical windows. Low W porch. Arcades of five bays with banded ironstone and limestone columns and foliate capitals. – PULPIT. Designed 1932 by *F. E. Howard*. Painted with a tester. The chancel STALLS are the same date. – SCREEN in the Perp style with Rood 1918 the figures 1922 by *Talbot Brown & Fisher*. – REREDOS and apse panelling by *Kempe* 1897–8. – STAINED GLASS. Several by *Kempe*. Apse 1887, S aisle 1893, chancel N 1903. – S aisle 1907 and 1918 by *Heaton, Butler & Bayne*. – N aisle two by *J. Powell & Sons* 1922. – N aisle centre by *Clayton & Bell* 1907. – N chapel one by *Francis Skeat* 1961, and one by *F. C. Eden* 1927. – S aisle 2012 by *Rachael Aldridge*. – CHURCH HALL built 1974.

ST ANDREW, Queensway. 1935–6 by *Talbot Brown & Panter*. Very much of its time. Long brick hall form with three- and two-light rectangular windows in its low side walls. Two transept-like projections at either end with blank round arches in their fronts. Tall slender tower attached to the r.-hand projection with recessed panel and conical roof.

ST BARNABAS, St Barnabas Street. 1951–3 by *Paul J. Panter &
Eric A. Roberts*, replacing a church of 1893–4 by *Talbot Brown
& Fisher* destroyed by fire in 1949. Light brown brick with a
square SW tower, block shapes altogether, and square-headed
slender windows. Light, airy and white interior. Low, passage-
like aisles, round-arched openings towards them. Square E end
with a small circular window above the altar, crossed by a large
cross outside. The glass has a Crown of Thorns. Altogether
simple, honest and very satisfying.

ST MARK, Berrymoor Road. 1968 by *Paul Panter*. Built as a
combined multi-purpose hall with overhanging arched canopy.
Short mono-pitch tower.

ST MARY, Knox Road. One of the most thrilling churches in the
county. *Ninian Comper*'s most complete and, it is said, favourite
achievement. The money was given by the Misses Sharman.
Begun with the N chapel in 1908 and built gradually, until the
nave was reached in 1930. The furnishing never entirely completed, but it glistens and reveals and conceals to one's heart's
delight. The building is severe, the furnishings are full of
fantasy and fearless of the mixing of Gothic and classical styles.
Every detail inside and outside, right down to the iron gates
from the street, is by Comper. The external style is Perp, the
material ironstone. Severely simple W tower. Nave with clerestory. Two-storeyed N porch with a tall polygonal turret, open
in its top stage. It is placed unusually far to the E. The interior
has eight bays of tall concave-sided octagonal piers with capitals decorated with lilies. They carry a most flamboyant lierne
vault of plaster with pendants. It was intended to be all blue
and gold. At present only the W bay, the E bay and the part
above the rood screen are painted but that somehow adds to
the impact of the interior. Of furnishings there is more than
one can enumerate: a ROOD SCREEN with gilded and painted
Tuscan columns and Gothic loft and rood, a SIDE SCREEN to
the N chapel, a SCREEN round the lobby past the porch, the
ORGAN CASE above this lobby, the BALDACCHINO over the
altar, with gilded Corinthian columns, the gilded FRONTAL,
the gilded SCREEN round the font. The FONT CANOPY, blue
and gold, with Tuscan columns, spire and bulgy pinnacles, is
by *J. S. Comper*, 1969. – STAINED GLASS. The N chapel E
window is a memorial to Mrs Comper †1932. Her ashes are
buried in the N chapel. The chancel E window is of 1919–21.
All by *Comper*, except a vestry window, which is by *J. Bucknall*.
It should be recorded that the ashes of Comper's partner
Arthur Bucknall (†1952), together with those of his wife, are
also buried here. Comper also wished to be buried here but
the State intervened and he is in Westminster Abbey.

OUR LADY OF THE SACRED HEART (R.C.), Ranelagh Road.
1885–6 by *S. J. Nicholl*. Ironstone and limestone, in the Late
Dec style with elements of Perpendicular. It was designed to
have an elaborate tower and small spire at the SW corner, but
that was not built. Its site is marked by a tall pine tree. The
building is orientated N–S. Finely carved doorway with two

113

106 segmental arches and rich foliage carving. The interior starts off with an orthodox rectangular nave. This breaks into two arches over transepts. Tie-beam with rood cross. The E end is marked by a triple arch, the tallest forming, as it were, the chancel arch, but surprisingly the transept arches cut across the middle of the two side arches, their abutments forming positions for small side altars with statues and decorative canopies. Nicely carved foliage capitals. The choir is even more bizarre. It has arcades and on the E a narrow aisle, with three big Perp windows, joined to the arcade by horizontal castellated flying buttresses, the central ones angled. On the W side the arcade gives onto side areas, now filled by the organ but designed as the Lady Chapel. (The organ was originally in the E transept, but that is now the baptistery. The font was originally at the S end of the church.) Beyond are vestries and other rooms. The altar has an elaborate canopied reredos, attached to the side arcades by slim flying buttresses. Rose window at the E end. *Minton* tiled floor. The choir has been slightly reordered and part of its original alabaster and marble altar rail is now at the W end of the church. Choir stalls have been dismantled but their four carved ends now form the ends of both the front and back pews in the nave. Despite its somewhat quirky forms the interior is decidedly impressive. The church was largely funded by Robert Arkwright of Knuston Hall, Irchester (q.v.), and the two small side altars are memorials to his wife, Sophia †1888, and his daughter, Diana †1892. – STAINED GLASS. E choir aisle, grisaille with heraldry for original donors, and W transept two windows, one a memorial for Baron Edward Howard of Glossop †1883. They are all by *Lavers, Barraud & Westlake.*

OUR LADY'S R.C. CHURCH AND INFANT SCHOOL, Henshaw Road, by the *Ellis Williams Partnership*, 1971–2. A combined church and school. The church is the taller windowless part, with simple top-lit interior. The plan is L-shaped, with one arm that can be partitioned off as a school hall. Beyond this are central teaching areas surrounded by partly open classrooms.

105 UNITED REFORMED CHURCH (former Congregational), High Street. Built in 1874–5 by *Edward Sharman* to a plan by *Caleb Archer*. Ironstone in C14 Gothic style. Carved decoration by *H. Hems*. Egg-shaped plan with projections. These are gabled, and the windows are pointed, and that does not marry with the curves of the oval. But as a plan it remains interesting. Inside a long oval shape with a U-shaped balcony on Gothic cast iron columns. Flat panelled ceiling. At the E end an elaborate platform and organ case, a central section and two further arrangements of pipes in two little galleries, all in impeccable woodwork, just enough Gothic to be called so. Charming small animals at the corners of the stalls, a cross between a fox and a beaver with a leafy tail. In 1925 it was called 'the most successful experiment in free church architecture in this country' and it remains as interesting today. – WAR MEMORIAL in the porch with a fine figure of the Angel of Peace, erected 1920.

Behind the church in Salem Lane a former chapel of 1812. Brick with pairs of round-arched windows.

BAPTIST CHURCH, Mill Road. 1905 by *George Baines & Son*. Spirited version of Perpendicular with a touch of Art Nouveau, equally reflected in the glazing and the railings. The tower looks odd because it has been capped, having formerly had a small spire.

TABERNACLE BAPTIST CHURCH, Great Park Street/Park Road. Yellow brick with a double Baroque doorway with the date 1901. Pastor's house in Park Road, also yellow brick.

WESLEYAN CHAPEL, Great Park Street. Built in 1872 as a Methodist church. Red and yellow brick with blue bands. Lombardic in style with arcaded portal and small tower. HALL alongside of 1914 and just beyond PARK JUNIOR SCHOOL, 1873 and typical Victorian Gothic.

FRIENDS' MEETING HOUSE, St John's Street. 1819. A delightful little building of ironstone. Four arched windows and a modest porch. Hipped roof.

SWAMINARAYAN MANDIR (Hindu Temple), Mill Road. A large white walled building of 2008–9 by *Amrish Patel* with ornamental windows and doorways with intricate decoration carved in India. Three shikharas.

CEMETERY, Castle Road. Two Gothic chapels with corner towers and broach type spires. 1857–8 by *E. F. Law*. Also a stone Lodge also with a short tower with pyramidal top.

PUBLIC BUILDINGS

POLICE STATION AND COURT HOUSE, Midland Road. The Court House of 1916 by *Law & Harris* in a red brick and stone Jacobean style, with a central pedimented block, the doorway set within a large mullioned-and-transomed window. Extension to the r. in a sympathetic manner, 2005.

Former PARK HOSPITAL, Irthlingborough Road. The former WORKHOUSE. The original large brick building with its cruciform wings is of 1835–6 by *G. G. Scott*. The complex was extended by further blocks later. It was converted into apartments 2008–9.

Former COTTAGE HOSPITAL, Doddington Road. Now SOUTHWOOD HOUSE (residential care home). Built 1899–1900 by *Sharman & Archer* in the Edwardian brick, stucco and half-timbered manner. Large house at the front and smaller blocks behind, all largely intact and sensitively modernized by *John Olley Architects* for Shaftesbury Society Housing, 1987–9.

CASTLE THEATRE, off Castle Way. Built 1993–5 as a theatre and arts centre by *PDD Architects* of Milton Keynes. Rather barn-like, with plain brickwork base, timber-clad upper parts and big tower, all with big gables. It adjoins on the s the former CATTLE MARKET OFFICES of 1881. Red brick and stone in the Tudor manner. Hall in the middle and two wings. Octagonal tower with pyramidal roof and weathervane. Rich carved panel with apple trees and wheat over its N entrance and clock above.

TRESHAM COLLEGE, N of the church. Built as a Technical College by the County Architect, *A. N. Harris*, 1960–8. Typical of its age and beginning to look dated. A group of different heights. The largest building, in plan two linked trapezia, has canted end walls faced with reconstituted ironstone (1964–6). Plans are in hand for a new building on a different site (2012).

WELLINGBOROUGH SCHOOL, London Road. The first buildings by *Talbot Brown*, 1879–95. The original block of brick, Queen Anne of 1880, with Headmaster's House at its S end. Garden setting. Extra blocks were added 1888 and 1895, the latter including the hall. Internally this has a barrel-vaulted ceiling with gilt Arts and Crafts flower motifs, a round-arched arcade on its inner wall and a balcony. The block behind the Headmaster's House with a tall baroque chimneystack of banded brick and stone and two slim round-arched shapes. – CHAPEL of 1908 also by *Talbot Brown*. Gothic in Late Perp manner. Bell-tower on the N side with decorative canopy. Low barrel-vault inside, the E end refurbished in a Neo-Wren manner as a 1914–18 war memorial. – STALLS. Brought from Weymouth College. *c.* 1920 with poppyheads and foliage carvings on their ends. – STAINED GLASS. E window by *F. C. Eden c.* 1930. W window of 1962 by *Harry Harvey*. – Delightful CRICKET PAVILION, 1928 again by *Talbot Brown*. Of chequer brick with thatched roof, a veranda and clock turret. It is a copy of one at Jesus College, Cambridge. The steps up to it include the threshold steps of W. G. Grace's house at Downend, Bristol, rescued when that was demolished in 1939. A considerable assembly of other buildings from 1912 onwards, including a dining hall of 1962 by *David Roberts*, junior classrooms of 1967, music school of 1971, dormitories of 1972, sports hall 1983, and the Robert Robinson Teaching Block 2002, all by *Sursham, Tompkins & Partners*.

WRENN SCHOOL. This has buildings on two sites and has absorbed previously separate establishments. They are the former County High School in London Road, 1912 by *Sharman & Archer*, Neo-Georgian, red brick with three segmental pedimented bays; and the former Grammar School in Doddington Road, in a similar but simpler design of 1930 by *Talbot Brown & Fisher*, also with three projecting bays, this time triangular pediments and a central cupola. Extensive additions to both.

FREEMAN'S ENDOWED C.E. SCHOOL, Westfield Road. Typical school manner of 1900 in red brick with decorative panels and lettering by *J. E. Cutlan* of Wellingborough.

VICTORIA SCHOOLS, Stanley Road and Mill Road. 1895 by *W. Talbot Brown*. An impressive ensemble in the Neo-Queen Anne manner, sadly unoccupied and becoming derelict. Red brick with stone dressings. Two detached buildings formerly for juniors and infants. The Mill Road elevation dominated by the roof-line of the central hall, which has a pretty balustrade bellcote, and behind an extraordinary campanile-like octagonal chimney tower with eight arched openings and conical top.

WEAVERS SCHOOL, Weavers Road. Original buildings of the 1930s were built as a clothing factory. Red brick with a long two storey range having a central staircase tower with vertical glazing. Simple Art Deco in manner. 1955–7 school buildings alongside. To the N three large and one smaller block, system-built, 1970–1 by the County Architect, *John Goff*.

STATION, Midland Road. 1857 by *C. H. Driver* for the Midland Railway. An especially good example and largely complete. Somewhat cottagey buildings of dark red brick, using yellow and blue brick as decoration, with round-arched windows, some with their original cast-iron diamond glazing and bargeboarded gables. Cast-iron columned platforms. Not only the station itself but other ancillary buildings survive including a rare LOCOMOTIVE ROUNDHOUSE of 1872, just off Mill Road.

PERAMBULATION

The planners have not been kind to Wellingborough and any Perambulation is a disjointed affair. Most of what is worth seeing is either side of the N–S route, from Broad Green, via High Street, past the Square and then into Silver Street and Sheep Street.

At the N end of High Street is the attractive, triangular BROAD GREEN with old trees. The best buildings are on the NW side. From l. to r.: the MANOR HOUSE, a small C17 two-storey house of ironstone, with early C19 doorcase and bargeboarded dormers. Octagonal brick chimneys. Then, set back, HATTON HALL, mostly late C18 Tudor Style. Only the façade remains, the rest altered when it was converted into flats. Further on, HATTON HOUSE, late C18, of ironstone, five bays and two and a half storeys. Arched doorway with fluted pilasters and round-headed windows above it. On the S edge of the green a WAR MEMORIAL, 1921 by *W. Talbot Brown*, with Ionic columns, coupled on the sides, and an arc wall of memorial plaques. Piers with heavy ball tops. In ROCK STREET to the W the former Gothic SCHOOL (Afro-Caribbean Centre) of 1873, first converted as a youth centre 1969–71 by the County Architect *John Goff*.

The area N of Broad Green was developed from the 1870s onwards and there are substantial villa-type residences in HATTON PARK ROAD and THE PROMENADE. On its W edge on HARDWICK ROAD is DYBDALE, a good brick residence in the Jacobethan manner built in 1879 as his own residence by *W. Talbot Brown*. Elaborate terracotta plaque above the doorway. Timber gable, bays, etc.

HIGH STREET is dominated by the United Reformed church (*see* above), and opposite ST HELIERS (Daylight Centre), 1887 and

QUEEN'S HALL (built as a Free Library 1902). Jacobean manner in ironstone. On the E side a row called the Parade (now Warwicks), with its sequence of triple arched windows, built as a shopping arcade in 1890. On the same side comes CHURCH STREET with a large ironstone building on its N side built as the Post Office in 1908. A little further on the S side is the OLD GRAMMAR SCHOOL, now the Church Hall. It was founded in 1595 but largely rebuilt in 1620 and remodelled 1904 by *Talbot Brown & Fisher*. Ironstone. Mullioned windows. Gables above the doorway and one dormer. Next door a pair of irregular cottages, dated on the rear wall 1608. On the N side Tresham College (*see* Public Buildings). Beyond the parish church, standing proudly in its oasis of green trees, are some pleasant Georgian stone houses including the former VICARAGE, a large three-bay stuccoed house of 1813 with castellations. An early C19 front onto an older house. At the S end of Church Street, just worth a glance, is the former WORKING MEN'S CLUB (now The Gloucester), 1882 by *E. Sharman*. Adjoining and forming the corner is the former PALACE CINEMA (now Cutting Room) of 1911 in a broad Early Georgian manner. Corner feature with arched doorcase and window with broken pediment above.

Back in High Street, on the W side, LEIGHTON HOUSE, early C19, of five bays and two and a half storeys. Doorcase and window frames of alternating rustication. The former stables are nicely Neoclassical. Next door the former Conservative Club (BRITISH LEGION), by *W. Talbot Brown*, 1882, aware of the Norman-Shaw revolution, i.e. with window aprons and two gables plastered and with incised ornament and inscription.

To the W from the S end of High Street a short diversion into OXFORD STREET. Nos. 61–62 is an early C19 double house of six bays. The two doorways adjoin and have one rather stretched-out door surround with Tuscan columns and an entablature. Opposite, the site has been overtaken by a supermarket. Tucked away in WEST STREET on the N side a former PRIMITIVE METHODIST CHAPEL with datestones of 1734 and 1794. Chequer brick of two storeys and a three-storey house attached. Back in Oxford Street comes WEST END HOUSE, Early Georgian, of five bays and two storeys with segment-headed windows, and somewhat further on WESTLANDS, late C18 with altered ground floor. Opposite a late C18 house with several Venetian windows. After that some small Victorian villas in their gardens, and on the l. KENROYAL, 1864 ironstone with a short Italianate tower. Even further out at the beginning of Northampton Road, on the N side, the former CONGREGATIONAL MISSION HALL (now Coral) of 1903 by *Sharman & Archer*. Red brick with a tall pointed gable and a wide Diocletian window whose uprights have delicate Art Nouveau garlands.

Back in High Street continuing S into SILVER STREET where there is variety but little of consequence. One façade on the W side does stand out, a large brick front with a big arched window and pilasters with wreaths at the top. This is all that remains of the former SILVER CINEMA of 1920 by *Talbot Brown & Fisher*. Continuing s one comes to the MARKET PLACE, one of Wellingborough's lost opportunities. It used to have as its centrepiece the CORN EXCHANGE, 1861, with a thoroughly debased but jolly tower, but this was sadly demolished in 1958 and what has replaced it and fills the square can only be described as nondescript. It is part shops, part Library and part offices, part concrete, part brick and glass, built 1972–3 by the *Architect's Department of the Greater London Council*. On the s side of the Square two distinctive banks, both rather surprisingly built in 1880 by the same architect, *Edward Sharman*. LLOYDS TSB (originally Northamptonshire Banking Co.) is Gothic with foliated capitals on the ground floor. Trefoiled windows above. HSBC (originally Northamptonshire Union Bank) is brick with decorative panels and a Dutch gable. Beyond SWANSGATE CENTRE a predictable shopping mall, but opposite NATIONWIDE, a stucco and half-timbered building in the Ipswich manner of 1907 originally built for Boots chemists. On the corner of MIDLAND ROAD the upper floors of the former TEMPERANCE HOTEL. Brick and stone 1883 by *W. T. Brown* of Northampton, with a stone corner domed feature. Just round the corner in Midland Road, on the l. is the former POST OFFICE, Neo-Georgian of the 1920s by the *Office of Works*. Attractive rusticated doorcase with garlanded *œil de boeuf*. Alongside the TELEPHONE EXCHANGE, a tall block with forceful projecting mullions across aggregate cladding, 1968–71 by *Gotch, Saunders & Surridge*. Both are now empty and threatened (2012).

On the w side of the Square, at the beginning of SHEEP STREET, one of Wellingborough's famous buildings, the HIND HOTEL.* Ironstone again, with three identical gables with windows of the later C17 type which are tripartite and straight-headed but include an arch for the middle light. The timber porch reaches over the pavement and has coupled fluted Ionic piers. The building had a considerable overhaul in 1878 by *E. Sharman*. Upstairs the Cromwell Room has flat panelling and a crossbeam made partly from a C15 bressumer with quatrefoil patterns. Another room has a fireplace flanked by giant Corinthian pilasters. The building adjoining to the s (No. 37) has amusing roundels in the gables dated 1886 titled 'The House that Jack built', for John Horden, a shopkeeper. The side of the hotel faces BURYSTEAD PLACE, where Nos. 2–3 are early C18, but with imitation C17 ground-floor windows and a shell-hooded doorway of 1902, when the building became *Talbot Brown*'s office. This leads into the grounds of CROYLAND ABBEY (Wellingborough Council), a large and rambling house, which stands on its s side. Ironstone with some banding, chiefly Jacobean and Victorian, but the remains of the medieval monastic

---

* The design is traditionally credited to William Batley †1664, whose memorial plaque in All Hallows describes him as 'Architect'.

grange are embedded in the w range. Big roof trusses on the first floor, probably of the original hall, arched-braced with castellated collars and wind-braces. Good Jacobean staircase with splat balusters with Ionic capitals and newels with turned baluster caps. The house was acquired by *Edward Sharman* and he was doubtless responsible for the 1868 alterations. The building was sensitively restored in 1973 by Wellingborough Council. On the N side of the grounds stands the former TITHE BARN, ironstone and limestone striped, of six bays divided by stepped buttresses, with two cart entrances. Converted for communal use. Nearby TITHEBARN OFFICES (Borough Council), partly Late Georgian, five-bay house with an early C20 veranda. The COUNCIL OFFICES of 1973, with s extension 1983, have a tall central tower with blue slate cladding, four bays on the r. and five on the l. Tinted glass. Nor can one ignore the 1970s former BEST DEAL INSURANCE offices. Large canted block, four floors of white and brown brick, with long canopied windows.

Moving back into Sheep Street, No. 29 on the w side is a timber-framed, much renovated house with an oversailing upper floor; then THE GOLDEN LION, again with a timber-framed oversailing gable, and No. 20, *c.* 1820, with a front chequered in red and yellow brick and with two shallow ground-floor bow windows. Finally, facing the s end of Sheep Street, SWANSPOOL HOUSE (Wellingborough Borough Council offices), plain Late Georgian *c.* 1770 with a chimney-stack dated 1799, rendered, of five bays and two and a half storeys with all the ground-floor windows in blank arches. The two upper middle windows are of the plainest Venetian kind. Gardens at the front, a pool and a bridge. Dismal 1967 rear addition. At the s end of the park behind, on the London Road edge is a fine 1929 PAVILION. Central hall with stepped gable over a large Venetian window. Lower wings with colonnade overlooking the park.

On the s edge of the town THE EMBANKMENT, created in the 1920s–30s as a long public park alongside the River Nene, famous for its swans. On its s side the buildings of VICTORIA MILLS, with the original five-storey brick and stone building of 1886 built for J. B. Whitworth by *Usher & Anthony* of Bedford and still part of Whitworth Bros. Despite its situation it was not originally a watermill but a steam roller mill. The first silos were built in 1912. New towers 2011. All too obvious on the ridge to the SE is the modern distribution centre of PROLOGIS PARK, which houses some of the largest warehouses in the county.

THE POPLARS, Gold Street, ¼ m. E of Broad Green. A double-fronted ironstone house, of C17 origin. Good late C18 s front of white ashlar, three storeys, rustic quoins and pedimented doorcase. The ground floor with added bays. A big Victorian yellow brick house, BEECHWOOD to its E.

STATUES OF SILVER LADIES, on the Wellingborough–Harrowden road (A5193). 2007 by *Rick Kirby*. On each side of the road, in threes, silver females with curvaceous bodies, arms outstretched, standing on cylindrical columns. Riveted aluminium squares.

WELTON

St Martin. Almost entirely Dec and Perp. Dec the w tower top, but the lower parts C13, and the N and S doorways. Open, light interior. Tall arcades of four bays, octagonal piers, double-chamfered arches. Perp many of the windows. The chancel has a black-and-white diamond stone floor of the C18, but the sanctuary was refurbished in a most elaborate fashion with coloured marbles laid in 1868. Even an inlaid cross in malachite which was a gift to Lady Emma Tulloch (memorial N wall chancel) by Czar Alexander II. There was a restoration 1866–7 by *E. F. Law* and further work in 1961 by *Caroe*. – PULPIT. Beautifully carved with traceried designs by five men in the village, 1899. The main carver being *Trevor Davys*. – ORGAN CASE. A most striking piece, with excellent gilded decorations in the Renaissance style. Good enough for a London City church. Formerly at Hengrave Hall, Suffolk, it came here in 1953. It is a 1910 Aeolian Organ from New York. – SCULPTURE. The corbel on the w wall of the nave is supported by a bearded head, probably C12. – STAINED GLASS. Chancel E of 1854, and other windows, by *Holland* of Warwick. – Small tower window by *Clayton & Bell*. – MONUMENTS. Many tablets, e.g. Isaac Astley †1757 by *William Cox*, John Clarke †1816 by *Samuel Cox Jun.* (still with sarcophagus and obelisk), and John Plomer Clarke †1826 (turned Gothic). – LEAD CISTERN, in the yard, S of the tower. Very fine, with the date 1673 and much ornamentation. It came from Welton Place, a mid-C18 house demolished in 1972. An ARCHWAY in the former garden wall, just SW of the church, must be mid-C17.

Manor House. Mid Georgian. The front has a canted bay window in the middle and Venetian windows, heavily detailed, to the l. and r. on both floors. Excellent staircase, from Daventry's Moot Hall, built in 1769. Three balusters to the tread, one columnar, the other two twisted to different patterns. Carved tread-ends.

WEST HADDON

All Saints. Early C13 arcades and S doorway. Tower arch also C13 with signs of early roof-line and a blocked opening above. The arcades have octagonal piers and double-chamfered arches. One has a capital decorated with fleur-de-lys. In the chancel one lowside lancet. Perp windows in the chancel. Most of the windows are altered or renewed, including several with ogee tops but plain leaded glass and no tracery. Dec w tower. s porch dated 1682. The medieval s aisle wall with random ironstone and limestone patterning. Fine timber roof. The principals rest on figures. A restoration is recorded in 1887. – FONT. Square, Norman, with well-preserved and interesting sculptured scenes on the four sides. They represent the Nativity, the Baptism of Christ, the Entry into Jerusalem, and Christ in Glory between the Eagle of St John and the Angel of St Matthew. The date proposed by Professor Zarnecki is *c.* 1120. It was discovered in 1887, having been built into a wall. – COMMUNION RAIL, C17, turned balusters. – SCREEN and REREDOS. 1910 in West Country manner, by *Bligh Bond*. – STAINED GLASS. Chancel E, 1897 by *Clayton & Bell*. – s aisle E by *J. Hardman & Co.* to a design by *Pugin*, 1850. – N aisle window of 1879 by *James Ballantine & Sons*. – Clerestory N by *Morris & Co.* – MONUMENTS. Several C19, in Gothic surrounds, for the Heygate family, one signed *Whiting* of Northampton.

BROWNSTONES, next to the church. The former rectory. Dated 1676. Stone front of three bays. Inside, a good staircase with turned balusters, and a chimneypiece said to be made up from an Elizabethan moulded stone handrail from Holdenby.

ALMSHOUSES, 1846, at the W end of the village. Red and blue brick dressings and pilasters. With porches and a bell-turret.

WEST HADDON HALL, Station Road. Late Georgian. The top storey removed in 1946. The original entrance was on the s. The present W entrance is C19.

WESTON
¾ m. w of Weedon Lois

BAPTIST CHAPEL. 1791. Plain three-bay front with very elongated windows and a pyramid roof. Simple interior. Enlarged in 1866.

WESTON HALL. Late C17 with a wing of 1776–7. The N front of this has been rendered, gabled and generally Tudorized *c.* 1825–30. The s front is in its original state. Fine fireplace in the drawing room. This comes from Greatworth Manor House, so presumably survived the fire there in 1793 which otherwise destroyed the house. It must be of *c.* 1740–50. The opening is flanked by cherubs in profile growing out of slender volutes. The staircase is partly of *c.* 1700 (strong twisted balusters), partly of the C18 (slender twisted balusters – two to a tread). The house is famous for its Sitwell connections and was for many years the home of the architectural writer Sir Sacheverell Sitwell (*see also* Weedon Lois).

ARMADA HOUSE, opposite. The house was dated 1588. A picturesque gabled and dormered building with mullioned-and-transomed windows. Sadly gutted by fire in 2011 but being restored.

STONEHOUSE FARM, Helmdon Road, SW of the chapel. Dated 1694. The windows are mullioned but arranged symmetrically (three bays) and have broad flat frames curving up slightly towards the outer border. Canopied doorway and nice early C19 railings.

A row of Victorian red brick COTTAGES in High Street with arched windows with yellow and blue brick infilling. The side gables likewise. At the W end of the street on the corner of Grove Lane a pair of mid-C19 COTTAGES with pretty latticed windows.

WESTON-BY-WELLAND

7090

ST MARY. Rebuilt by *R. C. Hussey*, 1863–6, 'in exact facsimile' of its medieval predecessor, so *Kelly's Directory* of 1890 says. In fact much of the medieval church is still evident. The W tower ashlar, the rest a mottled yellow and brown ironstone. Tall pairs of two-light bell-openings with Y-tracery, continuous circular mouldings, and shafts with rings i.e. late C13. A conspicuous date of 1865. The other external details Dec. S arcade with quatrefoil piers, N arcade with octagonal piers. Double-chamfered arches. Low tomb-recess in the N aisle. – REREDOS and STALLS, 1929–33, by *Traylen & Lenton*. – STAINED GLASS. Chancel E, 1865 by *Ward & Hughes*. – N aisle 1914–18 window signed by *A. K. Nicholson*, 1936.

Former SCHOOL and SCHOOL HOUSE, E of the church. 1871 by *H. Goddard* of Leicester.

No. 8 THE GREEN, a good mid-C17 house with canted bays and four-centred doorway.

WESTON FAVELL *see* OUTER NORTHAMPTON

WHILTON

6060

ST ANDREW. Unbuttressed C13 W tower with upper parts of *c.* 1769. Round-arched bell-openings with Y-tracery. Chancel, higher than the nave, of 1878–81, part of the all too obvious restoration by *J. P. St Aubyn*. The Perp chancel arch however is original. C13 arcades of two bays with circular piers, circular abaci and double-chamfered arches. The E bays are narrow to connect with the chancel. – REREDOS. A most elaborate affair with painted tiles and mosaics. Last Supper panel in centre, part of the 1877–8 restoration. – STAINED GLASS. Chancel E,

1877 by *Burlison & Grylls*. – MONUMENT. Tall memorial to Richard Freeman †1749 with Ionic pilasters and urn at the top. Rococo cartouche at the foot. Some elements of coloured marbles. A good piece and of a type made by the *Smiths* of Warwick Marble Yard.

OLD RECTORY, N of the church. Late C18, stuccoed. Five bays with a three-bay centre with pediment and a doorcase, likewise with a pediment. COACH HOUSE of red brick with three arched carriage entrances and a pediment with a circle, now a separate residence.

HOME FARMHOUSE. Georgian, of brick, five bays, two storeys. Several other pleasant houses, including by the churchyard gate a late C17 ironstone COTTAGE with an oversize brick chimney-stack. Cob wall to its yard.

GRAND UNION CANAL, between the A5 and M1. There is a sequence of six LOCKS at Whilton originally built in 1796 and a number of buildings survive. Several of the locks have side ponds built in 1805 to save water. Close to the M1 bridge is SPOTTED COW LANE with at its end the former early C19 inn, red brick of two storeys with archway for horses.

WHILTON LODGE, 1 m. W, off the A5. A large mansion in the Elizabethan style by *Frederick Chancellor*, 1867. It incorporates an earlier house of *c*. 1840. The S front with two gables and a long veranda. Big semicircular bay at the W end. There were considerable alterations and additions by *Law & Harris* in 1909. Now apartments. Pretty bargeboarded LODGES, early C19.

WHISTON

ST MARY. On a hill, quite on its own, only to be reached on foot, and worth the climb. One of the most perfect essays in the Perp style in the Midlands and one of the most beautiful churches in Northamptonshire. It is indeed a monument, built by one man, Anthony Catesby, it seems within about twenty or thirty years, and not altered since. The monument to Thomas Catesby (*see* below) mentions the date 1534 – a last-minute date, even if it represents the completion of the church. A lost inscription in the glass, recorded by John Bridges, also mentions the date 1534, and states that Anthony Catesby, his wife and son 'hanc ecclesiam cindiderunt'. The early C16 anyway fits the design. The tower must have been built first and separate, as the aisle walls overlap the base corners of the tower, and inside there are buttresses on either side of the tower arch. There are also other differences between the tower and the body of the church: the tower is much more elaborately ornamented and is of ironstone and limestone; the body of the church only of limestone. It is splendid enough for Somerset. Golden brown and silver ashlar bands. Friezes of quatrefoils at the base and below the bell-stage. Buttresses first of the clasping type, then turning to the set-back type, then developing into pairs of square pinnacles set diagonally. The bell-openings are pairs of two lights each with transom. All four are under one hoodmould with ornamented spandrels. Battlements with tracery panelling, tall pinnacles, many gargoyles. At the base of the tower these are demons and grotesques, higher up they are angels, some with symbols of the Passion. Enormous water spouts at the battlement stage: two monkeys to the S and a bearded figure to the E (a replica – *see* below). W doorway with a continuously moulded arch. Odd patches of rough stone either side. Why? The Catesby arms in a lozenge above.

The body of the church immaculately built. The quality is such that it is considered that royal masons could have been involved. A near comparison is St Margaret's Westminster. Nave and aisles and slightly projecting chancel. Windows of three, four and five lights, all with varieties of the same tracery – monotonous but incisive. Shallow embattled S porch, beautifully proportioned, below the second window (artfully, the window has been raised a few inches higher than the others in the aisle to make room for it). Attractive open interior, airy with stone-flagged floor. Arcades with slender piers (four-shafts-four-hollows section), shafts on angel corbels carrying the roof principals, traceried spandrels, and no clerestory or chancel arch. Good roofs with moulded and carved beams of a type more often found in East Anglia. Shields with emblems at the end of each beam, with in the nave on one side the Catesby shield and on the other their symbol, a cat encircled with the motto 'Gras be howr gyd (Grace be our guide)'. – FONT. Octagonal, Perp, with panelled stem and shields in quatrefoils on the bowl. – FONT CANOPY. Of oak, with five turned corkscrew posts supporting a pyramidal top, an unusual design. Probably mid-C17. – BENCHES. All original, in several groups, square-topped with thin buttress-shafts. – CANDLE-STICKS on the benches. Pretty ironwork, with flowers, probably *c*. 1850. – COMMUNION RAIL. With turned balusters, early C18. – REREDOS. Carved wood with representation of the Last Supper, designed by *Mayer* of Munich and carved by *Habner*, 1886. – PULPIT and SCREENS of 1855. – COMMANDMENT BOARDS (vestry). Georgian. – CHANDELIER. Brass, Georgian. – SCULPTURES. Two gargoyles, one a grinning face found in the churchyard and perhaps a remnant from an earlier church; the other the original of that on the E face of the tower. A bearded figure with scissors in his belt and a cross-shaped implement. A connection with the wool trade is suggested. – STAINED GLASS. E window, 1858 by *O'Connor*, looking a little harsh in this setting. – W window by *Mayer* of Munich, 1885. – MONUMENTS. Thomas Catesby, erected 1700. A fine piece, attributed to *William Woodman* the elder (GF). Standing monument with two busts on supports carved with masks. The base showing in relief three kneeling daughters, a small child with a skull, and a baby in swaddling clothes. Ionic columns l. and

r. of the inscription panel, string of flowers and fruit, and open
pediment with shield. – 1st Lord Boston †1775. By *Nollekens*.
Standing monument. Mourning woman bent over an urn and
holding an extinguished torch. Grey obelisk behind. (Both
these in the chancel). – Mary Irby †1792. With a weeping putto
by an urn. Also by *Nollekens* (s aisle). – 2nd Lord Boston †1835.
By *W. Pitts*. With a relief of the praying family and a rising
angel (N aisle).

Former RECTORY, on the hill s of the church. Tudor, 1852.

MOAT HOUSE (formerly Place House). A medieval remnant of
uncertain origin. Oblong buttresses at one corner and some
windows with depressed-arched lights.

6030   WHITFIELD

ST JOHN EVANGELIST. By *H. Woodyer*, 1869–70. E.E. style,
with a rather convincing broach spire but the rest less orthodox. Odd N arcade with a corbelled effect rather than capitals
and hoodmoulds ending in conical corbels where the capitals
should be. Small N lancet windows connected outside by blank
arcading. – SEDILIA formed by a tall trefoil-headed niche. –
Elaborate REREDOS. – TILES. Sanctuary pavement by *Mintons*.
– STAINED GLASS. Almost every window by *Morris & Co.*,
c. 1898–1914. They are largely single figures within the lancet
windows.

6040   WHITTLEBURY

ST MARY. In effect a Victorian church owing to the heavy restoration in 1877–8 by *J. P. St Aubyn* for the patron, Sir Robert
Loder. C13 w tower. The arch towards the nave is pointed and
single-stepped. It has dogtooth decoration in the step and the
hoodmould. A nutmeg frieze higher up on the wall. The s
porch entrance seems *c.* 1300. Pretty floor of squares made of
slates standing on end and placed in alternating directions,
probably C19. The N windows are Late Perp. Arcades of three
bays with octagonal piers and double-chamfered arches. One
capital on the N side must be reused, as it is late C12. The SW
respond is triple-shafted and was probably built in the C13.
Chancel mostly of 1878. – CHEST. A huge long structure with
original ironwork. C13? – REREDOS. Elaborate with E.E. style
arcading and a painted ceramic and mosaic scene of the
Crucifixion. – STAINED GLASS. Chancel s by *Mayer & Co.* of
Munich, 1895. – N aisle of 1878 by *William Wailes*. – MONU-
MENT. Mrs Charlotte Bradshaw †1820, by *Chantrey*. Grecian.
She is rising gently to heaven. Interesting example of Latinized
name 'Carolette' to fit the Latin inscription.

WHITTLEBURY HOUSE, E of the church. Built for the Fitzroys in 1874 by *T. H. Vernon*. Elizabethan style.

The village has one or two pretty Victorian COTTAGES, just a few of which still retain delightful twiggy rustic porches.

WHITTLEBURY LODGE,* I m. s. 2009–10 by *Peregrine-Bryant & Partners*. A handsome creation in the East European schloss manner. A central block of three storeys with single-storey pavilions at each side. The main house of three bays with a central doorcase and on either side windows with segmental pediments. Hipped roof with a balustraded belvedere lit by a thermal window. The pavilions have single windows with pediments above lit by a lunette. Brick-rendered and quoins to all the elements.

WHITTLEBURY HALL, ¾ m. s. Neo-Georgian hotel of 2003 of brick and stone and hugely overstated. Three-bay centre with pediment and a sort of Venetian window below with a balustrade balcony. Projecting porch also with balustrading. Quoins and platband on the wings of four and five bays. Behind even more neo-work in yellow brick with lots of rounded arches. Opposite the ATRIUM (golf clubhouse) complex of 2005. An equally outlandish Georgian mannered façade with an overstretched Tuscan portico. The other façades are mostly glass.

SHOLEBROOKE LODGE, ½ m. ENE. A small but distinguished hunting lodge built *c.* 1807 for the Hon. Charles Fitzroy by *James Morgan*. Morgan was assistant to Nash as architect to the Department of Woods and Forests and the house was built as the residence for the deputy warden of Whittlebury Forest. A design for it was exhibited at the Royal Academy in 1807. Extraordinarily tall, being three storeys. Brick-rendered. On the entrance side a small porch, the garden side with a large curved bay the full height of the house. Wide bracketed eaves, the effect very Nash-like. The interior much altered *c.* 1900 following fire damage when the large open-well staircase hall was created, a big top-lit square space with balustraded stairs the whole height of the house. The elegant drawing room may retain some original decoration. A further *c.* 1900 wing on the N side was demolished *c.* 1970. Fine setting.

WICKEN

ST JOHN EVANGELIST. Tall w tower, said to be of 1617. There is a carved plaque with the arms of the Spencers of Wormleighton, Warwicks. The bell-openings are pairs of lancets. Parapet. Pinnacles which were there had to be removed for safety reasons. The rest of the church of 1758–70, and an

---

*A previous house of this name by *William Burn*, 1865–8, was demolished in 1972. The site, at the s end of the village on the E side of High Street, is a housing estate, but GATEPIERS and an Italianate LODGE survive.

Wicken, St John the Evangelist.
Drawing by G. Clarke, *c.* 1850

extremely interesting example from that period. According to an inscription in the N aisle it was 'designed and built' by *Thomas Prowse*, an amateur and friend of Sanderson Miller. The execution was left, it seems, in the hands of the architect *John Sanderson*. Prowse's church is a strange design. Nave and narrow aisles of the same height, tall quatrefoil piers with two shaft-bands rather than shaft-rings. Capitals with leaves in the French later C13 style. Abaci square with hollows at the angles. The aisles are groin-vaulted, the nave tunnel-vaulted with penetrations or groin-vaulted with disappearing groins. The chancel projects and is gaily fan-vaulted (in papier mâché) with pendants hanging from openwork ribs. Nave and chancel do not go together, it seems. Prowse died in 1767 and his widow and her mother finished the church, as is recorded in her diary, in 1770, so the chancel may be of that later date. The nave is a much less pretty but much more serious conception, reminiscent somehow of the work of the Jesuits in the early C17 in the Netherlands and Germany. The windows made correctly Gothic by *Matthew Holding* in 1897, when the S transept was added and the E end of the chancel rebuilt. The S porch, Tudor form, is dated 1839. A vestry was added in 1874 and an organ chamber in 1878, both by *E. Swinfen Harris*. The REREDOS is of 1897 and also by Holding. Gothic with gilded and painted panels. The carving is by *S. L. Reynolds* of Northampton and the painting by *Clayton & Bell*. – FONT. Square, C12, of Purbeck marble, with three shallow blank arches to each side. – STAINED GLASS. Chancel E window of 1873 by *Clayton & Bell*. – Chancel N designed by *Eleanor Brickdale* and made by *J. V. Cole* 1921. – S transept E window of 1908 by *Burlison & Grylls*, and S window of 1920 by *A. K. Nicholson*. – N aisle windows of 1886 and 1925 possibly by *Clayton & Bell*, who designed the tower

window, 1890. – MONUMENTS. Charles Hosier and wife,
Prowse's parents-in-law, erected 1758. It must be by *Sir Henry
Cheere*. Rococo, with an obelisk in front of an open pediment.
Urn and many garlands. Some coloured marbles. Extremely
pretty. – Mrs Sharp, daughter of Charles Hosier, †1747. With
a standing putto. Pediment at the top. It is identical with the
monument by *T. Bastard* in the cloister of Wells Cathedral and
since Prowse had connections in the West Country, it might
also be by him. – John Sharp †1726. With two seated putti and
an obelisk. – John Hosier Sharp †1734, simpler. – Elizabeth
Sharp †1810. Signed by *J. Bacon Jun*. Draped urn; relief on
the base. Weeping willow by its side.

WICKEN MANOR. Immediately SW of the church, C17 but much
renewed. Flat E front of three bays with mullioned windows.
Formerly the gatehouse to the manor of the Spencers of Wormleighton. It used to have a central archway and the lintel is still
there with a panel with the Spencer arms above. A Georgian
wing with a porch to the rear. The main house is thought to
have stood a little further W.

SCHOOL and SCHOOL HOUSE, opposite the church. 1878 in a
Tudorish style by *E. Swinfen Harris*. Sandstone and ironstone.
Two big chimneys and a large bellcote.

Former RECTORY, a little further SW. Built in 1703, it is said out
of the debris of the Spencer mansion. Seven bays, the first two
and last two gabled. Two storeys. Doorway with open segmental pediment. The upper windows all have open segmental
pediments ending in small volutes, except for the middle one,
which has scrolly double curves. The glazing bars on the
ground floor are original.

WICKEN PARK (Akely Wood Junior School). The present house
originated as a forest lodge. It was sold in 1716 to Charles
Hosier, who enlarged it. By marriage it then passed to the
architect *Thomas Prowse*, though he seems not to have done
anything to it. It remained in a family descent till 1860 when
it was bought by George Douglas-Pennent, Baron Penrhyn,
who added considerably to it and altered the interior. It has
since been enlarged more for the school. The house of Charles
Hosier seems to have been seven bays wide and two and a half
storeys high. Very plain. Lower two-bay wings to the garden.
To the entrance side they are treated as broad canted bay
windows. Hardly any of the Georgian interiors or fittings
survive save for the early C18 staircase, which was rearranged,
and some panelling in various rooms. Close by an older house,
dated 1614, with gables and mullioned windows. It was the
STABLES of the Spencer mansion.

WILBARSTON

8080

ALL SAINTS. Ironstone; much renewed. The church originates
from a late C12 building, but it is difficult to be sure of what

form. In the N arcade it is the W and E responds which are Norman. Upright leaves on the capitals. The E respond, like that on the S, has a roll moulding running continuously to its base on its edge. The priest's doorway has a round arch with a slight chamfer. All that then is of before 1200. It is when we come to consider the E bay of the S arcade that uncertainty arises. It has a wide and very tall round arch considered to be C12, which it is suggested once opened into a transept or a transeptal chapel. Its edges are formed of a continuous roll moulding and it must have been remodelled. Could it originally, as on the N side, have had a respond which was removed at some later date? Photographs taken before the 1884 restoration show just a simple impost moulding. Its arch rests on the W side on a respond which may represent a remodelled Norman piece with nook-shafts, two now but only one on the pre-1884 photograph. However, the shafts do not fit well, nor do they look medieval. Curious trefoil niche head in the E jamb. The capital is an odd shape: square towards the E and rounded into the arcade. The whole thing is somehow unconvincing and could easily be post-medieval. C13 the rest of the S arcade: circular piers and circular abaci; pointed arches with one chamfer and one hollow chamfer. The three regular arches of the N arcade with their sunk quadrant mouldings seem to be of *c.* 1300. Late C13 W tower, small. Twin bell-openings with separating shaft. Spire with low broaches. Two tiers of lucarnes. Tower arch with three slight chamfers. Good late C13 S doorway with a five-cusped arch, mouldings and shafts. Fine S aisle window of three lights with a big circle in bar tracery (filled in with Victorian trefoils). Internally with side shafts with fillets. Externally, there is a change in masonry just to its l. which could indicate an original transeptal chapel. Dec the N chapel two-bay arcade, the two ogee niches, and the REREDOS at the E end of the S aisle, a big cusped and sub-cusped niche with an ogee arch and patterned sill. There was a restoration in 1884 by *G. F. Bodley.* His are the PAINTED ROOFS throughout, the SCREEN, PULPIT and PEWS with linenfold and some renewed window tracery, such as the chancel E window of reticulated design. Judging from the pre-1884 photographs he also built up the floor level of the chancel and its very eastern portion may well be totally his. – FONT. A small round basin on a pillar, C17 or C18. – STAINED GLASS. Chancel E, Christ resurrected, 1885 by *J. Hardman & Co.* S aisle, 1938 by *A. K. Nicholson* (the 1951 date in the window is an addition).

SCHOOL, School Lane. The original ironstone building in Tudor manner *c.* 1846 by *J. G. Bland* stands just S of the new school.

The village has a good assembly of ironstone houses of varying dates, some with mullioned windows. The ironstone is of a specially attractive golden shade, quarried the other side of the Welland. In MAIN STREET, for example, a house with alternating courses of light and dark sandstone, dated 1633.

WILBY

St Mary. A remarkable and very beautiful Perp w tower and spire, so fine in fact that it almost looks Victorian. It starts square with diagonal buttresses and below the bell-stage turns octagonal. The buttresses develop into diagonally placed pinnacles. There is a quatrefoil frieze and a parapet. The pinnacles connect with the octagon by flying buttresses, pierced by quatrefoils. The octagon has two-light bell-openings in the cardinal directions. Then there is another quatrefoil frieze, a parapet with pinnacles, and a recessed spire connected again with the pinnacles by short flying buttresses. Two tiers of lucarnes. The w doorway has traceried spandrels and gabled niches with traceried tops l. and r. A small square upper w window with tracery in the form of the so-called four-petalled flower. Early c14 s arcade of four bays with octagonal piers and double-hollow-chamfered arches. The n wall three two-light Perp windows. Its wall externally overlaps the tower buttress rather clumsily and this results from the n wall being an infill from a previous aisle which was taken down in 1817. Tall chancel, rebuilt in 1853 by *Anthony Salvin*, except for the lowside window, which is original work of the c13. – pulpit. Jacobean, with two tiers of the usual flat, broad arches. – stained glass. Nave s, c14 foliage and grisaille. In the porch a Flemish c17 panel of St George. – Chancel s, *c.* 1854, signed by *A. Lusson* of Paris. Chancel e, Stockdale memorial (†1853) by *Clayton & Bell*, 1878. Lowside window of the Good Shepherd, 1908 by *C. E. Kempe*. Tower window of *c.* 1908 by *H. V. Milner*.

Wilby Hall (on the main road). Georgian. Ironstone, five bays, two storeys, pedimented doorway with Gibbs surround.

WINWICK

St Michael. A cruciform c13 church – witness the lancet windows and the tomb-recesses in the transepts – to which an ashlar-faced Perp w tower with clasping buttresses was added. Chancel replaced in 1853 by *E. F. Law*, who did a more general restoration in 1856. – font. 1821 by *Thomas Rickman*, the inventor of the terminology of E.E., Dec and Perp. Here he is designing in the Perp mode. Panelled stem widening towards the bowl. Angel heads against the underside of the bowl. Octagonal bowl with shields and quatrefoils. – tiles. Donated in 1852 by their manufacturer *Herbert Minton*. – stained glass. Chancel e, 1886 by *Burlison & Grylls*. Nave s of 1844 by *W. Wailes*, somewhat faded. Nave n of 1905 and n chapel of 1911 also by *Burlison & Grylls*. Fine w window 2003 by *Jane Campbell*. – monuments. Sir William Craven †1707, large architectural tablet, without effigies. Two putti at the top. In front of the altar step, black ledger stone for the same. The stone is known to be by *Edward Stanton*, so he was doubtless responsible for the monument as well. – Maria Craven, 1736. Similar architectural tablet, but simpler. Signed by *Samuel Huskisson* of London.

WINWICK MANOR HOUSE. In the C16 Winwick was owned by the Andrews of Charwelton, and the present house is thought to have been built by Thomas Andrews (†1594). By the early C17 it had passed to John, Lord Craven, and the Cravens continued to own it till the early C19. The house is built of brick, with vitrified brick diapering, gabled, C16. Only half of the house is preserved. It was originally of half-H shape, with the porch and probably the hall bay projecting in the re-entrant angles. The back doorway is preserved which corresponded to the front porch. The original windows are mullioned and have arched lights. Other windows straightforward C17 mullioned-and-transomed. The staircase has flat tapering balusters and is arranged around a square well and so goes with the later windows. A watercolour drawing of 1870 shows that the house had already been reduced but it was then redoubled in size with a further range on the E side by *Morley Horder c.* 1926 in a manner which matches the original. Further service rooms added in 1913 by *J. H. Liddington* of Rugby.

In line with the original entrance a GATEWAY in the S wall of the front garden. This is a very fine piece of Elizabethan display, tripartite with four Roman Doric columns. In the spaces between the outer columns panels with rosettes and strapwork in simple geometrical forms. In the centre a round-headed arch. In the spandrels medallions with demi-figures. The columns carry a metope frieze. In the metopes rosettes and bucrania. Semicircular pediment at the top. The back is treated so roughly that the question has been asked if the gateway was not originally a porch. In the N of the county this would be attributed to the *Thorpe* workshop, but the details and decoration, though similar, are more intricate and from a different source. Behind it a knot garden created in 1992. At right angles to the house and facing the former front garden the STABLES, also of diapered brick.

Former SCHOOL and SCHOOL HOUSE, just below the church. 1841 by *E. F. Law*, of chequer brick with ironstone windows, all in the Tudor manner. The school was enlarged in 1867.

WINWICK HALL (former vicarage), E of the church. A large brick and stone house of 1848–9 in the Italianate manner by *Law & Clarke* (i.e. *E. F. Law*). Later enlargements have kept to the same style.

WOLLASTON

A large village which had a lacemaking industry in the C17, replaced by boots and shoes in the C19, the latter causing some expansion of a suburban quality, so several terraces of brick cottages etc. There is hardly a trace of either industry today.

ST MARY. An odd-looking church, because the tower with its tall spire is a crossing tower and the nave is Georgian. The tower is Dec, with bands of ironstone and grey oolite below, ashlar from the bell-stage upwards. The bell-openings are pairs of two lights. The broaches of the spire are low and have pinnacles standing on them. Three tiers of lucarnes in alternating directions. The arches inside have many hollow chamfers and the capitals are therefore partly concave-sided. In the N transept is a double tomb-recess. The body of the church was built 1737–9, very probably by *Francis Smith* of Warwick. Externally the nave has three tall round-arched windows with flat intersected tracery, just like the ones Smith designed at Lamport. Nave and aisles are separated by giant Doric columns on high bases, formerly hidden by the box pews. Just the semblance of a Doric frieze with the guttae of triglyphs below the ceiling. The nave ceiling is flat; the aisle ceilings cove up to it. Broad W front with an arched doorway and a circular window over, reusing some of the ironstone from the earlier church. Instead of the S transept a lobby of 1737. The chancel was re-Gothicized in 1902 and the Georgian interior dismantled during restoration in 1894 both by *Talbot Brown & Fisher*. Galleries and a three-decker pulpit of 1841 were removed, and box pews were taken apart and their doors reused in a random way as pew-ends. Further pews removed 2011–12. Two watercolours in the church also show that the tower crossing had been infilled to create round classical archways through to the chancel. These were unblocked 1885–6 under the direction of *Edward Stephens*. – The PULPIT of *c.* 1737 with parquetry survives set on a Victorian stand. – Also the FONT. A stone baluster stem and heavily gadrooned bowl. – The central portion of the WEST GALLERY also, with Roman Doric pilasters. The interior is to be reordered under a scheme by *Stimpson & Walton* of Northampton, devised in 2009. – STAINED GLASS. E window, Christ in Majesty by *Jane Cummings*, 1961. – N chapel, 1885 by *Heaton, Butler & Bayne*.

BAPTIST CHURCH, Hinwick Road. 1867. Yellow brick with three round-arched windows under a pediment enclosing a circle.

WOLLASTON HALL, NE of the church. Built *c.* 1738 and attributed by Andor Gomme to *Francis Smith* of Warwick. Seven by six bays. One and a half storeys. Hipped roof. A pretty Victorian iron veranda to the S. Handsome staircase with plaster ceiling. Earlier range at the back. Contemporary STABLES with a three-arched centre, hipped roof and cupola. The house has belonged to the Scott Bader Company since 1940, and they have built a conference hall, laboratories, etc. The architects were *Sir John Brown, Henson & Partners*. THE COMMONWEALTH CENTRE conference hall of 1958–9, is a pavilion with a hyperbolic-paraboloid ('collapsed-tent') roof. It is of timber,

60 ft (18 metres) square. The dip is 12 ft (3.7 metres). Curtain walling and brick buttressing as a support.

A handsome group of houses to the SE and SW of the church, especially those at the start of the street called HICKMIRE, notably THE PRIORY, C17, on the site of a building attached to the nunnery of Delapré near Northampton. Considerably altered and extended. Some work was done by *Talbot Brown*, probably *c.* 1880. In HIGH STREET, in a yard, the former INDEPENDENT CHAPEL dated 1752 (now a museum). Further S, WOLLASTON HOUSE of 1856, said to have been built by *George Burnham*, a Wellingborough solicitor, for himself. Italianate, of L-shape, with a three-storey tower in the re-entrant angle, and typical windows of tall arched lights, as e.g. illustrated in Loudon's *Encyclopaedia*, bargeboarded eaves, low-pitched roofs. In the parallel COLLEGE STREET the SCHOOL, mild Gothic, 1874 by *E. Sharman* of Wellingborough, and its attached classical infants' building of 1894 by *Charles Dorman* of Northampton. Opposite, the unremarkable WESLEYAN CHAPEL of 1898 signed *J. Blunt*, architect.

CROMWELL HOUSE, London Road. A good stone house dated 1657. Staircase with turned balusters.

NPS SHOES LTD, Holyoake Road. The village's last remaining factory, established 1881. Six sloped gables with the office entrance given a pediment enclosing a circle and doorway below.

MOTTE, a short distance S of the church. Locally called Beacon Hill. Rather low: its use is uncertain but some evidence of C12 occupation has been detected.

9070

WOODFORD

A large village much enlarged since the C19 when ironstone furnaces were set up just to the N. Large green with the church below to the S, well set overlooking the river valley.

ST MARY. A walk around the outside with the regular pattern and array of Perp windows does not prepare one for what lies within. The interior is one of those standard archaeological puzzles which remains largely unsolved. Standing at the W end of the nave, the long arcades, the assembly of pillars and arches and the ominously varied details give a perplexing impression. The normally accepted version of the church's history is something like this. A Norman church had its W wall at the E end of the short first N bay. It received a N aisle of three bays *c.* 1200. This has circular piers and capitals with leaf characteristic of that date, circular abaci, and unmoulded round arches. At the same time the then chancel received a N chapel of two bays also with round arches. The position of the original chancel arch is clear, and the arch from the aisle into the chapel also remains. The arcade details are the same, except that the capitals are moulded and have some nailhead enrichment. After that a W tower was begun W of the Norman nave and connected with it on the N side by a short pointed arch. But can this be so? Yes, the two E pillars of the N arcade are reasonable, with stiff-leaf foliage capitals, but the W pillar? While its column seems original, what of its capital? It is a clumsy affair compared with the other two, with decidedly crude carving and surely not medieval. Then to be considered also are the marks either side of the tower externally. There are curious large patched areas, with various masonry joints and cut-off weatherings or string courses. On the S side the string course fits the aisle height and there is the faint mark of a wall profile, sliced through, on the l. edge of the patch. The evidence on the N side is less obvious as the N aisle was heightened in the C15. Does all this not mean that the aisles of the church overlapped the tower? So an alternative version of the story could be that the *c.* 1200 church did not have a tower at all, but just a nave with N and S aisles, of which the base of the tower is the former W end of the early nave. This could account for why it is the only part of the building to use so much ironstone. Then *c.* 1250 it was decided to contrive the tower and to do this the aisles were shortened and the remaining walls of the nave strengthened, so leaving the square of the tower separate. This would also explain the half-arch on the N arcade and why the base walls of the tower are so thick. The break in the masonry and weathering string on the N side fits exactly the position where a former respond would have been. There is no supporting evidence on the S side, that arcade having been rebuilt in the C14 respecting the new tower. As for the tower itself, its approximate date can be guessed from its lancet windows, two-light bell-openings with a shaft, trefoil top frieze,

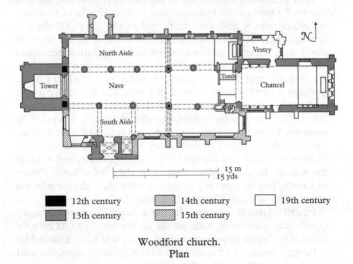

Woodford church.
Plan

shafted pinnacles, and spire, a broach rising behind a parapet with pinnacles and having three tiers of lucarnes. It must have been started before 1250 and the spire built into the C14.

Early in the C13 the s aisle had been built and connected with a new s chapel by an arch with circular piers and circular abaci and an unusual arch moulding with two hollows side by side. The over-restored s aisle doorway belongs to the same time, a handsome piece with odd scrolls of leaves along the roll moulding of the trefoiled doorway. The s porch again need not be later. Outer arch with columns with amulets. It has a quadripartite rib-vault. It was originally two-storeyed and its staircase now descends within a window recess inside; it had an E annexe which still has remnants of vaulting. Its E pier, though partly embedded in the wall, is of quatrefoil plan with a capital with stiff-leaf foliage. Further E, opposite the next arcade pillar, is a further quatrefoil pier, likewise embedded in the wall; all have transverse arches across the aisles. Just beyond this in the s chapel wall is a blocked window arch and under it a tomb-recess of late C13 date. What does all this mean? If they were full rounded piers, then an extra s aisle must have been intended, or even built. These complications probably arise because from the early medieval period, already by 1205, and right through to the 1740s, the advowson was split between two lordships and they seem to have operated separately with their own clergy etc. The architecture would suggest that they were responsible for different parts of the building. They were indeed referred to as Northern and Southern Moieties and this could explain the contrast between N and s aisles, with the more elaborate arrangements on the s side. The architecture again suggests some sort of agreement had been reached by the C14 as from then on the building is treated as a single unit. Further research is needed to clarify the story.

A new chancel was added in the late C13, with the old one becoming part of the nave and still leaving blocks of masonry on either side N and s at the E end of the nave. Of the old chancel there also remains, close to the E end of the nave on the N side, a large tomb-arch of the early C14 with a depressed two-centred arch. On its N side, i.e. at the E end of the N aisle, it cut into, and half destroyed, a richly moulded C13 arch, perhaps a SEDILIA. Of original C13 work are the C13 SEDILIA and PISCINA and the portions of the blank arcading on both sides. On the s side, before the chancel arch, a square of masonry hides the staircase to the rood loft, with its entrance turret in the s chapel, probably C15 like many of the windows in the aisles. The new chancel is now, in its details, and notably the E triple lancet window, largely of 1865–6 by *James Fowler* of Louth; but he was only responsible for that, the nave being restored by *William Slater* at the same time.

FURNISHINGS. – DOOR. In the s porch, C15 with tracery panels and two birds with scrolls at the top. – REREDOS (N aisle). De Capell Brooke memorial 1926, said to be painted by a French artist. – STAINED GLASS. N chapel. Apostles and prophets together with other fragments, all of *c.* 1425–50. –

Chancel E of 1893 and S of 1867 by *Heaton, Butler & Bayne*. By them also the tower window of 1867. – N aisle window of 1923 and three windows in the S aisle (1895, 1912 and 1936) all by *J. Hardman & Co.* – N aisle NW a Nativity by *Harry Harvey*, 1958. – MONUMENTS. Under the arch between N chapel and chancel, two effigies of oak, a knight and lady, he cross-legged, both very slender, early C14. – In the chancel a brass for Simon Mallory †1580. Figure in armour. – In the ringing chamber of the tower, Sir Roland St John, his wife (†1656) and son. A large architectural tablet of simple design with a cherub head at the top of the inscription plate. It would hardly be worth the note save that a contract exists for the sculptor *Thomas Cartwright* the elder (GF). – S aisle, the Rt Hon. Charles Arbuthnot of Woodford House (*see* below) †1850. Mundane white marble plaque signed by *Skelton* of York.

The village is somewhat spread but a number of buildings are worth noting. In CHURCH STREET, SW of the church, WOODFORD RISE, still a very typical stone-built Northamptonshire house with Collyweston and pantiled roofs and the fine chimneyshafts peculiar to the region. Originally a six-roomed cottage, probably C17, with direct front to back access. The datestone of 1729 refers to alterations and additions, which probably include not only the extension of the E front by an additional room on the ground and first floors, but also the transformation of the roof-space into attic bedrooms with dormer windows at the back. A later wing at right angles forms with it two sides of the courtyard; the remaining sides are defined by the stable block and a garden wall. Early C19 addition for kitchen and pantry with two rooms above. Finally, in 1930–5, a stone-built dining room was added to the N end of the main building and the old pantry enlarged by *Gotch, Saunders & Surridge*. At the same time many of the windows were replaced by stone mullions, and the ashlar porch introduced. The fine old oak staircase is said to have come from the former mansion, now demolished, which stood about 1 m. NE. In the garage a small Early Dec window which must have been brought from elsewhere. Further S, the OLD RECTORY, 1820 by *J. Teasdale*, with round-headed windows on its garden front and a closed-in porch of Doric columns. N of the church is RECTORY FARM (or Old Manor House). The S side has buttresses and a doorway of the C13 or early C14 with continuous mouldings. The centre range is a late C13 hall with stack inserted in the C16 against part of the screens passage. A wall with two arches with trefoil heads, their upper portions now within the first floor. Some C16 fireplaces and beams. RECTORY LANE leads W, along a wall with piers topped by balls, past an archway of *c.* 1700, enclosing the garden of the large DE CAPELL HOUSE, *c.* 1860, which stands on Church Green. N into Addington Road is MANOR HOUSE FARM, C17, half-H shape with renewed three-light transomed windows. Another GREEN with on the NE side the large front of the former INFANTS' SCHOOL of 1883 by *J. C. Traylen*, red and blue brick in the Gothic manner.

N into High Street, a long, much altered C17 row on the l., rendered stone but with several mullioned windows. Opposite a nice development of 1899–1900 with four houses on the street, at its corner SUNFLOWER COTTAGE and running back SUNNYSIDE, a terrace of ten houses. All these of yellow and red brick. A large HOUSE on the opposite corner, dated 1890 with a half-timbered gable. A little further N, on the l., is the former TEMPERANCE HALL of 1883, red brick and stone with round-arched windows, and further out on the r. is VIRGINIA LODGE. It appears to be an early C19 Gothic house extended in a Late Arts and Crafts manner in 1913.

WOODFORD HOUSE, 1¾ m. w. Originally a farmhouse. Bought early in the C19 by Charles Arbuthnot (a close friend of the Duke of Wellington), who demolished the farm buildings to re-erect them ¼ m. SE of the house, which he considerably enlarged. His architect was *Charles Bacon* (who died in 1818). To the w of the central block he built a commodious stable range and, to the E, a small wing with a billiard room – now the drawing room – and an ante-room, above which are bed and dressing rooms for the Duke, a frequent visitor. These alterations and additions (according to Mrs Arbuthnot's private journal) were completed by the autumn of 1826. Apparently, therefore, the building programme was spread over thirteen years, as the date above the main doorway is 1813. From the forecourt (on the s side) the house and stables, built of local stone and with low-pitched, deep-eaved roofs, form a delightful group of buildings, with the emphasis on the symmetrical centre block with its regular, typically sashed windows, and flanked by the two recessed but uneven wings on either side of it. The architectural balance of the N elevation has, however, been sadly upset by the protruding billiard room, which was built to the designs of *Blackwell & Thomson* in 1901–2.

ROUNDHOUSE, 1 m. SW of Woodford House, on the Finedon road. The inscription says 'Panorama – Waterloo Victory June 18 AD 1815'. This may be unexpected, but there is a tradition that Wellington remarked that the surrounding countryside was reminiscent of Waterloo. The main round tower is attached to a farmhouse. It has a circular window and a small railed prospect platform on its roof around the central chimney. The Burton Wolds Wind Farm has dramatically changed the view.

BARROWS. Line of three well-preserved mounds known as Three Hills, on the valley side overlooking the Nene, 1 km. s of the village above the road to Great Addington, public access from farm track.

WOODFORD HALSE

ST MARY. Of sandstone. Extensive restoration and partial rebuilding in 1878 by *Albert Hartshorne*, but apparently correctly done. N arcade of four bays, circular piers and octagonal abaci, pointed single-chamfered arches, *c.* 1200. It is noteworthy that one capital is still of the Late Norman multi-scalloped type. The S arcade with octagonal piers and double-chamfered arches is C14. Externally much of *c.* 1300, namely the W tower (cusped Y-tracery in the W window and bell-openings), the S doorway and the chancel (cusped Y- and cusped intersected tracery). N extension of 1999. – FONT. Octagonal bowl probably of the 1660s. – BENCH-ENDS. C15, some in the nave and two in the chancel, possibly C14, with poppyheads. – SCULPTURE. Bottom part of an image; nave E wall. – STAINED GLASS. A large selection including chancel E window 1884, S window (memorial †1851) also probably 1884 by *Burlison & Grylls* and another by a different hand. – S aisle E window of 1908, and side windows of 1878, 1907 and 1840 also *Burlison & Grylls*. – N aisle a good window of 1940. – MONUMENTS. Effigy of a lady, stone, early C14, unearthed during the 1877–8 restoration. – Brass to Nicholas Stafford, vicar, †1400 (chancel floor). The figure is 20 in. (51 cm.) long. – Catherine Knightley †1730, architectural, of variegated marbles with Ionic pilasters and a round-arched inscription panel, the familiar pattern which came from the *Smiths* of Warwick Marble Yard (*see* Lamport and Fawsley).

MORAVIAN CHAPEL, Hinton Road. 1906, of red brick in Dec Gothic style. Small tower with octagonal lancet top and porch below. Three-light lancet window with quatrefoil above. A frieze of terracotta below.

WESLEYAN CHAPEL, Hinton Road. 1879 in the lancet style, mainly red brick but with double-banded window arches of blue and yellow brick, and a circle in the gable which has bargeboarding. All rather jolly.

METHODIST CHAPEL, Hinton Road. 1902 of ironstone and limestone. Two two-light windows with tracery somewhere between Dec and Perp.

Former SCHOOL, E of the church. 1853 stone and brick in the Dec manner. Later buildings by *W. E. Mills*. The building to the r. was also a school building by *J. T. Blackwell* of Kettering, 1927.

PRIMARY SCHOOL, High Street. 1926–8 by *J. Blackwell* of Kettering. A long range with pedimented wings, mildly Neo-Georgian.

MANOR HOUSE, School Street, SE of the church. Of three bays only, of ironstone and sandstone. Originally two-storeyed, but a third added later. An elaborately framed doorway carrying a big segmental pediment with a flat urn between and tiny scroll supports. Sundial above dated 1858.

The junction between the Great Central Railway and the Stratford & Midland Railway was created in 1890, and this led to a rapid expansion of Woodford Halse, all too obvious as the village has a considerable early 1900s suburban brick air, whereas all around the villages take advantage of the plentiful local stone. This expansion overtook the adjoining S hamlet of

Hinton. The main building of the railway era is the former
Railwaymen's Club (now SOCIAL CLUB) in Hinton Road,
1898 by *Mosley & Anderson*. Large, black-and-white half-
timbered upper storeys on an ironstone base. Both porch and
a projecting wing have gables and oriels. N of this, set back
behind a small green, is the former HINTON MANOR HOUSE
(now a nursery). Basically one wing of a house begun *c.* 1695
but never completed. It was built for Richard Knightley and is
attributed to *William Smith* the elder and *Francis Smith* of
Warwick (see the monument in the church and, of course, the
connection with Fawsley). Of ironstone, with quoins and a
hipped roof. The SE façade of five bays has sash windows. The
SW facade is less regular, but has the original shape and framing
of the windows. Clarke drawings show them with mullion-
transom crosses. Doorway with segmental pediment on brackets. To the S, a stable range with mullioned windows.

HINTON HOUSE, 1½ m. NW, off the Byfield Road. A grand
mansion built in 1900 for Charles Church, J.P., by *James A.
Morris* of Ayr, who set up a London practice around 1890; this
is his only known work S of the border. In the Elizabethan style.
The two-storey entrance side has a porch on the r. with Doric
columns and a balustrade top. Angled sides with niches. To the
l. are two projecting gabled bays of three floors. Everywhere
mullioned windows. Several rooms with beamed ceilings and
a curved staircase with splat balusters of twisted shape.

WOODNEWTON

ST MARY. A church with a number of intriguing features, even if
one regrets the 1910 repointing of the interior walls. It is a cruciform church whose W tower was rebuilt in the C17, probably
at the same time as its N aisle was removed. The tower arch
towards the nave however looks like reused material. The double-stepped round (late C12) arch does not fit the later half-
octagonal C14 responds. At the top of the tower battlements and
pinnacles. (There is a document recording that 'Newton men'
bought battlement stone 'for their church' from the sale of
materials at Fotheringhay in 1573.) The oldest part of the church
is the indication of a nave S wall of before the arcades were
built. It appears at the W end in projections of wall and in the
fact that the S transept N wall is not in line with the S arcade.
Late C12 N arch of the S transept, single-stepped and round. This
may also be not totally in its original form. RCHME noted
its moulded capitals and bases have a 'classical' feel. A S aisle
was added a little later, say *c.* 1200–10. Three bays with one
round and one coarse quatrefoil pier, a little nailhead decoration
and, on the capital of the E respond, a series of human heads.
Double-chamfered arches. To the transept an arch of the same
type, resting on a corbel on the l., on a new or renewed pier on

the r. In the w wall of the aisle traces of a lancet window indicating that the aisle was formerly narrower. This has what appears to be one side of a triangular arch and it has been suggested it could be Saxon. If the aisle was narrower, the wall into the transept must also have been narrower. The respond seems too thick to assume that. If it was a corbel, as on the other side, it could have been so. Early C13 also the chancel s doorway with a zigzag surround to the round-headed opening, the round-headed lowside window to its w, the s doorway to the aisle, also still round-headed, but with much dogtooth, and the materials such as the pointed arch and the dogtooth which were used when the porch was remodelled in 1662. In the late C13 the s aisle was widened and the transept made part of it. Windows in the transept with intersected tracery (circular mullions) and that of the s aisle with (somewhat suspicious) bar tracery with foiled circles under a triangular head. It is a most odd form, but it does appear to be medieval. Perp clerestory and restored E window. The chancel was restored in 1910 by *W. Bassett-Smith* and the N transept rebuilt to contain the organ, and of this date are the STALLS, PANELLING and REREDOS, as well as the black-and-white MARBLE PAVING. – COFFIN-SLABS. Three in the porch, C13 or C14 with almost identical cross designs. – STAINED GLASS. Chancel E window of 1870 by *Heaton, Butler & Bayne.* – MONUMENT. Just N of the chancel the grave of Nicolai Polakovs, O.B.E., †1974, the famous 'CoCo the Clown' of C20 circus fame. Tiny bust in the headstone.

MANOR HOUSE. A most impressive façade to find in a modest village street. It was built *c.* 1740 by the Earl of Westmorland for one of his chief farm tenants and must therefore be from designs of *Roger Morris.* It is all façade, the building behind being a standard farmhouse. Only the façade is ashlar, the rest is rubble construction. The three-bay centre has three storeys, the outer bays only one and a half. These outer bays run their pediments up against the middle section, but in addition the ground floor of the centre has its own open pediment, and in the open part between the two shanks stands the first-floor centre window. The second-floor window is arched, as are the surrounds of the outer ground-floor windows. The crowning motif is a truncated pediment on which stands the chimney-stack. It is all very metropolitan. Extensions of 1895.

Among the nice stone houses in the village is FRANEY HOUSE, dated 1745 which was built by the mason *John Franey.*

WOOTTON

Northampton

7050

Despite now being part of outer Northampton, Wootton still has a village atmosphere at its centre, with a number of good stone houses, some thatched.

St George, Church Hill. The exterior too much renewed to be of interest. Restored by *Butterfield* in 1865 and his are the chancel arch, the chancel chapel arches and the tower arch. In the chancel a C13 lancet and three-light Perp windows. The s and N doorways are of 1300 or thereabouts. The w tower with battlements and pinnacles seems Dec. Two unusually large corbel heads N and S of the tower arch, C13 arcades of three bays with circular capitals, circular abaci and double-chamfered arches. The nave is to be reordered 2011–12 with new screens at the w end by *Stimpson Walton Bond*. – REREDOS. 1865 by *Butterfield*, E.E. style arcading with painted decoration. The CHANCEL ROOF also painted. *Minton* tiles. – FONT. Expensive, of various coloured marbles, by *G. E. Street*, 1874. – STAINED GLASS. Chancel E, 1840s by *Wailes*. – s aisle window with St George, 1909 by *Morris & Co*. Rather fine.

Former RECTORY, w of the church. Dated 1630. With mullioned windows and gables refronted in Tudor manner 1835.

PRIMARY SCHOOL, opposite the church. 1871–2, partly Gothic by *E. F. Law*.

CAROLINE CHISHOLM SCHOOL, Wooldale Road. By *BDP*, 2003–4. Central entrance building with a curved roof. Radiating from it five blocks of a curtailed triangular plan. Primary extension by the same architects, 2010.

In the centre, in HIGH STREET, THE WHITE HOUSE (No. 52) at the N end is early C19 with pretty Gothic windows. At the street's s end No. 3 of three storeys, rendered early C19 but older work at the rear and a date of 1736. No. 4 opposite is older although its datestone records 1763. Just below in BERRY LANE No. 4 has an especially good doorcase.

Former WORKHOUSE, Newport Pagnell Road. 1839 by *James Milne* for the Hardingstone Union. Late classical, of ironstone. One range only. A composition of seventeen bays, with a pedimented higher centre of three bays and two storeys, one-storey connecting links, and end pavilions. Handsomely converted for housing in 1972, when the rear buildings were demolished. It now looks more like a country house than a workhouse.

GRANGE PARK, s of Wootton before the M1 motorway. The development began in the late 1990s with building starting in 2001. Woodlands View Primary School was built 2002, the Community Centre 2003 and Medical Centre 2004. *Stephen George & Partners* have been the main designers. RICHMOND VILLAGE, Bridge Meadow way, is an attractive residential care complex by *Barchester* 2009–10 with housing part brick, part weatherboarded in pastel colour shades.

WOTHORPE

A hamlet with two main roads, known as the First and Second Drifts. On the E side of FIRST DRIFT is CLARE LODGE, built

c. 1850 by the architect *Bryan Browning* for himself and not
at all orthodox. It is a villa of stone in a vague medieval-
cum-Tudor manner. He apparently used some ecclesiastical
fragments. The main block is three storeys with its main rooms
on the first floor, where there is a large four-light Gothic
window on the l. and a two-storey open balcony on the r. under
a big timberwork gable. The l. wing is a bit more down to earth
with battlement cresting, mullioned-and-transomed windows,
more bays and timber gables. Timberwork tiled porch. Nearby
THE LAWNS, *c.* 1870 of yellow brick with round-arched
windows and a Tuscan porch. Further s, round the corner, is
TERRACOTTA HOUSE of 1879, built for himself by *Robert
Eldred.* A double-fronted red brick house with ground-floor
bays. Much terracotta ornament as rusticated quoins and surround, a foliage frieze and mask keystone for the doorway. It is
all reminiscent of *J. M. Blashfield*'s work in Stamford but he was
dead by this time. *Henry Lumby,* terracotta worker, is listed at
St Martins in Whellan's *Directory* of 1874, so perhaps his work.
A little further on a converted MALTINGS. The SECOND DRIFT
has a nice mid-Victorian terraced row of brick and stone with
pairs of houses with triple doorcases. Further on is WOTHORPE
HOUSE, like a Victorian Gothic vicarage.

WOTHORPE TOWERS.* One of the most intriguing buildings of   50
Jacobean England, made the more so because it survives only
as a ruin. It was built early in the C17, probably *c.* 1611–15, for
Thomas Cecil, Earl of Exeter, Lord Burghley's eldest son,

Wothorpe Towers.
Survey drawing by W. D. Legg, late C18

* This account derives extensively from the detailed researches and investigations
of Paul and Janet Griffin and their archaeologist Joe Prentice, to whom I am deeply
indebted.

within an estate which had been in Cecil hands since the time of Henry VIII. It was built for him, so Fuller says in his Worthies, 'to retire to while his great house at Burleigh was a sweeping'. Fuller also calls it 'the least of noble houses and the best of lodges'. It was indeed a spectacular lodge, with ancillary buildings of some extent and set within a series of formal walled enclosures and gardens and clearly designed for grand entertaining. The question arises as to whether there were already buildings on the site and to what extent portions of these might be incorporated in the present remains. The earliest surviving survey plan was drawn by *Thomas Thorpe Jun.* in 1615 and this shows the basic layout. After Cecil's death in 1623, Wothorpe seems to have been less used by the family and tended to be leased. For example, it was used for a time after the Restoration by George Villiers, second Duke of Buckingham. It was last occupied in the mid C18 by the widow of Brownlow 8th Earl of Exeter. However, in 1758–9 the main roof was removed and the W and E façades dismantled and the service ranges demolished. Fortunately the building was drawn in 1757 by the artist *John Haynes*. There are also undated survey drawings by the Stamford architect *W. D. Legg* (in both cases the drawings are at Burghley). The house survived then as a picturesque ruin and remained with the Burghley Estate until 2004 when the site was sold to the present owners who have consolidated the ruins and made huge efforts to reveal and conserve what remains of the building and to reinstate much of its garden layout.

Wothorpe is one of a type of Elizabethan and Jacobean lodges which is distinguished by specially compact and tall composition. It is difficult to find another of comparable plan and design. Sherborne Castle in Dorset, built by Sir Walter Raleigh in the late 1590s, is a near relative of Wothorpe but only in its basic concept. Comparison has also been made to the Smythson series of houses, but again the comparison is slight. What survive are four tall towers and the spine wall of the central block. The towers are square with octagonal top storeys and had until the C19 their original ogival roofs, just like those at Burghley.[*] The windows, of one tall rectangular light with the odd square supra-windows with flat volute decoration, are derived directly from Serlio. They are curiously reminiscent of Italian Mannerism and completely different from those at Burghley, or for that matter from Robert Cecil's work at Hatfield. The plan was a central square block with projections to l. and r. so forming a broad cross shape with the towers in the re-entrant angles. Once again a derivation from Serlio should be noted. The main façade facing W was of three bays and three storeys with gables above each bay and a central one-bay projection, the full height of the house, with a porch at ground level, no longer near one end, as was the medieval and Eliza-

[*] A number of mason's marks suggest that the builders were some of the same team who were working at Burghley. I am grateful to Kathryn Morrison for this reference.

bethan tradition. On the s side the projection housed a big
open-well staircase of similar form to that at Hatfield. There
was a secondary service stair in the sw tower. The Hall faced
a large forecourt flanked N and s by subsidiary wings of two
storeys. These had large gables at their ends and five smaller
gables facing the court. All the gables, both on the main block
and the wings, had elaborate crow-stepped profiles. The kitchens were in the base of the s wing which was joined onto the
house. The N wing was detached but balanced in design that
opposite. Excavation has revealed foundation walls. There were
cellars under the E and N part of the main block with access
from the main staircase. What is clear is that the towers are an
addition to the main building. They slightly overlap the lateral
walls and where they meet the windows of the main block a
slice of wall has been angled back to reveal the full frame.
Interestingly a similar situation occurred at Sherborne. At
Sherborne is a signed survey plan by *Simon Basil*. Basil (†1615)
is an enigmatic figure and little is known of his architecture,
but he rose to be Surveyor of the Royal Works. His chief patron
was Lord Exeter's brother, Robert, Earl of Salisbury at Hatfield, so an association with Wothorpe is not impossible. It is
also worth remembering that Robert Cecil himself was con-
structing a lodge at the same time at Cranborne, Dorset, not
very far from Sherborne, though here it was an enlargement
and alteration of a medieval house. Cranborne also has towers
of three storeys, one at either end of the s front, but here of a
more orthodox design. But these are digressions.

Of the ancillary buildings is an original though altered U-shaped
block marked on the 1615 plan as STALLS. This is as equally
intriguing as the main house and may have been of a higher
status than just stables. It consists of three ranges: a domestic
range, the N cross range containing stables with the remaining
range probably a substantial barn. Only the N end of the block
remains in anything like original form. It is of two storeys and
five bays with windows of a similar form to the main house,
that is a large rectangle below and a small square opening
above, but without the extra decoration seen on the main
building. The first floor had dormers above the windows. In
the centre is a grand Doric doorway, but judging from the
square window above, it is not *in situ*. The coursing of the
masonry is much finer on the ground floor, layers of narrow
and broad courses, than the first floor suggesting there were
two phases in construction. The W range of the block has been
severely altered but enough has been found to show that its
inner façade was originally of four bays with dormers and
doorways between bays one and two and three and four. The
rear façade was six bays with two large chimneystacks more or
less opposite the doorways on the front façade. The E range of
the court was totally rebuilt as a large barn when the whole
block was adapted as farm buildings in the C19. While the
general effect of this block reflects the main building one
wonders whether it might pre-date it.

The GARDEN layout consisted of formal plots on the E and W sides of which the outer walls largely remain and a more informal arrangement on the N with an enclosure behind the N wing of the house and a parterre beyond that. There is a considerable slope down from S to N. The formal approach to the house was from the W, via an avenue then into a walled court which ended at the forecourt of the house with a balustrade wall and steps, of which the foundations have been revealed. The E court behind the house had a gateway in its outer wall which survives. It has a stepped gable and niches to the l. and r. This court had across its lower area a curious zigzag water feature shown on the 1615 survey of which evidence was found during clearance of undergrowth. The S court, also walled, was the service court. It was cobbled with irregular pieces of stone. It had an oval centerpiece probably with a structure within it. One final feature needs to be considered. It is on the S side of the W entrance court and is a rare survival from the period when the site was used as farm premises: a large octagonal C19 POULETERIE. Its outer walls are stone but its internal compartments are of brick.

For the Stamford racecourse GRANDSTAND see Easton-on-the-Hill (p. 258).

YARDLEY GOBION

ST LEONARD. 1863–4 by *E. F. Law*. Nave and chancel of sandstone with ironstone dressings. Bellcote at the E end of the nave. Geometrical and Decorated detail. Internally the arches and windows have voussoirs of red and blue brick. The chancel arch on elaborate foliate capped pillar corbels. A good atmospheric interior of its time. – STAINED GLASS. Chancel E window of 1903 by *Mayer* of Munich, rather fine. – W window of 1865 by *Clayton & Bell*.

UNITED REFORMED CHURCH (former Congregational chapel). Built 1826 of rubble with red brick dressings to its round-arched windows. Tactful extension on its façade. It still has its gallery and pulpit.

SCHOOL, SE of the church. Patterned brick with red and blue bands. 1874 by *E. Swinfen Harris*.

Large spread village with a good many attractive thatched cottages and several Georgian houses with square-headed windows linked by platbands, e.g. the OLD PACKHORSE, opposite the church. A little further SE, PROSPECT HOUSE, dated 1757, of three bays with a hooded doorway. On the tiny green the old PUMP and former well, restored in 2000. Opposite is STONEBANK, a typical 1901 stone house with castellated bay and porch. Set back to the N is YARDLEY GOBION HOUSE, a mildly Italianate Victorian villa with a prospect tower. In MOOREND ROAD a pair of Victorian red and yellow brick

COTTAGES and beyond on the N side No. 48, THE MEADOWS (care home), a substantial c. 1900 house with a central bay with a first-floor Venetian-type window and rusticated opening in the attic. Wings with canted bays and oriel-type windows above. Sensitively extended for its current use.

YARDLEY HASTINGS

8050

ST ANDREW. Short early C13 W tower. Twin nook-shafted bell-openings with separating shaft, the whole under a round arch. The connexion between tower and nave is only a doorway with a slight chamfer. Of the Norman nave wall a little remains W of the arcades, which are of c. 1300. Three bays. Octagonal piers, moulded capitals, double-chamfered arches. The S capitals show a slightly earlier date than the N capitals. The E respond has a corbel with a bust of a man. His gesture is popularly interpreted as toothache, but probably means some obscene challenge. At the E end of the S aisle two brackets for images. The walls of the aisles and the general restoration were done 1883–8 under the direction of *George Sutherland*, clerk of works on the Castle Ashby Estate. The S aisle and porch were rebuilt 1883, the chancel 1884–5 and the N aisle 1887–8. The S porch retains its old door with decorative iron handle surround. C14? Dec chancel with straight-headed side windows but a C13 doorway. The westernmost chancel windows with their transom are in the form of the lowside variety. E window of four lights with reticulated tracery. Much restored. SEDILIA with Dec ogee arches but C13 shafts. S aisle PISCINA also C13. – CHANDELIER. Brass, two tiers, dated 1808. – PANELLING made from former box pews and some rather bizarre panelling forming the S aisle vestry. Gothic frieze with weird Ionic pilasters. Early C19. – STAINED GLASS. Chancel E of 1910 by *R. J. Newberry*. Chancel S, for Rev. Rigby †1893, but not made till 1901, by *Morris & Co.* S aisle, two windows of 1905 also by *Newberry*. – MONUMENTS. Several tablets by the local men *John Hunt* (Humfrey Betty †1737) and the *Coxes*, notably Rev. Edward Lye †1767 by *William Cox*. Lye is famous as an Anglo-Saxon and Gothic scholar. His memorial has a shelf with a book and an inkpot and quill.

YARDLEY CHAPEL (United Reformed Church). Originally 1718 but rebuilt after a fire in 1813. Quite grand, with four round-arched windows and a big pediment. The doorways and upper windows are arranged so that bays one and four carry the main accents. Two entrances since it was formerly Congregational.

MANOR HOUSE, immediately N of the church. The remains of the hall range of the Hastings mansion of c. 1320–40. A large barn-like structure, of two floors with a cellar. The N end of the fragment shows on the W side the r. jamb and the springing of the arch which led into the hall, and on the E side the simpler exit arch. The screens passage must have been to the l. To the r. four doorways, the two middle ones identical and probably leading into the offices; the l. one leads into the cellar, the r. one by a rough wooden stair to the upper storey of the fragment. Lancets and square-headed two-light windows with ogee-headed lights. On the upper floor a fireplace, and in the E wall a garderobe. Arched-braced roof with a collar and kingpost. It is thought that the house had a detached kitchen for which there is evidence within the present Manor House, which otherwise is C19.

OLD RECTORY, at the N end of the village. Dated 1701. Handsome brick front of five bays. Blank panels at each end on each floor. Two storeys and basement. Dormers in the roof with steep triangular and semicircular pediments. Doorway with a broad segmental pediment on brackets enclosing the date. The interior was much embellished c. 1950 with panelling and other items brought from Felling Hall, Newcastle and from Streatham Castle, Durham. Simple but good ironwork GATE of same date, which must be by *Thomas Warren* of Castle Ashby.

YARWELL

ST MARY MAGDALENE. Short unbuttressed W tower with small pyramid roof. The tower is largely an C18 remodelling, though the late C13 W window (two lights and a circle; circular mullions) is original. The aisles were both pulled down in 1782 but the shaved-down shapes still decorate the walls. Blocked Georgian doorway on the S side and plain Georgian square panel glazing. The alterations were made by *Mr Sanderson*, probably *William Sanderson* (†1803), whose gravestone with various decorations and the Masons' arms is on the S side of the churchyard. The arcade pillars survive inset within the walls, all C13, as are the surviving N and S chapel arcades. Circular piers with circular abaci, double-chamfered pointed arches. A little nailhead enrichment in the S arcade and the S chapel arcade. Both chancel chapels probably derive from the 1782 changes, but were rebuilt in 1892. There was a restoration 1910–11 by *H. F. Traylen*, with elegant new CHOIR STALLS of 1912 with Tudor rose scroll tops. WALL PAINTING. A fragment in the N chapel over the arcade. – ROYAL ARMS. On painted lozenge, 1790. – STAINED GLASS. Chancel E, 1963 by *G. Maile & Son*. – MONUMENT. A large table tomb in the N chapel with black marble ledger stone top, Humphrey Bellamy †1715.

The village has a number of good stone houses, several with mullioned windows, largely C17. The following are in MAIN STREET, almost opposite the church. MANOR FARM, L-shaped with windows of four and three mullions. C18 extension to the

r. Former barns to the rear, notably THE OLD BYRE, dated 1827, and SPRING BARN. Both have remains of little triangular ventilation holes. On the E side N of the church is SUNDIAL COTTAGE, C17 of one storey with attics. Two projecting bays, one with a doorway flanked by blind windows, the other much altered. Formerly mullioned but changed when the house was reduced in height. One of the best houses is MULLIONS, No. 57, further W, on the S side. C17, with one canted bay with gable, balanced by a dormer the other side of the entrance. At the top of the street on the N side, SUNNYSIDE, with one remaining three-light mullioned window but signs of others.

YARWELL MILL, ½ m. SW, is a big three-storey stone building of seven bays dated 1839. There are records of it being originally built 1730–1 for the Earl of Westmorland by the mason *John Dimbleby*. The MILL HOUSE of 1839 has three bays and two storeys with canted bays on the ground floor.

OLD SULEHAY LODGE, 1¼ m. WNW. Set within a small park. Main house demolished in the early C18. What remains is a GATEWAY and parts of STABLES, with three arches, mostly 1642, built by the 2nd Earl of Westmorland, of Apethorpe. Some mullioned windows. Altered 1851 by *Browning* of Stamford, and further enlarged 1892.

YELVERTOFT

ALL SAINTS. The strange thing about the church is the existence of an outer S aisle. There are thus three arcades in all. They have octagonal piers and double-chamfered arches. The N arcade is of three bays, the other two have four. The N and inner S arcade are Dec, the outer S arcade is Perp and the outer S aisle was probably built as a result of a bequest of the C15 rector (*see* below). Added to the inner aisle a one-bay S chapel. The arch towards the chancel on corbels, one with an animal head, the other with leaf. Dec S porch entrance with three orders of ballflower and fleurons and ogee hoodmould, which must have been rebuilt when the outer aisle was added. Dec the chancel too, see the (renewed) E window with reticulation and the curiously eroded SEDILIA with nodding ogee arches. The W tower has no feature of special interest, except the niche above the W window. Transomed two-light bell-openings with ogee-headed lights. The nave N aisle windows and its roof appear to be C17. Of special interest, however, is the sudden and lavish display of Perp decoration around the chancel N window. Four friezes of quatrefoil etc. below the window, and carried on across the framing buttresses. Their upper parts are moreover panelled. To this display, unaccountable from outside, corresponds a similar display inside, and its centre is the MONUMENT to John Dycson, rector from 1439 to 1445. Effigy of alabaster on a low tomb-chest with many small

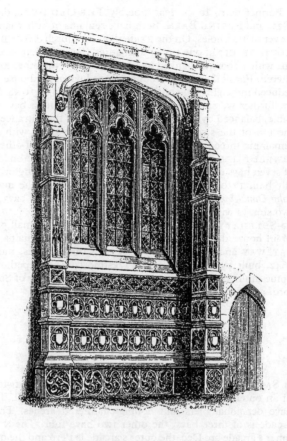

Yelvertoft, All Saints. Chancel window.
Engraving, 1849

quatrefoils. Two angels by his pillow. Low segmental arch, panelled back wall. Buttresses l. and r. with tiny niches one above the other. Broad cresting ending in a row of niches. – BENCHES. Broad, unbuttressed ends with very rich and varied traceried patterns. Lots of differently treated circles. They look C15 but there is a record of *Ruddle* of Peterborough providing carved open seats in the mid C19. – CANDELABRA. Of wrought iron in a swirling pattern, *c.* 2000. – STAINED GLASS. Chancel E, 1878 by *Burlison & Grylls*, somewhat faded. – S chapel E, 1904 by *Jones & Willis*. – MONUMENTS. John Dycson (*see* above). – Thomas Plampin †1770. By *William Cox Sen.* of Northampton. Very pretty. Also another of shield shape by the same in the S chapel.

CONGREGATIONAL CHAPEL, High Street. Founded *c.* 1792 but refronted in 1832. Red brick with a central later porch and a round-arched window on each side. Above in the centre a circular window and on either side two semicircular windows, like fanlights.

SCHOOL, High Street and School Lane. Mostly of 1874–6 by *E. F. Law* with a master's house on the r. with additions of 1906 by *Law & Harris*. The style is broadly Tudor but the fenestration has been much altered.

Six timber-framed houses in the village, unusual for Northamptonshire, but then we are on the border of Warwickshire. The best collection is at the w end of HIGH STREET, near the school. They include TUDOR COTTAGE and SCHOOL FARM, both of which are thatched, and both probably C17. Others are in ASHWELL LANE and ELKINGTON ROAD.

GLOSSARY

Numbers and letters refer to the illustrations (by John Sambrook)
on pp. 703–713.

ABACUS: flat slab forming the top of a capital (3a).

ACANTHUS: classical formalized leaf ornament (4b).

ACCUMULATOR TOWER: *see* Hydraulic power.

ACHIEVEMENT: a complete display of armorial bearings.

ACROTERION: plinth for a statue or ornament on the apex or ends of a pediment; more usually, both the plinth and what stands on it (4a).

AEDICULE (*lit.* little building): architectural surround, consisting usually of two columns or pilasters supporting a pediment.

AGGREGATE: *see* Concrete.

AISLE: subsidiary space alongside the body of a building, separated from it by columns, piers, or posts.

ALMONRY: a building from which alms are dispensed to the poor.

AMBULATORY (*lit.* walkway): aisle around the sanctuary (q.v.).

ANGLE ROLL: roll moulding in the angle between two planes (1a).

ANSE DE PANIER: *see* Arch.

ANTAE: simplified pilasters (4a), usually applied to the ends of the enclosing walls of a portico *in antis* (q.v.).

ANTEFIXAE: ornaments projecting at regular intervals above a Greek cornice, originally to conceal the ends of roof tiles (4a).

ANTHEMION: classical ornament like a honeysuckle flower (4b).

APRON: raised panel below a window or wall monument or tablet.

APSE: semicircular or polygonal end of an apartment, especially of a chancel or chapel. In classical architecture sometimes called an *exedra*.

ARABESQUE: non-figurative surface decoration consisting of flowing lines, foliage scrolls etc., based on geometrical patterns. Cf. Grotesque.

ARCADE: series of arches supported by piers or columns. *Blind arcade* or *arcading*: the same applied to the wall surface. *Wall arcade*: in medieval churches, a blind arcade forming a dado below windows. Also a covered shopping street.

ARCH: Shapes *see* 5c. *Basket arch* or *anse de panier* (basket handle): three-centred and depressed, or with a flat centre. *Nodding*: ogee arch curving forward from the wall face. *Parabolic*: shaped like a chain suspended from two level points, but inverted. Special purposes. *Chancel*: dividing chancel from nave or crossing. *Crossing*: spanning piers at a crossing (q.v.). *Relieving or discharging*: incorporated in a wall to relieve superimposed weight (5c). *Skew*: spanning responds not diametrically opposed. *Strainer*: inserted in an opening to resist inward pressure. *Transverse*: spanning a main axis (e.g. of a vaulted space). *See also* Jack arch, Triumphal arch.

ARCHITRAVE: formalized lintel, the lowest member of the classical entablature (3a). Also the moulded frame of a door or window (often borrowing the profile of a classical architrave). For *lugged* and *shouldered* architraves *see* 4b.

ARCUATED: dependent structurally on the arch principle. Cf. Trabeated.

ARK: chest or cupboard housing the

tables of Jewish law in a synagogue.

ARRIS: sharp edge where two surfaces meet at an angle (3a).

ASHLAR: masonry of large blocks wrought to even faces and square edges (6d).

ASTRAGAL: classical moulding of semicircular section (3f).

ASTYLAR: with no columns or similar vertical features.

ATLANTES: *see* Caryatids.

ATRIUM (plural: atria): inner court of a Roman or C20 house; in a multi-storey building, a toplit covered court rising through all storeys. Also an open court in front of a church.

ATTACHED COLUMN: *see* Engaged column.

ATTIC: small top storey within a roof. Also the storey above the main entablature of a classical façade.

AUMBRY: recess or cupboard to hold sacred vessels for the Mass.

BAILEY: *see* Motte-and-bailey.

BALANCE BEAM: *see* Canals.

BALDACCHINO: free-standing canopy, originally fabric, over an altar. Cf. Ciborium.

BALLFLOWER: globular flower of three petals enclosing a ball (1a). Typical of the Decorated style.

BALUSTER: pillar or pedestal of bellied form. *Balusters*: vertical supports of this or any other form, for a handrail or coping, the whole being called a *balustrade* (6c). *Blind balustrade*: the same applied to the wall surface.

BARBICAN: outwork defending the entrance to a castle.

BARGEBOARDS (corruption of 'vergeboards'): boards, often carved or fretted, fixed beneath the eaves of a gable to cover and protect the rafters.

BAROQUE: style originating in Rome *c.*1600 and current in England *c.*1680–1720, characterized by dramatic massing and silhouette and the use of the giant order.

BARROW: burial mound.

BARTIZAN: corbelled turret, square or round, frequently at an angle.

BASCULE: hinged part of a lifting (or bascule) bridge.

BASE: moulded foot of a column or pilaster. For *Attic* base *see* 3b.

BASEMENT: lowest, subordinate storey; hence the lowest part of a classical elevation, below the *piano nobile* (q.v.).

BASILICA: a Roman public hall; hence an aisled building with a clerestory.

BASTION: one of a series of defensive semicircular or polygonal projections from the main wall of a fortress or city.

BATTER: intentional inward inclination of a wall face.

BATTLEMENT: defensive parapet, composed of *merlons* (solid) and *crenels* (embrasures) through which archers could shoot; sometimes called *crenellation*. Also used decoratively.

BAY: division of an elevation or interior space as defined by regular vertical features such as arches, columns, windows etc.

BAY LEAF: classical ornament of overlapping bay leaves (3f).

BAY WINDOW: window of one or more storeys projecting from the face of a building. *Canted*: with a straight front and angled sides. *Bow window*: curved. *Oriel*: rests on corbels or brackets and starts above ground level; also the bay window at the dais end of a medieval great hall.

BEAD-AND-REEL: *see* Enrichments.

BEAKHEAD: Norman ornament with a row of beaked bird or beast heads usually biting into a roll moulding (1a).

BELFRY: chamber or stage in a tower where bells are hung.

BELL CAPITAL: *see* 1b.

BELLCOTE: small gabled or roofed housing for the bell(s).

BERM: level area separating a ditch from a bank on a hill-fort or barrow.

BILLET: Norman ornament of small half-cylindrical or rectangular blocks (1a).

BLIND: *see* Arcade, Baluster, Portico.

BLOCK CAPITAL: *see* 1a.

BLOCKED: columns, etc. interrupted by regular projecting

blocks (*blocking*), as on a Gibbs surround (4b).

BLOCKING COURSE: course of stones, or equivalent, on top of a cornice and crowning the wall.

BOLECTION MOULDING: covering the joint between two different planes (6b).

BOND: the pattern of long sides (*stretchers*) and short ends (*headers*) produced on the face of a wall by laying bricks in a particular way (6e).

BOSS: knob or projection, e.g. at the intersection of ribs in a vault (2c).

BOWTELL: a term in use by the C15 for a form of roll moulding, usually three-quarters of a circle in section (also called *edge roll*).

BOW WINDOW: *see* Bay window.

BOX FRAME: timber-framed construction in which vertical and horizontal wall members support the roof (7). Also concrete construction where the loads are taken on cross walls; also called *cross-wall construction*.

BRACE: subsidiary member of a structural frame, curved or straight. *Bracing* is often arranged decoratively e.g. quatrefoil, herringbone (7). *See also* Roofs.

BRATTISHING: ornamental crest, usually formed of leaves, Tudor flowers or miniature battlements.

BRESSUMER (*lit.* breast-beam): big horizontal beam supporting the wall above, especially in a jettied building (7).

BRICK: *see* Bond, Cogging, Engineering, Gauged, Tumbling.

BRIDGE: *Bowstring*: with arches rising above the roadway which is suspended from them. *Clapper*: one long stone forms the roadway. *Roving*: *see* Canal. *Suspension*: roadway suspended from cables or chains slung between towers or pylons. *Stay-suspension* or *stay-cantilever*: supported by diagonal stays from towers or pylons. *See also* Bascule.

BRISES-SOLEIL: projecting fins or canopies which deflect direct sunlight from windows.

BROACH: *see* Spire and 1c.

BUCRANIUM: ox skull used decoratively in classical friezes.

BULL-NOSED SILL: sill displaying a pronounced convex upper moulding.

BULLSEYE WINDOW: small oval window, set horizontally (cf. Oculus). Also called *œil de bœuf*.

BUTTRESS: vertical member projecting from a wall to stabilize it or to resist the lateral thrust of an arch, roof, or vault (1c, 2c). A *flying buttress* transmits the thrust to a heavy abutment by means of an arch or half-arch (1c).

CABLE OR ROPE MOULDING: originally Norman, like twisted strands of a rope.

CAMES: *see* Quarries.

CAMPANILE: free-standing bell-tower.

CANALS: *Flash lock*: removable weir or similar device through which boats pass on a flush of water. Predecessor of the *pound lock*: chamber with gates at each end allowing boats to float from one level to another. *Tidal gates*: single pair of lock gates allowing vessels to pass when the tide makes a level. *Balance beam*: beam projecting horizontally for opening and closing lock gates. *Roving bridge*: carrying a towing path from one bank to the other.

CANTILEVER: horizontal projection (e.g. step, canopy) supported by a downward force behind the fulcrum.

CAPITAL: head or crowning feature of a column or pilaster; for classical types *see* 3; for medieval types *see* 1b.

CARREL: compartment designed for individual work or study.

CARTOUCHE: classical tablet with ornate frame (4b).

CARYATIDS: female figures supporting an entablature; their male counterparts are *Atlantes* (*lit.* Atlas figures).

CASEMATE: vaulted chamber, with embrasures for defence, within a castle wall or projecting from it.

CASEMENT: side-hinged window.

CASTELLATED: with battlements (q.v.).

CAST IRON: hard and brittle, cast in a mould to the required shape.

Wrought iron is ductile, strong in tension, forged into decorative patterns or forged and rolled into e.g. bars, joists, boiler plates; *mild steel* is its modern equivalent, similar but stronger.

CATSLIDE: *See* 8a.

CAVETTO: concave classical moulding of quarter-round section (3f).

CELURE OR CEILURE: enriched area of roof above rood or altar.

CEMENT: *see* Concrete.

CENOTAPH (*lit.* empty tomb): funerary monument which is not a burying place.

CENTRING: wooden support for the building of an arch or vault, removed after completion.

CHAMFER (*lit.* corner-break): surface formed by cutting off a square edge or corner. For types of chamfers and *chamfer stops see* 6a. *See also* Double chamfer.

CHANCEL: part of the E end of a church set apart for the use of the officiating clergy.

CHANTRY CHAPEL: often attached to or within a church, endowed for the celebration of Masses principally for the soul of the founder.

CHEVET (*lit.* head): French term for chancel with ambulatory and radiating chapels.

CHEVRON: V-shape used in series or double series (later) on a Norman moulding (1a). Also (especially when on a single plane) called *zigzag*.

CHOIR: the part of a cathedral, monastic or collegiate church where services are sung.

CIBORIUM: a fixed canopy over an altar, usually vaulted and supported on four columns; cf. Baldacchino. Also a canopied shrine for the reserved sacrament.

CINQUEFOIL: *see* Foil.

CIST: stone-lined or slab-built grave.

CLADDING: external covering or skin applied to a structure, especially a framed one.

CLERESTORY: uppermost storey of the nave of a church, pierced by windows. Also high-level windows in secular buildings.

CLOSER: a brick cut to complete a bond (6e).

CLUSTER BLOCK: *see* Multi-storey.

COADE STONE: ceramic artificial stone made in Lambeth 1769–c.1840 by Eleanor Coade (†1821) and her associates.

COB: walling material of clay mixed with straw. Also called *pisé*.

COFFERING: arrangement of sunken panels (coffers), square or polygonal, decorating a ceiling, vault, or arch.

COGGING: a decorative course of bricks laid diagonally (6e). Cf. Dentilation.

COLLAR: *see* Roofs and 7.

COLLEGIATE CHURCH: endowed for the support of a college of priests.

COLONNADE: range of columns supporting an entablature. Cf. Arcade.

COLONNETTE: small medieval column or shaft.

COLOSSAL ORDER: *see* Giant order.

COLUMBARIUM: shelved, niched structure to house multiple burials.

COLUMN: a classical, upright structural member of round section with a shaft, a capital, and usually a base (3a, 4a).

COLUMN FIGURE: carved figure attached to a medieval column or shaft, usually flanking a doorway.

COMMUNION TABLE: unconsecrated table used in Protestant churches for the celebration of Holy Communion.

COMPOSITE: *see* Orders.

COMPOUND PIER: grouped shafts (q.v.), or a solid core surrounded by shafts.

CONCRETE: composition of *cement* (calcined lime and clay), *aggregate* (small stones or rock chippings), sand and water. It can be poured into *formwork* or *shuttering* (temporary frame of timber or metal) on site (*in-situ* concrete), or *pre-cast* as components before construction. *Reinforced*: incorporating steel rods to take the tensile force. *Pre-stressed*: with tensioned steel rods. Finishes include the impression of boards left by formwork (*board-marked* or *shuttered*), and texturing with steel brushes (*brushed*) or hammers (*hammer-dressed*). *See also* Shell.

CONSOLE: bracket of curved outline (4b).

COPING: protective course of masonry or brickwork capping a wall (6d).

CORBEL: projecting block supporting something above. *Corbel course*: continuous course of projecting stones or bricks fulfilling the same function. *Corbel table*: series of corbels to carry a parapet or a wall-plate or wall-post (7). *Corbelling*: brick or masonry courses built out beyond one another to support a chimney-stack, window, etc.

CORINTHIAN: *see* Orders and 3d.

CORNICE: flat-topped ledge with moulded underside, projecting along the top of a building or feature, especially as the highest member of the classical entablature (3a). Also the decorative moulding in the angle between wall and ceiling.

CORPS-DE-LOGIS: the main building(s) as distinct from the wings or pavilions.

COTTAGE ORNÉ: an artfully rustic small house associated with the Picturesque movement.

COUNTERCHANGING: of joists on a ceiling divided by beams into compartments, when placed in opposite directions in alternate squares.

COUR D'HONNEUR: formal entrance court before a house in the French manner, usually with flanking wings and a screen wall or gates.

COURSE: continuous layer of stones, etc. in a wall (6e).

COVE: a broad concave moulding, e.g. to mask the eaves of a roof. *Coved ceiling*: with a pronounced cove joining the walls to a flat central panel smaller than the whole area of the ceiling.

CRADLE ROOF: *see* Wagon roof.

CREDENCE: a shelf within or beside a piscina (q.v.), or a table for the sacramental elements and vessels.

CRENELLATION: parapet with crenels (*see* Battlement).

CRINKLE-CRANKLE WALL: garden wall undulating in a series of serpentine curves.

CROCKETS: leafy hooks. *Crocketing* decorates the edges of Gothic features, such as pinnacles, canopies, etc. *Crocket capital*: *see* 1b.

CROSSING: central space at the junction of the nave, chancel, and transepts. *Crossing tower*: above a crossing.

CROSS-WINDOW: with one mullion and one transom (qq.v.).

CROWN-POST: *see* Roofs and 7.

CROWSTEPS: squared stones set like steps, e.g. on a gable (8a).

CRUCKS (*lit.* crooked): pairs of inclined timbers (*blades*), usually curved, set at bay-lengths; they support the roof timbers and, in timber buildings, also support the walls (8b). *Base*: blades rise from ground level to a tie- or collar-beam which supports the roof timbers. *Full*: blades rise from ground level to the apex of the roof, serving as the main members of a roof truss. *Jointed*: blades formed from more than one timber; the lower member may act as a wall-post; it is usually elbowed at wall-plate level and jointed just above. *Middle*: blades rise from half-way up the walls to a tie- or collar-beam. *Raised*: blades rise from half-way up the walls to the apex. *Upper*: blades supported on a tie-beam and rising to the apex.

CRYPT: underground or half-underground area, usually below the E end of a church. *Ring crypt*: corridor crypt surrounding the apse of an early medieval church, often associated with chambers for relics. Cf. Undercroft.

CUPOLA (*lit.* dome): especially a small dome on a circular or polygonal base crowning a larger dome, roof, or turret.

CURSUS: a long avenue defined by two parallel earthen banks with ditches outside.

CURTAIN WALL: a connecting wall between the towers of a castle. Also a non-load-bearing external wall applied to a C20 framed structure.

CUSP: *see* Tracery and 2b.

CYCLOPEAN MASONRY: large irregular polygonal stones, smooth and finely jointed.

CYMA RECTA and CYMA REVERSA: classical mouldings with double curves (3f). Cf. Ogee.

DADO: the finishing (often with panelling) of the lower part of a wall in a classical interior; in origin a formalized continuous pedestal. *Dado rail*: the moulding along the top of the dado.

DAGGER: *see* Tracery and 2b.

DALLE-DE-VERRE (*lit.* glass-slab): a late C20 stained-glass technique, setting large, thick pieces of cast glass into a frame of reinforced concrete or epoxy resin.

DEC (DECORATED): English Gothic architecture *c.* 1290 to *c.* 1350. The name is derived from the type of window tracery (q.v.) used during the period.

DEMI- or HALF-COLUMNS: engaged columns (q.v.) half of whose circumference projects from the wall.

DENTIL: small square block used in series in classical cornices (3c). *Dentilation* is produced by the projection of alternating headers along cornices or stringcourses.

DIAPER: repetitive surface decoration of lozenges or squares flat or in relief. Achieved in brickwork with bricks of two colours.

DIOCLETIAN OR THERMAL WINDOW: semicircular with two mullions, as used in the Baths of Diocletian, Rome (4b).

DISTYLE: having two columns (4a).

DOGTOOTH: E.E. ornament, consisting of a series of small pyramids formed by four stylized canine teeth meeting at a point (1a).

DORIC: *see* Orders and 3a, 3b.

DORMER: window projecting from the slope of a roof (8a).

DOUBLE CHAMFER: a chamfer applied to each of two recessed arches (1a).

DOUBLE PILE: *see* Pile.

DRAGON BEAM: *see* Jetty.

DRESSINGS: the stone or brickwork worked to a finished face about an angle, opening, or other feature.

DRIPSTONE: moulded stone projecting from a wall to protect the lower parts from water. Cf. Hood-mould, Weathering.

DRUM: circular or polygonal stage supporting a dome or cupola. Also one of the stones forming the shaft of a column (3a).

DUTCH or FLEMISH GABLE: *see* 8a.

EASTER SEPULCHRE: tomb-chest used for Easter ceremonial, within or against the N wall of a chancel.

EAVES: overhanging edge of a roof; hence *eaves cornice* in this position.

ECHINUS: ovolo moulding (q.v.) below the abacus of a Greek Doric capital (3a).

EDGE RAIL: *see* Railways.

E.E. (EARLY ENGLISH): English Gothic architecture *c.* 1190–1250.

EGG-AND-DART: *see* Enrichments and 3f.

ELEVATION: any face of a building or side of a room. In a drawing, the same or any part of it, represented in two dimensions.

EMBATTLED: with battlements.

EMBRASURE: small splayed opening in a wall or battlement (q.v.).

ENCAUSTIC TILES: earthenware tiles fired with a pattern and glaze.

EN DELIT: stone cut against the bed.

ENFILADE: reception rooms in a formal series, usually with all doorways on axis.

ENGAGED or ATTACHED COLUMN: one that partly merges into a wall or pier.

ENGINEERING BRICKS: dense bricks, originally used mostly for railway viaducts etc.

ENRICHMENTS: the carved decoration of certain classical mouldings, e.g. the ovolo (qq.v.) with *egg-and-dart*, the cyma reversa with *waterleaf*, the astragal with *bead-and-reel* (3f).

ENTABLATURE: in classical architecture, collective name for the three horizontal members (architrave, frieze, and cornice) carried by a wall or a column (3a).

ENTASIS: very slight convex deviation from a straight line, used to prevent an optical illusion of concavity.

EPITAPH: inscription on a tomb.

EXEDRA: *see* Apse.

EXTRADOS: outer curved face of an arch or vault.

EYECATCHER: decorative building terminating a vista.

FASCIA: plain horizontal band, e.g. in an architrave (3c, 3d) or on a shopfront.

FENESTRATION: the arrangement of windows in a façade.

FERETORY: site of the chief shrine of a church, behind the high altar.

FESTOON: ornamental garland, suspended from both ends. Cf. Swag.

FIBREGLASS, or glass-reinforced polyester (GRP): synthetic resin reinforced with glass fibre. GRC: glass-reinforced concrete.

FIELD: see Panelling and 6b.

FILLET: a narrow flat band running down a medieval shaft or along a roll moulding (1a). It separates larger curved mouldings in classical cornices, fluting or bases (3c).

FLAMBOYANT: the latest phase of French Gothic architecture, with flowing tracery.

FLASH LOCK: see Canals.

FLÈCHE or SPIRELET (*lit.* arrow): slender spire on the centre of a roof.

FLEURON: medieval carved flower or leaf, often rectilinear (1a).

FLUSHWORK: knapped flint used with dressed stone to form patterns.

FLUTING: series of concave grooves (flutes), their common edges sharp (arris) or blunt (fillet) (3).

FOIL (*lit.* leaf): lobe formed by the cusping of a circular or other shape in tracery (2b). *Trefoil* (three), *quatrefoil* (four), *cinquefoil* (five), and *multifoil* express the number of lobes in a shape.

FOLIATE: decorated with leaves.

FORMWORK: see Concrete.

FRAMED BUILDING: where the structure is carried by a framework – e.g. of steel, reinforced concrete, timber – instead of by load-bearing walls.

FREESTONE: stone that is cut, or can be cut, in all directions.

FRESCO: *al fresco*: painting on wet plaster. *Fresco secco*: painting on dry plaster.

FRIEZE: the middle member of the classical entablature, sometimes ornamented (3a). *Pulvinated frieze* (*lit.* cushioned): of bold convex profile (3c). Also a horizontal band of ornament.

FRONTISPIECE: in C16 and C17 buildings the central feature of doorway and windows above linked in one composition.

GABLE: For types *see* 8a. *Gablet*: small gable. *Pedimental gable*: treated like a pediment.

GADROONING: classical ribbed ornament like inverted fluting that flows into a lobed edge.

GALILEE: chapel or vestibule usually at the W end of a church enclosing the main portal(s).

GALLERY: a long room or passage; an upper storey above the aisle of a church, looking through arches to the nave; a balcony or mezzanine overlooking the main interior space of a building; or an external walkway.

GALLETING: small stones set in a mortar course.

GAMBREL ROOF: see 8a.

GARDEROBE: medieval privy.

GARGOYLE: projecting water spout often carved into human or animal shape.

GAUGED or RUBBED BRICKWORK: soft brick sawn roughly, then rubbed to a precise (gauged) surface. Mostly used for door or window openings (5c).

GAZEBO (jocular Latin, 'I shall gaze'): ornamental lookout tower or raised summer house.

GEOMETRIC: English Gothic architecture c.1250–1310. *See also* Tracery. For another meaning, *see* Stairs.

GIANT or COLOSSAL ORDER: classical order (q.v.) whose height is that of two or more storeys of the building to which it is applied.

GIBBS SURROUND: C18 treatment of an opening (4b), seen particularly in the work of James Gibbs (1682–1754).

GIRDER: a large beam. *Box*: of hollow-box section. *Bowed*: with its top rising in a curve. *Plate*: of I-section, made from iron or steel

plates. *Lattice*: with braced framework.

GLAZING BARS: wooden or sometimes metal bars separating and
supporting window panes.

GRAFFITI: *see* Sgraffito.

GRANGE: farm owned and run by a
religious order.

GRC: *see* Fibreglass.

GRISAILLE: monochrome painting
on walls or glass.

GROIN: sharp edge at the meeting of
two cells of a cross-vault; *see* Vault
and 2c.

GROTESQUE (*lit.* grotto-esque): wall
decoration adopted from Roman
examples in the Renaissance. Its
foliage scrolls incorporate figur-
ative elements. Cf. Arabesque.

GROTTO: artificial cavern.

GRP: *see* Fibreglass.

GUILLOCHE: classical ornament of
interlaced bands (4b).

GUNLOOP: opening for a firearm.

GUTTAE: stylized drops (3b).

HALF-TIMBERING: archaic term for
timber-framing (q.v.). Sometimes
used for non-structural decorative
timberwork.

HALL CHURCH: medieval church
with nave and aisles of approximately equal height.

HAMMERBEAM: *see* Roofs and 7.

HAMPER: in C20 architecture, a visually distinct topmost storey or
storeys.

HEADER: *see* Bond and 6e.

HEADSTOP: stop (q.v.) carved with
a head (5b).

HELM ROOF: *see* IC.

HENGE: ritual earthwork.

HERM (*lit.* the god Hermes): male
head or bust on a pedestal.

HERRINGBONE WORK: *see* 7ii. Cf.
Pitched masonry.

HEXASTYLE: *see* Portico.

HILL-FORT: Iron Age earthwork enclosed by a ditch and bank system.

HIPPED ROOF: *see* 8a.

HOODMOULD: projecting moulding
above an arch or lintel to throw off
water (2b, 5b). When horizontal
often called a *label*. For label stop
see Stop.

HUSK GARLAND: festoon of stylized
nutshells (4b).

HYDRAULIC POWER: use of water
under high pressure to work
machinery. *Accumulator tower*:
houses a hydraulic accumulator
which accommodates fluctuations
in the flow through hydraulic mains.

HYPOCAUST (*lit.* underburning): Roman underfloor heating system.

IMPOST: horizontal moulding at the
springing of an arch (5c).

IMPOST BLOCK: block between
abacus and capital (1b).

IN ANTIS: *see* Antae, Portico and 4a.

INDENT: shape chiselled out of a
stone to receive a brass.

INDUSTRIALIZED or SYSTEM
BUILDING: system of manufac-
tured units assembled on site.

INGLENOOK (*lit.* fire-corner): recess
for a hearth with provision for
seating.

INTERCOLUMNATION: interval between columns.

INTERLACE: decoration in relief
simulating woven or entwined
stems or bands.

INTRADOS: *see* Soffit.

IONIC: *see* Orders and 3c.

JACK ARCH: shallow segmental vault
springing from beams, used for
fireproof floors, bridge decks, etc.

JAMB (*lit.* leg): one of the vertical
sides of an opening.

JETTY: in a timber-framed building,
the projection of an upper storey
beyond the storey below, made by
the beams and joists of the lower
storey oversailing the wall; on their
outer ends is placed the sill of the
walling for the storey above (7).
Buildings can be jettied on several
sides, in which case a *dragon beam*
is set diagonally at the corner to
carry the joists to either side.

JOGGLE: the joining of two stones to
prevent them slipping by a notch
in one and a projection in the other.

KEEL MOULDING: moulding used
from the late C12, in section like
the keel of a ship (1a).

KEEP: principal tower of a castle.

KENTISH CUSP: *see* Tracery and 2b.

KEY PATTERN: see 4b.

KEYSTONE: central stone in an arch or vault (4b, 5c).

KINGPOST: see Roofs and 7.

KNEELER: horizontal projecting stone at the base of each side of a gable to support the inclined coping stones (8a).

LABEL: see Hoodmould and 5b.

LABEL STOP: see Stop and 5b.

LACED BRICKWORK: vertical strips of brickwork, often in a contrasting colour, linking openings on different floors.

LACING COURSE: horizontal reinforcement in timber or brick to walls of flint, cobble, etc.

LADY CHAPEL: dedicated to the Virgin Mary (Our Lady).

LANCET: slender single-light, pointed-arched window (2a).

LANTERN: circular or polygonal windowed turret crowning a roof or a dome. Also the windowed stage of a crossing tower lighting the church interior.

LANTERN CROSS: churchyard cross with lantern-shaped top.

LAVATORIUM: in a religious house, a washing place adjacent to the refectory.

LEAN-TO: see Roofs.

LESENE (lit. a mean thing): pilaster without base or capital. Also called pilaster strip.

LIERNE: see Vault and 2c.

LIGHT: compartment of a window defined by the mullions.

LINENFOLD: Tudor panelling carved with simulations of folded linen. See also Parchemin.

LINTEL: horizontal beam or stone bridging an opening.

LOGGIA: gallery, usually arcaded or colonnaded; sometimes free-standing.

LONG-AND-SHORT WORK: quoins consisting of stones placed with the long side alternately upright and horizontal, especially in Saxon building.

LONGHOUSE: house and byre in the same range with internal access between them.

LOUVRE: roof opening, often protected by a raised timber structure, to allow the smoke from a central hearth to escape.

LOWSIDE WINDOW: set lower than the others in a chancel side wall, usually towards its w end.

LUCAM: projecting housing for hoist pulley on upper storey of warehouses, mills, etc., for raising goods to loading doors.

LUCARNE (lit. dormer): small gabled opening in a roof or spire.

LUGGED ARCHITRAVE: see 4b.

LUNETTE: semicircular window or blind panel.

LYCHGATE (lit. corpse-gate): roofed gateway entrance to a churchyard for the reception of a coffin.

LYNCHET: long terraced strip of soil on the downward side of prehistoric and medieval fields, accumulated because of continual ploughing along the contours.

MACHICOLATIONS (lit. mashing devices): series of openings between the corbels that support a projecting parapet through which missiles can be dropped. Used decoratively in post-medieval buildings.

MANOMETER or STANDPIPE TOWER: containing a column of water to regulate pressure in water mains.

MANSARD: see 8a.

MATHEMATICAL TILES: facing tiles with the appearance of brick, most often applied to timber-framed walls.

MAUSOLEUM: monumental building or chamber usually intended for the burial of members of one family.

MEGALITHIC TOMB: massive stone-built Neolithic burial chamber covered by an earth or stone mound.

MERLON: see Battlement.

METOPES: spaces between the triglyphs in a Doric frieze (3b).

MEZZANINE: low storey between two higher ones.

MILD STEEL: see Cast iron.

MISERICORD (lit. mercy): shelf on a carved bracket placed on the underside of a hinged choir stall seat to support an occupant when standing.

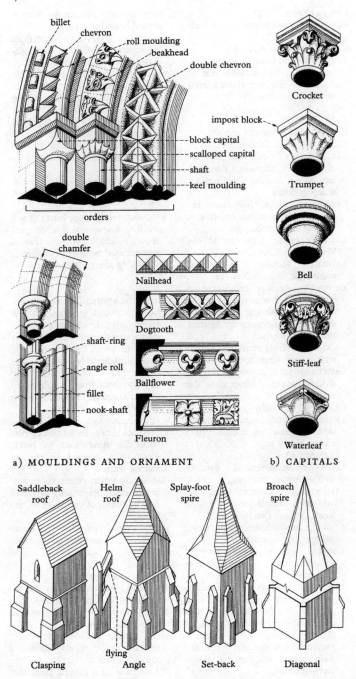

a) MOULDINGS AND ORNAMENT

b) CAPITALS

c) BUTTRESSES, ROOFS AND SPIRES

FIGURE I: MEDIEVAL

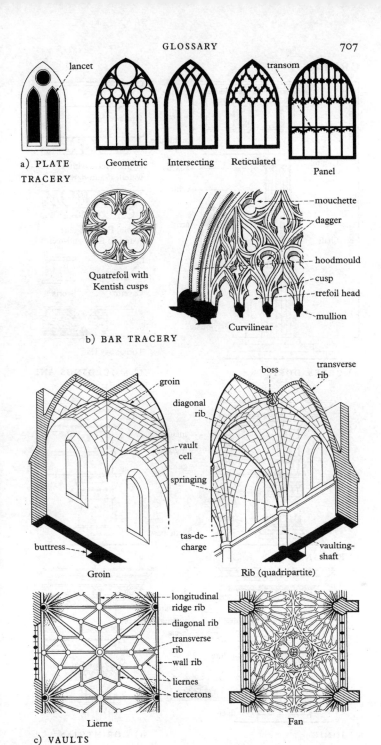

a) PLATE TRACERY

Geometric Intersecting Reticulated Panel

Quatrefoil with Kentish cusps

Curvilinear

b) BAR TRACERY

Groin

Rib (quadripartite)

Lierne

Fan

c) VAULTS

FIGURE 2: MEDIEVAL

ORDERS

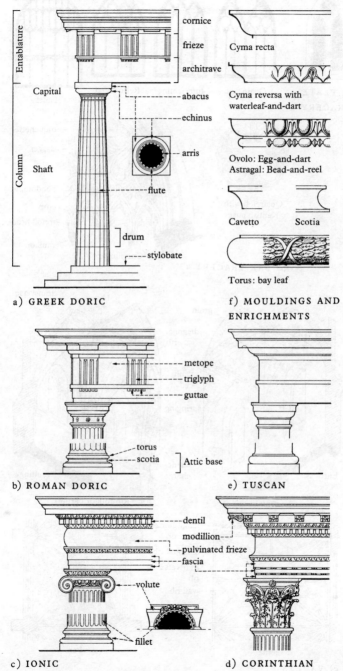

a) GREEK DORIC

Entablature
- cornice
- frieze
- architrave

Column
- Capital
  - abacus
  - echinus
- Shaft
  - arris
  - flute
- drum
- stylobate

b) ROMAN DORIC
- metope
- triglyph
- guttae
- torus
- scotia
- Attic base

c) IONIC
- dentil
- modillion
- pulvinated frieze
- fascia
- volute
- fillet

d) CORINTHIAN

e) TUSCAN

f) MOULDINGS AND ENRICHMENTS
- Cyma recta
- Cyma reversa with waterleaf-and-dart
- Ovolo: Egg-and-dart
- Astragal: Bead-and-reel
- Cavetto   Scotia
- Torus: bay leaf

FIGURE 3: CLASSICAL

a) PORTICO

Anthemion & Palmette

Guilloche

Key pattern

Rinceau

Husk garland

Vitruvian scroll

Console

Diocletian window

Acanthus

Broken pediment

Segmental pediment

Venetian window

Lugged architrave

Shouldered architrave

Open pediment

Swan-neck pediment

Gibbs surround

b) ORNAMENTS AND FEATURES

FIGURE 4: CLASSICAL

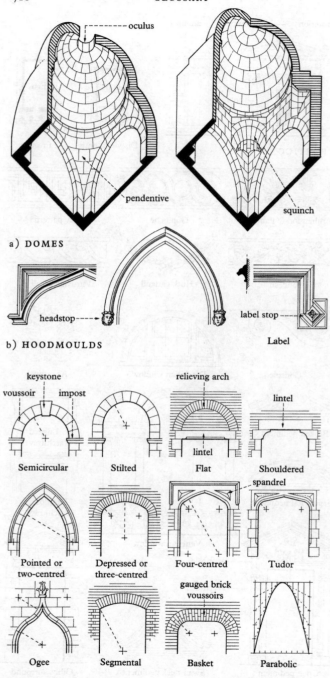

a) DOMES

b) HOODMOULDS

Label

c) ARCHES

FIGURE 5: CONSTRUCTION

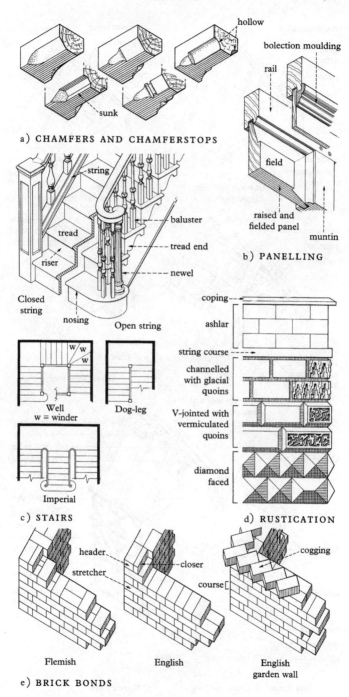

a) CHAMFERS AND CHAMFERSTOPS

b) PANELLING

c) STAIRS

d) RUSTICATION

e) BRICK BONDS

FIGURE 6: CONSTRUCTION

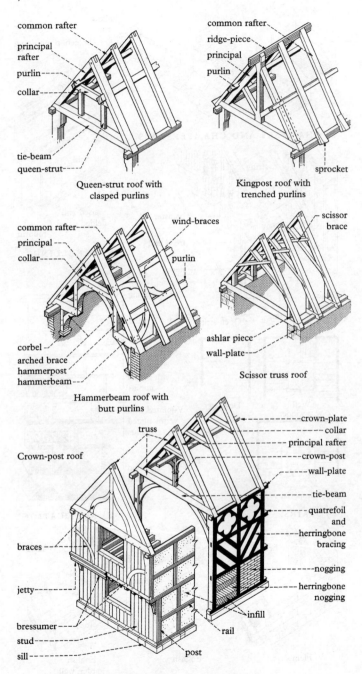

Queen-strut roof with clasped purlins

- common rafter
- principal rafter
- purlin
- collar
- tie-beam
- queen-strut

Kingpost roof with trenched purlins

- common rafter
- ridge-piece
- principal
- purlin
- sprocket

Hammerbeam roof with butt purlins

- common rafter
- principal
- collar
- wind-braces
- purlin
- corbel
- arched brace
- hammerpost
- hammerbeam

Scissor truss roof

- scissor brace
- ashlar piece
- wall-plate

Crown-post roof

- truss
- crown-plate
- collar
- principal rafter
- crown-post
- wall-plate
- tie-beam
- quatrefoil and herringbone bracing
- nogging
- herringbone nogging
- braces
- jetty
- bressumer
- stud
- sill
- post
- rail
- infill

Box frame: i) Close studding   ii) Square panel

FIGURE 7: ROOFS AND TIMBER-FRAMING

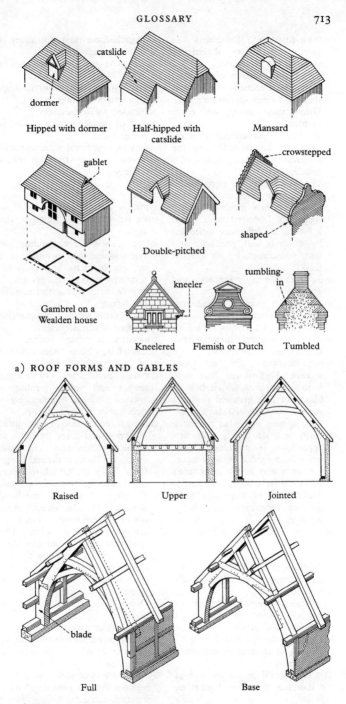

a) ROOF FORMS AND GABLES

b) CRUCK FRAMES

FIGURE 8: ROOFS AND TIMBER-FRAMING

MIXER-COURTS: forecourts to groups of houses shared by vehicles and pedestrians.

MODILLIONS: small consoles (q.v.) along the underside of a Corinthian or Composite cornice (3d). Often used along an eaves cornice.

MODULE: a predetermined standard size for co-ordinating the dimensions of components of a building.

MOTTE-AND-BAILEY: post-Roman and Norman defence consisting of an earthen mound (motte) topped by a wooden tower within a bailey, an enclosure defended by a ditch and palisade, and also, sometimes, by an internal bank.

MOUCHETTE: see Tracery and 2b.

MOULDING: shaped ornamental strip of continuous section; see e.g. Cavetto, Cyma, Ovolo, Roll.

MULLION: vertical member between window lights (2b).

MULTI-STOREY: five or more storeys. Multi-storey flats may form a *cluster block*, with individual blocks of flats grouped round a service core; a *point block*, with flats fanning out from a service core; or a *slab block*, with flats approached by corridors or galleries from service cores at intervals or towers at the ends (plan also used for offices, hotels etc.). *Tower block* is a generic term for any very high multi-storey building.

MUNTIN: see Panelling and 6b.

NAILHEAD: E.E. ornament consisting of small pyramids regularly repeated (1a).

NARTHEX: enclosed vestibule or covered porch at the main entrance to a church.

NAVE: the body of a church w of the crossing or chancel often flanked by aisles (q.v.).

NEWEL: central or corner post of a staircase (6c). Newel stair: see Stairs.

NIGHT STAIR: stair by which religious entered the transept of their church from their dormitory to celebrate night services.

NOGGING: see Timber-framing (7).

NOOK-SHAFT: shaft set in the angle of a wall or opening (1a).

NORMAN: see Romanesque.

NOSING: projection of the tread of a step (6c).

NUTMEG: medieval ornament with a chain of tiny triangles placed obliquely.

OCULUS: circular opening.

ŒIL DE BŒUF: see Bullseye window.

OGEE: double curve, bending first one way and then the other, as in an *ogee* or *ogival arch* (5c). Cf. Cyma recta and Cyma reversa.

OPUS SECTILE: decorative mosaic-like facing.

OPUS SIGNINUM: composition flooring of Roman origin.

ORATORY: a private chapel in a church or a house. Also a church of the Oratorian Order.

ORDER: one of a series of recessed arches and jambs forming a splayed medieval opening, e.g. a doorway or arcade arch (1a).

ORDERS: the formalized versions of the post-and-lintel system in classical architecture. The main orders are *Doric*, *Ionic*, and *Corinthian*. They are Greek in origin but occur in Roman versions. Tuscan is a simple version of Roman Doric. Though each order has its own conventions (3), there are many minor variations. The *Composite* capital combines Ionic volutes with Corinthian foliage. *Superimposed orders*: orders on successive levels, usually in the upward sequence of Tuscan, Doric, Ionic, Corinthian, Composite.

ORIEL: see Bay window.

OVERDOOR: painting or relief above an internal door. Also called a *sopraporta*.

OVERTHROW: decorative fixed arch between two gatepiers or above a wrought-iron gate.

OVOLO: wide convex moulding (3f).

PALIMPSEST: of a brass: where a metal plate has been reused by turning over the engraving on the back; of a wall painting: where one overlaps and partly obscures an earlier one.

PALLADIAN: following the examples and principles of Andrea Palladio (1508–80).

PALMETTE: classical ornament like a palm shoot (4b).

PANELLING: wooden lining to interior walls, made up of vertical members (*muntins*) and horizontals (*rails*) framing panels: also called *wainscot*. *Raised and fielded*: with the central area of the panel (*field*) raised up (6b).

PANTILE: roof tile of S section.

PARAPET: wall for protection at any sudden drop, e.g. at the wall-head of a castle where it protects the *parapet walk* or wall-walk. Also used to conceal a roof.

PARCLOSE: *see* Screen.

PARGETTING (*lit.* plastering): exterior plaster decoration, either in relief or incised.

PARLOUR: in a religious house, a room where the religious could talk to visitors; in a medieval house, the semi-private living room below the solar (q.v.).

PARTERRE: level space in a garden laid out with low, formal beds.

PATERA (*lit.* plate): round or oval ornament in shallow relief.

PAVILION: ornamental building for occasional use; or projecting subdivision of a larger building, often at an angle or terminating a wing.

PEBBLEDASHING: *see* Rendering.

PEDESTAL: a tall block carrying a classical order, statue, vase, etc.

PEDIMENT: a formalized gable derived from that of a classical temple; also used over doors, windows, etc. For variations *see* 4b.

PENDENTIVE: spandrel between adjacent arches, supporting a drum, dome or vault and consequently formed as part of a hemisphere (5a).

PENTHOUSE: subsidiary structure with a lean-to roof. Also a separately roofed structure on top of a C20 multi-storey block.

PERIPTERAL: *see* Peristyle.

PERISTYLE: a colonnade all round the exterior of a classical building, as in a temple which is then said to be *peripteral*.

PERP (PERPENDICULAR): English Gothic architecture *c.* 1335–50 to *c.* 1530. The name is derived from the upright tracery panels then used (*see* Tracery and 2a).

PERRON: external stair to a doorway, usually of double-curved plan.

PEW: loosely, seating for the laity outside the chancel; strictly, an enclosed seat. *Box pew*: with equal high sides and a door.

PIANO NOBILE: principal floor of a classical building above a ground floor or basement and with a lesser storey overhead.

PIAZZA: formal urban open space surrounded by buildings.

PIER: large masonry or brick support, often for an arch. *See also* Compound pier.

PILASTER: flat representation of a classical column in shallow relief. *Pilaster strip*: *see* Lesene.

PILE: row of rooms. *Double pile*: two rows thick.

PILLAR: free-standing upright member of any section, not conforming to one of the orders (q.v.).

PILLAR PISCINA: *see* Piscina.

PILOTIS: C20 French term for pillars or stilts that support a building above an open ground floor.

PISCINA: basin for washing Mass vessels, provided with a drain; set in or against the wall to the S of an altar or free-standing (*pillar piscina*).

PISÉ: *see* Cob.

PITCHED MASONRY: laid on the diagonal, often alternately with opposing courses (*pitched and counterpitched* or *herringbone*).

PLATBAND: flat horizontal moulding between storeys. Cf. stringcourse.

PLATE RAIL: *see* Railways.

PLATEWAY: *see* Railways.

PLINTH: projecting courses at the

foot of a wall or column, generally chamfered or moulded at the top.

PODIUM: a continuous raised platform supporting a building; or a large block of two or three storeys beneath a multi-storey block of smaller area.

POINT BLOCK: see Multi-storey.

POINTING: exposed mortar jointing of masonry or brickwork. Types include *flush*, *recessed* and *tuck* (with a narrow channel filled with finer, whiter mortar).

POPPYHEAD: carved ornament of leaves and flowers as a finial for a bench end or stall.

PORTAL FRAME: C20 frame comprising two uprights rigidly connected to a beam or pair of rafters.

PORTCULLIS: gate constructed to rise and fall in vertical grooves at the entry to a castle.

PORTICO: a porch with the roof and frequently a pediment supported by a row of columns (4a). A portico *in antis* has columns on the same plane as the front of the building. A *prostyle* porch has columns standing free. Porticoes are described by the number of front columns, e.g. tetrastyle (four), hexastyle (six). The space within the temple is the *naos*, that within the portico the *pronaos*. *Blind portico*: the front features of a portico applied to a wall.

PORTICUS (plural: porticūs): subsidiary cell opening from the main body of a pre-Conquest church.

POST: upright support in a structure (7).

POSTERN: small gateway at the back of a building or to the side of a larger entrance door or gate.

POUND LOCK: see Canals.

PRESBYTERY: the part of a church lying E of the choir where the main altar is placed; or a priest's residence.

PRINCIPAL: see Roofs and 7.

PRONAOS: see Portico and 4a.

PROSTYLE: see Portico and 4a.

PULPIT: raised and enclosed platform for the preaching of sermons. *Three-decker*: with reading desk below and clerk's desk below that. *Two-decker*: as above, minus the clerk's desk.

PULPITUM: stone screen in a major church dividing choir from nave.

PULVINATED: see Frieze and 3c.

PURLIN: see Roofs and 7.

PUTHOLES or PUTLOG HOLES: in the wall to receive putlogs, the horizontal timbers which support scaffolding boards; sometimes not filled after construction is complete.

PUTTO (plural: putti): small naked boy.

QUARRIES: square (or diamond) panes of glass supported by lead strips (*cames*); square floor slabs or tiles.

QUATREFOIL: see Foil and 2b.

QUEEN-STRUT: see Roofs and 7.

QUIRK: sharp groove to one side of a convex medieval moulding.

QUOINS: dressed stones at the angles of a building (6d).

RADBURN SYSTEM: vehicle and pedestrian segregation in residential developments, based on that used at Radburn, New Jersey, USA, by Wright and Stein, 1928–30.

RADIATING CHAPELS: projecting radially from an ambulatory or an apse (see Chevet).

RAFTER: see Roofs and 7.

RAGGLE: groove cut in masonry, especially to receive the edge of a roof-covering.

RAGULY: ragged (in heraldry). Also applied to funerary sculpture, e.g. *cross raguly*: with a notched outline.

RAIL: see Panelling and 6b; also 7.

RAILWAYS: *Edge rail*: on which flanged wheels can run. *Plate rail*: L-section rail for plain unflanged wheels. *Plateway*: early railway using plate rails.

RAISED AND FIELDED: see Panelling and 6b.

RAKE: slope or pitch.

RAMPART: defensive outer wall of stone or earth. *Rampart walk*: path along the inner face.

REBATE: rectangular section cut out of a masonry edge to receive a shutter, door, window, etc.

REBUS: a heraldic pun, e.g. a fiery cock for Cockburn.

REEDING: series of convex mouldings, the reverse of fluting (q.v.). Cf. Gadrooning.

RENDERING: the covering of outside walls with a uniform surface or skin for protection from the weather. *Limewashing*: thin layer of lime plaster. *Pebble-dashing*: where aggregate is thrown at the wet plastered wall for a textured effect. *Roughcast*: plaster mixed with a coarse aggregate such as gravel. *Stucco*: fine lime plaster worked to a smooth surface. *Cement rendering*: a cheaper substitute for stucco, usually with a grainy texture.

REPOUSSÉ: relief designs in metalwork, formed by beating it from the back.

REREDORTER (*lit.* behind the dormitory): latrines in a medieval religious house.

REREDOS: painted and/or sculptured screen behind and above an altar. Cf. Retable.

RESPOND: half-pier or half-column bonded into a wall and carrying one end of an arch. It usually terminates an arcade.

RETABLE: painted or carved panel standing on or at the back of an altar, usually attached to it.

RETROCHOIR: in a major church, the area between the high altar and E chapel.

REVEAL: the plane of a jamb, between the wall and the frame of a door or window.

RIB-VAULT: *see* Vault and 2C.

RINCEAU: classical ornament of leafy scrolls (4b).

RISER: vertical face of a step (6c).

ROACH: a rough-textured form of Portland stone, with small cavities and fossil shells.

ROCK-FACED: masonry cleft to produce a rugged appearance.

ROCOCO: style current *c.* 1720 and *c.* 1760, characterized by a serpentine line and playful, scrolled decoration.

ROLL MOULDING: medieval moulding of part-circular section (1a).

ROMANESQUE: style current in the C11 and C12. In England often called Norman. *See also* Saxo-Norman.

ROOD: crucifix flanked by the Virgin and St John, usually over the entry into the chancel, on a beam (*rood beam*) or painted on the wall. The *rood screen* below often had a walkway (*rood loft*) along the top, reached by a *rood stair* in the side wall.

ROOFS: Shape. For the main external shapes (hipped, mansard, etc.) *see* 8a. *Helm* and *Saddleback*: *see* 1C. *Lean-to*: single sloping roof built against a vertical wall; lean-to is also applied to the part of the building beneath.

Construction. *See* 7.

Single-framed roof: with no main trusses. The rafters may be fixed to the wall-plate or ridge, or longitudinal timber may be absent altogether.

Double-framed roof: with longitudinal members, such as purlins, and usually divided into bays by principals and principal rafters. Other types are named after their main structural components, e.g. *hammerbeam*, *crown-post* (*see* Elements below and 7).

Elements. *See* 7.

Ashlar piece: a short vertical timber connecting inner wall-plate or timber pad to a rafter.

Braces: subsidiary timbers set diagonally to strengthen the frame. *Arched braces*: curved pair forming an arch, connecting wall or post below with tie- or collar-beam above. *Passing braces*: long straight braces passing across other members of the truss. *Scissor braces*: pair crossing diagonally between pairs of rafters or principals. *Wind-braces*: short, usually curved braces connecting side purlins with principals; sometimes decorated with cusping.

Collar or *collar-beam*: horizontal transverse timber connecting a pair of rafter or cruck blades (q.v.), set between apex and the wall-plate.

Crown-post: a vertical timber set centrally on a tie-beam and supporting a collar purlin braced to it longitudinally. In an open truss lateral braces may rise to the collar-beam; in a closed truss they may descend to the tie-beam.

Hammerbeams: horizontal brackets projecting at wall-plate level like an interrupted tie-beam; the inner ends carry *hammerposts*, vertical timbers which support a purlin and are braced to a collar-beam above.

Kingpost: vertical timber set centrally on a tie- or collar-beam, rising to the apex of the roof to support a ridge-piece (cf. Strut).

Plate: longitudinal timber set square to the ground. *Wall-plate*: plate along the top of a wall which receives the ends of the rafters; cf. Purlin.

Principals: pair of inclined lateral timbers of a truss. Usually they support side purlins and mark the main bay divisions.

Purlin: horizontal longitudinal timber. *Collar purlin* or *crown plate*: central timber which carries collar-beams and is supported by crown-posts. *Side purlins*: pairs of timbers placed some way up the slope of the roof, which carry common rafters. *Butt* or *tenoned purlins* are tenoned into either side of the principals. *Through purlins* pass through or past the principal; they include *clasped purlins*, which rest on queenposts or are carried in the angle between principals and collar, and *trenched purlins* trenched into the backs of principals.

Queen-strut: paired vertical, or near-vertical, timbers placed symmetrically on a tie-beam to support side purlins.

Rafters: inclined lateral timbers supporting the roof covering. *Common rafters*: regularly spaced uniform rafters placed along the length of a roof or between principals. *Principal rafters*: rafters which also act as principals.

Ridge, ridge-piece: horizontal longitudinal timber at the apex supporting the ends of the rafters.

Sprocket: short timber placed on the back and at the foot of a rafter to form projecting eaves.

Strut: vertical or oblique timber between two members of a truss,

not directly supporting longitudinal timbers.

Tie-beam: main horizontal transverse timber which carries the feet of the principals at wall level.

Truss: rigid framework of timbers at bay intervals, carrying the longitudinal roof timbers which support the common rafters. *Closed truss*: with the spaces between the timbers filled, to form an internal partition.

See also Cruck, Wagon roof.

ROPE MOULDING: *see* Cable moulding.

ROSE WINDOW: circular window with tracery radiating from the centre. Cf. Wheel window.

ROTUNDA: building or room circular in plan.

ROUGHCAST: *see* Rendering.

ROVING BRIDGE: *see* Canals.

RUBBED BRICKWORK: *see* Gauged brickwork.

RUBBLE: masonry whose stones are wholly or partly in a rough state. *Coursed*: coursed stones with rough faces. *Random*: uncoursed stones in a random pattern. *Snecked*: with courses broken by smaller stones (snecks).

RUSTICATION: *see* 6d. Exaggerated treatment of masonry to give an effect of strength. The joints are usually recessed by V-section chamfering or square-section channelling (*channelled rustication*). *Banded rustication* has only the horizontal joints emphasized. The faces may be flat, but can be *diamond-faced*, like shallow pyramids, *vermiculated*, with a stylized texture like worm-casts, and *glacial* (frost-work), like icicles or stalactites.

SACRISTY: room in a church for sacred vessels and vestments.

SADDLEBACK ROOF: *see* 1C.

SALTIRE CROSS: with diagonal limbs.

SANCTUARY: area around the main altar of a church. Cf. Presbytery.

SANGHA: residence of Buddhist monks or nuns.

SARCOPHAGUS: coffin of stone or other durable material.

SAXO-NORMAN: transitional Romanesque style combining Anglo-Saxon and Norman features, current *c.* 1060–1100.

SCAGLIOLA: composition imitating marble.

SCALLOPED CAPITAL: *see* 1a.

SCOTIA: a hollow classical moulding, especially between tori (q.v.) on a column base (3b, 3f).

SCREEN: in a medieval church, usually at the entry to the chancel; *see* Rood (screen) and Pulpitum. A *parclose screen* separates a chapel from the rest of the church.

SCREENS or SCREENS PASSAGE: screened-off entrance passage between great hall and service rooms.

SECTION: two-dimensional representation of a building, moulding, etc., revealed by cutting across it.

SEDILIA (singular: sedile): seats for the priests (usually three) on the S side of the chancel.

SET-OFF: *see* Weathering.

SETTS: squared stones, usually of granite, used for paving or flooring.

SGRAFFITO: decoration scratched, often in plaster, to reveal a pattern in another colour beneath. *Graffiti*: scratched drawing or writing.

SHAFT: vertical member of round or polygonal section (1a, 3a). *Shaft-ring*: at the junction of shafts set *en delit* (q.v.) or attached to a pier or wall (1a).

SHEILA-NA-GIG: female fertility figure, usually with legs apart.

SHELL: thin, self-supporting roofing membrane of timber or concrete.

SHOULDERED ARCHITRAVE: *see* 4b.

SHUTTERING: *see* Concrete.

SILL: horizontal member at the bottom of a window or door frame; or at the base of a timber-framed wall into which posts and studs are tenoned (7).

SLAB BLOCK: *see* Multi-storey.

SLATE-HANGING: covering of overlapping slates on a wall. *Tile-hanging* is similar.

SLYPE: covered way or passage leading E from the cloisters between transept and chapter house.

SNECKED: *see* Rubble.

SOFFIT (*lit.* ceiling): underside of an arch (also called *intrados*), lintel, etc. *Soffit roll*: medieval roll moulding on a soffit.

SOLAR: private upper chamber in a medieval house, accessible from the high end of the great hall.

SOPRAPORTA: *see* Overdoor.

SOUNDING-BOARD: *see* Tester.

SPANDRELS: roughly triangular spaces between an arch and its containing rectangle, or between adjacent arches (5c). Also non-structural panels under the windows in a curtain-walled building.

SPERE: a fixed structure screening the lower end of the great hall from the screens passage. *Spere-truss*: roof truss incorporated in the spere.

SPIRE: tall pyramidal or conical feature crowning a tower or turret. *Broach*: starting from a square base, then carried into an octagonal section by means of triangular faces; and *splayed-foot*: variation of the broach form, found principally in the south-east, in which the four cardinal faces are splayed out near their base, to cover the corners, while oblique (or intermediate) faces taper away to a point (1c). *Needle spire*: thin spire rising from the centre of a tower roof, well inside the parapet: when of timber and lead often called a *spike*.

SPIRELET: *see* Flèche.

SPLAY: of an opening when it is wider on one face of a wall than the other.

SPRING or SPRINGING: level at which an arch or vault rises from its supports. *Springers*: the first stones of an arch or vaulting rib above the spring (2c).

SQUINCH: arch or series of arches thrown across an interior angle of a square or rectangular structure to support a circular or polygonal superstructure, especially a dome or spire (5a).

SQUINT: an aperture in a wall or through a pier usually to allow a view of an altar.

STAIRS: *see* 6c. *Dog-leg stair*: parallel flights rising alternately in opposite directions, without an open well. *Flying stair*: cantilevered from the walls of a stairwell, without newels; sometimes called a *Geometric* stair when the inner edge describes a curve. *Newel stair*: ascending round a central supporting newel (q.v.); called a *spiral stair* or *vice* when in a circular shaft, a *winder* when in a rectangular compartment. (Winder also applies to the steps on the turn.) *Well stair*: with flights round a square open well framed by newel posts. *See also* Perron.

STALL: fixed seat in the choir or chancel for the clergy or choir (cf. Pew). Usually with arm rests, and often framed together.

STANCHION: upright structural member, of iron, steel or reinforced concrete.

STANDPIPE TOWER: *see* Manometer.

STEAM ENGINES: *Atmospheric*: worked by the vacuum created when low-pressure steam is condensed in the cylinder, as developed by Thomas Newcomen. *Beam engine*: with a large pivoted beam moved in an oscillating fashion by the piston. It may drive a flywheel or be *non-rotative*. *Watt* and *Cornish*: single-cylinder; *compound*: two cylinders; *triple expansion*: three cylinders.

STEEPLE: tower together with a spire, lantern, or belfry.

STIFF-LEAF: type of E.E. foliage decoration. *Stiff-leaf capital see* 1b.

STOP: plain or decorated terminal to mouldings or chamfers, or at the end of hoodmoulds and labels (*label stop*), or stringcourses (5b, 6a); *see also* Headstop.

STOUP: vessel for holy water, usually near a door.

STRAINER: *see* Arch.

STRAPWORK: late C16 and C17 decoration, like interlaced leather straps.

STRETCHER: *see* Bond and 6e.

STRING: *see* 6c. Sloping member holding the ends of the treads and risers of a staircase. *Closed string*: a broad string covering the ends of the treads and risers. *Open string*: cut into the shape of the treads and risers.

STRINGCOURSE: horizontal course or moulding projecting from the surface of a wall (6d).

STUCCO: *see* Rendering.

STUDS: subsidiary vertical timbers of a timber-framed wall or partition (7).

STUPA: Buddhist shrine, circular in plan.

STYLOBATE: top of the solid platform on which a colonnade stands (3a).

SUSPENSION BRIDGE: *see* Bridge.

SWAG: like a festoon (q.v.), but representing cloth.

SYSTEM BUILDING: *see* Industrialized building.

TABERNACLE: canopied structure to contain the reserved sacrament or a relic; or architectural frame for an image or statue.

TABLE TOMB: memorial slab raised on free-standing legs.

TAS-DE-CHARGE: the lower courses of a vault or arch which are laid horizontally (2c).

TERM: pedestal or pilaster tapering downward, usually with the upper part of a human figure growing out of it.

TERRACOTTA: moulded and fired clay ornament or cladding.

TESSELLATED PAVEMENT: mosaic flooring, particularly Roman, made of *tesserae*, i.e. cubes of glass, stone, or brick.

TESTER: flat canopy over a tomb or pulpit, where it is also called a *sounding-board*.

TESTER TOMB: tomb-chest with effigies beneath a tester, either free-standing (tester with four or more columns), or attached to a wall (*half-tester*) with columns on one side only.

TETRASTYLE: *see* Portico.

THERMAL WINDOW: *see* Diocletian window.

THREE-DECKER PULPIT: *see* Pulpit.

TIDAL GATES: *see* Canals.

TIE-BEAM: *see* Roofs and 7.

TIERCERON: *see* Vault and 2c.

TILE-HANGING: *see* Slate-hanging.

TIMBER-FRAMING: *see* 7. Method of construction where the structural frame is built of interlocking timbers. The spaces are filled with non-structural material, e.g. *infill* of wattle and daub, lath and plaster, brickwork (known as *nogging*), etc. and may be covered by plaster, weatherboarding (q.v.), or tiles.

TOMB-CHEST: chest-shaped tomb, usually of stone. Cf. Table tomb, Tester tomb.

TORUS (plural: tori): large convex moulding usually used on a column base (3b, 3f).

TOUCH: soft black marble quarried near Tournai.

TOURELLE: turret corbelled out from the wall.

TOWER BLOCK: *see* Multi-storey.

TRABEATED: depends structurally on the use of the post and lintel. Cf. Arcuated.

TRACERY: openwork pattern of masonry or timber in the upper part of an opening. *Blind tracery* is tracery applied to a solid wall.
Plate tracery, introduced *c.* 1200, is the earliest form, in which shapes are cut through solid masonry (2a).
Bar tracery was introduced into England *c.* 1250. The pattern is formed by intersecting moulded ribwork continued from the mullions. It was especially elaborate during the Decorated period (q.v.). Tracery shapes can include circles, *daggers* (elongated ogee-ended lozenges), *mouchettes* (like daggers but with curved sides) and upright rectangular *panels*. They often have *cusps*, projecting points defining lobes or *foils* (q.v.) within the main shape: *Kentish* or *split-cusps* are forked (2b).
Types of bar tracery (*see* 2b) include *geometric(al)*: *c.* 1250–1310, chiefly circles, often foiled; *Y-tracery*: *c.* 1300, with mullions branching into a Y-shape; *intersecting*: *c.* 1300, formed by interlocking mullions; *reticulated*: early C14, net-like pattern of ogee-ended lozenges; *curvilinear*: C14, with uninterrupted flowing curves; *panel*: Perp, with straight-sided panels, often cusped at the top and bottom.

TRANSEPT: transverse portion of a church.

TRANSITIONAL: generally used for the phase between Romanesque and Early English (*c.* 1175–*c.* 1200).

TRANSOM: horizontal member separating window lights (2b).

TREAD: horizontal part of a step. The *tread end* may be carved on a staircase (6c).

TREFOIL: *see* Foil.

TRIFORIUM: middle storey of a church treated as an arcaded wall passage or blind arcade, its height corresponding to that of the aisle roof.

TRIGLYPHS (*lit.* three-grooved tablets): stylized beam-ends in the Doric frieze, with metopes between (3b).

TRIUMPHAL ARCH: influential type of Imperial Roman monument.

TROPHY: sculptured or painted group of arms or armour.

TRUMEAU: central stone mullion supporting the tympanum of a wide doorway. *Trumeau figure*: carved figure attached to it (cf. Column figure).

TRUMPET CAPITAL: *see* 1b.

TRUSS: braced framework, spanning between supports. *See also* Roofs and 7.

TUMBLING or TUMBLING-IN: courses of brickwork laid at right-angles to a slope, e.g. of a gable, forming triangles by tapering into horizontal courses (8a).

TUSCAN: *see* Orders and 3e.

TWO-DECKER PULPIT: *see* Pulpit.

TYMPANUM: the surface between a lintel and the arch above it or within a pediment (4a).

UNDERCROFT: usually describes the vaulted room(s), beneath the main room(s) of a medieval house. Cf. Crypt.

VAULT: arched stone roof (sometimes imitated in timber or plaster). For types see 2c.
Tunnel or *barrel vault*: continuous semicircular or pointed arch, often of rubble masonry.

Groin-vault: tunnel vaults intersecting at right angles. *Groins* are the curved lines of the intersections.

Rib-vault: masonry framework of intersecting arches (ribs) supporting *vault cells*, used in Gothic architecture. *Wall rib* or *wall arch*: between wall and vault cell. *Transverse rib*: spans between two walls to divide a vault into bays. *Quadripartite* rib-vault: each bay has two pairs of diagonal ribs dividing the vault into four triangular cells. *Sexpartite* rib-vault: most often used over paired bays, has an extra pair of ribs springing from between the bays. More elaborate vaults may include *ridge ribs* along the crown of a vault or bisecting the bays; *tiercerons*: extra decorative ribs springing from the corners of a bay; and *liernes*: short decorative ribs in the crown of a vault, not linked to any springing point. A *stellar* or *star* vault has liernes in star formation.

Fan-vault: form of barrel vault used in the Perp period, made up of halved concave masonry cones decorated with blind tracery.

VAULTING SHAFT: shaft leading up to the spring or springing (q.v.) of a vault (2c).

VENETIAN or SERLIAN WINDOW: derived from Serlio (4b). The motif is used for other openings.

VERMICULATION: *see* Rustication and 6d.

VESICA: oval with pointed ends.

VICE: *see* Stair.

VILLA: originally a Roman country house or farm. The term was revived in England in the C18 under the influence of Palladio and used especially for smaller, compact country houses. In the later C19 it was debased to describe any suburban house.

VITRIFIED: bricks or tiles fired to a darkened glassy surface.

VITRUVIAN SCROLL: classical running ornament of curly waves (4b).

VOLUTES: spiral scrolls. They occur on Ionic capitals (3c). *Angle volute*: pair of volutes, turned outwards to meet at the corner of a capital.

VOUSSOIRS: wedge-shaped stones forming an arch (5c).

WAGON ROOF: with the appearance of the inside of a wagon tilt; often ceiled. Also called *cradle roof*.

WAINSCOT: *see* Panelling.

WALL MONUMENT: attached to the wall and often standing on the floor. *Wall tablets* are smaller with the inscription as the major element.

WALL-PLATE: *see* Roofs and 7.

WALL-WALK: *see* Parapet.

WARMING ROOM: room in a religious house where a fire burned for comfort.

WATERHOLDING BASE: early Gothic base with upper and lower mouldings separated by a deep hollow.

WATERLEAF: *see* Enrichments and 3f.

WATERLEAF CAPITAL: Late Romanesque and Transitional type of capital (1b).

WATER WHEELS: described by the way water is fed on to the wheel. *Breastshot*: mid-height, falling and passing beneath. *Overshot*: over the top. *Pitchback*: on the top but falling backwards. *Undershot*: turned by the momentum of the water passing beneath. In a *water turbine*, water is fed under pressure through a vaned wheel within a casing.

WEALDEN HOUSE: type of medieval timber-framed house with a central open hall flanked by bays of two storeys, roofed in line; the end bays are jettied to the front, but the eaves are continuous (8a).

WEATHERBOARDING: wall cladding of overlapping horizontal boards.

WEATHERING or SET-OFF: inclined, projecting surface to keep water away from the wall below.

WEEPERS: figures in niches along the sides of some medieval tombs. Also called mourners.

WHEEL WINDOW: circular, with radiating shafts like spokes. Cf. Rose window.

WROUGHT IRON: *see* Cast iron.

INDEX OF ARCHITECTS, ARTISTS, PATRONS AND RESIDENTS

Names of architects and artists working in the area covered by this volume are given in *italic*. Entries for partnerships and group practices are listed after entries for a single name.

Also indexed here are names/titles of families and individuals (not of bodies or commercial firms) recorded in this volume as having commissioned architectural work or owned, lived in, or visited properties in the area. The index includes monuments to members of such families and other individuals where they are of particular interest.

INDEX OF PLACES

Principal references are in **bold** type; demolished buildings are shown in *italic*.

Northampton (pp. 429–501) is indexed in three entries: Northampton centre; Northampton inner areas; Northampton outer areas. The subdivisions are listed on pp. 429–30.